COMPACT WORLD ATLAS

T0322253

DK | Penguin Random House

FOR THE EIGHTH EDITION

DK London

Senior Cartographic Editor Simon Mumford
Jacket Design Development Sophia MTT
Jacket Designer Stephanie Cheng Hui Tan
Senior Production Controller Poppy David
Production Editor Robert Dunn
Publishing Director Jonathan Metcalf
Associate Publishing Director Liz Wheeler
Art Director Karen Self

DK Delhi

Desk Editor Saumya Agarwal
Assistant Editor Agey George
Managing Editor Saloni Singh
Senior Cartographer Subhashree Bharati
Manager Cartography Suresh Kumar
DTP Designer Rakesh Kumar
Senior DTP Designer Pushpak Tyagi
Senior Jackets Coordinator Priyanka Sharma Saddi

Placenames Consultant Juliette Koskinas
Authenticity Reader Bianca Hezekiah

First published in Great Britain in 2001 by
Dorling Kindersley Limited
DK, One Embassy Gardens, 8 Viaduct Gardens,
London, SW11 7BW

The authorised representative in the EEA is
Dorling Kindersley Verlag GmbH. Arnulfstr. 124,
80636 Munich, Germany

Copyright © 2001, 2002, 2003, 2004, 2005, 2009, 2012, 2015, 2018, 2023
Dorling Kindersley Limited
A Penguin Random House Company
10 9 8 7 6 5 4 3
004–334038–Sep/2023

A CIP catalogue record for this book is available from the British Library.
ISBN 978-0-2416-0154-9

Printed in India

www.dk.com

This book was made with Forest Stewardship
Council™ certified paper - one small step in
DK's commitment to a sustainable future.
For more information go to
www.dk.com/our-green-pledge

Key to map symbols

Physical features

Elevation

- 6000m/19,686ft
- 4000m/13,124ft
- 3000m/9843ft
- 2000m/6562ft
- 1,000m/3281ft
- 500m/1640ft
- 250m/820ft
- 0
- Below sea level

△   Mountain

▽   Depression

△   Volcano

)(Pass/tunnel

     Sandy desert

Drainage features

Major perennial river

Minor perennial river

Seasonal river

Canal

Waterfall

Perennial lake

Seasonal lake

Wetland

Ice features

Permanent ice cap/ice shelf

Winter limit of pack ice

Summer limit of pack ice

Borders

Full international border

Disputed de facto border

Territorial claim border

x x x   Cease-fire line

Undefined boundary

Internal administrative boundary

Communications

Major road

Minor road

Railway

✈   International airport

Settlements

◉   Above 500,000

◉   100,000 to 500,000

○   50,000 to 100,000

○   Below 50,000

●   National capital

●   Internal administrative capital

Miscellaneous features

+   Site of interest

⊓⊔⊓⊔   Ancient wall

Graticule features

Line of latitude/longitude/ Equator

Tropic/Polar circle

25°   Degrees of latitude/ longitude

Names

Physical features

Andes	
Sahara	Landscape features
Ardennes	
Land's End	Headland
Mont Blanc 4,807m	Elevation/volcano/pass
Blue Nile	River/canal/waterfall
Ross Ice Shelf	Ice feature
PACIFIC OCEAN	
Sulu Sea	Sea features
Palk Strait	
Chile Rise	Undersea feature

Regions

FRANCE	Country
BERMUDA (to UK)	Dependent territory
KANSAS	Administrative region
Dordogne	Cultural region

Settlements

PARIS	Capital city
SAN JUAN	Dependent territory capital city
Chicago	
Kettering	Other settlements
Burke	

Inset map symbols

Urban area

City

Park

Place of interest

Suburb/district

COMPACT WORLD ATLAS

Contents

The Political World 6-7
The Physical World 8-9
Standard Time Zones 10

The World's Regions

North & Central America

North & Central America 12-13
Western Canada & Alaska 14-15
Eastern Canada 16-17
USA: The Northeast 18-19
USA: The Southeast 20-21
    Bermuda
USA: Central States 22-23
USA: The West 24-25
    Los Angeles & Hawaii
USA: The Southwest 26-27
Mexico 28-29
Central America 30-31
The Caribbean 32-33
    Jamaica, St. Lucia & Barbados

South America

South America 34-35
Northern South America 36-37
Western South America 38-39
    Galápagos Islands
Brazil 40-41
Southern South America 42-43

The Atlantic Ocean 44-45

Africa

Africa 46-47
Northwest Africa 48-49
Northeast Africa 50-51
West Africa 52-53
Central Africa 54-55
    Sao Tome & Principe
Southern Africa 56-57

Europe

Europe 58-59
The North Atlantic 60-61
Scandinavia & Finland 62-63
The Low Countries 64-65
The British Isles 66-67
    London
France, Andorra & Monaco 68-69
    Paris, Andorra & Monaco
Spain & Portugal 70-71
    Azores & Gibraltar

Germany & the Alpine States....................72-73
   Liechtenstein
Italy 74-75
   San Marino & Vatican City
Central Europe....................................76-77
Southeast Europe................................78-79
   Bosnia & Herzegovina
The Mediterranean..............................80-81
   Malta & Cyprus
Bulgaria & Greece 82-83
The Baltic States & Belarus.....................84-85
Ukraine, Moldova & Romania...............86-87
European Russia...................................88-89

North India, Pakistan
   & Bangladesh 112-113
Mainland Southeast Asia 114-115
Maritime Southeast Asia.......................116-117
   Singapore

The Indian Ocean................................118-119

North & West Asia

North & West Asia.................................. 90-91
Russia & Kazakhstan.............................92-93
Turkey & the Caucasus............................ 94-95
The Near East..96-97
   West Bank
The Middle East.....................................98-99
Central Asia...................................... 100-101

South & East Asia

South & East Asia 102-103
Western China & Mongolia................. 104-105
Eastern China & Korea......................... 106-107
   Hong Kong
Japan 108-109
   Tokyo & Nansei-Shoto
South India & Sri Lanka 110-111

Australasia & Oceania

Australasia & Oceania.........................120-121
The Southwest Pacific.........................122-123
Western Australia...............................124-125
Eastern Australia 126-127
   Sydney
New Zealand......................................128-129

The Pacific Ocean...............................130-131

Antarctica 132

The Arctic Ocean 133

Index – Gazetteer

Countries Factfile...............................134-150
Overseas Territories
& Dependencies.................................150-151
Geographical Comparisons.................152-153
Index 154-192

The Political World

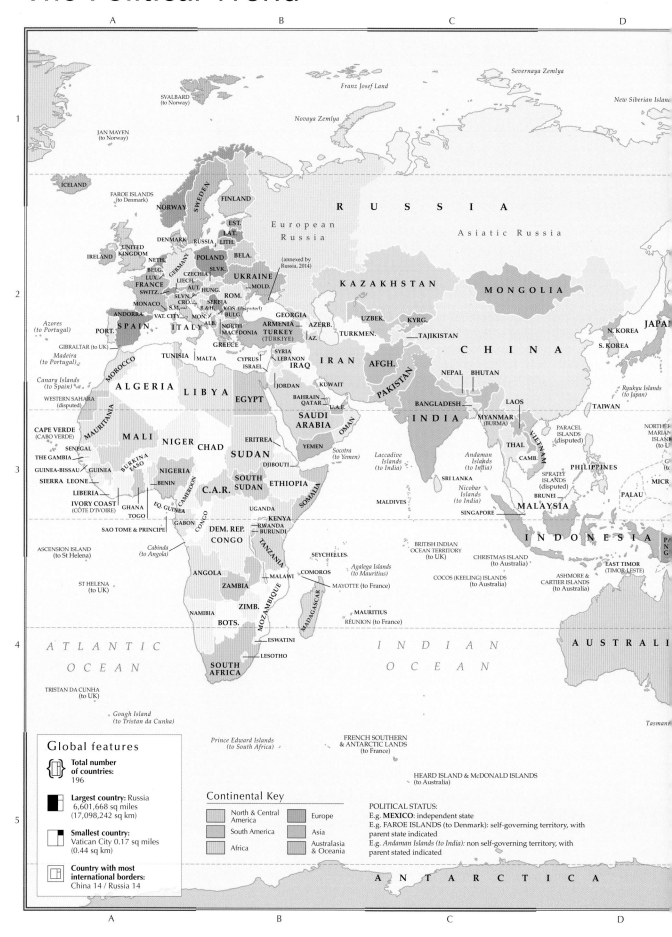

Global features

Total number of countries: 196

Largest country: Russia 6,601,668 sq miles (17,098,242 sq km)

Smallest country: Vatican City 0.17 sq miles (0.44 sq km)

Country with most international borders: China 14 / Russia 14

Continental Key

- North & Central America
- South America
- Africa
- Europe
- Asia
- Australasia & Oceania

POLITICAL STATUS:
E.g. **MEXICO**: independent state
E.g. FAROE ISLANDS (to Denmark): self-governing territory, with parent state indicated
E.g. *Andaman Islands (to India)*: non self-governing territory, with parent stated indicated

A R C T I C
O C E A N

Queen Elizabeth Islands

GREENLAND
(to Denmark)

Baffin Island

Arctic Circle

Alaska
(to US)

Aleutian Islands (to US)

Islands
ussia)

P A C I F I C
O C E A N

C A N A D A

A T L A N T I C
O C E A N

UNITED STATES
OF AMERICA

ST PIERRE
& MIQUELON
(to France)

MIDWAY ISLANDS
(to US)

Guadalupe
(to Mexico)

BERMUDA
(to UK)

PUERTO RICO (to US)
BRITISH VIRGIN ISLANDS (to UK)
VIRGIN ISLANDS (to US)
ANGUILLA (to UK)
ST KITTS & NEVIS

TURKS & CAICOS ISLANDS (to UK)
CAYMAN ISLANDS
(to UK)

DOM. REP.

Tropic of Cancer

WAKE ISLAND
(to US)

Hawaii
(to US)

Revillagigedo
Islands
(to Mexico)

THE
BAHAMAS
HONDURAS
BELIZE
CUBA

ANTIGUA & BARBUDA
MONTSERRAT (to UK)
GUADELOUPE (to France)
DOMINICA
MARTINIQUE (to France)
ST LUCIA
BARBADOS

JOHNSTON ATOLL (to US)

JAMAICA
NAVASSA I.
(to US)

MARSHALL
ISLANDS

WALLIS & FUTUNA
(to France)

KINGMAN REEF (to US)
PALMYRA ATOLL (to US)

CLIPPERTON ISLAND
(to France)

GUATEMALA
EL SALVADOR
NICARAGUA
COSTA RICA

HAITI
CURAÇAO
(Neth.)
ARUBA
(Neth.)

ST VINCENT & THE GRENADINES
GRENADA
TRINIDAD & TOBAGO

NAURU

HOWLAND ISLAND
(to US)
BAKER ISLAND
(to US)

JARVIS ISLAND
(to US)

PANAMA

VENEZUELA

FRENCH GUIANA
(to France)

Equator

COLOMBIA

K I R I B A T I

Galápagos Islands
(to Ecuador)

GUYANA
SURINAME

TUVALU

ECUADOR

B R A Z I L

OMON
ANDS

TOKELAU
(to NZ)

P
E
R
U

SAMOA

AMERICAN
SAMOA
(to US)

VANUATU

ONIA
ance)

FIJI

TONGA

COOK
ISLANDS
(to NZ)

FRENCH POLYNESIA
(to France)

BOLIVIA

PARAGUAY

Tropic of Capricorn

NIUE (to NZ)

A ISLANDS
ralia)

NORFOLK ISLAND
(to Australia)

Lord Howe Island
(to Australia)

PITCAIRN,
HENDERSON,
DUCIE & OENO
ISLANDS
(to UK)

Easter Island
(to Chile)

San Felix Island
(to Chile)

Sala y Gomez
(to Chile)

San Ambrosia
Island
(to Chile)

CHILE

A
R
G
E
N
T
I
N
A

URUGUAY

Juan Fernandez Island
(to Chile)

NEW
ZEALAND

Chatham Island
(to NZ)

P A C I F I C

O C E A N

Bounty Island
(to NZ)

FALKLAND ISLANDS
(to UK)

Campbell Island
(to NZ)

Macquarie Island (to Australia)

CHILE

SOUTH GEORGIA &
SOUTH SANDWICH ISLANDS
(to UK)

ABBREVIATIONS: AFGH. Afghanistan, ALB. Albania, AUT. Austria,
AZ. or AZERB. Azerbaijan, BELG. Belgium, BELA. Belarus,
B.&H. Bosnia & Herzegovina, BOTS. Botswana, BULG. Bulgaria,
CAMB. Cambodia, C.A.R. Central African Republic, CRO. Croatia,
DOM. REP. Dominican Republic, EST. Estonia, HUNG. Hungary,
KOS. Kosovo, KYRG. Kyrgyzstan, LAT. Latvia, LIECH. Liechtenstein,
LITH. Lithuania, LUX. Luxembourg,

MOLD. Moldova, MON. Montenegro, NETH. Netherlands,
PORT. Portugal, ROM. Romania, S.M. San Marino,
SLVK. Slovakia, SLVN. Slovenia, SWITZ. Switzerland,
THAI. Thailand, TURKMEN. Turkmenistan,
U.A.E. United Arab Emirates, UZBEK. Uzbekistan,
VAT. CITY Vatican City, ZIMB. Zimbabwe.

Antarctic Circle

ANTARCTICA

1
2
3
4
5

The Physical World

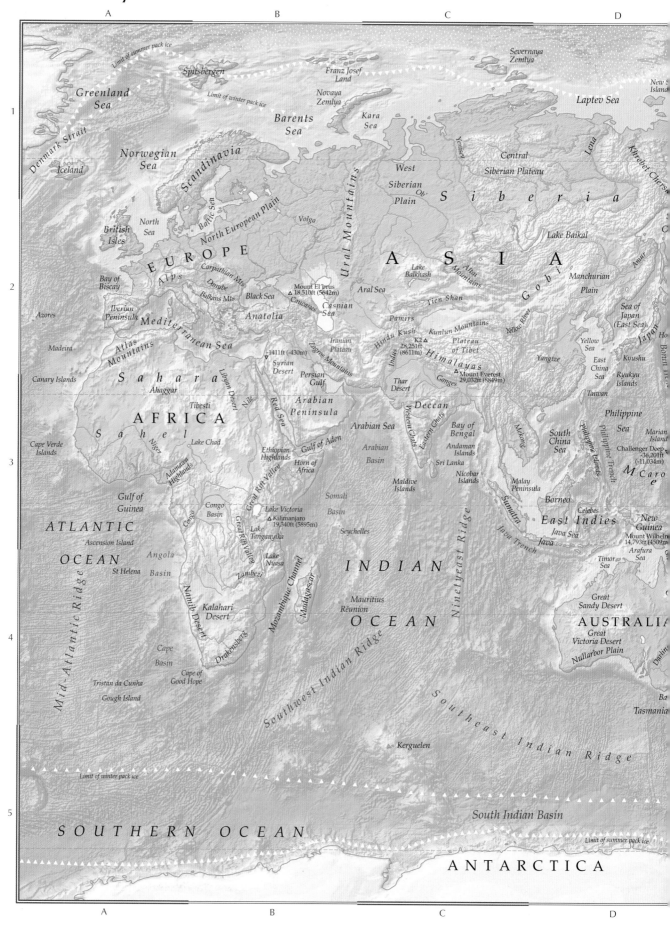

Greenland Sea

Denmark Strait

Iceland

Limit of summer pack ice

Spitsbergen

Limit of winter pack ice

Franz Josef Land

Novaya Zemlya

Severnaya Zemlya

New S Island

Laptev Sea

Norwegian Sea

Scandinavia

Barents Sea

Kara Sea

Lena

Central Siberian Plateau

Khrebet Chers

British Isles

North Sea

Baltic Sea

North European Plain

West Siberian Plain

Volga

Ob-

S i b e r i a

A S I A

Lake Baikal

Bay of Biscay

E U R O P E

Carpathian Mts

Danube

Balkans Mts

Alps

Black Sea

Mount El'brus 18,510ft (5642m)

Caucasus

Aral Sea

Lake Balkhash

Altai Mountains

Manchurian Plain

Amur

G o b i

Azores

Iberian Peninsula

Anatolia

Caspian Sea

Pamirs

Tien Shan

Sea of Japan (East Sea)

Madeira

Atlas Mountains

Mediterranean Sea

Iranian Plateau

Zagros Mountains

Hindu Kush

Kunlun Mountains

Plateau of Tibet

Yellow River

Yellow Sea

Japan

Canary Islands

S a h a r a

Ahaggar

-1411ft (-430m)

Syrian Desert

Libyan Desert

Persian Gulf

K2 28,251ft (8611m)

Indus

Himalayas

Mount Everest 29,032ft (8849m)

Ganges

Yangtze

East China Sea

Ryukyu Islands

Kyushu

Bonin Tre

Tibesti

A F R I C A

Nile

Red Sea

Arabian Peninsula

Thar Desert

Deccan

Taiwan

S a h e l

Niger

Lake Chad

Arabian Sea

Western Ghats

Eastern Ghats

Bay of Bengal

Andaman Islands

Mekong

South China Sea

Philippine Islands

Philippine Sea

Philippine Trench

Marian Island

Cape Verde Islands

Ethiopian Highlands

Gulf of Aden

Horn of Africa

Arabian Basin

Sri Lanka

Nicobar Islands

Malay Peninsula

Challenger Deep -36,201ft (-11,034m)

M C a r o

Gulf of Guinea

Adamawa Highlands

Congo

Great Rift Valley

Lake Victoria

Kilimanjaro 19,340ft (5895m)

Maldive Islands

Somali Basin

Borneo

Sumatra

Celebes

Java Sea

East Indies

New Guinea

ATLANTIC OCEAN

Ascension Island

Congo Basin

Lake Tanganyika

Seychelles

Java Trench

Java

Mount Wilhelm 14,793ft (4509m)

St Helena

Angola Basin

Lake Nyasa

I N D I A N

Timor Sea

Arafura Sea

Mid-Atlantic Ridge

Namib Desert

Zambezi

Mozambique Channel

Madagascar

O C E A N

Mauritius Réunion

Ninetyeast Ridge

Great Sandy Desert

AUSTRALIA

Cape Basin

Kalahari Desert

Drakensberg

Great Victoria Desert

Nullarbor Plain

Tristan da Cunha

Cape of Good Hope

Southwest Indian Ridge

Southeast Indian Ridge

Ba

Gough Island

Tasmania

Limit of winter pack ice

Kerguelen

South Indian Basin

Limit of summer pack ice

S O U T H E R N   O C E A N

A N T A R C T I C A

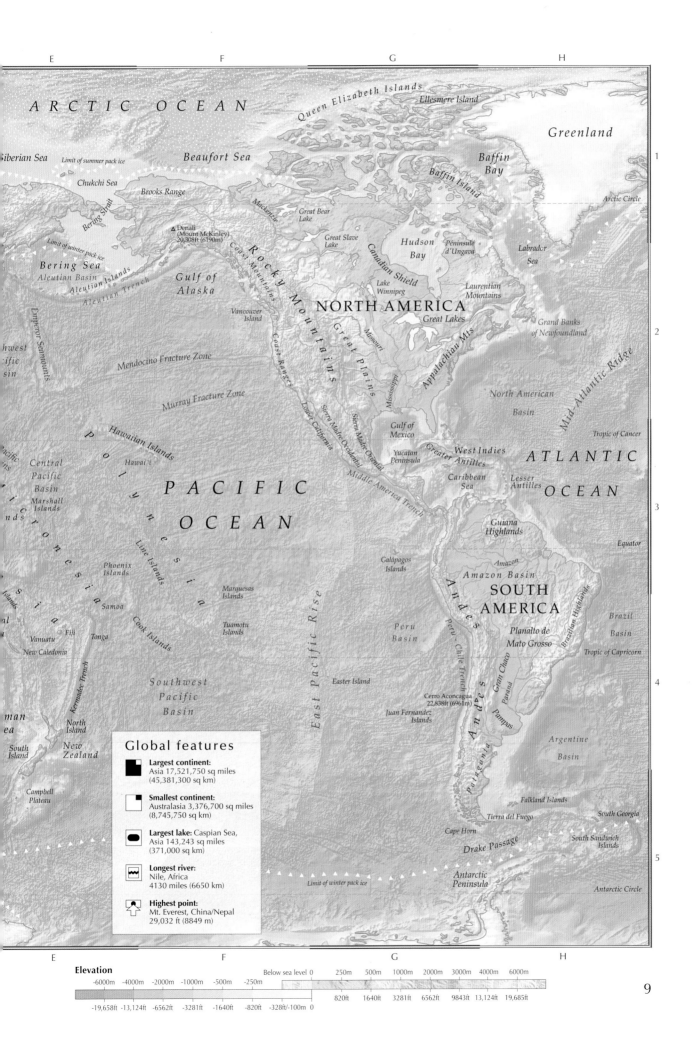

E   F   G   H

ARCTIC OCEAN

Siberian Sea   Limit of summer pack ice   *Beaufort Sea*   Queen Elizabeth Islands   Ellesmere Island

Greenland

1

Chukchi Sea   *Brooks Range*   *Baffin Island*   *Baffin Bay*

Mackenzie   Arctic Circle

Bering Strait   △ Denali   *Great Bear Lake*   Péninsule d'Ungava   *Labrador Sea*
     (Mount McKinley) 20,308ft (6190m)

Limit of winter pack ice   *Great Slave Lake*   *Hudson Bay*

Bering Sea   *Gulf of Alaska*   *Canadian Shield*

Aleutian Basin   *Laurentian Mountains*

Aleutian Islands   Aleutian Trench   *Vancouver Island*   *Lake Winnipeg*   *Grand Banks of Newfoundland*

Emperor Seamounts   **NORTH AMERICA**   *Great Lakes*

2

hwest ific sin   *Mendocino Fracture Zone*   Missouri   Appalachian Mts   *North American Basin*

Murray Fracture Zone   Mississippi   Mid-Atlantic Ridge

Hawaiian Islands   Sierra Madre Occidental   *Gulf of Mexico*   Tropic of Cancer

Central Pacific Basin   Hawai'i   Sierra Madre Oriental   Yucatan Peninsula   Greater Antilles   *West Indies*   **ATLANTIC**

Marshall Islands   *PACIFIC*   *Lower California*   *Caribbean Sea*   Lesser Antilles   **OCEAN**

3

nds   *P o l y n e s i a*   *OCEAN*   Middle America Trench   *Guiana Highlands*

Equator

Phoenix Islands   Line Islands   *Galápagos Islands*   Amazon   *Amazon Basin*

Marquesas Islands   **SOUTH AMERICA**   *Brazil Basin*

Samoa   *Peru Basin*   Andes   *Planalto de Mato Grosso*   *Brazil*

Vanuatu   Tonga   Cook Islands   *Tuamotu Islands*   Peru-Chile Trench   Brazilian Highlands   Tropic of Capricorn

Fiji   *New Caledonia*   *Southwest Pacific Basin*   *East Pacific Rise*   Easter Island   Gran Chaco   Paraná   *Argentine Basin*

4

man ea   Kermadec Trench   *North Island*   Cerro Aconcagua 22,838ft (6961m)   Pampas

South Island   *New Zealand*   Juan Fernandez Islands   Patagonia

Campbell Plateau   Falkland Islands

Global features

■ **Largest continent:**
Asia 17,521,750 sq miles
(45,381,300 sq km)

□ **Smallest continent:**
Australasia 3,376,700 sq miles
(8,745,750 sq km)

● **Largest lake:** Caspian Sea,
Asia 143,243 sq miles
(371,000 sq km)

〰 **Longest river:**
Nile, Africa
4130 miles (6650 km)

⊼ **Highest point:**
Mt. Everest, China/Nepal
29,032 ft (8849 m)

Tierra del Fuego   South Georgia

Cape Horn   South Sandwich Islands

Drake Passage

5

Limit of winter pack ice   *Antarctic Peninsula*   Antarctic Circle

E   F   G   H

Elevation

-6000m   -4000m   -2000m   -1000m   -500m   -250m   Below sea level 0   250m   500m   1000m   2000m   3000m   4000m   6000m

-19,658ft   -13,124ft   -6562ft   -3281ft   -1640ft   -820ft   -328ft/-100m   0   820ft   1640ft   3281ft   6562ft   9843ft   13,124ft   19,685ft

Standard Time Zones

The numbers at the top of the map indicate how many hours each time zone is ahead or behind Coordinated Universal Time (UTC). The row of clocks indicate the time in each zone when it is 12:00 noon UTC.

TIME ZONES

Because Earth is a rotating sphere, the Sun shines on only half of its surface at any one time. Thus, it is simultaneously morning, evening, and night time in different parts of the world. Because of these disparities, each country or part of a country adheres to a local time. A region of the Earth's surface within which a single local time is used is called a time zone.

COORDINATED UNIVERSAL TIME (UTC)

Coordinated Universal Time (UTC) is a reference by which the local time in each time zone is set. UTC is a successor to, and closely approximates, Greenwich Mean Time (GMT). However, UTC is based on an atomic clock, whereas GMT is determined by the Sun's position in the sky relative to the 0° longitudinal meridian, which runs through Greenwich, UK.

THE INTERNATIONAL DATELINE

The International Dateline is an imaginary line from pole to pole that roughly corresponds to the 180° longitudinal meridian. It is an arbitrary marker between calendar days. The dateline is needed because of the use of local times around the world rather than a single universal time.

The
WORLD
ATLAS

THE MAPS IN THIS ATLAS ARE ARRANGED CONTINENT BY CONTINENT, STARTING FROM THE
INTERNATIONAL DATE LINE, AND MOVING EASTWARD. THE MAPS PROVIDE A UNIQUE VIEW
OF TODAY'S WORLD, COMBINING TRADITIONAL CARTOGRAPHIC TECHNIQUES WITH THE
LATEST REMOTE-SENSED AND DIGITAL TECHNOLOGY.

North & Central America

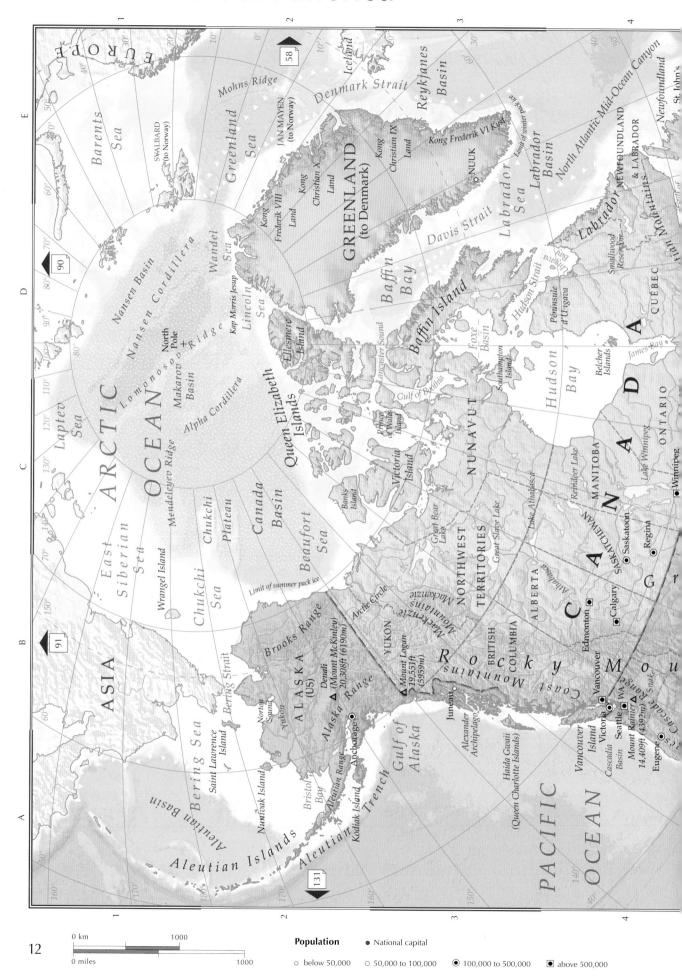

EUROPE

Barents Sea

SVALBARD (to Norway)

Mohns Ridge

Greenland Sea

JAN MAYEN (to Norway)

Iceland

Denmark Strait

Reykjanes Basin

Nansen Basin

Nansen Cordillera

Wandel Sea

Kong Frederik VIII Land

Kong Christian X Land

Kong Christian IX Land

Kong Frederik VI Kyst

North Atlantic Mid-Ocean Canyon

Newfoundland

St. John's

NUUK

GREENLAND (to Denmark)

NEWFOUNDLAND & LABRADOR

North Pole

Makarov Basin

Kap Morris Jesup

Lincoln Sea

Labrador Sea

Labrador Basin

Labrador

Alpha Cordillera

Queen Elizabeth Islands

Ellesmere Island

Baffin Bay

Baffin Island

Davis Strait

Smallwood Reservoir

QUÉBEC

Laptev Sea

East Siberian Sea

Wrangel Island

Chukchi Sea

Chukchi Plateau

Canada Basin

Beaufort Sea

Banks Island

Victoria Island

Prince of Wales Island

Lancaster Sound

Gulf of Boothia

Foxe Basin

Southampton Island

Péninsule d'Ungava

Hudson Bay

Belcher Islands

James Bay

Ungava Bay

ONTARIO

Reindeer Lake

Lake Winnipeg

Winnipeg

MANITOBA

Saskatoon

Regina

SASKATCHEWAN

Lake Athabasca

Great Slave Lake

Great Bear Lake

NUNAVUT

NORTHWEST TERRITORIES

Athabasca

ALBERTA

CANADA

Edmonton

Calgary

Mendeleyev Ridge

Limit of summer pack ice

ARCTIC OCEAN

ASIA

Bering Sea

Saint Lawrence Island

Nunivak Island

Norton Sound

Bristol Bay

Yukon

Arctic Circle

Brooks Range

ALASKA (US)

Alaska Range

Denali (Mount McKinley) 20,308ft (6190m)

Mackenzie Mountains

Mackenzie

BRITISH COLUMBIA

Rocky Mountains

Coast Mountains

Mount Logan 19,551ft (5959m)

YUKON

Juneau

Alexander Archipelago

Haida Gwaii (Queen Charlotte Islands)

Cascadia Basin

Vancouver Island

Victoria

Seattle WA

Mount Rainier 14,409ft (4392m)

Eugene

Cascade Range

Snake

Coast Ranges

Aleutian Range

Anchorage

Kodiak Island

Gulf of Alaska

Aleutian Trench

Aleutian Islands

Aleutian Basin

Bering Strait

PACIFIC OCEAN

Mou

Gr

58

90

91

131

0 km   1000

0 miles   1000

Population   ● National capital

○ below 50,000   ○ 50,000 to 100,000   ◉ 100,000 to 500,000   ◼ above 500,000

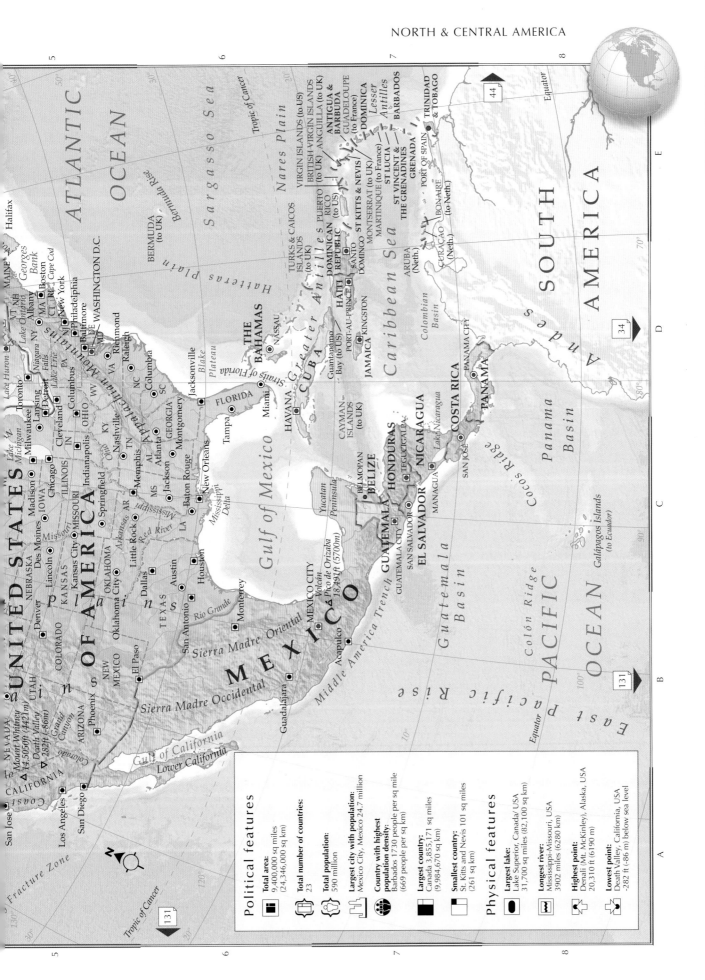

Political features

Total area:
9,400,000 sq miles
(24,346,000 sq km)

Total number of countries:
23

Total population:
590 million

Largest city with population:
Mexico City, Mexico 24.7 million

**Country with highest
population density:**
Barbados 1730 people per sq mile
(669 people per sq km)

Largest country:
Canada 3,855,171 sq miles
(9,984,670 sq km)

Smallest country:
St. Kitts and Nevis 101 sq miles
(261 sq km)

Physical features

Largest lake:
Lake Superior, Canada/ USA
31,700 sq miles (82,100 sq km)

Longest river:
Mississippi-Missouri, USA
3902 miles (6280 km)

Highest point:
Denali (Mt. McKinley), Alaska, USA
20,310 ft (6190 m)

Lowest point:
Death Valley, California, USA
-282 ft (-86 m) below sea level

Western Canada & Alaska

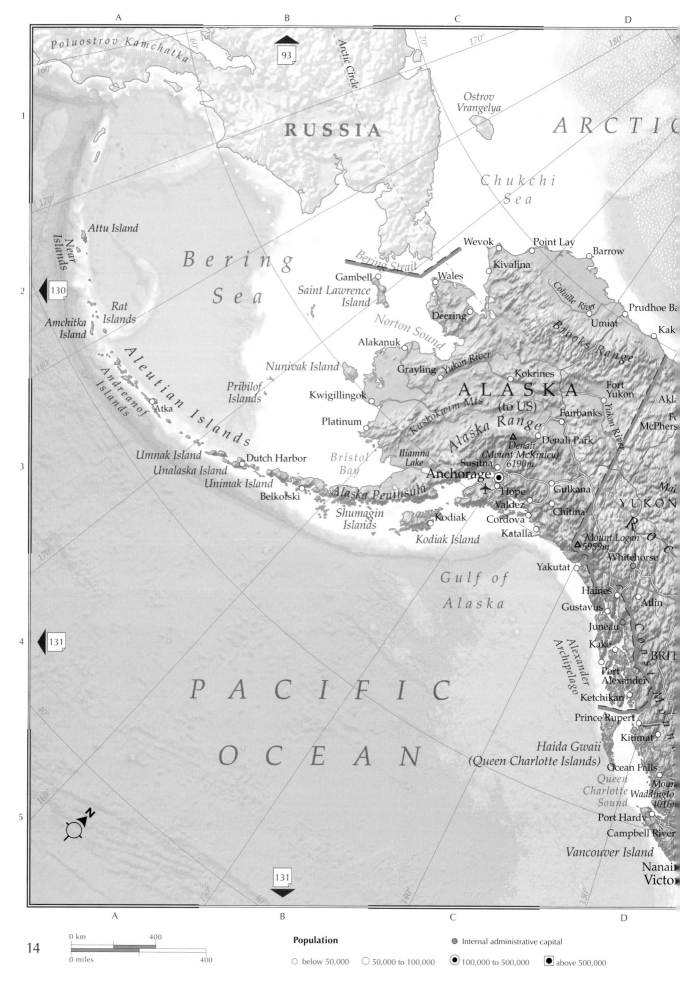

poluostrov Kamchatka

RUSSIA

Arctic Circle

Ostrov Vrangelya

A R C T I C

Chukchi Sea

Near Islands

Attu Island

Bering Sea

Rat Islands

Amchitka Island

Aleutian Islands

Andreanof Islands

Atka

Wevok
Point Lay
Barrow
Kivalina
Gambell
Wales
Deering
Bering Strait
Coville River
Umiat
Prudhoe Ba
Kak
Brooks Range

Saint Lawrence Island

Norton Sound

Alakanuk

Grayling *Yukon River*
Kokrines
Fort Yukon
Akla

Nunivak Island

Pribilof Islands

Kwigillingok

Platinum

Kuskokwim Mts

A L A S K A
(to US)

Fairbanks
Yukon River
McPhers
Fo

Alaska Range

Denali Park
△ *Denali (Mount McKinley) 6190m*

Bristol Bay

Iliamna Lake

Susita

Anchorage

Hope
Valdez
Cordova
Katalla
Gulkana
Chitina

Mau

YUKON

R O C

Alaska Peninsula

Shumagin Islands

Kodiak

Kodiak Island

△ *Mount Logan 5959m*

Whitehorse

Umnak Island
Unalaska Island
Unimak Island
Dutch Harbor
Belkofski

Yakutat

Gulf of Alaska

Haines
Gustavus
Juneau
Kake
Atlin

Alexander Archipelago

Consta

BRIT

Port Alexander
Ketchikan

Prince Rupert

P A C I F I C

O C E A N

Haida Gwaii (Queen Charlotte Islands)

Queen Charlotte Sound

Kitimat

Ocean Falls

Moun Wadd 4016

Port Hardy
Campbell River

Vancouver Island

Nanai
Victor

93
130
131
131

Population

○ below 50,000   ○ 50,000 to 100,000   ◉ 100,000 to 500,000   ■ above 500,000

● Internal administrative capital

0 km   400
0 miles   400

14

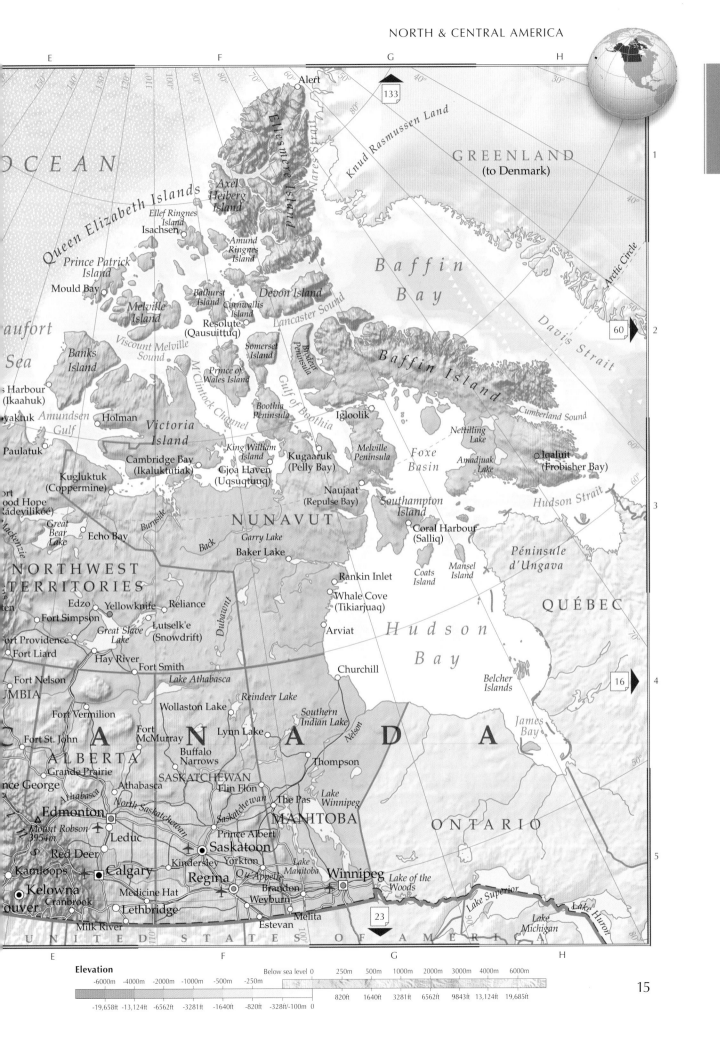

GREENLAND
(to Denmark)

*Baffin
Bay*

Knud Rasmussen Land

Alert

Ellesmere Island

Queen Elizabeth Islands

*Axel
Heiberg
Island*

Ellef Ringnes
Island
Isachsen

*Amund
Ringnes
Island*

Prince Patrick
Island

Mould Bay

*Bathurst
Island*
Cornwallis
Island

Devon Island

Lancaster Sound

*Melville
Island*

Resolute
(Qausuittuq)

*Viscount Melville
Sound*

Banks
Island

Somerset
Island

*Brodeur
Peninsula*

Baffin Island

Cumberland Sound

s Harbour
(Ikaahuk)

M'Clintock Channel

*Prince of
Wales Island*

Gulf of Boothia

Davis Strait

Arctic Circle

yaktuk
*Amundsen
Gulf*

Holman

*Victoria
Island*

*Boothia
Peninsula*

Igloolik

*Nettilling
Lake*

Paulatuk

King William
Island

Kugaaruk
(Pelly Bay)

*Melville
Peninsula*

*Foxe
Basin*

*Amadjuak
Lake*

Iqaluit
(Frobisher Bay)

Cambridge Bay
(Ikaluktutiak)

Gjoa Haven
(Uqsuqtuuq)

Kugluktuk
(Coppermine)

ort
ood Hope
Rádeyilikóé)

Naujaat
(Repulse Bay)

*Southampton
Island*

Hudson Strait

*Péninsule
d'Ungava*

*Great
Bear
Lake*

Echo Bay

Burnside

N U N A V U T

Coral Harbour
(Salliq)

Mackenzie

Back

Garry Lake

Baker Lake

*Coats
Island*

*Mansel
Island*

QUÉBEC

N O R T H W E S T
E R R I T O R I E S

Rankin Inlet

ten

Edzo

Yellowknife

Reliance

Dubawnt

Whale Cove
(Tikiarjuaq)

Fort Simpson

*Great Slave
Lake*

Lutselk'e
(Snowdrift)

Arviat

*H u d s o n
B a y*

ort Providence

Fort Liard

Hay River

Fort Smith

Churchill

*Belcher
Islands*

Fort Nelson

Lake Athabasca

*James
Bay*

MBIA

Reindeer Lake

Fort St. John

Fort Vermilion

Wollaston Lake

Nelson

Fort
McMurray

Lynn Lake

C A N A D A

*Southern
Indian Lake*

ALBERTA

Buffalo
Narrows

Grande Prairie

Thompson

O N T A R I O

nce George

Athabasca

SASKATCHEWAN

Flin Flon

*Lake
Winnipeg*

Athabasca

△Edmonton

North Saskatchewan

The Pas

Mount Robson
3954m

Leduc

Saskatchewan

MANITOBA

Prince Albert

Red Deer

Saskatoon

Kamloops

Calgary

Kindersley

Yorkton

*Lake
Manitoba*

Winnipeg

*Lake of the
Woods*

Kelowna

Medicine Hat

Regina

Qu'Appelle

Brandon

Lake Superior

ouver

Cranbrook

Lethbridge

Weyburn

Melita

*Lake
Michigan*

Lake Huron

Milk River

Estevan

U N I T E D   S T A T E S   O F   A M E R I C A

O C E A N

*aufort
Sea*

Elevation

							Below sea level 0	250m	500m	1000m	2000m	3000m	4000m	6000m

-6000m -4000m -2000m -1000m -500m -250m

820ft 1640ft 3281ft 6562ft 9843ft 13,124ft 19,685ft

-19,658ft -13,124ft -6562ft -3281ft -1640ft -820ft -328ft/-100m 0

Eastern Canada

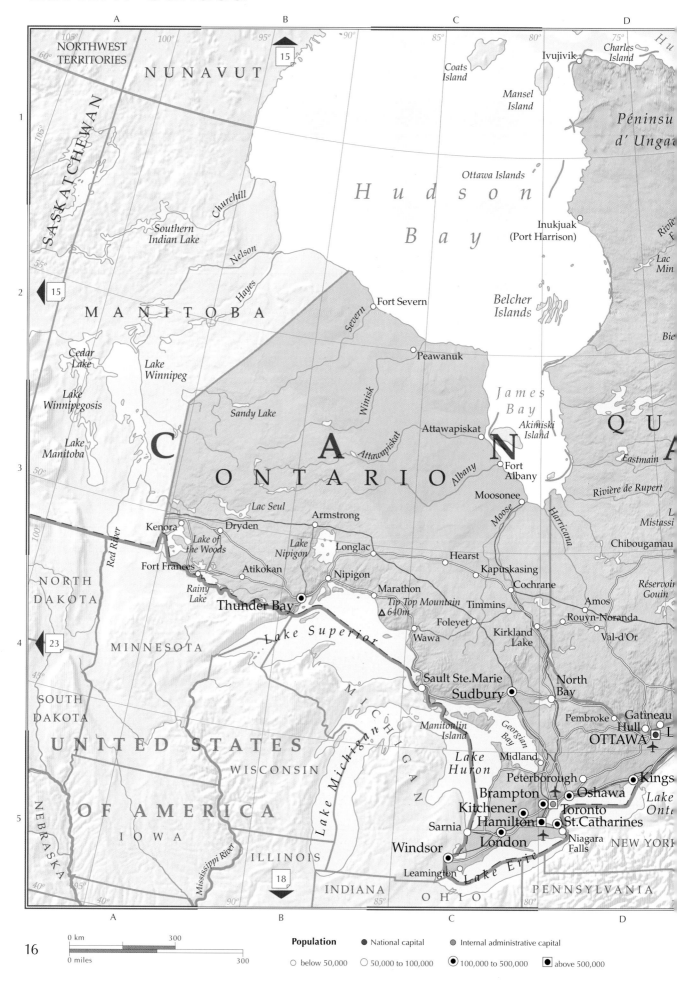

NORTHWEST TERRITORIES

N U N A V U T

S A S K A T C H E W A N

M A N I T O B A

Churchill

Southern Indian Lake

Nelson

Hayes

Cedar Lake

Lake Winnipeg

Lake Winnipegosis

Lake Manitoba

C

Sandy Lake

O N T A R I O

Lac Seul

Kenora

Dryden

Lake of the Woods

Red River

Fort Frances

Atikokan

Rainy Lake

N O R T H D A K O T A

M I N N E S O T A

S O U T H D A K O T A

Armstrong

Lake Nipigon

Longlac

Nipigon

Thunder Bay

Lake Superior

Marathon

Tip Top Mountain △640m

Foleyet

Wawa

M I C H I G A N

Sault Ste.Marie

Sudbury

Manitoulin Island

Georgian Bay

North Bay

Pembroke

Lake Michigan

U N I T E D   S T A T E S

O F   A M E R I C A

W I S C O N S I N

I O W A

N E B R A S K A

Mississippi River

I L L I N O I S

I N D I A N A

Leamington

Windsor

Lake Huron

Midland

Peterborough

Brampton

Kitchener

Sarnia

Hamilton

London

Lake Erie

Toronto

Oshawa

St.Catharines

Niagara Falls

Kings

Lake Onte

NEW YORK

PENNSYLVANIA

O H I O

Hudson

Charles Island

Ivujivik

Coats Island

Mansel Island

Péninsu d' Unga

Ottawa Islands

H u d s o n

B a y

Inukjuak (Port Harrison)

Rivié F

Lac Min

Fort Severn

Severn

Peawanuk

Winisk

Belcher Islands

Bie

A

N

Attawapiskat

Attawapiskat

J a m e s Bay

Akimiski Island

Fort Albany

Albany

Moosonee

Moose

Harricana

Hearst

Kapuskasing

Cochrane

Timmins

Kirkland Lake

Amos

Rouyn-Noranda

Val-d'Or

Q U

A

Eastmain

Rivière de Rupert

Chibougamau

Mistassi

Réservoir Gouin

Gatineau

Hull

OTTAWA

Population

● National capital   ● Internal administrative capital

○ below 50,000   ○ 50,000 to 100,000   ◉ 100,000 to 500,000   ◼ above 500,000

0 km   300

0 miles   300

USA: The Northeast

0 km   200

0 miles   200

Population · National capital · Internal administrative capital

○ below 50,000 ○ 50,000 to 100,000 ◉ 100,000 to 500,000 ◼ above 500,000

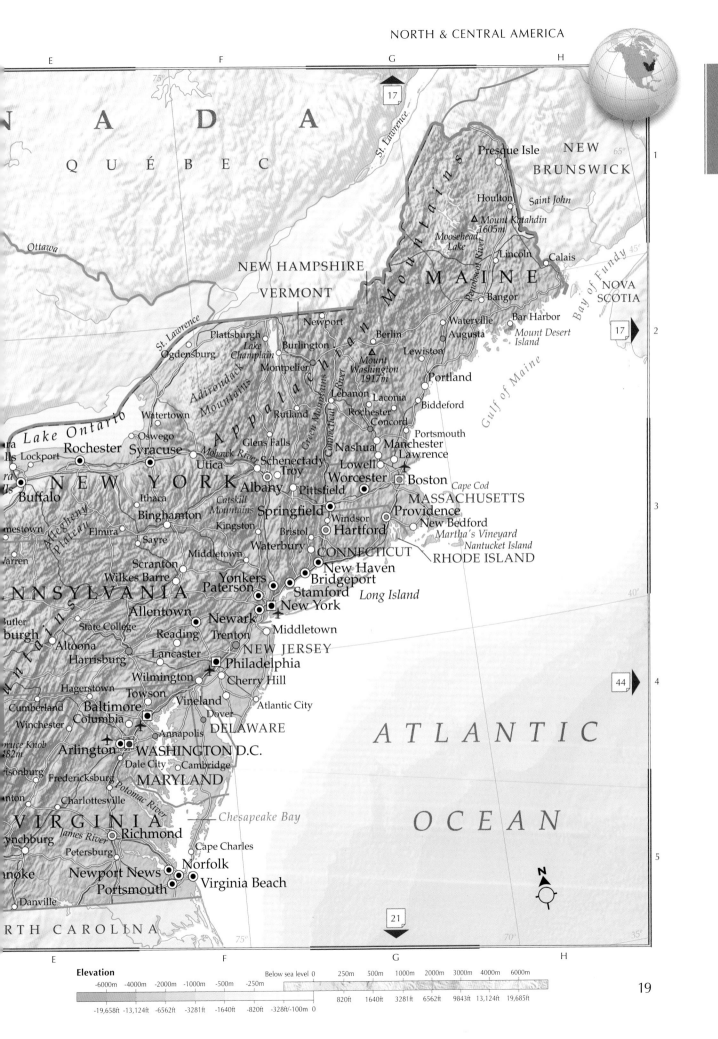

E   F   G   H

17

CANADA

QUÉBEC

1

NEW BRUNSWICK

Ottawa

St. Lawrence

Presque Isle

Houlton   Saint John

△ Mount Katahdin
1605m

Moosehead
Lake

Lincoln   Calais

NOVA
SCOTIA

Bay of Fundy

NEW HAMPSHIRE

VERMONT

Newport

Berlin

Waterville   Bar Harbor

Augusta

Bangor

MAINE

Plattsburgh

Burlington

Mount
Washington
1917m

Lewiston

Mount Desert
Island

2

St. Lawrence

Ogdensburg

Lake
Champlain

Montpelier

Lebanon

Laconia

Portland

Biddeford

Gulf of Maine

Adirondack
Mountains

Rutland

Rochester

Concord

Portsmouth

Watertown

Glens Falls

Nashua

Manchester

Oswego

Utica

Schenectady

Lowell

Lawrence

Appalachian Mountains

Green Mountains

Connecticut River

Rochester   Syracuse

Mohawk River

Troy

Worcester

Boston

Cape Cod

3

Buffalo

NEW YORK

Albany

Pittsfield

MASSACHUSETTS

Lockport

Ithaca

Catskill
Mountains

Springfield

Windsor

Providence

New Bedford

Binghamton

Kingston

Bristol

Hartford

Martha's Vineyard

Elmira

Sayre

Waterbury

CONNECTICUT

Nantucket Island

Allegheny
Plateau

Middletown

New Haven

RHODE ISLAND

Scranton

Yonkers

Bridgeport

Wilkes Barre

Paterson

Stamford

Long Island

40°

PENNSYLVANIA

Allentown

Newark

New York

Reading

Middletown

Altoona

Lancaster

Trenton

NEW JERSEY

Harrisburg

Philadelphia

44   4

Hagerstown

Wilmington

Cherry Hill

Cumberland

Towson

Vineland

Atlantic City

ATLANTIC

Winchester

Baltimore

Columbia

Dover

DELAWARE

Spruce Knob
482m

Arlington

Annapolis

WASHINGTON D.C.

Dale City   Cambridge

Fredericksburg

MARYLAND

Potomac River

Chesapeake Bay

OCEAN

VIRGINIA

Charlottesville

Richmond

James River

Cape Charles

5

Lynchburg

Petersburg

Roanoke

Newport News

Norfolk

Virginia Beach

Danville

Portsmouth

21

NORTH CAROLINA

75°   70°   35°

E   F   G   H

Elevation

| | | Below sea level 0 | 250m | 500m | 1000m | 2000m | 3000m | 4000m | 6000m |

-6000m   -4000m   -2000m   -1000m   -500m   -250m

820ft   1640ft   3281ft   6562ft   9843ft   13,124ft   19,685ft

-19,658ft   -13,124ft   -6562ft   -3281ft   -1640ft   -820ft   -328ft/-100m   0

USA: The Southeast

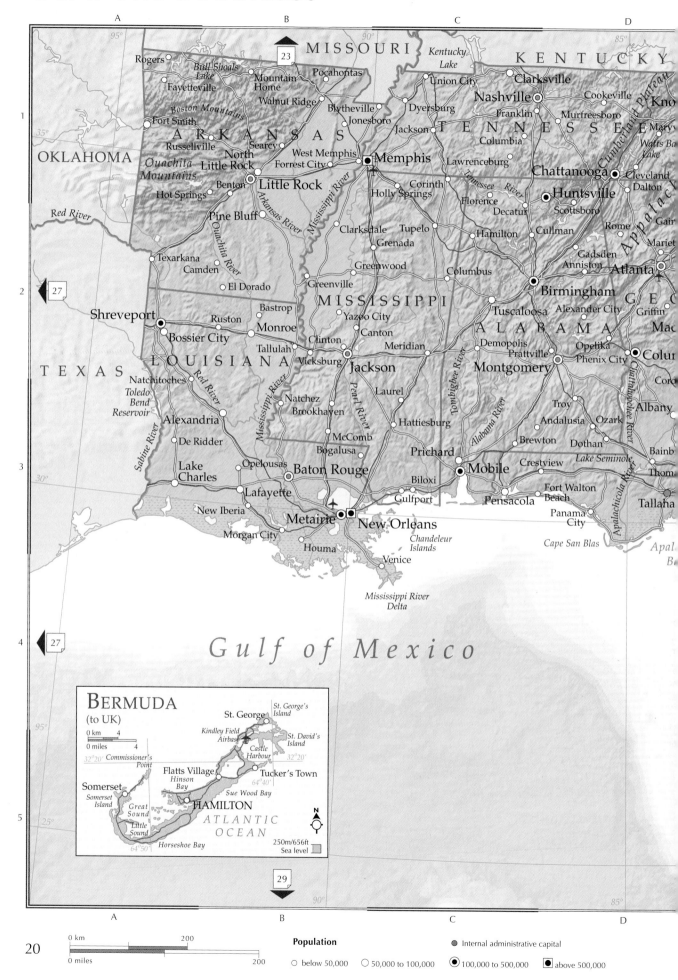

MISSOURI

KENTUCKY

Rogers
Bull Shoals Lake
Fayetteville
Mountain Home
Pocahontas
Walnut Ridge
Union City
Clarksville
Cookeville
Nashville
Knox
Blytheville
Dyersburg
Franklin
Murfreesboro
Boston Mountains
Jonesboro
Jackson
Fort Smith
Columbia
Mary
ARKANSAS
Watts Ba
Lake

OKLAHOMA
Russellville
Searcy
West Memphis
Memphis
Lawrenceburg
Ouachita Mountains
North Little Rock
Forrest City
Corinth
Chattanooga
Cleveland
Dalton
Benton
Little Rock
Holly Springs
Florence
Huntsville
Rome
Hot Springs
Clarksdale
Tupelo
Decatur
Scottsboro
Gai

Red River
Pine Bluff
Grenada
Hamilton
Cullman
Marie

Texarkana
Greenwood
Columbus
Gadsden
Anniston
Atlanta
Camden
Greenville
Birmingham
GEO
El Dorado
MISSISSIPPI
Tuscaloosa
Alexander City
Griffin

Shreveport
Bastrop
Yazoo City
Ala
Mac
Bossier City
Ruston
Monroe
Canton
ALABAMA
TEXAS
Tallulah
Clinton
Meridian
Demopolis
Opelika
Colu
LOUISIANA
Vicksburg
Jackson
Prattville
Phenix City
Cor
Natchitoches
Red River
Natchez
Laurel
Montgomery
Troy
Albany
Toledo Bend Reservoir
Brookhaven
Hattiesburg
Andalusia
Ozark
Alexandria
Dothan
Bain
De Ridder
McComb
Prichard
Brewton
Lake Seminole
Sabine River
Bogalusa
Mobile
Crestview
Thom
Lake Charles
Opelousas
Baton Rouge
Biloxi
Fort Walton Beach
Lafayette
Gulfport
Pensacola
Panama City
Talaha
New Iberia
Metairie
New Orleans
Morgan City
Houma
Chandeleur Islands
Cape San Blas
Apal
Venice
B

Gulf of Mexico

Mississippi River Delta

BERMUDA
(to UK)

0 km 4
0 miles 4

St. George's Island
St. George
St. David's Island
Kindley Field Airbase
Castle Harbour
Commissioner's Point
Flatts Village
Tucker's Town
Hinson Bay
Somerset
Sue Wood Bay
Somerset Island
Great Sound
HAMILTON
ATLANTIC OCEAN
Little Sound
Horseshoe Bay

N

250m/656ft
Sea level

0 km   200
0 miles   200

Population
○ below 50,000 ○ 50,000 to 100,000 ◉ 100,000 to 500,000 ◼ above 500,000
● Internal administrative capital

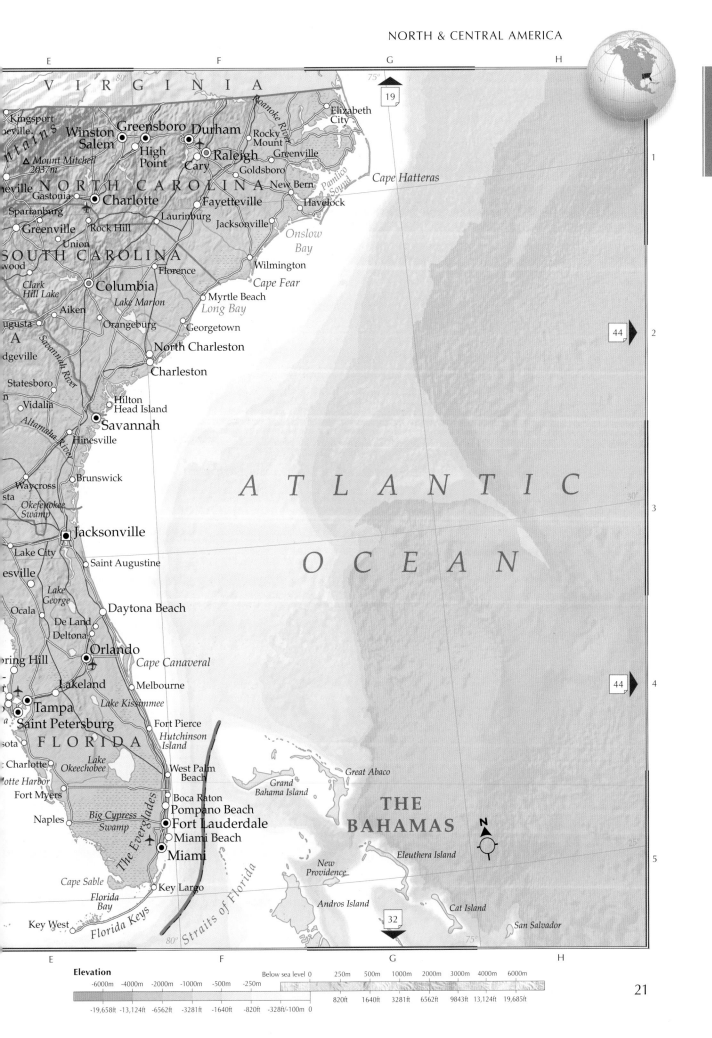

44

44

32

VIRGINIA

Kingsport
eville
Winston
Salem
Greensboro
Durham
Rocky
Mount
Elizabeth
City

High
Point
Raleigh
Greenville

△ Mount Mitchell
2037m
Cary
Goldsboro

NORTH CAROLINA
New Bern
Havelock
Cape Hatteras
Pamlico Sound

eville
Gastonia
Charlotte
Fayetteville

Spartanburg
Laurinburg
Jacksonville

Greenville
Rock Hill
Onslow
Bay

Union

SOUTH CAROLINA
Wilmington
Cape Fear

wood
Florence
Myrtle Beach

Clark
Hill Lake
Columbia
Long Bay

ugusta
Aiken
Lake Marion
Orangeburg
Georgetown

A
North Charleston

dgeville
Charleston

Statesboro

Vidalia
Hilton
Head Island

Savannah
Hinesville

Brunswick

ATLANTIC

Waycross
sta
Okefenokee
Swamp

Jacksonville

OCEAN

Lake City

esville
Saint Augustine

Lake
George

Ocala
Daytona Beach

De Land
Deltona

Orlando
Cape Canaveral

pring Hill

Lakeland
Melbourne

Tampa
Lake Kissimmee

Saint Petersburg

a
FLORIDA
Fort Pierce
Hutchinson
Island

sota

Charlotte
Lake
Okeechobee

otte Harbor
West Palm
Beach
Great Abaco

Fort Myers
Boca Raton
Grand
Bahama Island

Big Cypress
Swamp
Pompano Beach

Naples
Fort Lauderdale
THE

Miami Beach
BAHAMAS
N

Miami
New
Providence
Eleuthera Island

Cape Sable
Key Largo

Florida
Bay
Andros Island
Cat Island

Key West
San Salvador
Florida Keys
Straits of Florida

Altamaha River

Savannah River

Roanoke River

Elevation

Below sea level 0	250m	500m	1000m	2000m	3000m	4000m	6000m

-6000m -4000m -2000m -1000m -500m -250m

-19,658ft -13,124ft -6562ft -3281ft -1640ft -820ft -328ft/-100m 0

820ft 1640ft 3281ft 6562ft 9843ft 13,124ft 19,685ft

USA: Central States

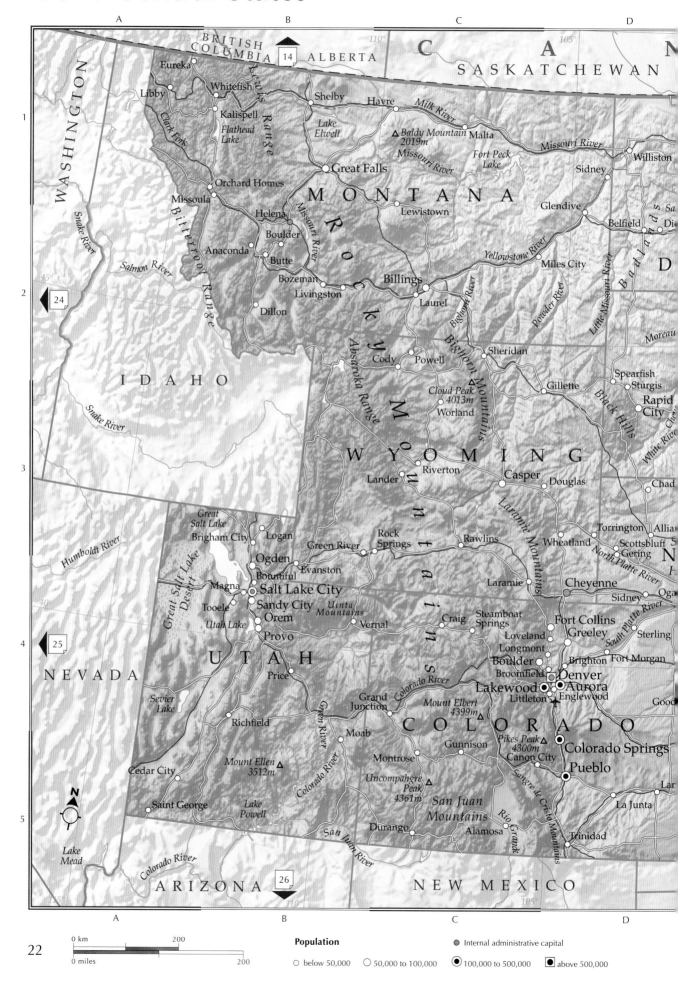

British Columbia · Alberta · CANADA · SASKATCHEWAN

Eureka
Libby
Whitefish
Kalispell
Shelby
Havre
Milk River
Lake Elwell
△ Baldy Mountain 2019m · Malta
Missouri River
Fort Peck Lake
Sidney
Williston
Flathead Lake
Lewis Range
Clark Fork
Orchard Homes
Great Falls
MONTANA
Lewistown
Glendive
Belfield
Di
Missoula
Helena
Boulder
Missouri River
Anaconda
Butte
Yellowstone River
Miles City
Little Missouri River
D
Bozeman
Livingston
Billings
Laurel
Powder River
Moreau
Dillon
Absaroka Range
Cody
Powell
Sheridan
Bighorn River
Bighorn Mountains
Spearfish
Sturgis
Cloud Peak 4013m △
Gillette
Rapid City
IDAHO
Worland
Black Hills
White Riv
Salmon River
Snake River
WYOMING
Mountains
Lander
Riverton
Casper
Douglas
Chad
Laramie Mountains
Torrington
Allia
North Platte River
Great Salt Lake
Logan
Rock Springs
Rawlins
Wheatland
Scottsbluff
Gering
N
Brigham City
Green River
Humboldt River
Ogden
Evanston
Laramie
Cheyenne
Oga
Bountiful
Uinta Mountains
Sidney
S Platte River
Magna
Salt Lake City
Craig
Steamboat Springs
Fort Collins
Greeley
Sterling
Great Salt Lake Desert
Sandy City
Orem
Vernal
Loveland
Longmont
South Platte River
Tooele
Utah Lake
Provo
Boulder
Brighton
Fort Morgan
Sevier Lake
Price
UTAH
Broomfield
Denver
Lakewood
Aurora
Littleton
Englewood
NEVADA
Colorado River
Grand Junction
Mount Elbert 4399m △
Good
Richfield
Moab
Pikes Peak △ 4300m
Colorado Springs
Mount Ellen 3512m △
COLORADO
Gunnison
Canon City
Pueblo
Green River
Montrose
Uncompahgre Peak 4361m △
Sangre de Cristo Mountains
Lar
Cedar City
Colorado River
San Juan Mountains
Rio Grande
La Junta
Saint George
Lake Powell
Durango
Alamosa
Trinidad
Lake Mead
San Juan River
Colorado River
ARIZONA
NEW MEXICO

0 km   200
0 miles   200

Population

○ below 50,000   ○ 50,000 to 100,000   ◉ 100,000 to 500,000   ■ above 500,000

● Internal administrative capital

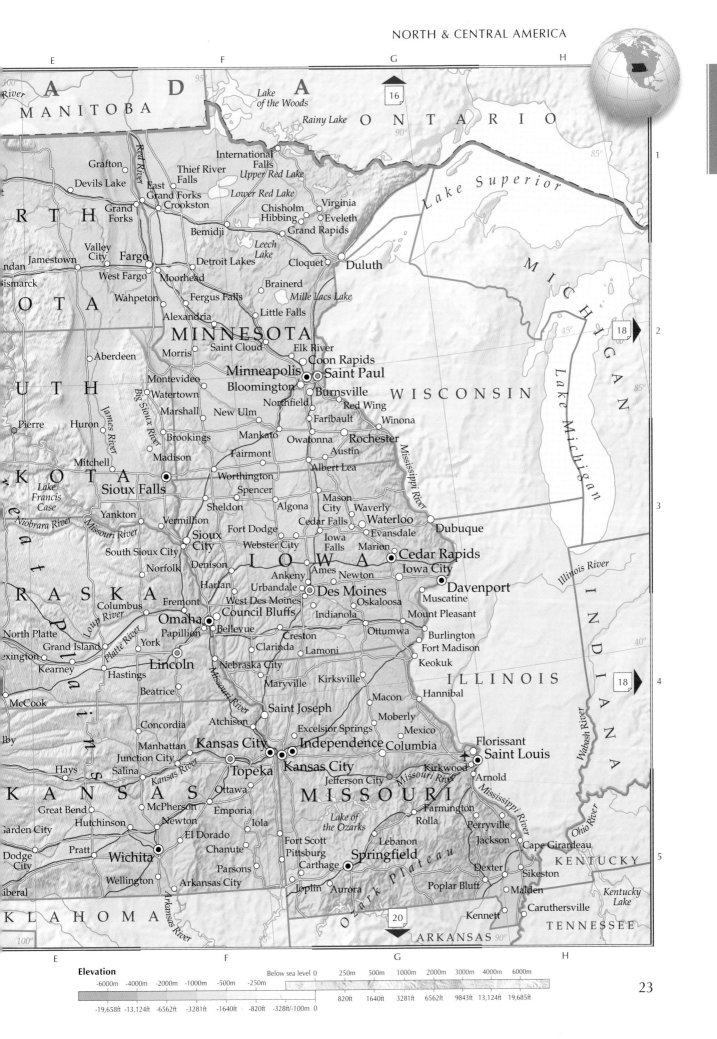

Elevation

USA: The West

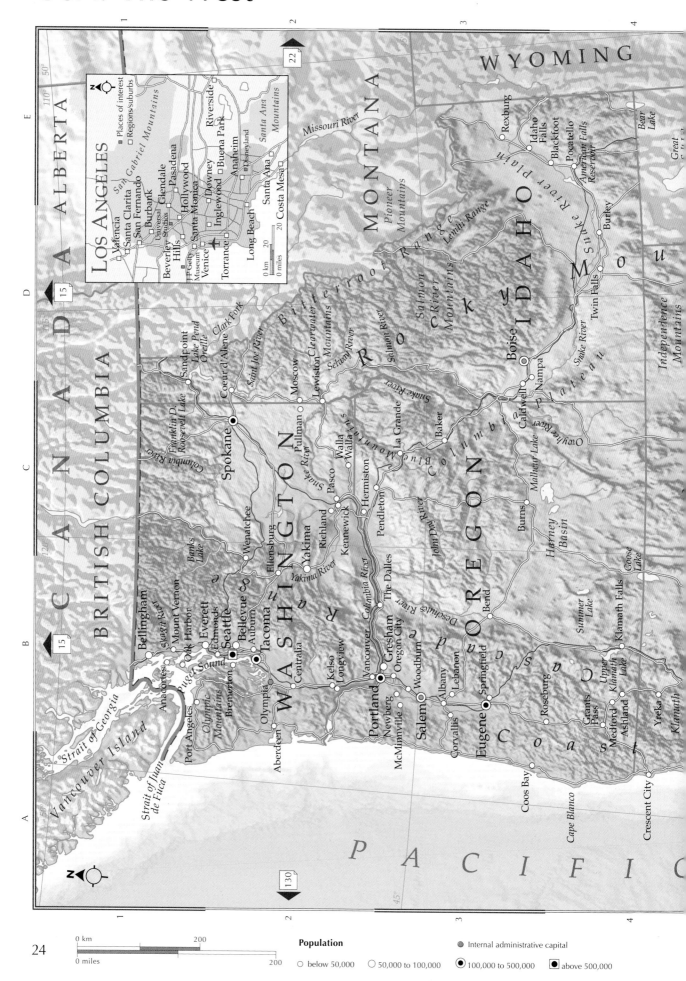

LOS ANGELES

Places of interest
Regions/suburbs

Valencia
Santa Clarita
San Fernando
Universal Studios
Burbank
Beverley Hills
P. Getty Museum
Venice
Santa Monica
Torrance
Glendale
Pasadena
Hollywood
Inglewood
Long Beach
Downey
Riverside
Buena Park
Anaheim
Disneyland
Santa Ana
Costa Mesa

San Gabriel Mountains
Santa Ana Mountains

WYOMING

MONTANA

IDAHO

Rexburg
Idaho Falls
Blackfoot
Pocatello
American Falls Reservoir
Burley
Twin Falls
Bear Lake
Great

Snake River Plain

Pioneer Mountains
Lemhi Range
Salmon River Mountains
Bitterroot Range
Clearwater Mountains
Selway River
Salmon River
Snake River

Rocky Mountains

Boise
Nampa
Caldwell
Malheur Lake
Independence Mountains

Missouri River

Sandpoint
Lake Pend Oreille
Clark Fork
Coeur d'Alene
Saint Joe River
Moscow
Lewiston
Pullman
Walla Walla
La Grande
Baker
Owyhee River
Burns
Harney Basin
Goose Lake

CANADA

ALBERTA

BRITISH COLUMBIA

Columbia River
Franklin D. Roosevelt Lake
Spokane
Banks Lake
Wenatchee
Ellensburg
Yakima
Yakima River
Snake River
Pasco
Richland
Kennewick
Hermiston
Pendleton
Blue Mountains
John Day River
Columbia Plateau

WASHINGTON

Bellingham
Skagit River
Mount Vernon
Oak Harbor
Everett
Edmonds
Anacortes
Puget Sound
Seattle
Bellevue
Auburn
Tacoma
Bremerton
Olympia
Centralia
Kelso
Longview
Vancouver
Columbia River
The Dalles
Deschutes River
Bend
Aberdeen

OREGON

Gresham
Oregon City
Portland
Newberg
McMinnville
Woodburn
Salem
Albany
Lebanon
Corvallis
Springfield
Eugene
Roseburg
Grants Pass
Medford
Ashland
Upper Klamath Lake
Klamath Falls
Summer Lake
Cascade Range

Olympic Mountains
Port Angeles
Strait of Juan de Fuca
Strait of Georgia
Vancouver Island

Coos Bay
Cape Blanco
Crescent City
Yreka
Klamath
Coast

PACIFIC

Population

○ below 50,000
○ 50,000 to 100,000
◉ 100,000 to 500,000
◼ above 500,000

● Internal administrative capital

0 km 200
0 miles 200

24

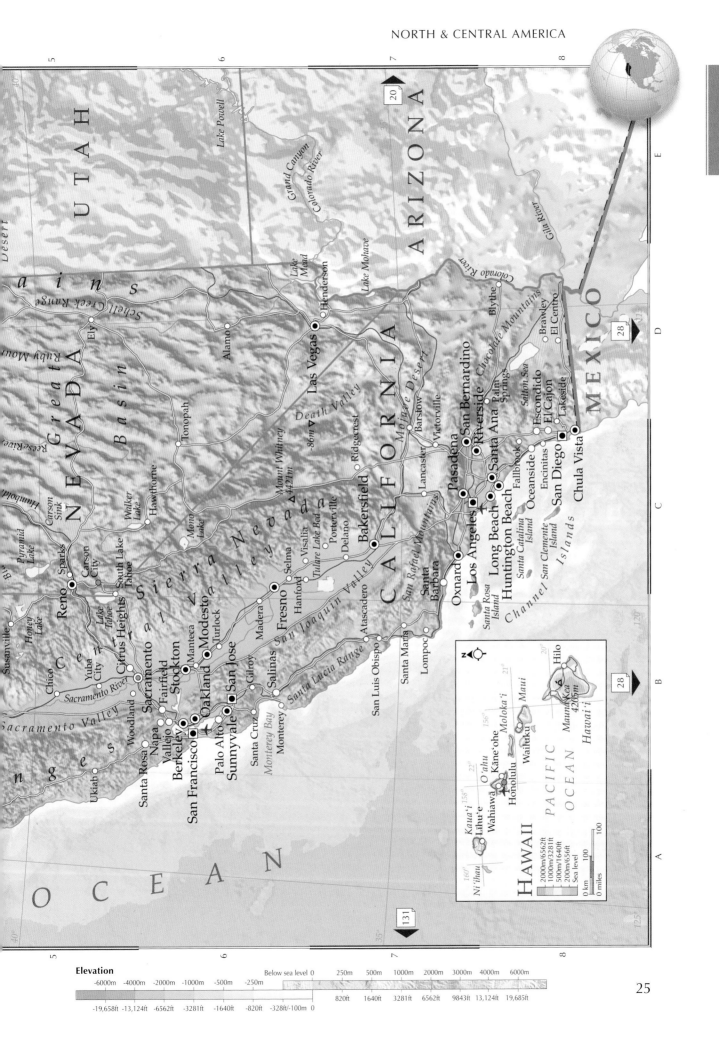

UTAH

Great Plains

Desert

Lake Powell

Grand Canyon

Colorado River

ARIZONA

Gila River

MEXICO

Schell Creek Range

Ruby Mountains

Ely

Alamo

Lake Mead

Henderson

Lake Mohave

Colorado River

Blythe

Chocolate Mountains

Brawley

El Centro

NEVADA

Great Basin

Reese River

Humboldt River

Tonopah

Death Valley -86m ▽

Mount Whitney △421m

Ridgecrest

Mojave Desert

Barstow

Victorville

Lancaster

San Bernardino

Riverside

Santa Ana

Palm Springs

Salton Sea

Escondido

El Cajon

Lakeside

San Diego

Chula Vista

CALIFORNIA

Pyramid Lake

Honey Lake

Susanville

Chico

Sacramento River

Sacramento Valley

Woodland

Ukiah

Santa Rosa

Napa

Vallejo

Fairfield

Berkeley

San Francisco

Palo Alto

Sunnyvale

Oakland

San Jose

Santa Cruz

Monterey Bay

Monterey

Salinas

Gilroy

Santa Lucia Range

San Luis Obispo

Santa Maria

Lompoc

San Rafael Mountains

Santa Barbara

Oxnard

Los Angeles

Pasadena

Long Beach

Huntington Beach

Fallbrook

Oceanside

Encinitas

Santa Catalina Island

San Clemente Island

Channel Islands

Santa Rosa Island

Carson Sink

Carson City

Reno

Sparks

South Lake Tahoe

Lake Tahoe

Citrus Heights

Sacramento

Stockton

Manteca

Modesto

Turlock

Madera

Fresno

Selma

Hanford

Visalia

Porterville

Delano

Tulare Lake Bed

Bakersfield

Atascadero

San Joaquin Valley

Central Valley

Sierra Nevada

Walker Lake

Hawthorne

Mono Lake

Chocolate Mountains

Yuba City

Sacramento Valley

Ranges

Reno

-86m ▽ Death Valley

OCEAN

Inset: HAWAII

Hilo

Mauna Kea 4205m

Hawai'i

Maui

Wailuku

Moloka'i

Kāne'ohe

O'ahu

Honolulu

Wahiawā

Kaua'i

Lihu'e

Ni'ihau

PACIFIC OCEAN

2000m/6562ft
1000m/3281ft
500m/1640ft
200m/656ft
Sea level

0 km 100
0 miles 100

Elevation

-6000m	-4000m	-2000m	-1000m	-500m	-250m	Below sea level 0	250m	500m	1000m	2000m	3000m	4000m	6000m	
-19,658ft	-13,124ft	-6562ft	-3281ft	-1640ft	-820ft	-328ft/-100m	0		820ft	1640ft	3281ft	6562ft	9843ft	13,124ft	19,685ft

USA: The Southwest

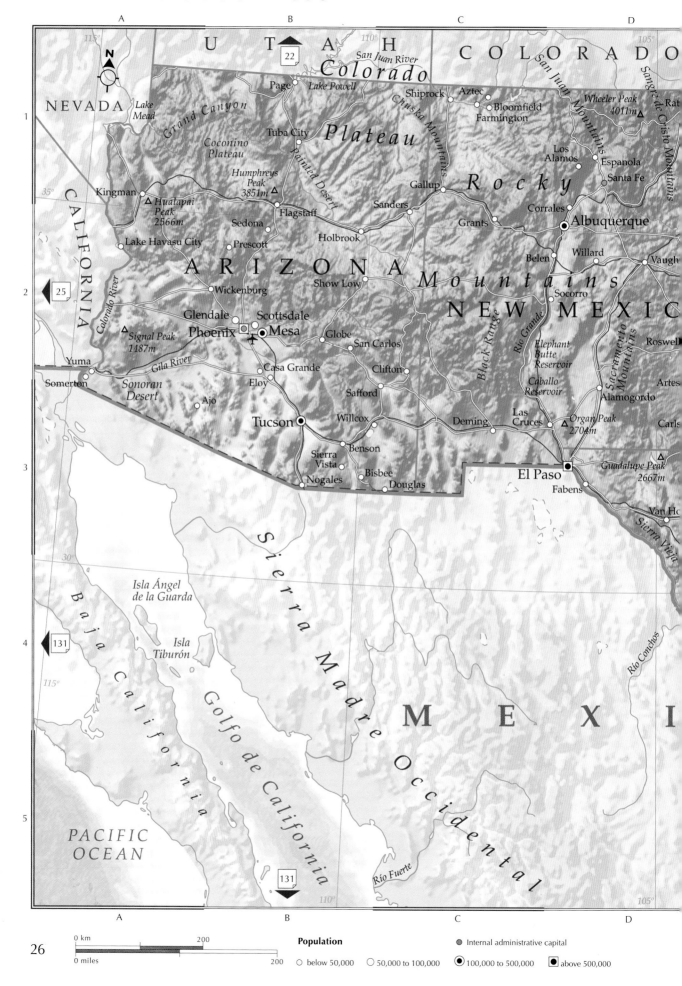

NEVADA

UTAH

COLORADO

San Juan River

Colorado

Page
Lake Powell

Lake Mead

Grand Canyon

Shiprock
Aztec
Bloomfield
Farmington

Wheeler Peak
4011m
Rat

Chuska Mountains

San Juan Mountains

Sangre de Cristo Mountains

Tuba City

Plateau

Coconino Plateau

Painted Desert

Los Alamos
Espanola
Santa Fe

Kingman

Humphreys Peak
3851m

Gallup

Rocky

Hualapai Peak
2566m

Sedona

Flagstaff

Sanders

Corrales

Grants

Albuquerque

Lake Havasu City

Prescott

Holbrook

Mountains

Belen

Willard

Vaugh

ARIZONA

Show Low

Socorro

NEW MEXICO

Wickenburg

Glendale
Scottsdale
Phoenix
Mesa

Signal Peak
1487m

Globe
San Carlos

Black Range

Rio Grande

Elephant Butte Reservoir

Roswell

Yuma

Gila River

Casa Grande
Eloy

Clifton

Caballo Reservoir

Artes

Somerton

Sonoran Desert

Safford

Las Cruces

Alamogordo

Sacramento Mountains

Ajo

Willcox

Deming

Organ Peak
2704m

Carls

Tucson

Benson

Sierra Vista

Nogales
Bisbee
Douglas

El Paso
Fabens

Guadalupe Peak
2667m

Colorado River

CALIFORNIA

Van Ho

Sierra Vieja

Isla Ángel de la Guarda

Isla Tiburón

Baja California

Sierra Madre Occidental

M E X I C

Golfo de California

Río Conchos

PACIFIC OCEAN

Río Fuerte

0 km   200
0 miles   200

Population

○ below 50,000   ○ 50,000 to 100,000   ◉ 100,000 to 500,000   ▣ above 500,000

● Internal administrative capital

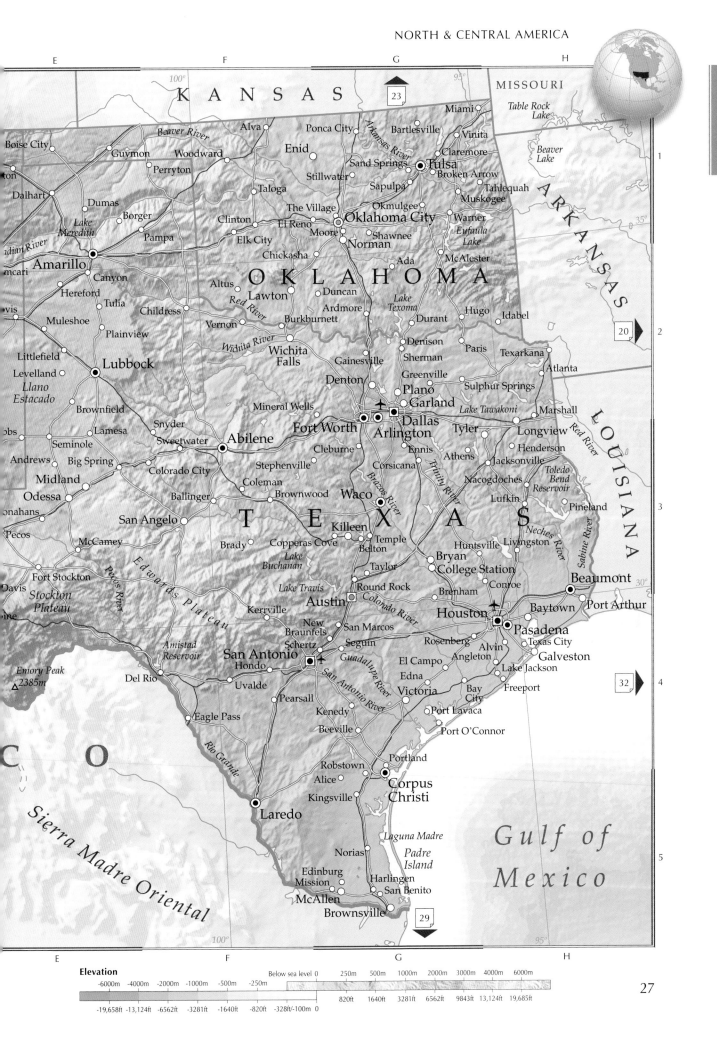

E | F | G | H

KANSAS

[23]

MISSOURI

Miami

Table Rock Lake

Boise City
Guymon
Woodward
Beaver River
Alva
Ponca City
Bartlesville
Vinita
Beaver Lake

Dalhart
Perryton
Enid
Sand Springs
Stillwater
Claremore
Tulsa
Broken Arrow

Dumas
Borger
Pampa
Clinton
El Reno
Taloga
The Village
Okmulgee
Sapulpa
Tahlequah
Muskogee

Amarillo
Lake Meredith
Indian River
Canyon
Elk City
Moore
Oklahoma City
Norman
Shawnee
Warner
Eufaula Lake
McAlester

Hereford
Altus
Chickasha
Ada
Idabel

mcari
Tulia
Lawton
Duncan
Red River
Ardmore
Lake Texoma
Durant
Hugo

Muleshoe
Childress
Vernon
Burkburnett
Denison
Sherman
Paris
Texarkana

Littlefield
Levelland
Wichita River
Wichita Falls
Gainesville
Greenville
Atlanta

Lubbock
Llano Estacado
Denton
Plano
Garland
Sulphur Springs
Marshall

Brownfield
Mineral Wells
Fort Worth
Dallas
Arlington
Lake Tawakoni
Longview

Lamesa
Snyder
Sweetwater
Abilene
Cleburne
Ennis
Tyler
Henderson

Seminole
Big Spring
Colorado City
Stephenville
Corsicana
Athens
Jacksonville

Andrews
Midland
Ballinger
Coleman
Brownwood
Waco
Brazos River
Nacogdoches
Toledo Bend Reservoir

Odessa
San Angelo
TEXAS
Killeen
Lufkin
Pineland

onahans
Pecos
McCamey
Brady
Copperas Cove
Temple
Belton
Trinity River
Huntsville
Livingston
Neches River

Davis
Fort Stockton
Pecos River
Edwards Plateau
Lake Buchanan
Taylor
Bryan
College Station
Sabine River
Beaumont

Stockton Plateau
Kerrville
Round Rock
Austin
Lake Travis
Colorado River
Brenham
Conroe
Houston
Baytown
Port Arthur

Emory Peak
△2385m
New Braunfels
Schertz
San Marcos
Seguin
Pasadena
Texas City

Del Rio
Amistad Reservoir
San Antonio
Hondo
San Antonio River
Guadalupe River
Rosenberg
Alvin
Angleton
Galveston
Lake Jackson

Uvalde
El Campo
Edna
Victoria
Bay City
Freeport

Eagle Pass
Pearsall
Kenedy
Port Lavaca
Port O'Connor

Rio Grande
Beeville
Portland
Corpus Christi

M E X I C O

Sierra Madre Oriental

Robstown
Alice
Kingsville

Norias
Laguna Madre
Padre Island

Gulf of Mexico

Edinburg
Mission
McAllen
Harlingen
San Benito
Brownsville

[29]

[32]

[20]

LOUISIANA
ARKANSAS

Elevation

Below sea level 0 | 250m | 500m | 1000m | 2000m | 3000m | 4000m | 6000m

-6000m -4000m -2000m -1000m -500m -250m

-19,658ft -13,124ft -6562ft -3281ft -1640ft -820ft -328ft/-100m 0

820ft 1640ft 3281ft 6562ft 9843ft 13,124ft 19,685ft

27

Mexico

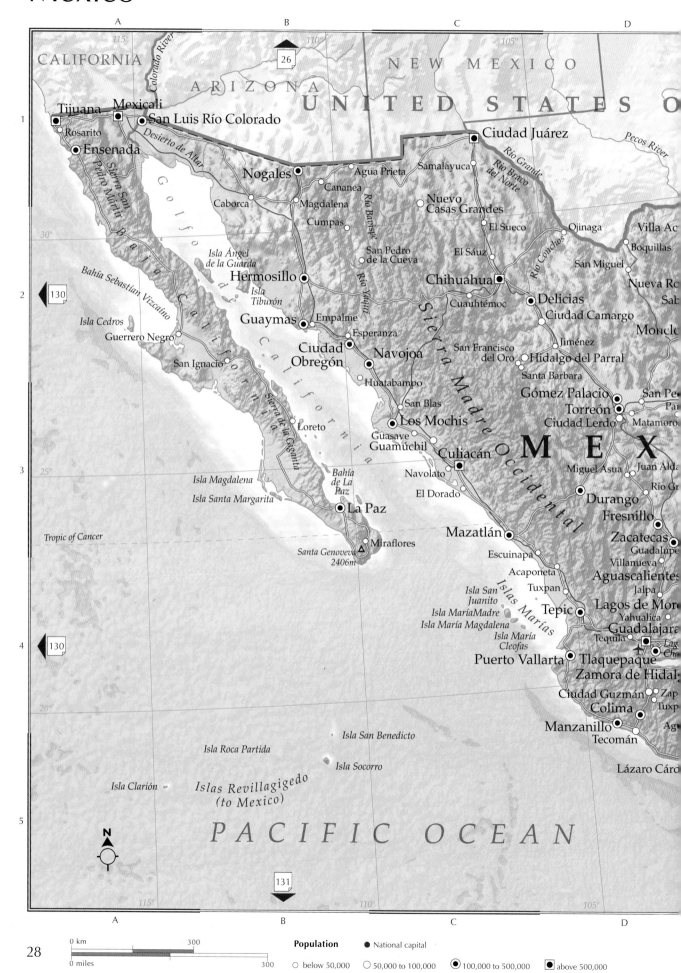

CALIFORNIA

ARIZONA

NEW MEXICO

UNITED STATES O

Colorado River
Desierto de Altar
Pecos River

Tijuana
Rosarito
Mexicali
San Luis Río Colorado
Ensenada
Ciudad Juárez
Nogales
Agua Prieta
Samalayuca
Cananea
Caborca
Magdalena
Cumpas
San Pedro de la Cueva
Nuevo Casas Grandes
El Sueco
Ojinaga
Villa Ac
Boquillas
San Miguel
Nueva Ro
Sab

Sierra San Pedro Mártir
Baja California
Bahía Sebastián Vizcaíno
Isla Cedros
Isla Ángel de la Guarda
Golfo de California
Isla Tiburón
Hermosillo
Río Bavispe
Río Yaqui
Chihuahua
Cuauhtémoc
Delicias
Ciudad Camargo
Monclo

Guerrero Negro
Guaymas
Empalme
Esperanza
San Francisco del Oro
Jiménez
Hidalgo del Parral
Santa Barbara

San Ignacio
Ciudad Obregón
Navojoa
Huatabampo

Sierra Madre Occidental

San Blas
Gómez Palacio
Torreón
Ciudad Lerdo
San Pe
Pa
Matamoro

Loreto
Los Mochis
Guasave
Guamúchil
Culiacán

Isla Magdalena
Isla Santa Margarita
Bahía de La Paz
Navolato
El Dorado

MEX

Miguel Asua
Juan Alda
Río Gr

La Paz
Durango
Fresnillo

Tropic of Cancer
Mazatlán
Escuinapa
Zacatecas
Guadalupe
Villanueva

Santa Genoveva 2406m
Miraflores
Acaponeta
Tuxpan

Aguascalientes
Jalpa

Isla San Juanito
Islas Marías
Isla MaríaMadre
Isla María Magdalena
Isla María Cleofas
Tepic
Lagos de Mor
Yahualica
Guadalajara
Tequila
Las
Cho

Puerto Vallarta
Tlaquepaque
Zamora de Hidal

Ciudad Guzmán
Zap
Colima
Tuxp

Manzanillo
Ag
Tecomán

Isla San Benedicto

Isla Roca Partida
Isla Socorro
Lázaro Cárd

Isla Clarión
Islas Revillagigedo (to Mexico)

PACIFIC OCEAN

N

0 km   300
0 miles   300

Population   ● National capital
○ below 50,000   ○ 50,000 to 100,000   ◉ 100,000 to 500,000   ▣ above 500,000

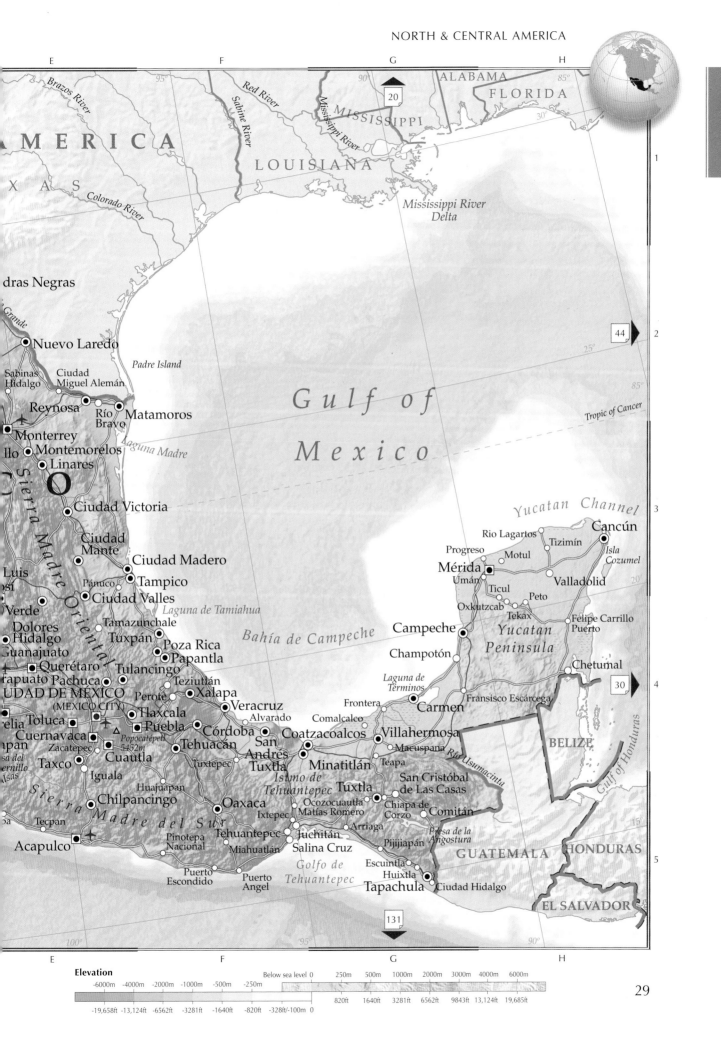

Elevation

Below sea level 0	250m	500m	1000m	2000m	3000m	4000m	6000m

-6000m	-4000m	-2000m	-1000m	-500m	-250m

-19,658ft	-13,124ft	-6562ft	-3281ft	-1640ft	-820ft	-328ft/-100m 0

820ft	1640ft	3281ft	6562ft	9843ft	13,124ft	19,685ft

Central America

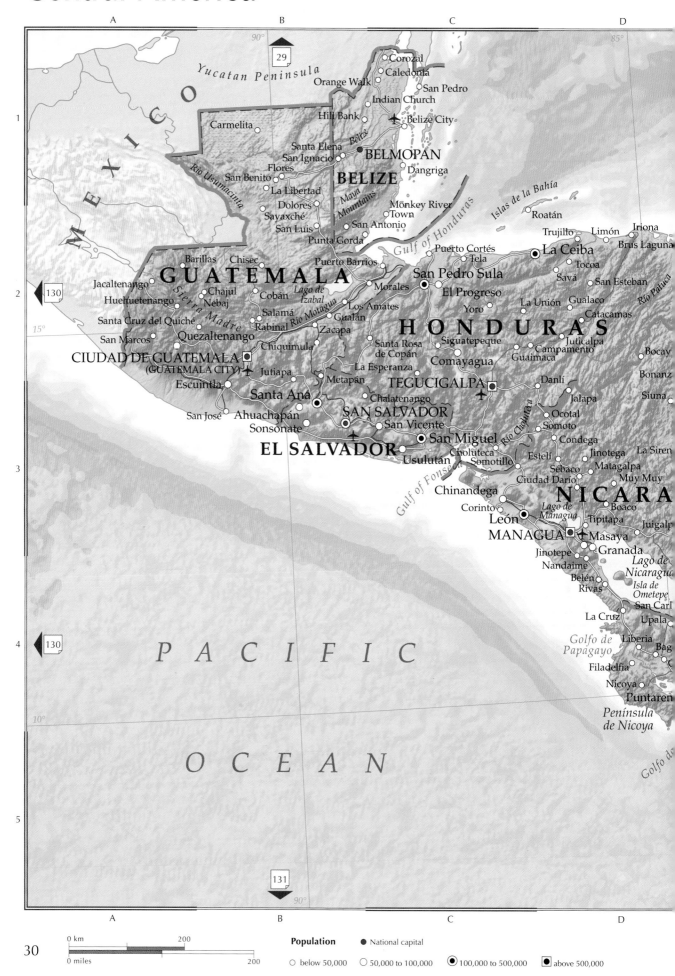

MEXICO

Yucatan Peninsula

Corozal
Caledonia
Orange Walk
San Pedro
Indian Church
Hill Bank
Belize City
Carmelita

Santa Elena
San Ignacio
BELMOPAN
Flores
San Benito
BELIZE
Dangriga
La Libertad
Dolores
Maya Mountains
Monkey River Town
Sayaxché
San Antonio
San Luis
Punta Gorda
Puerto Cortés

Río Usumacinta

Islas de la Bahía
Roatán

Barillas   Chisec
Puerto Barrios
Gulf of Honduras
Trujillo   Limón   Iriona
Brus Laguna
GUATEMALA
San Pedro Sula
La Ceiba
Jacaltenango   Chajul
Cobán   *Lago de Izabal*
Morales
Tocoa
Savá   San Esteban
Huehuetenango   Nebaj
Salamá
Los Amates
El Progreso
La Unión   Gualaco
Río Patuca
Santa Cruz del Quiché
Rabinal   *Río Motagua*
Gualán
Yoro
Catacamas
San Marcos
Quezaltenango   Chiquimula
Zacapa
HONDURAS
Sierra Madre
Santa Rosa de Copán
Siguatepeque
Juticalpa
Bocay
CIUDAD DE GUATEMALA
(GUATEMALA CITY)
Jutiapa
La Esperanza
Comayagua
Guaimaca
Campamento
Bonanz
Escuintla   Metapán
TEGUCIGALPA
Danlí
Siuna
Santa Ana
Chalatenango
Jalapa
San José   Ahuachapán
SAN SALVADOR
Ocotal
Ahuachapán   San Vicente
Somoto
Condega
Sonsonate   San Miguel
Estelí   Jinotega   La Siren
EL SALVADOR   Choluteca
Sébaco   Matagalpa
Usulután   Somotillo
Ciudad Darío
Muy Muy
Gulf of Fonseca
Chinandega
NICARA
Corinto
Lago de Managua
Boaco
León   Tipitapa   Juigalp
MANAGUA   Masaya
Jinotepe   Granada
Nandaime   *Lago de Nicaragua*
Belén
Rivas   *Isla de Ometepe*
La Cruz   San Carl
Upala
Liberia   Bag
Golfo de Papagayo
Filadelfia

Nicoya

Puntaren

P A C I F I C

Península de Nicoya

O C E A N

Golfo de

0 km   200
0 miles   200

Population   ● National capital

○ below 50,000   ○ 50,000 to 100,000   ◉ 100,000 to 500,000   ■ above 500,000

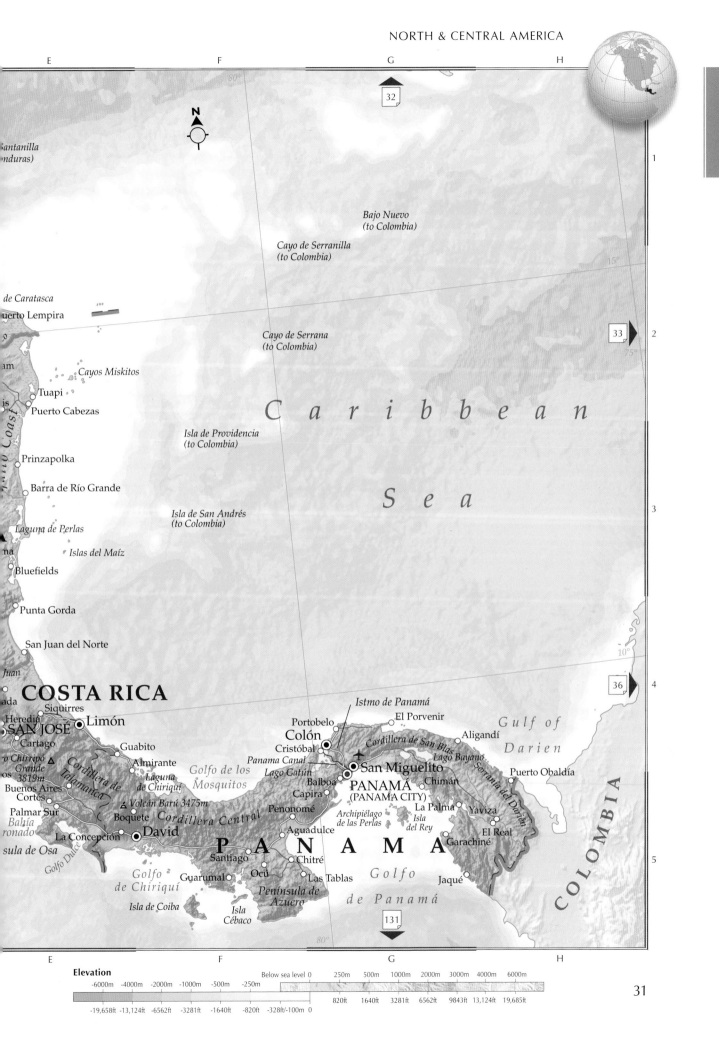

E F G H

N

1

Bajo Nuevo
(to Colombia)

Cayo de Serranilla
(to Colombia)

2

Cayo de Serrana
(to Colombia)

C a r i b b e a n

Cayos Miskitos

Isla de Providencia
(to Colombia)

S e a

3

Isla de San Andrés
(to Colombia)

antanilla
nduras)

de Caratasca
uerto Lempira

Tuapi
Puerto Cabezas

Prinzapolka

Barra de Río Grande

Laguna de Perlas

Islas del Maíz

Bluefields

Punta Gorda

San Juan del Norte

Juan

4

COSTA RICA

Siquirres
Limón

Heredia
SAN JOSÉ
Cartago
Guabito
Almirante

o Chirripó
Grande
3819m

Buenos Aires
Cortés

Palmar Sur

Bahía
ronado

sula de Osa

La Concepción
David
Boquete

Cordillera de
Talamanca

Laguna
de Chiriquí

Volcán Barú 3475m

Golfo de los
Mosquitos

Istmo de Panamá
El Porvenir

Portobelo
Colón
Cristóbal
Panama Canal
Lago Gatún
Balboa
PANAMÁ
Capira **(PANAMA CITY)**

Cordillera de San Blas
Aligandí

Lago Bayano
San Miguelito
Chimán

G u l f o f
D a r i e n

Puerto Obaldía

La Palma
Yaviza

Penonomé

Aguadulce

Archipiélago
de las Perlas

Isla
del Rey

El Real

Garachiné

P A N A M A

Santiago

Cordillera Central

Chitré

Golfo
de Panamá

Jaqué

Golfo
de Chiriquí

Guarumal
Ocú
Las Tablas

Península de
Azuero

Isla de Coiba

Isla
Cébaco

d e P a n a m á

5

COLOMBIA

Serranía del Darién

Elevation

| -6000m | -4000m | -2000m | -1000m | -500m | -250m | Below sea level 0 | 250m | 500m | 1000m | 2000m | 3000m | 4000m | 6000m |

-19,658ft -13,124ft -6562ft -3281ft -1640ft -820ft -328ft/-100m 0 820ft 1640ft 3281ft 6562ft 9843ft 13,124ft 19,685ft

The Caribbean

UNITED STATES OF AMERICA

The Everglades

Gulf of Mexico

Florida Keys

Straits of Florida

Tropic of Cancer

Yucatan Channel

LA HABANA (HAVANA)
Guanabacoa
Artemisa
Cárdenas
Matanzas
Pinar del Río
Consolación del Sur
La Fé
Cienfuegos
Santa Clara
Sagua la Grande
Nueva Gerona
Isla de la Juventud
Cayo Largo
Sancti Spíritus
Placetas
Morón
Ciego de Ávila
Archipiélago de los Canarreos
Bahía de Cochinos
Cay Sal
Anguilla Cays

C U B A

Camagüey
Nuevitas
Las Tunas
Holguín
Bayamo
Manzanillo
Palma Soriano
Santiago de Cuba
Guantánamo
Guantánamo Bay (to US)

Archipiélago de los Jardines de la Reina
Cayman Brac
Little Cayman

GEORGE TOWN
Grand Cayman
CAYMAN ISLANDS (to UK)

Montego Bay
Spanish Town
Portmore
KINGSTON
JAMAICA
Pedro Cays

Grand Bahama Island
Freeport
Marsh Harbour
Great Abaco
Bimini Islands
Berry Islands
Northeast Providence Channel
Nicholls Town
NASSAU
New Providence
Andros Town
Andros Island
Eleuthera Island
Rock Sound
Cat Island
Exuma Sound
Exuma Cays
George Town
San Salvador
Rum Cay
Long Island
Great Exuma Island
Clarence Town
Clarence Town
Archipiélago de Camagüey
Ragged Island Range
Crooked Island Passage
Crooked Island
Mayaguana Passage
Acklins Island
Caicos Pass
Little Inagua
Lake Rosa
Matthew Town
Great In
Windward Passage
Gonaïves
HA
Jérémie
PORT-AU-PRINCE
Cayes
Jac

THE BAHAMAS

NAVASSA ISLAND (to US)
Jamaica Channel
Haïti
Île de la Gonâve

A T

Great
G r e a t e r

C a r i b b e a n

HONDURAS
NICARAGUA
COSTA RICA
COLOMBIA

JAMAICA

Montego Bay
Lucea
Falmouth
Discovery Bay
St Ann's Bay
Ocho Rios
The Cockpit Country
Cambridge
Christiana
Ewarton
Annotto Bay
Buff Bay
Port Antonio
Savanna-La-Mar
Mandeville
Spanish Town
Blue Mountain Peak △2258m
Black River
May Pen
Old Harbour
KINGSTON
Portmore
Morant Bay

Caribbean Sea
Portland Bight
Caribbean Sea

2000m/6562ft	
1000m/3281ft	
500m/1640ft	
200m/656ft	
Sea level	

0 km   20
0 miles   20

0 km   200
0 miles   200

Population   ● National capital

○ below 50,000   ○ 50,000 to 100,000   ◉ 100,000 to 500,000   ▣ above 500,000

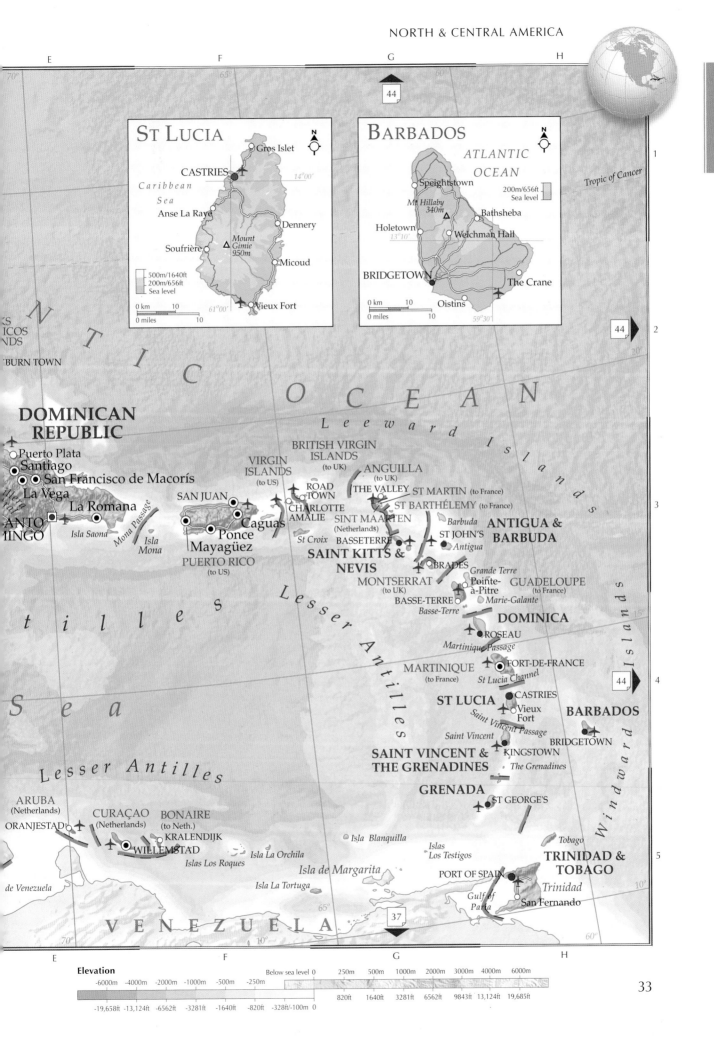

St Lucia

N

Gros Islet

CASTRIES

Caribbean Sea

Anse La Raye

Dennery

Soufrière

Mount Gimie 950m

Micoud

14°00'

63°

500m/1640ft
200m/656ft
Sea level

0 km 10
0 miles 10

61°00'

Vieux Fort

Barbados

N

ATLANTIC OCEAN

Speightstown

Mt Hillaby 340m

Bathsheba

Holetown

Welchman Hall

13°10'

200m/656ft
Sea level

BRIDGETOWN

The Crane

Oistins

59°30'

0 km 10
0 miles 10

44

44

Tropic of Cancer

20°

DOMINICAN REPUBLIC

Puerto Plata

Santiago

San Francisco de Macorís

La Vega

La Romana

SANTO DOMINGO

Isla Saona

Mona Passage

Isla Mona

SAN JUAN

Caguas

Ponce

Mayagüez

PUERTO RICO
(to US)

VIRGIN ISLANDS
(to US)

BRITISH VIRGIN ISLANDS
(to UK)

ROAD TOWN

CHARLOTTE AMALIE

St Croix

ANGUILLA
(to UK)

THE VALLEY

ST MARTIN (to France)

ST BARTHÉLEMY (to France)

SINT MAARTEN
(Netherlands)

BASSETERRE

SAINT KITTS & NEVIS

BRADES

MONTSERRAT
(to UK)

BASSE-TERRE

Basse-Terre

Barbuda

ST JOHN'S

Antigua

ANTIGUA & BARBUDA

Grande Terre

Pointe-à-Pitre

Marie-Galante

GUADELOUPE
(to France)

DOMINICA

ROSEAU

Martinique Passage

MARTINIQUE
(to France)

FORT-DE-FRANCE

St Lucia Channel

ST LUCIA

CASTRIES

Vieux Fort

Saint Vincent Passage

Saint Vincent

SAINT VINCENT & THE GRENADINES

KINGSTOWN

The Grenadines

GRENADA

ST GEORGE'S

BARBADOS

BRIDGETOWN

TRINIDAD & TOBAGO

Tobago

Islas Los Testigos

PORT OF SPAIN

Trinidad

Gulf of Paria

San Fernando

ARUBA
(Netherlands)

ORANJESTAD

CURAÇAO
(Netherlands)

BONAIRE
(to Neth.)

KRALENDIJK

WILLEMSTAD

Islas Los Roques

Isla La Orchila

Isla Blanquilla

Isla de Margarita

Isla La Tortuga

de Venezuela

VENEZUELA

ATLANTIC OCEAN

Leeward Islands

Lesser Antilles

Windward Islands

Sea

70°

65°

10°

60°

15°

44

37

Elevation

Below sea level 0   250m   500m   1000m   2000m   3000m   4000m   6000m

-6000m   -4000m   -2000m   -1000m   -500m   -250m

-19,658ft -13,124ft -6562ft -3281ft -1640ft -820ft -328ft/-100m 0

820ft   1640ft   3281ft   6562ft   9843ft 13,124ft 19,685ft

33

South America

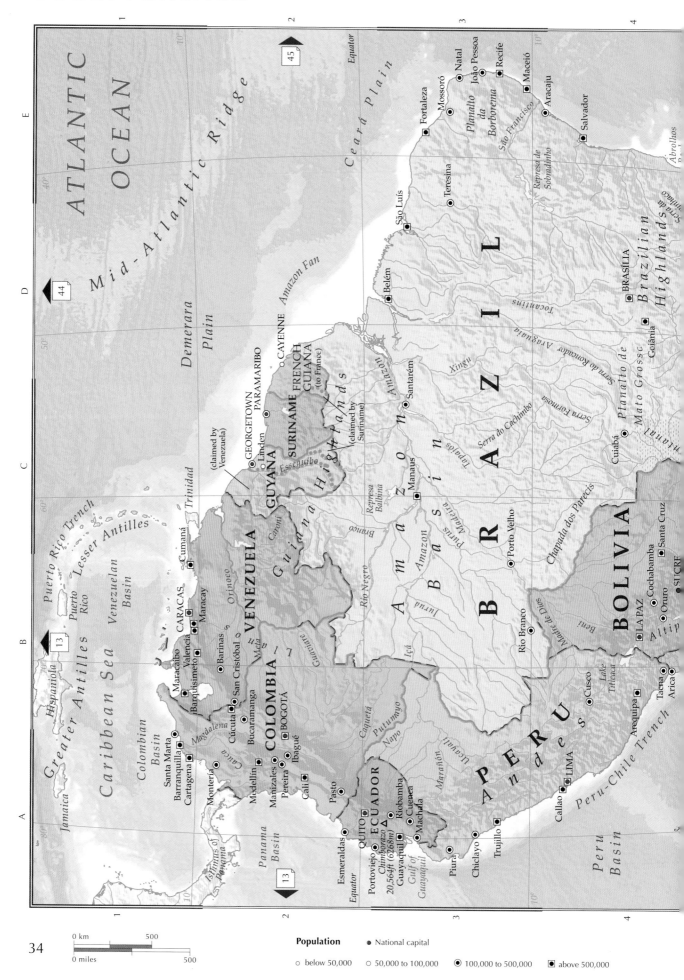

ATLANTIC OCEAN

Mid-Atlantic Ridge

Equator

45

44

13

13

ATLANTIC OCEAN

Mid-Atlantic Ridge

Demerara Plain

Amazon Fan

Puerto Rico Trench

Lesser Antilles

Venezuelan Basin

Greater Antilles

Caribbean Sea

Jamaica

Hispaniola

Puerto Rico

Colombian Basin

Santa Marta
Barranquilla
Cartagena

Monteria

Panama Basin

Isthmus of Panama

Gulf of Guayaquil

Esmeraldas

Equator

Portoviejo
QUITO
Guayaquil
Chimborazo
20,564ft (6268m)
ECUADOR
Riobamba
Cuenca
Machala

Piura

Chiclayo
Trujillo

Callao
LIMA

P E R U

Andes

Peru-Chile Trench

Peru Basin

Cumaná

CARACAS
Valencia
Maracay
Barquisimeto
Maracaibo

Barinas

San Cristóbal

VENEZUELA

Orinoco

Caroní

Meta

Cúcuta
Bucaramanga
BOGOTÁ
COLOMBIA
Ibagué
Pereira
Manizales
Medellín
Cali

Pasto

Magdalena

Cauca

Caquetá

Putumayo

Napo

Marañón

Ucayali

Guaviare

Icá

Japurá

Juruá

(claimed by Venezuela)

GEORGETOWN
Linden
GUYANA

PARAMARIBO
SURINAME

CAYENNE
FRENCH GUIANA
(to France)

(claimed by Suriname)

Essequibo

Guiana Highlands

Trinidad

Rio Branco

Rio Negro

A m a z o n   B a s i n

Amazon

Manaus
Represa Balbina

Branco

Santarém

Amazon

Madeira

Purus

Porto Velho

Rio Branco

Madre de Dios

Beni

BOLIVIA
LA PAZ
Cochabamba
Oruro
SUCRE
Santa Cruz

Altip

Lake Titicaca

Cusco

Arequipa

Tacna
Arica

Belém

São Luís

Teresina

Fortaleza

Mossoró
Natal
João Pessoa
Recife
Maceió
Aracaju
Salvador

Ceará Plain

Planalto da Borborema

São Francisco

Represa de Sobradinho

Abrolhos

B R A Z I L

BRASÍLIA

Goiânia

Cuiabá

Mato Grosso

Brazilian Highlands

Serra do Cachimbo

Serra Formosa

Chapada dos Parecis

Chapada do Roncador

Tocantins

Araguaia

Xingu

Tapajós

Planalto de

Serra do Aripuanã

Itanuá

Population

● National capital

○ below 50,000 ○ 50,000 to 100,000 ◉ 100,000 to 500,000 ◼ above 500,000

0 km   500
0 miles   500

34

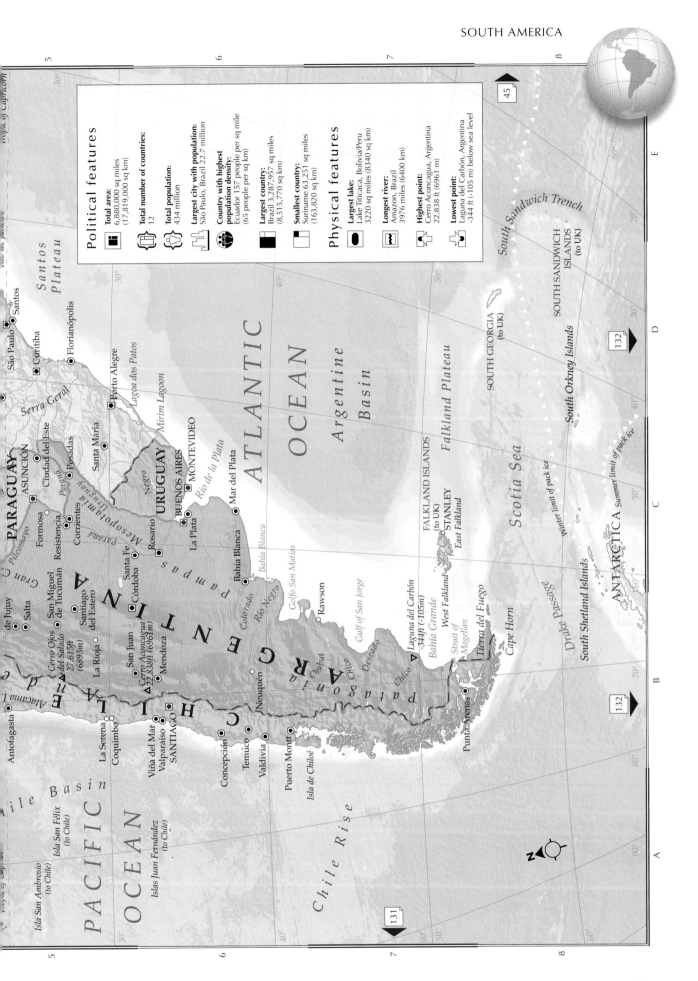

Political features

Total area:
6,880,000 sq miles
(17,819,000 sq km)

Total number of countries:
12

Total population:
434 million

Largest city with population:
São Paulo, Brazil 22.7 million

Country with highest population density:
Ecuador 157 people per sq mile
(65 people per sq km)

Largest country:
Brazil 3,287,957 sq miles
(8,515,770 sq km)

Smallest country:
Suriname 63,251 sq miles
(163,820 sq km)

Physical features

Largest lake:
Lake Titicaca, Bolivia/Peru
3220 sq miles, (8340 sq km)

Longest river:
Amazon, Brazil
3976 miles (6400 km)

Highest point:
Cerro Aconcagua, Argentina
22,838 ft (6961 m)

Lowest point:
Laguna del Carbón, Argentina
-344 ft (-105 m) below sea level

PACIFIC OCEAN

ATLANTIC OCEAN

Chile Basin

Chile Rise

Isla San Ambrosio
(to Chile)

Isla San Félix
(to Chile)

Islas Juan Fernández
(to Chile)

Antofagasta

Atacama

Cerro Ojos del Salado
22,615ft (6893m)

Cerro Aconcagua
22,838ft (6961m)

La Serena

Coquimbo

San Juan

Mendoza

Viña del Mar
Valparaíso
SANTIAGO

Concepción

Temuco

Valdivia

Puerto Montt

Isla de Chiloé

CHILE

ARGENTINA

Patagonia

Neuquén

Río Negro

Colorado

Chico

Chico

Chubut

Desvido

Laguna del Carbón
-344ft (-105m)

Bahía Grande

Strait of Magellan

Tierra del Fuego

Cape Horn

Drake Passage

Punta Arenas

Rawson

Gulf of San Jorge

Golfo San Matías

Bahía Blanca

Bahía Blanca

La Plata

BUENOS AIRES

Rosario

Santa Fe

Córdoba

Santiago del Estero

San Miguel de Tucumán

La Rioja

de Jujuy

Salta

Gran Chaco

Pilcomayo

Formosa

Resistencia

Corrientes

Paraná

PARAGUAY

ASUNCIÓN

Ciudad del Este

Posadas

Mesopotamia

Santa María

Paraná

Uruguay

URUGUAY

MONTEVIDEO

Mar del Plata

Río de la Plata

Negro

Pampas

Lagoa dos Patos

Mirim Lagoon

Porto Alegre

Santa Maria

Serra Geral

Florianópolis

Curitiba

São Paulo
Santos

Santos Plateau

Tropic of Capricorn

ARGENTINE Basin

Argentine Basin

FALKLAND ISLANDS
(to UK)

STANLEY

West Falkland

East Falkland

Falkland Plateau

SOUTH GEORGIA
(to UK)

Scotia Sea

Winter limit of pack ice

South Orkney Islands

South Sandwich Trench

SOUTH SANDWICH ISLANDS
(to UK)

South Shetland Islands

ANTARCTICA

Summer limit of pack ice

N

131

132

132

45

ATLANTIC

OCEAN

SAINT VINCENT &
THE GRENADINES

BARBADOS

GRENADA

Isla Blanquilla

*Isla de
Margarita*

Tobago

La Asunción

Carúpano

TRINIDAD &
TOBAGO

Güiria

Cariaco *Gulf of
Paria*

The Serpent's Mouth

Trinidad

Puerto La Cruz

Barcelona

San Mateo

Maturín

Anaco

Cantaura

Tucupita

El Tigre

Río Orinoco

Ciudad Guayana

Ciudad
Bolívar

Upata

Embalse de Guri

Matthews
Ridge

Charity

U E L A

El Callao

Spring Garden

GEORGETOWN

Cuyuni River

Parika

El Dorado

Aurora

New
Amsterdam

Río Paragua

Peters Mine

Bartica

PARAMARIBO

Totness

Nieuw Amsterdam

*Salto
Angel*

Rockstone

Linden

St-Laurent-du-Maroni

Kamarang

Nieuw
Nickerie

Sinnamary

Río Caroní

GUYANA

Kaaimanston

SURINAME

Kourou

Mount Roraima
2810m

Orealla

Apoera

*W. J. van
Blommesteinmeer*

CAYENNE

Pakaraima Mountains

Kurupukari

△ *Juliana Top*
1230m

Grand-
Santi

Ouanary

FRENCH
GUIANA
(to France)

St-Georges

Essequibo River

(Venezuela claims all
of Guyana west of
Essequibo River)

Lethem

Camopi

Courantyne River

Tumuc-Humac Mountains

(claimed by
Suriname)

G u i a n a

Acarai Mountains

(claimed by
Suriname)

H i g h l a n d s

Orinoco

(claimed by
Suriname)

Equator

Negro

B   R   A   Z   I   L

Amazon

z   o   n   B   a   s   i   n

Amazon

Amazon

Río Purus

Río Tapajós

Elevation

-6000m	-4000m	-2000m	-1000m	-500m	-250m	Below sea level 0	250m	500m	1000m	2000m	3000m	4000m	6000m
-19,658ft	-13,124ft	-6562ft	-3281ft	-1640ft	-820ft	-328ft/-100m 0		820ft	1640ft	3281ft	6562ft	9843ft 13,124ft	19,685ft

Western South America

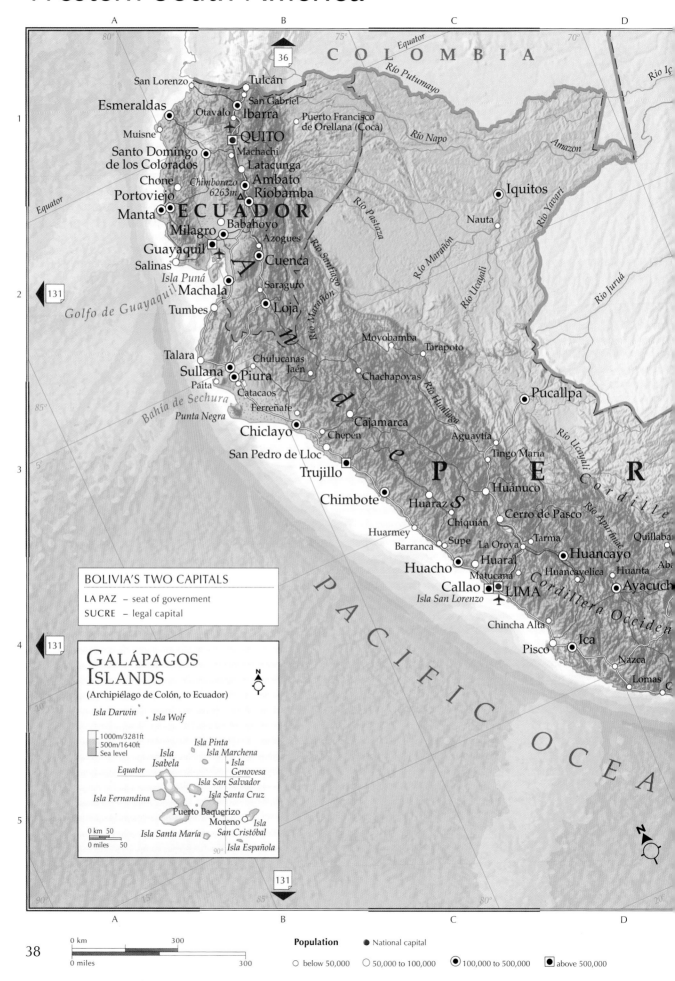

C O L O M B I A

Equator

Río Putumayo

San Lorenzo

Tulcán

Esmeraldas

San Gabriel

Muisne

Otavalo · Ibarra

Puerto Francisco
de Orellana (Coca)

Río Napo

QUITO

Machachi

Amazon

Santo Domingo
de los Colorados

Latacunga

Iquitos

Chone

*Chimborazo
6263m*

Ambato

Riobamba

Río Pastaza

Nauta

Portoviejo

E C U A D O R

Río Santiago

Manta

Río Marañón

Río Yavari

Milagro

Babahoyo

Río Ucayali

Guayaquil

Azogues

Cuenca

Río Juruá

Salinas

A

Isla Puná

Saraguro

Machala

Golfo de Guayaquil

Loja

Tumbes

n

Moyobamba

Tarapoto

Río Marañón

Talara

Chulucanas

Jaén

Chachapoyas

Sullana

Piura

d

Río Huallaga

Pucallpa

Paita

Catacaos

Ferreñafe

Cajamarca

Aguaytía

Río Ucayali

Bahía de Sechura

Punta Negra

Chiclayo

Chepén

e

P E R Ú

San Pedro de Lloc

Tingo María

Quillabamba

Trujillo

s

Huánuco

Cordille

Chimbote

Huaraz

Cerro de Pasco

Río Apurímac

Chiquián

Tarma

Aba

Huarmey

La Oroya

Huancayo

Barranca

Supe

Huancavelica

Huanta

Huacho

Huaral

Matucana

Ayacucho

Callao

LIMA

Isla San Lorenzo

Chincha Alta

P A C I F I C

Pisco

Ica

Nazca

131

GALÁPAGOS
ISLANDS

(Archipiélago de Colón, to Ecuador)

N

Isla Darwin · *Isla Wolf*

	1000m/3281ft
	500m/1640ft
	Sea level

Isla Pinta

Isla Marchena

*Isla
Isabela*

*Isla
Genovesa*

Equator

Isla San Salvador

Isla Fernandina

Isla Santa Cruz

Puerto Baquerizo
Moreno

*Isla
San Cristóbal*

0 km	50
0 miles	50

Isla Santa María

Isla Española

O C E A

131

N

0 km	300
0 miles	300

Population ● National capital

○ below 50,000 ○ 50,000 to 100,000 ◉ 100,000 to 500,000 ▣ above 500,000

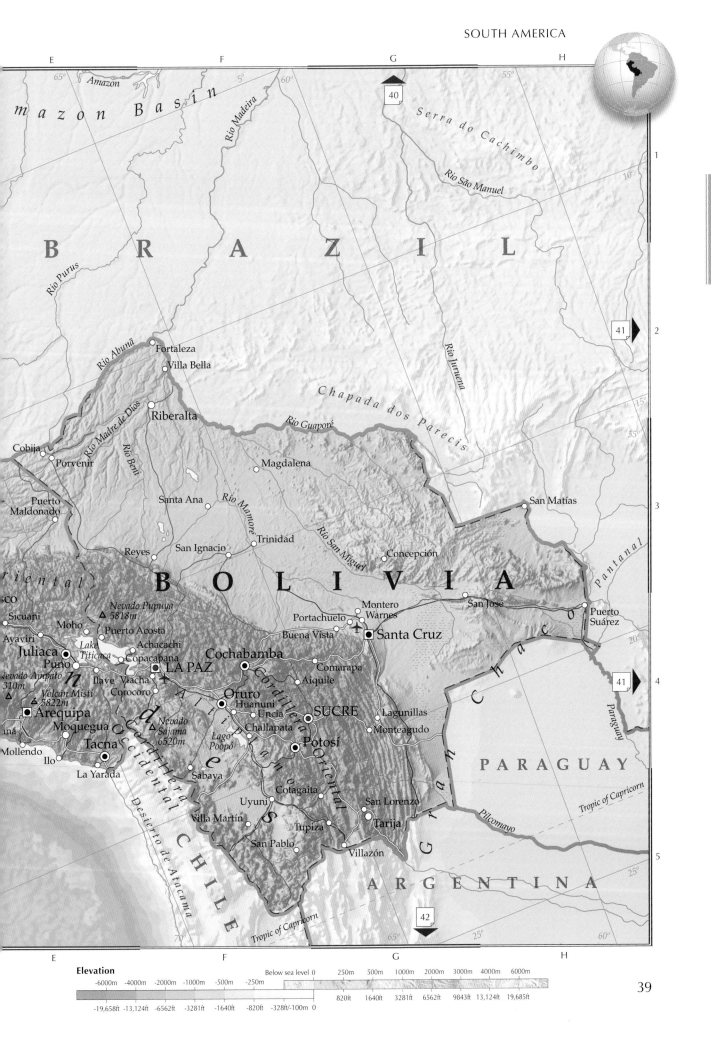

E 65° *Amazon* 5° 60° G 55° H

40

Serra do Cachimbo

Rio São Manuel 10° 1

B R A Z I L

Rio Purus

Rio Madeira

Rio Juruena

41 2

Fortaleza
Rio Abunã
Villa Bella

Chapada dos Parecis 15°

Riberalta
Rio Guaporé 55°

Cobija
Rio Madre de Dios
Porvenir

Magdalena

Rio Beni

San Matías

Puerto
Maldonado

Santa Ana
Rio Mamoré

Concepción 3

Reyes
San Ignacio
Trinidad
Rio San Miguel

Pantanal

B O L I V I A

SCO
Sicuani
Nevado Pupuya
△ 5818m

Montero
Warnes

San José
Puerto
Suárez

Moho
Puerto Acosta
Achacachi

Portachuelo

Ayaviri
Lake Titicaca
Copacabana

Buena Vista
Santa Cruz 20°

Juliaca
Cochabamba

Nevado Ampato 310m
△
Puno
Ilave Viacha

Oruro
Comarapa
Aiquile

41 4

Volcán Misti 5822m
△
Corocoro
LA PAZ

Huanuni
Uncia

SUCRE
Lagunillas

Paraguay

Arequipa
Nevado Sajama 6520m

Challapata

Monteagudo

Moquegua
Lago Poopó

Potosí

ana
Tacna
Sabaya

P A R A G U A Y

Mollendo
Ilo

Cotagaita
San Lorenzo

Tropic of Capricorn

La Yarada

Uyuni

Tarija

Villa Martín

Tupiza

Pilcomayo

San Pablo
Villazón 25° 5

Desierto de Atacama

C H I L E

A R G E N T I N A

42

70° *Tropic of Capricorn* 65° G 25° 60°

E F G H

Elevation

| -6000m | -4000m | -2000m | -1000m | -500m | -250m | Below sea level 0 | 250m | 500m | 1000m | 2000m | 3000m | 4000m | 6000m |

-19,658ft -13,124ft -6562ft -3281ft -1640ft -820ft -328ft/-100m 0 820ft 1640ft 3281ft 6562ft 9843ft 13,124ft 19,685ft

Brazil

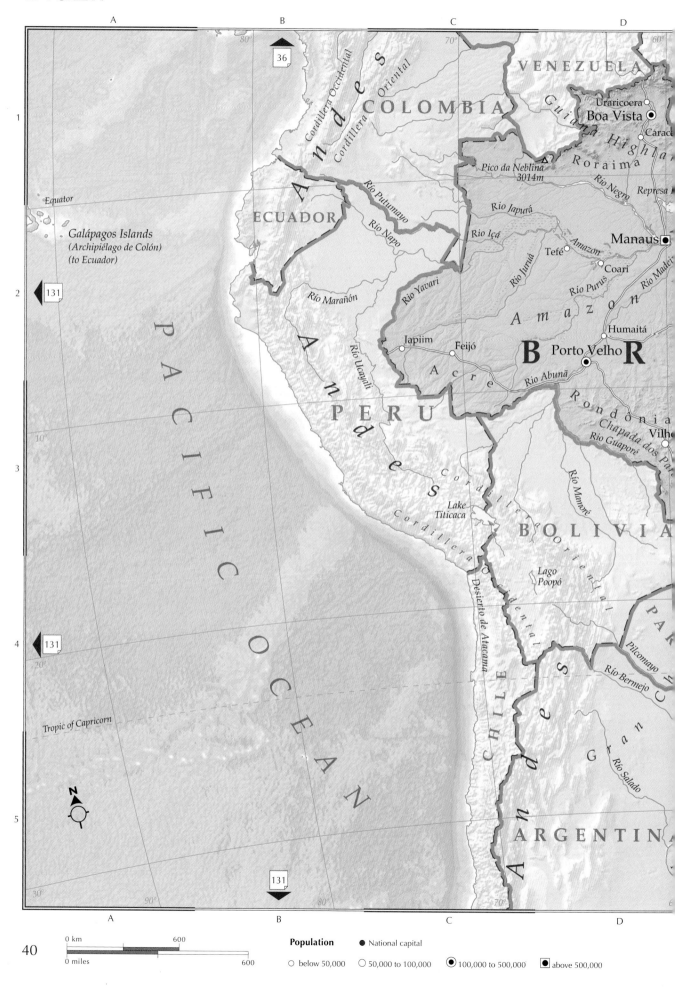

VENEZUELA

COLOMBIA

Cordillera Occidental

Cordillera Oriental

Uraricoera
Boa Vista
Caraca

Guiana Highlan

Río Negro

Roraima

Pico da Neblina
3014m

Represa

A n d e s

Equator

ECUADOR

Río Putumayo

Río Napo

Río Japurá

Río Içá

Río Juruá

Tefé

Amazon

Manaus

Coari

Río Madeir

Galápagos Islands
(Archipiélago de Colón)
(to Ecuador)

Río Marañón

Río Yavari

A m a z o n

Río Purus

Humaitá

Iapiim

Feijó

B Porto Velho **R**

Río Abuná

Rondônia

Vilhe

Chapada dos Par

Río Guaporé

A n d e s

P E R U

Río Llcayali

A c r e

Río Mamoré

PACIFIC

Cordillera

Lake
Titicaca

Cordillera Oriental

BOLIVIA

10°

Cordillera Occidental

Lago
Poopó

PAR

Desierto de Atacama

Pilcomayo

Río Bermejo

20°

OCEAN

A n d e s

G r a n

Tropic of Capricorn

C h i l e

Río Salado

N

5

ARGENTINA

30°   90°   80°   70°

A   B   C   D

0 km   600
0 miles   600

Population   ● National capital

○ below 50,000   ○ 50,000 to 100,000   ◉ 100,000 to 500,000   ◼ above 500,000

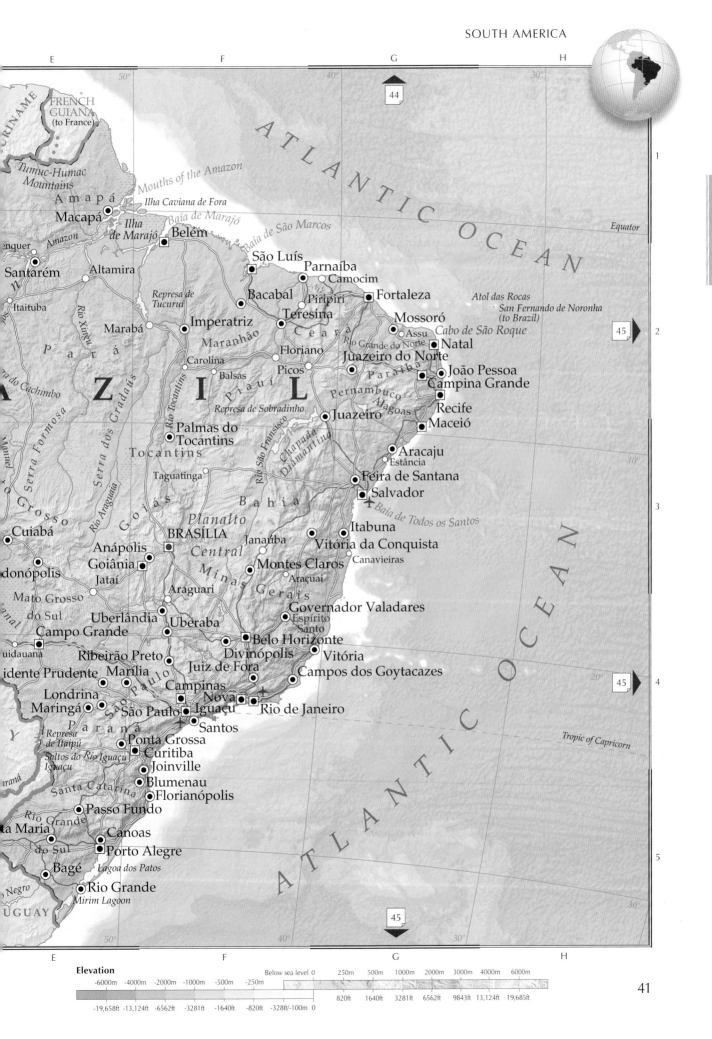

ATLANTIC OCEAN

FRENCH GUIANA (to France)

Tumuc-Humac Mountains

Mouths of the Amazon

Amapá

Ilha Caviana de Fora

Macapá

Baía de Marajó

Ilha de Marajó

Belém

Baía de São Marcos

enquer

Amazon

Santarém

São Luís

Parnaíba

Camocim

Equator

Itaituba

Altamira

Bacabal

Píripíri

Fortaleza

Atol das Rocas

Represa de Tucuruí

Imperatriz

Teresina

Mossoró

San Fernando de Noronha (to Brazil)

Marabá

Maranhão

Ceará

Assu

Cabo de São Roque

Rio Grande do Norte

Natal

Pa rá

Carolina

Floriano

Juazeiro do Norte

Paraíba

João Pessoa

Balsas

Picos

Piauí

Pernambuco

Campina Grande

Serra do Cachimbo

BRAZIL

Serra dos Gradaús

Represa de Sobradinho

Alagoas

Recife

Rio Tocantins

Palmas do Tocantins

Juazeiro

Maceió

Chapada Diamantina

Tocantins

Rio São Fransisco

Aracaju

Serra Formosa

Taguatinga

Estância

Rio Araguaia

Goiás

Bahia

Feira de Santana

Grosso

Planalto

Salvador

Cuiabá

BRASÍLIA

Janaúba

Itabuna

Baía de Todos os Santos

Anápolis

Central

Vitória da Conquista

donópolis

Goiânia

Montes Claros

Canavieiras

Mato Grosso do Sul

Jataí

Araçuai

Minas Gerais

Araguari

Governador Valadares

uidauana

Uberlândia

Espírito Santo

Campo Grande

Uberaba

Belo Horizonte

Ribeirão Preto

Divinópolis

Vitória

idente Prudente

Marília

Juiz de Fora

Campos dos Goytacazes

Y

Londrina

São Paulo

Campinas

Tropic of Capricorn

Maringá

Nova

Paraná

São Paulo

Iguaçu

Rio de Janeiro

Represa de Itaipu

Santos

Saltos do Rio Iguaçu

Ponta Grossa

Iguaçu

Curitiba

Paraná

Joinville

Blumenau

Santa Catarina

Florianópolis

Passo Fundo

a Maria

Rio Grande

Canoas

do Sul

Porto Alegre

Bagé

Lagoa dos Patos

Negro

Rio Grande

UGUAY

Mirim Lagoon

ATLANTIC OCEAN

Elevation

| -6000m | -4000m | -2000m | -1000m | -500m | -250m | Below sea level 0 | 250m | 500m | 1000m | 2000m | 3000m | 4000m | 6000m |

-19,658ft -13,124ft -6562ft -3281ft -1640ft -820ft -328ft/-100m 0   820ft 1640ft 3281ft 6562ft 9843ft 13,124ft 19,685ft

Southern South America

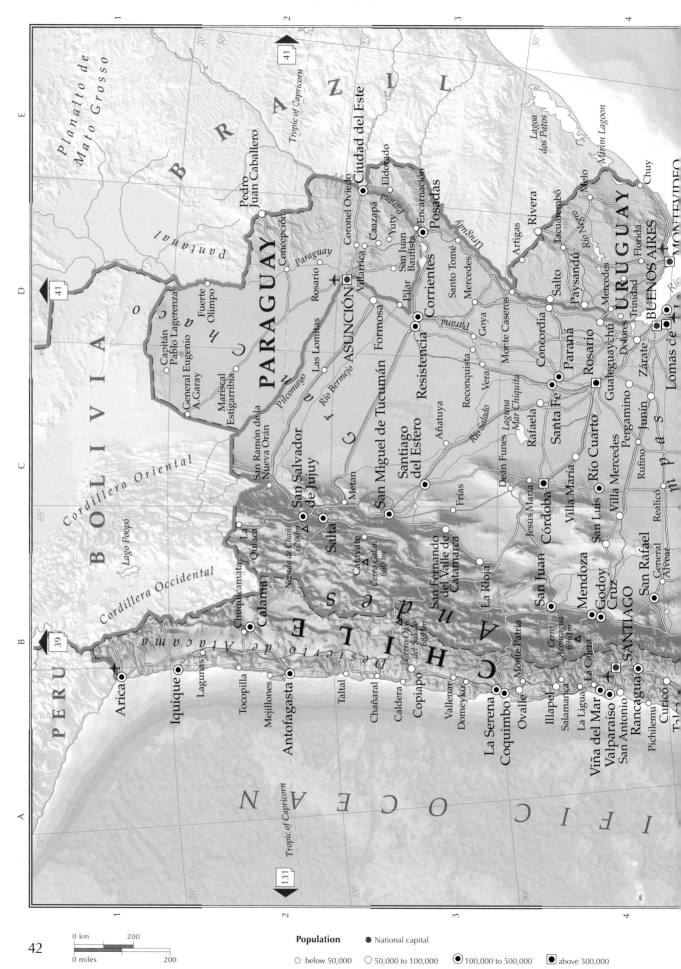

Population   ● National capital

○ below 50,000   ○ 50,000 to 100,000   ◉ 100,000 to 500,000   ◼ above 500,000

0 km   200

0 miles   200

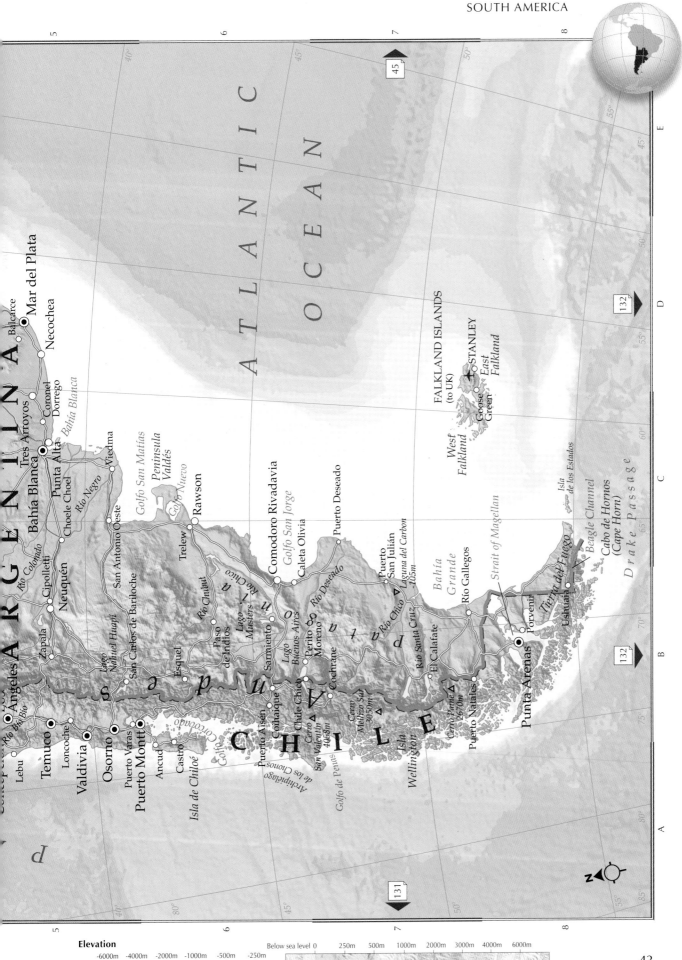

ATLANTIC

OCEAN

ARGENTINA

CHILE

Mar del Plata
Balcarce
Necochea
Coronel
Dorrego
Tres Arroyos
Bahía Blanca
Punta Alta
Bahía Blanca
Choele Choel
Viedma
Cipolletti
Neuquén
San Antonio Oeste
Río Negro
Río Colorado
Zapala
San Carlos de Bariloche
Lago Nahuel Huapi
Esquel
Manuel Huapi
Angeles
Río Bío Bío
Lebu
Temuco
Loncoche
Valdivia
Osorno
Puerto Varas
Puerto Montt
Ancud
Castro
Isla de Chiloé
Golfo Corcovado
Archipiélago de los Chonos
Puerto Aisén
Coihaique
Chile Chico
Cochrane
Paso de Indios
Lago Musters
Sarmiento
Lago Buenos Aires
Perito Moreno
Cerro San Valentín 4058m
Golfo de Penas
Isla Wellington

Peninsula Valdés
Golfo San Matías
Golfo Nuevo
Rawson
Trelew
Río Chubut
Río Chico
Comodoro Rivadavia
Golfo San Jorge
Caleta Olivia
Puerto Deseado
Río Deseado
Río Chico
Puerto San Julián
Laguna del Carbon -105m
Río Santa Cruz
El Calafate
Río Gallegos
Bahía Grande
Puerto Natales
Cerro Paine 2670m
Cerro Melliza Sur 3050m

FALKLAND ISLANDS
(to UK)
STANLEY
East Falkland
Goose Green
West Falkland

Strait of Magellan
Isla de los Estados
Beagle Channel
Cabo de Hornos (Cape Horn)
Drake Passage
Tierra del Fuego
Porvenir
Ushuaia
Punta Arenas

45

132

132

131

z

Elevation

-6000m	-4000m	-2000m	-1000m	-500m	-250m	Below sea level 0	250m	500m	1000m	2000m	3000m	4000m	6000m
-19,658ft	-13,124ft	-6562ft	-3281ft	-1640ft	-820ft	-328ft/-100m 0	820ft	1640ft	3281ft	6562ft	9843ft	13,124ft	19,685ft

The Atlantic Ocean

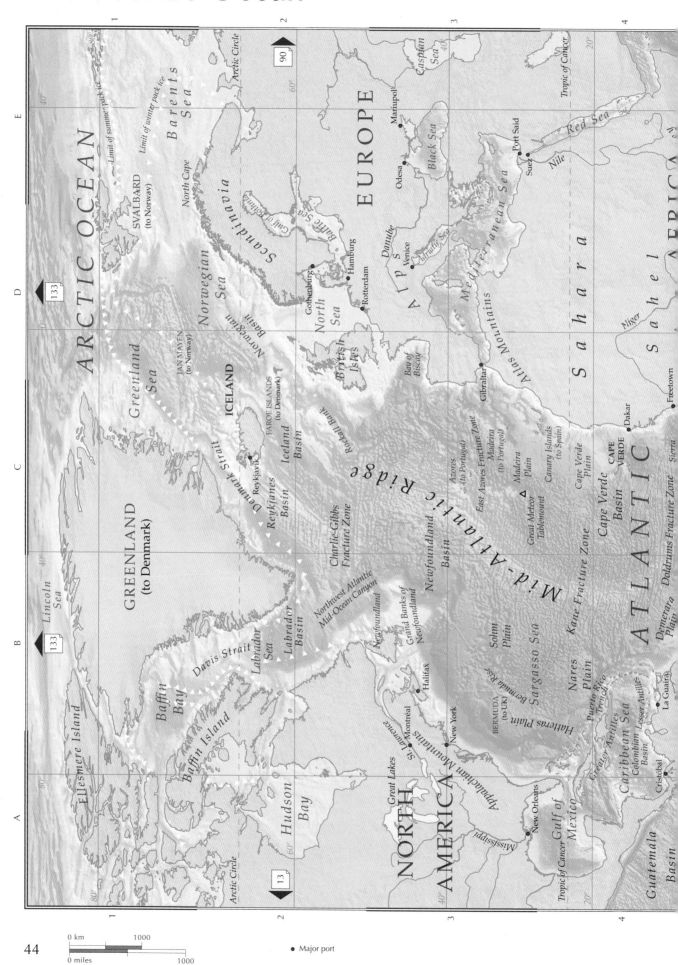

ARCTIC OCEAN

Limit of summer pack ice
Limit of winter pack ice
Arctic Circle

Barents Sea

SVALBARD (to Norway)
North Cape
Scandinavia
Gulf of Bothnia
Baltic Sea

EUROPE

Mariupol
Black Sea
Odesa
Port Said
Red Sea
Suez
Nile

Norwegian Sea

JAN MAYEN (to Norway)
Greenland Sea

ICELAND
Reykjavik
Denmark Strait

Norwegian Basin

North Sea
Gothenburg
Hamburg
Rotterdam

Danube
Venice
Adriatic Sea
Alps
Mediterranean Sea
Gibraltar
Atlas Mountains

Sahara

Sahel

AFRICA

Tropic of Cancer

FAROE ISLANDS (to Denmark)
Iceland Basin
Reykjanes Basin

British Isles
Bay of Biscay
Rockall Bank

Azores (to Portugal)
East Azores Fracture Zone
Madeira (to Portugal)
Madeira Plain
Canary Islands (to Spain)
Great Meteor Tablemount

Cape Verde Plain

Niger
Freetown
Dakar

CAPE VERDE

GREENLAND (to Denmark)

Lincoln Sea

Baffin Bay
Davis Strait
Baffin Island

Labrador Sea
Labrador Basin

Charlie-Gibbs Fracture Zone
Northwest Atlantic Mid-Ocean Canyon

Newfoundland Basin

Mid-Atlantic Ridge

Cape Verde Basin

ATLANTIC

Doldrums Fracture Zone
Sierra

Ellesmere Island

Hudson Bay

Newfoundland
Grand Banks of Newfoundland
Halifax

Sohm Plain
Sargasso Sea
Bermuda Rise
BERMUDA (to UK)
Hatteras Plain

Nares Plain
Kane Fracture Zone

Puerto Rico Trench
Greater Antilles
Lesser Antilles

Demerara Plain

La Guaira

NORTH AMERICA

Great Lakes
St. Lawrence
Montréal
New York

Appalachian Mountains
New Orleans
Mississippi
Gulf of Mexico
Tropic of Cancer

Caribbean Sea
Colombian Basin
Cristóbal

Guatemala Basin

Arctic Circle

Scale

0 km — 1000
0 miles — 1000

● Major port

44

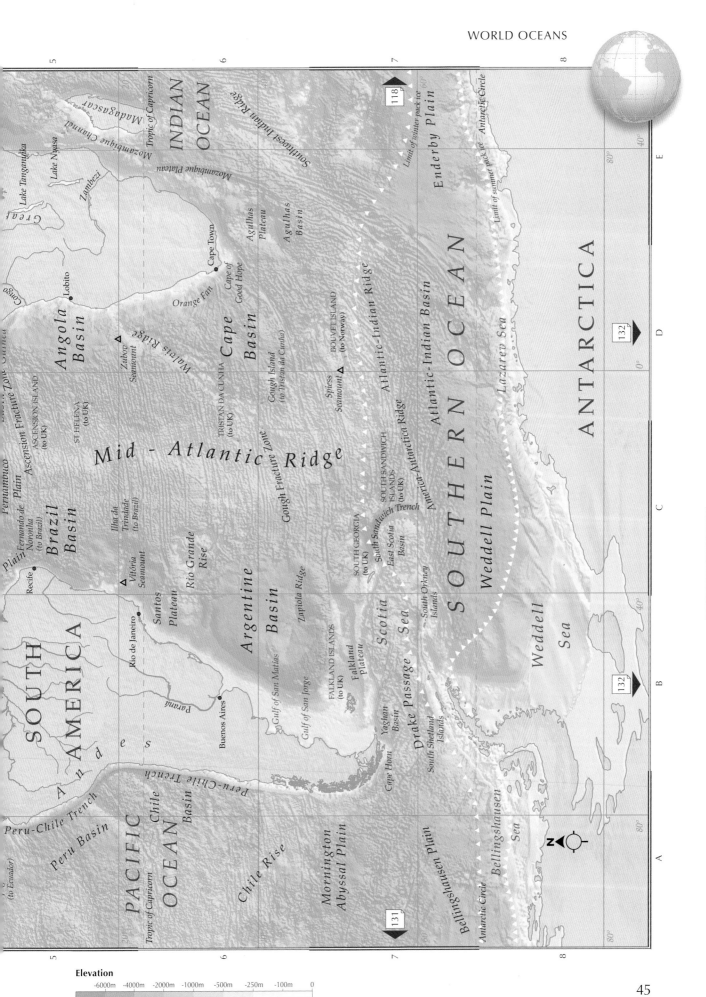

INDIAN OCEAN

Madagascar

Mozambique Channel

Lake Tanganyika

Lake Nyasa

Zambezi

Great

Tropic of Capricorn

Mozambique Plateau

Southwest Indian Ridge

118

Limit of winter pack ice

Enderby Plain

Antarctic Circle

Agulhas Plateau

Agulhas Basin

Cape Town

Cape of Good Hope

Orange Fan

Congo

Lobito

Angola Basin

Walvis Ridge

Zubov Seamount

Cape Basin

Gough Island (to Tristan da Cunha)

BOUVET ISLAND (to Norway)

Spiess Seamount

Atlantic-Indian Ridge

SOUTHERN OCEAN

132

Lazarev Sea

ANTARCTICA

ST. HELENA (to UK)

ASCENSION ISLAND (to UK)

Ascension Fracture Zone Guinea

Pernambuco

Mid – Atlantic Ridge

TRISTAN DA CUNHA (to UK)

Gough Fracture Zone

SOUTH SANDWICH ISLANDS (to UK)

America-Antarctica Ridge

Atlantic-Indian Basin

Weddell Plain

Pernambuco Plain

Brazil Basin

Ilha da Trindade (to Brazil)

Rio Grande Rise

South Sandwich Trench

Fernando de Noronha (to Brazil)

Recife

Vitória Seamount

Santos Plateau

Argentine Basin

Zapiola Ridge

SOUTH GEORGIA (to UK)

East Scotia Basin

Scotia Sea

South Orkney Islands

Weddell Sea

SOUTH AMERICA

Rio de Janeiro

Buenos Aires

Paraná

Gulf of San Matías

Gulf of San Jorge

FALKLAND ISLANDS (to UK)

Falkland Plateau

Yaghan Basin

Drake Passage

South Shetland Islands

Andes

Peru-Chile Trench

Cape Horn

132

Chile Basin

Mornington Abyssal Plain

Bellingshausen Plain

PACIFIC OCEAN

Tropic of Capricorn

Peru Basin

Peru-Chile Trench

(to Ecuador)

Chile Rise

131

Bellingshausen

Bellingshausen Sea

Antarctic Circle

Limit of summer pack ice

N

S

5 6 7 8

E

D

C

B

A

80° 80° 40° 0° 40° 80° 80°

60° 60°

Elevation

-6000m -4000m -2000m -1000m -500m -250m -100m 0

-19,658ft -13,124ft -6562ft -3281ft -1640ft -820ft -328ft/-100m 0

Africa

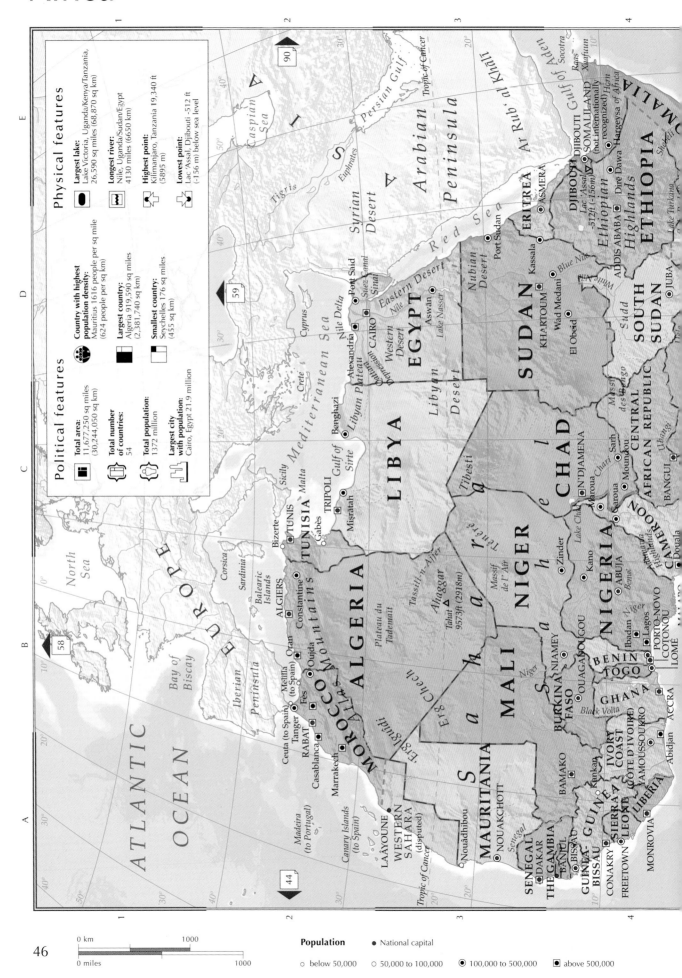

Political features

Total area:
11,677,250 sq miles
(30,244,050 sq km)

Total number of countries:
54

Total population:
1372 million

Largest city with population:
Cairo, Egypt 21.9 million

Physical features

Largest lake:
Lake Victoria, Uganda/Kenya/Tanzania, 26,590 sq miles (68,870 sq km)

Longest river:
Nile, Uganda/Sudan/Egypt 4130 miles (6650 km)

Highest point:
Kilimanjaro, Tanzania 19,340 ft (5895 m)

Lowest point:
Lac 'Assal, Djibouti -512 ft (-156 m) below sea level

Country with highest population density:
Mauritius 1616 people per sq mile (624 people per sq km)

Largest country:
Algeria 919,590 sq miles (2,381,740 sq km)

Smallest country:
Seychelles 176 sq miles (455 sq km)

ATLANTIC

OCEAN

North Sea

EUROPE

Bay of Biscay

Iberian Peninsula

Mediterranean Sea

Corsica

Sardinia

Balearic Islands

Sicily

Malta

Crete

Cyprus

Syrian Desert

Caspian Sea

Tigris

Euphrates

Persian Gulf

Arabian Peninsula

Ar Rub' al Khālī

Gulf of Aden

Socotra

Ras Xaafuun

Tropic of Cancer

Madeira (to Portugal)

Canary Islands (to Spain)

Ceuta (to Spain)

Tanger

Melilla (to Spain)

Oran

Oujda

Fes

Casablanca

RABAT

Marrakech

MOROCCO

Atlas Mountains

Constantine

ALGIERS

Oran

TUNIS

Bizerte

TUNISIA

Gabes

Misrātah

TRIPOLI

Gulf of Sirte

Benghazi

LIBYA

ALGERIA

Plateau du Tademaït

Erg Chech

Er-g-Iguidi

Tanezrouft

Sahara

Tassili-n-Ajjer

Ahaggar

Tahat 9573ft (2918m)

Massif de l'Aïr

Tibesti

Libyan Desert

Alexandria

CAIRO

Nile Delta

Port Said

Suez Canal

Sinai

Qattara Depression

Western Desert

EGYPT

Aswān

Lake Nasser

Nubian Desert

Eastern Desert

Nile

Red Sea

Port Sudan

Kassala

Khartoum

Wad Medani

El Obeid

SUDAN

Blue Nile

White Nile

Sudd

Massif des Bongo

SOUTH SUDAN

JUBA

ERITREA

ASMERA

DJIBOUTI

DJIBOUTI

Lac 'Assal -512ft (-156m)

SOMALILAND (not internationally recognized)

Hargeysa

Dire Dawa

ADDIS ABABA

Ethiopian Highlands

ETHIOPIA

Lake Turkana

Shebeli

SOMALIA

Horn of Africa

CENTRAL AFRICAN REPUBLIC

BANGUI

Ubangi

CAMEROON

Douala

Adamawa Highlands

Sarh

Moundou

N'DJAMENA

Maroua

Garoua

CHAD

Lake Chad

Chari

Logone

NIGER

Zinder

Kano

NIGERIA

ABUJA

Benue

Niger

IBADAN

Lagos

PORTO-NOVO

COTONOU

LOMÉ

BENIN

TOGO

ACCRA

GHANA

Black Volta

Sahel

MALI

Niger

NIAMEY

OUAGADOUGOU

BURKINA FASO

BAMAKO

IVORY COAST (CÔTE D'IVOIRE)

YAMOUSSOUKRO

Abidjan

Kankan

GUINEA

CONAKRY

SIERRA LEONE

FREETOWN

LIBERIA

MONROVIA

GUINEA-BISSAU

BISSAU

THE GAMBIA

BANJUL

SENEGAL

DAKAR

Senegal

MAURITANIA

NOUAKCHOTT

Nouâdhibou

WESTERN SAHARA (disputed)

LAÂYOUNE

Tropic of Cancer

0 km   1000

0 miles   1000

Population   ● National capital

○ below 50,000   ◉ 50,000 to 100,000   ◉ 100,000 to 500,000   ■ above 500,000

Northwest Africa

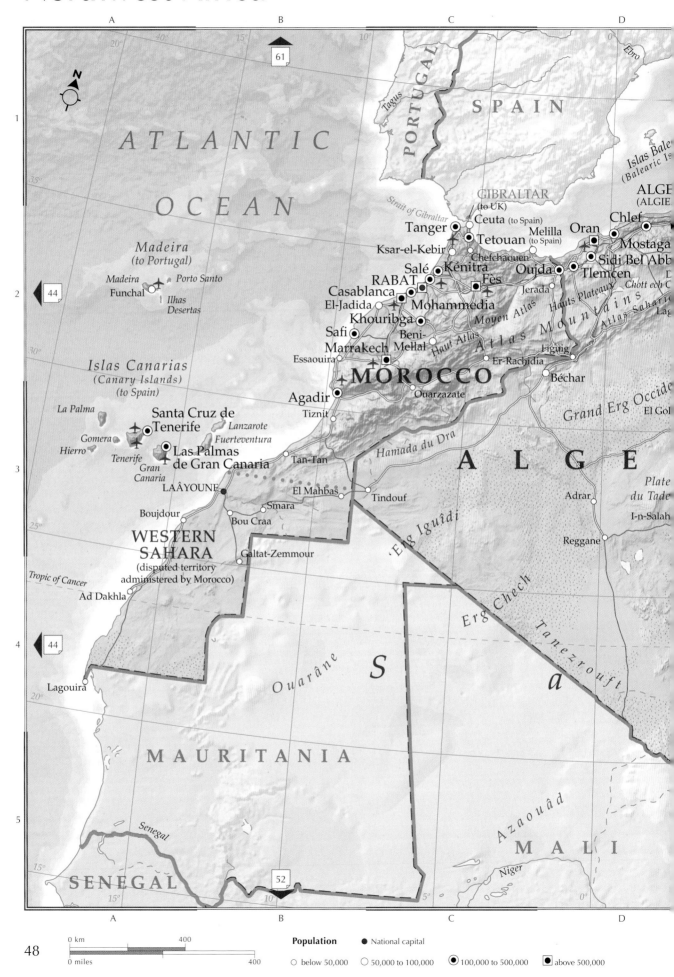

ATLANTIC

OCEAN

PORTUGAL

SPAIN

Tagus

GIBRALTAR
(to UK)

Strait of Gibraltar

Ceuta (to Spain)

Tanger
Tetouan
Ksar-el-Kebir

Chefchaouen

Melilla
(to Spain)

Oran

Chlef

ALGE
(ALGIE

Mostaga

Madeira
(to Portugal)

Madeira
Funchal
*Ilhas
Desertas*

Porto Santo

Salé
Kénitra
RABAT
Casablanca
El-Jadida
Mohammedia
Khouribga
Safi
Marrakech
Essaouira

Fès

Oujda
Tlemcen

Sidi Bel Abb

Jerada

Moyen Atlas

Hauts Plateaux

Atlas Sahari

Chott ech C

La

Islas Canarias
(Canary Islands)
(to Spain)

Beni-
Mellal

Haut Atlas

Atlas Mountains

Figuig

MOROCCO

Er-Rachidia

Béchar

La Palma

Santa Cruz de
Tenerife

Lanzarote

Fuerteventura

Agadir

Ouarzazate

Gomera

Hierro

Tenerife

Las Palmas
de Gran Canaria

Tiznit

Islas Bale
(Balearic Is

ALGE

Grand Erg Occide

El Gol

*Plate
du Tade*

*Gran
Canaria*

Tan-Tan

Hamada du Dra

Adrar

I-n-Salah

LAÂYOUNE

El Mahbas

Tindouf

Reggane

Boujdour

Smara

Bou Craa

'Erg Iguîdi

WESTERN
SAHARA
*(disputed territory
administered by Morocco)*

Galtat-Zemmour

Tropic of Cancer

Ad Dakhla

Erg Chech

Tanezrouft

Lagouira

Ouarâne

S

a

MAURITANIA

Azouâd

MALI

Senegal

Niger

SENEGAL

0 km   400

0 miles   400

Population   ● National capital

○ below 50,000   ◎ 50,000 to 100,000   ◉ 100,000 to 500,000   ▣ above 500,000

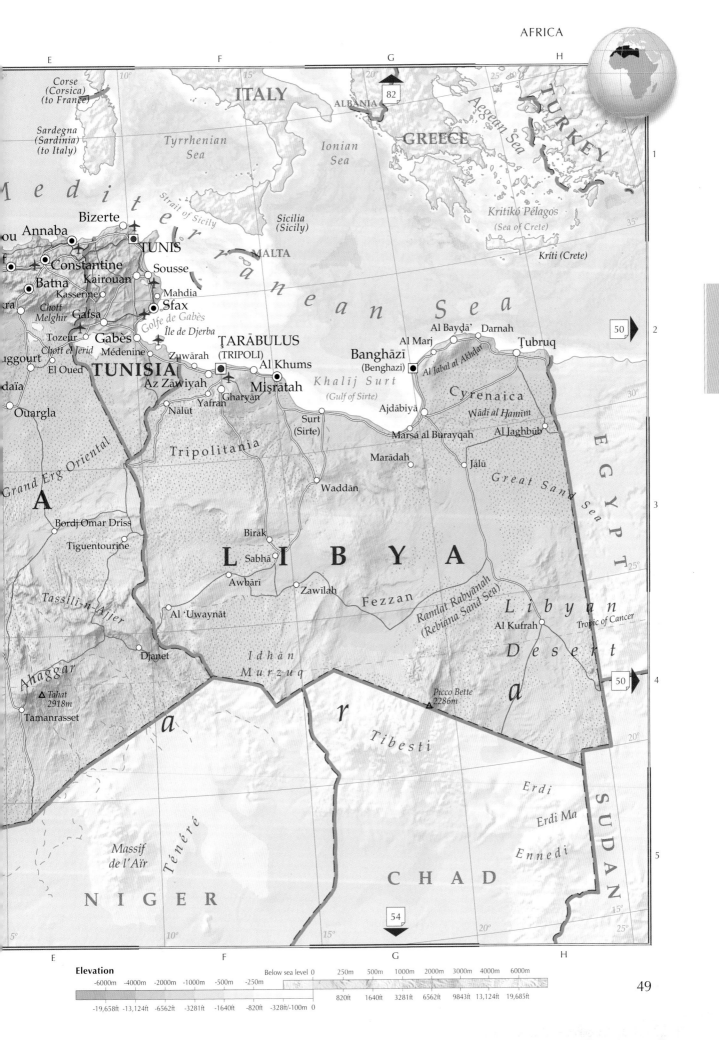

ITALY

82

ALBANIA

GREECE

TURKEY

Corse
(Corsica)
(to France)

Sardegna
(Sardinia)
(to Italy)

Tyrrhenian
Sea

Ionian
Sea

Aegean
Sea

Kritikó Pélagos
(Sea of Crete)

Kríti (Crete)

Bizerte

Annaba

ou

TUNIS

Strait of Sicily

Sicilia
(Sicily)

MALTA

Sousse

Constantine

f

Batna

Kairouan

Kasserine

Mahdia

Al Baydā'

Darnah

50

Chott
Melghir

Gafsa

Sfax

Golfe de Gabès

ŢARĀBULUS
(TRIPOLI)

Al Marj

Banghāzī
(Benghazi)

Ţubruq

kra

Tozeur

Gabès

Île de Djerba

Zuwārah

Al Khums

Al Jabal al Akhḍar

Chott el Jerid

Médenine

TUNISIA

Az Zāwiyah

Miṣrātah

Khalīj Surt
(Gulf of Sirte)

Cyrenaica

El Oued

Yafran

Gharyān

Ajdābiyā

Wādi al Ḥamīm

daïa

Ouargla

Nālūt

Surt
(Sirte)

Marsá al Burayqah

Al Jaghbūb

Grand Erg Oriental

Tripolitania

Marādah

Jālū

A

Waddān

Great Sand Sea

EGYPT

Bordj Omar Driss

Birāk

L   I   B   Y   A

Tiguentourine

Sabhā

Tassili-n-Ajjer

Awbārī

Zawīlah

Fezzan

Ramlat Rabyānah
(Rebiana Sand Sea)

Libyan

Al 'Uwaynāt

Al Kufrah

Tropic of Cancer

50

Djanet

Idhān
Murzuq

Desert

Ahaggar

△ Tahat
2918m

a

r

Picco Bette
2286m △

Tamanrasset

Tibesti

Erdi

SUDAN

Massif
de l'Aïr

Ténéré

Erdi Ma

Ennedi

N   I   G   E   R

C   H   A   D

54

Elevation

| | | | | | | Below sea level 0 | 250m | 500m | 1000m | 2000m | 3000m | 4000m | 6000m |

-6000m   -4000m   -2000m   -1000m   -500m   -250m

-19,658ft   -13,124ft   -6562ft   -3281ft   -1640ft   -820ft   -328ft/-100m   0

820ft   1640ft   3281ft   6562ft   9843ft   13,124ft   19,685ft

Northeast Africa

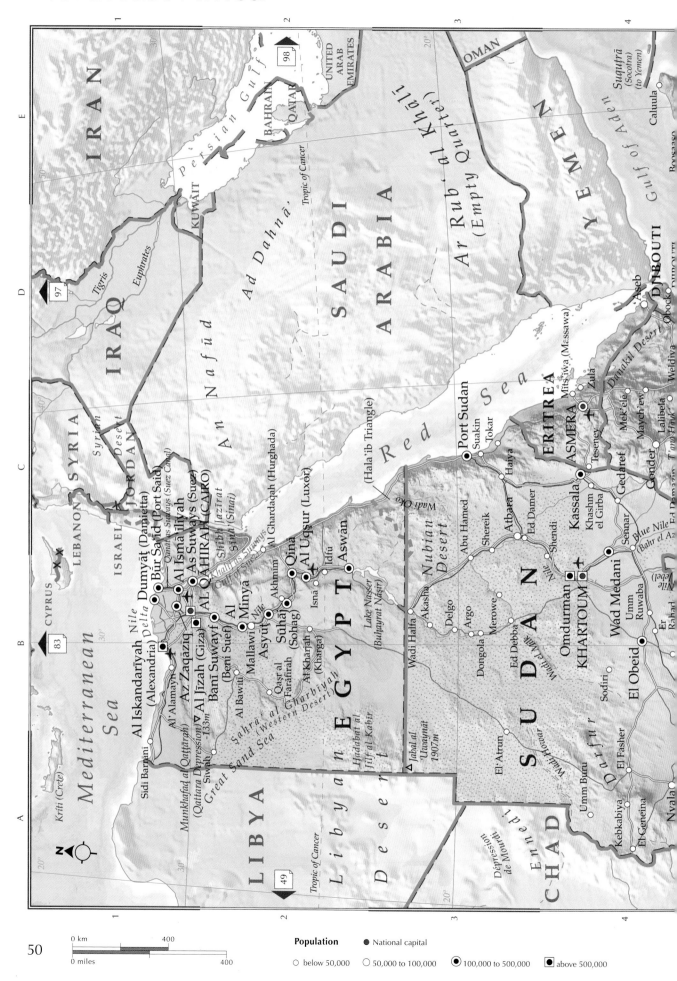

Population

● National capital

○ below 50,000
◯ 50,000 to 100,000
◉ 100,000 to 500,000
▣ above 500,000

50

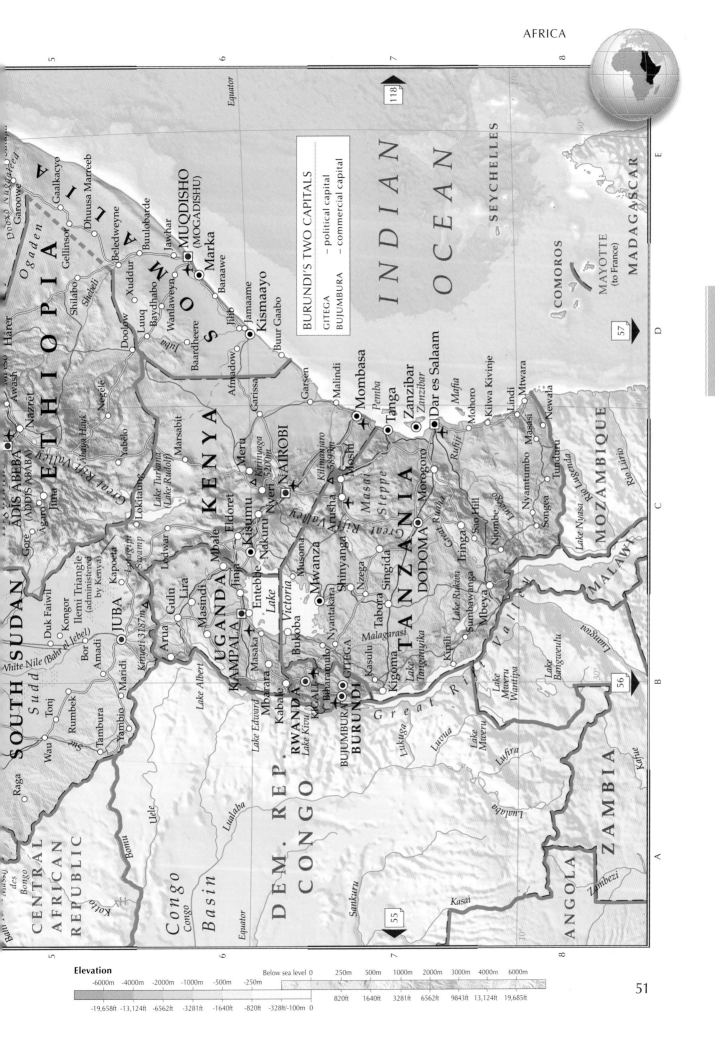

BURUNDI'S TWO CAPITALS
GITEGA – political capital
BUJUMBURA – commercial capital

Elevation

-6000m	-4000m	-2000m	-1000m	-500m	-250m	Below sea level 0	250m	500m	1000m	2000m	3000m	4000m	6000m	
-19,658ft	-13,124ft	-6562ft	-3281ft	-1640ft	-820ft	-328ft/-100m 0		820ft	1640ft	3281ft	6562ft	9843ft	13,124ft	19,685ft

West Africa

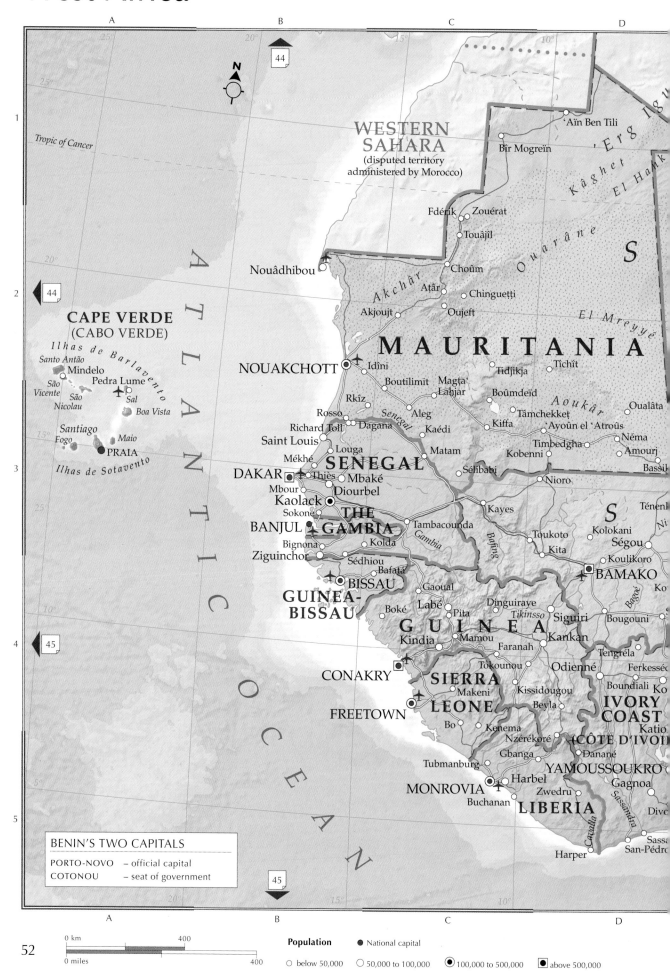

WESTERN
SAHARA
(disputed territory
administered by Morocco)

Tropic of Cancer

Aïn Ben Tili

Bîr Mogreïn

Fdérik · Zouérat

Touâjîl

Nouâdhibou

Choûm

Atâr · Chinguetti

Akjoujt

Akchâr

Oujeft

El Mreyyé

MAURITANIA

Ouarâne

S

CAPE VERDE
(CABO VERDE)

Ilhas de Barlavento

Santo Antão

Mindelo

Pedra Lume

São
Vicente

São
Nicolau

Sal

Boa Vista

Santiago

Fogo

Maio

PRAIA

Ilhas de Sotavento

A
T
L
A
N
T
I
C

NOUAKCHOTT

Idîni

Boutilimit

Magta'
Lahjar

Tidjikja

Tîchît

Boûmdeïd

Aoukâr

Oualâta

Rkîz

Rosso

Aleg

Kaédi

Tâmchekket

'Ayoûn el 'Atroûs

Néma

Richard Toll

Dagana

Kiffa

Timbedgha

Amourj

Saint Louis

Sénégal

Kobenni

Bassik

Louga

Matam

Sélibabi

Nioro

S

Mékhé

SENEGAL

DAKAR

Thiès

Mbaké

Ténenk

Mbour

Diourbel

Kayes

Kolokani

Ni

Kaolack

Toukoto

Ségou

Sokone

THE

Tambacounda

Kita

Koulikoro

BANJUL

GAMBIA

Gambia

Bafing

BAMAKO

Bignona

Kolda

Ziguinchor

Sédhiou

Bafatá

Ko

BISSAU

Gaoual

Bagoé

**GUINEA-
BISSAU**

Boké

Labé

Dinguiraye

Pita

Tikinsso

Siguiri

Bougouni

G U I N E A

Mamou

Kankan

Kindia

Faranah

Tengréla

Odienné

Ferkessé

CONAKRY

Tokounou

SIERRA

Makeni

Kissidougou

Boundiali

Ko

FREETOWN

LEONE

Beyla

**IVORY
COAST**

Bo

Konema

Katio

Nzérékoré

(CÔTE D'IVOI

Gbanga

Đanané

YAMOUSSOUKRO

Tubmanburg

Gagnoa

Harbel

Zwedru

MONROVIA

Buchanan

LIBERIA

Divo

Cavalla

Sassa
San-Pédro

Harper

Sassandra

O
C
E
A
N

BENIN'S TWO CAPITALS

PORTO-NOVO   – official capital
COTONOU   – seat of government

---

0 km   400

0 miles   400

Population   ● National capital

○ below 50,000   ○ 50,000 to 100,000   ◉ 100,000 to 500,000   ◼ above 500,000

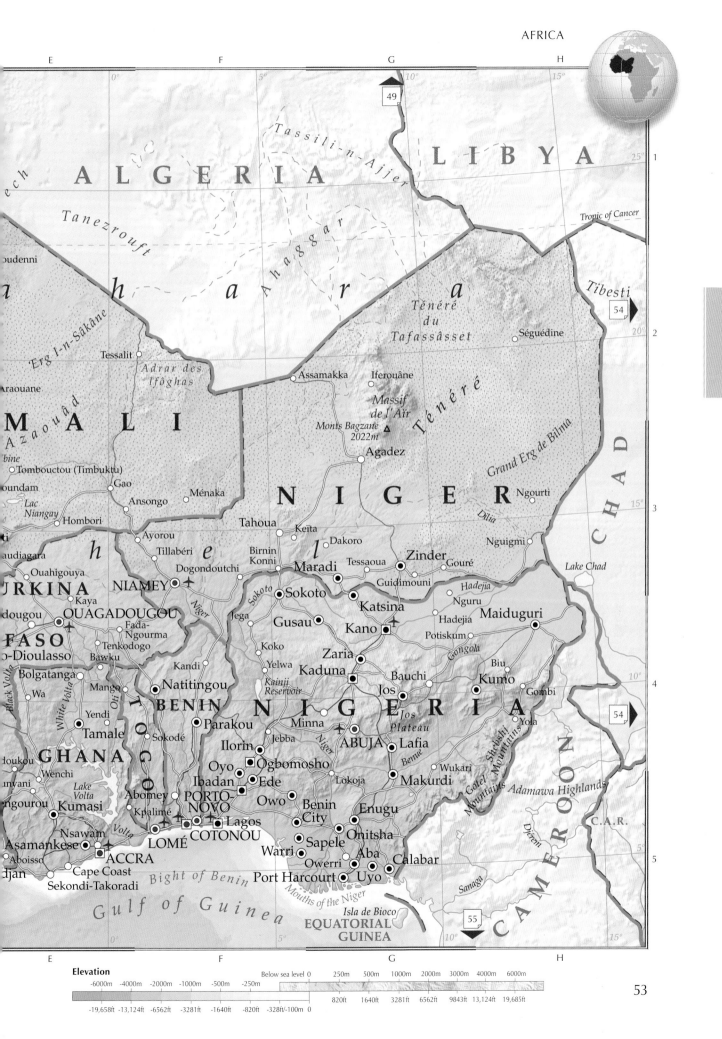

ALGERIA

LIBYA

Tassili-n-Ajjer

25°

Tanezrouft

Ahaggar

S a h a r a

Tibesti

54

Tropic of Cancer

Ténéré
du
Tafassâsset

Séguédine

20°

'Erg I-n-Sâkâne

Tessalit

Adrar des
Ifôghas

Assamakka

Iferouâne

Massif
de l' Air

Ténéré

Grand Erg de Bilma

oudenni

Araouane

MALI

Azaouâd

Tombouctou (Timbuktu)

Monts Bagzane
2022m

Agadez

bine

oundam

Lac
Niangay

Gao

Ménaka

NIGER

Ngourti

Ansongo

Ngourti

15°

Hombori

Tahoua

Keïta

Dakoro

Dilia

Nguigmi

3

audiagara

Ayorou

Tillabéri

Birnin
Konni

Maradi

Tessaoua

Zinder

Gouré

Lake Chad

Ouahigouya

Dogondoutchi

Maradi

Guidimouni

Hadejia

URKINA

Kaya

NIAMEY

Niger

Jega

Sokoto

Sokoto

Katsina

Nguru

Maiduguri

dougou

OUAGADOUGOU

Fada-
Ngourma

Koko

Gusau

Kano

Hadejia

Potiskum

FASO

Tenkodogo

Yelwa

Zaria

Biu

Kumo

o-Dioulasso

Bawku

Kandi

Kaduna

Bauchi

Gongola

Gombi

Bolgatanga

Mango

Oti

Kainji
Reservoir

Jos

Jos
Plateau

Yola

Wa

BENIN

Minna

ABUJA

Lafia

Shebshi Mountains

Yendi

Parakou

Jebba

Benue

Wukari

Tamale

Sokodé

Ilorin

Niger

Makurdi

Gotel
Mountains

Adamawa Highlands

GHANA

TOGO

Oyo

Ogbomosho

Lokoja

C.A.R.

oukou

Wenchi

Ibadan

Ede

Abomey

PORTO-
NOVO

Owo

Benin
City

Enugu

Djerem

myani

Lake
Volta

Kpalimé

Owo

Onitsha

CAMEROON

ngourou

Kumasi

LOMÉ

COTONOU

Lagos

Sapele

Aba

Calabar

Nsawam

Warri

Owerri

Uyo

Asamankese

ACCRA

Port Harcourt

Sanaga

Aboisso

Cape Coast

Bight of Benin

Mouths of the Niger

Ijan

Sekondi-Takoradi

Gulf of Guinea

Isla de Bioco

EQUATORIAL
GUINEA

55

Elevation

Below sea level 0   250m   500m   1000m   2000m   3000m   4000m   6000m

-6000m   -4000m   -2000m   -1000m   -500m   -250m

-19,658ft   -13,124ft   -6562ft   -3281ft   -1640ft   -820ft   -328ft/-100m   0

820ft   1640ft   3281ft   6562ft   9843ft   13,124ft   19,685ft

Central Africa

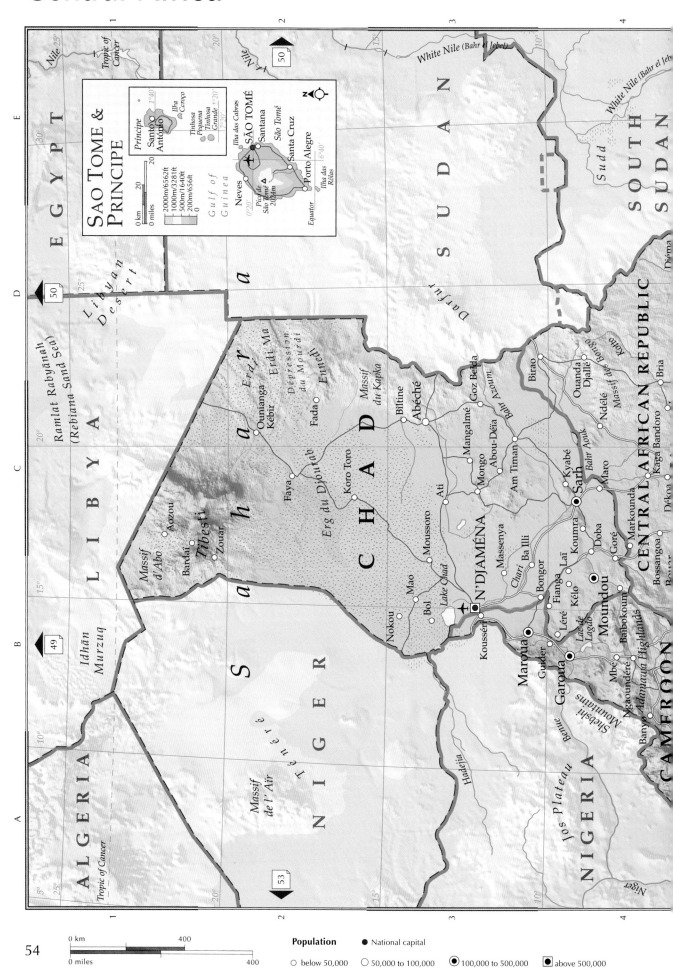

Sao Tome & Principe

Príncipe
Santo António
Ilha Cerejo
Tinhosa Pequena
Tinhosa Grande

Ilha das Cabras
SÃO TOMÉ
Santana
Santa Cruz
São Tomé
Neves
Pico de São Tomé 2024m
Porto Alegre
Ilha das Rôlas
Equator

Gulf of Guinea

2000m/6562ft
1000m/3281ft
500m/1640ft
200m/656ft

0 km
0 miles

EGYPT

Nile

Tropic of Cancer

Libyan Desert

Ramlat Rabyānah
(Rebiana Sand Sea)

LIBYA

Idhān Murzuq

ALGERIA

Tropic of Cancer

S a h a r a

Massif d'Abo
Aozou
Bardaï
Tibesti
Zouar

Massif de l'Aïr

Ténéré

NIGER

Nokou
Bol
Mao
Lake Chad

Massif du Kapka

Erdi Ma
Erdi
Ennedi
Depression du Mourdi

Ounianga Kébir
Fada
Koro Toro
Faya
Erg du Djourab

CHAD

Ati
Moussoro
Massenya
Chari
Bongor

Biltine
Abéché
Mangalmé
Mongo
Abou-Déia
Am Timan
Ba Illi

N'DJAMÉNA
Kousséri

Hadejia

Niger

NIGERIA

Jos Plateau

CAMEROON

Maroua
Guider
Garoua
Ngaoundéré
Banyo
Adamaua Highlands
Shebshi Mountains
Benue
Mbé
Baïbokoum
Moundou
Lac de Léré
Léré
Fianga
Kélo
Laï

Doba
Goré
Koumra

Sarh
Kyabé
Maro
Bahr Aouk

Markounda
Ndélé
Ouanda Djallé
Bria
Raga
Bandoro
Dékoa
Bossangoa
Déma

CENTRAL AFRICAN REPUBLIC

Massif des Bongo
Kōtō

Birao

Goz Beïda

Bahr Azoum

SUDAN

Darfur

White Nile (Bahr el Jebel)

White Nile (Bahr el Jebel)

Sudd

SOUTH SUDAN

0 km   400
0 miles   400

Population ● National capital

○ below 50,000   ○ 50,000 to 100,000   ◉ 100,000 to 500,000   ◼ above 500,000

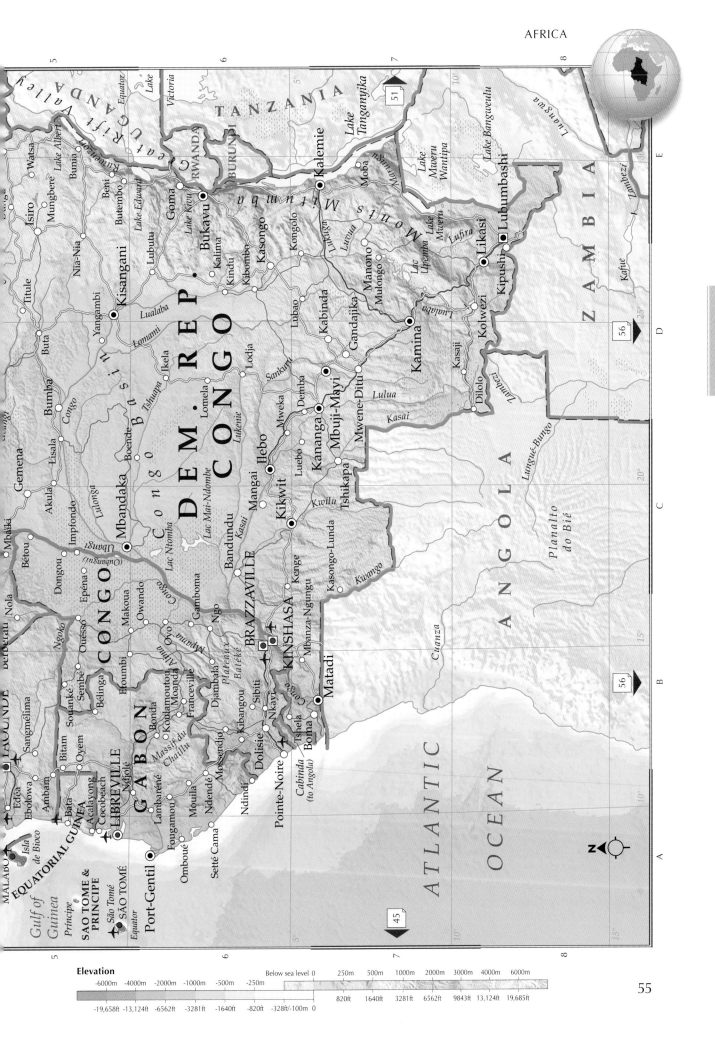

Southern Africa

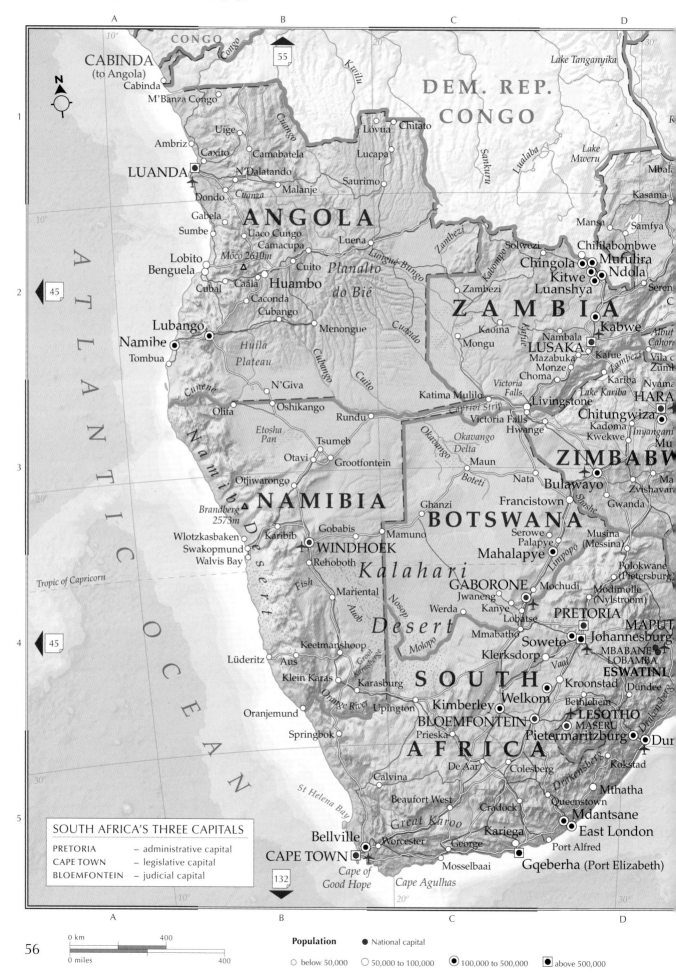

CABINDA
(to Angola)
Cabinda

M'Banza Congo

CONGO

DEM. REP.
CONGO

Lake Tanganyika

Uíge
Ambriz
Caxito
Camabatela
Lóvua
Chitato

LUANDA
N'Dalatando
Lucapa
Mbala

Dondo
Cuanza
Saurimo
Kasama

Gabela
Malanje
ANGOLA
Mansa
Samfya

Sumbe
Uaco Cungo
Camacupa
Luena
Solwezi
Chililabombwe

Lobito
Benguela
Môco 2610m
Cuito
Planalto
do Bié
Zambezi
Chingola
Mufulira
Kitwe
Ndola

Cubal
Caála
Huambo
Lungué-Bungo
Zambezi
Luanshya
Seren

Caconda
Cubango
ZAMBIA
Kabwe
Albuf
Cahore

Lubango
Menongue
Cuando
Kaoma
Mongu
Nambala
LUSAKA
Vila
Zúm

Namibe
Tombua
Cubango
Mazabuka
Monze
Choma
Kafue
Zambezi
Kariba

N'Giva
Cuito
Victoria
Falls
Lake Kariba
Nyama
HARA

Olifa
Oshikango
Katima Mulilo
Caprivi Strip
Livingstone
Chitungwiza

Cunene
Rundu
Victoria Falls
Hwange
Kadoma
Kwekwe
Inyangani
Mu

Etosha
Pan
Tsumeb
Okavango
Okavango
Delta
ZIMBABW

Otavi
Grootfontein
Maun
Boteti
Nata
Bulawayo
Ma
Zvishavan

Otjiwarongo
Ghanzi
Francistown
Gwanda

Brandberg
2573m
NAMIBIA
BOTSWANA
Shashe
Musina
(Messina)

Karibib
Gobabis
Mamuno
Serowe
Palapye
Limpopo
Polokwane
(Pietersburg)

Wlotzkasbaken
Swakopmund
Walvis Bay
WINDHOEK
Rehoboth
Mahalapye
Modimolle
(Nylstroom)

Fish
Kalahari
GABORONE
Mochudi
PRETORIA

Mariental
Jwaneng
Kanye
Lobatse
MAPUT

Werda
Mmabatho
Johannesburg
MBABANE
LOBAMBA

Keetmanshoop
Nosop
Desert
Soweto
ESWATINI

Lüderitz
Aus
Klein Karas
Molopo
Klerksdorp
Kroonstad
Dundee

Karasburg
SOUTH
Vaal
Welkom
Bethlehem

Oranjemund
Orange River
Upington
Kimberley
BLOEMFONTEIN
LESOTHO
MASERU
Pietermaritzburg
Dur

Springbok
Prieska
AFRICA
Colesberg
Kokstad

Calvina
De Aar
Mthatha
Queenstown
Mdantsane

Beaufort West
Cradock
Kariega
East London

St Helena Bay
Great Karoo
Port Alfred

Bellville
Worcester
George
Mosselbaai
Gqeberha (Port Elizabeth)

CAPE TOWN
Cape of
Good Hope
Cape Agulhas

ATLANTIC OCEAN

Namib Desert

Huíla Plateau

Tropic of Capricorn

SOUTH AFRICA'S THREE CAPITALS

PRETORIA – administrative capital
CAPE TOWN – legislative capital
BLOEMFONTEIN – judicial capital

0 km   400
0 miles   400

Population   ● National capital
○ below 50,000   ○ 50,000 to 100,000   ◉ 100,000 to 500,000   ■ above 500,000

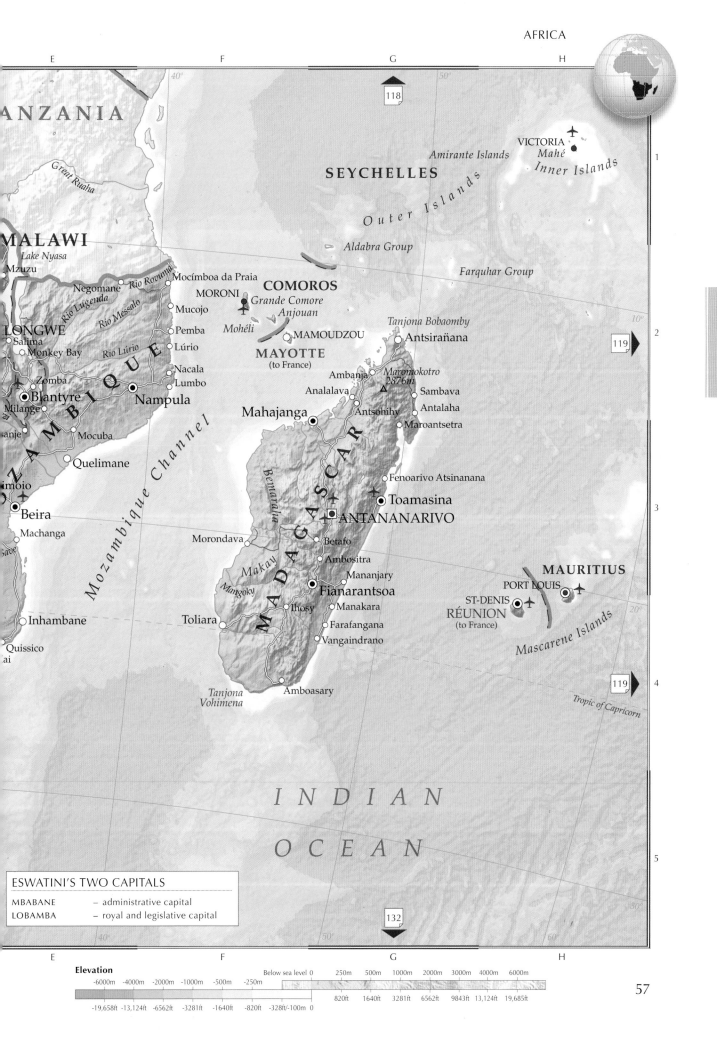

ANZANIA

MALAWI

SEYCHELLES

Amirante Islands

VICTORIA
Mahé
Inner Islands

Outer Islands

Aldabra Group

Farquhar Group

Great Ruaha

Mzuzu
Negomane
Rio Rovuma
Mocímboa da Praia

LONGWE
Salima
Monkey Bay
Zomba
Blantyre
Milange
anje
Mocuba

Rio Lugenda
Rio Messalo
Mucojo
Pemba
Lúrio
Nacala
Lumbo
Nampula

COMOROS
MORONI
Grande Comore
Anjouan
Mohéli
MAMOUDZOU
MAYOTTE
(to France)

Tanjona Bobaomby
Antsirañana

Ambanja
Analalava
Maromokotro
2876m
Sambava
Antalaha
Antsohihy
Maroantsetra

Mahajanga

Bemaraha

MADAGASCAR

Fenoarivo Atsinanana

Toamasina
ANTANANARIVO

Morondava
Betafo
Ambositra
Mananjary
Fianarantsoa
Ihosy
Manakara
Farafangana
Vangaindrano

Toliara

Makay
Mangoky

Tanjona
Vohimena
Amboasary

MAURITIUS
PORT LOUIS
ST-DENIS
RÉUNION
(to France)

Mascarene Islands

Tropic of Capricorn

Quelimane
imoio
Beira
Machanga
Save
Inhambane
Quissico
ai

MOZAMBIQUE

Mozambique Channel

INDIAN

OCEAN

Lake Nyasa

Zomba
Blantyre

118

119

119

132

118

ESWATINI'S TWO CAPITALS

| MBABANE | – administrative capital |
| LOBAMBA | – royal and legislative capital |

Elevation

						Below sea level 0	250m	500m	1000m	2000m	3000m	4000m	6000m
-6000m	-4000m	-2000m	-1000m	-500m	-250m								

							820ft	1640ft	3281ft	6562ft	9843ft	13,124ft	19,685ft
-19,658ft	-13,124ft	-6562ft	-3281ft	-1640ft	-820ft	-328ft/-100m 0							

Europe

Political features

Total area:
4,809,200 sq miles
(12,456,000 sq km)

Total number of countries:
44

Total population:
723 million

Largest city with population:
Moscow, European Russia 17.4 million

Country with highest population density:
Monaco 50,145 people per sq mile
(19,497 people per sq km)

Largest country:
European Russia 1,527,341 sq miles
(3,955,818 sq km)

Smallest country:
Vatican City, Italy 0.17 sq miles
(0.44 sq km)

Physical features

Largest lake:
Lake Lagoda, European Russia
6800 sq miles (17,700 sq km)

Longest river:
Volga, European Russia
2194 miles (3531 km)

Highest point:
El'brus, Caucasus, European Russia
18,510ft (5642 m)

Lowest point:
Volga Delta, Caspian Sea, European
Russia -92ft (-28m) below sea level

133
44
44
46

REYKJAVÍK
ICELAND
Vatnajökull

Reykjanes Ridge

Limit of winter pack ice

Arctic Circle

Iceland Basin

Norwegian Basin

Norwegian Sea

Hatton Ridge

Faroe-Iceland Ridge

FAROE ISLANDS
(to Denmark)

Trondheim

Faroe-Shetland Trough

Shetland Islands

Bergen

Stavanger

OSLO

Rockall Bank

Rockall Trough

Outer Hebrides

Orkney Islands

British Isles

Glasgow

Edinburgh

North Sea

Gothenburg
Aalborg
Jönkö

Porcupine Plain

Ireland

Belfast

Isle of Man

UNITED KINGDOM

DENMARK

Jutland

IRELAND

DUBLIN

Liverpool

Manchester

Britain

Birmingham

Hamburg

Odense

Mal

COPENHA

Celtic Sea

Cardiff

LONDON

NETHERLANDS

THE HAGUE

AMSTERDAM

Rotterdam

Elbe

Hanover

N

Celtic Shelf

English Channel

Channel Islands

le Havre

BELGIUM

BRUSSELS

Düsseldorf

BERLIN

ATLANTIC

Azores-Biscay Rise

Charcot Seamounts

Biscay Plain

Rennes

Seine

Liège

Bonn

LUXEMBOURG

GERMANY

Wroc

OCEAN

PARIS

LUXEMBOURG

Rhine

Frankfurt am Main

PRAGU

CZECHIA

(CZECH REPU

Nantes

Loire

Orléans

Strasbourg

Stuttgart

BRA

Bay of Biscay

A Coruña

Galicia Bank

FRANCE

Zurich

Munich

VIENNA

Salzburg

AUSTRI

Iberian Plain

Cordillera Cantábrica

Bordeaux

Bilbao

Massif Central

Mont Blanc
15,774ft
(4808m)

BERN

Lyon

SWITZERLAND

Innsbruck

LIECH

Milan

SLOVENIA

Porto

Duero

Rhône

Toulouse

Turin

LJUBLJANA

Venice

Trieste

PORTUGAL

Pyrenees

ANDORRA

Nice

Bologna

CRO

Iberian

Zaragoza

Ebro

Nantes

Marseille

MONACO

Pisa

SAN MARINO

Tagus Plain

LISBON

Tagus

MADRID

I T A L Y

Apennines

B

SAR

Mo

Adriatic S

SPAIN

Peninsula

Barcelona

Corsica

VATICAN CITY

ROME

Madeira
(to Portugal)

Seville

Guadalquivir

Valencia

Sardinia

Naples

Bari

Strait of Gibraltar

Málaga

Palma

Algerian Basin

Cagliari

Tyrrhenian Sea

Cosenza

GIBRALTAR
(to UK)

Ceuta
(to Spain)

Balearic Islands

M e d i t e r r a n e a

Palermo

I

Canary Islands
(to Spain)

Melilla
(to Spain)

Mount Etna
10,922ft
(3329m)

Catania

Sicily

Io

Atlas Mountains

AFRICA

MALTA

VALLETTA

0 km 500
0 miles 500

Population   ● National capital

○ below 50,000   ◎ 50,000 to 100,000   ◉ 100,000 to 500,000   ▣ above 500,000

Barents Sea

North Cape

Ostrov Kolguyev

133

Arctic Circle

Ob'

Irtysh

Murmansk

Kola
Peninsula

FINLAND

White
Sea

Archangel

Northern Dvina

R U S S I A

Tampere

Lake Onega

Perm'

90

Turku

HELSINKI

Lake Ladoga

Vologda

Ufa

TALLINN

Saint Petersburg

Yaroslavl'

Kazan'

ESTONIA

Nizhniy
Novgorod

Ul'yanovsk

Orenburg

LATVIA

MOSCOW

Samara

Ural

Syr Darya

RIGA

Volga Uplands

Volga

LITHUANIA

Vitsyebsk/
Vitebsk

Central
Russian
Upland

Aral Sea

KALININGRAD
(to Russia)

VILNIUS

Kaunas

Amu Darya

MINSK

Babruysk/
Bobruysk

Homyel'/
Gomel'

Voronezh

Ural

WARSAW

BELARUS

Brest

Pripyat
Marshes

Dnieper Lowland

Don

Volgograd

Kraków

Lviv

UKRAINE

Dnieper

Kharkiv

Astrakhan'

Volga Delta
98ft (-28m)

Dniester

KYIV

Dnipro

Donetsk

Rostov-na-Donu

Chernivtsi

MOLDOVA

Caspian Sea

CHIŞINĂU

Sea of
Azov

Stavropol'

Cluj-Napoca

ROMANIA

Odesa

Crimea

Caucasus

BELGRADE

Braşov

Simferopol

El'brus 18,510ft
(5642m)

BUCHAREST

Constanţa

(since 2014 the Ukrainian
territory of Crimea has been
annexed by Russia)

Danube

Black
Sea

BULGARIA

Varna

Balkan Mountains

Burgas

KOSOVO
(disputed)

PRISTINA

SOFIA

NORTH
MACEDONIA

TURKEY
(TÜRKIYE)

Aegean
Sea

Anatolia

GREECE

ATHENS

Piraeus

Peloponnese

Zagros Mountains

Crete

Irákleio

Cyprus

96

Tigris

Euphrates

The North Atlantic

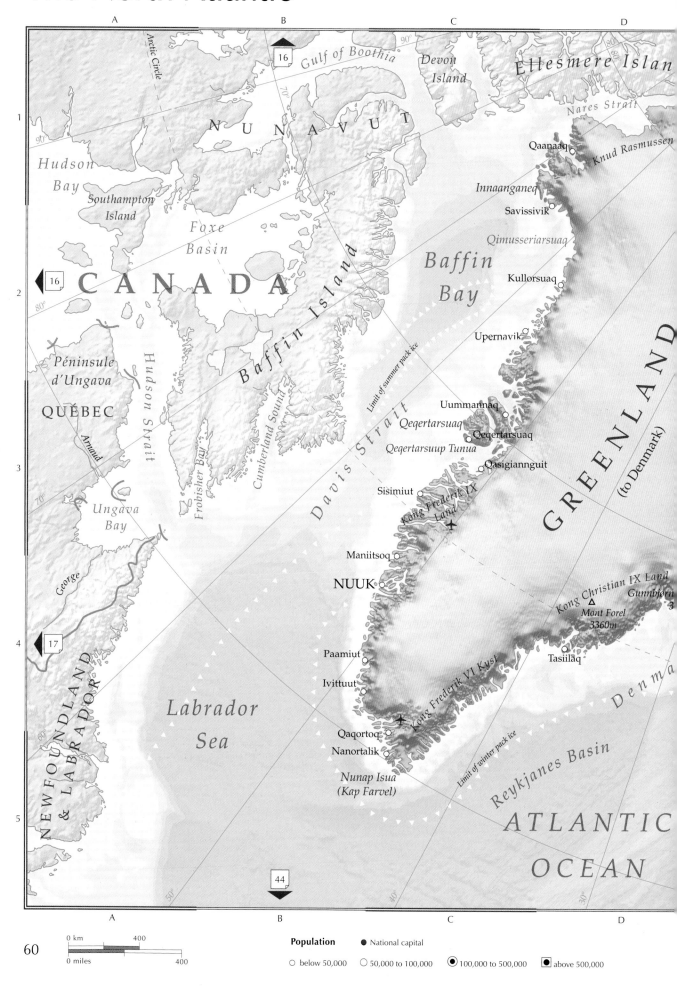

Gulf of Boothia

Devon Island

Ellesmere Islan

Nares Strait

NUNAVUT

Hudson Bay

Southampton Island

Foxe Basin

CANADA

Baffin Island

Qaanaaq

Knud Rasmussen

Innaanganeq

Savissivik

Qimusseriarsuaq

Baffin Bay

Kullorsuaq

Upernavik

Péninsule d'Ungava

QUÉBEC

Hudson Strait

Cumberland Sound

Frobisher Bay

Arnaud

Limit of summer pack ice

Davis Strait

Uummannaq

Qeqertarsuaq

Qeqertarsuaq

Qeqertarsuup Tunua

Qasigianguit

GREENLAND

(to Denmark)

Ungava Bay

Sisimiut

Kong Frederik IX Land

George

Maniitsoq

NUUK

Kong Christian IX Land

Gunnbjørn

Mont Forel 3360m

Paamiut

Ivittuut

Tasiilaq

Kong Frederik VI Kyst

NEWFOUNDLAND & LABRADOR

Labrador Sea

Qaqortoq

Nanortalik

Nunap Isua (Kap Farvel)

Limit of winter pack ice

Denma

Reykjanes Basin

ATLANTIC

OCEAN

Arctic Circle

0 km   400
0 miles   400

Population   National capital

○ below 50,000   ○ 50,000 to 100,000   ◉ 100,000 to 500,000   ■ above 500,000

ARCTIC
OCEAN

*Zemlya
Frantsa-Iosifa*

Kap Morris Jesup

*Wandel
Sea*

Kvitøya

Independence Fjord

*Novaya
Zemlya*

Nord

SVALBARD
(to Norway)

Nordaustlandet

Kong Karls Land

Spitsbergen

Barentsøya

*Barents
Sea*

Edgeøya

LONGYEARBYEN
Barentsburg

Storfjorden

88

*Greenland
Sea*

Limit of winter pack ice

*Peternann Bjerg
2940m*

Daneborg

Limit of summer pack ice

*Bjørnøya
(to Norway)*

*Nordkapp
(North Cape)*

Mohns Ridge

FINLAND

Kong Oscar Fjord

Ittoqqortoormiit

Kangertittivaq

Kangikajik

JAN MAYEN
(to Norway)

Arctic Circle

Vestfjorden

62

*Norwegian
Sea*

ICELAND

olungarvík
Siglufjörður   Raufarhöfn
rður
Húsavík
Akureyri
Seyðisfjörður
Stykkishólmur   Neskaupstaður
REYKJAVÍK
Selfoss   Vatnajökull
orlákshöfn   Djúpivogur
rtsey   Hvannadalshnúkur
2119m
Vestmannaeyjar

Norwegian Basin

S
W
E
D
E
N

*Gulf
of
Bothnia*

FAROE ISLANDS
(to Denmark)

N O R W A Y

N

TÓRSHAVN

63

*Shetland
Islands*

E   F   G   H

Elevation

| Below sea level 0 | 250m | 500m | 1000m | 2000m | 3000m | 4000m | 6000m |

-6000m   -4000m   -2000m   -1000m   -500m   -250m

820ft   1640ft   3281ft   6562ft   9843ft   13,124ft   19,685ft

-19,658ft   -13,124ft   -6562ft   -3281ft   -1640ft   -820ft   -328ft/-100m   0

Scandinavia & Finland

Barents Sea

RUSSIA

Arctic Ocean

Nordkapp (North Cape)

Magerøya

Varangerhalvøya

Varangerfjorden

Porsangerfjorden

Søroya

Kirkenes

Tana Bru

Lakselv

Alta

Talvik

Deatnu

Vadisjohka

Kaaresvuohka (Garasavon)

Kautokeino (Fanašjohka)

Karigasniemi (Čáregasnjárga)

Inarijärvi

Kaamanen

Ivalo (Avvil, Avveel)

Saariselkä (Skoločielgi)

Sodankylä

Sattanen

Kitinen

Kemijärvi

Kuusamo

Pudasjärvi

Suomussalmi

Kuhmo

Sotkamo

Ringvassøya

Kvaløya

Senja

Tromsø

Andøya

Harstad

Narvik

Hinnøya

Vesterålen

Lofoten

Vestfjorden

Saltfjorden

Bodø

Vega

Namsos

Steinkjer

Mosjøen

Mo i Rana

Fauske

Kebnekaise 2117m

Kiruna

Malmberget

Gällivare

Skalka

Jokkmokk

Arvidsjaur

Storuman

Vilhelmina

Storliden

Dorotea

Lycksele

Angermanälven

Umeälven

Skellefteälven

Borgefjell

Lapland

Kvänangen

Kaaresvanto

Muonio

Kolari

Muonionjoki

Tornetrask

Visttasjohka

Tornionjoki

Ounasjoki

Rovaniemi

Kemijoki

Kemi

Tornio

Haparanda

Kalix

Boden

Luleå

Luleälven

Piteå

Skellefteå

Kokkola (Karleby)

Kokkola (Karleby)

Kvitojoki

Oulu

Oulujoki

Oulu (Uleåborg)

Hailuoto

Kempele

Raahe

Kajaani (Kajana)

Oulujärvi

FINLAND

Gulf of Bothnia

Barents Sea

Norwegian Sea

Arctic Circle

Arctic Circle

Population ● National capital

0 km   200
0 miles   200

○ below 50,000   ○ 50,000 to 100,000   ◉ 100,000 to 500,000   ◼ above 500,000

RUSSIA

Ladozhskoye Ozero

Lappeenranta
(Villmanstrand)
Varkaus
Haukivesi
Imatra
Joutseno
Jyväskylä
Saimaa
Kotka
Kouvola
Lahti (Lahtis)
Porvoo (Borgå)
Riihimäki
HELSINKI/HELSINGFORS

RUSSIA

ESTONIA

Lake Peipus

LATVIA

Western Dvina

LITHUANIA

BELARUS

Gulf of Riga

Tampere (Tammerfors)
Nokia
Hämeenlinna (Tavastehus)
Hyvinkää
Salo
Vantaa (Vanda)
Espoo (Esbo)

Seinäjoki
Keuruu
Näsijärvi
Pori (Björneborg)
Rauma

Hiiumaa

Saaremaa

Hanko (Hangö)

KALININGRAD (to Russia)

Turku (Åbo)

Gulf of Finland

Courland Lagoon

POLAND

Gulf of Gdansk

Åland

Ålands Hav

SWEDEN

STOCKHOLM

Uppsala
Täby
Sollentuna
Norrtälje

Gotland

Wisla

Härnösand
Sundsvall
Hudiksvall
Söderhamn
Gävle
Sandviken
Tierp
Sala
Västerås
Nora
Örebro
Askersund
Nyköping
Norrköping
Linköping

Visby

Borgholm
Öland
Kalmar

Baltic Sea

Kramfors
Timrå
Ånge
Bollnäs
Rättvik
Leksand
Falun
Ludvika
Borlänge
Mora
Malung
Klarälven
Filipstad
Karlstad
Säffle
Mariestad
Vättern
Jönköping
Oskarshamn
Växjö
Karlskrona
Kristianstad

Hjälmaren
Hanöbukten

Liusnan
Ljusdal
Sveg
Idre
Svenstavik
Rätan

Grums
Åmål
Mellerud
Lidköping
Vänern
Borås
Mölndal
Kungsbacka
Varberg
Ljungby
Lakolp
Helsingborg
Lund
Malmö
Rønne
Bornholm

Ringebu
Roros
Dombås
Fokstua
Hamar
Lillehammer
Gjøvik
Mjøsa
Lillestrøm
OSLO
Ski
Moss
Sarpsborg
Halden
Uddevalla
Trollhättan
Göteborg (Gothenburg)
Halmstad
Halmstad
Kattegat
KØBENHAVN (Copenhagen)
Møn
Falster
Nykøbing
Lolland

NORWAY

Jotunheimen
Glittertind 2472m

Setesdal

Stavanger
Sandnes
Liknes
Moi
Evje
Kristiansand

Skagerrak

North Sea

Hjørring
Aalborg
Holstebro
Hobro
Viborg
Randers
Aarhus
Varde
Esbjerg
Rømø
Kolding
Odense
Slagelse
Storebælt
Fyn
Sjælland
Lolland

DENMARK

Jylland

Ringkøbing Fjord

GERMANY

Elbe

Weser

Ems

Oder

The Low Countries

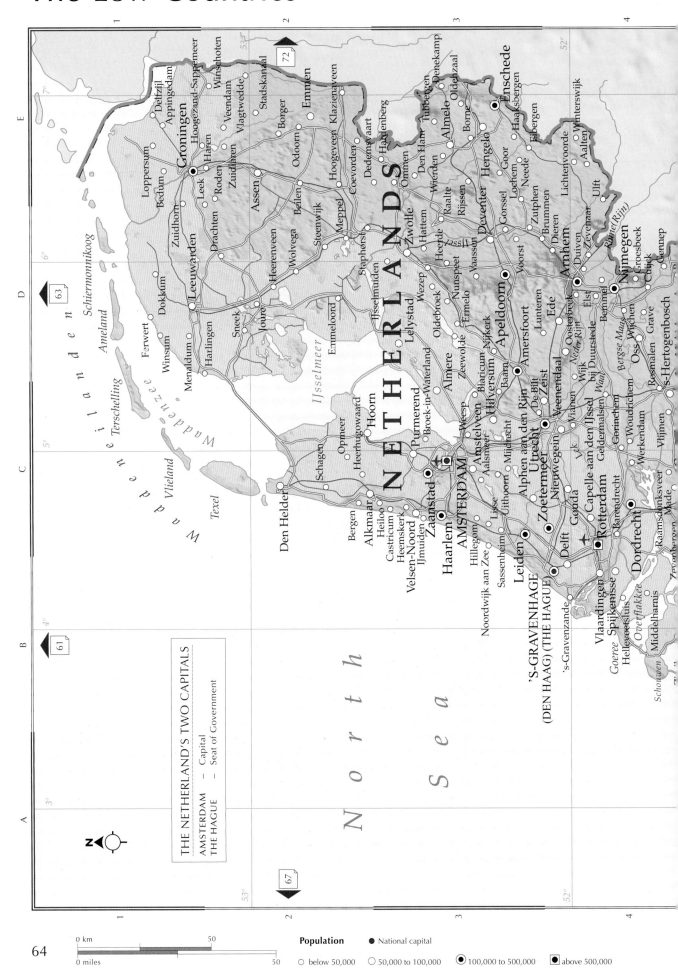

THE NETHERLAND'S TWO CAPITALS

AMSTERDAM – Capital
THE HAGUE – Seat of Government

Population

- National capital
- ○ below 50,000
- ○ 50,000 to 100,000
- ◉ 100,000 to 500,000
- ▣ above 500,000

0 km   50
0 miles   50

Elevation

						Below sea level 0	250m	500m	1000m	2000m	3000m	4000m	6000m
-6000m	-4000m	-2000m	-1000m	-500m	-250m								
-19,658ft	-13,124ft	-6562ft	-3281ft	-1640ft	-820ft	-328ft/-100m 0		820ft	1640ft	3281ft	6562ft	9843ft 13,124ft 19,685ft	

The British Isles

North Sea

ATLANTIC OCEAN

Shetland Islands

Unst
Yell
Fetlar
Mainland
Lerwick

Fair Isle

Sanday
Orkney Islands
Kirkwall
Mainland
Hoy
John o'Groats

Thurso

Ben Hope
927m △

North West Highlands

The Minch

Ullapool

The Little Minch

Isle of Lewis
Stornoway

Harris

North Uist

South Uist

Barra

St Kilda

Outer Hebrides

Isle of Skye
Strometerry

Rhum
Eigg
Coll
Tiree

Isle of Mull

Mallaig
Fort William

Oban

Firth of Lorn

Jura

Islay

Kintyre

Inner Hebrides

Isle of Arran

Fraserburgh
Peterhead
Aberdeen

Elgin
Moray Firth

Spey
Dee

Inverness
Loch Ness
Aviemore

Ben Nevis
1343m △

SCOTLAND

Grampian Mountains

Montrose
Arbroath
Dundee
St Andrews

Forfar

Tay

Perth
Forth Dunfermline
Stirling
Firth of Forth
Edinburgh

Loch
Lomond
Greenock
Paisley
Glasgow
Hamilton
Clyde

East Kilbride
Kilmarnock
Prestwick
Ayr

Berwick-upon-Tweed

Galashiels
Hawick

Newcastle upon Tyne

0 km   100

0 miles   100

Population ● National capital   ● Internal administrative capital

○ below 50,000   ○ 50,000 to 100,000   ◉ 100,000 to 500,000   ▣ above 500,000

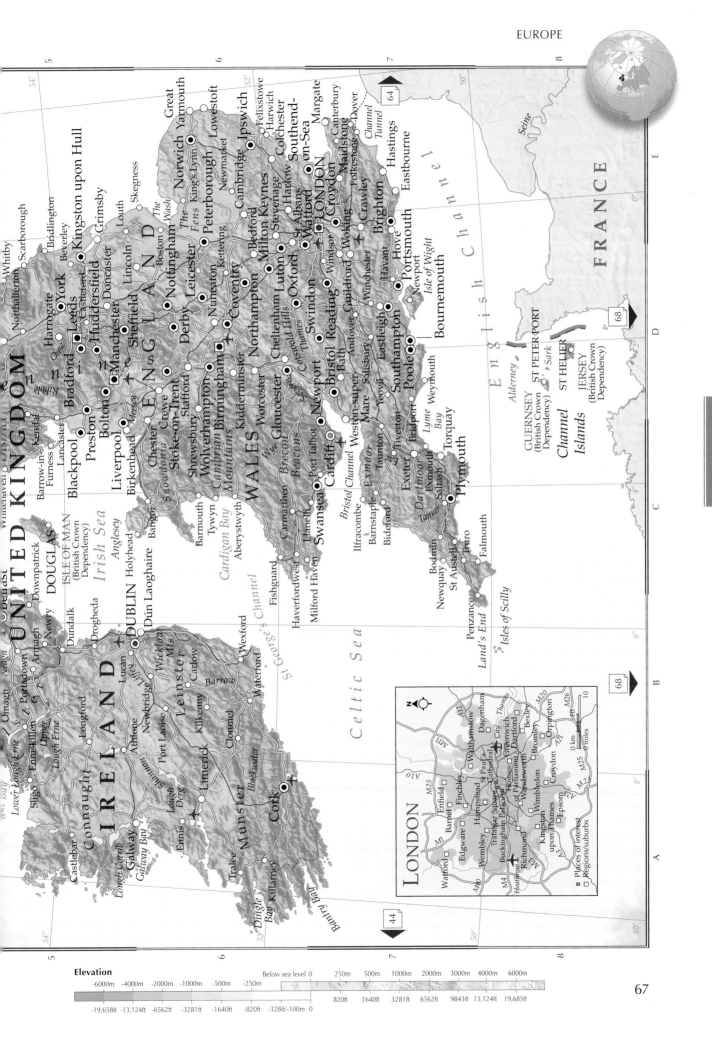

UNITED KINGDOM

ENGLAND

WALES

IRELAND

Connaught
Leinster
Munster

FRANCE

Celtic Sea

Irish Sea

English Channel

ISLE OF MAN
(British Crown Dependency)

GUERNSEY
(British Crown Dependency)

JERSEY
(British Crown Dependency)

Channel Islands

LONDON

Places of interest
Regions/suburbs

Elevation

Below sea level	0	250m	500m	1000m	2000m	3000m	4000m	6000m

-6000m	-4000m	-2000m	-1000m	-500m	-250m			

| -19,658ft | -13,124ft | -6562ft | -3281ft | -1640ft | -820ft | -328ft/-100m | 0 | 820ft | 1640ft | 3281ft | 6562ft | 9843ft | 13,124ft | 19,685ft |

France, Andorra & Monaco

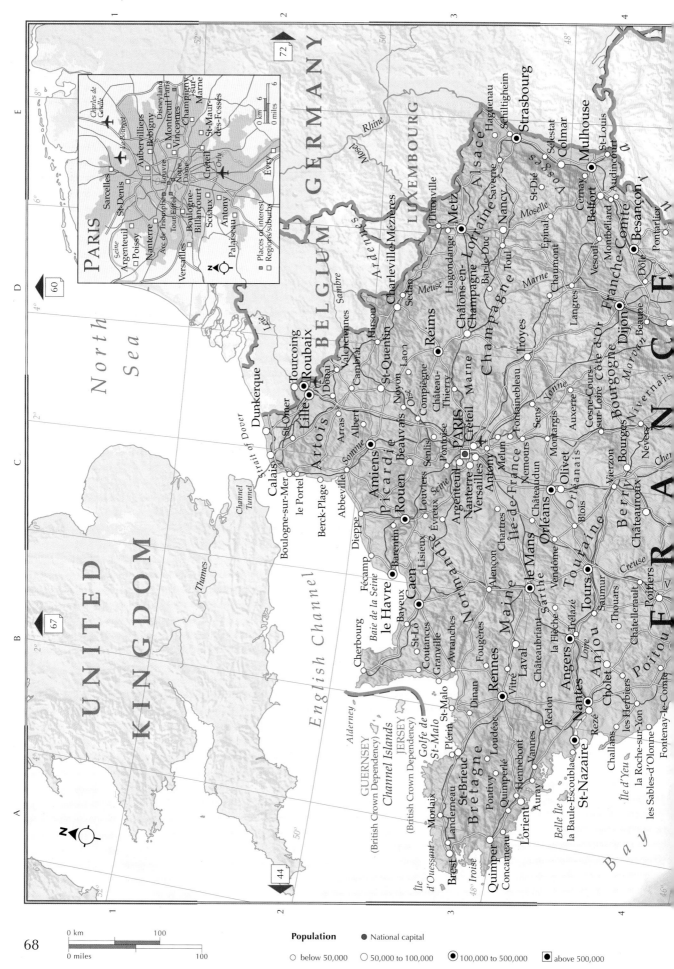

Population   ● National capital

○ below 50,000   ○ 50,000 to 100,000   ◉ 100,000 to 500,000   ◼ above 500,000

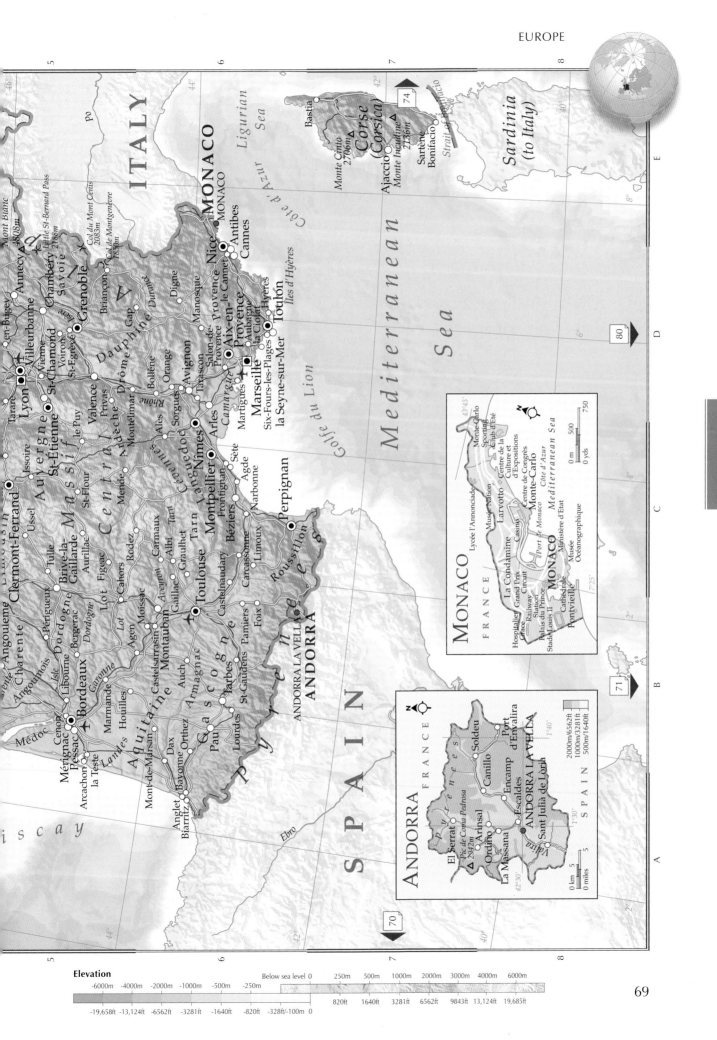

ITALY

Mont Blanc 4808m △
Col du Mont Cenis 2083m
Little St-Bernard Pass
St-Bernard Pass
Col de Montgenèvre 1850m 2188m

MONACO

Ligurian Sea

Bastia
Corse (Corsica)
Monte Cinto 2706m △
Monte Incudine △ 2136m
Ajaccio
Sartène
Bonifacio
Strait of Bonifacio

Sardinia (to Italy)

Annecy △
Villeurbanne
Chambéry
Savoie
Grenoble
Voiron
St-Egrève
Briançon
Gap
Digne
Manosque
Salon-de-Provence
Aix-en-Provence
Antibes
Nice
Cannes
MONACO
Côte d'Azur

Mediterranean Sea

Tarare
Lyon
Vienne
St-Chamond
St-Étienne
Le Puy
Valence
Privas
Montélimar
Orange
Avignon
Tarascon
Arles
Martigues
Marseille
Six-Fours-les-Plages
la Seyne-sur-Mer
Toulon
Hyères
Îles d'Hyères
la Ciotat
Aubagne
Camargue

Issoire
Clermont-Ferrand
Auvergne
St-Flour
Mende
Alès
Nîmes
Sète
Agde
Narbonne
Béziers
Montpellier
Languedoc
Frontignan
Golfe du Lion

Ussel
Tulle
Brive-la-Gaillarde
Aurillac
Rodez
Massif Central
Figeac
Albi
Gaillac
Carmaux
Castres
Mazamet
Tarn
Montauban
Toulouse
Castelnaudary
Carcassonne
Limoux
Foix
Pamiers
Roussillon
Perpignan

Liousin
Angoulême
Périgueux
Bergerac
Dordogne
Cahors
Agen
Moissac
Castelsarrasin
Auch
Armagnac
St-Gaudens
Lourdes
Pau
Tarbes
Gascogne

Charente
Angoulins
Libourne
Bordeaux
Cenon
Mérignac
Pessac
Aquitaine
Marmande
Houilles
Dax
Mont-de-Marsan
Orthez
Bayonne
Anglet
Biarritz

Dauphiné
Drôme
Durance
Bollène
Sorgues
Vaucluse

Po

44°
46°
42°
40°

SPAIN
Ebro

Pyrénées
ANDORRA LA VELLA
ANDORRA

Medoc
la Teste
Arcachon
Landes

Biscay

74
80
71
70

MONACO inset

MONACO

F R A N C E

43°45'

Mediterranean Sea

Monte-Carlo
Sporting Club d'Été
Musée National
Larvotto
Centre de la Culture et d'Expositions
Lycée l'Annonciade
Casino
Centre de Congrès
Monte-Carlo
La Condamine
Grand Prix Circuit
Hospitalier Grace
Railway Station
Palais du Prince
Stade Louis II
Port de Monaco
MONACO
Cathédrale
Fontvieille
Ministère d'État
Musée Océanographique

7°25'
7°25'

0 m 500 750
0 yds 500 750

2°
4°
6°
8°

ANDORRA inset

ANDORRA

F R A N C E

Soldeu
El Serrat
Pic de Coma Pedrosa 2942m △
Arinsal
Ordino
La Massana
Arcalis
Canillo
Encamp
Escaldes
ANDORRA LA VELLA
Sant Julià de Lòria
Port d'Envalira
Valira
Pyrénées

S P A I N

1°40'
1°30'
42°30'

2000m/6562ft
1000m/3281ft
500m/1640ft

0 km 5
0 miles 5

Elevation

| Below sea level 0 | 250m | 500m | 1000m | 2000m | 3000m | 4000m | 6000m |

-6000m -4000m -2000m -1000m -500m -250m

-19,658ft -13,124ft -6562ft -3281ft -1640ft -820ft -328ft/-100m 0

820ft 1640ft 3281ft 6562ft 9843ft 13,124ft 19,685ft

Spain & Portugal

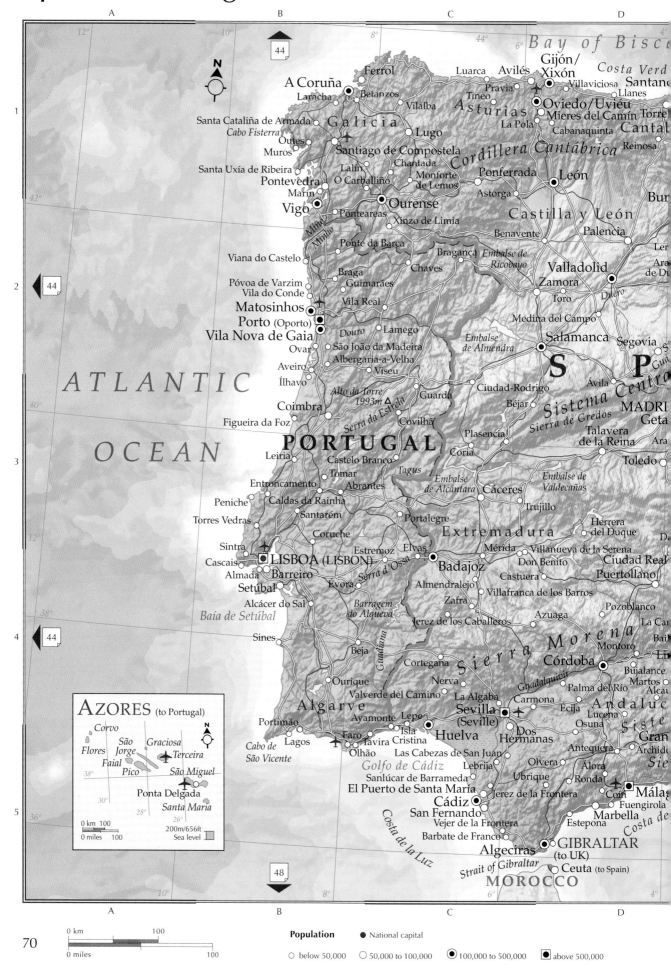

ATLANTIC

OCEAN

Bay of Biscay

Ferrol
A Coruña
Laracha
Betanzos
Luarca Avilés
Pravia
Tineo
Gijón/Xixón
Villaviciosa
Santan
Costa Verd
Llanes
Oviedo/Uvieu
Mieres del Camín
Torre

Santa Cataliña de Armada
Cabo Fisterra
Outes
Muros
Galicia
Lugo
La Pola
Cabanaquinta
Cantab

Santiago de Compostela
Chantada
Monforte de Lemos
Cordillera Cantábrica
Ponferrada
León
Reinosa

Santa Uxía de Ribeira
Lalín
O Carballiño
Astorga
Bur

Pontevedra
Marín
Ourense
Castilla y León
Palencia

Vigo
Ponteareas
Xinzo de Limia
Benavente

Miño
Ponte da Barca
Bragança
Embalse de Ricobayo
Valladolid
Zamora
Ara
de Du

Viana do Castelo
Braga
Chaves
Toro
Duero

Póvoa de Varzim
Vila do Conde
Guimarães
Vila Real
Medina del Campo
Ler

Matosinhos
Porto (Oporto)
Vila Nova de Gaia
Lamego
Embalse de Almendra
Salamanca
Segovia

Ovar
São João da Madeira
Albergaria-a-Velha
Viseu
Ciudad-Rodrigo
Ávila
S   P

Aveiro
Douro
Béjar
Sistema
MADRI
Geta

Ílhavo
Alto da Torre
1993m
Guarda
Sierra de Gredos
Central

Coimbra
Serra da Estrela
Covilhã
Plasencia
Talavera de la Reina
Ara

Figueira da Foz
PORTUGAL
Coria
Toledo

Leiria
Castelo Branco
Tagus
Embalse de Alcántara
Cáceres
Embalse de Valdecañas

Entroncamento
Tomar
Abrantes
Trujillo
Herrera del Duque
Da

Peniche
Caldas da Rainha
Santarém
Portalegre
Extremadura

Torres Vedras
Coruche
Mérida
Villanueva de la Serena
Ciudad Real

Sintra
Estremoz
Elvas
Don Benito
Puertollano

Cascais
LISBOA (LISBON)
Badajoz
Castuera
Pozoblanco
La Ca

Almada
Barreiro
Évora
Serra d'Ossa
Almendralejo
Villafranca de los Barros
Bai

Setúbal
Zafra
Azuaga
Sierra   Morena

Alcácer do Sal
Barragem do Alqueva
Jerez de los Caballeros
Montoro
Li

Baía de Setúbal
Guadiana
Córdoba
Bujalance
Martos
Alca

Sines
Beja
Cortegana
Guadalquivir
Palma del Río
Andaluc

Ourique
Nerva
La Algaba
Écija
Lucena
Siste
Gran

Valverde del Camino
Carmona
Osuna
Sierra
Gra

Algarve
Sevilla (Seville)
Antequera
Archid
Sie

Portimão
Ayamonte
Lepe
Huelva
Dos Hermanas
Olvera
Álora

Lagos
Faro
Isla Cristina
Ubrique
Ronda
Coín
Málaga

Cabo de São Vicente
Tavira
Olhão
Golfo de Cádiz
Las Cabezas de San Juan
Lebrija
Jerez de la Frontera
Fuengirola
Marbella
Costa de

Sanlúcar de Barrameda
El Puerto de Santa María
Cádiz
San Fernando
Vejer de la Frontera
Barbate de Franco
Estepona

Costa de la Luz
Algeciras
GIBRALTAR (to UK)
Ceuta (to Spain)

Strait of Gibraltar
MOROCCO

Azores (to Portugal)

Corvo
Flores
Faial
São Jorge
Pico
Graciosa
Terceira
São Miguel
Ponta Delgada
Santa María

0 km 100
0 miles 100
200m/656ft
Sea level

0 km   100
0 miles   100

Population   ● National capital

○ below 50,000   ○ 50,000 to 100,000   ◉ 100,000 to 500,000   ◼ above 500,000

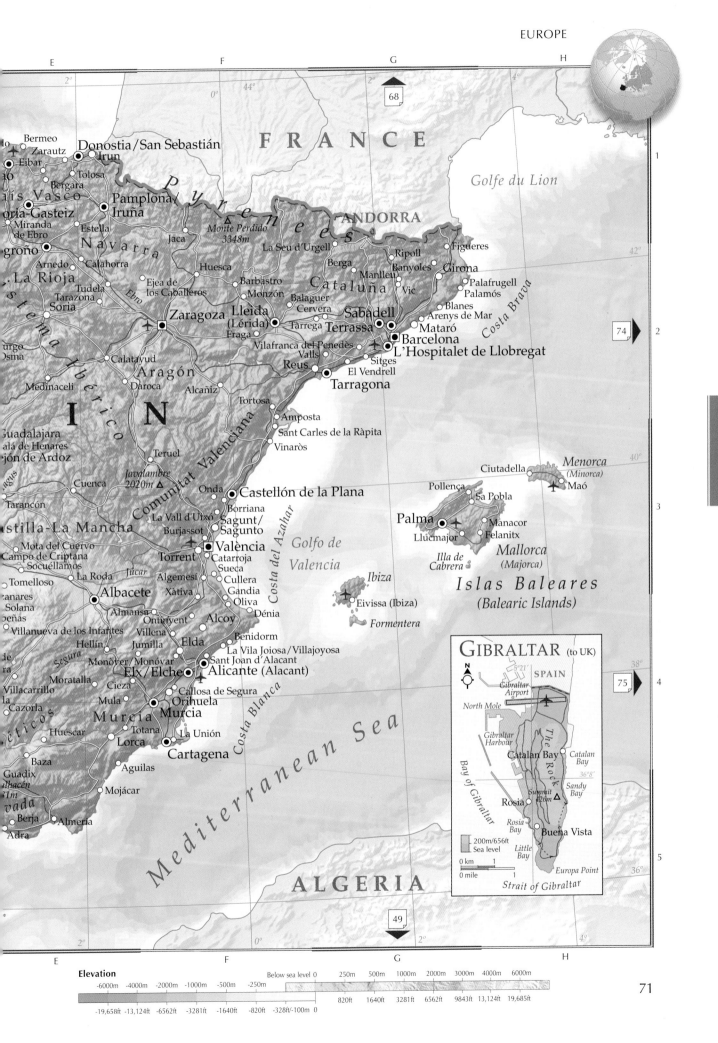

FRANCE

Golfe du Lion

ANDORRA

Pyrenees

Monte Perdido
3348m

Navarra

La Seu d'Urgell

Ripoll

Figueres

Berga

Banyoles

Girona

Cataluña

Manlleu

Vic

Palafrugell
Palamós

Costa Brava

I N

Aragón

Balaguer

Cervera

Sabadell

Blanes

Arenys de Mar

Terrassa

Mataró

Lleida
(Lérida)

Tàrrega

Barcelona

Vilafranca del Penedès

L'Hospitalet de Llobregat

Fraga

Valls

Reus

Sitges

El Vendrell

Tarragona

Tortosa

Amposta

Sant Carles de la Ràpita

Comunitat Valenciana

Vinaròs

Javalambre
2020m

Onda

Castellón de la Plana

Ciutadella

Menorca
(Minorca)

Maó

Borriana

Pollença

Sa Pobla

La Vall d'Uixó
Sagunt/
Saguntó

Palma

Manacor

Felanitx

Burjassot

València

Llucmajor

Mallorca
(Majorca)

Torrent

Catarroja

Golfo de
Valencia

Sueca

Costa del Azahar

Algemesí

Cullera

Xàtiva

Gandia

Oliva

Ibiza

Islas Baleares
(Balearic Islands)

Illa de
Cabrera

Albacete

Almansa

Ontinyent

Villena

Alcoy

Dénia

Eivissa (Ibiza)

Elda

Benidorm

Formentera

Hellín

Jumilla

La Vila Joiosa/Villajoyosa

Monòver/Monóvar

Sant Joan d'Alacant

Segura

Elx/Elche

Alicante (Alacant)

Mula

Callosa de Segura

Moratalla

Cieza

Orihuela

Murcia

Murcia

Costa Blanca

Totana

La Unión

Lorca

Cartagena

Mediterranean Sea

Aguilas

Mojácar

ALGERIA

GIBRALTAR (to UK)

N

5°21'

SPAIN

Gibraltar
Airport

North Mole

Gibraltar
Harbour

The Rock

Catalan Bay

Catalan
Bay

36°8'

Bay of Gibraltar

Rosia

Summit
426m

Sandy
Bay

Rosia
Bay

Buena Vista

Little
Bay

Europa Point

200m/656ft
Sea level

0 km   1

0 mile   1

Strait of Gibraltar

Elevation

| Below sea level 0 | 250m | 500m | 1000m | 2000m | 3000m | 4000m | 6000m |

-6000m -4000m -2000m -1000m -500m -250m

-19,658ft -13,124ft -6562ft -3281ft -1640ft -820ft -328ft/-100m 0

820ft 1640ft 3281ft 6562ft 9843ft 13,124ft 19,685ft

Germany & The Alpine States

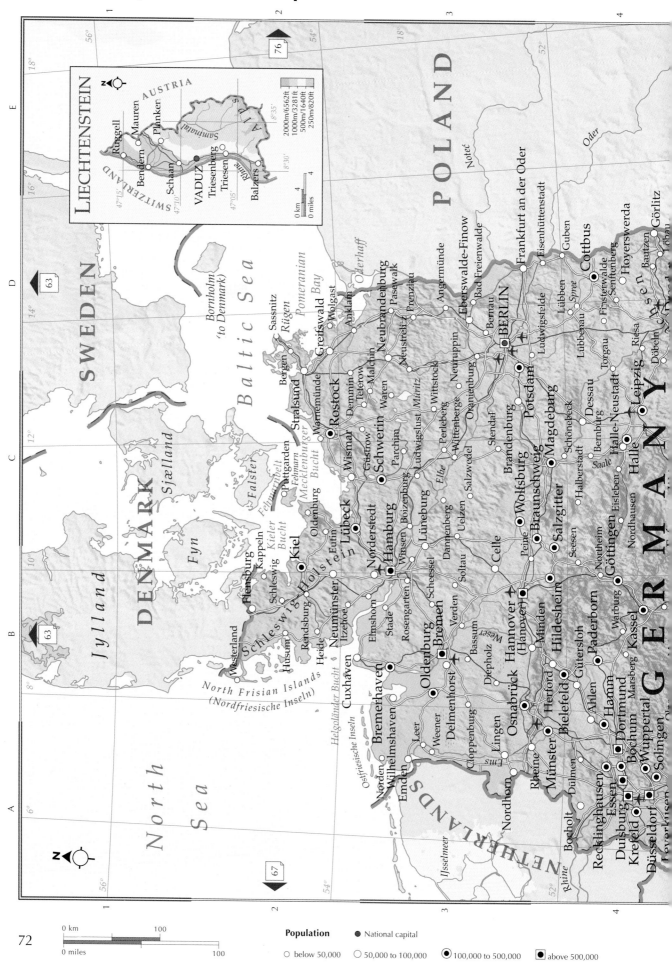

LIECHTENSTEIN

AUSTRIA

SWITZERLAND

Ruggell
Mauren
Bendern
Planken
Schaan
VADUZ
Triesenberg
Triesen
Balzers

Saminatal
Alps
Rhine

2000m/6562ft
1000m/3281ft
500m/1640ft
250m/820ft

8°35'
18°30'
47°15'
47°10'
47°05'

4
0 km   4
0 miles

POLAND

SWEDEN

DENMARK

Bornholm
('to Denmark')

Baltic Sea

Sassnitz
Rügen
Bergen
Pomeranian
Greifswald Bay
Wolgast

Oderhaff

North Sea

Jylland

Sjælland

Fyn

Falster

Fehmarn
Fehmbelt
Mecklenburger Bucht
Kieler Bucht

Westerland

Flensburg
Kappeln
Schleswig
Randsburg
Husum
Heide

Schleswig-Holstein

Neumünster
Itzehoe
Elmshorn
Stade
Rosengarten

Kiel
Eutin
Lübeck

Norderstedt
Hamburg
Winsen
Wrsen
Scheessel
Soltau

Wismar
Güstrow
Schwerin
Parchim

Rostock
Demmin
Malchin
Waren
Teterow

Anklam

Warnemünde
Stralsund

Neubrandenburg
Pasewalk
Prenzlau
Neustrelitz

Angermünde
Eberswalde-Finow
Bad Freienwalde

Frankfurt an der Oder
Eisenhüttenstadt
Guben
Cottbus
Hoyerswerda
Senftenberg
Görlitz
Bautzen

Ludwigslust
Müritz
Wittstock
Wittenberge
Oranienburg
Perleberg

Neuruppin

BERLIN
Potsdam
Ludwigsfelde
Lübben
Lübbenau
Spree
Finsterwalde
Torgau
Riesa
Döbeln

Elbe
Salzwedel
Stendal
Brandenburg
Magdeburg
Schönebeck
Halberstadt
Bernburg
Dessau
Wittenberg
Bernau

Uelzen
Lüneburg
Dannenberg
Boizenburg

Celle

Wolfsburg
Braunschweig
Salzgitter
Peine
Seesen

Nordhausen
Halle-Neustadt
Halle
Eisleben
Saale
Leipzig
Sachsen

North Frisian Islands
(Nordfriesische Inseln)

Helgoländer Bucht
Cuxhaven

Bremerhaven
Wilhelmshaven
Norden
Emden

Oldenburg
Delmenhorst
Bremen
Bassum
Diepholz
Verden
Weser

Cloppenburg
Leer
Weener
Lingen
Rheine
Nordhorn
Lohne

Osnabrück
Herford
Bielefeld
Gütersloh

Hannover
(Hanover)
Minden
Hildesheim
Paderborn
Warburg
Marsberg
Kassel
Northeim
Göttingen

Münster
Dülmen
Ahlen
Hamm
Dortmund
Bochum
Essen
Wuppertal
Solingen
Leverkusen
Düsseldorf
Krefeld
Duisburg
Recklinghausen
Bocholt

GERMANY

NETHERLANDS

Ijsselmeer
Rhine
Ems

Ostfriesische Inseln

72

Population   ● National capital

○ below 50,000   ◎ 50,000 to 100,000   ◉ 100,000 to 500,000   ■ above 500,000

SLOVAKIA

HUNGARY

CZECHIA
(CZECH REPUBLIC)

AUSTRIA

SLOVENIA

CROATIA

ITALY

FRANCE

SWITZERLAND

BELGIUM

LUX.

Elbe

Mistelbach an
der Zaya
Hollabrunn
Tulln
WIEN
(VIENNA)
Traiskirchen
Neusiedler
See
Murska Sobota
Maribor
Ptuj
Drava
Novo mesto
Krško
Eisenstadt
Bad Vöslau
Wiener-Neustadt
Graz
Mur
Velenje
Celje
Sava
Trbovlje
Kočevje
Istra

Markredwitz
Münchberg
Hof
Kronach
Lichtenfels
Coburg
Bayreuth
Forchheim
Schweinfurt
Würzburg
Bamberg
Erlangen
Fürth
Nürnberg
(Nuremberg)

Zwettl

Sankt Pölten
Linz
Danub.
(Donau)
Haulzenberg
Passau
Deggendorf
Danube
(Donau)
Straubing
Regensburg
Regenstauf
Schwandorf
Schwäbische Alb
Weissenburg
Aalen
Ingolstadt
Donauwörth

Wels
Ried im
Innkreis
Vöcklabruck
Ebensee
Bad Ischl
Liezen
Salzburg
Steyr
Enns
Mürzzuschlag
Leoben
Judenburg
Fischbacher
Alpen
Wolfsberg
Klagenfurt
Loibl Pass
1367m
Jesenice
LJUBLJANA
Nova Gorica
Koper
Kranj
Tolmin
Postojna

Bohemian Forest
Fränkische Alb

Heidenheim an
der Brenz
Augsburg
Mindelheim
Kempten
Memmingen
Kaufbeuren
Füssen
München
(Munich)
Rosenheim
Bayern
Bavarian Alps
Zugspitze 2962m
Innsbruck
Schwaz
Hohe Tauern
Grossglockner
3798m
Kitzbüheler
Alpen
Lienz
Plöckener Pass
1357m
Villach
Gurktaler
Alpen
Gailtaler Alpen
Plöcken Pass
Brenner Pass
1374m
Tirol
Alps

Heilbronn
Ludwigsburg
Göppingen
Stuttgart
Sindelfingen
Reutlingen
Ulm
Neu-Ulm
Schwennigen
Singen
Rottweil
Villingen
Lahr
Offenburg
Emmendingen
Freiburg im Breisgau
Bad Krozingen
Müllheim
Lörrach
Basel
Schwäbische Alb
Friedrichshafen
Bregenz
Konstanz
Lake Constance
Stockach
Schaffhausen
Sankt Gallen
Bülach
Winterthur
Zürich
Zürichsee
Zug
Luzern
Schwyz
LIECHTENSTEIN
VADUZ
Chur
Klosters
St.Moritz
Bellinzona
Locarno
Lugano
Lake Maggiore
Bodensee
Po
Po Valley

Heidelberg
Mannheim
Ludwigshafen
Sinsheim
Neckar
Neustadt an
der Weinstrasse
Karlsruhe
Pforzheim
Baden-Baden
Kehl
Schwarzwald

Wetzlar
Bad Homburg vor der Höhe
Frankfurt am Main
Offenbach
Darmstadt
Pfungstadt
Main
Worms
Mainz
Wiesbaden
Hessen

Neuwied
Koblenz
Boppard
Rhine
(Rhein)
Kaiserslautern
Neunkirchen
Saarbrücken
Mosel

Trier
Birkenfeld
Merzig
Bitburg
Wittlich
Eifel
Rheinische
Rhône

Vosges
Montbéliard
La Chaux-de-Fonds
Neuchâtel
Lac de
Neuchâtel
Biel
BERN
Thun
Thuner See
Brig
Simplon Pass
2005m
Egau
Rhine
(Rhein)
Berner Alpen
Sion
Monthey
Pennine Alps
Matterhorn
4478m
Great Saint
Bernard Pass
2469m
San
Bernardino Pass
3070m
Lugano
Lausanne
Lake
Geneva
Genève
(Geneva)
Onex
Lake
Geneva
Rhône

Da
Bad

SWITZERLAND

ITALY

77
78
74
69

Elevation

-6000m	-4000m	-2000m	-1000m	-500m	-250m	Below sea level 0	250m	500m	1000m	2000m	3000m	4000m	6000m

-19,658ft -13,124ft -6562ft -3281ft -1640ft -820ft -328ft/-100m 0   820ft 1640ft 3281ft 6562ft 9843ft 13,124ft 19,685ft

Italy

Population

- ○ below 50,000
- ○ 50,000 to 100,000
- ◉ 100,000 to 500,000
- ■ above 500,000
- ● National capital

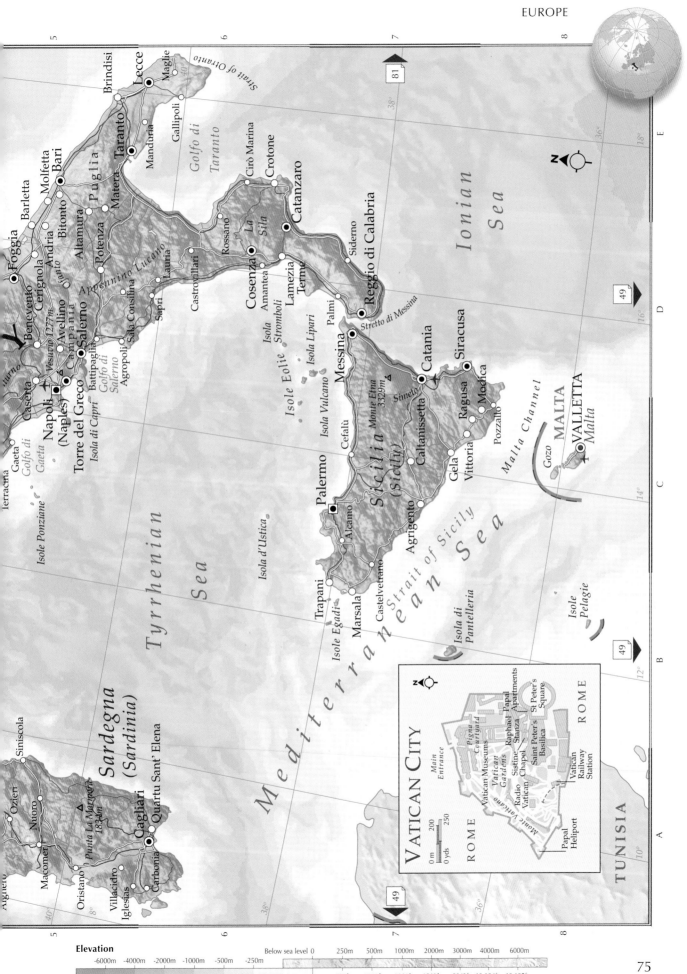

Elevation

Below sea level 0   250m   500m   1000m   2000m   3000m   4000m   6000m

-6000m   -4000m   -2000m   -1000m   -500m   -250m

-19,658ft   -13,124ft   -6562ft   -3281ft   -1640ft   -820ft   -328ft/-100m   0

820ft   1640ft   3281ft   6562ft   9843ft   13,124ft   19,685ft

Map labels

Brindisi • Lecce • Maglie
Strait of Otranto
Taranto • Manduria • Gallipoli
Molfetta • Bari
Barletta • Bitonto • Golfo di Taranto
Andria • Altamura • Ciro Marina
Foggia • Cerignola • Potenza • Matera • Crotone
Benevento • Avellino • Puglia • Catanzaro
Caserta • Salerno • Appennino Lucano • La Sila
Vesuvio 1277m • Battipaglia • Rossano • Reggio di Calabria
Napoli (Naples) • Campania • Sala Consilina • Castrovillari • Siderno
Torre del Greco • Golfo di Salerno • Sapri • Cosenza • Lamezia Terme
Isola di Capri • Agropoli • Laurìa • Amantea • Stretto di Messina
Terracina • Gaeta • Golfo di Gaeta • Isola Stromboli • Palmi
Isole Ponziane • Isole Eolie • Isola Lipari • Messina
Isola d'Ustica • Isola Vulcano • Monte Etna 3329m • Catania
Cefalù • Sicilia (Sicily) • Simeto • Siracusa
Palermo • Calanissetta • Ragusa • Modica
Alcamo • Agrigento • Gela • Vittoria • Pozzallo
Trapani • Marsala • Castelvetrano • Strait of Sicily
Isole Egadi • Isola di Pantelleria
Isole Pelagie

Tyrrhenian Sea
Ionian Sea
Mediterranean Sea
Malta Channel
Gozo • MALTA • VALLETTA • Malta

Sardegna (Sardinia)
Siniscola • Ozieri • Nuoro • Punta La Marmora 1834m
Macomer • Cagliari • Quartu Sant'Elena
Oristano • Villacidro • Carbonia
Iglesias

TUNISIA

Vatican City inset

VATICAN CITY

ROME

Main Entrance
Pigna Courtyard
Vatican Museums
Raphael Stanza
Papal Apartments
St Peter's Square
Vatican Gardens
Sistine Chapel
Saint Peter's Basilica
Radio Vatican
Monte Vaticano
Vatican Railway Station
Papal Heliport

ROME

0 m   200
0 yds   250

75

Central Europe

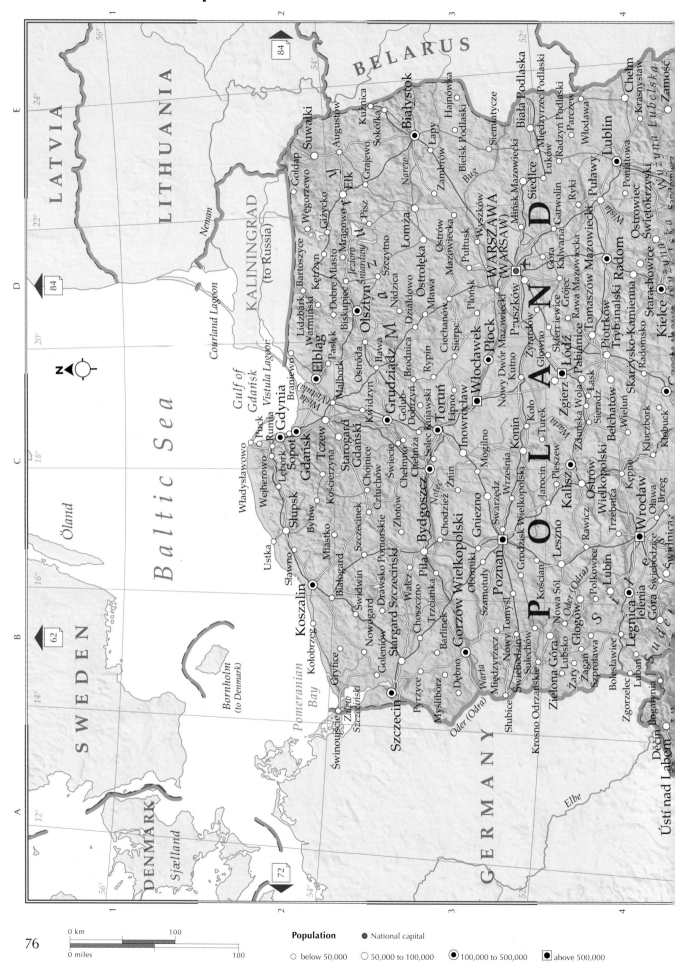

LATVIA

LITHUANIA

BELARUS

KALININGRAD
(to Russia)

SWEDEN

Baltic Sea

Öland

Bornholm
(to Denmark)

DENMARK

Sjælland

Neman

Courland Lagoon

POLAND

GERMANY

Pomeranian
Bay

Gulf of
Gdańsk

Vistula Lagoon

Wisła (Vistula)

Elbe

Oder (Odra)

Warta

Noteć

Odra

Wisła

Narew

Bug

Wisła

Cities and towns:

Suwałki · Goldap · Gołdap · Augustów · Kuźnica · Sokółka · Białystok · Łapy · Siemiatycze · Hajnówka · Bielsk Podlaski · Zambrów · Międzyrzec Podlaski · Biała Podlaska · Radzyń Podlaski · Parczew · Włodawa · Chełm · Krasnystaw · Zamość · Lublin · Poniatowa · Puławy · Świdnik · Lubelska · Kielce · Starachowice · Świętokrzyski · Radom · Ostrowiec · Skarżysko-Kamienna · Radomsko · Bełchatów · Piotrków Trybunalski · Tomaszów Mazowiecki · Rawa Mazowiecka · Łowicz · Głowno · Zgierz · Łódź · Pabianice · Łask · Zduńska Wola · Sieradz · Wieluń · Wieruszów · Kępno · Ostrzeszów · Kluczbork · Olesno · Kłobuck

Wejherowo · Rumia · Gdynia · Sopot · Gdańsk · Tczew · Starogard Gdański · Puck · Władysławowo · Ustka · Słupsk · Lębork · Bytów · Kościerzyna · Chojnice · Człuchów · Złotów · Miastko · Szczecinek · Drawsko Pomorskie · Świdwin · Białogard · Koszalin · Kołobrzeg · Gryfice · Goleniów · Nowogard · Stargard Szczeciński · Świecie · Chełmno · Chełmża · Grudziądz · Kwidzyn · Malbork · Elbląg · Braniewo · Pasłęk · Lidzbark Warmiński · Bartoszyce · Kętrzyn · Węgorzewo · Giżycko · Mrągowo · Ełk · Pisz · Dobre Miasto · Biskupiec · Olsztyn · Ostróda · Iława · Nidzica · Działdowo · Mława · Ciechanów · Sierpc · Rypin · Brodnica · Golub-Dobrzyń · Lipno · Toruń · Włocławek · Płock · Nowy Dwór Mazowiecki · Ciechanów

Smardy · Jezioro Śniardwy · Szczytno · Łomża · Ostrołęka · Ostrów Mazowiecka · Pułtusk · Wyszków · Płońsk · Wąbrzeźno · WARSZAWA (WARSAW) · Pruszków · Żyrardów · Skierniewice · Grójec · Góra Kalwaria · Garwolin · Ryki · Dęblin · Łuków · Siedlce · Mińsk Mazowiecki · Kołbiel

Myślibórz · Pyrzyce · Szczecin · Świnoujście · Złota · Szczeciński · Gryfino · Chojna · Dębno · Międzyrzecz · Gorzów Wielkopolski · Barlinek · Choszczno · Wałcz · Piła · Trzcianka · Chodzież · Czarnków · Obornik · Szamotuły · Oborniki · Poznań · Swarzędz · Września · Środa Wielkopolska · Gniezno · Mogilno · Żnin · Bydgoszcz · Inowrocław · Konin · Koło · Turek · Kalisz · Jarocin · Pleszew · Ostrów Wielkopolski · Krotoszyn · Rawicz · Trzebnica · Oleśnica · Wrocław · Oława · Brzeg · Oborniki Śląskie

Słubice · Krosno Odrzańskie · Sulechów · Świebodzin · Nowy Tomyśl · Zbąszyń · Wolsztyn · Nowa Sól · Zielona Góra · Lubsko · Żary · Żagań · Szprotawa · Głogów · Polkowice · Lubin · Legnica · Złotoryja · Bolesławiec · Zgorzelec · Lubań · Jelenia Góra · Bogatynia · Góra Śląska · Gostyń · Leszno · Kościan · Grodzisk Wielkopolski · Wschowa · Świdnica · Jawor · Świebodzice · Wałbrzych

Ústí nad Labem · Děčín

Scale markers: 84 · 62 · 72

Wisła · Pilica · Sudety

0 km   100

0 miles   100

Population   ● National capital

○ below 50,000   ◌ 50,000 to 100,000   ◉ 100,000 to 500,000   ▣ above 500,000

24° · 22° · 20° · 18° · 16° · 14° · 12°

56° · 54° · 52°

E · D · C · B · A

1 · 2 · 3 · 4

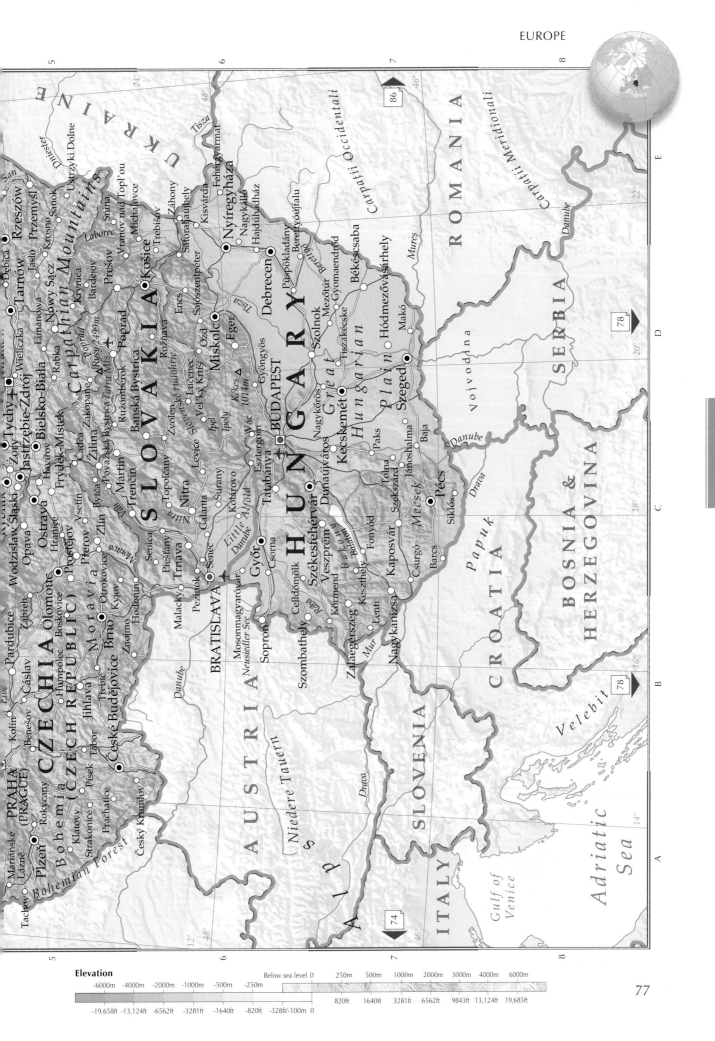

Elevation

| Below sea level 0 | 250m | 500m | 1000m | 2000m | 3000m | 4000m | 6000m |

-6000m -4000m -2000m -1000m -500m -250m

820ft 1640ft 3281ft 6562ft 9843ft 13,124ft 19,685ft

-19,658ft -13,124ft -6562ft -3281ft -1640ft -820ft -328ft/-100m 0

Southeast Europe

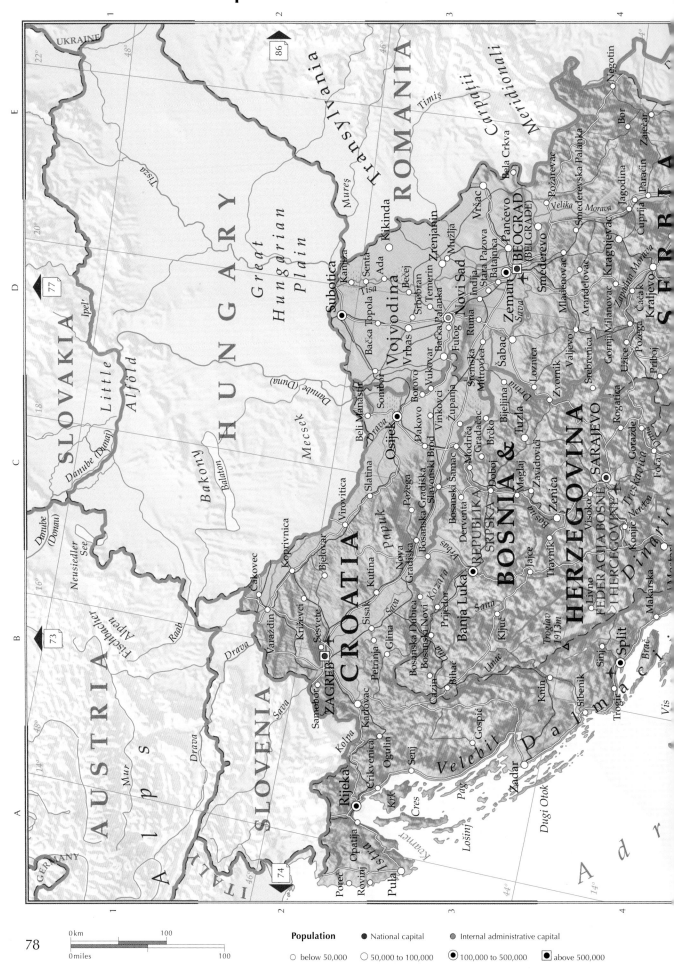

Population   ● National capital   ● Internal administrative capital

○ below 50,000   ◉ 50,000 to 100,000   ◉ 100,000 to 500,000   ■ above 500,000

BULGARIA

GREECE

Aegean Sea

Évvoia (Euboea)

Thermaïkós Kólpos

Strymónas

Pineiós

Píndos (Pindus Mountains)

PRISHTINË/PRISTINA (PRISTINA) (disputed)

KOSOVO (disputed)

NORTH MACEDONIA

SKOPJE

Vardar

Crna Reka

Ohrid

Bitola

Lake Prespa

Lake Ohrid

ALBANIA

TIRANË (TIRANA)

North Albanian Alps

Gjeravicë 2658m

Black Drin

Lumi i Shkumbinit

Lumi i Devollit

Lumi i Osumit

Lumi i Vjosës

Korçë

Konispol

Sarandë

Gjirokastër

Tepelenë

Vlorë

Fier

Berat

Lushnjë

Kuçovë

Pogradec

Elbasan

Struga

Debar

Kičevo

Prilep

Kavadarci

Gevgelija

Strumica

Radoviš

Kočani

Štip

Sveti Nikole

Bregalnica

Veles

Gostivar

Tetovo

Kumanovo

Kriva Palanka

Pirot

Vlasotince

Surdulica

Vranje

Bujanovac

Preševo

Gnjilane

Gjilan

Ferizaj/Uroševac

Kačanik

Prizren

Rahovec

Gjakovë/Đakovica

Peshkopi

Burrel

Kukës

Bajram Curri

Lumi i Drinit

Giakovë

Pejë/Peć

Fushë Kosovë

Mitrovicë Mitrovica

Vushtrri/Vučitrn

Podujevë

Leskovac

Kuršumlija

Žitni

Žna Morava

Prokuplje

Kursenik

Berane

Novi Pazar

MONTENEGRO

PODGORICA

Cetinje

Nikšić

Niksić

Bar

Shkodër

Lezhë

Laç

Krujë

Kavajë

Durrës

Lake Scutari

Lake Skadar

Lake Shkodër

Lake Ohrid

Dubrovnik

Palagruža

Kefalloniá

Kérkyra (Corfu)

Ió n i a   N i s i á (Ionian Islands)

Ionian Sea

Strait of Otranto

Adriatic Sea

ITALY

Golfo di Taranto

Appennino Lucano

Strait of Otranto

In February 2008, Kosovo (a UN Protectorate within Serbia since 1999) declared independence. Although recognized by several countries, this decision has proved controversial with other states wary of setting a precedent for separatist groups within their own borders. It is therefore likely to be some time before Kosovo becomes universally recognized.

BOSNIA & HERZEGOVINA

CROATIA

SERBIA

MONTENEGRO

CROATIA

Sava

Una

Bosna

Drina

Bihać

Banja Luka

Brčko

Tuzla

Sarajevo

Goražde

Mostar

Dubrovnik

Split

Adriatic Sea

Territorial extent
Republika Srpska
Federacija Bosne i Hercegovine

0   50 km
0   50 miles

N

Elevation

-6000m	-4000m	-2000m	-1000m	-500m	-250m	Below sea level 0	250m	500m	1000m	2000m	3000m	4000m	6000m
-19,658ft	-13,124ft	-6562ft	-3281ft	-1640ft	-820ft	-328ft/-100m 0	820ft	1640ft	3281ft	6562ft	9843ft	13,124ft	19,685ft

The Mediterranean

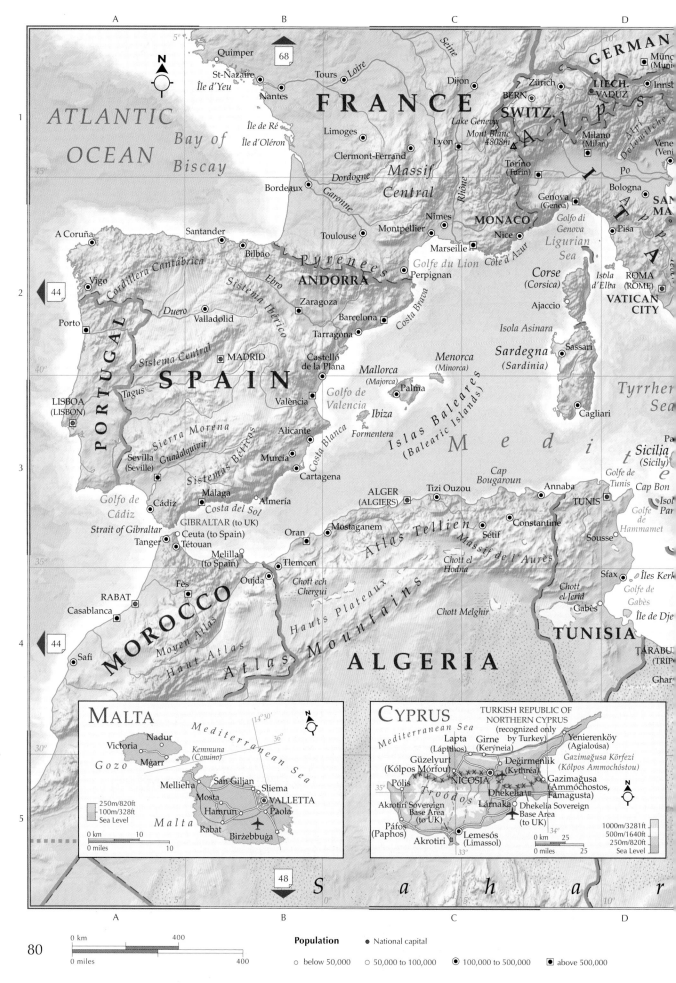

ATLANTIC
OCEAN

Bay of
Biscay

FRANCE

GERMANY

Quimper
St-Nazaire
Île d'Yeu
Nantes
Tours
Loire
Limoges
Clermont-Ferrand
Bordeaux
Dordogne
Garonne
Toulouse
Massif
Central
Nîmes
Montpellier
Marseille
Perpignan
Golfe du Lion

Seine
Dijon
Lyon
Lake Geneva
Mont Blanc
4808m
Rhône
MONACO
Nice
Côte d'Azur

Zürich
BERN
SWITZ.
Torino
(Turin)
Genova
(Genoa)
Ligurian
Sea

LIECH.
VADUZ
Milano
(Milan)
Po
Bologna

Innst
Münç
(Muni
Vene
(Veni

Ligurian
Sea
Corse
(Corsica)
Ajaccio

Isola
d'Elba
ROMA
(ROME)
VATICAN
CITY

SAN
MA

Isola Asinara
Sardegna
(Sardinia)
Sassari

Cagliari

Tyrrher
Sea

A Coruña
Santander
Bilbao
Cordillera Cantábrica
Vigo
Porto
Duero
Valladolid
PORTUGAL
Sistema Central
MADRID
SPAIN
LISBOA
(LISBON)
Tagus
Sierra Morena
Guadalquivir
Sevilla
(Seville)
Sistemas Béticos
Málaga
Cádiz
Costa del Sol
Golfo de
Cádiz
Strait of Gibraltar
GIBRALTAR (to UK)
Tanger
Ceuta (to Spain)
Tétouan
Melilla
(to Spain)

Pyrenees
ANDORRA
Ebro
Zaragoza
Sistema Ibérico
Barcelona
Tarragona
Castelló
de la Plana
València
Golfo de
Valencia
Alicante
Costa Blanca
Murcia
Cartagena
Almería
Costa Brava

Mallorca
(Majorca)
Palma
Ibiza
Formentera
Islas Baleares
(Balearic Islands)
Menorca
(Minorca)

Medi

ALGER
(ALGIERS)
Tizi Ouzou
Cap
Bougaroun
Annaba
TUNIS
Golfe de
Tunis
Cap Bon
Sicilia
(Sicily)

Oran
Mostaganem
Constantine
Sétif
Atlas Tellien
Massif de l'Aurès
Chott el
Hodna
Sousse

Golfe
de
Hammamet
Isol
Par

RABAT
Casablanca
Fès
Oujda
Tlemcen
MOROCCO
Moyen Atlas
Haut Atlas
Chott ech
Chergui
Hauts Plateaux
Atlas Mountains
Chott Melghir
ALGERIA
Safi

Sfax
Chott
el Jerid
Gabès
Golfe de
Gabès
Île de Dje
TUNISIA
ȚARABU
(TRIP
Ghar

Îles Kerk

MALTA

Mediterranean Sea

Victoria
Nadur
Gozo
Mġarr
Kemmuna
(Comino)
Mellieħa
Mosta
San Ġiljan
Sliema
VALLETTA
Hamrun
Paola
Malta
Rabat
Birżebbuġa

250m/820ft
100m/328ft
Sea Level

0 km   10
0 miles   10

CYPRUS

TURKISH REPUBLIC OF
NORTHERN CYPRUS
(recognized only by Turkey)

Mediterranean Sea
Lapta
(Lápithos)
Girne
(Kerýneia)
Yenierenköy
(Agialoúsa)
Güzelyurt
(Kólpos Mórfou)
Değirmenlik
(Kythréa)
Gazimağusa Körfezi
(Kólpos Ammochóstou)
Pólis
NICOSIA
Gazimağusa
(Ammóchostos,
Famagusta)
Troódos
Akrotíri Sovereign
Base Area
(to UK)
Dhekelia
Lárnaka
Dhekelia Sovereign
Base Area
(to UK)
Páfos
(Paphos)
Lemesós
(Limassol)
Akrotíri

1000m/3281ft
500m/1640ft
250m/820ft
Sea Level

0 km   25
0 miles   25

S a h a r a

0 km   400
0 miles   400

Population   ● National capital

○ below 50,000   ○ 50,000 to 100,000   ◉ 100,000 to 500,000   ▣ above 500,000

SLOVAKIA
WIEN
(NNA)
RIA
Danube
BUDAPEST
HUNGARY
Tisza
Satu Mare
Târgu Mures
Carpathian Mountains
Bâlti
86
U K R A I N E
Kakhovske
Vodoskhovyshche
MOLD.
CHIŞINĂU
Dnister
Odesa
Dnieper
Berdiansk
Sea of Azov
Krym
(Crimea)
Kerch
RUSS.
Novorossiysk
1

Great
Hungarian
Plain
R O M A N I A
Carpaţii Meridonali
Galaţi
ZAGREB
CROATIA
Novi Sad
Sava
BOSNIA
& HERZ.
SARAJEVO
BEOGRAD
(BELGRADE)
SERBIA
BUCUREŞTI
(BUCHAREST)
Danube
Constanţa
B U L G A R I A
PRISHTINË/PRIŠTINA
(PRISTINA)
Balkan Mountains
Varna
Black
Sea
Sevastopol'
(since 2014 the Ukrainian
territory of Crimea has
been annexed by Russia)

MON.
KOSOVO
(disputed)
SOFIA
Burgas
95
2
PODGORICA
SKOPJE
Edirne
İstanbul
Boğazı
(Bosporus)
Küre Dağları
Samsun
Ordu
TIRANË
(TIRANA)
NORTH
MACEDONIA
Rhodope
Mountains
İstanbul
Zonguldak
Kızıl Irmak
Bari
(Naples)
Thessaloníki
(Salonica)
Marmara
Denizi
Bursa
ANKARA
esuvio 1277m
Lecce
Golfo di
Taranto
Strait of
Otranto
ALBANIA
Pindos
Mts
Límnos
Aegean
Sea
Balıkesir
T U R K E Y
Kérkyra
(Corfu)
GREECE
Lárisa
(T Ü R K I Y E)
senza
Ionian
Kefalloniá
Chíos
İzmir
Tuz
Gölü
Kayseri
Catanzaro
ATHÍNA
(ATHENS)
Sámos
3
Zákynthos
Sea
Kýklades
(Cyclades)
Dodekánisa
(Dodecanese)
Antalya
Toros Dağları
Adana
Gaziantep
Euphrates
Siracusa
Monte Etna
329m
Catania
Kýthira
Kritikó Pélagos
(Sea of Crete)
Ródos
(Rhodes)
Antalya
Körfezi
İskenderun Körfezi
Halab
(Aleppo)
LLETTA
TA
Irákleio
Kárpathos
NICOSIA
Ródos
CYPRUS
SYRIA
Kríti
(Crete)
Lárnaka
Lemesós
(Limassol)
LEBANON
BEYROUTH
(BEIRUT)
DIMASHQ
(DAMASCUS)
97
4
n
e
a
n
S
e
a
Hefa
(Haifa)
ISRAEL
Tel Aviv-Yafo
JERUSALEM
Gaza
Dead Sea
'AMMĀN
Darnah
Banghāzī
(Benghazi)
Ţubruq
Al Iskandarīyah
(Alexandria)
Nile
Delta
Bûr Sa'īd
(Port Said)
Qanāt as Suways
(Suez Canal)
JORDAN
Mişrātah
In 1974 Turkey occupied the northern part
of Cyprus while Greek Cypriots remained in
control of the south. Cyprus was effectively
partitioned and a UN buffer zone currently
divides the two areas. In 1983 the north of
the island proclaimed itself the Turkish
Republic of North Cyprus. It was only
recognized by Turkey.
Libyan
Plateau
Munkhafad al Qattārah
(Qatara Depression)
AL QĀHIRAH
(CAIRO)
Al Jīzah
(Giza)
Nile
Suez
(As Suways)
Qanāt as Suways
Al 'Aqabah
Elat
Shibh
Jazīrat
Sīnā'
(Sinai)
SAUDI
ARABIA
5

L I B Y A
Great
Sand
Sea
Libyan
Desert
E G Y P T
50
Red
Sea

Elevation
-6000m   -4000m   -2000m   -1000m   -500m   -250m   Below sea level 0   250m   500m   1000m   2000m   3000m   4000m   6000m
-19,658ft -13,124ft -6562ft -3281ft -1640ft -820ft -328ft/-100m 0   820ft   1640ft   3281ft   6562ft   9843ft   13,124ft 19,685ft

Bulgaria & Greece

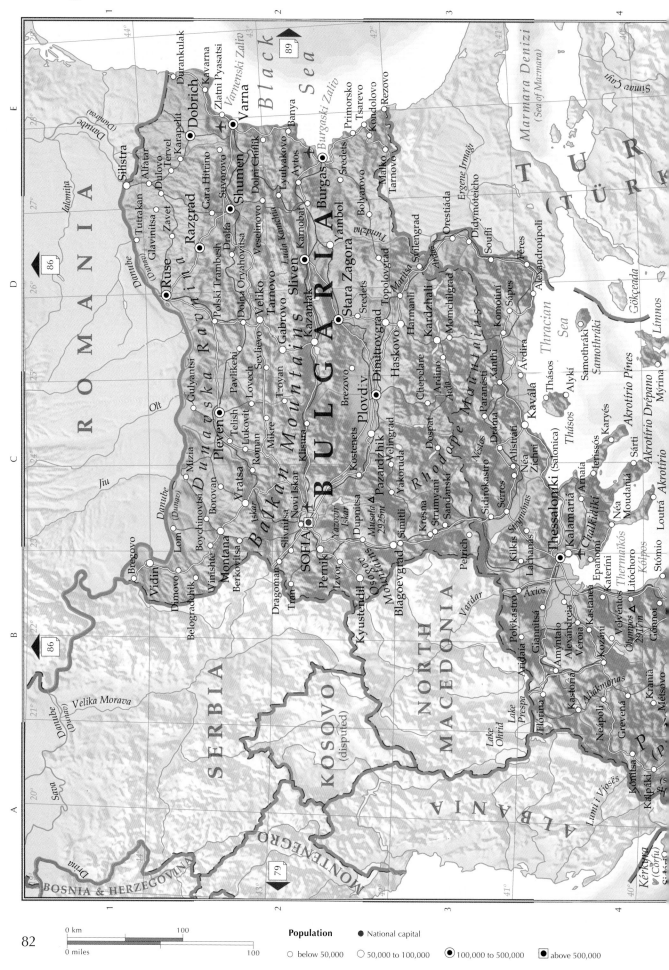

Population   ● National capital

○ below 50,000   ○ 50,000 to 100,000   ◉ 100,000 to 500,000   ◼ above 500,000

0 km   100

0 miles   100

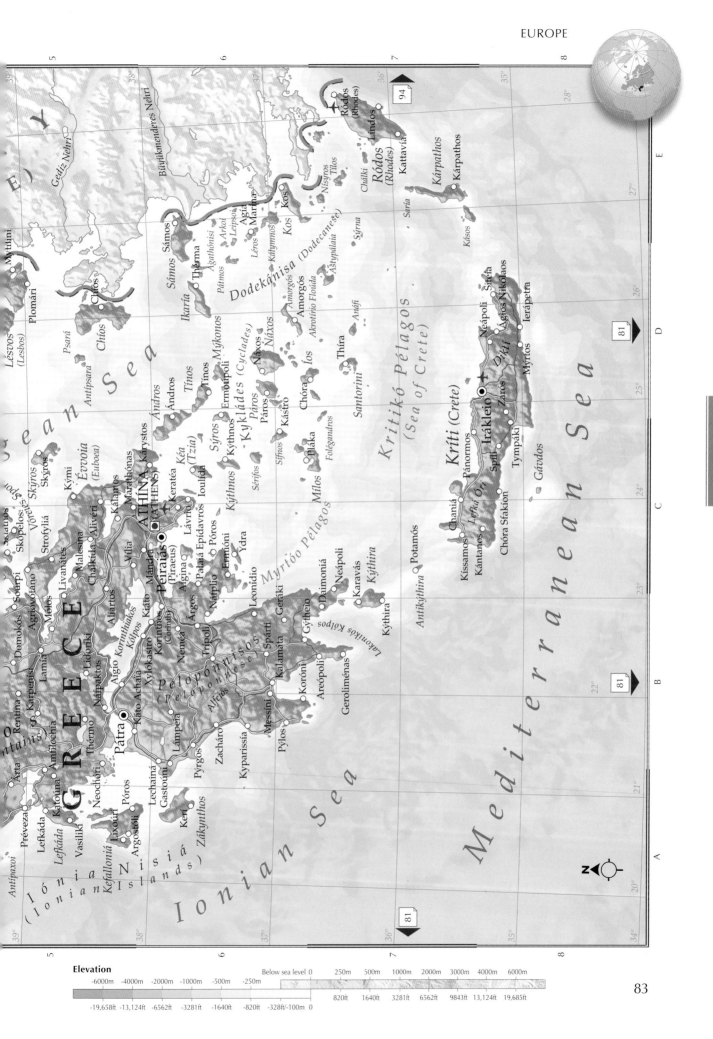

Elevation

-6000m	-4000m	-2000m	-1000m	-500m	-250m	Below sea level 0	250m	500m	1000m	2000m	3000m	4000m	6000m
-19,658ft	-13,124ft	-6562ft	-3281ft	-1640ft	-820ft	-328ft/-100m	0	820ft	1640ft	3281ft	6562ft	9843ft	13,124ft	19,685ft

The Baltic States & Belarus

SWEDEN
FINLAND
RUSSIA
ESTONIA
LATVIA
LITHUANIA
KALININGRAD (to Russia)

Gulf of Finland
Narva Bay
Lake Peipus
Lake Pskov
Gulf of Riga
BALTIC SEA
Ålands Hav
Skiftet
Gotland
Öland
Gotska Sandön
Courland Lagoon

TALLINN
RĪGA
Kaliningrad

Narva
Sillamäe
Narva Reservoir
Kunda
Loksa
Rakvere
Kohtla-Järve
Kalläste
Palamuse
Puurmani
Tartu
Võnnu
Rapina
Maardu
Aegviidu
Raasiku
Tapa
Rakke
Põltsamaa
Otepää
Põlva
Võru
Keila
Paldiski
Risti
Rapla
Paide
Viljandi
Rõngu
Tõrva
Valga
Valka
Smiltene
Ape
Alūksne
Balvi
Viļaka
Rugāji
Kārsava
Ludza
Rēzekne
Malta
Špoģi
Haapsalu
Lihula
Pärnu-Jaagupi
Sindi
Pärnu
Kilingi-Nõmme
Mõisaküla
Rūjiena
Staicele
Valmiera
Cēsis
Gauja
Jaunpiebalga
Gulbene
Madona
Lubāns
Varakļāni
Viļāni
Līvāni
Jēkabpils
Plaviņas
Western Dvina
Kärdla
Emmaste
Vormsi
Väinameri
Virtsu
Audru
Kihnu
Ruhnu
Ainaži
Salacgrīva
Saulkrasti
Aloja
Burtnieks
Iecava
Bauska
Aizkraukle
Biržai
Pasvalys
Viesīte
Nereta
Rokiškis
Obeliai
Hiiumaa
Orissaare
Kuressaare
Säärе
Kolkasrags
Kolka
Roja
Mērsrags
Engure
Tukums
Jūrmala
Jelgava
Pakruojis
Panevėžys
Subačius
Naujamiestis
Dotnuva
Saaremaa
Mazirbe
Ugāle
Talsi
Kandava
Engures Ezers
Brocēni
Saldus
Mažeikiai
Papilė
Joniškis
Šiauliai
Radviliškis
Žemaičių Aukštumas
Naujamiestis
Ventspils
Pāvilosta
Usmas Ezers
Kuldīga
Durbe
Venta
Skuodas
Plungė
Telšiai
Kelmė
Šiaulė
Skaudvilė
Raseiniai
Jurbarkas
Chernyakhovsk
Liepāja
Grobiņa
Salantai
Gargždai
Šilalė
Tauragė
Neman
Gusev
Rucava
Kretinga
Priekulė
Šilutė
Neman
Klaipėda
Nida
Zelenogradsk
Gvardeysk
Kaliningrad
Pionerskiy
Primorsk
Mamonovo
Bagrationovsk
Zheleznodorozhnyy

Suur Munamägi 318m
Gaiziņkalns 311m

0 km   100
0 miles   100

Population
○ below 50,000
◉ 50,000 to 100,000
◉ 100,000 to 500,000
■ above 500,000
● National capital

Elevation

Below sea level 0	250m	500m	1000m	2000m	3000m	4000m	6000m

-6000m	-4000m	-2000m	-1000m	-500m	-250m

820ft	1640ft	3281ft	6562ft	9843ft	13,124ft	19,685ft

-19,658ft	-13,124ft	-6562ft	-3281ft	-1640ft	-820ft	-328ft/-100m 0

Ukraine, Moldova & Romania

BELARUS

Pripyat

POLAND

Małopolska

Wyżyna Lubelska

Kovel
Sarny
Olevsk

Volodymyr-Volynskyi
Novovolynsk
Kivertsi
Korosten
Sokal
Lutsk
Rivne
Chervonohrad
Dubno
Novohrad-Volynskyi
Radomys
Zhovkva
Slavuta
Shepetivka
Yavoriv
Lviv
Zolochiv
Kremenets
Polonne
Zhytom
Horodok
Iziaslav
Berdy
Sambir
Khodoriv
Zbarazh
Starokostiantyniv
Drohobych
Berezhany
Ternopil
Khmelnytskyi
Ko
Boryslav
Stryi
Zhydachiv
U
K
R
Kalush
Chortkiv
Vinnytsia
Dolyna
Lypo
Uzhhorod
Nadvirna
Ivano-Frankivsk
Zhmerynka
Haiś
Mukachevo
Kamianets-Podilskyi
Tulc
Berehove
Kolomyia
Chernivtsi
Mohyliv-Podilskyi
Vynohradiv
Khust
Hora Hoverla 2061m
Negreşti-Oaş
Darabani
Soroca
Satu Mare
Rădăuţi
Dorohoi
Bălţi
Carei
Baia Mare
Solca
Botoşani
Rîbniţa
Marghita
Baia Sprie
Borşa
Suceava
Şimleu Silvaniei
Năsăud
Fălticeni
MOLDOVA
Oradea
Zalău
Dej
Bistriţa
Topliţa
Târgu-Neamţ
Paşcani
Călăraşi
Aleşd
Beiuş
Cluj-Napoca
Bicaz
Iaşi
Ungheni
Orhei
Străşeni
Salonta
Reghin
Roman
Curtici
Ineu
Turda
Luduş
Gheorgheni
Piatra-Neamţ
CHIŞINĂU
Ben
Muntii Apuseni
Aiud
Târgu Mureş
Bacău
Hînceşti
Sânnicolau Mare
Abrud
Cristuru Secuiesc
Miercurea-Ciuc
Vaslui
Tiraspo
Arad
Alba Iulia
Medias
Secuiesc
Târgu Ocna
Bârlad
Comrat
Basara
Jimbolia
Lipova
Deva
Rupea
Sfântu Gheorghe
Adjud
Ciadîr-Lu
Timişoara
Hunedoara
Vârful Moldoveanu 2544m
Târgu Secuiesc
Cahul
Artsyz
Lugoj
Cisnădie
Sibiu
Făgăraş
Codlea
Braşov
Focşani
Tecuci
Bolhrad
Oţelu Roşu
Haţeg
Câmpulung
Râşnov
Ozero Yalpuh
R O M A N I A
Bocşa
Petroşani
Sinaia
Câmpina
Râmnicu Sărat
Galaţi
Reni
Kil
Reşiţa
Carpaţii Meridionali
Curtea de Argeş
Buzău
Brăila
Izmayil
Orăviţa
Anina
Târgu Jiu
Câmpina
Mizil
Măcin
Tulcea
Moldova Nouă
Călimăneşti
Moreni
Isaccea
Orşova
Râmnicu Vâlcea
Pitesti
Târgovişte
Ploieşti
Babadag
Drobeta-Turnu-Severin
Motru
Strehaia
Titu
Urziceni
Ilăndărei
Hârşova
Laeut Razi
Drăgăşani
Buftea
Ialomiţa
Lacul Sinoie
Filiaşi
W a l l a c h i a
Slobozia
SERBIA
Craiova
Slatina
BUCUREŞTI (BUCHAREST)
Feteşti
Medgidia
Balş
Caracal
Oltenita
Călăraşi
Calafat
Băileşti
Alexandria
Constanţa
Roşiori de Vede
Turnu
Techirghiol
Corabia
Măgurele
Giurgiu
Eforie-Sud
Danube (Dunărea)
Zimnicea
Mangalia
Dunavska Ravnina
BULGARIA

SLOVAKIA
Tatra Mountains
Slovenské Rudohorie
Carpathian Mountains

HUNGARY
Great Hungarian Plain
Tisza

Transylvania

Bug
Styr
Sluch
Pripyat Marshes
Podilska Vysochyna
Dniester
Transnistria
Seret
Someş
Mureş
Timiş
Danube
Velika Morava
Jiu
Olt

18° *20°* *22°* *52°* *24°* *26°* *28°*
50°
48°
46°
44°

A B C D

1
2
3
4
5

0 km 100
0 miles 100

Population ● National capital
○ below 50,000   ○ 50,000 to 100,000   ◉ 100,000 to 500,000   ■ above 500,000

RUSSIA

Srednerusskaya Vozvyshennost'

Don

88

Kyivske Vodoskhovyshche

Horodnia
Snovsk
Shostka
Hlukhiv
Chernihiv
Krolevets
Konotop
Nizhyn
Bakhmach
Sumy
Oster
Nosivka
Romny
IV
Brovary
Pryluky
Lebedyn
Yahotyn
Pyriatyn
Okhtyrka
Zolochiv
rka
Vasylkiv
stiv
Hrebinka
Lubny
Myrhorod
Liubotyn
Derhachi
Kharkiv
Kupiansk
Kanivske Vodoskhovyshche
Kaniv
Psel
Mereta
Starobilsk
Bila Tserkva
Zolotonosha
I   N   E
Poltava
Siverskyi Donets
Izium
Kreminna
Bohuslav
Cherkasy
Hlobyne
Rubizhne
Horodyshche
Smila
Svitlovodsk
Kremenchuk
Kreminchutske Vodoskhovyshche
Sloviansk
Sievierodonetsk
nyhorodka
Kramatorsk
Lysychansk
Shpola
Chyhyryn
Talne
Znamianka
Dniprodzerzhynske Vodoskhovyshche
Zolote
Luhansk
Mala Vyska
Oleksandrivka
Kamianske
Novomoskovsk
Kostiantynivka
Kadiivka
Sorokyne
vanivsk
Oleksandriia
(Dniprodzerzhynsk)
(Krasnodon)
Zhovti Vody
(Stakhanov)
Kropyvnytskyi
Dnipro
Pavlohrad
Horlivka
Khrustalnyi
vyshchenske
Piatykhatky
Yenakiieve
(Kirovohrad)
Synelnykove
Makiivka
(Krasnyi Luch)
novka)
Dolynska
Pokrovske
Chystiakove
Pervomaisk
Kryvyi Rih
Donetsk
Bobrynets
(Torez)
ve Ozero
Arbuzynka
Inhulets
Pokrov
Nikopol
Zaporizhzhia
Orikhiv
Dokuchaievsk
Ambrosiivka
Novyy Buh
(Ordzhonikidze)
Marhanets
Volnovakha
Voznesensk
Kamianka-Dniprovska
Dniprorudne
Polohy
Don
Tokmak
Mariupol
Novoazovsk
Kamianka-Dniprovska
Kakhovske Vodoskhovyshche
Molochansk
Bila
Piidennyi Buh
Mykolaiv
Nova
Melitopol
Gulf of Taganrog
Posad-Pokrovske
Kakhovka
Kakhovka
Prymorsk
Berdiansk
Yeya
Ochakiv
Kherson
Yakymivka
a
S
Oleshky (Tsiurupynsk)
Odesa
Hola Prystan
Novotroitske
L
Chaplynka
Henichesk
88
Chornomorsk
(Illichivsk)
Kalanchak
Bilhorod-
Armiansk
Sea of Azov
Dnistrovskyi
Yany Kapu
(Krasnoperekopsk)
RUSSIA
Karkinitska Zatoka
Rozdolne
Kurman
Dzhankoi
Kerch Strait
Chornomorske
(Krasnohvardiiske)
Nyzhnohirskyi
Zatoka Syvash
Kerch
Kuban'
Yevpatoriia
Krym (Crimea)
Yedy Kuiu
Saky
(Lenine)
Simferopol
Feodosiia
Bakhchysarai
Krymski Hory
Sudak
(since 2014 the Ukrainian territory of Crimea has been annexed by Russia)
Sevastopol
Alushta
Yalta
Alupka

B l a c k   S e a

94

European Russia

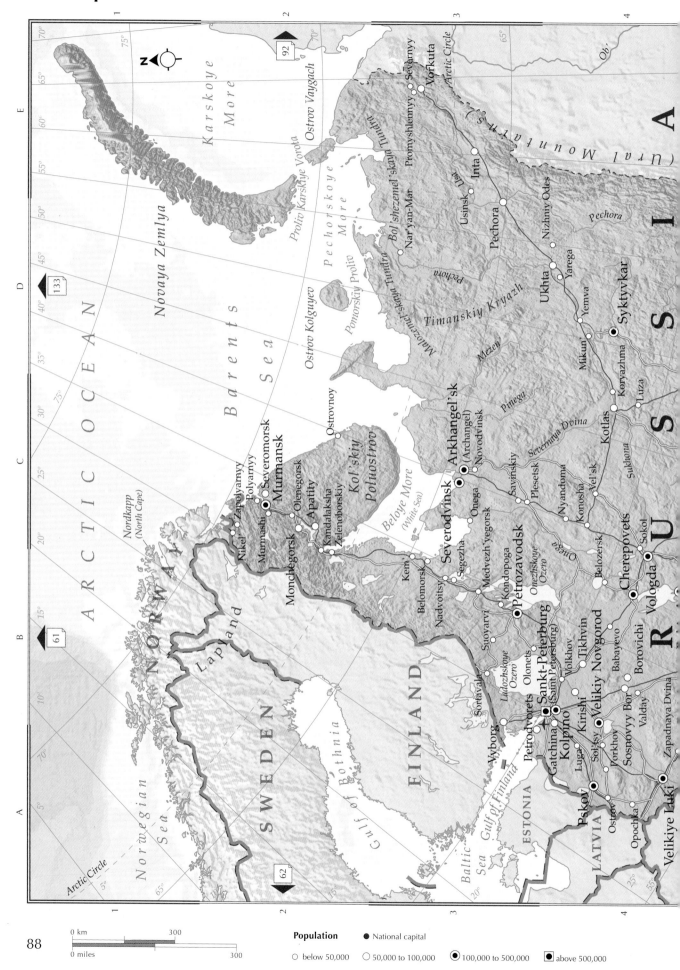

88

0 km 300
0 miles 300

Population

● National capital

○ below 50,000
○ 50,000 to 100,000
◉ 100,000 to 500,000
■ above 500,000

ARCTIC OCEAN

Karskoye More

Novaya Zemlya

Ostrov Vaygach

Proliv Karskiye Vorota

Pechorskoye More

Ostrov Kolguyev

Pomorskiy Proliv

Barents Sea

NORWAY

Nordkapp (North Cape)

SWEDEN

Norwegian Sea

Arctic Circle

Lapland

FINLAND

Gulf of Bothnia

Baltic Sea

Gulf of Finland

ESTONIA

LATVIA

Kol'skiy Poluostrov

Beloye More (White Sea)

Nikel'
Zapolyarnyy
Polyarnyy
Murmashi
Severomorsk
Murmansk
Olenegorsk
Monchegorsk
Apatity
Kandalaksha
Zelenoborskiy

Ostrovnoy

Kem'
Belomorsk
Nadvoitsy
Segezha
Medvezh'yegorsk
Suoyarvi
Olonets
Sortavala
Lidozhskoye Ozero
Petrozavodsk
Kondopoga
Onezhskoye Ozero
Vyborg
Petrodvorets
Sankt-Peterburg (Saint Petersburg)
Gatchina
Kolpino
Luga
Kirishi
Sol'tsy
Porkhov
Sosnovyy Bor
Valday
Zapadnaya Dvina
Velikiye Luki
Pskov
Ostrov
Opochka
Velikiy Novgorod
Volkhov
Tikhvin
Babayevo
Borovichi

Arkhangel'sk (Archangel)
Novodvinsk
Severodvinsk
Onega
Plesetsk
Savinskiy
Nyandoma
Konosha
Vel'sk
Belozersk
Cherepovets
Vologda
Sokol

Promyshlennyy
Severnyy
Vorkuta
Arctic Circle
Inta
Usinsk
Usa
Nar'yan-Mar
Bol'shezemel'skaya Tundra
Malozemel'skaya Tundra
Pechora
Pechora
Pechora
Nizhniy Odes
Yarega
Ukhta
Yemva
Mikun'
Koryazhma
Luza
Syktyvkar
Kotlas
Sukhona
Severnaya Dvina
Pinega
Mezen'
Mezen'
Timanskiy Kryazh

Ural Mountains

R U S S I A

92
133
61
62

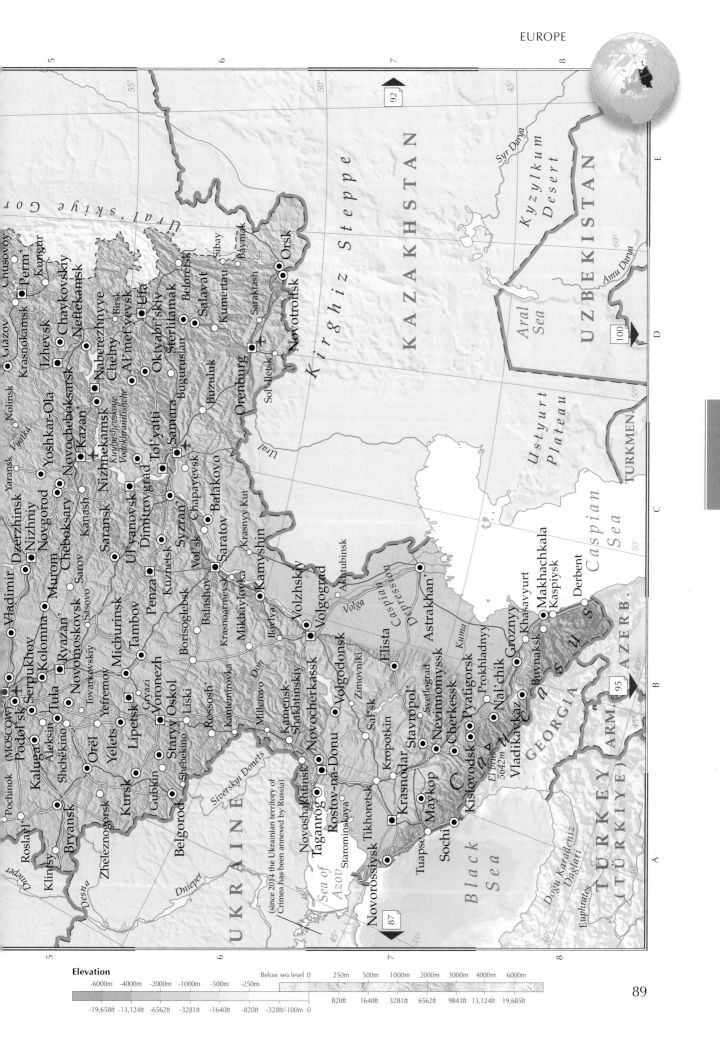

Elevation

| -6000m | -4000m | -2000m | -1000m | -500m | -250m | Below sea level 0 | 250m | 500m | 1000m | 2000m | 3000m | 4000m | 6000m |

-19,658ft   -13,124ft   -6562ft   -3281ft   -1640ft   -820ft   -328ft/-100m 0   820ft   1640ft   3281ft   6562ft   9843ft   13,124ft   19,685ft

North & West Asia

Franz Josef Land

ARCTIC

Severnaya Z

Ostrov Komsomolets

Ostrov Oktyabr'skoy Revolyutsii
Ostrov Bol'shevik

Summer limit of pack ice

Winter limit of pack ice

Norwegian Sea North Cape

Barents Sea

Novaya Zemlya

East Novaya Zemlya Trench

Kara Sea

Ostrov Kolguyev

Poluostrov Yamal

North Sibe

Kheta

Poluostrov Taymi

Noril'sk

Centra
Siberia
Platea

Kureyka

White Sea

Murmansk
Kola Peninsula

Arctic Circle

Archangel

Gulf of Ob

Northern Dvina

Lake Onega

Ural Mountains

R U S S i

West Siberian Plain

Ob'

Lower Tunguska

Ob'

Stony Tunguska

Angara

Lake Ladoga

Gulf of Bothnia

Saint Petersburg
Vologda
Yaroslavl'

Nizhniy Novgorod

Volga

Perm'

Yekaterinburg

Irtysh

Yenisey

Tomsk

Chulym

Krasnoyarsk

Baltic Sea

MOSCOW

Central Russian Upland

Kazan'
Ufa
Samara

Chelyabinsk

Ishim

Irtysh

Omsk

Novosibirsk

Novokuznetsk

Kaliningrad

KALININGRAD
(to Russia)

Ul'yanovsk

Saratov

Orenburg

Oral/Ural'sk

ASTANA

Kazakh Steppe

Qaraghandy
(Karagandy)

Semey

Sayanskiy Khrebet

Irk

Voronezh

E U R O P E

(since 2014 the Ukrainian territory of Crimea has been annexed by Russia)

Volgograd

Ural

Kazakh Uplands

KAZAKHSTAN

Ozero Zaysan

Altai Mountains

Danube

Don

Rostov-na-Donu

Stavropol'

Astrakhan'

Aktau

Aral Sea

Syr Darya

Aral/Aral'sk

Lake Balkhash

Ili

S

Black Sea

El'brus
18,510ft
(5642m)

Caucasus

Caspian Sea

Ustyurt Plateau

Kyzyl Kum

Qyzylorda/Kyzylorda

Taraz

Almaty

Tien Shan

Istanbul

Küre Dağları

GEORGIA

TBILISI

Dasoguz

UZBEKISTAN

Amu Darya

BISHKEK

Jengish Chokusu/Tömür Feng
24,406ft (7439m)

ANKARA

TURKEY
(TÜRKIYE)

ARMENIA

YEREVAN

AZERB.

BAKU

TURKMENISTAN

Garagum

TASHKENT

KYRGYZSTAN

DUSHANBE

TAJIKISTAN

Lake Van

Gaziantep

Tabriz

ASHGABAT

Kunlun Mountains

Adana

Aleppo
Mosul

Qom

TEHRAN

KABUL

Jalalabad

Hindu Kush

CYPRUS

SYRIA/IRAQ

Isfahan

IRAN

Herat

AFGHANISTAN

Khyber Pass

Himalayas

BEIRUT
LEBANON

DAMASCUS
BAGHDAD

Euphrates

Tigris

Zagros Mountains

Iranian Plateau

Thar Desert

Ganges

ISRAEL

JERUSALEM

AMMAN

Syrian Desert

Basra

Zahedan

Indus Fan

Mediterranean Sea

Dead Sea
-1411ft
(- 430m)

JORDAN

KUWAIT

Shiraz

Bandar-e 'Abbas

An Nafud

KUWAIT CITY

MANAMA

Persian Gulf

Dubai

Murray Ridge

Ganges Fan

SAUDI
ARABIA

BAHRAIN

DOHA

U.A.E.

MUSCAT

Tropic of Cancer

RIYADH

QATAR

Arabian Peninsula

Nile

Jedda

At Ta'if

AFRICA

Red Sea

Ar Rub' al Khali

OMAN

DHABI

Sur

Gulf of Oman

Arabian Sea

Bay of Bengal

SANAA

YEMEN

Ta'izz

Aden

Socotra (to Yemen)

Gulf of Aden

N

0 km   800

0 miles   800

Population   ● National capital

○ below 50,000   ⊙ 50,000 to 100,000   ◉ 100,000 to 500,000   ▣ above 500,000

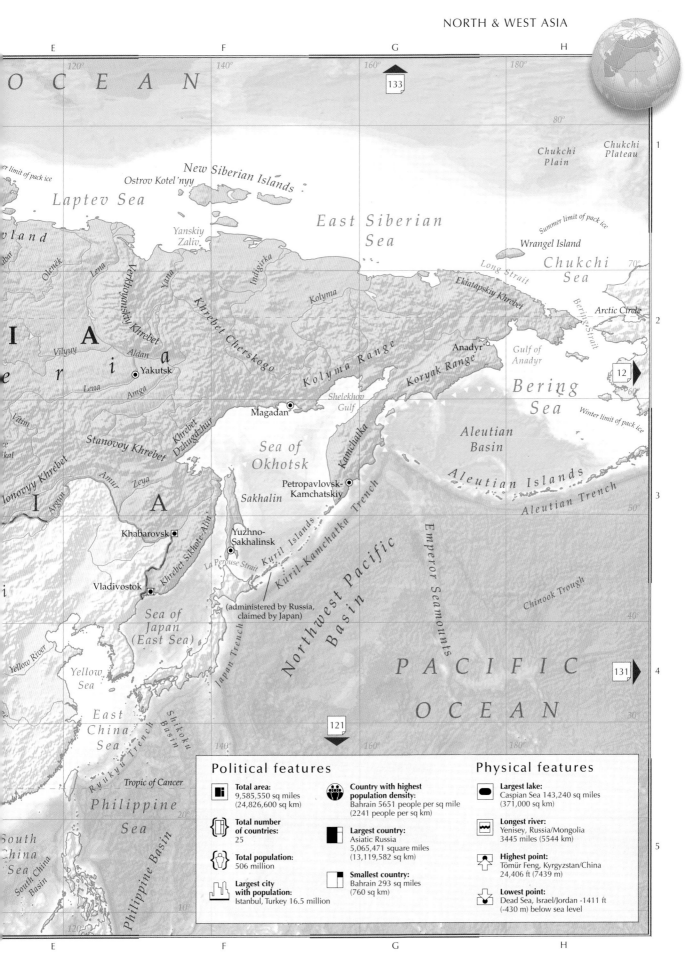

O C E A N

133

120°　　　　　　*140°*　　　　　　*160°*　　　　　　*180°*

80°

1

Chukchi Plain

Chukchi Plateau

upper limit of pack ice

New Siberian Islands

Ostrov Kotel'nyy

Laptev Sea

East Siberian Sea

Summer limit of pack ice

Wrangel Island

Yanskiy Zaliv.

Chukchi Sea

70°

Olenek　*Lena*　*Verkhoyanskiy Khrebet*　*Yana*　*Indigirka*　*Kolyma*　*Khrebet Cherskogo*　*Long Strait*　*Ekiatapskiy Khrebet*

Arctic Circle

2

I A

Vilyuy　*Aldan*

Kolyma Range

Koryak Range

Anadyr

Bering Strait

Gulf of Anadyr

12

60°

Lena　⊙ Yakutsk　*Amga*

Shelekhov Gulf

Bering Sea

Winter limit of pack ice

Magadan ⊙

Aleutian Basin

Stanovoy Khrebet　*Khrebet Dzhugdzhur*

Sea of Okhotsk

Kamchatka

Aleutian Islands

Aleutian Trench

3

Amur　*Zeya*

Petropavlovsk-Kamchatskiy ⊙

Sakhalin

Kuril-Kamchatka Trench

Emperor Seamounts

50°

Khabarovsk ◙

Yuzhno-Sakhalinsk

Kuril Islands

Khrebet Sikhote-Alin'

La Perouse Strait

Northwest Pacific Basin

Chinook Trough

Vladivostok ◙

(administered by Russia, claimed by Japan)

40°

Sea of Japan (East Sea)

Japan Trench

P A C I F I C

131

4

Yellow River

Yellow Sea

O C E A N

30°

121

East China Sea

Shikoku Basin

Ryukyu Trench

Tropic of Cancer

20°

Philippine Sea

South China Sea

Philippine Basin

South China Basin

10°

5

120°　　　*140°*　　　*160°*　　　*180°*

Political features

▤ **Total area:**
9,585,550 sq miles
(24,826,600 sq km)

▥ **Total number of countries:**
25

▧ **Total population:**
506 million

▤ **Largest city with population:**
Istanbul, Turkey 16.5 million

⬤ **Country with highest population density:**
Bahrain 5651 people per sq mile
(2241 people per sq km)

◼ **Largest country:**
Asiatic Russia
5,065,471 square miles
(13,119,582 sq km)

◧ **Smallest country:**
Bahrain 293 sq miles
(760 sq km)

Physical features

⬬ **Largest lake:**
Caspian Sea 143,240 sq miles
(371,000 sq km)

〰 **Longest river:**
Yenisey, Russia/Mongolia
3445 miles (5544 km)

⬆ **Highest point:**
Tömür Feng, Kyrgyzstan/China
24,406 ft (7439 m)

⬇ **Lowest point:**
Dead Sea, Israel/Jordan -1411 ft
(-430 m) below sea level

E　　F　　G　　H

Russia & Kazakhstan

NETH.

NORWAY

DENMARK

GERMANY

SWEDEN

FINLAND

SVALBARD
(to Norway)

Zemlya Fran
Iosifa

Arctic Circle

Winter limit of pack ice

Summer limit of pack ice

A R C T

Barents
Sea

Nordkapp
(North Cape)

Novaya Zemlya

Karskoye More

Ostrov Belyt

Diks

Murmansk

Kandalaksha

Kol'skiy
Poluostrov

Ostrov
Kolguyev

Gulf of Bothnia

Baltic Sea

Gulf of Finland

KALININGRAD
(to Russia)

Kaliningrad

POLAND

LITH.   LAT.   EST.

Sankt-Peterburg

Pskov

Velikiy Novgorod

BELARUS

Smolensk

Ladozhskoye
Ozero

Petrozavodsk

Onezhskoye
Ozero

Cherepovets

Vel'sk

Beloye More

Severodvinsk

Arkhangel'sk

Severnaya Dvina

Nar'yan-Mar

Pechora

Poluostrov Yamal

MOSKVA
(MOSCOW)

Tver'

Vologda

Kotlas

Ukhta

Vorkuta

UKRAINE

MOLDOVA

(since 2014
the Ukrainian
territory of
Crimea has been
annexed by
Russia)

Bryansk

Tula

Yaroslavl'

Kineshma

Vladimir

Nizhniy Novgorod

Kirov

Syktyvkar

Salekhard

Tal'

Noril'

Belgorod

Ryazan'

Tambov

Kazan'

Glazov

Solikamsk'

U r a l ' s k i y e   G o r y

Ob'

Igarka

Voronezh

Penza

Ul'yanovsk

Izhevsk

Perm'

Serov

Nadym

Nyagan'

Zapadno-

Sea of
Azov

Mikhaylovka

Saratov

Tol'yatti

Naberezhnyye
Chelny

Khanty-Mansiysk

Sibirskaya

Rostov-na-
Donu

Balakovo

Samara

Ufa

Yekaterinburg

Surgut

Nizhnevartovsk

Ravnina

Krasnodar

Volgograd

Sterlitamak

Lesnoy

Sochi

Stavropol'

El'brus
5642m

Oral/Ural'sk

Ural

Tyumen'

Tobol'sk

R   U

Black Sea

GEORGIA

CAUCASUS

Nal'chik

Astrakhan'

Orenburg

Ural
(Zhayyk)

Chelyabinsk

Ishim

Ob'

Chulym

Vladikavkaz

Groznyy

Volga

Aqtöbe

Orsk

Tobol

Qostanay/Kostanay

Ishim

Irtysh

Omsk

Seversk

Tomsk

St

Makhachkala

Atyraū/Atyrau

Alga

Rudnyy

Petropavlovsk

Novosibirsk

Krasnoy

ARM.

AZERBAIJAN

Aktobe

Emba

Shalqar/Shalkar

Magnitogorsk

Kökshetaū/
Kökshetau

Atbasar

Shchuchinsk

Kemerov

Fort-Shevchenko

Aqtaū/Aktau

Zhangaözen/
Zhanaozen

Ustyurt
Plateau

KAZAKHSTAN

ASTANA

Pavlodar

Barnaul

Novokuznetsk

Ab

Caspian Sea

Aral
Sea

Syr Darya

Aral/Aral'sk

Ayteke Bi

Temirtau

Saran'

Qaraghandy/
Karagandy

Semey

Rïdder/
Ridder

Zyryanovsk

K

TURKMENISTAN

UZBEKISTAN

Kyzyl
Kum

Zhezqazghan/
Zhezkazgan

Zhosaly

Qyzylorda/
Kyzylorda

Saryarqa/Kazakhskiy
Melkosopochnik

Shar

Öskemen/Ust'-Kamenogorsk

Balqash/
Balkash

Ayagoz

Ozero
Zaysan

Gora Belukha
4506m

Altai
Mountain

Zap

IRAN

Amu Darya

Türkistan/
Turkestan

Kentau

Karatau

Arys'

Shu

Balqash Köli/
Ozero Balkash

Taldyqorghan/Taldykorgan

Tekeli

AFGHANISTAN

TAJIKISTAN

Shymkent

Taraz

Almaty

Kirghiz Range

KYRGYZSTAN

Tien Shan

CHINA

0 km   600

0 miles   600

Population

○ below 50,000

◉ 50,000 to 100,000

● National capital

◉ 100,000 to 500,000

■ above 500,000

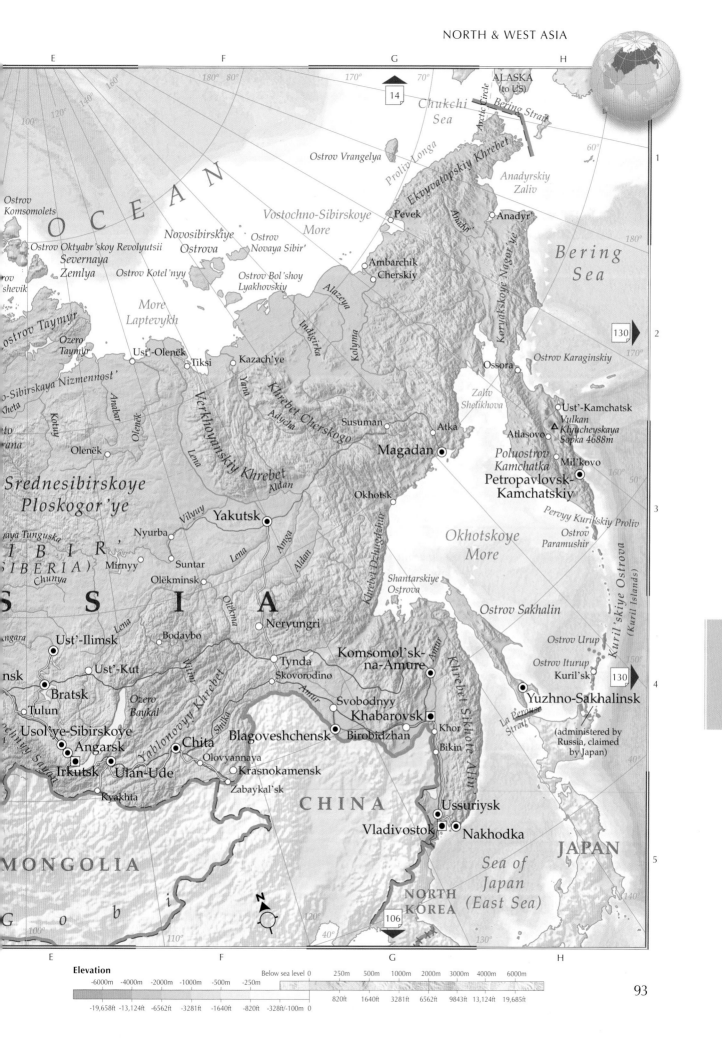

ALASKA
(to US)

*Chukchi
Sea*

Ostrov Vrangelya

Pevek

Ekvyvatapskiy Khrebet

*Anadyrskiy
Zaliv*

Anadyr'

O C E A N

*Vostochno-Sibirskoye
More*

*Bering
Sea*

*Novosibirskiye
Ostrova*

*Ostrov
Novaya Sibir'*

Ambarchik
Cherskiy

130

*Ostrov
Komsomolets*

Ostrov Oktyabr'skoy Revolyutsii

Ostrova

*Severnaya
Zemlya*

Ostrov Kotel'nyy

*Ostrov Bol'shoy
Lyakhovskiy*

Ossora

Ostrov Karaginskiy

*rov
shevik*

*More
Laptevykh*

Alazeya

Indigirka

Kolyma

*Zaliv
Shelikhova*

Ust'-Kamchatsk
*Vulkan
Klyucheyskaya
Sopka 4688m*

Ostrov Taymyr

*Ozero
Taymyr*

Ust'-Olenëk

Tiksi

Kazach'ye

Yana

Adycha

Khrebet Cherskogo

Susuman

Atka

Atlasovo

*Poluostrov
Kamchatka*

Mil'kovo

Sibirskaya Nizmennost'

Kheta

Anabar

Olenëk

Verkhoyanskiy Khrebet

Lena

Magadan

Okhotsk

Petropavlovsk-
Kamchatskiy

Pervyy Kuril'skiy Proliv

Kotuy

Olenëk

Aldan

Pervyy Kuril'skiy Proliv

Srednesibirskoye
Ploskogor'ye

Vilyuy

Nyurba

Yakutsk

Amga

*Okhotskoye
More*

*Ostrov
Paramushir*

aya Tunguska

Mirnyy

Suntar

Lena

Aldan

Khrebet Dzhugdzhur

*Shantarskiye
Ostrova*

Ostrov Sakhalin

I B I R '

(S I B E R I A)

Chunya

Olëkminsk

I

A

Kuril'skiye Ostrova

(Kuril Islands)

S

S

I

A

Olëkma

Neryungri

Ostrov Urup

Angara

Ust'-Ilimsk

Bodaybo

Tynda
Skovorodino

Komsomol'sk-
na-Amure

Amur

Ostrov Iturup
Kuril'sk

La Pérouse Strait

130

Ust'-Kut

Vilyuy

Khrebet Sikhote Alin'

Yuzhno-Sakhalinsk

nsk

Bratsk

*Ozero
Baykal*

Yablonovyy Khrebet

Olëkma

Svobodnyy

Khabarovsk

Khor

(administered by
Russia, claimed
by Japan)

Tulun

Amur

Birobidzhan

Bikin

Usol'ye-Sibirskoye

Angarsk

Chita

Blagoveshchensk

Shilka

chnyy Sayan

Irkutsk

Ulan-Ude

Olovyannaya

Krasnokamensk

Ussuriysk

Kyakhta

Zabaykal'sk

C H I N A

Vladivostok

Nakhodka

J A P A N

M O N G O L I A

*Sea of
Japan
(East Sea)*

G o b i

106

NORTH
KOREA

G

Elevation

| -6000m | -4000m | -2000m | -1000m | -500m | -250m | Below sea level 0 | 250m | 500m | 1000m | 2000m | 3000m | 4000m | 6000m |

| -19,658ft | -13,124ft | -6562ft | -3281ft | -1640ft | -820ft | -328ft/-100m 0 | 820ft | 1640ft | 3281ft | 6562ft | 9843ft | 13,124ft | 19,685ft |

93

Turkey & The Caucasus

ROMANIA

Lacul Sinoie

UKRAINE

Krym (Crimea)

(since 2014 the Ukrainian territory of Crimea has been annexed by Russia)

Danube

BULGARIA

Varnenski Zaliv

B l a c k   S e a

Burgaski Zaliv

Maritsa

Kırklareli

Edirne

Ergene Çayı

Çorlu

Tekirdag

İstanbul

Zonguldak

İnebolu

Cide

Sinop

Gerze

Bartın

Küre Dağları

Kastamonu

Bafra

Samsun

Devrek

Karabük

Kargı

Çerkeş

Merzifon

Çanık Dağları

Ü

Or

İzmit

Adapazarı

Marmara Denizi (Sea of Marmara)

Bandırma

Yalova

İznik Gölü

Bolu

Gerede

Çankırı

Kızıl Irmak

Çorum

Tokat

Çanakkale

Simav Çayı

Bursa

Bilecik

ANKARA

Kırıkkale

Kalecik

Alaca

Yıldızeli

Çanakkale Boğazı (Dardanelles)

Balıkesir

Bozüyük

Eskişehir

T U R K E Y

Polatlı

Sorgun

Boğazlıyan

Şarkışla

Siv

Edremit

Ayvalık

Kütahya

Simav

Gediz

Hirfanli Baraji

Kulu

(T Ü R K İ Y E)

Bünyan

Gürün

Lésvos

Akhisar

Tuz Gölü

Manisa

Uşak

Afyon

Cihanbeyli

Nevşehir

İncesu

Kayseri

Chios

Gediz Nehri

Menemen

İzmir

Ödemiş

Alaşehir

A n a t o l i a

Akşehir

Aksaray

Göksun

Gü

Sámos

Aydın

Nazilli

Dinar

Beyşehir Gölü

Konya

Niğde

İsparta

Burdur

Söke

Büyükmenderes Nehri

Denizli

Burdur Gölü

Ereğli

Kahramann

Milas

Tavas

Suğla Gölü

Karaman

Gazi

Muğla

T o r o s   D a ğ l a r ı

Ceyhan

Bodrum

Marmaris

Dalaman

Antalya

Manavgat

Tarsus

Mersin (İçel)

Adana

Osmaniye

Fethiye

Alanya

İskenderun

Kilis

Kaş

Finike

Mut

Antakya

Kırıkhan

Doðekánisa (Dodecánese)

Ródos (Rhodes)

Antalya Körfezi

Silifke

Anamur

Orontes

Kárpathos

CYPRUS

TURKISH REPUBLIC OF NORTHERN CYPRUS (recognized only by Turkey)

M e d i t e r r a n e a n

S e a

LEBANON

0 km   200

0 miles   200

Population   ● National capital

○ below 50,000   ○ 50,000 to 100,000   ◉ 100,000 to 500,000   ◼ above 500,000

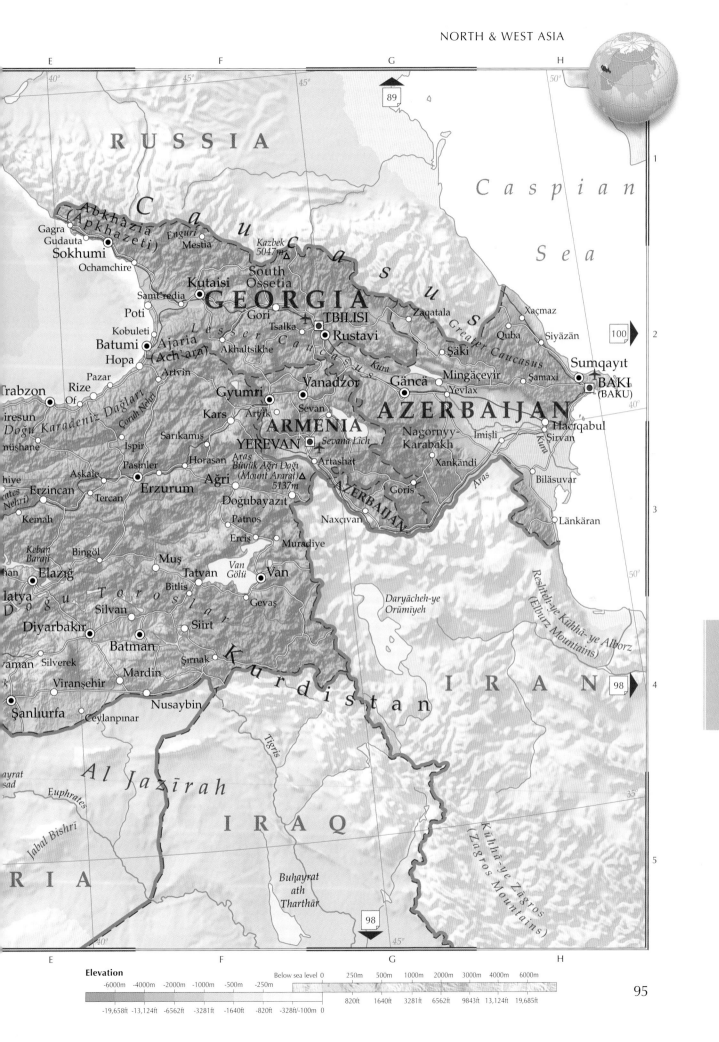

Elevation

| Below sea level 0 | 250m | 500m | 1000m | 2000m | 3000m | 4000m | 6000m |

| -6000m | -4000m | -2000m | -1000m | -500m | -250m |

| -19,658ft | -13,124ft | -6562ft | -3281ft | -1640ft | -820ft | -328ft/-100m | 0 |

| 820ft | 1640ft | 3281ft | 6562ft | 9843ft | 13,124ft | 19,685ft |

The Near East

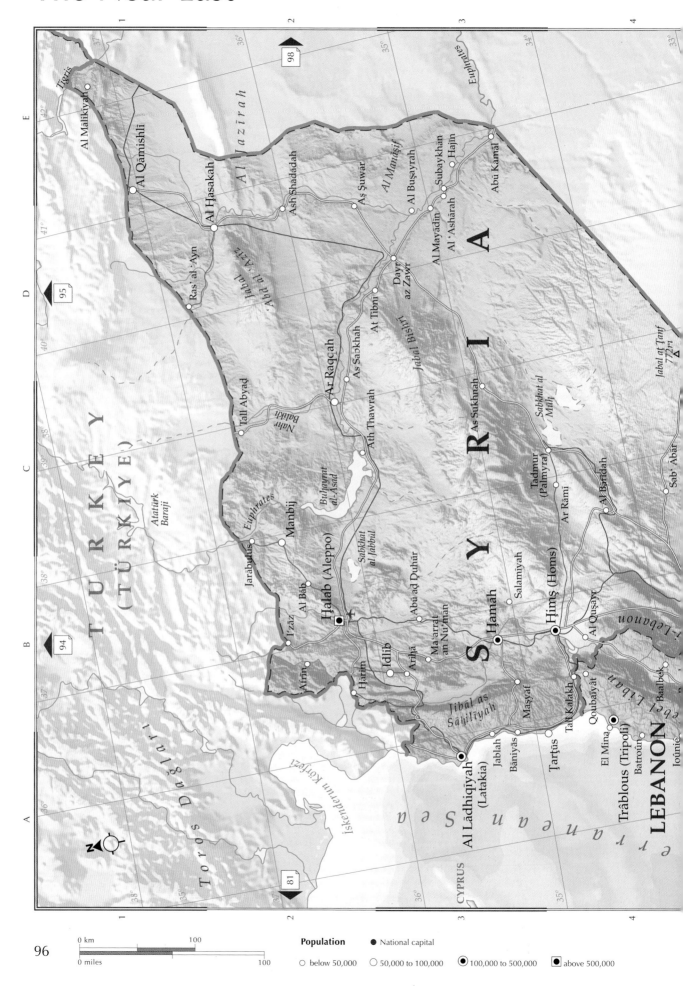

TURKEY (TÜRKİYE)

SYRIA

LEBANON

CYPRUS

Mediterranean Sea

Tigris

Al Malikiyah

Al Qāmishli

Al Ḥasakah

Al Jazīrah

Ash Shadādah

As Suwār

Al Manūṣif

Al Buṣayrah

Subaykhān

Hajīn

Abū Kamāl

Al Mayādīn

Al 'Ashārah

Dayr az Zawr

At Tibnī

Jabal Bishrī

Ras al 'Ayn

Jabal 'Abd al 'Azīz

Jabal aṭ Ṭanf
772 m

Ar Raqqah

As Sabkhah

Ath Thawrah

Tall Abyad

Nahr Balīkh

Buḥayrat al-Asad

As Sukhnah

Sabkhat al Mūḥ

Sab' Ābār

Tadmur (Palmyra)

Ar Rāmī

Al Baridah

Atatürk Barajı

Euphrates

Manbij

Jarābulus

A'zāz

Al Bāb

Ḥalab (Aleppo)

Sabkhat al Jabbūl

Abū aḍ Ḍuhūr

Ma'arrat an Nu'mān

Salamiyah

Ḥamāh

Ḥimṣ (Homs)

Al Quṣayr

Afrin

Ḥārim

Idlib

Arīḥā

Jibāl as Sāḥilīyah

Masyāf

Tall Kalakh

Qoubaïyât

Baalbek

Jebel Liban

Anti-Lebanon

Al Lādhiqīyah (Latakia)

Jablah

Bāniyās

Ṭarṭūs

El Mina

Trâblous (Tripoli)

Batroûn

Joûnié

İskenderun Körfezi

Toros Dağları

N

Population

● National capital
○ below 50,000
◎ 50,000 to 100,000
◉ 100,000 to 500,000
▣ above 500,000

0 km 100
0 miles 100

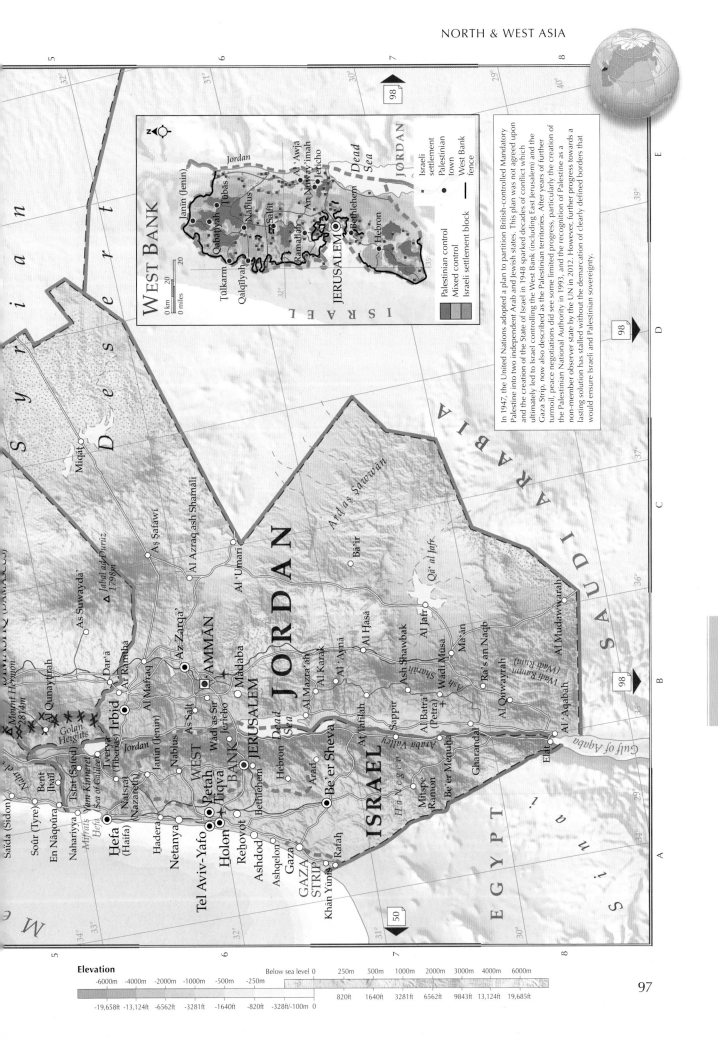

WEST BANK

In 1947, the United Nations adopted a plan to partition British-controlled Mandatory Palestine into two independent Arab and Jewish states. This plan was not agreed upon and the creation of the State of Israel in 1948 sparked decades of conflict which ultimately led to Israel controlling the West Bank (including East Jerusalem) and the Gaza Strip, now also described as the Palestinian territories. After years of further turmoil, peace negotiations did see some limited progress, particularly the creation of the Palestinian National Authority in 1993, and the recognition of Palestine as a non-member observer state by the UN in 2012. However, further progress towards a lasting solution has stalled without the demarcation of clearly defined borders that would ensure Israeli and Palestinian sovereignty.

Palestinian control
Mixed control
Israeli settlement block

▪ Israeli settlement
● Palestinian town
— West Bank fence

0 km   20
0 miles 20

Elevation

						Below sea level 0	250m	500m	1000m	2000m	3000m	4000m	6000m
-6000m	-4000m	-2000m	-1000m	-500m	-250m								

| -19,658ft | -13,124ft | -6562ft | -3281ft | -1640ft | -820ft | -328ft/-100m 0 | 820ft | 1640ft | 3281ft | 6562ft | 9843ft | 13,124ft | 19,685ft |

The Middle East

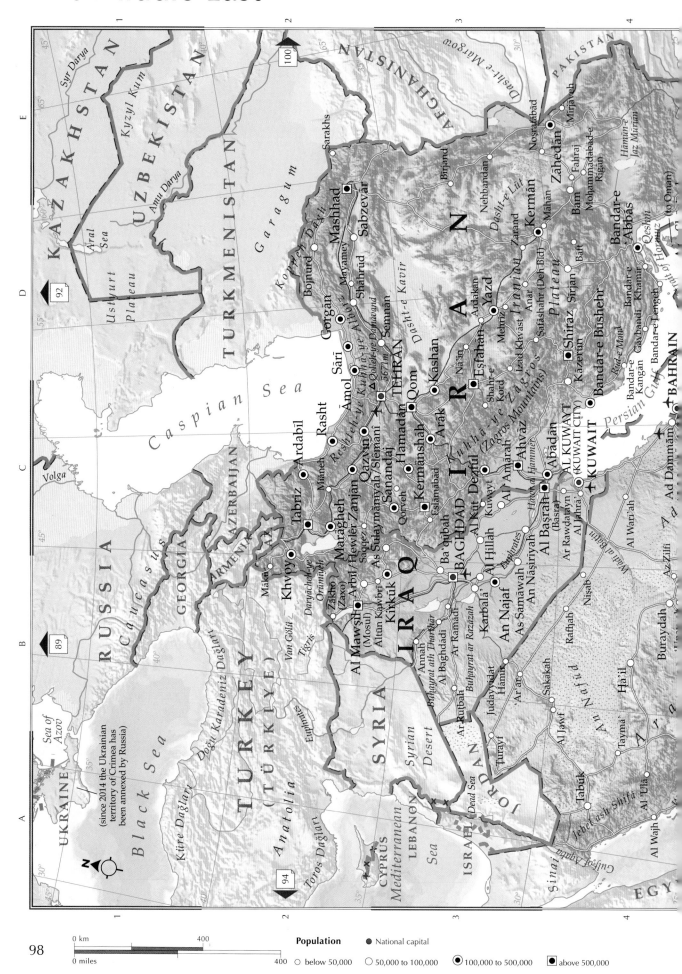

0 km   400
0 miles   400

Population   ● National capital

○ below 50,000   ○ 50,000 to 100,000   ◉ 100,000 to 500,000   ■ above 500,000

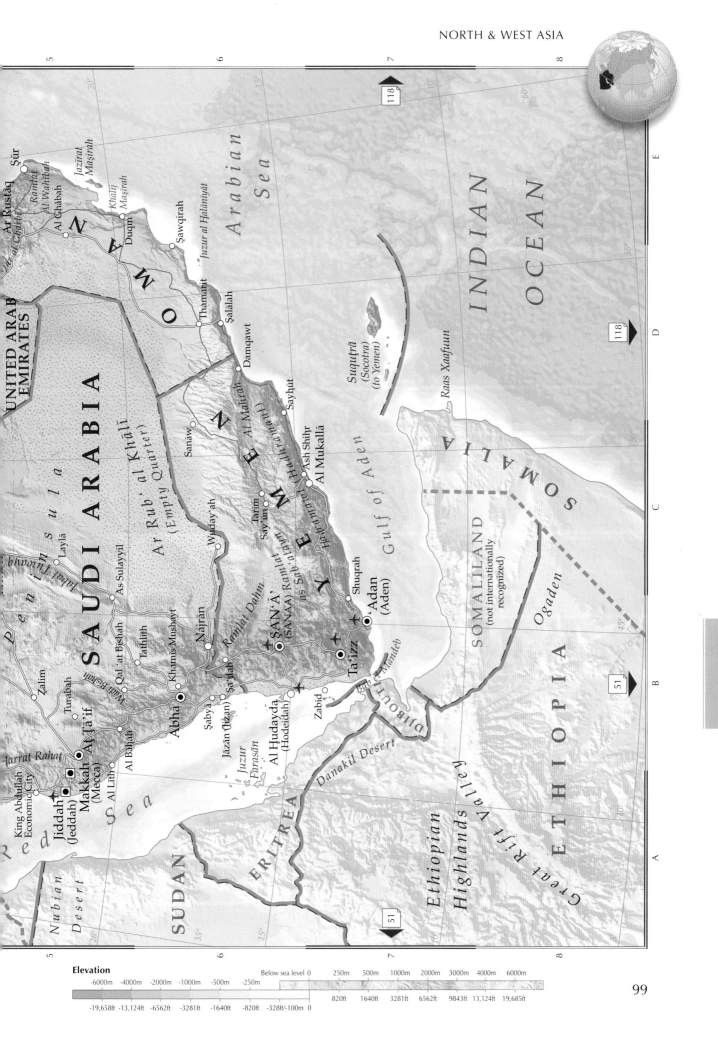

Elevation

Below sea level 0	250m	500m	1000m	2000m	3000m	4000m	6000m

-6000m -4000m -2000m -1000m -500m -250m

820ft 1640ft 3281ft 6562ft 9843ft 13,124ft 19,685ft

-19,658ft -13,124ft -6562ft -3281ft -1640ft -820ft -328ft/-100m 0

Central Asia

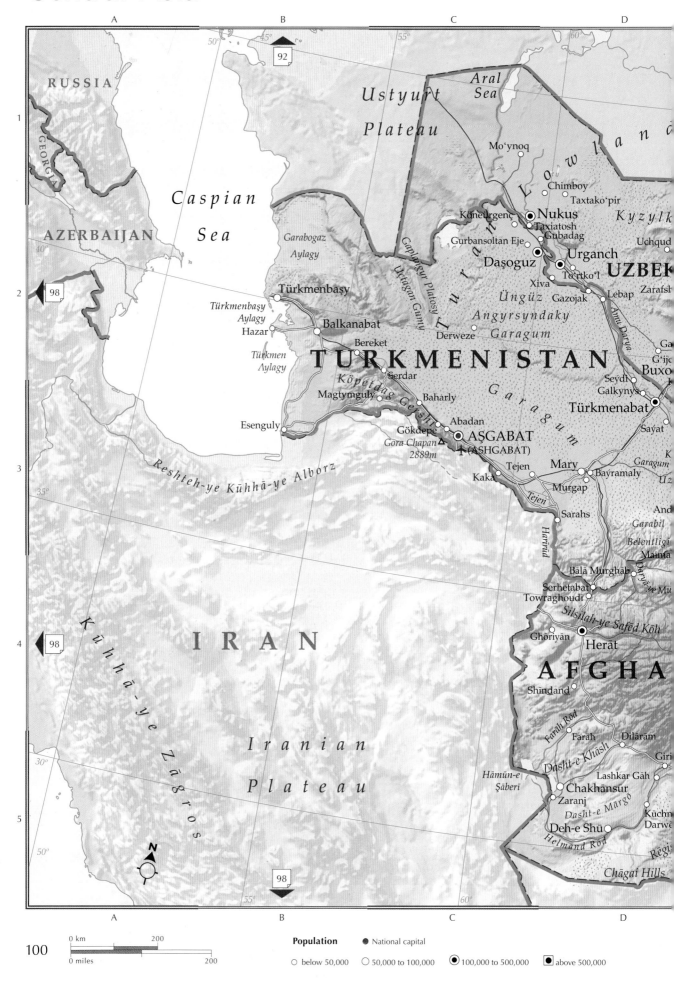

RUSSIA

GEORGIA

AZERBAIJAN

Caspian
Sea

Ustyurt
Plateau

Aral
Sea

Mo'ynoq

Chimboy
Taxtako'pir

Köneürgenç
Nukus
Taxiatosh
Gubadag
Gurbansoltan Eje
Daşoguz
Urganch
UZBEK
Xiva
To'rtko'l
Gazojak
Lebap
Zarafsh
Uchqud

Kyzylk

Garabogaz
Aylagy

Türkmenbaşy

Türkmenbaşy
Aylagy
Hazar

Balkanabat

Bereket

Türkmen
Aylagy

Esenguly

Magtymguly

Köpetdag Gershi

Serdar

Baharly

Gökdepe
Abadan
Gora Chapan
2889m

AŞGABAT
(ASHGABAT)

Kaka

Tejen

Üngüz
Angyrsyndaky
Garagum
Derweze

TURKMENISTAN

G a r a g u m

Mary
Murgap

Anmu Darya
Ga
G'ijc
Seydi
Galkynys
Türkmenabat
Saýat
Buxo

Bayramaly

Garagum
Uz

Reshteh-ye Kūhhā-ye Alborz

Sarahs

Tejen

Harīrūd

And
Garabil
Belentligi
Maima

Bālā Murghāb

Serhetabat
Towraghoudī

Silshlah-ye Safēd Kōh

Ghōriyān
Herāt

AFGHA

Kūhhā-ye Zağros

I R A N

Iranian
Plateau

Shīndand

Farāh Rōd
Farāh
Dilāram

Dasht-e Khāsh
Lashkar Gāh
Giri

Hāmūn-e
Şāberī
Chakhānsur
Zaranj

Dasht-e Mārgō
Kūchm
Darwē

Deh-e Shū

Helmand Rōd

Rēgi

Chāgai Hills

N

0 km   200

0 miles   200

Population   ● National capital

○ below 50,000   ◉ 50,000 to 100,000   ◉ 100,000 to 500,000   ◼ above 500,000

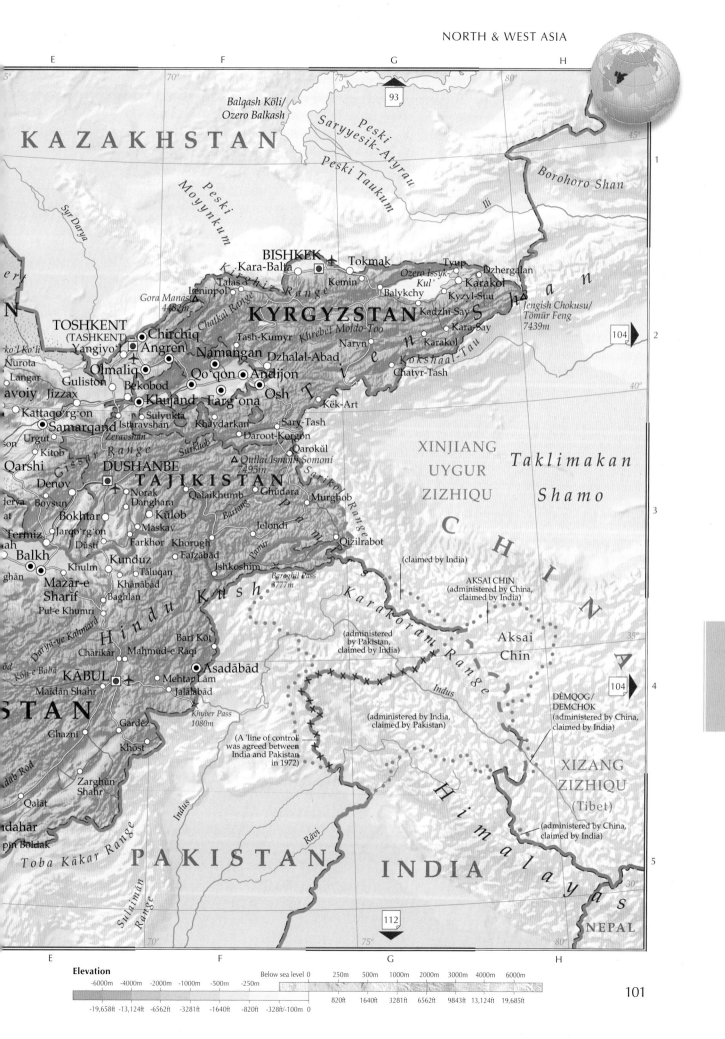

KAZAKHSTAN

Balqash Köli/
Ozero Balkash

Peski Saryyesik-Atyrau

Peski Taukum

Peski Moyynkum

Syr Darya

Borohoro Shan

Ili

BISHKEK
Kara-Balta
Tokmak
Tyup
Dzhergalan
Kemin
Ozero Issyk-Kul'
Karakol
Kara-Balta
Talas
Balykchy
Kyzyl-Suu
Leninpol
Gora Manas
4482m
Chatkal Range
Kirghiz Range
Kadzhi-Say
Jengish Chokusu/
Tömür Feng
7439m

KYRGYZSTAN
TOSHKENT
(TASHKENT)
Chirchiq
Tash-Kumyr
Khrebet Moldo-Too
Kara-Say
Yangiyo'l
Angren
Namangan
Dzhalal-Abad
Naryn
Karakol
Kokshaal-Tau
ko'l Ko'li
Olmaliq
Qo'qon
Andijon
Chatyr-Tash
Nurota
Bekobod
Osh
T
Langar
Khujand
Farg'ona
Këk-Art
avoiy
Jizzax
Sulyukta
Zeravshan
Kattaqo'rg'on
Istaravshan
Khaydarkan
Sary-Tash
Samarqand
Daroot-Korgon
Urgut
Surkhob
Qarokül

XINJIANG
UYGUR
ZIZHIQU
Taklimakan
Shamo

Qarshi
Kitob
Cissar Range
DUSHANBE
TAJIKISTAN
Qullai Ismoili Somoni
7495m
Sarikol Range

Denov
Norak
Danghara
Qalaikhumb
Ghudara
Murghob

Boysun
Kŭlob
Bartang
C H I N A

Bokhtar
Maskav
Jelondi

Jarqo'rg'on
Dŭsti
Farkhor
Khorugh
Pamir
Qizilrabot
(claimed by India)

Balkh
Kunduz
Faïzābād
Ishkoshim
AKSAI CHIN
(administered by China,
claimed by India)

Khulm
Tāluqān
Baroghil Pass
3777m
(administered
by Pakistan,
claimed by India)
Aksai
Chin

Mazār-e
Sharîf
Khānābād
Hindu Kush
Karakoram Range

ghān
Baghlān

Pul-e Khumri
Indus
DÊMQOG /
DEMCHOK
(administered by China,
claimed by India)

Daryā-ye Kahmard
Barī Kōt

Chārikār
Mahmūd-e Rāqi
(administered
by India,
claimed by Pakistan)

Kōh-e Bābā
KĀBUL
Asadābād
Mehtar Lām
XIZANG
ZIZHIQU
(Tibet)

ōd
Maīdān Shahr
Jalālābād
Khyber Pass
1080m
(A 'line of control'
was agreed between
India and Pakistan
in 1972)
(administered by China,
claimed by India)

STAN
Ghazni
Gardēz
Khōst
Indus
Himalayas

Zarghūn
Shahr
Ravi

Qalāt
PAKISTAN
INDIA

dahār
Toba Kākar Range
Sulaimān Range

pin Boldak
NEPAL

Elevation

| -6000m | -4000m | -2000m | -1000m | -500m | -250m | Below sea level 0 | 250m | 500m | 1000m | 2000m | 3000m | 4000m | 6000m |

-19,658ft   -13,124ft   -6562ft   -3281ft   -1640ft   -820ft   -328ft/-100m 0

820ft   1640ft   3281ft   6562ft   9843ft   13,124ft   19,685ft

South & East Asia

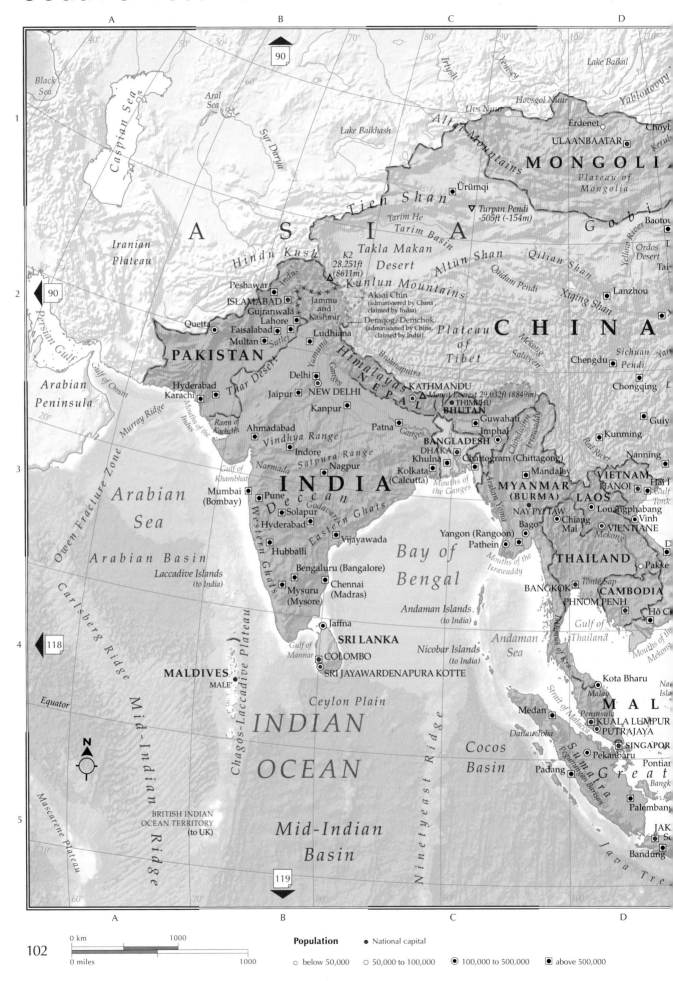

Black Sea

Caspian Sea

Aral Sea

Syr Darya

Lake Balkhash

Irtysh

Yenisey

Lake Baikal

ASIA

Iranian Plateau

Hindu Kush

Tien Shan

Tarim He

Tarim Basin

Takla Makan Desert

Altai Mountains

Uvs Nuur

Hovsgol Nuur

Yablonovyy

Erdenet

Choyt

ULAANBAATAR

MONGOLIA

Plateau of Mongolia

Gobi

Ürümqi

▽ Turpan Pendi -505ft (-154m)

Baotou

Yellow River

Ordos Desert

Tai

Lanzhou

Altun Shan

Qilian Shan

Qaidam Pendi

Xiqing Shan

Persian Gulf

Peshawar

ISLAMABAD

Gujranwala

Lahore

Quetta

Faisalabad

Multan

K2 28,251ft (8611m)

Jammu and Kashmir

Aksai Chin (administered by China, claimed by India)

Demqog/Demchok (administered by China, claimed by India)

Kunlun Mountains

Plateau of Tibet

CHINA

Mekong

Salween

Chengdu

Sichuan Pendi

Yar

PAKISTAN

Thar Desert

Sutlej

Ludhiana

Delhi

Yamuna

Ganges

Himalayas

NEPAL

KATHMANDU

△ Mount Everest 29,032ft (8849m)

THIMPHU

BHUTAN

Guwahati

Imphal

Chongqing

L

Guiy

Arabian Peninsula

Arabian Sea

Gulf of Oman

Murray Ridge

Mouths of the Indus

Karachi

Hyderabad

Rann of Kachchh

Gulf of Khambhat

Ahmadabad

Jaipur

NEW DELHI

Kanpur

Vindhya Range

Narmada

Satpura Range

Indore

Nagpur

Patna

Ganges

BANGLADESH

DHAKA

Khulna

Chattogram (Chittagong)

Kolkata (Calcutta)

Mouths of the Ganges

Mandalay

MYANMAR (BURMA)

Chindwin

Irrawaddy

Brahmaputra

NAY PYI TAW

Red River

Kunming

Nanning

VIETNAM

HANOI

Hai P

Gulf of Tonk

LAOS

Mumbai (Bombay)

Pune

INDIA

DECCAN

Godavari

Solapur

Hyderabad

Eastern Ghats

Vijayawada

Western Ghats

Hubballi

Bengaluru (Bangalore)

Mysuru (Mysore)

Chennai (Madras)

Bay of Bengal

Yangon (Rangoon)

Pathein

Bago

Mouths of the Irrawaddy

Louangphabang

Chiang Mai

Vinh

VIENTIANE

Mekong

THAILAND

Pakxe

D

Arabian Basin

Laccadive Islands (to India)

Carlsberg Ridge

Chagos-Laccadive Plateau

Jaffna

SRI LANKA

Gulf of Mannar

COLOMBO

SRI JAYAWARDENAPURA KOTTE

Andaman Islands (to India)

Nicobar Islands (to India)

Andaman Sea

BANGKOK

Tônlé Sap

CAMBODIA

PHNOM PENH

Hô C

Gulf of Thailand

Mouths of the Mekong

MALDIVES

MALE

Equator

Mid-Indian Ridge

Ceylon Plain

INDIAN OCEAN

Ninetyeast Ridge

Cocos Basin

Kota Bharu

Malay Peninsula

Medan

Danau Toba

Strait of Malacca

Na Isla

MAL

KUALA LUMPUR

PUTRAJAYA

SINGAPOR

Pekanbaru

Sumatra

Pontiar

Great

Mascarene Plateau

BRITISH INDIAN OCEAN TERRITORY (to UK)

Mid-Indian Basin

N

Padang

Palemban

Bangk

JAK

S

Bandung

Java Tre

102

0 km   1000

0 miles   1000

Population   ● National capital

○ below 50,000   ◎ 50,000 to 100,000   ◉ 100,000 to 500,000   ▣ above 500,000

Political features

Total area:
7,936,200 sq miles
(20,554,700 sq km)

Total number of countries:
24

Total population:
4156 million

Largest city with population:
Guangzhou, China 65.1 million

Country with highest population density:
Singapore 20,769 people per sq mile
(7692 people per sq km)

Largest country:
China 3,705,386 sq miles
(9,596,960 sq km)

Smallest country:
Maldives 120 sq miles
(300 sq km)

Physical features

Largest lake:
Tônlé Sap, Cambodia
1042 sq miles (2850 sq km)

Longest river:
Chang Jiang (Yangtze), China
3917 miles (6300 km)

Highest point:
Mount Everest, China/Nepal
29,032ft (8849m)

Lowest point:
Turpan Pendi (Turfan Basin), China
-505 ft (-154 m) below sea level

Western China & Mongolia

KAZAKHSTAN

Saryarqa/
Kazakhskiy Melkosopchnik

Kulunda Steppe

R U S S

Zapadnyy Sayan

Yenisey

Hövsgöl Nuur

Ozero Zaysan

Uvs Nuur

Ulaangom

Ölgiy

Altai

Har-Us Nuur

Hyargas Nuur

Hovd

Har Nuur

Hangayn Nuru

Tsetserle

M O N

Mc

*Balqash Köli
(Ozero Balkash)*

Ulungur Hu

Gurbantünggüt Shamo

Karamay

Kuytun

Fukang

Jimsar

Altay

Bayanhongor

△ *Aj Bogd Uul 3802m*

Atas Bogd △ *2695m*

G

Yining

Borohoro Shan

Shihezi

Ürümqi

Qitai

Turpan

Turpan Pendi

Hami

Dalain H

KYRGYZSTAN

Ozero Issyk-Kul'

T i e n   S h a n

△ *Jengish Chokusu/Tömür Feng 7439m*

Korla

Bosten Hu

Kuruktag

Xingxingxia

TAJIKISTAN

Kashi

Tarim He

T a r i m   B a s i n

Lop Nur

GANSU

Qilian Shan

AFGH.

Yengisar

Shache

XINJIANG UYGUR

ZIZHIQU

Ruoqiang

A l t u n   S h a n

Danghe Nanshan

Qaidam Pendi

Qinghai

Yecheng

(claimed by India)

Pishan

Moyu

Taklimakan Shamo

Qira

Burhan Budai Shan

Golmud

Dulan

Karakoram Range

K2 △ 8611m

Hotan

K u n l u n   S h a n

C

H

Kashmir

×××××

AKSAI CHIN

AKSAI CHIN
(administered by China, claimed by India)

QINGHAI

Bayan Har Sh

PAKISTAN

JAMMU AND KASHMIR

Indus

Rutog

*Qingzang Gaoyuan
(Plateau of Tibet)*

Tongtian He

Yushu

Mekong

Anyemaqen

DEMQOG/DEMCHOK
(administered by China, claimed by India)

Gar Xincun

Zanda

XIZANG

ZIZHIQU

(T i b e t)

Gozhê

Siling Co

Amdo

Tanggula Shan

Nagqu

Salween

Qamdo

Jinsha Jiang

Tangra Yumco

Gyaring Co

Nam Co

Damxung

Ngangzê Co

Nyainqêntanglha Shan

Maizhokunggar

Yamuna

Ganges

HIMALA

Brahmaputra

NEPAL

Lhazê

Xigazê

Gonggar

Lhasa

Gyangzê

△ *Mount Everest 8849m*

H e g d u a n s h a n

ARUNACHAL PRADESH
(claimed by China)

BHUTAN

INDIA

MYANMAR (BURMA)

I N D I A

0 km   400
0 miles   400

Population

● National capital
◉ Internal administrative capital
○ below 50,000
○ 50,000 to 100,000
◉ 100,000 to 500,000
◼ above 500,000

RUSSIA

HEILONGJIANG

Ozero Baykal

zero Baykal

Shilka

Ergun (Ergun He)

Amur (Heilong Jiang)

93

Ergun

Jagdaqi

Onon

Hulun Buir (Hailar)

Manzhouli

Hulun Nur

Sühbaatar

Darhan

rdenet

Onon Gol

Choybalsan

ULAANBAATAR

Dzuunmod

Öndörhaan

Menengiyn Tal

Baruun-Urt

Holin Gol

Kerulen

JILIN

106

LIA

Xilinhot

Tongliao

I A

Saynshand

Erenhot

Chifeng (Ulanhad)

Liao He

LIAONING

NORTH KOREA

Sea of Japan (East Sea)

Dalandzadgad

n Nuruu

Ulan Qab (Jining)

Korea Bay

SOUTH KOREA

Lake Khanka

Lang Shan

Hohhot

Baotou

Liaodong Wan

Bo Hai

BEIJING

TIANJIN

Korea Wan

EI MONGOL ZIZHIQU

(Inner Mongolia)

Da Hinggan Ling

Wuhai (Haibowan)

Huang He (Yellow River)

Mu Us Shadi

ing

Tengger Shamo

Sham

HEBEI

Great Wall of China

NINGXIA

SHANXI

SHANDONG

Yellow Sea

JAPAN

108

N A

GANSU

SHAANXI

Han Shui

Huang He (Yellow River)

HENAN

JIANGSU

ANHUI

SHANGHAI SHI

East China Sea

HUBEI

ZHEJIANG

Nansei-shotō (to Japan)

ICHUAN

Chang Jiang (Yangtze)

CHONGQING

JIANGXI

HUNAN

FUJIAN

107

Tropic of Cancer

YUNNAN

GUIZHOU

TAIWAN

Elevation

Below sea level 0   250m   500m   1000m   2000m   3000m   4000m   6000m

-6000m -4000m -2000m -1000m -500m -250m

820ft 1640ft 3281ft 6562ft 9843ft 13,124ft 19,685ft

-19,658ft -13,124ft -6562ft -3281ft -1640ft -820ft -328ft/-100m 0

Eastern China & Korea

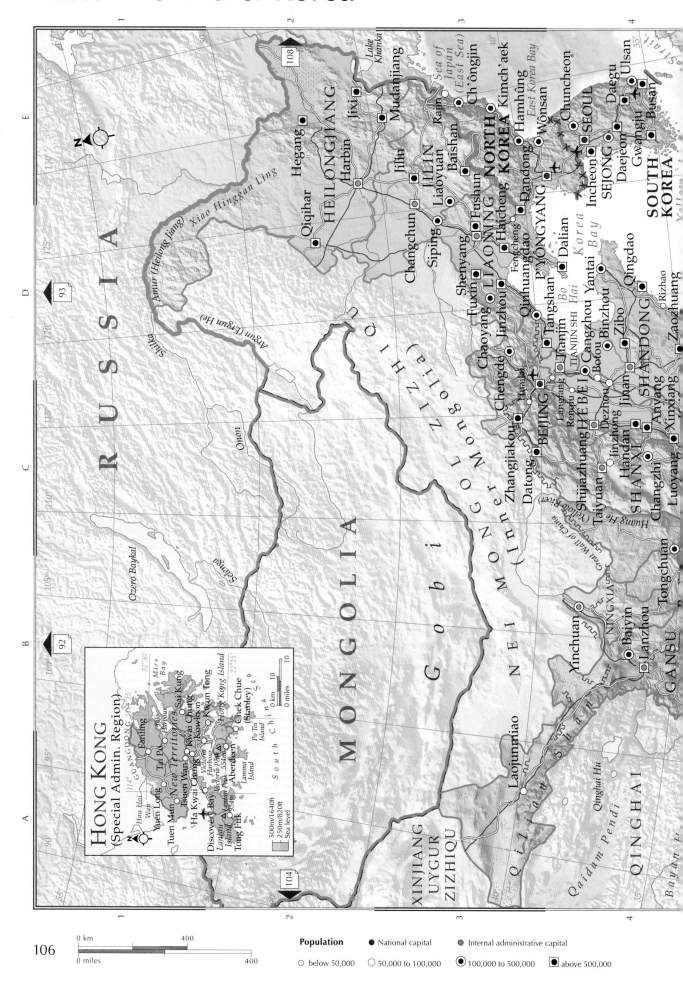

Population

○ below 50,000   ○ 50,000 to 100,000   ◉ 100,000 to 500,000   ◼ above 500,000

● National capital   ● Internal administrative capital

0 km _____ 400

0 miles _____ 400

Map labels

RUSSIA

MONGOLIA

NEI MONGOL (Inner Mongolia)

HEILONGJIANG

JILIN

LIAONING

NORTH KOREA

SOUTH KOREA

HEBEI

SHANXI

SHANDONG

SHAANXI

NINGXIA

GANSU

QINGHAI

XINJIANG UYGUR ZIZHIQU

Hegang
Qiqihar
Harbin
Jixi
Mudanjiang
Jilin
Changchun
Siping
Liaoyuan
Baishan
Fushun
Shenyang
Fuxin
Chaoyang
Jinzhou
Haicheng
Fengcheng
Dandong
Dalian
Hamhŭng
Wŏnsan
PYONGYANG
Namp'o
Ch'ŏngjin
Kimch'aek
Chuncheon
SEOUL
Incheon
SEJONG
Daejeon
Daegu
Ulsan
Busan
Gwangju
Qinhuangdao
Tangshan
Tianjin
TIANJIN SHI
Cangzhou
Yantai
Binzhou
Botou
Dezhou
Zibo
Jinan
Qingdao
Rizhao
Zaozhuang
Anyang
Xinxiang
Handan
Jinzhong
Taiyuan
Changzhi
Luoyang
Chengde
Zhangjiakou
Datong
BEIJING
Langfang
Renqiu
Shijiazhuang
Baoding
Yinchuan
Baiyin
Lanzhou
Tongchuan
Laojunmiao

Lake Khanka
Sea of Japan (East Sea)
East Korea Bay
West Korea Bay
Bo Hai
Yellow Sea
South China Sea
Ozero Baykal
Qinghai Hu
Qaidam Pendi

Amur (Heilong Jiang)
Xiao Hinggan Ling
Shilka
Argun (Ergun He)
Onon
Selenga
Gobi
Huang He (Yellow River)
Great Wall of China
Qilian Shan
Bayan K.

Inset map

HONG KONG
(Special Admin. Region)

GUANGDONG

Fanling
Yuen Long
Tai Po
Tuen Mun
New Territories
Sai Kung
Tsuen Wan
Kwai Chung
Kowloon
Kwun Tong
Ha Kwai Chung
Victoria Harbour
Hong Kong Island
Discovery Bay
Lantau Island
Lantau Peak 934m
Victoria Peak 554m
Aberdeen
Tong Fuk
Lamma Island
Po Toi Island
Chek Chue (Stanley)

Hau Hoi Wan
Mirs Bay
South China Sea

22°30′
22°15′
114°

500m/1640ft
250m/820ft
Sea level

0 km   10
0 miles   10

Elevation

| Below sea level 0 | 250m | 500m | 1000m | 2000m | 3000m | 4000m | 6000m |

-6000m -4000m -2000m -1000m -500m -250m

-19,658ft -13,124ft -6562ft -3281ft -1640ft -820ft -328ft/-100m 0

820ft 1640ft 3281ft 6562ft 9843ft 13,124ft 19,685ft

Japan

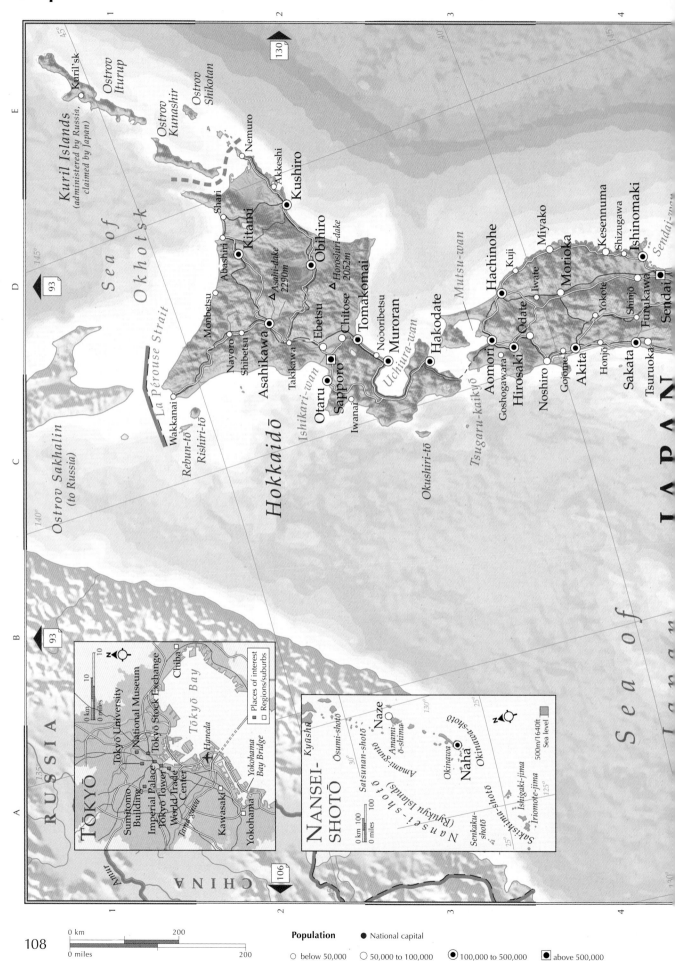

Kuril'sk
Ostrov Iturup

Kuril Islands
(administered by Russia, claimed by Japan)

Ostrov Kunashir
Ostrov Shikotan

Sea of Okhotsk

Nemuro
Akkeshi
Shari
Kushiro

Abashiri
Kitami

Monbetsu

△ *Asahi-dake 2290m*

Obihiro
△ *Horoshiri-dake 2052m*

Nayoro
Shibetsu

Takikawa
Asahikawa

La Pérouse Strait

Ebetsu
Chitose
Tomakomai
Nooribetsu
Muroran

Ostrov Sakhalin
(to Russia)

Wakkanai

Rebun-tō
Rishiri-tō

Otaru
Sapporo
Iwanai

Ishikari-wan

Uchiura-wan

Hakodate

Okushiri-tō

Tsugaru-kaikyō

Hokkaidō

Goshogawara
Aomori
Hirosaki
Noshiro
Gojome
Akita
Honjō
Sakata
Tsuruoka

Mutsu-wan

Hachinohe
Kuji
Iwate
Odate
Yokote
Shinjō
Furukawa

Miyako
Morioka
Kesennuma
Shizugawa
Ishinomaki
Sendai

Sendai-wan

JAPAN

Sea of Japan

RUSSIA

CHINA

Amur

TŌKYŌ

- Places of interest ■
- Regions/suburbs □

Z

Chiba

Tōkyō University
National Museum
Tōkyō Stock Exchange

Tōkyō Bay

Haneda

Sumitomo Building
Imperial Palace
Tōkyō Tower
World Trade Center

Tama-gawa

Yokohama
Yokohama Bay Bridge

Kawasaki

Yokohama

0 km 10
0 miles 10

NANSEI-SHOTŌ

Z

500m/1640ft
Sea level

Kyūshū

Ōsumi-shotō
Satsunan-shotō

Naze
Amami-gunto
Amami-ō-shima

Okinawa
Naha
Okinawa-shotō

Nansei-shotō (Ryūkyū Islands)

Sakishima-shotō
Ishigaki-jima
Iriomote-jima
Senkaku-shotō

0 km 100
0 miles 100

0 km   200
0 miles   200

Population   ● National capital

○ below 50,000   ◎ 50,000 to 100,000   ◉ 100,000 to 500,000   ▣ above 500,000

Honshū

Iwaki
Hitachi
Utsunomiya
Mito
Oyama
Chōshi
Chiba
Kawagoe
Yokohama
TOKYO
Kawasaki
Maebashi
Matsumoto
Nagano
Toyama
Kōfu
Fuji
Fuji-san 3776m
Shizuoka
Hamamatsu
Toyota
Nagaoka
Jōetsu
Itoigawa
Takaoka
Kanazawa
Komatsu
Gifu
Nakatsugawa
Ōgaki
Nagoya
Okazaki
Ōtsu
Tsu
Ise
Owase
Shingū
Tanabe
Gobō
Wakayama
Fukui
Tsuruga
Kyōto
Kōbe
Himeji
Osaka
Tottori
Matsue
Yonago
Okayama
Kurashiki
Tokushima
Niihama
Matsuyama
Kōchi
Nakamura
Sukumo
Kure
Hiroshima
Iwakuni
Hōfu
Ube
Ōita
Nobeoka
Miyazaki
Miyakonojō
Yatsushiro
Kagoshima
Satsuma-Sendai
Kumamoto
Ōmuta
Kurume
Fukuoka
Nagasaki
Sasebo
Shimonoseki
Yamaguchi
Kitakyūshū
Nagato
Masuda
Hamada
Gōtsu

Shinano-gawa
Toyama-wan
Hida-sanmyaku
Mikuni-sammyaku
Kusatsu-gawa
Wakasa-wan
Biwa-ko
Awaji-shima
Harima-nada
Iyo-nada
Bingo-nada
Suō-nada
Chūgoku-sanchi
Suzuka-sammyaku
Ise-wan
Surugu-wan
Izu-hantō
Kōzu-shima
Ō-shima
Nii-jima
Sagami-nada
Bōsō-hantō
Izu-shotō
Miyake-jima
Mikura-jima
Hachijō-jima

Liancourt Rocks
(under South
Korean control)

Oki-shotō
Dōgo
Dōzen

SOUTH
KOREA

Korea Strait
Tsushima
Iki
Kō-saki

Shikoku
Tosa-wan
Bungo-suidō
Kii-suidō

Kyūshū
Shibushi-wan
Tanega-shima
Yaku-shima
Ōsumi-shotō
Ōsumi-kaikyō
Kagoshima-wan
Satsuma-hantō
Amakusa-nada
Koshikijima-rettō
Gotō-rettō

PACIFIC OCEAN

East China Sea

130°
135°
140°
30°
35°

106
130
130

Z

109

Elevation

							Below sea level 0	250m	500m	1000m	2000m	3000m	4000m	6000m
-6000m	-4000m	-2000m	-1000m	-500m	-250m									

-19,658ft -13,124ft -6562ft -3281ft -1640ft -820ft -328ft/-100m 0
820ft 1640ft 3281ft 6562ft 9843ft 13,124ft 19,685ft

South India & Sri Lanka

Arabian Sea

112
Mumbai (Bombay)
Pune
Kalyan
Ahmadnagar
Nizāmabād
Nānded
Telangana
Karimnagar
Jagdalpu
Bārāmati
Solāpur
Hyderābād
Secunderābād
Vizianagaram
Sangli
Kolhāpur
Kalaburagi (Gulbarga)
Visākhapat
Belagāvi
Karnataka
Rāichūr
Andhra
Deccan
Rajahmu
Kākin
Gadag
Kurnool
Krishna
Vijayawāda
Machilipatn
Panaji
Nandyāl
Pradesh
Chirāla
Hubballi
Tungabhadra Reservoir
Tādpatri
Ongole
Kāvali
Dāvangere
Anantapur
Kadapa (Cuddapah)
Nellore
Shivamogga
Bhadrāvati
Bengalūru (Bangalore)
Udupi
Tumakūru
Chennai (Madras)
Mangalūru (Mangalore)
Mandya
Vellore
Kanchīpuram
Kāsaragod
Krishnagiri
Tiruppattūr
Kannur (Cannanore)
Mysūru (Mysore)
Puducherry (Pondicherry)
Kozhikode (Calicut)
Erode
Salem
Neyveli
Tamil Nādu
Coimbatore
Thrissur (Trichūr)
Tiruchchirāppalli
Ernākulam
Dindigul
Madurai
Kochi (Cochin)
Jaffna
Alappuzha (Alleppey)
Rājapālaiyam
SRI LANK
Kollam (Quilon)
Mannar
Vavuniya
Thiruvananthapuram (Trivandrum)
Tuticorin (Thoothukudi)
Trincomalee
Nāgercoil
Puttalam
Anurādhapura
Gulf of Mannar
Batticaloa
Matale
Negombo
Kandy
SRI JAYAWARDENAPURA KOTTE
COLOMBO
Ratnapura
Kalutara
Galle
Matara

Godavari
Western Ghats
Eastern Ghats
Coromandel Coast
Palk Strait

Lakshadweep (Laccadive Islands) (to India)
Amindivi Islands
Kavaratti Island
Kalpeni Island
Nine Degree Channel
Minicoy Island
Eight Degree Channel

Ihavandhippolhu Atoll

MALDIVES

Faadhippolhu Atoll
Horsburgh Atoll
Ari Atoll
Male'Atoll
MAALE (MALE')
Felidhu Atoll
Mulakatholhu
Kolhumadulu
Hadhdhunmathi Atoll
North Huvadhu Atoll

INDIAN

Equator

South Huvadhu Atoll

Gan
118
Addu Atoll

99

51

110

0 km   300
0 miles   300

Population   ● National capital

○ below 50,000   ◎ 50,000 to 100,000   ◉ 100,000 to 500,000   ◼ above 500,000

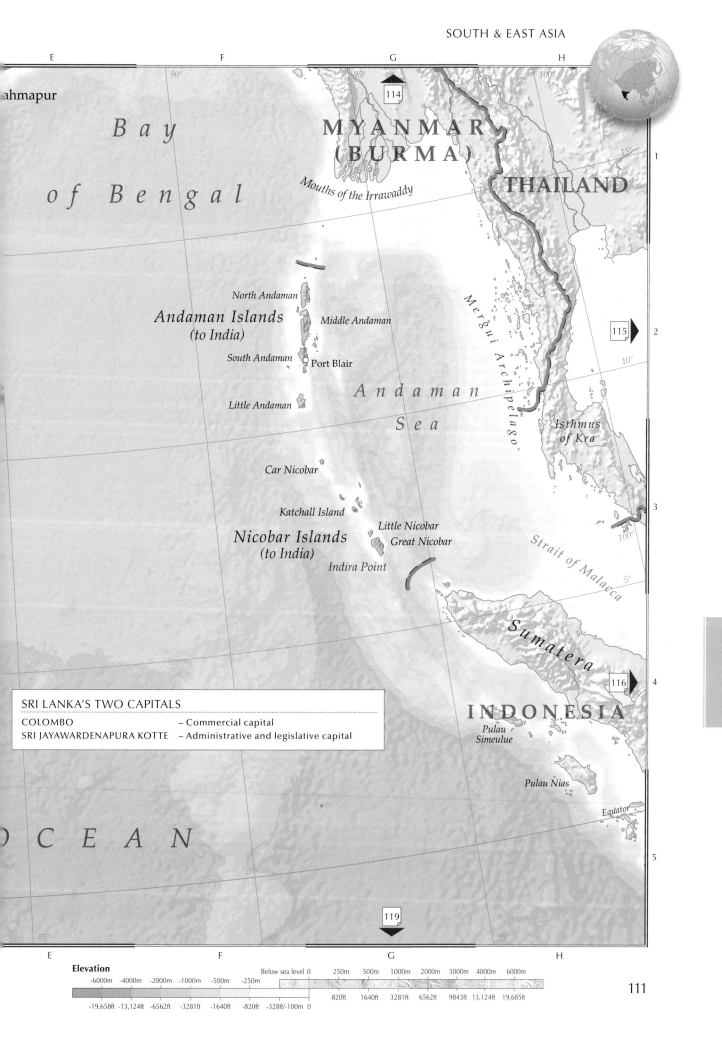

ahmapur

Bay

of Bengal

MYANMAR
(BURMA)

Mouths of the Irrawaddy

THAILAND

North Andaman

Andaman Islands
(to India)

Middle Andaman

Mergui Archipelago

South Andaman

○ Port Blair

A n d a m a n

S e a

Little Andaman

Isthmus
of Kra

Car Nicobar

Katchall Island

Little Nicobar

Nicobar Islands
(to India)

Great Nicobar

Strait of Malacca

Indira Point

Sumatera

INDONESIA

SRI LANKA'S TWO CAPITALS
COLOMBO — Commercial capital
SRI JAYAWARDENAPURA KOTTE — Administrative and legislative capital

Pulau
Simeulue

Pulau Nias

O C E A N

Equator

Elevation

						Below sea level 0	250m	500m	1000m	2000m	3000m	4000m	6000m
-6000m	-4000m	-2000m	-1000m	-500m	-250m								
-19,658ft	-13,124ft	-6562ft	-3281ft	-1640ft	-820ft	-328ft/-100m 0		820ft	1640ft	3281ft	6562ft	9843ft 13,124ft 19,685ft

Northern India, Pakistan & Bangladesh

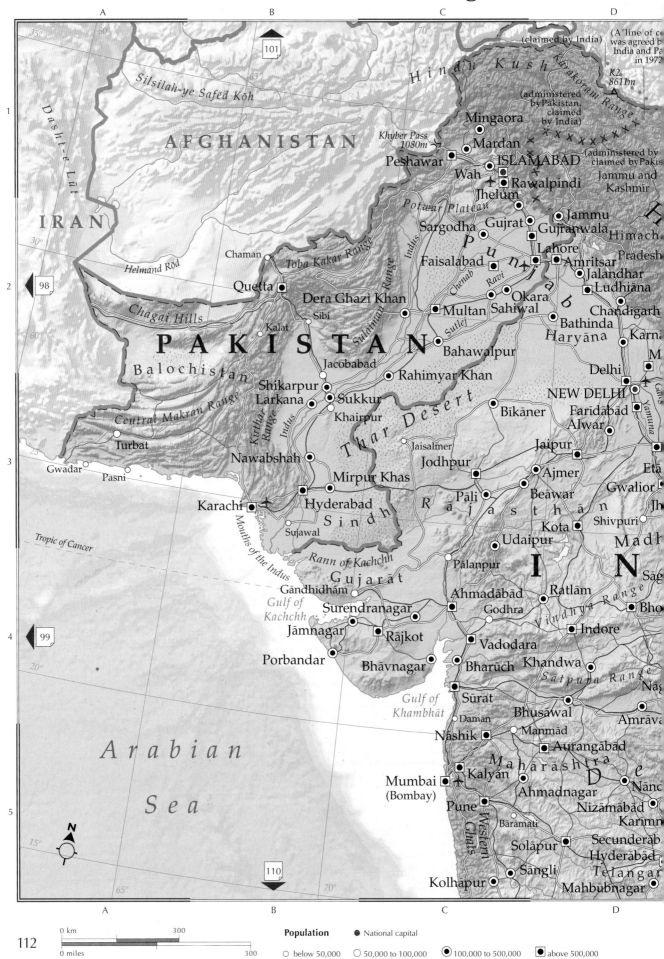

AFGHANISTAN

IRAN

Dasht-e Lūt

Silsilah-ye Safēd Kōh

Helmand Rōd

Chaman

Quetta

Toba Kakar Range

Chagai Hills

Kalat

Sibi

PAKISTAN

Balochistan

Central Makran Range

Kirthar Range

Turbat

Gwadar · Pasni

Nawabshah

Shikarpur

Larkana · Sukkur

Khairpur

Jacobabad

Dera Ghazi Khan

Karachi

Hyderabad

Sindh

Sujawal

Mouths of the Indus

Tropic of Cancer

Arabian

Sea

Hindu Kush

Karakoram Range

(claimed by India)

(A"line of c
was agreed b
India and Pa
in 1972

K2
8611m

(administered
by Pakistan,
claimed
by India)

(administered by
claimed by Pakis

Mingaora

Mardan

*Khyber Pass
1080m*

Peshawar

Wah

ISLAMABAD

Rawalpindi

Jhelum

Jammu and
Kashmir

Jammu

Sargodha

Gujrat

Gujranwala

Himach.

Lahore

Pradesh

Faisalabad

Amritsar

Jalandhar

Ludhiāna

P u n j a b

Indus

Chenab

Ravi

Okara

Sahiwal

Chandīgarh

Sulaimān Range

Multan

Sutlej

Bathinda

Haryāna

Karn

Bahawalpur

Delhi

Rahimyar Khan

M

NEW DELHI

Thar Desert

Bīkāner

Faridābād

Alwar

Yamuna

Ganç

Jaisalmer

Jaipur

Jodhpur

Ajmer

I

Eta

Pāli

Beāwar

Gwalior

Jh

Kota

Shivpuri

Rā · jasthān

Udaipur

Madh

Pālanpur

Sāg

Rann of Kachchh

Gujarāt

Ahmadābād

Ratlām

N

Gāndhīdhām

Godhra

Bho

*Gulf of
Kachchh*

Surendranagar

Vindhya Range

Indore

Jāmnagar

Rājkot

Vadodara

Khandwa

Porbandar

Bhāvnagar

Bharūch

Sātpura Range

Nāg

*Gulf of
Khambhāt*

Sūrat

Bhusāwal

Amrāva

Daman

Nāshik · Manmād

Aurangābād

Mahārāshtra

D e

Mumbai
(Bombay)

Kalyān

Ahmadnagar

Nānd

Pune

Nizāmābād

Karīm

Bārāmati

Western Ghats

Secunderāb

Solāpur

Hyderābād

Sangli

Telangar

Kolhapur

Mahbūbnagar

N

0 km   300

0 miles   300

Population   ● National capital

○ below 50,000   ○ 50,000 to 100,000   ◉ 100,000 to 500,000   ■ above 500,000

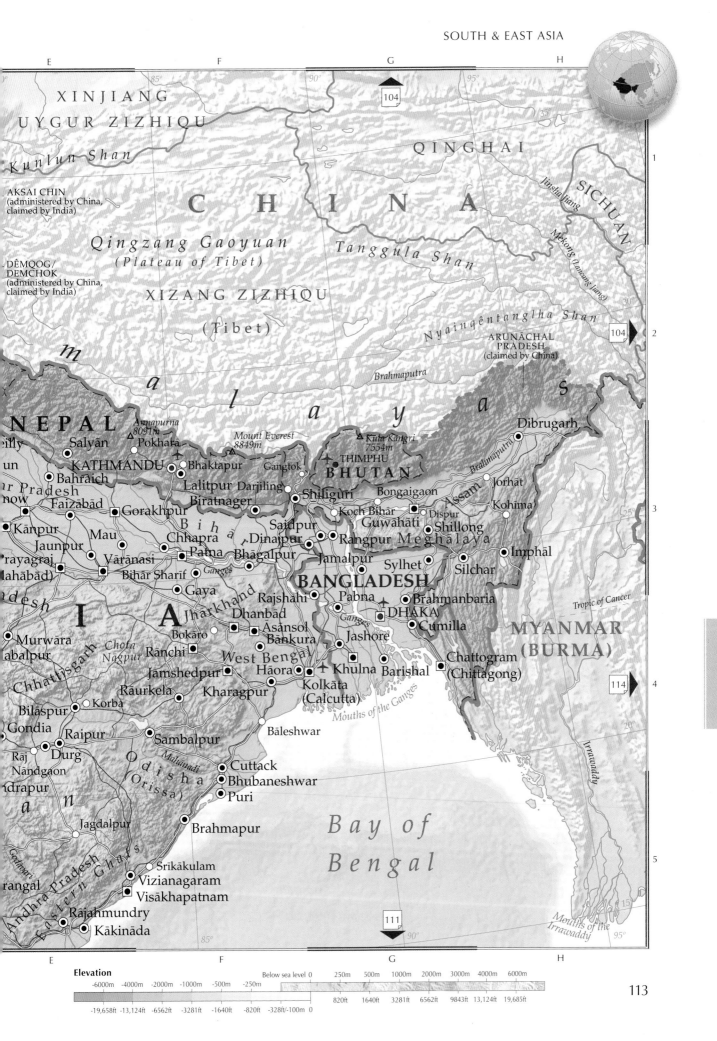

Map labels

XINJIANG
UYGUR ZIZHIQU
Kunlun Shan

QINGHAI

Jinsha Jiang

SICHUAN

AKSAI CHIN
(administered by China,
claimed by India)

C H I N A

Mekong (Lancang Jiang)

Qingzang Gaoyuan
(Plateau of Tibet)

Tanggula Shan

DÊMQOG/
DEMCHOK
(administered by China,
claimed by India)

XIZANG ZIZHIQU

(Tibet)

Nyainqêntanglha Shan

ARUNACHAL
PRADESH
(claimed by China)

m

Brahmaputra

NEPAL
a
Annapurna
8091m
Salyān Pokharā
l
Mount Everest
8849m
△ Kula Kangri
7554m

Dibrugarh

a

y

Brahmaputra

s

THIMPHU
Bhaktapur
KATHMANDU Bhaktapur Gangtok
BHUTAN
Assam Jorhāt

Bahraich Lalitpur Darjiling
Pradesh Biratnager
Shiligūri
Bongaigaon

un Faizabad Gorakhpur
Koch Bihār Dispur Kohima
Lucknow Guwāhāti Shillong

Kānpur
Mau B i h ā r
Saidpur Rangpur Meghālaya

Jaunpur Chhapra Dinajpur Imphāl

rayagraj Vārānasi Patna Bhāgalpur
Jamalpur Silchar

Mahābād) Bihar Sharif Ganges
Sylhet

Gaya
Rajshahi Pabna Brahmanbaria
Tropic of Cancer

I A Jharkhand Dhanbād
DHAKA
MYANMAR
(BURMA)

Murwāra Chota Bokāro Āsānsol
Cumilla

Jabalpur Nagpur Rānchi Bānkura
Ganges
Jashore

Bilāspur Korba Jamshedpur
Hāora Khulna Barishal
Chattogram
(Chittagong)

Gondia Rāurkela Kharagpur
Kolkāta
(Calcutta)

Raj Raipur Sambalpur
Mouths of the Ganges

Nāndgaon Durg
Bāleshwar

andrapur O d i s h a
Mahanadi
Cuttack

a n (Orissa)
Bhubaneshwar

Puri

Jagdalpur Brahmapur

Bay of

rangal Srīkākulam
Bengal

Andhra Pradesh Vizianagaram

Eastern Ghats Visākhapatnam

Rājahmundry
Kākināda

Mouths of the
Irrawaddy

Elevation

-6000m -4000m -2000m -1000m -500m -250m

-19,658ft -13,124ft -6562ft -3281ft -1640ft -820ft -328ft/-100m 0

820ft 1640ft 3281ft 6562ft 9843ft 13,124ft 19,685ft

Mainland Southeast Asia

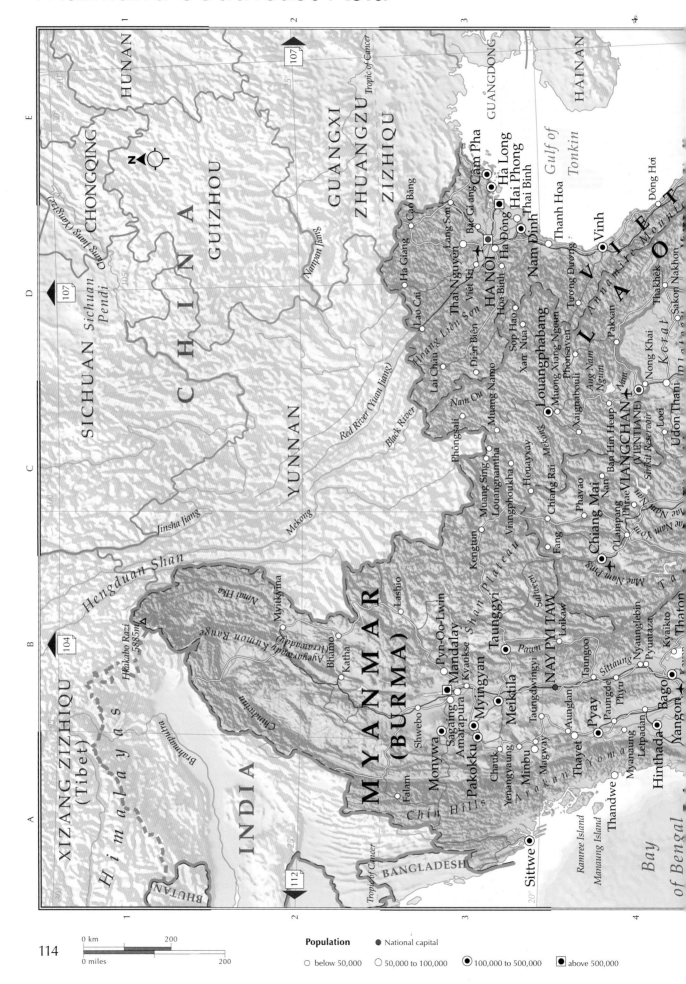

0 km 200
0 miles 200

Population ● National capital
○ below 50,000 ○ 50,000 to 100,000 ◉ 100,000 to 500,000 ■ above 500,000

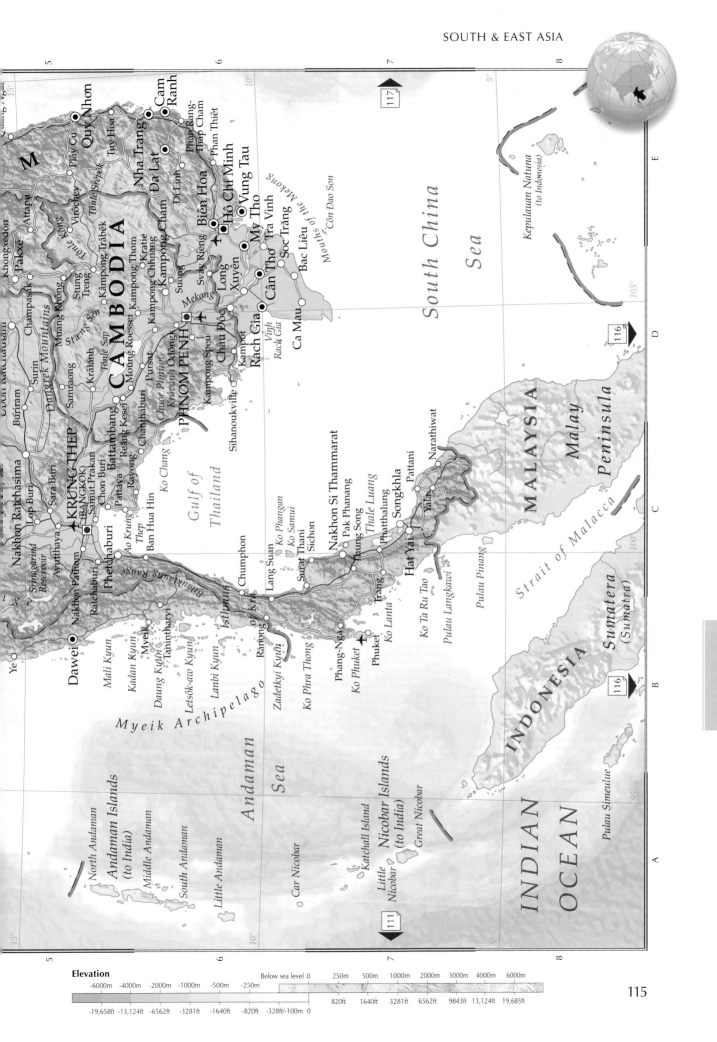

M

CAMBODIA

Quy Nhon
Cam Ranh
Plây Cu
Tuy Hoa
Nha Trang
Da Lat
Di Linh
Phan Rang-Tháp Cham
Phan Thiêt
Pakxe
Attapu
Viróchey
Kampong Cham
Biên Hoa
Hô Chí Minh
Vung Tau
My Tho
Tra Vinh
Soc Trang
Bac Liêu
Côn Dao Son
Khongxedon
Champasak
Stung Treng
Mtang Khong
Kampong Thom
Suong
Svay Rieng
Long Xuyên
Cân Tho
Ca Mau
Mouths of the Mekong
Surin
Samraong
Moung Roessei
Kampong Chhnang
Châu Dôc
Rach Gia
Vinh Rach Gia
Buriram
Krâlánh
Pursat
Kampong Speu
Kâmpôt
Nakhon Ratchasima
Lop Buri
Sara Buri
Battambang
Rêláng Kesei
Chanthaburi
Chuor Phnum Krâvanh Odóngk
PHNOM PENH
KRUNG THEP (BANGKOK)
Samut Prakan
Chon Buri
Pattaya
Rayong
Ko Chung
Sihanoukville
Srinagarind Reservoir
Ayutthaya
Nakhon Pathom
Ratchaburi
Phetchaburi
Ban Hua Hin
Ao Krung Thep
Gulf of Thailand
Bilauktaung Range
Isthmus of Kra
Chumphon
Lang Suan
Ko Phangan
Ko Samui
Nakhon Si Thammarat
Pak Phanang
Thale Luang
Phatthalung
Songkhla
Pattani
Narathiwat
MALAYSIA
Malay Peninsula
Ye
Dawei
Mali Kyun
Kadan Kyun
Myeik
Daung Kyun
Taninthayi
Letsôk-aw Kyun
Lanbi Kyun
Zadetkyi Kyun
Ko Phra Thong
Phang-Nga
Ko Phuket
Phuket
Ko Lanta
Trang
Hat Yai
Yala
Ko Ta Ru Tao
Pulau Langkawi
Pulau Pinang
Strait of Malacca
Sumatera (Sumatra)
Myeik Archipelago
Andaman Sea
North Andaman
Andaman Islands (to India)
Middle Andaman
South Andaman
Little Andaman
Car Nicobar
Katchall Island
Little Nicobar
Nicobar Islands (to India)
Great Nicobar
INDIAN OCEAN
INDONESIA
Pulau Simeulue

South China Sea

Kepulauan Natuna (to Indonesia)

Ranong

Damrek Mountains
Tônle Kong
Tônle Sab
Mekong
Stœng Sèn
Tônle Srêpôk
Kratie
Kampong Trâbêk

117
116
116
111

Elevation

-6000m	-4000m	-2000m	-1000m	-500m	-250m	Below sea level 0	250m	500m	1000m	2000m	3000m	4000m	6000m
-19,658ft	-13,124ft	-6562ft	-3281ft	-1640ft	-820ft	-328ft/-100m 0		820ft	1640ft	3281ft	6562ft	9843ft 13,124ft	19,685ft

Maritime Southeast Asia

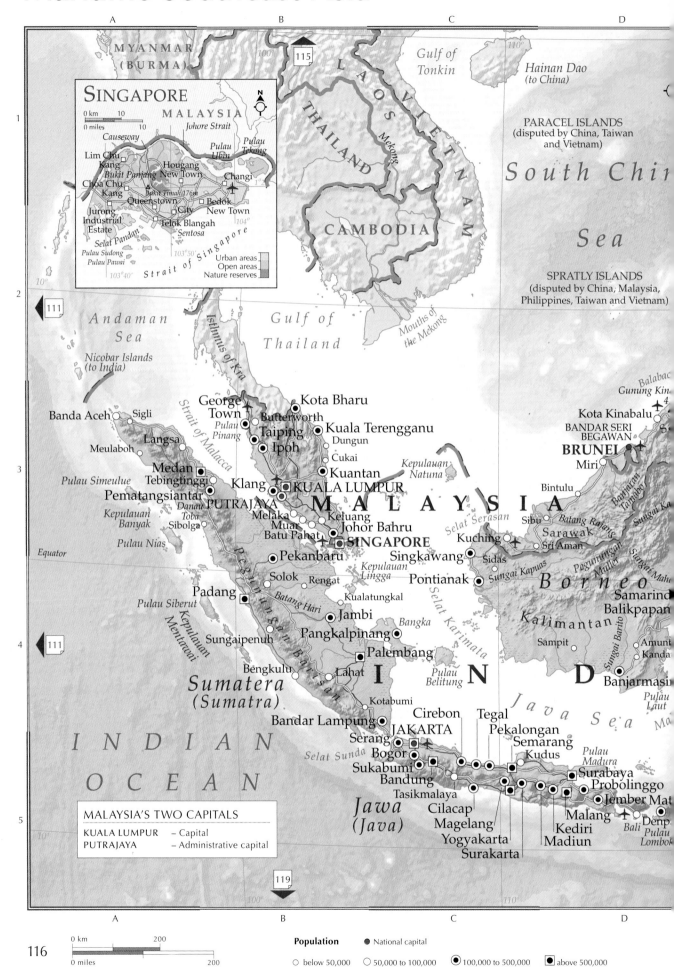

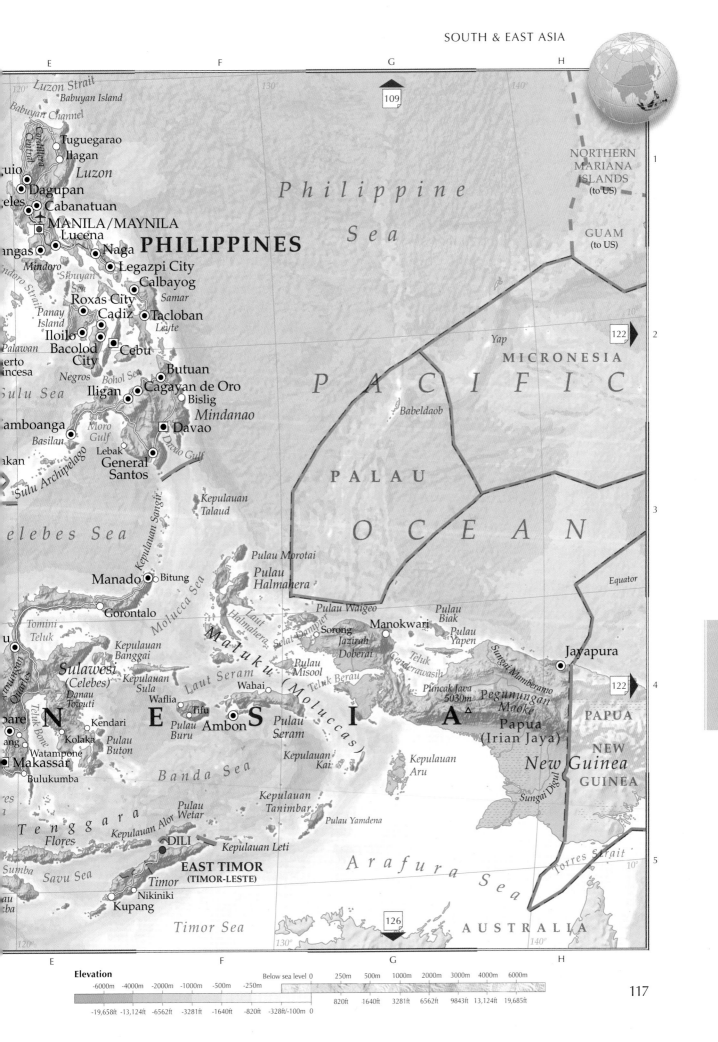

Luzon Strait
Babuyan Island
Babuyan Channel
Cordillera Central
Tuguegarao
Ilagan
uio
Luzon
Dagupan
eles
Cabanatuan
MANILA/MAYNILA
Lucena
angas
Naga
PHILIPPINES
Mindoro
Legazpi City
Sibuyan
Calbayog
Mindoro Strait
Sea
Samar
Roxas City
Panay Island
Cadiz
Tacloban
Leyte
Iloilo
Palawan
Bacolod City
Cebu
erto cesa
Negros
Bohol Sea
Butuan
Iligan
Cagayan de Oro
Bislig
Sulu Sea
Mindanao
amboanga
Moro Gulf
Davao
Basilan
Lebak
Davao Gulf
akan
General Santos
Sulu Archipelago

Philippine Sea

109

1

GUAM (to US)

10°

Yap

122

2

MICRONESIA

P A C I F I C

Babeldaob

P A L A U

3

O C E A N

Equator

Celebes Sea

Kepulauan Talaud

Pulau Morotai
Pulau Halmahera

Manado
Bitung

Gorontalo

Tomini Teluk
u

Molucca Sea

Laut Halmahera

Pulau Waigeo
Sorong
Jazirah Doberai
Manokwari
Pulau Biak
Pulau Yapen

Jayapura

122

4

Maluku

Pulau Misool
Teluk Berau

Teluk Cenderawasih

Sungai Mamberamo

PAPUA

Kepulauan Banggai
Sulawesi (Celebes)
Kepulauan Sula
Laut Seram
Wahai

Selat Dampier

Puncak Jaya 5030m

Pegunungan Maoke

Papua (Irian Jaya)

NEW

Danau Towuti
Waflia
Tifu

(Moluccas)

pare
N
Kendari
Pulau Buru
E
Ambon
S
Pulau Seram
I
A

New Guinea

GUINEA

ang
Kolaka
Pulau Buton
Watampone
Makassar
Bulukumba

Banda Sea

Kepulauan Kai

Kepulauan Aru

Sungai Digul

es

Kepulauan Tanimbar

Pulau Yamdena

T e n g g a r a
Flores
Pulau Wetar
Kepulauan Alor
DILI
Kepulauan Leti

A r a f u r a   S e a

Torres Strait

10°

5

Sumba

Savu Sea
Timor
Nikiniki
EAST TIMOR (TIMOR-LESTE)

ba
Kupang

Timor Sea

126

A U S T R A L I A

120°   130°   140°

E   F   G   H

Elevation

Below sea level 0   250m   500m   1000m   2000m   3000m   4000m   6000m

-6000m -4000m -2000m -1000m -500m -250m

-19,658ft -13,124ft -6562ft -3281ft -1640ft -820ft -328ft/-100m 0

820ft 1640ft 3281ft 6562ft 9843ft 13,124ft 19,685ft

The Indian Ocean

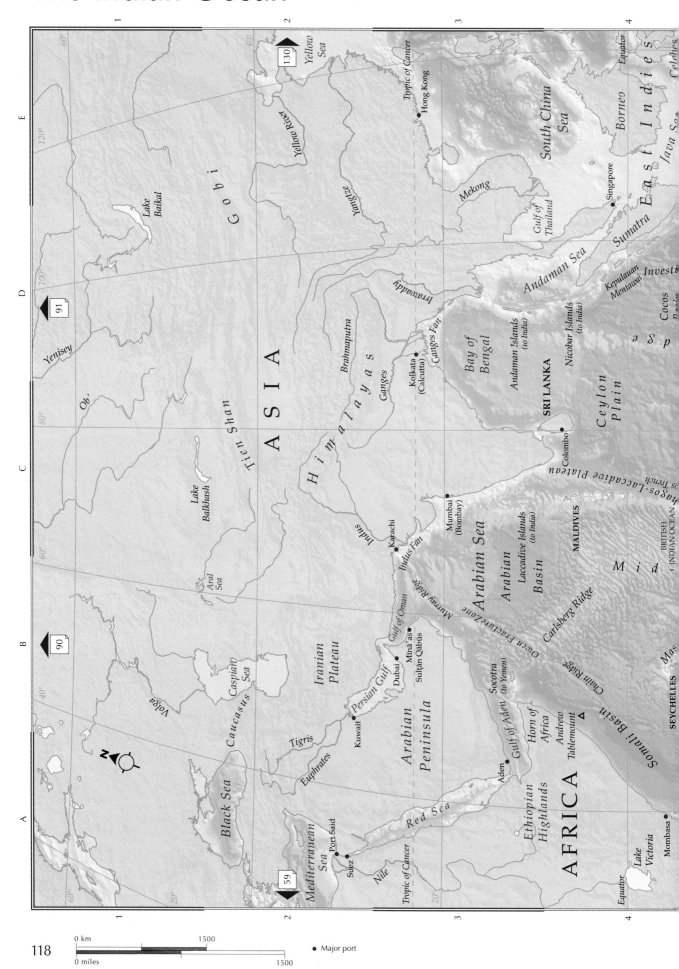

0 km   1500

0 miles   1500

● Major port

AUSTRALIA

Fremantle

Tropic of Capricorn

North Australian Basin

Exmouth Plateau

Cuvier Plateau

Perth Basin

Naturaliste Plateau

Wharton Basin

East Indian Ridge

Diamantina Fracture Zone

130

130

Limit of winter pack ice

Limit of summer pack ice

Antarctic Circle

Broken Ridge

Ninetyeast Ridge

(to Australia)

Osborn Plateau

INDIAN

OCEAN

Southeast Indian Ridge

South Indian Basin

SOUTHERN OCEAN

132

Egeria Fracture Zone

Indian Ridge

Amsterdam Island

St-Paul Island

ANTARCTICA

132

Argo Plain

Plateau

MAURITIUS

RÉUNION (to France)

Crozet Basin

FRENCH SOUTHERN & ANTARCTIC ISLANDS (to France)

Kerguelen Plateau

Kerguelen

Banzare Seamounts

Basin

Mascarene Plain

Madagascar Basin

Indomed Fracture Zone

Crozet Islands

HEARD ISLAND AND McDONALD ISLANDS (to Australia)

Southwest Indian Ridge

Farafangana

MADAGASCAR

MAYOTTE (to France)

Madagascar Plateau

Crozet Plateau

Lena Tablemount

Enderby Plain

132

Davie Ridge

Natal Basin

Prince Edward Islands (to South Africa)

Ob' Tablemount

Mozambique Plateau

Mozambique Channel

Zambezi

Tropic of Capricorn

Durban

Africana Seamount

Agulhas Plateau

Agulhas Basin

Atlantic-Indian Basin

Antarctic Circle

45

Antarctic Circle

Elevation

-6000m	-4000m	-2000m	-1000m	-500m	-250m	-100m	0
-19,658ft	-13,124ft	-6562ft	-3281ft	-1640ft	-820ft	-328ft/-100m	0

Australasia & Oceania

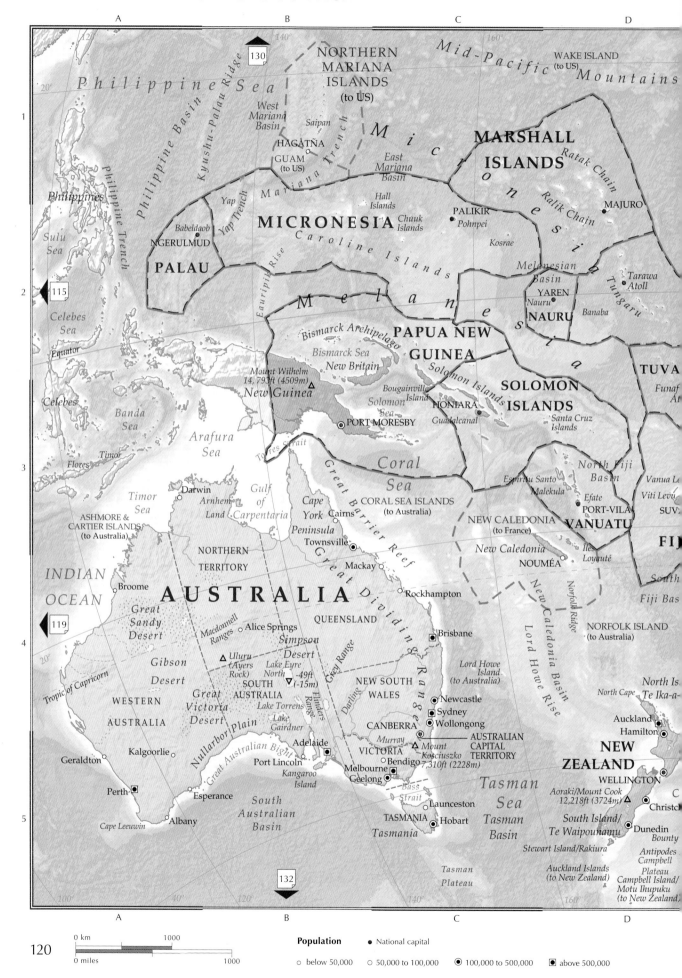

Philippine Sea

Mid-Pacific Mountains

NORTHERN MARIANA ISLANDS (to US)

WAKE ISLAND (to US)

Philippine Basin Ridge

Kyushu-Palau Ridge

West Mariana Basin

Saipan

Mariana Trench

Micronesia

MARSHALL ISLANDS

Ratak Chain

Philippines

HAGÁTÑA
GUAM (to US)

East Mariana Basin

Ralik Chain

MAJURO

Yap Trench

Hall Islands

Sulu Sea

Babeldaob

Yap Trench

Chuuk Islands

PALIKIR
Pohnpei

Kosrae

Melanesian Basin

Tarawa Atoll

NGERULMUD

MICRONESIA

Caroline Islands

Tungaru

Celebes Sea

PALAU

Eauripik Rise

Melanesia

YAREN
Nauru

NAURU

Banaba

Equator

Celebes

Banda Sea

Bismarck Archipelago

Bismarck Sea
New Britain

PAPUA NEW GUINEA

Solomon Islands

TUVA

Mount Wilhelm 14,793ft (4509m)

New Guinea

Bougainville Island

SOLOMON ISLANDS

Funaf At

Timor

Flores

Solomon Sea

HONIARA

Guadalcanal

Santa Cruz Islands

North Fiji Basin

Vanua Le

Arafura Sea

PORT MORESBY

Espíritu Santo
Malekula

Viti Levu

Timor Sea

Torres Strait

Coral Sea

Efate

PORT-VILA

SUV

Darwin

Gulf of Carpentaria

Cape York

Cairns

Great Barrier Reef

CORAL SEA ISLANDS (to Australia)

NEW CALEDONIA (to France)

VANUATU

FIJ

ASHMORE & CARTIER ISLANDS (to Australia)

Arnhem Land

Peninsula

Townsville

New Caledonia

NOUMÉA

Îles Loyauté

South Fiji Bas

INDIAN OCEAN

NORTHERN TERRITORY

AUSTRALIA

Great Dividing Range

New Caledonia Ridge

Norfolk Ridge

NORFOLK ISLAND (to Australia)

Broome

Great Sandy Desert

Macdonnell Ranges

Alice Springs

Simpson Desert

QUEENSLAND

Mackay

Rockhampton

Lord Howe Basin

Tropic of Capricorn

Gibson Desert

Uluru (Ayers Rock)

Lake Eyre North

-49ft (-15m)

Grey Range

Brisbane

Lord Howe Island (to Australia)

Lord Howe Rise

North Cape

North Is Te Ika-a-

WESTERN AUSTRALIA

Great Victoria Desert

SOUTH AUSTRALIA

Lake Torrens

NEW SOUTH WALES

Darling

Newcastle

Auckland

Hamilton

Geraldton

Kalgoorlie

Lake Gairdner

Flinders Range

Sydney

Wollongong

Nullarbor Plain

Adelaide

CANBERRA

AUSTRALIAN CAPITAL TERRITORY

NEW ZEALAND

Perth

Port Lincoln

Murray

Mount Kosciuszko 7,310ft (2228m)

Esperance

Great Australian Bight

Kangaroo Island

VICTORIA

Bendigo

Melbourne

Geelong

Bass Strait

Tasman Sea

Aoraki/Mount Cook 12,218ft (3724m)

WELLINGTON

Christc

Cape Leeuwin

Albany

South Australian Basin

Launceston

Tasman Basin

South Island/ Te Waipounamu

Dunedin
Bounty

TASMANIA

Hobart

Tasmania

Stewart Island/Rakiura

Antipodes Campbell Plateau

Tasman Plateau

Auckland Islands (to New Zealand)

Campbell Island/ Motu Ihupuku (to New Zealand)

0 km   1000

0 miles   1000

Population   ● National capital

○ below 50,000   ◎ 50,000 to 100,000   ◉ 100,000 to 500,000   ◼ above 500,000

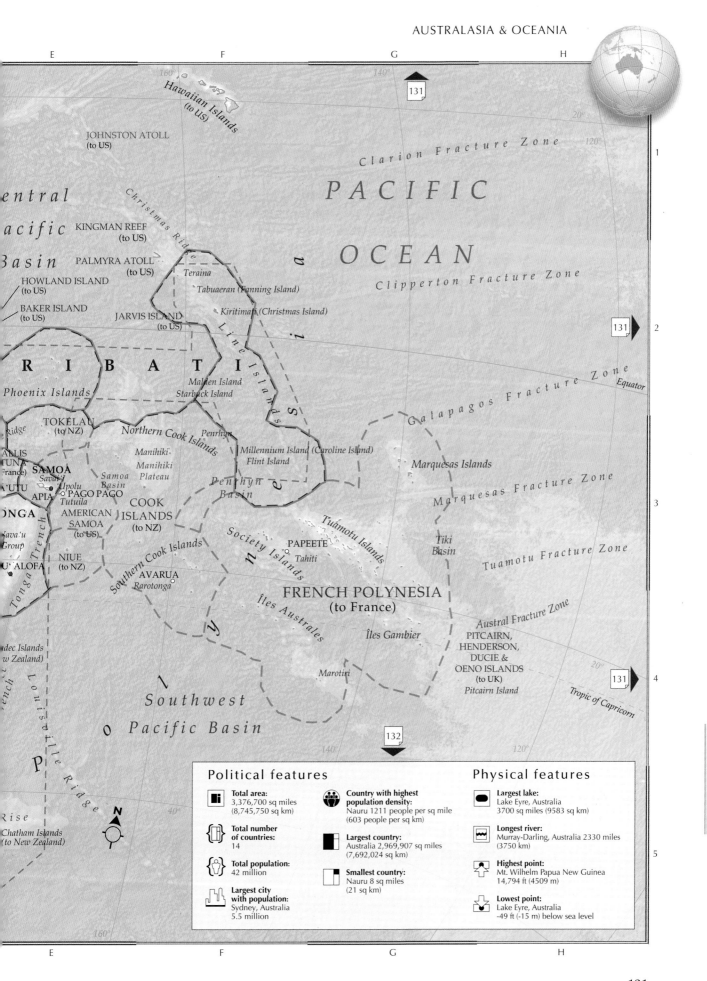

131

131

PACIFIC

OCEAN

Clarion Fracture Zone

Clipperton Fracture Zone

JOHNSTON ATOLL
(to US)

KINGMAN REEF
(to US)

PALMYRA ATOLL
(to US)

HOWLAND ISLAND
(to US)

BAKER ISLAND
(to US)

JARVIS ISLAND
(to US)

Hawaiian Islands
(to US)

Christmas Ridge

Teraina

Tabuaeran (Fanning Island)

Kiritimati (Christmas Island)

Line Islands

Galapagos Fracture Zone

Equator

entral

acific

Basin

RIBATI

Phoenix Islands

Malden Island

Starback Island

TOKELAU
(to NZ)

Northern Cook Islands

Penrhyn

Manihiki
Manihiki
Plateau

Millennium Island (Caroline Island)
Flint Island

*Penrhyn
Basin*

Marquesas Islands

Marquesas Fracture Zone

Ridge

ALLIS
UTUNA
rance)

SAMOA

Savai'i

Upolu

PAGO PAGO

APIA

Tutuila

Samoa
Basin

COOK
ISLANDS
(to NZ)

AMERICAN
SAMOA
(to US)

ONGA

ava'u
Group

NIUE
(to NZ)

U'ALOFA

Tuamotu Islands

Society Islands

PAPEETE

Tahiti

Tiki
Basin

Tuamotu Fracture Zone

Southern Cook Islands

AVARUA
Rarotonga

FRENCH POLYNESIA
(to France)

Îles Australes

Îles Gambier

Austral Fracture Zone

PITCAIRN,
HENDERSON,
DUCIE &
OENO ISLANDS
(to UK)
Pitcairn Island

Tropic of Capricorn

dec Islands
w Zealand)

Tonga Trench

Marotiri

Southwest

Pacific Basin

131

132

Louisville Ridge

Rise

Chatham Islands
(to New Zealand)

N

Political features

Total area:
3,376,700 sq miles
(8,745,750 sq km)

**Total number
of countries:**
14

Total population:
42 million

**Largest city
with population:**
Sydney, Australia
5.5 million

**Country with highest
population density:**
Nauru 1211 people per sq mile
(603 people per sq km)

Largest country:
Australia 2,969,907 sq miles
(7,692,024 sq km)

Smallest country:
Nauru 8 sq miles
(21 sq km)

Physical features

Largest lake:
Lake Eyre, Australia
3700 sq miles (9583 sq km)

Longest river:
Murray-Darling, Australia 2330 miles
(3750 km)

Highest point:
Mt. Wilhelm Papua New Guinea
14,794 ft (4509 m)

Lowest point:
Lake Eyre, Australia
-49 ft (-15 m) below sea level

The Southwest Pacific

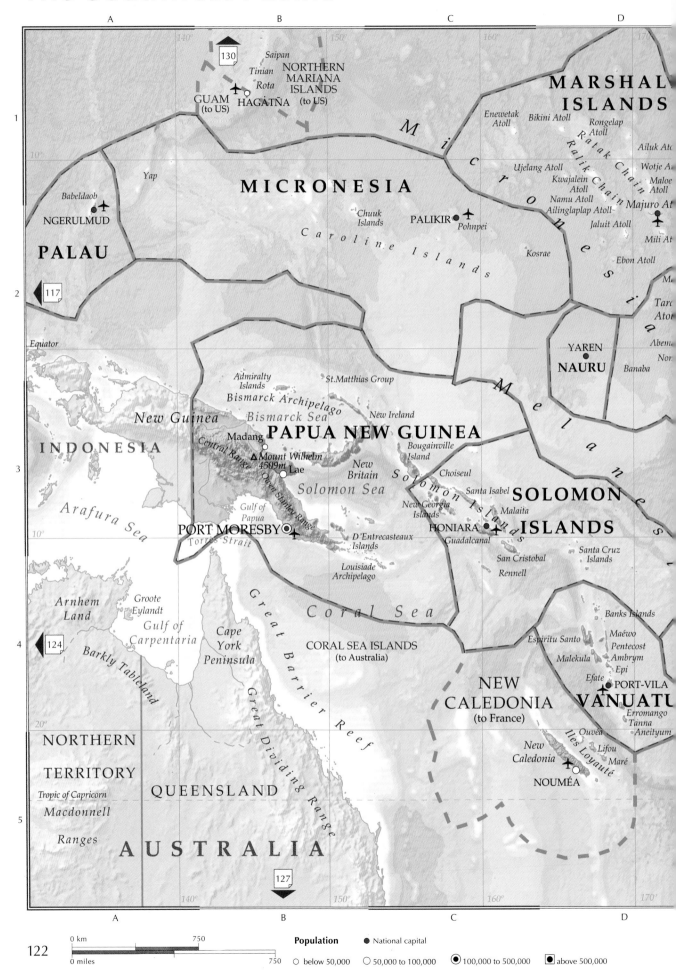

A B C D

130

Saipan
Tinian
Rota

NORTHERN
MARIANA
ISLANDS
(to US)

GUAM
(to US) HAGÅTÑA

**MARSHALL
ISLANDS**

1

Enewetak
Atoll Bikini Atoll Rongelap
Atoll

Ailuk Ato

Yap

Ujelang Atoll Wotje
Atoll

MICRONESIA

Babeldaob

NGERULMUD

Kwajalein
Atoll Maloe
Atoll

Namu Atoll
Ailinglaplap Atoll Majuro At

Chuuk
Islands PALIKIR Pohnpei

Jaluit Atoll

Mili At

PALAU

Caroline Islands

Kosrae

Ebon Atoll

M

117

Tara
Ator

2

Equator

YAREN
NAURU

Abem

Banaba

Nor

Admiralty
Islands St.Matthias Group

New Guinea

Bismarck Archipelago

Bismarck Sea

New Ireland

INDONESIA

Central Range Madang

△ Mount Wilhelm
4509m Lae

PAPUA NEW GUINEA

Bougainville
Island

New
Britain

Solomon Sea

Choiseul
Santa Isabel

SOLOMON

3

Owen Stanley Range

Gulf of
Papua

New Georgia
Islands Malaita

PORT MORESBY

Arafura Sea

Torres Strait

D'Entrecasteaux
Islands

HONIARA
Guadalcanal

ISLANDS

Louisiade
Archipelago

San Cristobal
Rennell

Santa Cruz
Islands

Arnhem
Land

Groote
Eylandt

Gulf of
Carpentaria

Cape
York
Peninsula

Coral Sea

Banks Islands

Espiritu Santo

Maéwo
Pentecost

4

124

Barkly Tableland

CORAL SEA ISLANDS
(to Australia)

Malekula Ambrym
Epi

Efate PORT-VILA

**NEW
CALEDONIA**
(to France)

VANUATU

Erromango
Tanna Aneityum

20°

NORTHERN

Ouvéa

New
Caledonia

Iles Loyauté

Lifou
Maré

TERRITORY

Tropic of Capricorn

Macdonnell

QUEENSLAND

NOUMÉA

5

Ranges

AUSTRALIA

127

A B C D

0 km   750

0 miles   750

Population ● National capital

○ below 50,000 ○ 50,000 to 100,000 ◉ 100,000 to 500,000 ◼ above 500,000

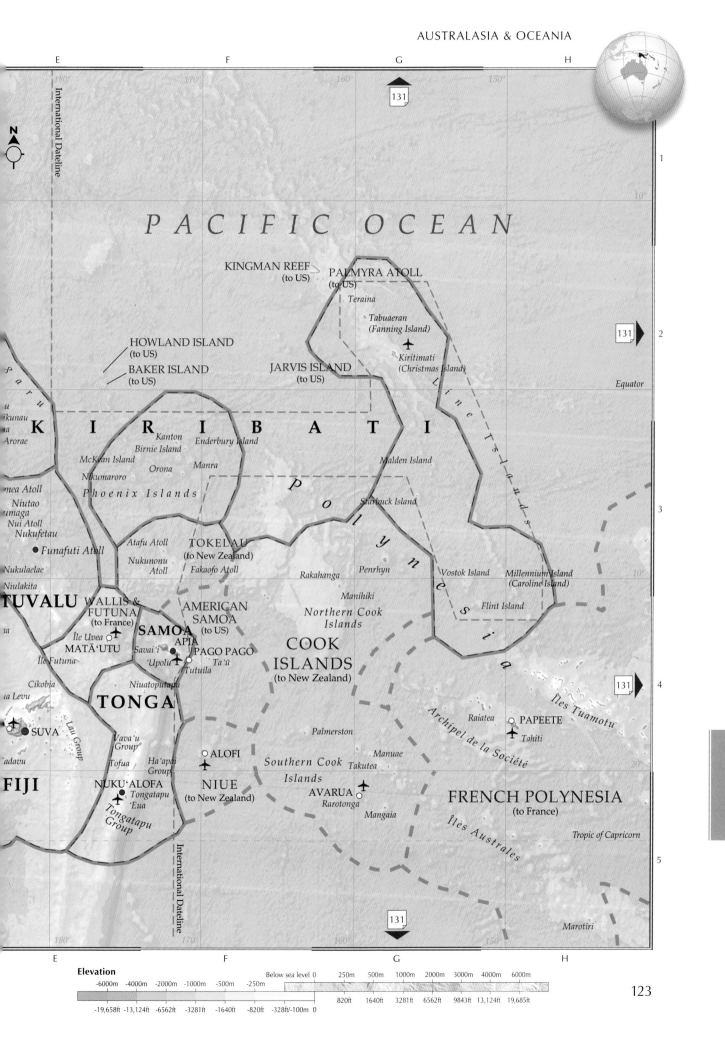

N

International Dateline

PACIFIC OCEAN

KINGMAN REEF
(to US)

PALMYRA ATOLL
(to US)

Teraina

*Tabuaeran
(Fanning Island)*

HOWLAND ISLAND
(to US)

BAKER ISLAND
(to US)

JARVIS ISLAND
(to US)

*Kiritimati
(Christmas Island)*

Equator

paru

ukunau

a

Arorae

K I R I B A T I

Kanton

Birnie Island

Enderbury Island

McKean Island

Orona

Manra

Nikumaroro

Malden Island

mea Atoll

Niutao

umaga

Nui Atoll

Nukufetau

Phoenix Islands

Starbuck Island

P

o

l

y

n

e

s

i

a

Funafuti Atoll

Nukulaelae

Niulakita

Atafu Atoll

TOKELAU
(to New Zealand)

*Nukunonu
Atoll*

Fakaofo Atoll

Rakahanga

Penrhyn

Vostok Island

*Millennium Island
(Caroline Island)*

Manihiki

Flint Island

TUVALU

WALLIS &
FUTUNA
(to France)

AMERICAN
SAMOA
(to US)

*Northern Cook
Islands*

ua

Île Uvea

SAMOA

APIA

COOK
ISLANDS
(to New Zealand)

Savai'i

PAGO PAGO

MATĀ'UTU

Île Futuna

Upolu

Ta'ū

Tutuila

Cikobia

ua Levu

Niuatoputapu

TONGA

SUVA

Lau Group

*Vava'u
Group*

Palmerston

Manuae

Raiatea

PAPEETE

Tahiti

Archipel de la Société

Îles Tuamotu

Tofua

*Ha'apai
Group*

*Southern Cook
Islands*

ALOFI

Takutea

FIJI

adavu

NUKU'ALOFA

Tongatapu

'Eua

NIUE
(to New Zealand)

AVARUA

Rarotonga

Mangaia

FRENCH POLYNESIA
(to France)

*Tongatapu
Group*

International Dateline

Îles Australes

Tropic of Capricorn

Marotiri

Elevation

Below sea level 0   250m   500m   1000m   2000m   3000m   4000m   6000m

-6000m -4000m -2000m -1000m -500m -250m

-19,658ft -13,124ft -6562ft -3281ft -1640ft -820ft -328ft/-100m 0

820ft 1640ft 3281ft 6562ft 9843ft 13,124ft 19,685ft

Western Australia

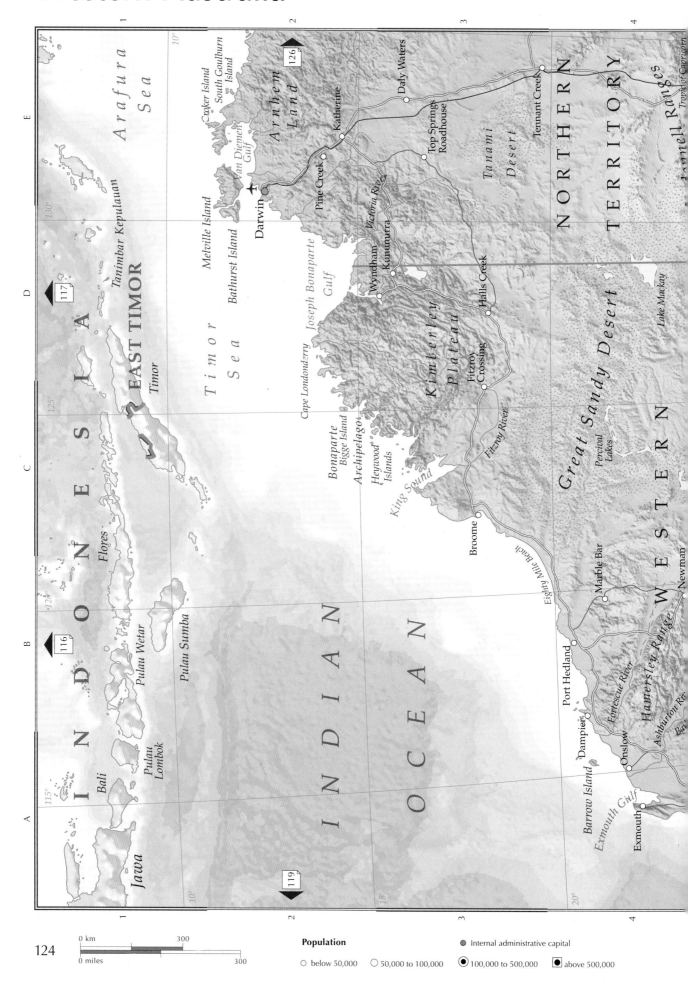

Arafura Sea

Croker Island
South Goulburn Island
Taninbar Kepulauan
Tanimbar

EAST TIMOR
Timor

INDONESIA

Jawa
Bali
Pulau Lombok
Pulau Sumba
Pulau Wetar
Flores

Melville Island
Bathurst Island
Van Diemen Gulf

Darwin

Arnhem Land

Pine Creek
Katherine
Daly Waters
Top Springs Roadhouse
Tennant Creek

NORTHERN TERRITORY

Tanami Desert

Victoria River
Kununurra
Wyndham
Halls Creek

Kimberley Plateau

Fitzroy Crossing
Fitzroy River

Great Sandy Desert

Percival Lakes
Lake Mackay

Tropic of Capricorn

Timor Sea

Joseph Bonaparte Gulf

Cape Londonderry
Bonaparte Archipelago
Bigge Island
Heywood Islands
King Sound

Broome

Eighty Mile Beach

Marble Bar

WESTERN

Hamersley Range
Newman

Port Hedland
Dampier
Onslow
Barrow Island
Exmouth Gulf
Exmouth

Fortescue River
Ashburton River

INDIAN OCEAN

0 km   300
0 miles   300

Population

⦿ Internal administrative capital

○ below 50,000   ○ 50,000 to 100,000   ◉ 100,000 to 500,000   ◼ above 500,000

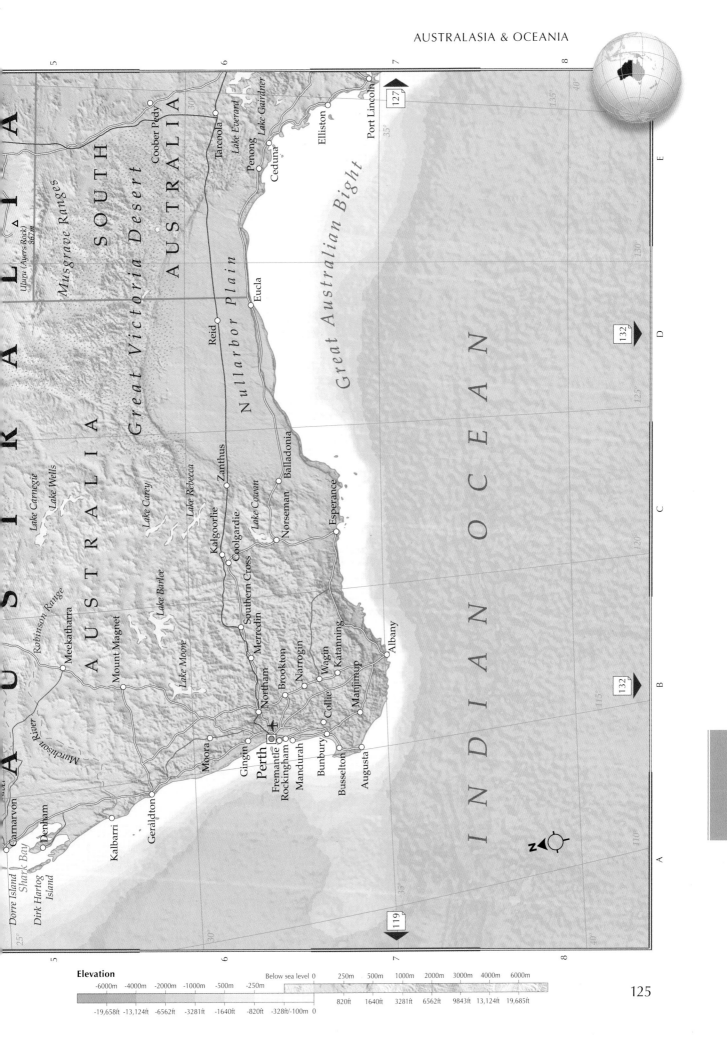

AUSTRALIA

SOUTH

AUSTRALIA

Musgrave Ranges

Uluru (Ayers Rock)
867m

Coober Pedy

Tarcoola

Lake Everard

Lake Gairdner

Penong

Ceduna

Elliston

Port Lincoln

Eucla

Reid

Nullarbor Plain

Great Victoria Desert

Great Australian Bight

WESTERN AUSTRALIA

Lake Carnegie

Lake Wells

Lake Carey

Lake Rebecca

Zanthus

Balladonia

Lake Barlee

Lake Cowan

Kalgoorlie

Coolgardie

Norseman

Esperance

Robinson Range

Meekatharra

Lake Moore

Mount Magnet

Southern Cross

Merredin

Northam

Brookton

Narrogin

Wagin

Katanning

Manjimup

Albany

Murchison River

Moora

Gingin

Perth

Fremantle

Rockingham

Mandurah

Collie

Bunbury

Busselton

Augusta

Carnarvon

Denham

Shark Bay

Dorre Island

Dirk Hartog Island

Kalbarri

Geraldton

INDIAN OCEAN

N

Elevation

-6000m	-4000m	-2000m	-1000m	-500m	-250m	Below sea level 0	250m	500m	1000m	2000m	3000m	4000m	6000m

-19,658ft -13,124ft -6562ft -3281ft -1640ft -820ft -328ft/-100m 0   820ft 1640ft 3281ft 6562ft 9843ft 13,124ft 19,685ft

Eastern Australia

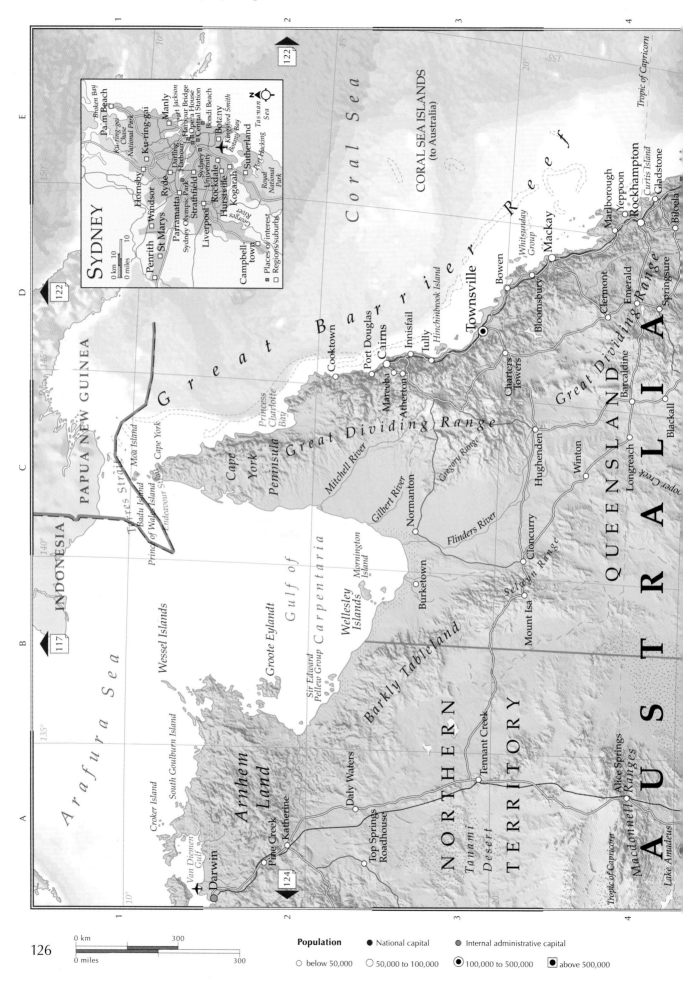

SYDNEY

Broken Bay
Palm Beach
Ku-ring-gai Chase
Ku-ring-gai
National Park
Manly
Port Jackson
Harbour Bridge
Darling Harbour
Opera House
Central Station
Bondi Beach
Hornsby
Windsor
Ryde
Sydney
Parramatta
Sydney Olympic Park
University
Botany
Kingsford Smith
Strathfield
Penrith
St Marys
Liverpool
Rockdale
Hurstville
Kogarah
Sutherland
Port Hacking
Royal National Park
George River
Campbell town

Tasman Sea
Botany Bay

0 km 10
0 miles 10

■ Places of interest
□ Regions/suburbs

Coral Sea

CORAL SEA ISLANDS
(to Australia)

Tropic of Capricorn

Great Barrier Reef

PAPUA NEW GUINEA

Torres Strait
Moa Island
Cape York
Badu Island
Prince of Wales Island
Endeavour Strait

Cape York Peninsula

INDONESIA

Great Dividing Range

Princess Charlotte Bay

Cooktown
Port Douglas
Cairns
Mareeba
Atherton
Innisfail
Tully
Hinchinbrook Island
Townsville
Bowen
Bloomsbury
Whitsunday Group
Mackay

Marlborough
Yeppoon
Rockhampton
Curtis Island
Gladstone
Biloela

Charters Towers
Clermont
Emerald
Springsure

Great Dividing Range

Mitchell River

Gregory Range

Hughenden

Winton
Barcaldine
Longreach
Blackall

QUEENSLAND

Gilbert River

Normanton

Flinders River

Cooper Creek

Burketown

Cloncurry
Selwyn Range
Mount Isa

Gulf of Carpentaria

Wellesley Islands
Mornington Island

Sir Edward Pellew Group

Groote Eylandt

Barkly Tableland

Arafura Sea

Wessel Islands

Croker Island
South Goulburn Island

Van Diemen Gulf

Darwin
Pine Creek

Arnhem Land

Katherine

Daly Waters

Top Springs Roadhouse

Tanami Desert

Tennant Creek

NORTHERN TERRITORY

AUSTRALIA

Alice Springs
Macdonnell Ranges
Lake Amadeus

Tropic of Capricorn

126

0 km 300
0 miles 300

Population ● National capital ● Internal administrative capital

○ below 50,000 ○ 50,000 to 100,000 ◉ 100,000 to 500,000 ■ above 500,000

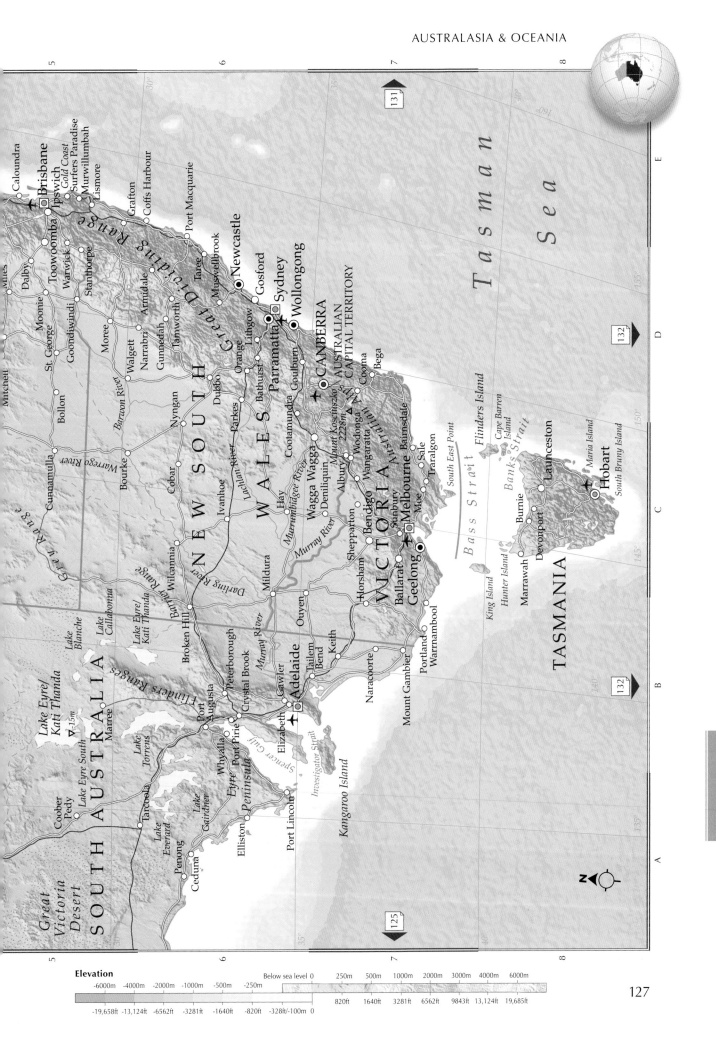

Elevation

-6000m	-4000m	-2000m	-1000m	-500m	-250m	

Below sea level 0 | 250m | 500m | 1000m | 2000m | 3000m | 4000m | 6000m

-19,658ft | -13,124ft | -6562ft | -3281ft | -1640ft | -820ft | -328ft/-100m | 0

820ft | 1640ft | 3281ft | 6562ft | 9843ft | 13,124ft | 19,685ft

New Zealand

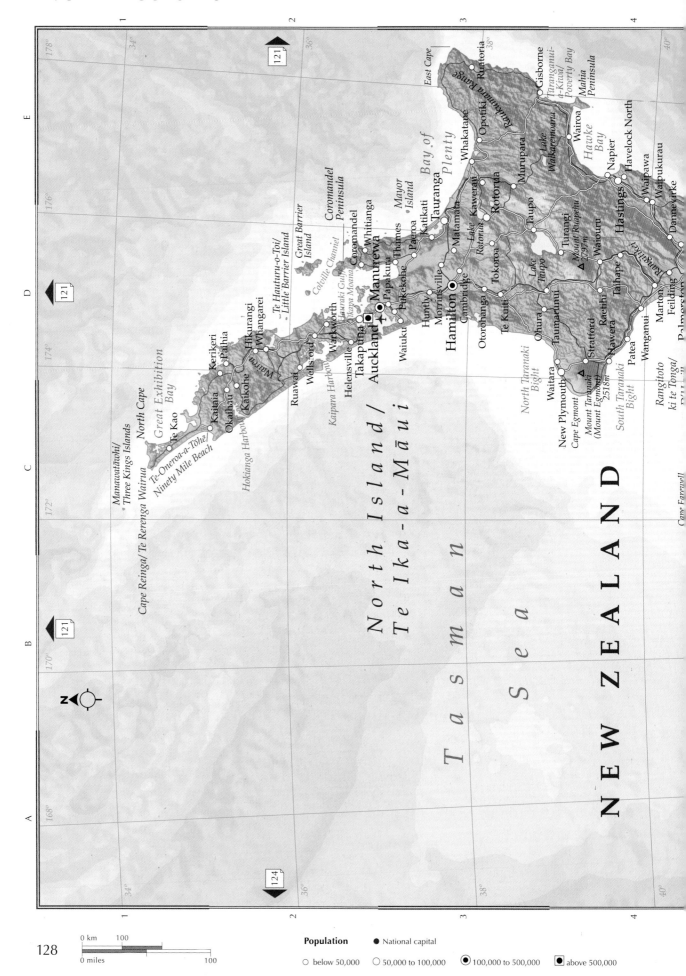

Population   ● National capital

○ below 50,000   ○ 50,000 to 100,000   ◉ 100,000 to 500,000   ◼ above 500,000

0 km   100

0 miles   100

Map labels:

N E W   Z E A L A N D

North Island /
Te Ika-a-Māui

Tasman Sea

Cities and towns:
Te Kao, Kaitaia, Okaihau, Kaikohe, Kerikeri, Paihia, Hikurangi, Whangarei, Ruawai, Wellsford, Helensville, Warkworth, Takapuna, Auckland, Manurewa, Papakura, Pukekohe, Waiuku, Huntly, Morrinsville, Cambridge, Hamilton, Otorohanga, Te Kuiti, Te Awamutu, Ohura, Taumarunui, Stratford, Raetihi, Hawera, Patea, Wanganui, Marton, Feilding, Palmerston, New Plymouth, Waitara, Cape Egmont

Manurewa, Papakura, Paeroa, Thames, Coromandel, Whitianga, Katikati, Tauranga, Matamata, Rotorua, Tokoroa, Taupo, Turangi, Waiouru, Taihape

Whakatane, Opotiki, Murupara, Wairoa, Napier, Hastings, Havelock North, Waipawa, Waipukurau, Dannevirke, Gisborne, Ruatoria

Physical features:
Manaoatitohi / Three Kings Islands, North Cape, Cape Reinga / Te Rerenga Wairua, Great Exhibition Bay, Te Oneroa-a-Tōhē / Ninety Mile Beach, Hokianga Harbour, Kaipara Harbour, Wairau, Te Hauturu-o-Toi / Little Barrier Island, Great Barrier Island, Coville Channel, Coromandel Peninsula, Hauraki Gulf, Tikapa Moana, Mayor Island, Bay of Plenty, East Cape, Kaimanawa Range, Raukumara Range, Tūranganui-a-Kiwa / Poverty Bay, Mahia Peninsula, Hawke Bay, Lake Waikaremoana, Lake Rotorua, Lake Rotoiti, Lake Kawerau, Lake Taupo, Mount Ruapehu 2797m, Mount Taranaki (Mount Egmont) 2518m, North Taranaki Bight, South Taranaki Bight, Rangitoto ki te Tonga / D'Urville, Rangitikei, Ruahine, Cape Farewell

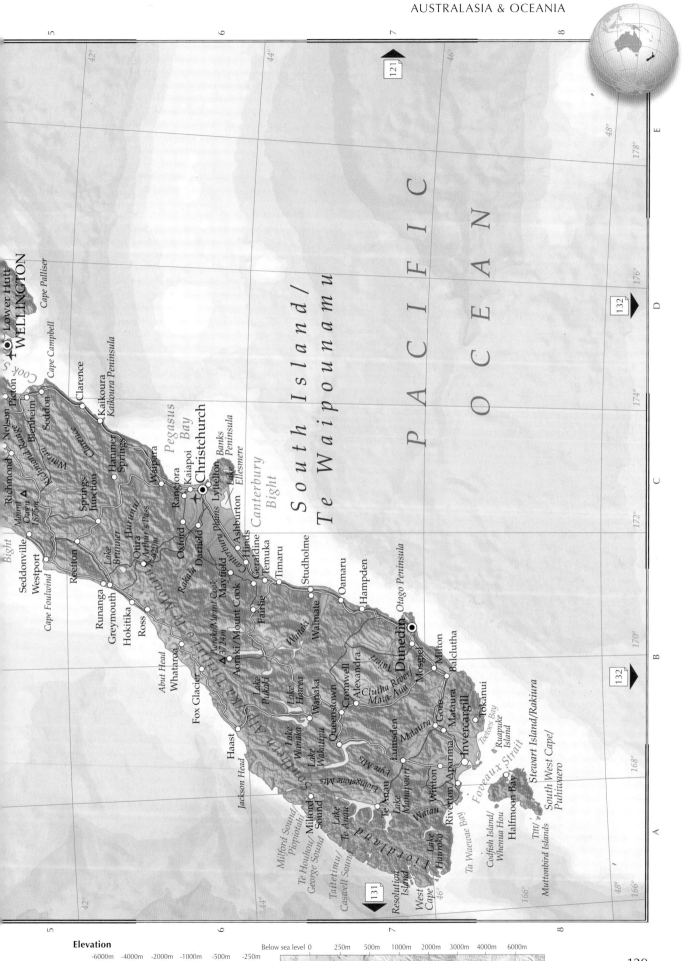

PACIFIC

OCEAN

South Island /
Te Waipounamu

WELLINGTON
Lower Hutt
Cape Palliser
Cape Campbell
Cook's
Strait
Nelson
Picton
Richmond
Blenheim
Seddon
Clarence
Kaikoura
Kaikoura Peninsula
Richmond Range
Mount
Owen
1875m
Wairau
Hanmer
Springs
Springs
Junction
Pegasus
Bay
Waiau
Rangiora
Kaiapoi
Christchurch
Lyttelton
Banks
Peninsula
Lake
Ellesmere
Seddonville
Westport
Cape Foulwind
Reefton
Lake
Brunner
Huriunui
Otira
Arthur's Pass
920m
Oxford
Darfield
Canterbury Plains
Rakaia
Ashburton
Hinds
Canterbury
Bight
Runanga
Greymouth
Hokitika
Ross
Abut Head
Whataroa
Aoraki/Mount Cook
Mayfield
Geraldine
Temuka
Timaru
Studholme
Oamaru
Hampden
Otago Peninsula
Fox Glacier
Southern Alps
Aoraki/Mount Cook
3724m
Fairlie
Waihki
Waimate
Dunedin
Milton
Balclutha
Jackson Head
Haast
Lake
Pukaki
Lake
Hawea
Wanaka
Cromwell
Alexandra
Clutha River/
Mata-Au
Taieri
Mosgiel
Lake
Wanaka
Lake
Wakatipu
Queenstown
Eyre Mts
Lumsden
Mataura
Gore
Tokanui
Stewart Island/Rakiura
Te Anau
Lake
Te Anau
Livingstone Mts
Lake
Manapouri
Waiau
Riverton/Aparima
Winton
Invercargill
Mataura
Foveaux Strait
South West Cape/
Puhiwaero
Milford Sound/
Piopiotahi
Te Houhou/ Milford
Sound
George Sound
Taitetimu/
Castell Sound
Resolution
Island
West
Cape
Lake
Hauroko
Waiau
Ta Waewae Bay
Codfish Island/
Whenua Hou
Halfmoon Bay
Ruapuke
Island
Toetoes Bay
Muttonbird Islands
Fiordland

121
132
132
131

42°
44°
46°
48°
48°
46°
44°
42°
166°
168°
170°
172°
174°
176°
178°
166°
168°
170°
172°
174°
176°
178°

5   6   7   8

E
D
C
B
A

Elevation

-6000m	-4000m	-2000m	-1000m	-500m	-250m	Below sea level 0	250m	500m	1000m	2000m	3000m	4000m	6000m

-19,658ft -13,124ft -6562ft -3281ft -1640ft -820ft -328ft/-100m 0   820ft 1640ft 3281ft 6562ft 9843ft 13,124ft 19,685ft

129

The Pacific Ocean

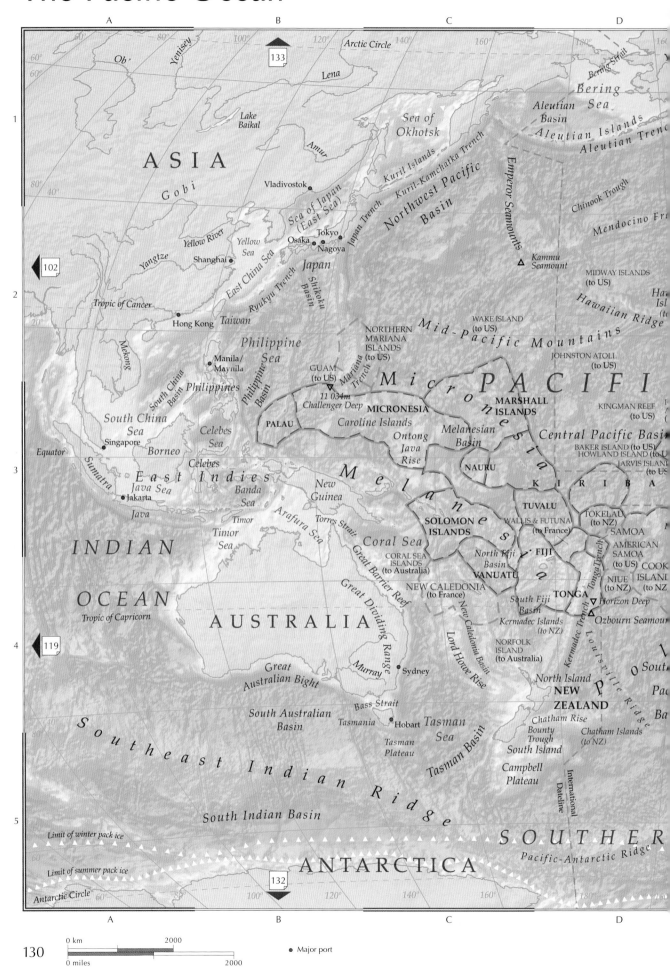

133

102

119

132

A B C D

Arctic Circle

Ob'
Yenisey
Lena
Bering Strait
Bering Sea
Aleutian Basin
Aleutian Islands
Aleutian Trench

Lake Baikal
Amur
Sea of Okhotsk
Chinook Trough
Mendocino Fra

ASIA
Gobi
Vladivostok
Kuril Islands
Kuril-Kamchatka Trench
Northwest Pacific Basin
Emperor Seamounts

Yellow River
Yellow Sea
Osaka Tokyo
Nagoya
Japan
Japan Trench
Kammu Seamount
MIDWAY ISLANDS (to US)

Yangtze
Shanghai
Sea of Japan (East Sea)
Shikoku Basin
Ryukyu Trench
Hawaiian Ridge
Hai Isl (to

Tropic of Cancer
Hong Kong
Taiwan
East China Sea
Mid-Pacific Mountains
WAKE ISLAND (to US)

Philippine Sea
NORTHERN MARIANA ISLANDS (to US)
GUAM (to US)
Mariana Trench
Micronesia
PACIFI
JOHNSTON ATOLL (to US)

Manila/ Maynila
Philippines
Philippine Basin
11 034m
Challenger Deep
MICRONESIA
MARSHALL ISLANDS
KINGMAN REEF (to US)

South China Basin
PALAU
Caroline Islands
Melanesian Basin
Central Pacific Basi

South China Sea
Celebes Sea
Ontong Java Rise
NAURU
BAKER ISLAND (to US)
HOWLAND ISLAND (to US)

Singapore
Borneo
Celebes
New Guinea
Melanesia
K I R I B A
JARVIS ISLAN (to US

Equator
East Indies
Banda Sea
TUVALU
TOKELAU (to NZ)

Sumatra
Java Sea
Timor
Arafura Sea
Torres Strait
SOLOMON ISLANDS
WALLIS & FUTUNA (to France)
SAMOA

Jakarta
Timor Sea
Melanesia
North Fiji Basin
FIJI
AMERICAN SAMOA (to US)
COOK

INDIAN
Coral Sea
CORAL SEA ISLANDS (to Australia)
VANUATU
NIUE (to NZ)
ISLANI (to NZ)

NEW CALEDONIA (to France)
New Caledonia Basin
South Fiji Basin
TONGA
Horizon Deep

OCEAN
Great Barrier Reef
Great Dividing Range
Kermadec Islands (to NZ)
Ozbourn Seamou

Tropic of Capricorn
AUSTRALIA
Lord Howe Rise
NORFOLK ISLAND (to Australia)
North Island
NEW ZEALAND
Louisville Ridge

Murray
Sydney
Tasman Sea
Chatham Rise
Pa
Ba

Great Australian Bight
Bass Strait
Bounty Trough
Chatham Islands (to NZ)

South Australian Basin
Tasmania
Hobart
Tasman Sea
South Island

Tasman Plateau
Tasman Basin
Campbell Plateau
International Dateline

Southeast Indian Ridge

South Indian Basin

Limit of winter pack ice
SOUTHER

Limit of summer pack ice
Pacific-Antarctic Ridge

Antarctic Circle
ANTARCTICA

0 km ———— 2000
0 miles ———— 2000
● Major port

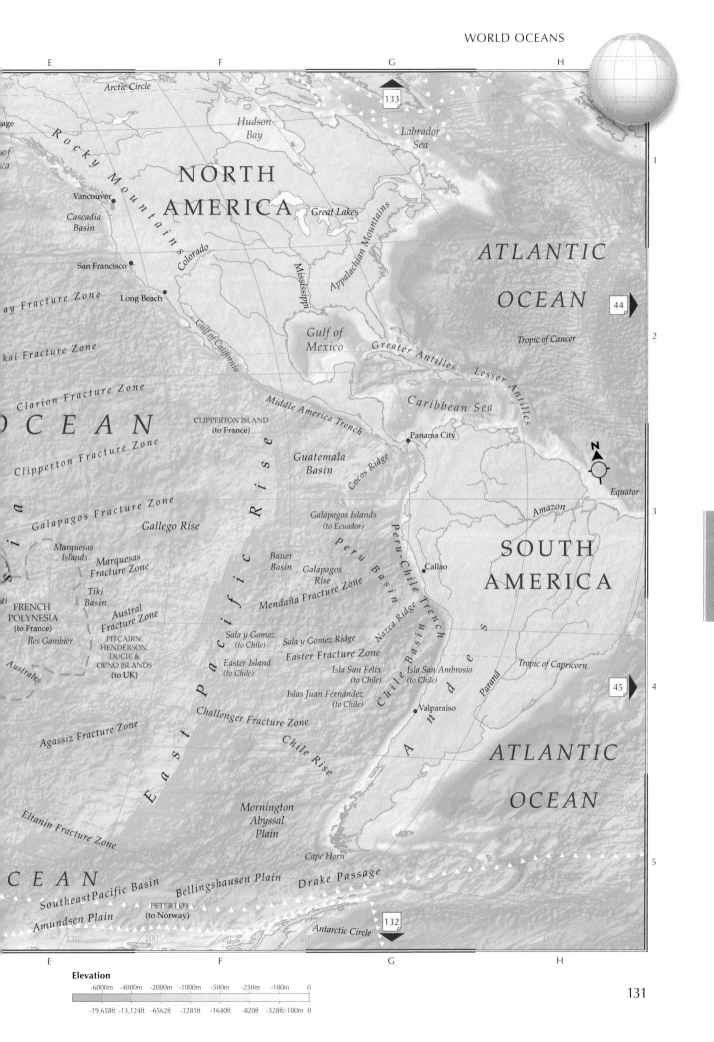

Arctic Circle

Rocky Mountains

Hudson
Bay

Labrador
Sea

NORTH
AMERICA

Vancouver

Cascadia
Basin

Great Lakes

ATLANTIC

San Francisco

Colorado

OCEAN

ay Fracture Zone

Long Beach

Appalachian Mountains

Mississippi

kai Fracture Zone

Gulf of California

Gulf of
Mexico

Greater Antilles

Tropic of Cancer

Clarion Fracture Zone

OCEAN

Caribbean Sea

Lesser Antilles

Middle America Trench

CLIPPERTON ISLAND
(to France)

Clipperton Fracture Zone

Panama City

Guatemala
Basin

Cocos Ridge

N

Galapagos Fracture Zone

Galápagos Islands
(to Ecuador)

Equator

Gallego Rise

Amazon

Marquesas
Islands

Marquesas
Fracture Zone

Bauer
Basin

Galapagos
Rise

Peru Basin

SOUTH
AMERICA

Callao

Tiki
Basin

Mendaña Fracture Zone

FRENCH
POLYNESIA
(to France)

Austral
Fracture Zone

Sala y Gomez
(to Chile)

Sala y Gomez Ridge

Nazca Ridge

Peru-Chile Trench

Îles Gambier

PITCAIRN,
HENDERSON,
DUCIE &
OENO ISLANDS
(to UK)

Easter Fracture Zone

Tropic of Capricorn

Australes

Easter Island
(to Chile)

Isla San Félix
(to Chile)

Isla San Ambrosio
(to Chile)

Chile Basin

Andes

Paraná

Islas Juan Fernández
(to Chile)

Valparaiso

Agassiz Fracture Zone

Challenger Fracture Zone

Chile Rise

ATLANTIC

Eltanin Fracture Zone

Mornington
Abyssal
Plain

OCEAN

Cape Horn

OCEAN

Drake Passage

SoutheastPacific Basin

Bellingshausen Plain

Amundsen Plain

PETER I ØY
(to Norway)

Antarctic Circle

East Pacific Rise

Elevation

-6000m	-4000m	-2000m	-1000m	-500m	-250m	-100m	0

| -19,658ft | -13,124ft | -6562ft | -3281ft | -1640ft | -820ft | -328ft/-100m | 0 |

Antarctica

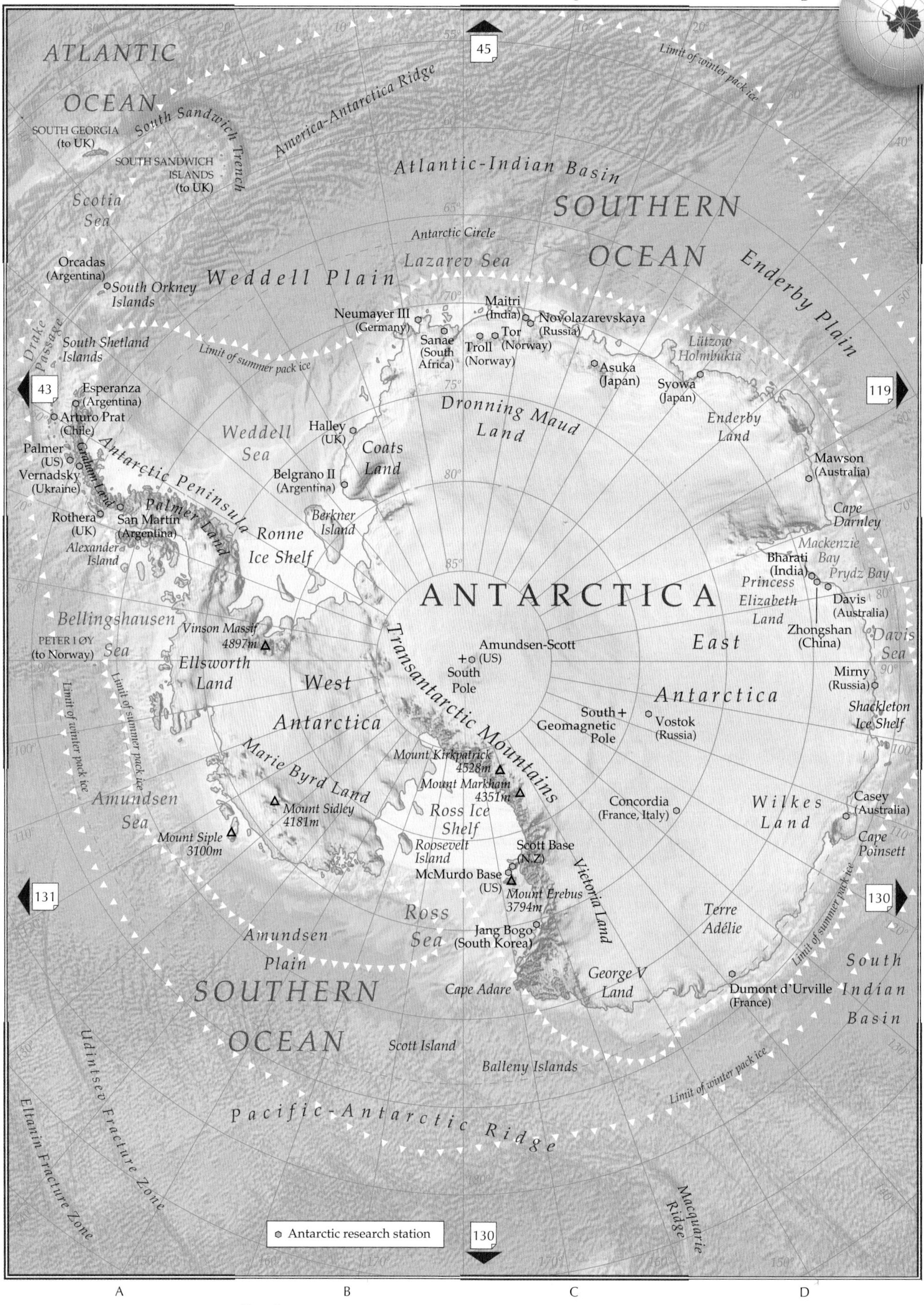

ATLANTIC

OCEAN

SOUTH GEORGIA
(to UK)

SOUTH SANDWICH
ISLANDS
(to UK)

South Sandwich Trench

America-Antarctica Ridge

Atlantic-Indian Basin

Limit of winter pack ice

SOUTHERN

OCEAN

Enderby Plain

45

Scotia
Sea

Antarctic Circle

Lazarev Sea

Orcadas
(Argentina)

South Orkney
Islands

Weddell Plain

Neumayer III
(Germany)

Maitri
(India)

Novolazarevskaya
(Russia)

Lützow
Holmbukta

Drake Passage

South Shetland
Islands

Limit of summer pack ice

Sanae
(South
Africa)

Troll
(Norway)

Tor
(Norway)

Asuka
(Japan)

Syowa
(Japan)

Enderby
Land

43

119

Esperanza
(Argentina)

Arturo Prat
(Chile)

Weddell
Sea

Halley
(UK)

Dronning Maud
Land

Mawson
(Australia)

Palmer
(US)

Vernadsky
(Ukraine)

Coats
Land

Cape
Darnley

Rothera
(UK)

San Martin
(Argentina)

Graham Land

Antarctic Peninsula

Belgrano II
(Argentina)

Berkner
Island

Mackenzie
Bay

Prydz Bay

Bharati
(India)

Alexander
Island

Palmer Land

Ronne
Ice Shelf

Princess
Elizabeth
Land

Davis
(Australia)

Zhongshan
(China)

Bellingshausen
Sea

ANTARCTICA

East

Davis
Sea

PETER I ØY
(to Norway)

Vinson Massif
4897m

Amundsen-Scott
+ o (US)
South
Pole

Antarctica

Mirny
(Russia)

Ellsworth
Land

West

Transantarctic Mountains

South +
Geomagnetic
Pole

Vostok
(Russia)

Shackleton
Ice Shelf

Amundsen
Sea

Antarctica

Marie Byrd Land

Mount Sidley
4181m

Mount Kirkpatrick
4528m

Mount Markham
4351m

Ross Ice
Shelf

Concordia
(France, Italy)

Wilkes
Land

Casey
(Australia)

Mount Siple
3100m

Roosevelt
Island

Scott Base
(N.Z.)

Cape
Poinsett

McMurdo Base
(US)

Victoria Land

Terre
Adélie

131

130

Amundsen

Ross
Sea

Mount Erebus
3794m

Jang Bogo
(South Korea)

George V
Land

Dumont d'Urville
(France)

South
Indian

Plain

SOUTHERN

Cape Adare

Basin

OCEAN

Scott Island

Balleny Islands

Macquarie
Ridge

Pacific-Antarctic Ridge

Udintsev Fracture Zone

Eltanin Fracture Zone

⬢ Antarctic research station

130

0 km 500

0 miles 500

Elevation

| -6000m | -4000m | -2000m | -1000m | -500m | -250m | Below sea level 0 | 250m | 500m | 1000m | 2000m | 3000m | 4000m | 6000m |

-19,658ft -13,124ft -6562ft -3281ft -1640ft -820ft -328ft/-100m 0   820ft 1640ft 3281ft 6562ft 9843ft 13,124ft 19,685ft

Arctic Ocean

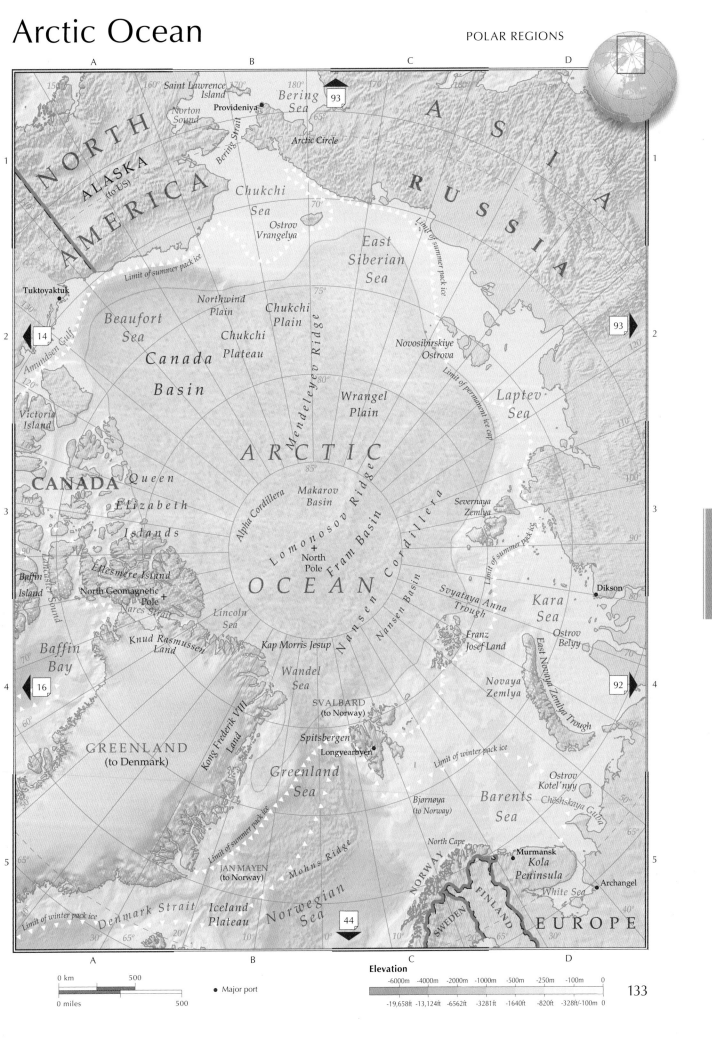

NORTH AMERICA

ALASKA (to US)

Saint Lawrence Island

Norton Sound

Provideniya

Bering Sea

Arctic Circle

Bering Strait

ASIA

RUSSIA

93

Chukchi Sea

Ostrov Vrangelya

Limit of summer pack ice

Tuktoyaktuk

Northwind Plain

Chukchi Plain

East Siberian Sea

Limit of summer pack ice

14

Beaufort Sea

Chukchi Plateau

Mendeleyev Ridge

93

Canada Basin

Wrangel Plain

Novosibirskiye Ostrova

Laptev Sea

Limit of permanent ice cap

Victoria Island

Amundsen Gulf

A R C T I C

CANADA

Queen Elizabeth Islands

Alpha Cordillera

Makarov Basin

Lomonosov Ridge

Severnaya Zemlya

Limit of summer pack ice

Dikson

North Geomagnetic Pole

North Pole

Fram Basin

Nansen Cordillera

Svyataya Anna Trough

Kara Sea

Baffin Island

Ellesmere Island

Nares Strait

O C E A N

Franz Josef Land

Ostrov Belyy

Lancaster Sound

Knud Rasmussen Land

Lincoln Sea

Kap Morris Jesup

Nansen Basin

East Novaya Zemlya Trough

Baffin Bay

Wandel Sea

SVALBARD (to Norway)

Novaya Zemlya

92

Kong Frederik VIII Land

Spitsbergen

Longyearbyen

Limit of winter pack ice

Ostrov Kotel'nyy

Chëshskaya Guba

GREENLAND (to Denmark)

Greenland Sea

Bjørnøya (to Norway)

Barents Sea

North Cape

Murmansk

Kola Peninsula

Archangel

NORWAY

White Sea

Limit of summer pack ice

Mohns Ridge

JAN MAYEN (to Norway)

Norwegian Sea

44

SWEDEN

FINLAND

EUROPE

Limit of winter pack ice

Denmark Strait

Iceland Plateau

16

Scale / Legend

0 km   500

0 miles   500

● Major port

Elevation

-6000m -4000m -2000m -1000m -500m -250m -100m 0

-19,658ft -13,124ft -6562ft -3281ft -1640ft -820ft -328ft/-100m 0

Country Profiles

This Factfile is intended as a guide to a world that is continually changing as political fashions and personalities come and go. Nevertheless, all the material in these factfiles has been researched from the most up-to-date and authoritative sources to give an incisive portrait of the geographical, political, and social characteristics that make each country so unique.

There are currently 196 independent countries in the world – more than at any previous time – and over 50 dependencies. Antarctica is the only land area on Earth that is not officially part of, and does not belong to, any single country.

AFGHANISTAN
Central Asia

Page 100 D4

Landlocked in Central Asia, Afghanistan has suffered decades of conflict. After the US-led coalition withdrew troops in 2021, the Taliban movement overthrew the government, leading to global isolation.

Official name Islamic Republic of Afghanistan
Formation 1919 / 1919
Capital Kabul
Population 38.3 million / 152 people per sq mile (59 people per sq km)
Total area 251,827 sq miles (652,230 sq km)
Languages Pashto*, Tajik, Dari*, Farsi, Uzbek, Turkmen, Urdu
Religions Muslim 99% (Sunni 87%, Shi'a 12%), Other 1%
Demographics Pashtun 38%, Tajik 25%, Hazara 19%, Uzbek and Turkmen 15%, Other 3%
Government Nonparty system
Currency Afghani = 100 puls
Literacy rate 37%
Life expectancy 54 years

ALBANIA
Southeast Europe

Page 79 C6

Lying at the southeastern end of the Adriatic Sea, Albania - or the "land of the eagles" - held its first multiparty elections in 1991. It joined NATO in 2009 and became an EU candidate in 2014.

Official name Republic of Albania
Formation 1912 / 1921
Capital Tirana
Population 3 million / 270 people per sq mile (104 people per sq km)
Total area 11,100 sq miles (28,748 sq km)
Languages Albanian*, Greek
Religions Muslim (mainly Sunni) 68%, Roman Catholic 12%, Albanian Orthodox 8%, Nonreligious 6%, Other 6%
Demographics Albanian 83%, Other 17%
Government Parliamentary system
Currency Lek = 100 qindarka (qintars)
Literacy rate 98%
Life expectancy 79 years

ALGERIA
North Africa

Page 48 C3

Set on the Mediterranean coast, Algeria, the largest country in Africa, is rich in natural resources, particularly oil and gas. It has huge potential for solar-power generation from the vast Sahara desert.

Official name People's Democratic Republic of Algeria
Formation 1962 / 1962
Capital Algiers
Population 44.1 million / 48 people per sq mile (19 people per sq km)
Total area 919,590 sq miles (2,381,740 sq km)
Languages Arabic*, Tamazight* (Kabyle, Shawia, Tamashek), French
Religions Muslim (mainly Sunni) 99%, Other 1%
Demographics Arab 75%, Amazigh 24%, European & Jewish 1%
Government Presidential system
Currency Algerian dinar = 100 centimes
Literacy rate 81%
Life expectancy 78 years

ANDORRA
Southwest Europe

Page 69 B6

A tiny landlocked principality, Andorra lies between France and Spain, high in the eastern Pyrenees. Its economy, based on tourism, also features low tax and duty-free shopping.

Official name Principality of Andorra
Formation 1278 / 1278
Capital Andorra la Vella
Population 85,560 / 473 people per sq mile (183 people per sq km)
Total area 181 sq miles (468 sq km)
Languages Spanish, Catalan*, French, Portuguese, Castilian
Religions Christian (mainly Roman Catholic) 90%, Other 10%
Demographics Andorran 48%, Spanish 25%, Portuguese 11%, French 5%, Other 11%
Government Parliamentary system
Currency Euro = 100 cents
Literacy rate 100%
Life expectancy 83 years

ANGOLA
Southern Africa

Page 56 B2

Emerging from decades of devastating civil war in 2002, Angola has enormous natural resources, particularly minerals, oil, and gemstones. It is the third largest producer of diamonds in Africa.

Official name Republic of Angola
Formation 1975 / 1975
Capital Luanda
Population 34.7 million / 72 people per sq mile (28 people per sq km)
Total area 481,354 sq miles (1,246,700 sq km)
Languages Portuguese*, Kimbundu, Umbundu, Chokwe, Kikongo
Religions Roman Catholic 40%, Protestant 38%, Nonreligious 12%, Other (including animist) 10%
Demographics Ovimbundu 37%, Ambundu 25%, Bakongo 13%, Other African 21%, Other 4%
Government Presidential system
Currency Kwanza = 100 centimos
Literacy rate 71%
Life expectancy 62 years

ANTIGUA & BARBUDA
West Indies

Page 33 H3

Lying on the Atlantic edge of the Leeward Islands, tourism is vital to the economy here but it is vulnerable to seasonal storm damage, notably hurricane Irma in 2017 which devastated the island of Barbuda.

Official name Antigua and Barbuda
Formation 1981 / 1981
Capital St. John's
Population 100,335 / 587 people per sq mile (226 people per sq km)
Total area 171 sq miles (443 sq km)
Languages English*, English patois
Religions Other Christian 49%, Anglican 19%, Seventh-day Adventist 13%, Other 19%
Demographics Black 87%, Mixed race 5%, Hispanic 3%, White 2%, Other 3%
Government Parliamentary system
Currency East Caribbean dollar = 100 cents
Literacy rate 98%
Life expectancy 78 years

ARGENTINA
South America

Page 43 B5

This vast country ranges from semiarid lowlands, through fertile grasslands, to the glacial southern tip of South America. This diversity allows for key agricultural exports such as soybeans, corn, and beef.

Official name Argentine Republic
Formation 1816 / 1898
Capital Buenos Aires
Population 46.2 million / 43 people per sq mile (17 people per sq km)
Total area 1,073,518 sq miles (2,780,400 sq km)
Languages Spanish*, Italian, English, German, French, Indigenous (Mapudungun, Quechua)
Religions Roman Catholic 63%, Evangelical 15%, Nonreligious 19%, Other 3%
Demographics European and mixed race 97%, Indigenous 2%, Other 1%
Government Presidential system
Currency Argentine peso = 100 centavos
Literacy rate 99%
Life expectancy 78 years

ARMENIA
Southwest Asia

Page 95 F3

Set at the crossroads between Europe and Asia in the Caucasus Mountains, Armenia is rich in ancient history and culture. It was the first country to adopt Christianity as the state religion, in the 4th century CE.

Official name Republic of Armenia
Formation 1991 / 1991
Capital Yerevan
Population 3 million / 261 people per sq mile (101 people per sq km)
Total area 11,484 sq miles (29,743 sq km)
Languages Armenian*, Azeri, Russian, Kurdish
Religions Orthodox Christian 89%, Nonreligious 2%, Armenian Catholic Church 1%, Other 8%
Demographics Armenian 98%, Yezidi 1%, Other 1%
Government Parliamentary system
Currency Dram = 100 luma
Literacy rate 100%
Life expectancy 76 years

AUSTRALIA
Australasia & Oceania

Page 125 B5

An island continent between the Pacific and Indian oceans, Australia has a highly urbanized population that is concentrated on the coast. The economy is dominated by the service sector underpinned by vast mineral wealth.

Official name Commonwealth of Australia
Formation 1901 / 1901
Capital Canberra
Population 26.1 million / 8 people per sq mile (3 people per sq km)
Total area 2,969,907 sq miles (7,692,024 sq km)
Languages English*, Italian, Cantonese, Greek, Arabic, Vietnamese, Mandarin
Religions Roman Catholic 28%, Nonreligious 24%, Other Christian 20%, Anglican 19%, Other 9%,
Demographics British 33%, Australian 30%, Irish 9%, Scottish 9%, Chinese 5%, Indigenous 3%, Other 11%
Government Parliamentary system
Currency Australian dollar = 100 cents
Literacy rate 99%
Life expectancy 83 years

AUSTRIA
Central Europe

Page 73 D7

Nestled in the eastern Alps of Central Europe, Austria has developed a varied, high-tech, industrialized economy with well over half of its electricity demand now met by renewable resources.

Official name Republic of Austria
Formation 1918 / 1920
Capital Vienna
Population 8.9 million / 275 people per sq mile (106 people per sq km)
Total area 32,383 sq miles (83,871 sq km)
Languages German*, Turkish, Serbian, Croatian, Slovenian, Hungarian (Magyar)
Religions Roman Catholic 55%, None 26%, Other Christian 9%, Muslim 8%, Other 2%
Demographics Austrian 81%, German 3%, Turkish 2%, Other 14%
Government Parliamentary system
Currency Euro = 100 cents
Literacy rate 98%
Life expectancy 82 years

AZERBAIJAN
Southwest Asia

Page 95 G2

Situated on the west coast of the Caspian Sea, Azerbaijan was one of the world's first oil producing nations. The economy is still dominated by oil and gas, accounting for almost 90 percent of total exports.

Official name Republic of Azerbaijan
Formation 1991 / 1991
Capital Baku
Population 10.3 million / 308 people per sq mile (119 people per sq km)
Total area 33,436 sq miles (86,600 sq km)
Languages Azeri*, Russian, Armenian
Religions Muslim (mainly Shi'a) 97%, Christian 3%
Demographics Azeri 92%, Lezgin 2%, Other 6%
Government Presidential system
Currency Manat = 100 gopik
Literacy rate 100%
Life expectancy 74 years

BAHAMAS, THE
West Indies

Page 32 C1

Located off the Florida coast, The Bahamas comprise over 3,000 islands and cays, only 30 of which are inhabited. Tourism and financial services are key sectors in the economy.

Official name Commonwealth of The Bahamas
Formation 1973 / 1973
Capital Nassau
Population 355,608 / 66 people per sq mile (26 people per sq km)
Total area 5359 sq miles (13,880 sq km)
Languages English*, English Creole, French Creole
Religions Baptist 36%, Anglican 14%, Roman Catholic 12%, Pentecostal 9%, Seventh-day Adventist 5%, Methodist 4%, Other 20%
Demographics Black 90%, White 5%, Mixed race 2%, Other 3%
Government Parliamentary system
Currency Bahamian dollar = 100 cents
Literacy rate 96%
Life expectancy 76 years

BAHRAIN
Southwest Asia

Page 98 C4

Once famed for its pearl fisheries, this island nation set on the Persian Gulf has relied heavily on petroleum products for its wealth. Steps have been taken to diversify the economy.

Official name Kingdom of Bahrain
Formation 1971 / 2001
Capital Manama
Population 1.5 million / 5651 people per sq mile (2241 people per sq km)
Total area 293 sq miles (760 sq km)
Languages Arabic*, English, Farsi, Urdu
Religions Muslim (mainly Shi'a) 74%, Christian 9%, Other 17%
Demographics Bahraini 46%, Asian 46%, Other Arab 5%, Other 3%
Government Monarchical / parliamentary system
Currency Bahraini dinar = 1000 fils
Literacy rate 100%
Life expectancy 78 years

BANGLADESH
South Asia

Page 113 G3

The geography of this low-lying nation is dominated by the Ganges delta which makes it prone to flooding. However, this also makes it a fertile land, able to produce three rice crops a year in some areas.

Official name People's Republic of Bangladesh
Formation 1971 / 2015
Capital Dhaka
Population 166 million / 3276 people per sq mile (1278 people per sq km)
Total area 57,321 sq miles (148,460 sq km)
Languages Bengali*, Urdu, Chakma, Marma (Magh), Garo, Khasi, Santhali, Tripuri, Mro
Religions Muslim (mainly Sunni) 91%, Hindu 8%, Other 1%
Demographics Bengali 98%, Other indigenous ethnic groups 2%
Government Parliamentary system
Currency Taka = 100 poisha
Literacy rate 78%
Life expectancy 73 years

BARBADOS
West Indies

Page 33 H4

The most easterly of the Windward Islands, Barbados was once a major sugar producer, but this densely populated island now has a diverse economy based on manufacturing, tourism, and financial services.

Official name Barbados
Formation 1966 / 1966
Capital Bridgetown
Population 302,674 / 1730 people per sq mile (669 people per sq km)
Total area 166 sq miles (430 sq km)
Languages Bajan (Barbadian English), English*
Religions Anglican 24%, Nonreligious 21%, Pentecostal 20%, Seventh-day Adventist 6%, Methodist 4%, Roman Catholic 4%, Other 21%
Demographics Black 93%, Mixed race 3%, White 3%, Other 1%
Government Parliamentary system
Currency Barbados dollar = 100 cents
Literacy rate 100%
Life expectancy 81 years

BELARUS
Eastern Europe

Page 85 B6

Landlocked in eastern Europe, Belarus continues to exert heavy state-control over many aspects of media, politics, and the economy. It is closely aligned with Russia, its powerful neighbor and ally.

Official name Republic of Belarus
Formation 1991 / 1991
Capital Minsk
Population 9.4 million / 117 people per sq mile (45 people per sq km)
Total area 80,155 sq miles (207,600 sq km)
Languages Belarussian*, Russian*
Religions Orthodox Christian 73%, Roman Catholic 12%, Nonreligious 3%, Other 12%
Demographics Belarussian 86%, Russian 8%, Polish 3%, Ukrainian 1%, Other 2%
Government Presidential system
Currency Belarussian ruble = 100 kopeks
Literacy rate 100%
Life expectancy 80 years

BELGIUM
Northwest Europe

Page 65 B6

Located in Northwest Europe, Belgium is host to many international organizations and institutions of the European Union (EU). The diamond trade is a key part of a diverse and productive economy.

Official name Kingdom of Belgium
Formation 1830 / 1919
Capital Brussels
Population 11.8 million / 1001 people per sq mile (387 people per sq km)
Total area 11,787 sq miles (30,528 sq km)
Languages Dutch*, French*, German*
Religions Roman Catholic 57%, Nonreligious 30%, Muslim 7%, Other Christian 4%, Other 2%
Demographics Belgian 75%, Italian 4%, Moroccan 4%, French 2%, Turkish 2%, Dutch 2%, Other 11%
Government Parliamentary system
Currency Euro = 100 cents
Literacy rate 99%
Life expectancy 85 years

BELIZE
Central America

Page 30 B1

Lying on the eastern shore of the Yucatan Peninsula, Belize is close to the world's second largest barrier reef, which includes the Great Blue Hole, a giant marine sinkhole popular with recreational divers.

Official name Belize
Formation 1981 / 1981
Capital Belmopan
Population 412,387 / 47 people per sq mile (18 people per sq km)
Total area 8867 sq miles (22,966 sq km)
Languages English Creole, Spanish, English*, Mayan, Garifuna (Carib), German
Religions Roman Catholic 40%, Other Christian 34%, Nonreligious 16%, Other 10%,
Demographics Mixed race 49%, Creole 24%, Maya 10%, Garifuna 6%, Asian Indian 4%, Other 7%
Government Parliamentary system
Currency Belizean dollar = 100 cents
Literacy rate 75%
Life expectancy 76 years

BENIN
West Africa

Page 53 F4

Set on the West African coast, the economy of Benin is dominated by agricultural products. It is the twelfth largest cotton producer and fifth largest cashew nut producer in the world.

Official name Republic of Benin
Formation 1960 / 1960
Capital Porto-Novo; Cotonou
Population 13.7 million / 315 people per sq mile (122 people per sq km)
Total area 43,484 sq miles (112,622 sq km)
Languages Fon, Bariba, Yoruba, Adja, Houeda, Somba, French*
Religions Muslim 28%, Roman Catholic 26%, Other Christian 24%, Vodoun 12%, Other 10%
Demographics Fon 38%, Adja 15%, Yoruba 12%, Bariba 10%, Fulani 9%, Other 16%
Government Presidential system
Currency CFA franc = 100 centimes
Literacy rate 42%
Life expectancy 62 years

BHUTAN
South Asia

Page 113 G3

This landlocked Buddhist kingdom, perched in the eastern Himalayas between India and China, announced the draft of its first constitution in 2005 and held its first parliamentary election in 2008.

Official name Kingdom of Bhutan
Formation 1907 / 2006
Capital Thimphu
Population 867,775 / 59 people per sq mile (23 people per sq km)
Total area 14,824 sq miles (38,394 sq km)
Languages Dzongkha*, Sharchopkha, Lhotshamkha
Religions Mahayana Buddhist 75%, Hindu 22%, Other 3%
Demographics Ngalop 50%, Nepali 35%, Tribal groups 15%
Government Monarchical / parliamentary system
Currency Ngultrum = 100 chetrum
Literacy rate 67%
Life expectancy 72 years

BOLIVIA
South America

Page 39 F3

Landlocked high in central South America, Bolivia is renowned for its vast mineral wealth, which drives the economy, including the world's largest reserves of lithium.

Official name Plurinational State of Bolivia
Formation 1825 / 1938
Capital La Paz (administrative); Sucre (judicial)
Population 12 million / 28 people per sq mile (11 people per sq km)
Total area 424,164 sq miles (1,098,581 sq km)
Languages Aymara*, Quechua*, Spanish*, Guarani
Religions Roman Catholic 70%, Evangelical 15%, Adventist 2%, Church of Jesus Christ 1%, Other 12%
Demographics Mixed race 70%, Indigenous 20%, White 5%, African 1%, Other 4%
Government Presidential system
Currency Boliviano = 100 centavos
Literacy rate 93%
Life expectancy 73 years

BOSNIA & HERZEGOVINA
Southeast Europe

Page 78 B3

Set in the western Balkans, this state has a complex history born out of the differences between its three main ethnic groups. With its spectacular alpine scenery, tourism is a fast growing sector.

Official name Bosnia and Herzegovina
Formation 1992 / 1992
Capital Sarajevo
Population 3.8 million / 192 people per sq mile (74 people per sq km)
Total area 19,767 sq miles (51,197 sq km)
Languages Bosnian*, Serbian*, Croatian*
Religions Muslim (mainly Sunni) 53%, Orthodox Christian 35%, Roman Catholic 8%, Nonreligious 3%, Other 1%
Demographics Bosniak 50%, Serb 31%, Croat 15%, Other 4%
Government Parliamentary system
Currency Marka = 100 pfeninga
Literacy rate 99%
Life expectancy 78 years

BOTSWANA
Southern Africa

Page 56 C3

Botswana lies landlocked in Southern Africa. The Orapa diamond mine is one of the largest in the world and this, along with other mineral resources, helps to provide a relatively prosperous economy.

Official name Republic of Botswana
Formation 1966 / 1966
Capital Gaborone
Population 2.3 million / 13 people per sq mile (5 people per sq km)
Total area 224,607 sq miles (581,730 sq km)
Languages Setswana, English*, Sekalanga, Shona, San, Khoikhoi, isiNdebele
Religions Christian (mainly Protestant) 80%, Nonreligious 15%, Traditional beliefs 4%, Other (including Muslim) 1%
Demographics Tswana (or Setswana) 79%, Kalanga 11%, Basarwa 3%, Other 7%
Government Parliamentary system
Currency Pula = 100 thebe
Literacy rate 89%
Life expectancy 66 years

BRAZIL
South America

Page 40 C2

Brazil covers about half of South America and has immense natural resources. As well as a diverse, high-tech industrial base and a burgeoning service sector, it produces a third of the world's coffee.

Official name Federative Republic of Brazil
Formation 1822 / 1909
Capital Brasília
Population 214 million / 65 people per sq mile (25 people per sq km)
Total area 3,287,957 sq miles (8,515,770 sq km)
Languages Portuguese*, German, Italian, Spanish, Polish, Japanese, Amerindian languages
Religions Roman Catholic 61%, Protestant 26%, Nonreligious 8%, Other 5%
Demographics White 48%, Mixed race 43%, Black 8%, Other 1%
Government Presidential system
Currency Real = 100 centavos
Literacy rate 93%
Life expectancy 76 years

BRUNEI
Southeast Asia

Page 116 D3

Located on the island of Borneo, Brunei has a high standard of living due to oil and gas revenues. The Sultan of Brunei was crowned in 1967, making him one of the world's longest reigning monarchs.

Official name Brunei Darussalam
Formation 1984 / 1984
Capital Bandar Seri Begawan
Population 474,054 / 213 people per sq mile (82 people per sq km)
Total area 2226 sq miles (5765 sq km)
Languages Malay*, English, Chinese dialects
Religions Muslim (mainly Sunni) 79%, Christian 9%, Buddhist 8%, Other 4%
Demographics Malay 66%, Chinese 10%, Indigenous 4%, Other 20%
Government Monarchy
Currency Bruneian dollar = 100 cents
Literacy rate 97%
Life expectancy 78 years

BULGARIA
Southeast Europe

Page 82 C2

Located on the western shore of the Black Sea, Bulgaria is rich in history and culture. It was here that the Cyrillic script was developed in the 9th century CE. EU membership was achieved in 2007.

Official name Republic of Bulgaria
Formation 1908 / 1947
Capital Sofia
Population 6.8 million / 159 people per sq mile (61 people per sq km)
Total area 42,811 sq miles (110,879 sq km)
Languages Bulgarian*, Turkish, Romani
Religions Orthodox Christian 75%, Muslim 15%, Nonreligious 5%, Protestant 1%, Roman Catholic 1%, Other 3%
Demographics Bulgarian 85%, Turkish 9%, Roma 5%, Other 1%
Government Parliamentary system
Currency Lev = 100 stotinki
Literacy rate 98%
Life expectancy 76 years

BURKINA FASO
West Africa

Page 53 E4

Burkina Faso is landlocked in the semiarid Sahel of West Africa. Often struggling with political instability, it is the fourth largest producer of gold in Africa, which makes up over 75 percent of the country's exports.

Official name Burkina Faso
Formation 1960 / 2016
Capital Ouagadougou
Population 21.9 million / 207 people per sq mile (80 people per sq km)
Total area 105,869 sq miles (274,200 sq km)
Languages Mossi, Fulani, French*, Tuareg, Dyula, Songhai
Religions Muslim 60% Christian 23%, Indigenous beliefs 15%, Other 2%
Demographics Mossi 52%, Fulani 8%, Gurma 7%, Bobo 5%, Gurunsi 5%, Senufo 5%, Bissa 4%, Lobi 2%, Dagara 2%, Other 10%
Government Presidential system
Currency CFA franc = 100 centimes
Literacy rate 39%
Life expectancy 63 years

BURUNDI
Central Africa

Page 51 B7

Landlocked in central Africa, Burundi has a predominantly rural society with an emphasis on agriculture. Ethnic tensions led to brutal conflict but peace efforts have since brought greater stability.

Official name Republic of Burundi
Formation 1962 / 1962
Capital Bujumbura; Gitega
Population 12.6 million / 1173 people per sq mile (453 people per sq km)
Total area 10,745 sq miles (27,830 sq km)
Languages Kirundi*, French*, Kiswahili, English
Religions Roman Catholic 65%, Protestant 23%, Muslim 3%, Seventh-day Adventist 2%, Other 7%
Demographics Hutu 85%, Tutsi 14%, Twa 1%
Government Presidential system
Currency Burundian franc = 100 centimes
Literacy rate 68%
Life expectancy 67 years

CAMBODIA
Southeast Asia

Page 115 D5

This ancient Southeast Asian kingdom suffered years of brutal totalitarian rule but is now recovering, with recent economic growth helping to dramatically reduce poverty.

Official name Kingdom of Cambodia
Formation 1953 / 1953
Capital Phnom Penh
Population 16.7 million/ 239 people per sq mile (92 people per sq km)
Total area 69,898 sq miles (181,035 sq km)
Languages Khmer*, French, Chinese, Vietnamese, Cham
Religions Buddhist 97%, Muslim 2%, Other (mostly Christian) 1%
Demographics Khmer 95%, Cham 2%, Chinese 2%, Other 1%
Government Parliamentary system
Currency Riel = 100 sen
Literacy rate 81%
Life expectancy 71 years

CAMEROON
Central Africa

Page 54 A4

Set on the central West African coast, Cameroon has a hugely diverse geography, including extensive tropical forests. Small-scale agriculture, forestry, and fishing are key economic activities.

Official name Republic of Cameroon
Formation 1960 / 2006
Capital Yaoundé
Population 29.3 million / 160 people per sq mile (62 people per sq km)
Total area 183,568 sq miles (475,440 sq km)
Languages Bamileke, Fang, Fulani, French*, English*
Religions Roman Catholic 38%, Protestant 26%, Other Christian 7%, Muslim 24%, Other 5%
Demographics Bamileke-Bamu 24%, Beti/Bassa, Mbam 21%, Biu-Mandara 14%, Arab-Choa/Hausa/Kanuri 11%, Adamawa-Ubangi 9%, Other 21%
Government Presidential system
Currency CFA franc = 100 centimes
Literacy rate 77%
Life expectancy 63 years

CANADA
North America

Page 15 E4

The world's second largest country spans six time zones and is rich in natural resources. Huge oil and gas reserves allow a net export of energy, contributing to a well-developed and high-tech globalized economy.

Official name Canada
Formation 1867 / 1949
Capital Ottawa
Population 38.2 million / 10 people per sq mile (4 people per sq km)
Total area 3,855,171 sq miles (9,984,670 sq km)
Languages English*, French*, Pubjabi, Cantonese, Spanish, Arabic,Tagalog, Italian, German
Religions Roman Catholic 39%, Other Christian 28%, Nonreligious 24%, Muslim 3%, Other 6%
Demographics European descent 80%, Asian 15%, First Nations, Métis, and Inuit 5%
Government Parliamentary system
Currency Canadian dollar = 100 cents
Literacy rate 99%
Life expectancy 84 years

CAPE VERDE (CABO VERDE)
Atlantic Ocean

Page 52 A2

A group of mainly volcanic islands off the west coast of Africa, Cape Verde has limited natural resources. The economy relies on fisheries and tourists attracted by its warm climate and unspoilt beaches.

Official name Republic of Cabo Verde
Formation 1975 / 1975
Capital Praia
Population 596,707 / 383 people per sq mile (148 people per sq km)
Total area 1557 sq miles (4033 sq km)
Languages Portuguese Creole, Portuguese*
Religions Roman Catholic 77%, Protestant 5%, other Christian 3%, Muslim 2%, Other 13%
Demographics Mixed race 71%, African 28%, European 1%
Government Presidential / parliamentary system
Currency Escudo = 100 centavos
Literacy rate 87%
Life expectancy 74 years

CENTRAL AFRICAN REPUBLIC
Central Africa

Page 54 C4

Set on a landlocked plateau dividing the Chad and Congo river basins, the CAR has suffered from years of political instability and conflict. It is rich in diamonds, gold, oil, and uranium.

Official name Central African Republic
Formation 1960 / 1960
Capital Bangui
Population 5.4 million / 22 people per sq mile (9 people per sq km)
Total area 240,535 sq miles (622,984 sq km)
Languages Sango, Banda, Gbaya, French*
Religions Christian 89%, Muslim 9%, Folk Religion 1%, Unaffiliated 1%
Demographics Baya 29%, Banda 23%, Mandjia 10%, Sara 8%, M'Baka-Bantu 8%, Mbum 6%, Arab-Fulani 6%, Ngbanki 6%, Other 4%
Government Presidential system
Currency CFA franc = 100 centimes
Literacy rate 37%
Life expectancy 56 years

CHAD
Central Africa

Page 54 C3

Landlocked in Central Africa, with desert to the north, Chad has been troubled by periods of civil war. The majority of its people rely on small-scale farming. It became a net oil exporter in 2003.

Official name Republic of Chad
Formation 1960 / 1960
Capital N'Djaména
Population 17.9 million / 36 people per sq mile (14 people per sq km)
Total area 495,755 sq miles (1,284,000 sq km)
Languages French*, Sara, Arabic*, Maba
Religions Muslim 52%, Protestant 24%, Roman Catholic 20%, None 3%, Other 1%
Demographics Sara 31%, Arab 10%, Kanembu 9%, Masalit 7%, Gorane 6%, Other Indigenous groups 34%, Other 3%
Government Presidential system
Currency CFA franc = 100 centimes
Literacy rate 22%
Life expectancy 59 years

CHILE
South America

Page 42 B3

Chile extends in a thin ribbon down the Pacific coast of South America. Rich in mineral resources, it is the world's largest copper producer supplying about a third of the global market.

Official name Republic of Chile
Formation 1810 / 1898
Capital Santiago
Population 18.4 million / 63 people per sq mile (24 people per sq km)
Total area 291,933 sq miles (756,120 sq km)
Languages Spanish*, Amerindian languages
Religions Roman Catholic 60%, Evangelical 18%, Atheist or Agnostic 4%, None 17%
Demographics White and mixed race 89%, Mapuche 9%, Aymara 1%, Other Indigenous 1%
Government Presidential system
Currency Chilean peso = 100 centavos
Literacy rate 96%
Life expectancy 80 years

CHINA
East Asia

Page 104 C4

This vast East Asian country, home to a fifth of the global population, became a communist state in 1949. It has now emerged as one of the world's major political and economic powers.

Official name People's Republic of China
Formation 1949 / 2011
Capital Beijing
Population 1.41 billion / 381 people per sq mile (147 people per sq km)
Total area 3,705,386 sq miles (9,596,960 sq km)
Languages Mandarin*, Wu, Cantonese, Hsiang, Min, Hakka, Kan
Religions Folk religion 22%, Buddhist 18%, Christian 5%, Muslim 2%, Unaffiliated 52%, Hindu, Jewish, and other 1%
Demographics Han Chinese 91%, Ethnic minorities 9%
Government One-party state
Currency Renminbi (or yuan) = 10 jiao = 100 fen
Literacy rate 97%
Life expectancy 78 years

COLOMBIA
South America

Page 36 B3

Lying in northwest South America, Colombia is rich in biodiversity with around 45,000 plant species. Exports of petroleum and agricultural products are driving rapid economic growth.

Official name Republic of Colombia
Formation 1810 / 1903
Capital Bogotá
Population 49.1 million / 112 people per sq mile (43 people per sq km)
Total area 439,736 sq miles (1,138,910 sq km)
Languages Spanish*, Amerindian languages
Religions Christian 92% (mainly Roman Catholic), Unspecified 7%, Other 1%
Demographics Mixed race and White 88%, Indigenous 4%, Afro-Colombian 7%, Unspecified 1%
Government Presidential system
Currency Colombian peso = 100 centavos
Literacy rate 96%
Life expectancy 75 years

COMOROS
Indian Ocean

Page 57 F2

Comoros sits between Mozambique and Madagascar. A volatile political history and limited natural resources have restricted economic growth. Spices, particularly cloves, are the main export.

Official name Union of the Comoros
Formation 1975 / 1975
Capital Moroni
Population 876,437 / 1016 people per sq mile (392 people per sq km)
Total area 863 sq miles (2235 sq km)
Languages Arabic*, Comoran*, French*
Religions Sunni Muslim 98%, Other 2%
Demographics Comoran 97%, Other 3%
Government Presidential system
Currency Comoros franc = 100 centimes
Literacy rate 59%
Life expectancy 67 years

CONGO
Central Africa

Page 55 B5

This country straddles the equator in Central Africa. Decades of political instability have restricted growth. Oil accounts for over 90 percent of export values but there is great untapped mineral wealth.

Official name Republic of the Congo
Formation 1960 / 1960
Capital Brazzaville
Population 5.5 million/ 42 people per sq mile (16 people per sq km)
Total area 132,047 sq miles (342,000 sq km)
Languages Kongo, Teke, Lingala, French*
Religions Roman Catholic 34%, Awakening Churches/Christian Revival 22%, Protestant 20%, None 12%, Other 12%
Demographics Kongo 41%, Teke 17%, Mbochi 13%, Sangha 6%, Mbere/Mbeti/Kele 4%, Punu 4%, Other 15%
Government Presidential system
Currency CFA franc = 100 centimes
Literacy rate 80%
Life expectancy 62 years

CONGO, DEM. REP.
Central Africa

Page 55 C6

Straddling the equator in east Central Africa, this mineral-rich country is the second largest in Africa. Years of political instability and conflict have restricted its potential and led to widespread poverty.

Official name Democratic Republic of the Congo
Formation 1960 / 1960
Capital Kinshasa
Population 108.4 million/ 120 people per sq mile (46 people per sq km)
Total area 905,355 sq miles (2,344,858 sq km)
Languages Kiswahili, Tshiluba, Kikongo, Lingala, French*
Religions Roman Catholic 31%, Protestant 28%, Other Christian 37%, Muslim 1%, Other 3%
Demographics Mongo, Luba, Kongo, and Mangbetu-Azande 45%, Other African ethnic groups 55%
Government Semi-Presidential system
Currency Congolese franc = 100 centimes
Literacy rate 77%
Life expectancy 62 years

COSTA RICA
Central America

Page 31 E4

Set in Central America, Costa Rica abolished its army in 1948 in favour of spending on education and welfare. Its pristine forests and many national parks encourage the principles of ecotourism.

Official name Republic of Costa Rica
Formation 1821 / 1941
Capital San José
Population 5.2 million / 264 people per sq mile (102 people per sq km)
Total area 19,730 sq miles (51,100 sq km)
Languages Spanish*, English Creole, Bribri, Cabecar
Religions Roman Catholic 48%, Evangelical and Pentecostal 20%, Jehovah's Witness 1%, Other Protestant 1%, None 27%, Other 3%
Demographics Mixed race and European 96%, Indigenous 3%, Black 1%
Government Presidential system
Currency Costa Rican colón = 100 céntimos
Literacy rate 98%
Life expectancy 80 years

CROATIA
Southeast Europe

Page 78 B2

Croatia emerged from bitter conflict in the 1990s to develop into a stable, democratic society, eventually joining the EU in 2013. It is set on the eastern Adriatic coast and tourism is a key part of the economy.

Official name Republic of Croatia
Formation 1991 / 1991
Capital Zagreb
Population 4.1 million / 188 people per sq mile (72 people per sq km)
Total area 21,851 sq miles (56,594 sq km)
Languages Croatian*
Religions Roman Catholic 84%, Nonreligious 7%, Orthodox Christian 4%, Muslim 2%, Other 3%
Demographics Croat 92%, Serb 4%, Bosniak 1%, Other 3%
Government Parliamentary system
Currency Kuna = 100 lipa
Literacy rate 99%
Life expectancy 77 years

CUBA
West Indies

Page 32 C2

The largest of the Caribbean islands, an archipelago of about 1,600 islands, islets, and cays, Cuba is the only communist state in the Americas. A rich cultural history helps to attract millions of tourists.

Official name Republic of Cuba
Formation 1902 / 1902
Capital Havana
Population 11 million / 257 people per sq mile (99 people per sq km)
Total area 42,803 sq miles (110,860 sq km)
Languages Spanish
Religions Christian 58%, Folk religion 16%, Buddhist 1%, Hindu 1%, Jewish 1%, Muslim 1%, None 22%
Demographics White 65%, Mixed race 25%, Black 10%
Government One-party state
Currency Cuban peso = 100 centavos
Literacy rate 100%
Life expectancy 80 years

CYPRUS
Southeast Europe

Page 80 C5

With a strategic location in the eastern Mediterranean, Cyprus has a rich legacy of antiquities and architecture dating back thousands of years. Shipping and tourism are key economic sectors.

Official name Republic of Cyprus
Formation 1960 / 1960
Capital Nicosia
Population 1.2 million / 336 people per sq mile (130 people per sq km)
Total area 3572 sq miles (9251 sq km)
Languages Greek*, Turkish*, English, Romanian, Russian, Bulgarian, Arabic, Filipino
Religions Orthodox Christian 89%, Roman Catholic 3%, Protestant/Anglican 2%, Muslim 2%, Other 4%
Demographics Greek 99%, Other 1%
Government Presidential system
Currency Euro = 100 cents (In TRNC, Turkish lira = 100 kurus)
Literacy rate 99%
Life expectancy 80 years

CZECHIA
Central Europe

Page 77 A5

Landlocked in Central Europe, and formerly part of Czechoslovakia, this country peacefully dissolved its federal union with Slovakia in 1993. It joined NATO in 1999 and the EU in 2004.

Official name Czech Republic
Formation 1993 / 1993
Capital Prague
Population 10.7 million/ 351 people per sq mile (136 people per sq km)
Total area 30,450 sq miles (78,867 sq km)
Languages Czech*, Slovak, Hungarian
Religions Roman Catholic 9%, Other Christian 2%, Nonreligious 57%, Unspecified 32%
Demographics Czech 57%, Moravian 3%, Unspecified 32%, Other 8%
Government Parliamentary system
Currency Czech koruna = 100 haleru
Literacy rate 99%
Life expectancy 80 years

DENMARK
Northern Europe

Page 63 A7

Denmark occupies the Jutland peninsula at the entrance to the Baltic Sea. In the 1930s, it set up one of the first welfare systems supported by a highly diverse and successful industrial economy.

Official name Kingdom of Denmark
Formation 965 / 1944
Capital Copenhagen
Population 5.9 million / 355 people per sq mile (137 people per sq km)
Total area 16,639 sq miles (43,094 sq km)
Languages Danish*, English, Faroese
Religions Evangelical Lutheran 75%, Muslim 5%, Other 20%,
Demographics Danish 86%, Turkish 1%, Other 13%
Government Parliamentary system
Currency Danish krone = 100 øre
Literacy rate 99%
Life expectancy 82 years

DJIBOUTI
East Africa

Page 50 D4

This city state with a desert hinterland lies on the coast of the Horn of Africa. Its economy relies on its Red Sea container port, which handles 95 percent of seaborne trade for neighboring landlocked Ethiopia.

Official name Republic of Djibouti
Formation 1977 / 1977
Capital Djibouti
Population 957,273 / 107 people per sq mile (41 people per sq km)
Total area 8958 sq miles (23,200 sq km)
Languages Somali, Afar, French*, Arabic*
Religions Muslim (mainly Sunni) 94%, Other 6%
Demographics Somali 60%, Afar 35%, Other 5%
Government Presidential system
Currency Djibouti franc = 100 centimes
Literacy rate 68%
Life expectancy 65 years

DOMINICA
West Indies

Page 33 H4

Known for its lush flora and fauna, this Caribbean island is home to a number of endemic species, notably the Sisserou Parrot. Agriculture, particularly bananas and coffee, and tourism are important.

Official name Commonwealth of Dominica
Formation 1978 / 1978
Capital Roseau
Population 72,170 / 249 people per sq mile (96 people per sq km)
Total area 290 sq miles (751 sq km)
Languages French Creole, English*
Religions Roman Catholic 62%, Protestant 30%, Nonreligious 6%, Other 2%
Demographics African 84%, Mixed 9%, Indigenous 4%, Other 3%
Government Parliamentary system
Currency East Caribbean dollar = 100 cents
Literacy rate 94%
Life expectancy 78 years

DOMINICAN REPUBLIC
West Indies

Page 33 F2

Occupying the eastern part of the island of Hispaniola, the Dominican Republic is the Caribbean's top tourist destination and largest economy. The Pueblo Viejo gold mine is the third largest in the world.

Official name Dominican Republic
Formation 1844 / 1936
Capital Santo Domingo
Population 10.6 million / 564 people per sq mile (218 people per sq km)
Total area 18,792 sq miles (48,670 sq km)
Languages Spanish*, French Creole
Religions Roman Catholic 44%, Evangelical 14%, Protestant 8%, None 29%, Unspecified 2%, Other 3%
Demographics Mixed race 70%, Black 16%, White 13%, Other 1%
Government Presidential system
Currency Dominican Republic peso = 100 centavos
Literacy rate 94%
Life expectancy 73 years

EAST TIMOR (TIMOR-LESTE)
Southeast Asia

Page 116 F5

Set on the eastern part of the island of Timor in the East Indies, this nation emerged from a turbulent transition to gain independence from Indonesia in 2002. Exports are dominated by oil and gas.

Official name Democratic Republic of Timor-Leste
Formation 2002 / 2002
Capital Dili
Population 1.4 million / 244 people per sq mile (94 people per sq km)
Total area 5743 sq miles (14,874 sq km)
Languages Tetum* (Portuguese/Austronesian), Bahasa Indonesia, Portuguese*
Religions Roman Catholic 96%, Protestant/ Evangelical 2%, Muslim 1%, Other 1%
Demographics Papuan groups approx. 85%, Indonesian groups approx. 13%, Chinese 2%
Government Semi-presidential system
Currency US dollar = 100 cents
Literacy rate 58%
Life expectancy 70 years

ECUADOR
South America

Page 38 A2

Once part of the Inca heartland on the northwest coast of South America, Ecuador is the world's leading banana exporter. Its territory includes the wildlife-rich Galápagos Islands.

Official name Republic of Ecuador
Formation 1822 / 1942
Capital Quito
Population 17.2 million / 157 people per sq mile (61 people per sq km)
Total area 109,484 sq miles (283,561 sq km)
Languages Spanish*, Quechua, Other Amerindian languages
Religions Roman Catholic 69%, Evangelical 16%, Adventist 1%, Agnostic or Atheist 2%, None 10%, Other 2%
Demographics Mixed race 79%, Black 7%, Indigenous 7%, White 6%, Other 1%
Government Presidential system
Currency US dollar = 100 cents
Literacy rate 94%
Life expectancy 78 years

EGYPT
North Africa

Page 50 B2

Egypt lies in the northeast corner of Africa, where arid deserts are split by the Nile valley. Vast natural gas reserves, agriculture, and tourism underpin the economy. The Suez Canal is a key global transport link.

Official name Arab Republic of Egypt
Formation 1953 / 2017
Capital Cairo
Population 107.7 million/ 279 people per sq mile (108 people per sq km)
Total area 386,662 sq miles (1,001,450 sq km)
Languages Arabic*, French, English, Berber
Religions Muslim (mainly Sunni) 90%, Coptic Christian 9%, Other Christian 1%
Demographics Egyptian 99%, Other 1%
Government Presidential system
Currency Egyptian pound = 100 piastres
Literacy rate 71%
Life expectancy 74 years

EL SALVADOR
Central America

Page 30 B3

El Salvador is Central America's smallest country. Conservation efforts are ongoing to protect the abundant natural biodiversity, including 1,000 species of butterflies and 400 types of orchid.

Official name Republic of El Salvador
Formation 1821 / 1998
Capital San Salvador
Population 6.5 million / 800 people per sq mile (309 people per sq km)
Total area 8124 sq miles (21,041 sq km)
Languages Spanish*, Nawat
Religions Roman Catholic 50%, Protestant 36%, Nonreligious 12%, Other 2%
Demographics Mixed race 86%, White 13%, Indigenous and other 1%
Government Presidential system
Currency Salvadorean colón = 100 centavos; US dollar = 100 cents
Literacy rate 89%
Life expectancy 75 years

EQUATORIAL GUINEA
Central Africa

Page 55 A5

Equatorial Guinea comprises the Rio Muni mainland in west Central Africa and five islands. Large oil and gas reserves dominate exports and the tropical climate helps to support the rural economy.

Official name Republic of Equatorial Guinea
Formation 1968 / 1968
Capital Malabo
Population 1.6 million / 148 people per sq mile (57 people per sq km)
Total area 10,830 sq miles (28,051 sq km)
Languages Spanish*, Fang, Bubi, French*
Religions Roman Catholic 88%, Protestant 5%, Muslim 2%, Other 5%
Demographics Fang 86%, Bubi 6%, Other 8%
Government Presidential system
Currency CFA franc = 100 centimes
Literacy rate 95%
Life expectancy 64 years

ERITREA
East Africa

Page 50 C4

Eritrea lies on the southern shores of the Red Sea. Gold and copper from the Bisha mine currently account for the majority of export values, while 70 percent of the country's workforce is engaged in agriculture.

Official name State of Eritrea
Formation 1993 / 2002
Capital Asmara
Population 6.2 million / 137 people per sq mile (53 people per sq km)
Total area 45,406 sq miles (117,600 sq km)
Languages Tigrinya*, English*, Tigre, Afar, Arabic*, Saho, Bilen, Kunama, Nara, Hadareb
Religions Christian 50%, Muslim 48%, Other 2%
Demographics Tigrinya 50%, Tigre 30%, Saho 4%, Afar 4%, Kunama 4%, Bilen 3%, Other 5%
Government Presidential system
Currency Nakfa = 100 cents
Literacy rate 77%
Life expectancy 70 years

ESTONIA
Northeast Europe

Page 84 D2

Situated toward the eastern end of the Baltic Sea, Estonia's ancient capital city, Tallinn, is rich in medieval architecture. A fast-growing, high-tech economy has seen numerous successful IT start-ups.

Official name Republic of Estonia
Formation 1991 / 1991
Capital Tallinn
Population 1.2 million/ 69 people per sq mile (27 people per sq km)
Total area 17,463 sq miles (45,228 sq km)
Languages Estonian*, Russian, Ukranian
Religions Nonreligious 45%, Orthodox Christian 25%, Lutheran 20%, Other 10%
Demographics Estonian 70%, Russian 25%, Ukrainian 2%, Belarussian 1%, Other 2%
Government Parliamentary system
Currency Euro = 100 cents
Literacy rate 100%
Life expectancy 78 years

ESWATINI
Southern Africa

Page 56 D4

Formerly known as Swaziland, this small, land-locked kingdom is one of the world's last remaining absolute monarchies. The economy is closely linked to South Africa for the majority of its trade.

Official name Kingdom of Eswatini
Formation 1968 / 1968
Capital Mbabane; Lobamba
Population 1.1 million / 164 people per sq mile (63 people per sq km)
Total area 6704 sq miles (17,364 sq km)
Languages English*, siSwati*, isiZulu, Xitsonga
Religions Christian 90%, Muslim 2%, Other 8%
Demographics Swazi 97%, Other 3%
Government Absolute monarchy
Currency Swazi lilangeni = 100 cents; South African rand = 100 cents
Literacy rate 83%
Life expectancy 58 years

ETHIOPIA
East Africa

Page 51 C5

Landlocked Ethiopia is the largest and most populous country in the Horn of Africa. It was a founding member of the UN. Coffee production and extensive hydro-electric schemes bolster the economy.

Official name Federal Democratic Republic of Ethiopia
Formation 1896 / 2002
Capital Addis Ababa
Population 113 million / 265 people per sq mile (102 people per sq km)
Total area 426,373 sq miles (1,104,300 sq km)
Languages Amharic*, Oromo, Tigrinya, Galla, Sidamo, Somali, English, Arabic
Religions Christian 62%, Muslim 34%, Other 4%
Demographics Oromo 36%, Amhara 24%, Somali 7%, Tigray 6%, Sidama 4%, Guragie 3%, Welaita 2%, Afar 2%, Other 16%
Government Parliamentary system
Currency Birr = 100 santim
Literacy rate 57%
Life expectancy 68 years

FIJI
Australasia & Oceania

Page 123 E5

Fiji is a volcanic archipelago of 882 islands in the southern Pacific Ocean. Abundant natural resources, including minerals, forestry, and fisheries, are supplemented by significant levels of tourism.

Official name Republic of Fiji
Formation 1970 / 1970
Capital Suva
Population 943,737 / 134 people per sq mile (52 people per sq km)
Total area 7056 sq miles (18,274 sq km)
Languages Fijian, English*, Hindi, Urdu, Tamil, Telugu
Religions Methodist 35%, Hindu 28%, Other Christian 21%, Roman Catholic 9%, Muslim 6%, Other and nonreligious 1%
Demographics Melanesian 57%, Indian 38%, Other 5%
Government Parliamentary system
Currency Fiji dollar = 100 cents
Literacy rate 99%
Life expectancy 74 years

FINLAND
Northern Europe

Page 62 D4

A low-lying country of forests and lakes, Finland was the first to adopt full gender equality, granting men and women the right to both vote and stand for election, in 1906. It joined NATO in 2023.

Official name Republic of Finland
Formation 1917 / 1947
Capital Helsinki / Helsingfors
Population 5.6 million / 43 people per sq mile (17 people per sq km)
Total area 130,127 sq miles (338,145 sq km)
Languages Finnish*, Swedish*, Russian
Religions Lutheran 67%, Greek Orthodox 1%, None 30%, Other 2%
Demographics Finnish 93%, Other (including Sámi) 7%
Government Parliamentary system
Currency Euro = 100 cents
Literacy rate 100%
Life expectancy 82 years

FRANCE
Western Europe

Page 68 B4

Straddling Western Europe from the English Channel to the Mediterranean Sea, France was Europe's first modern republic. It is now one of the world's leading industrial powers.

Official name French Republic
Formation 987 / 1947
Capital Paris
Population 68.3 million / 321 people per sq mile (124 people per sq km)
Total area 212,935 sq miles (551,500 sq km)
Languages French*, Provençal, German, Breton, Catalan, Basque
Religions Roman Catholic 47%, Muslim 4%, None 33%, Protestant 2%, Unspecified 9%, Other 5%
Demographics French 86%, Black 10%, German (Alsace) 2%, Breton 1%, Other 1%
Government Presidential / Parliamentary system
Currency Euro = 100 cents
Literacy rate 99%
Life expectancy 83 years

GABON
Central Africa

Page 55 A5

Gabon straddles the Equator on Africa's west coast. 80 percent of its export revenues come from oil, although planning is now underway to diversify the economy as reserves are declining.

Official name Gabonese Republic
Formation 1960 / 1960
Capital Libreville
Population 2.3 million / 22 people per sq mile (9 people per sq km)
Total area 103,347 sq miles (267,667 sq km)
Languages Fang, French*, Punu, Sira, Nzebi, Mpongwe, Bandjabi
Religions Roman Catholic 42%, Protestant 12%, other Christian 27%, Muslim 10%, Animist 1%, None 7%, Other 1%
Demographics Gabonese 80%, Cameroonian 5%, Malian 2%, Beninese 2%, Togolese 2%, Other 9%
Government Presidential system
Currency CFA franc = 100 centimes
Literacy rate 85%
Life expectancy 70 years

GAMBIA, THE
West Africa

Page 52 B3

A narrow state along the Gambia River on Africa's west coast and surrounded by Senegal, Gambia has a warm, tropical climate which supports a mainly rural economy, with the key activity being nut production.

Official name Republic of The Gambia
Formation 1965 / 1965
Capital Banjul
Population 2.4 million / 550 people per sq mile (212 people per sq km)
Total area 4363 sq miles (11,300 sq km)
Languages Mandinka, Fulani, Wolof, Jola, Soninke, English*
Religions Muslim 96%, Christian 3%, Other 1%
Demographics Mandinka/Jahanka 33%, Fulani/Tukulur/Lorobo 18%, Wolof 13%, Jola/Karoninka 11%, Non-Gambian 10%, Other 15%
Government Presidential system
Currency Dalasi = 100 butut
Literacy rate 51%
Life expectancy 68 years

GEORGIA
Southwest Asia

Page 95 F2

Set in the Caucasus on the Black Sea's eastern shore, Georgia is one of the world's oldest wine producers. Efforts are being made to encourage tourism to numerous spas, ski resorts, and historic sites.

Official name Georgia
Formation 1991 / 1991
Capital Tbilisi
Population 4.9 million / 182 people per sq mile (70 people per sq km)
Total area 26,911 sq miles (69,700 sq km)
Languages Georgian*, Russian, Azeri, Armenian, Mingrelian, Ossetian, Abkhazian (* in Abkhazia)
Religions Orthodox Christian 89%, Muslim 9%, Roman Catholic 1%, Other 1%
Demographics Georgian 87%, Azeri 6%, Armenian 4%, Russian 1%, Other 2%
Government Presidential / Parliamentary system
Currency Lari = 100 tetri
Literacy rate 100%
Life expectancy 78 years

GERMANY
Northern Europe

Page 72 B4

At the heart of Europe, Germany is a global economic power. An efficient, diverse, and highly skilled industrial economy is increasingly using renewable energy sources to reduce dependency on fossil fuels.

Official name Federal Republic of Germany
Formation 1871 / 1990
Capital Berlin
Population 84.3 million / 612 people per sq mile (236 people per sq km)
Total area 137,847 sq miles (357,022 sq km)
Languages German*, Turkish
Religions Roman Catholic 27%, Protestant 24%, Muslim 3%, None 41%, Other 5%
Demographics German 86%, Turkish 2%, Polish 1%, Syrian 1%, Romanian 1%, Other 9%
Government Parliamentary system
Currency Euro = 100 cents
Literacy rate 99%
Life expectancy 82 years

GHANA
West Africa

Page 83 A5

Set on the coast of West Africa, Ghana is a major gold producer. Lake Volta is the largest artificial reservoir in the world and provides enough hydro-electricity to allow exports to neighboring countries.

Official name Republic of Ghana
Formation 1957 / 1957
Capital Accra
Population 33.1 million / 359 people per sq mile (139 people per sq km)
Total area 92,098 sq miles (238,533 sq km)
Languages Twi, Fanti, Ewe, Ga, Adangbe, Gurma, Dagomba (Dagbani), English*, Asante
Religions Christian 71%, Muslim 20%, Traditionalist 3%, None 1%, Other 5%
Demographics Akan 46%, Mole-Dagbani 18%, Ewe 13%, Ga-Dangme 7%, Other 16%
Government Presidential system
Currency Cedi = 100 pesewas
Literacy rate 79%
Life expectancy 69 years

GREECE
Southeast Europe

Page 83 A5

Situated at the eastern end of the Mediterranean, Greece has more than 2000 islands. It is rich in culture and historic architecture. Shipping and tourism are key economic drivers.

Official name Hellenic Republic
Formation 1830 / 1947
Capital Athens
Population 10.5 million / 206 people per sq mile (80 people per sq km)
Total area 50,949 sq miles (131,957 sq km)
Languages Greek*, Turkish, Macedonian, Albanian
Religions Orthodox Christian 90%, Nonreligious 4%, Muslim 2%, Other 4%
Demographics Greek 92%, Albanian 4%, Other 4%
Government Parliamentary system
Currency Euro = 100 cents
Literacy rate 98%
Life expectancy 80 years

GRENADA
West Indies

Page 33 G5

Also known as the "Island of Spice", Grenada is the most southerly of the Windward Islands. Historically one of the world's largest nutmeg producers, its main economic resource is now tourism.

Official name Grenada
Formation 1974 / 1974
Capital St. George's
Population 113,949 / 857 people per sq mile (331 people per sq km)
Total area 133 sq miles (344 sq km)
Languages English*, English Creole
Religions Protestant 49%, Roman Catholic 36%, Jehovah's Witness 1%, Rastafarian 1%, None 6%, Unspecified 1%, Other 6%
Demographics African 82%, Mixed 14%, East Indian 2%, Unspecified 1%, Other 1%
Government Parliamentary system
Currency East Caribbean dollar = 100 cents
Literacy rate 99%
Life expectancy 76 years

GUATEMALA
Central America

Page 30 A2

Once the heart of the Mayan civilization on the Central American isthmus, Guatemala has emerged from years of conflict into a thriving democracy. Agricultural products and tourism are key economic sectors.

Official name Republic of Guatemala
Formation 1821 / 1838
Capital Guatemala City
Population 17.7 million / 421 people per sq mile (163 people per sq km)
Total area 42,042 sq miles (108,889 sq km)
Languages Quiché, Mam, Cakchiquel, Kekchí, Spanish*, Maya Languages
Religions Roman Catholic 42%, Evangelical 39%, None 14%, Unspecified 2%, Other 3%
Demographics Mixed race 56%, Maya 42%, Xinca 1%, Other 1%
Government Presidential system
Currency Quetzal = 100 centavos
Literacy rate 81%
Life expectancy 73 years

GUINEA
West Africa

Page 52 C4

Set on the west coast of Africa, Guinea is rich in mineral resources, notably bauxite, with over 25 percent of the world's known reserves. Iron-ore, gold, and diamonds are also valuable exports.

Official name Republic of Guinea
Formation 1958 / 1958
Capital Conakry
Population 13.2 million / 139 people per sq mile (54 people per sq km)
Total area 94,926 sq miles (245,857 sq km)
Languages Pulaar, Malinké, Soussou, French*
Religions Muslim 89%, Christian 7%, Nonreligious 2%, Traditional beliefs and other 2%
Demographics Fulani (Peuhl) 33%, Malinke 30%, Susu 21%, Guerze 8%, Kissi 6%, Other 2%
Government Presidential system
Currency Guinea franc = 100 centimes
Literacy rate 40%
Life expectancy 64 years

GUINEA-BISSAU
West Africa

Page 52 B4

Situated on Africa's west coast, Guinea-Bissau has seen considerable political and military upheaval since independence in 1974. Agricultural products, particularly cashew nuts, are the main exports.

Official name Republic of Guinea-Bissau
Formation 1974 / 1974
Capital Bissau
Population 2 million/ 143 people per sq mile (55 people per sq km)
Total area 13,948 sq miles (36,125 sq km)
Languages Portuguese Creole, Balante, Fulani, Malinké, Portuguese*
Religions Muslim 46%, Folk religions 31%, Christian 19%, Unaffiliated or Other 4%
Demographics Balante 30%, Fulani 30%, Papel 7%, Mandyako 14%, Mandinka 13%, Other 6%
Government Semi-presidential system
Currency CFA franc = 100 centimes
Literacy rate 60%
Life expectancy 64 years

GUYANA
South America

Page 37 F3

A land of rainforest, mountains, coastal plains, and savanna, Guyana is rich in natural resources that make agriculture a key economic activity. Large oil reserves were discovered off the coast in 2015.

Official name Cooperative Republic of Guyana
Formation 1966 / 1966
Capital Georgetown
Population 789,683 / 10 people per sq mile (4 people per sq km)
Total area 83,000 sq miles (214,969 sq km)
Languages English Creole, Hindi, Tamil, Amerindian languages, English*
Religions Protestant 35%, Hindu 25%, Roman Catholic 7%, Muslim 7%, Other Christian 20%, None 3%, Other 3%
Demographics East Indian 40%, African 29%, Mixed race 20%, Indigenous 11%
Government Parliamentary system
Currency Guyanese dollar = 100 cents
Literacy rate 89%
Life expectancy 72 years

HAITI
West Indies

Page 32 D3

Set on the western side of Hispaniola, Haiti has struggled with both political instability and damage caused by natural disasters. It is a leading producer of vetiver, a plant used in perfume manufacturing.

Official name Republic of Haiti
Formation 1804 / 1936
Capital Port-au-Prince
Population 11.3 million / 1055 people per sq mile (407 people per sq km)
Total area 10,714 sq miles (27,750 sq km)
Languages French Creole*, French*
Religions Catholic 55%, Protestant 28%, Vodou 2%, None 10%, Other 5%
Demographics Black 95%, Mixed race 5%
Government Semi-presidential system
Currency Gourde = 100 centimes
Literacy rate 62%
Life expectancy 66 years

HONDURAS
Central America

Page 30 C2

Straddling the Central American isthmus, Honduras returned to civilian rule in 1984, after a series of military regimes. The country is known for its rich natural resources, including minerals, coffee, and sugarcane.

Official name Republic of Honduras
Formation 1821 / 1998
Capital Tegucigalpa
Population 9.4 million / 217 people per sq mile (84 people per sq km)
Total area 43,278 sq miles (112,090 sq km)
Languages Spanish*, Garífuna (Carib), English Creole
Religions Evangelical/Protestant 48%, Roman Catholic 34%, None 17%, Other 1%
Demographics Mixed race 90%, Black 2%, Indigenous 7%, White 1%
Government Presidential system
Currency Lempira = 100 centavos
Literacy rate 89%
Life expectancy 75 years

HUNGARY
Central Europe

Page 77 C6

This landlocked country is home to the largest lake in Central Europe, Lake Balaton. Hungary returned to democratic rule in 1984, after a period of military government, and joined the EU in 2004.

Official name Hungary
Formation 1918 / 1947
Capital Budapest
Population 9.7 million / 270 people per sq mile (104 people per sq km)
Total area 35,922 sq miles (93,038 sq km)
Languages Hungarian* (Magyar), English, German, Russian
Religions Roman Catholic 56%, Nonreligious 21%, Presbyterian 13%, Other 10%
Demographics Magyar 92%, Roma 3%, German 2%, Other 3%
Government Parliamentary system
Currency Forint = 100 fillér
Literacy rate 99%
Life expectancy 77 years

ICELAND
Northwest Europe

Page 61 E4

This northerly island outpost of Europe has stunning, sparsely inhabited volcanic terrain. Although its economy crashed heavily in the 2008 global credit crunch, it is now powered by a tourism and construction boom.

Official name Republic of Iceland
Formation 1944 / 1944
Capital Reykjavík
Population 357,603 / 10 people per sq mile (4 people per sq km)
Total area 39,769 sq miles (103,000 sq km)
Languages Icelandic*, English, Nordic languages
Religions The Evangelical Lutheran Church of Iceland 63%, Other Christian 8%, Nonreligious 7%, Roman Catholic 4%, Other 18%
Demographics Icelandic 81%, Polish 6%, Danish 1%, Other 12%
Government Parliamentary system
Currency Icelandic króna = 100 aurar
Literacy rate 99%
Life expectancy 84 years

INDIA
South Asia

Page 112 D4

The Indian subcontinent, divided from the rest of Asia by the Himalayas, is home to some of the world's most ancient civilizations. India is the world's largest democracy and second most populous country.

Official name Republic of India
Formation 1947 / 2015
Capital New Delhi
Population 1.39 billion / 1095 people per sq mile (423 people per sq km)
Total area 1,269,219 sq miles (3,287,263 sq km)
Languages Hindi*, English*, Urdu, Bengali, Marathi, Telugu, Tamil, Bihari, Gujarati
Religions Hindu 80%, Muslim 14%, Christian 2%, Sikh 2%, Unspecified or Other 2%
Demographics Indo-Aryan 72%, Dravidian 25%, Other 3%
Government Parliamentary system
Currency Indian rupee = 100 paise
LLiteracy rate 74%
Life expectancy 67 years

INDONESIA
Southeast Asia

Page 116 C4

The world's largest archipelago spans over 3,100 miles (5,000 km), from the Indian to the Pacific Ocean. It has Southeast Asia's largest economy and is home to some of the world's most active volcanoes.

Official name Republic of Indonesia
Formation 1945 / 1999
Capital Jakarta
Population 276 million / 375 people per sq mile (145 people per sq km)
Total area 735,358 sq miles (1,904,569 sq km)
Languages Javanese, Sundanese, Madurese, Bahasa Indonesia*, Dutch, English
Religions Sunni Muslim 87%, Protestant 7%, Roman Catholic 3%, Hindu 2%, Buddhist 1%
Demographics Javanese 40%, Sundanese 16%, Malay 4%, Batak 4%, Madurese 3%, Betawi 3%, Minangkabau 3%, Buginese 3%, Other 24%
Government Presidential system
Currency Rupiah = 100 sen
Literacy rate 96%
Life expectancy 73 years

IRAN
Southwest Asia

Page 98 C3

After the 1979 Islamist revolution deposed the Shah, this ethnically diverse Middle Eastern country became the world's largest theocracy. It has large oil and natural gas reserves.

Official name Islamic Republic of Iran
Formation 1979 / 1990
Capital Tehran
Population 86.7 million / 136 people per sq mile (53 people per sq km)
Total area 636,372 sq miles (1,648,195 sq km)
Languages Farsi*, Azeri, Luri, Gilaki, Mazanderani, Kurdish, Turkmen, Arabic, Baluchi
Religions Shi'a Muslim 90%, Sunni Muslim 9%, Other 1%
Demographics Persian 51%, Azari 24%, Lur and Bakhtiari 8%, Kurdish 7%, Other 10%
Government Islamic theocracy
Currency Iranian rial = 100 dinars
Literacy rate 86%
Life expectancy 75 years

IRAQ
Southwest Asia

Page 98 B3

Political instability in this central Middle Eastern country has hindered its economic growth. Rich with natural resources, Iraq notably has the world's second largest oil reserves.

Official name Republic of Iraq
Formation 1932 / 1991
Capital Baghdad
Population 40.4 million / 239 people per sq mile (92 people per sq km)
Total area 169,235 sq miles (438,317 sq km)
Languages Arabic*, Kurdish*, Turkic languages, Armenian, Assyrian
Religions Muslim 97%, Christian 1%, Other 2%
Demographics Arab 80%, Kurdish 15%, Turkmen 3%, Other 2%
Government Parliamentary system
Currency New Iraqi dinar = 1000 fils
Literacy rate 86%
Life expectancy 73 years

IRELAND
Northwest Europe

Page 67 A6

Ireland transformed from a largely agricultural society into a modern, high-technology economy after joining the European Economic Community in 1973. It has a strong indigenous Celtic culture.

Official name Ireland
Formation 1922 / 1922
Capital Dublin
Population 5.2 million / 192 people per sq mile (74 people per sq km)
Total area 27,133 sq miles (70,273 sq km)
Languages English*, Irish*
Religions Roman Catholic 86%, Other Christian 6%, Nonreligious 6%, Muslim 1%, Other 1%
Demographics Irish 86%, Other White 9%, Asian 2%, Black 1%, Other 2%
Government Parliamentary system
Currency Euro = 100 cents
Literacy rate 99%
Life expectancy 82 years

ISRAEL
Southwest Asia

Page 97 A7

Set on the eastern shore of the Mediterranean Sea, Israel has been in conflict with its Arab neighbors since its inception in 1948. It is home to some of the world's most holy religious sites.

Official name State of Israel
Formation 1948 / 1994
Capital Jerusalem (not internationally recognized)
Population 8.9 million / 1051 people per sq mile (406 people per sq km)
Total area 8470 sq miles (21,937 sq km)
Languages Hebrew*, Arabic*, Yiddish, German, Russian, Polish, Romanian, Persian, English
Religions Jewish 74%, Muslim 18%, Christian 2%, Druze 2%, Other 4%
Demographics Jewish 74%, Arab 21%, Other 5%
Government Parliamentary system
Currency Shekel = 100 agorot
Literacy rate 98%
Life expectancy 83 years

ITALY
Southern Europe

Page 74 B3

Jutting into the central Mediterranean, and once at the heart of the Roman Empire, Italy is a world leader in product design, fashion, and textiles, and is renowned for its art, operas, and architecture.

Official name Italian Republic
Formation 1861 / 1954
Capital Rome
Population 61 million/ 524 people per sq mile (202 people per sq km)
Total area 116,348 sq miles (301,340 sq km)
Languages Italian*, German, French, Rhaeto-Romanic, Sardinian, Slovene
Religions Christian 81%, Muslim 5%, Unaffiliated 13%, Other 1%
Demographics Italian 92%, Other European 5%, African 1%, Other 2%
Government Parliamentary system
Currency Euro = 100 cents
Literacy rate 99%
Life expectancy 83 years

IVORY COAST (CÔTE D'IVOIRE)
West Africa

Page 52 D4

One of the larger countries on the West African coast, Ivory Coast is the world's biggest cocoa producer. Two recent conflicts have damaged its previous reputation for stability.

Official name Republic of Côte d'Ivoire
Formation 1960 / 1960
Capital Yamoussoukro
Population 28.7 million / 231 people per sq mile (89 people per sq km)
Total area 124,504 sq miles (322,463 sq km)
Languages Akan, French*, Krou, Voltaïque, Dioula
Religions Muslim 43%, Nonreligious or traditional beliefs 23%, Roman Catholic 17%, Evangelical 12%, Other Christian 4%, Other 1%
Demographics Akan 29%, Voltaique or Gur 16%, Northern Mande 15%, Kru 8%, Southern Mande 7%, Non-Ivoirian 24%, Other 1%
Government Presidential system
Currency CFA franc = 100 centimes
Literacy rate 90%
Life expectancy 62 years

JAMAICA
West Indies

Page 32 C3

Set in the central Caribbean, Jamaica is the birthplace of Rastafarianism. A strong cultural identity includes reggae and ska music, while tourism, agricultural products, and mining are key economic sectors.

Official name Jamaica
Formation 1962 / 1962
Capital Kingston
Population 2.8 million / 660 people per sq mile (255 people per sq km)
Total area 4244 sq miles (10,991 sq km)
Languages English Creole, English*
Religions Church of God 26%, Nonreligious 22%, Other Christian 21%, Seventh-day Adventist 12%, Pentecostal 11%, Other 8%
Demographics Black 92%, Mixed race 6%, East Indian 1%, Other 1%
Government Parliamentary system
Currency Jamaican dollar = 100 cents
Literacy rate 89%
Life expectancy 76 years

JAPAN
East Asia

Page 108 C4

Japan has four main islands and over 3,000 smaller ones. It has the world's third largest economy, led by high-tech industries and vehicle manufacturing. It retains its emperor as head of state.

Official name Japan
Formation 1890 / 1972
Capital Tokyo
Population 124 million / 850 people per sq mile (328 people per sq km)
Total area 145,914 sq miles (377,915 sq km)
Languages Japanese*, Korean, Chinese
Religions Shintoism 71%, Buddhism 67%, Christianity 2%, Other 6%
Demographics Japanese 98%, Chinese and Korean 1%, Other 1%
Government Parliamentary system
Currency Yen = 100 sen
Literacy rate 99%
Life expectancy 85 years

JORDAN
Southwest Asia

Page 97 B6

This Middle Eastern kingdom provides sanctuary to millions of refugees from neighboring conflicts, which has put great strain on the economy. It is rich in ancient culture and architecture.

Official name Hashemite Kingdom of Jordan
Formation 1946 / 1967
Capital Amman
Population 10.9 million / 316 people per sq mile (122 people per sq km)
Total area 34,495 sq miles (89,342 sq km)
Languages Arabic*, English
Religions Muslim 97% (official; predominantly Sunni), Christian 2% , Other 1%
Demographics Jordanian 69%, Syrian 13%, Palestinian 7%, Egyptian 7%, Iraqi 1%, Other 3%
Government Monarchy
Currency Jordanian dinar = 1000 fils
Literacy rate 98%
Life expectancy 76 years

KAZAKHSTAN
Central Asia

Page 92 B4

Kazakhstan was the last of the former Soviet republics to declare independence in 1991. It has a diverse landscape with vast mineral and oil resources, making it the major economic power in the region.

Official name Republic of Kazakhstan
Formation 1991 / 1991
Capital Astana
Population 19.3 million / 18 people per sq mile (7 people per sq km)
Total area 1,052,089 sq miles (2,724,900 sq km)
Languages Kazakh*, Russian, Ukrainian, German, Uzbek, Tatar, Uighur
Religions Muslim (mainly Sunni) 71%, Christian (mainly Orthodox) 26%, Nonreligious 3%
Demographics Kazakh 68%, Russian 19%, Uzbek 3%, Ukrainian 2%, Uighur 2%, Other 6%
Government Presidential system
Currency Tenge = 100 tiyn
Literacy rate 100%
Life expectancy 73 years

KENYA
East Africa

Page 51 C6

Straddling the equator on Africa's east coast, Kenya is famous for its scenic landscapes and vast wildlife reserves. Tea and coffee production, along with tourism, are important economic activities.

Official name Republic of Kenya
Formation 1963 / 1963
Capital Nairobi
Population 55.8 million / 249 people per sq mile (96 people per sq km)
Total area 224,081 sq miles (580,367 sq km)
Languages Kiswahili*, English*, Kikuyu, Luo, Kalenjin, Kamba
Religions Christian 86%, Muslim 11%, Other 3%
Demographics Kikuyu 17%, Luhya 14%, Kalenjin 13%, Luo 11%, Kamba 10%, Somali 6%, Kisii 6%, Mijikenda 5%, Meru 4%, Maasai 3%, Turkana 2%, Non-Kenyan 1%, Other 8%
Government Presidential system
Currency Kenya shilling = 100 cents
Literacy rate 82%
Life expectancy 70 years

KIRIBATI
Australasia & Oceania

Page 123 F3

Home to the South Pacific's largest marine reserve, the 33 low-lying atolls that make up Kiribati are at risk from rising sea levels. The economy is largely dependent on exports of fish products and coconut oil.

Official name Republic of Kiribati
Formation 1979 / 2012
Capital Tarawa Atoll
Population 114,189 / 365 people per sq mile (141 people per sq km)
Total area 313 sq miles (811 sq km)
Languages English*, Kiribati
Religions Roman Catholic 59%, Kiribati Uniting Church 21%, Kiribati Protestant Church 8%, Church of Jesus Christ 6%, Other 6%
Demographics I-Kiribati 95%, Mixed race 3%, Other 2%
Government Presidential system
Currency Australian dollar = 100 cents
Literacy rate 99%
Life expectancy 68 years

KOSOVO
Southeast Europe

Page 79 D5

NATO intervention in 1999 ended the brutal ethnic violence which ultimately led to a unilateral declaration of independence from Serbia in 2008. Forestry, minerals, and agriculture are key to the economy.

Official name Republic of Kosovo
Formation 2008 / 2008
Capital Prishtinë/Priština (Pristina)
Population 1.9 million / 452 people per sq mile (175 people per sq km)
Total area 4203 sq miles (10,887 sq km)
Languages Albanian*, Serbian*, Bosniak, Gorani, Roma, Turkish
Religions Muslim 96%, Roman Catholic 2%, Orthodox 1%, Other 1%
Demographics Albanians 93%, Bosniaks 1%, Serbs 1%, Turk 1%, Other 4%
Government Parliamentary system
Currency Euro = 100 cents
Literacy rate 92%
Life expectancy 71 years

KUWAIT
Southwest Asia

Page 98 C4

Nestled at the top of the Persian Gulf, Kuwait has large oil and gas reserves which have brought great wealth. An Iraqi invasion in 1990 triggered the Gulf War, but a US-led coalition quickly restored the ruling power.

Official name State of Kuwait
Formation 1961 / 1969
Capital Kuwait City
Population 4.1 million / 596 people per sq mile (230 people per sq km)
Total area 6880 sq miles (17,818 sq km)
Languages Arabic*, English
Religions Muslim (official) 75%, Christian 18%, Unspecified or Other 7%
Demographics Kuwaiti 30%, Other Arab 28%, Asian 40%, African 1%, Other 1%
Government Monarchy
Currency Kuwaiti dinar = 1000 fils
Literacy rate 97%
Life expectancy 79 years

KYRGYZSTAN
Central Asia

Page 101 F2

A mountainous landlocked state in Central Asia, Kyrgyzstan has an economy that revolves around agriculture. Gold and minerals are key exports but it relies on imports for most of its energy needs.

Official name Kyrgyz Republic
Formation 1991 / 1991
Capital Bishkek
Population 6 million / 78 people per sq mile (30 people per sq km)
Total area 77,202 sq miles (199,951 sq km)
Languages Kyrgyz*, Russian*, Uzbek, Tatar, Ukrainian
Religions Muslim 90% (majority Sunni), Christian 7%, Other 3%
Demographics Kyrgyz 74%, Uzbek 15%, Russian 5%, Dungan 1%, Other 5%
Government Presidential / Parliamentary system
Currency Som = 100 tyiyn
Literacy rate 100%
Life expectancy 72 years

LAOS
Southeast Asia

Page 114 D4

Landlocked Laos is one of the world's few remaining communist states. A rural economy supports the majority of its people but a huge capacity for hydro-electric power allows net exports of energy.

Official name Lao People's Democratic Republic
Formation 1953 / 1953
Capital Viangchan (Vientiane)
Population 7.7 million / 84 people per sq mile (33 people per sq km)
Total area 91,429 sq miles (236,800 sq km)
Languages Lao*, Mon-Khmer, Yao, Vietnamese, Chinese, French, English
Religions Buddhist 65%, Christian 2%, None 31%, Other 2%
Demographics Lao 53%, Khmou 11%, Hmong 9%, Phouthay 3%, Tai 3%, Makong 3%, Katong 2%, Lue 2%, Akha 2%, Other 12%
Government One-party state
Currency Kip = 100 att
Literacy rate 85%
Life expectancy 68 years

LATVIA
Northeast Europe

Page 84 C3

Situated on the low-lying eastern shores of the Baltic Sea, Latvia has a diverse economy based on agricultural products and manufacturing. It joined both the EU and NATO in 2004.

Official name Republic of Latvia
Formation 1991 / 1991
Capital Riga
Population 1.8 million/ 72 people per sq mile (28 people per sq km)
Total area 24,938 sq miles (64,589 sq km)
Languages Latvian*, Russian
Religions Lutheran 36%, Roman Catholic 19%, Orthodox 19%, Other Christian 2%, Unspecified 24%
Demographics Latvian 63%, Russian 25%, Belarusian 3%, Ukrainian 2%, Polish 2%, Unspecified 2%, Other 3%
Government Parliamentary system
Currency Euro = 100 cents
Literacy rate 100%
Life expectancy 76 years

LEBANON
Southwest Asia

Page 96 A4

Situated in the eastern Mediterranean, Lebanon has served as a busy commercial and cultural hub for centuries. The country had emerged from decades of conflict but recently, instability has returned.

Official name Lebanese Republic
Formation 1943 / 1941
Capital Beirut
Population 5.2 million/ 1728 people per sq mile (662 people per sq km)
Total area 4015 sq miles (10,400 sq km)
Languages Arabic*, French, Armenian, Assyrian, English
Religions Muslim 64%, Christian 31%, Druze 4%, Other 1%
Demographics Arab 95%, Armenian 4%, Other 1%
Government Parliamentary system
Currency Lebanese pound = 100 piastres
Literacy rate 95%
Life expectancy 79 years

LESOTHO
Southern Africa

Page 56 D5

Lesotho lies within South Africa, on whom it is economically dependent as it has limited agricultural capacity. Hydro-electric power and its diamond industry have helped grow the economy.

Official name Kingdom of Lesotho
Formation 1966 / 1966
Capital Maseru
Population 2.2 million / 188 people per sq mile (72 people per sq km)
Total area 11,720 sq miles (30,355 sq km)
Languages English*, Sesotho*, isiZulu, Xhosa
Religions Protestant 48%, Roman Catholic 40%, Other Christian 9%, Non-Christian 1%, None 2%
Demographics Sotho 99%, European and Asian 1%
Government Parliamentary system
Currency Loti = 100 lisente; South African rand = 100 cents
Literacy rate 79%
Life expectancy 60 years

LIBERIA
West Africa

Page 52 C5

Facing the Atlantic Ocean, Liberia is Africa's oldest republic. Ellen Johnson Sirleaf was the first woman to be elected a head of state in Africa when she was voted president in 2005.

Official name Republic of Liberia
Formation 1847 / 1911
Capital Monrovia
Population 5.3 million / 123 people per sq mile (48 people per sq km)
Total area 43,000 sq miles (111,369 sq km)
Languages Kpelle, Vai, Bassa, Kru, Grebo, Kissi, Gola, Loma, English*
Religions Christian 86%, Muslim 12%, Nonreligious 1%, Traditional beliefs and other 1%
Demographics Indigenous tribes (12 groups) 40%, Kpellé 20%, Bassa 14%, Grebo 10%, Gio 8%, Krou 6%, Other 2%
Government Presidential system
Currency Liberian dollar = 100 cents
Literacy rate 48%
Life expectancy 65 years

LIBYA
North Africa

Page 49 F3

Situated on the Mediterranean coast, most of Libya lies in the Sahara Desert. Emphasis on agricultural and industrial developments aims to reduce the country's dependence on oil revenues.

Official name State of Libya
Formation 1951 / 1951
Capital Tripoli
Population 7.1 million / 11 people per sq mile (4 people per sq km)
Total area 679,362 sq miles (1,759,540 sq km)
Languages Arabic*, Tuareg, English, Italian
Religions Muslim 96%, Christian 2%, Other 2%
Demographics Arab and Berber 97%, Other 3%
Government Transitional regime
Currency Libyan dinar = 1000 dirhams
Literacy rate 91%
Life expectancy 77 years

LIECHTENSTEIN
Central Europe

Page 73 B7

Tucked high in the Alps, Liechtenstein's diverse, industrialized economy is dominated by financial services that benefit from its tax-haven status. Switzerland handles its foreign affairs and defense.

Official name Principality of Liechtenstein
Formation 1719 / 1719
Capital Vaduz
Population 38,250 / 617 people per sq mile (239 people per sq km)
Total area 62 sq miles (160 sq km)
Languages German*, Alemannish dialect, Italian, Turkish, Portuguese
Religions Roman Catholic 78%, Protestant 9%, Muslim 6%, Nonreligious 5%, Orthodox Christian 1%, Other 1%
Demographics Liechtensteiner 65%, German 5%, Austrian 6%, Swiss 10%, Italian 3%, Other 11%
Government Monarchy
Currency Swiss franc = 100 rappen/centimes
Literacy rate 100%
Life expectancy 83 years

LITHUANIA
Northeast Europe

Page 84 B4

Mostly low-lying, Lithuania is the largest of the three Baltic states. It was the first former Soviet republic to declare independence in 1990 and went on to join the EU and NATO in 2004.

Official name Republic of Lithuania
Formation 1991 / 2003
Capital Vilnius
Population 2.6 million / 103 people per sq mile (40 people per sq km)
Total area 25,212 sq miles (65,300 sq km)
Languages Lithuanian*, Russian, Polish
Religions Roman Catholic 74%, Russian Orthodox 4%, None 6%, Unspecified 14%, Other 2%
Demographics Lithuanian 85%, Polish 6%, Russian 5%, Belarusian 1%, Other 3%
Government Semi-presidential system
Currency Euro = 100 cents
Literacy rate 100%
Life expectancy 76 years

LUXEMBOURG
Northwest Europe

Page 65 D8

Part of the forested Ardennes plateau in Northwest Europe, Luxembourg is Europe's last independent duchy and one of its richest states. It is a banking center and hosts EU institutions.

Official name Grand Duchy of Luxembourg
Formation 1839 / 1867
Capital Luxembourg
Population 650,364 / 652 people per sq mile (251 people per sq km)
Total area 998 sq miles (2586 sq km)
Languages Luxembourgish*, Portuguese, Italian, German*, French*, English
Religions Christian 71%, Muslim 2%, Unaffiliated 27%
Demographics Luxembourger 53%, Portuguese 15%, French 8%, Italian 4%, Belgian 3%, German 2%, Spanish 1%, Romania 1%, Other 13%
Government Monarchy
Currency Euro = 100 cents
Literacy rate 100%
Life expectancy 83 years

MADAGASCAR
Indian Ocean

Page 79 D6

Off Africa's southeast coast, Madagascar is the world's fourth largest island. An abundance of unique flora and fauna has generated a boom in ecotourism, but economic problems persist.

Official name Republic of Madagascar
Formation 1960 / 1960
Capital Antananarivo
Population 28 million / 124 people per sq mile (48 people per sq km)
Total area 226,658 sq miles (587,042 sq km)
Languages Malagasy*, French*, English*
Religions Traditional beliefs 52%, Christian 41%, Muslim 7%
Demographics Malay 46%, Merina 26%, Betsimisaraka 15%, Betsileo 12%, Other 1%
Government Semi-presidential system
Currency Ariary = 5 iraimbilanja
Literacy rate 77%
Life expectancy 68 years

MALAWI
Southern Africa

Page 57 F4

Landlocked Malawi lies along the Great Rift Valley and Lake Nyasa, Africa's third largest lake. Its rural society depends on the mainly agricultural economy, with tobacco and tea being the principal exports.

Official name Republic of Malawi
Formation 1964 / 1964
Capital Lilongwe
Population 21 million / 459 people per sq mile (177 people per sq km)
Total area 45,746 sq miles (118,484 sq km)
Languages Chewa, Lomwe, Yao, Ngoni, English*
Religions Christian (mainly Protestant) 50%, Other Christian 27%, Muslim 14%, Traditionalist 1%, none 2%, Other 6%
Demographics Chewa 34%, Lomwe 19%, Yao 13%, Ngoni 10%, Tumbuka 9%, Sena 4%, Mang'anja 3%, Tonga 2%, Nyanja 2%, Nkhonde 1%, Other 3%
Government Presidential system
Currency Malawi kwacha = 100 tambala
Literacy rate 62%
Life expectancy 72 years

MALAYSIA
Southeast Asia

Page 57 E1

Spread across two separate regions, Malaysia has built upon its abundant natural resources to create a diverse industrialized economy. Its rich biodiversity attracts huge numbers of tourists.

Official name Malaysia
Formation 1957 / 1965
Capital Kuala Lumpur; Putrajaya (administrative)
Population 33.1 million / 259 people per sq mile (100 people per sq km)
Total area 127,723 sq miles (330,803 sq km)
Languages Bahasa Malaysia*, Malay, Chinese, Tamil, English
Religions Muslim (mainly Sunni) 61%, Buddhist 20%, Christian 9%, Hindu 6%, Other 3%
Demographics Malay 50%, Chinese 22%, Indigenous tribes 12%, Indian 7%, Other 9%
Government Parliamentary system
Currency Ringgit = 100 sen
Literacy rate 95%
Life expectancy 76 years

MALTA
Southern Europe

Page 53 E2

A central Mediterranean location has made Malta an important strategic port throughout history. Financial services underpin the economy and the warm climate attracts large numbers of tourists.

Official name Republic of Malta
Formation 1964 / 1964
Capital Valletta
Population 464,186/ 4252 people per sq mile (1615 people per sq km)
Total area 122 sq miles (316 sq km)
Languages Maltese*, English*
Religions Roman Catholic 98%, Nonreligious and other 2%
Demographics Maltese 96%, Other 4%
Government Parliamentary system
Currency Euro = 100 cents
Literacy rate 95%
Life expectancy 83 years

MAURITIUS
Indian Ocean

Page 52 C2

This Indian Ocean archipelago has one of Africa's highest per capita incomes. Once dependent on sugar exports, the country now has a diverse economy that includes luxury tourism and financial services.

Official name Republic of Mauritius
Formation 1968 / 1968
Capital Port Louis
Population 1.3 million / 1616 people per sq mile (624 people per sq km)
Total area 787 sq miles (2040 sq km)
Languages French Creole, Hindi, Urdu, Tamil, Chinese, English*, French
Religions Hindu 48%, Roman Catholic 26%, Muslim 17%, Other Christian 7%, Other 2%
Demographics Indo-Mauritian 68%, Creole 27%, Sino-Mauritian 3%, Franco-Mauritian 2%
Government Parliamentary system
Currency Mauritian rupee = 100 cents
Literacy rate 91%
Life expectancy 75 years

MOLDOVA
Southeast Europe

Page 122 B1

The smallest of the ex-Soviet republics, Moldova has strong linguistic and cultural ties with its neighbor, Romania. Although it exports tobacco, wine, and fruit, the service sector drives the economy.

Official name Republic of Moldova
Formation 1991 / 1991
Capital Chisinau
Population 3.2 million / 245 people per sq mile (95 people per sq km)
Total area 13,069 sq miles (33,851 sq km)
Languages Moldovan*, Ukrainian, Russian
Religions Orthodox Christian 90%, Nonreligious 2%, Other 8%
Demographics Moldovan 75%, Ukrainian 7%, Russian 4%, Gagauz 5%, Romanian 7%, Bulgarian 2%, Other 1%
Government Parliamentary system
Currency Moldovan leu = 100 bani
Literacy rate 99%
Life expectancy 72 years

MALDIVES
Indian Ocean

Page 116 B3

This low-lying group of over 1,000 coral islands in the Indian Ocean is vulnerable to rising sea levels. Idyllic tropical beaches and reefs have boosted growth in luxury tourism.

Official name Republic of Maldives
Formation 1965 / 1965
Capital Maale (Male')
Population 390,164 / 4667 people per sq mile (1812 people per sq km)
Total area 120 sq miles (300 sq km)
Languages Dhivehi* (Maldivian), Sinhala, Tamil, Arabic, English
Religions Sunni Muslim 94%, Hindu 3%, Christian 2%, Buddhist 1%
Demographics Arab-Sinhalese-Malay 100%
Government Presidential system
Currency Rufiyaa = 100 laari
Literacy rate 98%
Life expectancy 77 years

MARSHALL ISLANDS
Australasia & Oceania

Page 80 A5

This group of 34 low-lying coral atolls is spread across a vast area of the Pacific Ocean. The nation was the first to try to make cryptocurrency legal tender by launching the "Sovereign" in 2018.

Official name Republic of the Marshall Islands
Formation 1986 / 1986
Capital Majuro Atoll
Population 59,620 / 852 people per sq mile (329 people per sq km)
Total area 70 sq miles (181 sq km)
Languages Marshallese*, English*, Japanese, German
Religions Protestant 81%, Roman Catholic 8%, Other 11%
Demographics Micronesian 90%, Other 10%
Government Presidential system
Currency US dollar = 100 cents
Literacy rate 98%
Life expectancy 75 years

MEXICO
North America

Page 57 H3

The third largest country in Latin America, Mexico is a major oil exporter but still suffers from social inequality. The highly diversified industrial economy is the second largest in Latin America.

Official name United Mexican States
Formation 1821 / 1848
Capital Mexico City
Population 130 million / 171 people per sq mile (66 people per sq km)
Total area 758,449 sq miles (1,964,375 sq km)
Languages Spanish*, Nahuatl, Mayan, Zapotec, Mixtec, Otomi, Totonac, Tzotzil, Tzeltal
Religions Roman Catholic 78%, Protestant 11%, Nonreligious 11%, Other 1%
Demographics Mixed race 62%, Indigenous 21%, Other 10%
Government Presidential system
Currency Mexican peso = 100 centavos
Literacy rate 95%
Life expectancy 72 years

MONACO
Southern Europe

Page 86 D3

This tiny enclave on France's Côte d'Azur has built a thriving financial services and banking sector based on its tax-haven status. It is famous for its expensive property and jet-set lifestyle.

Official name Principality of Monaco
Formation 1419 / 1861
Capital Monaco
Population 39,520 / 50,145 people per sq mile (19,497 people per sq km)
Total area 0.77 sq miles (2 sq km)
Languages French*, Italian, Monégasque, English
Religions Roman Catholic 89%, Protestant 6%, Other 5%
Demographics French 20%, Italian 15%, Monégasque 32%, British 5%, Belgian 2%, Swiss 2%, German 2%, Russian 2%, American 1%, Dutch 1%, Moroccan 1%, Other 17%
Government Monarchical / parliamentary system
Currency Euro = 100 cents
Literacy rate 99%
Life expectancy 90 years

MALI
West Africa

Page 110 A4

Once at the heart of a trans-Saharan trading empire, Mali is geographically dominated by the Sahara Desert. Mining activities yield a third of Africa's gold production while cotton is the main agricultural export.

Official name Republic of Mali
Formation 1960 / 1986
Capital Bamako
Population 20.7 million / 43 people per sq mile (17 people per sq km)
Total area 478,840 sq miles (1,240,192 sq km)
Languages Bambara, Fulani, Senufo, Soninke, French*
Religions Muslim (mainly Sunni) 93%, Traditional beliefs 6%, Christian 4%
Demographics Bambara 33%, Fulani 13%, Sarakole/ Soninke/Marka 10%, Senufo/Manianka 10%, Malinke 9%, Dogon 9%, Sonrai 6%, Other 10%
Government Presidential system
Currency CFA franc = 100 centimes
Literacy rate 36%
Life expectancy 62 years

MAURITANIA
West Africa

Page 122 D1

Mauritania is one of Africa's newest oil producers. Four-fifths of its area lies within the Sahara Desert. Extensive mineral deposits and rich fishing grounds in the Atlantic Ocean are key economic contributors.

Official name Islamic Republic of Mauritania
Formation 1960 / 1960
Capital Nouakchott
Population 4.1 million / 13 people per sq mile (5 people per sq km)
Total area 397,953 sq miles (1,030,700 sq km)
Languages Arabic*, Hassaniyah Arabic, Wolof, Pular, Soninke, French
Religions Sunni Muslim 100%
Demographics Maure 81%, Wolof 7%, Tukolor 5%, Soninka 3%, Other 4%
Government Presidential system
Currency Ouguiya = 5 khoums
Literacy rate 52%
Life expectancy 65 years

MICRONESIA
Australasia & Oceania

Page 28 D3

The Federated States of Micronesia, situated in the western Pacific, comprises 607 islands and atolls. Exports are almost entirely made up of fish products with some tourism, mainly recreational diving.

Official name Federated States of Micronesia
Formation 1986 / 1986
Capital Palikir (Pohnpei Island)
Population 101,009 / 373 people per sq mile (144 people per sq km)
Total area 271 sq miles (702 sq km)
Languages English, Chuukese, Kosraean, Pohnpeian, Yapese, Ulithian, Woleaian, Nukuoro, Kapingamarangi
Religions Roman Catholic 55%, Protestant 41%, Nonreligious 1%, Other 3%
Demographics Chuukese 49%, Pohnpeian 30%, Kosraean 6%, Yapese 5%, Asian 2%, Other 14%
Government Nonparty system
Currency US dollar = 100 cents
Literacy rate 72%
Life expectancy 74 years

MONGOLIA
East Asia

Page 69 E6

Once the center of the Mongol empire, Mongolia is a sparsely populated, landlocked country on the edge of the Gobi Desert. Huge mineral resources have attracted foreign investment.

Official name Mongolia
Formation 1921 / 1924
Capital Ulaanbaatar
Population 3.3 million / 5 people per sq mile (2 people per sq km)
Total area 603,908 sq miles (1,564,116 sq km)
Languages Khalkha Mongolian*, Kazakh, Chinese, Russian
Religions Tibetan Buddhist 52%, Nonreligious 41%, Muslim 4%, Shamanist 2%, Christian 1%, Other 1%
Demographics Khalkh 84%, Kazakh 4%, Dorvod 3%, Bayad 2%, Other 4%
Government Presidential / Parliamentary system
Currency Tugrik (tögrög) = 100 möngo
Literacy rate 99%
Life expectancy 71 years

MONTENEGRO
Southeast Europe

Page 104 D2

The complex history of this region of SE Europe eventually led to Montenegro declaring independence from Serbia in 2006. The Tara River canyon here is the deepest and longest in Europe.

Official name Montenegro
Formation 2006 / 2006
Capital Podgorica
Population 604,966 / 113 people per sq mile (44 people per sq km)
Total area 5332 sq miles (13,812 sq km)
Languages Montenegrin*, Serbian, Albanian, Bosnian, Croatian
Religions Orthodox Christian 74%, Muslim 20%, Roman Catholic 4%, Nonreligious 1%, Other 1%
Demographics Montenegrin 45%, Serb 29%, Bosniak 9%, Albanian 5%, Other 12%
Government Parliamentary system
Currency Euro = 100 cents
Literacy rate 99%
Life expectancy 78 years

MOROCCO
North Africa

Page 79 C5

The mountainous country of Morocco sits on the northwest African coast. Its rich history and culture attract large numbers of tourists. Recent moves have been made to tap the huge solar energy potential.

Official name Kingdom of Morocco
Formation 1956 / 1969
Capital Rabat
Population 36.7 million / 133 people per sq mile (51 people per sq km)
Total area 276,661 sq miles (716,550 sq km)
Languages Arabic*, Tamazight* (Berber), French, Spanish
Religions Muslim (mainly Sunni) 99%, Other 1%
Demographics Arab 70%, Berber 29%, European 1%
Government Monarchical / parliamentary system
Currency Moroccan dirham = 100 centimes
Literacy rate 74%
Life expectancy 74 years

MOZAMBIQUE
Southern Africa

Page 48 C2

Mozambique, on the southeast African coast, is rich in natural resources but remains underdeveloped. The discovery of gas fields off its coast in 2011 has the potential to transform the economy.

Official name Republic of Mozambique
Formation 1975 / 1975
Capital Maputo
Population 31.6 million / 102 people per sq mile (40 people per sq km)
Total area 308,642 sq miles (799,380 sq km)
Languages Makua, Xitsonga, Sena, Nyanja, Chuwabo, Ndau, Tswa, Lomwe, Portuguese*
Religions Roman Catholic 27%, Muslim 19%, Christian 16%, Evangelical/Pentecostal 15%, None 14%, Other 9%
Demographics Makua Lomwe 47%, Tsonga 23%, Malawi 12%, Shona 11%, Yao 4%, Other 3%
Government Presidential system
Currency New metical = 100 centavos
Literacy rate 61%
Life expectancy 57 years

MYANMAR (BURMA)
Southeast Asia

Page 57 E3

Myanmar, set on the Bay of Bengal, underwent gradual liberalization after 2010 before the civilian government was overthrown in a coup in 2021. The rural economy is dominated by rice production.

Official name Republic of the Union of Myanmar
Formation 1948 / 1948
Capital Nay Pyi Taw
Population 57.5 million / 220 people per sq mile (85 people per sq km)
Total area 261,228 sq miles (676,578 sq km)
Languages Burmese* (Myanmar), Shan, Karen, Rakhine, Chin, Yangbye, Kachin, Mon
Religions Buddhist 88%, Christian 6%, Muslim 4%, Animist 1%, Other 1%
Demographics Burman (Bamah) 68%, Chinese 3%, Shan 9%, Karen 7%, Rakhine 4%, Indian 2%, Mon 2%, Other 5%
Government Parliamentary system
Currency Kyat = 100 pyas
Literacy rate 89%
Life expectancy 70 years

NAMIBIA
Southern Africa

Page 114 A3

On Africa's southwest coast, this large and sparsely populated country is dominated geographically by the Namib Desert. It is rich in minerals, particularly uranium, and is a significant diamond producer.

Official name Republic of Namibia
Formation 1990 / 1994
Capital Windhoek
Population 2.7 million / 8 people per sq mile (3 people per sq km)
Total area 318,260 sq miles (824,292 sq km)
Languages Ovambo, Kavango, English*, Bergdama, German, Afrikaans
Religions Christian 98%, Traditional beliefs 2%
Demographics Ovambo 50%, Other tribes 22%, Kavango 9%, Herero 7%, Damara 7%, Other 5%
Government Presidential system
Currency Namibian dollar = 100 cents; South African rand = 100 cents
Literacy rate 92%
Life expectancy 66 years

NAURU
Australasia & Oceania

Page 56 B3

This small island nation sits in the Pacific Ocean. It was once dependent on phosphate mining, until viable deposits ran out in the 1980s, causing an economic crisis from which it is only just starting to recover.

Official name Republic of Nauru
Formation 1968 / 1968
Capital None (Yaren de facto capital)
Population 10,870 / 1359 people per sq mile (518 people per sq km)
Total area 8 sq miles (21 sq km)
Languages Nauruan*, Kiribati, Chinese, Tuvaluan, English
Religions Nauruan Congregational Church 60%, Roman Catholic 35%, Other 5%
Demographics Nauruan 93%, Chinese 5%, Other Pacific islanders 1%, European 1%
Government Parliamentary system
Currency Australian dollar = 100 cents
Literacy rate 95%
Life expectancy 68 years

NEPAL
South Asia

Page 122 D3

Nestled in the Himalayas, Nepal is home to eight of the world's highest mountains including Mount Everest, known locally as Sagarmatha. Its rural economy is boosted by a rapid growth in tourism.

Official name Nepal
Formation 1768 / 1768
Capital Kathmandu
Population 30 million / 528 people per sq mile (204 people per sq km)
Total area 56,826 sq miles (147,181 sq km)
Languages Nepali*, Maithili, Bhojpuri
Religions Hindu 81%, Buddhist 9%, Muslim 4%, Other 5%
Demographics Chhetri 17%, Hill Brahman 12%, Magar 7%, Tharu 7%, Tamang 6%, Newar 5%, Kami 5%, Muslim 4%, Yadav 4%, Other 33%
Government Parliamentary system
Currency Nepalese rupee = 100 paisa
Literacy rate 68%
Life expectancy 72 years

NETHERLANDS
Northwest Europe

Page 113 E3

Astride the delta of four major rivers, this low-lying nation (a quarter of its land is below sea-level) is one of the world's foremost maritime trading nations with Rotterdam being Europe's largest port.

Official name Kingdom of the Netherlands
Formation 1648 / 1839
Capital Amsterdam; The Hague (administrative)
Population 17.4 million / 1085 people per sq mile (419 people per sq km)
Total area 16,039 sq miles (41,543 sq km)
Languages Dutch*, Frisian
Religions Roman Catholic 20%, Protestant 15%, Muslim 5%, None 54%, Other 6%
Demographics Dutch 82%, Surinamese 2%, Turkish 2%, Moroccan 2%, Other 12%
Government Parliamentary system
Currency Euro = 100 cents
Literacy rate 99%
Life expectancy 82 years

NEW ZEALAND
Australasia & Oceania

Page 64 C3

This progressive nation on the southwest Pacific rim was the first in the world to give women the vote, in 1893. The high-tech economy is heavily reliant on international trade, particularly in agricultural products.

Official name New Zealand
Formation 1907 / 1947
Capital Wellington
Population 5 million / 48 people per sq mile (19 people per sq km)
Total area 103,798 sq miles (268,838 sq km)
Languages English*, Maori*
Religions Nonreligious 48%, Christian 15%, Anglican 7%, Roman Catholic 10%, Presbyterian 5%, Other 8%
Demographics European 64%, Maori 17%, Chinese 5%, Samoan 4%, Other 14%
Government Parliamentary system
Currency New Zealand dollar = 100 cents
Literacy rate 99%
Life expectancy 83 years

NICARAGUA
Central America

Page 128 A4

Nicaragua, at the heart of Central America, has traditionally relied on agricultural exports to sustain its economy. Its lush rainforests and spectacular scenery are attracting a large growth in ecotourism.

Official name Republic of Nicaragua
Formation 1821 / 1838
Capital Managua
Population 6.3 million / 125 people per sq mile (48 people per sq km)
Total area 50,336 sq miles (130,370 sq km)
Languages Spanish*, English Creole, Miskito
Religions Roman Catholic 50%, Protestant 33%, Nonreligious 1%, Other 16%
Demographics Mixed race 69%, White 17%, Black 9%, Indigenous 5%
Government Presidential system
Currency Córdoba oro = 100 centavos
Literacy rate 83%
Life expectancy 75 years

NIGER
West Africa

Page 30 D3

A vast, arid state on the edge of the Sahara Desert, landlocked Niger is linked to the sea by the Niger River. It is focusing on increased oil exploration and gold mining to help modernize its economy.

Official name Republic of Niger
Formation 1960 / 2016
Capital Niamey
Population 24.4 million / 50 people per sq mile (19 people per sq km)
Total area 489,188 sq miles (1,267,000 sq km)
Languages Hausa, Djerma, Fulani, Tuareg, Teda, French*
Religions Muslim 99%, Other 1%
Demographics Hausa 53%, Djerma and Songhai 21%, Tuareg 11%, Peul 7%, Kanuri 6%, Other 1%
Government Semi-presidential system
Currency CFA franc = 100 centimes
Literacy rate 35%
Life expectancy 60 years

NIGERIA
West Africa

Page 53 G3

Nigeria has both the largest population and economy in Africa. The Niger Delta holds some of the world's largest proven oil and gas reserves. The cinema industry is one of the largest film producers in the world.

Official name Federal Republic of Nigeria
Formation 1960 / 2006
Capital Abuja
Population 211 million / 592 people per sq mile (228 people per sq km)
Total area 356,667 sq miles (923,768 sq km)
Languages Hausa, English*, Yoruba, Ibo
Religions Muslim 54%, Christian 45%, Traditional beliefs 1%
Demographics Hausa 30%, Yoruba 16%, Ibo 15%, Fulani 6%, Tiv 2%, Kanuri/Beriberi 2%, Ibibio 2%, Ijaw/Izon 2% Other 25%
Government Presidential system
Currency Naira = 100 kobo
Literacy rate 62%
Life expectancy 61 years

NORTH KOREA
East Asia

Page 53 G4

The communist state in Korea's northern half has been largely isolated from the outside world since 1948. The capital and largest city of the country, P'yŏngyang, is a major industrial and transport center.

Official name Democratic People's Republic of Korea
Formation 1945 / 1953
Capital Pyongyang
Population 25.9 million / 557 people per sq mile (215 people per sq km)
Total area 46,539 sq miles (120,538 sq km)
Languages Korean*
Religions Atheist 100%
Demographics Korean 100%
Government One-party state
Currency North Korean won = 100 chon
Literacy rate 100%
Life expectancy 72 years

NORTH MACEDONIA
Southeast Europe

Page 106 E3

Landlocked in the southern Balkans, this state changed its name to North Macedonia in 2019 to settle a long-standing dispute with neighboring Greece and pave the way for EU and NATO candidacy.

Official name Republic of North Macedonia
Formation 1991 / 1991
Capital Skopje
Population 2.1 million / 212 people per sq mile (82 people per sq km)
Total area 9928 sq miles (25,713 sq km)
Languages Macedonian*, Albanian*, Turkish, Romani, Serbian
Religions Orthodox Christian 65%, Muslim 33%, Other 2%
Demographics Macedonian 64%, Albanian 25%, Turkish 4%, Roma 3%, Serb 2%, Other 2%
Government Parliamentary system
Currency Macedonian denar = 100 deni
Literacy rate 98%
Life expectancy 77%

NORWAY
Northern Europe

Page 63 A5

Norway lies on the rugged western coast of Scandinavia, and most people live in southern, coastal areas. Extensive oil and gas reserves give it one of the world's highest standards of living.

Official name Kingdom of Norway
Formation 1905 / 1905
Capital Oslo
Population 5.5 million / 44 people per sq mile (17 people per sq km)
Total area 125,020 sq miles (323,802 sq km)
Languages Norwegian* (Bokmål "book language" and Nynorsk "new Norsk"), Sámi
Religions Evangelical Lutheran 68%, Roman Catholic 3%, Other Christian 4%, Muslim 3%, Unspecified 20%, Other 2%
Demographics Norwegian 81%, Other European 19%
Government Parliamentary system
Currency Norwegian krone = 100 øre
Literacy rate 99%
Life expectancy 83 years

OMAN
Southwest Asia

Page 99 D6

Situated on the eastern corner of the Arabian Peninsula, Oman is the oldest independent state in the Arab world. Oil was discovered here in 1964 and oil and gas products still dominate the economy.

Official name Sultanate of Oman
Formation 1650 / 1955
Capital Muscat
Population 3.7 million / 31 people per sq mile (12 people per sq km)
Total area 119,498 sq miles (309,500 sq km)
Languages Arabic*, Baluchi, Farsi, Hindi, Punjabi
Religions Ibadi Muslim 86%, Other 14%
Demographics Arab 88%, Baluchi 4%, Indian and Pakistani 3%, Persian 3%, African 2%
Government Monarchy
Currency Omani rial = 1000 baisa
Literacy rate 96%
Life expectancy 77 years

PAKISTAN
South Asia

Page 112 B2

Pakistan was created as a Muslim state out of the partition of the Indian sub-continent in 1947. The service sector dominates the economy with burgeoning information technology and internet use.

Official name Islamic Republic of Pakistan
Formation 1947 / 1971
Capital Islamabad
Population 225 million / 732 people per sq mile (283 people per sq km)
Total area 307,373 sq miles (796,095 sq km)
Languages Punjabi, Sindhi, Pashtu, Urdu*, Baluchi, Brahui
Religions Sunni Muslim 77%, Shi'a Muslim 20%, Hindu 2%, Christian 1%
Demographics Punjabi 45%, Pathan (Pashtun) 15%, Sindhi 14%, Mohajir 8%, Baluchi 4%, Other 18%
Government Parliamentary system
Currency Pakistani rupee = 100 paisa
Literacy rate 58%
Life expectancy 70 years

PALAU
Australasia & Oceania

Page 122 A2

This archipelago of over 200 volcanic and coral islands, only ten of which are inhabited, lies in the western Pacific Ocean. The economy relies on fisheries and sustainable tourism.

Official name Republic of Palau
Formation 1994 / 1994
Capital Ngerulmud
Population 18,170 / 103 people per sq mile (40 people per sq km)
Total area 177 sq miles (459 sq km)
Languages Palauan*, English*, Japanese, Angaur, Tobi, Sonsorolese
Religions Roman Catholic 45%, Protestant 35%, Modekngei 6%, Muslim 3%, Other 11%
Demographics Palauan 73%, Filipino 16%, Other Asian 7%, Other Micronesian 3%, Other 2%
Government Nonparty system
Currency US dollar = 100 cents
Literacy rate 97%
Life expectancy 75 years

PANAMA
Central America

Page 31 F5

The southernmost country in Central America, Panama is rich in biodiversity. The Panama Canal, a vital shortcut for shipping between the Atlantic and Pacific oceans, is an important economic contributor.

Official name Republic of Panama
Formation 1903 / 1941
Capital Panama City
Population 4.3 million / 148 people per sq mile (57 people per sq km)
Total area 29,119 sq miles (75,420 sq km)
Languages English Creole, Spanish*, Amerindian languages, Chibchan languages
Religions Roman Catholic 49%, Protestant 30%, Nonreligious 12%, Other 9%
Demographics Mixed race 71%, Black 9%, White 7%, Indigenous 12%, Other 1%
Government Presidential system
Currency Balboa = 100 centésimos; US dollar
Literacy rate 96%
Life expectancy 78 years

PAPUA NEW GUINEA
Australasia & Oceania

Page 122 B3

The world's most linguistically diverse country, mineral-rich PNG occupies the east of the island of New Guinea and several other island groups. Most people make their livelihood from agriculture.

Official name Independent State of Papua New Guinea
Formation 1975 / 1975
Capital Port Moresby
Population 9.5 million / 53 people per sq mile (21 people per sq km)
Total area 178,703 sq miles (462,840 sq km)
Languages Pidgin English, Papuan, English*, Motu, 800 (est.) native languages
Religions Protestant 64%, Roman Catholic 26%, Other 9%
Demographics Melanesian and mixed race 100%
Government Parliamentary system
Currency Kina = 100 toea
Literacy rate 64%
Life expectancy 69 years

PARAGUAY
South America

Page 42 D2

South America's longest dictatorship held power in landlocked Paraguay from 1954 to 1989. Now under democratic government, the country's economy is reliant on agriculture and hydro-electric power.

Official name Republic of Paraguay
Formation 1811 / 1938
Capital Asunción
Population 7.3 million / 46 people per sq mile (18 people per sq km)
Total area 157,047 sq miles (406,752 sq km)
Languages Guaraní*, Spanish*, German
Religions Roman Catholic 90%, Protestant 6%, Other Christian 1%, Other 3%
Demographics Mixed race 95%, Other 5%
Government Presidential system
Currency Guaraní = 100 céntimos
Literacy rate 95%
Life expectancy 78 years

PERU
South America

Page 38 C3

On the Pacific coast of South America, Peru was once the heart of the Inca empire. The country is home to Lake Titicaca, the world's highest navigable lake. Mineral wealth drives the economy.

Official name Republic of Peru
Formation 1821 / 1941
Capital Lima
Population 32.2 million / 65 people per sq mile (25 people per sq km)
Total area 496,224 sq miles (1,285,216 sq km)
Languages Spanish*, Quechua*, Aymara
Religions Roman Catholic 60%, Protestant 15%, Nonreligious 4%, Other 21%
Demographics Indigenous 26%, Mixed race 60%, White 6%, Black 4%, Other 4%
Government Presidential system
Currency New sol = 100 céntimos
Literacy rate 95%
Life expectancy 69 years

PHILIPPINES
Southeast Asia

Page 117 E1

This 7,500-island archipelago between the South China Sea and the Pacific is prone to earthquakes and volcanic activity. Founded in 1611, the University of Santo Tomas in Manila is the oldest in Asia.

Official name Republic of the Philippines
Formation 1946 / 1946
Capital Manila
Population 114 million / 984 people per sq mile (380 people per sq km)
Total area 115,830 sq miles (300,000 sq km)
Languages Filipino*, English*, Tagalog, Cebuano, Ilocano, Hiligaynon, many other local languages
Religions Roman Catholic 80%, Other Christian 6%, Muslim 6%, Other 8%
Demographics Tagalog 24%, Cebuano 10%, Ilocano 9%, Hiligaynon 8%, Bisaya 11%, Bikol 7%, Waray 4%, Other 27%
Government Presidential system
Currency Philippine peso = 100 centavos
Literacy rate 96%
Life expectancy 70 years

POLAND
Northern Europe

Page 76 B3

Extending from the Baltic Sea into the heart of Europe, Poland has a diverse, industrialized economy which supports an extensive health, education, and welfare system. It joined NATO in 1999 and the EU in 2004.

Official name Republic of Poland
Formation 1918 / 1945
Capital Warsaw
Population 38 million / 315 people per sq mile (122 people per sq km)
Total area 120,728 sq miles (312,685 sq km)
Languages Polish*, Silesian
Religions Roman Catholic 85%, Orthodox Christian 1%, Protestant 1%, Other 13%
Demographics Polish 97%, Silesian 1%, Other 2%
Government Parliamentary system
Currency Zloty = 100 groszy
Literacy rate 100%
Life expectancy 79 years

PORTUGAL
Southwest Europe

Page 70 B3

Portugal, on the Iberian Peninsula, is the westernmost country in mainland Europe. A highly developed, diverse economy is supported by a sizeable tourist industry with over 20 million visitors a year.

Official name Portuguese Republic
Formation 1143 / 1640
Capital Lisbon
Population 10.2 million / 287 people per sq mile (111 people per sq km)
Total area 35,556 sq miles (92,090 sq km)
Languages Portuguese*, Mirandese
Religions Roman Catholic 81%, Nonreligious 7%, Other Christian 3%, Unspecified 8%, Other 1%
Demographics Portuguese 95%, Other 5%
Government Parliamentary system
Currency Euro = 100 cents
Literacy rate 96%
Life expectancy 82 years

QATAR
Southwest Asia

Page 98 C4

Projecting north from the Arabian Peninsula into the Persian Gulf, Qatar is mostly flat, semiarid desert. Massive reserves of oil and gas have made it one of the world's wealthiest states.

Official name State of Qatar
Formation 1971 / 2001
Capital Doha
Population 2.5 million / 559 people per sq mile (216 people per sq km)
Total area 4473 sq miles (11,586 sq km)
Languages Arabic*
Religions Muslim (mainly Sunni) 65%, Christian 14%, Other 14%
Demographics Qatari 12%, Other Arab 20%, Indian 20%, Nepalese 13%, Filipino 10%, Pakistani 7%, Other 10%
Government Monarchy
Currency Qatar riyal = 100 dirhams
Literacy rate 94%
Life expectancy 80 years

ROMANIA
Southeast Europe

Page 86 B4

Romania lies on the western shores of the Black Sea. Reforms have allowed a diverse, high-tech economy to develop with an emphasis on electronics and vehicle manufacturing. It joined the EU in 2007.

Official name Romania
Formation 1878 / 2009
Capital Bucharest
Population 18.5 million / 201 people per sq mile (78 people per sq km)
Total area 92,043 sq miles (238,391 sq km)
Languages Romanian*, Hungarian (Magyar), Romani, German
Religions Orthodox Christian 82%, Roman Catholic 4%, Nonreligious 1% , Other 13%
Demographics Romanian 83%, Magyar 6%, Roma 3%, Other 7%
Government Presidential / Parliamentary system
Currency New Romanian leu = 100 bani
Literacy rate 99%
Life expectancy 76 years

RUSSIA
Europe / Asia

Page 92 D4

Russia is the world's largest country, with vast mineral and energy reserves. It is a major global power with a rich cultural heritage that includes many notable writers, composers, and philosophers.

Official name Russian Federation
Formation 1547 / 2008
Capital Moscow
Population 143 million / 22 people per sq mile (8 people per sq km)
Total area 6,601,668 sq miles (17,098,242 sq km)
Languages Russian*, Tatar, Ukrainian, Chavash, various other national languages
Religions Russian Orthodox 20%, Muslim 15%, Other Christian 2%
Demographics Russian 78%, Tatar 4%, Ukrainian 1%, Bashkir 1%, Chavash 1%, Chechen 1%, Other 10%
Government Presidential / parliamentary system
Currency Russian rouble = 100 kopeks
Literacy rate 100%
Life expectancy 72 years

RWANDA
Central Africa

Page 51 B6

A small landlocked country, Rwanda lies just south of the Equator in Central Africa. Recovering from ethnic violence that flared into genocide in 1994, the country is now rebuilding both politically and economically.

Official name Republic of Rwanda
Formation 1962 / 1962
Capital Kigali
Population 13.1 million / 1288 people per sq mile (497 people per sq km)
Total area 10,169 sq miles (26,338 sq km)
Languages Kinyarwanda*, French*, Kiswahili, English*
Religions Roman Catholic 38%, Protestant 38%, Seventh-day Adventist 13%, Muslim 2%, Other 2%
Demographics Hutu 85%, Tutsi 14%, Other 1%
Government Presidential system
Currency Rwanda franc = 100 centimes
Literacy rate 73%
Life expectancy 66 years

ST KITTS AND NEVIS
West Indies

Page 33 G3

Saint Kitts and Nevis are part of the Caribbean Leeward Islands. Once a major sugar exporter, they are now a popular tourist destination while offshore finance is also a key contributor to the economy.

Official name Federation of Saint Christopher and Nevis
Formation 1983 / 1983
Capital Basseterre
Population 53,550 / 530 people per sq mile (205 people per sq km)
Total area 101 sq miles (261 sq km)
Languages English*, English Creole
Religions Protestant 76%, Roman Catholic 6%, Hindu 2%, Jehovah's Witness 1%, Rastafarian 1%, None 9%, Other 5%
Demographics Black 93%, Mixed race 3%, White 2%, Indigenous and other 2%
Government Parliamentary system
Currency East Caribbean dollar = 100 cents
Literacy rate 98%
Life expectancy 77 years

ST LUCIA
West Indies

Page 33 G4

Part of the Caribbean Windward Islands, Saint Lucia boasts beaches, mountains, exotic plants, and the Qualibou volcano with its boiling sulfur springs. Tourism and fruit production dominate the economy.

Official name Saint Lucia
Formation 1979 / 1979
Capital Castries
Population 167,122 / 705 people per sq mile (271 people per sq km)
Total area 237 sq miles (616 sq km)
Languages English*, French Creole
Religions Roman Catholic 62%, Seventh-day Adventist 10%, Other Christian 3%, Pentecostal 9%, Nonreligious 6%, Rastafarian 2%, Other 1%
Demographics Black 85%, Mixed race 11%, Asian 2%, Other 2%
Government Parliamentary system
Currency East Caribbean dollar = 100 cents
Literacy rate 95%
Life expectancy 79 years

ST VINCENT & THE GRENADINES
West Indies

Page 33 G4

Home to La Soufriere, an active volcano, this multi-island country forms part of the Caribbean Windward Islands. The economy relies on tourism and banana production, which is susceptible to seasonal storms.

Official name Saint Vincent and the Grenadines
Formation 1979 / 1979
Capital Kingstown
Population 100,969 / 673 people per sq mile (260 people per sq km)
Total area 150 sq miles (389 sq km)
Languages English*, English Creole
Religions Other Christian 48%, Anglican 18%, Pentecostal 18%, Nonreligious 9%, Other 7%
Demographics Black 71%, Mixed race 23%, Carib 4%, Asian 2%, Other 1%
Government Parliamentary system
Currency East Caribbean dollar = 100 cents
Literacy rate %
Life expectancy 77 years

SAMOA
Australasia & Oceania

Page 123 F4

Samoa is a small island group in the Southern Pacific, and the traditional, communal way of life is still strong here. The economy depends on fishing and agriculture while 60% of its electricity comes from renewables.

Official name Independent State of Samoa
Formation 1962 / 1962
Capital Apia
Population 206,179 / 189 people per sq mile (73 people per sq km)
Total area 1093 sq miles (2,831 sq km)
Languages Samoan*, English*
Religions Other Christian 78%, Roman Catholic 19%, Other 3%
Demographics Samoan 96%, Samoan/New Zealander 2%, Other 2%
Government Parliamentary system
Currency Tala = 100 sene
Literacy rate 99%
Life expectancy 75 years

SAN MARINO
Southern Europe

Page 74 C3

Perched on the slopes of Monte Titano in the Italian Appennino, San Marino has been a city-state since the 4th century CE. Beneficial tax arrangements attract businesses, chiefly banking and electronics.

Official name Republic of San Marino
Formation 301 / 1631
Capital San Marino
Population 34,010 / 1417 people per sq mile (558 people per sq km)
Total area 24 sq miles (61 sq km)
Languages Italian*
Religions Roman Catholic 93%, Nonreligious and other 7%
Demographics Sammarinese 88%, Italian 10%, Other 2%
Government Parliamentary system
Currency Euro = 100 cents
Literacy rate 100%
Life expectancy 84 years

SÃO TOMÉ & PRÍNCIPE
West Africa

Page 55 A5

São Tomé and Príncipe, once a leading cocoa producer, consists of two main volcanic islands off the west coast of Africa. It has plans to reduce its reliance on imports by capitalizing on offshore oil potential.

Official name Democratic Republic of São Tomé and Príncipe
Formation 1975 / 1975
Capital São Tomé
Population 217,164 / 584 people per sq mile (225 people per sq km)
Total area 372 sq miles (964 sq km)
Languages Portuguese Creole, Portuguese*
Religions Roman Catholic 56%, Nonreligious 21%, Other Christian 16%, Other 7%
Demographics Black 90%, Portuguese and Creole 10%
Government Parliamentary system
Currency Dobra = 100 céntimos
Literacy rate 93%
Life expectancy 67 years

SAUDI ARABIA
Southwest Asia

Page 99 B5

This vast desert kingdom is one of the world's leading oil and gas producers. It is home to Islam's two holiest cities, Medina and Mecca, the latter of which is the focus of the annual Hajj pilgrimage.

Official name Kingdom of Saudi Arabia
Formation 1932 / 2017
Capital Riyadh
Population 35.3 million / 43 people per sq mile (16 people per sq km)
Total area 829,999 sq miles (2,149,690 sq km)
Languages Arabic*
Religions Sunni Muslim 85%, Shi'a Muslim 15%
Demographics Arab 90%, Afro-Asian 10%
Government Monarchy
Currency Saudi riyal = 100 halalat
Literacy rate 98%
Life expectancy 77 years

SENEGAL
West Africa

Page 52 B3

Senegal, and its capital, Dakar, sit on the westernmost coast of Africa. Its mainly rural economy is sensitive to the effects of climate change with fish products, cotton, and groundnuts being the main exports.

Official name Republic of Senegal
Formation 1960 / 1960
Capital Dakar
Population 17.9 million / 236 people per sq mile (91 people per sq km)
Total area 75,954 sq miles (196,722 sq km)
Languages Wolof, Pulaar, Serer, Diola, Mandinka, Malinké, Soninké, French*
Religions Sunni Muslim 97%, Christian 3%
Demographics Wolof 40%, Serer 16%, Peul 14%, Toucouleur 9%, Diola 5%, Other 14%
Government Presidential system
Currency CFA franc = 100 centimes
Literacy rate 52%
Life expectancy 70 years

SIERRA LEONE
West Africa

Page 52 C4

This West African country has undergone significant economic growth recently. With a mainly rural economy, the country is rich in minerals and now carefully managed, ethical diamond mining is on the rise.

Official name Republic of Sierra Leone
Formation 1961 / 1961
Capital Freetown
Population 8.6 million / 310 people per sq mile (120 people per sq km)
Total area 27,698 sq miles (71,740 sq km)
Languages Mende, Temne, Krio, English*
Religions Muslim 77%, Christian 23%,
Demographics Mende 31%, Temne 35%, Limba 9%, Kono 4%, Kurankoh 4%, Fullah 4%, Other 13%
Government Presidential system
Currency Leone = 100 cents
Literacy rate 32%
Life expectancy 59 years

SLOVENIA
Central Europe

Page 73 D8

This small country in Central Europe was the first to break away from the former Yugoslavia in 1991 and was subsequently also the first of the ex-republics to join NATO and the EU in 2004.

Official name Republic of Slovenia
Formation 1991 / 1991
Capital Ljubljana
Population 2.1 million / 268 people per sq mile (104 people per sq km)
Total area 7827 sq miles (20,273 sq km)
Languages Slovenian*
Religions Roman Catholic 58%, Nonreligious 36%, Muslim 2%, Orthodox Christian 2%, Other 1%
Demographics Slovene 83%, Serb 2%, Croat 2%, Bosniak 1%, Other 12%
Government Parliamentary system
Currency Euro = 100 cents
Literacy rate 100%
Life expectancy 82 years

SOUTH AFRICA
Southern Africa

Page 56 C4

Mineral-rich South Africa has one of the biggest economies on the continent. The country has undergone a dramatic political shift to become a liberal democracy after decades of apartheid rule ended in 1994.

Official name Republic of South Africa
Formation 1910 / 1994
Capital Pretoria; Cape Town; Bloemfontein
Population 57.5 million / 122 people per sq mile (47 people per sq km)
Total area 470,693 sq miles (1,219,090 sq km)
Languages English*, isiZulu*, isiXhosa*, Afrikaans*, Sepedi*, Setswana*, Sesotho*, Xitsonga*, siSwati*, Tshivenda*, isiNdebele*
Religions Christian 86%, Nonreligious 11%, Muslim 2%, Other 1%
Demographics Black 81%, White 8%, Colored 9%, Asian 3%
Government Presidential system
Currency Rand = 100 cents
Literacy rate 95%
Life expectancy 65 years

SERBIA
Southeast Europe

Page 78 D4

Once a key part of the former Yugoslavia, Serbia faced ethnic tensions and conflict in the 1990s, which held back development. Fertile agricultural conditions allow for significant exports of fruit, maize, and wheat.

Official name Republic of Serbia
Formation 2006 / 2008
Capital Belgrade
Population 6.7 million / 224 people per sq mile (86 people per sq km)
Total area 29,912 sq miles (77,474 sq km)
Languages Serbian*, Hungarian (Magyar)
Religions Orthodox Christian 85%, Roman Catholic 5%, Nonreligious 5%, Muslim 3%, Other 1%
Demographics Serb 83%, Magyar 4%, Roma 2%, Bosniak 2%, Croat 1%, Slovak 1%, Other 3%
Government Parliamentary system
Currency Serbian dinar = 100 para
Literacy rate 99%
Life expectancy 74 years

SINGAPORE
Southeast Asia

Page 116 A1

A city state linked to the southern tip of the Malay Peninsula by a causeway, Singapore is one of Asia's major commercial and financial hubs with a high standard of living and generous social care.

Official name Republic of Singapore
Formation 1965 / 1965
Capital Singapore
Population 5.9 million / 20,769 people per sq mile (7692 people per sq km)
Total area 277 sq miles (719 sq km)
Languages Mandarin*, Malay*, Tamil*, English*
Religions Christian 19%, Buddhist 31%, Nonreligious 20%, Muslim 15%, Taoist 9%, Hindu 5%, Other 1%
Demographics Chinese 74%, Malay 14%, Indian 9%, Other 3%
Government Parliamentary system
Currency Singapore dollar = 100 cents
Literacy rate 98%
Life expectancy 86 years

SOLOMON ISLANDS
Australasia & Oceania

Page 122 C3

This archipelago of around 1,000 volcanic islands scattered in the southwest Pacific has mountainous and heavily forested terrain. Most people are involved with the rural economy, particularly fishing.

Official name Solomon Islands
Formation 1978 / 1978
Capital Honiara
Population 702,694 / 63 people per sq mile (24 people per sq km)
Total area 11,156 sq miles (28,896 sq km)
Languages English*, Pidgin English, Melanesian Pidgin, around 120 native languages
Religions Protestant 73%, Roman Catholic 20%, Other Christian 3%, Other 4%
Demographics Melanesian 95%, Polynesian 3%, Micronesian 1%, Other 1%
Government Parliamentary system
Currency Solomon Islands dollar = 100 cents
Literacy rate 77%
Life expectancy 77 years

SOUTH KOREA
East Asia

Page 106 E4

The southern half of the Korean peninsula was separated from the communist North in 1948. The country is one of the world's major economies and a leading exporter of automotive and electronic goods.

Official name Republic of Korea
Formation 1945 / 1953
Capital Seoul; Sejong (administrative)
Population 51 million / 1325 people per sq mile (511 people per sq km)
Total area 38,502 sq miles (99,720 sq km)
Languages Korean*, English
Religions Nonreligious 57%, Mahayana Buddhist 16%, Other Christian 20%, Roman Catholic 8%, Other 1%
Demographics Korean 100%
Government Presidential system
Currency South Korean won = 100 chon
Literacy rate 99%
Life expectancy 83 years

SEYCHELLES
Indian Ocean

Page 57 G1

The tropical location of the Seychelles in the Indian Ocean creates a thriving tourist industry which engenders good health care and education. Its diverse flora includes the world's largest seed, the coco-de-mer.

Official name Republic of Seychelles
Formation 1976 / 1976
Capital Victoria
Population 97,017 / 551 people per sq mile (213 people per sq km)
Total area 176 sq miles (455 sq km)
Languages French Creole*, English*, French*
Religions Roman Catholic 76%, Anglican 6%, Other Christian 7%, Hindu 2%, Muslim 2%, Nonreligious and other 7%
Demographics Creole 89%, Indian 5%, Chinese 2%, Other 4%
Government Presidential system
Currency Seychelles rupee = 100 cents
Literacy rate 96%
Life expectancy 76 years

SLOVAKIA
Central Europe

Page 77 C6

Slovakia was part of Czechoslovakia until the "Velvet Divorce" with the Czech Republic in 1993, and went on to join the EU in 2004. Its vibrant economy is one of the world's largest automotive producers.

Official name Slovak Republic
Formation 1993 / 1993
Capital Bratislava
Population 5.4 million / 285 people per sq mile (110 people per sq km)
Total area 18,932 sq miles (49,035 sq km)
Languages Slovak*, Hungarian (Magyar), Czech
Religions Roman Catholic 56%, Nonreligious 24%, Other Christian 7%, Greek Catholic (Uniate) 4%, Other 8%
Demographics Slovak 84%, Magyar 9%, Roma 2%, Other 5%
Government Parliamentary system
Currency Euro = 100 cents
Literacy rate 99%
Life expectancy 78 years

SOMALIA
East Africa

Page 51 E5

This semiarid state on the Horn of Africa is working toward a democratic system of government after decades of instability. Agriculture dominates the economy, particularly livestock farming and fisheries.

Official name Federal Republic of Somalia
Formation 1960 / 1960
Capital Mogadishu
Population 12.3 million / 50 people per sq mile (19 people per sq km)
Total area 246,199 sq miles (637,657 sq km)
Languages Somali*, Arabic*, English, Italian
Religions Sunni Muslim 99%, Christian 1%
Demographics Somali 85%, Other 15%
Government Parliamentary system
Currency Somali shilin = 100 senti
Literacy rate 38%
Life expectancy 56 years

SOUTH SUDAN
East Africa

Page 51 B5

This landlocked country seceded from Sudan in 2011 after years of conflict. Apart from the domestic rural economy, revenues from oil production generate almost the entire government budget.

Official name Republic of South Sudan
Formation 2011 / 2011
Capital Juba
Population 11.5 million / 46 people per sq mile (18 people per sq km)
Total area 248,777 sq miles (644,329 sq km)
Languages Arabic, Dinka, Nuer, Zande, Bari, Shilluk, Lotuko, English*
Religions Christian 60% traditional beliefs 33%, Muslim 6%, Other 1%
Demographics Dinka 40%, Nuer 15%, Shilluk 10%, Azande 10%, Arab 10%, Bari 10%, Other 5%
Government Presidential system
Currency South Sudan Pound = 100 piastres
Literacy rate 35%
Life expectancy 59 years

SPAIN
Southwest Europe

Page 70 D2

At the gateway to the Mediterranean, Spain has a rich cultural and historical heritage. The high-tech industrialized economy is led by a number of global companies, particularly in telecoms and construction.

Official name Kingdom of Spain
Formation 1492 / 1713
Capital Madrid
Population 47.1 million / 241 people per sq mile (93 people per sq km)
Total area 195,124 sq miles (505,370 sq km)
Languages Spanish*, Catalan*, Galician*, Basque*
Religions Roman Catholic 58%, Nonreligious 16%, Other 3%
Demographics Castilian Spanish 72%, Catalan 17%, Galician 6%, Basque 2%, Roma 1%, Other 2%
Government Parliamentary system
Currency Euro = 100 cents
Literacy rate 99%
Life expectancy 83 years

SRI LANKA
South Asia

Page 110 D3

Once known as Ceylon, the island republic of Sri Lanka is separated from India by the narrow Palk Strait. A severe economic crisis was declared in 2019, which has led to social unrest.

Official name Democratic Socialist Republic of Sri Lanka
Formation 1948 / 1948
Capital Colombo; Sri Jayawardenapura Kotte
Population 23.1 million / 912 people per sq mile (352 people per sq km)
Total area 25,332 sq miles (65,610 sq km)
Languages Sinhala*, Tamil*, Sinhala-Tamil, English
Religions Buddhist 70%, Hindu 13%, Muslim 10%, Christian (mainly Roman Catholic) 7%
Demographics Sinhalese 75%, Tamil 15%, Moor 9%, Other 1%
Government Presidential system
Currency Sri Lankan rupee = 100 cents
Literacy rate 92%
Life expectancy 78 years

SUDAN
East Africa

Page 50 B4

Once the largest country in Africa, Sudan was reduced to two thirds its size following the secession of South Sudan in 2011. Agricultural products and mineral extraction are key economic activities.

Official name Republic of the Sudan
Formation 1956 / 2011
Capital Khartoum
Population 47.9 million / 67 people per sq mile (26 people per sq km)
Total area 718,723 sq miles (1,861,484 sq km)
Languages Arabic*, English, Nubian, Beja, Fur
Religions Muslim (mainly Sunni) 99%, Other 1%
Demographics Arab 70%, Nubian 3%, Beja 6%, Fur 2%, Egyptian 1%, Fulani 1%, Coptic 1%, Other 16%
Government Presidential system
Currency Sudanese pound = 100 piastres
Literacy rate 60%
Life expectancy 67 years

SURINAME
South America

Page 37 G3

Suriname is one of South America's smallest countries. The tropical rainforest of the Central Suriname Nature Reserve is a World Heritage site. Gold and oil are important contributors to the economy.

Official name Republic of Suriname
Formation 1975 / 1975
Capital Paramaribo
Population 632,000 / 10 people per sq mile (4 people per sq km)
Total area 63,251 sq miles (163,820 sq km)
Languages Sranang Tongo (creole), Dutch*, Caribbean Hindustani , Javanese
Religions Christian 50%, Hindu 23%, Muslim 14%, Other 13%
Demographics East Indian 27%, Creole 16%, Black 37%, Javanese 14%, Mixed race 13%, Other 8%
Government Presidential system
Currency Surinamese dollar = 100 cents
Literacy rate 94%
Life expectancy 72 years

SWEDEN
Northern Europe

Page 62 B4

Forests cover over two-thirds of this large and densly populated Scandinavian country. A strong economy helps fund the extensive welfare system. It applied to join NATO in 2022.

Official name Kingdom of Sweden
Formation 1523 / 1921
Capital Stockholm
Population 10.4 million / 60 people per sq mile (23 people per sq km)
Total area 173,860 sq miles (450,295 sq km)
Languages Swedish*, Finnish, Sámi
Religions Evangelical Lutheran 58%, Muslim 2%, Other 40%
Demographics Swedish 80%, Syrian 2%, Iraqi 2%, Finnish 1%, Other 15%
Government Parliamentary constitutional monarchy
Currency Swedish krona = 100 öre
Literacy rate 99%
Life expectancy 83 years

SWITZERLAND
Central Europe

Page 73 A7

One of the world's richest countries with a long tradition of neutrality, this mountainous nation lies at the center of Europe geographically, but outside it politically, having chosen not to join the EU.

Official name Swiss Confederation
Formation 1291 / 1857
Capital Bern
Population 8.5 million / 533 people per sq mile (206 people per sq km)
Total area 15,937 sq miles (41,277 sq km)
Languages German*, Swiss-German, French*, Italian*, Portuguese, Romansch*
Religions Roman Catholic 34%, Protestant 23%, Muslim 5%, Other Christian 6%, Other 32%
Demographics Swiss 69%, German 4%, French 2%, Italian 3%, Portuguese 3%, Kosovo 1%, Turkish 1%, Other 17%
Government Federal republic
Currency Swiss franc = 100 rappen/centimes
Literacy rate 99%
Life expectancy 83 years

SYRIA
Southwest Asia

Page 96 B3

Situated at the eastern end of the Mediterranean, Syria contains an abundance of important, ancient historical sites. Recent political unrest has led to a brutally oppressed civil war.

Official name Syrian Arab Republic
Formation 1946 / 1967
Capital Damascus
Population 21.5 million / 297 people per sq mile (117 people per sq km)
Total area 72,370 sq miles (184,437 sq km)
Languages Arabic*, French, Kurdish, Armenian, Circassian, Turkic languages, Assyrian, Aramaic
Religions Muslim 87%, Christian 10%, Druze 3%
Demographics Arab 50%, Kurd 10%, Alawite 15%, Levantine 10%, Other 15%
Government Presidential system
Currency Syrian pound = 100 piastres
Literacy rate 86%
Life expectancy 74 years

TAIWAN
East Asia

Page 107 D6

Following a period of rapid industrial growth in the 1960s, Taiwan is now one of the world's leading economies. Complex relations with China dominate domestic and international politics.

Official name Republic of China (ROC)
Formation 1945 / 1945
Capital Taipei
Population 23.5 million / 1692 people per sq mile (653 people per sq km)
Total area 13,892 sq miles (35,980 sq km)
Languages Amoy Chinese, Mandarin Chinese*, Hakka Chinese
Religions Buddhist 35%, Taoist 33%, Christian 4%, Indigenous 10%, Other 18%
Demographics Han Chinese 95%, Indigenous 2%, Other 3%
Government Semi-presidential system
Currency New Taiwan dollar = 100 cents
Literacy rate 99%
Life expectancy 81 years

TAJIKISTAN
Central Asia

Page 101 F3

This landlocked ex-Soviet republic lies on the western slopes of the Pamirs in Central Asia. Rich mineral deposits, particularly gold and aluminium, and cotton production are the main economic exports.

Official name Republic of Tajikistan
Formation 1991 / 2011
Capital Dushanbe
Population 9.1 million / 164 people per sq mile (63 people per sq km)
Total area 55,637 sq miles (144,100 sq km)
Languages Tajik*, Uzbek, Russian
Religions Sunni Muslim 95%, Shi'a Muslim 3%, Other 2%
Demographics Tajik 84%, Uzbek 14%, Other 2%
Government Presidential system
Currency Somoni = 100 diram
Literacy rate 100%
Life expectancy 69 years

TANZANIA
East Africa

Page 51 B7

This East African state was formed in 1964 by the union of Tanganyika and Zanzibar. A third of its area is game reserve or national park, including Africa's highest peak, Mt. Kilimanjaro.

Official name United Republic of Tanzania
Formation 1964 / 1964
Capital Dodoma
Population 63.8 million / 174 people per sq mile (67 people per sq km)
Total area 365,754 sq miles (947,300 sq km)
Languages Kiswahili*, Sukuma, Chagga, Nyamwezi, Hehe, Makonde, Yao, Sandawe, English*
Religions Christian 63%, Muslim 34%, Other 3%
Demographics Indigenous tribes 99%, Other 1%
Government Presidential system
Currency Tanzanian shilling = 100 cents
Literacy rate 78%
Life expectancy 70 years

THAILAND
Southeast Asia

Page 115 C5

Thailand lies at the heart of the Indochinese Peninsula. Formerly Siam, it has been an independent kingdom for most of its history. The military has frequently intervened in politics.

Official name Kingdom of Thailand
Formation 1238 / 1907
Capital Bangkok
Population 69.6 million / 351 people per sq mile (136 people per sq km)
Total area 198,117 sq miles (513,120 sq km)
Languages Thai*, Chinese, Malay, Khmer, Mon, Karen, Miao
Religions Buddhist 94%, Muslim 4%, Other 2%
Demographics Thai 98%, Burmese 1%, Other 1%
Government Constitutional monarchy
Currency Baht = 100 satang
Literacy rate 94%
Life expectancy 78 years

TOGO
West Africa

Page 53 F4

Togo lies sandwiched between Ghana and Benin in West Africa. Mining activities, including the world's fourth largest phosphate deposits, and agricultural products underpin the economy.

Official name Togolese Republic
Formation 1960 / 1960
Capital Lomé
Population 8.4 million / 383 people per sq mile (148 people per sq km)
Total area 21,925 sq miles (56,785 sq km)
Languages Ewe and Mina, Kabye, Gurma, French*
Religions Christian 42%, Indigenous 37%, Muslim 14%, Other 7%
Demographics Ewe 42%, Other African 41%, Kabye 12%, Foreigners 5%
Government Presidential system
Currency West African CFA franc = 100 centimes
Literacy rate 67%
Life expectancy 71 years

TONGA
Australasia & Oceania

Page 123 E4

Northeast of New Zealand, Tonga is a 170-island archipelago, 45 of which are inhabited. In 2010, political reforms allowed more representative elections but the monarchy retains its influence.

Official name Kingdom of Tonga
Formation 1970 / 1970
Capital Nuku'alofa
Population 100,000/ 347 people per sq mile (134 people per sq km)
Total area 288 sq miles (747 sq km)
Languages English*, Tongan*, Other
Religions Free Wesleyan 38%, Roman Catholic 16%, Church of Jesus Christ of Latter-day Saints 17%, Other Christian 16%, Free Church of Tonga 12%, Other 1%
Demographics Tongan 97%, Other 3%
Government Constitutional monarchy
Currency Pa'anga = 100 seniti
Literacy rate 99%
Life expectancy 78 years

TRINIDAD AND TOBAGO
West Indies

Page 33 H5

The most southerly of the Caribbean islands lie just 9 miles (15km) off the coast of South America. An industrialized economy based on oil and gas generates substantial wealth.

Official name Republic of Trinidad and Tobago
Formation 1962 / 1962
Capital Port of Spain
Population 1.4 million / 707 people per sq mile (273 people per sq km)
Total area 1980 sq miles (5128 sq km)
Languages English Creole, Trinidadian Creole, English*, Caribbean Hindustani, French, Spanish
Religions Protestant 32%, Roman Catholic 22%, Hindu 18%, Muslim 5%, Jehovah's Witness 2%, Other 21%
Demographics East Indian 38%, Black 36%, Mixed race 24%, Other 2%
Government Parliamentary system
Currency Trinidad and Tobago dollar = 100 cents
Literacy rate 99%
Life expectancy 76 years

TUNISIA
North Africa

Page 49 E2

This northernmost country in Africa has long been an important center of trade and culture. It was the seat of the Arab Spring movement in 2011, and mass civil protests led to successful democratic elections.

Official name Republic of Tunisia
Formation 1956 / 1956
Capital Tunis
Population 11.8 million / 187 people per sq mile (72 people per sq km)
Total area 63,170 sq miles (163,610 sq km)
Languages Arabic*, French, Berber
Religions Muslim (mainly Sunni) 99%, Other 1%
Demographics Arab 98%, European 1%, Jewish and other 1%
Government Parliamentary system
Currency Tunisian dinar = 1000 millimes
Literacy rate 90%
Life expectancy 77 years

TURKEY (TÜRKIYE)
Asia / Europe

Page 94 B3

With land in Europe and Asia, Turkey controls the entrance to the Black Sea. The balance between secular and religious influences is key to its politics. It has been a NATO member since 1952 with hopes to join the EU.

Official name Republic of Turkey
Formation 1923 / 1939
Capital Ankara
Population 83 million / 274 people per sq mile (106 people per sq km)
Total area 302,535 sq miles (783,562 sq km)
Languages Turkish*, Kurdish, Arabic, Circassian, Armenian, Greek, Georgian, Ladino
Religions Muslim (mainly Sunni) 99%, Other 1%
Demographics Turkish 73%, Kurdish 17%, Other 10%
Government Presidential system
Currency Turkish lira = 100 kuruş
Literacy rate 97%
Life expectancy 76 years

TURKMENISTAN
Central Asia

Page 100 B2

Stretching from the Caspian Sea to the deserts of central Asia, this vast nation holds the world's sixth largest reserves of natural gas, which was supplied free to its citizens between 1993 and 2017.

Official name Turkmenistan
Formation 1991 / 1991
Capital Ashgabat
Population 5.6 million / 30 people per sq mile (11 people per sq km)
Total area 188,456 sq miles (488,100 sq km)
Languages Turkmen*, Uzbek, Russian, Kazakh, Tatar
Religions Muslim 93%, Christian 6%, Other 2%
Demographics Turkmen 85%, Uzbek 5%, Russian 4%, Other 6%
Government Presidential system / authoritarian
Currency Manat = 100 tenge
Literacy rate 100%
Life expectancy 72 years

TUVALU
Australasia & Oceania

Page 123 E3

Tuvalu is a chain of nine atolls in the Central Pacific. It has the world's smallest Gross National Income (GNI), but has made substantial earnings leasing its ".tv" internet suffix.

Official name Tuvalu
Formation 1978 / 2012
Capital Funafuti Atoll
Population 11,930 / 1193 people per sq mile (459 people per sq km)
Total area 10 sq miles (26 sq km)
Languages Tuvaluan, Kiribati, Samoan, English*
Religions Church of Tuvalu 91%, Seventh-day Adventist 2%, Baha'i 2%, Other 5%
Demographics Tuvaluan 97%, Other 3%
Government Parliamentary democracy
Currency Australian dollar = 100 cents; Tuvaluan dollar = 100 cents
Literacy rate 95%
Life expectancy 68 years

UGANDA
East Africa

Page 51 B6

Landlocked and abundantly fertile, Uganda is home to a variety of ecosystems, ranging from volcanic mountains to forested swamps and rainforests. Coffee is the mainstay of its agricultural economy.

Official name Republic of Uganda
Formation 1962 / 1962
Capital Kampala
Population 46.2 million / 496 people per sq mile (192 people per sq km)
Total area 93,065 sq miles (241,038 sq km)
Languages Luganda, Nkole, Chiga, Lango, Acholi, Teso, Lugbara, English*
Religions Roman Catholic 42%, Protestant 42%, Muslim (mainly Sunni) 12%, Other 4%
Demographics Baganda 17%, Banyakole 10%, Basoga 9%, Bakiga 7%, Iteso 7%, Langi 6%, Bagisu 5%, Acholi 4%, Lugbara 3%, Other 32%
Government Presidential system
Currency Ugandan shilling
Literacy rate 77%
Life expectancy 69 years

UKRAINE
Eastern Europe

Page 86 C2

This vast, fertile nation is one of the world's leading grain producers. In 2022, following years of escalating tension, neighboring Russia launched an unprovoked invasion.

Official name Ukraine
Formation 1991 / 2009
Capital Kyiv
Population 43.5 million / 187 people per sq mile (72 people per sq km)
Total area 233,032 sq miles (603,550 sq km)
Languages Ukrainian*, Russian, Tatar, Other
Religions Orthodox Christian 78%, Roman Catholic 10%, Nonreligious 7%, Other 5%
Demographics Ukrainian 78%, Russian 17%, Belarussian 1%, Other 4%
Government Semi-presidential system
Currency Hryvnia = 100 kopiykas
Literacy rate 100%
Life expectancy 73 years

UNITED ARAB EMIRATES
Southwest Asia

Page 99 D5

Situated on the Persian Gulf, this federation of seven states is trying to move away from its past reliance on oil and gas exports by encouraging tourism and financial services.

Official name United Arab Emirates
Formation 1971 / 1974
Capital Abu Dhabi
Population 9.9 million / 307 people per sq mile (118 people per sq km)
Total area 32,278 sq miles (83,600 sq km)
Languages Arabic*, Farsi, Indian and Pakistani languages, English
Religions Muslim (mainly Sunni) 76%, Christian 9%, Other 15%
Demographics South Asian 59%, Emirati 12%, Filipino 6%, Egyptian 10%, Other 13%
Government Federation of monarchies
Currency UAE dirham = 100 fils
Literacy rate 98%
Life expectancy 80 years

UNITED KINGDOM
Northwest Europe

Page 67 C5

The UK comprises England, Scotland, Wales, and Northern Ireland and is one of the world's leading economies. Following a referendum in 2016, the UK left the EU in 2020.

Official name United Kingdom of Great Britain and Northern Ireland
Formation 1707 / 1922
Capital London
Population 67.7 million / 720 people per sq mile (278 people per sq km)
Total area 94,058 sq miles (243,610 sq km)
Languages English*, Welsh (* in Wales), Gaelic, Irish
Religions Christian 64%, Nonreligious 28%, Muslim 5%, Hindu 1%, Other 2%
Demographics White 87%, Indian and Pakistani 4%, Black 3%, Other Asian 2%, Bengali 1%, Other 3%
Government Parliamentary constitutional monarchy
Currency Pound sterling = 100 pence
Literacy rate 99%
Life expectancy 82 years

UNITED STATES
North America

Page 13 B5

Bestowed with an abundance of natural resources, this vast nation has the world's largest economy, which helps cement its status as a global superpower.

Official name United States of America
Formation 1776 / 1959
Capital Washington D.C.
Population 332 million / 90 people per sq mile (35 people per sq km)
Total area 3,677,649 sq miles (9,525,067 sq km)
Languages English*, Spanish, Chinese, French, Polish, German, Tagalog, Vietnamese, Italian, Korean, Russian
Religions Protestant 47%, Nonreligious 23%, Roman Catholic 21%, Jewish 2%, Muslim 1%, Other 6%
Demographics White 62%, Black 12%, Asian 6%, Indigenous 2%, Mixed race 10%, Other 8%
Government Constitutional federal republic
Currency US dollar = 100 cents
Literacy rate 99%
Life expectancy 81 years

URUGUAY
South America

Page 42 D4

Due to Uruguay's wealth of fertile pasture and a temperate climate, agriculture is a major part of its economy. After a period of military rule in the 1980s, it transitioned to a thriving democracy.

Official name Oriental Republic of Uruguay
Formation 1828 / 1828
Capital Montevideo
Population 3.4 million / 50 people per sq mile (19 people per sq km)
Total area 68,037 sq miles (176,215 sq km)
Languages Spanish*
Religions Roman Catholic 42%, Nonreligious 37%, Protestant 15%, Other 6%
Demographics White 87%, Black 7%, Mixed race 5%, Other 1%
Government Presidential system
Currency Uruguayan peso = 100 centésimos
Literacy rate 99%
Life expectancy 78 years

UZBEKISTAN
Central Asia

Page 100 D2

Uzbekistan lies on the ancient Silk Road route between Asia and Europe. Its main exports today are cotton, oil, copper, and gold. It ranks 7th in the world for gold production.

Official name Republic of Uzbekistan
Formation 1991 / 1991
Capital Tashkent
Population 31.1million / 180 people per sq mile (70 people per sq km)
Total area 172,742 sq miles (447,400 sq km)
Languages Uzbek*, Russian, Tajik, Kazakh
Religions Sunni Muslim 88%, Orthodox Christian 9%, Other 3%
Demographics Uzbek 84%, Russian 2%, Tajik 5%, Kazakh 3%, Other 6%
Government Presidential system / authoritarian
Currency So'm = 100 tiyin
Literacy rate 100%
Life expectancy 75 years

VATICAN CITY
Southern Europe

Page 75 A8

The Vatican City, seat of the Roman Catholic Church, is a walled enclave in Rome. It is the world's smallest country. Its head, the pope, is elected for life by a college of cardinals.

Official name Vatican City State
Formation 1929 / 1929
Capital Vatican City
Population 825 / 4852 people per sq mile (1875 people per sq km)
Total area 0.17 sq miles (0.44 sq km)
Languages Italian*, Latin*, French
Religions Roman Catholic 100%
Demographics Clergy 9%, Diplomats 39%, Swiss Guard 13%, Other 39%
Government Papal state
Currency Euro = 100 cents
Literacy rate 99%
Life expectancy 78 years

VIETNAM
Southeast Asia

Page 114 D4

After Vietnam emerged from years of bitter conflict in the 1970s, recent economic reforms have resulted in a remarkable growth in GDP, accompanied by a huge surge in tourism.

Official name Socialist Republic of Viet Nam
Formation 1945 / 1976
Capital Hanoi
Population 103.8 million / 812 people per sq mile (313 people per sq km)
Total area 127,881 sq miles (331,210 sq km)
Languages Vietnamese*, English, French, Chinese, Thai, Khmer
Religions Catholic 6%, Buddhist 6%, Protestant 1%, None 86%, Other 1%
Demographics Vietnamese 85%, Tay 2%, Thai 2%, Muong 2%, Other 8%
Government Communist state
Currency Đông
Literacy rate 96%
Life expectancy 76 years

ZAMBIA
Southern Africa

Page 56 C2

This landlocked nation in the heart of southern Africa is rich in natural resources, including minerals (particularly copper), forestry, and wildlife, all of which have led to economic growth.

Official name Republic of Zambia
Formation 1964 / 1964
Capital Lusaka
Population 19.6 million / 67 people per sq mile (26 people per sq km)
Total area 290,587 sq miles (752,618 sq km)
Languages Bemba, Tonga, Nyanja, Lozi, Lala-Bisa, Nsenga, English*
Religions Protestant 75%, Roman Catholic 20%, Nonreligious 2%, Other 3%
Demographics Bemba 21%, Tonga 14%, Chewa 7%, Lozi 6%, Nsenga 5%, Tumbuka 4%, Ngoni 4%, Lala 3%, Kaonde 3%, Lunda 3%, Other 30%
Government Presidential system
Currency New Zambian kwacha = 100 ngwee
Literacy rate 87%
Life expectancy 66 years

VANUATU
Australasia & Oceania

Page 122 D4

This South Pacific archipelago of 82 islands and islets boasts over 100 indigenous languages, each with an average of only around 2,000 speakers. Its favorable tax status attracts financial services.

Official name Republic of Vanuatu
Formation 1980 / 1980
Capital Port Vila
Population 300,000 / 63 people per sq mile (25 people per sq km)
Total area 4706 sq miles (12,189 sq km)
Languages Bislama*, English*, French*, Other indigenous languages
Religions Protestant 45%, Presbyterian 35%, Roman Catholic 14%. Indigenous 4%, Other 2%
Demographics ni-Vanuatu 99%, Other 1%
Government Parliamentary system
Currency Vanuatu Vatu
Literacy rate 88%
Life expectancy 75 years

VENEZUELA
South America

Page 36 D2

Located on the Caribbean coast of South America, Venezuela has the continent's most urbanized society. It has the world's largest known oil reserves that have yet to reach their full production potential.

Official name Bolivarian Republic of Venezuela
Formation 1811 / 1811
Capital Caracas
Population 29.7 million / 84 people per sq mile (33 people per sq km)
Total area 352,144 sq miles (912,050 sq km)
Languages Spanish*, Indigenous languages
Religions Roman Catholic 73%, Protestant 17%, Nonreligious 7%, Other 3%
Demographics Mixed race 69%, White 20%, Black 9%, Indigenous 2%
Government Federal presidential republic
Currency Venezuelan bolívar = 100 céntimos
Literacy rate 97%
Life expectancy 73 years

YEMEN
Southwest Asia

Page 99 C7

Located near the Red Sea, Yemen sits at the crossroads of ancient and modern trade and communications routes. However, it remains one of the world's least developed countries.

Official name Republic of Yemen
Formation 1990 / 2000
Capital Sanaa
Population 30.9 million / 152 people per sq mile (59 people per sq km)
Total area 203,850 sq miles (527,968 sq km)
Languages Arabic*
Religions Muslim 99% (Sunni 65%, Shi'a 35%), Other 1%
Demographics Arab 99%, Other 1%
Government Transitional regime
Currency Yemeni rial = 100 fils
Literacy rate 70%
Life expectancy 68 years

ZIMBABWE
Southern Africa

Page 56 D3

Zimbabwe is rich in natural resources but mismanagement, hyper inflation and drought have caused economic difficulties. Gold and diamonds are key exports while Victoria Falls is a major tourist attraction.

Official name Republic of Zimbabwe
Formation 1980 / 1980
Capital Harare
Population 15.1 million / 100 people per sq mile (39 people per sq km)
Total area 150,872 sq miles (390,757 sq km)
Languages Shona, isiNdebele, English*
Religions Protestant 75%, Roman Catholic 7%, Other Christian 5%, Traditional 2%, None 10%, Other 1%
Demographics Black 99%, Other 1%
Government Presidential system
Currency RTGS dollar = 100 cents; multiple foreign currencies
Literacy rate 87%
Life expectancy 63 years

Overseas Territories and Dependencies

Despite the rapid process of decolonization since the end of the Second World War, around 7.5 million people in more than 50 territories around the world continue to live under the protection of a parent state.

AUSTRALIA

ASHMORE & CARTIER ISLANDS
Indian Ocean
Claimed 1931
Capital not applicable
Area 2 sq miles (5 sq km)
Population None

CHRISTMAS ISLAND
Indian Ocean
Claimed 1958
Capital The Settlement (Flying Fish Cove)
Area 52 sq miles (135 sq km)
Population 1692

COCOS (KEELING) ISLANDS
Indian Ocean
Claimed 1955
Capital West Island
Area 5.5 sq miles (14 sq km)
Population 544

CORAL SEA ISLANDS
Southwest Pacific
Claimed 1969
Capital None
Area Less than 1.2 sq miles (3 sq km)
Population below 10 (scientists)

HEARD ISLAND & McDONALD ISLANDS
Indian Ocean
Claimed 1947
Capital not applicable
Area 159 sq miles (412 sq km)
Population None

NORFOLK ISLAND
Southwest Pacific
Claimed 1914
Capital Kingston
Area 14 sq miles (36 sq km)
Population 2188

DENMARK

FAROE ISLANDS
North Atlantic
Claimed 1380
Capital Tórshavn
Area 538 sq miles (1393 sq km)
Population 52,269

GREENLAND
North Atlantic
Claimed 1380
Capital Nuuk
Area 822,700 sq miles (2,130,783 sq km)
Population 57,792

FRANCE

CLIPPERTON ISLAND
East Pacific
Claimed 1935
Capital not applicable
Area 2 sq miles (6 sq km)
Population None

FRENCH GUIANA
South America
Claimed 1946
Capital Cayenne
Area 32,252 sq miles (83,534 sq km)
Population 304,641

FRENCH POLYNESIA
South Pacific
Claimed 1842
Capital Papeete
Area 1609 sq miles (4167 sq km)
Population 299,356

FRENCH SOUTHERN & ANTARCTIC LANDS
Indian Ocean
Claimed 1924
Capital Port-aux-Français
Area 169,800 sq miles (439,781 sq km)
Population 150

GUADELOUPE
West Indies
Claimed 1635
Capital Basse-Terre
Area 629 sq miles (1628 sq km)
Population 395,752

MARTINIQUE
West Indies
Claimed 1635
Capital Fort-de-France
Area 436 sq miles (1128 sq km)
Population 367,507

MAYOTTE
Indian Ocean
Claimed 1843
Capital Mamoudzou
Area 144 sq miles (374 sq km)
Population 326,206

NEW CALEDONIA
Southwest Pacific
Claimed 1853
Capital Nouméa
Area 7172 sq miles (18,575 sq km)
Population 297,160

RÉUNION
Indian Ocean
Claimed 1638
Capital Saint-Denis
Area 970 sq miles (2511 sq km)
Population 974,157

ST. BARTHÉLEMY
West Indies
Claimed 1878
Capital Gustavia
Area 10 sq miles (25 sq km)
Population 10,000

ST. MARTIN
West Indies
Claimed 1648
Capital Marigot
Area 20 sq miles (53 sq km)
Population 32,500

ST. PIERRE & MIQUELON
North America
Claimed 1604
Capital Saint-Pierre
Area 93 sq miles (242 sq km)
Population 5257

WALLIS & FUTUNA
South Pacific
Claimed 1842
Capital Matā'utu
Area 55 sq miles (142 sq km)
Population 15,891

NETHERLANDS

ARUBA
West Indies
Claimed 1636
Capital Oranjestad
Area 69 sq miles (180 sq km)
Population 122,320

BONAIRE
West Indies
Claimed 1816
Capital Kralendijk
Area 111 sq miles (288 sq km)
Population 22,573

CURAÇAO
West Indies
Claimed 1815
Capital Willemstad
Area 171 sq miles (444 sq km)
Population 152,379

SABA
West Indies
Claimed 1816
Capital The Bottom
Area 5 sq miles (13 sq km)
Population 1911

SINT-EUSTATIUS
West Indies
Claimed 1784
Capital Oranjestad
Area 8 sq miles (21 sq km)
Population 3242

SINT-MAARTEN
West Indies
Claimed 1648
Capital Philipsburg
Area 13 sq miles (34 sq km)
Population 45,126

NEW ZEALAND

COOK ISLANDS
South Pacific
Claimed 1901
Capital Avarua
Area 91 sq miles (236 sq km)
Population 8128

NIUE
South Pacific
Claimed 1901
Capital Alofi
Area 100 sq miles (260 sq km)
Population 2000

TOKELAU
South Pacific
Claimed 1925
Capital not applicable
Area 5 sq miles (12 sq km)
Population 1871

NORWAY

BOUVET ISLAND
South Atlantic
Claimed 1929
Capital not applicable
Area 19 sq miles (49 sq km)
Population None

JAN MAYEN
North Atlantic
Claimed 1929
Capital not applicable
Area 146 sq miles (377 sq km)
Population 35 (military personnel / scientists)

PETER I ISLAND
Antarctica
Claimed 1931
Capital not applicable
Area 60 sq miles (156 sq km)
Population None

SVALBARD
Arctic Ocean
Claimed 1920
Capital Longyearbyen
Area 23,956 sq miles (62,045 sq km)
Population 2926

UNITED KINGDOM

ANGUILLA
West Indies
Claimed 1650
Capital The Valley
Area 35 sq miles (91 sq km)
Population 18,741

ASCENSION ISLAND
South Atlantic
Claimed 1815
Capital Georgetown
Area 34 sq miles (88 sq km)
Population 880

BERMUDA
North Atlantic
Claimed 1612
Capital Hamilton
Area 21 sq miles (54 sq km)
Population 72,337

BRITISH INDIAN OCEAN TERRITORY
Indian Ocean
Claimed 1814
Capital not applicable
Area 23 sq miles (60 sq km)
Population 4000 (UK/US air base)

BRITISH VIRGIN ISLANDS
West Indies
Claimed 1672
Capital Road Town
Area 58 sq miles (151 sq km)
Population 38,632

CAYMAN ISLANDS
West Indies
Claimed 1670
Capital George Town
Area 102 sq miles (264 sq km)
Population 64,309

FALKLAND ISLANDS
South Atlantic
Claimed 1833
Capital Stanley
Area 4699 sq miles (12,173 sq km)
Population 3780

GIBRALTAR
Southwest Europe
Claimed 1713
Capital Gibraltar
Area 3 sq miles (7 sq km)
Population 29,573

GUERNSEY
Northwest Europe
Claimed 1066
Capital St Peter Port
Area 30 sq miles (78 sq km)
Population 67,491

ISLE OF MAN
Northwest Europe
Claimed 1765
Capital Douglas
Area 221 sq miles (572 sq km)
Population 91,382

JERSEY
Northwest Europe
Claimed 1066
Capital St. Helier
Area 45 sq miles (116 sq km)
Population 102,146

MONTSERRAT
West Indies
Claimed 1632
Capital Plymouth (de jure); Brades Estate (de facto)
Area 40 sq miles (102 sq km)
Population 5414

PITCAIRN GROUP OF ISLANDS
South Pacific
Claimed 1838
Capital Adamstown
Area 18 sq miles (47 sq km)
Population 50

ST. HELENA
South Atlantic
Claimed 1657
Capital Jamestown
Area 47 sq miles (122 sq km)
Population 4217

SOUTH GEORGIA &
THE SOUTH SANDWICH ISLANDS
South Atlantic
Claimed 1775
Capital not applicable
Area 1507 sq miles (3903 sq km)
Population None

TRISTAN DA CUNHA
South Atlantic
Claimed 1816
Capital Edinburgh of the Seven Seas
Area 38 sq miles (98 sq km)
Population 242

TURKS & CAICOS ISLANDS
West Indies
Claimed 1799
Capital Grand Turk (Cockburn Town)
Area 366 sq miles (948 sq km)
Population 58,286

UNITED STATES OF AMERICA

AMERICAN SAMOA
South Pacific
Claimed 1900
Capital Pago Pago
Area 86 sq miles (224 sq km)
Population 45,443

BAKER ISLAND
Central Pacific
Claimed 1856
Capital not applicable
Area 0.8 sq miles (1.2 sq km)
Population None

GUAM
West Pacific
Claimed 1898
Capital Hagåtña
Area 210 sq miles (544 sq km)
Population 169,086

HOWLAND ISLAND
Central Pacific
Claimed 1856
Capital not applicable
Area 1 sq mile (2.6 sq km)
Population None

JARVIS ISLAND
Central Pacific
Claimed 1935
Capital not applicable
Area 2 sq miles (5 sq km)
Population None

JOHNSTON ATOLL
Central Pacific
Claimed 1858
Capital not applicable
Area 1 sq mile (2.6 sq km)
Population None

KINGMAN REEF
Central Pacific
Claimed 1856
Capital not applicable
Area 0.4 sq miles (1 sq km)
Population None

MIDWAY ATOLL
Central Pacific
Claimed 1867
Capital not applicable
Area 2 sq miles (5.2 sq km)
Population 40 (US air base)

NAVASSA ISLAND
Central Pacific
Claimed 1856
Capital not applicable
Area 2 sq miles (5.2 sq km)
Population None

NORTHERN MARIANA ISLANDS
West Pacific
Claimed 1944
Capital Saipan
Area 179 sq miles (464 sq km)
Population 51,475

PALMYRA ATOLL
Central Pacific
Claimed 1898
Capital not applicable
Area 2 sq miles (4 sq km)
Population 20

PUERTO RICO
West Indies
Claimed 1898
Capital San Juan
Area 3515 sq miles (9104 sq km)
Population 3.1 million

VIRGIN ISLANDS
West Indies
Claimed 1917
Capital Charlotte Amalie
Area 134 sq miles (346 sq km)
Population 105,413

WAKE ISLAND
Central Pacific
Claimed 1899
Capital not applicable
Area 3 sq miles (7 sq km)
Population 150 (US air base)

Geographical comparisons

Largest countries

Russia	6,601,668 sq miles	(17,098,242 sq km)
Canada	3,855,171 sq miles	(9,984,670 sq km)
China	3,705,386 sq miles	(9,596,960 sq km)
USA	3,677,649 sq miles	(9,525,067 sq km)
Brazil	3,287,957 sq miles	(8,515,770 sq km)
Australia	2,969,907 sq miles	(7,692,024 sq km)
India	1,269,219 sq miles	(3,287,263 sq km)
Argentina	1,073,518 sq miles	(2,780,400 sq km)
Kazakhstan	1,052,089 sq miles	(2,724,900 sq km)
Algeria	919,590 sq miles	(2,381,740 sq km)

Smallest countries

Vatican City	0.17 sq miles	(0.44 sq km)
Monaco	0.77 sq miles	(2 sq km)
Nauru	8 sq miles	(21 sq km)
Tuvalu	10 sq miles	(26 sq km)
San Marino	24 sq miles	(61 sq km)
Liechtenstein	62 sq miles	(160 sq km)
Marshall Islands	70 sq miles	(181 sq km)
St. Kitts & Nevis	101 sq miles	(261 sq km)
Maldives	120 sq miles	(300 sq km)
Malta	122 sq miles	(316 sq km)

Largest islands

Greenland	822,700 sq miles (2,130,783 sq km)
New Guinea	303,381 sq miles (785,753 sq km)
Borneo	288,869 sq miles (748,167 sq km)
Madagascar	226,658 sq miles (587,042 sq km)
Baffin Island	195,928 sq miles (507,451 sq km)
Sumatra	171,068 sq miles (443,064 sq km)
Honshu	87,200 sq miles (225,847 sq km)
Victoria Island	83,897 sq miles (217,292 sq km)
Britain	80,823 sq miles (209,331 sq km)
Ellesmere Island	75,767 sq miles (196,236 sq km)

Richest countries
(GNI per capita, in US$)

Liechtenstein	116,540
Switzerland	90,360
Norway	84,490
Luxembourg	81,110
Ireland	74,520
USA	70,430
Denmark	68,110
Iceland	64,410
Singapore	64,010
Sweden	58,890

Poorest countries
(GNI per capita, in US$)

Burundi	240
Somalia	450
Mozambique	480
Madagascar	500
Afghanistan	500
Sierra Leone	510
Central African Republic	530
Congo, Dem. Republic	580
Niger	590
Eritrea	600

Most populous countries

China	1.41 billion
India	1.39 billion
USA	332 million
Indonesia	276 million
Pakistan	225 million
Brazil	214 million

Most populous countries *continued*

Nigeria	211 million
Bangladesh	166 million
Russia	143 million
Mexico	130 million

Least populous countries

Vatican City	825
Nauru	10,870
Tuvalu	11,930
Palau	18,170
San Marino	34,010
Liechtenstein	38,250
Monaco	39,520
St. Kitts & Nevis	53,550
Marshall Islands	59,620
Dominica	72,170

Most densely populated countries

Monaco	50,145 people per sq mile (19,497 per sq km)
Singapore	20,769 people per sq mile (7692 per sq km)
Bahrain	5651 people per sq mile (2241 per sq km)
Vatican City	4852 people per sq mile (1875 per sq km)
Maldives	4667 people per sq mile (1812 per sq km)
Malta	4252 people per sq mile (1615 per sq km)
Bangladesh	3276 people per sq mile (1278 per sq km)
Barbados	1730 people per sq mile (669 per sq km)
Lebanon	1728 people per sq mile (662 per sq km)
Mauritius	1616 people per sq mile (624 per sq km)

Most sparsely populated countries

Mongolia	5 people per sq mile (2 per sq km)
Namibia	8 people per sq mile (3 per sq km)
Australia	8 people per sq mile (3 per sq km)
Iceland	10 people per sq mile (4 per sq km)
Guyana	10 people per sq mile (4 per sq km)
Suriname	10 people per sq mile (4 per sq km)
Canada	10 people per sq mile (4 per sq km)
Libya	11 people per sq mile (4 per sq km)
Botswana	13 people per sq mile (5 per sq km)
Mauritania	13 people per sq mile (5 per sq km)

Most widely spoken languages
(Native speakers)

1. Chinese (Mandarin)	6. Portuguese
2. Spanish	7. Bengali
3. English	8. Russian
4. Hindi	9. Japanese
5. Arabic	10. Western Punjabi

Largest conurbations*

Guangzhou (China)	65,100,000
Tokyo (Japan)	40,700,000
Shanghai (China)	39,300,000
Delhi (India)	32,400,000
Jakarta (Indonesia)	28,600,000
Manila (Philippines)	26,400,000
Mumbai (India)	26,100,000
Seoul (South Korea)	24,800,000
Mexico City (Mexico)	24,700,000
New York (USA)	23,000,000
São Paulo (Brazil)	22,700,000
Cairo (Egypt)	21,900,000
Dhaka (Bangladesh)	20,900,000
Lagos (Nigeria)	20,700,000
Beijing (China)	20,500,000
Bangkok (Thailand)	19,900,000
Karachi (Pakistan)	18,600,000
Osaka (Japan)	17,700,000

* Largest conurbations source: Thomas Brinkhoff: City Population, http://www.citypopulation.de

Largest conurbations *continued*

Los Angeles (USA)	17,500,000
Moscow (Russia)	17,400,000
Kolkata (India)	17,200,000
Buenos Aires (Argentina)	16,800,000
Istanbul (Turkey)	16,500,000
Tehran (Iran)	15,800,000
Chengdu (China)	15,200,000

Longest river systems

Nile (Northeast Africa)	4130 miles	(6650 km)
Amazon (South America)	3976 miles	(6400 km)
Yangtze (China)	3917 miles	(6300 km)
Mississippi/Missouri (USA)	3902 miles	(6280 km)
Yenisey (Russia)	3445 miles	(5544 km)
Yellow River (China)	3395 miles	(5464 km)
Ob (Russia)	3364 miles	(5414 km)
Parana (South America)	3030 miles	(4876 km)
Congo (Central Africa)	2922 miles	(4703 km)
Amur (East Asia)	2763 miles	(4447 km)

Highest mountains   (Height above sea level)

Everest	29,032 ft	(8849 m)
K2	28,251 ft	(8611 m)
Kanchenjunga	28,169 ft	(8586 m)
Lhotse	27,940 ft	(8516 m)
Makalu	27,838 ft	(8485 m)
Cho Oyu	26,864 ft	(8188 m)
Dhaulagiri I	26,795 ft	(8167 m)
Manaslu	26,781 ft	(8163 m)
Nanga Parbat	26,660 ft	(8126 m)
Annapurna I	26,545 ft	(8091 m)

Largest bodies of inland water   (Area & depth)

Caspian Sea	143,240 sq miles (371,000 sq km)	3363 ft (1025 m)
Lake Superior	31,700 sq miles (82,100 sq km)	1332 ft (406 m)
Lake Victoria	26,590 sq miles (68,870 sq km)	276 ft (84 m)
Lake Huron	23,000 sq miles (59,600 sq km)	751 ft (229 m)
Lake Michigan	22,400 sq miles (58,000 sq km)	922 ft (281 m)
Lake Tanganyika	12,600 sq miles (32,600 sq km)	4820 ft (1470 m)
Lake Baikal	12,200 sq miles (31,500 sq km)	5371 ft (1637 m)
Great Bear Lake	12,000 sq miles (31,000 sq km)	1463 ft (446 m)
Lake Malawi	11400 sq miles (29,500 sq km)	2316 ft (706 m)
Great Slave Lake	10,000 sq miles (27,000 sq km)	2014 ft (614 m)

Deepest ocean features

Challenger Deep, Mariana Trench (Pacific)	36,197 ft (11,034 m)
Horizon Deep, Tonga Trench (Pacific)	35,702 ft (10,882 m)
Galathea Depth, Philippine Trench (Pacific)	34,580 ft (10,545 m)
Kuril-Kamchatka Trench (Pacific)	34,449 ft (10,542 m)
Kermadec Trench (Pacific)	32,963 ft (10,047 m)
Izu–Ogasawara Trench (Pacific)	32,087 ft (9810 m)
Japan Trench (Pacific)	29,527 ft (9000 m)
Milwaukee Deep, Puerto Rico Trench (Atlantic)	28,232 ft (8605 m)
Yap Trench (Pacific)	27,976 ft (8527 m)
Meteor Deep, South Sandwich Trench (Atlantic)	27,651 ft (8428 m)

Greatest waterfalls   (Mean flow of water)

Boyoma (Congo, Dem. Rep.)	600,000 cu. ft/sec (16,990 cu.m/sec)
Khone (Laos/Cambodia)	410,000 cu. ft/sec (11,600 cu.m/sec)
Pará (Venezuela)	125,000 cu. ft/sec (3540 cu.m/sec)
Paulo Afonso (Brazil)	100,000 cu. ft/sec (2800 cu.m/sec)
Niagara (USA/Canada)	85,000 cu. ft/sec (2407 cu.m/sec)
Vermilion (Canada)	64,000 cu. ft/sec (1800 cu.m/sec)
Iguaçu (Argentina/Brazil)	61,800 cu. ft/sec (1750 cu.m/sec)
Limestone (Canada)	51,600 cu. ft/sec (1460 cu.m/sec)
Pyrite (Canada)	51,600 cu. ft/sec (1460 cu.m/sec)
Victoria (Zimbabwe)	39,000 cu. ft/sec (1100 cu.m/sec)

Greatest waterfalls *continued*

Virginia (Canada)	35,300 cu. ft/sec (1000 cu.m/sec)
Shivanasamudra (India)	33,000 cu. ft/sec (930 cu.m/sec)

Highest waterfalls

Angel (Venezuela)	3212 ft	(979 m)
Tugela (South Africa)	3110 ft	(948 m)
Tres Hermanas (Peru)	2999 ft	(914 m)
Olo'upena (USA)	2953 ft	(900 m)
Yumbilla (Peru)	2940 ft	(896 m)
Skorga (Norway)	2871 ft	(875 m)
Vinnufossen (Norway)	2822 ft	(860 m)
Balåifossen (Norway)	2789 ft	(850 m)
Mattenbachfall (Switzerland)	2756 ft	(840 m)
Pu'uka'oku (USA)	2756 ft	(840 m)
James Bruce (Canada)	2756 ft	(840 m)
Browne (New Zealand)	2743 ft	(836 m)

Largest deserts

Sahara	3,552,140 sq miles (9,200,000 sq km)
Gobi	500,000 sq miles (1,295,000 sq km)
Kalahari	347,492 sq miles (900,000 sq km)
Patagonian	259,847 sq miles (673,000 sq km)
Ar Rub al Khali	250,000 sq miles (650,000 sq km)
Great Basin	190,000 sq miles (492,098 sq km)
Chihuahuan	175,000 sq miles (453,248 sq km)
Karakum	135,136 sq miles (350,000 sq km)
Great Victorian	134,653 sq miles (348,750 sq km)
Sonoran	130,116 sq miles (337,000 sq km)

NB – Most of Antarctica is a polar desert, with only 2 inches (50 mm) of precipitation annually

Hottest inhabited places   (Average annual temperature)

Abéché (Chad)	90.0°F	(32.2°C)
Mecca (Saudi Arabia)	89.8°F	(32.1°C)
Kaédi (Mauritania)	89.2°F	(31.7°C)
Yélimané (Mali)	88.7°F	(31.5°C)
Jizan (Saudi Arabia)	88.0°F	(31.1°C)
Kiffa (Mauritania)	87.9°F	(31.0°C)
Atbara (Sudan)	87.7°F	(30.9°C)
Matam (Senegal)	87.6°F	(30.8°C)
Ayoun al Atrous (Mauritania)	87.2°F	(30.6°C)
Coro (Venezuela)	87.2°F	(30.6°C)

Driest inhabited places   (Average annual rainfall)

Al Jawf (Libya)	<0.10 in	(2.5 mm)
Chimbote (Peru)	<0.10 in	(2.5 mm)
Kaktovik (AK, USA)	<0.10 in	(2.5 mm)
Pisco (Peru)	<0.10 in	(2.5 mm)
Wadi Halfa (Sudan)	<0.10 in	(2.5 mm)
Siwa Oasis (Egypt)	<0.10 in	(2.5 mm)
Kharga Oasis (Egypt)	0.10 in	(2.5 mm)
Aswan (Egypt)	0.10 in	(2.5 mm)
Nok Kundi (Pakistan)	0.10 in	(2.5 mm)
Altos del Mar (Chile)	0.10 in	(2.5 mm)

Wettest inhabited places   (Average annual rainfall)

Mawsynram (India)	467 in	(11871 mm)
Cherrapunji (India)	464 in	(11777 mm)
Tutunendo (Colombia)	463 in	(11770 mm)
San Antonio de Ureca (Equatorial Guinea)	418 in	(10450 mm)
Debundscha (Cameroon)	405 in	(10299 mm)
Quibdó City (Colombia)	289 in	(7328 mm)
Buenaventura (Colombia)	247 in	(6276 mm)
Mawlamyine (Myanmar)	188 in	(4772 mm)
Monrovia (Liberia)	179 in	(4540 mm)
Hilo (Hawaii)	127 in	(3219 mm)

A

Aa see Gauja
Aachen 72 A4 Dut. Aken, Fr. Aix-la-Chapelle; anc. Aquae Grani, Aquisgranum. Nordrhein-Westfalen, W Germany
Aaiún see Laâyoune
Aalborg 63 B7 var. Ålborg, Ålborg-Nørresundby; anc. Alburgum. Nordjylland, N Denmark
Aalen 73 B6 Baden-Württemberg, S Germany
Aalsmeer 64 C3 Noord-Holland, C Netherlands
Aalst 65 B6 Oost-Vlaanderen, C Belgium
Aalten 64 E4 Gelderland, E Netherlands
Aalter 65 B5 Oost-Vlaanderen, NW Belgium
Aanaarjärvi see Inarijärvi
Äänekoski 63 D5 Keski-Suomi, W Finland
Aar see Aare
Aare 73 A7 var. Aar. river W Switzerland
Aarhus 63 B7 var. Århus, C Denmark
Aarlen see Arlon
Aassi, Nahr El see Orontes
Aat see Ath
Aba 55 E5 Orientale, NE Dem. Rep. Congo
Aba 53 G5 Abia, S Nigeria
Abā as Su'ūd see Najrān
Abaco Island see Great Abaco, N The Bahamas
Ābādān 98 C4 Khūzestān, SW Iran
Abadan 100 C3 prev. Bezmein, Büzmeýin, Rus. Byuzmeyin. Ahal Welaýaty, C Turkmenistan
Abai see Blue Nile
Abakan 92 D4 Respublika Khakasiya, S Russia
Abancay 38 D4 Apurímac, SE Peru
Abariringa see Kanton
Abashiri 108 D2 var. Abasiri. Hokkaidō, NE Japan
Abasiri see Abashiri
Ābay Wenz see Blue Nile
Abbaia see Ābaya Hāyk'
Abbatis Villa see Abbeville
Abbazia see Opatija
Abbeville 68 C2 anc. Abbatis Villa. Somme, N France
'Abd al 'Azīz, Jabal 96 D2 mountain range NE Syria
Abéché 54 C3 var. Abécher, Abeshr. Ouaddaï, SE Chad
Abécher see Abéché
Abela see Ávila
Abellinum see Avellino
Abemama 122 D2 var. Apamama; prev. Roger Simpson Island. atoll Tungaru, W Kiribati
Abengourou 53 E5 E Ivory Coast
Aberbrothock see Arbroath
Abercorn see Mbala
Aberdeen 66 D3 anc. Devana. NE Scotland, United Kingdom
Aberdeen 23 E2 South Dakota, N USA
Aberdeen 24 B2 Washington, NW USA
Abergwaun see Fishguard
Abertawe see Swansea
Aberystwyth 67 C6 W Wales, United Kingdom
Abeshr see Abéché
Abhā 99 B6 'Asīr, SW Saudi Arabia
Abidavichy 85 D7 Rus. Obidovichi. Mahilyowskaya Voblasts', E Belarus
Abidjan 53 E5 S Ivory Coast
Abilene 27 F3 Texas, SW USA
Abingdon see Pinta, Isla
Abkhazia 95 E1 var. Apkhazeti. autonomous republic NW Georgia
Åbo see Turku
Aboisso 53 E5 SE Ivory Coast
Abo, Massif d' 54 B1 mountain range NW Chad
Abomey 53 F5 S Benin
Abou-Déïa 54 C3 Salamat, SE Chad
Aboudouhour see Abū aḑ Ḑuhūr
Abou Kémal see Abū Kamāl
Abrantes 70 B3 var. Abrántes. Santarém, C Portugal
Abrashlare see Brezovo
Abrolhos Bank 34 E4 undersea bank W Atlantic Ocean
Abrova 85 B6 Rus. Obrovo. Brestskaya Voblasts', SW Belarus
Abrud 86 B4 Ger. Gross-Schlatten, Hung. Abrudbánya. Alba, SW Romania
Abrudbánya see Abrud
Abruzzese, Appennino 74 C4 mountain range C Italy
Absaroka Range 22 B2 mountain range Montana/Wyoming, NW USA
Abū aḑ Ḑuhūr 96 B3 Fr. Aboudouhour. Idlib, NW Syria
Abu Dhabi see Abū Ẓabī
Abu Hamed 50 C3 River Nile, N Sudan
Abū Ḩardān see Hajîn
Abuja 53 G4 country capital (Nigeria) Federal Capital District, C Nigeria
Abū Kamāl 96 E3 Fr. Abou Kémal. Dayr az Zawr, E Syria
Abula see Ávila
Abunã, Rio 40 C2 var. Río Abuná. river Bolivia/Brazil
Abut Head 129 B6 headland South Island, New Zealand
Abuye Meda 50 D4 mountain C Ethiopia
Abū Ẓabī 99 C5 var. Abū Ẓabī, Eng. Abu Dhabi. country capital (United Arab Emirates) Abū Ẓaby, C United Arab Emirates
Abū Ẓabī see Abū Ẓabī
Abyaḑ, Al Baḩr al see White Nile
Abyla see Ávila
Abyssinia see Ethiopia
Acalayong 55 A5 SW Equatorial Guinea
Acaponeta 28 D4 Nayarit, C Mexico
Acapulco 29 E5 var. Acapulco de Juárez. Guerrero, S Mexico
Acapulco de Juárez see Acapulco
Acarai Mountains 37 F4 Sp. Serra Acaraí. mountain range Brazil/Guyana
Acaraí, Serra see Acarai Mountains
Acarigua 36 D2 Portuguesa, N Venezuela
Accra 53 E5 country capital (Ghana) SE Ghana
Achacachi 39 E4 La Paz, W Bolivia
Ach'ara see Ajaria
Acklins Island 32 C2 island SE The Bahamas
Aconcagua, Cerro 42 B4 mountain W Argentina
Açores/Açores, Arquipélago dos/Açores, Ilhas dos see Azores
A Coruña 70 B1 Cast. La Coruña, Eng. Corunna; anc. Caronium. Galicia, NW Spain
Acre 40 C2 off. Estado do Acre. state/region W Brazil
Açu see Assu
Acunum Acusio see Montélimar
Ada 78 D3 Vojvodina, N Serbia
Ada 27 G2 Oklahoma, C USA
Ada Bazar see Adapazarı
Adalia see Antalya
Adalia, Gulf of see Antalya Körfezi
Adama see Nazrēt
'Adan 99 B7 Eng. Aden. SW Yemen
Adana 94 D4 var. Seyhan. Adana, S Turkey (Türkiye)
Adâncata see Horlivka
Adapazarı 94 B2 prev. Ada Bazar. Sakarya, NW Turkey (Türkiye)
Adare, Cape 132 B4 cape Antarctica
Ad Dahna 98 C4 desert E Saudi Arabia
Ad Dakhla 48 A4 var. Dakhla. SW Western Sahara
Ad Dalanj see Dilling
Ad Damar see Ed Damer
Ad Damazīn see Ed Damazin
Ad Dāmir see Ed Damer
Ad Dammām 98 C4 Ash Sharqīyah, NE Saudi Arabia
Ad Dāmūr see Damoûr
Ad Dawḩah 98 C4 Eng. Doha. country capital (Qatar) C Qatar
Aḑ Ḑiffah see Libyan Plateau
Addis Ababa see Ādīs Ābeba
Addoo Atoll see Addu Atoll
Addu Atoll 110 A5 var. Addoo Atoll, Seenu Atoll. atoll S Maldives
Adelaide 127 B6 state capital South Australia
Adelsberg see Postojna
Aden see 'Adan
Aden, Gulf of 99 C7 gulf SW Arabian Sea
Adige 74 C2 Ger. Etsch. river N Italy
Adirondack Mountains 19 F2 mountain range New York, NE USA
Ādīs Ābeba 51 C5 Eng. Addis Ababa. country capital (Ethiopia) Ādīs Ābeba, C Ethiopia
Adıyaman 95 E4 Adıyaman, SE Turkey (Türkiye)
Adjud 86 C4 Vrancea, E Romania
Admiralty Islands 122 B3 island group N Papua New Guinea
Adra 71 E5 Andalucía, S Spain
Adrar 48 D3 C Algeria
Adrian 18 C3 Michigan, N USA
Adrianople/Adrianopolis see Edirne
Adriatico, Mare see Adriatic Sea
Adriatic Sea 81 E2 Alb. Deti Adriatik, It. Mare Adriatico, Croatian Jadransko More, Slvn. Jadransko Morje. sea N Mediterranean Sea
Adriatik, Deti see Adriatic Sea
Adycha 93 F2 river NE Russia
Aegean Sea 83 C5 Gk. Aigaíon Pélagos, Aigaío Pélagos, Turk. Ege Denizi. sea NE Mediterranean Sea
Aegviidu 84 D2 Ger. Charlottenhof. Harjumaa, NW Estonia
Aegyptus see Egypt
Aelana see Al 'Aqabah
Aelok see Ailuk Atoll
Aelōnlaplap see Ailinglaplap Atoll
Aemona see Ljubljana
Aeolian Islands 75 C6 var. Isole Lipari, Eng. Aeolian Islands, Lipari Islands. island group S Italy
Aeolian Islands see Eolie, Isole
Æsernia see Isernia
Afar Depression see Danakil Desert
Afars et des Issas, Territoire Français des see Djibouti
Afghanistan 100 C4 off. Islamic Republic of Afghanistan; var. Dari as Jamhūrī-ye Islāmī-ye Afghānistān, Pash. Dē Afghānistān Islāmī Jumhūriyat, prev. Republic of Afghanistan. country C Asia
Afghānistān, Dari as Jamhūrī-ye Islāmī-ye see Afghanistan
Afmadow 51 D6 Jubbada Hoose, S Somalia
Africa 46 continent
Africa, Horn of 46 E4 physical region Ethiopia/Somalia
Africana Seamount 119 A6 seamount SW Indian Ocean
'Afrīn 96 B2 Ḩalab, N Syria
Afyon 94 B3 prev. Afyonkarahisar. Afyon, W Turkey (Türkiye)
Agadès see Agadez
Agadez 53 G3 prev. Agadès. Agadez, C Niger
Agadir 48 B3 SW Morocco
Agana/Agaña see Hagåtña
Āgaro 51 C5 Oromīya, C Ethiopia
Agassiz Fracture Zone 121 G5 fracture zone S Pacific Ocean
Agatha see Agde
Agathónisi 83 D6 island Dodekánisa, Greece, Aegean Sea
Agde 69 C6 anc. Agatha. Hérault, S France
Agedabia see Ajdābiyā
Agen 69 B5 anc. Aginnum. Lot-et-Garonne, SW France
Agendicum see Sens
Agiá 82 B4 var. Ayiá. Thessalía, C Greece
Agialoúsa see Yenierenköy
Agía Marína 83 E6 Léros, Dodekánisa, Greece, Aegean Sea
Aginnum see Agen
Ágios Efstrátios 82 D4 var. Áyios Evstrátios, Hagios Evstrátios. island E Greece
Ágios Nikólaos 83 D8 var. Áyios Nikólaos. Kríti, Greece, E Mediterranean Sea
Āgra 112 D3 Uttar Pradesh, N India
Agra and Oudh, United Provinces of see Uttar Pradesh
Agram see Zagreb
Ağrı 95 F3 var. Karaköse; prev. Karakılısse. Ağrı, NE Turkey (Türkiye)
Ağrı Dağı see Büyük Ağrı Dağı
Agrigento 75 C7 Gk. Akragas; prev. Girgenti. Sicilia, Italy, C Mediterranean Sea
Agriovótano 83 C5 Évvoia, C Greece
Agropoli 75 D5 Campania, S Italy
Aguachica 36 B2 Cesar, N Colombia
Aguadulce 31 F5 Coclé, S Panama
Agua Prieta 28 B1 Sonora, NW Mexico
Aguascalientes 28 D4 Aguascalientes, C Mexico
Aguaytía 38 C3 Ucayali, C Peru
Aguilas 71 E4 Murcia, SE Spain
Aguililla 28 D4 Michoacán, SW Mexico
Agulhas Basin 47 D8 undersea basin SW Indian Ocean
Agulhas, Cape 56 C5 headland SW South Africa
Agulhas Plateau 45 D6 undersea plateau SW Indian Ocean
Ahaggar 53 F2 high plateau region SE Algeria
Ahlen 72 B4 Nordrhein-Westfalen, W Germany
Ahmadābād 112 C4 var. Ahmedabad. Gujarāt, W India
Ahmadnagar 112 C5 var. Ahmednagar. Mahārāshtra, W India
Ahmedabad see Ahmadābād
Ahmednagar see Ahmadnagar
Ahuachapán 30 B3 Ahuachapán, W El Salvador
Ahvāz 98 C3 var. Ahwāz; prev. Nāsiri. Khūzestān, SW Iran
Ahvenanmaa see Åland
Ahwāz see Ahvāz
Aigaíon Pélagos/Aigaío Pélagos see Aegean Sea
Aígina 83 C6 var. Aíyina, Egina. Aígina, C Greece
Aígio 83 B5 var. Egio; prev. Aíyion. Dytikí Ellás, S Greece
Aiken 21 E2 South Carolina, SE USA
Ailinglaplap Atoll 122 D2 var. Aelōnlaplap. atoll Ralik Chain, S Marshall Islands
Ailuk Atoll 122 D1 var. Aelok. atoll Ratak Chain, NE Marshall Islands
Ainaži 84 D3 Est. Heinaste, Ger. Hainasch. Limbaži, N Latvia
'Aïn Ben Tili 52 D1 Tiris Zemmour, N Mauritania
Aintab see Gaziantep
Aïoun el Atrous/Aïoun el Atroûss see 'Ayoûn el 'Atroûs
Aiquile 39 F4 Cochabamba, C Bolivia
Aïr see Aïr, Massif de l'
Air du Azbine see Aïr, Massif de l'
Aïr, Massif de l' 53 G2 var. Aïr, Air du Azbine, Asben. mountain range NC Niger
Aiud 86 B4 Ger. Strassburg, Hung. Nagyenyed; prev. Engeten. Alba, SW Romania
Aix see Aix-en-Provence
Aix-en-Provence 69 D6 var. Aix; anc. Aquae Sextiae. Bouches-du-Rhône, SE France
Aix-la-Chapelle see Aachen
Aíyina see Aígina
Aíyion see Aígio
Aizkraukle 84 C4 Aizkraukle, S Latvia
Ajaccio 69 E7 Corse, France, C Mediterranean Sea
Ajaria 95 F2 var. Ach'ara. autonomous republic SW Georgia
Aj Bogd Uul 104 D2 mountain SW Mongolia
Ajdābiyā 49 G2 var. Agedabia, Ajdābiyah. NE Libya
Ajdābiyah see Ajdābiyā
Ajjinena see El Geneina
Ajmer 112 D3 var. Ajmere. Rājasthān, N India
Ajo 26 A3 Arizona, SW USA
Akaba see Al 'Aqabah
Akamagaseki see Shimonoseki
Akasha 50 B3 Northern, N Sudan
Akchâr 52 C2 desert W Mauritania
Aken see Aachen
Akermanceaster see Bath
Akhaltsikhe 95 F2 prev. Akhalts'ikhe. SW Georgia
Akhalts'ikhe see Akhaltsikhe
Akhisar 94 A3 Manisa, W Turkey (Türkiye)
Akhmīm 50 B2 var. Akhmîm; anc. Panopolis. C Egypt
Akhtubinsk 89 C7 Astrakhanskaya Oblast', SW Russia
Akhtyrka see Okhtyrka
Akimiski Island 16 C3 island Nunavut, C Canada
Akinovka 87 F4 Zaporiz'ka Oblast', S Ukraine
Akita 108 D4 Akita, Honshū, C Japan
Akjoujt 52 C2 prev. Fort-Repoux. Inchiri, W Mauritania
Akkerman see Bilhorod-Dnistrovskyi
Akkeshi 108 E2 Hokkaidō, NE Japan
Aklavik 14 D3 Northwest Territories, NW Canada
Akmola see Nur-Sultan
Akmolinsk see Nur-Sultan
Aknavásár see Târgu Ocna
Akpatok Island 17 E1 island Nunavut, E Canada
Akragas see Agrigento
Akron 18 D4 Ohio, N USA
Akrotiri 80 C5 var. Akrotírion. UK Sovereign Base Area S Cyprus
Akrotírion see Akrotiri
Akrotirion Aksai Chin 102 B2 Chin. Aksayqin. disputed region China/India
Aksaray 94 C4 Aksaray, C Turkey (Türkiye)
Aksayqin see Aksai Chin
Akşehir 94 B4 Konya, W Turkey (Türkiye)
Aktash see Oqtosh
Aktau see Aqtaū
Aktjubinsk/Aktyubinsk see Aqtöbe
Aktobe see Aqtöbe
Aktsyabrski 85 C7 Rus. Oktyabr'skiy; prev. Karpilovka. Homyel'skaya Voblasts', SE Belarus
Aktyubinsk see Aqtöbe
Akula 55 C5 Equateur, NW Dem. Rep. Congo
Akureyri 61 E4 Nordhurland Eystra, N Iceland
Akyab see Sittwe
Alabama 20 C2 off. State of Alabama, also known as Camellia State, Heart of Dixie, The Cotton State, Yellowhammer State. state S USA
Alabama River 20 C3 river Alabama, S USA
Alaca 94 C3 Çorum, N Turkey (Türkiye)
Alacant see Alicante
Alagoas 41 G2 off. Estado de Alagoas. state/region E Brazil
Alais see Alès
Alajuela 31 E4 Alajuela, C Costa Rica
Alakanuk 14 C2 Alaska, USA
Al 'Alamayn 50 B1 var. El 'Alamein. N Egypt
Al 'Amārah 98 C3 var. Amara. Maysān, E Iraq
Alamo 25 D6 Nevada, W USA
Alamogordo 26 D3 New Mexico, SW USA
Alamosa 22 C5 Colorado, C USA
Åland 63 C6 var. Aland Islands, Fin. Ahvenanmaa. island group SW Finland
Aland Islands see Åland
Aland Sea see Ålands Hav
Ålands Hav 63 C6 var. Aland Sea. strait Baltic Sea/Gulf of Bothnia
Alanya 94 C4 Antalya, S Turkey (Türkiye)
Alappuzha 110 C3 var. Alleppey. Kerala, SW India
Al 'Aqabah 97 B8 var. Akaba, Aqaba, 'Aqaba; anc. Aelana, Elath. Al 'Aqabah, SW Jordan
Al 'Arabīyah as Su'ūdīyah see Saudi Arabia
Alasca, Golfo de see Alaska, Gulf of
Alaşehir 94 A4 Manisa, W Turkey (Türkiye)
Al 'Ashārah 96 E3 var. Ashara. Dayr az Zawr, E Syria
Alaska 14 C3 off. State of Alaska, also known as Land of the Midnight Sun, The Last Frontier, Seward's Folly; prev. Russian America. state NW USA
Alaska, Gulf of 14 C4 var. Golfo de Alasca. gulf Canada/USA
Alaska Peninsula 14 C3 peninsula Alaska, USA
Alaska Range 12 B2 mountain range Alaska, USA
Al-Asnam see Chlef
Alattio see Alta
Al Awaynāt see Al 'Uwaynāt
Al 'Awjā 97 E7 E West Bank, Middle East
Alaykel'/Alay-Kuu see Këk-Art
Al 'Aynā 97 B7 Al Karak, W Jordan
Alazeya 93 G2 river NE Russia
Al Bāb 96 B2 Ḩalab, N Syria
Albacete 71 E3 Castilla-La Mancha, C Spain
Al Baghdādī 98 B3 var. Khān al Baghdādī. Al Anbār, SW Iraq
Al Bāha see Al Bāḩah
Al Bāḩah 99 B5 var. Al Bāha. Al BāḨah, SW Saudi Arabia
Al Baḩrayn see Bahrain
Alba Iulia 86 B4 Ger. Weissenburg, Hung. Gyulafehérvár; prev. Bălgrad, Karlsburg, Károly-Fehérvár. Alba, W Romania
Albania 79 C7 off. Republic of Albania, Alb. Republika e Shqipqërisë, Shqipëria; prev. People's Socialist Republic of Albania. country SE Europe
Albania see Aubagne
Albany 125 B7 Western Australia
Albany 20 D3 Georgia, SE USA
Albany 19 F3 state capital New York, NE USA
Albany 24 B3 Oregon, NW USA
Albany 16 C3 river Ontario, S Canada
Alba Regia see Székesfehérvár
Al Bāridah 96 C4 var. Bāridah. Ḩimş, C Syria
Al Başrah 98 C3 Eng. Basra, hist. Busra, Bussora. Al Başrah, SE Iraq
Al Batrūn see Batroûn
Al Bawītī 50 B2 var. Bawīṭi C Egypt
Al Bayḑā' 49 G2 var. Beida. NE Libya
Albemarle Island see Isabela, Isla
Albemarle Sound 21 G1 inlet W Atlantic Ocean
Albergaria-a-Velha 70 B2 Aveiro, N Portugal
Albert 68 C3 Somme, N France
Alberta 15 E4 province SW Canada
Albert Edward Nyanza see Edward, Lake
Albert, Lake 51 B6 var. Albert Nyanza, Lac Mobutu Sese Seko. lake Uganda/Dem. Rep. Congo
Albert Lea 23 F3 Minnesota, N USA
Albert Nyanza see Albert, Lake
Albertville see Kalemie
Albi 69 C6 anc. Albiga. Tarn, S France
Albiga see Albi
Ålborg see Aalborg
Ålborg-Nørresundby see Aalborg
Alborz, Reshteh-ye Kūhhā-ye 98 C2 Eng. Elburz Mountains. mountain range N Iran
Albuquerque 26 D2 New Mexico, SW USA
Al Burayqah see Marsá al Burayqah
Alburgum see Aalborg
Albury 127 C7 New South Wales, SE Australia
Al Buşayrah 96 D3 Dayr az Zawr, E Syria
Alcácer do Sal 70 B4 Setúbal, W Portugal
Alcalá de Henares 71 E3 Ar. Alkal'a; anc. Complutum. Madrid, C Spain
Alcamo 75 C7 Sicilia, Italy, C Mediterranean Sea
Alcañiz 71 F2 Aragón, NE Spain
Alcántara, Embalse de 70 C3 reservoir W Spain
Alcaudete 70 D4 Andalucía, S Spain
Alcázar see Ksar-el-Kebir
Alcazarquivir see Ksar-el-Kebir
Alcoi see Alcoy
Alcoy 71 F4 Cat. Alcoi. Comunitat Valenciana, E Spain
Aldabra Group 57 G2 island group SW Seychelles
Aldan 93 F3 river NE Russia
al Dar al Baida see Rabat
Alderney 68 A2 island Channel Islands
Aleg 52 C3 Brakna, SW Mauritania
Aleksandriya see Oleksandriia
Aleksandropol' see Gyumri
Aleksandrovka see Oleksandrivka
Aleksandrovsk see Zaporizhzhia
Aleksin 89 B5 Tul'skaya Oblast', W Russia
Aleksinac 78 E4 Serbia, SE Serbia
Alençon 68 B3 Orne, N France
Alenquer 41 E2 Pará, NE Brazil
Alep/Aleppo see Ḩalab
Alert 15 F1 Ellesmere Island, Nunavut, N Canada
Alès 69 C6 prev. Alais. Gard, S France
Aleşd 86 B3 Hung. Élesd. Bihor, SW Romania
Alessandria 74 B2 Fr. Alexandrie. Piemonte, N Italy
Ålesund 63 A5 Møre og Romsdal, S Norway
Aleutian Basin 91 G3 undersea basin Bering Sea
Aleutian Islands 14 A3 island group Alaska, USA
Aleutian Range 12 A2 mountain range Alaska, USA
Aleutian Trench 91 H3 trench S Bering Sea
Alexander Archipelago 14 D4 island group Alaska, USA
Alexander City 20 D2 Alabama, S USA
Alexander Island 132 A3 island Antarctica
Alexander Range see Kirghiz Range
Alexandra 129 B7 Otago, South Island, New Zealand
Alexándreia 82 B4 var. Alexándria. Kentrikí Makedonía, N Greece
Alexandreta see İskenderun
Alexandretta, Gulf of see İskenderun Körfezi
Alexandria see Al Iskandarīyah
Alexandria 86 C5 Teleorman, S Romania
Alexandria 20 B3 Louisiana, S USA
Alexandria 23 F2 Minnesota, N USA
Alexándria see Alexándreia
Alexandrie see Alessandria
Alexandroúpoli 82 D3 var. Alexandroúpolis, Turk. Dedeagaç, Dedeagach. Anatolikí Makedonía kai Thráki, NE Greece
Alexandroúpolis see Alexandroúpoli
Al Fāshir see El Fasher
Alfatar 82 E1 Silistra, NE Bulgaria
Alfeiós 83 B6 prev. Alfiós; anc. Alpheius, Alpheus. river S Greece
Alfiós see Alfeiós
Alföld see Great Hungarian Plain
Al-Furāt see Euphrates
Alga 92 B4 Kaz. Algha. Aktyubinsk, NW Kazakhstan
Algarve 70 B4 cultural region S Portugal
Algeciras 70 C5 Andalucía, SW Spain
Algemesí 71 F3 Comunitat Valenciana, E Spain
Al-Genain see El Geneina
Alger 49 E1 var. Algiers, El Djazaïr, Al Jazair. country capital (Algeria) N Algeria
Algeria 48 C3 off. People's Democratic Republic of Algeria. prev. Democratic and Popular Republic of Algeria. country N Africa
Algeria, Democratic and Popular Republic of see Algeria
Algeria, People's Democratic Republic of see Algeria
Algerian Basin 58 C5 var. Balearic Plain. undersea basin W Mediterranean Sea
Algha see Alga
Al Ghābah 99 E5 var. Ghaba. C Oman
Alghero 75 A5 Sardegna, Italy, C Mediterranean Sea
Al Ghardaqah 50 C2 var. Hurghada, Ghurdaqah. E Egypt
Algiers see Alger
Al Golea see El Goléa
Algona 23 F3 Iowa, C USA
Al Hajar al Gharbi 99 D5 mountain range N Oman
Al Hamad see Syrian Desert
Al Ḩasakah 96 D2 var. Al Hasijah, Al Haseke, Fr. Hassetché. Al Ḩasakah, NE Syria
Al Hasijah see Al Ḩasakah
Al Ḩillah 98 B3 var. Hilla. Bābil, C Iraq
Al Ḩisā 97 B7 Aṭ Ṭafīlah, W Jordan
Al Ḩudaydah 99 B6 Eng. Hodeidah. W Yemen
Al Hufūf 98 C4 var. Hofuf. Ash Sharqīyah, NE Saudi Arabia
Aliákmon see Aliákmonas
Aliákmonas 82 B4 prev. Aliákmon; anc. Haliacmon. river N Greece
Alíartos 83 C5 Stereá Ellás, C Greece
Āli-Bayramı see Şirvan
Alicante 71 F4 Cat. Alacant, Lat. Lucentum. Comunitat Valenciana, SE Spain
Alice 27 G5 Texas, SW USA
Alice Springs 126 A4 Northern Territory, C Australia
Alifu Atoll see Ari Atoll
Aligandí 31 G4 Kuna Yala, NE Panama
Aliki see Alykí
Alima 55 B6 river C Congo
Al Imārāt al 'Arabīyah al Muttaḩidah see United Arab Emirates
Alindao 54 C4 Basse-Kotto, S Central African Republic
Aliquippa 18 D4 Pennsylvania, NE USA
Al Iskandarīyah 50 B1 Eng. Alexandria. N Egypt
Al Ismā'īlīya 50 B1 var. Ismailia, Ismâ'ilîya. N Egypt
Alistráti 82 C3 Kentrikí Makedonía, NE Greece
Alivéri 83 C5 var. Alivérion. Évvoia, C Greece
Alivérion see Alivéri
Al Jabal al Akhḑar 49 G2 mountain range NE Libya
Al Jafr 97 B7 Ma'ān, S Jordan
Al Jaghbūb 49 H3 NE Libya
Al Jahrā' 98 C4 var. Al Jahrah, Jahra. C Kuwait
Al Jahrah see Al Jahrā'
Al Jawf 98 B4 off. Jauf. Al Jawf, NW Saudi Arabia
Al Jawlān see Golan Heights
Al Jazair see Alger
Al Jazīrah 96 E2 physical region Iraq/Syria
Al Jīzah 50 B1 var. El Gîza, Gizeh; Eng. Giza. N Egypt
Al Junaynah see El Geneina
Alkal'a see Alcalá de Henares
Al Karak 97 B7 var. El Kerak, Karak, Kerak; anc. Kir Moab, Kir of Moab. Al Karak, W Jordan
Al-Kasr al-Kebir see Ksar-el-Kebir
Al Khalīl see Hebron
Al Khārjah 50 B2 var. El Khârga; Eng. Kharga. C Egypt
Al Khums 49 F2 var. Homs, Khoms, Khums. NW Libya
Alkmaar 64 C2 Noord-Holland, NW Netherlands
Al Kufrah 49 H4 SE Libya
Al Kūt 98 C3 var. Kūt al 'Amārah, Kut al Imara. Wāsiṭ, E Iraq
Al-Kuwait see Al Kuwayt
Al Kuwayt 98 C4 var. Al-Kuwait, Eng. Kuwait, Kuwait City; prev. Qurein. country capital (Kuwait) E Kuwait
Al Lādhiqīyah 96 A3 Eng. Latakia, Fr. Lattaquié; anc. Laodicea, Laodicea ad Mare. Al Lādhiqīyah, W Syria
Allahābād see Prayagraj
Allanmyo see Aunglan
Allegheny Plateau 19 E3 mountain range New York/Pennsylvania, NE USA
Allenstein see Olsztyn
Allentown 19 F4 Pennsylvania, NE USA
Alleppey see Alappuzha
Alliance 22 D3 Nebraska, C USA
Al Līth 99 B5 Makkah, SW Saudi Arabia
Alma-Ata see Almaty
Almada 70 B4 Setúbal, W Portugal
Al Madīnah 99 A5 Eng. Medina. Al Madīnah, W Saudi Arabia
Al Mafraq 97 B6 var. Mafraq. Al Mafraq, N Jordan
Al Maghrib see Morocco
Al Mahdīyah see Mahdia
Al Mahrah 99 C6 mountain range E Yemen
Al Majma'ah 98 B4 Ar Riyāḑ, C Saudi Arabia
Al Mālikīyah 96 E1 var. Malkiye. Al Ḩasakah, N Syria
Almalyk see Olmaliq
Al Mamlaka al Urdunīya al Hashemīyah see Jordan
Al Manāmah 98 C4 Eng. Manama. country capital (Bahrain) N Bahrain
Al Manāşif 96 E3 mountain range E Syria
Almansa 71 F4 Castilla-La Mancha, C Spain
Al-Mariyya see Almería
Al Marj 49 G2 var. Barka, It. Barce. NE Libya
Almaty 92 C5 var. Alma-Ata. Almaty, SE Kazakhstan
Al Mawşil 98 B2 Eng. Mosul. Nīnawá, N Iraq
Al Mayādīn 96 D3 var. Mayadin, Fr. Meyadine. Dayr az Zawr, E Syria
Al Mazra' see Al Mazra'ah
Al Mazra'ah 97 B6 var. Al Mazra', Mazra'a. Al Karak, W Jordan
Almelo 64 E3 Overijssel, E Netherlands
Almendra, Embalse de 70 C2 reservoir Castilla y León, NW Spain
Almendralejo 70 C4 Extremadura, W Spain

Almere 64 C3 var. Almere-stad. Flevoland, C Netherlands
Almere-stad see Almere
Almería 71 E5 Ar. Al-Mariyya; anc. Unci, Lat. Portus Magnus. Andalucía, S Spain
Al'met'yevsk 89 D5 Respublika Tatarstan, W Russia
Al Mīnā' see El Mina
Al Minyā 50 B2 var. El Minya, Minya. C Egypt
Almirante 31 E4 Bocas del Toro, NW Panama
Al Mudawwarah 97 B8 Ma'ān, SW Jordan
Al Mukallā 99 C6 var. Mukalla. SE Yemen
Al Obayyid see El Obeid
Alofi 123 F4 dependent territory capital (Niue) W Niue
Aloha State see Hawaii
Aloja 84 D3 Limbaži, N Latvia
Alónnisos 83 C5 island Vóreies Sporádes, Greece, Aegean Sea
Álora 70 D5 Andalucía, S Spain
Alor, Kepulauan 117 E5 island group E Indonesia
Al Oued see El Oued
Alpen see Alps
Alpena 18 D2 Michigan, N USA
Alpes see Alps
Alpha Cordillera 133 B3 var. Alpha Ridge. seamount range Arctic Ocean
Alpha Ridge see Alpha Cordillera
Alpheius see Alfeiós
Alphen see Alphen aan den Rijn
Alphen aan den Rijn 64 C3 var. Alphen. Zuid-Holland, C Netherlands
Alpheus see Alfeiós
Alpi see Alps
Alpine 27 E4 Texas, SW USA
Alps 80 C1 Fr. Alpes, Ger. Alpen, It. Alpi. mountain range C Europe
Al Qaḍārif see Gedaref
Al Qāhirah 50 B2 var. El Qâhira, Eng. Cairo. country capital (Egypt) N Egypt
Al Qāmishlī 96 E1 var. Kamishli, Qamishly. Al Ḥasakah, NE Syria
Al Qaṣrayn see Kasserine
Al Qayrawān see Kairouan
Al-Qsar al-Kbir see Ksar-el-Kebir
Al Qubayyāt see Qoubaïyât
Al Quds/Al Quds ash Sharif see Jerusalem
Alqueva, Barragem do 70 C4 reservoir Portugal/Spain
Al Qunayṭirah 97 B5 var. El Kuneitra, El Quneitra, Kuneitra, Qunaytra. Al Qunayṭirah, SW Syria
Al Quṣayr 96 B4 var. El Quseir, Quṣayr, Fr. Kousseir. Ḥimṣ, W Syria
Al Quwayrah 97 B8 var. El Quweira. Al 'Aqabah, SW Jordan
Alsace 68 E3 Ger. Elsass; anc. Alsatia. cultural region NE France
Alsatia see Alsace
Alsdorf 72 A4 Nordrhein-Westfalen, W Germany
Alt see Olt
Alta 62 D2 Fin. Alattio. Finnmark, N Norway
Altai see Altai Mountains
Altai Mountains 104 C2 var. Altai, Chin. Altay Shan, Rus. Altay. mountain range Asia/Europe
Altamaha River 21 E3 river Georgia, SE USA
Altamira 41 E2 Pará, NE Brazil
Altamura 75 E5 anc. Lupatia. Puglia, SE Italy
Altar, Desierto de 28 A1 var. Sonoran Desert. desert Mexico/USA
Altar, Desierto de see Sonoran Desert
Altay 104 C2 Xinjiang Uygur Zizhiqu, NW China
Altay 104 D2 prev. Yösönbulag. Govĭ-Altay, W Mongolia
Altay Altai Mountains, Asia/Europe
Altay Shan see Altai Mountains
Altbetsche see Bečej
Altenburg see Bucureşti, Romania
Altin Köprü see Āltūn Kawbrī
Altiplano 39 F4 physical region W South America
Altkanischa see Kanjiža
Alton 18 B4 Illinois, C USA
Altoona 19 E4 Pennsylvania, NE USA
Alto Paraná see Paraná
Altpasua see Stara Pazova
Alt-Schwanenburg see Gulbene
Altsohl see Zvolen
Āltūn Kawbrī 98 B3 var. Altin Köprü, Altun Kupri. Kirkūk, N Iraq
Altun Kupri see Āltūn Kawbrī
Altun Shan 104 C3 var. Altyn Tagh. mountain range NW China
Altus 27 F2 Oklahoma, C USA
Altyn Tagh see Altun Shan
Al Ubayyiḍ see El Obeid
Alūksne 84 D3 Ger. Marienburg. Alūksne, NE Latvia
Al 'Ulā 98 A4 Al Madīnah, NW Saudi Arabia
Al 'Umarī 97 C6 'Ammān, E Jordan
Alupka 87 F5 Respublika Krym, S Ukraine
Al Uqṣur 50 B2 Eng. Luxor. E Egypt
Al Urdunn see Jordan
Alushta 87 F5 Respublika Krym, S Ukraine
Al 'Uwaynāt 49 F4 var. Al Awaynāt. SW Libya
Alva 27 F1 Oklahoma, C USA
Alvarado 29 F4 Veracruz-Llave, E Mexico
Alvin 27 H4 Texas, SW USA
Al Wajh 98 A4 Tabūk, NW Saudi Arabia
Alwar 112 D3 Rājasthān, N India
Al Wari'ah 98 C4 Ash Sharqīyah, N Saudi Arabia
Al Yaman see Yemen
Alykí 82 C4 var. Aliki. Thásos, N Greece
Alytus 85 B5 Pol. Olita. Alytus, S Lithuania
Alzette 65 D8 river S Luxembourg
Amadeus, Lake 125 D5 seasonal lake Northern Territory, C Australia
Amadi 51 B5 W Equatoria, S South Sudan
Amadjuak Lake 15 G3 lake Baffin Island, Nunavut, N Canada
Amakusa-nada 109 A7 gulf SW Japan
Åmål 63 B6 Västra Götaland, S Sweden
Amami-gunto 108 A3 island group SW Japan
Amami-o-shim 108 A3 island S Japan
Amantea 75 D6 Calabria, SW Italy
Amapá 41 E1 off. Estado de Amapá; prev. Território de Amapá. state/region NE Brazil
Amapá, Estado de see Amapá
Amapá, Território de see Amapá
Amara see Al 'Amārah
Amarapura 114 B3 Mandalay, C Myanmar (Burma)
Amarillo 27 E2 Texas, SW USA
Amay 65 C6 Liège, E Belgium
Amazon 41 E1 Sp. Amazonas. river Brazil/Peru
Amazonas see Amazon
Amazon Basin 40 D2 basin N South America
Amazonía 36 B4 region S Colombia
Amazon, Mouths of the 41 F1 delta NE Brazil
Ambam 55 B5 Sud, S Cameroon
Ambanja 57 G2 Antsirañana, N Madagascar
Ambarchik 93 G2 Respublika Sakha (Yakutiya), NE Russia
Ambato 38 B1 Tungurahua, C Ecuador
Ambérieu-en-Bugey 69 D5 Ain, E France
Ambianum see Amiens
Amboasary 57 F4 Toliara, S Madagascar
Amboina see Ambon
Ambon 117 F4 prev. Amboina, Amboyna. Pulau Ambon, E Indonesia
Ambositra 57 G3 Fianarantsoa, SE Madagascar
Amboyna see Ambon
Ambracia see Árta
Ambre, Cap d' see Bobaomby, Tanjona
Ambrim see Ambrym
Ambriz 56 A1 Bengo, NW Angola
Ambrym 122 D4 var. Ambrim. island C Vanuatu
Amchitka Island 14 A2 island Aleutian Islands, Alaska, USA
Amdo 104 C5 Xizang Zizhiqu, W China
Ameland 64 D1 Fris. It Amelân. island Waddeneilanden, N Netherlands
Amelân, It see Ameland
America see United States of America
America-Antarctica Ridge 45 C7 undersea ridge S Atlantic Ocean
America in Miniature see Maryland
American Falls Reservoir 24 E4 reservoir Idaho, NW USA
American Samoa 123 E4 US unincorporated territory W Polynesia
Amersfoort 64 D3 Utrecht, C Netherlands
Ames 23 F3 Iowa, C USA
Amfilochía 83 A5 var. Amfilokhía. Dytikí Ellás, C Greece
Amfilokhía see Amfilochía
Amga 93 F3 river NE Russia
Amherst 17 F4 Nova Scotia, SE Canada
Amherst see Kyaikkami
Amida see Diyarbakır
Amiens 68 C3 anc. Ambianum, Samarobriva. Somme, N France
Amíndaion/Amindeo see Amýntaio
Amindivi Islands 110 A2 island group Lakshadweep, India, N Indian Ocean
Amirante Islands 57 G1 var. Amirantes Group. island group C Seychelles
Amirantes Group see Amirante Islands
Amistad, Presa de la see Amistad Reservoir
Amistad Reservoir 27 F4 var. Presa de la Amistad. reservoir Mexico/USA
Amisus see Samsun
Ammaia see Portalegre
'Ammān 97 B6 anc. Philadelphia, Bibl. Rabbah Ammon, Rabbath Ammon. country capital (Jordan) 'Ammān, NW Jordan
Ammassalik see Tasiilaq
Ammóchostos see Gazimağusa
Ammóchostos, Kólpos see Gazimağusa Körfezi
Amnok-kang see Yalu
Amoea see Portalegre
Amoentai see Amuntai
Āmol 98 D2 var. Amul. Māzandarān, N Iran
Amorgós 83 D6 Amorgós, Kykládes, Greece, Aegean Sea
Amorgós 83 D6 island Kykládes, Greece, Aegean Sea
Amos 16 D4 Québec, SE Canada
Amourj 52 D3 Hodh ech Chargui, SE Mauritania
Amoy see Xiamen
Ampato, Nevado 39 E4 mountain S Peru
Amposta 71 F2 Cataluña, NE Spain
Amraoti see Amrāvati
Amrāvati 112 D4 prev. Amraoti. Mahārāshtra, C India
Amritsar 112 D2 Punjab, N India
Amstelveen 64 C3 Noord-Holland, C Netherlands
Amsterdam 64 C3 country capital (Netherlands) Noord-Holland, C Netherlands
Amsterdam Island 119 C6 island NE French Southern and Antarctic Lands
Am Timan 54 C3 Salamat, SE Chad
Amu Darya 100 D2 Rus. Amudar'ya, Taj. Dar"yoi Amu, Turkm. Amyderya, Uzb. Amudaryo; anc. Oxus. river C Asia
Amu-Dar'ya see Amyderýa
Amudar'ya/Amudaryo/Amu, Dar"yoi see Amu Darya
Amul see Āmol
Amund Ringnes Island 15 F2 Island Nunavut, N Canada
Amundsen Basin see Fram Basin
Amundsen Plain 132 A4 abyssal plain S Pacific Ocean
Amundsen-Scott 132 B3 US research station Antarctica
Amundsen Sea 132 A4 sea S Pacific Ocean
Amuntai 116 D4 prev. Amoentai. Borneo, C Indonesia
Amur 93 G4 Chin. Heilong Jiang. river China/Russia
Amvrosiivka 87 H3 prev. Amvrosiyivka, Rus. Amvrosiyevka. Donets'ka Oblast', SE Ukraine
Amvrosiyevka see Amvrosiivka
Amvrosiyivka see Amvrosiivka
Amyderýa 101 E3 Rus. Amu-Dar'ya. Lebap Welaýaty, NE Turkmenistan
Amyderya see Amu Darya
Amýntaio 82 B4 var. Amindeo; prev. Amíndaion. Dytikí Makedonía, N Greece
Anabar 93 E2 river NE Russia
An Abhainn Mhór see Blackwater
Anaco 37 E2 Anzoátegui, NE Venezuela
Anaconda 22 B2 Montana, NW USA
Anacortes 24 B1 Washington, NW USA
Anadolu Dağları see Doğu Karadeniz Dağları
Anadyr' 93 H1 Chukotskiy Avtonomnyy Okrug, NE Russia
Anadyr' 93 G1 river NE Russia
Anadyr, Gulf of see Anadyrskiy Zaliv
Anadyrskiy Zaliv 93 H1 Eng. Gulf of Anadyr. gulf NE Russia
Anáfi 83 D7 anc. Anaphe. island Kykládes, Greece, Aegean Sea
'Ānah see 'Annah
Anaheim 24 E2 California, W USA
Anaiza see 'Unayzah
Analalava 57 G2 Mahajanga, NW Madagascar
Anamur 94 C5 İçel, S Turkey (Türkiye)
Anantapur 110 C2 Andhra Pradesh, S India
Anaphe see Anáfi
Anápolis 41 F3 Goiás, C Brazil
Anār 98 D3 Kermān, C Iran
Anatolia 94 C4 plateau C Turkey (Türkiye)
Anatom see Aneityum
Añatuya 42 C3 Santiago del Estero, N Argentina
An Bhearú see Barrow
Anchorage 14 C3 Alaska, USA
Ancona 74 C3 Marche, C Italy
Ancud 43 B6 prev. San Carlos de Ancud. Los Lagos, S Chile
Ancyra see Ankara
Åndalsnes 63 A5 Møre og Romsdal, S Norway
Andalucía 70 D4 cultural region S Spain
Andalusia 20 C3 Alabama, S USA
Andaman Islands 102 B4 island group India, NE Indian Ocean
Andaman Sea 102 C4 sea NE Indian Ocean
Andenne 65 C6 Namur, SE Belgium
Anderlues 65 B7 Hainaut, S Belgium
Anderson 18 C4 Indiana, N USA
Andes 42 B3 mountain range W South America
Andhra Pradesh 113 E5 cultural region E India
Andijon 101 F2 Rus. Andizhan. Andijon Viloyati, E Uzbekistan
Andikíthira see Antikýthira
Andipaxi see Antípaxoi
Andípsara see Antípsara
Ándissa see Ántissa
Andizhan see Andijon
Andkhvoy 100 D3 Fāryāb, N Afghanistan
Andorra 69 A7 off. Principality of Andorra, Cat. Valls d'Andorra, Fr. Vallée d'Andorre. country SW Europe
Andorra see Andorra la Vella
Andorra la Vella 69 A8 var. Andorra, Fr. Andorre la Vielle, Sp. Andorra la Vieja. country capital (Andorra) C Andorra
Andorra la Vieja see Andorra la Vella
Andorra, Principality of see Andorra
Andorra, Valls d'/Andorra, Vallée d' see Andorra
Andorre la Vielle see Andorra la Vella
Andover 67 D7 S England, United Kingdom
Andøya 62 C2 island C Norway
Andreanof Islands 14 A3 island group Aleutian Islands, Alaska, USA
Andrews 27 E3 Texas, SW USA
Andrew Tablemount 118 A4 var. Gora Andryu. seamount W Indian Ocean
Andria 75 D5 Puglia, SE Italy
An Droichead Nua see Newbridge
Andropov see Rybinsk
Ándros 83 D6 Ándros, Kykládes, Greece, Aegean Sea
Ándros 83 C6 island Kykládes, Greece, Aegean Sea
Andros Island 32 B2 island NW The Bahamas
Andros Town 32 C1 Andros Island, NW The Bahamas
Andryu, Gora see Andrew Tablemount
Aneityum 122 D5 var. Anatom; prev. Kéamu. island S Vanuatu
Ānewetak see Enewetak Atoll
Angara 93 E4 river C Russia
Angarsk 93 E4 Irkutskaya Oblast', S Russia
Ånge 63 C5 Västernorrland, C Sweden
Ángel de la Guarda, Isla 28 B2 island NW Mexico
Angeles 117 E1 off. Angeles City. Luzon, N Philippines
Angeles City see Angeles
Angel Falls 37 E3 Eng. Angel Falls. waterfall E Venezuela
Angel Falls see Ángel, Salto
Angerburg see Węgorzewo
Ångermanälven 62 C4 river N Sweden
Angermünde 72 D3 Brandenburg, NE Germany
Angers 68 B4 anc. Juliomagus. Maine-et-Loire, NW France
Anglesey 67 C5 island NW Wales, United Kingdom
Anglet 69 A6 Pyrénées-Atlantiques, SW France
Angleton 27 H4 Texas, SW USA
Anglia see England
Anglo-Egyptian Sudan see Sudan
Angmagssalik see Tasiilaq
Ang Nam Ngum 114 C4 lake C Laos
Angola 56 B2 off. Republic of Angola; prev. People's Republic of Angola, Portuguese West Africa. country SW Africa
Angola Basin 47 B5 undersea basin E Atlantic Ocean
Angola, People's Republic of see Angola
Angola, Republic of see Angola
Angora see Ankara
Angostura see Ciudad Bolívar
Angostura, Presa de la 29 G5 reservoir SE Mexico
Angoulême 69 B5 anc. Iculisma. Charente, W France
Angoumois 69 B5 cultural region W France
Angra Pequena see Lüderitz
Angren 101 F2 Toshkent Viloyati, E Uzbekistan
Anguilla 33 G3 UK Overseas Territory E West Indies
Anguilla Cays 32 B2 islets SW The Bahamas
Anhui 106 C5 var. Anhui Sheng, Anhwei, Wan. province E China
AnhuiSheng/Anhwei Wan see Anhui
Anicium see le Puy
Anina 86 A4 Ger. Steierdorf, Hung. Stájerlakanina; prev. Ştaierdorf-Anina, Steierdorf-Anina, Steyerlak-Anina. Caraş-Severin, SW Romania
Anjou 68 B4 cultural region NW France
Anjouan 57 F2 var. Ndzouani, Nzwani. island SE Comoros
Ankara 94 C3 prev. Angora; anc. Ancyra. country capital (Turkey) Ankara, C Turkey (Türkiye)
Ankeny 23 F3 Iowa, C USA
Anklam 72 D2 Mecklenburg-Vorpommern, NE Germany
An Mhuir Cheilteach see Celtic Sea
Annaba 49 E1 prev. Bône. NE Algeria
An Nafud 98 B4 desert NW Saudi Arabia
'Annah 98 B3 var. 'Ānah. Al Anbār, NW Iraq
An Najaf 98 B3 var. Najaf. An Najaf, S Iraq
Annamite Mountains 114 D4 Fr. Annamitique, Chaîne. mountain range C Laos
Annamitique, Chaîne see Annamite Mountains
Annapolis 19 F4 state capital Maryland, NE USA
Annapurṇa 113 E3 mountain C Nepal
An Nāqūrah see En Nâqoûra
Ann Arbor 18 C3 Michigan, N USA
An Nāṣirīyah 98 C3 var. Nasiriya. Dhī Qār, SE Iraq
Anneciacum see Annecy
Annecy 69 D5 anc. Anneciacum. Haute-Savoie, E France
An Nīl al Abyaḍ see White Nile
An Nīl al Azraq see Blue Nile
Anniston 20 D2 Alabama, S USA
Annotto Bay 32 B4 C Jamaica
An Nuway'imah 97 E7 E West Bank, Middle East
An Ómaigh see Omagh
Anqing 106 D5 Anhui, E China
Anse La Raye 33 F1 NW Saint Lucia
Anshun 106 B6 Guizhou, S China
Ansongo 53 E3 Gao, E Mali
An Srath Bán see Strabane
Antakya 94 D4 anc. Antioch, Antiochia. Hatay, S Turkey (Türkiye)
Antalaha 57 G2 Antsirañana, NE Madagascar
Antalya 94 B4 prev. Adalia; anc. Attaleia, Bibl. Attalia. Antalya, SW Turkey (Türkiye)
Antalya, Gulf of 94 B4 var. Gulf of Adalia, Eng. Gulf of Antalya. gulf SW Turkey (Türkiye)
Antalya, Gulf of see Antalya Körfezi
Antananarivo 57 G3 prev. Tananarive. country capital (Madagascar) Antananarivo, C Madagascar
Antarctica 132 B3 continent
Antarctic Peninsula 132 A2 peninsula Antarctica
Antep see Gaziantep
Antequera 70 D5 anc. Anticaria, Antiquaria. Andalucía, S Spain
Antequera see Oaxaca
Antibes 69 D6 anc. Antipolis. Alpes-Maritimes, SE France
Anticaria see Antequera
Anticosti, Île d' 17 F3 Eng. Anticosti Island. island Québec, E Canada
Anticosti Island see Anticosti, Île d'
Antigua 33 G3 island S Antigua and Barbuda, Leeward Islands
Antigua and Barbuda 33 G3 country E West Indies
Antikythira 83 B7 var. Andikíthira. island S Greece
Anti-Lebanon 96 B4 var. Jebel esh Sharqi, Ar. Al Jabal ash Sharqī, Fr. Anti-Liban. mountain range Lebanon/Syria
Anti-Liban see Anti-Lebanon
Antioch see Antakya
Antiochia see Antakya
Antípaxoi 83 A5 var. Andipaxi. island Iónia Nísiá, Greece, C Mediterranean Sea
Antipodes Islands 120 D5 island group S New Zealand
Antipolis see Antibes
Antípsara 83 D5 var. Andípsara. island E Greece
Antiquaria see Antequera
Ántissa 83 D5 var. Ándissa. Lésvos, E Greece
An tIúr see Newry
Antivari see Bar
Antofagasta 42 B2 Antofagasta, N Chile
Antony 68 E2 Hauts-de-Seine, N France
An tSionainn see Shannon
Antsirañana 57 G2 province N Madagascar
Antsohihy 57 G2 Mahajanga, NW Madagascar
An-tung see Dandong
Antwerpen 65 C5 Eng. Antwerp, Fr. Anvers. Antwerpen, N Belgium
Anuradhapura 110 D3 North Central Province, C Sri Lanka
Anvers see Antwerpen
Anyang 106 C4 Henan, C China
A'nyêmaqên Shan 104 D4 mountain range C China
Anykščiai 84 C4 Utena, E Lithuania
Anzio 75 C5 Lazio, C Italy
Aomori 108 D3 Aomori, Honshū, C Japan
Aóos see Vjosës, Lumi i
Aoraki 129 B6 var. Mount Cook. South Island, New Zealand
Aoraki 129 B6 prev. Aorangi, var. Mount Cook. mountain South Island, New Zealand
Aorangi see Aoraki
Aosta 74 A1 anc. Augusta Praetoria. Valle d'Aosta, NW Italy
Aotearoa see New Zealand
Aoukâr 52 D3 var. Aouker. plateau C Mauritania
Aouk, Bahr 54 C4 river Central African Republic/Chad
Aouker see Aoukâr
Aozou 54 C1 Borkou-Ennedi-Tibesti, N Chad
Apalachee Bay 20 D3 bay Florida, SE USA
Apalachicola River 20 D3 river Florida, SE USA
Apamama see Abemama
Apaporis, Río 36 C4 river Brazil/Colombia
Aparima see Riverton
Apatity 88 C2 Murmanskaya Oblast', NW Russia
Ape 84 D3 Alūksne, NE Latvia
Apeldoorn 64 D3 Gelderland, E Netherlands
Apennines 74 E2 Eng. Apennines. mountain range Italy/San Marino
Apennines see Appennino
Āpia 123 F4 country capital (Samoa) Upolu, SE Samoa
Apkhazeti see Abkhazia
Apoera 37 G3 Sipaliwini, NW Suriname
Apostle Islands 18 B1 island group Wisconsin, N USA
Appalachian Mountains 13 D5 mountain range E USA
Appingedam 64 E1 Groningen, NE Netherlands
Appleton 18 B2 Wisconsin, N USA
Apulia see Puglia
Apure, Río 36 C2 river W Venezuela
Apurímac, Río 38 D3 river S Peru
Apuseni, Munţii 86 A4 mountain range W Romania
Aqaba/'Aqaba see Al 'Aqabah
Aqaba, Gulf of 98 A4 var. Gulf of Elat, Ar. Khalīj al 'Aqabah; anc. Sinus Aelaniticus. gulf NE Red Sea
'Aqabah, Khalīj al see Aqaba, Gulf of
Āqchah 101 E3 var. Āqcheh. Jowzjān, N Afghanistan
Āqcheh see Āqchah
Aqmola see Nur-Sultan
Aqtaū 92 A4 var. Aktau; prev. Shevchenko. Mangistau, W Kazakhstan
Aqtöbe 92 B4 var. Aktobe; prev. Aktjubinsk, Aktyubinsk. Aktyubinsk, NW Kazakhstan
Aquae Augustae see Dax
Aquae Calidae see Bath
Aquae Flaviae see Chaves
Aquae Grani see Aachen
Aquae Sextiae see Aix-en-Provence
Aquae Solis see Bath
Aquae Tarbelicae see Dax
Aquidauana 41 E4 Mato Grosso do Sul, S Brazil
Aquila/Aquila degli Abruzzi see L'Aquila
Aquisgranum see Aachen
Aquitaine 69 B6 cultural region SW France
'Arabah, Wadi al 97 B7 Heb. Ha'Arava. dry watercourse Israel/Jordan
Arabian Basin 102 A4 undersea basin N Arabian Sea
Arabian Desert see Sahara el Sharqîya
Arabian Peninsula 99 B5 peninsula SW Asia
Arabian Sea 102 A3 sea NW Indian Ocean
Arabicus, Sinus see Red Sea
'Arabī, Khalīj al see Persian Gulf
'Arabīyah as Su'ūdīyah, Al Mamlakah al see Saudi Arabia
'Arabīyah Jumhūrīyat, Miṣr al see Egypt
Arab Republic of Egypt see Egypt
Aracaju 41 G3 state capital Sergipe, E Brazil
Araçuai 41 F3 Minas Gerais, SE Brazil
Arad 97 B7 Southern, S Israel
Arad 86 A4 Arad, W Romania
Arafura Sea 120 A3 Ind. Laut Arafuru. sea W Pacific Ocean
Arafuru, Laut see Arafura Sea
Aragón 71 E2 autonomous community E Spain
Araguaia, Río 41 E3 var. Araguaya. river C Brazil
Araguari 41 F3 Minas Gerais, SE Brazil
Araguaya see Araguaia, Río
Ara Jovis see Aranjuez
Arāk 98 C3 prev. Sultānābād. Markazī, W Iran
Arakan Yoma 114 A3 mountain range W Myanmar (Burma)
Araks/Arak's see Aras
Aral 92 B4 var. Aral'sk. Kzylorda, SW Kazakhstan
Aral Sea 100 C1 Kaz. Aral Tengizi, Rus. Aral'skoye More, Uzb. Orol Dengizi. inland sea Kazakhstan/Uzbekistan
Aral'sk see Aral
Aral'skoye More/Aral Tengizi see Aral Sea
Aranda de Duero 70 D2 Castilla y León, N Spain
Aranđelovac 78 D4 prev. Arandjelovac. Serbia, C Serbia
Arandjelovac see Aranđelovac
Aranjuez 70 D3 anc. Ara Jovis. Madrid, C Spain
Araouane 53 E2 Tombouctou, N Mali
'Ar'ar 98 B3 Al Ḥudūd ash Shamālīyah, NW Saudi Arabia
Ārārat-e Bozorg, Kūh-e see Büyük Ağrı Dağı
Ararat, Mount see Büyük Ağrı Dağı
Aras 95 G3 Arm. Arak's, Az. Araz Nehri, Per. Rūd-e Aras, Rus. Araks; prev. Araxes. river SW Asia
Aras, Rūd-e see Aras
Arauca 36 C2 Arauca, NE Colombia
Arauca, Río 36 C2 river Colombia/Venezuela
Arausio see Orange
Araxes see Aras
Araz Nehri see Aras
Arbela see Arbil
Arbīl 98 B2 var. Erbil, Irbīl, Kurd. Hewlêr; anc. Arbela. Arbīl/Hewlêr, N Iraq
Arbroath 66 D3 anc. Aberbrothock. E Scotland, United Kingdom
Arbuzinka see Arbuzynka
Arbuzynka 87 E3 Rus. Arbuzinka. Mykolayivs'ka Oblast', S Ukraine
Arcachon 69 B5 Gironde, SW France
Arcae Remorum see Châlons-en-Champagne
Arcata 24 A4 California, W USA
Archangel see Arkhangel'sk
Archangel Bay see Chëshskaya Guba
Archidona 70 D5 Andalucía, S Spain
Arco 74 C2 Trentino-Alto Adige, N Italy
Arctic Mid Oceanic Ridge see Nansen Cordillera
Arctic Ocean 133 B3 ocean
Arda 82 C3 var. Ardhas, Gk. Ardas. river Bulgaria/Greece
Ardabīl 98 C2 var. Ardebil. Ardabīl, NW Iran
Ardakān 98 D3 Yazd, C Iran
Ardas 82 D3 var. Ardhas, Bul. Arda. river Bulgaria/Greece
Arḍ aş Şawwān 97 C7 var. Ardh es Suwwān. plain S Jordan
Ardeal see Transylvania
Ardebil see Ardabīl
Ardèche 69 C5 cultural region E France
Ardennes 65 C8 physical region Belgium/France
Ardhas see Arda/Ardas
Ardh es Suwwān see Arḍ aş Şawwān
Ardino 82 D3 Kardzhali, S Bulgaria
Ard Mhacha see Armagh
Ardmore 27 G2 Oklahoma, C USA
Arel see Arlon
Arelas/Arelate see Arles
Arendal 63 A6 Aust-Agder, S Norway
Arensburg see Kuressaare
Arenys de Mar 71 G2 Cataluña, NE Spain
Areópoli 83 B7 prev. Areópolis. Pelopónnisos, S Greece
Areópolis see Areópoli
Arequipa 39 E4 Arequipa, SE Peru
Arezzo 74 C3 anc. Arretium. Toscana, C Italy
Argalastí 83 C5 Thessalía, C Greece
Argenteuil 68 D1 Val-d'Oise, N France
Argentina 43 B5 off. Argentine Republic. country S South America
Argentina Basin see Argentine Basin
Argentine Basin 35 C7 var. Argentina Basin. undersea basin SW Atlantic Ocean
Argentine Republic see Argentina
Argentine Rise see Falkland Plateau
Argentoratum see Strasbourg
Arghandab, Darya-ye see Arghandāb Rōd
Arghandāb Rōd 101 E5 var. Darya-ye Arghandab. river SE Afghanistan
Argirocastro see Gjirokastër
Argo 50 B3 Northern, N Sudan
Argo Fracture Zone 119 C5 tectonic Feature C Indian Ocean
Árgos 83 B6 Pelopónnisos, S Greece
Argostóli 83 A5 var. Argostólion. Kefallonía, Iónia Nísiá, Greece, C Mediterranean Sea
Argostólion see Argostóli
Argun 103 E1 Chin. Ergun He, Rus. Argun'. river China/Russia
Argyrokastron see Gjirokastër
Århus see Aarhus
Aria see Herāt

Ari Atoll 110 A4 var. Alifu Atoll. atoll C Maldives
Arica 42 B1 hist. San Marcos de Arica. Tarapacá, N Chile
Aridaía 82 B3 var. Aridea, Aridhaía. Dytikí Makedonía, N Greece
Aridea see Aridaía
Aridhaía see Aridaía
Arīḩā 96 B3 Al Karak, W Jordan
Arīḩā see Jericho
Ariminum see Rimini
Arinsal 69 A7 NW Andorra Europe
Arizona 26 A2 off. State of Arizona, also known as Copper State, Grand Canyon State. state SW USA
Arkansas 20 A1 off. State of Arkansas, also known as The Land of Opportunity. state S USA
Arkansas City 23 F5 Kansas, C USA
Arkansas River 27 G1 river C USA
Arkhangel'sk 92 B2 Eng. Archangel. Arkhangel'skaya Oblast', NW Russia
Arkoí 83 E6 island Dodekánisa, Greece, Aegean Sea
Arles 69 D6 var. Arles-sur-Rhône; anc. Arelas, Arelate. Bouches-du-Rhône, SE France
Arles-sur-Rhône see Arles
Arlington 27 G2 Texas, SW USA
Arlington 19 E4 Virginia, NE USA
Arlon 65 D8 Dut. Aarlen, Ger. Arel, Lat. Orolaunum. Luxembourg, SE Belgium
Armagh 67 B5 Ir. Ard Mhacha. S Northern Ireland, United Kingdom
Armagnac 69 B6 cultural region S France
Armenia 36 B3 Quindío, W Colombia
Armenia 95 F3 off. Republic of Armenia, var. Hayastan, Arm. Hayastani Hanrapetut'yun; prev. Armenian Soviet Socialist Republic. country SW Asia
Armenian Soviet Socialist Republic see Armenia
Armenia, Republic of see Armenia
Armiansk 87 F4 prev. Armyans'k, Rus. Armyansk. Respublika Krym, S Ukraine
Armidale 127 D6 New South Wales, SE Australia
Armstrong 16 B3 Ontario, S Canada
Armyansk see Armiansk
Armyans'k see Armiansk
Arnaía 82 C4 Cont. Arnea. Kentrikí Makedonía, N Greece
Arnaud 60 A3 river Québec, E Canada
Arnea see Arnaía
Arnedo 71 E2 La Rioja, N Spain
Arnhem 64 D4 Gelderland, SE Netherlands
Arnhem Land 126 A2 physical region Northern Territory, N Australia
Arno 74 B3 river C Italy
Arnold 23 G4 Missouri, C USA
Arnswalde see Choszczno
Aroe Islands see Aru, Kepulauan
Arorae 123 E3 atoll Tungaru, W Kiribati
Arrabona see Győr
Ar Rahad see Er Rahad
Ar Ramādī 98 B3 var. Ramadi, Rumadiya. Al Anbār, SW Iraq
Ar Rāmī 96 C4 Ḩimş, C Syria
Ar Ramthā 97 B5 var. Ramtha. Irbid, N Jordan
Arran, Isle of 66 C4 island SW Scotland, United Kingdom
Ar Raqqah 96 C2 var. Rakka; anc. Nicephorium. Ar Raqqah, N Syria
Arras 68 C2 anc. Nemetocenna. Pas-de-Calais, N France
Ar Rawḑatayn 98 C4 var. Raudhatain. N Kuwait
Arretium see Arezzo
Arriaca see Guadalajara
Arriaga 29 G5 Chiapas, SE Mexico
Ar Riyāḑ 99 C5 Eng. Riyadh. country capital (Saudi Arabia) Ar Riyāḑ, C Saudi Arabia
Ar Rub 'al Khali 99 C6 Eng. Empty Quarter, Great Sandy Desert. desert SW Asia
Ar Rustāq 99 E5 var. Rostak, Rustaq. N Oman
Ar Ruţbah 98 B3 var. Rutba. Al Anbār, SW Iraq
Árta 83 A5 anc. Ambracia. Ípeiros, W Greece
Artashat 95 F3 S Armenia
Artemisa 32 B2 La Habana, W Cuba
Artesia 26 D3 New Mexico, SW USA
Arthur's Pass 129 C6 pass South Island, New Zealand
Artigas 42 D3 prev. San Eugenio, San Eugenio del Cuareim. Artigas, N Uruguay
Art'ik 95 F2 W Armenia
Artois 68 C2 cultural region N France
Artsiz see Artsyz
Artsyz 86 D4 Rus. Artsiz. Odes'ka Oblast', SW Ukraine
Arturo Prat 132 A2 Chilean research station South Shetland Islands, Antarctica
Artvin 95 F2 Artvin, NE Turkey (Türkiye)
Arua 51 B6 NW Uganda
Aruba 36 C1 var. Oruba. Dutch self-governing territory S West Indies
Aru Islands see Aru, Kepulauan
Aru, Kepulauan 117 G4 Eng. Aru Islands; prev. Aroe Islands. island group E Indonesia
Arunāchal Pradesh 113 G3 prev. North East Frontier Agency, North East Frontier Agency of Assam. cultural region NE India
Arusha 51 C7 Arusha, N Tanzania
Arviat 15 G4 prev. Eskimo Point. Nunavut, C Canada
Arvidsjaur 62 C4 Norrbotten, N Sweden
Arys' 92 B5 Kaz. Arys. Türkistan/Turkestan, S Kazakhstan
Arys see Arys'
Asadābād 101 F4 var. Asaḏābād; prev. Chaghasarāy. Konar, E Afghanistan
Asaḏābād see Asadābād
Asad, Buḩayrat al 96 C2 Eng. Lake Assad. lake N Syria
Asahi-dake 108 D2 mountain Hokkaidō, N Japan
Asahikawa 108 D2 Hokkaidō, N Japan
Asamankese 53 E5 SE Ghana
Āsānsol 113 F4 West Bengal, NE India
Asben see Aïr, Massif de l'
Ascension Fracture Zone 47 A5 tectonic Feature C Atlantic Ocean
Ascension Island see St Helena, Ascension and Tristan da Cunha
Ascoli Piceno 74 C4 anc. Asculum Picenum. Marche, C Italy
Asculum Picenum see Ascoli Piceno
'Aseb 50 D4 var. Assab, Amh. Āseb. SE Eritrea
Assen 64 E2 Drenthe, NE Netherlands
Aşgabat 100 C3 prev. Ashgabat, Ashkhabad, Poltoratsk. country capital (Turkmenistan) Ahal Welaýaty, C Turkmenistan
Ashara see Al 'Ashārah
Ashburton 129 C6 Canterbury, South Island, New Zealand
Ashburton River 124 A4 river Western Australia
Ashdod 97 A6 anc. Azotos, Lat. Azotus. Central, W Israel
Asheville 21 E1 North Carolina, SE USA
Ashgabat see Aşgabat
Ashkelon 97 A6 prev. Ashqelon. Southern, C Israel
Ashkhabad see Aşgabat
Ashland 24 B4 Oregon, NW USA
Ashland 18 B1 Wisconsin, N USA
Ashmore and Cartier Islands 120 A3 Australian external territory E Indian Ocean
Ashmyany 85 C5 Rus. Oshmyany. Hrodzyenskaya Voblasts', W Belarus
Ashqelon see Ashkelon
Ash Shadādah 96 D2 var. Ash Shaddādah, Jisr ash Shadadi, Shaddādī, Shedadi, Tell Shedadi. Al Ḩasakah, NE Syria
Ash Shaddādah see Ash Shadādah
Ash Sharah 97 B7 var. Esh Sharā. mountain range W Jordan
Ash Shāriqah 98 D4 Eng. Sharjah. Ash Shāriqah, NE United Arab Emirates
Ash Shawbak 97 B7 Ma'ān, W Jordan
Ash Shiḩr 99 C6 SE Yemen
Asia 90 continent
'Āşī, Nahr Al see Orontes
Asinara 74 A4 island W Italy
Asi Nehri see Orontes
Asipovichy 85 D6 Rus. Osipovichi. Mahilyowskaya Voblasts', C Belarus
Aşkale 95 E3 Erzurum, NE Turkey (Türkiye)
Askersund 63 C6 Örebro, C Sweden
Asmara see Asmera
Asmera 50 C4 var. Asmara. country capital (Eritrea) C Eritrea
Aspadana see Eşfahān
Asphaltites, Lacus see Dead Sea
Aspinwall see Colón
Assab see 'Aseb
As Sabkhah 96 D2 var. Sabkha. Ar Raqqah, NE Syria
Assad, Lake see Asad, Buḩayrat al
Aş Şafāwī 97 C6 Al Mafraq, N Jordan
Aş Şaḩrā' ash Sharqīyah see Sahara el Sharqîya
As Salamīyah see Salamīyah
'Assal, Lac 46 E4 lake C Djibouti
As Salt 97 B6 var. Salt. Al Balqā', NW Jordan
Assamaka see Assamakka
Assamakka 53 F2 var. Assamaka. Agadez, NW Niger
As Samāwah 98 B3 var. Samawa. Al Muthannā, S Iraq
Assenede 65 B5 Oost-Vlaanderen, NW Belgium
Assiout see Asyūţ
Assiut see Asyūţ
Assling see Jesenice
Assouan see Aswān
Assu 41 G2 var. Açu. Rio Grande do Norte, E Brazil
Assuan see Aswān
As Sukhnah 96 C3 var. Sukhne, Fr. Soukhné. Ḩimş, C Syria
As Sulaymānīyah 98 C3 var. Sulaimaniya, Kurd. Slêmanî. As Sulaymānīyah/Slêmanî, NE Iraq
As Sulayyil 99 B5 Ar Riyāḑ, S Saudi Arabia
Aş Şuwār 96 D2 var. Şuwār. Dayr az Zawr, E Syria
As Suwaydā' 97 B5 var. El Suweida, Es Suweida, Suweida, Fr. Soueida. As Suwaydā', SW Syria
As Suways 50 B1 var. Suez; Ar. El Suweis. NE Egypt
Asta Colonia see Asti
Astacus see İzmit
Astana see Nur-Sultan
Asta Pompeia see Asti
Astarabad see Gorgān
Asterābād see Gorgān
Asti 74 A2 anc. Asta Colonia, Asta Pompeia, Hasta Colonia, Hasta Pompeia. Piemonte, NW Italy
Astigi see Écija
Astipálaia see Astypálaia
Astorga 70 C1 anc. Asturica Augusta. Castilla y León, N Spain
Astrabad see Gorgān
Astrakhan' 89 C7 Astrakhanskaya Oblast', SW Russia
Asturias 70 C1 autonomous community NW Spain
Asturias see Oviedo
Asturica Augusta see Astorga
Astypálaia 83 D7 var. Astipálaia, It. Stampalia. island Kykládes, Greece, Aegean Sea
Asunción 42 D2 country capital (Paraguay) Central, S Paraguay
Asuka 132 C2 Japanese research station Antarctica
Aswān 50 B2 var. Assouan, Assuan, Aswân; anc. Syene. SE Egypt
Aswân see Aswān
Asyūţ 50 B2 var. Assiout, Assiut, Asyût, Siut; anc. Lycopolis. C Egypt
Asyût see Asyūţ
Atacama Desert 42 B2 Eng. Atacama Desert. desert N Chile
Atacama Desert see Atacama, Desierto de
Atafu Atoll 123 E3 island NW Tokelau
Atamyrat 100 D3 prev. Kerki. Lebap Welaýaty, E Turkmenistan
Aţâr 52 C2 Adrar, W Mauritania
Atas Bogd 104 D3 mountain SW Mongolia
Atascadero 25 B7 California, W USA
Atatürk Baraji 95 E4 reservoir S Turkey (Türkiye)
Atbara 50 C3 var. 'Aţbārah. River Nile, NE Sudan
'Aţbārah/'Aţbarah, Nahr see Atbara
Atbasar 92 C4 Akmola, N Kazakhstan
Atchison 23 F4 Kansas, C USA
Aternum see Pescara
Ath 65 B6 var. Aat. Hainaut, SW Belgium
Athabasca 15 E5 Alberta, SW Canada
Athabasca 15 E5 var. Athabaska. river Alberta, SW Canada
Athabasca, Lake 15 F4 lake Alberta/Saskatchewan, SW Canada
Athabaska see Athabasca
Athenae see Athína
Athens 21 E2 Georgia, SE USA
Athens 18 D4 Ohio, N USA
Athens 27 G3 Texas, SW USA
Athens see Athína
Atherton 126 D3 Queensland, NE Australia
Athína 83 C6 Eng. Athens, prev. Athínai; anc. Athenae. country capital (Greece) Attikí, C Greece
Athínai see Athína
Athlone 67 B5 Ir. Baile Átha Luain. C Ireland
Ath Thawrah 96 C2 var. Madīnat ath Thawrah. Ar Raqqah, N Syria
Ati 54 C3 Batha, C Chad
Atikokan 16 B4 Ontario, S Canada
Atka 93 G3 Magadanskaya Oblast', E Russia
Atka 14 A3 Atka Island, Alaska, USA
Atlanta 20 D2 state capital Georgia, SE USA
Atlanta 27 H2 Texas, SW USA
Atlantic City 19 F4 New Jersey, NE USA
Atlantic-Indian Basin 45 D7 undersea basin SW Indian Ocean
Atlantic-Indian Ridge 47 B8 undersea ridge SW Indian Ocean
Atlantic Ocean 44 B4 ocean
Atlas Mountains 48 C2 mountain range NW Africa
Atlasovo 93 H3 Kamchatskaya Oblast', E Russia
Atlas Saharien 48 D2 var. Saharan Atlas. mountain range Algeria/Morocco
Atlas, Tell see Atlas Tellien
Atlas Tellien 80 C3 Eng. Tell Atlas. mountain range N Algeria
Atlin 14 D4 British Columbia, W Canada
Aţ Ţafīlah 97 B7 var. Et Tafila, Tafila. Aţ Ţafīlah, W Jordan
Aţ Ţā'if 99 B5 Makkah, W Saudi Arabia
Attaleia/Attalia see Antalya
At Tall al Abyaḑ see Tall Abyaḑ
At Ţanf 96 D4 Ḩimş, S Syria
Attapu 115 E5 var. Samakhixai, Attopeu. Attapu, S Laos
Attawapiskat 16 C3 Ontario, C Canada
Attawapiskat 16 C3 river Ontario, S Canada
At Tibnī 96 D2 var. Tibnī. Dayr az Zawr, NE Syria
Attopeu see Attapu
Attu Island 14 A2 island Aleutian Islands, Alaska, USA
Atyraū 92 B4 var. Atyrau, prev. Gur'yev. Atyrau, W Kazakhstan
Atyrau see Atyraū
Aubagne 69 D6 anc. Albania. Bouches-du-Rhône, SE France
Aubange 65 D8 Luxembourg, SE Belgium
Aubervilliers 68 E1 Seine-St-Denis, Île-de-France, N France Europe
Auburn 24 B2 Washington, NW USA
Auch 69 B6 Lat. Augusta Auscorum, Elimberrum. Gers, S France
Auckland 128 D2 Auckland, North Island, New Zealand
Auckland Islands 120 C5 island group S New Zealand
Audern see Audru
Audincourt 68 E4 Doubs, E France
Audru 84 D2 Ger. Audern. Pärnumaa, SW Estonia
Augathella 127 D5 Queensland, E Australia
Augsbourg see Augsburg
Augsburg 73 C6 Fr. Augsbourg; anc. Augusta Vindelicorum. Bayern, S Germany
Augusta 125 A7 Western Australia
Augusta 21 E2 Georgia, SE USA
Augusta 19 G2 state capital Maine, NE USA
Augusta see London
Augusta Auscorum see Auch
Augusta Emerita see Mérida
Augusta Praetoria see Aosta
Augusta Trajana see Stara Zagora
Augusta Treverorum see Trier
Augusta Vangionum see Worms
Augusta Vindelicorum see Augsburg
Augustobona Tricassium see Troyes
Augustodurum see Bayeux
Augustoritum Lemovicensium see Limoges
Augustów 76 E2 Rus. Avgustov. Podlaskie, NE Poland
Aulie Ata/Auliye-Ata see Taraz
Aunglan 114 B4 var. Allanmyo, Myaydo. Magway, C Myanmar (Burma)
Auob 56 B4 var. Oup. river Namibia/South Africa
Aurangābād 112 D5 Mahārāshtra, C India
Auray 68 A3 Morbihan, NW France
Aurelia Aquensis see Baden-Baden
Aurelianum see Orléans
Aurès, Massif de l' 80 C4 mountain range NE Algeria
Aurillac 69 C5 Cantal, C France
Aurium see Ourense
Aurora 37 F2 NW Guyana
Aurora 22 D4 Colorado, C USA
Aurora 18 B3 Illinois, N USA
Aurora 23 G5 Missouri, C USA
Aurora see Maéwo, Vanuatu
Aus 56 B4 Karas, SW Namibia
Ausa see Vic
Aussig see Ústí nad Labem
Austin 23 G3 Minnesota, N USA
Austin 27 G3 state capital Texas, SW USA
Australes, Archipel des see Australes, Îles
Australes et Antarctiques Françaises, Terres see French Southern and Antarctic Lands
Australes, Îles 121 F4 var. Archipel des Australes, Îles Tubuai, Tubuai Islands, Eng. Austral Islands. island group SW French Polynesia
Austral Fracture Zone 121 H4 tectonic feature S Pacific Ocean
Australia 120 A4 off. Commonwealth of Australia. country
Australia, Commonwealth of see Australia
Australian Alps 127 C7 mountain range SE Australia
Australian Capital Territory 127 D7 prev. Federal Capital Territory. territory SE Australia
Australie, Bassin Nord de l' see North Australian Basin
Austral Islands see Australes, Îles
Austrava see Ostrov
Austria 73 D7 off. Republic of Austria, Ger. Österreich. country C Europe
Austria, Republic of see Austria
Autesiodorum see Auxerre
Autissiodorum see Auxerre
Autricum see Chartres
Auvergne 69 C5 cultural region C France
Auxerre 68 C4 anc. Autesiodorum, Autissiodorum. Yonne, C France
Avaricum see Bourges
Avarua 123 G5 dependent territory capital (Cook Islands) Rarotonga, S Cook Islands
Avasfelsőfalu see Negreşti-Oaş
Ávdira 82 C3 Anatolikí Makedonía kai Thráki, NE Greece
Aveiro 70 B2 anc. Talabriga. Aveiro, W Portugal
Avela see Ávila
Avellino 75 D5 anc. Abellinum. Campania, S Italy
Avenio see Avignon
Avesta 63 C6 Dalarna, C Sweden
Aveyron 69 C6 river S France
Avezzano 74 C4 Abruzzo, C Italy
Avgustov see Augustów
Aviemore 66 C3 N Scotland, United Kingdom
Avignon 69 D6 anc. Avenio. Vaucluse, SE France
Ávila 70 D3 var. Avila; anc. Abela, Abula, Abyla, Avela. Castilla y León, C Spain
Avilés 70 C1 Asturias, NW Spain
Avranches 68 B3 Manche, N France
Avveel see Ivalo, Finland
Avvil see Ivalo
Awaji-shima 109 C6 island SW Japan
Āwash 51 D5 Āfar, NE Ethiopia
Awbārī 49 F3 SW Libya
Ax see Dax
Axel 65 B5 Zeeland, SW Netherlands
Axel Heiberg Island 15 E1 var. Axel Heiburg. island Nunavut, N Canada
Axel Heiburg see Axel Heiberg Island
Áxios see Vardar
Ayacucho 38 D4 Ayacucho, S Peru
Ayagoz 92 C5 var. Ayaguz, Kaz. Ayakoz. river E Kazakhstan
Ayamonte 70 C4 Andalucía, S Spain
Ayaviri 39 E4 Puno, S Peru
Aydarko'l Ko'li 101 E2 Rus. Ozero Aydarkul'. lake C Uzbekistan
Aydarkul', Ozero see Aydarko'l Ko'li
Aydın 94 A4 var. Aidin; anc. Tralles Aydin. Aydın, SW Turkey (Türkiye)
Ayers Rock see Uluru
Ayeyarwady 114 B2 var. Irrawaddy. river W Myanmar (Burma)
Ayiá see Agiá
Áyios Evstrátios see Ágios Efstrátios
Áyios Nikólaos see Ágios Nikólaos
Ayorou 53 E3 Tillabéri, W Niger
'Ayoûn el 'Atroûs 52 D3 var. Aïoun el Atrous, Aïoun el Atroûss. Hodh el Gharbi, SE Mauritania
Ayr 66 C4 W Scotland, United Kingdom
Ayteke Bi 92 B4 Kaz. Zhangaqazaly; prev. Novokazalinsk. Kzylorda, SW Kazakhstan
Aytos 82 E2 Burgas, E Bulgaria
Ayutthaya 115 C5 var. Phra Nakhon Si Ayutthaya. Phra Nakhon Si Ayutthaya, C Thailand
Ayvalık 94 A3 Balıkesir, W Turkey (Türkiye)
Azahar, Costa del 71 F3 coastal region E Spain
Azaouâd 53 E3 desert C Mali
Azärbaycan/Azärbaycan Respublikasī see Azerbaijan
A'zāz see I'zāz
Azerbaijan 95 G2 off. Republic of Azerbaijan, Az. Azärbaycan, Azärbaycan Respublikası; prev. Azerbaijan SSR. country SE Asia
Azerbaijan, Republic of see Azerbaijan
Azerbaijan SSR see Azerbaijan
Azimabad see Patna
Azizie see Telish
Azogues 38 B2 Cañar, S Ecuador
Azores 70 A4 var. Açores, Ilhas dos Açores, Port. Arquipélago dos Açores. island group Portugal, NE Atlantic Ocean
Azores-Biscay Rise 58 A3 undersea rise E Atlantic Ocean
Azotos/Azotus see Ashdod
Azoum, Bahr 54 C3 seasonal river SE Chad
Azov, Sea of 81 H1 Rus. Azovskoye More, Ukr. Azovs'ke More. sea NE Black Sea
Azovske More/Azovskoye More see Azov, Sea of
Azraq, Wāḩat al 97 C6 oasis N Jordan
Aztec 26 C1 New Mexico, SW USA
Azuaga 70 C4 Extremadura, W Spain
Azuero, Península de 31 F5 peninsula S Panama
Azul 43 D5 Buenos Aires, E Argentina
Azur, Côte d' 69 E6 coastal region SE France
'Azza see Gaza
Az Zaqāzīq 50 B1 var. Zagazig. N Egypt
Az Zarqā' 97 B6 NW Jordan
Az Zāwiyah 49 F2 var. Zawia. NW Libya
Az Zilfī 98 B4 Ar Riyāḑ, N Saudi Arabia

B

Baalbek 96 B4 var. Ba'labakk; anc. Heliopolis. E Lebanon
Baardheere 51 D6 var. Bardere, It. Bardera. Gedo, SW Somalia
Baarle-Hertog 65 C5 Antwerpen, N Belgium
Baarn 64 C3 Utrecht, C Netherlands
Babadag 86 D5 Tulcea, SE Romania
Babahoyo 38 B2 prev. Bodegas. Los Ríos, C Ecuador
Bābā, Kōh-e 101 E4 mountain range C Afghanistan
Babayevo 88 B4 Vologodskaya Oblast', NW Russia
Babeldaob 122 A1 var. Babeldaop, Babelthuap. island N Palau
Babeldaop see Babeldaob
Bab el Mandeb 99 B7 strait Gulf of Aden/Red Sea
Babelthuap see Babeldaob
Babian Jiang see Black River
Babruysk 85 D7 Rus. Bobruysk. Mahilyowskaya Voblasts', E Belarus
Babuyan Channel 117 E1 channel N Philippines
Babuyan Islands 117 E1 island group N Philippines
Bacabal 41 F2 Maranhão, E Brazil
Bacău 86 C4 Hung. Bákó. Bacău, NE Romania
Bắc Bộ, Vịnh see Tonkin, Gulf of
Bắc Giang 114 D3 Ha Bắc, N Vietnam
Bacheykava 85 D5 Rus. Bocheykovo. Vitsyebskaya Voblasts', N Belarus
Back 15 F3 river Nunavut, N Canada
Bačka Palanka 78 D3 prev. Palanka. Serbia, NW Serbia
Bačka Topola 78 D3 Hung. Topolya; prev. Hung. Bácstopolya. Vojvodina, N Serbia
Bac Liêu 115 D6 var. Vinh Loi. Minh Hai, S Vietnam
Bacolod 103 E4 off. Bacolod City. Negros, C Philippines
Bacolod City see Bacolod
Bácsszenttamás see Srbobran
Bácstopolya see Bačka Topola
Bactra see Balkh
Badajoz 70 C4 anc. Pax Augusta. Extremadura, W Spain
Baden-Baden 73 B6 anc. Aurelia Aquensis. Baden-Württemberg, SW Germany
Bad Freienwalde 72 D3 Brandenburg, NE Germany
Badger State see Wisconsin
Bad Hersfeld 72 B4 Hessen, C Germany
Bad Homburg see Bad Homburg vor der Höhe
Bad Homburg vor der Höhe 73 B5 var. Bad Homburg. Hessen, W Germany
Bad Ischl 73 D7 Oberösterreich, N Austria
Bad Krozingen 73 A6 Baden-Württemberg, SW Germany
Badlands 22 D2 physical region North Dakota/South Dakota, N USA
Badu Island 126 C1 island Queensland, NE Australia
Bad Vöslau 73 E6 Niederösterreich, NE Austria
Baeterrae/Baeterrae Septimanorum see Béziers
Baetic Cordillera/Baetic Mountains see Béticos, Sistemas
Bafatá 52 C4 C Guinea-Bissau
Baffin Bay 15 G2 bay Canada/Greenland
Baffin Island 15 G2 island Nunavut, NE Canada
Bafing 52 C3 river W Africa
Bafoussam 54 A4 Ouest, W Cameroon
Bafra 94 D2 Samsun, N Turkey (Türkiye)
Bāft 98 D4 Kermān, S Iran
Bagaces 30 D4 Guanacaste, NW Costa Rica
Bagdad see Baghdād
Bagé 41 E5 Rio Grande do Sul, S Brazil
Baghdād 98 B3 var. Bagdad. country capital (Iraq) Baghdād, C Iraq
Baghlān 101 E3 Baghlān, NE Afghanistan
Bago 114 B4 var. Pegu. Bago, SW Myanmar (Burma)
Bagoé 52 D4 river Ivory Coast/Mali
Bagrationovsk 84 A4 Ger. Preussisch Eylau. Kaliningradskaya Oblast', W Russia
Bagrax Hu see Bosten Hu
Baguio 117 E1 off. Baguio City. Luzon, N Philippines
Baguio City see Baguio
Bagzane, Monts 53 F3 mountain N Niger
Bahama Islands see Bahamas, The
Bahamas, The 32 C2 off. Commonwealth of The Bahamas. country N West Indies
Bahamas 13 D6 var. Bahama Islands. island group N West Indies
Bahamas, Commonwealth of The see Bahamas, The
Baharly 100 C3 var. Bäherden, Rus. Bakharden; prev. Bakherden. Ahal Welaýaty, C Turkmenistan
Bahawalpur 112 C2 Punjab, E Pakistan
Bäherden see Baharly
Bahia 41 F3 off. Estado da Bahia. state/region E Brazil
Bahía Blanca 43 C5 Buenos Aires, E Argentina
Bahia, Estado da see Bahia
Bahir Dar 50 C4 var. Bahr Dar, Bahrdar Giyorgis. Āmara, N Ethiopia
Bahraich 113 E3 Uttar Pradesh, N India
Bahrain 98 C4 off. Kingdom of Bahrain, Mamlakat al Baḩrayn, Ar. Al Baḩrayn, prev. Bahrein; anc. Tylos, Tyros. country SW Asia
Bahrain, Kingdom of see Bahrain
Bahrayn, Mamlakat al see Bahrain
Bahr Dar/Bahrdar Giyorgis see Bahir Dar
Bahrein see Bahrain
Bahr el, Azraq see Blue Nile
Bahr Tabariya, Sea of see Kinneret, Yam
Bahushewsk 85 E6 Rus. Bogushëvsk. Vitsyebskaya Voblasts', NE Belarus
Baia Mare 86 B3 Ger. Frauenbach, Hung. Nagybánya; prev. Neustadt. Maramureş, NW Romania
Baia Sprie 86 B3 Ger. Mittelstadt, Hung. Felsőbánya. Maramureş, NW Romania
Baïbokoum 54 B4 Logone-Oriental, SW Chad
Baidoa see Baydhabo
Baie-Comeau 17 E3 Québec, SE Canada
Baikal, Lake 93 E4 Eng. Lake Baikal. lake S Russia
Baikal, Lake see Baykal, Ozero
Baile Átha Cliath see Dublin
Baile Átha Luain see Athlone
Bailén 70 D4 Andalucía, S Spain
Baile na Mainistreach see Newtownabbey
Băileşti 86 B5 Dolj, SW Romania
Ba Illi 54 B3 Chari-Baguirmi, SW Chad
Bainbridge 20 D3 Georgia, SE USA
Bā'ir see Bāyir
Baireuth see Bayreuth
Bairnsdale 127 C7 Victoria, SE Australia
Baishan 107 E3 prev. Hunjiang. Jilin, NE China
Baiyin 106 B4 Gansu, C China
Baja 77 C7 Bács-Kiskun, S Hungary
Baja California 26 A4 Eng. Lower California. peninsula NW Mexico
Baja California Norte 28 B2 state NW Mexico
Bajo Boquete see Boquete
Bajram Curri 79 D5 Kukës, N Albania
Bakala 54 C4 Ouaka, C Central African Republic
Bakan see Shimonoseki
Baker 24 C3 Oregon, NW USA
Baker Island 123 E2 US unincorporated territory W Polynesia
Baker Lake 15 F3 Nunavut, N Canada
Bakersfield 25 C7 California, W USA
Bakharden see Baharly
Bakhchisaray see Bakhchysarai
Bakhchysarai 87 F5 prev. Bakhchysaray, Rus. Bakhchisaray. Respublika Krym, S Ukraine
Bakhchysaray see Bakhchysarai
Bakherden see Baharly
Bakhmach 87 F1 Chernihivs'ka Oblast', N Ukraine
Bākhtarān see Kermānshāh
Bakı 95 H2 Eng. Baku. country capital (Azerbaijan) E Azerbaijan
Bákó see Bacău
Bakony 77 C7 Eng. Bakony Mountains, Ger. Bakonywald. mountain range W Hungary
Bakony Mountains/Bakonywald see Bakony
Baku see Bakı
Bakwanga see Mbuji-Mayi
Balabac Island 107 C8 island W Philippines
Balabac, Selat see Balabac Strait
Balabac Strait 116 D2 var. Selat Balabac. strait Malaysia/Philippines
Ba'labakk see Baalbek
Balaguer 71 F2 Cataluña, NE Spain
Balakovo 89 C6 Saratovskaya Oblast', W Russia
Bālā Morghāb see Bālā Murghāb
Bālā Murghāb 100 D4 prev. Bālā Morghāb. Laghmān, NW Afghanistan
Balashov 89 B6 Saratovskaya Oblast', W Russia
Balasore see Bāleshwar

Balaton, Lake 77 C7 var. Lake Balaton, Ger. Plattensee. lake W Hungary
Balaton, Lake see Balaton
Balbina, Represa 40 D1 reservoir NW Brazil
Balboa 31 G4 Panamá, C Panama
Balcarce 43 D5 Buenos Aires, E Argentina
Balclutha 129 B7 Otago, South Island, New Zealand
Baldy Mountain 22 C1 mountain Montana, NW USA
Bâle see Basel
Balearic Plain see Algerian Basin
Baleares Major see Mallorca
Balearic Islands 71 G3 Eng. Balearic Islands. island group Spain, W Mediterranean Sea
Balearic Islands see Baleares, Islas
Balearis Minor see Menorca
Baleine, Rivière à la 17 E2 river Québec, E Canada
Balen 65 C5 Antwerpen, N Belgium
Bāleshwar 113 F4 prev. Balasore. Odisha, E India
Bălgrad see Alba Iulia
Bali 116 D5 island C Indonesia
Balıkesir 94 A3 Balıkesir, W Turkey (Türkiye)
Balīkh, Nahr 96 C2 river N Syria
Balikpapan 116 D4 Borneo, C Indonesia
Balkanabat 100 B2 Rus. Nebitdag. Balkan Welaýaty, W Turkmenistan
Balkan Mountains 82 C2 Bul./Croatian Stara Planina. mountain range Bulgaria/Serbia
Balkash see Balqash
Balkash, Ozero see Balqash Köli
Balkh 101 E3 anc. Bactra. Balkh, N Afghanistan
Balkhash, Lake see Balqash Köli
Balladonia 125 C6 Western Australia
Ballarat 127 C7 Victoria, SE Australia
Balleny Islands 132 B5 island group Antarctica
Ballinger 27 F3 Texas, SW USA
Balochistan see Baluchistan
Balqash 92 C5 Rus. Balkash. Karagandy, SE Kazakhstan see Balkhash
Balqash Köli 92 C5 Eng. Lake Balkhash, Rus. Ozero Balkash. lake SE Kazakhstan
Balş 86 B5 Olt, S Romania
Balsas 41 F2 Maranhão, E Brazil
Balsas, Río 29 E5 var. Río Mexcala. river S Mexico
Bal'shavik 85 D7 Rus. Bol'shevik. Homyel'skaya Voblasts', SE Belarus
Balta 86 D3 Odes'ka Oblast', SW Ukraine
Bălţi 86 D3 Rus. Bel'tsy. N Moldova
Baltic Port see Paldiski
Baltic Sea 63 C7 Ger. Ostee, Rus. Baltiskoye More. sea N Europe
Baltimore 19 F4 Maryland, NE USA
Baltischport/Baltiski see Paldiski
Baltiskoye More see Baltic Sea
Baltkrievija see Belarus
Baluchistan 112 B3 var. Balochistan, Beluchistan. province SW Pakistan
Balvi 84 D4 Balvi, NE Latvia
Balykchy 101 G2 Kir. Ysyk-Köl; prev. Issyk-Kul', Rybach'ye. Issyk-Kul'skaya Oblast', NE Kyrgyzstan
Balzers 72 E2 S Liechtenstein
Bam 98 E4 Kermān, SE Iran
Bamako 52 D4 country capital (Mali) Capital District, SW Mali
Bambari 54 C4 Ouaka, C Central African Republic
Bamberg 73 C5 Bayern, SE Germany
Bamenda 54 A4 Nord-Ouest, W Cameroon
Banaba 122 D2 var. Ocean Island. island Tungaru, W Kiribati
Banaras see Vārānasi
Bandaaceh 116 A3 var. Banda Atjeh; prev. Koetaradja, Kutaradja, Kutaraja. Sumatera, W Indonesia
Banda Atjeh see Bandaaceh
Banda, Laut see Banda Sea
Bandama 52 D5 var. Bandama Fleuve. river S Ivory Coast
Bandama Fleuve see Bandama
Bandar 'Abbās see Bandar-e 'Abbās
Bandarbeyla 51 E5 var. Bender Beila, Bender Beyla. Bari, NE Somalia
Bandar-e 'Abbās 98 D4 var. Bandar 'Abbās; prev. Gombroon. Hormozgān, S Iran
Bandar-e Būshehr 98 C4 var. Būshehr, Eng. Bushire. Būshehr, S Iran
Bandar-e Kangān 98 D4 var. Kangān. Būshehr, S Iran
Bandar-e Khamīr 98 D4 Hormozgān, S Iran
Bandar-e Langeh see Bandar-e Lengeh
Bandar-e Lengeh 98 D4 var. Bandar-e Langeh, Lingeh. Hormozgān, S Iran
Bandar Kassim see Boosaaso
Bandar Lampung 116 C4 var. Bandarlampung, Tanjungkarang-Telukbetung; prev. Tandjoengkarang, Tanjungkarang, Teloekbetoeng, Telukbetung. Sumatera, W Indonesia
Bandarlampung see Bandar Lampung
Bandar Maharani see Muar
Bandar Masulipatnam see Machilipatnam
Bandar Penggaram see Batu Pahat
Bandar Seri Begawan 116 D3 prev. Brunei Town. country capital (Brunei) N Brunei
Banda Sea 117 F5 var. Laut Banda. sea E Indonesia
Bandiagara 53 E3 Mopti, C Mali
Bandırma 94 A3 var. Penderma. Balıkesir, NW Turkey (Türkiye)
Bandjarmasin see Banjarmasin
Bandoeng see Bandung
Bandundu 55 C6 prev. Banningville. Bandundu, W Dem. Rep. Congo
Bandung 116 C5 prev. Bandoeng. Jawa, C Indonesia
Bangalore see Bengalūru
Bangassou 54 D4 Mbomou, SE Central African Republic
Banggai, Kepulauan 117 E4 island group C Indonesia
Banghāzī 49 G2 Eng. Bengazi, Benghazi, It. Bengasi. NE Libya
Bangka, Pulau 116 C4 island W Indonesia
Bangkok see Krung Thep
Bangkok, Bight of see Krung Thep, Ao
Bangladesh 113 G3 off. People's Republic of Bangladesh; prev. East Pakistan. country S Asia
Bangladesh, People's Republic of see Bangladesh
Bangor 67 C6 NW Wales, United Kingdom
Bangor 67 B5 Ir. Beannchar. E Northern Ireland, United Kingdom
Bangor 19 G2 Maine, NE USA
Bang Pla Soi see Chon Buri
Bangui 55 B5 country capital (Central African Republic) Ombella-Mpoko, SW Central African Republic
Bangweulu, Lake 51 B8 var. Lake Bengweulu. lake N Zambia
Ban Hat Yai see Hat Yai
Ban Hin Heup 114 C4 Viangchan, C Laos
Ban Houayxay/Ban Houei Sai see Houayxay
Ban Hua Hin 115 C6 var. Hua Hin. Prachuap Khiri Khan, SW Thailand
Bani 52 D3 river S Mali
Banias see Bāniyās
Banijska Palanka see Glina
Banī Suwayf 50 B2 var. Beni Suef. N Egypt
Bāniyās 96 B3 var. Banias, Baniyas, Paneas. Tarṭūs, W Syria
Banjak, Kepulauan see Banyak, Kepulauan
Banja Luka 78 B3 Republika Srpska, NW Bosnia and Herzegovina
Banjarmasin 116 D4 prev. Bandjarmasin. Borneo, C Indonesia
Banjul 52 B3 prev. Bathurst. country capital (The Gambia) W The Gambia
Banks, Îles see Banks Islands
Banks Island 15 E2 island Northwest Territories, NW Canada
Banks Islands 122 D4 Fr. Îles Banks. island group N Vanuatu
Banks Lake 24 B1 reservoir Washington, NW USA
Banks Peninsula 129 C6 peninsula South Island, New Zealand
Banks Strait 127 C8 strait SW Tasman Sea
Bānkura 113 F4 West Bengal, NE India
Ban Mak Khaeng see Udon Thani
Banmo see Bhamo
Banningville see Bandundu
Bañolas see Banyoles
Ban Pak Phanang see Pak Phanang
Ban Sichon see Sichon
Banská Bystrica 77 C6 Ger. Neusohl, Hung. Besztercebánya. Banskobystricky Kraj, C Slovakia
Bantry Bay 67 A7 Ir. Bá Bheanntraí. bay SW Ireland
Banya 82 E2 Burgas, E Bulgaria
Banyak, Kepulauan 116 A3 prev. Kepulauan Banjak. island group NW Indonesia
Banyo 54 B4 Adamaoua, NW Cameroon
Banyoles 71 G2 var. Bañolas. Cataluña, NE Spain
Banzare Seamounts 119 C7 seamount range S Indian Ocean
Banzart see Bizerte
Baoji 106 B4 var. Pao-chi, Paoki. Shaanxi, C China
Baoro 54 B4 Nana-Mambéré, W Central African Republic
Baoshan 106 A6 var. Pao-shan. Yunnan, SW China
Baotou 105 F3 var. Pao-t'ou, Paotow. Nei Mongol Zizhiqu, N China
Ba'qūbah 98 B3 var. Qubba. Diyālá, C Iraq
Baquerizo Moreno see Puerto Baquerizo Moreno
Bar 79 C5 It. Antivari. S Montenegro
Baraawe 51 D6 It. Brava. Shabeellaha Hoose, S Somalia
Bārāmati 112 C5 Mahārāshtra, W India
Baranavichy 85 B6 Pol. Baranowicze, Rus. Baranovichi. Brestskaya Voblasts', SW Belarus
Baranovichi/Baranowicze see Baranavichy
Barbados 33 G1 country SE West Indies
Barbastro 71 F2 Aragón, NE Spain
Barbate de Franco 70 C5 Andalucía, S Spain
Barbuda 33 G3 island N Antigua and Barbuda
Barcaldine 126 C4 Queensland, E Australia
Barcarozsnyó see Râşnov
Barcău see Berettyó
Barce see Al Marj
Barcelona 71 G2 anc. Barcino, Barcinona. Cataluña, E Spain
Barcelona 37 E2 Anzoátegui, NE Venezuela
Barcino/Barcinona see Barcelona
Barcoo see Cooper Creek
Barcs 77 C7 Somogy, SW Hungary
Bardaï 54 C1 Borkou-Ennedi-Tibesti, N Chad
Bardejov 77 D5 Ger. Bartfeld, Hung. Bártfa. Presovský Kraj, E Slovakia
Bardera/Bardere see Baardheere
Barduli see Barletta
Bareilly 113 E3 var. Bareli. Uttar Pradesh, N India
Bareli see Bareilly
Barendrecht 64 C4 Zuid-Holland, SW Netherlands
Barentin 68 C3 Seine-Maritime, N France
Barentsburg 61 G2 Spitsbergen, W Svalbard
Barentsevo More/Barents Havet see Barents Sea
Barentsøya 61 G2 island E Svalbard
Barents Sea 88 C2 Nor. Barents Havet, Rus. Barentsevo More. sea Arctic Ocean
Bar Harbor 19 H2 Mount Desert Island, Maine, NE USA
Bari 75 E5 var. Bari delle Puglie; anc. Barium. Puglia, SE Italy
Bāridah see Al Bāridah
Bari delle Puglie see Bari
Barikot see Barī Kōṭ
Barī Kōṭ 101 F4 var. Barikot, Barīkowṭ. Konar, NE Afghanistan
Barīkowṭ see Barī Kōṭ
Barillas 30 A2 var. Santa Cruz Barillas. Huehuetenango, NW Guatemala
Barinas 36 C2 Barinas, W Venezuela
Barisal see Barishal
Barisan, Pegunungan 116 B4 mountain range Sumatera, W Indonesia
Barishal 113 G4 prev. Barisal. Barishal, S Bangladesh
Barito, Sungai 116 D4 river Borneo, C Indonesia
Barium see Bari
Barka see Al Marj
Barkly Tableland 126 B3 plateau Northern Territory/Queensland, N Australia
Bârlad 86 D4 prev. Bîrlad. Vaslui, E Romania
Barlavento, Ilhas de 52 A2 var. Windward Islands. island group N Cape Verde (Cabo Verde)
Bar-le-Duc 68 D3 var. Bar-sur-Ornain. Meuse, NE France
Barlee, Lake 125 B6 lake Western Australia
Barlee Range 124 A4 mountain range Western Australia
Barletta 75 D5 anc. Barduli. Puglia, SE Italy
Barlinek 76 B3 Ger. Berlinchen. Zachodnio-pomorskie, NW Poland
Barmen-Elberfeld see Wuppertal
Barmouth 67 C6 NW Wales, United Kingdom
Barnaul 92 D4 Altayskiy Kray, C Russia
Barnet 67 A7 United Kingdom
Barnstaple 67 C7 SW England, United Kingdom
Baroda see Vadodara
Baroghil Pass 101 F3 var. Kowtal-e Barowghil. pass Afghanistan/Pakistan
Baron'ki 85 E7 Rus. Boron'ki. Mahilyowskaya Voblasts', E Belarus
Barowghil, Kowtal-e see Baroghil Pass
Barquisimeto 36 C2 Lara, NW Venezuela
Barra 66 B3 island NW Scotland, United Kingdom
Barra de Río Grande 31 E3 Región Autónoma Atlántico Sur, E Nicaragua
Barranca 38 C3 Lima, W Peru
Barrancabermeja 36 B2 Santander, N Colombia
Barranquilla 36 B1 Atlántico, N Colombia
Barreiro 70 B4 Setúbal, W Portugal
Barrier Range 127 C6 hill range New South Wales, SE Australia
Barrow 14 D2 Alaska, USA
Barrow 67 B6 Ir. An Bhearú. river SE Ireland
Barrow-in-Furness 67 C5 NW England, United Kingdom
Barrow Island 124 A4 island Western Australia
Barstow 25 C7 California, W USA
Bar-sur-Ornain see Bar-le-Duc
Bartang 101 F3 river SE Tajikistan
Bartenstein see Bartoszyce
Bártfa/Bartfeld see Bardejov
Bartica 37 F3 N Guyana
Bartın 94 C2 Bartın, NW Turkey (Türkiye)
Bartlesville 27 G1 Oklahoma, C USA
Bartoszyce 76 D2 Ger. Bartenstein. Warmińsko-mazurskie, NE Poland
Baruun-Urt 105 F2 Sühbaatar, E Mongolia
Barú, Volcán 31 E5 var. Volcán de Chiriquí. volcano W Panama
Barwon River 127 D5 river New South Wales, SE Australia
Barysaw 85 D6 Rus. Borisov. Minskaya Voblasts', NE Belarus
Basarabeasca 86 D4 Rus. Bessarabka. SE Moldova
Basel 73 A7 Eng. Basle, Fr. Bâle. Basel-Stadt, NW Switzerland
Basilan 117 E3 island Sulu Archipelago, SW Philippines
Basle see Basel
Basra see Al Başrah
Bassano del Grappa 74 C2 Veneto, NE Italy
Bassein see Pathein
Basseterre 33 G4 country capital (Saint Kitts and Nevis) Saint Kitts, Saint Kitts and Nevis
Basse-Terre 33 G3 dependent territory capital (Guadeloupe) Basse Terre, SW Guadeloupe
Basse Terre 33 G4 island W Guadeloupe
Bassikounou 52 D3 Hodh ech Chargui, SE Mauritania
Bass, Îlots de see Marotiri
Bass Strait 127 C7 strait SE Australia
Bassum 72 B3 Niedersachsen, NW Germany
Bastia 69 E7 Corse, France, C Mediterranean Sea
Bastogne 65 D7 Luxembourg, SE Belgium
Bastrop 20 B2 Louisiana, S USA
Bastyn' 85 B7 Rus. Bostyn'. Brestskaya Voblasts', SW Belarus
Basuo see Dongfang
Basutoland see Lesotho
Bata 55 A5 NW Equatorial Guinea
Batae Coritanorum see Leicester
Batajnica 78 D3 Vojvodina, N Serbia
Batangas 117 E2 off. Batangas City. Luzon, N Philippines
Batangas City see Batangas
Batavia see Jakarta
Bătdâmbâng see Battambang
Batéké, Plateaux 55 B6 plateau S Congo
Bath 67 D7 hist. Akermanceaster; anc. Aquae Calidae, Aquae Solis. SW England, United Kingdom
Bathinda 112 D2 Punjab, NW India
Bathsheba 33 G1 E Barbados
Bathurst 127 D6 New South Wales, SE Australia
Bathurst 17 F4 New Brunswick, SE Canada
Bathurst see Banjul
Bathurst Island 124 D2 island Northern Territory, N Australia
Bathurst Island 15 F2 island Parry Islands, Nunavut, N Canada
Batin, Wadi al 98 C4 dry watercourse SW Asia
Batman 95 E4 var. Iluh. Batman, SE Turkey (Türkiye)
Batna 49 E2 NE Algeria
Baton Rouge 20 B3 state capital Louisiana, S USA
Batroûn 96 A4 var. Al Batrūn. N Lebanon
Battambang 115 C5 Khmer. Bătdâmbâng, NW Cambodia
Batticaloa 110 D3 Eastern Province, E Sri Lanka
Battipaglia 75 D5 Campania, S Italy
Battle Born State see Nevada
Batumi 95 F2 prev. Bat'umi. W Georgia
Bat'umi see Batumi
Batu Pahat 116 B3 prev. Bandar Penggaram. Johor, Peninsular Malaysia
Bauchi 53 G4 Bauchi, NE Nigeria
Bauer Basin 131 F3 undersea basin E Pacific Ocean
Bauska 84 C3 Ger. Bauske. Bauska, S Latvia
Bauske see Bauska
Bautzen 72 D4 Lus. Budyšin. Sachsen, E Germany
Bauzanum see Bolzano
Bavaria see Bayern
Bavarian Alps 73 C7 Ger. Bayrische Alpen. mountain range Austria/Germany
Bavière see Bayern
Bavispe, Río 28 C2 river NW Mexico
Bawīṭī see Al Bawīṭī
Bawku 53 E4 N Ghana
Bayamo 32 C3 Granma, E Cuba
Bayan Har Shan 104 D4 var. Bayan Khar. mountain range C China
Bayanhongor 104 D2 Bayanhongor, C Mongolia
Bayan Khar see Bayan Har Shan
Bayano, Lago 31 G4 lake E Panama
Bay City 18 C3 Michigan, N USA
Bay City 27 G4 Texas, SW USA
Baydhabo 51 D6 var. Baydhowa, Isha Baydhabo, It. Baidoa. Bay, SW Somalia
Baydhowa see Baydhabo
Bayern 73 C6 Eng. Bavaria, Fr. Bavière. state SE Germany
Bayeux 68 B3 anc. Augustodurum. Calvados, N France
Bāyir 97 C7 var. Bā'ir. Ma'ān, S Jordan
Bay Islands 30 C1 Eng. Bay Islands. island group N Honduras
Bay Islands see Bahía, Islas de la
Baymak 89 D6 Respublika Bashkortostan, W Russia
Bayonne 69 A6 anc. Lapurdum. Pyrénées-Atlantiques, SW France
Bayou State see Mississippi
Bayram-Ali see Baýramaly
Baýramaly 100 D3 var. Bayramaly; prev. Bayram-Ali. Mary Welaýaty, S Turkmenistan
Bayreuth 73 C5 var. Baireuth. Bayern, SE Germany
Bayrische Alpen see Bavarian Alps
Bayrūt see Beyrouth
Bay State see Massachusetts
Baysun see Boysun
Bayt Laḥm see Bethlehem
Baytown 27 H4 Texas, SW USA
Baza 71 E4 Andalucía, S Spain
Bazargic see Dobrich
Bazin see Pezinok
Beagle Channel 43 C8 channel Argentina/Chile
Béal Feirste see Belfast
Beannchar see Bangor, Northern Ireland, UK
Bear Island see Bjørnøya
Bear Lake 24 E4 lake Idaho/Utah, NW USA
Beas de Segura 71 E4 Andalucía, S Spain
Beata, Isla 33 E3 island SW Dominican Republic
Beatrice 23 F4 Nebraska, C USA
Beaufort Sea 14 D2 sea Arctic Ocean
Beaufort-Wes see Beaufort West
Beaufort West 56 C5 Afr. Beaufort-Wes. Western Cape, SW South Africa
Beaumont 27 H3 Texas, SW USA
Beaune 68 D4 Côte d'Or, C France
Beauvais 68 C3 anc. Bellovacum, Caesaromagus. Oise, N France
Beaver Island 18 C2 island Michigan, N USA
Beaver Lake 27 H1 reservoir Arkansas, C USA
Beaver River 27 F1 river Oklahoma, C USA
Beaver State see Oregon
Beāwar 112 C3 Rājasthān, N India
Bečej 78 D3 Ger. Altbetsche, Hung. Óbecse, Rácz-Becse; prev. Magyar-Becse, Stari Bečej. Vojvodina, N Serbia
Béchar 48 D2 prev. Colomb-Béchar. W Algeria
Beckley 18 D5 West Virginia, NE USA
Bécs see Wien
Bedford 67 D6 E England, United Kingdom
Bedum 64 E1 Groningen, NE Netherlands
Beehive State see Utah
Be'er Menuha 97 B7 prev. Be'ér Menuḥa. Southern, S Israel
Be'ér Menuḥa see Be'er Menuha
Beernem 65 A5 West-Vlaanderen, NW Belgium
Beersheba see Be'er Sheva
Be'er Sheva 97 A7 var. Beersheba, Ar. Bir es Saba; prev. Be'ér Sheva'. Southern, S Israel
Be'ér Sheva' see Be'er Sheva
Beesel 65 D5 Limburg, SE Netherlands
Beeville 27 G4 Texas, SW USA
Bega 127 D7 New South Wales, SE Australia
Begoml' see Byahoml'
Begovat see Bekobod
Behagle see Laï
Behar see Bihār
Beibu Wan see Tonkin, Gulf of
Beida see Al Bayḍā'
Beihai 106 B6 Guangxi Zhuangzu Zizhiqu, S China
Beijing 106 C3 var. Pei-ching, Peking; prev. Pei-p'ing. country capital (China) Beijing Shi, E China
Beilen 64 E2 Drenthe, NE Netherlands
Beira 57 E3 Sofala, C Mozambique
Beirut see Beyrouth
Beit Lekhem see Bethlehem
Beiuş 86 B3 Hung. Belényes. Bihor, NW Romania
Beja 70 B4 anc. Pax Julia. Beja, SE Portugal
Béjar 70 C3 Castilla y León, N Spain
Bejraburi see Phetchaburi
Bekabad see Bekobod
Békás see Bicaz
Bek-Budi see Qarshi
Békéscsaba 77 D7 Rom. Bichiş-Ciaba. Békés, SE Hungary
Bekobod 101 E2 Rus. Bekabad; prev. Begovat. Toshkent Viloyati, E Uzbekistan
Bela Crkva 78 E3 Ger. Weisskirchen, Hung. Fehértemplom. Vojvodina, W Serbia
Belagāvi 110 B1 prev. Belgaum. Karnātaka, W India
Belarus 85 B6 off. Republic of Belarus, var. Belorussia, Latv. Baltkrievija; prev. Belorussian SSR, Rus. Belorusskaya SSR. country E Europe
Belarus, Republic of see Belarus
Belau see Palau
Belaya Tserkov' see Bila Tserkva
Bełchatów 76 C4 var. Belchatow. Łódzski, C Poland
Belchatow see Bełchatów
Belcher, Îles see Belcher Islands
Belcher Islands 16 C2 Fr. Îles Belcher. island group Nunavut, SE Canada
Beledweyne 51 D5 var. Belet Huen, It. Belet Uen. Hiiraan, C Somalia
Belém 41 F1 var. Pará. state capital Pará, N Brazil
Belén 30 D4 Rivas, SW Nicaragua
Belen 26 D2 New Mexico, SW USA
Belényes see Beiuş
Belet Huen/Belet Uen see Beledweyne
Belfast 67 B5 Ir. Béal Feirste. national capital E Northern Ireland, United Kingdom
Belfield 22 D2 North Dakota, N USA
Belfort 68 E4 Territoire-de-Belfort, E France
Belgard see Białogard
Belgaum see Belagāvi
Belgian Congo see Congo (Democratic Republic of)
België/Belgique see Belgium
Belgium 65 B6 off. Kingdom of Belgium, Dut. België, Fr. Belgique. country NW Europe
Belgium, Kingdom of see Belgium
Belgorod 89 A6 Belgorodskaya Oblast', W Russia
Belgorod-Dnestrovskiy see Bilhorod-Dnistrovskyi
Belgrano II 132 A2 Argentinian research station Antarctica
Belice see Belize/Belize City
Beligrad see Berat
Beli Manastir 78 C3 Hung. Pélmonostor; prev. Monostor. Osijek-Baranja, NE Croatia
Bélinga 55 B5 Ogooué-Ivindo, NE Gabon
Belitung, Pulau 116 C4 island W Indonesia
Belize 30 B1 Sp. Belice; prev. British Honduras, Colony of Belize. country Central America
Belize 30 B1 river Belize/Guatemala
Belize see Belize City
Belize City 30 C1 var. Belize, Sp. Belice. Belize, NE Belize
Belize, Colony of see Belize
Beljak see Villach
Belkofski 14 B3 Alaska, USA
Belle Île 68 A4 island NW France
Belle Isle, Strait of 17 G3 strait Newfoundland and Labrador, E Canada
Bellenz see Bellinzona
Belleville 18 B4 Illinois, N USA
Bellevue 23 F4 Iowa, C USA
Bellevue 24 B2 Washington, NW USA
Bellingham 24 B1 Washington, NW USA
Belling Hausen Mulde see Southeast Pacific Basin
Bellingshausen Abyssal Plain see Bellingshausen Plain
Bellingshausen Plain 131 F5 var. Bellingshausen Abyssal Plain. abyssal plain SE Pacific Ocean
Bellingshausen Sea 132 A3 sea Antarctica
Bellinzona 73 B8 Ger. Bellenz. Ticino, S Switzerland
Bello 36 B2 Antioquia, W Colombia
Bello Horizonte see Belo Horizonte
Bellovacum see Beauvais
Bellville 56 B5 Western Cape, SW South Africa
Belmopan 30 C1 country capital (Belize) Cayo, C Belize
Belogradchik 82 B1 Vidin, NW Bulgaria
Belo Horizonte 41 F4 prev. Bello Horizonte. state capital Minas Gerais, SE Brazil
Belomorsk 88 B3 Respublika Kareliya, NW Russia
Beloretsk 89 D6 Respublika Bashkortostan, W Russia
Belorussia/Belorussian SSR see Belarus
Belorusskaya Gryada see Byelaruskaya Hrada
Belorusskaya SSR see Belarus
Beloshchel'ye see Nar'yan-Mar
Belostok see Białystok
Belovár see Bjelovar
Beloye More 88 C3 Eng. White Sea. sea NW Russia
Belozërsk 88 B4 Vologodskaya Oblast', NW Russia
Belton 27 G3 Texas, SW USA
Bel'tsy see Bălţi
Beluchistan see Baluchistan
Belukha, Gora 92 D5 mountain Kazakhstan/Russia
Belynichi see Byalynichy
Belyy, Ostrov 92 D2 island N Russia
Bemaraha 57 F3 var. Plateau du Bemaraha. mountain range W Madagascar
Bemaraha, Plateau du see Bemaraha
Bemidji 23 F1 Minnesota, N USA
Bemmel 64 D4 Gelderland, SE Netherlands
Benaco see Garda, Lago di
Benares see Vārānasi
Benavente 70 D2 Castilla y León, N Spain
Bend 24 B3 Oregon, NW USA
Bender 86 D4 Rus. Bendery; var. Tighina. E Moldova
Bender Beila/Bender Beyla see Bandarbeyla
Bender Cassim/Bender Qaasim see Boosaaso
Bendern 72 E1 NW Liechtenstein Europe
Bendery see Bender
Bendigo 127 C7 Victoria, SE Australia
Beneschau see Benešov
Beneški Zaliv see Venice, Gulf of
Benešov 77 B5 Ger. Beneschau. Středočeský Kraj, W Czechia (Czech Republic)
Benevento 75 D5 anc. Beneventum, Malventum. Campania, S Italy
Beneventum see Benevento
Bengal, Bay of 102 C4 bay N Indian Ocean
Bengalūru 110 C2 prev. Bangalore. state capital Karnātaka, S India
Bengasi see Banghāzī
Bengbu 106 D5 var. Peng-pu. Anhui, E China
Benghazi see Banghāzī
Bengkulu 116 B4 prev. Bengkoeloe, Benkoelen, Benkulen. Sumatera, W Indonesia
Benguela 56 A2 var. Benguella. Benguela, W Angola
Benguella see Benguela
Bengweulu, Lake see Bangweulu, Lake
Ben Hope 66 B2 mountain N Scotland, United Kingdom
Beni 55 E5 Nord-Kivu, NE Dem. Rep. Congo
Benidorm 71 F4 Comunitat Valenciana, SE Spain
Beni-Mellal 48 C2 C Morocco
Benin 53 F4 off. Republic of Benin; prev. Dahomey. country W Africa
Benin, Bight of 53 F5 gulf W Africa
Benin City 53 F5 Edo, SW Nigeria
Benin, Republic of see Benin
Beni, Río 39 E3 river N Bolivia
Beni Suef see Banī Suwayf
Ben Nevis 66 C3 mountain N Scotland, United Kingdom
Bénoué see Benue
Benson 26 B3 Arizona, SW USA
Bent Jbaïl 97 A5 var. Bint Jubayl. S Lebanon
Benton 20 B1 Arkansas, C USA
Benue 54 B4 Fr. Bénoué. river Cameroon/Nigeria
Beograd 78 D3 Eng. Belgrade. Serbia, N Serbia
Berane 79 D5 prev. Ivangrad. E Montenegro
Berat 79 C6 var. Berati, Croatian Beligrad. Berat, C Albania
Berătău see Berettyó
Berati see Berat
Berau, Teluk 117 G4 var. MacCluer Gulf. bay Papua, E Indonesia
Berbera 50 D4 Sahil, NW Somalia
Berbérati 55 B5 Mambéré-Kadéï, SW Central African Republic
Berck-Plage 68 C2 Pas-de-Calais, N France
Berdiansk 87 G4 var. Berdyans'k, Rus. Berdyansk; prev. Osipenko. Zaporiz'ka Oblast', SE Ukraine
Berdichev see Berdychiv
Berdyans'k/Berdyansk see Berdiansk
Berdychiv 86 D2 Rus. Berdichev. Zhytomyrs'ka Oblast', N Ukraine
Beregovo/Beregszász see Berehove
Berehove 86 B3 Cz. Berehovo, Hung. Beregszász, Rus. Beregovo. Zakarpats'ka Oblast', W Ukraine
Berehovo see Berehove
Bereket 100 B2 prev. Rus. Gazandzhyk, Kazandzhik, Turkm. Gazanjyk. Balkan Welaýaty, W Turkmenistan
Beretău see Berettyó
Berettyó 77 D7 Rom. Barcău; prev. Berătău, Beretău. river Hungary/Romania
Berettyóújfalu 77 D6 Hajdú-Bihar, E Hungary

Berezhany 86 C2 Pol. Brzeżany. Ternopil's'ka Oblast', W Ukraine
Berezina see Byerezino
Berezniki 89 D5 Permskaya Oblast', NW Russia
Berga 71 G2 Cataluña, NE Spain
Bergamo 74 B2 anc. Bergomum. Lombardia, N Italy
Bergara 71 E1 País Vasco, N Spain
Bergen 72 D2 Mecklenburg-Vorpommern, NE Germany
Bergen 64 C2 Noord-Holland, NW Netherlands
Bergen 63 A5 Hordaland, S Norway
Bergen see Mons
Bergerac 69 B5 Dordogne, SW France
Bergeyk 65 C5 Noord-Brabant, S Netherlands
Bergomum see Bergamo
Bergse Maas 64 D4 river S Netherlands
Beringen 65 C5 Limburg, NE Belgium
Beringov Proliv see Bering Strait
Bering Sea 14 A2 sea N Pacific Ocean
Bering Strait 14 C2 Rus. Beringov Proliv. strait Bering Sea/Chukchi Sea
Berja 71 E5 Andalucía, S Spain
Berkeley 25 B6 California, W USA
Berkner Island 132 A2 island Antarctica
Berkovitsa 82 C2 Montana, NW Bulgaria
Berlin 72 D3 country capital (Germany) Berlin, NE Germany
Berlin 19 G2 New Hampshire, NE USA
Berlinchen see Barlinek
Bermejo, Río 42 C2 river N Argentina
Bermeo 71 E1 País Vasco, N Spain
Bermuda 13 D6 var. Bermuda Islands, Bermudas; prev. Somers Islands. UK Overseas Territory NW Atlantic Ocean
Bermuda Islands see Bermuda
Bermuda Rise 13 E6 undersea rise C Sargasso Sea
Bermudas see Bermuda
Bern 73 A7 Fr. Berne. country capital (Switzerland) Bern, W Switzerland
Bernau 72 D3 Brandenburg, NE Germany
Bernburg 72 C4 Sachsen-Anhalt, C Germany
Berne see Bern
Berner Alpen 73 A7 var. Berner Oberland, Eng. Bernese Oberland. mountain range SW Switzerland
Berner Oberland/Bernese Oberland see Berner Alpen
Bernier Island 125 A5 island Western Australia
Beroea see Ḩalab
Berry 68 C4 cultural region C France
Berry Islands 32 C1 island group N The Bahamas
Bertoua 55 B5 Est, E Cameroon
Beru 123 E2 var. Peru. atoll Tungaru, W Kiribati
Berwick-upon-Tweed 66 D4 N England, United Kingdom
Berytus see Beyrouth
Besançon 68 D4 anc. Besontium, Vesontio. Doubs, E France
Beskra see Biskra
Besontium see Besançon
Bessarabka see Basarabeasca
Beszterce see Bistriţa
Besztercebánya see Banská Bystrica
Betafo 57 G3 Antananarivo, C Madagascar
Betanzos 70 B1 Galicia, NW Spain
Bethlehem 56 D4 Free State, C South Africa
Bethlehem 97 B6 var. Beit Lekhem, Ar. Bayt Laḩm, Heb. Bet Leḥem. C West Bank, Middle East
Béticos, Sistemas 70 D4 var. Sistema Penibético, Eng. Baetic Cordillera, Baetic Mountains. mountain range S Spain
Bet Leḥem see Bethlehem
Bétou 55 C5 Likouala, N Congo
Bette, Picco 49 G4 var. Bikkū Bittī, It. Picco Bette. mountain S Libya
Bette, Picco see Bette, Picco
Beulah 18 C2 Michigan, N USA
Beuthen see Bytom
Beveren 65 B5 Oost-Vlaanderen, N Belgium
Beverley 67 D5 E England, United Kingdom
Bexley 67 B8 Bexley, SE England, United Kingdom
Beyla 52 D4 SE Guinea
Beyrouth 96 A4 var. Bayrūt, Eng. Beirut; anc. Berytus. country capital (Lebanon) W Lebanon
Beyşehir 94 B4 Konya, SW Turkey (Türkiye)
Beyşehir Gölü 94 B4 lake C Turkey (Türkiye)
Béziers 69 C6 anc. Baeterrae, Baeterrae Septimanorum, Julia Beterrae. Hérault, S France
Bezmein see Abadan
Bezwada see Vijayawāda
Bhadrāvati 110 C2 Karnātaka, SW India
Bhāgalpur 113 F3 Bihār, NE India
Bhaktapur 113 F3 Central, C Nepal
Bhamo 114 B2 var. Banmo. Kachin State, N Myanmar (Burma)
Bhārat see India
Bharati 132 D3 Indian research station. Antarctica
Bharūch 112 C4 Gujarāt, W India
Bhaunagar see Bhāvnagar
Bhāvnagar 112 C4 prev. Bhaunagar. Gujarāt, W India
Bheanntraí, Bá see Bantry Bay
Bhopāl 112 D4 state capital Madhya Pradesh, C India
Bhubaneshwar 113 F5 prev. Bhubaneswar, Bhuvaneshwar. state capital Odisha, E India
Bhubaneswar see Bhubaneshwar
Bhuket see Phuket
Bhusaval see Bhusāwal
Bhusāwal 112 D4 prev. Bhusaval. Mahārāshtra, C India
Bhutan 113 G3 off. Kingdom of Bhutan, var. Druk-yul. country S Asia
Bhutan, Kingdom of see Bhutan
Bhuvaneshwar see Bhubaneshwar
Biak, Pulau 117 G4 island E Indonesia
Biała Podlaska 76 E3 Lubelskie, E Poland
Białogard 76 B2 Ger. Belgard. Zachodnio-pomorskie, NW Poland
Białystok 76 E3 Rus. Belostok, Bielostok. Podlaskie, NE Poland
Bianco, Monte see Blanc, Mont
Biarritz 69 A6 Pyrénées-Atlantiques, SW France
Bicaz 86 C3 Hung. Békás. Neamţ, NE Romania
Bichiş-Ciaba see Békéscsaba
Biddeford 19 G2 Maine, NE USA
Bideford 67 C7 SW England, United Kingdom
Biel 73 A7 Fr. Bienne. Bern, W Switzerland
Bielefeld 72 B4 Nordrhein-Westfalen, NW Germany
Bielitz/Bielitz-Biala see Bielsko-Biała
Bielostok see Białystok
Bielsko-Biała 77 C5 Ger. Bielitz, Bielitz-Biala. Śląskie, S Poland
Bielsk Podlaski 76 E3 Białystok, E Poland
Bien Bien see Điện Biên
Biên Hoa 115 E6 Đông Nai, S Vietnam
Bienne see Biel
Bienville, Lac 16 D2 lake Québec, C Canada
Bié, Planalto do 56 B2 var. Bié Plateau. plateau C Angola
Bié Plateau see Bié, Planalto do
Big Cypress Swamp 21 E5 wetland Florida, SE USA
Bigge Island 124 C2 island Western Australia
Bighorn Mountains 22 C2 mountain range Wyoming, C USA
Bighorn River 22 C2 river Montana/Wyoming, NW USA
Bignona 52 B3 SW Senegal
Bigorra see Tarbes
Bigosovo see Bihosava
Big Sioux River 23 E2 river Iowa/South Dakota, N USA
Big Spring 27 E3 Texas, SW USA
Bihać 78 B3 Federacija Bosna I Hercegovina, NW Bosnia and Herzegovina
Bihār 113 F3 prev. Behar. cultural region N India
Bihār see Bihār Sharīf
Biharamulo 51 B7 Kagera, NW Tanzania
Bihār Sharīf 113 F3 var. Bihār. Bihār, N India
Bihosava 85 D5 Rus. Bigosovo. Vitsyebskaya Voblasts', NW Belarus
Bijeljina 78 C3 Republika Srpska, NE Bosnia and Herzegovina
Bijelo Polje 79 D5 E Montenegro
Bikāner 112 C3 Rājasthān, NW India
Bikin 93 G4 Khabarovskiy Kray, SE Russia
Bikini Atoll 122 C1 var. Pikinni. atoll Ralik Chain, NW Marshall Islands
Bikkū Bittī see Bette, Picco
Bilāspur 113 E4 Chhattīsgarh, C India
Biläsuvar 95 H3 Rus. Bilyasuvar; prev. Pushkino. SE Azerbaijan
Bila Tserkva 87 E2 Rus. Belaya Tserkov'. Kyivska Oblast, N Ukraine
Bilauktaung Range 115 C6 var. Thanintari Taungdan. mountain range Myanmar (Burma)/ Thailand
Bilbao 71 E1 Basq. Bilbo. País Vasco, N Spain
Bilbo see Bilbao
Bilecik 94 B3 Bilecik, NW Turkey (Türkiye)
Bilhorod-Dnistrovskyi 87 E4 prev. Akkerman, Rus. Belgorod-Dnestrovskiy, Rom. Cetatea Albă, anc. Tyras. SW Ukraine
Billings 22 C2 Montana, NW USA
Bilma, Grand Erg de 53 H3 desert NE Niger
Biloela 126 D4 Queensland, E Australia
Biloxi 20 C3 Mississippi, S USA
Biltine 54 C3 Biltine, E Chad
Bilwi see Puerto Cabezas
Bilyasuvar see Biläsuvar
Bilzen 65 D6 Limburg, NE Belgium
Bimini Islands 32 C1 island group W The Bahamas
Binche 65 B7 Hainaut, S Belgium
Bindloe Island see Marchena, Isla
Bin Ghalfān, Jazā'ir see Ḩalāniyāt, Juzur al
Binghamton 19 F3 New York, NE USA
Bingöl 95 E3 Bingöl, E Turkey (Türkiye)
Bint Jubayl see Bent Jbail
Bintulu 116 D3 Sarawak, East Malaysia
Binzhou 106 D4 Shandong, E China
Bío Bío, Río 43 B5 river C Chile
Bioco, Isla de 55 A5 var. Bioko, Eng. Fernando Po, Sp. Fernando Póo; prev. Macías Nguema Biyogo. island NW Equatorial Guinea
Bioko see Bioco, Isla de
Birāk 49 F3 var. Brak. C Libya
Birao 54 D3 Vakaga, NE Central African Republic
Birātnagar 113 F3 Eastern, SE Nepal
Bir es Saba see Be'er Sheva
Bīrjand 98 E3 Khorāsān-e Janūbī, E Iran
Birkenfeld 73 A5 Rheinland-Pfalz, SW Germany
Birkenhead 67 C5 NW England, United Kingdom
Birlad see Bârlad
Birmingham 67 C6 C England, United Kingdom
Birmingham 20 C2 Alabama, S USA
Bir Moghrein see Bîr Mogreïn
Bîr Mogreïn 52 C1 var. Bir Moghrein; prev. Fort-Trinquet. Tiris Zemmour, N Mauritania
Birnie Island 123 E3 atoll Phoenix Islands, C Kiribati
Birnin Konni 53 F3 var. Birni-Nkonni. Tahoua, SW Niger
Birni-Nkonni see Birnin Konni
Birobidzhan 93 G4 Yevreyskaya Avtonomnaya Oblast', SE Russia
Birsen see Biržai
Birsk 89 D5 Respublika Bashkortostan, W Russia
Biržai 84 C4 Ger. Birsen. Panevėžys, NE Lithuania
Birżebbuġa 80 B5 SE Malta
Bisanthe see Tekirdağ
Bisbee 26 B3 Arizona, SW USA
Biscaia, Baía de see Biscay, Bay of
Biscay, Bay of 58 B4 Sp. Golfo de Vizcaya, Port. Baía de Biscaia. bay France/Spain
Biscay Plain 58 B3 abyssal plain SE Bay of Biscay
Bischofsburg see Biskupiec
Bishah, Wadi 99 B5 dry watercourse C Saudi Arabia
Bishkek 101 G2 var. Pishpek; prev. Frunze. country capital (Kyrgyzstan) Chuyskaya Oblast', N Kyrgyzstan
Bishop's Lynn see King's Lynn
Bishrī, Jabal 96 D3 mountain range E Syria
Biskara see Biskra
Biskra 49 E2 var. Beskra, Biskara. NE Algeria
Biskupiec 76 D2 Ger. Bischofsburg. Warmińsko-Mazurskie, NE Poland
Bislig 117 F2 Mindanao, S Philippines
Bismarck 23 E2 state capital North Dakota, N USA
Bismarck Archipelago 122 B3 island group NE Papua New Guinea
Bismarck Sea 122 B3 sea W Pacific Ocean
Bisnulok see Phitsanulok
Bissau 52 B4 country capital (Guinea-Bissau) W Guinea-Bissau
Bistriţa 86 B3 Ger. Bistritz, Hung. Beszterce; prev. Nösen. Bistriţa-Năsăud, N Romania
Bistritz see Bistriţa
Bitam 55 B5 Woleu-Ntem, N Gabon
Bitburg 73 A5 Rheinland-Pfalz, SW Germany
Bitlis 95 F3 Bitlis, SE Turkey (Türkiye)
Bitoeng see Bitung
Bitola 79 D6 Turk. Monastir; prev. Bitolj. S North Macedonia
Bitolj see Bitola
Bitonto 75 D5 anc. Butuntum. Puglia, SE Italy
Bitterroot Range 24 D2 mountain range Idaho/ Montana, NW USA
Bitung 117 F3 prev. Bitoeng. Sulawesi, C Indonesia
Biu 53 H4 Borno, E Nigeria
Biwa-ko 109 C6 lake Honshū, SW Japan
Bizerta see Bizerte
Bizerte 49 E1 Ar. Banzart, Eng. Bizerta. N Tunisia
Bjelovar 78 B2 Hung. Belovár. Bjelovar-Bilogora, N Croatia
Bjeshkët e Namuna see North Albanian Alps
Björneborg see Pori
Bjørnøya 61 F3 Eng. Bear Island. island N Norway
Blackall 126 C4 Queensland, E Australia
Black Drin 79 D6 Alb. Lumi i Drinit të Zi, Croatian Crni Drim. river Albania/ North Macedonia
Blackfoot 24 E4 Idaho, NW USA
Black Forest 73 B6 Eng. Black Forest. mountain range SW Germany
Black Forest see Schwarzwald
Black Hills 22 D3 mountain range South Dakota/ Wyoming, N USA
Blackpool 67 C5 NW England, United Kingdom
Black Range 26 C2 mountain range New Mexico, SW USA
Black River 32 A5 W Jamaica
Black River 114 C3 Chin. Babian Jiang, Lixian Jiang, Fr. Rivière Noire, Vtn. Sông Đa. river China/Vietnam
Black Rock Desert 25 C5 desert Nevada, W USA
Black Sand Desert see Garagum
Black Sea 94 B1 var. Euxine Sea, Bul. Cherno More, Rom. Marea Neagră, Rus. Chernoye More, Turk. Karadeniz, Ukr. Chorne More. sea Asia/Europe
Black Sea Lowland 87 E4 Ukr. Prychornomor'ska Nyzovyna. depression SE Europe
Black Volta 53 E4 var. Borongo, Mouhoun, Moun Hou, Fr. Volta Noire. river W Africa
Blackwater 67 A6 Ir. An Abhainn Mhór. river S Ireland
Blackwater State see Nebraska
Blagoevgrad 82 C3 prev. Gorna Dzhumaya. Blagoevgrad, W Bulgaria
Blagoveshchensk 93 G4 Amurskaya Oblast', SE Russia
Blahovishchenske 87 E3 prev. Ulianovka, Rus. Ulyanovka. Kirovohrads'ka Oblast', C Ukraine
Blake Plateau 13 D6 var. Blake Terrace. undersea plateau W Atlantic Ocean
Blake Terrace see Blake Plateau
Blanca, Bahía 43 C5 bay E Argentina
Blanca, Costa 71 F4 physical region SE Spain
Blanche, Lake 127 B5 lake South Australia
Blanc, Mont 69 D5 It. Monte Bianco. mountain France/Italy
Blanco, Cape 24 A4 headland Oregon, NW USA
Blanes 71 G2 Cataluña, NE Spain
Blankenberge 65 A5 West-Vlaanderen, NW Belgium
Blankenheim 73 A5 Nordrhein-Westfalen, W Germany
Blanquilla, Isla 37 E1 var. La Blanquilla. island N Venezuela
Blanquilla, La see Blanquilla, Isla
Blantyre 57 E2 var. Blantyre-Limbe. Southern, S Malawi
Blantyre-Limbe see Blantyre
Blaricum 64 C3 Noord-Holland, C Netherlands
Blatnitsa see Durankulak
Blenheim 129 C5 Marlborough, South Island, New Zealand
Blesae see Blois
Blida 48 D2 var. El Boulaida, El Boulaïda. N Algeria
Bloemfontein 56 C4 var. Mangaung. country capital (South Africa-judicial capital) Free State, C South Africa
Blois 68 C4 anc. Blesae. Loir-et-Cher, C France
Bloomfield 26 C1 New Mexico, SW USA
Bloomington 18 B4 Illinois, N USA
Bloomington 18 C4 Indiana, N USA
Bloomington 23 F2 Minnesota, N USA
Bloomsbury 126 D3 Queensland, NE Australia
Bluefield 18 D5 West Virginia, NE USA
Bluefields 31 E3 Región Autónoma Atlántico Sur, SE Nicaragua
Bluegrass State see Kentucky
Blue Hen State see Delaware
Blue Law State see Connecticut
Blue Mountain Peak 32 B5 mountain E Jamaica
Blue Mountains 24 C3 mountain range Oregon/ Washington, NW USA
Blue Nile 50 C4 var. Abai, Bahr el, Azraq, Amh. Ābay Wenz, Ar. An Nīl al Azraq. river Ethiopia/Sudan
Blumenau 41 E5 Santa Catarina, S Brazil
Blythe 25 D8 California, W USA
Blytheville 20 C1 Arkansas, C USA
Bo 52 C4 S Sierra Leone
Boaco 30 D3 Boaco, S Nicaragua
Boa Vista 40 D1 state capital Roraima, NW Brazil
Boa Vista 52 A3 island Ilhas de Barlavento, E Cape Verde (Cabo Verde)
Bobaomby, Tanjona 57 G2 Fr. Cap d'Ambre. headland N Madagascar
Bobigny 68 E1 Seine-St-Denis, N France
Bobo-Dioulasso 52 D4 SW Burkina
Bobrinets see Bobrynets
Bobruysk see Babruysk
Bobrynets 87 E3 Rus. Bobrinets. Kirovohrads'ka Oblast', C Ukraine
Boca Raton 21 F5 Florida, SE USA
Bocay 30 D2 Jinotega, N Nicaragua
Bocheykovo see Bacheykava
Bocholt 72 A4 Nordrhein-Westfalen, W Germany
Bochum 72 A4 Nordrhein-Westfalen, W Germany
Bocşa 86 A4 Ger. Bokschen, Hung. Boksánbánya. Caraş-Severin, SW Romania
Bodaybo 93 F4 Irkutskaya Oblast', E Russia
Bodegas see Babahoyo
Boden 62 D4 Norrbotten, N Sweden
Bodensee see Constance, Lake, C Europe
Bodmin 67 C7 SW England, United Kingdom
Bodø 62 C3 Nordland, C Norway
Bodrum 94 A4 Muğla, SW Turkey (Türkiye)
Boeloekoemba see Bulukumba
Boende 55 C5 Equateur, C Dem. Rep. Congo
Boeroe see Buru, Pulau
Boetoeng see Buton, Pulau
Bogale 114 B4 Ayeyarwady, SW Myanmar (Burma)
Bogalusa 20 B3 Louisiana, S USA
Bogatynia 76 B4 Ger. Reichenau. Dolnośląskie, SW Poland
Boğazlıyan 94 D3 Yozgat, C Turkey (Türkiye)
Bogendorf see Łuków
Bogor 116 C5 Dut. Buitenzorg. Jawa, C Indonesia
Bogotá 36 B3 prev. Santa Fe, Santa Fe de Bogotá. country capital (Colombia) Cundinamarca, C Colombia
Bogushëvsk see Bahushewsk
Boguslav see Bohuslav
Bo Hai 106 D4 var. Gulf of Chihli. gulf NE China
Bohemia 77 A5 Cz. Čechy, Ger. Böhmen. W Czechia (Czech Republic)
Bohemian Forest 73 C5 Cz. Český Les, Šumava, Ger. Böhmerwald. mountain range C Europe
Böhmen see Bohemia
Böhmerwald see Bohemian Forest
Böhmisch-Krumau see Český Krumlov
Bohol Sea 117 E2 var. Mindanao Sea. sea S Philippines
Bohuslav 87 E2 Rus. Boguslav. Kyivska Oblast, N Ukraine
Boise 24 D3 var. Boise City. state capital Idaho, NW USA
Boise City 27 E1 Oklahoma, C USA
Boise City see Boise
Bois, Lac des see Woods, Lake of the
Bois-le-Duc see 's-Hertogenbosch
Boiarka 87 E2 prev. Boyarka. Kyivska Oblast, N Ukraine
Boizenburg 72 C3 Mecklenburg-Vorpommern, N Germany
Bojador see Boujdour
Bojnūrd 98 D2 var. Bujnurd. Khorāsān-e Shemālī, N Iran
Bokāro 113 F4 Jhārkhand, N India
Boké 52 C4 W Guinea
Bokhara see Buxoro
Bokhtar 101 E3 prev. Qŭrghonteppa, Rus. Kurgan-Tyube. SW Tajikistan
Boksánbánya/Bokschen see Bocşa
Bol 54 B3 Lac, W Chad
Bolgatanga 53 E4 N Ghana
Bolgrad see Bolhrad
Bolhrad 86 D4 Rus. Bolgrad. Odes'ka Oblast', SW Ukraine
Bolívar, Pico 36 C2 mountain W Venezuela
Bolivia 39 F3 off. Plurinational Republic of Bolivia. country W South America
Bolivia, Plurinational Republic of see Bolivia
Bollène 69 D6 Vaucluse, SE France
Bollnäs 63 C5 Gävleborg, C Sweden
Bollon 127 D5 Queensland, C Australia
Bologna 74 C3 Emilia-Romagna, N Italy
Bol'shevik see Bal'shavik
Bol'shevik, Ostrov 93 E2 island Severnaya Zemlya, N Russia
Bol'shezemel'skaya Tundra 88 E3 physical region NW Russia
Bol'shoy Lyakhovskiy, Ostrov 93 F2 island NE Russia
Bolton 67 D5 prev. Bolton-le-Moors. NW England, United Kingdom
Bolton-le-Moors see Bolton
Bolu 94 B3 Bolu, NW Turkey (Türkiye)
Bolungarvík 61 E4 Vestfirdhir, NW Iceland
Bolyarovo 82 D3 prev. Pashkeni. Yambol, E Bulgaria
Bolzano 74 C1 Ger. Bozen; anc. Bauzanum. Trentino-Alto Adige, N Italy
Boma 55 B6 Bas-Congo, W Dem. Rep. Congo
Bombay see Mumbai
Bomu 54 D4 var. Mbomou, Mbomu, M'Bomu. river Central African Republic/Dem. Rep. Congo
Bonaire 33 F5 Dutch special municipality S West Indies
Bonanza 30 D2 Región Autónoma Atlántico Norte, NE Nicaragua
Bonaparte Archipelago 124 C2 island group Western Australia
Bon, Cap 80 D3 headland N Tunisia
Bonda 55 B6 Ogooué-Lolo, C Gabon
Bondoukou 53 E4 E Ivory Coast
Bône see Annaba, Algeria
Bone see Watampone, Indonesia
Bone, Teluk 117 E4 bay Sulawesi, C Indonesia
Bongaigaon 113 G3 Assam, NE India
Bongo, Massif des 54 D4 var. Chaîne des Mongos. mountain range NE Central African Republic
Bongor 54 B3 Mayo-Kébbi, SW Chad
Bonifacio 69 E7 Corse, France, C Mediterranean Sea
Bonifacio, Bocche de/Bonifacio, Bouches de see Bonifacio, Strait of
Bonifacio, Strait of 74 A4 Fr. Bouches de Bonifacio, It. Bocche di Bonifacio. strait C Mediterranean Sea
Bonn 73 A5 Nordrhein-Westfalen, W Germany
Bononia see Vidin, Bulgaria
Bononia see Boulogne-sur-Mer, France
Boosaaso 50 E4 var. Bandar Kassim, Bender Qaasim, Bosaso, It. Bender Cassim. Bari, N Somalia
Boothia Felix see Boothia Peninsula
Boothia, Gulf of 15 F2 gulf Nunavut, NE Canada
Boothia Peninsula 15 F2 prev. Boothia Felix. peninsula Nunavut, NE Canada
Boppard 73 A5 Rheinland-Pfalz, W Germany
Boquete 31 E5 var. Bajo Boquete. Chiriquí, W Panama
Boquillas 28 D2 var. Boquillas del Carmen. Coahuila, NE Mexico
Boquillas del Carmen see Boquillas
Bor 78 E4 Serbia, E Serbia
Bor 51 B5 Jonglei, C South Sudan
Borås 63 B7 Västra Götaland, S Sweden
Borbetomagus see Worms
Borborema, Planalto da 34 E3 plateau NE Brazil
Bordeaux 69 B5 anc. Burdigala. Gironde, SW France
Bordj Omar Driss 49 E3 E Algeria
Borgå see Porvoo
Børgefjelt 62 C4 mountain range C Norway
Borger 64 E2 Drenthe, NE Netherlands
Borger 27 E1 Texas, SW USA
Borgholm 63 C7 Kalmar, S Sweden
Borgo Maggiore 74 E1 NW San Marino
Borislav see Boryslav
Borisoglebsk 89 B6 Voronezhskaya Oblast', W Russia
Borisov see Barysaw
Borlänge 63 C6 Dalarna, C Sweden
Borne 64 E3 Overijssel, E Netherlands
Borneo 116 C4 island Brunei/Indonesia/Malaysia
Bornholm 63 B8 island E Denmark
Borohoro Shan 104 B2 mountain range NW China
Borongo see Black Volta
Boron'ki see Baron'ki
Borosjenő see Ineu
Borovan 82 C2 Vratsa, NW Bulgaria
Borovichi 88 B4 Novgorodskaya Oblast', W Russia
Borovo 78 C3 Vukovar-Srijem, NE Croatia
Borriana 71 F3 var. Burriana. Comunitat Valenciana, E Spain
Borşa 86 C3 Hung. Borsa. Maramureş, N Romania
Boryslav 86 B2 Pol. Borysław, Rus. Borislav. L'vivs'ka Oblast', NW Ukraine
Borysław see Boryslav
Bosanska Dubica 78 B3 var. Kozarska Dubica. Republika Srpska, NW Bosnia and Herzegovina
Bosanska Gradiška 78 B3 var. Gradiška. Republika Srpska, N Bosnia and Herzegovina
Bosanski Novi 78 B3 var. Novi Grad. Republika Srpska, NW Bosnia and Herzegovina
Bosanski Šamac 78 C3 var. Šamac. Republika Srpska, N Bosnia and Herzegovina
Bosaso see Boosaaso
Bösing see Pezinok
Boskovice 77 B5 Ger. Boskowitz. Jihomoravský Kraj, SE Czechia (Czech Republic)
Boskowitz see Boskovice
Bosna 78 C4 river N Bosnia and Herzegovina
Bosnia and Herzegovina 78 B3 country SE Europe
Boso-hanto 109 D6 peninsula Honshū, S Japan
Bosphorus/Bosporus see İstanbul Boğazı
Bosporus Cimmerius see Kerch Strait
Bosporus Thracius see İstanbul Boğazı
Bossangoa 54 C4 Ouham, C Central African Republic
Bossembélé 54 C4 Ombella-Mpoko, C Central African Republic
Bossier City 20 A2 Louisiana, S USA
Bosten Hu 104 C3 var. Bagrax Hu. lake NW China
Boston 67 E6 prev. St.Botolph's Town. E England, United Kingdom
Boston 19 G3 state capital Massachusetts, NE USA
Boston Mountains 20 B1 mountain range Arkansas, C USA
Bostyn' see Bastyn'
Botany 126 E2 New South Wales, E Australia
Botany Bay 126 E2 inlet New South Wales, SE Australia
Boteti 56 C3 var. Botletle. river N Botswana
Bothnia, Gulf of 63 D5 Fin. Pohjanlahti, Swe. Bottniska Viken. gulf N Baltic Sea
Botletle see Boteti
Botoşani 86 C3 Hung. Botosány. Botoşani, NE Romania
Botosány see Botoşani
Botou 106 C4 prev. Bozhen. Hebei, E China
Botrange 65 D6 mountain E Belgium
Botswana 56 C3 off. Republic of Botswana. country S Africa
Botswana, Republic of see Botswana
Bottniska Viken see Bothnia, Gulf of
Bouar 54 B4 Nana-Mambéré, W Central African Republic
Bou Craa 48 B3 var. Bu Craa. NW Western Sahara
Bougainville Island 120 B3 island NE Papua New Guinea
Bougaroun, Cap 80 C3 headland NE Algeria
Bougouni 52 D4 Sikasso, SW Mali
Boujdour 48 A3 var. Bojador. W Western Sahara
Boulder 22 C4 Colorado, C USA
Boulder 22 B2 Montana, NW USA
Boulogne see Boulogne-sur-Mer
Boulogne-Billancourt 68 D1 Île-de-France, N France Europe
Boulogne-sur-Mer 68 C2 var. Boulogne; anc. Bononia, Gesoriacum, Gessoriacum. Pas-de-Calais, N France
Boûmdeïd 52 C3 var. Boumdeït. Assaba, S Mauritania
Boumdeït see Boûmdeïd
Boundiali 52 D4 N Ivory Coast
Bountiful 22 B4 Utah, W USA
Bounty Basin see Bounty Trough
Bounty Islands 120 D5 island group S New Zealand
Bounty Trough 130 C5 var. Bounty Basin. trough S Pacific Ocean
Bourbonnais 68 C4 cultural region C France
Bourbon Vendée see la Roche-sur-Yon
Bourg see Bourg-en-Bresse
Bourgas see Burgas
Bourge-en-Bresse see Bourg-en-Bresse
Bourg-en-Bresse 69 D5 var. Bourg, Bourge-en-Bresse. Ain, E France
Bourges 68 C4 anc. Avaricum. Cher, C France
Bourgogne 68 C4 Eng. Burgundy. cultural region E France
Bourke 127 C5 New South Wales, SE Australia
Bournemouth 67 D7 S England, United Kingdom
Boutilimit 52 C3 Trarza, SW Mauritania
Bouvet Island 45 D7 Norwegian dependency S Atlantic Ocean
Bowen 126 D3 Queensland, NE Australia
Bowling Green 18 B5 Kentucky, S USA
Bowling Green 18 C3 Ohio, N USA
Boxmeer 64 D4 Noord-Brabant, SE Netherlands
Boyarka see Boiarka
Boychinovtsi 82 C2 prev. Lekhchevo. Montana, NW Bulgaria
Boysun 101 E3 Rus. Baysun. Surkhondaryo Viloyati, S Uzbekistan
Bozeman 22 B2 Montana, NW USA
Bozen see Bolzano
Bozhen see Botou
Bozüyük 94 B3 Bilecik, NW Turkey (Türkiye)
Brač 78 B4 var. Brach, It. Brazza; anc. Brattia. island S Croatia
Bracara Augusta see Braga
Brach see Brač
Brades 33 G3 de facto dependent territory capital, de jure capital, Plymouth, destroyed by volcano in 1995 (Montserrat) SW Montserrat
Bradford 67 D5 N England, United Kingdom
Brady 27 F3 Texas, SW USA
Braga 70 B2 anc. Bracara Augusta. Braga, NW Portugal
Bragança 70 C2 Eng. Braganza; anc. Julio Briga. Bragança, NE Portugal
Braganza see Bragança
Brahestad see Raahe
Brahmanbaria 113 G4 Chattogram, E Bangladesh

Brahmapur 113 F5 Odisha, E India
Brahmaputra 113 H3 var. Padma, Tsangpo, Ben. Jamuna, Chin. Yarlung Zangbo Jiang, Ind. Bramaputra, Dihang, Siang. river S Asia
Brăila 86 D4 Brăila, E Romania
Braine-le-Comte 65 B6 Hainaut, SW Belgium
Brainerd 23 F2 Minnesota, N USA
Brak see Birāk
Bramaputra see Brahmaputra
Brampton 16 D5 Ontario, S Canada
Branco, Rio 34 C3 river N Brazil
Brandberg 56 A3 mountain NW Namibia
Brandenburg 72 C3 var. Brandenburg an der Havel. Brandenburg, NE Germany
Brandenburg an der Havel see Brandenburg
Brandon 15 F5 Manitoba, S Canada
Braniewo 76 D2 Ger. Braunsberg. Warmińsko-mazurskie, N Poland
Brasil see Brazil
Brasília 41 F3 country capital (Brazil) Distrito Federal, C Brazil
Brasil, República Federativa do see Brazil
Braşov 86 C4 Ger. Kronstadt, Hung. Brassó; prev. Oraşul Stalin. Braşov, C Romania
Brassó see Braşov
Bratislava 77 C6 Ger. Pressburg, Hung. Pozsony. country capital (Slovakia) Bratislavský Kraj, W Slovakia
Bratsk 93 E4 Irkutskaya Oblast', C Russia
Brattia see Brač
Braunsberg see Braniewo
Braunschweig 72 C4 Eng./Fr. Brunswick. Niedersachsen, N Germany
Brava see Baraawe
Brava, Costa 71 H2 coastal region NE Spain
Bravo del Norte, Río/Bravo, Río see Grande, Rio
Bravo, Río 28 C1 river Mexico/USA North America
Brawley 25 D8 California, W USA
Brazil 40 C2 off. Federative Republic of Brazil, Port. República Federativa do Brasil, Sp. Brasil; prev. United States of Brazil. country South America
Brazil Basin 45 C5 var. Brazilian Basin, Brazil'skaya Kotlovina. undersea basin W Atlantic Ocean
Brazil, Federative Republic of see Brazil
Brazilian Basin see Brazil Basin
Brazilian Highlands see Central, Planalto
Brazil'skaya Kotlovina see Brazil Basin
Brazil, United States of see Brazil
Brazos River 27 G3 river Texas, SW USA
Brazza see Brač
Brazzaville 55 B6 country capital (Congo) Capital District, S Congo
Brčko 78 C3 Republika Srpska, NE Bosnia and Herzegovina
Brecht 65 C5 Antwerpen, N Belgium
Brecon Beacons 67 C6 mountain range S Wales, United Kingdom
Breda 64 C4 Noord-Brabant, S Netherlands
Bree 65 D5 Limburg, NE Belgium
Bregalnica 79 E6 river E North Macedonia
Bregenz 73 B7 anc. Brigantium. Vorarlberg, W Austria
Bregovo 82 B1 Vidin, NW Bulgaria
Bremen 72 B3 Fr. Brême. Bremen, NW Germany
Bremerhaven 72 B3 Bremen, NW Germany
Bremerton 24 B2 Washington, NW USA
Brenham 27 G3 Texas, SW USA
Brenner, Col du/Brennero, Passo del see Brenner Pass
Brenner Pass 74 C1 var. Brenner Sattel, Fr. Col du Brenner, Ger. Brennerpass, It. Passo del Brennero. pass Austria/Italy
Brennerpass see Brenner Pass
Brenner Sattel see Brenner Pass
Brescia 74 B2 anc. Brixia. Lombardia, N Italy
Breslau see Wrocław
Bressanone 74 C1 Ger. Brixen. Trentino-Alto Adige, N Italy
Brest 85 A6 Pol. Brześć nad Bugiem, Rus. Brest-Litovsk; prev. Brześć Litewski. Brestskaya Voblasts', SW Belarus
Brest 68 A3 Finistère, NW France
Brest-Litovsk see Brest
Bretagne 68 A3 Eng. Brittany, Lat. Britannia Minor. cultural region NW France
Brewster, Kap see Kangikajik
Brewton 20 C3 Alabama, S USA
Brezhnev see Naberezhnyye Chelny
Brezovo 82 D2 prev. Abrashlare. Plovdiv, C Bulgaria
Bria 54 D4 Haute-Kotto, C Central African Rep.
Briançon 69 D5 anc. Brigantio. Hautes-Alpes, SE France
Bricgstow see Bristol
Bridgeport 19 F3 Connecticut, NE USA
Bridgetown 33 G2 country capital (Barbados) SW Barbados
Bridlington 67 D5 E England, United Kingdom
Bridport 67 D7 S England, United Kingdom
Brieg see Brzeg
Brig 73 A7 Fr. Brigue, It. Briga. Valais, SW Switzerland
Briga see Brig
Brigantio see Briançon
Brigantium see Bregenz
Brigham City 22 B3 Utah, W USA
Brighton 67 E7 SE England, United Kingdom
Brighton 22 D4 Colorado, C USA
Brigue see Brig
Brindisi 75 E5 anc. Brundisium, Brundusium. Puglia, SE Italy
Briovera see St-Lô
Brisbane 127 E5 state capital Queensland, E Australia
Bristol 67 D7 anc. Bricgstow. SW England, United Kingdom
Bristol 19 F3 Connecticut, NE USA
Bristol 18 D5 Tennessee, S USA
Bristol Bay 14 B3 bay Alaska, USA
Bristol Channel 67 C7 inlet England/Wales, United Kingdom
Britain 58 C3 var. Great Britain. island United Kingdom
Britannia Minor see Bretagne
British Columbia 14 D4 Fr. Colombie-Britannique. province SW Canada
British Guiana see Guyana
British Honduras see Belize
British Indian Ocean Territory 119 B5 UK Overseas Territory C Indian Ocean
British Isles 67 island group NW Europe
British North Borneo see Sabah
British Solomon Islands Protectorate see Solomon Islands
British Virgin Islands 33 F3 var. Virgin Islands. UK Overseas Territory E West Indies
Brittany see Bretagne
Briva Curretia see Brive-la-Gaillarde
Briva Isarae see Pontoise
Brive see Brive-la-Gaillarde
Brive-la-Gaillarde 69 C5 prev. Brive; anc. Briva Curretia. Corrèze, C France
Brixen see Bressanone
Brixia see Brescia
Brno 77 B5 Ger. Brünn. Jihomoravský Kraj, SE Czechia (Czech Republic)
Broceni 84 B3 Saldus, SW Latvia
Brod/Bród see Slavonski Brod
Brodeur Peninsula 15 F2 peninsula Baffin Island, Nunavut, NE Canada
Brod na Savi see Slavonski Brod
Brodnica 76 C3 Ger. Buddenbrock. Kujawski-pomorskie, C Poland
Broek-in-Waterland 64 C3 Noord-Holland, C Netherlands
Broken Arrow 27 G1 Oklahoma, C USA
Broken Bay 126 E1 bay New South Wales, SE Australia
Broken Hill 127 B6 New South Wales, SE Australia
Broken Ridge 119 D6 undersea plateau S Indian Ocean
Bromberg see Bydgoszcz
Bromley 67 B8 United Kingdom
Brookhaven 20 B3 Mississippi, S USA
Brookings 23 F3 South Dakota, N USA
Brooks Range 14 D2 mountain range Alaska, USA
Brookton 125 B6 Western Australia
Broome 124 B3 Western Australia
Broomfield 22 D4 Colorado, C USA
Broucsella see Brussel/Bruxelles
Brovary 87 E2 Kyivska Oblast, N Ukraine
Brownfield 27 E2 Texas, SW USA
Brownsville 27 G5 Texas, SW USA
Brownwood 27 F3 Texas, SW USA
Brozha 85 D7 Mahilyowskaya Voblasts', E Belarus
Bruges see Brugge
Brugge 65 A5 Fr. Bruges. West-Vlaanderen, NW Belgium
Brummen 64 D3 Gelderland, E Netherlands
Brundisium/Brundusium see Brindisi
Brunei 116 D3 off. Brunei Darussalam, Mal. Negara Brunei Darussalam. country SE Asia
Brunei Darussalam see Brunei
Brunei Town see Bandar Seri Begawan
Brünn see Brno
Brunner, Lake 129 C5 lake South Island, New Zealand
Brunswick 21 E3 Georgia, SE USA
Brunswick see Braunschweig
Brusa see Bursa
Brus Laguna 30 D2 Gracias a Dios, E Honduras
Brussa see Bursa
Brussel 65 C6 var. Brussels, Fr. Bruxelles, Ger. Brüssel; anc. Broucsella. country capital (Belgium) Brussels, C Belgium
Brüssel/Brussels see Brussel/Bruxelles
Brüx see Most
Bruxelles see Brussel
Bryan 27 G3 Texas, SW USA
Bryansk 89 A5 Bryanskaya Oblast', W Russia
Brzeg 76 C4 Ger. Brieg; anc. Civitas Altae Ripae. Opolskie, S Poland
Brześć Litewski/Brześć nad Bugiem see Brest
Brzeżany see Berezhany
Bucaramanga 36 B2 Santander, N Colombia
Buchanan 52 C5 prev. Grand Bassa. SW Liberia
Buchanan, Lake 27 F3 reservoir Texas, SW USA
Bucharest see Bucureşti
Buckeye State see Ohio
Bu Craa see Bou Craa
Bucureşti 86 C5 Eng. Bucharest, Ger. Bukarest, prev. Altenburg; anc. Cetatea Damboviţei. country capital (Romania) Bucureşti, S Romania
Buda-Kashalyova 85 D7 Rus. Buda-Koshelëvo. Homyel'skaya Voblasts', SE Belarus
Buda-Koshelëvo see Buda-Kashalyova
Budapest 77 C6 off. Budapest Főváros, Croatian Budimpešta. country capital (Hungary) Pest, N Hungary
Budapest Főváros see Budapest
Budaun 112 D3 Uttar Pradesh, N India
Buddenbrock see Brodnica
Budimpešta see Budapest
Budweis see České Budějovice
Budyšin see Bautzen
Buena Park 24 E2 California, W USA North America
Buenaventura 36 A3 Valle del Cauca, W Colombia
Buena Vista 39 G4 Santa Cruz, C Bolivia
Buena Vista 71 H5 S Gibraltar Europe
Buenos Aires 42 D4 hist. Santa Maria del Buen Aire. country capital (Argentina) Buenos Aires, E Argentina
Buenos Aires 31 E5 Puntarenas, SE Costa Rica
Buenos Aires, Lago 43 B6 var. Lago General Carrera. lake Argentina/Chile
Buffalo 19 E3 New York, NE USA
Buffalo Narrows 15 F4 Saskatchewan, C Canada
Buff Bay 32 B5 E Jamaica
Buftea 86 C5 Ilfov, S Romania
Bug 59 E3 Bel. Zakhodni Buh, Eng. Western Bug, Rus. Zapadnyy Bug, Ukr. Zakhidnyi Buh. river E Europe
Buga 36 B3 Valle del Cauca, W Colombia
Bughotu see Santa Isabel
Buguruslan 89 D6 Orenburgskaya Oblast', W Russia
Buitenzorg see Bogor
Bujalance 70 D4 Andalucía, S Spain
Bujanovac 79 E5 SE Serbia
Bujnurd see Bojnūrd
Bujumbura 51 B7 prev. Usumbura. country capital (Burundi - commercial) W Burundi
Bucureşti
Bukavu 55 E6 prev. Costermansville. Sud-Kivu, E Dem. Rep. Congo
Bukhara see Buxoro
Bukoba 51 B6 Kagera, NW Tanzania
Bülach 73 B7 Zürich, NW Switzerland
Bulawayo 56 D3 Matabeleland North, SW Zimbabwe
Bulgan 105 E2 Bulgan, N Mongolia
Bulgaria 82 C2 off. Republic of Bulgaria, Bul. Republika Bulgaria; prev. People's Republic of Bulgaria. country SE Europe
Bulgaria, People's Republic of see Bulgaria
Bulgaria, Republic of see Bulgaria
Bulgaria, Republika see Bulgaria
Bullion State see Missouri
Bull Shoals Lake 20 B1 reservoir Arkansas/Missouri, C USA
Bulukumba 117 E4 prev. Boeloekoemba. Sulawesi, C Indonesia
Bumba 55 D5 Equateur, N Dem. Rep. Congo
Bunbury 125 A7 Western Australia
Bundaberg 126 E4 Queensland, E Australia
Bungo-suido 109 B7 strait SW Japan
Bunia 55 E5 Orientale, NE Dem. Rep. Congo
Bünyan 94 D3 Kayseri, C Turkey (Türkiye)
Buraida see Buraydah
Buraydah 98 B4 var. Buraida. Al Qaşīm, N Saudi Arabia
Burdigala see Bordeaux
Burdur 94 B4 var. Buldur. Burdur, SW Turkey (Türkiye)
Burdur Gölü 94 B4 salt lake SW Turkey (Türkiye)
Burē 50 C4 Āmara, N Ethiopia
Burgas 82 E2 var. Bourgas. Burgas, E Bulgaria
Burgaski Zaliv 82 E2 gulf E Bulgaria
Burgos 70 D2 Castilla y León, N Spain
Burgundy see Bourgogne
Burhan Budai Shan 104 D4 mountain range C China
Buriram 115 D5 var. Buri Ram, Puriramya. Buri Ram, E Thailand
Buri Ram see Buriram
Burjassot 71 F3 Comunitat Valenciana, E Spain
Burkburnett 27 F2 Texas, SW USA
Burketown 126 B3 Queensland, NE Australia
Burkina see Burkina Faso
Burkina Faso 53 E4 off. Burkina Faso; var. Burkina; prev. Upper Volta. country W Africa
Burley 24 D4 Idaho, NW USA
Burlington 23 G4 Iowa, C USA
Burlington 19 F2 Vermont, NE USA
Burma see Myanmar
Burnie 127 C8 Tasmania, SE Australia
Burns 24 C3 Oregon, NW USA
Burnside 15 F3 river Nunavut, NW Canada
Burnsville 23 F2 Minnesota, N USA
Burrel 79 D6 var. Burreli. Dibër, C Albania
Burreli see Burrel
Burriana see Borriana
Bursa 94 B3 var. Brussa, prev. Brusa; anc. Prusa. Bursa, NW Turkey (Türkiye)
Būr Sa'īd 50 B1 var. Port Said. N Egypt
Burtnieks 84 C3 var. Burtnieks Ezers. lake N Latvia
Burtnieks Ezers see Burtnieks
Burundi 51 B7 off. Republic of Burundi; prev. Kingdom of Burundi, Urundi. country C Africa
Burundi, Kingdom of see Burundi
Burundi, Republic of see Burundi
Buru, Pulau 117 F4 prev. Boeroe. island E Indonesia
Busan 107 E4 off. Busan Gwang-yeoksi, prev. Pusan, Jap. Fusan. SE South Korea
Busan Gwang-yeoksi see Busan
Būshehr/Bushire see Bandar-e Būshehr
Busra see Al Başrah, Iraq
Busselton 125 A7 Western Australia
Bussora see Al Başrah
Buta 55 D5 Orientale, N Dem. Rep. Congo
Butembo 55 E5 Nord-Kivu, NE Dem. Rep. Congo
Butler 19 E4 Pennsylvania, NE USA
Buton, Pulau 117 E4 var. Pulau Butung; prev. Boetoeng. island C Indonesia
Bütow see Bytów
Butte 22 B2 Montana, NW USA
Butterworth 116 B3 Pinang, Peninsular Malaysia
Button Islands 17 E1 island group Nunavut, NE Canada
Butuan 117 F2 off. Butuan City. Mindanao, S Philippines
Butuan City see Butuan
Butung, Pulau see Buton, Pulau
Butuntum see Bitonto
Buulobarde 51 D5 var. Buulo Berde. Hiiraan, C Somalia
Buulo Berde see Buulobarde
Buur Gaabo 51 D6 Jubbada Hoose, S Somalia
Buxoro 100 D2 var. Bokhara, Rus. Bukhara. Buxoro Viloyati, C Uzbekistan
Buynaksk 89 B8 Respublika Dagestan, SW Russia
Büyük Ağrı Dağı 95 F3 var. Ağrı Dağı, Kūh-e Ārārat-e Bozorg, Masis, Eng. Great Ararat, Mount Ararat. mountain E Turkey (Türkiye)
Büyükmenderes Nehri 94 A4 river SW Turkey (Türkiye)
Buzău 86 C4 Buzău, SE Romania
Büzmeýin see Abadan
Buzuluk 89 D6 Orenburgskaya Oblast', W Russia
Byahoml' 85 D5 Rus. Begoml'. Vitsyebskaya Voblasts', N Belarus
Byalynichy 85 D6 Rus. Belynichi. Mahilyowskaya Voblasts', E Belarus
Byan Tumen see Choybalsan
Byarezina 85 D6 prev. Byerezino, Rus. Berezina. river C Belarus
Bydgoszcz 76 C3 Ger. Bromberg. Kujawski-pomorskie, C Poland
Byelaruskaya Hrada 85 B6 Rus. Belorusskaya Gryada. ridge N Belarus
Byerezino see Byarezina
Byron Island see Nikunau
Bystrovka see Kemin
Bytča 77 C5 Žilinský Kraj, N Slovakia
Bytom 77 C5 Ger. Beuthen. Śląskie, S Poland
Bytów 76 C2 Ger. Bütow. Pomorskie, N Poland
Byuzmeyin see Abadan
Byval'ki 85 D8 Homyel'skaya Voblasts', SE Belarus
Byzantium see Istanbul

C

Caála 56 B2 var. Kaala, Robert Williams, Port. Vila Robert Williams. Huambo, C Angola
Caazapá 42 D3 Caazapá, S Paraguay
Caballo Reservoir 26 C3 reservoir New Mexico, SW USA
Cabanaquinta 70 D1 var. Cabañaquinta. Asturias, N Spain
Cabañaquinta see Cabanaquinta
Cabanatuan 117 E1 off. Cabanatuan City. Luzon, N Philippines
Cabanatuan City see Cabanatuan
Cabillonum see Chalon-sur-Saône
Cabimas 36 C1 Zulia, NW Venezuela
Cabinda 56 A1 var. Kabinda. Cabinda, NW Angola
Cabinda 56 A1 var. Kabinda. province NW Angola
Cabo Verde, Republic of see Cape Verde
Cahora Bassa, Albufeira de 56 D2 var. Lake Cabora Bassa. reservoir NW Mozambique
Cabora Bassa, Lake see Cahora Bassa, Albufeira de
Caborca 28 B1 Sonora, NW Mexico
Cabot Strait 17 G4 strait E Canada
Cabo Verde, Ilhas do see Cape Verde
Cabras, Ilha das 54 E2 island S Sao Tome and Principe, Africa, E Atlantic Ocean
Cabrera, Illa de 71 G3 island E Spain
Cáceres 70 C3 Ar. Qazris. Extremadura, W Spain
Cachimbo, Serra do 41 E2 mountain range C Brazil
Caconda 56 B2 Huíla, C Angola
Čadca 77 C5 Hung. Csaca. Žilinský Kraj, N Slovakia
Cadillac 18 C2 Michigan, N USA
Cadiz 117 E2 off. Cadiz City. Negros, C Philippines
Cádiz 70 C5 anc. Gades, Gadier, Gadir, Gadire. Andalucía, SW Spain
Cadiz City see Cadiz
Cádiz, Golfo de 70 B5 Eng. Gulf of Cadiz. gulf Portugal/Spain
Cadiz, Gulf of see Cádiz, Golfo de
Cadurcum see Cahors
Caen 68 B3 Calvados, N France
Caene/Caenepolis see Qinā
Caerdydd see Cardiff
Caer Glou see Gloucester
Caer Gybi see Holyhead
Caerleon see Chester
Caer Luel see Carlisle
Caesaraugusta see Zaragoza
Caesarea Mazaca see Kayseri
Caesarobriga see Talavera de la Reina
Caesarodunum see Tours
Caesaromagus see Beauvais
Caesena see Cesena
Cafayate 42 C2 Salta, N Argentina
Cagayan de Oro 117 E2 off. Cagayan de Oro City. Mindanao, S Philippines
Cagayan de Oro City see Cagayan de Oro
Cagliari 75 A6 anc. Caralis. Sardegna, Italy, C Mediterranean Sea
Caguas 33 F3 E Puerto Rico
Cahors 69 C5 anc. Cadurcum. Lot, S France
Cahul 86 D4 Rus. Kagul. S Moldova
Caicos Passage 32 D2 strait The Bahamas/Turks and Caicos Islands
Caiffa see Hefa
Cailungo 74 E1 N San Marino
Caiphas see Hefa
Cairns 126 D3 Queensland, NE Australia
Cairo see Al Qāhirah
Cairo 18 B5 Illinois, N USA
Caisleán an Bharraigh see Castlebar
Cajamarca 38 B3 prev. Caxamarca. Cajamarca, NW Peru
Čakovec 78 B2 Ger. Csakathurn, Hung. Csáktornya; prev. Ger. Tschakathurn. Medimurje, N Croatia
Calabar 53 G5 Cross River, S Nigeria
Calabozo 36 D2 Guárico, C Venezuela
Calafat 86 B5 Dolj, SW Romania
Calafate see El Calafate
Calahorra 71 E2 La Rioja, N Spain
Calais 68 C2 Pas-de-Calais, N France
Calais 19 H2 Maine, NE USA
Calais, Pas de see Dover, Strait of
Calama 42 B2 Antofagasta, N Chile
Călăras see Călăraşi
Călăraşi 86 D3 var. Călăras, Rus. Kalarash. C Moldova
Călăraşi 86 C5 Călăraşi, SE Romania
Calatayud 71 E2 Aragón, NE Spain
Calbayog 117 E2 off. Calbayog City. Samar, C Philippines
Calbayog City see Calbayog
Calcutta see Kolkāta
Caldas da Rainha 70 B3 Leiria, W Portugal
Caldera 42 B3 Atacama, N Chile
Caldwell 24 C3 Idaho, NW USA
Caledonia 30 C1 Corozal, N Belize
Caleta Olivia 43 B6 Santa Cruz, SE Argentina
Calgary 15 E5 Alberta, SW Canada
Cali 36 B3 Valle del Cauca, W Colombia
Calicut see Kozhikode
California 25 B7 off. State of California, also known as El Dorado, The Golden State. state W USA
California, Golfo de 28 B2 Eng. Gulf of California; prev. Sea of Cortez. gulf W Mexico
California, Gulf of see California, Golfo de
Călimăneşti 86 B4 Vâlcea, SW Romania
Calisia see Kalisz
Callabonna, Lake 127 B5 lake South Australia
Callao 38 C4 Callao, W Peru
Callatis see Mangalia
Callosa de Segura 71 F4 Comunitat Valenciana, E Spain
Calmar see Kalmar
Caloundra 127 E5 Queensland, E Australia
Caltanissetta 75 C7 Sicilia, Italy, C Mediterranean Sea
Caluula 50 E4 Bari, NE Somalia
Calvinia 56 C5 W South Africa
Camabatela 56 B1 Cuanza Norte, NW Angola
Camacupa 56 B2 var. General Machado, Port. Vila General Machado. Bié, C Angola
Camagüey 32 C2 prev. Puerto Príncipe. Camagüey, C Cuba
Camagüey, Archipiélago de 32 C2 island group C Cuba
Camana 39 E4 var. Camaná. Arequipa, SW Peru
Camargue 69 D6 physical region SE France
Ca Mau 115 D6 var. Quan Long. Minh Hai, S Vietnam
Cambay, Gulf of see Khambhāt, Gulf of
Camberia see Chambéry
Cambodia 115 D5 off. Kingdom of Cambodia, var. Democratic Kampuchea, Roat Kampuchea, Cam. Kampuchea; prev. People's Democratic Republic of Kampuchea. country SE Asia
Cambodia, Kingdom of see Cambodia
Cambrai 68 C2 Flem. Kambryk, prev. Cambray; anc. Cameracum. Nord, N France
Cambray see Cambrai
Cambrian Mountains 67 C6 mountain range C Wales, United Kingdom
Cambridge 32 A4 W Jamaica
Cambridge 128 D3 Waikato, North Island, New Zealand
Cambridge 67 E6 Lat. Cantabrigia. E England, United Kingdom
Cambridge 19 F4 Maryland, NE USA
Cambridge 18 D4 Ohio, NE USA
Cambridge Bay 15 F3 var. Ikaluktutiak. Victoria Island, Nunavut, NW Canada
Camden 20 B2 Arkansas, C USA
Camellia State see Alabama
Cameracum see Cambrai
Cameroon 54 A4 off. Republic of Cameroon, Fr. Cameroun. country W Africa
Cameroon, Republic of see Cameroon
Cameroun see Cameroon
Camocim 41 F2 Ceará, E Brazil
Camopi 37 H3 E French Guiana
Campamento 30 C2 Olancho, C Honduras
Campania 75 D5 Eng. Champagne. region S Italy
Campbell, Cape 129 D5 headland South Island, New Zealand
Campbell Island 120 D5 var. Motu Ihupuku island S New Zealand
Campbell Plateau 120 D5 undersea plateau SW Pacific Ocean
Campbell River 14 D5 Vancouver Island, British Columbia, SW Canada
Campeche 29 G4 Campeche, SE Mexico
Campeche, Bahía de 29 F4 Eng. Bay of Campeche. bay E Mexico
Campeche, Bay of see Campeche, Bahía de
Câm Pha 114 E3 Quang Ninh, N Vietnam
Câmpina 86 C4 prev. Cîmpina. Prahova, SE Romania
Campina Grande 41 G2 Paraíba, E Brazil
Campinas 41 F4 São Paulo, S Brazil
Campobasso 75 D5 Molise, C Italy
Campo Criptana see Campo de Criptana
Campo de Criptana 71 E3 var. Campo Criptana. Castilla-La Mancha, C Spain
Campo dos Goytacazes 41 F4 var. Campos. Rio de Janeiro, SE Brazil
Campo Grande 41 E4 state capital Mato Grosso do Sul, SW Brazil
Campos see Campo dos Goytacazes
Câmpulung 86 B4 prev. Câmpulung-Muşcel, Cîmpulung. Argeş, S Romania
Câmpulung-Muşcel see Câmpulung
Campus Stellae see Santiago de Compostela
Cam Ranh 115 E6 Khanh Hoa, S Vietnam
Canada 12 B4 country N North America
Canada Basin 12 C2 undersea basin Arctic Ocean
Canadian River 27 E2 river SW USA
Çanakkale 94 A3 var. Dardanelli; prev. Chanak, Kale Sultanie. Çanakkale, W Turkey (Türkiye)
Cananea 28 B1 Sonora, NW Mexico
Canarreos, Archipiélago de los 32 B2 island group W Cuba
Canary Islands 48 A2 Eng. Canary Islands. island group Spain, NE Atlantic Ocean
Canary Islands see Canarias, Islas
Cañas 30 D4 Guanacaste, NW Costa Rica
Canaveral, Cape 21 E4 headland Florida, SE USA
Canavieiras 41 G3 Bahia, E Brazil
Canberra 120 C4 country capital (Australia) Australian Capital Territory, SE Australia
Cancún 29 H3 Quintana Roo, SE Mexico
Candia see Irákleio
Canea see Chaniá
Cangzhou 106 D4 Hebei, E China
Caniapiscau 17 E2 river Québec, E Canada
Caniapiscau, Réservoir de 16 D3 reservoir Québec, C Canada
Canik Dağları 94 D2 mountain range N Turkey (Türkiye)
Canillo 69 A7 Canillo, C Andorra Europe
Çankırı 94 C3 var. Chankiri; anc. Gangra, Germanicopolis. Çankırı, N Turkey (Türkiye)
Cannanore see Kannur
Cannes 69 D6 Alpes-Maritimes, SE France
Canoas 41 E5 Rio Grande do Sul, S Brazil
Canon City 22 C5 Colorado, C USA
Cantabria 70 D1 autonomous community N Spain
Cantábrica, Cordillera 70 C1 mountain range N Spain
Cantabrigia see Cambridge
Cantaura 37 E2 Anzoátegui, NE Venezuela
Canterbury 67 E7 hist. Cantwaraburh; anc. Durovernum, Lat. Cantuaria. SE England, United Kingdom
Canterbury Bight 129 C6 bight South Island, New Zealand
Canterbury Plains 129 C6 plain South Island, New Zealand
Cần Thơ 115 E6 Cần Thơ, S Vietnam
Canton 20 B2 Mississippi, S USA
Canton 18 D4 Ohio, N USA
Canton see Guangzhou
Canton Island see Kanton
Cantuaria/Cantwaraburh see Canterbury
Canyon 27 E2 Texas, SW USA
Cao Băng 114 D3 var. Caobang. Cao Băng, N Vietnam
Caobang see Cao Băng
Cap-Breton, Île du see Cape Breton Island
Cape Barren Island 127 C8 island Furneaux Group, Tasmania, SE Australia
Cape Basin 47 B7 undersea basin S Atlantic Ocean
Cape Breton Island 17 G4 Fr. Île du Cap-Breton. island Nova Scotia, SE Canada
Cape Charles 19 F5 Virginia, NE USA
Cape Coast 53 E5 prev. Cape Coast Castle. S Ghana
Cape Coast Castle see Cape Coast
Cape Girardeau 23 H5 Missouri, C USA
Capelle aan den IJssel 64 C4 Zuid-Holland, SW Netherlands
Cape Palmas see Harper
Cape Saint Jacques see Vung Tau
Cape Town 56 B5 var. Ekapa, Afr. Kaapstad, Kapstad. country capital (South Africa-legislative capital) Western Cape, SW South Africa
Cape Verde 52 A2 off. Republic of Cabo Verde, Port. Cabo Verde, Ilhas do Cabo Verde. country E Atlantic Ocean
Cape Verde Basin 44 C4 undersea basin E Atlantic Ocean
Cape Verde Plain 44 C4 abyssal plain E Atlantic Ocean
Cape York Peninsula 126 C2 peninsula Queensland, N Australia
Cap-Haïtien 32 D3 var. Le Cap. N Haiti

Capira 31 G5 Panamá, C Panama
Capitán Pablo Lagerenza 42 D1 var. Mayor Pablo Lagerenza. Chaco, N Paraguay
Capodistria see Koper
Capri 75 C5 island S Italy
Caprivi Concession see Caprivi Strip
Caprivi Strip 56 C3 Ger. Caprivizipfel; prev. Caprivi Concession. cultural region NE Namibia
Caprivizipfel see Caprivi Strip
Cap Saint-Jacques see Vung Tau
Caquetá, Río 36 C5 var. Rio Japurá, Yapurá. river Brazil/Colombia
Caquetá, Río see Japurá, Rio
CAR see Central African Republic
Caracal 86 B5 Olt, S Romania
Caracaraí 40 D1 Rondônia, W Brazil
Caracas 36 D1 country capital (Venezuela) Distrito Federal, N Venezuela
Caralis see Cagliari
Caratasca, Laguna de 31 E2 lagoon NE Honduras
Carballiño see O Carballiño
Carbón, Laguna del 43 B7 physical feature SE Argentina
Carbondale 18 B5 Illinois, N USA
Carbonia 75 A6 var. Carbonia Centro. Sardegna, Italy, C Mediterranean Sea
Carbonia Centro see Carbonia
Carcaso see Carcassonne
Carcassonne 69 C6 anc. Carcaso. Aude, S France
Cardamomes, Chaîne des see Krâvanh, Chuŏr Phnum
Cardamom Mountains see Krâvanh, Chuŏr Phnum
Cárdenas 32 B2 Matanzas, W Cuba
Cardiff 67 C7 Wel. Caerdydd. national capital S Wales, United Kingdom
Cardigan Bay 67 C6 bay W Wales, United Kingdom
Carei 86 B3 Ger. Gross-Karol, Karol, Hung. Nagykároly; prev. Careii-Mari. Satu Mare, NW Romania
Careii-Mari see Carei
Carey, Lake 125 B6 lake Western Australia
Cariaco 37 E1 Sucre, NE Venezuela
Caribbean Sea 32 C4 sea W Atlantic Ocean
Caribrod see Dimitrovgrad
Carlisle 66 C4 anc. Caer Luel, Luguvallium, Luguvallum. NW England, United Kingdom
Carlow 67 B6 Ir. Ceatharlach. SE Ireland
Carlsbad 26 D3 New Mexico, SW USA
Carlsbad see Karlovy Vary
Carlsberg Ridge 118 B4 undersea ridge S Arabian Sea
Carlsruhe see Karlsruhe
Carmana/Carmania see Kermān
Carmarthen 67 C6 SW Wales, United Kingdom
Carmaux 69 C6 Tarn, S France
Carmel 18 C4 Indiana, N USA
Carmelita 30 B1 Petén, N Guatemala
Carmen 29 G4 var. Ciudad del Carmen. Campeche, SE Mexico
Carmona 70 C4 Andalucía, S Spain
Carmona see Uíge
Carnaro see Kvarner
Carnarvon 125 A5 Western Australia
Carnegie, Lake 125 B5 salt lake Western Australia
Car Nicobar 111 F3 island Nicobar Islands, India, NE Indian Ocean
Caroạo, Ilha 54 E1 island N Sao Tome and Principe, Africa, E Atlantic Ocean
Carolina 41 F2 Maranhão, E Brazil
Caroline Island see Millennium Island
Caroline Islands 122 B2 island group C Micronesia
Carolopois see Châlons-en-Champagne
Caroní, Río 37 E3 river E Venezuela
Caronium see A Coruña
Carora 36 C1 Lara, N Venezuela
Carpathian Mountains 59 E4 var. Carpathians, Cz./Pol. Karpaty, Ger. Karpaten. mountain range E Europe
Carpathians see Carpathian Mountains
Carpathos/Carpathus see Kárpathos
Carpații Meridionali 86 B4 var. Alpi Transilvaniei, Carpații Sudici, Eng. South Carpathians, Transylvanian Alps, Ger. Südkarpaten, Transsylvanische Alpen, Hung. Déli-Kárpátok, Erdélyi-Havasok. mountain range C Romania
Carpații Sudici see Carpații Meridionali
Carpentaria, Gulf of 126 B2 gulf N Australia
Carpi 74 C2 Emilia-Romagna, N Italy
Carrara 74 B3 Toscana, C Italy
Carson City 25 C5 state capital Nevada, W USA
Carson Sink 25 C5 salt flat Nevada, W USA
Carstensz, Puntjak see Jaya, Puncak
Cartagena 36 B1 var. Cartagena de los Indes. Bolívar, NW Colombia
Cartagena 71 F4 anc. Carthago Nova. Murcia, SE Spain
Cartagena de los Indes see Cartagena
Cartago 31 E4 Cartago, C Costa Rica
Carthage 23 F5 Missouri, C USA
Carthago Nova see Cartagena
Cartwright 17 F2 Newfoundland and Labrador, E Canada
Carúpano 37 E1 Sucre, NE Venezuela
Carusbur see Cherbourg
Caruthersville 23 H5 Missouri, C USA
Cary 21 F1 North Carolina, SE USA
Casablanca 48 C2 Ar. Dar-el-Beida. NW Morocco
Casa Grande 26 B2 Arizona, SW USA
Cascade Range 24 B3 mountain range Oregon/Washington, NW USA
Cascadia Basin 12 A4 undersea basin NE Pacific Ocean
Cascais 70 B4 Lisboa, C Portugal
Caserta 75 D5 Campania, S Italy
Casey 132 D4 Australian research station Antarctica
Čáslav 77 B5 Ger. Tschaslau. Střední Čechy, C Czechia (Czech Republic)
Casper 22 C3 Wyoming, C USA
Caspian Depression 89 B7 Kaz. Kaspiy Mangy Oypaty, Rus. Prikaspiyskaya Nizmennost'. depression Kazakhstan/Russia
Caspian Sea 92 A4 Az. Xäzär Dänizi, Kaz. Kaspiy Tengizi, Per. Baḩr-e Khazar, Daryā-ye Khazar, Rus. Kaspiyskoye More. inland sea Asia/Europe
Cassai see Kasai
Cassel see Kassel
Castamoni see Kastamonu
Casteggio 74 B2 Lombardia, N Italy
Castelló de la Plana see Castellón de la Plana
Castellón/Castellón de la Plana see Castelló de la Plana
Castelló de la Plana 71 F3 var. Castellón, Castellón de la Plana. Comunitat Valenciana, E Spain
Castelnaudary 69 C6 Aude, S France
Castelo Branco 70 C3 Castelo Branco, C Portugal
Castelsarrasin 69 B6 Tarn-et-Garonne, S France
Castelvetrano 75 C7 Sicilia, Italy, C Mediterranean Sea
Castilla-La Mancha 71 E3 autonomous community NE Spain
Castilla y León 70 C2 autonomous community NW Spain
Castlebar 67 A5 Ir. Caisleán an Bharraigh. W Ireland
Castleford 67 D5 N England, United Kingdom
Castle Harbour 20 B5 inlet Bermuda, NW Atlantic Ocean
Castra Regina see Regensburg
Castricum 64 C3 Noord-Holland, W Netherlands
Castries 33 F1 country capital (Saint Lucia) N Saint Lucia
Castro 43 B6 Los Lagos, W Chile
Castrovillari 75 D6 Calabria, SW Italy
Castuera 70 D4 Extremadura, W Spain
Caswell Sound see Taitetimu
Catacamas 30 D2 Olancho, C Honduras
Catacaos 38 B3 Piura, NW Peru
Catalan Bay 71 H4 bay E Gibraltar, Mediterranean Sea
Cataluña 71 G2 N Spain
Catamarca see San Fernando del Valle de Catamarca
Catania 75 D7 Sicilia, Italy, C Mediterranean Sea
Catanzaro 75 D6 Calabria, SW Italy
Catarroja 71 F3 Comunitat Valenciana, E Spain
Cat Island 32 C1 island C The Bahamas
Catskill Mountains 19 F3 mountain range New York, NE USA
Cattaro see Kotor
Cauca, Río 36 B2 river N Colombia
Caucasia 36 B2 Antioquia, NW Colombia
Caucasus 59 G4 Rus. Kavkaz. mountain range Georgia/Russia
Caura, Río 37 E3 river C Venezuela
Cavaia see Kavajë
Cavalla 52 D5 var. Cavally, Cavally Fleuve. river Ivory Coast/Liberia
Cavally/Cavally Fleuve see Cavalla
Caviana de Fora, Ilha 41 E1 var. Ilha Caviana. island N Brazil
Caviana, Ilha see Caviana de Fora, Ilha
Cawnpore see Kānpur
Caxamarca see Cajamarca
Caxito 56 B1 Bengo, NW Angola
Cayenne 37 H3 dependent territory/arrondissement capital (French Guiana) NE French Guiana
Cayes 32 D3 var. Les Cayes. SW Haiti
Cayman Brac 32 B3 island E Cayman Islands
Cayman Islands 32 B3 UK Overseas Territory W West Indies
Cayo see San Ignacio
Cay Sal 32 B2 islet SW The Bahamas
Cazin 78 B3 Federacija Bosna I Hercegovina, NW Bosnia and Herzegovina
Cazorla 71 E4 Andalucía, S Spain
Ceadâr-Lunga see Ciadîr-Lunga
Ceará 41 F2 off. Estado do Ceará. state/region C Brazil
Ceará see Fortaleza
Ceara Abyssal Plain see Ceará Plain
Ceará, Estado do see Ceará
Ceará Plain 34 E3 var. Ceara Abyssal Plain. abyssal plain W Atlantic Ocean
Ceatharlach see Carlow
Cébaco, Isla 31 F5 island SW Panama
Cebu 117 E2 off. Cebu City. Cebu, C Philippines
Cebu City see Cebu
Čechy see Bohemia
Cecina 74 B3 Toscana, C Italy
Cedar City 22 A5 Utah, W USA
Cedar Falls 23 G3 Iowa, C USA
Cedar Lake 16 A2 lake Manitoba, C Canada
Cedar Rapids 23 G3 Iowa, C USA
Cedros, Isla 28 A2 island W Mexico
Ceduna 127 A6 South Australia
Cefalù 75 C7 anc. Cephaloedium. Sicilia, Italy, C Mediterranean Sea
Celebes see Sulawesi
Celebes Sea 117 E3 Ind. Laut Sulawesi. sea Indonesia/Philippines
Celje 73 E7 Ger. Cilli. C Slovenia
Celldömölk 77 C6 Vas, W Hungary
Celle 72 B3 var. Zelle. Niedersachsen, N Germany
Celovec see Klagenfurt
Celtic Sea 67 B7 Ir. An Mhuir Cheilteach. sea SW British Isles
Celtic Shelf 58 B3 continental shelf E Atlantic Ocean
Cenderawasih, Teluk 117 G4 var. Teluk Irian, Teluk Sarera. bay W Pacific Ocean
Cenon 69 B5 Gironde, SW France
Centennial State see Colorado
Centrafricaine, République see Central African Republic
Central African Republic 54 C4 var. République Centrafricaine, abbrev. CAR; prev. Ubangi-Shari, Oubangui-Chari, Territoire de l'Oubangui-Chari. country C Africa
Central, Cordillera 36 B3 mountain range W Colombia
Cordillera Central 33 E3 mountain range C Dominican Republic
Cordillera Central 31 F5 mountain range C Panama
Central, Cordillera 117 E1 mountain range Luzon, N Philippines
Central Group see Inner Islands
Centralia 24 B2 Washington, NW USA
Central Indian Ridge see Mid-Indian Ridge
Central Makran Range 112 A3 mountain range W Pakistan
Central Pacific Basin 120 D1 undersea basin C Pacific Ocean
Central, Planalto 41 F3 var. Brazilian Highlands. mountain range E Brazil
Central Provinces and Berar see Madhya Pradesh
Central Range 122 B3 mountain range NW Papua New Guinea
Central Russian Upland see Srednerusskaya Vozvyshennost'
Central Siberian Plateau 92 D3 var. Central Siberian Uplands, Eng. Central Siberian Plateau. mountain range N Russia
Central Siberian Plateau/Central Siberian Uplands see Srednesibirskoye Ploskogor'ye
Central, Sistema 70 D3 mountain range C Spain
Central Valley 25 B6 valley California, W USA
Centum Cellae see Civitavecchia
Ceos see Tziá
Cephaloedium see Cefalù
Ceram see Seram, Pulau
Ceram Sea see Laut Seram
Cerasus see Giresun
Cereté 36 B2 Córdoba, NW Colombia
Cergy-Pontoise see Pontoise
Cerignola 75 D5 Puglia, SE Italy
Çerkeş 94 C2 Çankin, N Turkey (Türkiye)
Cernăuți see Chernivtsi
Cernay 68 E4 Haut-Rhin, NE France
Cerro de Pasco 38 C3 Pasco, C Peru
Cervera 71 F2 Cataluña, NE Spain
Cervino, Monte see Matterhorn
Cesena 74 C3 anc. Caesena. Emilia-Romagna, N Italy
Cēsis 84 D3 Ger. Wenden. Cēsis, C Latvia
České Budějovice 77 B5 Ger. Budweis. Jihočeský Kraj, S Czechia (Czech Republic)
Česko see Czechia (Czech Republic)
Český Krumlov 77 A5 var. Böhmisch-Krumau, Ger. Krummau. Jihočeský Kraj, S Czech Republic (Czechia)
Ceský Les see Bohemian Forest
Cetatea Albă see Bilhorod-Dnistrovskyi
Cetatea Damboviței see București
Cetinje 79 C5 It. Cettigne. S Montenegro
Cette see Sète
Cettigne see Cetinje
Ceuta 48 C2 autonomous city of Spain Spain, N Africa
Cévennes 69 C6 mountain range S France
Ceyhan 94 D4 Adana, S Turkey (Türkiye)
Ceylanpınar 95 E4 Şanlıurfa, SE Turkey (Türkiye)
Ceylon see Sri Lanka
Ceylon Plain 102 B4 abyssal plain N Indian Ocean
Ceyre to the Caribs see Marie-Galante
Chachapoyas 38 B2 Amazonas, NW Peru
Chachevichy 85 D6 Rus. Chechevichi. Mahilyowskaya Voblasts', E Belarus
Chaco see Gran Chaco
Chad 54 C3 off. Republic of Chad, Fr. Tchad. country C Africa
Chad, Lake 54 B3 Fr. Lac Tchad. lake C Africa
Chad, Republic of see Chad
Chadron 22 D3 Nebraska, C USA
Chadyr-Lunga see Ciadîr-Lunga
Chāgai Hills 112 A2 var. Chah Gay. mountain range Afghanistan/Pakistan
Chaghasarāy see Asadābād
Chagos-Laccadive Plateau 102 B4 undersea plateau N Indian Ocean
Chagos Trench 119 C5 trench N Indian Ocean
Chah Gay see Chāgai Hills
Chaillu, Massif du 55 B6 mountain range C Gabon
Chain Ridge 118 B4 undersea ridge W Indian Ocean
Chajul 30 B2 Quiché, W Guatemala
Chakhānsūr 100 D5 Nīmrūz, SW Afghanistan
Chala 38 D4 Arequipa, SW Peru
Chalatenango 30 C3 Chalatenango, N El Salvador
Chalcidice see Chalkidikí
Chalcis see Chalkída
Chalki 83 E7 island Dodekánisa, Greece, Aegean Sea
Chalkída 83 C5 var. Halkida, prev. Khalkís; anc. Chalcis. Evvoia, E Greece
Chalkidikí 82 C4 var. Khalkidhikí; anc. Chalcidice. peninsula NE Greece
Challans 68 B4 Vendée, NW France
Challapata 39 F4 Oruro, SW Bolivia
Challenger Deep 130 B3 trench W Pacific Ocean
Challenger Fracture Zone 131 F4 tectonic feature SE Pacific Ocean
Châlons-en-Champagne 68 D3 prev. Châlons-sur-Marne, hist. Arcae Remorum; anc. Carolopois. Marne, NE France
Châlons-sur-Marne see Châlons-en-Champagne
Chalon-sur-Saône 68 D4 anc. Cabillonum. Saône-et-Loire, C France
Cha Mai see Thung Song
Chaman 112 B2 Baluchistan, SW Pakistan
Chambéry 69 D5 anc. Camberia. Savoie, E France
Champagne 68 D3 cultural region N France
Champagne see Campania
Champaign 18 B4 Illinois, N USA
Champasak 115 D5 Champasak, S Laos
Champlain, Lake 19 F2 lake Canada/USA
Champotón 29 G4 Campeche, SE Mexico
Chanak see Çanakkale
Chañaral 42 B3 Atacama, N Chile
Chan-chiang/Chanchiang see Zhanjiang
Chandeleur Islands 20 C3 island group Louisiana, S USA
Chandigarh 112 D2 state capital Punjab, N India
Chandrapur 113 E5 Mahārāshtra, C India
Changan see Xi'an, Shaanxi, C China
Changane 57 E3 river S Mozambique
Changchun 106 D3 var. Ch'angch'un, Ch'ang-ch'un; prev. Hsinking. province capital Jilin, NE China
Ch'angch'un/Ch'ang-ch'un see Changchun
Chang Jiang 106 A5 Eng. Yangtze; var. Yangtze Kiang. river SW China
Changkiakow see Zhangjiakou
Chang, Ko 115 C6 island S Thailand
Changsha 106 C5 var. Ch'angsha, Ch'ang-sha. province capital Hunan, S China
Ch'angsha/Ch'ang-sha see Changsha
Changzhi 106 C4 Shanxi, C China
Chaniá 83 C7 var. Hania, Khaniá, Eng. Canea; anc. Cydonia. Kríti, Greece, E Mediterranean Sea
Chañi, Nevado de 42 B2 mountain NW Argentina
Chankiri see Çankırı
Channel Islands 67 C8 Fr. Iles Normandes. island group S English Channel
Channel Islands 25 B8 island group California, W USA
Channel-Port aux Basques 17 G4 Newfoundland and Labrador, SE Canada
Channel, The see English Channel
Channel Tunnel 68 C2 tunnel France/United Kingdom
Chantabun/Chantaburi see Chanthaburi
Chantada 70 C1 Galicia, NW Spain
Chanthaburi 115 C6 var. Chantabun, Chantaburi. Chantaburi, S Thailand
Chanute 23 F5 Kansas, C USA
Chaouèn see Chefchaouen
Chaoyang 106 D3 Liaoning, NE China
Chapala, Lago de 28 D4 lake C Mexico
Chapan, Gora 100 B3 mountain C Turkmenistan
Chapayevsk 89 C6 Samarskaya Oblast', W Russia
Chaplynka 87 F4 Khersons'ka Oblast', S Ukraine
Chapra see Chhapra
Charcot Seamounts 58 B3 seamount range E Atlantic Ocean
Chardzhev see Türkmenabat
Chardzhou/Chardzhui see Türkmenabat
Charente 69 B5 cultural region W France
Charente 69 B5 river W France
Chari 54 B3 var. Shari. river Central African Republic/Chad
Chārīkār 101 E4 Parvān, NE Afghanistan
Charity 37 F2 NW Guyana
Chärjew see Türkmenabat
Charkhlik/Charkhliq see Ruoqiang
Charleroi 65 C7 Hainaut, S Belgium
Charlesbourg 17 E4 Québec, SE Canada
Charles de Gaulle 68 E1 (Paris) Seine-et-Marne, N France
Charles Island 16 D1 island Nunavut, NE Canada
Charles Island see Santa María, Isla
Charleston 21 F2 South Carolina, SE USA
Charleston 18 D5 state capital West Virginia, NE USA
Charleville 127 D5 Queensland, E Australia
Charleville-Mézières 68 D3 Ardennes, N France
Charlie-Gibbs Fracture Zone 44 C2 tectonic feature N Atlantic Ocean
Charlotte 21 E1 North Carolina, SE USA
Charlotte Amalie 33 F3 prev. Saint Thomas. dependent territory capital (Virgin Islands (US)) Saint Thomas, N Virgin Islands (US)
Charlotte Harbor 21 E5 inlet Florida, SE USA
Charlottenhof see Aegviidu
Charlottesville 19 E5 Virginia, NE USA
Charlottetown 17 F4 province capital Prince Edward Island, Prince Edward Island, SE Canada
Charlotte Town see Roseau, Dominica
Charsk see Shar
Charters Towers 126 D3 Queensland, NE Australia
Chartres 68 C3 anc. Autricum, Civitas Carnutum. Eure-et-Loir, C France
Chashniki 85 D5 Vitsyebskaya Voblasts', N Belarus
Châteaubriant 68 B4 Loire-Atlantique, NW France
Châteaudun 68 C3 Eure-et-Loir, C France
Châteauroux 68 C4 prev. Indreville. Indre, C France
Château-Thierry 68 C3 Aisne, N France
Châtelet 65 C7 Hainaut, S Belgium
Châtelherault see Châtellerault
Châtellerault 68 B4 var. Châtelherault. Vienne, W France
Chatham Island see San Cristóbal, Isla
Chatham Island Rise see Chatham Rise
Chatham Islands 121 E5 island group New Zealand, SW Pacific Ocean
Chatham Rise 120 D5 var. Chatham Island Rise. undersea rise S Pacific Ocean
Chatkal Range 101 F2 Rus. Chatkal'skiy Khrebet. mountain range Kyrgyzstan/Uzbekistan
Chatkal'skiy Khrebet see Chatkal Range
Chāttagām see Chattogram
Chattahoochee River 20 D3 river SE USA
Chattanooga 20 D1 Tennessee, S USA
Chattogram 113 G4 Ben. Chāttagām, prev. Chittagong. Chattogram, SE Bangladesh
Chatyr-Tash 101 G2 Narynskaya Oblast', C Kyrgyzstan
Châu Đốc 115 D6 var. Chauphu, Chau Phu. An Giang, S Vietnam
Chauk 114 A3 Magway, W Myanmar (Burma)
Chaumont 68 D4 prev. Chaumont-en-Bassigny. Haute-Marne, N France
Chaumont-en-Bassigny see Chaumont
Chau Phu see Châu Đốc
Chausy see Chavusy
Chaves 70 C2 anc. Aquae Flaviae. Vila Real, N Portugal
Chávez, Isla see Santa Cruz, Isla
Chavusy 85 E6 Rus. Chausy. Mahilyowskaya Voblasts', E Belarus
Chaykovskiy 89 D5 Permskaya Oblast', NW Russia
Cheb 77 A5 Ger. Eger. Karlovarský Kraj, W Czechia (Czech Republic)
Cheboksary 89 C5 Chuvashskaya Respublika, W Russia
Cheboygan 18 C2 Michigan, N USA
Chechaouèn see Chefchaouen
Chech, Erg 52 D1 desert Algeria/Mali
Chechevichi see Chachevichy
Che-chiang see Zhejiang
Cheduba Island see Manaung Island)
Chefchaouen 48 C2 var. Chaouèn, Chechaouèn, Sp. Xauen. N Morocco
Chefoo see Yantai
Cheju-do see Jeju-do
Cheju Strait see Jeju Strait
Chekiang see Zhejiang
Cheleken see Hazar
Chelkar see Shalqar
Chełm 76 E4 Rus. Kholm. Lubelskie, SE Poland
Chełmno 76 C3 Ger. Culm, Kulm. Kujawski-pomorskie, C Poland
Chełmża 76 C3 Ger. Culmsee, Kulmsee. Kujawski-pomorskie, C Poland
Cheltenham 67 D6 C England, United Kingdom
Chelyabinsk 92 C3 Chelyabinskaya Oblast', C Russia
Chemnitz 72 D4 prev. Karl-Marx-Stadt. Sachsen, E Germany
Chemulpo see Incheon
Chenab 112 C2 river India/Pakistan
Chengchiatun see Liaoyuan
Ch'eng-chou/Chengchow see Zhengzhou
Chengde 106 D3 var. Jehol. Hebei, E China
Chengdu 106 B5 var. Chengtu, Ch'eng-tu. province capital Sichuan, C China
Chenghsien see Zhengzhou
Chengtu/Ch'eng-tu see Chengdu
Chennai 110 D2 prev. Madras. state capital Tamil Nādu, S India
Chenstokhov see Częstochowa
Chen Xian/Chenxian/Chen Xiang see Chenzhou
Chenzhou 106 C6 var. Chenxian, Chen Xian, Chen Xiang. Hunan, S China
Chepelare 82 C3 Smolyan, S Bulgaria
Chepén 38 B3 La Libertad, C Peru
Cher 68 C4 river C France
Cherbourg 68 B3 anc. Carusbur. Manche, N France
Cherepovets 88 B4 Vologodskaya Oblast', NW Russia
Chergui, Chott ech 48 D2 salt lake NW Algeria
Cherikov see Cherykaw
Cherkassy see Cherkasy
Cherkasy 87 E2 Rus. Cherkassy. Cherkas'ka Oblast', C Ukraine
Cherkessk 89 B7 Karachayevo-Cherkesskaya Respublika, SW Russia
Chernigov see Chernihiv
Chernihiv 87 E1 Rus. Chernigov. Chernihivs'ka Oblast', NE Ukraine
Chernivtsi 86 C3 Ger. Czernowitz, Rom. Cernăuți, Rus. Chernovtsy. Chernivets'ka Oblast', W Ukraine
Cherno More see Black Sea
Chernomorskoye see Chornomorske
Chernovtsy see Chernivtsi
Chernoye More see Black Sea
Chernyakhovsk 84 A4 Ger. Insterburg. Kaliningradskaya Oblast', W Russia
Cherry Hill 19 F4 New Jersey, NE USA
Cherski Range see Cherskogo, Khrebet
Cherskiy 93 G2 Respublika Sakha (Yakutiya), NE Russia
Cherskogo, Khrebet 93 F2 var. Cherski Range. mountain range NE Russia
Cherso see Cres
Cherven' see Chervyen'
Chervonograd see Chervonohrad
Chervonohrad 86 C2 Rus. Chervonograd. L'vivs'ka Oblast', NW Ukraine
Chervyen' 85 D6 Rus. Cherven'. Minskaya Voblasts', C Belarus
Cherykaw 85 E7 Rus. Cherikov. Mahilyowskaya Voblasts', E Belarus
Chesapeake Bay 19 F5 inlet NE USA
Chesha Bay see Chëshskaya Guba
Chëshskaya Guba 133 D5 var. Archangel Bay, Chesha Bay, Dvina Bay. bay NW Russia
Chester 67 C6 Wel. Caerleon, hist. Legaceaster, Lat. Deva, Devana Castra. C England, United Kingdom
Chetumal 29 H4 var. Payo Obispo. Quintana Roo, SE Mexico
Cheviot Hills 66 D4 hill range England/Scotland, United Kingdom
Cheyenne 22 D4 state capital Wyoming, C USA
Cheyenne River 22 D3 river South Dakota/Wyoming, N USA
Chezdi-Oșorheiu see Târgu Secuiesc
Chhapra 113 F3 prev. Chapra. Bihār, N India
Chhattīsgarh 113 E4 cultural region E India
Chiai see Chiayi
Chia-i see Chiayi
Chiang-hsi see Jiangxi
Chiang Mai 114 B4 var. Chiangmai, Chiengmai, Kiangmai. Chiang Mai, NW Thailand
Chiangmai see Chiang Mai
Chiang Rai 114 C3 var. Chianpai, Chienrai, Muang Chiang Rai. Chiang Rai, NW Thailand
Chiang-su see Jiangsu
Chianning/Chian-ning see Nanjing
Chianpai see Chiang Rai
Chianti 74 C3 cultural region C Italy
Chiapa see Chiapa de Corzo
Chiapa de Corzo 29 G5 var. Chiapa. Chiapas, SE Mexico
Chiayi 106 D6 var. Chiai, Chia-i, Kiayi, Jiayi, Jap. Kagi. C Taiwan
Chiba 108 B1 var. Tiba. Chiba, Honshū, S Japan
Chibougamau 16 D3 Québec, SE Canada
Chicago 18 B3 Illinois, N USA
Ch'i-ch'i-ha-erh see Qiqihar
Chickasha 27 G2 Oklahoma, C USA
Chiclayo 38 B3 Lambayeque, NW Peru
Chico 25 B5 California, W USA
Chico, Río 43 B7 river SE Argentina
Chico, Río 43 B6 river S Argentina
Chicoutimi 17 E4 Québec, SE Canada
Chiengmai see Chiang Mai
Chienrai see Chiang Rai
Chiesanuova 74 D2 SW San Marino
Chieti 74 D4 var. Teate. Abruzzo, C Italy
Chifeng 105 G2 var. Ulanhad. Nei Mongol Zizhiqu, N China
Chigirin see Chyhyryn
Chih-fu see Yantai
Chihli see Hebei
Chihli, Gulf of see Bo Hai
Chihuahua 28 C2 Chihuahua, NW Mexico
Childress 27 F2 Texas, SW USA
Chile 42 B3 off. Republic of Chile. country SW South America
Chile Basin 35 A5 undersea basin E Pacific Ocean
Chile Chico 43 B6 Aisén, W Chile
Chile, Republic of see Chile
Chile Rise 35 A7 undersea rise SE Pacific Ocean
Chilia-Nouă see Kiliya
Chililabombwe 56 D2 Copperbelt, C Zambia
Chi-lin see Jilin
Chillán 43 B5 Bío Bío, C Chile
Chillicothe 18 D4 Ohio, N USA
Chill Mhantáin, Sléibhte see Wicklow Mountains
Chiloé, Isla de 43 A6 var. Isla Grande de Chiloé. island W Chile
Chilpancingo 29 E5 var. Chilpancingo de los Bravos. Guerrero, S Mexico
Chilpancingo de los Bravos see Chilpancingo
Chilung see Keelung
Chimán 31 G5 Panamá, E Panama
Chimbay see Chimboy
Chimborazo 38 A1 volcano C Ecuador
Chimbote 38 C3 Ancash, W Peru
Chimboy 100 D1 Rus. Chimbay. Qoraqalpog'iston Respublikasi, NW Uzbekistan
Chimkent see Shymkent
Chimoio 57 E3 Manica, C Mozambique
China 102 C2 off. People's Republic of China, Chin. Chung-hua Jen-min Kung-ho-kuo, Zhonghua Renmin Gongheguo; prev. Chinese Empire. country E Asia
Chi-nan/Chinan see Jinan
Chinandega 30 C3 Chinandega, NW Nicaragua

China, People's Republic of see China
China, Republic of see Taiwan
Chincha Alta 38 D4 Ica, SW Peru
Chin-chiang see Quanzhou
Chin-chou/Chinchow see Jinzhou
Chindwin see Chindwinn
Chindwinn 114 B2 var. Chindwin. river N Myanmar (Burma)
Chinese Empire see China
Ch'ing Hai see Qinghai Hu, China
Chinghai see Qinghai
Chingola 56 D2 Copperbelt, C Zambia
Ching-Tao/Ch'ing-tao see Qingdao
Chinguețți 52 C2 var. Chinguetti. Adrar, C Mauritania
Chin Hills 114 A3 mountain range W Myanmar (Burma)
Chinhsien see Jinzhou
Chinnereth see Kinneret, Yam
Chinook Trough 91 H4 trough N Pacific Ocean
Chioggia 74 C2 anc. Fossa Claudia. Veneto, NE Italy
Chíos 83 D5 var. Hios, Khíos, It. Scio, Turk. Sakiz-Adasi. Chíos, E Greece
Chíos 83 D5 var. Khíos. island E Greece
Chipata 56 D2 prev. Fort Jameson. Eastern, E Zambia
Chiquián 38 C3 Ancash, W Peru
Chiquimula 30 B2 Chiquimula, SE Guatemala
Chīrāla 110 D1 Andhra Pradesh, E India
Chirchik see Chirchiq
Chirchiq 101 E2 Rus. Chirchik. Toshkent Viloyati, E Uzbekistan
Chiriqui Gulf 31 E5 Eng. Chiriqui Gulf. gulf SW Panama
Chiriqui Gulf see Chiriquí, Golfo de
Chiriquí, Laguna de 31 E5 lagoon NW Panama
Chiriquí, Volcán de see Barú, Volcán
Chirripó, Cerro see Chirripó Grande, Cerro
Chirripó Grande, Cerro 30 D4 var. Cerro Chirripó. mountain SE Costa Rica
Chisec 30 B2 Alta Verapaz, C Guatemala
Chisholm 23 F1 Minnesota, N USA
Chisimaio/Chisimayu see Kismaayo
Chişinău 86 D4 Rus. Kishinev. country capital (Moldova) C Moldova
Chita 93 F4 Chitinskaya Oblast', S Russia
Chitangwiza see Chitungwiza
Chitato 56 C1 Lunda Norte, NE Angola
Chitina 14 D3 Alaska, USA
Chitose 108 D2 var. Titose. Hokkaidō, NE Japan
Chitré 31 F5 Herrera, S Panama
Chittagong see Chattogram
Chitungwiza 56 D3 prev. Chitangwiza. Mashonaland East, NE Zimbabwe
Chkalov see Orenburg
Chlef 48 D2 var. Ech Cheliff, Ech Chleff; prev. Al-Asnam, El Asnam, Orléansville. NW Algeria
Chocolate Mountains 25 D8 mountain range California, W USA
Chodorów see Khodoriv
Chodzież 76 C3 Wielkopolskie, C Poland
Choele Choel 43 C5 Río Negro, C Argentina
Choiseul 122 C3 var. Lauru. island NW Solomon Islands
Chojnice 76 C2 Ger. Konitz. Pomorskie, N Poland
Ch'ok'ē 50 C4 var. Choke Mountains. mountain range NW Ethiopia
Choke Mountains see Ch'ok'ē
Cholet 68 B4 Maine-et-Loire, NW France
Choluteca 30 C3 Choluteca, S Honduras
Choluteca, Río 30 C3 river SW Honduras
Choma 56 D2 Southern, S Zambia
Chomutov 76 A4 Ger. Komotau. Ústecký Kraj, NW Czechia (Czech Republic)
Chona 91 E2 river C Russia
Chon Buri 115 C5 prev. Bang Pla Soi. Chon Buri, S Thailand
Chone 38 A1 Manabí, W Ecuador
Ch'ŏngjin 107 E3 NE North Korea
Chongqing 107 B5 var. Ch'ung-ching, Ch'ung-ch'ing, Chungking, Pahsien, Tchongking, Yuzhou. Chongqing, C China
Chongqing 107 B5 province C China
Chonnacht see Connaught
Chonos, Archipiélago de los 43 A6 island group S Chile
Chóra 83 D7 Kykládes, Greece, Aegean Sea
Chóra Sfakíon 83 C8 var. Sfákia. Kríti, Greece, E Mediterranean Sea
Chorne More see Black Sea
Chornomorsk 87 E4 prev. Illichivsk. Odes'ka Oblast', SW Ukraine
Chornomorske 87 E4 Rus. Chernomorskoye. Respublika Krym, S Ukraine
Chorokh/Chorokhi see Çoruh Nehri
Chortkiv 86 C2 Rus. Chortkov. Ternopil's'ka Oblast', W Ukraine
Chortkov see Chortkiv
Chorzów 77 C5 Ger. Königshütte; prev. Królewska Huta. Śląskie, S Poland
Chośebuz see Cottbus
Chōsen-kaikyō see Korea Strait
Chōshi 109 D5 var. Tyôsi. Chiba, Honshū, S Japan
Chosŏn-minjujuŭi-inmin-kanghwaguk see North Korea
Choszczno 76 B3 Ger. Arnswalde. Zachodnio-pomorskie, NW Poland
Chota Nagpur 113 E4 plateau N India
Choûm 52 C2 Adrar, C Mauritania
Choybalsan 105 F2 prev. Byan Tumen. Dornod, E Mongolia
Christchurch 129 C6 Canterbury, South Island, New Zealand
Christiana 32 B5 C Jamaica
Christiania see Oslo
Christiansand see Kristiansand
Christianshåb see Qasigiannguit
Christiansund see Kristiansund
Christmas Island 119 D5 Australian external territory E Indian Ocean
Christmas Island see Kiritimati
Christmas Ridge 121 E1 undersea ridge C Pacific Ocean
Chuan see Sichuan
Ch'uan-chou see Quanzhou
Chubek see Maskav
Chubut, Río 43 B6 river SE Argentina
Ch'u-chiang see Shaoguan
Chudskoye Ozero see Peipus, Lake
Chugoku-sanchi 109 B6 mountain range Honshū, SW Japan
Chuí see Chuy
Chukai see Cukai
Chukchi Plain 133 B2 abyssal plain Arctic Ocean
Chukchi Plateau 12 C2 undersea plateau Arctic Ocean
Chukchi Sea 12 B2 Rus. Chukotskoye More. sea Arctic Ocean
Chukotskoye More see Chukchi Sea
Chula Vista 25 C8 California, W USA
Chulucanas 38 B2 Piura, NW Peru
Chulym 92 D4 river C Russia
Chumphon 115 C6 var. Jumporn. Chumphon, SW Thailand
Chuncheon 107 E4 prev. Ch'unch'ŏn, Jap. Shunsen. N South Korea
Ch'unch'ŏn see Chuncheon
Ch'ung-ch'ing/Ch'ung-ching see Chongqing
Chung-hua Jen-min Kung-ho-kuo see China
Chungking see Chongqing
Chunya 93 E3 river C Russia
Chuquicamata 42 B2 Antofagasta, N Chile
Chuquisaca see Sucre
Chur 73 B7 Fr. Coire, It. Coira, Rmsch. Cuera, Quera; anc. Curia Rhaetorum. Graubünden, E Switzerland
Churchill 15 G4 Manitoba, C Canada
Churchill 16 B2 river Manitoba/Saskatchewan, C Canada
Churchill 17 F2 river Newfoundland and Labrador, E Canada
Chuska Mountains 26 C1 mountain range Arizona/New Mexico, SW USA
Chusovoy 89 D5 Permskaya Oblast', NW Russia
Chust see Khust
Chuuk Islands 122 B2 var. Hogoley Islands; prev. Truk Islands. island group Caroline Islands, C Micronesia
Chuy 42 E4 var. Chuí. Rocha, E Uruguay
Chyhyryn 87 E2 Rus. Chigirin. Cherkas'ka Oblast', N Ukraine
Chystiakove 87 H3 prev. Chystyakove, Rus. Torez. Donets'ka Oblast', SE Ukraine
Chystyakove see Chystiakove
Ciadîr-Lunga 86 D4 var. Ceadâr-Lunga, Rus. Chadyr-Lunga. S Moldova
Cide 94 C2 Kastamonu, N Turkey (Türkiye)
Ciechanów 76 D3 prev. Zichenau. Mazowieckie, C Poland
Ciego de Ávila 32 C2 Ciego de Ávila, C Cuba
Ciénaga 36 B1 Magdalena, N Colombia
Cienfuegos 32 B2 Cienfuegos, C Cuba
Cieza 71 E4 Murcia, SE Spain
Cihanbeyli 94 C3 Konya, C Turkey (Türkiye)
Cikobia 123 E4 prev. Thikombia. island N Fiji
Cilacap 116 C5 prev. Tjilatjap. Jawa, C Indonesia
Cill Airne see Killarney
Cill Chainnigh see Kilkenny
Cilli see Celje
Cill Mhantáin see Wicklow
Cimpina see Câmpina
Cimpulung see Câmpulung
Cincinnati 18 C4 Ohio, N USA
Ciney 65 C7 Namur, SE Belgium
Cinto, Monte 69 E7 mountain Corse, France, C Mediterranean Sea
Cintra see Sintra
Cipolletti 43 B5 Río Negro, C Argentina
Cirebon 116 C4 prev. Tjirebon. Jawa, S Indonesia
Cirkvenica see Crikvenica
Cirò Marina 75 E6 Calabria, S Italy
Cirquenizza see Crikvenica
Cisnădie 86 B4 Ger. Heltau, Hung. Nagydisznód. Sibiu, SW Romania
Citharista see la Ciotat
Citlaltépetl see Orizaba, Volcán Pico de
Citrus Heights 25 B5 California, W USA
Ciudad Acuña see Villa Acuña
Ciudad Bolívar 37 E2 prev. Angostura. Bolívar, E Venezuela
Ciudad Camargo 28 D2 Chihuahua, N Mexico
Ciudad Cortés see Cortés
Ciudad Darío 30 D3 var. Dario. Matagalpa, W Nicaragua
Ciudad de Dolores Hidalgo see Dolores Hidalgo
Ciudad de Guatemala 30 B2 Eng. Guatemala City; prev. Santiago de los Caballeros. country capital (Guatemala) Guatemala, C Guatemala
Ciudad del Carmen see Carmen
Ciudad del Este 42 E2 prev. Ciudad Presidente Stroessner, Presidente Stroessner, Puerto Presidente Stroessner. Alto Paraná, SE Paraguay
Ciudad Delicias see Delicias
Ciudad de México see México
Ciudad de Panamá see Panamá
Ciudad Guayana 37 E2 prev. San Tomé de Guayana, Santo Tomé de Guayana. Bolívar, NE Venezuela
Ciudad Guzmán 28 D4 Jalisco, SW Mexico
Ciudad Hidalgo 29 G5 Chiapas, SE Mexico
Ciudad Juárez 28 C1 Chihuahua, N Mexico
Ciudad Lerdo 28 D3 Durango, C Mexico
Ciudad Madero 29 E3 var. Villa Cecilia. Tamaulipas, C Mexico
Ciudad Mante 29 E3 Tamaulipas, C Mexico
Ciudad Miguel Alemán 29 E2 Tamaulipas, C Mexico
Ciudad Obregón 28 B2 Sonora, NW Mexico
Ciudad Ojeda 36 C1 Zulia, NW Venezuela
Ciudad Porfirio Díaz see Piedras Negras
Ciudad Presidente Stroessner see Ciudad del Este
Ciudad Quesada see Quesada
Ciudad Real 70 D3 Castilla-La Mancha, C Spain
Ciudad-Rodrigo 70 C3 Castilla y León, N Spain
Ciudad Trujillo see Santo Domingo
Ciudad Valles 29 E3 San Luis Potosí, C Mexico
Ciudad Victoria 29 E3 Tamaulipas, C Mexico
Ciutadella 71 H3 var. Ciutadella de Menorca. Menorca, Spain, W Mediterranean Sea
Ciutadella de Menorca see Ciutadella
Civitanova Marche 74 D3 Marche, C Italy
Civitas Altae Ripae see Brzeg
Civitas Carnutum see Chartres
Civitas Eburovicum see Évreux
Civitavecchia 74 C4 anc. Centum Cellae, Trajani Portus. Lazio, C Italy
Claremore 27 G1 Oklahoma, C USA
Clarence 129 C5 Canterbury, South Island, New Zealand
Clarence 129 C5 river South Island, New Zealand
Clarence Town 32 D2 Long Island, C The Bahamas
Clarinda 23 F4 Iowa, C USA
Clarion Fracture Zone 131 E2 tectonic feature NE Pacific Ocean
Clarión, Isla 28 A5 island W Mexico
Clark Fork 22 A1 river Idaho/Montana, NW USA
Clark Hill Lake 21 E2 var. J.Storm Thurmond Reservoir. reservoir Georgia/South Carolina, SE USA
Clarksburg 18 D4 West Virginia, NE USA
Clarksdale 20 B2 Mississippi, S USA
Clarksville 20 C1 Tennessee, S USA
Clausentum see Southampton
Clayton 27 E1 New Mexico, SW USA
Clearwater 21 E4 Florida, SE USA
Clearwater Mountains 24 D2 mountain range Idaho, NW USA
Cleburne 27 G3 Texas, SW USA
Clermont 126 D4 Queensland, E Australia
Clermont-Ferrand 69 C5 Puy-de-Dôme, C France
Cleveland 18 D3 Ohio, N USA
Cleveland 20 D1 Tennessee, S USA
Clifton 26 C2 Arizona, SW USA
Clinton 20 B2 Mississippi, S USA
Clinton 27 F1 Oklahoma, C USA
Clipperton Fracture Zone 131 E3 tectonic feature E Pacific Ocean
Clipperton Island 131 F3 administered from France E Pacific Ocean
Cloncurry 126 B3 Queensland, C Australia
Clonmel 67 B6 Ir. Cluain Meala. S Ireland
Cloppenburg 72 B3 Niedersachsen, NW Germany
Cloquet 23 G2 Minnesota, N USA
Cloud Peak 22 C3 mountain Wyoming, C USA
Clovis 27 E2 New Mexico, SW USA
Cluain Meala see Clonmel
Cluj see Cluj-Napoca
Cluj-Napoca 86 B3 Ger. Klausenburg, Hung. Kolozsvár; prev. Cluj. Cluj, NW Romania
Clutha River 129 B7 var. Mata-Au. river South Island, New Zealand
Clyde 66 C4 river W Scotland, United Kingdom
Coari 40 D2 Amazonas, N Brazil
Coast Mountains 14 D4 Fr. Chaîne Côtière. mountain range Canada/USA
Coast Ranges 24 A4 mountain range W USA
Coats Island 15 G3 island Nunavut, NE Canada
Coats Land 132 B2 physical region Antarctica
Coatzacoalcos 29 G4 var. Quetzalcoalco; prev. Puerto México. Veracruz-Llave, E Mexico
Cobán 30 B2 Alta Verapaz, C Guatemala
Cobar 127 C6 New South Wales, SE Australia
Cobija 39 E3 Pando, NW Bolivia
Coblence/Coblenz see Koblenz
Coburg 73 C5 Bayern, SE Germany
Coca see Puerto Francisco de Orellana
Cocanada see Kākināda
Cochabamba 39 F4 hist. Oropeza. Cochabamba, C Bolivia
Cochin see Kochi
Cochinos, Bahía de 32 B2 Eng. Bay of Pigs. bay SE Cuba
Cochrane 16 C4 Ontario, S Canada
Cochrane 43 B7 Aisén, S Chile
Cocibolca see Nicaragua, Lago de
Cockade State see Maryland
Cockburn Town 33 E2 San Salvador, E The Bahamas
Cockpit Country, The 32 A4 physical region W Jamaica
Cocobeach 55 A5 Estuaire, NW Gabon
Coconino Plateau 26 B1 plain Arizona, SW USA
Coco, Río 31 E2 var. Río Wanki, Segoviao Wangkí. river Honduras/Nicaragua
Cocos Basin 102 C5 undersea basin E Indian Ocean
Cocos Island Ridge see Cocos Ridge
Cocos Islands 119 D5 island group E Indian Ocean
Cocos Ridge 13 C8 var. Cocos Island Ridge. undersea ridge E Pacific Ocean
Cod, Cape 19 G3 headland Massachusetts, NE USA
Codfish Island 129 A8 var. Whenua Hou. island SW New Zealand
Codlea 86 C4 Ger. Zeiden, Hung. Feketehalom. Brașov, C Romania
Cody 22 C2 Wyoming, C USA
Coeur d'Alene 24 C2 Idaho, NW USA
Coevorden 64 E2 Drenthe, NE Netherlands
Coffs Harbour 127 E6 New South Wales, SE Australia
Cognac 69 B5 anc. Compniacum. Charente, W France
Cohalm see Rupea
Coiba, Isla de 31 E5 island SW Panama
Coihaique 43 B6 var. Coyhaique. Aisén, S Chile
Coimbatore 110 C3 Tamil Nādu, S India
Coimbra 70 B3 anc. Conimbria, Conimbriga. Coimbra, W Portugal
Coín 70 D5 Andalucía, S Spain
Coira/Coire see Chur
Coirib, Loch see Corrib, Lough
Colby 23 E4 Kansas, C USA
Colchester 67 E6 Connecticut, NE USA
Coleman 27 F3 Texas, SW USA
Coleraine 66 B4 Ir. Cúil Raithin. N Northern Ireland, United Kingdom
Colesberg 56 C5 Northern Cape, C South Africa
Colima 28 D4 Colima, S Mexico
Coll 66 B3 island W Scotland, United Kingdom
College Station 27 G3 Texas, SW USA
Collie 125 A7 Western Australia
Collipo see Leiria
Colmar 68 E4 Ger. Kolmar. Haut-Rhin, NE France
Cöln see Köln
Cologne see Köln
Colomb-Béchar see Béchar
Colombia 36 B3 off. Republic of Colombia. country N South America
Colombian Basin 34 A1 undersea basin SW Caribbean Sea
Colombia, Republic of see Colombia
Colombie-Britannique see British Columbia
Colombo 110 C4 commercial capital (Sri Lanka) Western Province, W Sri Lanka
Colón 31 G4 prev. Aspinwall. Colón, C Panama
Colón, Archipiélago de see Galápagos Islands
Colón Ridge 13 B8 undersea ridge E Pacific Ocean
Colorado 22 C4 off. State of Colorado, also known as Centennial State, Silver State. state C USA
Colorado City 27 F3 Texas, SW USA
Colorado Plateau 26 B1 plateau W USA
Colorado, Río 43 C5 river E Argentina
Colorado, Río see Colorado River
Colorado River 13 B5 var. Río Colorado. river Mexico/USA
Colorado River 27 G4 river Texas, SW USA
Colorado Springs 22 D5 Colorado, C USA
Columbia 19 E4 Maryland, NE USA
Columbia 23 G4 Missouri, C USA
Columbia 21 E2 state capital South Carolina, SE USA
Columbia 20 C1 Tennessee, S USA
Columbia River 24 B3 river Canada/USA
Columbia Plateau 24 C3 plateau Idaho/Oregon, NW USA
Columbus 20 D2 Georgia, SE USA
Columbus 18 C4 Indiana, N USA
Columbus 20 C2 Mississippi, S USA
Columbus 23 F4 Nebraska, C USA
Columbus 18 D4 state capital Ohio, N USA
Colville Channel 128 D2 channel North Island, New Zealand
Colville River 14 D2 river Alaska, USA
Comacchio 74 C3 var. Commachio; anc. Comactium. Emilia-Romagna, N Italy
Comactium see Comacchio
Comalcalco 29 G4 Tabasco, SE Mexico
Coma Pedrosa, Pic de 69 A7 mountain NW Andorra
Comarapa 39 F4 Santa Cruz, C Bolivia
Comayagua 30 C2 Comayagua, W Honduras
Comer See see Como, Lago di
Comilla see Cumilla
Comino see Kemmuna
Comitán 29 G5 var. Comitán de Domínguez. Chiapas, SE Mexico
Comitán de Domínguez see Comitán
Commachio see Comacchio
Commissioner's Point 20 A5 headland W Bermuda
Communism Peak 101 F3 prev. Qullai Kommunizm. mountain E Tajikistan
Como 74 B2 anc. Comum. Lombardia, N Italy
Comodoro Rivadavia 43 B6 Chubut, SE Argentina
Como, Lake 74 B2 var. Lario, Eng. Lake Como, Ger. Comer See. lake N Italy
Como, Lake see Como, Lago di
Comores, Union des see Comoros
Comoros 57 F2 off. Union of the Comoros, Fr. Union des Comores. country W Indian Ocean
Comoros, Union of the see Comoros
Compiègne 68 C3 Oise, N France
Complutum see Alcalá de Henares
Compniacum see Cognac
Compostella see Santiago de Compostela
Comrat 86 D4 Rus. Komrat. S Moldova
Comum see Como
Conakry 52 C4 country capital (Guinea) SW Guinea
Conca see Cuenca
Concarneau 68 A3 Finistère, NW France
Concepción 39 G3 Santa Cruz, E Bolivia
Concepción 43 B5 Bío Bío, C Chile
Concepción 42 D2 var. Villa Concepción. Concepción, C Paraguay
Concepción see La Concepción
Concepción de la Vega see La Vega
Conchos, Río 26 D4 river NW Mexico
Conchos, Río 28 D2 river C Mexico
Concord 19 G3 state capital New Hampshire, NE USA
Concordia 42 D4 Entre Ríos, E Argentina
Concordia 23 E4 Kansas, C USA
Concordia 132 C4 French/Italian research station Antarctica
Côn Đao see Côn Đao Son
Côn Đao Son 115 E7 var. Côn Đao, Con Son. island S Vietnam
Condate see Rennes, Ille-et-Vilaine, France
Condate see St-Claude, Jura, France
Condega 30 D3 Estelí, NW Nicaragua
Condivincum see Nantes
Confluentes see Koblenz
Công Hoa Xa Hôi Chu Nghia Việt Nam see Vietnam
Congo 55 D5 off. Republic of the Congo, Fr. Moyen-Congo; prev. Middle Congo. country C Africa
Congo 55 C6 off. Democratic Republic of Congo; prev. Zaire, Belgian Congo, Congo (Kinshasa). country C Africa
Congo 55 C6 var. Kongo, Fr. Zaire. river C Africa
Congo Basin 55 C6 drainage basin W Dem. Rep. Congo
Congo/Congo (Kinshasa) see Congo (Democratic Republic of)
Coni see Cuneo
Conimbria/Conimbriga see Coimbra
Conjeeveram see Kānchipuram
Connacht see Connaught
Connaught 67 A5 var. Connacht, Ir. Chonnacht, Cúige. province W Ireland
Connecticut 19 F3 off. State of Connecticut, also known as Blue Law State, Constitution State, Land of Steady Habits, Nutmeg State. state NE USA
Connecticut 19 G3 river Canada/USA
Conroe 27 G3 Texas, SW USA
Consentia see Cosenza
Consolación del Sur 32 A2 Pinar del Río, W Cuba
Con Son see Côn Đao Son
Constance see Konstanz
Constance, Lake 73 B7 Ger. Bodensee. lake C Europe
Constanța 86 D5 var. Küstendje, Eng. Constanza, Ger. Konstanza, Turk. Küstence. Constanța, SE Romania
Constantia see Coutances
Constantia see Konstanz
Constantine 49 E2 var. Qacentina, Ar. Qoussantina. NE Algeria
Constantinople see İstanbul
Constantiola see Oltenița
Constanz see Konstanz
Constanza see Constanța
Constitution State see Connecticut
Coo see Kos
Coober Pedy 127 A5 South Australia
Cookeville 20 D1 Tennessee, S USA
Cook Islands 123 F4 self-governing territory in free association with New Zealand S Pacific Ocean
Cook, Mount see Aoraki
Cook Strait 129 D5 var. Raukawa. strait New Zealand
Cooktown 126 D2 Queensland, NE Australia
Coolgardie 125 B6 Western Australia
Cooma 127 D7 New South Wales, SE Australia
Coomassie see Kumasi
Coon Rapids 23 F2 Minnesota, N USA
Cooper Creek 126 C4 var. Barcoo, Cooper's Creek. seasonal river Queensland/ South Australia, Australia
Cooper's Creek see Cooper Creek
Coos Bay 24 A3 Oregon, NW USA
Cootamundra 127 D6 New South Wales, SE Australia
Copacabana 39 E4 La Paz, W Bolivia
Copenhagen see København
Copiapó 42 B3 Atacama, N Chile
Copperas Cove 27 G3 Texas, SW USA
Coppermine see Kugluktuk
Copper State see Arizona
Coquilhatville see Mbandaka
Coquimbo 42 B3 Coquimbo, N Chile
Corabia 86 B5 Olt, S Romania
Coral Harbour 15 G3 var. Salliq. Southampton Island, Nunavut, NE Canada
Coral Sea 120 B3 sea SW Pacific Ocean
Coral Sea Islands 122 B4 Australian external territory SW Pacific Ocean
Corantijn River see Courantyne River
Corcovado, Golfo 43 B6 gulf S Chile
Corcyra Nigra see Korčula
Cordele 20 D3 Georgia, SE USA
Córdoba 42 C3 Córdoba, C Argentina
Córdoba 29 F4 Veracruz-Llave, E Mexico
Córdoba 70 D4 var. Cordoba, Eng. Cordova; anc. Corduba. Andalucía, SW Spain
Cordova 14 C3 Alaska, USA
Cordova/Cordoba see Córdoba
Corduba see Córdoba
Corentyne River see Courantyne River
Corfu see Kérkyra
Coria 70 C3 Extremadura, W Spain
Corinth 20 C1 Mississippi, S USA
Corinth see Kórinthos
Corinth, Gulf of/Corinthiacus Sinus see Korinthiakós Kólpos
Corinthus see Kórinthos
Corinto 30 C3 Chinandega, NW Nicaragua
Cork 67 A6 Ir. Corcaigh. S Ireland
Çorlu 94 A2 Tekirdağ, NW Turkey (Türkiye)
Corner Brook 17 G3 Newfoundland, Newfoundland and Labrador, E Canada
Cornhusker State see Nebraska
Corn Islands 31 E3 var. Corn Islands. island group SE Nicaragua
Corn Islands see Maíz, Islas del
Cornwallis Island 15 F2 Island Nunavut, N Canada
Coro 36 C1 prev. Santa Ana de Coro. Falcón, NW Venezuela
Corocoro 39 F4 La Paz, W Bolivia
Coromandel 128 D2 Waikato, North Island, New Zealand
Coromandel Coast 110 D2 coast E India
Coromandel Peninsula 128 D2 peninsula North Island, New Zealand
Coronado, Bahía de 30 D5 bay S Costa Rica
Coronel Dorrego 43 C5 Buenos Aires, E Argentina
Coronel Oviedo 42 D2 Caaguazú, SE Paraguay
Corozal 30 C1 Corozal, N Belize
Corpus Christi 27 G4 Texas, SW USA
Corrales 26 D2 New Mexico, SW USA
Corrib, Lough 67 A5 Ir. Loch Coirib. lake W Ireland
Corrientes 42 D3 Corrientes, NE Argentina
Corriza see Korçë
Corsica 69 E7 Eng. Corsica. island France, C Mediterranean Sea
Corsica see Corse
Corsicana 27 G3 Texas, SW USA
Cortegana 70 C4 Andalucía, S Spain
Cortés 31 E5 var. Ciudad Cortés. Puntarenas, SE Costa Rica
Cortez, Sea of see California, Golfo de
Cortina d'Ampezzo 74 C1 Veneto, NE Italy
Coruche 70 B3 Santarém, C Portugal
Çoruh Nehri 95 E3 Geor. Chorokh, Rus. Chorokhi. river Georgia/Turkey (Türkiye)
Çorum 94 D3 var. Chorum. Çorum, N Turkey (Türkiye)
Corunna see A Coruña
Corvallis 24 B3 Oregon, NW USA
Corvo 70 A5 var. Ilha do Corvo. island Azores, Portugal, NE Atlantic Ocean
Corvo, Ilha do see Corvo
Cos see Kos
Cosenza 75 D6 anc. Consentia. Calabria, SW Italy
Cosne-Cours-sur-Loire 68 C4 Nièvre, Bourgogne, C France Europe
Costa Mesa 24 D2 California, W USA North America
Costa Rica 31 E4 off. Republic of Costa Rica. country Central America
Costa Rica, Republic of see Costa Rica
Costermansville see Bukavu
Cotagaita 39 F5 Potosí, S Bolivia
Côte d'Ivoire see Ivory Coast
Côte d'Ivoire, République de la see Ivory Coast
Côte d'Or 68 D4 cultural region C France
Côte Française des Somalis see Djibouti
Côtière, Chaine see Coast Mountains
Cotonou 53 F5 var. Kotonu. country capital (Benin - seat of government) S Benin
Cotrone see Crotone
Cotswold Hills 67 D6 var. Cotswolds. hill range S England, United Kingdom
Cotswolds see Cotswold Hills
Cottbus 72 D4 Lus. Chośebuz; prev. Kottbus. Brandenburg, E Germany
Cotton State, The see Alabama
Cotyora see Ordu
Couentrey see Coventry
Council Bluffs 23 F4 Iowa, C USA
Courantyne River 37 G4 var. Corantijn Rivier, Corentyne River. river Guyana/Suriname
Courland Lagoon 84 A4 Ger. Kurisches Haff, Rus. Kurskiy Zaliv. lagoon Lithuania/Russia
Courtrai see Kortrijk
Coutances 68 B3 anc. Constantia. Manche, N France
Couvin 65 C7 Namur, S Belgium
Coventry 67 D6 anc. Couentrey. C England, United Kingdom
Covilhã 70 C3 Castelo Branco, E Portugal
Cowan, Lake 125 B6 lake Western Australia
Coxen Hole see Roatán
Coxin Hole see Roatán
Coyhaique see Coihaique
Coyote State, The see South Dakota
Cozhê 104 C5 Xizang Zizhiqu, W China
Cozumel, Isla 29 H3 island SE Mexico
Cracovia/Cracow see Kraków
Cradock 56 C5 Eastern Cape, S South Africa

Craig *22 C4* Colorado, C USA
Craiova *86 B5* Dolj, SW Romania
Cranbrook *15 E5* British Columbia, SW Canada
Crane *see* The Crane
Cranz *see* Zelenogradsk
Crawley *67 E7* SE England, United Kingdom
Cremona *74 B2* Lombardia, N Italy
Creole State *see* Louisiana
Cres *78 A3 It.* Cherso; *anc.* Crexa. *island* W Croatia
Crescent City *24 A4* California, W USA
Crescent Group *106 C7 island group* C Paracel Islands
Creston *23 F4* Iowa, C USA
Crestview *20 D3* Florida, SE USA
Crete *see* Kríti
Créteil *68 E2* Val-de-Marne, N France
Crete, Sea of/Creticum, Mare *see* Kritikó Pélagos
Creuse *68 B4 river* C France
Crewe *67 D6* C England, United Kingdom
Crexa *see* Cres
Crikvenica *78 A3 It.* Cirquenizza; *prev.* Cirkvenica, Crjkvenica. Primorje-Gorski Kotar, NW Croatia
Crimea *see* Krym
Cristóbal *31 G4* Colón, C Panama
Cristóbal Colón, Pico *36 B1 mountain* N Colombia
Cristur/Cristuru Săcuiesc *see* Cristuru Secuiesc
Cristuru Secuiesc *86 C4 prev.* Cristur, Cristuru Săcuiesc, Sitaş Cristuru, *Ger.* Kreutz, *Hung.* Székelykeresztúr, Szitás-Keresztúr. Harghita, C Romania
Crjkvenica *see* Crikvenica
Crna Gora *see* Montenegro
Crna Reka *79 D6 river* S North Macedonia
Crni Drim *see* Black Drin
Croatia *78 B3 off.* Republic of Croatia, *Cro.* Hrvatska, Republika Hrvatska. *country* SE Europe
Croatia, Republic of *see* Croatia
Crocodile *see* Limpopo
Croia *see* Krujë
Croker Island *124 E2 island* Northern Territory, N Australia
Cromwell *129 B7* Otago, South Island, New Zealand
Crooked Island *32 D2 island* SE The Bahamas
Crooked Island Passage *32 D2 channel* SE The Bahamas
Crookston *23 F1* Minnesota, N USA
Crossen *see* Krosno Odrzańskie
Croton/Crotona *see* Crotone
Crotone *75 E6 var.* Cotrone; *anc.* Croton, Crotona. Calabria, SW Italy
Croydon *67 A8* SE England, United Kingdom
Crozet Basin *119 B6 undersea basin* S Indian Ocean
Crozet Islands *119 B7 island group* French Southern and Antarctic Lands
Crozet Plateau *119 B7 var.* Crozet Plateaus. *undersea plateau* SW Indian Ocean
Crozet Plateaus *see* Crozet Plateau
Crystal Brook *127 B6* South Australia
Csaca *see* Čadca
Csakathurn/Csáktornya *see* Čakovec
Csíkszereda *see* Miercurea-Ciuc
Csorna *77 C6* Győr-Moson-Sopron, NW Hungary
Csurgó *77 C7* Somogy, SW Hungary
Cuando *56 C2 var.* Kwando. *river* S Africa
Cuango *see* Kwango
Cuanza *56 B1 var.* Kwanza. *river* C Angola
Cuauhtémoc *28 C2* Chihuahua, N Mexico
Cuautla *29 E4* Morelos, S Mexico
Cuba *32 B2 off.* Republic of Cuba. *country* W West Indies
Cubal *56 B2* Benguela, W Angola
Cubango *56 B2 var.* Kuvango, *Port.* Vila Artur de Paiva, Vila da Ponte. Huíla, SW Angola
Cubango *56 B2 var.* Kavango, Kavengo, Kubango, Okavango, Okavanggo. *river* S Africa
Cuba, Republic of *see* Cuba
Cúcuta *36 C2 var.* San José de Cúcuta. Norte de Santander, N Colombia
Cuddapah *see* Kadapa
Cuenca *38 B2* Azuay, S Ecuador
Cuenca *71 E3 anc.* Conca. Castilla-La Mancha, C Spain
Cuera *see* Chur
Cuernavaca *29 E4* Morelos, S Mexico
Cuiabá *41 E3 prev.* Cuyabá. *state capital* Mato Grosso, SW Brazil
Cúige *see* Connaught
Cúige Laighean *see* Leinster
Cúige Mumhan *see* Munster
Cuijck *64 D4* Noord-Brabant, SE Netherlands
Cúil Raithin *see* Coleraine
Cuito *56 B2 var.* Kuito; *Port.* Silva Porto. Bié, C Angola
Cuito *56 B2 var.* Kwito. *river* SE Angola
Cukai *116 B3 var.* Chukai, Kemaman. Terengganu, Peninsular Malaysia
Cularo *see* Grenoble
Culiacán *28 C3 var.* Culiacán Rosales, Culiacán-Rosales. Sinaloa, C Mexico
Culiacán-Rosales/Culiacán Rosales *see* Culiacán
Cullera *71 F3* Comunitat Valenciana, E Spain
Cullman *20 C2* Alabama, S USA
Culm *see* Chełmno
Culmsee *see* Chełmża
Cumaná *37 E1* Sucre, NE Venezuela
Cumbal, Nevado de *36 A4 elevation* S Colombia
Cumberland *19 E4* Maryland, NE USA
Cumberland Plateau *20 D1 plateau* E USA
Cumberland Sound *15 H3 inlet* Baffin Island, Nunavut, NE Canada
Cumilla *113 G4 prev.* Comilla, *Ben.* Kumillā. Chattogram, E Bangladesh
Cumpas *28 B2* Sonora, NW Mexico
Cuneo *74 A2 Fr.* Coni. Piemonte, NW Italy
Cunnamulla *127 C5* Queensland, E Australia
Ćuprija *78 E4* Serbia, E Serbia
Curaçao *33 E5 Dutch self-governing territory* S West Indies
Curia Rhaetorum *see* Chur
Curicó *42 B4* Maule, C Chile
Curieta *see* Krk
Curitiba *41 E4 prev.* Curytiba. *state capital* Paraná, S Brazil
Curtbunar *see* Tervel
Curtea de Argeş *86 C4 var.* Curtea-de-Arges. Argeş, S Romania
Curtea-de-Arges *see* Curtea de Argeş
Curtici *86 A4 Ger.* Kurtitsch, *Hung.* Kürtös. Arad, W Romania
Curtis Island *126 E4 island* Queensland, SE Australia
Curytiba *see* Curitiba
Curzola *see* Korčula
Cusco *39 E4 var.* Cuzco. Cusco, C Peru
Cusset *69 C5* Allier, C France
Cutch, Gulf of *see* Kachchh, Gulf of
Cuttack *113 F4* Odisha, E India
Cuvier Plateau *119 E6 undersea plateau* E Indian Ocean
Cuxhaven *72 B2* Niedersachsen, NW Germany
Cuyabá *see* Cuiabá
Cuyuni, Río *see* Cuyuni River
Cuyuni River *37 F3 var.* Río Cuyuni. *river* Guyana/Venezuela
Cuzco *see* Cusco
Cyclades *see* Kykládes
Cydonia *see* Chaniá
Cymru *see* Wales
Cyprus *80 C4 off.* Republic of Cyprus, *Gk.* Kypriakí Dimokratía, Kýpros, *Turk.* Kıbrıs, Kıbrıs Cumhuriyeti. *country* E Mediterranean Sea
Cyprus, Republic of *see* Cyprus
Cyrenaica *49 H2 region* NE Libya
Cythnos *see* Kýthnos
Czech Republic *see* Czechia
Czechia *77 A5 off.* Czech Republic, *Cz.* Česko. *country* C Europe
Czenstochau *see* Częstochowa
Czernowitz *see* Chernivtsi
Częstochowa *76 C4 Ger.* Czenstochau, Tschenstochau, *Rus.* Chenstokhov. Śląskie, S Poland
Człuchów *76 C3 Ger.* Schlochau. Pomorskie, NW Poland

D

Dabajuro *36 C1* Falcón, NW Venezuela
Dabeiba *36 B2* Antioquia, NW Colombia
Dąbrowa Tarnowska *77 D5* Małopolskie, S Poland
Dabryn' *85 C8 Rus.* Dobryn'. Homyel'skaya Voblasts', SE Belarus
Dacca *see* Dhaka
Daegu *107 E4 off.* Daegu Gwang-yeoksi, *prev.* Taegu, *Jap.* Taikyū. SE South Korea
Daegu Gwang-yeoksi *see* Daegu
Dagana *52 B3* N Senegal
Dagda *84 D4* Krāslava, SE Latvia
Dagden *see* Hiiumaa
Dagenham *67 B8* United Kingdom
Dağlıq Qarabağ *see* Nagornyy-Karabakh
Dagö *see* Hiiumaa
Dagupan *117 E1 off.* Dagupan City. Luzon, N Philippines
Dagupan City *see* Dagupan
Da Hinggan Ling *105 G1 Eng.* Great Khingan Range. *mountain range* NE China
Dahm, Ramlat *99 B6 desert* NW Yemen
Dahomey *see* Benin
Daihoku *see* Taibei
Daimiel *70 D3* Castilla-La Mancha, C Spain
Daimoniá *83 B7* Pelopónnisos, S Greece
Dainan *see* Tainan
Daingin, Bá an *see* Dingle Bay
Dairen *see* Dalian
Daejeon *107 E4 off.* Daejeon Gwang-yeoksi, *prev.* Taejŏn, *Jap.* Taiden. C South Korea
Daejeon Gwang-yeoksi *see* Daejeon
Dakar *52 B3 country capital* (Senegal) W Senegal
Dakhla *see* Ad Dakhla
Dakoro *53 G3* Maradi, S Niger
Đakovica *see* Gjakovë
Đakovo *78 C3 var.* Djakovo, *Hung.* Diakovár. Osijek-Baranja, E Croatia
Dakshin *see* Deccan
Dalain Hob *104 D3 var.* Ejin Qi. Nei Mongol Zizhiqu, N China
Dalai Nor *see* Hulun Nur
Dalaman *94 A4* Muğla, SW Turkey (Türkiye)
Dalandzadgad *105 E3* Ömnögovĭ, S Mongolia
Đa Lat *115 E6* Lâm Đồng, S Vietnam
Dalby *127 D5* Queensland, E Australia
Dale City *19 E4* Virginia, NE USA
Dalhart *27 E1* Texas, SW USA
Dali *106 A6 var.* Xiaguan. Yunnan, SW China
Dalian *106 D4 var.* Dairen, Dalien, Jay Dairen, Lüda, Ta-lien, *Rus.* Dalny. Liaoning, NE China
Dalien *see* Dalian
Dallas *27 G2* Texas, SW USA
Dalmacija *78 B4 Eng.* Dalmatia, *Ger.* Dalmatien, *It.* Dalmazia. *cultural region* S Croatia
Dalmatia/Dalmatien/Dalmazia *see* Dalmacija
Dalny *see* Dalian
Dalton *20 D1* Georgia, SE USA
Dálvvadis *see* Jokkmokk
Daly Waters *126 A2* Northern Territory, N Australia
Damachava *85 A6 var.* Damachova, *Pol.* Domaczewo, *Rus.* Domachëvo. Brestskaya Voblasts', SW Belarus
Damachova *see* Damachava
Damān *112 C4* Damān and Diu, W India
Damara *54 C4* Ombella-Mpoko, S Central African Republic
Damas *see* Dimashq
Damasco *see* Dimashq
Damascus *see* Dimashq
Damavand, Qolleh-ye *98 D3 mountain* N Iran
Damietta *see* Dumyāţ
Dammām *see* Ad Dammān
Damoûr *97 A5 var.* Ad Dāmūr. W Lebanon
Dampier *124 A4* Western Australia
Dampier, Selat *117 F4 strait* Papua, E Indonesia
Damqawt *99 D6 var.* Damqut. E Yemen
Damqut *see* Damqawt
Damxung *104 C5 var.* Gongtang. Xizang Zizhiqu, W China
Danakil Desert *50 D4 var.* Afar Depression, Danakil Plain. *desert* E Africa
Danakil Plain *see* Danakil Desert
Danané *52 D5* W Ivory Coast
Đă Năng *115 E5 prev.* Tourane. Quang Nam-Đa Năng, C Vietnam
Danborg *see* Daneborg
Dandong *106 D3 var.* Tan-tung; *prev.* An-tung. Liaoning, NE China
Daneborg *61 E3 var.* Danborg. NE Greenland
Dänew *see* Galkynyş
Dangara *see* Danghara
Dangerous Archipelago *see* Tuamotu, Îles
Danghara *101 E3 Rus.* Dangara. SW Tajikistan
Danghe Nanshan *104 D3 mountain range* W China
Dangrek, Chaîne des *see* Dangrek Mountains
Dângrêk, Chuŏr Phnum *see* Dangrek Mountains
Dangrek Mountains *115 D5 Cam.* Chuŏr Phnum Dângrêk, *Thai.* Thiu Khao Phanom Dong Rak, *Fr.* Chaîne des Dangrek. *mountain range* Cambodia/Thailand
Dangriga *30 C1 prev.* Stann Creek. Stann Creek, E Belize
Danish West Indies *see* Virgin Islands (US)
Danlí *30 D2* El Paraíso, S Honduras
Danmark *see* Denmark
Danmarksstraedet *see* Denmark Strait
Dannenberg *72 C3* Niedersachsen, N Germany
Dannevirke *128 D4* Manawatu-Wanganui, North Island, New Zealand
Dantzig *see* Gdańsk
Danube *59 E4 Bul., Croatian, Serb.* Dunav, *Cz., Slov.* Dunaj, *Ger.* Donau, *Hung.* Duna, *Rom.* Dunărea, *Ukr.* Dunai. *river* C Europe
Danubian Plain *see* Dunavska Ravnina
Danum *see* Doncaster
Danville *19 E5* Virginia, NE USA
Danxian/Dan Xian *see* Danzhou
Danzhou *106 C7 prev.* Danxian, Dan Xian, Nada. Hainan, S China
Danzig *see* Gdańsk
Danziger Bucht *see* Gdańsk, Gulf of
Danzig, Gulf of *see* Gdańsk, Gulf of
Daqm *see* Duqm
Dar'ā *97 B5 var.* Der'a, *Fr.* Déraa. Dar'ā, SW Syria
Darabani *86 C3* Botoşani, NW Romania
Daraut-Kurgan *see* Daroot-Korgon
Dardanelles *94 A2 Eng.* Dardanelles. *strait* NW Turkey (Türkiye)
Dardanelles *see* Çanakkale Boğazı
Dardanelli *see* Çanakkale
Dar-el-Beida *see* Casablanca
Dar es Salaam *51 C7* Dar es Salaam, E Tanzania
Darfield *129 C6* Canterbury, South Island, New Zealand
Darfur *50 A4 var.* Darfur Massif. *cultural region* W Sudan
Darfur Massif *see* Darfur
Darhan *105 E2* Darhan Uul, N Mongolia
Darién, Golfo del *see* Darien, Gulf of
Darien, Gulf of *36 A2 Sp.* Golfo del Darién. *gulf* S Caribbean Sea
Darien, Isthmus of *see* Panama, Istmo de
Darién, Serranía del *31 H5 mountain range* Colombia/Panama
Dario *see* Ciudad Darío
Dariorigum *see* Vannes
Darjeeling *see* Dārjiling
Dārjiling *113 F3 prev.* Darjeeling. West Bengal, NE India
Darling River *127 C6 river* New South Wales, SE Australia
Darlington *67 D5* N England, United Kingdom
Darmstadt *73 B5* Hessen, SW Germany
Darnah *49 G2 var.* Dérna. NE Libya
Darnley, Cape *132 D2 cape* Antarctica
Daroca *71 E2* Aragón, NE Spain
Daroot-Korgon *101 F3 var.* Daraut-Kurgan. Oshskaya Oblast', SW Kyrgyzstan
Dartford *67 B8* SE England, United Kingdom
Dartmoor *67 C7 moorland* SW England, United Kingdom
Dartmouth *17 F4* Nova Scotia, SE Canada
Darvaza *see* Derweze, Turkmenistan
Darwin *124 D2 prev.* Palmerston, Port Darwin. *territory capital* Northern Territory, N Australia
Darwin, Isla *38 A4 island* Galápagos Islands, W Ecuador
Dashhowuz *see* Daşoguz
Dashkawka *85 D6 Rus.* Dashkovka. Mahilyowskaya Voblasts', E Belarus
Dashkovka *see* Dashkawka
Daşoguz *100 C2 Rus.* Dashkhovuz, *Turkm.* Dashhowuz; *prev.* Tashauz. Daşoguz Welaýaty, N Turkmenistan
Đa, Sông *see* Black River
Datong *106 C3 var.* Tatung, Ta-t'ung. Shanxi, C China
Daugava *see* Western Dvina
Daugavpils *84 D4 Ger.* Dünaburg; *prev. Rus.* Dvinsk. Daugvapils, SE Latvia
Daung Kyun *115 B6 island* S Myanmar (Burma)
Dauphiné *69 D5 cultural region* E France
Dāvangere *110 C2* Karnātaka, W India
Davao *117 F3 off.* Davao City. Mindanao, S Philippines
Davao City *see* Davao
Davao Gulf *117 F3 gulf* Mindanao, S Philippines
Davenport *23 G3* Iowa, C USA
David *31 E5* Chiriquí, W Panama
Davie Ridge *119 A5 undersea ridge* W Indian Ocean
Davis *132 D3 Australian research station* Antarctica
Davis Sea *132 D3 sea* Antarctica
Davis Strait *60 B3 strait* Baffin Bay/Labrador Sea
Dawei *115 B5 var.* Tavoy, Htawei. Tanintharyi, S Myanmar (Burma)
Dawlat Qaṭar *see* Qatar
Dax *69 B6 var.* Ax; *anc.* Aquae Augustae, Aquae Tarbelicae. Landes, SW France
Dayr az Zawr *96 D3 var.* Deir ez Zor. Dayr az Zawr, E Syria
Dayton *18 C4* Ohio, N USA
Daytona Beach *21 E4* Florida, SE USA
De Aar *56 C5* Northern Cape, C South Africa
Dead Sea *97 B6 var.* Bahret Lut, Lacus Asphaltites, *Ar.* Al Baḩr al Mayyit, Baḩrat Lūṭ, *Heb.* Yam HaMelaḥ. *salt lake* Israel/Jordan
Dē Afghānistān Islāmī Jumhūriyat *see* Afghanistan
Deán Funes *42 C3* Córdoba, C Argentina
Death Valley *25 C7 valley* California, W USA
Deatnu *62 D2 Fin.* Tenojoki, *Nor.* Tana. *river* Finland/Norway
Debar *79 D6 Ger.* Dibra, *Turk.* Debre. W North Macedonia
De Behagle *see* Laï
Dębica *77 D5* Podkarpackie, SE Poland
De Bildt *see* De Bilt
De Bilt *64 C3 var.* De Bildt. Utrecht, C Netherlands
Dębno *76 B3* Zachodnio-pomorskie, NW Poland
Debre *see* Debar
Debrecen *77 D6 Ger.* Debreczin, *Rom.* Debreţin; *prev.* Debreczen. Hajdú-Bihar, E Hungary
Debreczen/Debreczin *see* Debrecen
Debreţin *see* Debrecen
Decatur *20 C1* Alabama, S USA
Decatur *18 B4* Illinois, N USA
Deccan *112 D5 Hind.* Dakshin. *plateau* C India
Děčín *76 B4 Ger.* Tetschen. Ústecký Kraj, NW Czechia (Czech Republic)
Dedeagaç/Dedeagach *see* Alexandroúpoli
Dedemsvaart *64 E3* Overijssel, E Netherlands
Dee *66 C3 river* NE Scotland, United Kingdom
Deering *14 C2* Alaska, USA
Deés *see* Dej
Deggendorf *73 D6* Bayern, SE Germany
Değirmenlik *80 C5 Gk.* Kythréa. N Cyprus
Deh Bīd *see* Şafāshahr
Dehli *see* Delhi
Deh-e Shū *100 D5 prev.* Deh Shū, *var.* Deshu, Dishū. Helmand, S Afghanistan
Deh Shū *see* Deh-e Shū
Deinze *65 B5* Oost-Vlaanderen, NW Belgium
Deir ez Zor *see* Dayr az Zawr
Deirgeirt, Loch *see* Derg, Lough
Dej *86 B3 Hung.* Dés; *prev.* Deés. Cluj, NW Romania
De Jouwer *see* Joure
Dekéleia *see* Dhekelia
Dékoa *54 C4* Kémo, C Central African Republic
De Land *21 E4* Florida, SE USA
Delano *25 C7* California, W USA
Delārām *see* Dilārām
Delaware *18 D4* Ohio, N USA
Delaware *19 F4 off.* State of Delaware, *also known as* Blue Hen State, Diamond State, First State. *state* NE USA
Delft *64 B4* Zuid-Holland, W Netherlands
Delfzijl *64 E1* Groningen, NE Netherlands
Delgo *50 B3* Northern, N Sudan
Delhi *112 D3 var.* Dehli, *Hind.* Dilli, *hist.* Shahjahanabad. *union territory capital* Delhi, N India
Delicias *28 D2 var.* Ciudad Delicias. Chihuahua, N Mexico
Déli-Kárpátok *see* Carpaţii Meridionali
Delmenhorst *72 B3* Niedersachsen, NW Germany
Del Rio *27 F4* Texas, SW USA
Deltona *21 E4* Florida, SE USA
Demba *55 D6* Kasai-Occidental, C Dem. Rep. Congo
Dembia *54 D4* Mbomou, SE Central African Rep.
Demchok *see* Dêmqog
Demerara Plain *34 C2 abyssal plain* W Atlantic Ocean
Deming *26 C3* New Mexico, SW USA
Demmin *72 C2* Mecklenburg-Vorpommern, NE Germany
Demopolis *20 C2* Alabama, S USA
Dêmqog *104 A5 var.* Demchok. *disputed region* China/India
Denali *14 C3 var.* Mount McKinley. *mountain* Alaska, USA
Denali Park *14 C3 prev.* McKinley Park, Alaska, USA
Denau *see* Denov
Dender *65 B6 Fr.* Dendre. *river* W Belgium
Dendre *see* Dender
Denekamp *64 E3* Overijssel, E Netherlands
Den Haag *see* 's-Gravenhage
Denham *125 A5* Western Australia
Den Ham *64 E3* Overijssel, E Netherlands
Den Helder *64 C2* Noord-Holland, NW Netherlands
Dénia *71 F4* Comunitat Valenciana, E Spain
Deniliquin *127 C7* New South Wales, SE Australia
Denison *23 F3* Iowa, C USA
Denison *27 G2* Texas, SW USA
Denizli *94 B4* Denizli, SW Turkey (Türkiye)
Denmark *63 A7 off.* Kingdom of Denmark, *Dan.* Danmark; *anc.* Hafnia. *country* N Europe
Denmark, Kingdom of *see* Denmark
Denmark Strait *60 D4 var.* Danmarksstraedet. *strait* Greenland/Iceland
Dennery *33 F1* E Saint Lucia
Denov *101 E3 Rus.* Denau. Surkhondaryo Viloyati, S Uzbekistan
Denpasar *116 D5 prev.* Paloe. Bali, C Indonesia
Denton *27 G2* Texas, SW USA
D'Entrecasteaux Islands *122 B3 island group* SE Papua New Guinea
Denver *22 D4 state capital* Colorado, C USA
Der'a/Derá/Déraa *see* Dar'ā
Dera Ghazi Khan *112 C2 var.* Dera Ghazikhan. Punjab, C Pakistan
Dera Ghazikhan *see* Dera Ghazi Khan
Đeravica *79 D5 mountain* S Serbia
Derbent *89 B8* Respublika Dagestan, SW Russia
Derby *67 D6* C England, United Kingdom
Dereĭ *see* Gónnoi
Dergachi *see* Derhachi
Derg, Lough *67 A6 Ir.* Loch Deirgeirt. *lake* W Ireland
Derhachi *87 G2 Rus.* Dergachi. Kharkivs'ka Oblast', E Ukraine
De Ridder *20 A3* Louisiana, S USA
Dérna *see* Darnah
Derry *see* Londonderry
Dertosa *see* Tortosa
Derventa *78 B3* Republika Srpska, N Bosnia and Herzegovina
Derweze *100 C2 Rus.* Darvaza. Ahal Welaýaty, C Turkmenistan
Dés *see* Dej
Deschutes River *24 B3 river* Oregon, NW USA
Desē *50 C4 var.* Desse, *It.* Dessie. Āmara, N Ethiopia
Deseado, Río *43 B7 river* S Argentina
Desertas, Ilhas *48 A2 island group* Madeira, Portugal, NE Atlantic Ocean
Deshu *see* Deh-e Shū
Des Moines *23 F3 state capital* Iowa, C USA
Desna *87 E2 river* Russia/Ukraine
Dessau *72 C4* Sachsen-Anhalt, E Germany
Desse *see* Desē
Dessie *see* Desē
Destêrro *see* Florianópolis
Detroit *18 D3* Michigan, N USA
Detroit Lakes *23 F2* Minnesota, N USA
Deurne *65 D5* Noord-Brabant, SE Netherlands
Deutschendorf *see* Poprad
Deutsch-Eylau *see* Iława
Deutsch Krone *see* Wałcz
Deutschland/Deutschland, Bundesrepublik *see* Germany
Deutsch-Südwestafrika *see* Namibia
Deva *86 B4 Ger.* Diemrich, *Hung.* Déva. Hunedoara, W Romania
Déva *see* Deva
Deva *see* Chester
Devana *see* Aberdeen
Devana Castra *see* Chester
Đevđelija *see* Gevgelija
Deventer *64 D3* Overijssel, E Netherlands
Devils Lake *23 E1* North Dakota, N USA
Devoll *see* Devollit, Lumi i
Devollit, Lumi i *79 D6 var.* Devoll. *river* SE Albania
Devon Island *15 F2 prev.* North Devon Island. *island* Parry Islands, Nunavut, NE Canada
Devonport *127 C8* Tasmania, SE Australia
Devrek *94 C2* Zonguldak, N Turkey (Türkiye)
Dexter *23 H5* Missouri, C USA
Deynau *see* Galkynyş
Dezfūl *98 C3 var.* Dizful. Khūzestān, SW Iran
Dezhou *106 D4* Shandong, E China
Dhaka *113 G4 prev.* Dacca. *country capital* (Bangladesh) Dhaka, C Bangladesh
Dhanbād *113 F4* Jhārkhand, NE India
Dhekelia *80 C5 Gk.* Dekéleia. *UK Sovereign Base Area* SE Cyprus
Dhidhimótikhon *see* Didymóteicho
Dhíkti Ori *see* Díkti
Dhodhekánisos *see* Dodekánisa
Dhomokós *see* Domokós
Dhráma *see* Dráma
Dhrepanon, Akrotírio *see* Drépano, Akrotírio
Dhún na nGall, Bá *see* Donegal Bay
Dhuusa Marreeb *51 E5 var.* Dusa Marreb, *It.* Dusa Mareb. Galguduud, C Somalia
Diakovár *see* Đakovo
Diamantina, Chapada *41 F3 mountain range* E Brazil
Diamantina Fracture Zone *119 E6 tectonic feature* E Indian Ocean
Diamond State *see* Delaware
Diaoyutai Lieyu/ Diaoyutai Qundao *see* Senkaku-shoto
Diarbekr *see* Diyarbakır
Dibio *see* Dijon
Dibra *see* Debar
Dibrugarh *113 H3* Assam, NE India
Dickinson *22 D2* North Dakota, N USA
Dicle *see* Tigris
Didimotiho *see* Didymóteicho
Didymóteicho *82 D3 var.* Dhidhimótikhon, Didimotiho. Anatolikí Makedonía kai Thráki, NE Greece
Diedenhofen *see* Thionville
Diekirch *65 D7* Diekirch, C Luxembourg
Diemrich *see* Deva
Điện Biên *114 D3 var.* Bien Bien, Dien Bien Phu. Lai Châu, N Vietnam
Dien Bien Phu *see* Điện Biên
Diepenbeek *65 D6* Limburg, NE Belgium
Diepholz *72 B3* Niedersachsen, NW Germany
Dieppe *68 C2* Seine-Maritime, N France
Dieren *64 D4* Gelderland, E Netherlands
Differdange *65 D8* Luxembourg, SW Luxembourg
Digne *69 D6 var.* Digne-les-Bains. Alpes-de-Haute-Provence, SE France
Digne-les-Bains *see* Digne
Digoel *see* Digul, Sungai
Digoin *68 C4* Saône-et-Loire, C France
Digul, Sungai *117 H5 prev.* Digoel. *river* Papua, E Indonesia
Dihang *see* Brahmaputra
Dijlah *see* Tigris
Dijon *68 D4 anc.* Dibio. Côte d'Or, C France
Dikhil *50 D4* SW Djibouti
Dikson *92 D2* Taymyrskiy (Dolgano-Nenetskiy) Avtonomnyy Okrug, N Russia
Díkti *83 D8 var.* Dhíkti Ori. *mountain range* Kríti, Greece, E Mediterranean Sea
Dilārām *100 D5 prev.* Delārām. Nīmrūz, SW Afghanistan
Dili *117 F5 var.* Dilli, Dilly. *country capital* (East Timor) N East Timor (Timor-Leste)
Dilia *53 G3 var.* Dillia. *river* SE Niger
Di Linh *115 E6* Lâm Đồng, S Vietnam
Dilli *see* Dili, East Timor (Timor-Leste)
Dilli *see* Delhi, India
Dillia *see* Dilia
Dilling *50 B4 var.* Ad Dalanj. Southern Kordofan, C Sudan
Dillon *22 B2* Montana, NW USA
Dilly *see* Dili
Dilolo *55 D7* Katanga, S Dem. Rep. Congo
Dimashq *97 B5 var.* Ash Shām, Esh Sham, *Eng.* Damascus, *Fr.* Damas, *It.* Damasco. *country capital* (Syria) Dimashq, SW Syria
Dimitrovgrad *82 D3* Haskovo, S Bulgaria
Dimitrovgrad *89 C6 prev.* Caribrod. Serbia, SE Serbia
Dimitrovo *see* Pernik
Dimovo *82 B1* Vidin, NW Bulgaria
Dinajpur *113 F3* Rajshahi, NW Bangladesh
Dinan *68 B3* Côtes d'Armor, NW France
Dinant *65 C7* Namur, S Belgium
Dinar *94 B4* Afyon, SW Turkey (Türkiye)
Dinara *see* Dinaric Alps
Dinaric Alps *78 C4 var.* Dinara. *mountain range* Bosnia and Herzegovina/Croatia
Dindigul *110 C3* Tamil Nādu, SE India
Dingle Bay *67 A6 Ir.* Bá an Daingin. *bay* SW Ireland
Dinguiraye *52 C4* N Guinea
Diourbel *52 B3* W Senegal
Dīrē Dawa *51 D5* Dīrē Dawa, E Ethiopia
Dirk Hartog Island *125 A5 island* Western Australia
Dirschau *see* Tczew
Disappointment, Lake *124 C4 salt lake* Western Australia
Discovery Bay *32 B4* Middlesex, Jamaica, Greater Antilles, C Jamaica Caribbean Sea
Dishū *see* Deh-e Shū
Disko Bugt *see* Qeqertarsuup Tunua
Dispur *113 G3 state capital* Assam, NE India
Divinópolis *41 F4* Minas Gerais, SE Brazil
Divo *52 D5* S Ivory Coast
Divodurum Mediomatricum *see* Metz
Diyarbakır *95 E4 var.* Diarbekr; *anc.* Amida. Diyarbakır, SE Turkey (Türkiye)

Dizful see Dezfūl
Djailolo see Halmahera, Pulau
Djajapura see Jayapura
Djakarta see Jakarta
Djakovo see Đakovo
Djambala 55 B6 Plateaux, C Congo
Djambi see Jambi
Djambi see Hari, Batang
Djanet 49 E4 prev. Fort Charlet. SE Algeria
Djéblé see Jablah
Djelfa 48 D2 var. El Djelfa. N Algeria
Djéma 54 D4 Haut-Mbomou, E Central African Republic
Djember see Jember
Djérablous see Jarābulus
Djerba, Île de 49 F2 var. Djerba, Jazīrat Jarbah. island E Tunisia
Djerba see Djerba, Île de
Djérem 54 B4 river C Cameroon
Djevdjelija see Gevgelija
Djibouti 50 D4 var. Jibuti. country capital (Djibouti) E Djibouti
Djibouti 50 D4 off. Republic of Djibouti, var. Jibuti; prev. French Somaliland, French Territory of the Afars and Issas, Fr. Côte Française des Somalis, Territoire Français des Afars et des Issas. country E Africa
Djibouti, Republic of see Djibouti
Djokjakarta see Yogyakarta
Djourab, Erg du 54 C2 desert N Chad
Djúpivogur 61 E5 Austurland, SE Iceland
Dmitriyevsk see Makiivka
Dnepr see Dnieper
Dneprodzerzhinskoye Vodokhranilishche see Dniprodzerzhynske Vodoskhovyshche
Dneprorudnoye see Dniprorudne
Dnestr see Dniester
Dnieper 59 F4 Bel. Dnyapro, Rus. Dnepr, Ukr. Dnipro. river E Europe
Dnieper Lowland 87 E2 Bel. Prydnyaprowskaya Nizina, Ukr. Prydniprovska Nyzovyna. lowlands Belarus/Ukraine
Dniester 59 E4 Rom. Nistru, Rus. Dnestr, Ukr. Dnister; anc. Tyras. river Moldova/Ukraine
Dnipro see Dnieper
Dnipro 87 F3 prev. Dnipropetrovsk, Yekaterinoslav. Dnipropetrovska Oblast, E Ukraine
Dniprodzerzhyns'k see Kamianske
Dniprodzerzhynske Vodoskhovyshche 87 F3 Rus. Dneprodzerzhinskoye Vodokhranilishche. reservoir C Ukraine
Dnipropetrovsk see Dnipro
Dniprorudne 87 F3 Rus. Dneprorudnoye. Zaporiz'ka Oblast', SE Ukraine
Dnister see Dniester
Dnyapro see Dnieper
Doba 54 C4 Logone-Oriental, S Chad
Döbeln 72 D4 Sachsen, E Germany
Doberai Peninsula 117 G4 Dut. Vogelkop. peninsula Papua, E Indonesia
Doboj 78 C3 Republiks Srpska, N Bosnia and Herzegovina
Dobre Miasto 76 D2 Ger. Guttstadt. Warmińsko-mazurskie, NE Poland
Dobrich 82 E1 Rom. Bazargic; prev. Tolbukhin. Dobrich, NE Bulgaria
Dobrush 85 D7 Homyel'skaya Voblasts', SE Belarus
Dobryn' see Dabryn'
Dodecanese see Dodekánisa
Dodekánisa 83 D6 var. Nóties Sporádes, Eng. Dodecanese; prev. Dhodhekánisos, Dodekanisos. island group SE Greece
Dodekanisos see Dodekánisa
Dodge City 23 E5 Kansas, C USA
Dodoma 47 D5 country capital (Tanzania) Dodoma, C Tanzania
Dogana 74 E1 NE San Marino Europe
Dogo 109 B6 island Oki-shotō, SW Japan
Dogondoutchi 53 F3 Dosso, SW Niger
Dogrular see Pravda
Doğubayazıt 95 F3 Ağrı, E Turkey (Türkiye)
Doğu Karadeniz Dağları 95 E3 var. Anadolu Dağları. mountain range NE Turkey (Türkiye)
Doha see Ad Dawḩah
Doire see Londonderry
Dokdo see Liancourt Rocks
Dokkum 64 D1 Fryslân, N Netherlands
Dokuchaievsk 87 G3 prev. Dokuchayevs'k, var. Dokuchayevsk. Donets'ka Oblast', SE Ukraine
Dokuchayevsk/Dokuchayevs'k see Dokuchaievsk
Doldrums Fracture Zone 44 C4 fracture zone W Atlantic Ocean
Dôle 68 D4 Jura, E France
Dolina see Dolyna
Dolinskaya see Dolynska
Dolisie 55 B6 prev. Loubomo. Niari, S Congo
Dolna Oryahovitsa 82 D2 prev. Polikrayshte. Veliko Tarnovo, N Bulgaria
Dolni Chiflik 82 E2 prev. Rudnik. Varna, E Bulgaria
Dolomites 74 C1 var. Dolomiti, Eng. Dolomites. mountain range NE Italy
Dolomites/Dolomiti see Dolomitiche, Alpi
Dolores 42 D4 Buenos Aires, E Argentina
Dolores 30 B1 Petén, N Guatemala
Dolores 42 D4 Soriano, SW Uruguay
Dolores Hidalgo 29 E4 var. Ciudad de Dolores Hidalgo. Guanajuato, C Mexico
Dolyna 86 B2 Rus. Dolina. Ivano-Frankivs'ka Oblast', W Ukraine
Dolynska 87 F3 Rus. Dolinskaya. Kirovohrads'ka Oblast', S Ukraine
Domachëvo/Domaczewo see Damachava
Dombås 63 B5 Oppland, S Norway
Domel Island see Letsôk-aw Kyun
Domesnes, Cape see Kolkasrags
Domeyko 42 B3 Atacama, N Chile
Dominica 33 H4 off. Commonwealth of Dominica. country E West Indies
Dominica Channel see Martinique Passage
Dominica, Commonwealth of see Dominica
Dominican Republic 33 E2 country C West Indies
Domokós 83 B5 var. Dhomokós. Stereá Ellás, C Greece
Don 89 B6 var. Duna, Tanais. river SW Russia
Donau see Danube
Donauwörth 73 C6 Bayern, S Germany
Don Benito 70 C3 Extremadura, W Spain
Doncaster 67 D5 anc. Danum. N England, United Kingdom
Dondo 56 B1 Cuanza Norte, NW Angola
Donegal 67 B5 Ir. Dún na nGall. Donegal, NW Ireland
Donegal Bay 67 A5 Ir. Bá Dhún na nGall. bay NW Ireland
Donets see Siverskyi Donets
Donetsk 87 G3 prev. Stalino. Donets'ka Oblast', E Ukraine
Dongfang 106 B7 var. Basuo. Hainan, S China
Dongguan 106 C6 Guangdong, S China
Đông Ha 114 E4 Quang Tri, C Vietnam
Dong Hai see East China Sea
Đông Hơi 114 D4 Quang Binh, C Vietnam
Dongliao see Liaoyuan
Dongola 50 B3 var. Donqola, Dunqulah. Northern, N Sudan
Dongou 55 C5 Likouala, NE Congo
Dong Rak, Thiu Khao Phanom see Dangrak Mountains
Dongting Hu 106 C5 var. Tung-t'ing Hu. lake S China
Donostia 71 E1 País Vasco, N Spain see also San Sebastián
Donqola see Dongola
Doolow 51 D5 Sumalē, E Ethiopia
Doornik see Tournai
Door Peninsula 18 C2 peninsula Wisconsin, N USA
Dooxo Nugaaleed 51 E5 var. Nogal Valley. valley E Somalia
Dordogne 69 B5 cultural region SW France
Dordogne 69 B5 river W France
Dordrecht 64 C4 var. Dordt, Dort. Zuid-Holland, SW Netherlands
Dordt see Dordrecht
Dorohoi 86 C3 Botoşani, NE Romania
Dorotea 62 C4 Västerbotten, N Sweden
Dorpat see Tartu
Dorre Island 125 A5 island Western Australia
Dort see Dordrecht
Dortmund 72 A4 Nordrhein-Westfalen, W Germany
Dos Hermanas 70 C4 Andalucía, S Spain
Dospad Dagh see Rhodope Mountains
Dospat 82 C3 Smolyan, S Bulgaria
Dothan 20 D3 Alabama, S USA
Dotnuva 84 B4 Kaunas, C Lithuania
Douai 68 C2 prev. Douay; anc. Duacum. Nord, N France
Douala 55 A5 var. Duala. Littoral, W Cameroon
Douay see Douai
Douglas 67 C5 dependent territory capital (Isle of Man) E Isle of Man
Douglas 26 C3 Arizona, SW USA
Douglas 22 D3 Wyoming, C USA
Douma see Dūmā
Douro see Duero
Douvres see Dover
Dover 67 E7 Fr. Douvres, Lat. Dubris Portus. SE England, United Kingdom
Dover 19 F4 state capital Delaware, NE USA
Dover, Strait of 68 C2 var. Straits of Dover, Fr. Pas de Calais. strait England, United Kingdom/France
Dover, Straits of see Dover, Strait of
Dovrefjell 63 B5 plateau S Norway
Downpatrick 67 B5 Ir. Dún Pádraig. SE Northern Ireland, United Kingdom
Dozen 109 B6 island Oki-shotō, SW Japan
Drâa, Hammada du see Dra, Hamada du
Drač/Draç see Durrës
Drachten 64 D2 Fryslân, N Netherlands
Drăgăşani 86 B5 Vâlcea, SW Romania
Dragoman 82 B2 Sofiya, W Bulgaria
Dra, Hamada du 48 C3 var. Hammada du Drâa, Haut Plateau du Dra. plateau W Algeria
Dra, Haut Plateau du see Dra, Hamada du
Drahichyn 85 B6 Pol. Drohiczyn Poleski, Rus. Drogichin. Brestskaya Voblasts', SW Belarus
Drakensberg 56 D5 mountain range Lesotho/South Africa
Drake Passage 35 B8 passage Atlantic Ocean/Pacific Ocean
Dralfa 82 D2 Tŭrgovishte, N Bulgaria
Dráma 82 C3 var. Dhráma. Anatolikí Makedonía kai Thráki, NE Greece
Dramburg see Drawsko Pomorskie
Drammen 63 B6 Buskerud, S Norway
Drau see Drava
Drava 78 C3 var. Drau, Eng. Drave, Hung. Dráva. river C Europe
Dráva/Drave see Drau/Drava
Drawsko Pomorskie 76 B3 Ger. Dramburg. Zachodnio-pomorskie, NW Poland
Drépano, Akrotírio 82 C4 var. Akrotírio Dhrepanon. headland N Greece
Drepanum see Trapani
Dresden 72 D4 Sachsen, E Germany
Drin see Drinit, Lumi i
Drina 78 C3 river Bosnia and Herzegovina/Serbia
Drinit, Lumi i 79 D5 var. Drin. river NW Albania
Drinit të Zi, Lumi i see Black Drin
Drissa see Drysa
Drobeta-Turnu Severin 86 B5 prev. Turnu Severin. Mehedinţi, SW Romania
Drogheda 67 B5 Ir. Droichead Átha. NE Ireland
Drogichin see Drahichyn
Drogobych see Drohobych
Drohiczyn Poleski see Drahichyn
Drohobych 86 B2 Pol. Drohobycz, Rus. Drogobych. L'vivs'ka Oblast', NW Ukraine
Drohobycz see Drohobych
Droichead Átha see Drogheda
Drôme 69 D5 cultural region E France
Dronning Maud Land 132 B2 physical region Antarctica
Drontheim see Trondheim
Drug see Durg
Druk-yul see Bhutan
Drummondville 17 E4 Québec, SE Canada
Druskieniki see Druskininkai
Druskininkai 85 B5 Pol. Druskienniki. Alytus, S Lithuania
Dryden 16 B3 Ontario, C Canada
Drysa 85 D5 Rus. Drissa. river N Belarus
Duacum see Douai
Duala see Douala
Dubai see Dubayy
Dubăsari 86 D3 Rus. Dubossary. NE Moldova
Dubawnt 15 F4 river Nunavut, NW Canada
Dubayy 98 D4 Eng. Dubai. Dubayy, NE United Arab Emirates
Dubbo 127 D6 New South Wales, SE Australia
Dublin 67 B5 Ir. Baile Átha Cliath; anc. Eblana. country capital (Ireland) Dublin, E Ireland
Dublin 21 E2 Georgia, SE USA
Dubno 86 C2 Rivnens'ka Oblast', NW Ukraine
Dubossary see Dubăsari
Dubris Portus see Dover
Dubrovnik 79 B5 It. Ragusa. Dubrovnik-Neretva, SE Croatia
Dubuque 23 G3 Iowa, C USA
Dudelange 65 D8 var. Forge du Sud, Ger. Dudelingen. Luxembourg, S Luxembourg
Dudelingen see Dudelange
Duero 70 D2 Port. Douro. river Portugal/Spain
Duesseldorf see Düsseldorf
Duffel 65 C5 Antwerpen, C Belgium
Dugi Otok 78 A4 var. Isola Grossa, It. Isola Lunga. island W Croatia
Duinekerke see Dunkerque
Duisburg 72 A4 prev. Duisburg-Hamborn. Nordrhein-Westfalen, W Germany
Duisburg-Hamborn see Duisburg
Duiven 64 D4 Gelderland, E Netherlands
Duk Faiwil 51 B5 Jonglei, C South Sudan
Dulan 104 D4 var. Qagan Us. Qinghai, C China
Dulce, Golfo 31 E5 gulf S Costa Rica
Dulce, Golfo see Izabal, Lago de
Dülmen 72 A4 Nordrhein-Westfalen, W Germany
Dulovo 82 E1 Silistra, NE Bulgaria
Duluth 23 G2 Minnesota, N USA
Dūmā 97 B5 Fr. Douma. Dimashq, SW Syria
Dumas 27 E1 Texas, SW USA
Dumfries 66 C4 S Scotland, United Kingdom
Dumont d'Urville 132 C4 French research station Antarctica
Dumyāṭ 50 B1 Eng. Damietta. N Egypt
Duna see Danube, C Europe
Düna see Western Dvina
Duna see Don
Dünaburg see Daugavpils
Dunai see Danube
Dunaj see Wien, Austria
Dunaj see Danube, C Europe
Dunapentele see Dunaújváros
Dunărea see Danube
Dunaújváros 77 C7 prev. Dunapentele, Sztálinváros. Fejér, C Hungary
Dunav see Danube
Dunavska Ravnina 82 C2 Eng. Danubian Plain. lowlands N Bulgaria
Duncan 27 G2 Oklahoma, C USA
Dundalk 67 B5 Ir. Dún Dealgan. Louth, NE Ireland
Dún Dealgan see Dundalk
Dundee 56 D4 KwaZulu/Natal, E South Africa
Dundee 66 C4 E Scotland, United Kingdom
Dunedin 129 B7 Otago, South Island, New Zealand
Dunfermline 66 C4 C Scotland, United Kingdom
Dungu 55 E5 Orientale, NE Dem. Rep. Congo
Dungun 116 B3 var. Kuala Dungun. Terengganu, Peninsular Malaysia
Dunholme see Durham
Dunkerque 68 C2 Eng. Dunkirk, Flem. Duinekerke; prev. Dunquerque. Nord, N France
Dunkirk see Dunkerque
Dún Laoghaire 67 B6 Eng. Dunleary; prev. Kingstown. E Ireland
Dunleary see Dún Laoghaire
Dún Pádraig see Downpatrick
Dunquerque see Dunkerque
Dunqulah see Dongola
Dupnitsa 82 C2 prev. Marek, Stanke Dimitrov. Kyustendil, W Bulgaria
Duqm 99 E5 var. Daqm. E Oman
Durance 69 D6 river SE France
Durango 28 D3 var. Victoria de Durango. Durango, W Mexico
Durango 22 C5 Colorado, C USA
Durankulak 82 E1 Rom. Răcari; prev. Blatnitsa, Duranulac. Dobrich, NE Bulgaria
Durant 27 G2 Oklahoma, C USA
Duranulac see Durankulak
Durazzo see Durrës
Durban 56 D4 var. Port Natal. KwaZulu/Natal, E South Africa
Durbe 84 B3 Ger. Durben. Liepāja, W Latvia
Durben see Durbe
Durg 113 E4 prev. Drug. Chhattīsgarh, C India
Durham 67 D5 hist. Dunholme. N England, United Kingdom
Durham 21 F1 North Carolina, SE USA
Durocortorum see Reims
Durostorum see Silistra
Durovernum see Canterbury
Durrës 79 C6 var. Durrësi, Dursi, It. Durazzo, Croatian Drač, Turk. Draç. Durrës, W Albania
Durrësi see Durrës
Dursi see Durrës
Durūz, Jabal ad 97 C5 mountain SW Syria
D'Urville Island see Rangitoto ki te Tonga
Dusa Mareb/Dusa Marreb see Dhuusa Marreeb
Dushanbe 101 E3 var. Dyushambe; prev. Stalinabad, Taj. Stalinobod. country capital (Tajikistan) W Tajikistan
Düsseldorf 72 A4 var. Duesseldorf. Nordrhein-Westfalen, W Germany
Düsti 101 E3 Rus. Dusti. SW Tajikistan
Dutch East Indies see Indonesia
Dutch Guiana see Suriname
Dutch Harbor 14 B3 Unalaska Island, Alaska, USA
Dutch New Guinea see Papua
Duzdab see Zāhedān
Dvina Bay see Chëshskaya Guba
Dvinsk see Daugavpils
Dyanev see Galkynyş
Dyersburg 20 C1 Tennessee, S USA
Dyushambe see Dushanbe
Dza Chu see Mekong
Dzaudzhikau see Vladikavkaz
Dzerzhinsk 89 C5 Nizhegorodskaya Oblast', W Russia
Dzerzhinskiy see Nar'yan-Mar
Dzhalal-Abad 101 F2 Kir. Jalal-Abad. Dzhalal-Abadskaya Oblast', W Kyrgyzstan
Dzhambul see Taraz
Dzhankoi 87 F4 prev. Dzhankoy, Respublika Krym, S Ukraine
Dzhankoy see Dzhankoi
Dzharkurgan see Jarqo'rg'on
Dzhelandy see Jelondi
Dzhergalan 101 G2 Kir. Jyrgalan. Issyk-Kul'skaya Oblast', NE Kyrgyzstan
Dzhezkazgan see Zhezqazghan
Dzhizak see Jizzax
Dzhugdzhur, Khrebet 93 G3 mountain range E Russia
Dzhusaly see Zhosaly
Działdowo 76 D3 Warmińsko-Mazurskie, C Poland
Dzuunmod 105 E2 Töv, C Mongolia
Dzüün Soyonï Nuruu see Vostochnyy Sayan
Dzvina see Western Dvina

E

Eagle Pass 27 F4 Texas, SW USA
East Açores Fracture Zone see East Azores Fracture Zone
East Antarctica 132 C3 var. Greater Antarctica. physical region Antarctica
East Australian Basin see Tasman Basin
East Azores Fracture Zone 44 C3 var. East Açores Fracture Zone. tectonic feature E Atlantic Ocean
Eastbourne 67 E7 SE England, United Kingdom
East Cape 128 E3 headland North Island, New Zealand
East China Sea 103 E2 Chin. Dong Hai. sea W Pacific Ocean
Easter Fracture Zone 131 G4 tectonic feature E Pacific Ocean
Easter Island see Pascua, Isla de
Eastern Desert see Ṣaḥrā' ash Sharqīyah
Eastern Ghats 102 B3 mountain range SE India
Eastern Sayans see Vostochnyy Sayan
Eastern Sierra Madre see Madre Oriental, Sierra
East Falkland 43 D8 var. Isla Soledad. island E Falkland Islands
East Frisian Islands 72 A3 Eng. East Frisian Islands. island group NW Germany
East Frisian Islands see Ostfriesische Inseln
East Grand Forks 23 E1 Minnesota, N USA
East Indiaman Ridge 119 D6 undersea ridge E Indian Ocean
East Indies 130 A3 island group SE Asia
East Kilbride 66 C4 S Scotland, United Kingdom
East Korea Bay 107 E3 bay E North Korea
Eastleigh 67 D7 S England, United Kingdom
East London 56 D5 Afr. Oos-Londen; prev. Emonti, Port Rex. Eastern Cape, S South Africa
Eastmain 16 D3 river Québec, C Canada
East Mariana Basin 120 B1 undersea basin W Pacific Ocean
East Novaya Zemlya Trough 90 C1 var. Novaya Zemlya Trough. trough W Kara Sea
East Pacific Rise 131 F4 undersea rise E Pacific Ocean
East Pakistan see Bangladesh
East Saint Louis 18 B4 Illinois, N USA
East Scotia Basin 45 C7 undersea basin SE Scotia Sea
East Sea 108 A4 var. Sea of Japan, Rus. Yapanskoye More. Sea NW Pacific Ocean
East Siberian Sea see Vostochno-Sibirskoye More
East Timor 117 F5 var. Timor Lorosa'e, Port. Timor-Leste, prev. Portuguese Timor, Timor Timur. country S Indonesia
Eau Claire 18 A2 Wisconsin, N USA
Eau Claire, Lac à L' see St. Clair, Lake
Eauripik Rise 120 B2 undersea rise W Pacific Ocean
Ebensee 73 D6 Oberösterreich, N Austria
Eberswalde-Finow 72 D3 Brandenburg, E Germany
Ebetsu 108 D2 var. Ebetu. Hokkaidō, NE Japan
Ebetu see Ebetsu
Eblana see Dublin
Ebolowa 55 A5 Sud, S Cameroon
Ebon Atoll 122 D2 var. Epoon. atoll Ralik Chain, S Marshall Islands
Ebora see Évora
Eboracum see York
Ebro 71 E2 river NE Spain
Eburacum see York
Ebusus see Eivissa
Ecbatana see Hamadān
Ech Cheliff/Ech Chleff see Chlef
Echo Bay 15 E3 Northwest Territories, NW Canada
Echt 65 D5 Limburg, SE Netherlands
Écija 70 D4 anc. Astigi. Andalucía, SW Spain
Eckengraf see Viesīte
Ecuador 38 B1 off. Republic of Ecuador. country NW South America
Ecuador, Republic of see Ecuador
Ed Da'ein 50 A4 Southern Darfur, W Sudan
Ed Damazin 50 C4 var. Ad Damazīn. Blue Nile, E Sudan
Ed Damer 50 C3 var. Ad Dāmir, Ad Damar. River Nile, NE Sudan
Ed Debba 50 B3 Northern, N Sudan
Ede 64 D4 Gelderland, C Netherlands
Ede 53 F5 Osun, SW Nigeria
Edéa 55 A5 Littoral, SW Cameroon
Edessa see Şanlıurfa
Edfu see Idfū
Edgeøya 61 G2 island S Svalbard
Edgware 67 A7 Harrow, SE England, United Kingdom
Edinburg 27 G5 Texas, SW USA
Edinburgh 66 C4 national capital S Scotland, United Kingdom
Edingen see Enghien
Edirne 94 A2 Eng. Adrianople; anc. Adrianopolis, Hadrianopolis. Edirne, NW Turkey (Türkiye)
Edmonds 24 B2 Washington, NW USA
Edmonton 15 E5 province capital Alberta, SW Canada
Edmundston 17 E4 New Brunswick, SE Canada
Edna 27 G4 Texas, SW USA
Edolo 74 B1 Lombardia, N Italy
Edremit 94 A3 Balıkesir, NW Turkey (Türkiye)
Edward, Lake 55 E5 var. Albert Edward Nyanza, Edward Nyanza, Lac Idi Amin, Lake Rutanzige. lake Uganda/Dem. Rep. Congo
Edward Nyanza see Edward, Lake
Edwards Plateau 27 F3 plain Texas, SW USA
Edzo 31 E4 prev. Rae-Edzo. Northwest Territories, NW Canada
Eeklo 65 B5 var. Eekloo. Oost-Vlaanderen, NW Belgium
Eekloo see Eeklo
Eems see Ems
Eersel 65 C5 Noord-Brabant, S Netherlands
Eesti Vabariik see Estonia
Efate 122 D4 var. Efate, Fr. Vaté; prev. Sandwich Island. island C Vanuatu
Efate see Efate
Effingham 18 B4 Illinois, N USA
Eforie-Sud 86 D5 Constanţa, E Romania
Egadi Is. 75 B7 island group S Italy
Ege Denizi see Aegean Sea
Eger 77 D6 Ger. Erlau. Heves, NE Hungary
Eger see Cheb, Czechia (Czech Republic)
Egeria Fracture Zone 119 C5 tectonic feature W Indian Ocean
Éghezèe 65 C6 Namur, C Belgium
Egina see Aígina
Egio see Aígio
Egmont see Taranaki, Mount
Egmont, Cape 128 C4 headland North Island, New Zealand
Egoli see Johannesburg
Egypt 50 B2 off. Arab Republic of Egypt, Ar. Jumhūrīyat Miṣr al 'Arabīyah, Miṣr, prev. United Arab Republic; anc. Aegyptus. country NE Africa
Eibar 71 E1 País Vasco, N Spain
Eibergen 64 E3 Gelderland, E Netherlands
Eidfjord 63 A5 Hordaland, S Norway
Eier-Berg see Suur Munamägi
Eifel 73 A5 plateau W Germany
Eiger 73 B7 mountain C Switzerland
Eigg 66 B3 island W Scotland, United Kingdom
Eight Degree Channel 110 B3 channel India/Maldives
Eighty Mile Beach 124 B4 beach Western Australia
Eijsden 65 D6 Limburg, SE Netherlands
Eilat see Elat
Eindhoven 65 D5 Noord-Brabant, S Netherlands
Eipel see Ipel'
Éire see Ireland
Éireann, Muir see Irish Sea
Eisenhüttenstadt 72 D4 Brandenburg, E Germany
Eisenmarkt see Hunedoara
Eisenstadt 73 E6 Burgenland, E Austria
Eisleben 72 C4 Sachsen-Anhalt, C Germany
Eivissa 71 G3 var. Iviza, Cast. Ibiza; anc. Ebusus. Ibiza, Spain, W Mediterranean Sea
Ejea de los Caballeros 71 E2 Aragón, NE Spain
Ejin Qi see Dalain Hob
Ekapa see Cape Town
Ekaterinodar see Krasnodar
Ekvyvatapskiy Khrebet 93 G1 mountain range NE Russia
El 'Alamein see Al 'Alamayn
El Asnam see Chlef
Elat 97 B8 var. Eilat, Elath. Southern, S Israel
Elat, Gulf of see Aqaba, Gulf of
Elath see Elat, Israel
Elath see Al 'Aqabah, Jordan
El'Atrun 50 B3 Northern Darfur, NW Sudan
Elâzığ 95 E3 var. Elazig, Elâziz. Elâzığ, E Turkey (Türkiye)
Elba 74 B4 island Archipelago Toscano, C Italy
Elbasan 79 D6 var. Elbasani. Elbasan, C Albania
Elbasani see Elbasan
Elbe 58 D3 Cz. Labe. river Czechia (Czech Republic) /Germany
Elbert, Mount 22 C4 mountain Colorado, C USA
Elbing see Elbląg
Elbląg 76 C2 var. Elblag, Ger. Elbing. Warmińsko-Mazurskie, NE Poland
El Boulaida/El Bouläida see Blida
El'brus 89 A8 var. Gora El'brus. mountain SW Russia
El'brus, Gora see El'brus
El Burgo de Osma 71 E2 Castilla y León, C Spain
Elburz Mountains see Alborz, Reshteh-ye Kūhhā-ye
El Cajon 25 C8 California, W USA
El Calafate 43 B7 var. Calafate. Santa Cruz, S Argentina
El Callao 37 E2 Bolívar, E Venezuela
El Campo 27 G4 Texas, SW USA
El Carmen de Bolívar 36 B2 Bolívar, NW Colombia
El Cayo see San Ignacio
El Centro 25 D8 California, W USA
Elche see Elx
Elda 71 F4 Comunitat Valenciana, E Spain
El Djazaïr see Alger
El Djelfa see Djelfa
Eldorado 42 E3 Misiones, NE Argentina
El Dorado 28 C3 Sinaloa, C Mexico
El Dorado 20 B2 Arkansas, C USA
El Dorado 23 F5 Kansas, C USA
El Dorado 37 F2 Bolívar, E Venezuela
El Dorado see California
Eldoret 51 C6 Rift Valley, W Kenya
Elektrostal' 89 B5 Moskovskaya Oblast', W Russia
Elephant Butte Reservoir 26 C2 reservoir New Mexico, SW USA
Élesd see Aleşd
Eleuthera Island 32 C1 island N The Bahamas
El Fasher 50 A4 var. Al Fāshir. Northern Darfur, W Sudan
El Ferrol/El Ferrol del Caudillo see Ferrol
El Gedaref see Gedaref
El Geneina 50 A4 var. Ajjinena, Al-Genain, Al Junaynah. Western Darfur, W Sudan
Elgin 66 C3 NE Scotland, United Kingdom
Elgin 18 B3 Illinois, N USA
El Gîza see Al Jīzah
El Goléa 48 D3 var. Al Golea. C Algeria
El Ḩank 52 D1 cliff N Mauritania
El Haseke see Al Ḩasakah
Elimberrum see Auch
Eliocroca see Lorca
Élisabethville see Lubumbashi
Elista 89 B7 Respublika Kalmykiya, SW Russia
Elizabeth 127 B6 South Australia
Elizabeth City 21 G1 North Carolina, SE USA
Elizabethtown 18 C5 Kentucky, S USA
El-Jadida 48 C2 prev. Mazagan. W Morocco
Ełk 76 E2 Ger. Lyck. Warmińsko-mazurskie, NE Poland
Elk City 27 F1 Oklahoma, C USA
El Khalil see Hebron
El Khârga see Al Khārjah
Elkhart 18 C3 Indiana, N USA
El Khartûm see Khartoum
Elk River 23 F2 Minnesota, N USA
El Kuneitra see Al Qunayṭirah
Ellás see Greece
Elláda see Greece
Ellef Ringnes Island 15 E1 island Nunavut, N Canada
Ellen, Mount 22 B5 mountain Utah, W USA
Ellensburg 24 B2 Washington, NW USA
Ellesmere Island 15 F1 island Queen Elizabeth Islands, Nunavut, N Canada
Ellesmere, Lake 129 C6 lake South Island, New Zealand
Ellice Islands see Tuvalu

Ellinikí Dimokratía *see* Greece
Elliston *127 A6* South Australia
Ellsworth Land *132 A3 physical region* Antarctica
El Mahbas *48 B3 var.* Mahbés. SW Western Sahara
El Mina *96 B4 var.* Al Mīnā'. N Lebanon
El Minya *see* Al Minyā
Elmira *19 E3* New York, NE USA
El Mreyyé *52 D2 desert* E Mauritania
Elmshorn *72 B3* Schleswig-Holstein, N Germany
El Muglad *50 B4* Western Kordofan, C Sudan
El Obeid *50 B4 var.* Al Obayyid, Al Ubayyiḍ. Northern Kordofan, C Sudan
El Ouâdi *see* El Oued
El Oued *49 E2 var.* Al Oued, El Ouâdi, El Wad. NE Algeria
Eloy *26 B2* Arizona, SW USA
El Paso *26 D3* Texas, SW USA
El Porvenir *31 G4* Kuna Yala, N Panama
El Progreso *30 C2* Yoro, NW Honduras
El Puerto de Santa María *70 C5* Andalucía, S Spain
El Qâhira *see* Al Qāhirah
El Quneitra *see* Al Qunayṭirah
El Quseir *see* Al Quṣayr
El Quweira *see* Al Quwayrah
El Rama *31 E3* Región Autónoma Atlántico Sur, SE Nicaragua
El Real *31 H5 var.* El Real de Santa María. Darién, SE Panama
El Real de Santa María *see* El Real
El Reno *27 F1* Oklahoma, C USA
El Salvador *30 B3 off.* Republic of El Salvador, *Sp.* República de El Salvador. *country* Central America
El Salvador, Republic of *see* El Salvador
El Salvador, República de *see* El Salvador
Elsass *see* Alsace
El Sáuz *28 C2* Chihuahua, N Mexico
El Serrat *69 A7* N Andorra Europe
Elst *64 D4* Gelderland, E Netherlands
El Sueco *28 C2* Chihuahua, N Mexico
El Suweida *see* As Suwaydā'
El Suweis *see* As Suways
Eltanin Fracture Zone *131 E5 tectonic feature* SE Pacific Ocean
El Tigre *37 E2* Anzoátegui, NE Venezuela
Elvas *70 C4* Portalegre, C Portugal
El Vendrell *71 G2* Cataluña, NE Spain
El Vigía *36 C2* Mérida, NW Venezuela
El Wad *see* El Oued
Elwell, Lake *22 B1 reservoir* Montana, NW USA
Elx *71 F4 var.* Elche; *anc.* Ilici, *Lat.* Illicis. Comunitat Valenciana, E Spain
Ely *25 D5* Nevada, W USA
El Yopal *see* Yopal
Emajõgi *84 D3 Ger.* Embach. *river* SE Estonia
Emāmrūd *see* Shāhrūd
Emāmshahr *see* Shāhrūd
Emba *92 B4 Kaz.* Embi. Aktyubinsk, W Kazakhstan
Embach *see* Emajõgi
Embi *see* Emba
Emden *72 A3* Niedersachsen, NW Germany
Emerald *126 D4* Queensland, E Australia
Emerald Isle *see* Montserrat
Emesa *see* Ḥimṣ
Emmaste *84 C2* Hiiumaa, W Estonia
Emmeloord *64 D2* Flevoland, N Netherlands
Emmen *64 E2* Drenthe, NE Netherlands
Emmendingen *73 A6* Baden-Württemberg, SW Germany
Emona *see* Ljubljana
Emonti *see* East London
Emory Peak *27 E4 mountain* Texas, SW USA
Empalme *28 B2* Sonora, NW Mexico
Emperor Seamounts *91 G3 seamount range* NW Pacific Ocean
Empire State of the South *see* Georgia
Emporia *23 F5* Kansas, C USA
Empty Quarter *see* Ar Rub 'al Khālī
Ems *72 A3 Dut.* Eems. *river* NW Germany
Enaretträsk *see* Inarijärvi
Encamp *69 A8* Encamp, C Andorra Europe
Encarnación *42 D3* Itapúa, S Paraguay
Encinitas *25 C8* California, W USA
Encs *77 D6* Borsod-Abaúj-Zemplén, NE Hungary
Endeavour Strait *126 C1 strait* Queensland, NE Australia
Enderbury Island *123 F3 atoll* Phoenix Islands, C Kiribati
Enderby Land *132 C2 physical region* Antarctica
Enderby Plain *132 D2 abyssal plain* S Indian Ocean
Endersdorf *see* Jędrzejów
Enewetak Atoll *122 C1 var.* Ānewetak, Eniwetok. *atoll* Ralik Chain, W Marshall Islands
Enfield *67 A7* United Kingdom
Engeten *see* Aiud
Enghien *65 B6 Dut.* Edingen. Hainaut, SW Belgium
England *67 D5 Lat.* Anglia. *cultural region* England, United Kingdom
Englewood *22 D4* Colorado, C USA
English Channel *67 D8 var.* The Channel, *Fr.* la Manche. *channel* NW Europe
Engure *84 C3* Tukums, W Latvia
Engures Ezers *84 B3 lake* NW Latvia
Enguri *95 F1 Rus.* Inguri. *river* NW Georgia
Enid *27 F1* Oklahoma, C USA
Enikale Strait *see* Kerch Strait
Eniwetok *see* Enewetak Atoll
En Nâqoûra *97 A5 var.* An Nāqūrah. SW Lebanon
En Nazira *see* Natzrat
Ennedi *54 D2 plateau* E Chad
Ennis *67 A6 Ir.* Inis. Clare, W Ireland
Ennis *27 G3* Texas, SW USA
Enniskillen *67 B5 var.* Inniskilling, *Ir.* Inis Ceithleann. SW Northern Ireland, United Kingdom
Enns *73 D6 river* C Austria
Enschede *64 E3* Overijssel, E Netherlands
Ensenada *28 A1* Baja California Norte, NW Mexico
Entebbe *51 B6* S Uganda
Entroncamento *70 B3* Santarém, C Portugal
Enugu *53 G5* Enugu, S Nigeria
Epanomí *82 B4* Kentrikí Makedonía, N Greece
Epéna *55 B5* Likouala, NE Congo
Eperies/Eperjes *see* Prešov
Epi *122 D4 var.* Épi. *island* C Vanuatu
Épi *see* Epi
Épinal *68 D4* Vosges, NE France
Epiphania *see* Ḥamāh
Epoon *see* Ebon Atoll
Epsom *67 A8* United Kingdom
Equality State *see* Wyoming
Equatorial Guinea *55 A5 off.* Equatorial Guinea, Republic of. *country* C Africa
Equatorial Guinea, Republic of *see* Equatorial Guinea
Erautini *see* Johannesburg
Erbil *see* Arbīl
Erciş *95 F3* Van, E Turkey (Türkiye)
Erdély *see* Transylvania
Erdélyi-Havasok *see* Carpaţii Meridionali
Erdenet *105 E2* Orhon, N Mongolia
Erdi *54 C2 plateau* NE Chad
Erdi Ma *54 D2 desert* NE Chad
Erebus, Mount *132 B4 volcano* Ross Island, Antarctica
Ereğli *94 C4* Konya, S Turkey (Türkiye)
Erenhot *105 F2 var.* Erlian. Nei Mongol Zizhiqu, NE China
Erfurt *72 C4* Thüringen, C Germany
Ergene Çayı *see* Ergene Irmaği
Ergene Irmaği *94 A2 var.* Ergene Çayı. *river* NW Turkey (Türkiye)
Ergun *105 F1 var.* Labudalin; *prev.* Ergun Youqi. Nei Mongol Zizhiqu, N China
Ergun He *see* Argun
Ergun Youqi *see* Ergun
Erie *18 D3* Pennsylvania, NE USA
Érié, Lac *see* Erie, Lake
Erie, Lake *18 D3 Fr.* Lac Érié. *lake* Canada/USA
Eritrea *50 C4 off.* State of Eritrea, Iertra. *country* E Africa
Eritrea, State of *see* Eritrea
Erivan *see* Yerevan
Erlangen *73 C5* Bayern, S Germany
Erlau *see* Eger
Erlian *see* Erenhot
Ermelo *64 D3* Gelderland, C Netherlands
Ermióni *83 C6* Pelopónnisos, S Greece
Ermoúpoli *83 D6 var.* Hermoupolis; *prev.* Ermoúpolis. Sýyros, Kykládes, Greece, Aegean Sea
Ermoúpolis *see* Ermoúpoli
Ernākulam *110 C3* Kerala, SW India
Erode *110 C2* Tamil Nādu, SE India
Erquelinnes *65 B7* Hainaut, S Belgium
Er-Rachidia *48 C2 var.* Ksar al Soule. E Morocco
Er Rahad *50 B4 var.* Ar Rahad. Northern Kordofan, C Sudan
Erromango *122 D4 island* S Vanuatu
Ertis *see* Irtysh, C Asia
Erzerum *see* Erzurum
Erzgebirge *73 C5 Cz.* Krušné Hory, *Eng.* Ore Mountains. *mountain range* Czechia (Czech Republic) /Germany
Erzincan *95 E3 var.* Erzinjan. Erzincan, E Turkey (Türkiye)
Erzinjan *see* Erzincan
Erzurum *95 E3 prev.* Erzerum. Erzurum, NE Turkey (Türkiye)
Esbjerg *63 A7* Ribe, W Denmark
Esbo *see* Espoo
Escaldes *69 A8* Escaldes Engordany, C Andorra Europe
Escanaba *18 C2* Michigan, N USA
Escaut *see* Scheldt
Esch-sur-Alzette *65 D8* Luxembourg, S Luxembourg
Esclaves, Grand Lac des *see* Great Slave Lake
Escondido *25 C8* California, W USA
Escuinapa *28 D3 var.* Escuinapa de Hidalgo. Sinaloa, C Mexico
Escuinapa de Hidalgo *see* Escuinapa
Escuintla *30 B2* Escuintla, S Guatemala
Escuintla *29 G5* Chiapas, SE Mexico
Esenguly *100 B3 Rus.* Gasan-Kuli. Balkan Welaýaty, W Turkmenistan
Eşfahān *98 C3 Eng.* Isfahan; *anc.* Aspadana. Eşfahān, C Iran
Esh Sharā *see* Ash Sharāh
Esil *see* Ishim, Kazakhstan/Russia
Eskimo Point *see* Arviat
Eskişehir *94 B3 var.* Eskishehr. Eskişehir, W Turkey (Türkiye)
Eskishehr *see* Eskişehir
Eslāmābād *98 C3 var.* Eslāmābād-e Gharb; *prev.* Harunabad, Shāhābād. Kermānshāhān, W Iran
Eslāmābād-e Gharb *see* Eslāmābād
Esmeraldas *38 A1* Esmeraldas, N Ecuador
Esna *see* Isnā
España *see* Spain
Espanola *26 D1* New Mexico, SW USA
Esperance *125 B7* Western Australia
Esperanza *28 B2* Sonora, NW Mexico
Esperanza *132 A2 Argentinian research station* Antarctica
Espinal *36 B3* Tolima, C Colombia
Espinhaço, Serra do *34 D4 mountain range* SE Brazil
Espírito Santo *41 F4 off.* Estado do Espírito Santo. *region* E Brazil
Espírito Santo *41 F4 off.* Estado do Espírito Santo. *state* E Brazil
Espírito Santo, Estado do *see* Espírito Santo
Espiritu Santo *122 C4 var.* Santo. *island* W Vanuatu
Espoo *63 D6 Swe.* Esbo. Uusimaa, S Finland
Esquel *43 B6* Chubut, SW Argentina
Essaouira *48 B2 prev.* Mogador. W Morocco
Esseg *see* Osijek
Es Semara *see* Smara
Essen *65 C5* Antwerpen, N Belgium
Essen *72 A4 var.* Essen an der Ruhr. Nordrhein-Westfalen, W Germany
Essen an der Ruhr *see* Essen
Essequibo River *37 F3 river* C Guyana
Es Suweida *see* As Suwaydā'
Estacado, Llano *27 E2 plain* New Mexico/Texas, SW USA
Estados, Isla de los *43 C8 prev. Eng.* Staten Island. *island* S Argentina
Estância *41 G3* Sergipe, E Brazil
Estelí *30 D3* Estelí, NW Nicaragua
Estella *71 E1 Bas.* Lizarra. Navarra, N Spain
Estepona *70 D5* Andalucía, S Spain
Estevan *15 F5* Saskatchewan, S Canada
Estland *see* Estonia
Estonia *84 D2 off.* Republic of Estonia, *Est.* Eesti Vabariik, *Ger.* Estland, *Latv.* Igaunija; *prev.* Estonian SSR, *Rus.* Estonskaya SSR. *country* NE Europe
Estonian SSR *see* Estonia
Estonia, Republic of *see* Estonia
Estonskaya SSR *see* Estonia
Estrela, Serra da *70 C3 mountain range* C Portugal
Estremadura *see* Extremadura
Estremoz *70 C4* Évora, S Portugal
Eswatini *56 D4 off.* Kingdom of Eswatini; *prev.* Swaziland. *country* S Africa
Eswatini, Kingdom of *see* Eswatini
Eszék *see* Osijek
Esztergom *77 C6 Ger.* Gran; *anc.* Strigonium. Komárom-Esztergom, N Hungary
Étalle *65 D8* Luxembourg, SE Belgium
Etāwah *112 D3* Uttar Pradesh, N India
Ethiopia *51 C5 off.* Federal Democratic Republic of Ethiopia; *prev.* Abyssinia, People's Democratic Republic of Ethiopia. *country* E Africa
Ethiopia, Federal Democratic Republic of *see* Ethiopia
Ethiopian Highlands *51 C5 var.* Ethiopian Plateau. *plateau* N Ethiopia
Ethiopian Plateau *see* Ethiopian Highlands
Ethiopia, People's Democratic Republic of *see* Ethiopia
Etna, Monte *75 C7 Eng.* Mount Etna. *volcano* Sicilia, Italy, C Mediterranean Sea
Etna, Mount *see* Etna, Monte
Etosha Pan *56 B3 salt lake* N Namibia
Etoumbi *55 B5* Cuvette Ouest, NW Congo
Etsch *see* Adige
Et Tafila *see* Aṭ Ṭafīlah
Ettelbrück *65 D8* Diekirch, C Luxembourg
'Eua *123 E5 prev.* Middleburg Island. *island* Tongatapu Group, SE Tonga
Euboea *see* Évvoia
Euboea *see* Évvoia
Eucla *125 D6* Western Australia
Euclid *18 D3* Ohio, N USA
Eufaula Lake *27 G1 var.* Eufaula Reservoir. *reservoir* Oklahoma, C USA
Eufaula Reservoir *see* Eufaula Lake
Eugene *24 B3* Oregon, NW USA
Eumolpias *see* Plovdiv
Eupen *65 D6* Liège, E Belgium
Euphrates *90 B4 Ar.* Al-Furāt, *Turk.* Firat Nehri. *river* SW Asia
Eureka *25 A5* California, W USA
Eureka *22 A1* Montana, NW USA
Europa Point *71 H5 headland* S Gibraltar
Europe *58 continent*
Eutin *72 C2* Schleswig-Holstein, N Germany
Euxine Sea *see* Black Sea
Evansdale *23 G3* Iowa, C USA
Evanston *18 B3* Illinois, N USA
Evanston *22 B4* Wyoming, C USA
Evansville *18 B5* Indiana, N USA
Eveleth *23 G1* Minnesota, N USA
Everard, Lake *127 A6 salt lake* South Australia
Everest, Mount *104 B5 Chin.* Qomolangma Feng, *Nep.* Sagarmāthā. *mountain* China/Nepal
Everett *24 B2* Washington, NW USA
Everglades, The *21 F5 wetland* Florida, SE USA
Evje *63 A6* Aust-Agder, S Norway
Evmolpia *see* Plovdiv
Évora *70 B4 anc.* Ebora, *Lat.* Liberalitas Julia. Évora, C Portugal
Évreux *68 C3 anc.* Civitas Eburovicum. Eure, N France
Évros *see* Maritsa
Évry *68 E2* Essonne, N France
Évvoia *83 C5 var.* Euboea, *Lat.* Euboea. *island* C Greece
Ewarton *32 B5* C Jamaica
Excelsior Springs *23 F4* Missouri, C USA
Exe *67 C7 river* SW England, United Kingdom
Exeter *67 C7 anc.* Isca Damnoniorum. SW England, United Kingdom
Exmoor *67 C7 moorland* SW England, United Kingdom
Exmouth *124 A4* Western Australia
Exmouth *67 C7* SW England, United Kingdom
Exmouth Gulf *124 A4 gulf* Western Australia
Exmouth Plateau *119 E5 undersea plateau* E Indian Ocean
Extremadura *70 C3 var.* Estremadura. *autonomous community* W Spain
Exuma Cays *32 C1 islets* C The Bahamas
Exuma Sound *32 C1 sound* C The Bahamas
Eyre Mountains *129 A7 mountain range* South Island, New Zealand
Eyre, Lake *127 A5 var.* Kati Thanda. *salt lake* South Australia
Eyre Peninsula *127 A6 peninsula* South Australia
Eyre South, Lake *127 A5 salt lake* South Australia
Ezo *see* Hokkaidō

F

Faadhippolhu Atoll *110 B4 var.* Fadiffolu, Lhaviyani Atoll. *atoll* N Maldives
Fabens *26 D3* Texas, SW USA
Fada *54 C2* Borkou-Ennedi-Tibesti, E Chad
Fada-Ngourma *53 E4* E Burkina
Fadiffolu *see* Faadhippolhu Atoll
Faenza *74 C3 anc.* Faventia. Emilia-Romagna, N Italy
Faeroe Islands *see* Faero Islands
Færøerne *see* Faroe Islands
Faetano *74 E2* E San Marino
Făgăraş *86 C4 Ger.* Fogarasch, *Hung.* Fogaras. Braşov, C Romania
Fagibina, Lake *see* Faguibine, Lac
Fagne *65 C7 hill range* S Belgium
Faguibine, Lac *53 E3 var.* Lake Fagibina. *lake* NW Mali
Fahlun *see* Falun
Fahraj *98 E4* Kermān, SE Iran
Faial *70 A5 var.* Ilha do Faial. *island* Azores, Portugal, NE Atlantic Ocean
Faial, Ilha do *see* Faial
Faifo *see* Hôi An
Fairbanks *14 D3* Alaska, USA
Fairfield *25 B6* California, W USA
Fair Isle *66 D2 island* NE Scotland, United Kingdom
Fairlie *129 B6* Canterbury, South Island, New Zealand
Fairmont *23 F3* Minnesota, N USA
Faisalabad *112 C2 prev.* Lyallpur. Punjab, NE Pakistan
Faizābād *113 E3* Uttar Pradesh, N India
Faiẓābād *101 F3 var.* Feyẓābād, Fyzabad. Badakhshān, NE Afghanistan
Fakaofo Atoll *123 F3 island* SE Tokelau
Falam *114 A3* Chin State, W Myanmar (Burma)
Falconara Marittima *74 C3* Marche, C Italy
Falkenau an der Eger *see* Sokolov
Falkland Islands *43 D7 var.* Falklands, Islas Malvinas. *UK Overseas Territory* SW Atlantic Ocean
Falkland Plateau *35 D7 var.* Argentine Rise. *undersea feature* SW Atlantic Ocean
Falklands *see* Falkland Islands
Falknov nad Ohří *see* Sokolov
Fallbrook *25 C8* California, W USA
Falmouth *32 A4* W Jamaica
Falmouth *67 C7* SW England, United Kingdom
Falster *63 B8 island* SE Denmark
Fălticeni *86 C3 Hung.* Falticsén. Suceava, NE Romania
Falticsén *see* Fălticeni
Falun *63 C6 var.* Fahlun. Kopparberg, C Sweden
Famagusta *see* Gazimağusa
Famagusta Bay *see* Gazimağusa Körfezi
Famenne *65 C7 physical region* SE Belgium
Fang *114 C3* Chiang Mai, NW Thailand
Fanning Island *see* Tabuaeran
Fanø *63 A7 island* W Denmark
Farafangana *57 G4* Fianarantsoa, SE Madagascar
Farāh *100 D4 var.* Farah, Fararud. Farāh, W Afghanistan
Farāh Rōd *100 D4 river* W Afghanistan
Faranah *52 C4* Haute-Guinée, S Guinea
Fararud *see* Farāh
Farasan Islands *see* Farasān, Jazur
Farasān, Jazur *99 A6 var.* Farasan Islands. *island group* SW Saudi Arabia
Farewell, Cape *128 C4 headland* South Island, New Zealand
Farewell, Cape *see* Nunap Isua
Fargo *23 F2* North Dakota, N USA
Farg'ona *101 F2 Rus.* Fergana; *prev.* Novyy Margilan. Farg'ona Viloyati, E Uzbekistan
Faribault *23 F2* Minnesota, N USA
Farīdābād *112 D3* Haryāna, N India
Farkhor *101 E3 Rus.* Parkhar. SW Tajikistan
Farmington *23 G5* Missouri, C USA
Farmington *26 C1* New Mexico, SW USA
Faro *70 B5* Faro, S Portugal
Faroe-Iceland Ridge *58 C1 undersea ridge* NW Norwegian Sea
Faroe Islands *61 E5 var.* Faero Islands, *Dan.* Færøerne, *Far.* Føroyar. *Self-governing territory of Denmark* N Atlantic Ocean
Faroe-Shetland Trough *58 C2 trough* NE Atlantic Ocean
Farquhar Group *57 G2 island group* S Seychelles
Fars, Khalij-e *see* Persian Gulf
Farvel, Kap *see* Nunap Isua
Fastiv *87 E2 Rus.* Fastov. Kyivska Oblast, NW Ukraine
Fastov *see* Fastiv
Fauske *62 C3* Nordland, C Norway
Faventia *see* Faenza
Faxa Bay *see* Faxaflói
Faxaflói *60 D5 Eng.* Faxa Bay. *bay* W Iceland
Faya *54 C2 prev.* Faya-Largeau, Largeau. Borkou-Ennedi-Tibesti, N Chad
Faya-Largeau *see* Faya
Fayetteville *20 A1* Arkansas, C USA
Fayetteville *21 F1* North Carolina, SE USA
Fdérick *see* Fdérik
Fdérik *52 C2 var.* Fdérick, *Fr.* Fort Gouraud. Tiris Zemmour, NW Mauritania
Fear, Cape *21 F2 headland* Bald Head Island, North Carolina, SE USA
Fécamp *68 B3* Seine-Maritime, N France
Fédala *see* Mohammedia
Federal Capital Territory *see* Australian Capital Territory
Fehérgyarmat *77 E6* Szabolcs-Szatmár-Bereg, E Hungary
Fehértemplom *see* Bela Crkva
Fehmarn *72 C2 island* N Germany
Fehmarn Belt *72 C2 Dan.* Femern Bælt, *Ger.* Fehmarnbelt. *strait* Denmark /Germany
Fehmarnbelt Fehmarn Belt/Femer Bælt
Feijó *40 C2* Acre, W Brazil
Feilding *128 D4* Manawatu-Wanganui, North Island, New Zealand
Feira *see* Feira de Santana
Feira de Santana *41 G3 var.* Feira. Bahia, E Brazil
Feketehalom *see* Codlea
Felanitx *71 G3* Mallorca, Spain, W Mediterranean Sea
Felicitas Julia *see* Lisboa
Felidhu Atoll *110 B4 atoll* C Maldives
Felipe Carrillo Puerto *29 H4* Quintana Roo, SE Mexico
Felixstowe *67 E6* E England, United Kingdom
Fellin *see* Viljandi
Felsőbánya *see* Baia Sprie
Felsőmuzslya *see* Mužlja
Femunden *63 B5 lake* S Norway
Fénérive *see* Fenoarivo Atsinanana
Fengcheng *106 D3 var.* Feng-cheng, Fenghwangcheng. Liaoning, NE China
Feng-cheng *see* Fengcheng
Fenghwangcheng *see* Fengcheng
Fengtien *see* Shenyang, China
Fengtien *see* Liaoning, China
Fenoarivo Atsinanana *57 G3 Fr.* Fénérive. Toamasina, E Madagascar
Fens, The *67 E6 wetland* E England, United Kingdom
Feodosiia *87 F5 prev.* Feodosiya, *var.* Kefe, *It.* Kaffa; *anc.* Theodosia. Respublika Krym, S Ukraine
Feodosiya *see* Feodosiia
Ferdinand *see* Montana, Bulgaria
Ferdinandsberg *see* Oţelu Roşu
Féres *82 D3* Anatolikí Makedonía kai Thráki, NE Greece
Fergana *see* Farg'ona
Fergus Falls *23 F2* Minnesota, N USA
Ferizaj *79 D5 Serb.* Uroševac. C Kosovo
Ferkessédougou *52 D4* N Ivory Coast
Fermo *74 C4 anc.* Firmum Picenum. Marche, C Italy
Fernandina, Isla *38 A5 var.* Narborough Island. *island* Galápagos Islands, Ecuador, E Pacific Ocean
Fernando de Noronha *41 H2 island* E Brazil
Fernando Po/Fernando Póo *see* Bioco, Isla de
Ferrara *74 C2 anc.* Forum Alieni. Emilia-Romagna, N Italy
Ferreñafe *38 B3* Lambayeque, W Peru
Ferro *see* Hierro
Ferrol *70 B1 var.* El Ferrol; *prev.* El Ferrol del Caudillo. Galicia, NW Spain
Fertő *see* Neusiedler See
Ferwerd *see* Ferwert
Ferwert *64 D1 Dutch.* Ferwerd. Fryslân, N Netherlands
Fès *48 C2 Eng.* Fez. N Morocco
Feteşti *86 D5* Ialomiţa, SE Romania
Fethiye *94 B4* Muğla, SW Turkey (Türkiye)
Fetlar *66 D1 island* NE Scotland, United Kingdom
Feuilles, Rivière aux *16 D2 river* Québec, E Canada
Feyẓābād *see* Faiẓābād
Fez *see* Fès
Fezzan *49 G4 region* S Libya
Fianarantsoa *57 F3* Fianarantsoa, C Madagascar
Fianga *54 B4* Mayo-Kébbi, SW Chad
Fier *79 C6 var.* Fieri. Fier, SW Albania
Fieri *see* Fier
Figeac *69 C5* Lot, S France
Figig *see* Figuig
Figueira da Foz *70 B3* Coimbra, W Portugal
Figueres *71 G2* Cataluña, E Spain
Figuig *48 D2 var.* Figig. E Morocco
Fiji *123 E5 off.* Republic of Fiji, *Fij.* Viti. *country* SW Pacific Ocean
Fiji, Republic of *see* Fiji
Filadelfia *30 D4* Guanacaste, W Costa Rica
Filiaşi *86 B5* Dolj, SW Romania
Filipstad *63 B6* Värmland, C Sweden
Finale Ligure *74 A3* Liguria, NW Italy
Finchley *67 A7* United Kingdom
Findlay *18 C4* Ohio, N USA
Finike *94 B4* Antalya, SW Turkey (Türkiye)
Finland *62 D4 off.* Republic of Finland, *Fin.* Suomen Tasavalta, Suomi. *country* N Europe
Finland, Gulf of *63 D6 Est.* Soome Laht, *Fin.* Suomenlahti, *Ger.* Finnischer Meerbusen, *Rus.* Finskiy Zaliv, *Swe.* Finska Viken. *gulf* E Baltic Sea
Finland, Republic of *see* Finland
Finnischer Meerbusen *see* Finland, Gulf of
Finnmarksvidda *62 D2 physical region* N Norway
Finska Viken/Finskiy Zaliv *see* Finland, Gulf of
Finsterwalde *72 D4* Brandenburg, E Germany
Fiordland *129 A7 physical region* South Island, New Zealand
Fiorina *74 E1* NE San Marino
Firat Nehri *see* Euphrates
Firenze *74 C3 Eng.* Florence; *anc.* Florentia. Toscana, C Italy
Firmum Picenum *see* Fermo
First State *see* Delaware
Fischbacher Alpen *73 E7 mountain range* E Austria
Fischhausen *see* Primorsk
Fish *56 B4 var.* Vis. *river* S Namibia
Fishguard *67 C6 Wel.* Abergwaun. SW Wales, United Kingdom
Fisterra, Cabo *70 B1 headland* NW Spain
Fitzroy Crossing *124 C3* Western Australia
Fitzroy River *124 C3 river* Western Australia
Fiume *see* Rijeka
Flagstaff *26 B2* Arizona, SW USA
Flanders *65 A6 Dut.* Vlaanderen, *Fr.* Flandre. *cultural region* Belgium/France
Flandre *see* Flanders
Flathead Lake *22 B1 lake* Montana, NW USA
Flat Island *106 C8 island* NE Spratly Islands
Flatts Village *20 B5 var.* The Flatts Village. C Bermuda
Flensburg *72 B2* Schleswig-Holstein, N Germany
Flessingue *see* Vlissingen
Flickertail State *see* North Dakota
Flinders Island *127 C8 island* Furneaux Group, Tasmania, SE Australia
Flinders Ranges *127 B6 mountain range* South Australia
Flinders River *126 C3 river* Queensland, NE Australia
Flin Flon *15 F5* Manitoba, C Canada
Flint *18 C3* Michigan, N USA
Flint Island *123 G4 island* Line Islands, E Kiribati
Floreana, Isla *see* Santa María, Isla
Florence *20 C1* Alabama, S USA
Florence *21 F2* South Carolina, SE USA
Florence *see* Firenze
Florencia *36 B4* Caquetá, S Colombia
Florentia *see* Firenze
Flores *30 B1* Petén, N Guatemala
Flores *117 E5 island* Nusa Tenggara, C Indonesia
Flores *70 A5 island* Azores, Portugal, NE Atlantic Ocean
Flores, Laut *see* Flores Sea
Flores Sea *116 D5 Ind.* Laut Flores. *sea* C Indonesia
Floriano *41 F2* Piauí, E Brazil
Florianópolis *41 F5 prev.* Destêrro. *state capital* Santa Catarina, S Brazil
Florida *42 D4* Florida, S Uruguay
Florida *21 E4 off.* State of Florida, *also known as* Peninsular State, Sunshine State. *state* SE USA
Florida Bay *21 E5 bay* Florida, SE USA
Florida Keys *21 E5 island group* Florida, SE USA
Florida, Straits of *32 B1 strait* Atlantic Ocean/ Gulf of Mexico
Flórina *82 B4 var.* Phlórina. Dytikí Makedonía, N Greece
Florissant *23 G4* Missouri, C USA
Floúda, Akrotírio *83 D7 headland* Astypálaia, Kykládes, Greece, Aegean Sea
Flushing *see* Vlissingen
Flylân *see* Vlieland
Foča *78 C4 var.* Srbinje. SE Bosnia and Herzegovina
Focşani *86 C4* Vrancea, E Romania
Fogaras/Fogarasch *see* Făgăraş
Foggia *75 D5* Puglia, SE Italy
Fogo *52 A3 island* Ilhas de Sotavento, SW Cape Verde (Cabo Verde)
Foix *69 B6* Ariège, S France
Folégandros *83 C7 island* Kykládes, Greece, Aegean Sea
Foleyet *16 C4* Ontario, S Canada
Foligno *74 C4* Umbria, C Italy
Folkestone *67 E7* SE England, United Kingdom
Fond du Lac *18 B2* Wisconsin, N USA
Fonseca, Golfo de *see* Fonseca, Gulf of
Fonseca, Gulf of *30 C3 Sp.* Golfo de Fonseca. *gulf* C Central America
Fontainebleau *68 C3* Seine-et-Marne, N France
Fontenay-le-Comte *68 B4* Vendée, NW France
Fontvieille *69 B8* SW Monaco Europe
Fonyód *77 C7* Somogy, W Hungary

Foochow see Fuzhou
Forchheim 73 C5 Bayern, SE Germany
Forel, Mont 60 D4 mountain SE Greenland
Forfar 66 C3 E Scotland, United Kingdom
Forge du Sud see Dudelange
Forlì 74 C3 anc. Forum Livii. Emilia-Romagna, N Italy
Formentera 71 G4 anc. Ophiusa, Lat. Frumentum. island Islas Baleares, Spain, W Mediterranean Sea
Formosa 42 D2 Formosa, NE Argentina
Formosa/Formo'sa see Taiwan
Formosa, Serra 41 E3 mountain range C Brazil
Formosa Strait see Taiwan Strait
Føroyar see Faroe Islands
Forrest City 20 B1 Arkansas, C USA
Fort Albany 16 C3 Ontario, C Canada
Fortaleza 39 F2 Pando, N Bolivia
Fortaleza 41 G2 prev. Ceará. state capital Ceará, NE Brazil
Fort-Archambault see Sarh
Fort-Bayard see Zhanjiang
Fort-Cappolani see Tidjikja
Fort Charlet see Djanet
Fort-Chimo see Kuujjuaq
Fort Collins 22 D4 Colorado, C USA
Fort-Crampel see Kaga Bandoro
Fort Davis 27 E3 Texas, SW USA
Fort-de-France 33 H4 prev. Fort-Royal. dependent territory capital (Martinique) W Martinique
Fort Dodge 23 F3 Iowa, C USA
Fortescue River 124 A4 river Western Australia
Fort-Foureau see Kousséri
Fort Frances 16 B4 Ontario, S Canada
Fort Good Hope 15 E3 var. Rádeyilikóé. Northwest Territories, NW Canada
Fort Gouraud see Fdérik
Forth 66 C4 river C Scotland, United Kingdom
Forth, Firth of 66 C4 estuary E Scotland, United Kingdom
Fortín General Eugenio Garay see General Eugenio A. Garay
Fort Jameson see Chipata
Fort-Lamy see Ndjamena
Fort Lauderdale 21 F5 Florida, SE USA
Fort Liard 15 E4 var. Liard. Northwest Territories, W Canada
Fort Madison 23 G4 Iowa, C USA
Fort McMurray 15 E4 Alberta, C Canada
Fort McPherson 14 D3 var. McPherson. Northwest Territories, NW Canada
Fort Morgan 22 D4 Colorado, C USA
Fort Myers 21 E5 Florida, SE USA
Fort Nelson 15 E4 British Columbia, W Canada
Fort Peck Lake 22 C1 reservoir Montana, NW USA
Fort Pierce 21 F4 Florida, SE USA
Fort Providence 15 E4 var. Providence. Northwest Territories, W Canada
Fort-Repoux see Akjoujt
Fort Rosebery see Mansa
Fort Rousset see Owando
Fort-Royal see Fort-de-France
Fort St. John 15 E4 British Columbia, W Canada
Fort Scott 23 F5 Kansas, C USA
Fort Severn 16 C2 Ontario, C Canada
Fort-Shevchenko 92 A4 Mangistau, W Kazakhstan
Fort-Sibut see Sibut
Fort Simpson 15 E4 var. Simpson. Northwest Territories, W Canada
Fort Smith 15 E4 Northwest Territories, W Canada
Fort Smith 20 B1 Arkansas, C USA
Fort Stockton 27 E3 Texas, SW USA
Fort-Trinquet see Bîr Mogreïn
Fort Vermilion 15 E4 Alberta, W Canada
Fort Victoria see Masvingo
Fort Walton Beach 20 C3 Florida, SE USA
Fort Wayne 18 C4 Indiana, N USA
Fort William 66 C3 N Scotland, United Kingdom
Fort Worth 27 G2 Texas, SW USA
Fort Yukon 14 D3 Alaska, USA
Forum Alieni see Ferrara
Forum Livii see Forlì
Fossa Claudia see Chioggia
Fougamou 55 A6 Ngounié, C Gabon
Fougères 68 B3 Ille-et-Vilaine, NW France
Fou-hsin see Fuxin
Foulwind, Cape 129 B5 headland South Island, New Zealand
Foumban 54 A4 Ouest, NW Cameroon
Fou-shan see Fushun
Foveaux Strait 129 A8 strait S New Zealand
Foxe Basin 15 G3 sea Nunavut, N Canada
Fox Glacier 129 B6 West Coast, South Island, New Zealand
Fraga 71 F2 Aragón, NE Spain
Fram Basin 133 C3 var. Amundsen Basin. undersea basin Arctic Ocean
France 68 B4 off. French Republic, It./Sp. Francia; prev. Gaul, Gaule, Lat. Gallia. country W Europe
Franceville 55 B6 var. Massoukou, Masuku. Haut-Ogooué, E Gabon
Francfort see Frankfurt am Main
Franche-Comté 68 D4 cultural region E France
Francia see France
Francis Case, Lake 23 E3 reservoir South Dakota, N USA
Francisco Escárcega 29 G4 Campeche, SE Mexico
Francistown 56 D3 North East, NE Botswana
Franconian Jura see Fränkische Alb
Frankenalb see Fränkische Alb
Frankenstein/Frankenstein in Schlesien see Ząbkowice Śląskie
Frankfort 18 C5 state capital Kentucky, S USA
Frankfort on the Main see Frankfurt am Main
Frankfurt see Frankfurt am Main, Germany
Frankfurt see Słubice, Poland
Frankfurt am Main 73 B5 var. Frankfurt, Fr. Francfort; prev. Eng. Frankfort on the Main. Hessen, SW Germany
Frankfurt an der Oder 72 D3 Brandenburg, E Germany
Fränkische Alb 73 C6 var. Frankenalb, Eng. Franconian Jura. mountain range S Germany
Franklin 20 C1 Tennessee, S USA
Franklin D. Roosevelt Lake 24 C1 reservoir Washington, NW USA
Franz Josef Land 92 D1 Eng. Franz Josef Land. island group N Russia
Franz Josef Land see Frantsa-Iosifa, Zemlya
Fraserburgh 66 D3 NE Scotland, United Kingdom
Fraser Island 126 E4 var. Great Sandy Island. island Queensland, E Australia
Frauenbach see Baia Mare
Frauenburg see Saldus, Latvia
Fredericksburg 19 E5 Virginia, NE USA
Fredericton 17 F4 province capital New Brunswick, SE Canada
Frederikshåb see Paamiut
Fredrikshald see Halden
Fredrikstad 63 B6 Østfold, S Norway
Freeport 32 C1 Grand Bahama Island, N The Bahamas
Freeport 27 H4 Texas, SW USA
Free State see Maryland
Freetown 52 C4 country capital (Sierra Leone) W Sierra Leone
Freiburg see Freiburg im Breisgau, Germany
Freiburg im Breisgau 73 A6 var. Freiburg, Fr. Fribourg-en-Brisgau. Baden-Württemberg, SW Germany
Freiburg in Schlesien see Świebodzice
Fremantle 125 A6 Western Australia
Fremont 23 F4 Nebraska, C USA
French Guiana 37 H3 var. Guiana, Guyane. French overseas department N South America
French Guinea see Guinea
French Polynesia 121 F4 Overseas Country of France S Pacific Ocean
French Republic see France
French Somaliland see Djibouti
French Southern and Antarctic Lands 119 B7 Fr. Terres Australes et Antarctiques Françaises. French overseas territory S Indian Ocean
French Sudan see Mali
French Territory of the Afars and Issas see Djibouti
French Togoland see Togo
Fresnillo 28 D3 var. Fresnillo de González Echeverría. Zacatecas, C Mexico
Fresnillo de González Echeverría see Fresnillo
Fresno 25 C6 California, W USA
Frías 42 C3 Catamarca, N Argentina
Fribourg-en-Brisgau see Freiburg im Breisgau
Friedek-Mistek see Frýdek-Místek
Friedrichshafen 73 B7 Baden-Württemberg, S Germany
Friendly Islands see Tonga
Frisches Haff see Vistula Lagoon
Frobisher Bay 60 B3 inlet Baffin Island, Nunavut, NE Canada
Frobisher Bay see Iqaluit
Frohavet 62 B4 sound C Norway
Frome, Lake 127 B6 salt lake South Australia
Frontera 29 G4 Tabasco, SE Mexico
Frontignan 69 C6 Hérault, S France
Frostviken see Kvarnbergsvattnet
Frøya 62 A4 island W Norway
Frumentum see Formentera
Frunze see Bishkek
Frýdek-Místek 77 C5 Ger. Friedek-Mistek. Moravskoslezský Kraj, E Czechia (Czech Republic)
Fu-chien see Fujian
Fu-chou see Fuzhou
Fuengirola 70 D5 Andalucía, S Spain
Fuerte Olimpo 42 D2 var. Olimpo. Alto Paraguay, NE Paraguay
Fuerte, Río 26 C5 river C Mexico
Fuerteventura 48 B3 island Islas Canarias, Spain, NE Atlantic Ocean
Fuhkien see Fujian
Fu-hsin see Fuxin
Fuji 109 D6 var. Huzi. Shizuoka, Honshū, S Japan
Fujian 106 D6 var. Fu-chien, Fuhkien, Fukien, Min, Fujian Sheng. province SE China
Fujian Sheng see Fujian
Fuji, Mount/Fujiyama see Fuji-san
Fuji-san 109 C6 var. Fujiyama, Eng. Mount Fuji. mountain Honshū, SE Japan
Fukang 104 C2 Xinjiang Uygur Zizhiqu, W China
Fukien see Fujian
Fukui 109 C6 var. Hukui. Fukui, Honshū, SW Japan
Fukuoka 109 A7 var. Hukuoka, hist. Najima. Fukuoka, Kyūshū, SW Japan
Fukushima 108 D4 var. Hukusima. Fukushima, Honshū, C Japan
Fulda 73 B5 Hessen, C Germany
Funafuti Atoll 123 E3 atoll and capital (Tuvalu) C Tuvalu
Funchal 48 A2 Madeira, Portugal, NE Atlantic Ocean
Fundy, Bay of 17 F5 bay Canada/USA
Fünen see Fyn
Fünfkirchen see Pécs
Furnes see Veurne
Fürth 73 C5 Bayern, S Germany
Furukawa 108 D4 var. Hurukawa, Ōsaki. Miyagi, Honshū, C Japan
Fusan see Busan
Fushë Kosovë 79 D5 Serb. Kosovo Polje. C Kosovo
Fushun 106 D3 var. Fou-shan, Fu-shun. Liaoning, NE China
Fu-shun see Fushun
Fusin see Fuxin
Füssen 73 C7 Bayern, S Germany
Futog 78 D3 Vojvodina, NW Serbia
Futuna, Île 123 E4 island S Wallis and Futuna
Fuxin 106 D3 var. Fou-hsin, Fu-hsin, Fusin. Liaoning, NE China
Fuzhou 106 D6 var. Foochow, Fu-chou. province capital Fujian, SE China
Fyn 63 B8 Ger. Fünen. island C Denmark
Fyzabad see Faizābād

G

Gaafu Alifu Atoll see North Huvadhu Atoll
Gaalkacyo 51 E5 var. Galka'yo, It. Galcaio. Mudug, C Somalia
Gabela 56 B2 Cuanza Sul, W Angola
Gaberones see Gaborone
Gabès 49 E2 var. Qābis. E Tunisia
Gabès, Golfe de 49 F2 Ar. Khalīj Qābis. gulf E Tunisia
Gabon 55 B6 off. Gabonese Republic. country C Africa
Gabonese Republic see Gabon
Gaborone 56 C4 prev. Gaberones. country capital (Botswana) South East, SE Botswana
Gabrovo 82 D2 Gabrovo, N Bulgaria
Gadag 110 C1 Karnātaka, W India
Gades/Gadier/Gadir/Gadire see Cádiz
Gadsden 20 D2 Alabama, S USA
Gaeta 75 C5 Lazio, C Italy
Gaeta, Golfo di 75 C5 var. Gulf of Gaeta. gulf C Italy
Gaeta, Gulf of see Gaeta, Golfo di
Gäfle see Gävle
Gafsa 49 E2 var. Qafṣah. W Tunisia
Gagnoa 52 D5 C Ivory Coast
Gagra 95 E1 NW Georgia
Gaillac 69 C6 var. Gaillac-sur-Tarn. Tarn, S France
Gaillac-sur-Tarn see Gaillac
Gaillimh see Galway
Gaillimhe, Cuan na see Galway Bay
Gainesville 21 E3 Florida, SE USA
Gainesville 20 D2 Georgia, SE USA
Gainesville 27 G2 Texas, SW USA
Lake Gairdner 127 A6 salt lake South Australia
Gaizina Kalns see Gaiziņkalns
Gaiziņkalns 84 C3 var. Gaizina Kalns. mountain E Latvia
Galán, Cerro 42 B3 mountain NW Argentina
Galanta 77 C6 Hung. Galánta. Trnavský Kraj, W Slovakia
Galapagos Fracture Zone 131 E3 tectonic feature E Pacific Ocean
Galápagos Islands 131 F3 var. Islas de los Galápagos, Sp. Archipiélago de Colón, Eng. Galapagos Islands, Tortoise Islands. island group Ecuador, E Pacific Ocean
Galapagos Islands see Galápagos Islands
Galápagos, Islas de los see Galápagos Islands
Galapagos Rise 131 F3 undersea rise E Pacific Ocean
Galashiels 66 C4 SE Scotland, United Kingdom
Galați 86 D4 Ger. Galatz. Galați, E Romania
Galatz see Galați
Galcaio see Gaalkacyo
Galesburg 18 B3 Illinois, N USA
Galicia 70 B1 anc. Gallaecia. autonomous community NW Spain
Galicia Bank 58 B4 undersea bank E Atlantic Ocean
Galilee, Sea of see Kinneret, Yam
Galka'yo see Gaalkacyo
Galkynyş 100 D3 prev. Rus. Deynau, Dyanev, Turkm. Dänew. Lebap Welaýaty, NE Turkmenistan
Gallaecia see Galicia
Galle 110 D4 prev. Point de Galle. Southern Province, SW Sri Lanka
Gallego Rise 131 F3 undersea rise E Pacific Ocean
Gallegos see Río Gallegos
Gallia see France
Gallipoli 75 E6 Puglia, SE Italy
Gällivare 62 C3 Lapp. Váhtjer. Norrbotten, N Sweden
Gallup 26 C1 New Mexico, SW USA
Galtat-Zemmour 48 B3 C Western Sahara
Galveston 27 H4 Texas, SW USA
Galway 67 A5 Ir. Gaillimh. W Ireland
Galway Bay 67 A6 Ir. Cuan na Gaillimhe. bay W Ireland
Gámas see Kaamanen
Gambell 14 C2 Saint Lawrence Island, Alaska, USA
Gambia see Gambia, The
Gambia 52 C3 Fr. Gambie. river W Africa
Gambia, Republic of The see Gambia, The
Gambia, The 52 B3 off. Republic of The Gambia var. Gambia. country W Africa
Gambie see Gambia, The
Gambier, Îles 121 G4 island group E French Polynesia
Gamboma 55 B6 Plateaux, E Congo
Gamlakarleby see Kokkola
Gan 110 B5 Addu Atoll, C Maldives
Gan see Gansu, China
Gan see Jiangxi, China
Ganaane see Juba
Gäncä 95 G2 Rus. Gyandzha; prev. Kirovabad, Yelisavetpol. W Azerbaijan
Gand see Gent
Gandajika 55 D7 Kasai-Oriental, S Dem. Rep. Congo
Gander 17 G3 Newfoundland and Labrador, SE Canada
Gāndhīdhām 112 C4 Gujarāt, W India
Gandía 71 F3 prev. Gandia. Comunitat Valenciana, E Spain
Gandia see Gandía
Ganges 113 F3 Ben. Padma. river Bangladesh/India
Ganges Cone see Ganges Fan
Ganges Fan 118 D3 var. Ganges Cone. undersea fan N Bay of Bengal
Ganges, Mouths of the 113 G4 delta Bangladesh/India
Gangra see Çankırı
Gangtok 113 F3 state capital Sikkim, N India
Gansos, Lago dos see Goose Lake
Gansu 106 B4 var. Gan, Gansu Sheng, Kansu. province N China
Gansu Sheng see Gansu
Gantsevichi see Hantsavichy
Ganzhou 106 D6 Jiangxi, S China
Gao 53 E3 Gao, E Mali
Gaocheng see Litang
Gaoual 52 C4 N Guinea
Gaoxiong see Kaohsiung
Gap 69 D5 anc. Vapincum. Hautes-Alpes, SE France
Gaplaňgyr Platosy 100 C2 Rus. Plato Kaplangky. ridge Turkmenistan/Uzbekistan
Gar see Gar Xincun
Garabil Belentligi 100 D3 Rus. Vozvyshennost' Karabil'. mountain range S Turkmenistan
Garabogaz Aylagy 100 B2 Rus. Zaliv Kara-Bogaz-Gol. bay NW Turkmenistan
Garachiné 31 G5 Darién, SE Panama
Garagum 100 C3 var. Garagumy, Qara Qum, Eng. Black Sand Desert, Kara Kum; prev. Peski Karakumy. desert C Turkmenistan
Garagum Canal 100 D3 var. Kara Kum Canal, Rus. Karagumskiy Kanal, Karakumskiy Kanal. canal C Turkmenistan
Garagumy see Garagum
Gara Hitrino 82 D2 var. Gara Khitrino. Shumen, NE Bulgaria
Gara Khitrino see Gara Hitrino
Gárasavon see Kaaresuvanto
Garda, Lago di 74 C2 var. Benaco, Eng. Lake Garda, Ger. Gardasee. lake NE Italy
Garda, Lake see Garda, Lago di
Gardasee see Garda, Lago di
Garden City 23 E5 Kansas, C USA
Garden State, The see New Jersey
Gardēz 101 E4 prev. Gardīz. E Afghanistan
Gardīz see Gardēz
Gardner Island see Nikumaroro
Garegegasnjárga see Karigasniemi
Gargždai 84 B3 Klaipėda, W Lithuania
Garissa 51 D6 Coast, E Kenya
Garland 27 G2 Texas, SW USA
Garoe see Garoowe
Garonne 69 B5 anc. Garumna. river S France
Garoowe 51 E5 var. Garoe. Nugaal, N Somalia
Garoua 54 B4 var. Garua. Nord, N Cameroon
Garrygala see Magtymguly
Garry Lake 15 F3 lake Nunavut, N Canada
Garsen 51 D6 Coast, S Kenya
Garua see Garoua
Garumna see Garonne
Garwolin 76 D4 Mazowieckie, E Poland
Gar Xincun 104 A4 prev. Gar. Xizang Zizhiqu, W China
Gary 18 B3 Indiana, N USA
Garzón 36 B4 Huila, S Colombia
Gasan-Kuli see Esenguly
Gascogne 69 B6 Eng. Gascony. cultural region S France
Gascony see Gascogne
Gascoyne River 125 A5 river Western Australia
Gaspé 17 F3 Québec, SE Canada
Gaspé, Péninsule de 17 E4 var. Péninsule de la Gaspésie. peninsula Québec, SE Canada
Gaspésie, Péninsule de la see Gaspé, Péninsule de
Gastonia 21 E1 North Carolina, SE USA
Gastoúni 83 B6 Dytikí Elláda, S Greece
Gatchina 88 B4 Leningradskaya Oblast', NW Russia
Gatineau 16 D4 Québec, SE Canada
Gatooma see Kadoma
Gatún, Lake 31 F4 reservoir C Panama
Gauhāti see Guwāhāti
Gauja 84 D3 Ger. Aa. river Estonia/Latvia
Gaul/Gaule see France
Gauteng see Johannesburg, South Africa
Gāvbandī 98 D4 Hormozgān, S Iran
Gávdos 83 C8 island SE Greece
Gavere 65 B6 Oost-Vlaanderen, NW Belgium
Gävle 63 C6 var. Gäfle; prev. Gefle. Gävleborg, C Sweden
Gawler 127 B6 South Australia
Gaya 113 F3 Bihār, N India
Gaya see Kyjov
Gayndah 127 E5 Queensland, E Australia
Gaysin see Haisyn
Gaza 97 A6 Ar. Ghazzah, Heb. 'Azza. NE Gaza Strip
Gaz-Achak see Gazojak
Gazandzhyk/Gazanjyk see Bereket
Gaza Strip 97 A7 Ar. Qita Ghazzah. disputed region SW Asia
Gaziantep 94 D4 var. Gazi Antep; prev. Aintab, Antep. Gaziantep, S Turkey (Türkiye)
Gazi Antep see Gaziantep
Gazimağusa 80 D5 var. Famagusta, Gk. Ammóchostos. E Cyprus
Gazimağusa Körfezi 80 C5 var. Famagusta Bay, Gk. Kólpos Ammóchostos. bay E Cyprus
Gazli 100 D2 Buxoro Viloyati, C Uzbekistan
Gazojak 100 D2 Rus. Gaz-Achak. Lebap Welaýaty, NE Turkmenistan
Gbanga 52 D5 var. Gbarnga. N Liberia
Gbarnga see Gbanga
Gdańsk 76 C2 Fr. Dantzig, Ger. Danzig. Pomorskie, N Poland
Gdańsk, Gulf of 76 C2 var. Gulf of Danzig, Ger. Danziger Bucht, Pol. Zakota Gdańska, Rus. Gdan'skaya Bukhta. gulf N Poland
Gdan'skaya Bukhta see Gdańsk, Gulf of
Gdańska, Zakota see Gdańsk, Gulf of
Gdingen see Gdynia
Gdynia 76 C2 Ger. Gdingen. Pomorskie, N Poland
Gedaref 50 C4 var. Al Qaḍārif, El Gedaref. Gedaref, E Sudan
Gediz 94 B3 Kütahya, W Turkey (Türkiye)
Gediz Nehri 94 A3 river W Turkey (Türkiye)
Geel 65 C5 var. Gheel. Antwerpen, N Belgium
Geelong 127 C7 Victoria, SE Australia
Ge'e'mu see Golmud
Gefle see Gävle
Geilo 63 A5 Buskerud, S Norway
Gejiu 106 B6 var. Kochiu. Yunnan, S China
Gëkdepe see Gökdepe
Gela 75 C7 prev. Terranova di Sicilia. Sicilia, Italy, C Mediterranean Sea
Geldermalsen 64 C4 Gelderland, C Netherlands
Geleen 65 D6 Limburg, SE Netherlands
Gelib see Jilib
Gellinsor 51 E5 Mudug, C Somalia
Gembloux 65 C6 Namur, Belgium
Gemena 55 C5 Equateur, NW Dem. Rep. Congo
Gem of the Mountains see Idaho
Gemona del Friuli 74 D2 Friuli-Venezia Giulia, NE Italy
Gem State see Idaho
Genalē Wenz see Juba
Genck see Genk
General Alvear 42 B4 Mendoza, W Argentina
General Carrera, Lago see Buenos Aires, Lago
General Eugenio A. Garay 42 C1 var. Fortín General Eugenio Garay; prev. Yrendagüé. Nueva Asunción, NW Paraguay
General José F.Uriburu see Zárate
General Machado see Camacupa
General Santos 117 F3 off. General Santos City. Mindanao, S Philippines
General Santos City see General Santos
Gênes see Genova
Geneva see Genève
Geneva, Lake 73 A7 Fr. Lac de Genève, Lac Léman, le Léman, Ger. Genfer See. lake France/Switzerland
Genève 73 A7 Eng. Geneva, Ger. Genf, It. Ginevra. Genève, SW Switzerland
Genève, Lac de see Geneva, Lake
Genf see Genève
Genfer See see Geneva, Lake
Genichesk see Henichesk
Genk 65 D6 var. Genck. Limburg, NE Belgium
Gennep 64 D4 Limburg, SE Netherlands
Genoa see Genova
Genoa, Gulf of 74 A3 Eng. Gulf of Genoa. gulf NW Italy
Genoa, Gulf of see Genova, Golfo di
Genova 80 D1 Eng. Genoa; anc. Genua, Fr. Gênes. Liguria, NW Italy
Genovesa, Isla 38 B5 var. Tower Island. island Galápagos Islands, Ecuador, E Pacific Ocean
Gent 65 B5 Eng. Ghent, Fr. Gand. Oost-Vlaanderen, NW Belgium
Genua see Genova
Geok-Tepe see Gökdepe
George 56 C5 Western Cape, S South Africa
George 60 A4 river Newfoundland and Labrador/Québec, E Canada
George, Lake 21 E3 lake Florida, SE USA
Georgenburg see Jurbarkas
Georges Bank 13 D5 undersea bank W Atlantic Ocean
George Sound see Te Houhou
Georges River 126 D2 river New South Wales, E Australia
Georgetown 37 F2 country capital (Guyana) N Guyana
George Town 32 C2 Great Exuma Island, C The Bahamas
George Town 32 B3 var. Georgetown. dependent territory capital (Cayman Islands) Grand Cayman, SW Cayman Islands
George Town 116 B3 var. Penang, Pinang. Pinang, Peninsular Malaysia
Georgetown 21 F2 South Carolina, SE USA
Georgetown see George Town
George V Land 132 C4 physical region Antarctica
Georgia 95 F2 off. Georgia, Geor. Sakartvelo, Rus. Gruzinskaya SSR, Gruziya. country SW Asia
Georgia 20 D2 off. State of Georgia, also known as Empire State of the South, Peach State. state SE USA
Georgian Bay 18 D2 lake bay Ontario, S Canada
Georgia, Strait of 24 A1 strait British Columbia, W Canada
Georgi Dimitrov see Kostenets
Georgiu-Dezh see Liski
Gera 72 C4 Thüringen, E Germany
Geráki 83 B6 Pelopónnisos, S Greece
Geraldine 129 B6 Canterbury, South Island, New Zealand
Geraldton 125 A6 Western Australia
Geral, Serra 35 D5 mountain range S Brazil
Gerede 94 C2 Bolu, N Turkey (Türkiye)
Gereshk see Girishk
Gering 22 D3 Nebraska, C USA
German East Africa see Tanzania
Germanicopolis see Çankırı
Germanicum, Mare/German Ocean see North Sea
German Southwest Africa see Namibia
Germany 72 B4 off. Federal Republic of Germany, Bundesrepublik Deutschland, Ger. Deutschland. country N Europe
Germany, Federal Republic of see Germany
Geroliménas 83 B7 Pelopónnisos, S Greece
Gerona see Girona
Gerpinnes 65 C7 Hainaut, S Belgium
Gerunda see Girona
Gerze 94 D2 Sinop, N Turkey (Türkiye)
Gesoriacum see Boulogne-sur-Mer
Gessoriacum see Boulogne-sur-Mer
Getafe 70 D3 Madrid, C Spain
Gevaş 95 F3 Van, SE Turkey (Türkiye)
Gevgeli see Gevgelija
Gevgelija 79 E6 var. Đevđelija, Djevdjelija, Turk. Gevgeli. SE North Macedonia
Ghaba see Al Ghābah
Ghana 53 E5 off. Republic of Ghana. country W Africa
Ghanzi 56 C3 var. Khanzi. Ghanzi, W Botswana
Gharandal 97 B7 Al'Aqabah, SW Jordan
Gharbt, Jabal al see Liban, Jebel
Ghardaïa 48 D2 N Algeria
Gharvān see Gharyān
Gharyān 49 F2 var. Gharvān. NW Libya
Ghawdex see Gozo
Ghaznī 101 E4 var. Ghazni. Ghaznī, E Afghanistan
Ghazzah see Gaza
Gheel see Geel
Ghent see Gent
Gheorgheni 86 C4 prev. Gheorghieni, Sîn-Miclăuş, Ger. Niklasmarkt, Hung. Gyergyószentmiklós. Harghita, C Romania
Gheorghieni see Gheorgheni
Ghōrīān see Ghōriyān
Ghōriyān 100 D4 var. Ghōrīān, Ghūrīān. Herāt, W Afghanistan
Ghŭdara 101 F3 var. Gudara, Rus. Kudara. SE Tajikistan
Ghurdaqah see Al Ghurdaqah
Ghūrīān see Ghōriyān
Giamame see Jamaame
Giannitsá 82 B4 var. Yiannitsá. Kentrikí Makedonía, N Greece
Gibraltar 71 G4 UK Overseas Territory SW Europe
Gibraltar, Bay of 71 G5 bay Gibraltar/Spain Europe Mediterranean Sea Atlantic Ocean
Gibraltar, Détroit de/Gibraltar, Estrecho de see Gibraltar, Strait of
Gibraltar, Strait of 70 C5 Fr. Détroit de Gibraltar, Sp. Estrecho de Gibraltar. strait Atlantic Ocean/Mediterranean Sea
Gibson Desert 125 B5 desert Western Australia
Giedraičiai 85 C5 Utena, E Lithuania
Giessen 73 B5 Hessen, W Germany
Gifu 109 C6 var. Gihu. Gifu, Honshū, SW Japan
Giganta, Sierra de la 28 B3 mountain range NW Mexico
Gihu see Gifu
G'ijduvon 100 D2 Rus. Gizhduvon. Buxoro Viloyati, C Uzbekistan
Gijón 70 D1 var. Xixón. Asturias, NW Spain
Gila River 26 A2 river Arizona, SW USA
Gilbert Islands see Tungaru
Gilbert River 126 C3 river Queensland, NE Australia
Gilf Kebir Plateau see Haḍabat al Jilf al Kabīr
Gillette 22 D3 Wyoming, C USA
Gilolo see Halmahera, Pulau
Gilroy 25 B6 California, W USA
Gimie, Mount 33 F1 mountain C Saint Lucia
Gimma see Jīma
Ginevra see Genève
Gingin 125 A6 Western Australia
Giohar see Jawhar
Gipeswic see Ipswich
Girardot 36 B3 Cundinamarca, C Colombia
Giresun 95 E2 var. Kerasunt; anc. Cerasus, Pharnacia. Giresun, NE Turkey (Türkiye)

Girgenti *see* Agrigento
Girin *see* Jilin
Girishk *100 D5 var.* Gereshk. Helmand, SW Afghanistan
Girne *80 C5 Gk.* Kerýneia, Kyrenia. N Cyprus
Giron *see* Kiruna
Girona *71 G2 var.* Gerona; *anc.* Gerunda. Cataluña, NE Spain
Gisborne *128 E3* Gisborne, North Island, New Zealand
Gissar Range *101 E3 Rus.* Gissarskiy Khrebet. *mountain range* Tajikistan/Uzbekistan
Gissarskiy Khrebet *see* Gissar Range
Gitega *51 B7 prev.* Kitega. *country capital* (Burundi - political) W Burundi
Githio *see* Gýtheio
Giulianova *74 D4* Abruzzi, C Italy
Giumri *see* Gyumri
Giurgiu *86 C5* Giurgiu, S Romania
Giza *see* Al Jīzah
Gizeh *see* Al Jīzah
Gizhduvon *see* G'ijduvon
Giżycko *76 D2 Ger.* Lötzen. Warmińsko-Mazurskie, NE Poland
Gjakovë *79 D5 Serb.* Đakovica. W Kosovo
Gjilan *79 D5 Serb.* Gnjilane. E Kosovo
Gjinokastër *see* Gjirokastër
Gjirokastër *79 C7 var.* Gjirokastra; *prev.* Gjinokastër, *Gk.* Argyrokastron, *It.* Argirocastro. Gjirokastër, S Albania
Gjirokastra *see* Gjirokastër
Gjoa Haven *15 F3 var.* Uqsuqtuuq. King William Island, Nunavut, NW Canada
Gjøvik *63 B5* Oppland, S Norway
Glace Bay *17 G4* Cape Breton Island, Nova Scotia, SE Canada
Gladstone *126 E4* Queensland, E Australia
Gláma *63 B5 var.* Glommen. *river* S Norway
Glasgow *66 C4* S Scotland, United Kingdom
Glavinitsa *82 D1 prev.* Pravda, Dogrular. Silistra, NE Bulgaria
Glavn'a Morava *see* Velika Morava
Glazov *89 D5* Udmurtskaya Respublika, NW Russia
Gleiwitz *see* Gliwice
Glendale *26 B2* Arizona, SW USA
Glendive *22 D2* Montana, NW USA
Glens Falls *19 F3* New York, NE USA
Glevum *see* Gloucester
Glina *78 B3 var.* Banijska Palanka. Sisak-Moslavina, NE Croatia
Glittertind *63 A5 mountain* S Norway
Gliwice *77 C5 Ger.* Gleiwitz. Śląskie, S Poland
Globe *26 B2* Arizona, SW USA
Globino *see* Hlobyne
Glogau *see* Głogów
Głogów *76 B4 Ger.* Glogau, Glogow. Dolnośląskie, SW Poland
Glogow *see* Głogów
Glomma *see* Gláma
Glommen *see* Gláma
Gloucester *67 D6 hist.* Caer Glou, *Lat.* Glevum. C England, United Kingdom
Głowno *76 D4* Łódź, C Poland
Glubokoye *see* Hlybokaye
Glukhov *see* Hlukhiv
Gnesen *see* Gniezno
Gniezno *76 C3 Ger.* Gnesen. Weilkopolskie, C Poland
Gnjilane *see* Gjilan
Gobabis *56 B3* Omaheke, E Namibia
Gobi *104 D3 desert* China/Mongolia
Gobō *109 C6* Wakayama, Honshū, SW Japan
Godāvari *102 B3 var.* Godavari. *river* C India
Godavari *see* Godāvari
Godhavn *see* Qeqertarsuaq
Godhra *112 C4* Gujarāt, W India
Göding *see* Hodonín
Godoy Cruz *42 B4* Mendoza, W Argentina
Godthaab/Godthåb *see* Nuuk
Godwin Austen, Mount *see* K2
Goede Hoop, Kaap de *see* Good Hope, Cape of
Goeie Hoop, Kaap die *see* Good Hope, Cape of
Goeree *64 B4 island* SW Netherlands
Goes *65 B5* Zeeland, SW Netherlands
Goettingen *see* Göttingen
Gogebic Range *18 B1 hill range* Michigan/Wisconsin, N USA
Goiânia *41 E3 prev.* Goyania. *state capital* Goiás, C Brazil
Goiás *41 E3 off.* Estado de Goiás; *prev.* Goiaz, Goyaz. *state/region* C Brazil
Goiás, Estado de *see* Goiás
Goiaz *see* Goiás
Goidhoo Atoll *see* Horsburgh Atoll
Gojōme *108 D4* Akita, Honshū, NW Japan
Gökçeada *82 D4 var.* Imroz Adasī, *Gk.* Imbros. *island* NW Turkey (Türkiye)
Gökdepe *100 C3 Rus.* Gëkdepe, Geok-Tepe. Ahal Welaýaty, C Turkmenistan
Göksun *94 D4* Kahramanmaraş, C Turkey (Türkiye)
Gol *63 A5* Buskerud, S Norway
Golan Heights *97 B5 Ar.* Al Jawlān, *Heb.* HaGolan. *mountain range* SW Syria
Golaya Pristan *see* Hola Prystan
Gołdap *76 E2 Ger.* Goldap. Warmińsko-Mazurskie, NE Poland
Gold Coast *127 E5 cultural region* Queensland, E Australia
Golden Bay *128 C4 var.* Mohua. *bay* South Island, New Zealand
Golden State, The *see* California
Goldingen *see* Kuldīga
Goldsboro *21 F1* North Carolina, SE USA
Goleniów *76 B3 Ger.* Gollnow. Zachodnio-pomorskie, NW Poland
Gollnow *see* Goleniów
Golmo *see* Golmud
Golmud *104 D4 var.* Ge'e'mu, Golmo, *Chin.* Ko-erh-mu. Qinghai, C China
Golovanevsk *see* Holovanivsk
Golub-Dobrzyń *76 C3* Kujawski-pomorskie, C Poland
Goma *55 E6* Nord-Kivu, NE Dem. Rep. Congo
Gombi *53 H4* Adamawa, E Nigeria
Gombroon *see* Bandar-e 'Abbās
Gomel' *see* Homyel'
Gomera *48 A3 island* Islas Canarias, Spain, NE Atlantic Ocean
Gómez Palacio *28 D3* Durango, C Mexico
Gonaïves *32 D3 var.* Les Gonaïves. N Haiti
Gonâve, Île de la *32 D3 island* C Haiti
Gondar *see* Gonder
Gonder *50 C4 var.* Gondar. Āmara, NW Ethiopia
Gondia *113 E4* Mahārāshtra, C India
Gonggar *104 C5 var.* Gyixong. Xizang Zizhiqu, W China
Gongola *53 G4 river* E Nigeria
Gongtang *see* Damxung
Gonni/Gónnos *see* Gónnoi
Gónnoi *82 B4 var.* Gonni, Gónnos; *prev.* Derelí. Thessalía, C Greece
Good Hope, Cape of *56 B5 Afr.* Kaap de Goede Hoop, Kaap die Goeie Hoop. *headland* SW South Africa
Goodland *22 D4* Kansas, C USA
Goondiwindi *127 D5* Queensland, E Australia
Goor *64 E3* Overijssel, E Netherlands
Goose Green *43 D7 var.* Prado del Ganso. East Falkland, Falkland Islands
Goose Lake *24 B4 var.* Lago dos Gansos. *lake* California/Oregon, W USA
Gopher State *see* Minnesota
Göppingen *73 B6* Baden-Württemberg, SW Germany
Góra Kalwaria *92 D4* Mazowieckie, C Poland
Gorakhpur *113 E3* Uttar Pradesh, N India
Gorany *see* Harany
Goražde *78 C4* Federacija Bosna I Hercegovina, SE Bosnia and Herzegovina
Gorbovichi *see* Harbavichy
Goré *54 C4* Logone-Oriental, S Chad
Gorē *51 C5* Oromīya, C Ethiopia
Gore *129 B7* Southland, South Island, New Zealand
Gorgān *98 D2 var.* Astarabad, Astrabad, Gurgan, *prev.* Asterābād; *anc.* Hyrcania. Golestān, N Iran
Gori *95 F2* C Georgia
Gorinchem *64 C4 var.* Gorkum. Zuid-Holland, C Netherlands
Goris *95 G3* SE Armenia
Gorki *see* Horki
Gor'kiy *see* Nizhniy Novgorod
Gorkum *see* Gorinchem
Görlitz *72 D4* Sachsen, E Germany
Görlitz *see* Zgorzelec
Gorlovka *see* Horlivka
Gorna Dzhumaya *see* Blagoevgrad
Gornja Mužlja *see* Mužlja
Gornji Milanovac *78 C4* Serbia, C Serbia
Gorodets *see* Haradzyets
Gorodishche *see* Horodyshche
Gorodnya *see* Horodnia
Gorodok *see* Haradok
Gorodok/Gorodok Yagellonski *see* Horodok
Gorontalo *117 E4* Sulawesi, C Indonesia
Gorontalo, Teluk *see* Tomini, Gulf of
Gorssel *64 D3* Gelderland, E Netherlands
Goryn *see* Horyn'
Gorzów Wielkopolski *76 B3 Ger.* Landsberg, Landsberg an der Warthe. Lubuskie, W Poland
Gosford *127 D6* New South Wales, SE Australia
Goshogawara *108 D3 var.* Gosyogawara. Aomori, Honshū, C Japan
Gospić *78 A3* Lika-Senj, C Croatia
Gostivar *79 D6* W Macedonia
Gosyogawara *see* Goshogawara
Göteborg *63 B7 Eng.* Gothenburg. Västra Götaland, S Sweden
Gotel Mountains *53 G5 mountain range* E Nigeria
Gotha *72 C4* Thüringen, C Germany
Gothenburg *see* Göteborg
Gotland *63 C7 island* SE Sweden
Goto-retto *109 A7 island group* SW Japan
Gotska Sandön *84 B1 island* SE Sweden
Gōtsu *109 B6 var.* Gôtu. Shimane, Honshū, SW Japan
Göttingen *72 B4 var.* Goettingen. Niedersachsen, C Germany
Gottschee *see* Kočevje
Gottwaldov *see* Zlín
Gôtu *see* Gōtsu
Gouda *64 C4* Zuid-Holland, C Netherlands
Gough Fracture Zone *45 C6 tectonic feature* S Atlantic Ocean
Gough Island *47 B8 island* Tristan da Cunha, S Atlantic Ocean
Gouin, Réservoir *16 D4 reservoir* Québec, SE Canada
Goulburn *127 D6* New South Wales, SE Australia
Goundam *53 E3* Tombouctou, NW Mali
Gouré *53 G3* Zinder, SE Niger
Goverla, Gora *see* Hoverla, Hora
Governador Valadares *41 F4* Minas Gerais, SE Brazil
Govi Altayn Nuruu *105 E3 mountain range* S Mongolia
Goya *42 D3* Corrientes, NE Argentina
Goyania *see* Goiânia
Goyaz *see* Goiás
Goz Beïda *54 C3* Ouaddaï, SE Chad
Gozo *75 C8 var.* Ghawdex. *island* N Malta
Gqeberha *56 C5 prev.* Port Elizabeth. Eastern Cape, S South Africa
Graciosa *70 A5 var.* Ilha Graciosa. *island* Azores, Portugal, NE Atlantic Ocean
Graciosa, Ilha *see* Graciosa
Gradačac *78 C3* Federacija Bosna I Hercegovina, N Bosnia and Herzegovina
Gradaús, Serra dos *41 E3 mountain range* C Brazil
Gradiška *see* Bosanska Gradiška
Grafton *127 E5* New South Wales, SE Australia
Grafton *23 E1* North Dakota, N USA
Graham Land *132 A2 physical region* Antarctica
Grajewo *76 E3* Podlaskie, NE Poland
Grampian Mountains *66 C3 mountain range* C Scotland, United Kingdom
Gran *see* Esztergom, Hungary
Granada *30 D3* Granada, SW Nicaragua
Granada *70 D5* Andalucía, S Spain
Gran Canaria *48 A3 var.* Grand Canary. *island* Islas Canarias, Spain, NE Atlantic Ocean
Gran Chaco *42 D2 var.* Chaco. *lowland plain* South America
Grand Bahama Island *32 B1 island* N The Bahamas
Grand Banks of Newfoundland *12 E4 undersea basin* NW Atlantic Ocean
Grand Bassa *see* Buchanan
Grand Canary *see* Gran Canaria
Grand Canyon *26 A1 canyon* Arizona, SW USA
Grand Canyon State *see* Arizona
Grand Cayman *32 B3 island* SW Cayman Islands
Grand Duchy of Luxembourg *see* Luxembourg
Grande, Bahía *43 B7 bay* S Argentina
Grande-Comore *see* Ngazidja
Grande de Chiloé, Isla *see* Chiloé, Isla de
Grande Prairie *15 E4* Alberta, W Canada
Grand Erg Occidental *48 D3 desert* W Algeria
Grand Erg Oriental *49 E3 desert* Algeria/Tunisia
Rio Grande *29 E2 var.* Río Bravo, *Sp.* Río Bravo del Norte, Bravo del Norte. *river* Mexico/USA
Grande Terre *33 G3 island* E West Indies
Grand Falls *17 G3* Newfoundland, Newfoundland and Labrador, SE Canada
Grand Forks *23 E1* North Dakota, N USA
Grandichi *see* Hrandzichy
Grand Island *23 E4* Nebraska, C USA
Grand Junction *22 C4* Colorado, C USA
Grand Paradis *see* Gran Paradiso
Grand Rapids *18 C3* Michigan, N USA
Grand Rapids *23 F1* Minnesota, N USA
Grand-Saint-Bernard, Col du *see* Great Saint Bernard Pass
Grand-Santi *37 G3* W French Guiana
Granite State *see* New Hampshire
Gran Lago *see* Nicaragua, Lago de
Gran Malvina *see* West Falkland
Gran Paradiso *74 A2 Fr.* Grand Paradis. *mountain* NW Italy
Gran San Bernardo, Passo di *see* Great Saint Bernard Pass
Gran Santiago *see* Santiago
Grants *26 C2* New Mexico, SW USA
Grants Pass *24 B4* Oregon, NW USA
Granville *68 B3* Manche, N France
Gratianopolis *see* Grenoble
Gratz *see* Graz
Graudenz *see* Grudziądz
Graulhet *69 C6* Tarn, S France
Grave *64 D4* Noord-Brabant, SE Netherlands
Grayling *14 C2* Alaska, USA
Graz *73 E7 prev.* Gratz. Steiermark, SE Austria
Great Abaco *32 C1 var.* Abaco Island. *island* N The Bahamas
Great Alfold *see* Great Hungarian Plain
Great Ararat *see* Büyük Ağrı Dağı
Great Australian Bight *125 D7 bight* S Australia
Great Barrier Island *128 D2 island* N New Zealand
Great Barrier Reef *126 D2 reef* Queensland, NE Australia
Great Basin *25 C5 basin* W USA
Great Bear Lake *15 E3 Fr.* Grand Lac de l'Ours. *lake* Northwest Territories, NW Canada
Great Belt *63 B8 var.* Store Bælt, *Eng.* Great Belt, Storebelt. *channel* Baltic Sea/Kattegat
Great Belt *see* Storebælt
Great Bend *23 E5* Kansas, C USA
Great Britain *see* Britain
Great Dividing Range *126 D4 mountain range* NE Australia
Greater Antilles *32 D3 island group* West Indies
Greater Caucasus *95 G2 mountain range* Azerbaijan/Georgia/Russia Asia/Europe
Greater Sunda Islands *102 D5 var.* Sunda Islands. *island group* Indonesia
Great Exhibition Bay *128 C1 inlet* North Island, New Zealand
Great Exuma Island *32 C2 island* C The Bahamas
Great Falls *22 B1* Montana, NW USA
Great Grimsby *see* Grimsby
Great Hungarian Plain *77 C7 var.* Great Alfold, Plain of Hungary, *Hung.* Alföld. *plain* SE Europe
Great Inagua *32 D2 var.* Inagua Islands. *island* S The Bahamas
Great Indian Desert *see* Thar Desert
Great Khingan Range *see* Da Hinggan Ling
Great Lake *see* Tônlé Sap
Great Lakes *13 C5 lakes* Ontario, Canada/USA
Great Lakes State *see* Michigan
Great Meteor Seamount *see* Great Meteor Tablemount
Great Meteor Tablemount *44 B3 var.* Great Meteor Seamount. *seamount* E Atlantic Ocean
Great Nicobar *111 G3 island* Nicobar Islands, India, NE Indian Ocean
Great Plain of China *103 E2 plain* E China
Great Plains *23 E3 var.* High Plains. *plains* Canada/USA
Great Rift Valley *51 C5 var.* Rift Valley. *depression* Asia/Africa
Great Ruaha *51 C7 river* S Tanzania
Great Saint Bernard Pass *74 A1 Fr.* Col du Grand-Saint-Bernard, *It.* Passo del Gran San Bernardo. *pass* Italy/Switzerland
Great Salt Desert *see* Kavīr, Dasht-e
Great Salt Lake *22 A3 salt lake* Utah, W USA
Great Salt Lake Desert *22 A4 plain* Utah, W USA
Great Sand Sea *49 H3 desert* Egypt/Libya
Great Sandy Desert *124 C4 desert* Western Australia
Great Sandy Desert *see* Ar Rub 'al Khālī
Great Sandy Island *see* Fraser Island
Great Slave Lake *15 E4 Fr.* Grand Lac des Esclaves. *lake* Northwest Territories, NW Canada
Great Socialist People's Libyan Arab Jamahiriya *see* Libya
Great Sound *20 A5 sound* Bermuda, NW Atlantic Ocean
Great Victoria Desert *125 C5 desert* South Australia/Western Australia
Great Wall of China *106 C4 ancient monument* N China Asia
Great Yarmouth *67 E6 var.* Yarmouth. E England, United Kingdom
Grebenka *see* Hrebinka
Gredos, Sierra de *70 D3 mountain range* W Spain
Greece *83 A5 off.* Hellenic Republic, *Gk.* Ellinikí Dimokratía, Elláda, Ellás; *anc.* Hellas. *country* SE Europe
Greeley *22 D4* Colorado, C USA
Green Bay *18 B2* Wisconsin, N USA
Green Bay *18 B2 lake bay* Michigan/Wisconsin, N USA
Greeneville *21 E1* Tennessee, S USA
Greenland *60 D3 Dan.* Grønland, *Inuit* Kalaallit Nunaat. *Danish self-governing territory* NE North America
Greenland Sea *61 F2 sea* Arctic Ocean
Green Mountains *19 G2 mountain range* Vermont, NE USA
Green Mountain State *see* Vermont
Greenock *66 C4* W Scotland, United Kingdom
Green River *22 B3* Wyoming, C USA
Green River *18 C5 river* Kentucky, C USA
Green River *22 B4 river* Utah, W USA
Greensboro *21 F1* North Carolina, SE USA
Greenville *20 B2* Mississippi, S USA
Greenville *21 F1* North Carolina, SE USA
Greenville *21 E1* South Carolina, SE USA
Greenville *27 G2* Texas, SW USA
Greenwich *67 B8* United Kingdom
Greenwood *20 B2* Mississippi, S USA
Greenwood *21 E2* South Carolina, SE USA
Gregory Range *126 C3 mountain range* Queensland, E Australia
Greifenberg/Greifenberg in Pommern *see* Gryfice
Greifswald *72 D2* Mecklenburg-Vorpommern, NE Germany
Grenada *20 C2* Mississippi, S USA
Grenada *33 G5 country* SE West Indies
Grenadines, The *33 H4 island group* Grenada/St Vincent and the Grenadines
Grenoble *69 D5 anc.* Cularo, Gratianopolis. Isère, E France
Gresham *24 B3* Oregon, NW USA
Grevená *82 B4* Dytikí Makedonía, N Greece
Grevenmacher *65 E8* Grevenmacher, E Luxembourg
Greymouth *129 B5* West Coast, South Island, New Zealand
Grey Range *127 C5 mountain range* New South Wales/Queensland, E Australia
Greytown *see* San Juan del Norte
Griffin *20 D2* Georgia, SE USA
Grimari *54 C4* Ouaka, C Central African Republic
Grimsby *67 E5 prev.* Great Grimsby. E England, United Kingdom
Grobin *see* Grobiņa
Grobiņa *84 B3 Ger.* Grobin. Liepāja, W Latvia
Gródek Jagielloński *see* Horodok
Grodno *see* Hrodna
Grodzisk Wielkopolski *76 B3* Wielkopolskie, C Poland
Groesbeek *64 D4* Gelderland, SE Netherlands
Grójec *76 D4* Mazowieckie, C Poland
Groningen *64 E1* Groningen, NE Netherlands
Grønland *see* Greenland
Groote Eylandt *126 B2 island* Northern Territory, N Australia
Grootfontein *56 B3* Otjozondjupa, N Namibia
Groot Karasberge *56 B4 mountain range* S Namibia
Gros Islet *33 F1* N Saint Lucia
Grossa, Isola *see* Dugi Otok
Grossbetschkerek *see* Zrenjanin
Grosse Morava *see* Velika Morava
Grosser Sund *see* Suur Väin
Grosseto *74 B4* Toscana, C Italy
Grossglockner *73 C7 mountain* W Austria
Grosskanizsa *see* Nagykanizsa
Gross-Karol *see* Carei
Grosskikinda *see* Kikinda
Grossmichel *see* Michalovce
Gross-Schlatten *see* Abrud
Grosswardein *see* Oradea
Groznyy *89 B8* Chechenskaya Respublika, SW Russia
Grudovo *see* Sredets
Grudziądz *76 C3 Ger.* Graudenz. Kujawsko-pomorskie, C Poland
Grums *63 B6* Värmland, C Sweden
Grünberg/Grünberg in Schlesien *see* Zielona Góra
Grüneberg *see* Zielona Góra
Gruzinskaya SSR/Gruziya *see* Georgia
Gryazi *89 B6* Lipetskaya Oblast', W Russia
Gryfice *76 B2 Ger.* Greifenberg, Greifenberg in Pommern. Zachodnio-pomorskie, NW Poland
Guabito *31 E4* Bocas del Toro, NW Panama
Guadalajara *28 D4* Jalisco, C Mexico
Guadalajara *71 E3 Ar.* Wad Al-Hajarah; *anc.* Arriaca. Castilla-La Mancha, C Spain
Guadalcanal *122 C3 island* C Solomon Islands
Guadalquivir *70 D4 river* W Spain
Guadalupe *28 D3* Zacatecas, C Mexico
Guadalupe Peak *26 D3 mountain* Texas, SW USA
Guadalupe River *27 G4 river* SW USA
Guadarrama, Sierra de *71 E2 mountain range* C Spain
Guadeloupe *33 H3 French overseas department* E West Indies
Guadiana *70 C4 river* Portugal/Spain
Guadix *71 E4* Andalucía, S Spain
Guaimaca *30 C2* Francisco Morazán, C Honduras
Guajira, Península de la *36 B1 peninsula* N Colombia
Gualaco *30 D2* Olancho, C Honduras
Gualán *30 B2* Zacapa, C Guatemala
Gualdicciolo *74 D1* NW San Marino
Gualeguaychú *42 D4* Entre Ríos, E Argentina
Guam *122 B1 US unincorporated territory* W Pacific Ocean
Guamúchil *28 C3* Sinaloa, C Mexico
Guanabacoa *32 B2* La Habana, W Cuba
Guanajuato *29 E4* Guanajuato, C Mexico
Guanare *36 C2* Portuguesa, N Venezuela
Guanare, Río *36 D2 river* W Venezuela
Guangdong *106 C6 var.* Guangdong Sheng, Kuang-tung, Kwangtung, Yue. *province* S China
Guangdong Sheng *see* Guangdong
Guangju *see* Gwangju
Guangxi *see* Guangxi Zhuangzu Zizhiqu
Guangxi Zhuangzu Zizhiqu *106 C6 var.* Guangxi, Gui, Kuang-hsi, Kwangsi, *Eng.* Kwangsi Chuang Autonomous Region. *autonomous region* S China
Guangyuan *106 B5 var.* Kuang-yuan, Kwangyuan. Sichuan, C China
Guangzhou *106 C6 var.* Kuang-chou, Kwangchow, *Eng.* Canton. *province capital* Guangdong, S China
Guantánamo *32 D3* Guantánamo, SE Cuba
Guantánamo, Bahía de *32 D3 Eng.* Guantanamo Bay. *US military base* SE Cuba
Guantanamo Bay *see* Guantánamo, Bahía de
Guaporé, Rio *40 D3 var.* Río Iténez. *river* Bolivia/Brazil
Guarda *70 C3* Guarda, N Portugal
Guarumal *31 F5* Veraguas, S Panama
Guasave *28 C3* Sinaloa, C Mexico
Guatemala *30 A2 off.* Republic of Guatemala. *country* Central America
Guatemala Basin *13 B7 undersea basin* E Pacific Ocean
Guatemala City *see* Ciudad de Guatemala
Guatemala, Republic of *see* Guatemala
Guaviare *34 B2 off.* Comisaría Guaviare. *province* S Colombia
Guaviare, Comisaría *see* Guaviare
Guaviare, Río *36 D3 river* E Colombia
Guayanas, Macizo de las *see* Guiana Highlands
Guayaquil *38 A2 var.* Santiago de Guayaquil. Guayas, SW Ecuador
Guayaquil, Golfo de *38 A2 var.* Gulf of Guayaquil. *gulf* SW Ecuador
Guayaquil, Gulf of *see* Guayaquil, Golfo de
Guaymas *28 B2* Sonora, NW Mexico
Gubadag *100 C2 Turkm.* Tel'man; *prev.* Tel'mansk. Daşoguz Welaýaty, N Turkmenistan
Guben *72 D4 var.* Wilhelm-Pieck-Stadt. Brandenburg, E Germany
Gudara *see* Ghŭdara
Gudauta *95 E1* NW Georgia
Guéret *68 C4* Creuse, C France
Guernsey *67 D8 British Crown Dependency* Channel Islands, NW Europe
Guerrero Negro *28 A2* Baja California Sur, NW Mexico
Gui *see* Guangxi Zhuangzu Zizhiqu
Guiana *see* French Guiana
Guiana Highlands *40 D1 var.* Macizo de las Guayanas. *mountain range* N South America
Guiba *see* Juba
Guidder *see* Guider
Guider *54 B4 var.* Guidder. Nord, N Cameroon
Guidimouni *53 G3* Zinder, S Niger
Guildford *67 D7* SE England, United Kingdom
Guilin *106 C6 var.* Kuei-lin, Kweilin. Guangxi Zhuangzu Zizhiqu, S China
Guimarães *70 B2 var.* Guimaráes. Braga, N Portugal
Guimaráes *see* Guimarães
Guinea *52 C4 off.* Republic of Guinea, *var.* Guinée; *prev.* French Guinea, People's Revolutionary Republic of Guinea. *country* W Africa
Guinea Basin *47 A5 undersea basin* E Atlantic Ocean
Guinea-Bissau *52 B4 off.* Republic of Guinea-Bissau, *Fr.* Guinée-Bissau, *Port.* Guiné-Bissau; *prev.* Portuguese Guinea. *country* W Africa
Guinea-Bissau, Republic of *see* Guinea-Bissau
Guinea, Gulf of *46 B4 Fr.* Golfe de Guinée. *gulf* E Atlantic Ocean
Guinea, People's Revolutionary Republic of *see* Guinea
Guinea, Republic of *see* Guinea
Guiné-Bissau *see* Guinea-Bissau
Guinée *see* Guinea
Guinée-Bissau *see* Guinea-Bissau
Guinée, Golfe de *see* Guinea, Gulf of
Güiria *37 E1* Sucre, NE Venezuela
Guiyang *106 B6 var.* Kuei-Yang, Kuei-yang, Kueyang, Kweiyang; *prev.* Kweichu. *province capital* Guizhou, S China
Guizhou *106 B6* Guangdong, SE China
Gujarāt *112 C4 var.* Gujerat. *cultural region* W India
Gujerat *see* Gujarāt
Gujranwala *112 D2* Punjab, NE Pakistan
Gujrat *112 D2* Punjab, E Pakistan
Gulbarga *see* Kalaburagi
Gulbene *84 D3 Ger.* Alt-Schwanenburg. Gulbene, NE Latvia
Gulf of Liaotung *see* Liaodong Wan
Gulfport *20 C3* Mississippi, S USA
Gulf, The *see* Persian Gulf
Gulistan *see* Guliston
Guliston *101 E2 Rus.* Gulistan. Sirdaryo Viloyati, E Uzbekistan
Gulja *see* Yining
Gulkana *14 D3* Alaska, USA
Gulu *51 B6* N Uganda
Gulyantsi *82 C1* Pleven, N Bulgaria
Guma *see* Pishan
Gumbinnen *see* Gusev
Gumpolds *see* Humpolec
Gümülcine/Gümüljina *see* Komotiní
Gümüşane *see* Gümüşhane
Gümüşhane *95 E3 var.* Gümüşane, Gumushkhane. Gümüşhane, NE Turkey (Türkiye)
Gumushkhane *see* Gümüşhane
Güney Doğu Toroslar *95 E4 mountain range* SE Turkey (Türkiye)
Gunnbjørn Fjeld *60 D4 var.* Gunnbjörns Bjerge. *mountain* C Greenland
Gunnbjörns Bjerge *see* Gunnbjørn Fjeld
Gunnedah *127 D6* New South Wales, SE Australia
Gunnison *22 C5* Colorado, C USA
Gurbansoltan Eje *100 C2 prev.* Ýylanly, *Rus.* Il'yaly. Daşoguz Welaýaty, N Turkmenistan
Gurbantünggüt Shamo *104 B2 desert* W China
Gurgan *see* Gorgān
Guri, Embalse de *37 E2 reservoir* E Venezuela
Gurkfeld *see* Krško
Gurktaler Alpen *73 D7 mountain range* S Austria
Gürün *94 D3* Sivas, C Turkey (Türkiye)
Gur'yev *see* Atyraū
Gusau *53 G4* Zamfara, NW Nigeria
Gusev *84 B4 Ger.* Gumbinnen. Kaliningradskaya Oblast', W Russia
Gustavus *14 D4* Alaska, USA
Güstrow *72 C3* Mecklenburg-Vorpommern, NE Germany
Guta/Gúta *see* Kolárovo
Gütersloh *72 B4* Nordrhein-Westfalen, W Germany
Gutta *see* Kolárovo
Guttstadt *see* Dobre Miasto
Guwāhāti *113 G3 prev.* Gauhāti. Assam, NE India
Guyana *37 F3 off.* Co-operative Republic of Guyana; *prev.* British Guiana. *country* N South America
Guyana, Co-operative Republic of *see* Guyana
Guyane *see* French Guiana
Guymon *27 E1* Oklahoma, C USA
Güzelyurt Körfezi *80 C5 Gk.* Kólpos Mórfu, Morphou. W Cyprus
Gvardeysk *84 A4 Ger.* Tapaiu. Kaliningradskaya Oblast', W Russia
Gwadar *112 A3 var.* Gwadur. Baluchistan, SW Pakistan
Gwadur *see* Gwādar
Gwalior *112 D3* Madhya Pradesh, C India
Gwanda *56 D3* Matabeleland South, SW Zimbabwe
Gwangju *107 E4 off.* Gwangju Gwang-yeoksi, *prev.* Kwangju, *var.* Guangju, Kwangchu, *Jap.* Kōshū. SW South Korea
Gwangju Gwang-yeoksi *see* Gwangju
Gwy *see* Wye
Gyandzha *see* Gäncä
Gyangzê *104 C5* Xizang Zizhiqu, W China
Gyaring Co *104 C5 lake* W China
Gyêgu *see* Yushu

Gyergyószentmiklós see Gheorgheni
Gyixong see Gonggar
Gympie 127 E5 Queensland, E Australia
Gyomaendrőd 77 D7 Békés, SE Hungary
Gyöngyös 77 D6 Heves, NE Hungary
Győr 77 C6 Ger. Raab, Lat. Arrabona. Győr-Moson-Sopron, NW Hungary
Gýtheio 83 B6 var. Githio; prev. Yíthion. Pelopónnisos, S Greece
Gyulafehérvár see Alba Iulia
Gyumri 95 F2 var. Giumri, Rus. Kumayri; prev. Aleksandropol', Leninakan. W Armenia
Gyzyrlabat see Serdar

H

Haabai see Ha'apai Group
Haacht 65 C6 Vlaams Brabant, C Belgium
Haaksbergen 64 E3 Overijssel, E Netherlands
Ha'apai Group 123 F4 var. Haabai. island group C Tonga
Haapsalu 84 D2 Ger. Hapsal. Läänemaa, W Estonia
Ha'Arava see 'Arabah, Wādī al
Haarlem 64 C3 prev. Harlem. Noord-Holland, W Netherlands
Haast 129 B6 West Coast, South Island, New Zealand
Hachijo-jima 109 D6 island Izu-shotō, SE Japan
Hachinohe 108 D3 Aomori, Honshū, C Japan
Hacıqabul 95 H3 prev. Qazimämmäd, Rus. Kazi Magomed. SE Azerbaijan
Haḍabat al Jilf al Kabīr 50 A2 var. Gilf Kebir Plateau. plateau SW Egypt
Hadama see Nazrēt
Hadejia 53 G4 Jigawa, N Nigeria
Hadejia 53 G3 river N Nigeria
Hadera 97 A6 var. Khadera; prev. Ḩadera. Haifa, C Israel
Ḩadera see Hadera
Hadhdhunmathi Atoll 110 A5 atoll S Maldives
Hadhramaut see Ḩaḑramawt
Ha Đông 114 D3 var. Hadong. Ha Tây, N Vietnam
Hadong see Ha Đông
Ḩaḑramawt 99 C6 Eng. Hadhramaut. mountain range S Yemen
Hadrianopolis see Edirne
Haerbin/Haerhpin/Ha-erh-pin see Harbin
Hafnia see Denmark
Hafnia see København
Hafren see Severn
Hafun, Ras see Xaafuun, Raas
Hagåtña 122 B1, var. Agaña. dependent territory capital (Guam) NW Guam
Hagerstown 19 E4 Maryland, NE USA
Ha Giang 114 D3 Ha Giang, N Vietnam
Hagios Evstrátios see Ágios Efstrátios
HaGolan see Golan Heights
Hagondange 68 D3 Moselle, NE France
Haguenau 68 E3 Bas-Rhin, NE France
Haibowan see Wuhai
Haicheng 106 D3 Liaoning, NE China
Haida Gwaii 14 C5 prev. Queen Charlotte Islands, Fr. Îles de la Reine-Charlotte. island group British Columbia, SW Canada
Haidarabad see Hyderabad
Haifa see Hefa
Haifa, Bay of see Mifrats Hefa
Haifong see Hai Phong
Haikou 106 C7 var. Hai-k'ou, Hoihow, Fr. Hoï-Hao. province capital Hainan, S China
Hai-k'ou see Haikou
Ḩā'il 98 B4 Ḩā'il, NW Saudi Arabia
Hailuoto 62 D4 Swe. Karlö. island W Finland
Hainan 106 B7 var. Hainan Sheng, Qiong. province S China
Hainan Dao 106 C7 island S China
Hainan Sheng see Hainan
Hainasch see Ainaži
Haines 14 D4 Alaska, USA
Hainichen 72 D4 Sachsen, E Germany
Hai Phong 114 D3 var. Haifong, Haiphong. N Vietnam
Haiphong see Hai Phong
Haisyn 86 D3 prev. Haysyn, Rus. Gaysin. Vinnyts'ka Oblast', C Ukraine
Haiti 32 D3 off. Republic of Haiti. country C West Indies
Haiti, Republic of see Haiti
Haiya 50 C3 Red Sea, NE Sudan
Hajdúhadház 77 D6 Hajdú-Bihar, E Hungary
Hajîn 96 E3 var. Abū Ḩardān, Hajîne. Dayr az Zawr, E Syria
Hajîne see Hajîn
Hajnówka 76 E3 Ger. Hermhausen. Podlaskie, NE Poland
Hakodate 108 D3 Hokkaidō, NE Japan
Hal see Halle
Ḩalab 96 B2 Eng. Aleppo, Fr. Alep; anc. Beroea. Ḩalab, NW Syria
Hala'ib Triangle 50 C3 region Egypt/Sudan
Ḩalāniyāt, Juzur al 99 D6 var. Jazā'ir Bin Ghalfān, Eng. Kuria Muria Islands. island group S Oman
Halberstadt 72 C4 Sachsen-Anhalt, C Germany
Halden 63 B6 prev. Fredrikshald. Østfold, S Norway
Halfmoon Bay 129 A8 var. Oban. Stewart Island, Southland, New Zealand
Haliacmon see Aliákmonas
Halifax 17 F4 province capital Nova Scotia, SE Canada
Halkida see Chalkída
Halle 65 B6 Fr. Hal. Vlaams Brabant, C Belgium
Halle 72 C4 var. Halle an der Saale. Sachsen-Anhalt, C Germany
Halle an der Saale see Halle
Halle-Neustadt 72 C4 Sachsen-Anhalt, C Germany
Halley 132 B2 UK research station Antarctica
Hall Islands 120 B2 island group C Micronesia
Halls Creek 124 C3 Western Australia
Halmahera, Laut 117 F3 Eng. Halmahera Sea; sea E Indonesia
Halmahera, Pulau 117 F3 prev. Djailolo, Gilolo, Jailolo. island E Indonesia
Halmahera Sea see Halmahera, Laut
Halmstad 63 B7 Halland, S Sweden
Ha Long 114 E3 prev. Hông Gai; var. Hon Gai, Hongay. Quang Ninh, N Vietnam
Hälsingborg see Helsingborg
Hamada 109 B6 Shimane, Honshū, SW Japan
Hamadān 98 C3 anc. Ecbatana. Hamadān, W Iran
Ḩamāh 96 B3 var. Hama; anc. Epiphania, Bibl. Hamath. Ḩamāh, W Syria
Hamamatsu 109 D6 var. Hamamatu. Shizuoka, Honshū, S Japan
Hamamatu see Hamamatsu
Hamar 63 B5 prev. Storhammer. Hedmark, S Norway
Hamath see Ḩamāh
Hamburg 72 B3 Hamburg, N Germany
Hamd, Wadi al 98 A4 dry watercourse W Saudi Arabia
Hämeenlinna 63 D5 Swe. Tavastehus. Kanta-Häme, S Finland
HaMela h, Yam see Dead Sea
Hamersley Range 124 A4 mountain range Western Australia
Hamhŭng 107 E3 C North Korea
Hami 104 C3 var. Ha-mi, Uigh. Kumul, Qomul. Xinjiang Uygur Zizhiqu, NW China
Ha-mi see Hami
Hamilton 20 A5 dependent territory capital (Bermuda) C Bermuda
Hamilton 16 D5 Ontario, S Canada
Hamilton 128 D3 Waikato, North Island, New Zealand
Hamilton 66 C4 S Scotland, United Kingdom
Hamilton 20 C2 Alabama, S USA
Hamim, Wadi al 49 G2 river NE Libya
Hamīs Musait see Khamīs Mushayt
Hamm 72 B4 var. Hamm in Westfalen. Nordrhein-Westfalen, W Germany
Ḩammāmāt, Khalīj al see Hammamet, Golfe de
Hammamet, Golfe de 80 D3 Ar. Khalīj al Ḩammāmāt. gulf NE Tunisia
Ḩammār, Hawr al 98 C3 lake SE Iraq
Hamm in Westfalen see Hamm
Hampden 129 B7 Otago, South Island, New Zealand
Hampstead 67 A7 Maryland, USA
Ħamrun 80 B5 C Malta
Hāmūn, Daryācheh-ye see Şāberī, Hāmūn-e/ Sīstān, Daryācheh-ye
Hamwih see Southampton
Hânceşti see Hînceşti
Hancewicze see Hantsavichy
Handan 106 C4 var. Han-tan. Hebei, E China
Haneda 108 A2 (Tōkyō) Tōkyō, Honshū, S Japan
HaNegev 97 A7 Eng. Negev. desert S Israel
Hanford 25 C6 California, W USA
Hangayn Nuruu 104 D2 mountain range C Mongolia
Hang-chou/Hangchow see Hangzhou
Hangö see Hanko
Hangzhou 106 D5 var. Hang-chou, Hangchow. province capital Zhejiang, SE China
Hania see Chaniá
Hanka, Lake see Khanka, Lake
Hanko 63 D6 Swe. Hangö. Uusimaa, SW Finland
Han-kou/Han-k'ou/Hankow see Wuhan
Hanmer Springs 129 C5 Canterbury, South Island, New Zealand
Hannibal 23 G4 Missouri, C USA
Hannover 72 B3 Eng. Hanover. Niedersachsen, NW Germany
Hanöbukten 63 B7 bay S Sweden
Ha Nôi 114 D3 Eng. Hanoi, Fr. Hanoï. country capital (Vietnam) N Vietnam
Hanover see Hannover
Han Shui 105 E4 river C China
Han-tan see Handan
Hantsavichy 85 B6 Pol. Hancewicze, Rus. Gantsevichi. Brestskaya Voblasts', SW Belarus
Hanyang see Wuhan
Hanzhong 106 B5 Shaanxi, C China
Hāora 113 F4 prev. Howrah. West Bengal, NE India
Haparanda 62 D4 Norrbotten, N Sweden
Hapsal see Haapsalu
Haradok 85 E5 Rus. Gorodok. Vitsyebskaya Voblasts', N Belarus
Haradzyets 85 B6 Rus. Gorodets. Brestskaya Voblasts', SW Belarus
Haramachi 108 D4 Fukushima, Honshū, E Japan
Harany 85 D5 Rus. Gorany. Vitsyebskaya Voblasts', N Belarus
Harare 56 D3 prev. Salisbury. country capital (Zimbabwe) Mashonaland East, NE Zimbabwe
Harbavichy 85 E6 Rus. Gorbovichi. Mahilyowskaya Voblasts', E Belarus
Harbel 52 C5 W Liberia
Harbin 107 E2 var. Haerbin, Ha-erh-pin, Kharbin; prev. Haerhpin, Pingkiang, Pinkiang. province capital Heilongjiang, NE China
Hardangerfjorden 63 A6 fjord S Norway
Hardangervidda 63 A6 plateau S Norway
Hardenberg 64 E3 Overijssel, E Netherlands
Harelbeke 65 A6 var. Harlebeke. West-Vlaanderen, W Belgium
Harem see Ḩārim
Haren 64 E2 Groningen, NE Netherlands
Hārer 51 D5 E Ethiopia
Hargeisa see Hargeysa
Hargeysa 51 D5 var. Hargeisa. Woqooyi Galbeed, NW Somalia
Hariana see Haryāna
Hari, Batang 116 B4 prev. Djambi. river Sumatera, W Indonesia
Ḩārim 96 B2 var. Harem. Idlib, W Syria
Harima-nada 109 B6 sea S Japan
Harī Rōd 101 E4 var. Harīrūd, Tedzhen, Turkm. Tejen. river Afghanistan/Iran
Harīrūd see Harī Rōd
Harlan 23 F3 Iowa, C USA
Harlebeke see Harelbeke
Harlem see Haarlem
Harlingen 64 D2 Fris. Harns. Fryslân, N Netherlands
Harlingen 27 G5 Texas, SW USA
Harlow 67 E6 E England, United Kingdom
Harney Basin 24 B4 basin Oregon, NW USA
Härnösand 63 C5 var. Hernösand. Västernorrland, C Sweden
Harns see Harlingen
Harper 52 D5 var. Cape Palmas. NE Liberia
Harricana 16 D3 river Québec, SE Canada
Harris 66 B3 physical region NW Scotland, United Kingdom
Harrisburg 19 E4 state capital Pennsylvania, NE USA
Harrisonburg 19 E4 Virginia, NE USA
Harrison, Cape 17 F2 headland Newfoundland and Labrador, E Canada
Harris Ridge see Lomonosov Ridge
Harrogate 67 D5 N England, United Kingdom
Hârşova 86 D5 prev. Hîrşova. Constanţa, SE Romania
Harstad 62 C2 Troms, N Norway
Hartford 19 G3 state capital Connecticut, NE USA
Hartlepool 67 D5 N England, United Kingdom
Harunabad see Eslāmābād
Har Us Gol 104 C2 lake Hovd, W Mongolia
Har Us Nuur 104 C2 lake NW Mongolia
Harwich 67 E6 E England, United Kingdom
Haryāna 112 D2 var. Hariana. cultural region N India
Hashemite Kingdom of Jordan see Jordan
Haskovo 82 D3 var. Khaskovo. Haskovo, S Bulgaria
Hasselt 65 C6 Limburg, NE Belgium
Hassetché see Al Ḩasakah
Hasta Colonia/Hasta Pompeia see Asti
Hastings 128 E4 Hawke's Bay, North Island, New Zealand
Hastings 67 E7 SE England, United Kingdom
Hastings 23 E4 Nebraska, C USA
Haţeg 86 B4 Ger. Wallenthal, Hung. Hátszeg; prev. Hatzeg, Hötzing. Hunedoara, SW Romania
Hátszeg see Haţeg
Hattem 64 D3 Gelderland, E Netherlands
Hatteras, Cape 21 G1 headland North Carolina, SE USA
Hatteras Plain 13 D6 abyssal plain Atlantic Ocean
Hattiesburg 20 C3 Mississippi, S USA
Hatton Bank see Hatton Ridge
Hatton Ridge 58 B2 var. Hatton Bank. undersea ridge N Atlantic Ocean
Hat Yai 115 C7 var. Ban Hat Yai. Songkhla, SW Thailand
Hatzeg see Haţeg
Hatzfeld see Jimbolia
Haugesund 63 A6 Rogaland, S Norway
Haukeligrend 63 A6 Telemark, S Norway
Haukivesi 63 E5 lake SE Finland
Hauraki Gulf 128 D2 var. Tikapa Moana. gulf North Island, N New Zealand
Hauroko, Lake 129 A7 lake South Island, New Zealand
Haut Atlas 48 C2 Eng. High Atlas. mountain range C Morocco
Hautes Fagnes 65 D6 Ger. Hohes Venn. mountain range E Belgium
Hauts Plateaux 48 D2 plateau Algeria/Morocco
Hauzenberg 73 D6 Bayern, SE Germany
Havana 13 D6 Illinois, N USA
Havana see La Habana
Havant 67 D7 S England, United Kingdom
Havelock 21 F1 North Carolina, SE USA
Havelock North 128 E4 Hawke's Bay, North Island, New Zealand
Haverfordwest 67 C6 SW Wales, United Kingdom
Havířov 77 C5 Moravskoslezský Kraj, E Czechia (Czech Republic)
Havre 22 C1 Montana, NW USA
Havre see le Havre
Havre-St-Pierre 17 F3 Québec, E Canada
Hawaii 25 A8 off. State of Hawaii, also known as Aloha State, Paradise of the Pacific, var. Hawai'i. state USA, C Pacific Ocean
Hawai'i 25 B8 var. Hawaii. island Hawaiian Islands, USA, C Pacific Ocean
Hawaiian Islands 130 D2 prev. Sandwich Islands. island group Hawaii, USA
Hawaiian Ridge 130 H4 undersea ridge N Pacific Ocean
Hawea, Lake 129 B6 lake South Island, New Zealand
Hawera 128 D4 Taranaki, North Island, New Zealand
Hawick 66 C4 SE Scotland, United Kingdom
Hawke Bay 128 E4 bay North Island, New Zealand
Hawkeye State see Iowa
Hawlēr see Arbil
Hawthorne 25 C6 Nevada, W USA
Hay 127 C6 New South Wales, SE Australia
HaYarden see Jordan
Hayastan see Armenia
Hayastani Hanrapetut'yun see Armenia
Hayes 16 B2 river Manitoba, C Canada
Hay River 15 E4 Northwest Territories, W Canada
Hays 23 E5 Kansas, C USA
Haysyn see Haisyn
Hazar 100 B2 prev. Rus. Cheleken. Balkan Welaýaty, W Turkmenistan
Heard Island and McDonald Islands 119 B7 Australian external territory S Indian Ocean
Hearst 16 C4 Ontario, S Canada
Heart of Dixie see Alabama
Heathrow 67 A8 (London) SE England, United Kingdom
Hebei 106 C4 var. Hebei Sheng, Hopeh, Hopei, Ji; prev. Chihli. province E China
Hebei Sheng see Hebei
Hebron 97 A6 var. Al Khalīl, El Khalil, Heb. Hevron; anc. Kiriath-Arba. S West Bank, Middle East
Heemskerk 64 C3 Noord-Holland, W Netherlands
Heerde 64 D3 Gelderland, E Netherlands
Heerenveen 64 D2 Fris. It Hearrenfean. Fryslân, N Netherlands
Heerhugowaard 64 C2 Noord-Holland, NW Netherlands
Heerlen 65 D6 Limburg, SE Netherlands
Heerwegen see Polkowice
Hefa 97 A5 var. Haifa, hist. Caiffa, Caiphas; anc. Sycaminum. Haifa, N Israel
Ḩefa, Mifraz see Mifrats Hefa
Hefei 106 D5 var. Hofei, hist. Luchow. province capital Anhui, E China
Hegang 107 E2 Heilongjiang, NE China
Hei see Heilongjiang
Heide 72 B2 Schleswig-Holstein, N Germany
Heidelberg 73 B5 Baden-Württemberg, SW Germany
Heidenheim see Heidenheim an der Brenz
Heidenheim an der Brenz 73 B6 var. Heidenheim. Baden-Württemberg, S Germany
Hei-ho see Nagqu
Heilbronn 73 B6 Baden-Württemberg, SW Germany
Heiligenbeil see Mamonovo
Heilongjiang 106 D2 var. Hei, Heilongjiang Sheng, Hei-lung-chiang, Heilungkiang. province NE China
Heilong Jiang see Amur
Heilongjiang Sheng see Heilongjiang
Heiloo 64 C3 Noord-Holland, NW Netherlands
Heilsberg see Lidzbark Warmiński
Hei-lung-chiang/Heilungkiang see Heilongjiang
Heimdal 63 B5 Sør-Trøndelag, S Norway
Heinaste see Ainaži
Hekimhan 94 D3 Malatya, C Turkey (Türkiye)
Helena 22 B2 state capital Montana, NW USA
Helensville 128 D2 Auckland, North Island, New Zealand
Helgoland Bay see Helgoländer Bucht
Helgoländer Bucht 72 A2 var. Helgoland Bay, Heligoland Bight. bay NW Germany
Heligoland Bight see Helgoländer Bucht
Heliopolis see Baalbek
Hellas see Greece
Hellenic Republic see Greece
Hellevoetsluis 64 B4 Zuid-Holland, SW Netherlands
Hellín 71 E4 Castilla-La Mancha, C Spain
Helmand, Darya-ye see Helmand Rōd
Helmand Rōd 100 D5 var. Daryā-ye Helmand, Rūd-e Hīrmand, Helmand Rūd. river Afghanistan/Iran
Helmand Rūd see Helmand Rōd
Helmantica see Salamanca
Helmond 65 D5 Noord-Brabant, S Netherlands
Helsingborg 63 B7 prev. Hälsingborg. Skåne, S Sweden
Helsingfors see Helsinki
Helsinki 63 D6 Swe. Helsingfors. country capital (Finland) Uusimaa, S Finland
Heltau see Cisnădie
Helvetia see Switzerland
Henan 106 C5 var. Henan Sheng, Honan, Yu. province C China
Henderson 18 B5 Kentucky, S USA
Henderson 25 D7 Nevada, W USA
Henderson 27 H3 Texas, SW USA
Hendū Kosh see Hindu Kush
Hengchow see Hengyang
Hengduan Shan 106 A5 mountain range SW China
Hengelo 64 E3 Overijssel, E Netherlands
Hengnan see Hengyang
Hengyang 106 C6 var. Hengnan, Heng-yang; prev. Hengchow. Hunan, S China
Heng-yang see Hengyang
Henichesk 87 F4 Rus. Genichesk. Khersons'ka Oblast', S Ukraine
Hennebont 68 A3 Morbihan, NW France
Henrique de Carvalho see Saurimo
Henzada see Hinthada
Herakleion see Irákleio
Herāt 100 D4 var. Herat; anc. Aria. Herāt, W Afghanistan
Heredia 31 E4 Heredia, C Costa Rica
Hereford 27 E2 Texas, SW USA
Herford 72 B4 Nordrhein-Westfalen, NW Germany
Héristal see Herstal
Herk-de-Stad 65 C6 Limburg, NE Belgium
Herlen Gol/Herlen He see Kerulen
Hermannstadt see Sibiu
Hermansverk 63 A5 Sogn Og Fjordane, S Norway
Hermhausen see Hajnówka
Hermiston 24 C2 Oregon, NW USA
Hermon, Mount 97 B5 Ar. Jabal ash Shaykh. mountain S Syria
Hermosillo 28 B2 Sonora, NW Mexico
Hermoupolis see Ermoúpoli
Hernösand see Härnösand
Herrera del Duque 70 D3 Extremadura, W Spain
Herselt 65 C5 Antwerpen, C Belgium
Herstal 65 D6 Fr. Héristal. Liège, E Belgium
Herzogenbusch see 's-Hertogenbosch
Hesse see Hessen
Hessen 73 B5 Eng./Fr. Hesse. state C Germany
Hevron see Hebron
Hewlêr see Arbil
Heydebrech see Kędzierzyn-Kozle
Heydekrug see Šilutė
Heywood Islands 124 C3 island group Western Australia
Hibbing 23 F1 Minnesota, N USA
Hibernia see Ireland
Hidalgo del Parral 28 C2 var. Parral. Chihuahua, N Mexico
Hida-sanmyaku 109 C5 mountain range Honshū, S Japan
Hierosolyma see Jerusalem
Hierro 48 A3 var. Ferro. island Islas Canarias, Spain, NE Atlantic Ocean
High Atlas see Haut Atlas
High Plains see Great Plains
High Point 21 E1 North Carolina, SE USA
Hiiumaa 84 C2 Ger. Dagden, Swe. Dagö. island W Estonia
Hikurangi 128 D2 Northland, North Island, New Zealand
Hildesheim 72 B4 Niedersachsen, N Germany
Hilla see Al Ḩillah
Hillaby, Mount 33 G1 mountain N Barbados
Hill Bank 30 C1 Orange Walk, N Belize
Hillegom 64 C3 Zuid-Holland, W Netherlands
Hilo 25 B8 Hawaii, USA, C Pacific Ocean
Hilton Head Island 21 E2 South Carolina, SE USA
Hilversum 64 C3 Noord-Holland, C Netherlands
Himalaya/Himalaya Shan see Himalayas
Himalayas 113 E2 var. Himalaya, Chin. Himalaya Shan. mountain range S Asia
Himeji 109 C6 var. Himezi. Hyōgo, Honshū, SW Japan
Himezi see Himeji
Ḩimş 96 B4 var. Homs; anc. Emesa. Ḩimş, C Syria
Hînceşti 86 D4 var. Hânceşti; prev. Kotovsk. C Moldova
Hinchinbrook Island 126 D3 island Queensland, NE Australia
Hinds 129 C6 Canterbury, South Island, New Zealand
Hindu Kush 101 F4 Per. Hendū Kosh. mountain range Afghanistan/Pakistan
Hinesville 21 E3 Georgia, SE USA
Hinnøya 62 C3 Lapp. Iinnasuolu. island C Norway
Hinson Bay 20 A5 bay W Bermuda, W Atlantic Ocean
Hinthada 114 B4 var. Henzada. Ayeyarwady, SW Myanmar (Burma)
Hios see Chíos
Hirfanlı Barajı 94 C3 reservoir C Turkey (Türkiye)
Hirmand, Rūd-e see Helmand Rōd
Hirosaki 108 D3 Aomori, Honshū, C Japan
Hiroshima 109 B6 var. Hirosima. Hiroshima, Honshū, SW Japan
Hirschberg/Hirschberg im Riesengebirge/ Hirschberg in Schlesien see Jelenia Góra
Hirson 68 D3 Aisne, N France
Hîrşova see Hârşova
Hispalis see Sevilla
Hispana/Hispania see Spain
Hispaniola 34 B1 island Dominion Republic/Haiti
Hitachi 109 D5 var. Hitati. Ibaraki, Honshū, S Japan
Hitati see Hitachi
Hitra 62 A4 prev. Hitteren. island S Norway
Hitteren see Hitra
Hjälmaren 63 C6 Eng. Lake Hjalmar. lake C Sweden
Hjalmar, Lake see Hjälmaren
Hjørring 63 B7 Nordjylland, N Denmark
Hkakabo Razi 114 B1 mountain Myanmar (Burma)/China
Hlobyne 87 F2 Rus. Globino. Poltavs'ka Oblast', NE Ukraine
Hlukhiv 87 F1 Rus. Glukhov. Sums'ka Oblast', NE Ukraine
Hlybokaye 85 D5 Rus. Glubokoye. Vitsyebskaya Voblasts', N Belarus
Hoa Binh 114 D3 Hoa Binh, N Vietnam
Hoang Lien Son 114 D3 mountain range N Vietnam
Hobart 127 C8 prev. Hobarton, Hobart Town. state capital Tasmania, SE Australia
Hobarton/Hobart Town see Hobart
Hobbs 27 E3 New Mexico, SW USA
Hobro 63 A7 Nordjylland, N Denmark
Hô Chi Minh 115 E6 var. Ho Chi Minh City; prev. Saigon. S Vietnam
Ho Chi Minh City see Hô Chi Minh
Hodeidah see Al Ḩudaydah
Hódmezővásárhely 77 D7 Csongrád, SE Hungary
Hodna, Chott El 80 C4 var. Chott el-Hodna, Ar. Shatt al-Hodna. salt lake N Algeria
Hodna, Chott el-/Hodna, Shatt al- see Hodna, Chott El
Hodonín 77 C5 Ger. Göding. Jihomoravský Kraj, SE Czechia (Czech Republic)
Hoei see Huy
Hoey see Huy
Hof 73 C5 Bayern, SE Germany
Hofei see Hefei
Hōfu 109 B7 Yamaguchi, Honshū, SW Japan
Hofuf see Al Hufūf
Hogoley Islands see Chuuk Islands
Hohensalza see Inowrocław
Hohenstadt see Zábřeh
Hohes Venn see Hautes Fagnes
Hohe Tauern 73 C7 mountain range W Austria
Hohhot 105 F3 var. Huhehot, Huhohaote, Mong. Kukukhoto; prev. Kweisui, Kwesui. Nei Mongol Zizhiqu, N China
Hôi An 115 E5 prev. Faifo. Quang Nam-Đa Năng, C Vietnam
Hoï-Hao/Hoihow see Haikou
Hokianga Harbour 128 C2 inlet SE Tasman Sea
Hokitika 129 B5 West Coast, South Island, New Zealand
Hokkaido 108 C2 prev. Ezo, Yeso, Yezo. island NE Japan
Hola Prystan 87 E4 Rus. Golaya Pristan. Khersons'ka Oblast', S Ukraine
Holbrook 26 B2 Arizona, SW USA
Holetown 33 G1 prev. Jamestown. W Barbados
Holguín 32 C2 Holguín, SE Cuba
Hollabrunn 73 E6 Niederösterreich, NE Austria
Holland see Netherlands
Hollandia see Jayapura
Holly Springs 20 C1 Mississippi, S USA
Holman 15 E3 Victoria Island, Northwest Territories, N Canada
Holmsund 62 D4 Västerbotten, N Sweden
Holon 97 A6 var. Kholon; prev. Ḩolon. Tel Aviv, C Israel
Ḩolon see Holon
Holovanivsk 87 E3 Rus. Golovanevsk. Kirovohrads'ka Oblast', C Ukraine
Holstebro 63 A7 Ringkøbing, W Denmark
Holsteinborg/Holsteinsborg/Holstenborg/ Holstensborg see Sisimiut
Holyhead 67 C5 Wel. Caer Gybi. NW Wales, United Kingdom
Hombori 53 E3 Mopti, S Mali
Homs see Al Khums, Libya
Homs see Ḩimş
Homyel' 85 D7 Rus. Gomel'. Homyel'skaya Voblasts', SE Belarus
Honan see Luoyang, China
Honan see Henan, China
Hondo 27 F4 Texas, SW USA
Hondo see Honshū
Honduras 30 C2 off. Republic of Honduras. country Central America
Honduras, Golfo de see Honduras, Gulf of
Honduras, Gulf of 30 C2 Sp. Golfo de Honduras. gulf W Caribbean Sea
Honduras, Republic of see Honduras
Hønefoss 63 B6 Buskerud, S Norway
Honey Lake 25 B5 lake California, W USA
Hon Gai see Ha Long
Hongay see Ha Long
Hông Gai see Ha Long
Hông Hà, Sông see Red River
Hong Kong 106 A1 Special administrative region Hong Kong, S China
Hong Kong Island 106 B2 island S China Asia
Honiara 122 C3 country capital (Solomon Islands) Guadalcanal, C Solomon Islands
Honjō 108 D4 var. Honzyô, Yurihonjō. Akita, Honshū, C Japan
Honolulu 25 A8 state capital O'ahu, Hawaii, USA, C Pacific Ocean
Honshu 109 E5 var. Hondo, Honsyû. island SW Japan
Honsyû see Honshū
Honte see Westerschelde
Honzyô see Honjō
Hoogeveen 64 E2 Drenthe, NE Netherlands
Hoogezand-Sappemeer 64 E2 Groningen, NE Netherlands
Hoorn 64 C2 Noord-Holland, NW Netherlands
Hoosier State see Indiana
Hopa 95 E2 Artvin, NE Turkey (Türkiye)
Hope 14 C3 British Columbia, SW Canada
Hopedale 17 F2 Newfoundland and Labrador, NE Canada
Hopeh/Hopei see Hebei
Hopkinsville 18 B5 Kentucky, S USA
Horasan 95 F3 Erzurum, NE Turkey (Türkiye)
Horizon Deep 130 D4 trench W Pacific Ocean

Horki *85 E6 Rus.* Gorki. Mahilyowskaya Voblasts', E Belarus
Horlivka *87 G3 Rom.* Adâncata, *Rus.* Gorlovka. Donets'ka Oblast', E Ukraine
Hormoz, Tangeh-ye *see* Hormuz, Strait of
Hormuz, Strait of *98 D4 var.* Strait of Ormuz, *Per.* Tangeh-ye Hormoz. *strait* Iran/Oman
Horn, Cape *see* Hornos, Cabo de
Hornos, Cabo de *43 C8 Eng.* Cape Horn. *headland* S Chile
Hornsby *126 E1* New South Wales, SE Australia
Horodnia *87 E1 prev.* Horodnya, *Rus.* Gorodnya. Chernihivs'ka Oblast', NE Ukraine
Horodnya *see* Horodnia
Horodok *86 B2 Pol.* Gródek Jagielloński, *Rus.* Gorodok, Gorodok Yagellonski. L'vivs'ka Oblast', NW Ukraine
Horodyshche *87 E2 Rus.* Gorodishche. Cherkas'ka Oblast', C Ukraine
Horoshiri-dake *108 D2 var.* Horosiri Dake. *mountain* Hokkaidō, N Japan
Horosiri Dake *see* Horoshiri-dake
Horsburgh Atoll *110 A4 var.* Goidhoo Atoll. *atoll* N Maldives
Horseshoe Bay *20 A5 bay* W Bermuda W Atlantic Ocean
Horseshoe Seamounts *58 A4 seamount range* E Atlantic Ocean
Horsham *127 B7* Victoria, SE Australia
Horst *65 D5* Limburg, SE Netherlands
Horten *63 B6* Vestfold, S Norway
Horyn' *85 B7 Rus.* Goryn. *river* NW Ukraine
Hosingen *65 D7* Diekirch, NE Luxembourg
Hospitalet *see* L'Hospitalet de Llobregat
Hotan *104 B4 var.* Khotan, *Chin.* Ho-t'ien. Xinjiang Uygur Zizhiqu, NW China
Ho-t'ien *see* Hotan
Hoting *62 C4* Jämtland, C Sweden
Hot Springs *20 B1* Arkansas, C USA
Hötzing *see* Haţeg
Houayxay *114 C3 var.* Ban Houayxay. Bokèo, N Laos
Houghton *18 B1* Michigan, N USA
Houilles *69 B5* Yvelines, Île-de-France, N France Europe
Houlton *19 H1* Maine, NE USA
Houma *20 B3* Louisiana, S USA
Houston *27 H4* Texas, SW USA
Hovd *104 C2 var.* Khovd, Kobdo; *prev.* Jirgalanta. Hovd, W Mongolia
Hove *67 E7* SE England, United Kingdom
Hoverla, Hora *86 C3 Rus.* Gora Goverla. *mountain* W Ukraine
Hovsgol, Lake *see* Hövsgöl Nuur
Hövsgöl Nuur *104 D1 var.* Lake Hovsgol. *lake* N Mongolia
Howa, Ouadi *see* Howar, Wādi
Howar, Wadi *50 A3 var.* Ouadi Howa. *river* Chad/Sudan
Howland Island *123 E2 US unincorporated territory* W Polynesia
Howrah *see* Hāora
Hoy *66 C2 island* N Scotland, United Kingdom
Hoyerswerda *72 D4 Lus.* Wojerecy. Sachsen, E Germany
Hpa-An *114 B4 var.* Pa-an. Kayin State, S Myanmar (Burma)
Hpyu *see* Phyu
Hradec Králové *77 B5 Ger.* Königgrätz. Královéhradecký Kraj, N Czechia (Czech Republic)
Hrandzichy *85 B5 Rus.* Grandichi. Hrodzyenskaya Voblasts', W Belarus
Hranice *77 C5 Ger.* Mährisch-Weisskirchen. Olomoucký Kraj, E Czechia (Czech Republic)
Hrebinka *87 E2 Rus.* Grebenka. Poltavs'ka Oblast', NE Ukraine
Hrodna *85 B5 Pol.* Grodno. Hrodzyenskaya Voblasts', W Belarus
Hrvatska/ Republika Hrvatska *see* Croatia
Hsia-men *see* Xiamen
Hsiang-t'an *see* Xiangtan
Hsi Chiang *see* Xi Jiang
Hsing-K'ai Hu *see* Khanka, Lake
Hsi-ning/Hsining *see* Xining
Hsinking *see* Changchun
Hsin-yang *see* Xinyang
Hsu-chou *see* Xuzhou
Htawei *see* Dawei
Huacho *38 C4* Lima, W Peru
Hua Hin *see* Ban Hua Hin
Huaihua *106 C5* Hunan, S China
Huailai *106 C3 var.* Shacheng. Hebei, E China
Huainan *106 D5 var.* Huai-nan, Hwainan. Anhui, E China
Huai-nan *see* Huainan
Huajuapan *29 F5 var.* Huajuapan de León. Oaxaca, SE Mexico
Huajuapan de León *see* Huajuapan
Hualapai Peak *26 A2 mountain* Arizona, SW USA
Huallaga, Río *38 C3 river* N Peru
Huambo *56 B2 Port.* Nova Lisboa. Huambo, C Angola
Huancavelica *38 D4* Huancavelica, SW Peru
Huancayo *38 D3* Junín, C Peru
Huang Hai *see* Yellow Sea
Huang He *106 C4 var.* Yellow River. *river* C China
Huangshi *106 C5 var.* Huang-shih, Hwangshih. Hubei, C China
Huang-shih *see* Huangshi
Huanta *38 D4* Ayacucho, C Peru
Huánuco *38 C3* Huánuco, C Peru
Huanuni *39 F4* Oruro, W Bolivia
Huaral *38 C4* Lima, W Peru
Huarás *see* Huaraz
Huaraz *38 C3 var.* Huarás. Ancash, W Peru
Huarmey *38 C3* Ancash, W Peru
Huatabampo *28 C2* Sonora, NW Mexico
Hubballi *102 B2 prev.* Hubli. Karnātaka, SW India
Hubli *see* Hubballi
Huddersfield *67 D5* N England, United Kingdom
Hudiksvall *63 C5* Gävleborg, C Sweden
Hudson Bay *15 G4 bay* NE Canada
Hudson, Détroit d' *see* Hudson Strait
Hudson Strait *15 H3 Fr.* Détroit d'Hudson. *strait* Northwest Territories/Québec, NE Canada
Hudur *see* Xuddur
Huê *114 E4* Th,a Thiên-Huê, C Vietnam
Huehuetenango *30 A2* Huehuetenango, W Guatemala
Huelva *70 C4 anc.* Onuba. Andalucía, SW Spain
Huesca *71 F2 anc.* Osca. Aragón, NE Spain
Huéscar *71 E4* Andalucía, S Spain
Hughenden *126 C3* Queensland, NE Australia
Hugo *27 G2* Oklahoma, C USA
Huhehot/Huhohaote *see* Hohhot
Huíla Plateau *56 B2 plateau* S Angola
Huixtla *29 G5* Chiapas, SE Mexico
Hulingol *105 G2 prev.* Huolin Gol. Nei Mongol Zizhiqu, N China
Hull *16 D4* Québec, SE Canada
Hull *see* Kingston upon Hull
Hull Island *see* Orona
Hulst *65 B5* Zeeland, SW Netherlands
Hulun *see* Hulun Buir
Hulun Buir *105 F1 var.* Hailar; *prev.* Hulun. Nei Mongol Zizhiqu, N China
Hu-lun Ch'ih *see* Hulun Nur
Hulun Nur *105 F1 var.* Hu-lun Ch'ih; *prev.* Dalai Nor. *lake* NE China
Humaitá *40 D2* Amazonas, N Brazil
Humboldt River *25 C5 river* Nevada, W USA
Humphreys Peak *26 B1 mountain* Arizona, SW USA
Humpolec *77 B5 Ger.* Gumpolds, Humpoletz. Vysočina, C Czechia (Czech Republic)
Humpoletz *see* Humpolec
Hunan *106 C6 var.* Hunan Sheng, Xiang. *province* S China
Hunan Sheng *see* Hunan
Hunedoara *86 B4 Ger.* Eisenmarkt, *Hung.* Vajdahunyad. Hunedoara, SW Romania
Hünfeld *73 B5* Hessen, C Germany
Hungarian People's Republic *see* Hungary
Hungary *77 C6 off.* Hungary, *Ger.* Ungarn, *Hung.* Magyarország, *Rom.* Ungaria, *Croatian* Madarska, *Ukr.* Uhorshchyna; *prev.* Hungarian People's Republic. *country* C Europe
Hungary, Plain of *see* Great Hungarian Plain
Hunjiang *see* Baishan
Hunter Island *127 B8 island* Tasmania, SE Australia
Huntington *18 D4* West Virginia, NE USA
Huntington Beach *25 B8* California, W USA
Huntly *128 D3* Waikato, North Island, New Zealand
Huntsville *20 D1* Alabama, S USA
Huntsville *27 G3* Texas, SW USA
Huolin Gol *see* Hulingol
Hurghada *see* Al Ghardaqah
Huron *23 E3* South Dakota, N USA
Huron, Lake *18 D2 lake* Canada/USA
Hurukawa *see* Furukawa
Hurunui *129 C5 river* South Island, New Zealand
Húsavík *61 E4* Nordhurland Eystra, NE Iceland
Husté *see* Khust
Husum *72 B2* Schleswig-Holstein, N Germany
Huszt *see* Khust
Hutchinson *23 E5* Kansas, C USA
Hutchinson Island *21 F4 island* Florida, SE USA
Huy *65 C6 Dut.* Hoei, Hoey. Liège, E Belgium
Huzi *see* Fuji
Hvannadalshnúkur *61 E5 volcano* S Iceland
Hvar *78 B4 It.* Lesina; *anc.* Pharus. *island* S Croatia
Hwainan *see* Huainan
Hwange *56 D3 prev.* Wankie. Matabeleland North, W Zimbabwe
Hwang-Hae *see* Yellow Sea
Hwangshih *see* Huangshi
Hyargas Nuur *104 C2 lake* NW Mongolia
Hyderābād *112 D5 var.* Haidarabad. *state capital* Telangana, C India
Hyderabad *112 B3 var.* Haidarabad. Sindh, SE Pakistan
Hyères *69 D6* Var, SE France
Hyères, Îles d' *69 D6 island group* S France
Hypanis *see* Kuban'
Hyrcania *see* Gorgān
Hyvinge *see* Hyvinkää
Hyvinkää *63 D5 Swe.* Hyvinge. Uusimaa, S Finland

I

Iader *see* Zadar
Ialomița *86 C5 river* SE Romania
Iași *86 D3 Ger.* Jassy. Iași, NE Romania
Ibadan *53 F5* Oyo, SW Nigeria
Ibagué *36 B3* Tolima, C Colombia
Ibar *78 D4 Alb.* Ibër. *river* C Serbia
Ibarra *38 B1 var.* San Miguel de Ibarra. Imbabura, N Ecuador
Ibër *see* Ibar
Iberia *see* Spain
Iberian Mountains *see* Ibérico, Sistema
Iberian Peninsula *58 B4 physical region* Portugal/Spain
Iberian Plain *58 B4 abyssal plain* E Atlantic Ocean
Ibérica, Cordillera *see* Ibérico, Sistema
Ibérico, Sistema *71 E2 var.* Cordillera Ibérica, *Eng.* Iberian Mountains. *mountain range* NE Spain
Ibiza *see* Eivissa
Ibo *see* Sassandra
Ica *38 D4* Ica, SW Peru
Icaria *see* Ikaría
Içá, Rio *see* Putumayo, Río
İçel *see* Mersin
Iceland *61 E4 off.* Republic of Iceland, *Dan.* Island, *Icel.* Ísland. *country* N Atlantic Ocean
Iceland Basin *58 B1 undersea basin* N Atlantic Ocean
Icelandic Plateau *see* Iceland Plateau
Iceland Plateau *133 B6 var.* Icelandic Plateau. *undersea plateau* S Greenland Sea
Iceland, Republic of *see* Iceland
Iconium *see* Konya
Iculisma *see* Angoulême
Idabel *27 H2* Oklahoma, C USA
Idaho *24 D3 off.* State of Idaho, *also known as* Gem of the Mountains, Gem State. *state* NW USA
Idaho Falls *24 E3* Idaho, NW USA
Idensalmi *see* Iisalmi
Idfū *50 B2 var.* Edfu. SE Egypt
Idi Amin, Lac *see* Edward, Lake
Idîni *52 B2* Trarza, W Mauritania
Idlib *96 B3* Idlib, NW Syria
Idre *63 B5* Dalarna, C Sweden
Iecava *84 C3* Bauska, S Latvia
Ieper *65 A6 Fr.* Ypres. West-Vlaanderen, W Belgium
Ierápetra *83 D8* Kríti, Greece, E Mediterranean Sea
Ierisós *see* Ierissós
Ierissós *82 C4 var.* Ierisós. Kentrikí Makedonía, N Greece
Iertra *see* Eritrea
Iferouâne *53 G2* Agadez, N Niger
Ifôghas, Adrar des *53 E2 var.* Adrar des Iforas. *mountain range* NE Mali
Iforas, Adrar des *see* Ifôghas, Adrar des
Igarka *92 D3* Krasnoyarskiy Kray, N Russia
Igaunija *see* Estonia
Iglau/Iglawa/Igława *see* Jihlava
Iglesias *75 A5* Sardegna, Italy, C Mediterranean Sea
Igloolik *15 G2* Nunavut, N Canada
Igoumenítsa *82 A4* Ípeiros, W Greece
Iguaçu, Rio *41 E4 Sp.* Río Iguazú. *river* Argentina/Brazil
Iguaçu, Saltos do *41 E4 Sp.* Cataratas del Iguazú; *prev.* Victoria Falls. *waterfall* Argentina/Brazil
Iguala *29 E4 var.* Iguala de la Independencia. Guerrero, S Mexico
Iguala de la Independencia *see* Iguala
Iguazú, Cataratas del *see* Iguaçu, Saltos do
Iguazú, Río *see* Iguaçu, Rio
Iguid, Erg *see* Iguîdi, 'Erg
Iguîdi, 'Erg *48 C3 var.* Erg Iguid. *desert* Algeria/Mauritania
Ihavandhippolhu Atoll *110 A3 var.* Ihavandiffulu Atoll. *atoll* N Maldives
Ihavandiffulu Atoll *see* Ihavandhippolhu Atoll
Ihosy *57 F4* Fianarantsoa, S Madagascar
Ihupuku, Motu *see* Campbell Island
Iinnasuolu *see* Hinnøya
Iisalmi *62 E4 var.* Idensalmi. Pohjois-Savo, C Finland
IJmuiden *64 C3* Noord-Holland, W Netherlands
IJssel *64 D3 var.* Yssel. *river* Netherlands
IJsselmeer *64 C2 prev.* Zuider Zee. *lake* N Netherlands
IJsselmuiden *64 D3* Overijssel, E Netherlands
Ijzer *65 A6 river* W Belgium
Ikaahuk *see* Sachs Harbour
Ikaluktutiak *see* Cambridge Bay
Ikaría *83 D6 var.* Kariot, Nicaria, Nikaria; *anc.* Icaria. *island* Dodekánisa, Greece, Aegean Sea
Ikela *55 D6* Equateur, C Dem. Rep. Congo
Iki *109 A7 island* SW Japan
Ilagan *117 E1* Luzon, N Philippines
Ilave *39 E4* Puno, S Peru
Iława *76 D3 Ger.* Deutsch-Eylau. Warmińsko-Mazurskie, NE Poland
Ilebo *55 C6 prev.* Port-Francqui. Kasai-Occidental, W Dem. Rep. Congo
Île-de-France *68 C3 cultural region* N France
Ilemi Triangle *51 B5 disputed region* Kenya/South Sudan
Ilerda *see* Lleida
Ilfracombe *67 C7* SW England, United Kingdom
Ílhavo *70 B2* Aveiro, N Portugal
Iliamna Lake *14 C3 lake* Alaska, USA
Ilici *see* Elx
Iligan *117 E2 off.* Iligan City. Mindanao, S Philippines
Iligan City *see* Iligan
Illapel *42 B4* Coquimbo, C Chile
Illichivsk *see* Chornomorsk
Illicis *see* Elx
Illinois *18 A4 off.* State of Illinois, *also known as* Prairie State, Sucker State. *state* C USA
Illinois River *18 B4 river* Illinois, N USA
Illurco *see* Lorca
Illuro *see* Mataró
Ilo *39 E4* Moquegua, SW Peru
Iloilo *117 E2 off.* Iloilo City. Panay Island, C Philippines
Iloilo City *see* Iloilo
Ilorin *53 F4* Kwara, W Nigeria
Ilovlya *89 B6* Volgogradskaya Oblast', SW Russia
Iluh *see* Batman
Il'yaly *see* Gurbansoltan Eje
Imatra *63 E5* Etelä-Kariala, SE Finland
Imbros *see* Gökçeada
Imishli *see* İmişli
İmişli *95 H3 Rus.* Imishli. C Azerbaijan
Imola *74 C3* Emilia-Romagna, N Italy
Imperatriz *41 F2* Maranhão, NE Brazil
Imperia *74 A3* Liguria, NW Italy
Impfondo *55 C5* Likouala, NE Congo
Imphāl *113 H3 state capital* Manipur, NE India
Imroz Adası *see* Gökçeada
Inagua Islands *see* Little Inagua
Inagua Islands *see* Great Inagua
Inarijärvi *62 D2 Lapp.* Aanaarjävri, *Swe.* Enareträsk. *lake* N Finland
Inău *see* Ineu
Inawashiro-ko *109 D5 var.* Inawasiro Ko. *lake* Honshū, C Japan
Inawasiro Ko *see* Inawashiro-ko
İncesu *94 D3* Kayseri, Turkey (Türkiye)
Incheon *107 E4 off.* Incheon Gwang-yeoksi, *prev.* Inch'ŏn, *Jap.* Jinsen; *prev.* Chemulpo. NW South Korea
Incheon-Gwang-yeoksi *see* Incheon
Inch'ŏn *see* Incheon
Incudine, Monte *69 E7 mountain* Corse, France, C Mediterranean Sea
Indefatigable Island *see* Santa Cruz, Isla
Independence *23 F4* Missouri, C USA
Independence Fjord *61 E1 fjord* N Greenland
Independence Island *see* Malden Island
Independence Mountains *24 C4 mountain range* Nevada, W USA
India *102 B3 off.* Republic of India, *var.* Indian Union, Union of India, *Hind.* Bhārat. *country* S Asia
India *see* Indija
Indiana *18 B4 off.* State of Indiana, *also known as* Hoosier State. *state* N USA
Indianapolis *18 C4 state capital* Indiana, N USA
Indian Church *30 C1* Orange Walk, N Belize
Indian Desert *see* Thar Desert
Indianola *23 F4* Iowa, C USA
Indian Union *see* India
India, Republic of *see* India
India, Union of *see* India
Indigirka *93 F2 river* NE Russia
Inđija *78 D3 Hung.* India; *prev.* Indjija. Vojvodina, N Serbia
Indira Point *110 G3 headland* Andaman and Nicobar Island, India, NE Indian Ocean
Indjija *see* Inđija
Indomed Fracture Zone *119 B6 tectonic feature* SW Indian Ocean
Indonesia *116 B4 off.* Republic of Indonesia, *Ind.* Republik Indonesia; *prev.* Dutch East Indies, Netherlands East Indies, United States of Indonesia. *country* SE Asia
Indonesian Borneo *see* Kalimantan
Indonesia, Republic of *see* Indonesia
Indonesia, Republik *see* Indonesia
Indonesia, United States of *see* Indonesia
Indore *112 D4* Madhya Pradesh, C India
Indreville *see* Châteauroux
Indus *112 C2 Chin.* Yindu He; *prev.* Yin-tu Ho. *river* S Asia
Indus Cone *see* Indus Fan
Indus Fan *90 C5 var.* Indus Cone. *undersea fan* N Arabian Sea
Indus, Mouths of the *112 B4 delta* S Pakistan
İnebolu *94 C2* Kastamonu, N Turkey (Türkiye)
Ineu *86 A4 Hung.* Borosjenő; *prev.* Inău. Arad, W Romania
Infiernillo, Presa del *29 E4 reservoir* S Mexico
Inglewood *24 D2* California, W USA
Ingolstadt *73 C6* Bayern, S Germany
Ingulets *see* Inhulets
Inguri *see* Enguri
Inhambane *57 E4* Inhambane, SE Mozambique
Inhulets *87 F3 Rus.* Ingulets. Dnipropetrovska Oblast, E Ukraine
I-ning *see* Yining
Inis *see* Ennis
Inis Ceithleann *see* Enniskillen
Inn *73 C6 river* C Europe
Innaanganeq *60 C1 var.* Kap York. *headland* NW Greenland
Inner Hebrides *66 B4 island group* W Scotland, United Kingdom
Inner Islands *57 H1 var.* Central Group. *island group* NE Seychelles
Innisfail *126 D3* Queensland, NE Australia
Inniskilling *see* Enniskillen
Innsbruch *see* Innsbruck
Innsbruck *73 C7 var.* Innsbruch. Tirol, W Austria
Inoucdjouac *see* Inukjuak
Inowrazlaw *see* Inowrocław
Inowrocław *76 C3 Ger.* Hohensalza; *prev.* Inowrazlaw. Kujawski-pomorskie, C Poland
I-n-Sakane, 'Erg *53 E2 desert* N Mali
I-n-Salah *48 D3 var.* In Salah. C Algeria
Insterburg *see* Chernyakhovsk
Insula *see* Lille
Inta *88 E3* Respublika Komi, NW Russia
Interamna *see* Teramo
Interamna Nahars *see* Terni
International Falls *23 F1* Minnesota, N USA
Inukjuak *16 D2 var.* Inoucdjouac; *prev.* Port Harrison. Québec, NE Canada
Inuuvik *see* Inuvik
Inuvik *14 D3 var.* Inuuvik. Northwest Territories, NW Canada
Invercargill *129 A7* Southland, South Island, New Zealand
Inverness *66 C3* N Scotland, United Kingdom
Investigator Ridge *119 D5 undersea ridge* E Indian Ocean
Investigator Strait *127 B7 strait* South Australia
Inyangani *56 D3 mountain* NE Zimbabwe
Ioánnina *82 A4 var.* Janina, Yannina. Ípeiros, W Greece
Iola *23 F5* Kansas, C USA
Ionia Basin *see* Ionian Basin
Ionian Basin *58 D5 var.* Ionia Basin. *undersea basin* Ionian Sea, C Mediterranean Sea
Ionian Islands *see* Iónia Nisiá
Ionian Sea *81 E3 Gk.* Iónio Pélagos, *It.* Mar Ionio. *sea* C Mediterranean Sea
Iónia Nisiá *83 A5 Eng.* Ionian Islands. *island group* W Greece
Ionio, Mar/Iónio Pélagos *see* Ionian Sea
Íos *83 D6 var.* Nio. *island* Kykládes, Greece, Aegean Sea
Ioulída *83 C6 prev.* Ioulís, Kykládes, Greece, Aegean Sea
Iowa *23 F3 off.* State of Iowa, *also known as* Hawkeye State. *state* C USA
Iowa City *23 G3* Iowa, C USA
Iowa Falls *23 G3* Iowa, C USA
Ipel' *77 C6 var.* Ipoly, *Ger.* Eipel. *river* Hungary/Slovakia
Ipiales *36 A4* Nariño, SW Colombia
Ipoh *116 B3* Perak, Peninsular Malaysia
Ipoly *see* Ipel'
Ippy *54 C4* Ouaka, C Central African Republic
Ipswich *127 E5* Queensland, E Australia
Ipswich *67 E6 hist.* Gipeswic. E England, United Kingdom
Iqaluit *15 H3 prev.* Frobisher Bay. *province capital* Baffin Island, Nunavut, NE Canada
Iquique *42 B1* Tarapacá, N Chile
Iquitos *38 C1* Loreto, N Peru
Irákleio *83 D7 var.* Herakleion, *Eng.* Candia; *prev.* Iráklion. Kríti, Greece, E Mediterranean Sea
Iráklion *see* Irákleio
Iran *98 C3 off.* Islamic Republic of Iran; *prev.* Persia. *country* SW Asia
Iranian Plateau *98 D3 var.* Plateau of Iran. *plateau* N Iran
Iran, Islamic Republic of *see* Iran
Iran, Plateau of *see* Iranian Plateau
Irapuato *29 E4* Guanajuato, C Mexico
Iraq *98 B3 off.* Republic of Iraq, *Ar.* 'Irāq. *country* SW Asia
'Irāq *see* Iraq
Iraq, Republic of *see* Iraq
Irbid *97 B5* Irbid, N Jordan
Irbil *see* Arbīl
Ireland *67 A5 off.* Ireland, *Ir.* Éire. *country* NW Europe
Ireland *58 C3 Lat.* Hibernia. *island* Ireland/United Kingdom
Irian *see* New Guinea
Irian Barat *see* Papua
Irian Jaya *see* Papua
Irian, Teluk *see* Cenderawasih, Teluk
Iringa *51 C7* Iringa, C Tanzania
Iriomote-jima *108 A4 island* Sakishima-shotō, SW Japan
Iriona *30 D2* Colón, NE Honduras
Irish Sea *67 C5 Ir.* Muir Éireann. *sea* C British Isles
Irkutsk *93 E4* Irkutskaya Oblast', S Russia
Irminger Basin *see* Reykjanes Basin
Iroise *68 A3 sea* NW France
Iron Mountain *18 B2* Michigan, N USA
Ironwood *18 B1* Michigan, N USA
Irrawaddy *see* Ayeyarwady
Irrawaddy, Mouths of the *115 A5 delta* SW Myanmar (Burma)
Irtish *see* Irtysh
Irtysh *92 C4 var.* Irtish, *Kaz.* Ertis. *river* C Asia
Irun *71 E1 Cast.* Irún. País Vasco, N Spain
Irún *see* Irun
Iruña *see* Pamplona
Isabela, Isla *38 A5 var.* Albemarle Island. *island* Galápagos Islands, Ecuador, E Pacific Ocean
Isaccea *86 D4* Tulcea, E Romania
Isachsen *15 F1* Ellef Ringnes Island, Nunavut, N Canada
Ísafjördur *61 E4* Vestfirdhir, NW Iceland
Isbarta *see* Isparta
Isca Damnoniorum *see* Exeter
Ise *109 C6* Mie, Honshū, SW Japan
Iseghem *see* Izegem
Isère *69 D5 river* E France
Isernia *75 D5 var.* Æsernia. Molise, C Italy
Ise-wan *109 C6 bay* S Japan
Isfahan *see* Eşfahān
Isha Baydhabo *see* Baydhabo
Ishigaki-jima *108 A4 island* Sakishima-shotō, SW Japan
Ishikari-wan *108 C2 bay* Hokkaidō, NE Japan
Ishim *92 C4* Tyumenskaya Oblast', C Russia
Ishim *92 C4 Kaz.* Esil. *river* Kazakhstan/Russia
Ishinomaki *108 D4 var.* Isinomaki. Miyagi, Honshū, C Japan
Ishkashim *see* Ishkoshim
Ishkoshim *101 F3 Rus.* Ishkashim. S Tajikistan
Isinomaki *see* Ishinomaki
Isiro *55 E5* Orientale, NE Dem. Rep. Congo
Iskar *82 C2 var.* Iskŭr. *river* NW Bulgaria
İskenderun *94 D4 Eng.* Alexandretta. Hatay, S Turkey (Türkiye)
İskenderun Körfezi *96 A2 Eng.* Gulf of Alexandretta. *gulf* S Turkey (Türkiye)
Iskŭr *see* Iskar
Iskar, Yazovir *82 B2 prev.* Yazovir Stalin. *reservoir* W Bulgaria
Isla Cristina *70 C4* Andalucía, S Spain
Isla de León *see* San Fernando
Islamabad *112 C1 country capital* (Pakistan) Federal Capital Territory Islamabad, NE Pakistan
Island/Ísland *see* Iceland
Islay *66 B4 island* SW Scotland, United Kingdom
Isle *69 B5 river* W France
Isle of Man *67 B5 British Crown Dependency* NW Europe
Isles of Scilly *67 B8 island group* SW England, United Kingdom
Ismailia *see* Al Ismā'īlīya
Ismâ'ilîya *see* Al Ismā'īlīya
Ismid *see* İzmit
Isnā *50 B2 var.* Esna. SE Egypt
Isoka *56 D1* Northern, NE Zambia
Isparta *94 B4 var.* Isbarta. Isparta, SW Turkey (Türkiye)
İspir *95 E3* Erzurum, NE Turkey (Türkiye)
Israel *97 A7 off.* State of Israel, *var.* Medinat Israel, *Heb.* Yisrael, Yisra'el. *country* SW Asia
Israel, State of *see* Israel
Issa *see* Vis
Issiq Köl *see* Issyk-Kul', Ozero
Issoire *69 C5* Puy-de-Dôme, C France
Issyk-Kul' *see* Balykchy
Issyk-Kul', Ozero *101 G2 var.* Issiq Köl, *Kir.* Ysyk-Köl. *lake* E Kyrgyzstan
İstanbul *94 B2 Bul.* Tsarigrad, *Eng.* Istanbul, *prev.* Constantinople; *anc.* Byzantium. Istanbul, NW Turkey (Türkiye)
İstanbul Boğazi *94 B2 var.* Bosporus Thracius, *Eng.* Bosphorus, Bosporus, *Turk.* Karadeniz Boğazi. *strait* NW Turkey (Türkiye)
Istaravshan *101 E2 prev.* Ŭroteppa, *Rus.* Ura-Tyube. NW Tajikistan
Istarska Županija *see* Istra
Istra *78 A3 off.* Istarska Županija. *province* NW Croatia
Istra *78 A3 Eng.* Istria, *Ger.* Istrien. *cultural region* NW Croatia
Istria/Istrien *see* Istra
Itabuna *41 G3* Bahia, E Brazil
Itagüí *36 B3* Antioquia, W Colombia
Itaipú, Represa de *41 E4 reservoir* Brazil/Paraguay
Itaituba *41 E2* Pará, NE Brazil
Italia/Italiana, Republica/Italian Republic, The *see* Italy
Italian Somaliland *see* Somalia
Italy *74 C3 off.* The Italian Republic, *It.* Italia, Repubblica Italiana. *country* S Europe
Iténez, Río *see* Guaporé, Rio
Ithaca *19 E3* New York, NE USA
It Hearrenfean *see* Heerenveen
Itoigawa *109 C5* Niigata, Honshū, C Japan
Itseqqortoormiit *see* Ittoqqortoormiit
Ittoqqortoormiit *61 E3 var.* Itseqqortoormiit, *Dan.* Scoresbysund, *Eng.* Scoresby Sound. Tunu, C Greenland
Iturup, Ostrov *108 E1 island* Kuril'skiye Ostrova, SE Russia
Itzehoe *72 B2* Schleswig-Holstein, N Germany
Ivalo *62 D2 Lapp.* Avveel, Avvil. Lappi, N Finland
Ivanava *85 B7 Pol.* Janów, Janów Poleski, *Rus.* Ivanovo. Brestskaya Voblasts', SW Belarus
Ivangrad *see* Berane
Ivanhoe *127 C6* New South Wales, SE Australia
Ivano-Frankivsk *86 C2 Ger.* Stanislau, *Pol.* Stanisławów, *Rus.* Ivano-Frankovsk; *prev.* Stanislav. Ivano-Frankivs'ka Oblast', W Ukraine
Ivano-Frankovsk *see* Ivano-Frankivsk
Ivanovo *89 B5* Ivanovskaya Oblast', W Russia
Ivanovo *see* Ivanava
Ivantsevichi/Ivatsevichi *see* Ivatsevichy
Ivatsevichy *85 B6 Pol.* Iwacewicze, *Rus.* Ivantsevichi, Ivatsevichi. Brestskaya Voblasts', SW Belarus
Ivigtut *see* Ivittuut
Ivittuut *60 B4 var.* Ivigtut. Sermersooq, S Greenland
Iviza *see* Eivissa\Ibiza
Ivory Coast *52 D4 off.* République de la Côte d'Ivoire. *country* W Africa
Ivujivik *16 D1* Québec, NE Canada
Iwacewicze *see* Ivatsevichy
Iwaki *109 D5* Fukushima, Honshū, N Japan
Iwakuni *109 B7* Yamaguchi, Honshū, SW Japan
Iwanai *108 C2* Hokkaidō, NE Japan
Iwate *108 D3* Iwate, Honshū, N Japan
Ixtapa *29 E5* Guerrero, S Mexico
Ixtepec *29 F5* Oaxaca, SE Mexico
Iyo-nada *109 B7 sea* S Japan
Izabal, Lago de *30 B2 prev.* Golfo Dulce. *lake* E Guatemala
Īzad Khvāst *98 D3* Fārs, C Iran
I'zāz *96 B2 var.* A'zāz. Ḩalab, NW Syria

Izegem *65 A6 prev.* Iseghem. West-Vlaanderen, W Belgium
Izhevsk *89 D5 prev.* Ustinov. Udmurtskaya Respublika, NW Russia
Iziaslav *86 C2 prev.* Izyaslav. Khmel'nyts'ka Oblast', W Ukraine
Izium *87 G2 prev.* Izyum. Kharkivs'ka Oblast', E Ukraine
Izmail *see* Izmayil
Izmayil *86 D4 Rus.* Izmail. Odes'ka Oblast', SW Ukraine
İzmir *94 A3 prev.* Smyrna. İzmir, W Turkey (Türkiye)
İzmit *94 B2 var.* Ismid; *anc.* Astacus. Kocaeli, NW Turkey (Türkiye)
İznik Gölü *94 B3 lake* NW Turkey (Türkiye)
Izu-hanto *109 D6 peninsula* Honshū, S Japan
Izu Shichito *see* Izu-shotō
Izu-shoto *109 D6 var.* Izu Shichito. *island group* S Japan
Izvor *82 B2* Pernik, W Bulgaria
Izyaslav *see* Iziaslav
Izyum *see* Izium

J

Jabal ash Shifa *98 A4 desert* NW Saudi Arabia
Jabalpur *113 E4 prev.* Jubbulpore. Madhya Pradesh, C India
Jabbūl, Sabkhat al *96 B2 sabkha* NW Syria
Jablah *96 A3 var.* Jeble, *Fr.* Djéblé. Al Lādhiqīyah, W Syria
Jaca *71 F1* Aragón, NE Spain
Jacaltenango *30 A2* Huehuetenango, W Guatemala
Jackson *20 B2 state capital* Mississippi, S USA
Jackson *23 H5* Missouri, C USA
Jackson *20 C1* Tennessee, S USA
Jackson Head *129 A6 headland* South Island, New Zealand
Jacksonville *21 E3* Florida, SE USA
Jacksonville *18 B4* Illinois, N USA
Jacksonville *21 F1* North Carolina, SE USA
Jacksonville *27 G3* Texas, SW USA
Jacmel *32 D3 var.* Jaquemel. S Haiti
Jacob *see* Nkayi
Jacobabad *112 B3* Sindh, SE Pakistan
Jadotville *see* Likasi
Jadransko More/Jadransko Morje *see* Adriatic Sea
Jaén *38 B2* Cajamarca, N Peru
Jaén *70 D4* Andalucía, SW Spain
Jaffna *110 D3* Northern Province, N Sri Lanka
Jagannath *see* Puri
Jagdalpur *113 E5* Chhattīsgarh, C India
Jagdaqi *105 G1* Nei Mongol Zizhiqu, N China
Jagodina *78 D4 prev.* Svetozarevo. Serbia, C Serbia
Jahra *see* Al Jahrā'
Jailolo *see* Halmahera, Pulau
Jaipur *112 D3 prev.* Jeypore. *state capital* Rājasthān, N India
Jaisalmer *112 C3* Rājasthān, NW India
Jajce *78 B3* Federacija Bosna I Hercegovina, W Bosnia and Herzegovina
Jakarta *116 C5 prev.* Djakarta, *Dut.* Batavia. *country capital* (Indonesia) Jawa, C Indonesia
Jakobstad *62 D4 Fin.* Pietarsaari. Österbotten, W Finland
Jakobstadt *see* Jēkabpils
Jalālābād *101 F4 var.* Jalalabad, Jelalabad. Nangarhār, E Afghanistan
Jalal-Abad *see* Dzhalal-Abad, Dzhalal-Abadskaya Oblast', Kyrgyzstan
Jalandhar *112 D2 prev.* Jullundur. Punjab, N India
Jalapa *30 D3* Nueva Segovia, NW Nicaragua
Jalpa *28 D4* Zacatecas, C Mexico
Jālū *49 G3 var.* Jūlā. NE Libya
Jaluit Atoll *122 D2 var.* Jālwōj. *atoll* Ralik Chain, S Marshall Islands
Jālwōj *see* Jaluit Atoll
Jamaame *51 D6 It.* Giamame; *prev.* Margherita. Jubbada Hoose, S Somalia
Jamaica *32 A4 country* W West Indies
Jamaica *34 A1 island* W West Indies
Jamaica Channel *32 D3 channel* Haiti/Jamaica
Jamālpur *113 F3* Bihār, NE India
Jambi *116 B4 var.* Telanaipura; *prev.* Djambi. Sumatera, W Indonesia
Jamdena *see* Yamdena, Pulau
James Bay *16 C3 bay* Ontario/Québec, E Canada
James River *23 E2 river* North Dakota/South Dakota, N USA
James River *19 E5 river* Virginia, NE USA
Jamestown *19 E3* New York, NE USA
Jamestown *23 E2* North Dakota, N USA
Jamestown *see* Holetown
Jammu *112 D2 prev.* Jummoo. *state capital* Jammu and Kashmir, NW India
Jammu and Kashmir *112 D1 disputed region* India/Pakistan
Jāmnagar *112 C4 prev.* Navanagar. Gujarāt, W India
Jamshedpur *113 F4* Jhārkhand, NE India
Jamuna *see* Brahmaputra
Janaúba *41 F3* Minas Gerais, SE Brazil
Janesville *18 B3* Wisconsin, N USA
Jang Bogo *132 C4 South Korean research station* Antarctica
Janina *see* Ioánnina
Janīn *97 E6* var. Jenin. N West Bank, Middle East
Janischken *see* Joniškis
Jankovac *see* Jánoshalma
Jan Mayen *61 F4 constituent part of Norway. island* N Atlantic Ocean
Jánoshalma *77 C7 Croatian* Jankovac. Bács-Kiskun, S Hungary
Janów *see* Ivanava, Belarus
Janow/Janów *see* Jonava, Lithuania
Janów Poleski *see* Ivanava
Japan *108 C4 var.* Nippon, *Jap.* Nihon. *country* E Asia
Japan, Sea of *108 A4 var.* East Sea, *Rus.* Yapanskoye More. *sea* NW Pacific Ocean
Japan Trench *103 F1 trench* NW Pacific Ocean
Japen *see* Yapen, Pulau
Japiim *40 C2 var.* Máncio Lima. Acre, W Brazil
Japurá, Rio *40 C2 var.* Río Caquetá, Yapurá. *river* Brazil/Colombia
Japurá, Rio *see* Caquetá, Río
Jaqué *31 G5* Darién, SE Panama
Jaquemel *see* Jacmel
Jarablos *see* Jarābulus
Jarābulus *96 C2 var.* Jarablos, Jerablus, *Fr.* Djérablous. Ḥalab, N Syria
Jarbah, Jazīrat *see* Djerba, Île de
Jardines de la Reina, Archipiélago de los *32 B2 island group* C Cuba
Jarīd, Shaṭṭ al *see* Jerid, Chott el
Jarocin *76 C4* Wielkopolskie, C Poland
Jaroslau *see* Jarosław
Jarosław *77 E5 Ger.* Jaroslau, *Rus.* Yaroslav. Podkarpackie, SE Poland
Jarqo'rg'on *101 E3 Rus.* Dzharkurgan. Surkhondaryo Viloyati, S Uzbekistan
Jarvis Island *123 G2 US unincorporated territory* C Pacific Ocean
Jashore *113 G4 prev.* Jessore. Khulna, W Bangladesh
Jasło *77 D5* Podkarpackie, SE Poland
Jastrzębie-Zdrój *77 C5* Śląskie, S Poland
Jataí *41 E3* Goiás, C Brazil
Jativa *see* Xàtiva
Jauf *see* Al Jawf
Jaunpiebalga *84 D3* Gulbene, NE Latvia
Jaunpur *113 E3* Uttar Pradesh, N India
Java *130 A3* South Dakota, N USA
Javalambre *71 E3 mountain* E Spain
Java Sea *116 D4 Ind.* Laut Jawa. *sea* W Indonesia
Java Trench *102 D5 var.* Sunda Trench. *trench* E Indian Ocean
Jawa, Laut *see* Java Sea
Jawhar *51 D6 var.* Jowhar, *It.* Giohar. Shabeellaha Dhexe, S Somalia
Jaworów *see* Yavoriv
Jaya, Puncak *117 G4 prev.* Puntjak Carstensz, Puntjak Sukarno. *mountain* Papua, E Indonesia
Jayapura *117 H4 var.* Djajapura, *Dut.* Hollandia; *prev.* Kotabaru, Sukarnapura. Papua, E Indonesia
Jay Dairen *see* Dalian
Jayhawker State *see* Kansas
Jaz Murian, Hamun-e *98 E4 lake* SE Iran
Jebba *53 F4* Kwara, W Nigeria
Jebel, Bahr el *see* White Nile
Jeble *see* Jablah
Jeddah *see* Jiddah
Jędrzejów *76 D4 Ger.* Endersdorf. Świętokrzyskie, C Poland
Jefferson City *23 G5 state capital* Missouri, C USA
Jega *53 F4* Kebbi, NW Nigeria
Jehol *see* Chengde
Jeju-do *107 E4 Jap.* Saishū; *prev.* Cheju-do, Quelpart. *island* S South Korea
Jeju Strait *107 E4 var.* Jeju-haehyŏp; *prev.* Cheju-Strait. *strait* S South Korea
Jeju-haehyŏp *see* Jeju Strait
Jēkabpils *84 D4 Ger.* Jakobstadt. Jēkabpils, S Latvia
Jelalabad *see* Jalālābād
Jelenia Góra *76 B4 Ger.* Hirschberg, Hirschberg im Riesengebirge, Hirschberg in Riesengebirge, Hirschberg in Schlesien. Dolnośląskie, SW Poland
Jelgava *84 C3 Ger.* Mitau. Jelgava, C Latvia
Jelondi *101 F3 prev.* Dzhelandy. SE Tajikistan
Jemappes *65 B6* Hainaut, S Belgium
Jember *116 D5 prev.* Djember. Jawa, C Indonesia
Jena *72 C4* Thüringen, C Germany
Jengish Chokusu *see* Tömür Feng
Jenin *see* Janīn
Jerablus *see* Jarābulus
Jerada *48 D2* NE Morocco
Jérémie *32 D3* SW Haiti
Jerez *see* Jeréz de la Frontera, Spain
Jerez de la Frontera *70 C5 var.* Jerez; *prev.* Xeres. Andalucía, SW Spain
Jerez de los Caballeros *70 C4* Extremadura, W Spain
Jericho *97 E7 var.* Arīḥā, Yeriẖo. C West Bank, Middle East
Jerid, Chott el *49 E2 var.* Shaṭṭ al Jarīd. *salt lake* SW Tunisia
Jersey *67 D8 British Crown Dependency* Channel Islands, NW Europe
Jerusalem *81 H4 Ar.* Al Quds, Al Quds ash Sharīf, *Heb.* Yerushalayim; *anc.* Hierosolyma. *country capital* (Israel - not internationally recognized) Jerusalem, NE Israel
Jesenice *73 D7 Ger.* Assling. NW Slovenia
Jesselton *see* Kota Kinabalu
Jessore *see* Jashore
Jesús María *42 C3* Córdoba, C Argentina
Jeypore *see* Jaipur, Rājasthān, India
Jhānsi *112 D3* Uttar Pradesh, N India
Jhārkhand *113 F4 cultural region* NE India
Jhelum *112 C2* Punjab, NE Pakistan
Ji *see* Hebei, China
Ji *see* Jilin, China
Jiangmen *106 C6* Guangdong, S China
Jiangsu *106 D4 var.* Chiang-su, Jiangsu Sheng, Kiangsu, Su. *province* E China
Jiangsu *see* Nanjing
Jiangsu Sheng *see* Jiangsu
Jiangxi *106 C6 var.* Chiang-hsi, Gan, Jiangxi Sheng, Kiangsi. *province* S China
Jiangxi Sheng *see* Jiangxi
Jiaxing *106 D5* Zhejiang, SE China
Jiayi *see* Chiayi
Jibuti *see* Djibouti
Jiddah *99 A5 Eng.* Jeddah. Makkah, W Saudi Arabia
Jih-k'a-tse *see* Xigazê
Jihlava *77 B5 Ger.* Iglau, *Pol.* Igława. Vysocina, S Czechia (Czech Republic)
Jilib *51 D6 It.* Gelib. Jubbada Dhexe, S Somalia
Jilin *106 E3 var.* Chi-lin, Girin, Kirin; *prev.* Yungki, Yunki. Jilin, NE China
Jilin *106 E3 var.* Chi-lin, Girin, Ji, Jilin Sheng, Kirin. *province* NE China
Jilin Sheng *see* Jilin
Jilong *see* Keelung
Jīma *51 C5 var.* Jimma, *It.* Gimma. Oromīya, C Ethiopia
Jimbolia *86 A4 Ger.* Hatzfeld, *Hung.* Zsombolya. Timiș, W Romania
Jiménez *28 D2* Chihuahua, N Mexico
Jimma *see* Jīma
Jimsar *104 C3* Xinjiang Uygur Zizhiqu, NW China
Jin *see* Shanxi
Jin *see* Tianjin Shi
Jinan *106 C4 var.* Chinan, Chi-nan, Tsinan. *province capital* Shandong, E China
Jingdezhen *106 C5* Jiangxi, S China
Jinghong *106 A6 var.* Yunjinghong. Yunnan, SW China
Jinhua *106 D5* Zhejiang, SE China
Jining *105 F3* Shandong, E China
Jinja *51 C6* S Uganda
Jinotega *30 D3* Jinotega, NW Nicaragua
Jinotepe *30 D3* Carazo, SW Nicaragua
Jinsen *see* Incheon
Jinzhong *106 C4 var.* Yuci. Shanxi, C China
Jinzhou *106 D3 var.* Chin-chou, Chinchow; *prev.* Chinhsien. Liaoning, NE China
Jirgalanta *see* Hovd
Jisr ash Shadadi *see* Ash Shadādah
Jiu *86 B5 Ger.* Schil, Schyl, *Hung.* Zsil, Zsily. *river* S Romania
Jiujiang *106 C5* Jiangxi, S China
Jixi *107 E2* Heilongjiang, NE China
Jizan *see* Jīzān
Jīzān *99 B6 var.* Qīzān, Jizan. Jīzān, SW Saudi Arabia
Jizzax *101 E2 Rus.* Dzhizak. Jizzax Viloyati, C Uzbekistan
João Belo *see* Xai-Xai
João Pessoa *41 G2 prev.* Paraíba. *state capital* Paraíba, E Brazil
Joazeiro *see* Juazeiro
Job'urg *see* Johannesburg
Jo-ch'iang *see* Ruoqiang
Jodhpur *112 C3* Rājasthān, NW India
Joensuu *63 E5* Pohjois-Karjala, SE Finland
Jōetsu *109 C5 var.* Zyôetu. Niigata, Honshū, C Japan
Jogjakarta *see* Yogyakarta
Johannesburg *56 D4 var.* Egoli, Erautini, Gauteng, *abbrev.* Job'urg. Gauteng, NE South Africa
Johannisburg *see* Pisz
John Day River *24 C3 river* Oregon, NW USA
John o'Groats *66 C2* N Scotland, United Kingdom
Johnston Atoll *121 E1 US unincorporated territory* C Pacific Ocean
Johor Baharu *see* Johor Bahru
Johor Bahru *116 B3 var.* Johor Baharu, Johore Bahru. Johor, Peninsular Malaysia
Johore Bahru *see* Johor Bahru
Johore Strait *116 A1 strait* Johor, Peninsular Malaysia, Malaysia/Singapore Asia Andaman Sea/ South China Sea
Joinvile *see* Joinville
Joinville *41 E4 var.* Joinvile. Santa Catarina, S Brazil
Jokkmokk *62 C3 Lapp.* Dálvvadis. Norrbotten, N Sweden
Jokyakarta *see* Yogyakarta
Joliet *18 B3* Illinois, N USA
Jonava *84 B4 Ger.* Janow, *Pol.* Janów. Kaunas, C Lithuania
Jonesboro *20 B1* Arkansas, C USA
Joniškis *84 C3 Ger.* Janischken. Šiaulai, N Lithuania
Jönköping *63 B7* Jönköping, S Sweden
Jonquière *17 E4* Québec, SE Canada
Joplin *23 F5* Missouri, C USA
Jordan *97 B6 off.* Hashemite Kingdom of Jordan, *Ar.* Al Mamlaka al Urdunīya al Hashemīyah, Al Urdunn; *prev.* Transjordan. *country* SW Asia
Jordan *97 B5 Ar.* Urdun, *Heb.* HaYarden. *river* SW Asia
Jorhāt *113 H3* Assam, NE India
Jos *53 G4* Plateau, C Nigeria
Joseph Bonaparte Gulf *124 D2 gulf* N Australia
Jos Plateau *53 G4 plateau* C Nigeria
Jotunheimen *63 A5 mountain range* S Norway
Joûnié *96 A4 var.* Junīyah. W Lebanon
Joure *64 D2 Fris.* De Jouwer. Fryslân, N Netherlands
Joutseno *63 E5* Etelä-Kariala, SE Finland
Jowhar *see* Jawhar
J.Storm Thurmond Reservoir *see* Clark Hill Lake
Juan Aldama *28 D3* Zacatecas, C Mexico
Juan de Fuca, Strait of *24 A1 strait* Canada/USA
Juan Fernández, Islas *35 A6 Eng.* Juan Fernandez Islands. *island group* W Chile
Juan Fernandez Islands *see* Juan Fernández, Islas
Juazeiro *41 G2 prev.* Joazeiro. Bahia, E Brazil
Juazeiro do Norte *41 G2* Ceará, E Brazil
Juba *51 B5 var.* Jūbā. *country capital* (South Sudan) Bahr el Gabel, S South Sudan
Juba *51 D6 Amh.* Genalē Wenz, *It.* Guiba, *Som.* Ganaane, Webi Jubba. *river* Ethiopia/Somalia
Jubba, Webi *see* Juba
Jubbulpore *see* Jabalpur
Júcar *71 E3 var.* Jucar. *river* C Spain
Juchitán *29 F5 var.* Juchitán de Zaragosa. Oaxaca, SE Mexico
Juchitán de Zaragosa *see* Juchitán
Judayyidat Hāmir *98 B3* Al Anbār, S Iraq
Judenburg *73 D7* Steiermark, C Austria
Juigalpa *30 D3* Chontales, S Nicaragua
Juiz de Fora *41 F4* Minas Gerais, SE Brazil
Jujuy *see* San Salvador de Jujuy
Jūlā *see* Jālū, Libya
Julia Beterrae *see* Béziers
Juliaca *39 E4* Puno, SE Peru
Juliana Top *37 G3 mountain* C Suriname
Julianehåb *see* Qaqortoq
Julio Briga *see* Bragança
Juliobriga *see* Logroño
Juliomagus *see* Angers
Jullundur *see* Jalandhar
Jumilla *71 E4* Murcia, SE Spain
Jummoo *see* Jammu
Jumna *see* Yamuna
Jumporn *see* Chumphon
Junction City *23 F4* Kansas, C USA
Juneau *14 D4 state capital* Alaska, USA
Junín *42 C4* Buenos Aires, E Argentina
Junīyah *see* Joûnié
Junkseylon *see* Phuket
Jur *51 B5 river* C Sudan
Jura *68 D4 cultural region* E France
Jura *73 A7 var.* Jura Mountains. *mountain range* France/Switzerland
Jura *66 B4 island* SW Scotland, United Kingdom
Jura Mountains *see* Jura
Jurbarkas *84 B4 Ger.* Georgenburg, Jurburg. Tauragė, W Lithuania
Jurburg *see* Jurbarkas
Jūrmala *84 C3* Rīga, C Latvia
Juruá, Rio *40 C2 var.* Río Yuruá. *river* Brazil/Peru
Juruena, Rio *40 D3 river* W Brazil
Jutiapa *30 B2* Jutiapa, S Guatemala
Juticalpa *30 D2* Olancho, C Honduras
Jutland *63 A7 Den.* Jylland. *peninsula* W Denmark
Juvavum *see* Salzburg
Juventud, Isla de la *32 A2 var.* Isla de Pinos, *Eng.* Isle of Youth; *prev.* The Isle of the Pines. *island* W Cuba
Južna Morava *79 E5 Ger.* Südliche Morava. *river* SE Serbia
Jwaneng *56 C4* Southern, S Botswana
Jylland *see* Jutland
Jyrgalan *see* Dzhergalan
Jyväskylä *63 D5* Keski-Suomi, C Finland

K

K2 *104 A4 Chin.* Qogir Feng, *Eng.* Mount Godwin Austen. *mountain* China/Pakistan
Kaafu Atoll *see* Male' Atoll
Kaaimanston *37 G3* Sipaliwini, N Suriname
Kaakhka *see* Kaka
Kaala *see* Caála
Kaamanen *62 D2 Lapp.* Gámas. Lappi, N Finland
Kaapstad *see* Cape Town
Kaaresuvanto *62 C3 Lapp.* Gárasavon. Lappi, N Finland
Kabale *51 B6* SW Uganda
Kabinda *55 D7* Kasai-Oriental, SE Dem. Rep. Congo
Kabinda *see* Cabinda
Kābol *see* Kābul
Kabompo *56 C2 river* W Zambia
Kābul *101 E4 prev.* Kābol, *Eng.* Kabul. *country capital* (Afghanistan) Kābul, E Afghanistan
Kabul *101 E4 var.* Daryā-ye Kābul. *river* Afghanistan/Pakistan
Kābul, Daryā-ye *see* Kabul
Kabwe *56 D2* Central, C Zambia
Kachchh, Gulf of *112 B4 var.* Gulf of Cutch, Gulf of Kutch. *gulf* W India
Kachchh, Rann of *112 B4 var.* Rann of Kachh, Rann of Kutch. *salt marsh* India/Pakistan
Kachh, Rann of *see* Kachchh, Rann of
Kadan Kyun *115 B5 prev.* King Island. *island* Myeik Archipelago, S Myanmar (Burma)
Kadapa *110 C2 prev.* Cuddapah. Andhra Pradesh, S India
Kadavu *123 E4 prev.* Kandavu. *island* S Fiji
Kadiivka *87 H3 prev.* Kadiyivka, *Rus.* Stakhanov. Luhans'ka Oblast', E Ukraine
Kadiyivka *see* Kadiivka
Kadoma *56 D3 prev.* Gatooma. Mashonaland West, C Zimbabwe
Kadugli *50 B4* Southern Kordofan, S Sudan
Kaduna *53 G4* Kaduna, C Nigeria
Kadzhi-Say *101 G2 Kir.* Kajisay. Issyk-Kul'skaya Oblast', NE Kyrgyzstan
Kaédi *52 C3* Gorgol, S Mauritania
Kaffa *see* Feodosiia
Kafue *56 D2* Lusaka, SE Zambia
Kafue *56 C2 river* C Zambia
Kaga Bandoro *54 C4 prev.* Fort-Crampel. Nana-Grébizi, C Central African Republic
Kagan *see* Kogon
Kâgheț *52 D1 var.* Karet. *physical region* N Mauritania
Kagi *see* Chiayi
Kagoshima *109 B8 var.* Kagosima. Kagoshima, Kyūshū, SW Japan
Kagoshima-wan *109 A8 bay* SW Japan
Kagosima *see* Kagoshima
Kagul *see* Cahul
Kharga *see* Al Khārjah
Kahmard, Darya-ye *101 E4 prev.* Darya-i-surkhab. *river* NE Afghanistan
Kahramanmaraş *94 D4 var.* Kahraman Maraş, Maraş, Marash. Kahramanmaraş, S Turkey (Türkiye)
Kaiapoi *129 C6* Canterbury, South Island, New Zealand
Kaifeng *106 C4* Henan, C China
Kai, Kepulauan *117 F4 prev.* Kei Islands. *island group* Maluku, SE Indonesia
Kaikohe *128 C2* Northland, North Island, New Zealand
Kaikoura *129 C5* Canterbury, South Island, New Zealand
Kaikoura Peninsula *129 C5 peninsula* South Island, New Zealand
Kainji Lake *see* Kainji Reservoir
Kainji Reservoir *53 F4 var.* Kainji Lake. *reservoir* W Nigeria
Kaipara Harbour *128 C2 harbour* North Island, New Zealand
Kairouan *49 E2 var.* Al Qayrawān. E Tunisia
Kaisaria *see* Kayseri
Kaiserslautern *73 A5* Rheinland-Pfalz, SW Germany
Kaišiadorys *85 B5* Kaunas, S Lithuania
Kaitaia *128 C2* Northland, North Island, New Zealand
Kajaani *62 E4 Swe.* Kajana. Kainuu, C Finland
Kajan *see* Kayan, Sungai
Kajana *see* Kajaani
Kajisay *see* Kadzhi-Say
Kaka *100 C2 Rus.* Kaakhka. Ahal Welaýaty, S Turkmenistan
Kake *14 D4* Kupreanof Island, Alaska, USA
Kakhovka *87 F4* Khersons'ka Oblast', S Ukraine
Kakhovske Vodoskhovyshche *87 F4 Rus.* Kakhovskoye Vodokhranilishche. *reservoir* SE Ukraine
Kakhovskoye Vodokhranilishche *see* Kakhovske Vodoskhovyshche
Kākināda *110 D1 prev.* Cocanada. Andhra Pradesh, E India
Kakshaal-Too, Khrebet *see* Kokshaal-Tau
Kaktovik *14 D2* Alaska, USA
Kalaallit Nunaat *see* Greenland
Kalaburagi *110 C1 prev.* Gulbarga. Karnātaka, C India
Kalahari Desert *56 B4 desert* Southern Africa
Kalaikhum *see* Qalaikhumb
Kalámai *see* Kalámata
Kalamariá *82 B4* Kentrikí Makedonía, N Greece
Kalamás *see* Thýamis
Kalámata *83 B6 prev.* Kalámai. Pelopónnisos, S Greece
Kalamazoo *18 C3* Michigan, N USA
Kalambaka *see* Kalampáka
Kálamos *83 C5* Attikí, C Greece
Kalampáka *82 B4 var.* Kalambaka. Thessalía, C Greece
Kalanchak *87 F4* Khersons'ka Oblast', S Ukraine
Kalarash *see* Călărași
Kalasin *114 D4 var.* Muang Kalasin. Kalasin, E Thailand
Kalat *112 B2 var.* Kelat, Khelat. Baluchistan, SW Pakistan
Kalāt *see* Qalāt
Kalbarri *125 A5* Western Australia
Kalecik *94 C3* Ankara, N Turkey (Türkiye)
Kalemie *55 E6 prev.* Albertville. Katanga, SE Dem. Rep. Congo
Kale Sultanie *see* Çanakkale
Kalgan *see* Zhangjiakou
Kalgoorlie *125 B6* Western Australia
Kalima *55 D6* Maniema, E Dem. Rep. Congo
Kalimantan *116 D4 Eng.* Indonesian Borneo. *geopolitical region* Borneo, C Indonesia
Kalinin *see* Tver'
Kaliningrad *84 A4* Kaliningradskaya Oblast', W Russia
Kaliningrad *see* Kaliningradskaya Oblast'
Kaliningradskaya Oblast' *84 B4 var.* Kaliningrad. *province and enclave* W Russia
Kalinkavichy *85 C7 Rus.* Kalinkovichi. Homyel'skaya Voblasts', SE Belarus
Kalinkovichi *see* Kalinkavichy
Kalisch/Kalish *see* Kalisz
Kalispell *22 B1* Montana, NW USA
Kalisz *76 C4 Ger.* Kalisch, *Rus.* Kalish; *anc.* Calisia. Wielkopolskie, C Poland
Kalix *62 D4* Norrbotten, N Sweden
Kalixälven *62 D3 river* N Sweden
Kallaste *84 E3 Ger.* Krasnogor. Tartumaa, SE Estonia
Kallavesi *63 E5 lake* SE Finland
Kalloní *83 D5* Lésvos, E Greece
Kalmar *63 C7 var.* Calmar. Kalmar, S Sweden
Kalmthout *65 C5* Antwerpen, N Belgium
Kalpáki *82 A4* Ípeiros, W Greece
Kalpeni Island *110 B3 island* Lakshadweep, India, N Indian Ocean
Kaltdorf *see* Pruszków
Kaluga *89 B5* Kaluzhskaya Oblast', W Russia
Kalush *86 C2 Pol.* Kałusz. Ivano-Frankivs'ka Oblast', W Ukraine
Kałusz *see* Kalush
Kalutara *110 D4* Western Province, SW Sri Lanka
Kalvarija *85 B5 Pol.* Kalwaria. Marijampolė, S Lithuania
Kalwaria *see* Kalvarija
Kalyān *112 C5* Mahārāshtra, W India
Kálymnos *83 D6 var.* Kálimnos. *island* Dodekánisa, Greece, Aegean Sea
Kama *88 D4 river* NW Russia
Kamarang *37 F3* W Guyana
Kambryk *see* Cambrai
Kamchatka *see* Kamchatka, Poluostrov
Kamchatka, Poluostrov *93 G3 Eng.* Kamchatka. *peninsula* E Russia
Kamenets-Podol'skiy *see* Kamianets-Podilskyi
Kamenka Dneprovskaya *see* Kamianka-Dniprovska
Kamenskoye *see* Kamianske
Kamensk-Shakhtinskiy *89 B6* Rostovskaya Oblast', SW Russia
Kamianets-Podilskyi *86 C3 prev.* Kam"yanets'-Podil's'kyy, *Rus.* Kamenets-Podol'skiy. Khmel'nyts'ka Oblast', W Ukraine
Kamianka-Dniprovska *87 F3 prev.* Kam"yanka-Dniprovs'ka, *Rus.* Kamenka Dneprovskaya. Zaporiz'ka Oblast', SE Ukraine
Kamianske *87 F3 prev.* Kam"yans'ke, Kamenskoye; *Rus.* Dniprodzerzhyns'k. Dnipropetrovska Oblast, E Ukraine
Kamina *55 D7* Katanga, S Dem. Rep. Congo
Kamishli *see* Al Qāmishlī
Kamloops *15 E5* British Columbia, SW Canada
Kammu Seamount *130 C2 guyot* N Pacific Ocean
Kampala *51 B6 country capital* (Uganda) S Uganda
Kampong Cham *115 D6 Khmer.* Kâmpóng Cham. Kampong Cham, C Cambodia
Kâmpóng Cham *see* Kampong Cham
Kampong Chhang *115 D6 Khmer.* Kâmpóng Chhnăng. Kampong Chhang, C Cambodia
Kâmpóng Chhnăng *see* Kampong Chhang
Kampong Speu *115 D6 Khmer.* Kâmpóng Spoe. Kampong Speu, S Cambodia
Kâmpóng Spoe *see* Kampong Speu
Kampong Thom *115 D5 Khmer.* Kâmpóng Thum, *prev.* Trâpeăng Vêng. Kampong Thom, C Cambodia
Kâmpóng Thum *see* Kampong Thom
Kâmpóng Trâbêk *115 D5 prev.* Phumĭ Kâmpóng Trâbêk, Phum Kompong Trabek. Kampong Thom, C Cambodia
Kampot *115 D6 Khmer.* Kâmpôt. Kampot, SW Cambodia
Kâmpôt *see* Kampot
Kampuchea *see* Cambodia
Kampuchea, Democratic *see* Cambodia
Kampuchea, People's Democratic Republic of *see* Cambodia
Kam"yanets'-Podil's'kyy *see* Kamianets-Podilskyi
Kam"yanka-Dniprovs'ka *see* Kamianka-Dniprovska
Kam"yans'ke *see* Kamianske
Kamyshin *89 B6* Volgogradskaya Oblast', SW Russia
Kanaky *see* New Caledonia
Kananga *55 D6 prev.* Luluabourg. Kasai-Occidental, S Dem. Rep. Congo
Kanara *see* Karnātaka
Kanash *89 C5* Chuvashskaya Respublika, W Russia
Kanazawa *109 C5* Ishikawa, Honshū, SW Japan
Kanbe *114 B4* Yangon, SW Myanmar (Burma)
Kānchīpuram *110 C2 prev.* Conjeeveram. Tamil Nādu, SE India
Kandahār *101 E5 Per.* Qandahār. Kandahār, S Afghanistan
Kandalakša *see* Kandalaksha
Kandalaksha *88 B2 var.* Kandalakša, *Fin.* Kantalahti. Murmanskaya Oblast', NW Russia
Kandangan *116 D4* Borneo, C Indonesia
Kandau *see* Kandava
Kandava *84 C3 Ger.* Kandau. Tukums, W Latvia
Kandavu *see* Kadavu
Kandi *53 F4* N Benin
Kandy *110 D3* Central Province, C Sri Lanka
Kane Fracture Zone *44 B4 fracture zone* NW Atlantic Ocean
Kāne'ohe *25 A8 var.* Kaneohe. O'ahu, Hawaii, USA, C Pacific Ocean
Kanestron, Akrotírio *see* Palioúri, Akrotírio
Kanëv *see* Kaniv
Kanevskoye Vodokhranilishche *see* Kanivske Vodoskhovyshche
Kangān *see* Bandar-e Kangān
Kangaroo Island *127 A7 island* South Australia
Kangertittivaq *61 E4 Dan.* Scoresby Sund. *fjord* E Greenland

Kangikajik 61 E4 var. Kap Brewster. headland E Greenland
Kaniv 87 E2 Rus. Kanëv. Cherkas'ka Oblast', C Ukraine
Kanivske Vodoskhovyshche 87 E2 prev. Kanivs'ke Vodoskhovyshche. Rus. Kanevskoye Vodokhranilishche. reservoir C Ukraine
Kanivs'ke Vodoskhovyshche see Kanivske Vodoskhovyshche
Kanjiža 78 D2 Ger. Altkanischa, Hung. Magyarkanizsa, Ókanizsa; prev. Stara Kanjiža. Vojvodina, N Serbia
Kankaanpää 63 D5 Satakunta, SW Finland
Kankakee 18 B3 Illinois, N USA
Kankan 52 D4 E Guinea
Kannur 110 B2 var. Cannanore. Kerala, SW India
Kano 53 G4 Kano, N Nigeria
Kānpur 113 E3 Eng. Cawnpore. Uttar Pradesh, N India
Kansas 23 F5 off. State of Kansas, also known as Jayhawker State, Sunflower State. state C USA
Kansas City 23 F4 Kansas, C USA
Kansas City 23 F4 Missouri, C USA
Kansas River 23 F5 river Kansas, C USA
Kansk 93 E4 Krasnoyarskiy Kray, S Russia
Kansu see Gansu
Kantalahti see Kandalaksha
Kántanos 83 C7 Kríti, Greece, E Mediterranean Sea
Kantemirovka 89 B6 Voronezhskaya Oblast', W Russia
Kantipur see Kathmandu
Kanton 123 F3 var. Abariringa, Canton Island; prev. Mary Island. atoll Phoenix Islands, C Kiribati
Kanye 56 C4 Southern, SE Botswana
Kaohsiung 106 D6 var. Gaoxiong, Jap. Takao, Takow. S Taiwan
Kaolack 52 B3 var. Kaolak. W Senegal
Kaolak see Kaolack
Kaolan see Lanzhou
Kaoma 56 C2 Western, W Zambia
Kapelle 65 B5 Zeeland, SW Netherlands
Kapellen 65 C5 Antwerpen, N Belgium
Kapka, Massif du 54 C2 mountain range E Chad
Kaplangky, Plato see Gaplaňgyr Platosy
Kapoeas see Kapuas, Sungai
Kapoeta 51 C5 E Equatoria, SE South Sudan
Kaposvár 77 C7 Somogy, SW Hungary
Kappeln 72 B2 Schleswig-Holstein, N Germany
Kapreoncza see Koprivnica
Kapstad see Cape Town
Kapsukas see Marijampolė
Kaptsevichy 85 C7 Rus. Koptsevichi. Homyel'skaya Voblasts', SE Belarus
Kapuas, Sungai 116 C4 prev. Kapoeas. river Borneo, C Indonesia
Kapuskasing 16 C4 Ontario, S Canada
Kapyl' 85 C6 Rus. Kopyl'. Minskaya Voblasts', C Belarus
Kara-Balta 101 F2 Chuyskaya Oblast', N Kyrgyzstan
Karabil', Vozvyshennost' see Garabil Belentligi
Kara-Bogaz-Gol, Zaliv see Garabogaz Aylagy
Karabük 94 C2 Karabük, NW Turkey (Türkiye)
Karachi 112 B3 Sindh, SE Pakistan
Karácsonkő see Piatra-Neamţ
Karadeniz see Black Sea
Karadeniz Boğazi see İstanbul Boğazı
Karaferiye see Véroia
Karagandy/Karaganda see Qaraghandy
Karaginskiy, Ostrov 93 H2 island E Russia
Karagumskiy Kanal see Garagum Kanaly
Karak see Al Karak
Kara-Kala see Magtymguly
Karakax see Moyu
Karakılısse see Ağrı
Karakol 101 G2 prev. Przheval'sk. Issyk-Kul'skaya Oblast', NE Kyrgyzstan
Karakol 101 G2 var. Karakolka. Issyk-Kul'skaya Oblast', NE Kyrgyzstan
Karakolka see Karakol
Karakoram Range 112 D1 mountain range C Asia
Karaköse see Ağrı
Karakul' see Qarokŭl, Tajikistan
Kara Kum see Garagum
Kara Kum Canal/Karakumskiy Kanal see Garagum Kanaly
Karakumy, Peski see Garagum
Karamai see Karamay
Karaman 94 C4 Karaman, S Turkey (Türkiye)
Karamay 104 B2 var. Karamai, Kelamayi; prev. Chin. K'o-la-ma-i. Xinjiang Uygur Zizhiqu, NW China
Karamea Bight 129 B5 gulf South Island, New Zealand
Karapelit 82 E1 Rom. Stejarul. Dobrich, NE Bulgaria
Kara-Say 101 G2 Issyk-Kul'skaya Oblast', NE Kyrgyzstan
Karasburg 56 B4 Karas, S Namibia
Kara Sea see Karskoye More
Kara Strait see Karskiye Vorota, Proliv
Karatau 92 C5 Kaz. Qarataū. Zhambyl, S Kazakhstan
Karavás 83 B7 Kýthira, S Greece
Karbalā' 98 B3 var. Kerbala, Kerbela. Karbalā', S Iraq
Kardeljevo see Ploče
Kardhítsa see Karditsa
Kardítsa 83 B5 var. Kardhítsa. Thessalía, C Greece
Kärdla 84 C2 Ger. Kertel. Hiiumaa, W Estonia
Kardzhali 82 D3 var. Kirdzhali, Kŭrdzhali. Kardzhali, S Bulgaria
Karet see Kâgheţ
Kargı 94 C2 Çorum, N Turkey (Türkiye)
Kargilik see Yecheng
Kariba 56 D2 Mashonaland West, N Zimbabwe
Kariba, Lake 56 D3 reservoir Zambia/Zimbabwe
Karibib 56 B3 Erongo, C Namibia
Kariega 56 C5 prev. Uitenhage. Eastern Cape, S South Africa
Karies see Karyés
Karigasniemi 62 D2 Lapp. Garegegasnjárga. Lappi, N Finland
Karimata, Selat 116 C4 strait W Indonesia
Karīmnagar 112 D5 Telangana, C India
Karin 50 D4 Sahil, N Somalia
Kariot see Ikaría
Káristos see Kárystos
Karkinitska Zatoka 87 E4 Rus. Karkinitskiy Zaliv. gulf S Ukraine
Karkinitskiy Zaliv see Karkinitska Zatoka
Karkūk see Kirkūk
Karleby see Kokkola
Karl-Marx-Stadt see Chemnitz
Karlō see Hailuoto
Karlovac 78 B3 Ger. Karlstadt, Hung. Károlyváros. Karlovac, C Croatia
Karlovy Vary 77 A5 Ger. Karlsbad; prev. Eng. Carlsbad. Karlovarský Kraj, W Czechia (Czech Republic)
Karlsbad see Karlovy Vary
Karlsburg see Alba Iulia
Karlskrona 63 C7 Blekinge, S Sweden
Karlsruhe 73 B6 var. Carlsruhe. Baden-Württemberg, SW Germany
Karlstad 63 B6 Värmland, C Sweden
Karlstadt see Karlovac
Karnāl 112 D2 Haryāna, N India
Karnātaka 110 C1 var. Kanara; prev. Maisur, Mysore. cultural region W India
Karnobat 82 D2 Burgas, E Bulgaria
Karnul see Kurnool
Karol see Carei
Károly-Fehérvár see Alba Iulia
Károlyváros see Karlovac
Karpaten see Carpathian Mountains
Kárpathos 83 E7 Kárpathos, SE Greece
Kárpathos 83 E7 It. Scarpanto; anc. Carpathos, Carpathus. island SE Greece
Karpaty see Carpathian Mountains
Karpenísi 83 B5 prev. Karpenision. Stereá Ellás, C Greece
Karpenision see Karpenísi
Karpilovka see Aktsyabrski
Kars 95 F2 var. Qars. Kars, NE Turkey (Türkiye)
Karsau see Kārsava
Kārsava 84 D4 Ger. Karsau; prev. Rus. Korsovka. Ludza, E Latvia
Karshi see Qarshi, Uzbekistan
Karskiye Vorota, Proliv 88 E2 Eng. Kara Strait. strait N Russia
Karskoye More 92 D2 Eng. Kara Sea. sea Arctic Ocean
Karyés 82 C4 var. Karies. Ágion Óros, N Greece
Kárystos 83 C6 var. Káristos. Évvoia, C Greece
Kasai 55 C6 var. Cassai, Kassai. river Angola/Dem. Rep. Congo
Kasaji 55 D7 Katanga, S Dem. Rep. Congo
Kasama 56 D1 Northern, N Zambia
Kasan see Koson
Kāsaragod 110 B2 Kerala, SW India
Kaschau see Košice
Kāshān 98 C3 Eşfahān, C Iran
Kashgar see Kashi
Kashi 104 A3 Chin. Kaxgar, K'o-shih, Uigh. Kashgar. Xinjiang Uygur Zizhiqu, NW China
Kasi see Vārānasi
Kasongo 55 D6 Maniema, E Dem. Rep. Congo
Kasongo-Lunda 55 C7 Bandundu, SW Dem. Rep. Congo
Kásos 83 D7 island S Greece
Kaspiy Mangy Oypaty see Caspian Depression
Kaspiysk 89 B8 Respublika Dagestan, SW Russia
Kaspiyskoye More/Kaspiy Tengizi see Caspian Sea
Kassa see Košice
Kassai see Kasai
Kassala 50 C4 Kassala, E Sudan
Kassel 72 B4 prev. Cassel. Hessen, C Germany
Kasserine 49 E2 var. Al Qaşrayn. W Tunisia
Kastamonu 94 C2 var. Castamoni, Kastamuni. Kastamonu, N Turkey (Türkiye)
Kastamuni see Kastamonu
Kastaneá 82 B4 Kentrikí Makedonía, N Greece
Kastélli see Kíssamos
Kastoriá 82 B4 Dytikí Makedonía, N Greece
Kástro 83 C6 Sífnos, Kykládes, Greece, Aegean Sea
Kastsyukovichy 85 E7 Rus. Kostyukovichi. Mahilyowskaya Voblasts', E Belarus
Kastsyukowka 85 D7 Rus. Kostyukovka. Homyel'skaya Voblasts', SE Belarus
Kasulu 51 B7 Kigoma, W Tanzania
Kasumiga-ura 109 D5 lake Honshū, S Japan
Katahdin, Mount 19 G1 mountain Maine, NE USA
Katalla 14 C3 Alaska, USA
Katana see Qaţanā
Katanning 125 B7 Western Australia
Katawaz see Zarghūn Shahr
Katchall Island 111 F3 island Nicobar Islands, India, NE Indian Ocean
Kateríni 82 B4 Kentrikí Makedonía, N Greece
Katha 114 B2 Sagaing, N Myanmar (Burma)
Katherine 126 A2 Northern Territory, N Australia
Kathmandu 102 C3 prev. Kantipur. country capital (Nepal) Central, C Nepal
Katikati 128 D3 Bay of Plenty, North Island, New Zealand
Katima Mulilo 56 C3 Caprivi, NE Namibia
Katiola 52 D4 C Ivory Coast
Kati Thanda see Eyre, Lake
Kā Tiritiri o Te Moana see Southern Alps
Káto Achaïa 83 B5 var. Kato Ahaia, Káto Akhaía. Dytikí Ellás, S Greece
Kato Ahaia/Káto Akhaía see Káto Achaïa
Katoúna 83 A5 Dytikí Ellás, C Greece
Katowice 77 C5 Ger. Kattowitz. Śląskie, S Poland
Katsina 53 G3 Katsina, N Nigeria
Kattakurgan see Kattaqo'rg'on
Kattaqo'rg'on 101 E2 Rus. Kattakurgan. Samarqand Viloyati, C Uzbekistan
Kattavía 83 E7 Ródos, Dodekánisa, Greece, Aegean Sea
Kattegat 63 B7 Dan. Kattegatt. strait N Europe
Kattegatt see Kattegat
Kattowitz see Katowice
Kaua'i 25 A7 var. Kauai. island Hawaiian Islands, Hawaii, USA, C Pacific Ocean
Kauai see Kaua'i
Kauen see Kaunas
Kaufbeuren 73 C6 Bayern, S Germany
Kaunas 84 B4 Ger. Kauen, Pol. Kowno; prev. Rus. Kovno. Kaunas, C Lithuania
Kavadar see Kavadarci
Kavadarci 79 E6 Turk. Kavadar. C Macedonia
Kavaja see Kavajë
Kavajë 79 C6 It. Cavaia, Kavaja. Tiranë, W Albania
Kavakli see Topolovgrad
Kavála 82 C3 prev. Kaválla. Anatolikí Makedonía kai Thráki, NE Greece
Kāvali 110 D2 Andhra Pradesh, E India
Kavālla see Kavála
Kavango see Cubango/Okavango
Kavaratti Island 110 A3 island Lakshadweep, Lakshadweep, SW India Asia N Indian Ocean
Kavarna 82 E2 Dobrich, NE Bulgaria
Kavengo see Cubango/Okavango
Kavir, Dasht-e 98 D3 var. Great Salt Desert. salt pan N Iran
Kavkaz see Caucasus
Kawagoe 109 D5 Saitama, Honshū, S Japan
Kawasaki 108 A2 Kanagawa, Honshū, S Japan
Kawerau 128 E3 Bay of Plenty, North Island, New Zealand
Kaxgar see Kashi
Kaya 53 E3 C Burkina
Kayan 114 B4 Yangon, SW Burma (Myanmar)
Kayan, Sungai 116 D3 prev. Kajan. river Borneo, C Indonesia
Kayes 52 C3 Kayes, W Mali
Kayseri 94 D3 var. Kaisaria; anc. Caesarea Mazaca, Mazaca. Kayseri, C Turkey (Türkiye)
Kazach'ye 93 F2 Respublika Sakha (Yakutiya), NE Russia
Kazakh Soviet Socialist Republic see Kazakhstan
Kazakhskiy Melkosopchnik see Saryarqa
Kazakhstan 92 B4 off. Republic of Kazakhstan, var. Kazakstan, Kaz. Qazaqstan, Qazaqstan Respūblīkasy; prev. Kazakh Soviet Socialist Republic, Rus. Respublika Kazakhstan. country C Asia
Kazakhstan, Republic of see Kazakhstan
Kazakhstan, Respublika see Kazakhstan
Kazakh Steppe 92 C4 var. Kirghiz Steppe. uplands C Kazakhstan
Kazakstan see Kazakhstan
Kazan' 89 C5 Respublika Tatarstan, W Russia
Kazandzhik see Bereket
Kazanlak 82 D2 var. Kazanlŭk, Kazanlik. Stara Zagora, C Bulgaria
Kazanlik see Kazanlak
Kazanlŭk see Kazanlak
Kazatin see Koziatyn
Kazbegi see Kazbek
Kazbek 95 F1 var. Kazbegi, Geor. Mqinvartsveri. mountain N Georgia
Kāzerūn 98 D4 Fārs, S Iran
Kazi Magomed see Hacıqabul
Kazvin see Qazvīn
Kéa 83 C6 var. Tziá, Kéos; anc. Ceos. island Kykládes, Greece, Aegean Sea
Kea, Mauna 25 B8 mountain Hawaii, USA
Kéamu see Aneityum
Kearney 23 E4 Nebraska, C USA
Keban Baraji 95 E3 reservoir C Turkey (Türkiye)
Kebkabiya 50 A4 Northern Darfur, W Sudan
Kebnekaise 62 C3 mountain N Sweden
Kecskemét 77 D7 Bács-Kiskun, C Hungary
Kediri 116 D5 Jawa, C Indonesia
Kędzierzyn-Kozle 77 C5 Ger. Heydebrech. Opolskie, S Poland
Keelung 106 D6 var. Chilung, Jilong; Jap. Kirun, Kirun'; prev. Sp. Santissima Trinidad. N Taiwan
Keetmanshoop 56 B4 Karas, S Namibia
Kefallinía see Kefalloniá
Kefalloniá 83 A5 var. Kefallinía. island Iónia Nisiá, Greece, C Mediterranean Sea
Kefe see Feodosiia
Kegel see Keila
Kehl 73 A6 Baden-Württemberg, SW Germany
Kei Islands see Kai, Kepulauan
Keijō see Seoul
Keila 84 D2 Ger. Kegel. Harjumaa, NW Estonia
Keïta 53 F3 Tahoua, C Niger
Keith 127 B7 South Australia
Kěk-Art 101 G2 prev. Alaykel', Alay-Kuu. Oshskaya Oblast', SW Kyrgyzstan
Kékes 77 C6 mountain N Hungary
Kelamayi see Karamay
Kelang see Klang
Kelat see Kālat
Kelifskiy Uzboy see Kelif Uzboýy
Kelif Uzboýy 100 D3 Rus. Kelifskiy Uzboy. salt marsh E Turkmenistan
Kelkit Çayı 95 E3 river N Turkey (Türkiye)
Kelmė 84 B4 Šiaulai, C Lithuania
Kélo 54 B4 Tandjilé, SW Chad
Kelowna 15 E5 British Columbia, SW Canada
Kelso 24 B2 Washington, NW USA
Keltsy see Kielce
Keluang 116 B3 var. Kluang. Johor, Peninsular Malaysia, Malaysia
Kem' 88 B3 Respublika Kareliya, NW Russia
Kemah 95 E3 Erzincan, E Turkey (Türkiye)
Kemaman see Cukai
Kemerovo 92 D4 prev. Shcheglovsk. Kemerovskaya Oblast', C Russia
Kemi 62 D4 Lappi, NW Finland
Kemijärvi 62 D3 Swe. Kemiträsk. Lappi, N Finland
Kemijoki 62 D3 river NW Finland
Kemin 101 G2 prev. Bystrovka. Chuyskaya Oblast', N Kyrgyzstan
Kemins Island see Nikumaroro
Kemiträsk see Kemijärvi
Kemmuna 80 A5 var. Comino. island C Malta
Kempele 62 D4 Pohjois-Pohjanmaa, C Finland
Kempten 73 B7 Bayern, S Germany
Kendal 67 D5 NW England, United Kingdom
Kendari 117 E4 Sulawesi, C Indonesia
Kenedy 27 G4 Texas, SW USA
Kenema 52 C4 SE Sierra Leone
Kéneurgench see Köneürgenç
Kenge 55 C6 Bandundu, SW Dem. Rep. Congo
Kengtung 114 C3 pev. Keng Tung. Shan State, E Myanmar (Burma)
Keng Tung see Kengtung
Kénitra 48 C2 prev. Port-Lyautey. NW Morocco
Kennett 23 H5 Missouri, C USA
Kennewick 24 C2 Washington, NW USA
Kenora 16 A3 Ontario, S Canada
Kenosha 18 B3 Wisconsin, N USA
Kentau 92 B5 Türkistan/Turkestan, S Kazakhstan
Kentucky 18 C5 off. Commonwealth of Kentucky, also known as Bluegrass State. state C USA
Kentucky Lake 18 B5 reservoir Kentucky/Tennessee, S USA
Kentung see Keng Tung
Kenya 51 C6 off. Republic of Kenya. country E Africa
Kenya, Mount see Kirinyaga
Kenya, Republic of see Kenya
Keokuk 23 G4 Iowa, C USA
Kéos see Keá
Kępno 76 C4 Wielkopolskie, C Poland
Keppel Island see Niuatoputapu
Kerak see Al Karak
Kerala 110 C2 cultural region S India
Kerasunt see Giresun
Keratéa 83 C6 var. Keratea. Attikí, C Greece
Keratea see Keratéa
Kerbala/Kerbela see Karbalā'
Kerch 87 G5 Rus. Kerch'. Respublika Krym, SE Ukraine
Kerch' see Kerch
Kerchens'ka Protska/Kerchenskiy Proliv see Kerch Strait
Kerch Strait 87 G4 var. Bosporus Cimmerius, Enikale Strait, Rus. Kerchenskiy Proliv, Ukr. Kerchens'ka Protska. strait Black Sea/Sea of Azov
Keremitlik see Lyulyakovo
Kerguelen 119 C7 island C French Southern and Antarctic Lands
Kerguelen Plateau 119 C7 undersea plateau S Indian Ocean
Kerí 83 A6 Zákynthos, Iónia Nisiá, Greece, C Mediterranean Sea
Kerikeri 128 D2 Northland, North Island, New Zealand
Kerkenah, Îles de 80 D4 var. Kerkennah Islands, Ar. Juzur Qarqannah. island group E Tunisia
Kerkennah Islands see Kerkenah, Îles de
Kerki see Atamyrat
Kérkira see Kérkyra
Kerkrade 65 D6 Limburg, SE Netherlands
Kerkuk see Kirkūk
Kérkyra 82 A4 var. Kérkira, Eng. Corfu. Kérkyra, Iónia Nisiá, Greece, C Mediterranean Sea
Kermadec Islands 130 C4 island group New Zealand, SW Pacific Ocean
Kermadec Trench 121 E4 trench SW Pacific Ocean
Kermān 98 D3 var. Kirman; anc. Carmana. Kermān, C Iran
Kermānshāh 98 C3 var. Qahremānshahr; prev. Bākhtarān. Kermānshāhān, W Iran
Kerrville 27 F4 Texas, SW USA
Kertel see Kärdla
Kerulen 105 E2 Chin. Herlen He, Mong. Herlen Gol. river China/Mongolia
Kerýneia see Girne
Kesennuma 108 D4 Miyagi, Honshū, C Japan
Keszthely 77 C7 Zala, SW Hungary
Ketchikan 14 D4 Revillagigedo Island, Alaska, USA
Kętrzyn 76 D2 Ger. Rastenburg. Warmińsko-Mazurskie, NE Poland
Kettering 67 D6 C England, United Kingdom
Kettering 18 C4 Ohio, N USA
Keupriya see Primorsko
Keuruu 63 D5 Keski-Suomi, C Finland
Keweenaw Peninsula 18 B1 peninsula Michigan, N USA
Key Largo 21 F5 Key Largo, Florida, SE USA
Keystone State see Pennsylvania
Key West 21 E5 Florida Keys, Florida, SE USA
Kezdivásárhely see Târgu Secuiesc
Khabarovsk 93 G4 Khabarovskiy Kray, SE Russia
Khachmas see Xaçmaz
Khadera see Hadera
Khairpur 112 B3 Sindh, SE Pakistan
Khalīj as Suways 50 B2 var. Suez, Gulf of. gulf NE Egypt
Khalkidhikí see Chalkidikí
Khalkís see Chalkída
Khambhat, Gulf of 112 C4 Eng. Gulf of Cambay. gulf W India
Khamīs Mushayt 99 B6 var. Hamīs Musait. 'Asīr, SW Saudi Arabia
Khānābād 101 E3 Kunduz, NE Afghanistan
Khān al Baghdādī see Al Baghdādī
Khandwa 112 D4 Madhya Pradesh, C India
Khanh Hung see Soc Trăng
Khaniá see Chaniá
Khanka, Lake 107 E2 var. Hsing-K'ai Hu, Lake Hanka, Chin. Xingkai Hu, Rus. Ozero Khanka. lake China/Russia
Khanka, Ozero see Khanka, Lake
Khankendi see Xankändi
Khanthabouli 114 D4 prev. Savannakhét. Savannakhét, S Laos
Khanty-Mansiysk 92 C3 prev. Ostyako-Voguls'k. Khanty-Mansiyskiy Avtonomnyy Okrug-Yugra, C Russia
Khān Yūnis 97 A7 var. Khān Yūnus. S Gaza Strip
Khān Yūnus see Khān Yūnis
Khanzi see Ghanzi
Kharagpur 113 F4 West Bengal, NE India
Kharbin see Harbin
Kharkiv 87 G2 Rus. Khar'kov. Kharkivs'ka Oblast', NE Ukraine
Khar'kov see Kharkiv
Kharmanli 82 D3 Haskovo, S Bulgaria
Khartoum 50 B4 var. El Khartûm, Khartum. country capital (Sudan) Khartoum, C Sudan
Khartum see Khartoum
Khasavyurt 89 B8 Respublika Dagestan, SW Russia
Khash, Dasht-e 100 D5 Eng. Khash Desert. desert SW Afghanistan
Khash Desert see Khāsh, Dasht-e
Khashim Al Qirba/Khashm al Qirbah see Khashm el Girba
Khashm el Girba 50 C4 var. Khashim Al Qirba, Khashm al Qirbah. Kassala, E Sudan
Khaskovo see Haskovo
Khaybar, Kowtal-e see Khyber Pass
Khaydarkan 101 F2 var. Khaydarken. Batkenskaya Oblast', SW Kyrgyzstan
Khaydarken see Khaydarkan
Khazar, Baḩr-e/Khazar, Daryā-ye see Caspian Sea
Khelat see Kālat
Kherson 87 E4 Khersons'ka Oblast', S Ukraine
Kheta 93 E2 river N Russia
Khios see Chíos
Khiva/Khiwa see Xiva
Khmel'nitskiy see Khmel 'nyts'kyy
Khmelnytskyi 86 C2 prev. Khmel'nyts'kyy, Rus. Khmel'nitskiy; prev. Proskurov. Khmel'nyts'ka Oblast', W Ukraine
Khmel 'nyts'kyy see Khmelnytskyi
Khodasy 85 E6 Rus. Khodosy. Mahilyowskaya Voblasts', E Belarus
Khodoriv 86 C2 Pol. Chodorów, Rus. Khodorov. L'vivs'ka Oblast', NW Ukraine
Khodorov see Khodoriv
Khodosy see Khodasy
Khodzhent see Khujand
Khoi see Khvoy
Khojend see Khujand
Khokand see Qo'qon
Kholm see Khulm
Kholm see Chełm
Kholon see Holon
Khoms see Al Khums
Khong Sedone see Muang Khôngxédôn
Khon Kaen 114 D4 var. Muang Khon Kaen. Khon Kaen, E Thailand
Khor 93 G4 Khabarovskiy Kray, SE Russia
Khorat see Nakhon Ratchasima
Khorog see Khorugh
Khorugh 101 F3 Rus. Khorog. S Tajikistan
Khōst 101 F4 prev. Khowst. Khōst, E Afghanistan
Khotan see Hotan
Khouribga 48 B2 C Morocco
Khovd see Hovd
Khowst see Khōst
Khoy see Khvoy
Khoyniki 85 D8 Homyel'skaya Voblasts', SE Belarus
Khrustalnyi 87 H3 prev. Khrustal'nyy, Krindachevka. Rus. Krasnyi Luch. Luhans'ka Oblast', E Ukraine
Khrustal'nyy see Khrustalnyi
Khudzhand see Khujand
Khujand 101 E2 var. Khodzhent, Khojend, Rus. Khudzhand; prev. Leninabad, Taj. Leninobod. N Tajikistan
Khulm 101 E3 var. Kholm, Tashqurghan. Balkh, N Afghanistan
Khulna 113 G4 Khulna, SW Bangladesh
Khums see Al Khums
Khust 86 B3 var. Husté, Cz. Chust, Hung. Huszt. Zakarpats'ka Oblast', W Ukraine
Khvoy 98 C2 var. Khoi, Khoy. Āẕarbāyjān-e Bākhtarī, NW Iran
Khyber Pass 112 C1 var. Kowtal-e Khaybar. pass Afghanistan/Pakistan
Kiangmai see Chiang Mai
Kiang-ning see Nanjing
Kiangsi see Jiangxi
Kiangsu see Jiangsu
Kiáto 83 B6 prev. Kiáton. Pelopónnisos, S Greece
Kiáton see Kiáto
Kiayi see Chiayi
Kibangou 55 B6 Niari, SW Congo
Kibombo 55 D6 Maniema, E Dem. Rep. Congo
Kıbrıs/Kıbrıs Cumhuriyeti see Cyprus
Kičevo 79 D6 SW Macedonia
Kidderminster 67 D6 C England, United Kingdom
Kiel 72 B2 Schleswig-Holstein, N Germany
Kielce 76 D4 Rus. Keltsy. Świętokrzyskie, C Poland
Kieler Bucht 72 B2 bay N Germany
Kiev see Kyiv
Kiffa 52 C3 Assaba, S Mauritania
Kigali 51 B6 country capital (Rwanda) C Rwanda
Kigoma 51 B7 Kigoma, W Tanzania
Kihnu 84 C2 var. Kihnu Saar, Ger. Kühnö. island SW Estonia
Kihnu Saar see Kihnu
Kii-suido 109 C7 strait S Japan
Kikinda 78 D3 Ger. Grosskikinda, Hung. Nagykikinda; prev. Velika Kikinda. Vojvodina, N Serbia
Kikládhes see Kykládes
Kikwit 55 C6 Bandundu, W Dem. Rep. Congo
Kilien Mountains see Qilian Shan
Kilimane see Quelimane
Kilimanjaro 47 E5 region E Tanzania
Kilimanjaro 51 C7 var. Uhuru Peak. volcano NE Tanzania
Kilingi-Nõmme 84 D3 Ger. Kurkund. Pärnumaa, SW Estonia
Kilis 94 D4 Kilis, S Turkey (Türkiye)
Kiliya 86 D4 Rom. Chilia-Nouă. Odes'ka Oblast', SW Ukraine
Kilkenny 67 B6 Ir. Cill Chainnigh. Kilkenny, S Ireland
Kilkís 82 B3 Kentrikí Makedonía, N Greece
Killarney 67 A6 Ir. Cill Airne. Kerry, SW Ireland
Killeen 27 G3 Texas, SW USA
Kilmain see Quelimane
Kilmarnock 66 C4 W Scotland, United Kingdom
Kilwa see Kilwa Kivinje
Kilwa Kivinje 51 C7 var. Kilwa. Lindi, SE Tanzania
Kimberley 56 C4 Northern Cape, C South Africa
Kimberley Plateau 124 C3 plateau Western Australia
Kimch'aek 107 E3 prev. Sŏngjin. E North Korea
Kími see Kými
Kinabalu, Gunung 116 D3 mountain East Malaysia
Kindersley 15 F5 Saskatchewan, S Canada
Kindia 52 C4 Guinée-Maritime, SW Guinea
Kindley Field 20 A4 air base E Bermuda
Kindu 55 D6 prev. Kindu-Port-Empain. Maniema, C Dem. Rep. Congo
Kindu-Port-Empain see Kindu
Kineshma 89 C5 Ivanovskaya Oblast', W Russia
King Abdullah Economic City 99 A5 W Saudi Arabia
King Charles Islands see Kong Karls Land
King Christian IX Land see Kong Christian IX Land
King Frederik VI Coast see Kong Frederik VI Kyst
King Frederik VIII Land see Kong Frederik VIII Land
King Island 127 B8 island Tasmania, SE Australia
King Island see Kadan Kyun
Kingissepp see Kuressaare
Kingman 26 A1 Arizona, SW USA
Kingman Reef 123 E2 US territory C Pacific Ocean
Kingsford Smith 126 E2 (Sydney) New South Wales, SE Australia
King's Lynn 67 E6 var. Bishop's Lynn, Kings Lynn, Lynn, Lynn Regis. E England, United Kingdom
Kings Lynn see King's Lynn
King Sound 124 B3 sound Western Australia
Kingsport 21 E1 Tennessee, S USA
Kingston 32 B5 country capital (Jamaica) E Jamaica
Kingston 16 D5 Ontario, SE Canada
Kingston 19 F3 New York, NE USA
Kingston upon Hull 67 D5 var. Hull. E England, United Kingdom
Kingston upon Thames 67 A8 SE England, United Kingdom
Kingstown 33 H4 country capital (Saint Vincent and the Grenadines) Saint Vincent, Saint Vincent and the Grenadines
Kingstown see Dún Laoghaire
Kingsville 27 F5 Texas, SW USA
King William Island 15 F3 island Nunavut, N Canada

Kinneret, Yam *97 B5 var.* Chinnereth, Sea of Bahr Tabariya, Sea of Galilee, Lake Tiberias, *Ar.* Bahrat Tabariya. *lake* N Israel
Kinrooi *65 D5* Limburg, NE Belgium
Kinshasa *55 B6 prev.* Léopoldville. *country capital* (Dem. Rep. Congo) Kinshasa, W Dem. Rep. Congo
Kintyre *66 B4 peninsula* W Scotland, United Kingdom
Kinyeti *51 B5 mountain* S South Sudan
Kiparissía *see* Kyparissía
Kipili *51 B7* Rukwa, W Tanzania
Kipushi *55 D8* Katanga, SE Dem. Rep. Congo
Kirdzhali *see* Kardzhali
Kirghizia *see* Kyrgyzstan
Kirghiz Range *101 F2 Rus.* Kirgizskiy Khrebet; *prev.* Alexander Range. *mountain range* Kazakhstan/Kyrgyzstan
Kirghiz SSR *see* Kyrgyzstan
Kirghiz Steppe *see* Kazakh Steppe
Kirgizskaya SSR *see* Kyrgyzstan
Kirgizskiy Khrebet *see* Kirghiz Range
Kiriath-Arba *see* Hebron
Kiribati *123 F2 off.* Republic of Kiribati. *country* C Pacific Ocean
Kiribati, Republic of *see* Kiribati
Kırıkhan *94 D4* Hatay, S Turkey (Türkiye)
Kırıkkale *94 C3 province* C Turkey (Türkiye)
Kirin *see* Jilin
Kirinyaga *51 C6 prev.* Mount Kenya. *volcano* C Kenya
Kirishi *88 B4 var.* Kirisi. Leningradskaya Oblast', NW Russia
Kirisi *see* Kirishi
Kiritimati *123 G2 prev.* Christmas Island. *atoll* Line Islands, E Kiribati
Kirkenes *62 E2 Fin.* Kirkkoniemi. Finnmark, N Norway
Kirk-Kilissa *see* Kırklareli
Kirkkoniemi *see* Kirkenes
Kirkland Lake *16 D4* Ontario, S Canada
Kırklareli *94 A2 prev.* Kirk-Kilissa. Kırklareli, NW Turkey (Türkiye)
Kirkpatrick, Mount *132 B3 mountain* Antarctica
Kirksville *23 G4* Missouri, C USA
Kirkūk *98 B3 var.* Karkūk, Kerkuk. At Ta'mīn, N Iraq
Kirkwall *66 C2* NE Scotland, United Kingdom
Kirkwood *23 G4* Missouri, C USA
Kir Moab/Kir of Moab *see* Al Karak
Kirov *89 C5 prev.* Vyatka. Kirovskaya Oblast', NW Russia
Kirovabad *see* Gäncä
Kirovakan *see* Vanadzor
Kirovo-Chepetsk *89 D5* Kirovskaya Oblast', NW Russia
Kirovohrad *see* Kropyvnytskyi
Kirovo *see* Kropyvnytskyi
Kirthar Range *112 B3 mountain range* S Pakistan
Kiruna *62 C3 Lapp.* Giron. Norrbotten, N Sweden
Kirun/Kirun' *see* Keelung
Kisalföld *see* Little Alföld
Kisangani *55 D5 prev.* Stanleyville. Orientale, NE Dem. Rep. Congo
Kishinev *see* Chişinău
Kislovodsk *89 B7* Stavropol'skiy Kray, SW Russia
Kismaayo *51 D6 var.* Chisimayu, Kismayu, *It.* Chisimaio. Jubbada Hoose, S Somalia
Kismayu *see* Kismaayo
Kíssamos *83 C7 prev.* Kastélli. Kríti, Greece, E Mediterranean Sea
Kissidougou *52 C4* Guinée-Forestière, S Guinea
Kissimmee, Lake *21 E4 lake* Florida, SE USA
Kistna *see* Krishna
Kisumu *51 C6 prev.* Port Florence. Nyanza, W Kenya
Kisvárda *77 E6 Ger.* Kleinwardein. Szabolcs-Szatmár-Bereg, E Hungary
Kita *52 D3* Kayes, W Mali
Kitab *see* Kitob
Kitakyūshū *109 A7 var.* Kitakyûsyû. Fukuoka, Kyūshū, SW Japan
Kitakyûsyû *see* Kitakyūshū
Kitami *108 D2* Hokkaidō, NE Japan
Kitchener *16 C5* Ontario, S Canada
Kitega *see* Gitega
Kíthnos *see* Kýthnos
Kitimat *14 D4* British Columbia, SW Canada
Kitinen *62 D3 river* N Finland
Kitob *101 E3 Rus.* Kitab. Qashqadaryo Viloyati, S Uzbekistan
Kitwe *56 D2 var.* Kitwe-Nkana. Copperbelt, C Zambia
Kitwe-Nkana *see* Kitwe
Kitzbüheler Alpen *73 C7 mountain range* W Austria
Kivalina *14 C2* Alaska, USA
Kivalo *62 D3 ridge* C Finland
Kivertsi *86 C1 Pol.* Kiwerce, *Rus.* Kivertsy. Volyns'ka Oblast', NW Ukraine
Kivertsy *see* Kivertsi
Kivu, Lac *see* Kivu, Lake
Kivu, Lake *55 E6 Fr.* Lac Kivu. *lake* Rwanda/Dem. Rep. Congo
Kiwerce *see* Kivertsi
Kiyev *see* Kyiv
Kiyevskoye Vodokhranilishche *see* Kyivske Vodoskhovyshche
Kızıl Irmak *94 C3 river* C Turkey (Türkiye)
Kizil Kum *see* Kyzylkum Desert
Kizyl-Arvat *see* Serdar
Kjølen *see* Kölen
Kladno *77 A5* Středočeský, NW Czechia (Czech Republic)
Klagenfurt *73 D7 Slvn.* Celovec. Kärnten, S Austria
Klaipėda *84 B3 Ger.* Memel. Klaipeda, NW Lithuania
Klamath Falls *24 B4* Oregon, NW USA
Klamath Mountains *24 A4 mountain range* California/Oregon, W USA
Klang *116 B3 var.* Kelang; *prev.* Port Swettenham. Selangor, Peninsular Malaysia
Klarälven *63 B6 river* Norway/Sweden
Klatovy *77 A5 Ger.* Klattau. Plzeňský Kraj, W Czechia (Czech Republic)
Klattau *see* Klatovy
Klausenburg *see* Cluj-Napoca
Klazienaveen *64 E2* Drenthe, NE Netherlands
Kleines Ungarisches Tiefland *see* Little Alföld
Klein Karas *56 B4* Karas, S Namibia
Kleinwardein *see* Kisvárda
Kleisoúra *83 A5* Ípeiros, W Greece
Klerksdorp *56 D4* North-West, N South Africa
Klimavichy *85 E7 Rus.* Klimovichi. Mahilyowskaya Voblasts', E Belarus
Klimovichi *see* Klimavichy
Klintsy *89 A5* Bryanskaya Oblast', W Russia
Klisura *82 C2* Plovdiv, C Bulgaria
Ključ *78 B3* Federacija Bosna I Hercegovina, NW Bosnia and Herzegovina
Kłobuck *76 C4* Śląskie, S Poland
Klosters *73 B7* Graubünden, SE Switzerland
Kluang *see* Keluang
Kluczbork *76 C4 Ger.* Kreuzburg, Kreuzburg in Oberschlesien. Opolskie, S Poland
Klyuchevskaya Sopka, Vulkan *93 H3 volcano* E Russia
Knin *78 B4* Šibenik-Knin, S Croatia
Knjaževac *78 E4* Serbia, E Serbia
Knokke-Heist *65 A5* West-Vlaanderen, NW Belgium
Knoxville *20 D1* Tennessee, S USA
Knud Rasmussen Land *60 D1 physical region* N Greenland
Kobdo *see* Hovd
Kōbe *109 C6* Hyōgo, Honshū, SW Japan
København *63 B7 Eng.* Copenhagen; *anc.* Hafnia. *country capital* (Denmark) Sjælland, København, E Denmark
Kobenni *52 D3* Hodh el Gharbi, S Mauritania
Koblenz *73 A5 prev.* Coblenz, *Fr.* Coblence; *anc.* Confluentes. Rheinland-Pfalz, W Germany
Kobrin *see* Kobryn
Kobryn *85 A6 Rus.* Kobrin. Brestskaya Voblasts', SW Belarus
Kobuleti *95 F2 prev.* K'obulet'i. W Georgia
K'obulet'i *see* Kobuleti
Kočani *79 E6* NE Macedonia
Kočevje *73 D8 Ger.* Gottschee. S Slovenia
Koch Bihār *113 G3* West Bengal, NE India
Kochchi *see* Kochi
Kochi *110 C3 var.* Cochin, Kochchi. Kerela SW India
Kōchi *109 B7 var.* Kôti. Kōchi, Shikoku, SW Japan
Kochiu *see* Gejiu
Kodiak *14 C3* Kodiak Island, Alaska, USA
Kodiak Island *14 C3 island* Alaska, USA
Koedoes *see* Kudus
Koeln *see* Köln
Koepang *see* Kupang
Ko-erh-mu *see* Golmud
Koetai *see* Mahakam, Sungai
Koetaradja *see* Bandaaceh
Kōfu *109 D5 var.* Kôhu. Yamanashi, Honshū, S Japan
Kogarah *126 E2* New South Wales, E Australia
Kogon *100 D2 Rus.* Kagan. Buxoro Viloyati, C Uzbekistan
Kőhalom *see* Rupea
Kohīma *113 H3 state capital* Nāgāland, E India
Kohtla-Järve *84 E2* Ida-Virumaa, NE Estonia
Kôhu *see* Kōfu
Kokand *see* Qo'qon
Kokchetav *see* Kökshetaū
Kokkola *62 D4 Swe.* Karleby; *prev. Swe.* Gamlakarleby. Österbotten, W Finland
Koko *53 F4* Kebbi, W Nigeria
Kokomo *18 C4* Indiana, N USA
Koko Nor *see* Qinghai, China
Koko Nor *see* Qinghai Hu, China
Kokrines *14 C2* Alaska, USA
Kokshaal-Tau *101 G2 Rus.* Khrebet Kakshaal-Too. *mountain range* China/Kyrgyzstan
Kokshetau *see* Kökshetaū
Kökshetaū *92 C4 var.* Kokshetau; *prev.* Kokchetav. Kokshetau, N Kazakhstan
Koksijde *65 A5* West-Vlaanderen, W Belgium
Koksoak *16 D2 river* Québec, E Canada
Kokstad *56 D5* KwaZulu/Natal, E South Africa
Kolaka *117 E4* Sulawesi, C Indonesia
K'o-la-ma-i *see* Karamay
Kola Peninsula *see* Kol'skiy Poluostrov
Kolari *62 D3* Lappi, NW Finland
Kolárovo *77 C6 Ger.* Gutta; *prev.* Guta, *Hung.* Gúta. Nitriansky Kraj, SW Slovakia
Kolberg *see* Kołobrzeg
Kolda *52 C3* S Senegal
Kolding *63 A7* Vejle, C Denmark
Kölen *59 E1 Nor.* Kjølen. *mountain range* Norway/Sweden
Kolguyev, Ostrov *88 C2 island* NW Russia
Kolhāpur *110 B1* Mahārāshtra, SW India
Kolhumadulu *110 A5 var.* Thaa Atoll. *atoll* S Maldives
Kolín *77 B5 Ger.* Kolin. Střední Čechy, C Czechia (Czech Republic)
Kolka *84 C2* Talsi, NW Latvia
Kolkasrags *84 C2 prev. Eng.* Cape Domesnes. *headland* NW Latvia
Kolkāta *113 G4 prev.* Calcutta. West Bengal, N India
Kollam *110 C3 var.* Quilon. Kerala, SW India
Kolmar *see* Colmar
Köln *72 A4 var.* Koeln, *Eng./Fr.* Cologne, *prev.* Cöln; *anc.* Colonia Agrippina, Oppidum Ubiorum. Nordrhein-Westfalen, W Germany
Koło *76 C3* Wielkopolskie, C Poland
Kołobrzeg *76 B2 Ger.* Kolberg. Zachodnio-pomorskie, NW Poland
Kolokani *52 D3* Koulikoro, W Mali
Kolomea *see* Kolomyia
Kolomna *89 B5* Moskovskaya Oblast', W Russia
Kolomyia *86 C3 prev.* Kolomyya, *Ger.* Kolomea. Ivano-Frankivs'ka Oblast', W Ukraine
Kolomyya *see* Kolomyia
Kolosjoki *see* Nikel'
Kolozsvár *see* Cluj-Napoca
Kolpa *78 A2 Ger.* Kulpa, *Croatian* Kupa. *river* Croatia/Slovenia
Kolpino *88 B4* Leningradskaya Oblast', NW Russia
Kólpos Mórfu *see* Güzelyurt Körfezi
Kol'skiy Poluostrov *88 C2 Eng.* Kola Peninsula. *peninsula* NW Russia
Kolwezi *55 D7* Katanga, S Dem. Rep. Congo
Kolyma *93 G2 river* NE Russia
Komatsu *109 C5 var.* Komatu. Ishikawa, Honshū, SW Japan
Komatu *see* Komatsu
Kommunizm, Qullai *see* Ismoili Somoní, Qullai
Komoé *53 E4 var.* Komoé Fleuve. *river* E Ivory Coast
Komoé Fleuve *see* Komoé
Komotau *see* Chomutov
Komotiní *82 D3 var.* Gümüljina, *Turk.* Gümülcine. Anatolikí Makedonía kai Thráki, NE Greece
Kompong Som *see* Sihanoukville
Komrat *see* Comrat
Komsomolets, Ostrov *93 E1 island* Severnaya Zemlya, N Russia
Komsomol'sk-na-Amure *93 G4* Khabarovskiy Kray, SE Russia
Kondolovo *82 E3* Burgas, E Bulgaria
Kondopoga *88 B3* Respublika Kareliya, NW Russia
Kondoz *see* Kunduz
Köneürgenç *100 C2 var.* Köneürgench, *Rus.* Këneurgench; *prev.* Kunya-Urgench. Daşoguz Welaýaty, N Turkmenistan
Kong Christian IX Land *60 D4 Eng.* King Christian IX Land. *physical region* SE Greenland
Kong Frederik IX Land *60 C3 physical region* SW Greenland
Kong Frederik VIII Land *61 E2 Eng.* King Frederik VIII Land. *physical region* NE Greenland
Kong Frederik VI Kyst *60 C4 Eng.* King Frederik VI Coast. *physical region* SE Greenland
Kong Karls Land *61 G2 Eng.* King Charles Islands. *island group* SE Svalbard
Kongo *see* Congo (river)
Kongolo *55 D6* Katanga, E Dem. Rep. Congo
Kongor *51 B5* Jonglei, E South Sudan
Kong Oscar Fjord *61 E3 fjord* E Greenland
Kongsberg *63 B6* Buskerud, S Norway
Kông, Tônle *115 E5 var.* Xê Kong. *river* Cambodia/Laos
Kong, Xê *see* Kông, Tônle
Königgrätz *see* Hradec Králové
Königshütte *see* Chorzów
Konin *76 C3 Ger.* Kuhnau. Weilkopolskie, C Poland
Koninkrijk der Nederlanden *see* Netherlands
Konispol *79 C7 var.* Konispoli. Vlorë, S Albania
Konispoli *see* Konispol
Kónitsa *82 A4* Ípeiros, W Greece
Konitz *see* Chojnice
Konjic *78 C4* Federacija Bosna I Hercegovina, S Bosnia and Herzegovina
Konosha *88 C4* Arkhangel'skaya Oblast', NW Russia
Konotop *87 F1* Sums'ka Oblast', NE Ukraine
Konstantinovka *see* Kostiantynivka
Konstanz *73 B7 var.* Constanz, *Eng.* Constance, *hist.* Kostnitz; *anc.* Constantia. Baden-Württemberg, S Germany
Konstanza *see* Constanța
Konya *94 C4 var.* Konieh, *prev.* Konia; *anc.* Iconium. Konya, C Turkey (Türkiye)
Kopaonik *79 D5 mountain range* S Serbia
Kopar *see* Koper
Koper *73 D8 It.* Capodistria; *prev.* Kopar. SW Slovenia
Köpetdag Gershi *100 C3 mountain range* Iran/Turkmenistan
Köpetdag Gershi/Kopetdag, Khrebet *see* Koppeh Dāgh
Koppeh Dagh *98 D2 Rus.* Khrebet Kopetdag, *Turkm.* Köpetdag Gershi. *mountain range* Iran/Turkmenistan
Kopreinitz *see* Koprivnica
Koprivnica *78 B2 Ger.* Kopreinitz, *Hung.* Kaproncza. Koprivnica-Križevci, N Croatia
Köprülü *see* Veles
Koptsevichi *see* Kaptsevichy
Kopyl' *see* Kapyl'
Korat *see* Nakhon Ratchasima
Korat Plateau *114 D4 plateau* E Thailand
Korba *113 E4* Chhattīsgarh, C India
Korça *see* Korçë
Korçë *79 D6 var.* Korça, *Gk.* Korytsa, *It.* Corriza; *prev.* Koritsa. Korçë, SE Albania
Korčula *78 B4 It.* Curzola; *anc.* Corcyra Nigra. *island* S Croatia
Korea Bay *105 G3 bay* China/North Korea
Korea, Democratic People's Republic of *see* North Korea
Korea, Republic of *see* South Korea
Korea Strait *109 A7 Jap.* Chōsen-kaikyō, *Kor.* Taehan-haehyŏp. *channel* Japan/South Korea
Korhogo *52 D4* N Ivory Coast
Korinthos *83 B6 anc.* Corinthus *Eng.* Corinth. Pelopónnisos, S Greece
Korinthiakós Kólpos *83 B5 Eng.* Gulf of Corinth; *anc.* Corinthiacus Sinus. *gulf* C Greece
Koritsa *see* Korçë
Kōriyama *109 D5* Fukushima, Honshū, C Japan
Korla *104 C3 Chin.* K'u-erh-lo. Xinjiang Uygur Zizhiqu, NW China
Körmend *77 B7* Vas, W Hungary
Koróni *83 B6* Pelopónnisos, S Greece
Koror *122 A2* (Palau) Oreor, N Palau
Kőrös *see* Križevci
Korosten' *86 D1* Zhytomyrs'ka Oblast', NW Ukraine
Koro Toro *54 C2* Borkou-Ennedi-Tibesti, N Chad
Korsovka *see* Kārsava
Kortrijk *65 A6 Fr.* Courtrai. West-Vlaanderen, W Belgium
Koryak Range *93 H2 var.* Koryakskiy Khrebet, *Eng.* Koryak Range. *mountain range* NE Russia
Koryak Range *see* Koryakskoye Nagor'ye
Koryakskiy Khrebet *see* Koryakskoye Nagor'ye
Koryazhma *88 C4* Arkhangel'skaya Oblast', NW Russia
Korytsa *see* Korçë
Kos *83 E6* Kos, Dodekánisa, Greece, Aegean Sea
Kos *83 E6 It.* Coo; *anc.* Cos. *island* Dodekánisa, Greece, Aegean Sea
Ko-saki *109 A7 headland* Nagasaki, Tsushima, SW Japan
Kościan *76 B4 Ger.* Kosten. Wielkopolskie, C Poland
Kościerzyna *76 C2* Pomorskie, NW Poland
Kosciusko, Mount *see* Kosciuszko, Mount
Kosciuszko, Mount *127 C7 prev.* Mount Kosciusko. *mountain* New South Wales, SE Australia
K'o-shih *see* Kashi
Koshikijima-retto *109 A8 var.* Kosikizima Rettô. *island group* SW Japan
Kōshū *see* Gwangju
Košice *77 D6 Ger.* Kaschau, *Hung.* Kassa. Košický Kraj, E Slovakia
Kosikizima Rettô *see* Koshikijima-rettō
Köslin *see* Koszalin
Koson *101 E3 Rus.* Kasan. Qashqadaryo Viloyati, S Uzbekistan
Kosovo *79 D5 prev.* Autonomous Province of Kosovo and Metohija. *country (not fully recognised)* SE Europe
Kosovo and Metohija, Autonomous Province of *see* Kosovo
Kosovo Polje *see* Fushë Kosovë
Kosovska Mitrovica *see* Mitrovicë
Kosrae *122 C2 prev.* Kusaie. *island* Caroline Islands, E Micronesia
Kossou, Lac de *52 D5 lake* C Ivory Coast
Kostanay *see* Qostanay
Kosten *see* Kościan
Kostenets *82 C2 prev.* Georgi Dimitrov. Sofiya, W Bulgaria
Kostiantynivka *87 G3 prev.* Kostyantynivka, *Rus.* Konstantinovka. Donets'ka Oblast', SE Ukraine
Kostnitz *see* Konstanz
Kostroma *88 B4* Kostromskaya Oblast', NW Russia
Kostyantynivka *see* Kostiantynivka
Kostyukovichi *see* Kastsyukovichy
Kostyukovka *see* Kastsyukovka
Koszalin *76 B2 Ger.* Köslin. Zachodnio-pomorskie, NW Poland
Kota *112 D3 prev.* Kotah. Rājasthān, N India
Kota Baharu *see* Kota Bharu
Kota Bahru *see* Kota Bharu
Kotabaru *see* Jayapura
Kota Bharu *116 B3 var.* Kota Baharu, Kota Bahru. Kelantan, Peninsular Malaysia
Kotaboemi *see* Kotabumi
Kotabumi *116 B4 prev.* Kotaboemi. Sumatera, W Indonesia
Kotah *see* Kota
Kota Kinabalu *116 D3 prev.* Jesselton. Sabah, East Malaysia
Kotel'nyy, Ostrov *93 E2 island* Novosibirskiye Ostrova, N Russia
Kotka *63 E5* Kymenlaakso, S Finland
Kotlas *88 C4* Arkhangel'skaya Oblast', NW Russia
Kotonu *see* Cotonou
Kotor *79 C5 It.* Cattaro. SW Montenegro
Kotovsk *see* Podilsk
Kotovsk *see* Hîncești
Kottbus *see* Cottbus
Kotto *54 D4 river* Central African Republic/Dem. Rep. Congo
Kotuy *93 E2 river* N Russia
Koudougou *53 E4* C Burkina
Koulamoutou *55 B6* Ogooué-Lolo, C Gabon
Koulikoro *52 D3* Koulikoro, SW Mali
Koumra *54 C4* Moyen-Chari, S Chad
Kourou *37 H3* N French Guiana
Kousseir *see* Al Quşayr
Kousséri *54 B3 prev.* Fort-Foureau. Extrême-Nord, NE Cameroon
Koutiala *52 D4* Sikasso, S Mali
Kouvola *63 E5* Kymenlaakso, S Finland
Kovel *86 C1 Pol.* Kowel. Volyns'ka Oblast', NW Ukraine
Kovno *see* Kaunas
Koweit *see* Kuwait
Kowel *see* Kovel
Kowloon *106 A2* Hong Kong, S China
Kowno *see* Kaunas
Kozáni *82 B4* Dytikí Makedonía, N Greece
Kozara *78 B3 mountain range* NW Bosnia and Herzegovina
Kozarska Dubica *see* Bosanska Dubica
Kozhikode *110 C2 var.* Calicut. Kerala, SW India
Koziatyn *86 D2 prev.* Kozyatyn, *Rus.* Kazatin. Vinnyts'ka Oblast', C Ukraine
Kozu-shima *109 D6 island* E Japan
Kozyatyn *see* Koziatyn
Kpalimé *53 E5 var.* Palimé. SW Togo
Krâchéh *see* Kratie
Kragujevac *78 D4* Serbia, C Serbia
Krainburg *see* Kranj
Kra, Isthmus of *115 B6 isthmus* Malaysia/Thailand
Krakau *see* Kraków
Kraków *77 D5 Eng.* Cracow, *Ger.* Krakau; *anc.* Cracovia. Małopolskie, S Poland
Krâlănh *115 D5* Siĕmréab, NW Cambodia
Kralendijk *33 E5 dependent territory capital* (Bonaire) Lesser Antilles, S Caribbean Sea
Kraljevo *78 D4 prev.* Rankovićevo. Serbia, C Serbia
Kramatorsk *87 G3* Donets'ka Oblast', SE Ukraine
Kramfors *63 C5* Västernorrland, C Sweden
Kranéa *see* Kraniá
Kraniá *82 B4 var.* Kranéa. Dytikí Makedonía, N Greece
Kranj *73 D7 Ger.* Krainburg. NW Slovenia
Kranz *see* Zelenogradsk
Krāslava *84 D4* Krāslava, SE Latvia
Krasnaye *85 C5 Rus.* Krasnoye. Minskaya Voblasts', C Belarus
Krasnoarmeysk *89 C6* Saratovskaya Oblast', W Russia
Krasnodar *89 A7 prev.* Ekaterinodar, Yekaterinodar. Krasnodarskiy Kray, SW Russia
Krasnodon *see* Sorokyne
Krasnogor *see* Kallaste
Krasnogvardeyskoye *see* Kurman
Krasnohvardiyske *see* Kurman
Krasnokamensk *93 F4* Chitinskaya Oblast', S Russia
Krasnokamsk *89 D5* Permskaya Oblast', W Russia
Krasnoperekopsk *see* Yany Kapu
Krasnostav *see* Krasnystaw
Krasnovodsk *see* Türkmenbaşy
Krasnovodskiy Zaliv *see* Türkmenbasy Aylagy
Krasnowodsk Aylagy *see* Türkmenbasy Aylagy
Krasnoyarsk *92 D4* Krasnoyarskiy Kray, S Russia
Krasnoye *see* Krasnaye
Krasnystaw *76 E4 Rus.* Krasnostav. Lubelskie, SE Poland
Krasnyy Kut *89 C6* Saratovskaya Oblast', W Russia
Krasnyi Luch *see* Khrustalnyi
Kratie *115 D6 Khmer.* Krâchéh. Kratie, E Cambodia
Krâvanh, Chuŏr Phnum *115 C6 Eng.* Cardamom Mountains, *Fr.* Chaîne des Cardamomes. *mountain range* W Cambodia
Krefeld *72 A4* Nordrhein-Westfalen, W Germany
Kreisstadt *see* Krosno Odrzańskie
Kremenchug *see* Kremenchuk
Kremenchugskoye Vodokhranilishche/Kremenchuk Reservoir *see* Kremenchutske Vodoskhovyshche
Kremenchuk *87 F2 Rus.* Kremenchug. Poltavs'ka Oblast', NE Ukraine
Kremenchuk Reservoir *see* Kremenchutske Vodoskhovyshche
Kremenchutske Vodoskhovyshche *87 F2 Eng.* Kremenchuk Reservoir, *Rus.* Kremenchugskoye Vodokhranilishche. *reservoir* C Ukraine
Kremenets *86 C2 Pol.* Krzemieniec. Ternopil's'ka Oblast', W Ukraine
Kremennaya *see* Kreminna
Kreminna *87 G2 Rus.* Kremennaya. Luhans'ka Oblast', E Ukraine
Kresena *see* Kresna
Kresna *82 C3 var.* Kresena. Blagoevgrad, SW Bulgaria
Kretikon Delagos *see* Kritikó Pélagos
Kretinga *84 B3 Ger.* Krottingen. Klaipėda, NW Lithuania
Kreutz *see* Cristuru Secuiesc
Kreuz *see* Križevci, Croatia
Kreuz *see* Risti, Estonia
Kreuzburg/Kreuzburg in Oberschlesien *see* Kluczbork
Krichëv *see* Krychaw
Krievija *see* Russia
Krindachevka *see* Khrustal'nyy
Krishna *110 C1 prev.* Kistna. *river* C India
Krishnagiri *110 C2* Tamil Nādu, SE India
Kristiania *see* Oslo
Kristiansand *63 A6 var.* Christiansand. Vest-Agder, S Norway
Kristianstad *63 B7* Skåne, S Sweden
Kristiansund *62 A4 var.* Christiansund. Møre og Romsdal, S Norway
Kríti *83 C7 Eng.* Crete. *island* Greece, Aegean Sea
Kritikó Pélagos *83 D7 var.* Kretikon Delagos, *Eng.* Sea of Crete; *anc.* Mare Creticum. *sea* Greece, Aegean Sea
Krivoy Rog *see* Kryvyi Rih
Križevci *78 B2 Ger.* Kreuz, *Hung.* Kőrös. Varaždin, NE Croatia
Krk *78 A3 It.* Veglia; *anc.* Curieta. *island* NW Croatia
Kroatien *see* Croatia
Krolevets *87 F1* Sums'ka Oblast', NE Ukraine
Królewska Huta *see* Chorzów
Kronach *73 C5* Bayern, E Germany
Kronstadt *see* Braşov
Kroonstad *56 D4* Free State, C South Africa
Kropotkin *89 A7* Krasnodarskiy Kray, SW Russia
Kropyvnytskyi *87 E3 prev.* Kropyvnyts'kyy, *Rus.* Kirovohrad; *prev.* Kirovo, Yelizavetgrad, Zinov'yevsk. Kirovohrads'ka Oblast', C Ukraine
Kropyvnyts'kyy *see* Kropyvnytskyi
Krosno *77 D5 Ger.* Krossen. Podkarpackie, SE Poland
Krosno Odrzańskie *76 B3 Ger.* Crossen, Kreisstadt. Lubuskie, W Poland
Krossen *see* Krosno
Krottingen *see* Kretinga
Krško *73 E8 Ger.* Gurkfeld; *prev.* Videm-Krško. E Slovenia
Krugloye *see* Kruhlaye
Kruhlaye *85 D6 Rus.* Krugloye. Mahilyowskaya Voblasts', E Belarus
Kruja *see* Krujë
Krujë *79 C6 var.* Kruja, *It.* Croia. Durrës, C Albania
Krummau *see* Český Krumlov
Krung Thep *115 C5 var.* Krung Thep Mahanakhon, *Eng.* Bangkok. *country capital* (Thailand) Bangkok, C Thailand
Krung Thep, Ao *115 C5 var.* Bight of Bangkok. *bay* S Thailand
Krung Thep Mahanakhon *see* Krung Thep
Krupki *85 D6* Minskaya Voblasts', C Belarus
Krušné Hory *see* Erzgebirge
Krychaw *85 E7 Rus.* Krichëv. Mahilyowskaya Voblasts', E Belarus
Krym *87 F5 prev.* Kryms'kyy Pivostriv, *Eng.* Crimea. (Ukrainian territory annexed by Russia since 2014). *peninsula* S Ukraine
Krymski Hory *87 F5 mountain range* S Ukraine
Kryms'kyy Pivostriv *see* Krym
Krynica *77 D5 Ger.* Tannenhof. Małopolskie, S Poland
Kryve Ozero *87 E3* Odes'ka Oblast', SW Ukraine
Kryvyi Rih *87 F3 prev.* Kryvyy Rih, *Rus.* Krivoy Rog. Dnipropetrovska Oblast, SE Ukraine
Kryvyy Rih *see* Kryvyi Rih
Krzemieniec *see* Kremenets
Ksar al Kabir *see* Ksar-el-Kebir
Ksar al Soule *see* Er-Rachidia
Ksar-el-Kebir *48 C2 var.* Alcázar, Ksar al Kabir, Ksar-el-Kébir, *Ar.* Al-Kasr al-Kebir, Al-Qsar al-Kbir, *Sp.* Alcazarquivir. NW Morocco
Ksar-el-Kébir *see* Ksar-el-Kebir
Kuala Dungun *see* Dungun
Kuala Lumpur *116 B3 country capital* (Malaysia) Kuala Lumpur, Peninsular Malaysia
Kuala Terengganu *116 B3 var.* Kuala Trengganu. Terengganu, Peninsular Malaysia
Kualatungkal *116 B4* Sumatera, W Indonesia
Kuang-chou *see* Guangzhou
Kuang-hsi *see* Guangxi Zhuangzu Zizhiqu
Kuang-tung *see* Guangdong
Kuang-yuan *see* Guangyuan
Kuantan *116 B3* Pahang, Peninsular Malaysia
Kuba *see* Quba
Kuban' *87 G5 var.* Hypanis. *river* SW Russia
Kubango *see* Cubango/Okavango
Kuching *116 C3 prev.* Sarawak. Sarawak, East Malaysia
Küchnay Darwāshān *100 D5 prev.* Küchnay Darweyshān. Helmand, S Afghanistan
Küchnay Darweyshān *see* Küchnay Darwāshān
Kuçova *see* Kuçovë
Kuçovë *79 C6 var.* Kuçova; *prev.* Qyteti Stalin. Berat, C Albania
Kudara *see* Ghūdara
Kudus *116 C5 prev.* Koedoes. Jawa, C Indonesia
Kuei-lin *see* Guilin
Kuei-Yang/Kuei-yang *see* Guiyang
K'u-erh-lo *see* Korla
Kueyang *see* Guiyang
Kugaaruk *15 G3 prev.* Pelly Bay. Nunavut, N Canada
Kugluktuk *31 E3 var.* Qurlurtuuq; *prev.* Coppermine. Nunavut, NW Canada
Kuhmo *62 E4* Kainuu, E Finland
Kuhnau *see* Konin
Kühnö *see* Kihnu
Kuibyshev *see* Kuybyshevskoye Vodokhranilishche
Kuito *see* Cuito
Kuji *108 D3 var.* Kuzi. Iwate, Honshū, C Japan

Kukës *79 D5* var. Kukësi. Kukës, NE Albania
Kukësi see Kukës
Kukong see Shaoguan
Kukukhoto see Hohhot
Kula Kangri *113 G3* var. Kulhakangri. mountain Bhutan/China
Kuldīga *84 B3* Ger. Goldingen. Kuldīga, W Latvia
Kuldja see Yining
Kulhakangri see Kula Kangri
Kullorsuaq *60 D2* var. Kuvdlorssuak. Avannaata, C Greenland
Kulm see Chełmno
Kulmsee see Chełmża
Kŭlob *101 F3* Rus. Kulyab. SW Tajikistan
Kulpa see Kolpa
Kulu *94 C3* Konya, W Turkey (Türkiye)
Kulunda Steppe *92 C4* Kaz. Qulyndy Zhazyghy, Rus. Kulundinskaya Ravnina. grassland Kazakhstan/Russia
Kulundinskaya Ravnina see Kulunda Steppe
Kulyab see Kŭlob
Kum see Qom
Kuma *89 B7* river SW Russia
Kumamoto *109 A7* Kumamoto, Kyūshū, SW Japan
Kumanova see Kumanovo
Kumanovo *79 E5* Turk. Kumanova. N Macedonia
Kumasi *53 E5* prev. Coomassie. C Ghana
Kumayri see Gyumri
Kumba *55 A5* Sud-Ouest, W Cameroon
Kumertau *89 D6* Respublika Bashkortostan, W Russia
Kumillā see Cumilla
Kumo *53 G4* Gombe, E Nigeria
Kumon Range *114 B2* mountain range N Myanmar (Burma)
Kumul see Hami
Kunashiri see Kunashir, Ostrov
Kunashir, Ostrov *108 E1* var. Kunashiri. island Kuril'skiye Ostrova, SE Russia
Kunda *84 E2* Lääne-Virumaa, NE Estonia
Kunduz *101 E3* prev. Kondoz. NE Afghanistan
Kunene *47 C6* var. Kunene. river Angola/Namibia
Kunene see Cunene
Kungsbacka *63 B7* Halland, S Sweden
Kungur *89 D5* Permskaya Oblast', NW Russia
Kunlun Mountains see Kunlun Shan
Kunlun Shan *104 B4* Eng. Kunlun Mountains. mountain range NW China
Kunming *106 B6* var. K'un-ming; prev. Yunnan. province capital Yunnan, SW China
K'un-ming see Kunming
Kununurra *124 D3* Western Australia
Kunya-Urgench see Köneürgenç
Kuopio *63 E5* Pohjois-Savo, C Finland
Kupa see Kolpa
Kupang *117 E5* prev. Koepang. Timor, C Indonesia
Kupiansk *87 G2* prev. Kup"yans'k, Rus. Kupyansk. Kharkivs'ka Oblast', E Ukraine
Kup"yans'k see Kupiansk
Kupyansk see Kupiansk
Kür see Kura
Kura *95 H3* Az. Kür, Geor. Mtkvari, Turk. Kura Nehri. river SW Asia
Kura Nehri see Kura
Kurashiki *109 B6* var. Kurasiki. Okayama, Honshū, SW Japan
Kurasiki see Kurashiki
Kurdistan *95 F4* cultural region SW Asia
Kŭrdzhali see Kardzhali
Kure *109 B7* Hiroshima, Honshū, SW Japan
Küre Dağları *94 C2* mountain range N Turkey (Türkiye)
Kuressaare *84 C2* Ger. Arensburg; prev. Kingissepp. Saaremaa, W Estonia
Kureyka *90 D2* river N Russia
Kurgan-Tyube see Bokhtar
Kuria Muria Islands see Ḩalāniyāt, Juzur al
Kuril'skiye Ostrova *93 H4* Eng. Kuril Islands. island group SE Russia
Kuril Islands see Kuril'skiye Ostrova
Kuril-Kamchatka Depression see Kuril-Kamchatka Trench
Kuril-Kamchatka Trench *91 F3* var. Kuril-Kamchatka Depression. trench NW Pacific Ocean
Kuril'sk *108 E1* Jap. Shana. Kuril'skiye Ostrova, Sakhalinskaya Oblats', SE Russia
Ku-ring-gai *126 E1* New South Wales, E Australia
Kurisches Haff see Courland Lagoon
Kurkund see Kilingi-Nõmme
Kurman *87 F4* prev. Krasnohvardiiske, Rus. Krasnogvardeyskoye. Respublika Krym, S Ukraine
Kurnool *110 C1* var. Karnul. Andhra Pradesh, S India
Kursk *89 A6* Kurskaya Oblast', W Russia
Kurskiy Zaliv see Courland Lagoon
Kuršumlija *79 D5* Serbia, S Serbia
Kurtbunar see Tervel
Kurtitsch/Kürtös see Curtici
Kuruktag *104 C3* mountain range NW China
Kurume *109 A7* Fukuoka, Kyūshū, SW Japan
Kurupukari *37 F3* C Guyana
Kusaie see Kosrae
Kushiro *108 D2* var. Kusiro. Hokkaidō, NE Japan
Kushka see Serhetabat
Kusiro see Kushiro
Kuskokwim Mountains *14 C3* mountain range Alaska, USA
Kustanay see Qostanay
Küstence/Küstendje see Constanța
Kütahya *94 B3* prev. Kutaia. Kütahya, W Turkey (Türkiye)
Kutai see Mahakam, Sungai
Kutaisi *95 F2* prev. K'ut'aisi *95 F2* W Georgia W Georgia
K'ut'aisi see Kutaisi
Kūt al 'Amārah see Al Kūt
Kut al Imara see Al Kūt
Kutaradja/Kutaraja see Bandaaceh
Kutch, Gulf of see Kachchh, Gulf of
Kutch, Rann of see Kachchh, Rann of
Kutina *78 B3* Sisak-Moslavina, NE Croatia
Kutno *76 C3* Łódzkie, C Poland
Kuujjuaq *17 E2* prev. Fort-Chimo. Québec, E Canada
Kuusamo *62 E3* Pohjois-Pohjanmaa, E Finland
Kuvango see Cubango
Kuvdlorssuak see Kullorsuaq
Kuwait *98 C4* off. State of Kuwait, var. Dawlat al Kuwait, Koweit, Kuweit. country SW Asia
Kuwait see Al Kuwayt
Kuwait City see Al Kuwayt
Kuwait, Dawlat al see Kuwait
Kuwait, State of see Kuwait
Kuwajleen see Kwajalein Atoll
Kuwayt *98 C3* Maysān, E Iraq
Kuweit see Kuwait
Kuybyshev see Samara
Kuybyshev Reservoir see Kuybyshevskoye Vodokhranilishche
Kuybyshevskoye Vodokhranilishche *89 C5* var. Kuibyshev, Eng. Kuybyshev Reservoir. reservoir W Russia
Kuytun *104 B2* Xinjiang Uygur Zizhiqu, NW China
Kuzi see Kuji
Kuznetsk *89 B6* Penzenskaya Oblast', W Russia
Kuźnica *76 E2* Białystok, NE Poland Europe
Kvaløya *62 C2* island N Norway
Kvarnbergsvattnet *62 B4* var. Frostviken. lake N Sweden
Kvarner *78 A3* var. Carnaro, It. Quarnero. gulf W Croatia
Kvitøya *61 G1* island NE Svalbard
Kwajalein Atoll *122 C1* var. Kuwajleen. atoll Ralik Chain, C Marshall Islands
Kwando see Cuando
Kwangchow see Guangzhou
Kwangchu see Gwangju
Kwangju see Gwangju
Kwango *55 C7* Port. Cuango. river Angola/Dem. Rep. Congo
Kwangsi/Kwangsi Chuang Autonomous Region see Guangxi Zhuangzu Zizhiqu
Kwangtung see Guangdong
Kwangyuan see Guangyuan
Kwanza see Cuanza
Kweichu see Guiyang
Kweilin see Guilin
Kweisui see Hohhot
Kweiyang see Guiyang
Kwekwe *56 D3* prev. Que Que. Midlands, C Zimbabwe
Kwesui see Hohhot
Kwidzyń *76 C2* Ger. Marienwerder. Pomorskie, N Poland
Kwigillingok *14 C3* Alaska, USA
Kwilu *55 C6* river W Dem. Rep. Congo
Kwito see Cuito
Kyabé *54 C4* Moyen-Chari, S Chad
Kyaikkami *115 B5* prev. Amherst. Mon State, S Myanmar (Burma)
Kyaiklat *114 B4* Ayeyarwady, SW Myanmar (Burma)
Kyaikto *114 B4* Mon State, S Myanmar (Burma)
Kyakhta *93 E5* Respublika Buryatiya, S Russia
Kyaukse *114 B3* Mandalay, C Myanmar (Burma)
Kyiv *87 E2* var. Kyyiv, Kiev, Rus. Kiyev. country capital (Ukraine) Kyivska Oblast, N Ukraine
Kyiv Reservoir see Kyivske Vodoskhovyshche
Kyivske Vodoskhovyshche *87 E1* var. Kyyivs'ke Vodoskhovyshche, Eng. Kyiv Reservoir, Rus. Kiyevskoye Vodokhranilishche. reservoir N Ukraine
Kyjov *77 C5* Ger. Gaya. Jihomoravský Kraj, SE Czechia (Czech Republic)
Kykládes *83 D6* var. Kikládhes, Eng. Cyclades. island group SE Greece
Kými *83 C5* prev. Kími. Évvoia, C Greece
Kyōngsōng see Seoul
Kyōto *109 C6* Kyōto, Honshū, SW Japan
Kyparissía *83 B6* var. Kiparissía. Pelopónnisos, S Greece
Kypriakí Dimokratía see Cyprus
Kýpros see Cyprus
Kyrá Panagía *83 C5* island Vóreies Sporádes, Greece, Aegean Sea
Kyrenia see Girne
Kyrgyz Republic see Kyrgyzstan
Kyrgyzstan *101 F2* off. Kyrgyz Republic, var. Kirghizia; prev. Kirgizskaya SSR, Kirghiz SSR, Republic of Kyrgyzstan. country C Asia
Kyrgyzstan, Republic of see Kyrgyzstan
Kythira *83 C7* var. Kíthira, It. Cerigo, Lat. Cythera. island S Greece
Kýthnos *83 C6* Kńythnos, Kykládes, Greece, Aegean Sea
Kythnos *83 C6* var. Kíthnos, Thermiá, It. Termia; anc. Cythnos. island Kykládes, Greece, Aegean Sea
Kythréa see Değirmenlik
Kyushu *109 B7* var. Kyûsyû. island SW Japan
Kyushu-Palau Ridge *103 F3* var. Kyusyu-Palau Ridge. undersea ridge W Pacific Ocean
Kyustendil *82 B2* anc. Pautalia. Kyustendil, W Bulgaria
Kyûsyû see Kyūshū
Kyusyu-Palau Ridge see Kyushu-Palau Ridge
Kyyiv see Kyiv
Kyyivs'ke Vodoskhovyshche see Kyivske Vodoskhovyshche
Kyzyl *92 D4* Respublika Tyva, C Russia
Kyzyl Kum see Kyzylkum Desert
Kyzylkum, Peski see Kyzylkum Desert
Kyzylkum Desert *100 D2* var. Kizil Kum, Kyzyl Kum, Qizil Qum, Uzb. Qizilqum, Kaz. Qyzylqum, Rus. Peski Kyzylkum. desert Kazakhstan/Uzbekistan
Kyzylrabot see Qizilrabot
Kyzyl-Suu *101 G2* prev. Pokrovka. Issyk-Kul'skaya Oblast', NE Kyrgyzstan
Kzylorda see Qyzylorda
Kzyl-Orda see Qyzylorda

L

Laaland see Lolland
La Algaba *70 C4* Andalucía, S Spain
Laarne *65 B5* Oost-Vlaanderen, NW Belgium
La Asunción *37 E1* Nueva Esparta, NE Venezuela
Laatokka see Ladozhskoye, Ozero
Laâyoune *48 B3* var. Aaiún. country capital (Western Sahara) NW Western Sahara
La Banda Oriental see Uruguay
la Baule-Escoublac *68 A4* Loire-Atlantique, NW France
Labé *52 C4* NW Guinea
Labe see Elbe
Laborca see Laborec
Laborec *77 E5* Hung. Laborca. river E Slovakia
Labrador *17 F2* cultural region Newfoundland and Labrador, SW Canada
Labrador Basin *12 E3* var. Labrador Sea Basin. undersea basin Labrador Sea
Labrador Sea *60 A4* sea NW Atlantic Ocean
Labrador Sea Basin see Labrador Basin
Labudalin see Ergun
Labutta *115 A5* Ayeyarwady, SW Myanmar (Burma)
Laç *79 C6* var. Laci. Lezhë, C Albania
La Calera *42 B4* Valparaíso, C Chile
La Carolina *70 D4* Andalucía, S Spain
Laccadive Islands *110 A3* Eng. Laccadive Islands. island group India, N Indian Ocean
Laccadive Islands/Laccadive Minicoy and Amindivi Islands, the see Lakshadweep
La Ceiba *30 D2* Atlántida, N Honduras
Lachanás *82 B3* Kentrikí Makedonía, N Greece
La Chaux-de-Fonds *73 A7* Neuchâtel, W Switzerland
Lachlan River *127 C6* river New South Wales, SE Australia
Laci see Laç
la Ciotat *69 D6* anc. Citharista. Bouches-du-Rhône, SE France
Lacobriga see Lagos
La Concepción *31 E5* var. Concepción. Chiriquí, W Panama
La Concepción *36 C1* Zulia, NW Venezuela
La Condamine *69 C8* W Monaco
Laconia *19 G2* New Hampshire, NE USA
La Crosse *18 A2* Wisconsin, N USA
La Cruz *30 D4* Guanacaste, NW Costa Rica
Ladoga, Lake see Ladozhskoye, Ozero
Ladozhskoye, Ozero *88 B3* Eng. Lake Ladoga, Fin. Laatokka. lake NW Russia
Ladysmith *18 B2* Wisconsin, N USA
Lae *122 B3* Morobe, W Papua New Guinea
La Esperanza *30 C2* Intibucá, SW Honduras
Lafayette *18 C4* Indiana, N USA
Lafayette *20 B3* Louisiana, S USA
La Fé *32 A2* Pinar del Río, W Cuba
Lafia *53 G4* Nassarawa, C Nigeria
la Flèche *68 B4* Sarthe, NW France
Lagdo, Lac de *54 B4* lake N Cameroon
Laghouat *48 D2* N Algeria
Lagos *53 F5* Lagos, SW Nigeria
Lagos *70 B5* anc. Lacobriga. Faro, S Portugal
Lagos de Moreno *29 E4* Jalisco, SW Mexico
Lagouira *48 A4* SW Western Sahara
La Grande *24 C3* Oregon, NW USA
La Guaira *44 B4* Distrito Federal, N Venezuela
Lagunas *42 B1* Tarapacá, N Chile
Lagunillas *39 G4* Santa Cruz, SE Bolivia
La Habana *32 B2* var. Havana. country capital (Cuba) Ciudad de La Habana, W Cuba
Lahat *116 B4* Sumatera, W Indonesia
La Haye see 's-Gravenhage
Laholm *63 B7* Halland, S Sweden
Lahore *112 D2* Punjab, NE Pakistan
Lahr *73 A6* Baden-Württemberg, S Germany
Lahti *63 D5* Swe. Lahtis. Päijät-Häme, S Finland
Lahtis see Lahti
Laï *54 B4* prev. Behagle, De Behagle. Tandjilé, S Chad
Laibach see Ljubljana
Lai Châu *114 D3* Lai Châu, N Vietnam
Laila see Laylā
La Junta *22 D5* Colorado, C USA
Lake Charles *20 A3* Louisiana, S USA
Lake City *21 E3* Florida, SE USA
Lake District *67 C5* physical region NW England, United Kingdom
Lake Havasu City *26 A2* Arizona, SW USA
Lake Jackson *27 H4* Texas, SW USA
Lakeland *21 E4* Florida, SE USA
Lakeside *25 C8* California, W USA
Lake State see Michigan
Lakewood *22 D4* Colorado, C USA
Lakhnau see Lucknow
Lakonikós Kólpos *83 B7* gulf S Greece
Lakselv *62 D2* Lapp. Leavdnja. Finnmark, N Norway
la Laon see Laon
Lalibela *50 C4* Āmara, Ethiopia
La Libertad *30 B1* Petén, N Guatemala
La Ligua *42 B4* Valparaíso, C Chile
Lalín *70 C1* Galicia, NW Spain
Lalitpur *113 F3* Central, C Nepal
la Louvière *65 B6* Hainaut, S Belgium
la Maddalena *74 A4* Sardegna, Italy, C Mediterranean Sea
la Manche see English Channel
Lamar *22 D5* Colorado, C USA
La Marmora, Punta *75 A5* mountain Sardegna, Italy, C Mediterranean Sea
La Massana *69 A8* La Massana, W Andorra Europe
Lambaréné *55 A6* Moyen-Ogooué, W Gabon
Lamego *70 C2* Viseu, N Portugal
Lamesa *27 E3* Texas, SW USA
Lamezia Terme *75 D6* Calabria, SE Italy
Lamía *83 B5* Stereá Ellás, C Greece
Lamoni *23 F4* Iowa, C USA
Lampang *114 C4* var. Muang Lampang. Lampang, NW Thailand
Lámpeia *83 B6* Dytikí Ellás, S Greece
Lanbi Kyun *115 B6* prev. Sullivan Island. island Myeik Archipelago, S Myanmar (Burma)
Lancang Jiang see Mekong
Lancaster *67 D5* NW England, United Kingdom
Lancaster *25 C7* California, W USA
Lancaster *19 F4* Pennsylvania, NE USA
Lancaster Sound *15 F2* sound Nunavut, N Canada
Lan-chou/Lan-chow/Lanchow see Lanzhou
Landao see Lantau Island
Landen *65 C6* Vlaams Brabant, C Belgium
Lander *22 C3* Wyoming, C USA
Landerneau *68 A3* Finistère, NW France
Landes *69 B5* cultural region SW France
Land of Enchantment see New Mexico
The Land of Opportunity see Arkansas
Land of Steady Habits see Connecticut
Land of the Midnight Sun see Alaska
Landsberg see Gorzów Wielkopolski, Lubuskie, Poland
Landsberg an der Warthe see Gorzów Wielkopolski
Land's End *67 B8* headland SW England, United Kingdom
Landshut *73 C6* Bayern, SE Germany
Langar *101 E2* Rus. Lyangar. Navoiy Viloyati, C Uzbekistan
Langfang *106 D4* Hebei, E China
Langkawi, Pulau *115 B7* island Peninsular Malaysia
Langres *68 D4* Haute-Marne, N France
Langsa *116 A3* Sumatera, W Indonesia
Lang Shan *105 E3* mountain range N China
Lang Sơn *114 D3* var. Langson. Lang Sơn, N Vietnam
Langson see Lang Sơn
Lang Suan *115 B6* Chumphon, SW Thailand
Languedoc *69 C6* cultural region S France
Länkäran *95 H3* Rus. Lenkoran'. S Azerbaijan
Lansing *18 C3* state capital Michigan, N USA
Lanta, Ko *115 B7* island S Thailand
Lantau Island *106 A2* Cant. Tai Yue Shan, Chin. Landao. island Hong Kong, S China
Lan-ts'ang Chiang see Mekong
Lantung, Gulf of see Liaodong Wan
Lanzarote *48 B3* island Islas Canarias, Spain, NE Atlantic Ocean
Lanzhou *106 B4* var. Lan-chou, Lanchow, Lan-chow; prev. Kaolan. province capital Gansu, C China
Lao Cai *114 D3* Lao Cai, N Vietnam
Laodicea/Laodicea ad Mare see Al Lādhiqīyah
Laoet see Laut, Pulau
Laojunmiao *106 A3* prev. Yumen. Gansu, N China
Laon *68 D3* var. la Laon; anc. Laudunum. Aisne, N France
Lao People's Democratic Republic see Laos
La Orchila, Isla *36 D1* island N Venezuela
La Oroya *38 C3* Junín, C Peru
Laos *114 D4* off. Lao People's Democratic Republic. country SE Asia
La Palma *31 G5* Darién, SE Panama
La Palma *48 A3* island Islas Canarias, Spain, NE Atlantic Ocean
La Paz *39 F4* var. La Paz de Ayacucho. country capital (Bolivia-seat of government) La Paz, W Bolivia
La Paz *28 B3* Baja California Sur, NW Mexico
La Paz, Bahía de *28 B3* bay NW Mexico
La Paz de Ayacucho see La Paz
La Pérouse Strait *108 D1* Jap. Sōya-kaikyō, Rus. Proliv Laperuza. strait Japan/Russia
Laperuza, Proliv see La Pérouse Strait
Lápithos see Lapta
Lapland *62 D3* Fin. Lappi, Swe. Lappland. cultural region N Europe
La Plata *42 D4* Buenos Aires, E Argentina
La Plata see Sucre
La Pola *70 D1* var. Pola de Lena. Asturias, N Spain
Lappeenranta *63 E5* Swe. Villmanstrand. Etelä-Karjala, SE Finland
Lappi/Lappland see Lapland
Lappo see Lapua
Lapta *80 C5* Gk. Lápithos. NW Cyprus
Laptev Sea see Laptevykh, More
Laptevykh, More *93 E2* Eng. Laptev Sea. sea Arctic Ocean
Lapua *63 D5* Swe. Lappo. Etelä-Pohjanmaa, W Finland
Lapurdum see Bayonne
Łapy *76 E3* Podlaskie, NE Poland
La Quiaca *42 C2* Jujuy, N Argentina
L'Aquila *74 C4* var. Aquila, Aquila degli Abruzzi. Abruzzo, C Italy
Laracha *70 B1* Galicia, NW Spain
Laramie *22 C4* Wyoming, C USA
Laramie Mountains *22 C3* mountain range Wyoming, C USA
Laredo *71 E1* Cantabria, N Spain
Laredo *27 F5* Texas, SW USA
La Réunion see Réunion
Largeau see Faya
Largo *21 E4* Florida, SE USA
Largo, Cayo *32 B2* island W Cuba
Lario see Como, Lago di
La Rioja *42 C3* La Rioja, NW Argentina
La Rioja *71 E2* autonomous community N Spain
Lárisa *82 B4* var. Larissa. Thessalía, C Greece
Larissa see Lárisa
Larkana *112 B3* var. Larkhana. Sindh, SE Pakistan
Larkhana see Lārkāna
Larnaca see Lárnaka
Lárnaka *80 C5* var. Larnaca, Larnax. SE Cyprus
Larnax see Lárnaka
la Rochelle *68 B4* anc. Rupella. Charente-Maritime, W France
la Roche-sur-Yon *68 B4* prev. Bourbon Vendée, Napoléon-Vendée. Vendée, NW France
La Roda *71 E3* Castilla-La Mancha, C Spain
La Romana *33 E3* E Dominican Republic
Larvotto *69 C8* N Monaco Europe
La-sa see Lhasa
Las Cabezas de San Juan *70 C5* Andalucía, S Spain
Las Cruces *26 D3* New Mexico, SW USA
La See d'Urgel see La Seu d'Urgell
La Serena *42 B3* Coquimbo, C Chile
La Seu d'Urgell *71 G1* prev. La See d'Urgel, Seo de Urgel. Cataluña, NE Spain
la Seyne-sur-Mer *69 D6* Var, SE France
Lashio *114 B3* Shan State, E Myanmar (Burma)
Lashkar Gāh *100 D5* var. Lash-Kar-Gar'. Helmand, S Afghanistan
Lash-Kar-Gar' see Lashkar Gāh
La Sila *75 D6* mountain range SW Italy
La Sirena *30 D3* Región Autónoma Atlántico Sur, E Nicaragua
Łask *76 C4* Łódzkie, C Poland
Las Lomitas *42 D2* Formosa, N Argentina
La Solana *71 E4* Castilla-La Mancha, C Spain
Las Palmas *48 A3* var. Las Palmas de Gran Canaria. Gran Canaria, Islas Canarias, Spain, NE Atlantic Ocean
Las Palmas de Gran Canaria see Las Palmas
La Spezia *74 B3* Liguria, NW Italy
Lassa see Lhasa
Las Tablas *31 F5* Los Santos, S Panama
Last Frontier, The see Alaska
Las Tunas *32 C2* var. Victoria de las Tunas. Las Tunas, E Cuba
La Suisse see Switzerland
Las Vegas *25 D7* Nevada, W USA
Latacunga *38 B1* Cotopaxi, C Ecuador
Latakia see Al Lādhiqīyah
la Teste *69 B5* Gironde, SW France
Latina *75 C5* prev. Littoria. Lazio, C Italy
La Tortuga, Isla *37 E1* var. Isla Tortuga. island N Venezuela
La Tuque *17 E4* Québec, SE Canada
Latvia *84 C3* off. Republic of Latvia, Ger. Lettland, Latv. Latvija, Latvijas Republika; prev. Latvian SSR, Rus. Latviyskaya SSR. country NE Europe
Latvian SSR/Latvija/Latvijas Republika/ Latviyskaya SSR see Latvia
Latvia, Republic of see Latvia
Laudunum see Laon
Laudus see St-Lô
Lauenburg/Lauenburg in Pommern see Lębork
Lau Group *123 E4* island group E Fiji
Lauis see Lugano
Launceston *127 C8* Tasmania, SE Australia
La Unión *30 C2* Olancho, C Honduras
La Unión *71 F4* Murcia, SE Spain
Laurel *20 C3* Mississippi, S USA
Laurel *22 C2* Montana, NW USA
Laurentian Highlands see Laurentian Mountains
Laurentian Mountains *17 E3* var. Laurentian Highlands, Fr. Les Laurentides. plateau Newfoundland and Labrador/Québec, Canada
Laurentides, Les see Laurentian Mountains
Lauria *75 D6* Basilicata, S Italy
Laurinburg *21 F1* North Carolina, SE USA
Lauru see Choiseul
Lausanne *73 A7* It. Losanna. Vaud, SW Switzerland
Laut, Pulau *116 D4* prev. Laoet. island Borneo, C Indonesia
Laval *16 D4* Québec, SE Canada
Laval *68 B3* Mayenne, NW France
La Vall d'Uixó *71 F3* var. Vall D'Uxó. Comunitat Valenciana, E Spain
La Vega *33 E3* var. Concepción de la Vega. C Dominican Republic
La Vila Joíosa *71 F4* var. Villajoyosa. Comunitat Valenciana, E Spain
Lávrio *83 C6* prev. Lávrion. Attikí, C Greece
Lávrion see Lávrio
Lawrence *19 G3* Massachusetts, NE USA
Lawrenceburg *20 C1* Tennessee, S USA
Lawton *27 F2* Oklahoma, C USA
La Yarada *39 E4* Tacna, SW Peru
Laylā *99 C5* var. Laila. Ar Riyāḑ, C Saudi Arabia
Lazarev Sea *132 B1* sea Antarctica
Lázaro Cárdenas *29 E5* Michoacán, SW Mexico
Leal see Lihula
Leamhcán see Lucan
Leamington *16 C5* Ontario, S Canada
Leavdnja see Lakselv
Lebak *117 E3* Mindanao, S Philippines
Lebanese Republic see Lebanon
Lebanon *23 G5* Missouri, C USA
Lebanon *19 G2* New Hampshire, NE USA
Lebanon *24 B3* Oregon, NW USA
Lebanon *96 A4* off. Lebanese Republic, Ar. Lubnān, Fr. Liban. country SW Asia
Lebanon, Mount see Lubnān, Jebel
Lebap *100 D2* Lebapskiy Velayat, NE Turkmenistan
Lebedin see Lebedyn
Lebedyn *87 F2* Rus. Lebedin. Sums'ka Oblast', NE Ukraine
Lębork *76 C2* var. Lębórk, Ger. Lauenburg, Lauenburg in Pommern. Pomorskie, N Poland
Lebrija *70 C5* Andalucía, S Spain
Lebu *43 A5* Bío Bío, C Chile
Le Cannet *69 D6* Alpes-Maritimes, SE France
Le Cap see Cap-Haïtien
Lecce *75 E6* Puglia, SE Italy
Lechainá *83 B6* var. Lehena, Lekhainá. Dytikí Ellás, S Greece
Ledo Salinarius see Lons-le-Saunier
Leduc *15 E5* Alberta, SW Canada
Leech Lake *23 F2* lake Minnesota, N USA
Leeds *67 D5* N England, United Kingdom
Leek *64 E2* Groningen, NE Netherlands
Leer *72 A3* Niedersachsen, NW Germany
Leeuwarden *64 D1* Fris. Ljouwert. Fryslân, N Netherlands
Leeuwin, Cape *120 A5* headland Western Australia
Leeward Islands *33 G3* island group E West Indies
Leeward Islands see Sotavento, Ilhas de
Lefkada *83 A5* prev. Levkás. Lefkáda, Iónia Nisiá, Greece, C Mediterranean Sea
Lefkáda *83 A5* It. Santa Maura, prev. Levkás; anc. Leucas. island Iónia Nisiá, Greece, C Mediterranean Sea
Lefká Óri *83 C7* mountain range Kríti, Greece, E Mediterranean Sea
Lefkímmi *83 A5* var. Levkímmi. Kérkyra, Iónia Nisiá, Greece, C Mediterranean Sea
Lefkosía/Lefkoşa see Nicosia
Legaceaster see Chester
Legaspi see Legazpi City
Legazpi City *117 E2* var. Legaspi. C Philippines
Leghorn see Livorno
Legnica *76 B4* Ger. Liegnitz. Dolnośląskie, SW Poland
le Havre *68 B3* Eng. Havre; prev. le Havre-de-Grâce. Seine-Maritime, N France
le Havre-de-Grâce see le Havre
Lehena see Lechainá
Leicester *67 D6* Lat. Batae Coritanorum. C England, United Kingdom
Leiden *64 B3* prev. Leyden; anc. Lugdunum Batavorum. Zuid-Holland, W Netherlands
Leie *68 D2* Fr. Lys. river Belgium/France
Leinster *67 B6* Ir. Cúige Laighean. cultural region E Ireland
Leipsic see Leipzig
Leipsoí *83 E6* island Dodekánisa, Greece, Aegean Sea
Leipzig *72 C4* Pol. Lipsk, hist. Leipsic; anc. Lipsia. Sachsen, E Germany
Leiria *70 B3* anc. Collipo. Leiria, C Portugal
Leirvik *63 A6* Hordaland, S Norway
Lek *64 C4* river SW Netherlands
Lekhainá see Lechainá
Lekhchevo see Boychinovtsi
Leksand *63 C5* Dalarna, C Sweden
Lel'chitsy see Lyel'chytsy
le Léman see Geneva, Lake
Lelystad *64 D3* Flevoland, C Netherlands
Léman, Lac see Geneva, Lake
le Mans *68 B3* Sarthe, NW France
Lemberg see Lviv
Lemesós *80 C5* var. Limassol. SW Cyprus
Lemhi Range *24 D3* mountain range Idaho, C USA North America
Lemnos see Límnos
Lemovices see Limoges
Lena *93 F3* river NE Russia
Lena Tablemount *119 B7* seamount S Indian Ocean
Len Dao *106 C8* island S Spratly Islands
Lengshuitan see Yongzhou
Leninabad see Khujand
Leninakan see Gyumri
Lenine see Yedy Kuiu
Leningrad see Sankt-Peterburg
Lenino see Yedy Kuiu
Leninobod see Khujand
Lenīnogor see Ridder/Ridder

Leninogorsk see Ridder/Ridder
Leninpol' 101 F2 Talasskaya Oblast', NW Kyrgyzstan
Lenin-Turkmenski see Türkmenabat
Lenkoran' see Länkäran
Lenti 77 B7 Zala, SW Hungary
Lentia see Linz
Leoben 73 E7 Steiermark, C Austria
León 29 E4 var. León de los Aldamas. Guanajuato, C Mexico
León 30 C3 León, NW Nicaragua
León 70 D1 Castilla y León, NW Spain
León de los Aldamas see León
Leonídi see Leonídio
Leonídio 83 B6 var. Leonídi. Pelopónnisos, S Greece
Léopold II, Lac see Mai-Ndombe, Lac
Léopoldville see Kinshasa
Lepe 70 C4 Andalucía, S Spain
Lepel' see Lyepyel'
le Portel 68 C2 Pas-de-Calais, N France
Le Puglie see Puglia
le Puy 69 C5 prev. le Puy-en-Velay, hist. Anicium, Podium Anicensis. Haute-Loire, C France
le Puy-en-Velay see le Puy
Léré 54 B4 Mayo-Kébbi, SW Chad
Lérida see Lleida
Lerma 70 D2 Castilla y León, N Spain
Lernayin Gharabagh see Nagornyy-Karabakh
Leros 83 D6 island Dodekánisa, Greece, Aegean Sea
Lerwick 66 D1 NE Scotland, United Kingdom
Lesbos see Lésvos
Les Cayes see Cayes
Les Gonaïves see Gonaïves
Leshan 106 B5 Sichuan, C China
les Herbiers 68 B4 Vendée, NW France
Lesh/Leshi see Lezhë
Lesina see Hvar
Leskovac 79 E5 Serbia, SE Serbia
Lesnoy 92 C3 Sverdlovskaya Oblast', C Russia
Lesotho 56 D4 off. Kingdom of Lesotho; prev. Basutoland. country S Africa
Lesotho, Kingdom of see Lesotho
les Sables-d'Olonne 68 B4 Vendée, NW France
Lesser Antarctica see West Antarctica
Lesser Antilles 33 G4 island group E West Indies
Lesser Caucasus 95 F2 Rus. Malyy Kavkaz. mountain range SW Asia
Lesser Khingan Range see Xiao Hinggan Ling
Lesser Sunda Islands 117 E5 Eng. Lesser Sunda Islands. island group C Indonesia
Lesser Sunda Islands see Nusa Tenggara
Lésvos 94 A3 anc. Lesbos. island E Greece
Leszno 76 B4 Ger. Lissa. Wielkopolskie, C Poland
Lethbridge 15 E5 Alberta, SW Canada
Lethem 37 F3 S Guyana
Leti, Kepulauan 117 F5 island group E Indonesia
Letpadan 114 B4 Bago, SW Myanmar (Burma)
Letsôk-aw Kyun 115 B6 var. Letsutan Island; prev. Domel Island. island Myeik Archipelago, S Myanmar (Burma)
Letsutan Island see Letsôk-aw Kyun
Lettland see Latvia
Lëtzebuerg see Luxembourg
Leucas see Lefkáda
Leuven 65 C6 Fr. Louvain, Ger. Löwen. Vlaams Brabant, C Belgium
Leuze see Leuze-en-Hainaut
Leuze-en-Hainaut 65 B6 var. Leuze. Hainaut, SW Belgium
Léva see Levice
Levanger 62 B4 Nord-Trøndelag, C Norway
Levelland 27 E2 Texas, SW USA
Leverkusen 72 A4 Nordrhein-Westfalen, W Germany
Levice 77 C6 Ger. Lewentz, Hung. Léva, Lewenz. Nitriansky Kraj, SW Slovakia
Levin 128 D4 Manawatu-Wanganui, North Island, New Zealand
Levkás see Lefkáda
Levkímmi see Lefkímmi
Lewentz/Lewenz see Levice
Lewis, Isle of 66 B2 island NW Scotland, United Kingdom
Lewis Range 22 B1 mountain range Montana, NW USA
Lewiston 24 C2 Idaho, NW USA
Lewiston 19 G2 Maine, NE USA
Lewistown 22 C1 Montana, NW USA
Lexington 18 C5 Kentucky, S USA
Lexington 23 E4 Nebraska, C USA
Leyden see Leiden
Leyte 117 F2 island C Philippines
Leżajsk 77 E5 Podkarpackie, SE Poland
Lezha see Lezhë
Lezhë 79 C6 var. Lezha; prev. Lesh, Leshi. Lezhë, NW Albania
Lhasa 104 C5 var. La-sa, Lassa. Xizang Zizhiqu, W China
Lhaviyani Atoll see Faadhippolhu Atoll
Lhazê 104 C5 var. Quxar. Xizang Zizhiqu, China E Asia
L'Hospitalet de Llobregat 71 G2 var. Hospitalet. Cataluña, NE Spain
Liancourt Rocks 109 A5 Jap. Takeshima, Kor. Dokdo. island group Japan/South Korea
Lianyungang 106 D4 var. Xinpu. Jiangsu, E China
Liao see Liaoning
Liaodong Wan 105 G3 Eng. Gulf of Lantung, Gulf of Liaotung. gulf NE China
Liao He 103 E1 river NE China
Liaoning 106 D3 var. Liao, Liaoning Sheng, Shengking, hist. Fengtien, Shenking. province NE China
Liaoning Sheng see Liaoning
Liaoyuan 107 E3 var. Dongliao, Shuang-liao, Jap. Chengchiatun. Jilin, NE China
Liard see Fort Liard
Liban see Lebanon
Liban, Jebel 96 B4 Ar. Jabal al Gharbt, Jabal Lubnān, Eng. Mount Lebanon. mountain range C Lebanon
Libau see Liepāja
Libby 22 A1 Montana, NW USA
Liberal 23 E5 Kansas, C USA
Liberalitas Julia see Évora
Liberec 76 B4 Ger. Reichenberg. Liberecký Kraj, N Czechia (Czech Republic)
Liberia 30 D4 Guanacaste, NW Costa Rica
Liberia 52 C5 off. Republic of Liberia. country W Africa
Liberia, Republic of see Liberia
Libian Desert see Libyan Desert
Lībīyah, Aş Şahrā' al see Libyan Desert
Lībiyā, Dawlat see Libya
Libourne 69 B5 Gironde, SW France
Libreville 55 A5 country capital (Gabon) Estuaire, NW Gabon
Libya 49 F3 off. State of Libya, Ar. Dawlat Lībiyā; prev. Libyan Arab Republic, Great Socialist People's Libyan Arab Jamahiriya. country N Africa
Libya, State of see Libya
Libyan Arab Republic see Libya
Libyan Desert 49 H4 var. Libian Desert, Ar. Aş Şahrā' al Lībīyah. desert N Africa
Libyan Plateau 81 F4 var. Aḍ Diffah. plateau Egypt/Libya
Lichtenfels 73 C5 Bayern, SE Germany
Lichtenvoorde 64 E4 Gelderland, E Netherlands
Lichuan 106 C5 Hubei, C China
Lida 85 B5 Hrodzyenskaya Voblasts', W Belarus
Lidhorikíon see Lidoríki
Lidköping 63 B6 Västra Götaland, S Sweden
Lidokhorikion see Lidoríki
Lidoríki 83 B5 prev. Lidhorikíon, Lidokhorikion. Stereá Ellás, C Greece
Lidzbark Warmiński 76 D2 Ger. Heilsberg. Olsztyn, N Poland
Liechtenstein 72 D1 off. Principality of Liechtenstein. country C Europe
Liechtenstein, Principality of see Liechtenstein
Liège 65 D6 Dut. Luik, Ger. Lüttich. Liège, E Belgium
Liegnitz see Legnica
Lienz 73 D7 Tirol, W Austria
Liepāja 84 B3 Ger. Libau. Liepāja, W Latvia
Lietuva see Lithuania
Lievenhof see Līvāni
Liezen 73 D7 Steiermark, C Austria
Liffey 67 B6 river Ireland
Lifou 122 D5 island Îles Loyauté, E New Caledonia
Liger see Loire
Ligure, Appennino 74 A2 Eng. Ligurian Mountains. mountain range NW Italy
Ligure, Mar see Ligurian Sea
Ligurian Mountains see Ligure, Appennino
Ligurian Sea 74 A3 Fr. Mer Ligurienne, It. Mar Ligure. sea N Mediterranean Sea
Ligurienne, Mer see Ligurian Sea
Līhu'e 25 A7 var. Lihue. Kaua'i, Hawaii, USA
Lihue see Līhu'e
Lihula 84 D2 Ger. Leal. Läänemaa, W Estonia
Liivi Laht see Riga, Gulf of
Likasi 55 D7 prev. Jadotville. Shaba, SE Dem. Rep. Congo
Liknes 63 A6 Vest-Agder, S Norway
Lille 68 C2 var. l'Isle, Dut. Rijssel, Flem. Ryssel, prev. Lisle; anc. Insula. Nord, N France
Lillehammer 63 B5 Oppland, S Norway
Lillestrøm 63 B6 Akershus, S Norway
Lilongwe 57 E2 country capital (Malawi) Central, W Malawi
Lilybaeum see Marsala
Lima 38 C4 country capital (Peru) Lima, W Peru
Limanowa 77 D5 Małopolskie, S Poland
Limassol see Lemesós
Limerick 67 A6 Ir. Luimneach. Limerick, SW Ireland
Límin Vathéos see Sámos
Límnos 81 F3 anc. Lemnos. island E Greece
Limoges 69 C5 anc. Augustoritum Lemovicensium, Lemovices. Haute-Vienne, C France
Limón 31 E4 var. Puerto Limón. Limón, E Costa Rica
Limón 30 D2 Colón, NE Honduras
Limonum see Poitiers
Limousin 69 C5 cultural region C France
Limoux 69 C6 Aude, S France
Limpopo 56 D3 var. Crocodile. river S Africa
Linares 42 B4 Maule, C Chile
Linares 29 E3 Nuevo León, NE Mexico
Linares 70 D4 Andalucía, S Spain
Lincoln 67 D5 anc. Lindum, Lindum Colonia. E England, United Kingdom
Lincoln 19 H2 Maine, NE USA
Lincoln 23 F4 state capital Nebraska, C USA
Lincoln Sea 12 D2 sea Arctic Ocean
Linden 37 F3 E Guyana
Líndhos see Líndos
Lindi 51 D8 Lindi, SE Tanzania
Líndos 83 E7 var. Líndhos. Ródos, Dodekánisa, Greece, Aegean Sea
Lindum/Lindum Colonia see Lincoln
Line Islands 123 G3 island group E Kiribati
Lingeh see Bandar-e Lengeh
Lingen 72 A3 var. Lingen an der Ems. Niedersachsen, NW Germany
Lingen an der Ems see Lingen
Lingga, Kepulauan 116 B4 island group W Indonesia
Linköping 63 C6 Östergötland, S Sweden
Linz 73 D6 anc. Lentia. Oberösterreich, N Austria
Lion, Golfe du 69 C7 Eng. Gulf of Lion, Gulf of Lions; anc. Sinus Gallicus. gulf S France
Lion, Gulf of/Lions, Gulf of see Lion, Golfe du
Liozno see Lyozna
Lipari 75 D6 island Isole Eolie, S Italy
Lipari Islands/Lipari, Isole see Eolie, Isole
Lipetsk 89 B5 Lipetskaya Oblast', W Russia
Lipno 76 C3 Kujawsko-pomorskie, C Poland
Lipova 86 A4 Hung. Lippa. Arad, W Romania
Lipovets see Lypovets
Lippa see Lipova
Lipsia/Lipsk see Leipzig
Lira 51 B6 N Uganda
Lisala 55 C5 Equateur, N Dem. Rep. Congo
Lisboa 70 B4 Eng. Lisbon; anc. Felicitas Julia, Olisipo. country capital (Portugal) Lisboa, W Portugal
Lisbon see Lisboa
Lisichansk see Lysychansk
Lisieux 68 B3 anc. Noviomagus. Calvados, N France
Liski 89 B6 prev. Georgiu-Dezh. Voronezhskaya Oblast', W Russia
Lisle/l'Isle see Lille
Lismore 127 E5 New South Wales, SE Australia
Lissa see Vis, Croatia
Lissa see Leszno, Poland
Lisse 64 C3 Zuid-Holland, W Netherlands
Litang 106 A5 var. Gaocheng. Sichuan, C China
Līṭani, Nahr el 97 B5 var. Nahr al Litant. river C Lebanon
Litant, Nahr al see Līṭani, Nahr el
Litauen see Lithuania
Lithgow 127 D6 New South Wales, SE Australia
Lithuania 84 B4 off. Republic of Lithuania, Ger. Litauen, Lith. Lietuva, Pol. Litwa, Rus. Litva; prev. Lithuanian SSR, Rus. Litovskaya SSR. country NE Europe
Lithuanian SSR see Lithuania
Lithuania, Republic of see Lithuania
Litóchoro 82 B4 var. Litohoro, Litókhoron. Kentrikí Makedonía, N Greece
Litohoro/Litókhoron see Litóchoro
Litovskaya SSR see Lithuania
Little Alföld 77 C6 Ger. Kleines Ungarisches Tiefland, Hung. Kisalföld, Slvk. Podunajská Rovina. plain Hungary/Slovakia
Little Andaman 111 F2 island Andaman Islands, India, NE Indian Ocean
Little Barrier Island see Te Hauturu-o-Toi
Little Bay 71 H5 bay Alboran Sea, Mediterranean Sea
Little Cayman 32 B3 island E Cayman Islands
Little Falls 23 F2 Minnesota, N USA
Littlefield 27 E2 Texas, SW USA
Little Inagua 32 D2 var. Inagua Islands. island S The Bahamas
Little Minch, The 66 B3 strait NW Scotland, United Kingdom
Little Missouri River 22 D2 river NW USA
Little Nicobar 111 G3 island Nicobar Islands, India, NE Indian Ocean
Little Rhody see Rhode Island
Little Rock 20 B1 state capital Arkansas, C USA
Little Saint Bernard Pass 69 D5 Fr. Col du Petit St-Bernard, It. Colle del Piccolo San Bernardo. pass France/Italy
Little Sound 20 A5 bay Bermuda, NW Atlantic Ocean
Littleton 22 D4 Colorado, C USA
Littoria see Latina
Litva/Litwa see Lithuania
Liubotyn 87 G2 prev. Lyubotyn, Rus. Lyubotin. Kharkivs'ka Oblast', E Ukraine
Liu-chou/Liuchow see Liuzhou
Liuzhou 106 C6 var. Liu-chou, Liuchow. Guangxi Zhuangzu Zizhiqu, S China
Livanátai see Livanátes
Livanátes 83 B5 prev. Livanátai. Stereá Ellás, C Greece
Līvāni 84 D4 Ger. Lievenhof. Preiļi, SE Latvia
Liverpool 17 F5 Nova Scotia, SE Canada
Liverpool 67 C5 NW England, United Kingdom
Livingston 22 B2 Montana, NW USA
Livingston 27 H3 Texas, SW USA
Livingstone 56 C3 var. Maramba. Southern, S Zambia
Livingstone Mountains 129 A7 mountain range South Island, New Zealand
Livno 78 B4 Federicija Bosna I Hercegovina, SW Bosnia and Herzegovina
Livojoki 62 D4 river C Finland
Livonia 18 D3 Michigan, N USA
Livorno 74 B3 Eng. Leghorn. Toscana, C Italy
Lixian Jiang see Black River
Lixoúri 83 A5 prev. Lixoúrion. Kefallinía, Iónia Nisiá, Greece, C Mediterranean Sea
Lixoúrion see Lixoúri
Lizarra see Estella
Ljouwert see Leeuwarden
Ljubelj see Loibl Pass
Ljubljana 73 D7 Ger. Laibach, It. Lubiana; anc. Aemona, Emona. country capital (Slovenia) C Slovenia
Ljungby 63 B7 Kronoberg, S Sweden
Ljusdal 63 C5 Gävleborg, C Sweden
Ljusnan 63 C5 river C Sweden
Llanelli 67 C6 prev. Llanelly. SW Wales, United Kingdom
Llanelly see Llanelli
Llanes 70 D1 Asturias, N Spain
Llanos 36 D2 physical region Colombia/Venezuela
Lleida 71 F2 Cast. Lérida; anc. Ilerda. Cataluña, NE Spain
Llucmajor 71 G3 Mallorca, Spain, W Mediterranean Sea
Loaita Island 106 C8 island W Spratly Islands
Loanda see Luanda
Lobamba 56 D4 country capital (Eswatini- royal and legislative) NW Eswatini
Lobatse 56 C4 var. Lobatsi. Kgatleng, SE Botswana
Lobatsi see Lobatse
Löbau 72 D4 Sachsen, E Germany
Lobito 56 B2 Benguela, W Angola
Lob Nor see Lop Nur
Lobositz see Lovosice
Loburi see Lop Buri
Locarno 73 B8 Ger. Luggarus. Ticino, S Switzerland
Lochem 64 E3 Gelderland, E Netherlands
Lockport 19 E3 New York, NE USA
Lodja 55 D6 Kasai-Oriental, C Dem. Rep. Congo
Lodwar 51 C6 Rift Valley, NW Kenya
Łódź 76 D4 Rus. Lodz. Łódź, C Poland
Loei 114 C4 var. Loey, Muang Loei. Loei, C Thailand
Loey see Loei
Lofoten 62 B3 var. Lofoten Islands. island group C Norway
Lofoten Islands see Lofoten
Logan 22 B3 Utah, W USA
Logan, Mount 14 D3 mountain Yukon, W Canada
Logroño 71 E1 anc. Vareia, Lat. Juliobriga. La Rioja, N Spain
Loibl Pass 73 D7 Ger. Loiblpass, Slvn. Ljubelj. pass Austria/Slovenia
Loiblpass see Loibl Pass
Loikaw 114 B4 Kayah State, C Myanmar (Burma)
Loire 68 B4 var. Liger. river C France
Loja 38 B2 Loja, S Ecuador
Lokitaung 51 C5 Rift Valley, NW Kenya
Lokoja 53 G4 Kogi, C Nigeria
Loksa 84 E2 Ger. Loxa. Harjumaa, NW Estonia
Lolland 63 B8 prev. Laaland. island S Denmark
Lom 82 C1 prev. Lom-Palanka. Montana, NW Bulgaria
Lomami 55 D6 river C Dem. Rep. Congo
Lomas 38 D4 Arequipa, SW Peru
Lomas de Zamora 42 D4 Buenos Aires, E Argentina
Lombamba 56 D4 country capital (Eswatini - royal and legislative) NW Eswatini
Lombardia 74 B2 Eng. Lombardy. region N Italy
Lombardy see Lombardia
Lombok, Pulau 116 D5 island Nusa Tenggara, C Indonesia
Lomé 53 F5 country capital (Togo) S Togo
Lomela 55 D6 Kasai-Oriental, C Dem. Rep. Congo
Lommel 65 C5 Limburg, N Belgium
Lomond, Loch 66 B4 lake C Scotland, United Kingdom
Lomonosov Ridge 133 B3 var. Harris Ridge, Rus. Khrebet Homonsova. undersea ridge Arctic Ocean
Lomonsova, Khrebet see Lomonosov Ridge
Lom-Palanka see Lom
Lompoc 25 B7 California, W USA
Lom Sak 114 C4 var. Muang Lom Sak. Phetchabun, C Thailand
Łomża 76 D3 Rus. Lomzha. Podlaskie, NE Poland
Lomzha see Łomża
Loncoche 43 B5 Araucanía, C Chile
Londinium see London
London 67 A7 anc. Augusta, Lat. Londinium. country capital (United Kingdom) SE England, United Kingdom
London 16 C5 Ontario, S Canada
London 18 C5 Kentucky, S USA
Londonderry 66 B4 var. Derry, Ir. Doire. NW Northern Ireland, United Kingdom
Londonderry, Cape 124 C2 cape Western Australia
Londrina 41 E4 Paraná, S Brazil
Lone Star State see Texas
Long Bay 21 F2 bay W Jamaica
Long Beach 25 C7 California, W USA
Longford 67 B5 Ir. An Longfort. Longford, C Ireland
Long Island 32 D2 island C The Bahamas
Long Island 19 G4 island New York, NE USA
Longlac 16 C3 Ontario, S Canada
Longmont 22 D4 Colorado, C USA
Longreach 126 C4 Queensland, E Australia
Long Strait 93 G1 Eng. Long Strait. strait NE Russia
Long Strait see Longa, Proliv
Longview 27 H3 Texas, SW USA
Longview 24 B2 Washington, NW USA
Long Xuyên 115 D6 var. Longxuyen. An Giang, S Vietnam
Longxuyen see Long Xuyên
Longyan 106 D6 Fujian, SE China
Longyearbyen 61 G2 dependent territory capital (Svalbard) Spitsbergen, W Svalbard
Lons-le-Saunier 68 D4 anc. Ledo Salinarius. Jura, E France
Lop Buri 115 C5 var. Loburi. Lop Buri, C Thailand
Lop Nor see Lop Nur
Lop Nur 104 C3 var. Lob Nor, Lop Nor, Lo-pu Po. seasonal lake NW China
Loppersum 64 E1 Groningen, NE Netherlands
Lo-pu Po see Lop Nur
Lorca 71 E4 Ar. Lurka; anc. Eliocroca, Lat. Illurco. Murcia, S Spain
Lord Howe Island 120 C4 island E Australia
Lord Howe Rise 120 C4 undersea rise SW Pacific Ocean
Loreto 28 B3 Baja California Sur, NW Mexico
Lorient 68 A3 prev. l'Orient. Morbihan, NW France
l'Orient see Lorient
Lorn, Firth of 66 B4 inlet W Scotland, United Kingdom
Lörrach 73 A7 Baden-Württemberg, S Germany
Lorraine 68 D3 cultural region NE France
Los Alamos 26 C1 New Mexico, SW USA
Los Amates 30 B2 Izabal, E Guatemala
Los Ángeles 43 B5 Bío Bío, C Chile
Los Angeles 25 C7 California, W USA
Losanna see Lausanne
Lošinj 78 A3 Ger. Lussin, It. Lussino. island W Croatia
Loslau see Wodzisław Śląski
Los Mochis 28 C3 Sinaloa, C Mexico
Losonc/Losontz see Lučenec
Los Roques, Islas 36 D1 island group N Venezuela
Lot 69 B5 cultural region S France
Lot 69 B5 river S France
Lotagipi Swamp 51 C5 wetland Kenya/ South Sudan
Lötzen see Giżycko
Loualaba see Lualaba
Louangnamtha 114 C3 var. Luong Nam Tha. Louang Namtha, N Laos
Louangphabang 102 D3 var. Louangphrabang, Luang Prabang. Louangphabang, N Laos
Louangphrabang see Louangphabang
Loubomo see Dolisie
Loudéac 68 A3 Côtes d'Armor, NW France
Loudi 106 C5 Hunan, S China
Louga 52 B3 NW Senegal
Louisiade Archipelago 122 B4 island group SE Papua New Guinea
Louisiana 20 A2 off. State of Louisiana, also known as Creole State, Pelican State. state S USA
Louisville 18 C5 Kentucky, S USA
Louisville Ridge 121 E4 undersea ridge S Pacific Ocean
Loup River 23 E4 river Nebraska, C USA
Lourdes 69 B6 Hautes-Pyrénées, S France
Lourenço Marques see Maputo
Louth 67 E5 E England, United Kingdom
Loutrá 82 C4 Kentrikí Makedonía, N Greece
Louvain see Leuven
Louvain-la Neuve 65 C6 Walloon Brabant, C Belgium
Louviers 68 C3 Eure, N France
Lovech 82 C2 Lovech, N Bulgaria
Loveland 22 D4 Colorado, C USA
Lovosice 76 A4 Ger. Lobositz. Ústecký Kraj, NW Czechia (Czech Republic)
Lóvua 56 C1 Moxico, E Angola
Lowell 19 G3 Massachusetts, NE USA
Löwen see Leuven
Lower California see Baja California
Lower Hutt 129 D5 Wellington, North Island, New Zealand
Lower Lough Erne 67 A5 lake SW Northern Ireland, United Kingdom
Lower Red Lake 23 F1 lake Minnesota, N USA
Lower Rhine see Neder Rijn
Lower Tunguska see Nizhnyaya Tunguska
Lowestoft 67 E6 E England, United Kingdom
Loxa see Loksa
Lo-yang see Luoyang
Loyauté, Îles 122 D5 island group S New Caledonia
Loyev see Loyew
Loyew 85 D8 Rus. Loyev. Homyel'skaya Voblasts', SE Belarus
Loznica 78 C3 Serbia, W Serbia
Lu see Shandong, China
Lualaba 55 D6 Fr. Loualaba. river SE Dem. Rep. Congo
Luanda 56 A1 var. Loanda, Port. São Paulo de Loanda. country capital (Angola) Luanda, NW Angola
Luang Prabang see Louangphabang
Luang, Thale 115 C7 lagoon S Thailand
Luangua, Rio see Luangwa
Luangwa 51 B8 var. Aruângua, Rio Luangua. river Mozambique/Zambia
Luanshya 56 D2 Copperbelt, C Zambia
Luarca 70 C1 Asturias, N Spain
Lubaczów 77 E5 var. Lúbaczów. Podkarpackie, SE Poland
Lubnān see Lebanon
L'uban' 76 B4 Leningradskaya Oblast', Russia
Lubānas Ezers see Lubāns
Lubango 56 B2 Port. Sá da Bandeira. Huíla, SW Angola
Lubāns 84 D4 var. Lubānas Ezers. lake E Latvia
Lubao 55 D6 Kasai-Oriental, C Dem. Rep. Congo
Lübben 72 D4 Brandenburg, E Germany
Lübbenau 72 D4 Brandenburg, E Germany
Lubbock 27 E2 Texas, SW USA
Lübeck 72 C2 Schleswig-Holstein, N Germany
Lubelska, Wyżyna 76 E4 plateau SE Poland
Lüben see Lubin
Lubiana see Ljubljana
Lubin 76 B4 Ger. Lüben. Dolnośląskie, SW Poland
Lublin 76 E4 Rus. Lyublin. Lubelskie, E Poland
Lubliniec 76 C4 Śląskie, S Poland
Lubnān, Jabal see Liban, Jebel
Lubny 87 F2 Poltavs'ka Oblast', NE Ukraine
Lubsko 76 B4 Ger. Sommerfeld. Lubuskie, W Poland
Lubumbashi 55 E8 prev. Élisabethville. Shaba, SE Dem. Rep. Congo
Lubutu 55 D6 Maniema, E Dem. Rep. Congo
Luca see Lucca
Lucan 67 B5 Ir. Leamhcán. Dublin, E Ireland
Lucanian Mountains see Lucano, Appennino
Lucano, Appennino 75 D5 Eng. Lucanian Mountains. mountain range S Italy
Lucapa 56 C1 var. Lukapa. Lunda Norte, NE Angola
Lucca 74 B3 anc. Luca. Toscana, C Italy
Lucea 32 A4 W Jamaica
Lucena 117 E1 off. Lucena City. Luzon, N Philippines
Lucena 70 D4 Andalucía, S Spain
Lucena City see Lucena
Lučenec 77 D6 Ger. Losontz, Hung. Losonc. Banskobystrický Kraj, C Slovakia
Lucentum see Alicante
Lucerna/Lucerne see Luzern
Luchow see Hefei
Łuck see Lutsk
Lucknow 113 E3 var. Lakhnau. state capital Uttar Pradesh, N India
Lüda see Dalian
Luda Kamchia 82 D2 river E Bulgaria
Ludasch see Luduş
Lüderitz 56 B4 prev. Angra Pequena. Karas, SW Namibia
Ludhiāna 112 D2 Punjab, N India
Ludington 18 C2 Michigan, N USA
Ludsan see Ludza
Luduş 86 B4 Ger. Ludasch, Hung. Marosludas. Mureş, C Romania
Ludvika 63 C6 Dalarna, C Sweden
Ludwigsburg 73 B6 Baden-Württemberg, SW Germany
Ludwigsfelde 72 D3 Brandenburg, NE Germany
Ludwigshafen 73 B5 var. Ludwigshafen am Rhein. Rheinland-Pfalz, W Germany
Ludwigshafen am Rhein see Ludwigshafen
Ludwigslust 72 C3 Mecklenburg-Vorpommern, N Germany
Ludza 84 D4 Ger. Ludsan. Ludza, E Latvia
Luebo 55 C6 Kasai-Occidental, SW Dem. Rep. Congo
Luena 56 C2 var. Lwena, Port. Luso. Moxico, E Angola
Lufira 55 E7 river SE Dem. Rep. Congo
Lufkin 27 H3 Texas, SW USA
Luga 88 A4 Leningradskaya Oblast', NW Russia
Lugano 73 B8 Ger. Lauis. Ticino, S Switzerland
Lugdunum see Lyon
Lugdunum Batavorum see Leiden
Lugenda, Rio 57 E2 river N Mozambique
Luggarus see Locarno
Lugh Ganana see Luuq
Lugo 70 C1 anc. Lugus Augusti. Galicia, NW Spain
Lugoj 86 A4 Ger. Lugosch, Hung. Lugos. Timiş, W Romania
Lugos/Lugosch see Lugoj
Lugus Augusti see Lugo
Luguvallium/Luguvallum see Carlisle
Luhansk 87 H3 Voroshilovgrad. Luhans'ka Oblast', E Ukraine
Luimneach see Limerick
Lukapa see Lucapa
Lukenie 55 C6 river C Dem. Rep. Congo
Lukovit 82 C2 Lovech, N Bulgaria
Łuków 76 E4 Ger. Bogendorf. Lubelskie, E Poland
Lukuga 55 D7 river SE Dem. Rep. Congo
Luleå 62 D4 Norrbotten, N Sweden
Luleälven 62 C3 river N Sweden
Lulonga 55 C5 river NW Dem. Rep. Congo
Lulua 55 D7 river S Dem. Rep. Congo
Luluabourg see Kananga
Lumber State see Maine
Lumbo 57 F2 Nampula, NE Mozambique
Lumsden 129 A7 Southland, South Island, New Zealand
Lund 63 B7 Skåne, S Sweden
Lüneburg 72 C3 Niedersachsen, N Germany
Lunga, Isola see Dugi Otok
Lungkiang see Qiqihar
Lungué-Bungo 56 C2 var. Lungwebungu. river Angola/Zambia
Lungwebungu see Lungué-Bungo
Luninets see Luninyets
Łuniniec see Luninyets
Luninyets 85 B7 Pol. Łuniniec, Rus. Luninets. Brestskaya Voblasts', SW Belarus
Lunteren 64 D4 Gelderland, C Netherlands

Luong Nam Tha see Louangnamtha
Luoyang 106 C4 var. Honan, Lo-yang. Henan, C China
Lupatia see Altamura
Lúrio 57 F2 Nampula, NE Mozambique
Lúrio, Rio 57 E2 river NE Mozambique
Lurka see Lorca
Lusaka 56 D2 country capital (Zambia) Lusaka, SE Zambia
Lushnja see Lushnjë
Lushnjë 79 C6 var. Lushnja. Fier, C Albania
Luso see Luena
Lussin/Lussino see Lošinj
Lūt, Baḩrat/Lut, Bahret see Dead Sea
Lut, Dasht-e 98 D3 var. Kavīr-e Lūt. desert E Iran
Lutetia/Lutetia Parisiorum see Paris
Lūt, Kavīr-e see Lūt, Dasht-e
Luton 67 D6 E England, United Kingdom
Łutselk'e 15 F4 prev. Snowdrift. Northwest Territories, W Canada
Lutsk 86 C1 Pol. Łuck. Volyns'ka Oblast', NW Ukraine
Lüttich see Liège
Lutzow-Holm Bay 132 C2 var. Lutzow-Holm Bay. bay Antarctica
Lutzow-Holm Bay see Lützow Holmbukta
Luuq 51 D6 It. Lugh Ganana. Gedo, SW Somalia
Luvua 55 D7 river SE Dem. Rep. Congo
Luwego 51 C8 river S Tanzania
Luxembourg 65 D8 country capital (Luxembourg) Luxembourg, S Luxembourg
Luxembourg 65 D8 off. Grand Duchy of Luxembourg, var. Lëtzebuerg, Luxemburg. country NW Europe
Luxemburg see Luxembourg
Luxor see Al Uqşur
Luza 88 C4 Kirovskaya Oblast', NW Russia
Luz, Costa de la 70 C5 coastal region SW Spain
Luzern 73 B7 Fr. Lucerne, It. Lucerna. Luzern, C Switzerland
Luzon 117 E1 island N Philippines
Luzon Strait 103 E3 strait Philippines/Taiwan
Lviv 86 B2 Ger. Lemberg, Pol. Lwów, Rus. L'vov. L'vivs'ka Oblast', W Ukraine
L'vov see Lviv
Lwena see Luena
Lwów see Lviv
Lyakhavichy 85 B6 Rus. Lyakhovichi. Brestskaya Voblasts', SW Belarus
Lyakhovichi see Lyakhavichy
Lyallpur see Faisalābād
Lyangar see Langar
Lyck see Ełk
Lycksele 62 C4 Västerbotten, N Sweden
Lycopolis see Asyūţ
Lyel'chytsy 85 C7 Rus. Lel'chitsy. Homyel'skaya Voblasts', SE Belarus
Lyepyel' 85 D5 Rus. Lepel'. Vitsyebskaya Voblasts', N Belarus
Lyme Bay 67 C7 bay S England, United Kingdom
Lynchburg 19 E5 Virginia, NE USA
Lynn see King's Lynn
Lynn Lake 15 F4 Manitoba, C Canada
Lynn Regis see King's Lynn
Lyon 69 D5 Eng. Lyons; anc. Lugdunum. Rhône, E France
Lyons see Lyon
Lyozna 85 E6 Rus. Liozno. Vitsyebskaya Voblasts', NE Belarus
Lypovets 86 D2 Rus. Lipovets. Vinnyts'ka Oblast', C Ukraine
Lys see Leie
Lysychansk 87 H3 Rus. Lisichansk. Luhans'ka Oblast', E Ukraine
Lyttelton 129 C6 South Island, New Zealand
Lyublin see Lublin
Lyubotin see Liubotyn
Lyubotyn see Liubotyn
Lyulyakovo 82 E2 prev. Keremitlik. Burgas, E Bulgaria
Lyusina 85 B6 Rus. Lyusino. Brestskaya Voblasts', SW Belarus
Lyusino see Lyusina

M

Maale 110 B4 var. Male'. country capital (Maldives) Male' Atoll, C Maldive
Ma'ān 97 B7 Ma'ān, SW Jordan
Maardu 84 D2 Ger. Maart. Harjumaa, NW Estonia
Ma'aret-en-Nu'man see Ma'arrat an Nu'mān
Ma'arrat an Nu'mān 96 B3 var. Ma'aret-en-Nu'man, Fr. Maarret enn Naamâne. Idlib, NW Syria
Maarret enn Naamâne see Ma'arrat an Nu'mān
Maart see Maardu
Maas see Meuse
Maaseik 65 D5 prev. Maeseyck. Limburg, NE Belgium
Maastricht 65 D6 var. Maestricht; anc. Traiectum ad Mosam, Traiectum Tungorum. Limburg, SE Netherlands
Macao 107 C6 Port. Macau. Special administrative region Guangdong, SE China
Macapá 41 E1 state capital Amapá, N Brazil
Macarsca see Makarska
Macassar see Makassar
Macău see Makó, Hungary
Macau see Macao
MacCluer Gulf see Berau, Teluk
Macdonnell Ranges 124 D4 mountain range Northern Territory, C Australia
Macedonia see North Macedonia
Maceió 41 G3 state capital Alagoas, E Brazil
Machachi 38 B1 Pichincha, C Ecuador
Machala 38 B2 El Oro, SW Ecuador
Machanga 57 E3 Sofala, E Mozambique
Machilīpatnam 110 D1 var. Bandar Masulipatnam. Andhra Pradesh, E India
Machiques 36 C2 Zulia, NW Venezuela
Macías Nguema Biyogo see Bioco, Isla de
Măcin 86 D5 Tulcea, SE Romania
Mackay 126 D4 Queensland, NE Australia
Mackay, Lake 124 C4 salt lake Northern Territory/Western Australia
Mackenzie 15 E3 river Northwest Territories, NW Canada
Mackenzie Bay 132 D3 bay Antarctica
Mackenzie Mountains 14 D3 mountain range Northwest Territories, NW Canada
Macleod, Lake 124 A4 lake Western Australia
Macomb 18 A4 Illinois, N USA
Macomer 75 A5 Sardegna, Italy, C Mediterranean Sea
Mâcon 69 D5 anc. Matisco, Matisco Ædourum. Saône-et-Loire, C France
Macon 20 D2 Georgia, SE USA
Macon 23 G4 Missouri, C USA
Macquarie Ridge 132 C5 undersea ridge SW Pacific Ocean
Macuspana 29 G4 Tabasco, SE Mexico
Ma'dabā 97 B6 var. Mādabā, Madeba; anc. Medeba. Ma'dabā, NW Jordan
Mādabā see Ma'dabā
Madagascar 57 F3 off. Republic of Madagascar, Malg. Madagasikara; prev. Democratic Republic of Madagascar, Malagasy Republic. country W Indian Ocean
Madagascar 57 F3 island W Indian Ocean
Madagascar Basin 47 E7 undersea basin W Indian Ocean
Madagascar, Democratic Republic of see Madagascar
Madagascar, Republic of see Madagascar
Madagascar Plateau 47 E7 var. Madagascar Ridge, Madagascar Rise, Rus. Madagaskarskiy Khrebet. undersea plateau W Indian Ocean
Madagascar Rise/Madagascar Ridge see Madagascar Plateau
Madagasikara see Madagascar
Madagaskarskiy Khrebet see Madagascar Plateau
Madang 122 B3 Madang, N Papua New Guinea
Madanīyīn see Médenine
Maďarska see Hungary
Made 64 C4 Noord-Brabant, S Netherlands
Madeba see Ma'dabā
Madeira 48 A2 var. Ilha de Madeira. island Madeira, Portugal, NE Atlantic Ocean
Madeira, Ilha de see Madeira
Madeira Plain 44 C3 abyssal plain E Atlantic Ocean
Madeira, Rio 40 D2 var. Río Madera. river Bolivia/Brazil
Madeleine, Îles de la 17 F4 Eng. Magdalen Islands. island group Québec, E Canada
Madera 25 B6 California, W USA
Madera, Río see Madeira, Rio
Madhya Pradesh 113 E4 prev. Central Provinces and Berar. cultural region C India
Madinat ath Thawrah see Ath Thawrah
Madioen see Madiun
Madison 23 F3 South Dakota, N USA
Madison 18 B3 state capital Wisconsin, N USA
Madiun 116 D5 prev. Madioen. Jawa, C Indonesia
Madoera see Madura, Pulau
Madona 84 D4 Ger. Modohn. Madona, E Latvia
Madras see Chennai
Madras see Tamil Nādu
Madre de Dios, Río 39 E3 river Bolivia/Peru
Madre del Sur, Sierra 29 E5 mountain range S Mexico
Madre, Laguna 29 F3 lagoon NE Mexico
Madre, Laguna 27 G5 lagoon Texas, SW USA
Madre Occidental, Sierra 28 C3 var. Western Sierra Madre. mountain range C Mexico
Madre Oriental, Sierra 29 E3 var. Eastern Sierra Madre. mountain range C Mexico
Madre, Sierra 30 B2 var. Sierra de Soconusco. mountain range Guatemala/Mexico
Madrid 70 D3 country capital (Spain) Madrid, C Spain
Madura see Madurai
Madurai 110 C3 prev. Madura, Mathurai. Tamil Nādu, S India
Madura, Pulau 116 D5 prev. Madoera. island C Indonesia
Maebashi 109 D5 var. Maebasi, Mayebashi. Gunma, Honshū, S Japan
Maebasi see Maebashi
Mae Nam Khong see Mekong
Mae Nam Nan 114 C4 river NW Thailand
Mae Nam Yom 114 C4 river W Thailand
Maeseyck see Maaseik
Maestricht see Maastricht
Maéwo 122 D4 prev. Aurora. island C Vanuatu
Mafia 51 D7 island E Tanzania
Mafraq/Muḩāfaẓat al Mafraq see Al Mafraq
Magadan 93 G3 Magadanskaya Oblast', E Russia
Magallanes see Punta Arenas
Magallanes, Estrecho de see Magellan, Strait of
Magangué 36 B2 Bolívar, N Colombia
Magdalena 39 F3 Beni, N Bolivia
Magdalena 28 B1 Sonora, NW Mexico
Magdalena, Isla 28 B3 island NW Mexico
Magdalena, Río 36 B2 river C Colombia
Magdalen Islands see Madeleine, Îles de la
Magdeburg 72 C4 Sachsen-Anhalt, C Germany
Magelang 116 C5 Jawa, C Indonesia
Magellan, Strait of 43 B8 Sp. Estrecho de Magallanes. strait Argentina/Chile
Magerøy see Magerøya
Magerøya 62 D1 var. Magerøy, Lapp. Máhkarávju. island N Norway
Maggiore, Lago see Maggiore, Lake
Maggiore, Lake 74 B1 It. Lago Maggiore. lake Italy/Switzerland
Maglaj 78 C3 Federacija Bosna I Hercegovina, N Bosnia and Herzegovina
Maglie 75 E6 Puglia, SE Italy
Magna 22 B4 Utah, W USA
Magnesia see Manisa
Magnitogorsk 92 B4 Chelyabinskaya Oblast', C Russia
Magnolia State see Mississippi
Magta' Lahjar 52 C3 var. Magta Lahjar, Magta' Lahjar, Magtá Lahjar. Brakna, SW Mauritania
Magtymguly 100 C3 prev. Garrygala; Rus. Kara-gala. W Turkmenistan
Magway 114 A3 var. Magwe. Magway, W Myanmar (Burma)
Magyar-Becse see Bečej
Magyarkanizsa see Kanjiža
Magyarország see Hungary
Mahajanga 57 F2 var. Majunga. Mahajanga, NW Madagascar
Mahakam, Sungai 116 D4 var. Koetai, Kutai. river Borneo, C Indonesia
Mahalapye 56 D3 var. Mahalatswe. Central, SE Botswana
Mahalatswe see Mahalapye
Māhān 98 D3 Kermān, E Iran
Mahanādi 113 F4 river E India
Mahārāshtra 112 D5 cultural region W India
Mahbés see El Mahbas
Mahbūbnagar 112 D5 Telangana, C India
Mahdia 49 F2 var. Al Mahdīyah, Mehdia. NE Tunisia
Mahé 57 H1 island Inner Islands, NE Seychelles
Mahia Peninsula 128 E4 peninsula North Island, New Zealand
Mahilyow 85 D6 Rus. Mogilëv. Mahilyowskaya Voblasts', E Belarus
Máhkarávju see Magerøya
Mahmūd-e 'Erāqī see Maḩmūd-e Rāqī
Maḩmūd-e Rāqī 101 E4 var. Mahmūd-e 'Erāqī. Kāpīsā, NE Afghanistan
Mahón see Maó
Mähren see Moravia
Mährisch-Weisskirchen see Hranice
Maicao 36 C1 La Guajira, N Colombia
Mai Ceu/Mai Chio see Maych'ew
Maīdān Shahr 101 E4 prev. Meydān Shahr. Vardak, E Afghanistan
Maidstone 67 E7 SE England, United Kingdom
Maiduguri 53 H4 Borno, NE Nigeria
Mailand see Milano
Maīmanah 100 D3 var. Meymaneh, Maymana. Fāryāb, NW Afghanistan
Main 73 B5 river C Germany
Mai-Ndombe, Lac 55 C6 prev. Lac Léopold II. lake W Dem. Rep. Congo
Maine 19 G2 off. State of Maine, also known as Lumber State, Pine Tree State. state NE USA
Maine 68 B3 cultural region NW France
Maine, Gulf of 19 H2 gulf NE USA
Mainland 66 C2 island N Scotland, United Kingdom
Mainland 66 D1 island NE Scotland, United Kingdom
Mainz 73 B5 Fr. Mayence. Rheinland-Pfalz, SW Germany
Maio 52 A3 var. Mayo. island Ilhas de Sotavento, SE Cape Verde (Cabo Verde)
Maisur see Mysūru, India
Maisur see Karnātaka, India
Maitri 132 C2 Indian research station Antarctica
Maizhokunggar 104 C5 Xizang Zizhiqu, W China
Majorca see Mallorca
Mājro see Majuro Atoll
Majunga see Mahajanga
Majuro Atoll 122 D2 var. Mājro. atoll and capital (Marshall Islands) Ratak Chain, SE Marshall Islands
Makale see Mek'elē
Makarov Basin 133 B3 undersea basin Arctic Ocean
Makarska 78 B4 It. Macarsca. Split-Dalmacija, SE Croatia
Makasar see Makassar
Makasar, Selat see Makassar Straits
Makassar 117 E4 var. Macassar, Makasar; prev. Ujungpandang. Sulawesi, C Indonesia
Makassar Straits 116 D4 Ind. Makasar Selat. strait C Indonesia
Makay 57 F3 var. Massif du Makay. mountain range SW Madagascar
Makay, Massif du see Makay
Makeni 52 C4 C Sierra Leone
Makeyevka see Makiivka
Makhachkala 92 A4 prev. Petrovsk-Port. Respublika Dagestan, SW Russia
Makiivka 87 G3 prev. Makiyivka, Rus. Makeyevka; prev. Dmitriyevsk. Donets'ka Oblast', E Ukraine
Makin 122 D2 prev. Pitt Island. atoll Tungaru, W Kiribati
Makira see San Cristobal
Makiyivka see Makiivka
Makkah 99 A5 Eng. Mecca. Makkah, W Saudi Arabia
Makkovik 17 F2 Newfoundland and Labrador, NE Canada
Makó 77 D7 Rom. Macău. Csongrád, SE Hungary
Makoua 55 B5 Cuvette, C Congo
Makran Coast 98 E4 coastal region SE Iran
Makrany 85 A6 Rus. Mokrany. Brestskaya Voblasts', SW Belarus
Mākū 98 B2 Āżarbāyjān-e Gharbī, NW Iran
Makurdi 53 G4 Benue, C Nigeria
Mala see Malaita, Solomon Islands
Malabār Coast 110 B3 coast SW India
Malabo 55 A5 prev. Santa Isabel. country capital (Equatorial Guinea) Isla de Bioco, NW Equatorial Guinea
Malaca see Málaga
Malacca, Strait of 116 B3 Ind. Selat Malaka. strait Indonesia/Malaysia
Malacka see Malacky
Malacky 77 C6 Hung. Malacka. Bratislavský Kraj, W Slovakia
Maladzyechna 85 C5 Pol. Molodeczno, Rus. Molodechno. Minskaya Voblasts', C Belarus
Málaga 70 D5 anc. Malaca. Andalucía, S Spain
Malagarasi River 51 B7 river W Tanzania Africa
Malagasy Republic see Madagascar
Malaita 122 C3 var. Mala. island N Solomon Islands
Malakal 51 B5 Upper Nile, NE South Sudan
Malakula see Malekula
Malang 116 D5 Jawa, C Indonesia
Malange see Malanje
Malanje 56 B1 var. Malange. Malanje, NW Angola
Mälaren 63 C6 lake C Sweden
Malatya 95 E4 anc. Melitene. Malatya, SE Turkey (Türkiye)
Mala Vyska 87 E3 Rus. Malaya Viska. Kirovohrads'ka Oblast', S Ukraine
Malawi 57 E1 off. Republic of Malawi; prev. Nyasaland, Nyasaland Protectorate. country S Africa
Malawi, Lake see Nyasa, Lake
Malawi, Republic of see Malawi
Malaya Viska see Mala Vyska
Malay Peninsula 102 D4 peninsula Malaysia/Thailand
Malaysia 116 B3 off. Malaysia, var. Federation of Malaysia; prev. the separate territories of Federation of Malaya, Sarawak and Sabah (North Borneo) and Singapore. country SE Asia
Malaysia, Federation of see Malaysia
Malbork 76 C2 Ger. Marienburg, Marienburg in Westpreussen. Pomorskie, N Poland
Malchin 72 C3 Mecklenburg-Vorpommern, N Germany
Malden 23 H5 Missouri, C USA
Malden Island 123 G3 prev. Independence Island. atoll E Kiribati
Maldives 110 A4 off. Republic of Maldives. country N Indian Ocean
Maldives, Republic of see Maldives
Male' see Maale
Male' Atoll 110 B4 var. Kaafu Atoll. atoll C Maldives
Malekula 122 D4 var. Malakula; prev. Mallicolo. island W Vanuatu
Malesína 83 C5 Stereá Ellás, E Greece
Malheur Lake 24 C3 lake Oregon, NW USA
Mali 53 E3 off. Republic of Mali, Fr. République du Mali; prev. French Sudan, Sudanese Republic. country W Africa
Malik, Wadi al see Milk, Wadi el
Mali Kyun 115 B5 var. Tavoy Island. island Myeik Archipelago, S Myanmar (Burma)
Malin see Malyn
Malindi 51 D7 Coast, SE Kenya
Malines see Mechelen
Mali, Republic of see Mali
Mali, République du see Mali
Malkiye see Al Mālikīyah
Malko Tarnovo 82 E3 var. Malko Tŭrnovo. Burgas, E Bulgaria
Malko Tŭrnovo see Malko Tarnovo
Mallaig 66 B3 N Scotland, United Kingdom
Mallawī 50 B2 var. Mallawi. C Egypt
Mallawi see Mallawī
Mallicolo see Malekula
Mallorca 71 G3 Eng. Majorca; anc. Baleares Major. island Islas Baleares, Spain, W Mediterranean Sea
Malmberget 62 C3 Lapp. Malmivaara. Norrbotten, N Sweden
Malmédy 65 D6 Liège, E Belgium
Malmivaara see Malmberget
Malmö 63 B7 Skåne, S Sweden
Maloelap see Maloelap Atoll
Maloelap Atoll 122 D1 var. Maloelap. atoll E Marshall Islands
Małopolska, Wyżyna 76 D4 plateau S Poland
Malozemel'skaya Tundra 88 D3 physical region NW Russia
Malta 84 D4 Rēzekne, SE Latvia
Malta 22 C1 Montana, NW USA
Malta 75 C8 off. Republic of Malta. country C Mediterranean Sea
Malta 75 C8 island Malta, C Mediterranean Sea
Malta, Canale di see Malta Channel
Malta Channel 75 C8 It. Canale di Malta. strait Italy/Malta
Malta, Republic of see Malta
Maluku 117 F4 Dut. Molukken, Eng. Moluccas; prev. Spice Islands. island group E Indonesia
Maluku, Laut see Molucca Sea
Malung 63 B6 Dalarna, C Sweden
Malventum see Benevento
Malvina, Isla Gran see West Falkland
Malvinas, Islas see Falkland Islands
Malyn 86 D2 Rus. Malin. Zhytomyrs'ka Oblast', N Ukraine
Malyy Kavkaz see Lesser Caucasus
Mamberamo, Sungai 117 H4 river Papua, E Indonesia
Mambij see Manbij
Mamonovo 84 A4 Ger. Heiligenbeil. Kaliningradskaya Oblast', W Russia
Mamoré, Rio 39 F3 river Bolivia/Brazil
Mamou 52 C4 W Guinea
Mamoudzou 57 F2 dependent territory capital (Mayotte) C Mayotte
Mamuno 56 C3 Ghanzi, W Botswana
Manacor 71 G3 Mallorca, Spain, W Mediterranean Sea
Manado 117 F3 prev. Menado. Sulawesi, C Indonesia
Managua 30 D3 country capital (Nicaragua) Managua, W Nicaragua
Managua, Lake 30 C3 var. Xolotlán. lake W Nicaragua
Manakara 57 G4 Fianarantsoa, SE Madagascar
Manama see Al Manāmah
Mananjary 57 G3 Fianarantsoa, SE Madagascar
Manáos see Manaus
Manapouri, Lake 129 A7 lake South Island, New Zealand
Manar see Mannar
Manas, Gora 101 E2 mountain Kyrgyzstan/Uzbekistan
Manaung Island 114 A4 prev. Cheduba Island. island W Myanmar (Burma)
Manaus 40 D2 prev. Manáos. state capital Amazonas, NW Brazil
Manavgat 94 B4 Antalya, SW Turkey (Türkiye)
Manawatāwhi 128 C1 var. Three Kings Islands. island group N New Zealand
Manbij 96 C2 var. Mambij, Fr. Membidj. Ḩalab, N Syria
Manchester 67 D5 Lat. Mancunium. NW England, United Kingdom
Manchester 19 G3 New Hampshire, NE USA
Man-chou-li see Manzhouli
Manchurian Plain 103 E1 plain NE China
Máncio Lima see Japiim
Mancunium see Manchester
Mand see Mand, Rūd-e
Mandalay 114 B3 Mandalay, C Myanmar (Burma)
Mandan 23 E2 North Dakota, N USA
Mandeville 32 B5 C Jamaica
Mándra 83 C6 Attikí, C Greece
Mand, Rud-e 98 D4 var. Mand. river S Iran
Mandurah 125 A6 Western Australia
Manduria 75 E5 Puglia, SE Italy
Mandya 110 C2 Karnātaka, C India
Manfredonia 75 D5 Puglia, SE Italy
Mangai 55 C6 Bandundu, W Dem. Rep. Congo
Mangaia 123 G5 island group S Cook Islands
Mangalia 86 D5 anc. Callatis. Constanța, SE Romania
Mangalmé 54 C3 Guéra, SE Chad
Mangalore see Mangalūru
Mangalūru 110 B2 prev. Mangalore. Karnātaka, W India
Mangaung see Bloemfontein
Mango 53 E4 var. Sansanné-Mango. N Togo
Mangoky 57 F3 river W Madagascar
Manhattan 23 F4 Kansas, C USA
Manicouagan, Réservoir 16 D3 lake Québec, E Canada
Manihiki 123 G4 atoll N Cook Islands
Manihiki Plateau 121 E3 undersea plateau C Pacific Ocean
Maniitsoq 60 C3 var. Manitsoq, Dan. Sukkertoppen. Qeqqata, S Greenland
Manila 117 E1 off. City of Manila; Fil. Maynila. country capital (Philippines) Luzon, N Philippines
Manila, City of see Manila
Manisa 94 A3 var. Manissa, prev. Saruhan; anc. Magnesia. Manisa, W Turkey (Türkiye)
Manissa see Manisa
Manitoba 15 F5 province S Canada
Manitoba, Lake 15 F5 lake Manitoba, S Canada
Manitoulin Island 16 C4 island Ontario, S Canada
Manitsoq see Maniitsoq
Manizales 36 B3 Caldas, W Colombia
Manjimup 125 A7 Western Australia
Mankato 23 F3 Minnesota, N USA
Manlleu 71 G2 Cataluña, NE Spain
Manly 126 E1 Iowa, C USA
Manmād 112 C5 Mahārāshtra, W India
Mannar 110 C3 var. Manar. Northern Province, NW Sri Lanka
Mannar, Gulf of 110 C3 gulf India/Sri Lanka
Mannheim 73 B5 Baden-Württemberg, SW Germany
Manokwari 117 G4 New Guinea, E Indonesia
Manono 55 E7 Shaba, SE Dem. Rep. Congo
Manosque 69 D6 Alpes-de-Haute-Provence, SE France
Manra 123 F3 prev. Sydney Island. atoll Phoenix Islands, C Kiribati
Mansa 56 D2 prev. Fort Rosebery. Luapula, N Zambia
Mansel Island 15 G3 island Nunavut, NE Canada
Mansfield 18 D4 Ohio, N USA
Manta 38 A2 Manabí, W Ecuador
Manteca 25 B6 California, W USA
Mantoue see Mantova
Mantova 74 B2 Eng. Mantua, Fr. Mantoue. Lombardia, NW Italy
Mantua see Mantova
Manuae 123 G4 island S Cook Islands
Manukau see Manurewa
Manurewa 128 D3 var. Manukau. Auckland, North Island, New Zealand
Manzanares 71 E3 Castilla-La Mancha, C Spain
Manzanillo 32 C3 Granma, E Cuba
Manzanillo 28 D4 Colima, SW Mexico
Manzhouli 105 F1 var. Man-chou-li. Nei Mongol Zizhiqu, N China
Mao 54 B3 Kanem, W Chad
Maó 71 H3 Cast. Mahón, Eng. Port Mahon; anc. Portus Magonis. Menorca, Spain, W Mediterranean Sea
Maoke, Pegunungan 117 H4 Dut. Sneeuw-gebergte, Eng. Snow Mountains. mountain range Papua, E Indonesia
Maoming 106 C6 Guangdong, S China
Mapmaker Seamounts 103 H2 seamount range N Pacific Ocean
Maputo 56 D4 prev. Lourenço Marques. country capital (Mozambique) Maputo, S Mozambique
Marabá 41 F2 Pará, NE Brazil
Maracaibo 36 C1 Zulia, NW Venezuela
Maracaibo, Gulf of see Venezuela, Golfo de
Maracaibo, Lago de 36 C2 var. Lake Maracaibo. inlet NW Venezuela
Maracaibo, Lake see Maracaibo, Lago de
Maracay 36 D2 Aragua, N Venezuela
Marada see Marādah
Marādah 49 G3 var. Marada. N Libya
Maradi 53 G3 Maradi, S Niger
Maragha see Marāgheh
Marāgheh 98 C2 var. Maragha. Āžarbāyjān-e Khāvarī, NW Iran
Marajó, Baía de 41 F1 bay N Brazil
Marajó, Ilha de 41 E1 island N Brazil
Marakesh see Marrakech
Maramba see Livingstone
Maranhão 41 F2 off. Estado do Maranhão. state/region E Brazil
Maranhão, Estado do see Maranhão
Marañón, Río 38 B2 river N Peru
Marathon 16 C4 Ontario, S Canada
Marathón see Marathónas
Marathónas 83 C5 prev. Marathón. Attikí, C Greece
Marbella 70 D5 Andalucía, S Spain
Marble Bar 124 B4 Western Australia
Marburg see Marburg an der Lahn, Germany
Marburg see Maribor, Slovenia
Marburg an der Lahn 72 B4 hist. Marburg. Hessen, W Germany
March see Morava
Marche 75 C4 Eng. Marches. region C Italy
Marche 69 C5 cultural region C France
Marche-en-Famenne 65 C7 Luxembourg, SE Belgium
Marchena, Isla 38 B5 var. Bindloe Island. island Galápagos Islands, Ecuador, E Pacific Ocean
Marches see Marche
Mar Chiquita, Laguna 42 C3 lake C Argentina
Marcounda see Markounda
Mardan 112 C1 North-West Frontier Province, N Pakistan
Mar del Plata 43 D5 Buenos Aires, E Argentina
Mardin 95 E4 Mardin, SE Turkey (Türkiye)
Maré 122 D5 island Îles Loyauté, E New Caledonia
Marea Neagră see Black Sea
Mareeba 126 D3 Queensland, NE Australia
Marek see Dupnitsa
Marganets see Marhanets
Margarita, Isla de 37 E1 island N Venezuela
Margate 67 E7 prev. Mergate. SE England, United Kingdom
Margherita see Jamaame
Margherita, Lake 51 C5 Eng. Lake Margherita, It. Abbaia. lake SW Ethiopia
Margherita, Lake see Ābaya Hāyk'
Marghita 86 B3 Hung. Margitta. Bihor, NW Romania
Margitta see Marghita
Mārgō, Dasht-e 100 D5 desert SW Afghanistan
Marhanets 87 F3 Rus. Marganets. Dnipropetrovska Oblast, E Ukraine
María Cleofas, Isla 28 C4 island C Mexico
Maria Island 127 C8 island Tasmania, SE Australia
María Madre, Isla 28 C4 island C Mexico
María Magdalena, Isla 28 C4 island C Mexico
Mariana Trench 103 G4 trench W Pacific Ocean
Mariánské Lázně 77 A5 Ger. Marienbad. Karlovarský Kraj, W Czechia (Czech Republic)
Marías, Islas 28 C4 island group C Mexico
Maria-Theresiopel see Subotica
Maribor 73 E7 Ger. Marburg. NE Slovenia
Marica see Maritsa

Maridi 51 B5 W Equatoria, S South Sudan
Marie Byrd Land 132 A3 physical region Antarctica
Marie-Galante 33 G4 var. Ceyre to the Caribs. island SE Guadeloupe
Marienbad see Mariánské Lázně
Marienburg see Alūksne, Latvia
Marienburg see Malbork, Poland
Marienburg in Westpreussen see Malbork
Marienhausen see Viļaka
Mariental 56 B4 Hardap, SW Namibia
Marienwerder see Kwidzyń
Mariestad 63 B6 Västra Götaland, S Sweden
Marietta 20 D2 Georgia, SE USA
Marijampolė 84 B4 prev. Kapsukas. Marijampolė, S Lithuania
Marília 41 E4 São Paulo, S Brazil
Marín 70 B1 Galicia, NW Spain
Mar'ina Gorka see Mar"ina Horka
Mar"ina Horka 85 C6 Rus. Mar'ina Gorka. Minskaya Voblasts', C Belarus
Maringá 41 E4 Paraná, S Brazil
Marion 23 G3 Iowa, C USA
Marion 18 D4 Ohio, N USA
Marion, Lake 21 E2 reservoir South Carolina, SE USA
Mariscal Estigarribia 42 D2 Boquerón, NW Paraguay
Maritsa 82 D3 var. Marica, Gk. Évros, Turk. Meriç; anc. Hebrus. river SW Europe
Maritzburg see Pietermaritzburg
Mariupol 87 G4 prev. Zhdanov. Donets'ka Oblast', SE Ukraine
Marka 51 D6 var. Merca. Shabeellaha Hoose, S Somalia
Markham, Mount 132 B4 mountain Antarctica
Markounda 54 C4 var. Marcounda. Ouham, NW Central African Republic
Marktredwitz 73 C5 Bayern, E Germany
Marlborough 126 D4 Queensland, E Australia
Marmanda see Marmande
Marmande 69 B5 anc. Marmanda. Lot-et-Garonne, SW France
Sea of Marmara 94 A2 Eng. Sea of Marmara. sea NW Turkey (Türkiye)
Marmara, Sea of see Marmara Denizi
Marmaris 94 A4 Muğla, SW Turkey (Türkiye)
Marne 68 C3 cultural region N France
Marne 68 D3 river N France
Maro 54 C4 Moyen-Chari, S Chad
Maroantsetra 57 G2 Toamasina, NE Madagascar
Maromokotro 57 G2 mountain N Madagascar
Maroni 37 G3 Dut. Marowijne. river French Guiana/Suriname
Maroshevíz see Toplița
Marosludas see Luduș
Marosvásárhely see Târgu Mureș
Marotiri 121 F4 var. Îlots de Bass, Morotiri. island group Îles Australes, SW French Polynesia
Maroua 54 B3 Extrême-Nord, N Cameroon
Marowijne see Maroni
Marquesas Fracture Zone 131 E3 fracture zone E Pacific Ocean
Marquette 18 B1 Michigan, N USA
Marrakech 48 C2 var. Marakesh, Eng. Marrakesh; prev. Morocco. W Morocco
Marrakesh see Marrakech
Marrawah 127 C8 Tasmania, SE Australia
Marree 127 B5 South Australia
Marsá al Burayqah 49 G3 var. Al Burayqah. N Libya
Marsabit 51 C6 Eastern, N Kenya
Marsala 75 B7 anc. Lilybaeum. Sicilia, Italy, C Mediterranean Sea
Marsberg 72 B4 Nordrhein-Westfalen, W Germany
Marseille 69 D6 Eng. Marseilles; anc. Massilia. Bouches-du-Rhône, SE France
Marseilles see Marseille
Marshall 23 F2 Minnesota, N USA
Marshall 27 H2 Texas, SW USA
Marshall Islands 122 C1 off. Republic of the Marshall Islands. country W Pacific Ocean
Marshall Islands, Republic of the see Marshall Islands
Marshall Seamounts 103 H3 seamount range SW Pacific Ocean
Marsh Harbour 32 C1 Great Abaco, W The Bahamas
Martaban see Mottama
Martha's Vineyard 19 G3 island Massachusetts, NE USA
Martigues 69 D6 Bouches-du-Rhône, SE France
Martin 77 C5 Ger. Sankt Martin, Hung. Turócszentmárton; prev. Turčianský Svätý Martin. Žilinský Kraj, N Slovakia
Martinique 33 G4 French overseas department E West Indies
Martinique Channel see Martinique Passage
Martinique Passage 33 G4 var. Dominica Channel, Martinique Channel. channel Dominica/Martinique
Marton 128 D4 Manawatu-Wanganui, North Island, New Zealand
Martos 70 D4 Andalucía, S Spain
Marungu 55 E7 mountain range SE Dem. Rep. Congo
Mary 100 D3 prev. Merv. Mary Welaýaty, S Turkmenistan
Maryborough 127 D4 Queensland, E Australia
Maryborough see Port Laoise
Mary Island see Kanton
Maryland 19 E5 off. State of Maryland, also known as America in Miniature, Cockade State, Free State, Old Line State. state NE USA
Maryland, State of see Maryland
Maryville 23 F4 Missouri, C USA
Maryville 20 D1 Tennessee, S USA
Masai Steppe 51 C7 grassland NW Tanzania
Masaka 51 B6 SW Uganda
Masallı 95 H3 Rus. Masally. S Azerbaijan
Masally see Masallı
Masasi 51 C8 Mtwara, SE Tanzania
Masawa/Massawa see Mits'iwa
Masaya 30 D3 Masaya, W Nicaragua
Mascarene Basin 119 B5 undersea basin W Indian Ocean
Mascarene Islands 57 H4 island group W Indian Ocean
Mascarene Plain 119 B5 abyssal plain W Indian Ocean
Mascarene Plateau 119 B5 undersea plateau W Indian Ocean
Maseru 56 D4 country capital (Lesotho) W Lesotho
Mashhad 98 E2 var. Meshed. Khorāsān-Razavī, NE Iran
Masindi 51 B6 W Uganda
Masīra see Maṣīrah, Jazīrat
Masira, Gulf of see Maṣīrah, Khalīj
Maṣīrah, Jazīrat 99 E5 var. Masīra. island E Oman
Maṣīrah, Khalīj 99 E5 var. Gulf of Masira. bay E Oman
Masis see Büyük Ağrı Dağı
Maskat see Masqaṭ
Maskav 101 E3 Rus. Moskovskiy; prev. Chubek, Moskva. SW Tajikistan
Mason City 23 F3 Iowa, C USA
Masqaṭ 99 E5 var. Maskat, Eng. Muscat. country capital (Oman) NE Oman
Massa 74 B3 Toscana, C Italy
Massachusetts 19 G3 off. Commonwealth of Massachusetts, also known as Bay State, Old Bay State, Old Colony State. state NE USA
Massenya 54 B3 Chari-Baguirmi, SW Chad
Massif Central 69 C5 plateau C France
Massilia see Marseille
Massoukou see Franceville
Mastanli see Momchilgrad
Masterton 129 D5 Wellington, North Island, New Zealand
Masty 85 B5 Rus. Mosty. Hrodzyenskaya Voblasts', W Belarus
Masuda 109 B6 Shimane, Honshū, SW Japan
Masuku see Franceville
Masvingo 56 D3 prev. Fort Victoria, Nyanda, Victoria. Masvingo, SE Zimbabwe
Maṣyāf 96 B3 Fr. Misiaf. Ḥamāh, C Syria
Mata-Au see Clutha River
Matadi 55 B6 Bas-Congo, W Dem. Rep. Congo
Matagalpa 30 D3 Matagalpa, C Nicaragua
Matale 110 D3 Central Province, C Sri Lanka
Matam 52 C3 NE Senegal
Matamata 128 D3 Waikato, North Island, New Zealand
Matamoros 28 D3 Coahuila, NE Mexico
Matamoros 29 E2 Tamaulipas, C Mexico
Matane 17 E4 Québec, SE Canada
Matanzas 32 B2 Matanzas, NW Cuba
Matara 110 D4 Southern Province, S Sri Lanka
Mataram 116 D5 Pulau Lombok, C Indonesia
Mataró 71 G2 anc. Illuro. Cataluña, E Spain
Mataura 129 B7 Southland, South Island, New Zealand
Mataura 129 B7 river South Island, New Zealand
Mata Uta see Matā'utu
Matā'utu 123 E4 var. Mata Uta. dependent territory capital (Wallis and Futuna) Île Uvea, Wallis and Futuna
Matera 75 E5 Basilicata, S Italy
Mathurai see Madurai
Matianus see Orūmīyeh, Daryācheh-ye
Matías Romero 29 F5 Oaxaca, SE Mexico
Matisco/Matisco Ædourum see Mâcon
Mato Grosso 41 E3 off. Estado de Mato Grosso; prev. Matto Grosso. state/region W Brazil
Mato Grosso do Sul 41 E4 off. Estado de Mato Grosso do Sul. state/region S Brazil
Mato Grosso do Sul, Estado de see Mato Grosso do Sul
Mato Grosso, Estado de see Mato Grosso
Mato Grosso, Planalto de 34 C4 plateau C Brazil
Matosinhos 70 B2 prev. Matozinhos. Porto, NW Portugal
Matozinhos see Matosinhos
Matsue 109 B6 var. Matsuye, Matue. Shimane, Honshū, SW Japan
Matsumoto 109 C5 var. Matumoto. Nagano, Honshū, S Japan
Matsuyama 109 B7 var. Matuyama. Ehime, Shikoku, SW Japan
Matsuye see Matsue
Matterhorn 73 A8 It. Monte Cervino. mountain Italy/Switzerland
Matthews Ridge 37 F2 N Guyana
Matthew Town 32 D2 Great Inagua, S The Bahamas
Matto Grosso see Mato Grosso
Matucana 38 C4 Lima, W Peru
Matue see Matsue
Matumoto see Matsumoto
Maturín 37 E2 Monagas, NE Venezuela
Matuyama see Matsuyama
Mau 113 E3 var. Maunāth Bhanjan. Uttar Pradesh, N India
Maui 25 B8 island Hawaii, USA, C Pacific Ocean
Maun 56 C3 North-West, C Botswana
Maunāth Bhanjan see Mau
Mauren 72 E1 NE Liechtenstein Europe
Maurice see Mauritius
Mauritania 52 C2 off. Islamic Republic of Mauritania, Ar. Mūrītānīyah. country W Africa
Mauritania, Islamic Republic of see Mauritania
Mauritius 57 H3 off. Republic of Mauritius, Fr. Maurice. country W Indian Ocean
Mauritius 119 B5 island W Indian Ocean
Mauritius, Republic of see Mauritius
Mawlamyaing see Mawlamyine
Mawlamyine 114 B4 var. Mawlamyaing, Moulmein. Mon State, S Myanmar (Burma)
Mawson 132 D2 Australian research station Antarctica
Mayadin see Al Mayādīn
Mayaguana 32 D2 island SE The Bahamas
Mayaguana Passage 32 D2 passage SE The Bahamas
Mayagüez 33 F3 W Puerto Rico
Mayamey 98 D2 Semnān, N Iran
Maya Mountains 30 B2 Sp. Montañas Mayas. mountain range Belize/Guatemala
Mayas, Montañas see Maya Mountains
Maych'ew 50 C4 var. Mai Chio, It. Mai Ceu. Tigray, N Ethiopia
Mayebashi see Maebashi
Mayence see Mainz
Mayfield 129 B6 Canterbury, South Island, New Zealand
Maykop 89 A7 Respublika Adygeya, SW Russia
Maymana see Maīmanah
Maymyo see Pyin-Oo-Lwin
Maynila see Manila
Mayo see Maio
Mayor Island 128 D3 island NE New Zealand
Mayor Pablo Lagerenza see Capitán Pablo Lagerenza
Mayotte 57 F2 French overseas department E Africa
May Pen 32 B5 C Jamaica
Mayyit, Al Baḥr al see Dead Sea
Mazabuka 56 D2 Southern, S Zambia
Mazaca see Kayseri
Mazagan see El-Jadida
Mazār-e Sharīf 101 E3 var. Mazār-i Sharif. Balkh, N Afghanistan
Mazār-i Sharif see Mazār-e Sharīf
Mazatlán 28 C3 Sinaloa, C Mexico
Mažeikiai 84 B3 Telšiai, NW Lithuania
Mazirbe 84 C2 Talsi, NW Latvia
Mazra'a see Al Mazra'ah
Mazury 76 D3 physical region NE Poland
Mazyr 85 C7 Rus. Mozyr'. Homyel'skaya Voblasts', SE Belarus
Mbabane 56 D4 country capital (Eswatini - administrative) NW Eswatini
Mbacké see Mbaké
Mbaïki 55 C5 var. M'Baiki. Lobaye, SW Central African Republic
M'Baiki see Mbaïki
Mbaké 52 B3 var. Mbacké. W Senegal
Mbala 56 D1 prev. Abercorn. Northern, NE Zambia
Mbale 51 C6 E Uganda
Mbandaka 55 C5 prev. Coquilhatville. Equateur, NW Dem. Rep. Congo
M'Banza Congo 56 B1 var. Mbanza Congo; prev. São Salvador, São Salvador do Congo. Dem. Rep. Congo, NW Angola
Mbanza-Ngungu 55 B6 Bas-Congo, W Dem. Rep. Congo
Mbarara 51 B6 SW Uganda
Mbé 54 B4 Nord, N Cameroon
Mbeya 51 C7 Mbeya, SW Tanzania
Mbomou/M'Bomu/Mbomu see Bomu
Mbour 52 B3 W Senegal
Mbuji-Mayi 55 D7 prev. Bakwanga. Kasai-Oriental, S Dem. Rep. Congo
McAlester 27 G2 Oklahoma, C USA
McAllen 27 G5 Texas, SW USA
McCamey 27 E3 Texas, SW USA
M'Clintock Channel 15 F2 channel Nunavut, N Canada
McComb 20 B3 Mississippi, S USA
McCook 23 E4 Nebraska, C USA
McKean Island 123 E3 island Phoenix Islands, C Kiribati
McKinley, Mount see Denali
McKinley Park see Denali Park
McMinnville 24 B3 Oregon, NW USA
McMurdo 132 B4 US research station Antarctica
McPherson 23 E5 Kansas, C USA
McPherson see Fort McPherson
Mdantsane 56 D5 Eastern Cape, SE South Africa
Mead, Lake 25 D6 reservoir Arizona/Nevada, W USA
Mecca see Makkah
Mechelen 65 C5 Eng. Mechlin, Fr. Malines. Antwerpen, C Belgium
Mechlin see Mechelen
Mecklenburger Bucht 72 C2 bay N Germany
Mecsek 77 C7 mountain range SW Hungary
Medan 116 B3 Sumatera, E Indonesia
Medeba see Ma'dabā
Medellín 36 B3 Antioquia, NW Colombia
Médenine 49 F2 var. Madanīyīn. SE Tunisia
Medeshamstede see Peterborough
Medford 24 B4 Oregon, NW USA
Medgidia 86 D5 Constanța, SE Romania
Medgyes see Mediaș
Mediaș 86 B4 Ger. Mediasch, Hung. Medgyes. Sibiu, C Romania
Mediasch see Mediaș
Medicine Hat 15 F5 Alberta, SW Canada
Medina see Al Madīnah
Medinaceli 71 E2 Castilla y León, N Spain
Medina del Campo 70 D2 Castilla y León, N Spain
Medinat Israel see Israel
Mediolanum see Saintes, France
Mediolanum see Milano, Italy
Mediomatrica see Metz
Mediterranean Sea 80 D3 Fr. Mer Méditerranée. sea Africa/Asia/Europe
Méditerranée, Mer see Mediterranean Sea
Médoc 69 B5 cultural region SW France
Medvezh'yegorsk 88 B3 Respublika Kareliya, NW Russia
Meekatharra 125 B5 Western Australia
Meemu Atoll see Mulakatholhu
Meerssen 65 D6 var. Mersen. Limburg, SE Netherlands
Meerut 112 D2 Uttar Pradesh, N India
Megáli Préspa, Límni see Prespa, Lake
Meghālaya 91 G3 cultural region NE India
Mehdia see Mahdia
Meheso see Mī'ēso
Me Hka see Nmai Hka
Mehrīz 98 D3 Yazd, C Iran
Mehtar Lām 101 F4 var. Mehtarlām, Meterlam, Methariam, Metharlam. Laghmān, E Afghanistan
Mehtarlām see Mehtar Lām
Meiktila 114 B3 Mandalay, C Myanmar (Burma)
Méjico see Mexico
Mejillones 42 B2 Antofagasta, N Chile
Mek'elē 50 C4 var. Makale. Tigray, N Ethiopia
Mékhé 52 B3 NW Senegal
Mekong 102 D3 var. Lan-ts'ang Chiang, Cam. Mékôngk, Chin. Lancang Jiang, Lao. Mènam Khong, Th. Mae Nam Khong, Tib. Dza Chu, Vtn. Sông Tiên Giang. river SE Asia
Mékôngk see Mekong
Mekong, Mouths of the 115 E6 delta S Vietnam
Melaka 116 B3 var. Malacca. Melaka, Peninsular Malaysia
Melaka, Selat see Malacca, Strait of
Melanesia 122 D3 island group W Pacific Ocean
Melanesian Basin 120 C2 undersea basin W Pacific Ocean
Melbourne 127 C7 state capital Victoria, SE Australia
Melbourne 21 E4 Florida, SE USA
Meleda see Mljet
Melghir, Chott 49 E2 var. Chott Melrhir. salt lake E Algeria
Melilla 58 B5 anc. Rusaddir, Russadir. Melilla, Spain, N Africa
Melilla 48 D2 autonomous city of Spain Spain, N Africa
Melita 15 F5 Manitoba, S Canada
Melita see Mljet
Melitene see Malatya
Melitopol 87 F4 Zaporiz'ka Oblast', SE Ukraine
Melle 65 B5 Oost-Vlaanderen, NW Belgium
Mellerud 63 B6 Västra Götaland, S Sweden
Mellieħa 80 B5 E Malta
Mellizo Sur, Cerro 43 A7 mountain S Chile
Melo 42 E4 Cerro Largo, NE Uruguay
Melodunum see Melun
Melrhir, Chott see Melghir, Chott
Melsungen 72 B4 Hessen, C Germany
Melun 68 C3 anc. Melodunum. Seine-et-Marne, N France
Melville Bay/Melville Bugt see Qimusseriarsuaq
Melville Island 124 D2 island Northern Territory, N Australia
Melville Island 15 E2 island Parry Islands, Northwest Territories, NW Canada
Melville, Lake 17 F2 lake Newfoundland and Labrador, E Canada
Melville Peninsula 15 G3 peninsula Nunavut, NE Canada
Melville Sound see Viscount Melville Sound
Membidj see Manbij
Memel see Neman, NE Europe
Memel see Klaipeda, Lithuania
Memmingen 73 B6 Bayern, S Germany
Memphis 20 C1 Tennessee, S USA
Menaam see Menaldum
Menado see Manado
Ménaka 53 F3 Goa, E Mali
Menaldum 64 D1 Fris. Menaam. Fryslân, N Netherlands
Mènam Khong see Mekong
Mendaña Fracture Zone 131 F4 fracture zone E Pacific Ocean
Mende 69 C5 anc. Mimatum. Lozère, S France
Mendeleyev Ridge 133 B2 undersea ridge Arctic Ocean
Mendocino Fracture Zone 130 D2 fracture zone NE Pacific Ocean
Mendoza 42 B4 Mendoza, W Argentina
Menemen 94 A3 İzmir, W Turkey (Türkiye)
Menengiyn Tal 105 F2 plain E Mongolia
Menongue 56 B2 var. Vila Serpa Pinto, Port. Serpa Pinto. Cuando Cubango, C Angola
Menorca 71 H3 Eng. Minorca; anc. Balearis Minor. island Islas Baleares, Spain, W Mediterranean Sea
Mentawai, Kepulauan 116 A4 island group W Indonesia
Meppel 64 D2 Drenthe, NE Netherlands
Meran see Merano
Merano 74 C1 Ger. Meran. Trentino-Alto Adige, N Italy
Merca see Marka
Mercedes 42 D3 Corrientes, NE Argentina
Mercedes 42 D4 Soriano, SW Uruguay
Meredith, Lake 27 E1 reservoir Texas, SW USA
Merefa 87 G2 Kharkivs'ka Oblast', E Ukraine
Mergate see Margate
Mergui see Myeik
Mergui Archipelago see Myeik Archipelago
Mérida 29 H3 Yucatán, SW Mexico
Mérida 70 C4 anc. Augusta Emerita. Extremadura, W Spain
Mérida 36 C2 Mérida, W Venezuela
Meridian 20 C2 Mississippi, S USA
Mérignac 69 B5 Gironde, SW France
Merín, Laguna see Mirim Lagoon
Merkulovichi see Myerkulavichy
Merowe 50 B3 Northern, N Sudan
Merredin 125 B6 Western Australia
Mersen see Meerssen
Mersey 67 D5 river NW England, United Kingdom
Mersin 94 C4 var. İçel. İçel, S Turkey (Türkiye)
Mērsrags 84 C3 Talsi, NW Latvia
Meru 51 C6 Eastern, C Kenya
Merv see Mary
Merzifon 94 D2 Amasya, N Turkey (Türkiye)
Merzig 73 A5 Saarland, SW Germany
Mesa 26 B2 Arizona, SW USA
Meseritz see Międzyrzecz
Meshed see Mashhad
Mesopotamia 35 C5 var. Mesopotamia Argentina. physical region NE Argentina
Mesopotamia Argentina see Mesopotamia
Messalo, Rio 57 E2 var. Mualo. river NE Mozambique
Messana/Messene see Messina
Messina see Musina
Messina, Strait of see Messina, Stretto di
Messina, Stretto di 75 D7 Eng. Strait of Messina. strait SW Italy
Messíni 83 B6 Pelopónnisos, S Greece
Mesta see Néstos
Mestghanem see Mostaganem
Mestia 95 F1 var. Mestiya. N Georgia
Mestiya see Mestia
Mestre 74 C2 Veneto, NE Italy
Metairie 20 B3 Louisiana, S USA
Metán 42 C2 Salta, N Argentina
Metapán 30 B2 Santa Ana, NW El Salvador
Meta, Río 36 D3 river Colombia/Venezuela
Meterlam see Mehtar Lām
Methariam/Metharlam see Mehtar Lām
Metis see Metz
Metković 78 B4 Dubrovnik-Neretva, SE Croatia
Métsovo 82 B4 prev. Métsovon. Ípeiros, C Greece
Métsovon see Métsovo
Metz 68 D3 anc. Divodurum Mediomatricum, Mediomatrica, Metis. Moselle, NE France
Meulaboh 116 A3 Sumatera, W Indonesia
Meuse 65 C6 Dut. Maas. river W Europe
Mexcala, Río see Balsas, Río
Mexicali 28 A1 Baja California Norte, NW Mexico
Mexicanos, Estados Unidos see Mexico
Mexico 23 G4 Missouri, C USA
Mexico 28 C3 off. United Mexican States, var. Méjico, México, Sp. Estados Unidos Mexicanos. country N Central America
México see Mexico
Mexico City see México, Ciudad de
México, Ciudad de 29 E4 var. Mexico City. country capital (Mexico) México, C Mexico
México, Golfo de see Mexico, Gulf of
Mexico, Gulf of 29 F2 Sp. Golfo de México. gulf W Atlantic Ocean
Meyadine see Al Mayādīn
Meydān Shahr see Maīdān Shahr
Meymaneh see Maīmanah
Mezen' 88 D3 river NW Russia
Mezőtúr 77 D7 Jász-Nagykun-Szolnok, E Hungary
Mġarr 80 A5 Gozo, N Malta
Miadzioł Nowy see Myadzyel
Miahuatlán 29 F5 var. Miahuatlán de Porfirio Díaz. Oaxaca, SE Mexico
Miahuatlán de Porfirio Díaz see Miahuatlán
Miami 21 F5 Florida, SE USA
Miami 27 G1 Oklahoma, C USA
Miami Beach 21 F5 Florida, SE USA
Miāneh 98 C2 var. Miyāneh. Āžarbāyjān-e Sharqī, NW Iran
Mianyang 106 B5 Sichuan, C China
Miastko 76 C2 Ger. Rummelsburg in Pommern. Pomorskie, N Poland
Mi Chai see Nong Khai
Michalovce 77 E5 Ger. Grossmichel, Hung. Nagymihály. Košický Kraj, E Slovakia
Michigan 18 C1 off. State of Michigan, also known as Great Lakes State, Lake State, Wolverine State. state N USA
Michigan, Lake 18 C2 lake N USA
Michurin see Tsarevo
Michurinsk 89 B5 Tambovskaya Oblast', W Russia
Micoud 33 F2 SE Saint Lucia
Micronesia 122 B1 off. Federated States of Micronesia. country W Pacific Ocean
Micronesia 122 C1 island group W Pacific Ocean
Micronesia, Federated States of see Micronesia
Mid-Atlantic Cordillera see Mid-Atlantic Ridge
Mid-Atlantic Ridge 44 C3 var. Mid-Atlantic Cordillera, Mid-Atlantic Rise, Mid-Atlantic Swell. undersea ridge Atlantic Ocean
Mid-Atlantic Rise/Mid-Atlantic Swell see Mid-Atlantic Ridge
Middelburg 65 B5 Zeeland, SW Netherlands
Middelharnis 64 B4 Zuid-Holland, SW Netherlands
Middelkerke 65 A5 West-Vlaanderen, W Belgium
Middle America Trench 13 B7 trench E Pacific Ocean
Middle Andaman 111 F2 island Andaman Islands, India, NE Indian Ocean
Middle Atlas 48 C2 Eng. Middle Atlas. mountain range N Morocco
Middle Atlas see Moyen Atlas
Middleburg Island see 'Eua
Middle Congo see Congo (Republic of)
Middlesboro 18 C5 Kentucky, S USA
Middlesbrough 67 D5 N England, United Kingdom
Middletown 19 F4 New Jersey, NE USA
Middletown 19 F3 New York, NE USA
Mid-Indian Basin 119 C5 undersea basin N Indian Ocean
Mid-Indian Ridge 119 C5 var. Central Indian Ridge. undersea ridge C Indian Ocean
Midland 16 D5 Ontario, S Canada
Midland 18 C3 Michigan, N USA
Midland 27 E3 Texas, SW USA
Mid-Pacific Mountains 130 C2 var. Mid-Pacific Seamounts. seamount range NW Pacific Ocean
Mid-Pacific Seamounts see Mid-Pacific Mountains
Midway Islands 130 D2 US unincorporated territory C Pacific Ocean
Miechów 77 D5 Małopolskie, S Poland
Międzyrzec Podlaski 76 E3 Lubelskie, E Poland
Międzyrzecz 76 B3 Ger. Meseritz. Lubuskie, W Poland
Mielec 77 D5 Podkarpackie, SE Poland
Miercurea-Ciuc 86 C4 Ger. Szeklerburg, Hung. Csíkszereda. Harghita, C Romania
Mieres del Camín 70 D1 var. Mieres del Camino. Asturias, NW Spain
Mieres del Camino see Mieres del Camín
Mī'ēso 51 D5 var. Meheso, Miesso. Oromīya, C Ethiopia
Miesso see Mī'ēso
Mifrats Hefa 97 A5 Eng. Bay of Haifa; prev. Mifraz Ḥefa. bay N Israel
Miguel Asua 28 D3 var. Miguel Auza. Zacatecas, C Mexico
Miguel Auza see Miguel Asua
Mijdrecht 64 C3 Utrecht, C Netherlands
Mikashevichi see Mikashevichy
Mikashevichy 85 C7 Pol. Mikaszewicze, Rus. Mikashevichi. Brestskaya Voblasts', SW Belarus
Mikaszewicze see Mikashevichy
Mikhaylovgrad see Montana
Mikhaylovka 89 B6 Volgogradskaya Oblast', SW Russia
Míkonos see Mýkonos
Mikre 82 C2 Lovech, N Bulgaria
Mikun' 88 D4 Respublika Komi, NW Russia
Mikuni-sanmyaku 109 D5 mountain range Honshū, N Japan Asia
Mikura-jima 109 D6 island E Japan
Milagro 38 B2 Guayas, SW Ecuador
Milan see Milano
Milange 57 E2 Zambézia, NE Mozambique
Milano 74 B2 Eng. Milan, Ger. Mailand; anc. Mediolanum. Lombardia, N Italy
Milas 94 A4 Muğla, SW Turkey (Türkiye)
Milashavichy 85 C7 Rus. Milashevichi. Homyel'skaya Voblasts', SE Belarus
Milashevichi see Milashavichy
Mildura 127 C6 Victoria, SE Australia
Mile see Mili Atoll
Miles 127 D5 Queensland, E Australia
Miles City 22 C2 Montana, NW USA
Milford see Milford Haven
Milford Haven 67 C6 prev. Milford. SW Wales, United Kingdom
Milford Sound 129 A6 var. Piopiotahi. Southland, South Island, New Zealand
Milford Sound 129 A6 inlet South Island, New Zealand
Milh, Bahr al see Razāzah, Buḥayrat ar
Mili Atoll 122 D2 var. Mile. atoll Ratak Chain, SE Marshall Islands
Mil'kovo 93 H3 Kamchatskaya Oblast', E Russia
Milk River 15 E5 Alberta, SW Canada
Milk River 22 C1 river Montana, NW USA
Milk, Wadi el 66 B4 var. Wadi al Malik. river C Sudan
Milledgeville 21 E2 Georgia, SE USA
Mille Lacs Lake 23 F2 lake Minnesota, N USA
Millennium Island 121 F3 prev. Caroline Island, Thornton Island. atoll Line Islands, E Kiribati
Millerovo 89 B6 Rostovskaya Oblast', SW Russia
Mílos 83 C7 island Kykládes, Greece, Aegean Sea
Milton 129 B7 Otago, South Island, New Zealand
Milton Keynes 67 D6 SE England, United Kingdom
Milwaukee 18 B3 Wisconsin, N USA
Mimatum see Mende
Min see Fujian
Mīnā' as Sulṭān Qābūs 118 B3 NE Oman

Minas Gerais 41 F3 off. Estado de Minas Gerais. state/region E Brazil
Minas Gerais, Estado de see Minas Gerais
Minatitlán 29 F4 Veracruz-Llave, E Mexico
Minbu 114 A3 Magway, W Myanmar (Burma)
Minch, The 66 B3 var. North Minch. strait NW Scotland, United Kingdom
Mindanao 117 F2 island S Philippines
Mindanao Sea see Bohol Sea
Mindelheim 73 C6 Bayern, S Germany
Mindello see Mindelo
Mindelo 52 A2 var. Mindello; prev. Porto Grande. São Vicente, N Cape Verde (Cabo Verde)
Minden 72 B4 anc. Minthun. Nordrhein-Westfalen, NW Germany
Mindoro 117 E2 island N Philippines
Mindoro Strait 117 E2 strait W Philippines
Mineral Wells 27 F2 Texas, SW USA
Mingäçevir 95 G2 Rus. Mingechaur, Mingechevir. C Azerbaijan
Mingechaur/Mingechevir see Mingäçevir
Mingora see Saidu Sharif
Minho 70 B2 former province N Portugal
Minho 70 B2 Sp. Miño. river Portugal/Spain
Minho, Rio see Miño
Minicoy Island 110 B3 island SW India
Minius see Miño
Minna 53 G4 Niger, C Nigeria
Minneapolis 23 F2 Minnesota, N USA
Minnesota 23 F2 off. State of Minnesota, also known as Gopher State, New England of the West, North Star State. state N USA
Miño 70 B2 var. Mino, Minius, Port. Rio Minho. river Portugal/Spain
Miño see Minho, Rio
Minorca see Menorca
Minot 23 E1 North Dakota, N USA
Minsk 85 C6 country capital (Belarus) Minskaya Voblasts', C Belarus
Minskaya Wzvyshsha 85 C6 mountain range C Belarus
Mińsk Mazowiecki 76 D3 var. Nowo-Minsk. Mazowieckie, C Poland
Minthun see Minden
Minto, Lac 16 D2 lake Québec, C Canada
Minya see Al Minyā
Miraflores 28 C3 Baja California Sur, NW Mexico
Miranda de Ebro 71 E1 La Rioja, N Spain
Mirgorod see Myrhorod
Miri 116 D3 Sarawak, East Malaysia
Mirim Lagoon 41 E5 var. Lake Mirim, Sp. Laguna Merín. lagoon Brazil/Uruguay
Mirim, Lake see Mirim Lagoon
Mírina see Mýrina
Mīrjāveh 98 E4 Sīstān va Balūchestān, SE Iran
Mirny 132 C3 Russian research station Antarctica
Mirnyy 93 F3 Respublika Sakha (Yakutiya), NE Russia
Mirpur Khas 112 B3 Sindh, SE Pakistan
Mirtóo Pélagos 83 C6 Eng. Myrtoan Sea; anc. Myrtoum Mare. sea S Greece
Misiaf see Maşyāf
Miskito Coast see Mosquito Coast
Miskitos, Cayos 31 E2 island group NE Nicaragua
Miskolc 77 D6 Borsod-Abaúj-Zemplén, NE Hungary
Misool, Pulau 117 F4 island Maluku, E Indonesia
Mişr see Egypt
Mişrātah 49 F2 var. Misurata. NW Libya
Mission 27 G5 Texas, SW USA
Mississippi 20 B2 off. State of Mississippi, also known as Bayou State, Magnolia State. state SE USA
Mississippi Delta 20 B4 delta Louisiana, S USA
Mississippi River 13 C6 river C USA
Missoula 22 B1 Montana, NW USA
Missouri 23 F5 off. State of Missouri, also known as Bullion State, Show Me State. state C USA
Missouri River 23 E3 river C USA
Mistassini, Lac 16 D3 lake Québec, SE Canada
Mistelbach an der Zaya 73 E6 Niederösterreich, NE Austria
Misti, Volcán 39 E4 volcano S Peru
Misurata see Mişrātah
Mitau see Jelgava
Mitchell 127 D5 Queensland, E Australia
Mitchell 23 E3 South Dakota, N USA
Mitchell, Mount 21 E1 mountain North Carolina, SE USA
Mitchell River 126 C2 river Queensland, NE Australia
Mi Tho see My Tho
Mitilíni see Mytilíni
Mito 109 D5 Ibaraki, Honshū, S Japan
Mitrovica see Mitrovicë
Mitrovica/Mitrowitz see Sremska Mitrovica, Serbia
Mitrovicë 79 D5 Serb. Mitrovica, prev. Kosovska Mitrovica, Titova Mitrovica. N Kosovo
Mits'iwa 50 C4 var. Masawa, Massawa. E Eritrea
Mitspe Ramon 97 A7 prev. Mizpe Ramon. Southern, S Israel
Mittelstadt see Baia Sprie
Mitú 36 C4 Vaupés, SE Colombia
Mitumba, Chaîne des/Mitumba Range see Mitumba, Monts
Mitumba Monts 55 E7 var. Chaîne des Mitumba, Mitumba Range. mountain range E Dem. Rep. Congo
Miueru Wantipa, Lake 55 E7 lake N Zambia
Miyake-jima 109 D6 island Sakishima-shotō, SW Japan
Miyako 108 D4 Iwate, Honshū, C Japan
Miyakonojō 109 B8 var. Miyakonzyô. Miyazaki, Kyūshū, SW Japan
Miyakonzyô see Miyakonojō
Miyāneh see Mīāneh
Miyazaki 109 B8 Miyazaki, Kyūshū, SW Japan
Mizia 82 C1 var. Miziya. Vratsa, NW Bulgaria
Mizil 86 C5 Prahova, SE Romania
Miziya see Mizia
Mizpe Ramon see Mitspe Ramon
Mjøsa 63 B6 var. Mjøsen. lake S Norway
Mjøsen see Mjøsa
Mladenovac 78 D4 Serbia, C Serbia
Mława 76 D3 Mazowieckie, C Poland
Mljet 79 B5 It. Meleda; anc. Melita. island S Croatia
Mmabatho 56 C4 North-West, N South Africa
Moab 22 B5 Utah, W USA
Moa Island 126 C1 island Queensland, NE Australia
Moanda 55 B6 var. Mouanda. Haut-Ogooué, SE Gabon
Moba 55 E7 Katanga, E Dem. Rep. Congo
Mobay see Montego Bay
Mobaye 55 C5 Basse-Kotto, S Central African Republic
Moberly 23 G4 Missouri, C USA
Mobile 20 C3 Alabama, S USA
Mobutu Sese Seko, Lac see Albert, Lake
Moçâmedes see Namibe
Mochudi 56 C4 Kgatleng, SE Botswana
Mocímboa da Praia 57 F2 var. Vila de Mocímboa da Praia. Cabo Delgado, N Mozambique
Môco 56 B2 var. Morro de Môco. mountain W Angola
Mocoa 36 A4 Putumayo, SW Colombia
Môco, Morro de see Môco
Mocuba 57 E3 Zambézia, NE Mozambique
Modena 74 B3 anc. Mutina. Emilia-Romagna, N Italy
Modesto 25 B6 California, W USA
Modica 75 C7 anc. Motyca. Sicilia, Italy, C Mediterranean Sea
Modimolle 56 D4 prev. Nylstroom. Limpopo, NE South Africa
Modohn see Madona
Modriča 78 C3 Republika Srpska, N Bosnia and Herzegovina
Moe 127 C7 Victoria, SE Australia
Möen see Møn, Denmark
Moero, Lac see Mweru, Lake
Moeskroen see Mouscron
Mogadiscio/Mogadishu see Muqdisho
Mogador see Essaouira
Mogilëv see Mahilyow
Mogilev-Podol'skiy see Mohyliv-Podilskyi
Mogilno 76 C3 Kujawsko-pomorskie, C Poland
Moḩammadābād-e Rīgān 98 E4 Kermān, SE Iran
Mohammedia 48 C2 prev. Fédala. NW Morocco
Mohave, Lake 25 D7 reservoir Arizona/Nevada, W USA
Mohawk River 19 F3 river New York, NE USA
Mohéli see Mwali
Mohns Ridge 61 F3 undersea ridge Greenland Sea/Norwegian Sea
Moho 39 E4 Puno, SE Peru
Mohoro 51 C7 Pwani, E Tanzania
Mohua see Golden Bay
Mohyliv-Podilskyi 86 D3 prev. Mohyliv-Podil's'kyy, Rus. Mogilev-Podol'skiy. Vinnyts'ka Oblast', C Ukrain
Mohyliv-Podil's'kyy see Mohyliv-Podilskyi
Moili see Mwali
Mo i Rana 62 C3 Nordland, C Norway
Mõisaküla 84 D3 Ger. Moiseküll. Viljandimaa, S Estonia
Moiseküll see Mõisaküla
Moissac 69 B6 Tarn-et-Garonne, S France
Mojácar 71 E5 Andalucía, S Spain
Mojave Desert 25 D7 plain California, W USA
Mokrany see Makrany
Moktama see Mottama
Mol 65 C5 prev. Moll. Antwerpen, N Belgium
Moldavia see Moldova
Moldavian SSR/Moldavskaya SSR see Moldova
Molde 63 A5 Møre og Romsdal, S Norway
Moldotau, Khrebet see Moldo-Too, Khrebet
Moldo-Too, Khrebet 101 G2 prev. Khrebet Moldotau. mountain range C Kyrgyzstan
Moldova 86 D3 off. Republic of Moldova, var. Moldavia; prev. Moldavian SSR, Rus. Moldavskaya SSR. country SE Europe
Moldova Nouă 86 A4 Ger. Neumoldowa, Hung. Újmoldova. Caraş-Severin, SW Romania
Moldova, Republic of see Moldova
Moldoveanul see Vârful Moldoveanu
Molfetta 75 E5 Puglia, SE Italy
Moll see Mol
Mollendo 39 E4 Arequipa, SW Peru
Mölndal 63 B7 Västra Götaland, S Sweden
Molochansk 87 G4 Zaporiz'ka Oblast', SE Ukraine
Molodechno/Molodeczno see Maladzyechna
Moloka'i 25 B8 var. Molokai. island Hawaiian Islands, Hawaii, USA
Molokai Fracture Zone 131 E2 tectonic feature NE Pacific Ocean
Molopo 56 C4 seasonal river Botswana/South Africa
Mólos 83 B5 Stereá Ellás, C Greece
Molotov see Severodvinsk, Arkhangel'skaya Oblast', Russia
Molotov see Perm', Permskaya Oblast', Russia
Moluccas see Maluku
Molucca Sea 117 F4 Ind. Laut Maluku. sea E Indonesia
Molukken see Maluku
Mombasa 51 D7 Coast, SE Kenya
Mombetsu see Monbetsu
Momchilgrad 82 D3 prev. Mastanli. Kardzhali, S Bulgaria
Møn 63 B8 prev. Möen. island SE Denmark
Mona, Canal de la see Mona Passage
Monaco 69 C7 var. Monaco-Ville; anc. Monoecus. country capital (Monaco) S Monaco
Monaco 69 E6 off. Principality of Monaco. country W Europe
Monaco see München
Monaco, Port de 69 C8 bay S Monaco W Mediterranean Sea
Monaco, Principality of see Monaco
Monaco-Ville see Monaco
Monahans 27 E3 Texas, SW USA
Mona, Isla 33 E3 island W Puerto Rico
Mona Passage 33 E3 Sp. Canal de la Mona. channel Dominican Republic/Puerto Rico
Monastir see Bitola
Monbetsu 108 D2 var. Mombetsu, Monbetu. Hokkaidō, NE Japan
Monbetu see Monbetsu
Moncalieri 74 A2 Piemonte, NW Italy
Monchegorsk 88 C2 Murmanskaya Oblast', NW Russia
Monclova 28 D2 Coahuila, NE Mexico
Moncton 17 F4 New Brunswick, SE Canada
Mondovì 74 A2 Piemonte, NW Italy
Monfalcone 74 D2 Friuli-Venezia Giulia, NE Italy
Monforte de Lemos 70 C1 Galicia, NW Spain
Mongo 54 C3 Guéra, C Chad
Mongolia 104 C2 Mong. Mongol Uls. country E Asia
Mongolia, Plateau of 102 D1 plateau E Mongolia
Mongol Uls see Mongolia
Mongora see Saidu Sharif
Mongos, Chaîne des see Bongo, Massif des
Mongu 56 C2 Western, W Zambia
Monkchester see Newcastle upon Tyne
Monkey Bay 57 E2 Southern, SE Malawi
Monkey River see Monkey River Town
Monkey River Town 30 C2 var. Monkey River. Toledo, SE Belize
Monoecus see Monaco
Mono Lake 25 C6 lake California, W USA
Monostor see Beli Manastir
Monóvar see Monòver
Monòver 71 F4 var. Monóvar. Comunitat Valenciana, E Spain
Monroe 20 B2 Louisiana, S USA
Monrovia 52 C5 country capital (Liberia) W Liberia
Mons 65 B6 Dut. Bergen. Hainaut, S Belgium
Monselice 74 C2 Veneto, NE Italy
Montana 82 C2 prev. Ferdinand, Mikhaylovgrad. Montana, NW Bulgaria
Montana 22 B1 off. State of Montana, also known as Mountain State, Treasure State. state NW USA
Montargis 68 C4 Loiret, C France
Montauban 69 B6 Tarn-et-Garonne, S France
Montbéliard 68 D4 Doubs, E France
Mont Cenis, Col du 69 D5 pass E France
Mont-de-Marsan 69 B6 Landes, SW France
Monteagudo 39 G4 Chuquisaca, S Bolivia
Montecarlo 69 C8 Misiones, NE Argentina
Monte Caseros 42 D3 Corrientes, NE Argentina
Monte Cristi 32 D3 var. San Fernando de Monte Cristi. NW Dominican Republic
Monte Croce Carnico, Passo di see Plöcken Pass
Montegiardino 74 E2 SE San Marino
Montego Bay 32 A4 var. Mobay. W Jamaica
Montélimar 69 D5 anc. Acunum Acusio, Montilium Adhemari. Drôme, E France
Montemorelos 29 E3 Nuevo León, NE Mexico
Montenegro 79 C5 Serb. Crna Gora. country SW Europe
Monte Patria 42 B3 Coquimbo, N Chile
Monterey 25 B6 California, W USA
Monterey see Monterrey
Monterey Bay 25 A6 bay California, W USA
Montería 36 B2 Córdoba, NW Colombia
Montero 39 G4 Santa Cruz, C Bolivia
Monterrey 29 E3 var. Monterey. Nuevo León, NE Mexico
Montes Claros 41 F3 Minas Gerais, SE Brazil
Montevideo 42 D4 country capital (Uruguay) Montevideo, S Uruguay
Montevideo 23 F2 Minnesota, N USA
Montgenèvre, Col de 69 D5 pass France/Italy
Montgomery 20 D2 state capital Alabama, S USA
Montgomery see Sahiwal
Monthey 73 A7 Valais, SW Switzerland
Montilium Adhemari see Montélimar
Montluçon 68 C4 Allier, C France
Montoro 70 D4 Andalucía, S Spain
Montpelier 19 G2 state capital Vermont, NE USA
Montpellier 69 C6 Hérault, S France
Montréal 17 E4 Eng. Montreal. Québec, SE Canada
Montrose 66 D3 E Scotland, United Kingdom
Montrose 22 C5 Colorado, C USA
Montserrat 33 G3 var. Emerald Isle. UK Overseas Territory E West Indies
Monywa 114 B3 Sagaing, C Myanmar (Burma)
Monza 74 B2 Lombardia, N Italy
Monze 56 D2 Southern, S Zambia
Monzón 71 F2 Aragón, NE Spain
Moonie 127 D5 Queensland, E Australia
Moon-Sund see Väinameri
Moora 125 A6 Western Australia
Moore 27 G1 Oklahoma, C USA
Moore, Lake 125 B6 lake Western Australia
Moorhead 23 F2 Minnesota, N USA
Moose 16 C3 river Ontario, S Canada
Moosehead Lake 19 G1 lake Maine, NE USA
Moosonee 16 C3 Ontario, SE Canada
Mopti 53 E3 Mopti, C Mali
Moquegua 39 E4 Moquegua, SE Peru
Mora 63 C5 Dalarna, C Sweden
Morales 30 C2 Izabal, E Guatemala
Morant Bay 32 B5 E Jamaica
Moratalla 71 E4 Murcia, SE Spain
Morava 77 C5 var. March. river C Europe
Morava see Moravia, Czechia (Czech Republic)
Morava see Velika Morava, Serbia
Moravia 77 B5 Cz. Morava, Ger. Mähren. cultural region E Czechia (Czech Republic)
Moray Firth 66 C3 inlet N Scotland, United Kingdom
Morea see Pelopónnisos
Moreau River 22 D2 river South Dakota, N USA
Moree 127 D5 New South Wales, SE Australia
Morelia 29 E4 Michoacán, S Mexico
Morena, Sierra 70 C4 mountain range S Spain
Moreni 86 C5 Dâmbovița, S Romania
Morgan City 20 B3 Louisiana, S USA
Morghab, Darya-ye 100 D3 Rus. Murgab, Murghab, Turkm. Murgap, Murgap Deryasy. river Afghanistan/Turkmenistan
Morioka 108 D4 Iwate, Honshū, C Japan
Morlaix 68 A3 Finistère, NW France
Mormon State see Utah
Mornington Abyssal Plain 45 A7 abyssal plain SE Pacific Ocean
Mornington Island 126 B2 island Wellesley Islands, Queensland, N Australia
Morocco 48 B3 off. Kingdom of Morocco, Ar. Al Maghrib. country N Africa
Morocco see Marrakech
Morocco, Kingdom of see Morocco
Morogoro 51 C7 Morogoro, E Tanzania
Moro Gulf 117 E3 gulf S Philippines
Morón 32 C2 Ciego de Ávila, C Cuba
Mörön 104 D2 Hövsgöl, N Mongolia
Morondava 57 F3 Toliara, W Madagascar
Moroni 57 F2 country capital (Comoros) Grande Comore, NW Comoros
Morotai, Pulau 117 F3 island Maluku, E Indonesia
Morotiri see Marotiri
Morphou see Güzelyurt
Morrinsville 128 D3 Waikato, North Island, New Zealand
Morris 23 F2 Minnesota, N USA
Morris Jesup, Kap 61 E1 headland N Greenland
Morvan 68 D4 physical region C France
Moscow 24 C2 Idaho, NW USA
Moscow see Moskva
Mosel 73 A5 Fr. Moselle. river W Europe
Mosel see Moselle
Moselle 65 E8 Ger. Mosel. river W Europe
Moselle see Mosel
Mosgiel 129 B7 Otago, South Island, New Zealand
Moshi 51 C7 Kilimanjaro, NE Tanzania
Mosjøen 62 B4 Nordland, C Norway
Moskovskiy see Maskav
Moskva 89 B5 Eng. Moscow. country capital (Russia) Gorod Moskva, W Russia
Moskva see Maskav
Moson and Magyaróvár see Mosonmagyaróvár
Mosonmagyaróvár 77 C6 Ger. Wieselburg-Ungarisch-Altenburg; prev. Moson and Magyaróvár, Ger. Wieselburg and Ungarisch-Altenburg. Győr-Moson-Sopron, NW Hungary
Mosquito Coast 31 E3 var. Miskito Coast, Eng. Mosquito Coast. coastal region E Nicaragua
Mosquito Coast see La Mosquitia
Mosquito Gulf 31 F4 Eng. Mosquito Gulf. gulf N Panama
Mosquito Gulf see Mosquitos, Golfo de los
Moss 63 B6 Østfold, S Norway
Mossâmedes see Namibe
Mosselbaai 56 C5 var. Mosselbai, Eng. Mossel Bay. Western Cape, SW South Africa
Mosselbai/Mossel Bay see Mosselbaai
Mossendjo 55 B6 Niari, SW Congo
Mossoró 41 G2 Rio Grande do Norte, NE Brazil
Most 76 A4 Ger. Brüx. Ústecký Kraj, NW Czechia (Czech Republic)
Mosta 80 B5 var. Musta. C Malta
Mostaganem 48 D2 var. Mestghanem. NW Algeria
Mostar 78 C4 Federacija Bosna I Hercegovina, S Bosnia and Herzegovina
Mosty see Masty
Mosul see Al Mawşil
Mota del Cuervo 71 E3 Castilla-La Mancha, C Spain
Motagua, Río 30 B2 river Guatemala/Honduras
Mother of Presidents/Mother of States see Virginia
Motril 70 D5 Andalucía, S Spain
Motru 86 B4 Gorj, SW Romania
Mottama 114 B4 prev. Martaban; var. Moktama. Mon State, S Myanmar (Burma)
Motueka 129 C5 Tasman, South Island, New Zealand
Motul 29 H3 var. Motul de Felipe Carrillo Puerto. Yucatán, SE Mexico
Motul de Felipe Carrillo Puerto see Motul
Motyca see Modica
Mouanda see Moanda
Mouhoun see Black Volta
Mouila 55 A6 Ngounié, C Gabon
Moukden see Shenyang
Mould Bay 15 E2 Prince Patrick Island, Northwest Territories, N Canada
Moulins 68 C4 Allier, C France
Moulmein see Mawlamyine
Moundou 54 B4 Logone-Occidental, SW Chad
Moŭng Roessei 115 D5 Battambang, W Cambodia
Moun Hou see Black Volta
Mountain Home 20 B1 Arkansas, C USA
Mountain State see Montana
Mountain State see West Virginia
Mount Cook see Aoraki (mountain)
Mount Cook see Aoraki (populated place)
Mount Desert Island 19 H2 island Maine, NE USA
Mount Gambier 127 B7 South Australia
Mount Isa 126 B3 Queensland, C Australia
Mount Magnet 125 B5 Western Australia
Mount Pleasant 23 G4 Iowa, C USA
Mount Pleasant 18 C3 Michigan, N USA
Mount Vernon 18 B5 Illinois, N USA
Mount Vernon 24 B1 Washington, NW USA
Mourdi, Dépression du 54 C2 desert lowland Chad/Sudan
Mouscron 65 A6 Dut. Moeskroen. Hainaut, W Belgium
Mouse River see Souris River
Moussoro 54 B3 Kanem, W Chad
Moyen-Congo see Congo (Republic of)
Mo'ynoq 100 C1 Rus. Muynak. Qoraqalpog'iston Respublikasi, NW Uzbekistan
Moyobamba 38 B2 San Martín, NW Peru
Moyu 104 B3 var. Karakax. Xinjiang Uygur Zizhiqu, NW China
Moyynkum, Peski 101 F1 Kaz. Moyynqum. desert S Kazakhstan
Moyynqum see Moyynkum, Peski
Mozambika, Lakandranon' i see Mozambique Channel
Mozambique 57 E3 off. Republic of Mozambique; prev. People's Republic of Mozambique, Portuguese East Africa. country S Africa
Mozambique Basin see Natal Basin
Mozambique, Canal de see Mozambique Channel
Mozambique Channel 57 E3 Fr. Canal de Mozambique, Mal. Lakandranon' i Mozambika. strait W Indian Ocean
Mozambique, People's Republic of see Mozambique
Mozambique Plateau 47 D7 var. Mozambique Rise. undersea plateau SW Indian Ocean
Mozambique, Republic of see Mozambique
Mozambique Rise see Mozambique Plateau
Mozyr' see Mazyr
Mpama 55 B6 river C Congo
Mpika 56 D2 Northern, NE Zambia
Mqinvartsveri see Kazbek
Mrągowo 76 D2 Ger. Sensburg. Warmińsko-Mazurskie, NE Poland
Mthatha 56 D5 prev. Umtata. Eastern Cape, SE South Africa
Mtkvari see Kura
Mtwara 51 D8 Mtwara, SE Tanzania
Mualo see Messalo, Rio
Muang Chiang Rai see Chiang Rai
Muang Kalasin see Kalasin
Muang Khammouan see Thakhèk
Muang Không 115 D5 Champasak, S Laos
Muang Khôngxédôn 115 D5 var. Khong Sedone. Salavan, S Laos
Muang Khon Kaen see Khon Kaen
Muang Lampang see Lampang
Muang Loei see Loei
Muang Lom Sak see Lom Sak
Muang Nakhon Sawan see Nakhon Sawan
Muang Namo 114 C3 Oudômxai, N Laos
Muang Nan see Nan
Muang Phalan 114 D4 var. Muang Phalane. Savannakhét, S Laos
Muang Phalane see Muang Phalan
Muang Phayao see Phayao
Muang Phitsanulok see Phitsanulok
Muang Phrae see Phrae
Muang Roi Et see Roi Et
Muang Sakon Nakhon see Sakon Nakhon
Muang Samut Prakan see Samut Prakan
Muang Sing 114 C3 Louang Namtha, N Laos
Muang Ubon see Ubon Ratchathani
Muang Xaignabouri see Xaignabouli
Muar 116 B3 var. Bandar Maharani. Johor, Peninsular Malaysia
Mucojo 57 F2 Cabo Delgado, N Mozambique
Mudanjiang 107 E3 var. Mu-tan-chiang. Heilongjiang, NE China
Mudon 115 B5 Mon State, S Myanmar (Burma)
Muenchen see München
Muenster see Münster
Mufulira 56 D2 Copperbelt, C Zambia
Mughla see Muğla
Muğla 94 A4 var. Mughla. Muğla, SW Turkey (Türkiye)
Mūḩ, Sabkhat al 96 C3 lake C Syria
Muhu Väin see Väinameri
Muisne 38 A1 Esmeraldas, NW Ecuador
Mukacheve see Mukachevo
Mukachevo 86 B3 prev. Mukacheve, Hung. Munkács. Zakarpats'ka Oblast', W Ukraine
Mukalla see Al Mukallā
Mukden see Shenyang
Mula 71 E4 Murcia, SE Spain
Mulakatholhu 110 B4 var. Meemu Atoll, Mulaku Atoll. atoll C Maldives
Mulaku Atoll see Mulakatholhu
Muleshoe 27 E2 Texas, SW USA
Mulhacén 71 E5 var. Cerro de Mulhacén. mountain S Spain
Mulhacén, Cerro de see Mulhacén
Mülhausen see Mulhouse
Mülheim 73 A6 var. Mulheim an der Ruhr. Nordrhein-Westfalen, W Germany
Mulheim an der Ruhr see Mülheim
Mulhouse 68 E4 Ger. Mülhausen. Haut-Rhin, NE France
Müller-gerbergte see Muller, Pegunungan
Muller, Pegunungan 116 D4 Dut. Müller-gerbergte. mountain range Borneo, C Indonesia
Mull, Isle of 66 B4 island W Scotland, United Kingdom
Mulongo 55 D7 Katanga, SE Dem. Rep. Congo
Multan 112 C2 Punjab, E Pakistan
Mumbai 112 C5 prev. Bombay. state capital Mahārāshtra, W India
Munamägi see Suur Munamägi
Münchberg 73 C5 Bayern, E Germany
München 73 C6 var. Muenchen, Eng. Munich, It. Monaco. Bayern, SE Germany
Muncie 18 C4 Indiana, N USA
Mungbere 55 E5 Orientale, NE Dem. Rep. Congo
Mu Nggava see Rennell
Munich see München
Munkács see Mukachevo
Münster 72 A4 var. Muenster, Münster in Westfalen. Nordrhein-Westfalen, W Germany
Munster 67 A6 Ir. Cúige Mumhan. cultural region S Ireland
Münster in Westfalen see Münster
Muong Xiang Ngeun 114 C4 var. Xieng Ngeun. Louangphabang, N Laos
Muonio 62 D3 Lappi, N Finland
Muonioälv/Muoniojoki see Muonionjoki
Muonionjoki 62 D3 var. Muoniojoki, Swe. Muonioälv. river Finland/Sweden
Muqāţ 97 C5 Al Mafraq, E Jordan
Muqdisho 51 D6 Eng. Mogadishu, It. Mogadiscio. country capital (Somalia) Banaadir, S Somalia
Mur 73 E7 Croatian Mura. river C Europe
Mura see Mur
Muradiye 95 F3 Van, E Turkey (Türkiye)
Murapara see Murupara
Murata 74 E2 S San Marino
Murchison River 125 A5 river Western Australia
Murcia 71 F4 Murcia, SE Spain
Murcia 71 E4 autonomous community SE Spain
Mureş 86 A4 river Hungary/Romania
Murfreesboro 20 D1 Tennessee, S USA
Murgab see Morghāb, Daryā-yeb
Murgap 100 D3 Mary Welaýaty, S Turkmenistan
Murgap see Morghāb, Daryā-ye
Murgap Deryasy see Morghāb, Daryā-ye
Murghab see Morghāb, Daryā-ye
Murghob 101 F3 Rus. Murgab. SE Tajikistan
Murgon 127 E5 Queensland, E Australia
Mūrītāniyah see Mauritania
Müritz 72 C3 var. Müritzee. lake NE Germany
Müritzee see Müritz
Murmansk 88 C2 Murmanskaya Oblast', NW Russia
Murmashi 88 C2 Murmanskaya Oblast', NW Russia
Murom 89 B5 Vladimirskaya Oblast', W Russia
Muroran 108 D3 Hokkaidō, NE Japan
Muros 70 B1 Galicia, NW Spain
Murray Fracture Zone 131 E2 fracture zone NE Pacific Ocean
Murray Range see Murray Ridge
Murray Ridge 90 C5 var. Murray Range. undersea ridge N Arabian Sea
Murray River 127 B6 river SE Australia
Murrumbidgee River 127 C6 river New South Wales, SE Australia
Murska Sobota 73 E7 Ger. Olsnitz. NE Slovenia
Murupara 128 E3 var. Murapara. Bay of Plenty, North Island, New Zealand
Murviedro see Sagunt
Murwāra 113 E4 Madhya Pradesh, N India
Murwillumbah 127 E5 New South Wales, SE Australia
Murzuq, Edeyin see Murzuq, Idhān
Murzuq, Idhan 49 F4 var. Edeyin Murzuq. desert SW Libya
Mürzzuschlag 73 E7 Steiermark, E Austria
Muş 95 F3 var. Mush. Muş, E Turkey (Türkiye)
Musa, Gebel 50 C2 var. Gebel Mûsa. mountain NE Egypt
Mûsa, Gebel see Mūsá, Jabal
Musala 82 B3 mountain W Bulgaria
Muscat see Masqaţ
Muscat and Oman see Oman
Muscatine 23 G3 Iowa, C USA
Musgrave Ranges 125 D5 mountain range South Australia
Musina 75 D7 var. Messana, Messene; anc. Zancle. Sicilia, Italy, C Mediterranean Sea

Musina *56 D3 prev.* Messina. Limpopo, NE South Africa
Muskegon *18 C3* Michigan, N USA
Muskogean *see* Tallahassee
Muskogee *27 G1* Oklahoma, C USA
Musoma *51 C6* Mara, N Tanzania
Musta *see* Mosta
Mustafa-Pasha *see* Svilengrad
Musters, Lago *43 B6 lake* S Argentina
Muswellbrook *127 D6* New South Wales, SE Australia
Mut *94 C4* İçel, S Turkey (Türkiye)
Mu-tan-chiang *see* Mudanjiang
Mutare *56 D3 var.* Mutari; *prev.* Umtali. Manicaland, E Zimbabwe
Mutari *see* Mutare
Mutina *see* Modena
Mutsu-wan *108 D3 bay* N Japan
Muttonbird Islands *see* Titi
Mu Us Shadi *105 E3 var.* Ordos Desert; *prev.* Mu Us Shamo. *desert* N China
Mu Us Shamo *see* Mu Us Shadi
Muy Muy *30 D3* Matagalpa, C Nicaragua
Muynak *see* Mo'ynoq
Mužlja *78 D3 Hung.* Felsőmuzslya; *prev.* Gornja Mužlja. Vojvodina, N Serbia
Mwali *57 F2 var.* Moili, *Fr.* Mohéli. *island* S Comoros
Mwanza *51 B6* Mwanza, NW Tanzania
Mweka *55 C6* Kasai-Occidental, C Dem. Rep. Congo
Mwene-Ditu *55 D7* Kasai-Oriental, S Dem. Rep. Congo
Mweru, Lake *55 D7 var.* Lac Moero. *lake* Dem. Rep. Congo/Zambia
Myadel' *see* Myadzyel
Myadzyel *85 C5 Pol.* Miadzioł Nowy, *Rus.* Myadel'. Minskaya Voblasts', N Belarus
Myanaung *114 B4* Ayeyarwady, SW Myanmar (Burma)
Myanmar *114 A3 off.* Republic of the Union of Myanmar; *prev.* Union of Myanmar, *var.* Burma. *country* SE Asia
Myanmar, Republic of the Union of *see* Myanmar
Myanmar, Union of *see* Myanmar
Myaungmya *114 A4* Ayeyarwady, SW Myanmar (Burma)
Myaydo *see* Aunglan
Myeik *115 B6 var.* Mergui. Tanintharyi, S Myanmar (Burma)
Myeik Archipelago *115 B6 prev.* Mergui Archipelago. *island group* S Myanmar (Burma)
Myerkulavichy *85 D7 Rus.* Merkulovichi. Homyel'skaya Voblasts', SE Belarus
Myingyan *114 B3* Mandalay, C Myanmar (Burma)
Myitkyina *114 B2* Kachin State, N Myanmar (Burma)
Mykolaiv *87 E4 prev.* Mykolayiv, *Rus.* Nikolayev. Mykolayivs'ka Oblast', S Ukraine
Mykolayiv *see* Mykolaiv
Mykonos *83 D6 var.* Míkonos. *island* Kykládes, Greece, Aegean Sea
Myrhorod *87 F2 Rus.* Mirgorod. Poltavs'ka Oblast', NE Ukraine
Mýrina *82 D4 var.* Mírina. Límnos, SE Greece
Myrtle Beach *21 F2* South Carolina, SE USA
Myrtoan Sea *see* Mirtóo Pélagos
Mýrtos *83 D8* Kríti, Greece, E Mediterranean Sea
Myrtoum Mare *see* Mirtóo Pélagos
Myślibórz *76 B3* Zachodnio-pomorskie, NW Poland
Mysore *see* Mysūru
Mysore *see* Karnātaka
Mysūru *110 C2 prev.* Mysore, *var.* Maisur. Karnātaka, W India
My Tho *115 E6 var.* Mi Tho. Tiền Giang, S Vietnam
Mytilene *see* Mytilíni
Mytilíni *83 D5 var.* Mitilíni; *anc.* Mytilene. Lésvos, E Greece
Mzuzu *57 E2* Northern, N Malawi

N

Naberezhnyye Chelny *89 D5 prev.* Brezhnev. Respublika Tatarstan, W Russia
Nāblus *97 A6 var.* Nābulus, *Heb.* Shekhem; *anc.* Neapolis, *Bibl.* Shechem. N West Bank, Middle East
Nābulus *see* Nāblus
Nacala *57 F2* Nampula, NE Mozambique
Na-Ch'ii *see* Nagqu
Nada *see* Danzhou
Nadi *123 E4 prev.* Nandi. Viti Levu, W Fiji
Nadur *80 A5* Gozo, N Malta
Nadvirna *86 C3 Pol.* Nadwórna, *Rus.* Nadvornaya. Ivano-Frankivs'ka Oblast', W Ukraine
Nadvoitsy *88 B3* Respublika Kareliya, NW Russia
Nadvornaya/Nadwórna *see* Nadvirna
Nadym *92 C3* Yamalo-Nenetskiy Avtonomnyy Okrug, N Russia
Náfpaktos *83 B5 var.* Návpaktos. Dytikí Elláś, C Greece
Náfplio *83 B6 prev.* Návplion. Pelopónnisos, S Greece
Naga *117 E2 off.* Naga City; *prev.* Nueva Caceres. Luzon, N Philippines
Naga City *see* Naga
Nagano *109 C5* Nagano, Honshū, S Japan
Nagaoka *109 D5* Niigata, Honshū, C Japan
Nagara Pathom *see* Nakhon Pathom
Nagara Sridharmaraj *see* Nakhon Si Thammarat
Nagara Svarga *see* Nakhon Sawan
Nagasaki *109 A7* Nagasaki, Kyūshū, SW Japan
Nagato *109 A7* Yamaguchi, Honshū, SW Japan
Nāgercoil *110 C3* Tamil Nādu, SE India
Nagorno-Karabakh *see* Nagornyy-Karabakh
Nagorno-Karabakhskaya Avtonomnaya Oblast *see* Nagornyy-Karabakh
Nagornyy Karabakh *95 G3 prev.* Nagorno-Karabakh, Nagorno-Karabakhskaya Avtonomnaya Oblast, *Arm.* Lernayin Gharabagh, *Az.* Dağlıq Qarabağ. *former autonomous region* SW Azerbaijan
Nagoya *109 C6* Aichi, Honshū, SW Japan
Nāgpur *112 D4* Mahārāshtra, C India
Nagqu *104 C5 Chin.* Na-Ch'ii; *prev.* Hei-ho. Xizang Zizhiqu, W China
Nagybánya *see* Baia Mare
Nagybecskerek *see* Zrenjanin
Nagydisznód *see* Cisnădie
Nagyenyed *see* Aiud
Nagykálló *77 E6* Szabolcs-Szatmár-Bereg, E Hungary
Nagykanizsa *77 C7 Ger.* Grosskanizsa. Zala, SW Hungary
Nagykároly *see* Carei
Nagykikinda *see* Kikinda
Nagykőrös *77 D7* Pest, C Hungary
Nagymihály *see* Michalovce
Nagysurány *see* Šurany
Nagyszalonta *see* Salonta
Nagyszeben *see* Sibiu
Nagyszentmiklós *see* Sânnicolau Mare
Nagyszöllös *see* Vynohradiv
Nagyszombat *see* Trnava
Nagytapolcsány *see* Topoľčany
Nagyvárad *see* Oradea
Naha *108 A3* Okinawa, Okinawa, SW Japan
Nahariya *97 A5 prev.* Nahariyya. Northern, N Israel
Nahariyya *see* Nahariya
Nahuel Huapí, Lago *43 B5 lake* W Argentina
Nain *17 F2* Newfoundland and Labrador, NE Canada
Nā'īn *98 D3* Eşfahān, C Iran
Nairobi *47 E5 country capital* (Kenya) Nairobi Area, S Kenya
Nairobi *51 C6* Nairobi Area, S Kenya
Naissus *see* Niš
Najaf *see* An Najaf
Najima *see* Fukuoka
Najin *see* Rajin
Najrān *99 B6 var.* Abā as Su'ūd. Najrān, S Saudi Arabia
Nakambé *see* White Volta
Nakamura *109 B7 var.* Shimanto. Kōchi, Shikoku, SW Japan
Nakatsugawa *109 C6 var.* Nakatugawa. Gifu, Honshū, SW Japan
Nakatugawa *see* Nakatsugawa
Nakhichevan' *see* Naxçıvan
Nakhodka *93 G5* Primorskiy Kray, SE Russia
Nakhon Pathom *115 C5 var.* Nagara Pathom, Nakorn Pathom. Nakhon Pathom, W Thailand
Nakhon Ratchasima *115 C5 var.* Khorat, Korat. Nakhon Ratchasima, E Thailand
Nakhon Sawan *115 C5 var.* Muang Nakhon Sawan, Nagara Svarga. Nakhon Sawan, W Thailand
Nakhon Si Thammarat *115 C7 var.* Nagara Sridharmaraj, Nakhon Sithammaraj. Nakhon Si Thammarat, SW Thailand
Nakhon Sithammaraj *see* Nakhon Si Thammarat
Nakorn Pathom *see* Nakhon Pathom
Nakuru *51 C6* Rift Valley, SW Kenya
Nal'chik *89 B8* Kabardino-Balkarskaya Respublika, SW Russia
Nālūt *49 F2* NW Libya
Namakan Lake *18 A1 lake* Canada/USA
Namangan *101 F2* Namangan Viloyati, E Uzbekistan
Nambala *56 D2* Central, C Zambia
Nam Co *104 C5 lake* W China
Nam Định *114 D3* Nam Ha, N Vietnam
Namib Desert *56 B3 desert* W Namibia
Namibe *56 A2 Port.* Moçâmedes, Mossâmedes. Namibe, SW Angola
Namibia *56 B3 off.* Republic of Namibia, *var.* South West Africa, *Afr.* Suidwes-Afrika, *Ger.* Deutsch-Südwestafrika; *prev.* German Southwest Africa, South-West Africa. *country* S Africa
Namibia, Republic of *see* Namibia
Namnetes *see* Nantes
Namo *see* Namu Atoll
Nam Ou *114 C3 river* N Laos
Nampa *24 D3* Idaho, NW USA
Nampula *57 E2* Nampula, NE Mozambique
Namsos *62 B4* Nord-Trøndelag, C Norway
Nam Tha *114 C4 river* N Laos
Namu Atoll *122 D2 var.* Namo. *atoll* Ralik Chain, C Marshall Islands
Namur *65 C6 Dut.* Namen. Namur, SE Belgium
Namyit Island *106 C8 island* S Spratly Islands
Nan *114 C4 var.* Muang Nan. Nan, NW Thailand
Nanaimo *14 D5* Vancouver Island, British Columbia, SW Canada
Nanchang *106 C5 var.* Nan-ch'ang, Nanch'ang-hsien. *province capital* Jiangxi, S China
Nan-ch'ang *see* Nanchang
Nanch'ang-hsien *see* Nanchang
Nan-ching *see* Nanjing
Nancy *68 D3* Meurthe-et-Moselle, NE France
Nandaime *30 D3* Granada, SW Nicaragua
Nānded *112 D5* Mahārāshtra, C India
Nandi *see* Nadi
Nándorhgy *see* Oţelu Roşu
Nandyāl *110 C1* Andhra Pradesh, E India
Naniwa *see* Ōsaka
Nanjing *106 D5 var.* Nan-ching, Nanking; *prev.* Chianning, Chian-ning, Kiang-ning, Jiangsu. *province capital* Jiangsu, E China
Nanking *see* Nanjing
Nanning *106 B6 var.* Nan-ning; *prev.* Yung-ning. Guangxi Zhuangzu Zizhiqu, S China
Nan-ning *see* Nanning
Nanortalik *60 C5* Kujalleq, S Greenland
Nanpan Jiang *114 D2 river* S China
Nanping *106 D6 var.* Nan-p'ing; *prev.* Yenping. Fujian, SE China
Nan-p'ing *see* Nanping
Nansei-shotō *108 A2 Eng.* Ryukyu Islands. *island group* SW Japan
Nansei Syotō Trench *see* Ryukyu Trench
Nansen Basin *133 C4 undersea basin* Arctic Ocean
Nansen Cordillera *133 B3 var.* Arctic Mid Oceanic Ridge, Nansen Ridge. *seamount range* Arctic Ocean
Nansen Ridge *see* Nansen Cordillera
Nanterre *68 D1* Hauts-de-Seine, N France
Nantes *68 B4 Bret.* Naoned; *anc.* Condivincum, Namnetes. Loire-Atlantique, NW France
Nantucket Island *19 G3 island* Massachusetts, NE USA
Nanumaga *123 E3 var.* Nanumanga. *atoll* NW Tuvalu
Nanumanga *see* Nanumaga
Nanumea Atoll *123 E3 atoll* NW Tuvalu
Nanyang *106 C5 var.* Nan-yang. Henan, C China
Nan-yang *see* Nanyang
Naoned *see* Nantes
Napa *25 B6* California, W USA
Napier *128 E4* Hawke's Bay, North Island, New Zealand
Naples *21 E5* Florida, SE USA
Naples *see* Napoli
Napo *34 A3 province* NE Ecuador
Napoléon-Vendée *see* la Roche-sur-Yon
Napoli *75 C5 Eng.* Naples, *Ger.* Neapel; *anc.* Neapolis. Campania, S Italy
Napo, Río *38 C1 river* Ecuador/Peru
Naracoorte *127 B7* South Australia
Naradhivas *see* Narathiwat
Narathiwat *115 C7 var.* Naradhivas. Narathiwat, SW Thailand
Narbada *see* Narmada
Narbo Martius *see* Narbonne
Narbonne *69 C6 anc.* Narbo Martius. Aude, S France
Narborough Island *see* Fernandina, Isla
Nares Abyssal Plain *see* Nares Plain
Nares Plain *13 E6 var.* Nares Abyssal Plain. *abyssal plain* NW Atlantic Ocean
Nares Stræde *see* Nares Strait
Nares Strait *60 D1 Dan.* Nares Stræde. *strait* Canada/Greenland
Narew *76 E3 river* E Poland
Narmada *102 B3 var.* Narbada. *river* C India
Narova *see* Narva
Narovlya *see* Narowlya
Narowlya *85 C8 Rus.* Narovlya. Homyel'skaya Voblasts', SE Belarus
Närpes *63 D5 Fin.* Närpiö. Österbotten, W Finland
Närpiö *see* Närpes
Narrabri *127 D6* New South Wales, SE Australia
Narrogin *125 B6* Western Australia
Narva *84 E2* Ida-Virumaa, NE Estonia
Narva *84 E2 prev.* Narova. *river* Estonia/Russia
Narva Bay *84 E2 Est.* Narva Laht, *Ger.* Narwa-Bucht, *Rus.* Narvskiy Zaliv. *bay* Estonia/Russia
Narva Laht *see* Narva Bay
Narva Reservoir *84 E2 Est.* Narva Veehoidla, *Rus.* Narvskoye Vodokhranilishche. *reservoir* Estonia/Russia
Narva Veehoidla *see* Narva Reservoir
Narvik *62 C3* Nordland, C Norway
Narvskiy Zaliv *see* Narva Bay
Narvskoye Vodokhranilishche *see* Narva Reservoir
Narwa-Bucht *see* Narva Bay
Nar'yan-Mar *88 D3 prev.* Beloshchel'ye, Dzerzhinskiy. Nenetskiy Avtonomnyy Okrug, NW Russia
Naryn *101 G2* Narynskaya Oblast', C Kyrgyzstan
Nassau *32 C1 country capital* (The Bahamas) New Providence, N The Bahamas
Năsăud *86 B3 Ger.* Nussdorf, *Hung.* Naszód. Bistriţa-Năsăud, N Romania
Nase *see* Naze
Nāshik *112 C5 prev.* Nāsik. Mahārāshtra, W India
Nashua *19 G3* New Hampshire, NE USA
Nashville *20 C1 state capital* Tennessee, S USA
Näsijärvi *63 D5 lake* SW Finland
Nāsik *see* Nāshik
Nasir, Buhayrat/Nâşir,Buḥeiret *see* Nasser, Lake
Nāsiri *see* Ahvāz
Nasiriya *see* An Nāşirīyah
Nasser, Lake *50 B3 var.* Buhayrat Nasir, Buḥayrat Nāşir, Buḥeiret Nâşir. *lake* Egypt/Sudan
Naszód *see* Năsăud
Nata *56 C3* Central, NE Botswana
Natal *41 G2 state capital* Rio Grande do Norte, E Brazil
Natal Basin *119 A6 var.* Mozambique Basin. *undersea basin* W Indian Ocean
Natanya *see* Netanya
Natchez *20 B3* Mississippi, S USA
Natchitoches *20 A2* Louisiana, S USA
Nathanya *see* Netanya
Natitingou *53 F4* NW Benin
Natsrat *see* Natzrat
Natuna Islands *see* Natuna, Kepulauan
Natuna, Kepulauan *102 D4 var.* Natuna Islands. *island group* W Indonesia
Naturaliste Plateau *119 E6 undersea plateau* E Indian Ocean
Natzrat *97 A5 var.* Natsrat, *Ar.* En Nazira, *Eng.* Nazareth; *prev.* Nazerat. Northern, N Israel
Naugard *see* Nowogard
Naujaat *15 G3 prev.* Repulse Bay. Nunavut, N Canada
Naujamiestis *84 C4* Panevėžys, C Lithuania
Nauru *122 D2 off.* Republic of Nauru; *prev.* Pleasant Island. *country* W Pacific Ocean
Nauru, Republic of *see* Nauru
Nauta *38 C2* Loreto, N Peru
Navahrudak *85 C6 Pol.* Nowogródek, *Rus.* Novogrudok. Hrodzyenskaya Voblasts', W Belarus
Navanagar *see* Jāmnagar
Navapolatsk *85 D5 Rus.* Novopolotsk. Vitsyebskaya Voblasts', N Belarus
Navarra *71 E2 Eng./Fr.* Navarre. *autonomous community* N Spain
Navarre *see* Navarra
Navassa Island *32 C3 US unincorporated territory* C West Indies
Navoi *see* Navoiy
Navoiy *101 E2 Rus.* Navoi. Navoiy Viloyati, C Uzbekistan
Navojoa *28 C2* Sonora, NW Mexico
Navolat *see* Navolato
Navolato *28 C3 var.* Navolat. Sinaloa, C Mexico
Návpaktos *see* Náfpaktos
Návplion *see* Náfplio
Nawabashah *see* Nawabshah
Nawabshah *112 B3 var.* Nawabashah. Sindh, S Pakistan
Naxçıvan *95 G3 Rus.* Nakhichevan'. SW Azerbaijan
Náxos *83 D6 var.* Naxos. Náxos, Kykládes, Greece, Aegean Sea
Náxos *83 D6 island* Kykládes, Greece, Aegean Sea
Nayoro *108 D2* Hokkaidō, NE Japan
Nay Pyi Taw *114 B4 country capital* Myanmar (Burma)) Mandalay, C Myanmar (Burma)
Nazareth *see* Natzrat
Nazca *38 D4* Ica, S Peru
Nazca Ridge *35 A5 undersea ridge* E Pacific Ocean
Naze *108 B3 var.* Nase. Kagoshima, Amami-ōshima, SW Japan
Nazerat *see* Natzrat
Nazilli *94 A4* Aydın, SW Turkey (Türkiye)
Nazrēt *51 C5 var.* Adama, Hadama. Oromīya, C Ethiopia
N'Dalatando *56 B1 Port.* Salazar, Vila Salazar. Cuanza Norte, NW Angola
Ndélé *54 C4* Bamingui-Bangoran, N Central African Republic
Ndendé *55 B6* Ngounié, S Gabon
Ndindi *55 A6* Nyanga, S Gabon
N'djaména *54 B3 var.* Ndjamena; *prev.* Fort-Lamy. *country capital* (Chad) Chari-Baguirmi, W Chad
Ndjamena *see* N'Djaména
Ndjolé *55 A5* Moyen-Ogooué, W Gabon
Ndola *56 D2* Copperbelt, C Zambia
Ndzouani *see* Anjouan
Neagh, Lough *67 B5 lake* E Northern Ireland, United Kingdom
Néa Moudaniá *82 C4 var.* Néa Moudhaniá. Kentrikí Makedonía, N Greece
Néa Moudhaniá *see* Néa Moudaniá
Neapel *see* Napoli
Neápoli *82 B4 prev.* Neápolis. Dytikí Makedonía, N Greece
Neápoli *83 D8* Kríti, Greece, E Mediterranean Sea
Neápoli *83 C7* Pelopónnisos, S Greece
Neápolis *see* Neápoli, Greece
Neapolis *see* Napoli, Italy
Neapolis *see* Nablus, West Bank
Near Islands *14 A2 island group* Aleutian Islands, Alaska, USA
Néa Zíchni *82 C3 var.* Néa Zíkhni; *prev.* Néa Zíkhna. Kentrikí Makedonía, NE Greece
Néa Zíkhna/Néa Zíkhni *see* Néa Zíchni
Nebaj *30 B2* Quiché, W Guatemala
Nebitdag *see* Balkanabat
Neblina, Pico da *40 C1 mountain* NW Brazil
Nebraska *22 D4 off.* State of Nebraska, *also known as* Blackwater State, Cornhusker State, Tree Planters State. *state* C USA
Nebraska City *23 F4* Nebraska, C USA
Neches River *27 H3 river* Texas, SW USA
Neckar *73 B6 river* SW Germany
Necochea *43 D5* Buenos Aires, E Argentina
Nederland *see* Netherlands
Neder Rijn *64 D4 Eng.* Lower Rhine. *river* C Netherlands
Nederweert *65 D5* Limburg, SE Netherlands
Neede *64 E3* Gelderland, E Netherlands
Neerpelt *65 D5* Limburg, NE Belgium
Neftekamsk *89 D5* Respublika Bashkortostan, W Russia
Neftezavodsk *see* Seýdi
Negara Brunei Darussalam *see* Brunei
Negēlē *51 D5 var.* Negelli, *It.* Neghelli. Oromīya, C Ethiopia
Negelli *see* Negēlē
Negev *see* HaNegev
Neghelli *see* Negēlē
Negomane *57 E2 var.* Negomano. Cabo Delgado, N Mozambique
Negomano *see* Negomane
Negombo *110 C3* Western Province, SW Sri Lanka
Negotin *78 E4* Serbia, E Serbia
Negra, Punto *38 A3 headland* NW Peru
Negreşti *see* Negreşti-Oaş
Negreşti-Oaş *86 B3 Hung.* Avasfelsőfalu; *prev.* Negreşti. Satu Mare, NE Romania
Negro, Río *43 C5 river* E Argentina
Negro, Río *40 D1 river* N South America
Negro, Río *42 D4 river* Brazil/Uruguay
Negros *117 E2 island* C Philippines
Nehbandān *98 E3* Khorāsān, E Iran
Neijiang *106 B5* Sichuan, C China
Neiva *36 B3* Huila, S Colombia
Nellore *110 D2* Andhra Pradesh, E India
Nelson *129 C5* Nelson, South Island, New Zealand
Nelson *15 G4 river* Manitoba, C Canada
Néma *52 D3* Hodh ech Chargui, SE Mauritania
Neman *84 B4 Ger.* Ragnit. Kaliningradskaya Oblast', W Russia
Neman *84 A4 Bel.* Nyoman, *Ger.* Memel, *Lith.* Nemunas, *Pol.* Niemen. *river* NE Europe
Nemausus *see* Nîmes
Neméa *83 B6* Pelopónnisos, S Greece
Nemetocenna *see* Arras
Nemours *68 C3* Seine-et-Marne, N France
Nemunas *see* Neman
Nemuro *108 E2* Hokkaidō, NE Japan
Neochóri *83 B5* Dytikí Elláś, C Greece
Nepal *113 E3 off.* Nepal. *country* S Asia
Nepal *see* Nepal
Nereta *84 C4* Aizkraukle, S Latvia
Neretva *78 C4 river* Bosnia and Herzegovina/ Croatia
Neris *85 C5 Bel.* Viliya, *Pol.* Wilia; *prev. Pol.* Wilja. *river* Belarus/Lithuania
Neris *see* Viliya
Nerva *70 C4* Andalucía, S Spain
Neryungri *93 F4* Respublika Sakha (Yakutiya), NE Russia
Neskaupstaður *61 E5* Austurland, E Iceland
Ness, Loch *66 C3 lake* N Scotland, United Kingdom
Nesterov *see* Zhovkva
Néstos *82 C3 Bul.* Mesta, *Turk.* Kara Su. *river* Bulgaria/Greece
Nesvizh *see* Nyasvizh
Netanya *97 A6 var.* Natanya, Nathanya. Central, C Israel
Netherlands *64 C3 off.* Kingdom of the Netherlands, *var.* Holland, *Dut.* Koninkrijk der Nederlanden, Nederland. *country* NW Europe
Netherlands East Indies *see* Indonesia
Netherlands Guiana *see* Suriname
Netherlands, Kingdom of the *see* Netherlands
Netherlands New Guinea *see* Papua
Nettilling Lake *15 G3 lake* Baffin Island, Nunavut, N Canada
Netze *see* Noteć
Neu Amerika *see* Puławy
Neubrandenburg *72 D3* Mecklenburg-Vorpommern, NE Germany
Neuchâtel *73 A7 Ger.* Neuenburg. Neuchâtel, W Switzerland
Neuchâtel, Lac de *73 A7 Ger.* Neuenburger See. *lake* W Switzerland
Neuenburger See *see* Neuchâtel, Lac de
Neufchâteau *65 D8* Luxembourg, SE Belgium
Neugradisk *see* Nova Gradiška
Neuhof *see* Zgierz
Neukuhren *see* Pionerskiy
Neumarkt *see* Târgu Secuiesc, Covasna, Romania
Neumarkt *see* Târgu Mureş
Neumayer III *132 A2 German research station* Antarctica
Neumoldowa *see* Moldova Nouă
Neumünster *72 B2* Schleswig-Holstein, N Germany
Neunkirchen *73 A5* Saarland, SW Germany
Neuquén *43 B5* Neuquén, SE Argentina
Neuruppin *72 C3* Brandenburg, NE Germany
Neusalz an der Oder *see* Nowa Sól
Neu Sandec *see* Nowy Sącz
Neusatz *see* Novi Sad
Neusiedler See *73 E6 Hung.* Fertő. *lake* Austria/ Hungary
Neusohl *see* Banská Bystrica
Neustadt *see* Baia Mare, Maramureş, Romania
Neustadt an der Haardt *see* Neustadt an der Weinstrasse
Neustadt an der Weinstrasse *73 B5 prev.* Neustadt an der Haardt, *hist.* Niewenstat; *anc.* Nova Civitas. Rheinland-Pfalz, SW Germany
Neustadtl *see* Novo mesto
Neustettin *see* Szczecinek
Neustrelitz *72 D3* Mecklenburg-Vorpommern, NE Germany
Neutra *see* Nitra
Neu-Ulm *73 B6* Bayern, S Germany
Neuwied *73 A5* Rheinland-Pfalz, W Germany
Neuzen *see* Terneuzen
Nevada *25 C5 off.* State of Nevada, *also known as* Battle Born State, Sagebrush State, Silver State. *state* W USA
Nevada, Sierra *70 D5 mountain range* S Spain
Nevada, Sierra *25 C6 mountain range* W USA
Nevers *68 C4 anc.* Noviodunum. Nièvre, C France
Neves *54 E2* São Tomé, S Sao Tome and Principe, Africa
Nevinnomyssk *89 B7* Stavropol'skiy Kray, SW Russia
Nevşehir *94 C3 var.* Nevshehr. Nevşehir, C Turkey (Türkiye)
Newala *51 C8* Mtwara, SE Tanzania
New Albany *18 C5* Indiana, N USA
New Amsterdam *37 G3* E Guyana
Newark *19 F4* New Jersey, NE USA
New Bedford *19 G3* Massachusetts, NE USA
Newberg *24 B3* Oregon, NW USA
New Bern *21 F1* North Carolina, SE USA
New Braunfels *27 G4* Texas, SW USA
Newbridge *67 B6 Ir.* An Droichead Nua. Kildare, C Ireland
New Britain *122 B3 island* E Papua New Guinea
New Brunswick *17 E4 Fr.* Nouveau-Brunswick. *province* SE Canada
New Caledonia *122 D4 var.* Kanaky, *Fr.* Nouvelle-Calédonie. *French self-governing territory of special status* SW Pacific Ocean
New Caledonia *122 C5 island* SW Pacific Ocean
New Caledonia Basin *120 C4 undersea basin* W Pacific Ocean
Newcastle *127 D6* New South Wales, SE Australia
Newcastle *see* Newcastle upon Tyne
Newcastle upon Tyne *66 D4 var.* Newcastle, *hist.* Monkchester, *Lat.* Pons Aelii. NE England, United Kingdom
New Delhi *112 D3 country capital* (India) Delhi, N India
New England of the West *see* Minnesota
Newfoundland *17 G3 Fr.* Terre-Neuve. *island* Newfoundland and Labrador, SE Canada
Newfoundland and Labrador *17 F2 Fr.* Terre Neuve. *province* E Canada
Newfoundland Basin *44 B3 undersea feature* NW Atlantic Ocean
New Georgia Islands *122 C3 island group* NW Solomon Islands
New Glasgow *17 F4* Nova Scotia, SE Canada
New Goa *see* Panaji
New Guinea *122 A3 Dut.* Nieuw Guinea, *Ind.* Irian. *island* Indonesia/Papua New Guinea
New Hampshire *19 F2 off.* State of New Hampshire, *also known as* Granite State. *state* NE USA
New Haven *19 G3* Connecticut, NE USA
New Hebrides *see* Vanuatu
New Iberia *20 B3* Louisiana, S USA
New Ireland *122 C3 island* NE Papua New Guinea
New Jersey *19 F4 off.* State of New Jersey, *also known as* The Garden State. *state* NE USA
Newman *124 B4* Western Australia
Newmarket *67 E6* E England, United Kingdom
New Mexico *26 C2 off.* State of New Mexico, *also known as* Land of Enchantment, Sunshine State. *state* SW USA
New Orleans *20 B3* Louisiana, S USA
New Plymouth *128 C4* Taranaki, North Island, New Zealand
Newport *67 C7* SE Wales, United Kingdom
Newport *18 C4* Kentucky, S USA
Newport *19 G2* Vermont, NE USA
Newport News *19 F5* Virginia, NE USA
New Providence *32 C1 island* N The Bahamas
Newquay *67 C7* SW England, United Kingdom
Newry *67 B5 Ir.* An tIúr. SE Northern Ireland, United Kingdom
New Sarum *see* Salisbury
New Siberian Islands *see* Novosibirskiye Ostrova
New South Wales *127 C6 state* SE Australia
Newton *23 G3* Iowa, C USA
Newton *23 F5* Kansas, C USA
Newtownabbey *67 B5 Ir.* Baile na Mainistreach. E Northern Ireland, United Kingdom
New Ulm *23 F2* Minnesota, N USA
New York *19 F4* New York, NE USA
New York *19 F3 state* NE USA
New Zealand *128 A4 var.* Aotearoa. *country* SW Pacific Ocean
Neyveli *110 C2* Tamil Nādu, SE India
Nezhin *see* Nizhyn
Ngangze Co *104 B5 lake* W China
Ngaoundéré *54 B4 var.* N'Gaoundéré. Adamaoua, N Cameroon
N'Gaoundéré *see* Ngaoundéré
Ngazidja *57 F2 Fr.* Grande-Comore. *island* NW Comoros
Ngerulmud *56 D4 country capital* (Palau) NW Pacific Ocean
N'Giva *56 B3 var.* Ondjiva, *Port.* Vila Pereira de Eça. Cunene, S Angola
Ngo *55 B6* Plateaux, SE Congo
Ngoko *55 B5 river* Cameroon/Congo
Ngourti *53 H3* Diffa, E Niger
Nguigmi *53 H3 var.* N'Guigmi. Diffa, SE Niger
N'Guigmi *see* Nguigmi
N'Gunza *see* Sumbe
Nguru *53 G3* Yobe, NE Nigeria
Nha Trang *115 E6* Khanh Hoa, S Vietnam

Niagara Falls *16 D5* Ontario, S Canada
Niagara Falls *19 E3* New York, NE USA
Niagara Falls *18 D3 waterfall* Canada/USA
Niamey *53 F3 country capital* (Niger) Niamey, SW Niger
Niangay, Lac *53 E3 lake* E Mali
Nia-Nia *55 E5* Orientale, NE Dem. Rep. Congo
Nias, Pulau *116 A3 island* W Indonesia
Nicaea *see* Nice
Nicaragua *30 D3 off.* Republic of Nicaragua. *country* Central America
Nicaragua, Lago de *30 D4 var.* Cocibolca, Gran Lago, *Eng.* Lake Nicaragua. *lake* S Nicaragua
Nicaragua, Lake *see* Nicaragua, Lago de
Nicaragua, Republic of *see* Nicaragua
Nicaria *see* Ikaría
Nice *69 D6 It.* Nizza; *anc.* Nicaea. Alpes-Maritimes, SE France
Nicephorium *see* Ar Raqqah
Nicholas II Land *see* Severnaya Zemlya
Nicholls Town *32 C1* Andros Island, NW The Bahamas
Nicobar Islands *102 B4 island group* India, E Indian Ocean
Nicosia *80 C5 Gk.* Lefkosía, *Turk.* Lefkoşa. *country capital* (Cyprus) C Cyprus
Nicoya *30 D4* Guanacaste, W Costa Rica
Nicoya, Golfo de *30 D5 gulf* W Costa Rica
Nicoya, Península de *30 D4 peninsula* NW Costa Rica
Nida *84 A3 Ger.* Nidden. Klaipėda, SW Lithuania
Nidaros *see* Trondheim
Nidden *see* Nida
Nidzica *76 D3 Ger.* Niedenburg. Warmińsko-Mazurskie, NE Poland
Niedenburg *see* Nidzica
Niedere Tauern *77 A6 mountain range* C Austria
Niemen *see* Neman
Nieśwież *see* Nyasvizh
Nieuw Amsterdam *37 G3* Commewijne, NE Suriname
Nieuw-Bergen *64 D4* Limburg, SE Netherlands
Nieuwegein *64 C4* Utrecht, C Netherlands
Nieuw Guinea *see* New Guinea
Nieuw Nickerie *37 G3* Nickerie, NW Suriname
Niewenstat *see* Neustadt an der Weinstrasse
Niğde *94 C4* Niğde, C Turkey (Türkiye)
Niger *53 F3 off.* Republic of Niger. *country* W Africa
Niger *53 F4 river* W Africa
Nigeria *53 F4 off.* Federal Republic of Nigeria. *country* W Africa
Nigeria, Federal Republic of *see* Nigeria
Niger, Mouths of the *53 F5 delta* S Nigeria
Niger, Republic of *see* Niger
Nihon *see* Japan
Niigata *109 D5* Niigata, Honshū, C Japan
Niihama *109 B7* Ehime, Shikoku, SW Japan
Ni'ihau *25 A7 var.* Niihau. *island* Hawaii, USA, C Pacific Ocean
Nii-jima *109 D6 island* E Japan
Nijkerk *64 D3* Gelderland, C Netherlands
Nijlen *65 C5* Antwerpen, N Belgium
Nijmegen *64 D4 Ger.* Nimwegen; *anc.* Noviomagus. Gelderland, SE Netherlands
Nikaria *see* Ikaría
Nikel' *88 C2 Finn.* Kolosjoki. Murmanskaya Oblast', NW Russia
Nikiniki *117 E5* Timor, S Indonesia
Niklasmarkt *see* Gheorgheni
Nikolainkaupunki *see* Vaasa
Nikolayev *see* Mykolayiv
Nikol'sk *see* Ussuriysk
Nikol'sk-Ussuriyskiy *see* Ussuriysk
Nikopol *87 F3* Dnipropetrovska Oblast, SE Ukraine
Nikšić *79 C5* C Montenegro
Nikumaroro *123 E3 ; prev.* Gardner Island. *atoll* Phoenix Islands, C Kiribati
Nikunau *123 E3 var.* Nukunau; *prev.* Byron Island. *atoll* Tungaru, W Kiribati
Nile *50 B2 former province* NW Uganda
Nile *46 D3 Ar.* Nahr an Nīl. *river* N Africa
Nile Delta *50 B1 delta* N Egypt
Nīl, Nahr an *see* Nile
Nîmes *69 C6 anc.* Nemausus, Nismes. Gard, S France
Nimwegen *see* Nijmegen
Nine Degree Channel *110 B3 channel* India/ Maldives
Ninetyeast Ridge *119 D5 undersea feature* E Indian Ocean
Ninety Mile Beach *see* Te-Oneroa-a-Tōhē
Ningbo *106 D5 var.* Ning-po, Yin-hsien; *prev.* Ninghsien. Zhejiang, SE China
Ning-hsia *see* Ningxia
Ninghsien *see* Ningbo
Ning-po *see* Ningbo
Ningsia/Ningsia Hui/Ningsia Hui Autonomous Region *see* Ningxia
Ningxia *106 B4 off.* Ningxia Huizu Zizhiqu, *var.* Ning-hsia, Ningsia, *Eng.* Ningsia Hui, Ningsia Hui Autonomous Region. *autonomous region* N China
Ningxia Huizu Zizhiqu *see* Ningxia
Nio *see* Íos
Niobrara River *23 E3 river* Nebraska/ Wyoming, C USA
Nioro *52 D3 var.* Nioro du Sahel. Kayes, W Mali
Nioro du Sahel *see* Nioro
Niort *68 B4* Deux-Sèvres, W France
Nipigon *16 B4* Ontario, S Canada
Nipigon, Lake *16 B3 lake* Ontario, S Canada
Nippon *see* Japan
Niš *79 E5 Eng.* Nish, *Ger.* Nisch; *anc.* Naissus. Serbia, SE Serbia
Nişab *98 B4* Al Ḩudūd ash Shamālīyah, N Saudi Arabia
Nisch/Nish *see* Niš
Nisibin *see* Nusaybin
Nisiros *see* Nísyros
Nisko *76 E4* Podkrapackie, SE Poland
Nismes *see* Nîmes
Nistru *see* Dniester
Nísyros *83 E7 var.* Nisiros. *island* Dodekánisa, Greece, Aegean Sea
Nitra *77 C6 Ger.* Neutra, *Hung.* Nyitra. Nitriansky Kraj, SW Slovakia
Nitra *77 C6 Ger.* Neutra, *Hung.* Nyitra. *river* W Slovakia
Niuatobutabu *see* Niuatoputapu
Niuatoputapu *123 E4 var.* Niuatobutabu; *prev.* Keppel Island. *island* N Tonga
Niue *123 F4 self-governing territory in free association with New Zealand* S Pacific Ocean
Niulakita *123 E3 var.* Nurakita. *atoll* S Tuvalu
Niutao *123 E3 atoll* NW Tuvalu
Nivernais *68 C4 cultural region* C France
Nizāmābād *112 D5* Telangana, C India
Nizhnegorskiy *see* Nyzhnohirskyi
Nizhnekamsk *89 C5* Respublika Tatarstan, W Russia
Nizhnevartovsk *92 D3* Khanty-Mansiyskiy Avtonomnyy Okrug-Yugra, C Russia
Nizhniy Novgorod *89 C5 prev.* Gor'kiy. Nizhegorodskaya Oblast', W Russia
Nizhniy Odes *88 D4* Respublika Komi, NW Russia
Nizhnyaya Tunguska *93 E3 Eng.* Lower Tunguska. *river* N Russia
Nizhyn *87 E1 Rus.* Nezhin. Chernihivs'ka Oblast', NE Ukraine
Nizza *see* Nice
Njombe *51 C8* Iringa, S Tanzania
Nkayi *55 B6 prev.* Jacob. Bouenza, S Congo
Nkongsamba *54 A4 var.* N'Kongsamba. Littoral, W Cameroon
N'Kongsamba *see* Nkongsamba
Nmai Hka *114 B2 var.* Me Hka. *river* N Myanmar (Burma)
Nobeoka *109 B7* Miyazaki, Kyūshū, SW Japan
Noboribetsu *108 D3 var.* Noboribetu. Hokkaidō, NE Japan
Noboribetu *see* Noboribetsu
Nogales *28 B1* Sonora, NW Mexico
Nogales *26 B3* Arizona, SW USA
Nogal Valley *see* Dooxo Nugaaleed
Noire, Rivi`ere *see* Black River
Nokia *63 D5* Pirkanmaa, W Finland
Nokou *54 B3* Kanem, W Chad
Nola *55 B5* Sangha-Mbaéré, SW Central African Republic
Nolinsk *89 C5* Kirovskaya Oblast', NW Russia
Nongkaya *see* Nong Khai
Nong Khai *114 C4 var.* Mi Chai, Nongkaya. Nong Khai, E Thailand
Nonouti *122 D2 prev.* Sydenham Island. *atoll* Tungaru, W Kiribati
Noord-Beveland *64 B4 var.* North Beveland. *island* SW Netherlands
Noordwijk aan Zee *64 C3* Zuid-Holland, W Netherlands
Noordzee *see* North Sea
Nora *63 C6* Örebro, C Sweden
Norak *101 E3 Rus.* Nurek. W Tajikistan
Nordaustlandet *61 G1 island* NE Svalbard
Norden *72 A3* Niedersachsen, NW Germany
Norderstedt *72 B3* Schleswig-Holstein, N Germany
Nordfriesische Inseln *see* North Frisian Islands
Nordhausen *72 C4* Thüringen, C Germany
Nordhorn *72 A3* Niedersachsen, NW Germany
Nord, Mer du *see* North Sea
Nord-Ouest, Territoires du *see* Northwest Territories
Nordsee/Nordsjøen/Nordsøen *see* North Sea
Norfolk *23 E3* Nebraska, C USA
Norfolk *19 F5* Virginia, NE USA
Norfolk Island *120 D4 Australian self-governing territory* SW Pacific Ocean
Norfolk Ridge *120 D4 undersea feature* W Pacific Ocean
Norge *see* Norway
Norias *27 G5* Texas, SW USA
Noril'sk *92 D3* Taymyrskiy (Dolgano-Nenetskiy) Avtonomnyy Okrug, N Russia
Norman *27 G1* Oklahoma, C USA
Normandes, Îles *see* Channel Islands
Normandie *68 B3 Eng.* Normandy. *cultural region* N France
Normandy *see* Normandie
Normanton *126 C3* Queensland, NE Australia
Norrköping *63 C6* Östergötland, S Sweden
Norrtälje *63 C6* Stockholm, C Sweden
Norseman *125 B6* Western Australia
Norske Havet *see* Norwegian Sea
North Albanian Alps *79 C5 Alb.* Bjeshkët e Namuna, *Croatian* Prokletije. *mountain range* SE Europe
Northallerton *67 D5* N England, United Kingdom
Northam *125 A6* Western Australia
North America *12 continent*
Northampton *67 D6* C England, United Kingdom
North Andaman *111 F2 island* Andaman Islands, India, NE Indian Ocean
North Australian Basin *119 E5 Fr.* Bassin Nord de l' Australie. *undersea feature* E Indian Ocean
North Bay *16 D4* Ontario, S Canada
North Beveland *see* Noord-Beveland
North Borneo *see* Sabah
North Cape *128 C1 headland* North Island, New Zealand
North Cape *62 D1 Eng.* North Cape. *headland* N Norway
North Cape *see* Nordkapp
North Carolina *21 E1 off.* State of North Carolina, *also known as* Old North State, Tar Heel State, Turpentine State. *state* SE USA
North Channel *18 D2 lake channel* Canada/USA
North Charleston *21 F2* South Carolina, SE USA
North Dakota *22 D2 off.* State of North Dakota, *also known as* Flickertail State, Peace Garden State, Sioux State. *state* N USA
North Devon Island *see* Devon Island
North East Frontier Agency/North East Frontier Agency of Assam *see* Arunāchal Pradesh
Northeast Providence Channel *32 C1 channel* N The Bahamas
Northeim *72 B4* Niedersachsen, C Germany
Northern Cook Islands *123 F4 island group* N Cook Islands
Northern Dvina *see* Severnaya Dvina
Northern Ireland *66 B4 var.* The Six Counties. *cultural region* Northern Ireland, United Kingdom
Northern Mariana Islands *120 B1 US commonwealth territory* W Pacific Ocean
Northern Rhodesia *see* Zambia
Northern Sporades *see* Vóreies Sporádes
Northern Territory *122 A5 territory* N Australia
North European Plain *59 E3 plain* N Europe
Northfield *23 F2* Minnesota, N USA
North Fiji Basin *120 D3 undersea feature* N Coral Sea
North Frisian Islands *72 B2 var.* Nordfriesische Inseln. *island group* N Germany
North Huvadhu Atoll *110 B5 var.* Gaafu Alifu Atoll. *atoll* S Maldives
North Island *128 B2 var.* Te Ika-a-Māui. *island* N New Zealand
North Korea *107 E3 off.* Democratic People's Republic of Korea, *Kor.* Chosŏn-minjujuŭi-inmin-kanghwaguk. *country* E Asia
North Little Rock *20 B1* Arkansas, C USA
North Macedonia *79 D6 off.* Republic of North Macedonia, *Mac.* Severna Makedonija, *prev.* Macedonia. *country* SE Europe
North Macedonia, Republic of *see* North Macedonia
North Minch *see* Minch, The
North Mole *71 G4 harbour wall* NW Gibraltar, Europe
North Platte *23 E4* Nebraska, C USA
North Platte River *22 D4 river* C USA
North Pole *133 B3 pole* Arctic Ocean
North Saskatchewan *15 F5 river* Alberta/ Saskatchewan, S Canada
North Sea *58 D3 Dan.* Nordsøen, *Dut.* Noordzee, *Fr.* Mer du Nord, *Ger.* Nordsee, *Nor.* Nordsjøen; *prev.* German Ocean, *Lat.* Mare Germanicum. *sea* NW Europe
North Siberian Lowland *93 E2 var.* North Siberian Plain, *Eng.* North Siberian Lowland. *lowlands* N Russia
North Siberian Lowland/North Siberian Plain *see* Severo-Sibirskaya Nizmennost'
North Star State *see* Minnesota
North Taranaki Bight *128 C3 gulf* North Island, New Zealand
North Uist *66 B3 island* NW Scotland, United Kingdom
Northwest Atlantic Mid-Ocean Canyon *12 E4 undersea feature* N Atlantic Ocean
North West Highlands *66 C3 mountain range* N Scotland, United Kingdom
Northwest Pacific Basin *91 G4 undersea feature* NW Pacific Ocean
Northwest Territories *15 E3 Fr.* Territoires du Nord-Ouest. *territory* NW Canada
Northwind Plain *133 B2 undersea feature* Arctic Ocean
Norton Sound *14 C2 inlet* Alaska, USA
Norway *63 A5 off.* Kingdom of Norway, *Nor.* Norge. *country* N Europe
Norway, Kingdom of *see* Norway
Norwegian Basin *61 F4 undersea feature* NW Norwegian Sea
Norwegian Sea *61 F4 var.* Norske Havet. *sea* NE Atlantic Ocean
Norwich *67 E6* E England, United Kingdom
Nösen *see* Bistrița
Noshiro *108 D4 var.* Nosiro; *prev.* Noshirominato. Akita, Honshū, C Japan
Noshirominato/Nosiro *see* Noshiro
Nosivka *87 E1 Rus.* Nosovka. Chernihivs'ka Oblast', NE Ukraine
Nosop *56 C4 river* E Namibia
Nosovka *see* Nosivka
Noşratābād *98 E3* Sīstān va Balūchestān, E Iran
Noteć *76 C3 Ger.* Netze. *river* NW Poland
Nóties Sporádes *see* Dodekánisa
Nottingham *67 D6* C England, United Kingdom
Nouâdhibou *52 B2 prev.* Port-Étienne. Dakhlet Nouâdhibou, W Mauritania
Nouakchott *52 B2 country capital* (Mauritania) Nouakchott District, SW Mauritania
Nouméa *122 C5 dependent territory capital* (New Caledonia) Province Sud, S New Caledonia
Nouveau-Brunswick *see* New Brunswick
Nouvelle-Calédonie *see* New Caledonia
Nouvelle Écosse *see* Nova Scotia
Nova Civitas *see* Neustadt an der Weinstrasse
Nova Gorica *73 D8* W Slovenia
Nova Gradiška *78 C3 Ger.* Neugradisk, *Hung.* Ujgradiska. Brod-Posavina, NE Croatia
Nova Iguaçu *41 F4* Rio de Janeiro, SE Brazil
Nova Kakhovka *87 F4* S Ukraine
Nova Lisboa *see* Huambo
Novara *74 B2 anc.* Novaria. Piemonte, NW Italy
Novaria *see* Novara
Nova Scotia *17 F4 Fr.* Nouvelle Écosse. *province* SE Canada
Nova Scotia *13 E5 physical region* SE Canada
Novaya Sibir', Ostrov *93 F1 island* Novosibirskiye Ostrova, NE Russia
Novaya Zemlya *88 D1 island group* N Russia
Novaya Zemlya Trough *see* East Novaya Zemlya Trough
Novgorod *see* Velikiy Novgorod
Novi Grad *see* Bosanski Novi
Novi Iskar *82 C2 var.* Novi Iksŭr. Sofia-Grad, W Bulgaria
Novi Iskŭr *see* Novi Iksar
Noviodunum *see* Nevers, Nièvre, France
Noviomagus *see* Lisieux, Calvados, France
Noviomagus *see* Nijmegen, Netherlands
Novi Pazar *79 D5 Turk.* Yenipazar. Serbia, S Serbia
Novi Sad *78 D3 Ger.* Neusatz, *Hung.* Újvidék. Vojvodina, N Serbia
Novoazovsk *87 G4* Donets'ka Oblast', E Ukraine
Novocheboksarsk *89 C5* Chuvashskaya Respublika, W Russia
Novocherkassk *89 B7* Rostovskaya Oblast', SW Russia
Novodvinsk *88 C3* Arkhangel'skaya Oblast', NW Russia
Novograd-Volynskiy *see* Novohrad-Volynskyi
Novogrudok *see* Navahrudak
Novohrad-Volynskyi *86 D2 prev.* Novohrad-Volyns'kyy, *Rus.* Novograd-Volynskiy. Zhytomyrs'ka Oblast', N Ukrain
Novohrad-Volyns'kyy *see* Novohrad-Volynskyi
Novokazalinsk *see* Ayteke Bi
Novokuznetsk *92 D4 prev.* Stalinsk. Kemerovskaya Oblast', S Russia
Novolazarevskaya *132 C2 Russian research station* Antarctica
Novo mesto *73 E8 Ger.* Rudolfswert; *prev. Ger.* Neustadtl. SE Slovenia
Novomoskovsk *89 B5* Tul'skaya Oblast', W Russia
Novomoskovsk *87 F3* Dnipropetrovska Oblast, E Ukraine
Novopolotsk *see* Navapolatsk
Novoradomsk *see* Radomsko
Novo Redondo *see* Sumbe
Novorossiysk *89 A7* Krasnodarskiy Kray, SW Russia
Novoshakhtinsk *89 B6* Rostovskaya Oblast', SW Russia
Novosibirsk *92 D4* Novosibirskaya Oblast', C Russia
Novosibirskiye Ostrova *93 F1 Eng.* New Siberian Islands. *island group* N Russia
Novotroitsk *89 D6* Orenburgskaya Oblast', W Russia
Novotroitskoye *see* Novotroyitske
Novotroyitske *87 F4 prev.* Novotroyits'ke, *Rus.* Novotroitskoye. Khersons'ka Oblast', S Ukraine
Novotroyits'ke *see* Novotroyitske
Novo-Urgench *see* Urganch
Novovolynsk *86 C1* Volyns'ka Oblast', NW Ukraine
Novy Dvor *85 B6 Rus.* Novyy Dvor. Hrodzyenskaya Voblasts', W Belarus
Novyy Bug *see* Novyy Buh
Novyy Buh *87 E3 Rus.* Novyy Bug. Mykolayivs'ka Oblast', S Ukraine
Novyy Dvor *see* Novy Dvor
Novyy Margilan *see* Farg'ona
Novyy Uzen' *see* Zhangaözen
Nowa Sól *76 B4 var.* Nowasól, *Ger.* Neusalz an der Oder. Lubuskie, W Poland
Nowasól *see* Nowa Sól
Nowogard *76 B2 var.* Nowógard, *Ger.* Naugard. Zachodnio-pomorskie, NW Poland
Nowogródek *see* Navahrudak
Nowo-Minsk *see* Mińsk Mazowiecki
Nowy Dwór Mazowiecki *76 D3* Mazowieckie, C Poland
Nowy Sącz *77 D5 Ger.* Neu Sandec. Małopolskie, S Poland
Nowy Tomyśl *76 B3 var.* Nowy Tomysl. Wielkopolskie, C Poland
Nowy Tomysl *see* Nowy Tomyśl
Noyon *68 C3* Oise, N France
Nsanje *57 E3* Southern, S Malawi
Nsawam *53 E5* SE Ghana
Ntomba, Lac *55 C6 var.* Lac Tumba. *lake* NW Dem. Rep. Congo
Nubian Desert *50 B3 desert* NE Sudan
Nu Chiang *see* Salween
Nueva Caceres *see* Naga
Nueva Gerona *32 B2* Isla de la Juventud, S Cuba
Nueva Rosita *28 D2* Coahuila, NE Mexico
Nuevitas *32 C2* Camagüey, E Cuba
Nuevo, Bajo *31 G1 island* NW Colombia South America
Nuevo Casas Grandes *28 C1* Chihuahua, N Mexico
Nuevo, Golfo *43 C6 gulf* S Argentina
Nuevo Laredo *29 E2* Tamaulipas, NE Mexico
Nui Atoll *123 E3 atoll* W Tuvalu
Nu Jiang *see* Salween
Nûk *see* Nuuk
Nukha *see* Şäki
Nuku'alofa *123 E5 country capital* (Tonga) Tongatapu, S Tonga
Nukufetau Atoll *123 E3 atoll* C Tuvalu
Nukulaelae Atoll *123 E3 var.* Nukulailai. *atoll* E Tuvalu
Nukulailai *see* Nukulaelae Atoll
Nukunau *see* Nikunau
Nukunonu Atoll *123 E3 island* C Tokelau
Nukus *100 C2* Qoraqalpog'iston Respublikasi, W Uzbekistan
Nullarbor Plain *125 C6 plateau* South Australia/ Western Australia
Nunap Isua *60 C5 var.* Uummannarsuaq, *Dan.* Kap Farvel, *Eng.* Cape Farewell. *cape* S Greenland
Nunavut *15 F3 territory* N Canada
Nuneaton *67 D6* C England, United Kingdom
Nunivak Island *14 B2 island* Alaska, USA
Nunspeet *64 D3* Gelderland, E Netherlands
Nuoro *75 A5* Sardegna, Italy, C Mediterranean Sea
Nuquí *36 A3* Chocó, W Colombia
Nurakita *see* Niulakita
Nurata *see* Nurota
Nurek *see* Norak
Nuremberg *see* Nürnberg
Nurmes *62 E4* Pohjois-Karjala, E Finland
Nürnberg *73 C5 Eng.* Nuremberg. Bayern, S Germany
Nurota *101 E2 Rus.* Nurata. Navoiy Viloyati, C Uzbekistan
Nur-Sultan *92 C4 prev.* Astana, Akmola, Akmolinsk, Tselinograd, Aqmola. *country capital* (Kazakhstan) Akmola, N Kazakhstan
Nusaybin *95 F4 var.* Nisibin. Manisa, SE Turkey (Türkiye)
Nussdorf *see* Năsăud
Nutmeg State *see* Connecticut
Nuuk *60 C4 var.* Nûk, *Dan.* Godthaab, Godthåb. *dependent territory capital* (Greenland) Sermersooq, SW Greenland
Nyagan' *92 C3* Khanty-Mansiyskiy Avtonomnyy Okrug-Yugra, N Russia
Nyainqentanglha Shan *104 C5 mountain range* W China
Nyala *50 A4* Southern Darfur, W Sudan
Nyamapanda *56 D3* Mashonaland East, NE Zimbabwe
Nyamtumbo *51 C8* Ruvuma, S Tanzania
Nyanda *see* Masvingo
Nyandoma *88 C4* Arkhangel'skaya Oblast', NW Russia
Nyantakara *51 B7* Kagera, NW Tanzania
Nyasa, Lake *57 E2 var.* Lake Malawi; *prev.* Lago Nyassa. *lake* E Africa
Nyasaland/Nyasaland Protectorate *see* Malawi
Nyassa, Lago *see* Nyasa, Lake
Nyasvizh *85 C6 Pol.* Nieśwież, *Rus.* Nesvizh. Minskaya Voblasts', C Belarus
Nyaunglebin *114 B4* Bago, SW Myanmar (Burma)
Nyeri *51 C6* Central, C Kenya
Nyíregyháza *77 D6* Szabolcs-Szatmár-Bereg, NE Hungary
Nyitra *see* Nitra
Nykøbing *63 B8* Storstrøm, SE Denmark
Nyköping *63 C6* Södermanland, S Sweden
Nylstroom *see* Modimolle
Nyngan *127 D6* New South Wales, SE Australia
Nyoman *see* Neman
Nyurba *93 F3* Respublika Sakha (Yakutiya), NE Russia
Nyzhnohirskyi *87 F4 prev.* Nyzhn'ohirs'kyy, *Rus.* Nizhnegorskiy. Respublika Krym, S Ukraine
Nyzhn'ohirs'kyy *see* Nyzhnohirskyi
NZ *see* New Zealand
Nzega *51 C7* Tabora, C Tanzania
Nzérékoré *52 D4* SE Guinea
Nzwani *see* Anjouan

O

Oa'hu *25 A7 var.* Oahu. *island* Hawaiian Islands, Hawaii, USA
Oak Harbor *24 B1* Washington, NW USA
Oakland *25 B6* California, W USA
Oamaru *129 B7* Otago, South Island, New Zealand
Oaxaca *29 F5 var.* Oaxaca de Juárez; *prev.* Antequera. Oaxaca, SE Mexico
Oaxaca de Juárez *see* Oaxaca
Ob' *90 C2 river* C Russia
Obal' *85 D5 Rus.* Obol'. Vitsyebskaya Voblasts', N Belarus
Oban *66 C4* W Scotland, United Kingdom
Oban *see* Halfmoon Bay
Obando *see* Puerto Inírida
Obdorsk *see* Salekhard
Óbecse *see* Bečej
Obeliai *84 C4* Panevėžys, NE Lithuania
Oberhollabrunn *see* Tulln
Ob', Gulf of *see* Obskaya Guba
Obidovichi *see* Abidavichy
Obihiro *108 D2* Hokkaidō, NE Japan
Obo *54 D4* Haut-Mbomou, E Central African Republic
Obock *50 D4* E Djibouti
Obol' *see* Obal'
Oborniki *76 C3* Wielkolpolskie, W Poland
Obrovo *see* Abrova
Obskaya Guba *92 D3 Eng.* Gulf of Ob. *gulf* N Russia
Ob' Tablemount *119 B7 undersea feature* S Indian Ocean
Ocala *21 E4* Florida, SE USA
Ocaña *36 B2* Norte de Santander, N Colombia
Ocaña *70 D3* Castilla-La Mancha, C Spain
O Carballiño *70 C1 Cast.* Carballiño. Galicia, NW Spain
Occidental, Cordillera *36 B2 mountain range* W South America
Occidental, Cordillera *39 E4 mountain range* Bolivia/Chile
Ocean Falls *14 D5* British Columbia, SW Canada
Ocean Island *see* Banaba
Oceanside *25 C8* California, W USA
Ocean State *see* Rhode Island
Ochakiv *87 E4 Rus.* Ochakov. Mykolayivs'ka Oblast', S Ukraine
Ochakov *see* Ochakiv
Ochamchire *95 E2 prev.* Och'amch'ire. W Georgia
Och'amch'ire *see* Ochamchire
Ocho Rios *32 B4* C Jamaica
Ochrida *see* Ohrid
Ochrida, Lake *see* Ohrid, Lake
Ocotal *30 D3* Nueva Segovia, NW Nicaragua
Ocozocuautla *29 G5* Chiapas, SE Mexico
October Revolution Island *see* Oktyabr'skoy Revolyutsii, Ostrov
Ocú *31 F5* Herrera, S Panama
Ōdate *108 D3* Akita, Honshū, C Japan
Oddur *see* Xuddur
Ödemiş *94 A4* İzmir, SW Turkey (Türkiye)
Ödenburg *see* Sopron
Odenpäh *see* Otepää
Odense *63 B7* Fyn, C Denmark
Oder *76 B3 Cz./Pol.* Odra. *river* C Europe
Oderhaff *see* Szczeciński, Zalew
Odesa *87 E4 Rus.* Odessa. Odes'ka Oblast', SW Ukraine
Odessa *27 E3* Texas, SW USA
Odessa *see* Odesa
Odessus *see* Varna
Odienné *52 D4* NW Ivory Coast
Odisha *113 F4 prev.* Orissa. *cultural region* NE India
Ŏdŏngk *115 D6* Kampong Speu, S Cambodia
Odoorn *64 E2* Drenthe, NE Netherlands
Odra *see* Oder
Oesel *see* Saaremaa
Of *95 E2* Trabzon, NE Turkey (Türkiye)
Ofanto *75 D5 river* S Italy
Offenbach *73 B5 var.* Offenbach am Main. Hessen, W Germany
Offenbach am Main *see* Offenbach
Offenburg *73 B6* Baden-Württemberg, SW Germany
Ogaadeen *see* Ogaden
Ogaden *51 D5 Som.* Ogaadeen. *plateau* Ethiopia/ Somalia
Ōgaki *109 C6* Gifu, Honshū, SW Japan
Ogallala *22 D4* Nebraska, C USA
Ogbomosho *53 F4 var.* Ogmoboso. Oyo, W Nigeria
Ogden *22 B4* Utah, W USA
Ogdensburg *19 F2* New York, NE USA
Ogmoboso *see* Ogbomosho
Ogulin *78 A3* Karlovac, NW Croatia
Ohio *18 C4 off.* State of Ohio, *also known as* Buckeye State. *state* N USA
Ohio River *18 C4 river* N USA
Ohlau *see* Oława
Ohri *see* Ohrid
Ohrid *79 D6 Turk.* Ochrida, Ohri. SW North Macedonia
Ohrid, Lake *79 D6 var.* Lake Ochrida, *Alb.* Liqeni i Ohrit, *Mac.* Ohridsko Ezero. *lake* Albania/ North Macedonia
Ohridsko Ezero/Ohrit, Liqeni i *see* Ohrid, Lake
Ohura *128 D3* Manawatu-Wanganui, North Island, New Zealand
Oirschot *65 C5* Noord-Brabant, S Netherlands
Oise *68 C3 river* N France
Oistins *33 G2* S Barbados
Ōita *109 B7* Ōita, Kyūshū, SW Japan
Ojinaga *28 D2* Chihuahua, N Mexico
Ojos del Salado, Cerro *42 B3 mountain* W Argentina
Okaihau *128 C2* Northland, North Island, New Zealand
Ókanizsa *see* Kanjiža
Okara *112 C2* Punjab, E Pakistan
Okavanggo *see* Cubango/Okavango
Okavango *see* Cubango
Okavango Delta *56 C3 wetland* N Botswana
Okayama *109 B6* Okayama, Honshū, SW Japan
Okazaki *109 C6* Aichi, Honshū, C Japan
Okeechobee, Lake *21 E4 lake* Florida, SE USA
Okefenokee Swamp *21 E3 wetland* Georgia, SE USA

Okhotsk 93 G3 Khabarovskiy Kray, E Russia
Okhotsk, Sea of 91 F3 sea NW Pacific Ocean
Okhtyrka 87 F2 Rus. Akhtyrka. Sums'ka Oblast', NE Ukraine
Oki-guntō see Oki-shotō
Okinawa 108 A3 island SW Japan
Okinawa-shoto 108 A3 island group Nansei-shotō, SW Japan Asia
Oki-shoto 109 B6 var. Oki-guntō. island group SW Japan
Oklahoma 27 F2 off. State of Oklahoma, also known as The Sooner State. state C USA
Oklahoma City 27 G1 state capital Oklahoma, C USA
Okmulgee 27 G1 Oklahoma, C USA
Oko, Wadi 50 C3 river NE Sudan
Oktyabr'skiy 89 D6 Volgogradskaya Oblast', SW Russia
Oktyabr'skiy see Aktsyabrski
Oktyabr'skoy Revolyutsii, Ostrov 93 E2 Eng. October Revolution Island. island Severnaya Zemlya, N Russia
Okulovka 88 B4 var. Okulovka. Novgorodskaya Oblast', W Russia
Okulovka see Okulovka
Okushiri-to 108 C3 var. Okusiri Tô. island NE Japan
Okusiri Tô see Okushiri-tō
Oláh-Toplicza see Toplița
Öland 63 C7 island S Sweden
Olavarría 43 D5 Buenos Aires, E Argentina
Oława 76 C4 Ger. Ohlau. Dolnośląskie, SW Poland
Olbia 75 A5 prev. Terranova Pausania. Sardegna, Italy, C Mediterranean Sea
Old Bay State/Old Colony State see Massachusetts
Old Dominion see Virginia
Oldebroek 64 D3 Gelderland, E Netherlands
Oldenburg 72 B3 Niedersachsen, NW Germany
Oldenburg 72 C2 var. Oldenburg in Holstein. Schleswig-Holstein, N Germany
Oldenburg in Holstein see Oldenburg
Oldenzaal 64 E3 Overijssel, E Netherlands
Old Harbour 32 B5 C Jamaica
Old Line State see Maryland
Old North State see North Carolina
Olëkma 93 F4 river C Russia
Olëkminsk 93 F3 Respublika Sakha (Yakutiya), NE Russia
Oleksandriia 87 F3 prev. Oleksandriya, Rus. Aleksandriya. Kirovohrads'ka Oblast', C Ukraine
Oleksandrivka 87 E3 Rus. Aleksandrovka. Kirovohrads'ka Oblast', C Ukraine
Oleksandriya see Oleksandriia
Olenegorsk 88 C2 Murmanskaya Oblast', NW Russia
Olenëk 93 E3 Respublika Sakha (Yakutiya), NE Russia
Olenëk 93 E3 river NE Russia
Oléron, Île d' 69 A5 island W France
Oleshky 87 E4 Rus. Tsiurupynsk. Khersons'ka Oblast', S Ukraine
Olevsk 86 D1 Zhytomyrs'ka Oblast', N Ukraine
Ölgiy 104 C2 Bayan-Ölgiy, W Mongolia
Olhão 70 B5 Faro, S Portugal
Olifa 56 B3 Kunene, NW Namibia
Ólimbos see Ólympos
Olimpo see Fuerte Olimpo
Olisipo see Lisboa
Olita see Alytus
Oliva 71 F4 Comunitat Valenciana, E Spain
Olivet 68 C4 Loiret, C France
Olmaliq 101 E2 Rus. Almalyk. Toshkent Viloyati, E Uzbekistan
Olmütz see Olomouc
Olomouc 77 C5 Ger. Olmütz, Pol. Ołomuniec. Olomoucký Kraj, E Czechia (Czech Republic)
Ołomuniec see Olomouc
Olonets 88 B3 Respublika Kareliya, NW Russia
Olovyannaya 93 F4 Chitinskaya Oblast', S Russia
Olpe 72 B4 Nordrhein-Westfalen, W Germany
Olsnitz see Murska Sobota
Olsztyn 76 D2 Ger. Allenstein. Warmińsko-Mazurskie, N Poland
Olt 86 B5 var. Oltul, Ger. Alt. river S Romania
Oltenița 86 C5 prev. Eng. Oltenitsa; anc. Constantiola. Călărași, SE Romania
Oltenitsa see Oltenița
Oltul see Olt
Olvera 70 D5 Andalucía, S Spain
Olviopol see Pervomaisk
Olympia 24 B2 state capital Washington, NW USA
Olympic Mountains 24 A2 mountain range Washington, NW USA
Olympus, Mount 82 B4 var. Ólimbos, Eng. Mount Olympus. mountain N Greece
Omagh 67 B5 Ir. An Ómaigh. W Northern Ireland, United Kingdom
Omaha 23 F4 Nebraska, C USA
Oman 99 D6 off. Sultanate of Oman, Ar. Salṭanat 'Umān; prev. Muscat and Oman. country SW Asia
Oman, Gulf of 98 E4 Ar. Khalīj 'Umān. gulf N Arabian Sea
Oman, Sultanate of see Oman
Omboué 55 A6 Ogooué-Maritime, W Gabon
Omdurman 50 B4 var. Umm Durmān. Khartoum, C Sudan
Ometepe, Isla de 30 D4 island S Nicaragua
Ommen 64 E3 Overijssel, E Netherlands
Omsk 92 C4 Omskaya Oblast', C Russia
Ōmuta 109 A7 Fukuoka, Kyūshū, SW Japan
Onda 71 F3 Comunitat Valenciana, E Spain
Ondjiva see N'Giva
Öndörhaan 105 E2 var. Undur Khan; prev. Tsetsen Khan. Hentiy, E Mongolia
Onega 88 C3 Arkhangel'skaya Oblast', NW Russia
Onega 88 B4 river NW Russia
Onega, Lake see Onezhskoye Ozero
Onex 73 A7 Genève, SW Switzerland
Onezhskoye Ozero 88 B4 Eng. Lake Onega. lake NW Russia
Ongole 110 D1 Andhra Pradesh, E India
Onitsha 53 G5 Anambra, S Nigeria
Onon Gol 105 E2 river N Mongolia
Onslow 124 A4 Western Australia
Onslow Bay 21 F1 bay North Carolina, E USA
Ontario 16 B3 province S Canada
Ontario, Lake 19 E3 lake Canada/USA
Onteniente see Ontinyent
Ontinyent 71 F4 var. Onteniente. Comunitat Valenciana, E Spain
Ontong Java Rise 103 H4 undersea feature W Pacific Ocean
Onuba see Huelva
Oodeypore see Udaipur
Oos-Londen see East London
Oostakker 65 B5 Oost-Vlaanderen, NW Belgium
Oostburg 65 B5 Zeeland, SW Netherlands
Oostende 65 A5 Eng. Ostend, Fr. Ostende. West-Vlaanderen, NW Belgium
Oosterbeek 64 D4 Gelderland, SE Netherlands
Oosterhout 64 C4 Noord-Brabant, S Netherlands
Opatija 78 A2 It. Abbazia. Primorje-Gorski Kotar, NW Croatia
Opava 77 C5 Ger. Troppau. Moravskoslezský Kraj, E Czechia (Czech Republic)
Ópazova see Stara Pazova
Opelika 20 D2 Alabama, S USA
Opelousas 20 B3 Louisiana, S USA
Ophiusa see Formentera
Opmeer 64 C2 Noord-Holland, NW Netherlands
Opochka 88 A4 Pskovskaya Oblast', W Russia
Opole 76 C4 Ger. Oppeln. Opolskie, S Poland
Oporto see Porto
Opotiki 128 E3 Bay of Plenty, North Island, New Zealand
Oppeln see Opole
Oppidum Ubiorum see Köln
Oqtosh 101 E2 Rus. Aktash. Samarqand Viloyati, C Uzbekistan
Oradea 86 B3 prev. Oradea Mare, Ger. Grosswardein, Hung. Nagyvárad. Bihor, NW Romania
Oradea Mare see Oradea
Orahovac see Rahovec
Oral 92 B3 var. Ural'sk. Zapadnyy Kazakhstan, NW Kazakhstan
Oran 48 D2 var. Ouahran, Wahran. NW Algeria
Orange 127 D6 New South Wales, SE Australia
Orange 69 D6 anc. Arausio. Vaucluse, SE France
Orangeburg 21 E2 South Carolina, SE USA
Orange Cone see Orange Fan
Orange Fan 47 C7 var. Orange Cone. undersea feature SW Indian Ocean
Orange Mouth/Orangemund see Oranjemund
Orange River 56 B4 Afr. Oranjerivier. river S Africa
Orange Walk 30 C1 Orange Walk, N Belize
Oranienburg 72 D3 Brandenburg, NE Germany
Oranjemund 56 B4 var. Orangemund; prev. Orange Mouth. Karas, SW Namibia
Oranjerivier see Orange River
Oranjestad 33 E5 dependent territory capital (Aruba) Lesser Antilles, S Caribbean Sea
Orantes see Orontes
Orany see Varėna
Orașul Stalin see Brașov
Oravicabánya see Oravița
Oravița 86 A4 Ger. Orawitza, Hung. Oravicabánya. Caraș-Severin, SW Romania
Orawitza see Oravița
Orbetello 74 B4 Toscana, C Italy
Orcadas 132 A1 Argentinian research station South Orkney Islands, Antarctica
Orchard Homes 22 B1 Montana, NW USA
Ordino 69 A8 Ordino, NW Andorra Europe
Ordos Desert see Mu Us Shadi
Ordu 94 D2 anc. Cotyora. Ordu, N Turkey (Türkiye)
Ordzhonikidze see Pokrov, Ukraine
Ordzhonikidze see Vladikavkaz, Russia
Ordzhonikidze see Yenakiieve
Orealla 37 G3 E Guyana
Örebro 63 C6 Örebro, C Sweden
Oregon 24 B3 off. State of Oregon, also known as Beaver State, Sunset State, Valentine State, Webfoot State. state NW USA
Oregon City 24 B3 Oregon, NW USA
Oregon, State of see Oregon
Orekhov see Orikhiv
Orël 89 B5 Orlovskaya Oblast', W Russia
Orem 22 B4 Utah, W USA
Ore Mountains see Erzgebirge/Krušné Hory
Orenburg 89 D6 prev. Chkalov. Orenburgskaya Oblast', W Russia
Orense see Ourense
Orestiáda 82 D3 prev. Orestiás. Anatolikí Makedonía kai Thráki, NE Greece
Orestiás see Orestiáda
Organ Peak 26 D3 mountain New Mexico, SW USA
Orgeyev see Orhei
Orhei 86 D3 var. Orheiu, Rus. Orgeyev. N Moldova
Orheiu see Orhei
Oriental, Cordillera 38 D3 mountain range Bolivia/Peru
Oriental, Cordillera 36 B3 mountain range C Colombia
Orihuela 71 F4 Comunitat Valenciana, E Spain
Orikhiv 87 G3 Rus. Orekhov. Zaporiz'ka Oblast', SE Ukraine
Orinoco, Río 37 E2 river Colombia/Venezuela
Orinoquía 36 C3 region NE Colombia
Orissa see Odisha
Orissaar see Orissaare
Orissaare 84 C2 Ger. Orissaar. Saaremaa, W Estonia
Oristano 75 A5 Sardegna, Italy, C Mediterranean Sea
Orito 36 A4 Putumayo, SW Colombia
Orizaba, Volcán Pico de 13 C7 var. Citlaltépetl. mountain S Mexico
Orkney see Orkney Islands
Orkney Islands 66 C2 var. Orkney, Orkneys. island group N Scotland, United Kingdom
Orkneys see Orkney Islands
Orlando 21 E4 Florida, SE USA
Orléanais 68 C4 cultural region C France
Orléans 68 C4 anc. Aurelianum. Loiret, C France
Orléansville see Chlef
Orly 68 E2 (Paris) Essonne, N France
Orlya 85 B6 Hrodzyenskaya Voblasts', W Belarus
Ormsö see Vormsi
Ormuz, Strait of see Hormuz, Strait of
Örnsköldsvik 63 C5 Västernorrland, C Sweden
Orolaunum see Arlon
Orol Dengizi see Aral Sea
Oromocto 17 F4 New Brunswick, SE Canada
Orona 123 F3 prev. Hull Island. atoll Phoenix Islands, C Kiribati
Orontes 94 D5 var. Orantes, Nahr El Aassi , Nahr Al 'Āṣī , Asi Nehri . river Lebanon/Syria/Turkey
Oropeza see Cochabamba
Oroseirá Rodópis see Rhodope Mountains
Orpington 67 B8 United Kingdom
Orschowa see Orșova
Orsha 85 E6 Vitsyebskaya Voblasts', NE Belarus
Orsk 92 B4 Orenburgskaya Oblast', W Russia
Orșova 86 A4 Ger. Orschowa, Hung. Orsova. Mehedinți, SW Romania
Ortelsburg see Szczytno
Orthez 69 B6 Pyrénées-Atlantiques, SW France
Ortona 74 D4 Abruzzo, C Italy
Oruba see Aruba
Orūmīyeh, Daryācheh-ye 99 C2 var. Matianus, Sha Hi, Urumi Yeh, Eng. Lake Urmia; prev. Daryācheh-ye Reẕā'īyeh. lake NW Iran
Oruro 39 F4 Oruro, W Bolivia
Oryokko see Yalu
Oss 64 D4 Noord-Brabant, S Netherlands
Ōsaka 109 C6 hist. Naniwa. Ōsaka, Honshū, SW Japan
Ōsaki see Furukawa
Osa, Península de 31 E5 peninsula S Costa Rica
Osborn Plateau 119 D5 undersea feature E Indian Ocean
Osca see Huesca
Ösel see Saaremaa
Osh 101 F2 Oshskaya Oblast', SW Kyrgyzstan
Oshawa 16 D5 Ontario, SE Canada
Oshikango 56 B3 Ohangwena, N Namibia
O-shima 109 D6 island S Japan
Oshkosh 18 B2 Wisconsin, N USA
Oshmyany see Ashmyany
Osiek see Osijek
Osijek 78 C3 prev. Osiek, Osjek, Ger. Esseg, Hung. Eszék. Osijek-Baranja, E Croatia
Osipenko see Berdiansk
Osipovichi see Asipovichy
Osjek see Osijek
Oskaloosa 23 G4 Iowa, C USA
Oskarshamn 63 C7 Kalmar, S Sweden
Öskemen 92 D5 var. Ust'-Kamenogorsk. Vostochnyy Kazakhstan, E Kazakhstan
Oskol see Oskil
Oskil 87 G2 Rus. Oskol. river Russia/Ukraine
Oslo 63 B6 prev. Christiania, Kristiania. country capital (Norway) Oslo, S Norway
Osmaniye 94 D4 Osmaniye, S Turkey (Türkiye)
Osnabrück 72 A3 Niedersachsen, NW Germany
Osogov Mountains 82 B3 var. Osogovske Planine, Osogovski Planina, Mac. Osogovski Planini. mountain range Bulgaria/North Macedonia
Osogovske Planine/Osogovski Planina/ Osogovski Planini see Osogov Mountains
Oșorhei see Târgu Mureș
Osorno 43 B5 Los Lagos, C Chile
Ossa, Serra d' 70 C4 mountain range SE Portugal
Ossora 93 H2 Koryakskiy Avtonomnyy Okrug, E Russia
Ostee see Baltic Sea
Ostend/Ostende see Oostende
Oster 87 E1 Chernihivs'ka Oblast', N Ukraine
Östermyra see Seinäjoki
Osterode/Osterode in Ostpreussen see Ostróda
Österreich see Austria
Östersund 63 C5 Jämtland, C Sweden
Ostia Aterni see Pescara
Ostiglia 74 C2 Lombardia, N Italy
Ostrava 77 C5 Moravskoslezský Kraj, E Czechia (Czech Republic)
Ostróda 76 D3 Ger. Osterode, Osterode in Ostpreussen. Warmińsko-Mazurskie, NE Poland
Ostrołęka 76 D3 Ger. Wiesenhof, Rus. Ostrolenka. Mazowieckie, C Poland
Ostrolenka see Ostrołęka
Ostrov 88 A4 Latv. Austrava. Pskovskaya Oblast', W Russia
Ostrovets see Ostrowiec Świętokrzyski
Ostrovnoy 88 C2 Murmanskaya Oblast', NW Russia
Ostrów see Ostrów Wielkopolski
Ostrowiec see Ostrowiec Świętokrzyski
Ostrowiec Świętokrzyski 76 D4 var. Ostrowiec, Rus. Ostrovets. Świętokrzyskie, C Poland
Ostrów Mazowiecka 76 D3 var. Ostrów Mazowiecki. Mazowieckie, NE Poland
Ostrów Mazowiecki see Ostrów Mazowiecka
Ostrowo see Ostrów Wielkopolski
Ostrów Wielkopolski 76 C4 var. Ostrów, Ger. Ostrowo. Wielkopolskie, C Poland
Ostyako-Voguls'k see Khanty-Mansiysk
Osum see Osumit, Lumi i
Osumi-shoto 109 A8 island group Kagoshima, Nansei-shotō, SW Japan Asia East China Sea Pacific Ocean
Osumit, Lumi i 79 D7 var. Osum. river SE Albania
Osuna 70 D4 Andalucía, S Spain
Oswego 19 F2 New York, NE USA
Otago Peninsula 129 B7 peninsula South Island, New Zealand
Otaki 128 D4 Wellington, North Island, New Zealand
Otaru 108 C2 Hokkaidō, NE Japan
Otavalo 38 B1 Imbabura, N Ecuador
Otavi 56 B3 Otjozondjupa, N Namibia
Oțelu Roșu 86 B4 Ger. Ferdinandsberg, Hung. Nándorhgy. Caras-Severin, SW Romania
Otepää 84 D3 Ger. Odenpäh. Valgamaa, SE Estonia
Oti 53 E4 river N Togo
Otira 129 C6 West Coast, South Island, New Zealand
Otjiwarongo 56 B3 Otjozondjupa, N Namibia
Otorohanga 128 D3 Waikato, North Island, New Zealand
Otranto, Canale d' see Otranto, Strait of
Otranto, Strait of 79 C6 It. Canale d'Otranto. strait Albania/Italy
Otrokovice 77 C5 Ger. Otrokowitz. Zlínský Kraj, E Czechia (Czech Republic)
Otrokowitz see Otrokovice
Ōtsu 109 C6 var. Ôtu. Shiga, Honshū, SW Japan
Ottawa 16 D5 country capital (Canada) Ontario, SE Canada
Ottawa 18 B3 Illinois, N USA
Ottawa 23 F5 Kansas, C USA
Ottawa 19 E2 Fr. Outaouais. river Ontario/ Québec, SE Canada
Ottawa Islands 16 C1 island group Nunavut, C Canada
Ottignies 65 C6 Wallon Brabant, C Belgium
Ottumwa 23 G4 Iowa, C USA
Ôtu see Ōtsu
Ouachita Mountains 20 A1 mountain range Arkansas/Oklahoma, C USA
Ouachita River 20 B2 river Arkansas/Louisiana, C USA
Ouagadougou 53 E4 var. Wagadugu. country capital (Burkina) C Burkina
Ouahigouya 53 E3 NW Burkina
Ouahran see Oran
Oualâta 52 D3 var. Oualata. Hodh ech Chargui, SE Mauritania
Ouanary 37 H3 E French Guiana
Ouanda Djallé 54 D4 Vakaga, NE Central African Republic
Ouarâne 52 D2 desert C Mauritania
Ouargla 49 E2 var. Wargla. NE Algeria
Ouarzazate 48 C3 S Morocco
Oubangui 55 C5 Fr. Oubangui. river C Africa
Oubangui see Ubangi
Oubangui-Chari see Central African Republic
Oubangui-Chari, Territoire de l' see Central African Republic
Oudjda see Oujda
Ouessant, Île d' 68 A3 Eng. Ushant. island NW France
Ouésso 55 B5 Sangha, NW Congo
Oujda 48 D2 Ar. Oudjda, Ujda. NE Morocco
Oujeft 52 C2 Adrar, C Mauritania
Oulu 62 D4 Swe. Uleåborg. Pohjois-Pohjanmaa, C Finland
Oulujärvi 62 D4 Swe. Uleträsk. lake C Finland
Oulujoki 62 D4 Swe. Uleälv. river C Finland
Ounasjoki 62 D3 river N Finland
Ounianga Kébir 54 C2 Borkou-Ennedi-Tibesti, N Chad
Oup see Auob
Oupeye 65 D6 Liège, E Belgium
Our 65 D6 river NW Europe
Ourense 70 C1 Cast. Orense, Lat. Aurium. Galicia, NW Spain
Ourique 70 B4 Beja, S Portugal
Ours, Grand Lac de l' see Great Bear Lake
Ourthe 65 D7 river E Belgium
Ouse 67 D5 river N England, United Kingdom
Outaouais see Ottawa
Outer Hebrides 66 B3 var. Western Isles. island group NW Scotland, United Kingdom
Outer Islands 57 G1 island group SW Seychelles Africa W Indian Ocean
Outes 70 B1 Galicia, NW Spain
Ouvéa 122 D5 island Îles Loyauté, NE New Caledonia
Ouyen 127 C6 Victoria, SE Australia
Ovalle 42 B3 Coquimbo, N Chile
Ovar 70 B2 Aveiro, N Portugal
Overflakkee 64 B4 island SW Netherlands
Overijse 65 C6 Vlaams Brabant, C Belgium
Oviedo 70 C1 var. Uviéu, anc. Asturias. Asturias, NW Spain
Ovilava see Wels
Ovruch 86 D1 Zhytomyrs'ka Oblast', N Ukraine
Owando 55 B5 prev. Fort Rousset. Cuvette, C Congo
Owase 109 C6 Mie, Honshū, SW Japan
Owatonna 23 F3 Minnesota, N USA
Owen Fracture Zone 118 B4 tectonic feature W Arabian Sea
Owen, Mount 129 C5 mountain South Island, New Zealand
Owensboro 18 B5 Kentucky, S USA
Owen Stanley Range 122 B3 mountain range S Papua New Guinea
Owerri 53 G5 Imo, S Nigeria
Owo 53 F5 Ondo, SW Nigeria
Owyhee River 24 C4 river Idaho/Oregon, NW USA
Oxford 129 C6 Canterbury, South Island, New Zealand
Oxford 67 D6 Lat. Oxonia. S England, United Kingdom
Oxkutzcab 29 H4 Yucatán, SE Mexico
Oxnard 25 B7 California, W USA
Oxonia see Oxford
Oxus see Amu Darya
Oyama 109 D5 Tochigi, Honshū, S Japan
Oyem 55 B5 Woleu-Ntem, N Gabon
Oyo 55 B6 Cuvette, C Congo
Oyo 53 F4 Oyo, W Nigeria
Ozark 20 D3 Alabama, S USA
Ozark Plateau 23 G5 plain Arkansas/Missouri, C USA
Ozarks, Lake of the 23 F5 reservoir Missouri, C USA
Ozbourn Seamount 130 D4 undersea feature W Pacific Ocean
Ózd 77 D6 Borsod-Abaúj-Zemplén, NE Hungary
Ozieri 75 A5 Sardegna, Italy, C Mediterranean Sea

P

Paamiut 60 B4 var. Pâmiut, Dan. Frederikshåb. S Greenland
Pa-an see Hpa-An
Pabianice 76 C4 Łódzski, Poland
Pabna 113 G4 Rajshahi, W Bangladesh
Pacaraima, Sierra/Pacaraim, Serra see Pakaraima Mountains
Pachuca 29 E4 var. Pachuca de Soto. Hidalgo, C Mexico
Pachuca de Soto see Pachuca
Pacific-Antarctic Ridge 132 B5 undersea feature S Pacific Ocean
Pacific Ocean 130 D3 ocean
Padalung see Phatthalung
Padang 116 B4 Sumatera, W Indonesia
Paderborn 72 B4 Nordrhein-Westfalen, NW Germany
Padma see Brahmaputra
Padma see Ganges
Padova 74 C2 Eng. Padua; anc. Patavium. Veneto, NE Italy
Padre Island 27 G5 island Texas, SW USA
Padua see Padova
Paducah 18 B5 Kentucky, S USA
Paeroa 128 D3 Waikato, North Island, New Zealand
Páfos 80 C5 var. Paphos. W Cyprus
Pag 78 A3 It. Pago. island Zadar, C Croatia
Page 26 B1 Arizona, SW USA
Pago see Pag
Pago Pago 123 F4 dependent territory capital (American Samoa) Tutuila, W American Samoa
Pahiatua 128 D4 Manawatu-Wanganui, North Island, New Zealand
Pahsien see Chongqing
Paide 84 D2 Ger. Weissenstein. Järvamaa, N Estonia
Paihia 128 D2 Northland, North Island, New Zealand
Päijänne 63 D5 lake S Finland
Paine, Cerro 43 A7 mountain S Chile
Painted Desert 26 B1 desert Arizona, SW USA
Paisance see Piacenza
Paisley 66 C4 W Scotland, United Kingdom
País Vasco 71 E1 cultural region N Spain
Paita 38 B3 Piura, NW Peru
Pakanbaru see Pekanbaru
Pakaraima Mountains 37 E3 var. Serra Pacaraim, Sierra Pacaraima. mountain range N South America
Pakistan 112 A2 off. Islamic Republic of Pakistan, var. Islami Jamhuriya e Pakistan. country S Asia
Pakistan, Islamic Republic of see Pakistan
Pakistan, Islami Jamhuriya e see Pakistan
Paknam see Samut Prakan
Pakokku 114 A3 Magway, C Myanmar (Burma)
Pak Phanang 115 C7 var. Ban Pak Phanang. Nakhon Si Thammarat, SW Thailand
Pakruojis 84 C4 Šiaulai, N Lithuania
Paks 77 C7 Tolna, S Hungary
Paksé see Pakxé
Pakxé 115 D5 var. Paksé. Champasak, S Laos
Palafrugell 71 G2 Cataluña, NE Spain
Palagruža 79 B5 It. Pelagosa. island SW Croatia
Palaiá Epídavros 83 C6 Pelopónnisos, S Greece
Palaiseau 68 D2 Essonne, N France
Palamós 71 G2 Cataluña, NE Spain
Palamuse 84 E2 Ger. Sankt-Bartholomäi. Jõgevamaa, E Estonia
Palanka see Bačka Palanka
Pālanpur 112 C4 Gujarāt, W India
Palantia see Palencia
Palapye 56 D3 Central, SE Botswana
Palau 122 A2 var. Belau. country W Pacific Ocean
Palawan 117 E2 island W Philippines
Palawan Passage 116 D2 passage W Philippines
Paldiski 84 D2 prev. Baltiski, Eng. Baltic Port, Ger. Baltischport. Harjumaa, NW Estonia
Palembang 116 B4 Sumatera, W Indonesia
Palencia 70 D2 anc. Palantia, Pallantia. Castilla y León, NW Spain
Palerme see Palermo
Palermo 75 C7 Fr. Palerme; anc. Panhormus, Panormus. Sicilia, Italy, C Mediterranean Sea
Palestine, State of see West Bank; Gaza Strip
Pāli 112 C3 Rājasthān, N India
Palikir 122 C2 country capital (Micronesia) Pohnpei, E Micronesia
Palimé see Kpalimé
Palioúri, Akrotírio 82 C4 var. Akrotírio Kanestron. headland N Greece
Palk Strait 110 C3 strait India/Sri Lanka
Pallantia see Palencia
Palliser, Cape 129 D5 headland North Island, New Zealand
Palma 71 G3 var. Palma de Mallorca. Mallorca, Spain, W Mediterranean Sea
Palma del Río 70 D4 Andalucía, S Spain
Palma de Mallorca see Palma
Palmar Sur 31 E5 Puntarenas, SE Costa Rica
Palma Soriano 32 C3 Santiago de Cuba, E Cuba
Palm Beach 126 E1 New South Wales, E Australia
Palmer 132 A2 US research station Antarctica
Palmer Land 132 A3 physical region Antarctica
Palmerston 123 F4 island S Cook Islands
Palmerston see Darwin
Palmerston North 128 D4 Manawatu-Wanganui, North Island, New Zealand
Palmetto State, The see South Carolina
Palmi 75 D7 Calabria, SW Italy
Palmira 36 B3 Valle del Cauca, W Colombia
Palm Springs 25 D7 California, W USA
Palmyra see Tadmur
Palmyra Atoll 123 G2 US incorporated territory C Pacific Ocean
Palo Alto 25 B6 California, W USA
Paloe see Denpasar, Bali, C Indonesia
Paloe see Palu
Palu 117 E4 prev. Paloe. Sulawesi, C Indonesia
Pamiers 69 B6 Ariège, S France
Pamir 101 F3 var. Daryā-ye Pāmīr, Taj. Dar"yoi Pomir. river Afghanistan/Tajikistan
Pāmīr, Daryā-ye see Pamir
Pamir/Pāmīr, Daryā-ye see Pamirs
Pamirs 101 F3 Pash. Daryā-ye Pāmīr, Rus. Pamir. mountain range C Asia
Pâmiut see Paamiut
Pamlico Sound 21 G1 sound North Carolina, SE USA
Pampa 27 E1 Texas, SW USA
Pampa Aullagas, Lago see Poopó, Lago
Pampas 42 C4 plain C Argentina
Pampeluna see Pamplona
Pamplona 36 C2 Norte de Santander, N Colombia
Pamplona 71 E1 Basq. Iruña, prev. Pampeluna; anc. Pompaelo. Navarra, N Spain
Panaji 110 B1 var. Pangim, Panjim, New Goa. state capital Goa, W India
Panamá 31 G4 var. Ciudad de Panama, Eng. Panama City. country capital (Panama) Panamá, C Panama
Panama 31 G5 off. Republic of Panama. country Central America
Panama Basin 13 C8 undersea feature E Pacific Ocean
Panama Canal 31 F4 canal E Panama
Panama City 20 D3 Florida, SE USA
Panama City see Panamá
Panamá, Golfo de 31 G5 var. Gulf of Panama. gulf S Panama
Panama, Gulf of see Panamá, Golfo de
Panama, Isthmus of see Panama, Istmo de
Panama, Istmo de 31 G4 Eng. Isthmus of Panama; prev. Isthmus of Darien. isthmus E Panama
Panama, Republic of see Panama
Panay Island 117 E2 island C Philippines
Pančevo 78 D3 Ger. Pantschowa, Hung. Pancsova. Vojvodina, N Serbia
Pancsova see Pančevo
Paneas see Bāniyās
Panevėžys 84 C4 Panevėžys, C Lithuania
Pangim see Panaji
Pangkalpinang 116 C4 Pulau Bangka, W Indonesia
Pang-Nga see Phang-Nga
Panhormus see Palermo
Panjim see Panaji
Panopolis see Akhmīm
Pánormos 83 C7 Kríti, Greece, E Mediterranean Sea

Panormus see Palermo
Pantanal 41 E3 var. Pantanalmato-Grossense. swamp SW Brazil
Pantanalmato-Grossense see Pantanal
Pantelleria, Isola di 75 B7 island SW Italy
Pantschowa see Pančevo
Pánuco 29 E3 Veracruz-Llave, E Mexico
Pao-chi/Paoki see Baoji
Paola 80 B5 E Malta
Pao-shan see Baoshan
Pao-t'ou/Paotow see Baotou
Papagayo, Golfo de 30 C4 gulf NW Costa Rica
Papakura 128 D3 Auckland, North Island, New Zealand
Papantla 29 F4 var. Papantla de Olarte. Veracruz-Llave, E Mexico
Papantla de Olarte see Papantla
Papeete 123 H4 dependent territory capital (French Polynesia) Tahiti, W French Polynesia
Paphos see Páfos
Papilė 84 B3 Šiaulai, NW Lithuania
Papillion 23 F4 Nebraska, C USA
Papua 117 H4 var. Irian Barat, West Irian, West New Guinea, West Papua; prev. Dutch New Guinea, Irian Jaya, Netherlands New Guinea. province E Indonesia
Papua and New Guinea, Territory of see Papua New Guinea
Papua, Gulf of 122 B3 gulf S Papua New Guinea
Papua New Guinea 122 B3 off. Independent State of Papua New Guinea; prev. Territory of Papua and New Guinea. country NW Melanesia
Papua New Guinea, Independent State of see Papua New Guinea
Papuk 78 C3 mountain range NE Croatia
Pará 41 E2 off. Estado do Pará. state/region NE Brazil
Pará see Belém
Paracel Islands 103 E3 disputed territory SE Asia
Paraćin 78 D4 Serbia, C Serbia
Paradise of the Pacific see Hawaii
Pará, Estado do see Pará
Paragua, Río 37 E3 river SE Venezuela
Paraguay 42 C2 country C South America
Paraguay 42 D2 var. Río Paraguay. river C South America
Paraguay, Río see Paraguay
Parahiba/Parahyba see Paraíba
Paraíba 41 G2 off. Estado da Paraíba; prev. Parahiba, Parahyba. state/region E Brazil
Paraíba see João Pessoa
Paraíba, Estado da see Paraíba
Parakou 53 F4 C Benin
Paramaribo 37 G3 country capital (Suriname) Paramaribo, N Suriname
Paramushir, Ostrov 93 H3 island SE Russia
Paraná 41 E4 Entre Ríos, E Argentina
Paraná 41 E5 off. Estado do Paraná. state/region S Brazil
Paraná 35 C5 var. Alto Paraná. river C South America
Paraná, Estado do see Paraná
Paranéstí 82 C3 var. Paranéstio. Anatolikí Makedonía kai Thráki, NE Greece
Paranéstio see Paranéstí
Paraparaumu 129 D5 Wellington, North Island, New Zealand
Parchim 72 C3 Mecklenburg-Vorpommern, N Germany
Parczew 76 E4 Lubelskie, E Poland
Pardubice 77 B5 Ger. Pardubitz. Pardubický Kraj, C Czechia (Czech Republic)
Pardubitz see Pardubice
Parechcha 85 B5 Pol. Porzecze, Rus. Porech'ye. Hrodzyenskaya Voblasts', W Belarus
Parecis, Chapada dos 40 D3 var. Serra dos Parecis. mountain range W Brazil
Parecis, Serra dos see Parecis, Chapada dos
Parenzo see Poreč
Parepare 117 E4 Sulawesi, C Indonesia
Párga 83 A5 Ípeiros, W Greece
Paria, Golfo de see Paria, Gulf of
Paria, Gulf of 37 E1 var. Golfo de Paria. gulf Trinidad and Tobago/Venezuela
Parika 37 F2 NE Guyana
Parikiá 83 D6 Kykládes, Greece, Aegean Sea
Paris 68 D1 anc. Lutetia, Lutetia Parisiorum, Parisii. country capital (France) Paris, N France
Paris 27 G2 Texas, SW USA
Parisii see Paris
Parkersburg 18 D4 West Virginia, NE USA
Parkes 127 D6 New South Wales, SE Australia
Parkhar see Farkhor
Parma 74 B2 Emilia-Romagna, N Italy
Parnahyba see Parnaíba
Parnaíba 41 F2 var. Parnahyba. Piauí, E Brazil
Pärnu 84 D2 Ger. Pernau, Latv. Pērnava; prev. Rus. Pernov. Pärnumaa, SW Estonia
Pärnu 84 D2 var. Parnu Jõgi, Ger. Pernau. river SW Estonia
Pärnu-Jaagupi 84 D2 Ger. Sankt-Jakobi. Pärnumaa, SW Estonia
Parnu Jõgi see Pärnu
Pärnu Laht 84 D2 Ger. Pernauer Bucht. bay SW Estonia
Paroikiá see Páros
Paropamisus Range see Safēd Kōh, Silsilah-ye
Páros 83 D6 var. Paroikiá. Páros, Greece
Páros 83 D6 island Kykládes, Greece, Aegean Sea
Parral 42 B4 Maule, C Chile
Parral see Hidalgo del Parral
Parramatta 126 D1 New South Wales, SE Australia
Parras 28 D3 var. Parras de la Fuente. Coahuila, NE Mexico
Parras de la Fuente see Parras
Parsons 23 F5 Kansas, C USA
Pasadena 25 C7 California, W USA
Pasadena 27 H4 Texas, SW USA
Paşcani 86 C3 Hung. Páskán. Iaşi, NE Romania
Pasco 24 C2 Washington, NW USA
Pascua, Isla de 131 F4 var. Rapa Nui, Easter Island. island E Pacific Ocean
Pasewalk 72 D3 Mecklenburg-Vorpommern, NE Germany
Pashkeni see Bolyarovo
Pasinler 95 F3 Erzurum, NE Turkey (Türkiye)
Páskán see Paşcani
Pasłęk 76 D2 Ger. Preußisch Holland. Warmińsko-Mazurskie, NE Poland
Pasni 112 A3 Baluchistan, SW Pakistan
Paso de Indios 43 B6 Chubut, S Argentina
Passarowitz see Požarevac
Passau 73 D6 Bayern, SE Germany
Passo Fundo 41 E5 Rio Grande do Sul, S Brazil
Pastavy 85 C5 Pol. Postawy, Rus. Postovy. Vitsyebskaya Voblasts', NW Belarus
Pastaza, Río 38 B2 river Ecuador/Peru
Pasto 36 A4 Nariño, SW Colombia
Pasvalys 84 C4 Panevėžys, N Lithuania
Patagonia 35 B7 physical region Argentina/Chile
Patalung see Phatthalung
Patani see Pattani
Patavium see Padova
Patea 128 D4 Taranaki, North Island, New Zealand
Paterson 19 F3 New Jersey, NE USA
Pathein 114 A4 var. Bassein. Ayeyarwady, SW Myanmar (Burma)
Pátmos 83 D6 island Dodekánisa, Greece, Aegean Sea
Patna 113 F3 var. Azimabad. state capital Bihār, N India
Patnos 95 F3 Ağrı, E Turkey (Türkiye)
Patos, Lagoa dos 41 E5 lagoon S Brazil
Pátra 83 B5 Eng. Patras; prev. Pátrai. Dytikí Ellás, S Greece
Pátrai/Patras see Pátra
Pattani 115 C7 var. Patani. Pattani, SW Thailand
Pattaya 115 C5 Chon Buri, S Thailand
Patuca, Río 30 D2 river E Honduras
Pau 69 B6 Pyrénées-Atlantiques, SW France
Paulatuk 15 E3 Northwest Territories, NW Canada
Paungde 114 B4 Bago, C Myanmar (Burma)
Pautalia see Kyustendil
Pavia 74 B2 anc. Ticinum. Lombardia, N Italy
Pāvilosta 84 B3 Liepāja, W Latvia
Pavlikeni 82 D2 Veliko Tarnovo, N Bulgaria
Pavlodar 92 C4 Pavlodar, NE Kazakhstan
Pavlograd see Pavlohrad
Pavlohrad 87 G3 Rus. Pavlograd. Dnipropetrovska Oblast, E Ukraine
Pawai, Pulau 116 A2 island SW Singapore Asia
Pawn 114 B3 river C Myanmar (Burma)
Pax Augusta see Badajoz
Pax Julia see Beja
Paxoí 83 A5 island Iónia Nisiá, Greece, C Mediterranean Sea
Payo Obispo see Chetumal
Paysandú 42 D4 Paysandú, W Uruguay
Pazar 95 E2 Rize, NE Turkey (Türkiye)
Pazardzhik 82 C3 prev. Tatar Pazardzhik. Pazardzhik, SW Bulgaria
Peace Garden State see North Dakota
Peach State see Georgia
Pearl Islands 31 G5 Eng. Pearl Islands. island group SE Panama
Pearl Islands see Perlas, Archipiélago de las
Pearl Lagoon see Perlas, Laguna de
Pearl River 20 B3 river Louisiana/Mississippi, S USA
Pearsall 27 F4 Texas, SW USA
Peawanuk 16 C2 Ontario, S Canada
Peć see Pejë
Pechora 88 D3 Respublika Komi, NW Russia
Pechora 88 D3 river NW Russia
Pechora Sea see Pechorskoye More
Pechorskoye More 88 D2 Eng. Pechora Sea. sea NW Russia
Pecos 27 E3 Texas, SW USA
Pecos River 27 E3 river New Mexico/Texas, SW USA
Pécs 77 C7 Ger. Fünfkirchen, Lat. Sopianae. Baranya, SW Hungary
Pedra Lume 52 A3 Sal, NE Cape Verde (Cabo Verde)
Pedro Cays 32 C3 island group Greater Antilles, S Jamaica North America N Caribbean Sea W Atlantic Ocean
Pedro Juan Caballero 42 D2 Amambay, E Paraguay
Peer 65 D5 Limburg, NE Belgium
Pegasus Bay 129 C6 bay South Island, New Zealand
Pegu see Bago
Pehuajó 42 C4 Buenos Aires, E Argentina
Pei-ching see Beijing/Beijing Shi
Peine 72 B3 Niedersachsen, C Germany
Pei-p'ing see Beijing/Beijing Shi
Peipsi Järv/Peipus-See see Peipus, Lake
Peipus, Lake 84 E3 Est. Peipsi Järv, Ger. Peipus-See, Rus. Chudskoye Ozero. lake Estonia/Russia
Peiraiás 83 C6 prev. Piraiévs, Eng. Piraeus. Attikí, C Greece
Pejë 79 D5 Serb. Peć. W Kosovo
Pèk see Phônsaven
Pekalongan 116 C4 Jawa, C Indonesia
Pekanbaru 116 B3 var. Pakanbaru. Sumatera, W Indonesia
Pekin 18 B4 Illinois, N USA
Peking see Beijing/Beijing Shi
Pelagie 75 B8 island group SW Italy
Pelagosa see Palagruža
Pelican State see Louisiana
Pelly Bay see Kugaaruk
Pélmonostor see Beli Manastir
Peloponnese 83 B6 var. Morea, Eng. Peloponnese; anc. Peloponnesus. peninsula S Greece
Peloponnese/Peloponnesus see Pelopónnisos
Pematangsiantar 116 B3 Sumatera, W Indonesia
Pemba 57 F2 prev. Port Amelia, Porto Amélia. Cabo Delgado, NE Mozambique
Pemba 51 D7 island E Tanzania
Pembroke 16 D4 Ontario, SE Canada
Penang see Pinang, Pulau, Peninsular Malaysia
Penang see George Town
Penas, Golfo de 43 A7 gulf S Chile
Penderma see Bandırma
Pendleton 24 C3 Oregon, NW USA
Pend Oreille, Lake 24 D2 lake Idaho, NW USA
Peneius see Pineiós
Peng-pu see Bengbu
Penibético, Sistema see Béticos, Sistemas
Peniche 70 B3 Leiria, W Portugal
Peninsular State see Florida
Penninae, Alpes/Pennine, Alpi see Pennine Alps
Pennine Alps 73 A8 Fr. Alpes Pennines, It. Alpi Pennine, Lat. Alpes Penninae. mountain range Italy/Switzerland
Pennine Chain see Pennines
Pennines 67 D5 var. Pennine Chain. mountain range N England, United Kingdom
Pennines, Alpes see Pennine Alps
Pennsylvania 19 E4 off. Commonwealth of Pennsylvania, also known as Keystone State. state NE USA
Penobscot River 19 G2 river Maine, NE USA
Penong 127 A6 South Australia
Penonomé 31 F5 Coclé, C Panama
Penrhyn 123 G3 atoll N Cook Islands
Penrhyn Basin 121 F3 undersea feature C Pacific Ocean
Penrith 126 D1 New South Wales, SE Australia
Penrith 67 D5 NW England, United Kingdom
Pensacola 20 C3 Florida, SE USA
Pentecost 122 D4 Fr. Pentecôte. island C Vanuatu
Pentecôte see Pentecost
Penza 89 C6 Penzenskaya Oblast', W Russia
Penzance 67 C7 SW England, United Kingdom
Peoria 18 B4 Illinois, N USA
Perchtoldsdorf 73 E6 Niederösterreich, NE Austria
Percival Lakes 124 C4 lakes Western Australia
Perdido, Monte 71 F1 mountain NE Spain
Perece Vela Basin see West Mariana Basin
Pereira 36 B3 Risaralda, W Colombia
Peremyshl see Przemyśl
Pergamino 42 C4 Buenos Aires, E Argentina
Périgueux 69 C5 anc. Vesuna. Dordogne, SW France
Perito Moreno 43 B6 Santa Cruz, S Argentina
Perlas, Laguna de 31 E3 Eng. Pearl Lagoon. lagoon E Nicaragua
Perleberg 72 C3 Brandenburg, N Germany
Perlepe see Prilep
Perm' 92 C3 prev. Molotov. Permskaya Oblast', NW Russia
Pernambuco 41 G2 off. Estado de Pernambuco. state/region E Brazil
Pernambuco see Recife
Pernambuco Abyssal Plain see Pernambuco Plain
Pernambuco, Estado de see Pernambuco
Pernambuco Plain 45 C5 var. Pernambuco Abyssal Plain. undersea feature E Atlantic Ocean
Pernau see Pärnu
Pernauer Bucht see Pärnu Laht
Pērnava see Pärnu
Pernik 82 B2 prev. Dimitrovo. Pernik, W Bulgaria
Pernov see Pärnu
Perote 29 F4 Veracruz-Llave, E Mexico
Pérouse see Perugia
Perovsk see Qyzylorda
Perpignan 69 C6 Pyrénées-Orientales, S France
Perryton 27 F1 Texas, SW USA
Perryville 23 H5 Missouri, C USA
Persia see Iran
Persian Gulf 98 C4 var. Gulf, The, Ar. Khalīj al 'Arabī, Per. Khalīj-e Fars. gulf SW Asia
Perth 125 B6 state capital Western Australia
Perth 66 C4 C Scotland, United Kingdom
Perth Basin 119 E6 undersea feature SE Indian Ocean
Peru 38 C3 off. Republic of Peru. country W South America
Peru see Beru
Peru Basin 45 A5 undersea feature E Pacific Ocean
Peru-Chile Trench 34 A4 undersea feature E Pacific Ocean
Perugia 74 C4 Fr. Pérouse; anc. Perusia. Umbria, C Italy
Perugia, Lake of see Trasimeno, Lago
Peru, Republic of see Peru
Perusia see Perugia
Péruwelz 65 B6 Hainaut, SW Belgium
Pervomaisk 87 E3 prev. Pervomays'k, Olviopol. Mykolayivs'ka Oblast', S Ukraine
Pervomays'k see Pervomaisk
Pervyy Kuril'skiy Proliv 93 H3 strait E Russia
Pesaro 74 C3 anc. Pisaurum. Marche, C Italy
Pescara 74 D4 anc. Aternum, Ostia Aterni. Abruzzo, C Italy
Peshawar 112 C1 North-West Frontier Province, N Pakistan
Peshkopi 79 C6 var. Peshkopia, Peshkopija. Dibër, NE Albania
Peshkopia/Peshkopija see Peshkopi
Pessac 69 B5 Gironde, SW France
Petach-Tikva see Petah Tikva
Petah Tikva 97 A6 var. Petach-Tikva, Petah Tiqva, Petakh Tikva; prev. Petah Tiqwa. Tel Aviv, C Israel
Petah Tiqwa see Petah Tikva
Petakh Tikva/Petah Tiqva see Petah Tikva
Pétange 65 D8 Luxembourg, SW Luxembourg
Petchaburi see Phetchaburi
Peterborough 127 B6 South Australia
Peterborough 16 D5 Ontario, SE Canada
Peterborough 67 E6 prev. Medeshamstede. E England, United Kingdom
Peterhead 66 D3 NE Scotland, United Kingdom
Peter I Øy 132 A3 Norwegian dependency Antarctica
Petermann Bjerg 61 E3 mountain C Greenland
Petersburg 19 E5 Virginia, NE USA
Peters Mine 37 F3 var. Peter's Mine. N Guyana
Petit St-Bernard, Col du see Little Saint Bernard Pass
Peto 29 H4 Yucatán, SE Mexico
Petoskey 18 C2 Michigan, N USA
Petra see Wādī Mūsā
Petrich 82 C3 Blagoevgrad, SW Bulgaria
Petrikau see Piotrków Trybunalski
Petrikov see Pyetrykaw
Petrinja 78 B3 Sisak-Moslavina, C Croatia
Petroaleksandrovsk see To'rtko'l
Petrodvorets 88 A4 Fin. Pietarhovi. Leningradskaya Oblast', NW Russia
Petrograd see Sankt-Peterburg
Petrokov see Piotrków Trybunalski
Petropavl see Petropavlovsk
Petropavlovsk 92 C4 Kaz. Petropavl. Severnyy Kazakhstan, N Kazakhstan
Petropavlovsk-Kamchatskiy 93 H3 Kamchatskaya Oblast', E Russia
Petroşani 86 B4 var. Petroşeni, Ger. Petroschen, Hung. Petrozsény. Hunedoara, W Romania
Petroschen/Petroşeni see Petroşani
Petroskoi see Petrozavodsk
Petrovgrad see Zrenjanin
Petrovsk-Port see Makhachkala
Petrozavodsk 92 B2 Fin. Petroskoi. Respublika Kareliya, NW Russia
Petrozsény see Petroşani
Pettau see Ptuj
Pevek 93 G1 Chukotskiy Avtonomnyy Okrug, NE Russia
Pezinok 77 C6 Ger. Bösing, Hung. Bazin. Bratislavský Kraj, W Slovakia
Pforzheim 73 B6 Baden-Württemberg, SW Germany
Pfungstadt 73 B5 Hessen, W Germany
Phangan, Ko 115 C6 island SW Thailand
Phang-Nga 115 B7 var. Pang-Nga, Phangnga. Phangnga, SW Thailand
Phangnga see Phang-Nga
Phan Rang/Phanrang see Phan Rang-Thap Cham
Phan Rang-Thap Cham 115 E6 var. Phanrang, Phan Rang, Phan Rang Thap Cham. Ninh Thuận, S Vietnam
Phan Thiết 115 E6 Bình Thuận, S Vietnam
Pharnacia see Giresun
Pharus see Hvar
Phatthalung 115 C7 var. Padalung, Patalung. Phatthalung, SW Thailand
Phayao 114 C4 var. Muang Phayao. Phayao, NW Thailand
Phenix City 20 D2 Alabama, S USA
Phet Buri see Phetchaburi
Phetchaburi 115 C5 var. Bejraburi, Petchaburi, Phet Buri. Phetchaburi, SW Thailand
Philadelphia 19 F4 Pennsylvania, NE USA
Philadelphia see 'Ammān
Philippine Basin 103 F3 undersea feature W Pacific Ocean
Philippine Islands 117 E1 island group W Pacific Ocean
Philippines 117 E1 off. Republic of the Philippines. country SE Asia
Philippine Sea 103 F3 sea W Pacific Ocean
Philippines, Republic of the see Philippines
Philippine Trench 120 A1 undersea feature W Philippine Sea
Philippopolis see Plovdiv
Phitsanulok 114 C4 var. Bisnulok, Muang Phitsanulok, Pitsanulok. Phitsanulok, C Thailand
Phlórina see Flórina
Phnom Penh 115 D6 Khmer. Phnum Pénh. country capital (Cambodia) Phnom Penh, S Cambodia
Phnum Pénh see Phnom Penh
Phoenix 26 B2 state capital Arizona, SW USA
Phoenix Islands 123 E3 island group C Kiribati
Phôngsali 114 C3 var. Phong Saly. Phôngsali, N Laos
Phong Saly see Phôngsali
Phônsaven 114 D4 var. Xieng Khouang; prev. Pèk, Xiangkhoang. Xiangkhoang, N Laos
Phrae 114 C4 var. Muang Phrae, Prae. Phrae, NW Thailand
Phra Nakhon Si Ayutthaya see Ayutthaya
Phra Thong, Ko 115 B6 island SW Thailand
Phuket 115 B7 var. Bhuket, Puket, Mal. Ujung Salang; prev. Junkseylon, Salang. Phuket, SW Thailand
Phuket, Ko 115 B7 island SW Thailand
Phumĭ Kâmpóng Trâbêk see Kâmpóng Trâbêk
Phumĭ Sâmraông see Samraong
Phum Kompong Trabek see Kâmpóng Trâbêk
Phum Samrong see Samraong
Phu Vinh see Tra Vinh
Phyu 114 B4 var. Hpyu, Pyu. Bago, C Myanmar (Burma)
Piacenza 74 B2 Fr. Paisance; anc. Placentia. Emilia-Romagna, N Italy
Piatra-Neamţ 86 C4 Hung. Karácsonkő. Neamţ, NE Romania
Piatykhatky 87 F3 prev. P"yatykhatky, Rus. Pyatikhatki. Dnipropetrovska Oblast, E Ukraine
Piauhy see Piauí
Piauí 41 F2 off. Estado do Piauí; prev. Piauhy. state/region E Brazil
Piauí, Estado do see Piauí
Picardie 68 C3 Eng. Picardy. cultural region N France
Picardy see Picardie
Piccolo San Bernardo, Colle di see Little Saint Bernard Pass
Pichilemu 42 B4 Libertador, C Chile
Pico 70 A5 var. Ilha do Pico. island Azores, Portugal, NE Atlantic Ocean
Pico, Ilha do see Pico
Picos 41 F2 Piauí, E Brazil
Picton 129 C5 Marlborough, South Island, New Zealand
Piedmont see Piemonte
Piedras Negras 29 E2 var. Ciudad Porfirio Díaz. Coahuila, NE Mexico
Pielavesi 62 D4 lake C Finland
Pielinen 62 E4 var. Pielisjärvi. lake E Finland
Pielisjärvi see Pielinen
Piemonte 74 A2 Eng. Piedmont. region NW Italy
Pierre 23 E3 state capital South Dakota, N USA
Piešťany 77 C6 Ger. Pistyan, Hung. Pöstyén. Tranavský Kraj, W Slovakia
Pietarhovi see Petrodvorets
Pietari see Sankt-Peterburg
Pietarsaari see Jakobstad
Pietermaritzburg 56 C5 var. Maritzburg. KwaZulu/Natal, E South Africa
Pietersburg see Polokwane
Pigs, Bay of see Cochinos, Bahía de
Pihkva Järv see Pskov, Lake
Pijijiapán 29 G5 Chiapas, SE Mexico
Pikes Peak 22 C5 mountain Colorado, C USA
Pikeville 18 D5 Kentucky, S USA
Pikinni see Bikini Atoll
Piła 76 B3 Ger. Schneidemühl. Wielkopolskie, C Poland
Pilar 42 D3 var. Villa del Pilar. Ñeembucú, S Paraguay
Pilcomayo, Rio 35 C5 river C South America
Pilos see Pýlos
Pilsen see Plzeň
Pilzno see Plzeň
Pinang see Pinang, Pulau, Peninsular Malaysia
Pinang see George Town
Pinang, Pulau 116 B3 var. Penang, Pinang; prev. Prince of Wales Island. island Peninsular Malaysia
Pinar del Río 32 A2 Pinar del Río, W Cuba
Píndhos/Píndhos Óros see Píndos
Píndos 82 A4 var. Píndhos Óros, Eng. Pindus Mountains; prev. Píndhos. mountain range C Greece
Pindus Mountains see Píndos
Pine Bluff 20 B2 Arkansas, C USA
Pine Creek 124 D2 Northern Territory, N Australia
Pinega 88 C3 river NW Russia
Pineiós 82 B4 var. Piniós; anc. Peneius. river C Greece
Pineland 27 H3 Texas, SW USA
Pínes, Akrotírio 82 C4 var. Akrotírio Pínnes. headland N Greece
Pines, The Isle of the see Juventud, Isla de la
Pine Tree State see Maine
Pingdingshan 106 C4 Henan, C China
Pingkiang see Harbin
Ping, Mae Nam 114 B4 river W Thailand
Piniós see Pineiós
Pinkiang see Harbin
Pínnes, Akrotírio see Pínes, Akrotírio
Pinos, Isla de see Juventud, Isla de la
Pinotepa Nacional 29 F5 var. Santiago Pinotepa Nacional. Oaxaca, SE Mexico
Pinsk 85 B7 Pol. Pińsk. Brestskaya Voblasts', SW Belarus
Pinta, Isla 38 A5 var. Abingdon. island Galápagos Islands, Ecuador, E Pacific Ocean
Piombino 74 B3 Toscana, C Italy
Pioneer Mountains 24 D3 mountain range Montana, N USA North America
Pionerskiy 84 A4 Ger. Neukuhren. Kaliningradskaya Oblast', W Russia
Piopiotahi see Milford Sound
Piotrków Trybunalski 76 D4 Ger. Petrikau, Rus. Petrokov. Łodzkie, C Poland
Piraeus/Piraiévs see Peiraías
Pírgos see Pýrgos
Pirineos see Pyrenees
Piripiri 41 F2 Piauí, E Brazil
Pirna 72 D4 Sachsen, E Germany
Pirot 79 E5 Serbia, SE Serbia
Piryatin see Pyriatyn
Pisa 74 B3 var. Pisae. Toscana, C Italy
Pisae see Pisa
Pisaurum see Pesaro
Pisco 38 D4 Ica, SW Peru
Písek 77 A5 Budějovický Kraj, S Czechia (Czech Republic)
Pishan 104 A3 var. Guma. Xinjiang Uygur Zizhiqu, NW China
Pishpek see Bishkek
Pistoia 74 B3 anc. Pistoria, Pistoriæ. Toscana, C Italy
Pistoria/Pistoriæ see Pistoia
Pistyan see Piešťany
Pisz 76 D3 Ger. Johannisburg. Warmińsko-Mazurskie, NE Poland
Pita 52 C4 NW Guinea
Pitalito 36 B4 Huila, S Colombia
Pitcairn Group of Islands see Pitcairn, Henderson, Ducie & Oeno Islands
Pitcairn Island 121 G4 island Pitcairn, Henderson, Ducie & Oeno Islands
Pitcairn, Henderson, Ducie & Oeno Islands 121 G4 var. Pitcairn Group of Islands. UK Overseas Territory C Pacific Ocean
Piteå 62 D4 Norrbotten, N Sweden
Piteşti 86 B5 Argeş, S Romania
Pitsanulok see Phitsanulok
Pitt Island see Makin
Pittsburg 23 F5 Kansas, C USA
Pittsburgh 19 E4 Pennsylvania, NE USA
Pittsfield 19 F3 Massachusetts, NE USA
Piura 38 B2 Piura, NW Peru
Pivdennyi Buh 87 E3 prev. Pivdennyy Buh, Rus. Yuzhnyy Bug. river S Ukraine
Pivdennyi Buh see Pivdennyi Buh
Placentia see Piacenza
Placetas 32 B2 Villa Clara, C Cuba
Plainview 27 E2 Texas, SW USA
Pláka 83 C7 Kykládes, Greece, Aegean Sea
Planeta Rica 36 B2 Córdoba, NW Colombia
Planken 72 E1 C Liechtenstein Europe
Plano 27 G2 Texas, SW USA
Plasencia 70 C3 Extremadura, W Spain
Plate, River 42 D4 var. River Plate. estuary Argentina/Uruguay
Plate, River see Plata, Río de la
Platinum 14 C3 Alaska, USA
Plattensee see Balaton
Platte River 23 E4 river Nebraska, C USA
Plattsburgh 19 F2 New York, NE USA
Plauen 73 C5 var. Plauen im Vogtland. Sachsen, E Germany
Plauen im Vogtland see Plauen
Pļaviņas 84 D4 Ger. Stockmannshof. Aizkraukle, S Latvia
Plây Cu 115 E5 var. Pleiku. Gia Lai, C Vietnam
Pleasant Island see Nauru
Pleiku see Plây Cu
Plenty, Bay of 128 E3 bay North Island, New Zealand
Plérin 68 A3 Côtes d'Armor, NW France
Plesetsk 88 C3 Arkhangel'skaya Oblast', NW Russia
Pleshchenitsy see Plyeshchanitsy
Pleskau see Pskov
Pleskauer See see Pskov, Lake
Pleskava see Pskov
Pleszew 76 C4 Wielkopolskie, C Poland
Pleven 82 C2 prev. Plevna. Pleven, N Bulgaria
Plevlja/Plevlje see Pljevlja
Plevna see Pleven
Pljevlja 78 C4 prev. Plevlja, Plevlje. N Montenegro
Plocce see Ploče
Ploče 78 B4 It. Plocce; prev. Kardeljevo. Dubrovnik-Neretva, SE Croatia
Płock 76 D3 Ger. Plozk. Mazowieckie, C Poland
Plöcken Pass 73 C7 Ger. Plöckenpass, It. Passo di Monte Croce Carnico. pass SW Austria
Plöckenpass see Plöcken Pass
Ploești see Ploiești
Ploiești 86 C5 prev. Ploești. Prahova, SE Romania
Plomári 83 D5 prev. Plomárion. Lésvos, E Greece
Plomárion see Plomári
Płońsk 76 D3 Mazowieckie, C Poland
Plovdiv 82 C3 prev. Eumolpias; anc. Evmolpia, Philippopolis, Lat. Trimontium. Plovdiv, C Bulgaria
Plozk see Płock
Plungė 84 B3 Telšiai, W Lithuania
Plyeshchanitsy 85 D5 Rus. Pleshchenitsy. Minskaya Voblasts', N Belarus
Plymouth 67 C7 SW England, United Kingdom
Plzeň 77 A5 Ger. Pilsen, Pol. Pilzno. Plzeňský Kraj, W Czechia (Czech Republic)
Po 58 D4 river N Italy
Pobedy, Pik see Tömür Feng
Po, Bocche del see Po, Foci del

Pocahontas *20 B1* Arkansas, C USA

Pocatello *24 E4* Idaho, NW USA

Pochinok *89 A5* Smolenskaya Oblast', W Russia

Pocking *73 D6* Bayern, SE Germany

Poděbrady *77 B5* *Ger.* Podiebrad. Středočeský Kraj, C Czechia (Czech Republic)

Podgorica *79 C5* *prev.* Titograd. *country capital* (Montenegro) S Montenegro

Podiebrad *see* Poděbrady

Podilsk *86 D3* *prev.* Kotovsk. Odes'ka Oblast', SW Ukraine

Podilska Vysochyna *86 D3* *prev.* Podil's'ka Vysochina. *plateau* W Ukraine

Podil's'ka Vysochina *see* Podilska Vysochyna

Podium Anicensis *see* le Puy

Podol'sk *89 B5* Moskovskaya Oblast', W Russia

Podravska Slatina *see* Slatina

Podujevë *79 D5* *Serb.* Podujevo. N Kosovo

Podujevo *see* Podujevë

Podunajská Rovina *see* Little Alföld

Poetovio *see* Ptuj

Pogradec *79 D6* *var.* Pogradeci. Korçë, SE Albania

Pogradeci *see* Pogradec

Pohjanlahti *see* Bothnia, Gulf of

Pohnpei *122 C2* *prev.* Ponape Ascension Island. *island* E Micronesia

Poictiers *see* Poitiers

Poinsett, Cape *132 D4* *headland* Antarctica

Point de Galle *see* Galle

Pointe-à-Pitre *33 G3* Grande Terre, C Guadeloupe

Pointe-Noire *55 B6* Kouilou, S Congo

Point Lay *14 C2* Alaska, USA

Poitiers *68 B4* *prev.* Poictiers; *anc.* Limonum. Vienne, W France

Poitou *68 B4* *cultural region* W France

Pokharā *113 E3* Western, C Nepal

Pokrov *87 F3* *Rus.* Ordzhonikidze. Dnipropetrovska Oblast, E Ukraine

Pokrovka *see* Kyzyl-Suu

Pokrovske *87 G3* *Rus.* Pokrovskoye. Dnipropetrovska Oblast, E Ukraine

Pokrovskoye *see* Pokrovske

Pola *see* Pula

Pola de Lena *see* La Pola

Poland *76 B4* *off.* Republic of Poland, *var.* Polish Republic, *Pol.* Polska, Rzeczpospolita Polska; *prev. Pol.* Polska Rzeczpospolita Ludowa, The Polish People's Republic. *country* C Europe

Poland, Republic of *see* Poland

Polatlı *94 C3* Ankara, C Turkey (Türkiye)

Polatsk *85 D5* *Rus.* Polotsk. Vitsyebskaya Voblasts', N Belarus

Pol-e Khomrī *see* Pul-e Khumrī

Poli *see* Pólis

Polikastro/Políkastron *see* Polýkastro

Polikrayshte *see* Dolna Oryahovitsa

Pólis *80 C5* *var.* Poli. W Cyprus

Polish People's Republic, The *see* Poland

Polish Republic *see* Poland

Polkowice *76 B4* *Ger.* Heerwegen. Dolnośląskie, W Poland

Pollença *71 G3* Mallorca, Spain, W Mediterranean Sea

Pologi *see* Polohy

Polohy *87 G3* *Rus.* Pologi. Zaporiz'ka Oblast', SE Ukraine

Polokwane *56 D4* *prev.* Pietersburg. Limpopo, NE South Africa

Polonne *86 D2* *Rus.* Polonnoye. Khmel'nyts'ka Oblast', NW Ukraine

Polonnoye *see* Polonne

Polotsk *see* Polatsk

Polska/Polska, Rzeczpospolita/Polska Rzeczpospolita Ludowa *see* Poland

Polski Trambesh *82 D2* *prev.* Polsko Kosovo, *var.* Polski Trŭmbesh. Ruse, N Bulgari

Polski Trŭmbesh *see* Polski Trambesh

Polsko Kosovo *see* Polski Trambesh

Poltava *87 F2* Poltavs'ka Oblast', NE Ukraine

Poltoratsk *see* Aşgabat

Põlva *84 E3* *Ger.* Pölwe. Põlvamaa, SE Estonia

Pölwe *see* Põlva

Polyarnyy *88 C2* Murmanskaya Oblast', NW Russia

Polýkastro *82 B3* *var.* Polikastro; *prev.* Políkastron. Kentrikí Makedonía, N Greece

Polynesia *121 F4* *island group* C Pacific Ocean

Pomeranian Bay *72 D2* *Ger.* Pommersche Bucht, *Pol.* Zatoka Pomorska. *bay* Germany/Poland

Pomir, Dar"yoi *see* Pamir/Pāmīr, Daryā-ye

Pommersche Bucht *see* Pomeranian Bay

Pomorska, Zatoka *see* Pomeranian Bay

Pomorskiy Proliv *88 D2* *strait* NW Russia

Po, Mouth of the *74 C2* *var.* Bocche del Po. *river* NE Italy

Pompaelo *see* Pamplona

Pompano Beach *21 F5* Florida, SE USA

Ponape Ascension Island *see* Pohnpei

Ponca City *27 G1* Oklahoma, C USA

Ponce *33 F3* C Puerto Rico

Pondicherry *see* Puducherry

Pondichéry *see* Puducherry

Ponferrada *70 C1* Castilla y León, NW Spain

Poniatowa *76 E4* Lubelskie, E Poland

Pons Aelii *see* Newcastle upon Tyne

Pons Vetus *see* Pontevedra

Ponta Delgada *70 B5* São Miguel, Azores, Portugal, NE Atlantic Ocean

Ponta Grossa *41 E4* Paraná, S Brazil

Pontarlier *68 D4* Doubs, E France

Ponteareas *70 B2* Galicia, NW Spain

Ponte da Barca *70 B2* Viana do Castelo, N Portugal

Pontevedra *70 B1* *anc.* Pons Vetus. Galicia, NW Spain

Pontiac *18 D3* Michigan, N USA

Pontianak *116 C4* Borneo, C Indonesia

Pontisarae *see* Pontoise

Pontivy *68 A3* Morbihan, NW France

Pontoise *68 C3* *anc.* Briva Isarae, Cergy-Pontoise, Pontisarae. Val-d'Oise, N France

Ponziane Island *75 C5* *island* C Italy

Poole *67 D7* S England, United Kingdom

Poona *see* Pune

Poopó, Lago *39 F4* *var.* Lago Pampa Aullagas. *lake* W Bolivia

Popayán *36 B4* Cauca, SW Colombia

Poperinge *65 A6* West-Vlaanderen, W Belgium

Poplar Bluff *23 G5* Missouri, C USA

Popocatépetl *29 E4* *volcano* S Mexico

Popper *see* Poprad

Poprad *77 D5* *Ger.* Deutschendorf, *Hung.* Poprád. Prešovský Kraj, E Slovakia

Poprád *77 D5* *Ger.* Popper, *Hung.* Poprád. *river* Poland/Slovakia

Porbandar *112 B4* Gujarāt, W India

Porcupine Plain *58 B3* *undersea feature* E Atlantic Ocean

Pordenone *74 C2* *anc.* Portenau. Friuli-Venezia Giulia, NE Italy

Poreč *78 A2* *It.* Parenzo. Istra, NW Croatia

Porech'ye *see* Parechcha

Pori *63 D5* *Swe.* Björneborg. Satakunta, SW Finland

Porirua *129 D5* Wellington, North Island, New Zealand

Porkhov *88 A4* Pskovskaya Oblast', W Russia

Porlamar *37 E1* Nueva Esparta, NE Venezuela

Póros *83 C6* Póros, S Greece

Póros *83 A5* Kefallinía, Iónia Nisiá, Greece, C Mediterranean Sea

Pors *see* Porsangenfijorden

Porsangenfijorden *62 D2* *Lapp.* Pors. *fjord* N Norway

Porsgrunn *63 B6* Telemark, S Norway

Portachuelo *39 G4* Santa Cruz, C Bolivia

Portadown *67 B5* *Ir.* Port An Dúnáin. S Northern Ireland, United Kingdom

Portalegre *70 C3* *anc.* Ammaia, Amoea. Portalegre, E Portugal

Port Alexander *14 D4* Baranof Island, Alaska, USA

Port Alfred *56 D5* Eastern Cape, S South Africa

Port Amelia *see* Pemba

Port An Dúnáin *see* Portadown

Port Angeles *24 B1* Washington, NW USA

Port Antonio *32 B5* NE Jamaica

Port Arthur *27 H4* Texas, SW USA

Port Augusta *127 B6* South Australia

Port-au-Prince *32 D3* *var.* Pòtoprens. *country capital* (Haiti) C Haiti

Port Blair *111 F2* Andaman and Nicobar Islands, SE India

Port Charlotte *21 E4* Florida, SE USA

Port Darwin *see* Darwin

Port d'Envalira *69 B8* E Andorra Europe

Port Douglas *126 D3* Queensland, NE Australia

Port Elizabeth *see* Gqeberha

Portenau *see* Pordenone

Porterville *25 C7* California, W USA

Port-Étienne *see* Nouâdhibou

Port Florence *see* Kisumu

Port-Francqui *see* Ilebo

Port-Gentil *55 A6* Ogooué-Maritime, W Gabon

Port Harcourt *53 G5* Rivers, S Nigeria

Port Hardy *14 D5* Vancouver Island, British Columbia, SW Canada

Port Harrison *see* Inukjuak

Port Hedland *124 B4* Western Australia

Port Huron *18 D3* Michigan, N USA

Portimão *70 B4* *var.* Vila Nova de Portimão. Faro, S Portugal

Port Jackson *126 E1* *harbour* New South Wales, E Australia

Portland *127 B7* Victoria, SE Australia

Portland *19 G2* Maine, NE USA

Portland *24 B3* Oregon, NW USA

Portland *27 G4* Texas, SW USA

Portland Bight *32 B5* *bay* S Jamaica

Portlaoighise *see* Port Laoise

Port Laoise *67 B6* *var.* Portlaoise, *Ir.* Portlaoighise; *prev.* Maryborough. C Ireland

Portlaoise *see* Port Laoise

Port Lavaca *27 G4* Texas, SW USA

Port Lincoln *127 A6* South Australia

Port Louis *57 H3* *country capital* (Mauritius) NW Mauritius

Port-Lyautey *see* Kénitra

Port Macquarie *127 E6* New South Wales, SE Australia

Port Mahon *see* Mahón

Portmore *32 B5* C Jamaica

Port Moresby *122 B3* *country capital* (Papua New Guinea) Central/National Capital District, SW Papua New Guinea

Port Natal *see* Durban

Porto *70 B2* *Eng.* Oporto; *anc.* Portus Cale. Porto, NW Portugal

Porto Alegre *41 E5* *var.* Pôrto Alegre. *state capital* Rio Grande do Sul, S Brazil

Porto Alegre *54 E2* São Tomé, S Sao Tome and Principe, Africa

Porto Alexandre *see* Tombua

Porto Amélia *see* Pemba

Porto Bello *see* Portobelo

Portobelo *31 G4* *var.* Porto Bello, Puerto Bello. Colón, N Panama

Port O'Connor *27 G4* Texas, SW USA

Porto Edda *see* Sarandë

Portoferraio *74 B4* Toscana, C Italy

Port of Spain *33 H5* *country capital* (Trinidad and Tobago) Trinidad, Trinidad and Tobago

Porto Grande *see* Mindelo

Portogruaro *74 C2* Veneto, NE Italy

Porto-Novo *53 F5* *country capital* (Benin - official) S Benin

Porto Rico *see* Puerto Rico

Porto Santo *48 A2* *var.* Ilha do Porto Santo. *island* Madeira, Portugal, NE Atlantic Ocean

Porto Santo, Ilha do *see* Porto Santo

Porto Torres *75 A5* Sardegna, Italy, C Mediterranean Sea

Porto Velho *40 D2* *var.* Velho. *state capital* Rondônia, W Brazil

Portoviejo *38 A2* *var.* Puertoviejo. Manabí, W Ecuador

Port Pirie *127 B6* South Australia

Port Rex *see* East London

Port Said *see* Būr Sa'īd

Portsmouth *67 D7* S England, United Kingdom

Portsmouth *19 G3* New Hampshire, NE USA

Portsmouth *18 D4* Ohio, N USA

Portsmouth *19 F5* Virginia, NE USA

Port Stanley *see* Stanley

Port Sudan *50 C3* Red Sea, NE Sudan

Port Swettenham *see* Klang/Pelabuhan Klang

Port Talbot *67 C7* S Wales, United Kingdom

Portugal *70 B3* *off.* Portuguese Republic. *country* SW Europe

Portuguese East Africa *see* Mozambique

Portuguese Guinea *see* Guinea-Bissau

Portuguese Republic *see* Portugal

Portuguese Timor *see* East Timor

Portuguese West Africa *see* Angola

Portus Cale *see* Porto

Portus Magnus *see* Almería

Portus Magonis *see* Mahón

Port-Vila *122 D4* *var.* Vila. *country capital* (Vanuatu) Éfaté, C Vanuatu

Porvenir *39 E3* Pando, NW Bolivia

Porvenir *43 B8* Magallanes, S Chile

Porvoo *63 E6* *Swe.* Borgå. Uusimaa, S Finland

Porzecze *see* Parechcha

Posadas *42 D3* Misiones, NE Argentina

Posad-Pokrovske *87 E4* Khersonska Oblast, S Ukraine

Poschega *see* Požega

Posen *see* Poznań

Posnania *see* Poznań

Postovy/Postawy *see* Pastavy

Posterholt *65 D5* Limburg, SE Netherlands

Postojna *73 D8* *Ger.* Adelsberg, *It.* Postumia. SW Slovenia

Postumia *see* Postojna

Pöstyén *see* Piešťany

Potamós *83 C7* Antikýthira, S Greece

Potentia *see* Potenza

Potenza *75 D5* *anc.* Potentia. Basilicata, S Italy

Poti *95 F2* *prev.* P'ot'i. W Georgia

P'ot'i *see* Poti

Potiskum *53 G4* Yobe, NE Nigeria

Potomac River *19 E5* *river* NE USA

Pòtoprens *see* Port-au-Prince

Potosí *39 F4* Potosí, S Bolivia

Potsdam *72 D3* Brandenburg, NE Germany

Potwar Plateau *112 C2* *plateau* NE Pakistan

Poŭthĭsăt *see* Pursat

Po, Valle del *see* Po Valley

Po Valley *74 C2* *It.* Valle del Po. *valley* N Italy

Považská Bystrica *77 C5* *Ger.* Waagbistritz, *Hung.* Vágbeszterce. Trenčiansky Kraj, W Slovakia

Poverty Bay *see* Tūranganui-a-Kiwa

Póvoa de Varzim *70 B2* Porto, NW Portugal

Powder River *22 D2* *river* Montana/Wyoming, NW USA

Powell *22 C2* Wyoming, C USA

Powell, Lake *22 B5* *lake* Utah, W USA

Požarevac *78 D4* *Ger.* Passarowitz. Serbia, NE Serbia

Poza Rica *29 F4* *var.* Poza Rica de Hidalgo. Veracruz-Llave, E Mexico

Poza Rica de Hidalgo *see* Poza Rica

Požega *78 D4* *prev.* Slavonska Požega, *Ger.* Poschega, *Hung.* Pozsega. Požega-Slavonija, NE Croatia

Požega *78 D4* Serbia

Poznań *76 C3* *Ger.* Posen, Posnania. Wielkolpolskie, C Poland

Pozoblanco *70 D4* Andalucía, S Spain

Pozsega *see* Požega

Pozsony *see* Bratislava

Pozzallo *75 C8* Sicilia, Italy, C Mediterranean Sea

Prachatice *77 A5* *Ger.* Prachatitz. Jihočeský Kraj, S Czechia (Czech Republic)

Prachatitz *see* Prachatice

Prado del Ganso *see* Goose Green

Prae *see* Phrae

Prag/Praga/Prague *see* Praha

Praha *77 A5* *Eng.* Prague, *Ger.* Prag, *Pol.* Praga. *country capital* (Czechia (Czech Republic)) Středočeský Kraj, NW Czechia (Czech Republic)

Praia *52 A3* *country capital* (Cape Verde) Santiago, S Cape Verde (Cabo Verde)

Prairie State *see* Illinois

Prathet Thai *see* Thailand

Prato *74 B3* Toscana, C Italy

Pratt *23 E5* Kansas, C USA

Prattville *20 D2* Alabama, S USA

Pravda *see* Glavinitsa

Pravia *70 C1* Asturias, N Spain

Prayagraj *113 E3* *prev.* Allahābād. Uttar Pradesh, N India

Preăh Seihânŭ *see* Sihanoukville

Preny *see* Prienai

Prenzlau *72 D3* Brandenburg, NE Germany

Prerau *see* Přerov

Přerov *77 C5* *Ger.* Prerau. Olomoucký Kraj, E Czechia (Czech Republic)

Preschau *see* Prešov

Prescott *26 B2* Arizona, SW USA

Preševo *79 D5* Serbia, SE Serbia

Presidente Epitácio *41 E4* São Paulo, S Brazil

Presidente Stroessner *see* Ciudad del Este

Prešov *77 D5* *var.* Preschau, *Ger.* Eperies, *Hung.* Eperjes. Prešovský Kraj, E Slovakia

Prespa, Lake *79 D6* *Alb.* Liqen i Prespës, *Gk.* Límni Megáli Préspa, Limni Prespa, *Mac.* Prespansko Ezero, *Serb.* Prespansko Jezero. *lake* SE Europe

Prespa, Limni/Prespansko Ezero/Prespansko Jezero/Prespës, Liqen i *see* Prespa, Lake

Presque Isle *19 H1* Maine, NE USA

Pressburg *see* Bratislava

Preston *67 D5* NW England, United Kingdom

Prestwick *66 C4* W Scotland, United Kingdom

Pretoria *56 D4* *var.* Epitoli. *country capital* (South Africa-administrative capital) Gauteng, NE South Africa

Preussisch Eylau *see* Bagrationovsk

Preußisch Holland *see* Pasłęk

Preussisch-Stargard *see* Starogard Gdański

Préveza *83 A5* Ípeiros, W Greece

Pribilof Islands *14 A3* *island group* Alaska, USA

Priboj *78 C4* Serbia, W Serbia

Price *22 B4* Utah, W USA

Prichard *20 C3* Alabama, S USA

Priekulė *84 B3* *Ger.* Prökuls. Klaipėda, W Lithuania

Prienai *85 B5* *Pol.* Preny. Kaunas, S Lithuania

Prieska *56 C4* Northern Cape, C South Africa

Prijedor *78 B3* Republika Srpska, NW Bosnia and Herzegovina

Prijepolje *78 D4* Serbia, W Serbia

Prikaspiyskaya Nizmennost' *see* Caspian Depression

Prilep *79 D6* *Turk.* Perlepe. S North Macedonia

Priluki *see* Pryluky

Primorsk *84 A4* *Ger.* Fischhausen. Kaliningradskaya Oblast', W Russia

Primorsko *82 E2* *prev.* Keupriya. Burgas, E Bulgaria

Primorskoye *see* Prymorsk

Prince Albert *15 F5* Saskatchewan, S Canada

Prince Edward Island *17 F4* *Fr.* Île-du Prince-Édouard. *province* SE Canada

Prince Edward Islands *47 E8* *island group* S South Africa

Prince George *15 E5* British Columbia, SW Canada

Prince of Wales Island *126 B1* *island* Queensland, E Australia

Prince of Wales Island *15 F2* *island* Queen Elizabeth Islands, Nunavut, NW Canada

Prince of Wales Island *see* Pinang, Pulau

Prince Patrick Island *15 E2* *island* Parry Islands, Northwest Territories, NW Canada

Prince Rupert *14 D4* British Columbia, SW Canada

Prince's Island *see* Príncipe

Princess Charlotte Bay *126 C2* *bay* Queensland, NE Australia

Princess Elizabeth Land *132 C3* *physical region* Antarctica

Príncipe *55 A5* *var.* Príncipe Island, *Eng.* Prince's Island. *island* N Sao Tome and Principe

Príncipe Island *see* Príncipe

Prinzapolka *31 E3* Región Autónoma Atlántico Norte, NE Nicaragua

Pripet *see* Pripyat

Pripiat *see* Pripyat

Pripyat *85 C7* *var.* Pripet, *Bel.* Prypyats', *Ukr.* Prypiat. *river* Belarus/Ukraine

Pripyat Marshes *85 B7* *Bel.* Prypyatskiya baloty, *Ukr.* Prypiatski bolota. *wetland* Belarus/Ukraine

Prishtinë *79 D5* *Eng.* Pristina, *Serb.* Priština. *country capital* (Kosovo) C Kosovo

Pristina/Priština *see* Prishtinë

Privas *69 D5* Ardèche, E France

Privolzhskaya Vozvyshennost' *59 G3* *var.* Volga Uplands. *mountain range* W Russia

Prizren *79 D5* S Kosovo

Probolinggo *116 D5* Jawa, C Indonesia

Probstberg *see* Wyszków

Progreso *29 H3* Yucatán, SE Mexico

Prokhladnyy *89 B8* Kabardino-Balkarskaya Respublika, SW Russia

Prokletije *see* North Albanian Alps

Prökuls *see* Priekulė

Prokuplje *79 D5* Serbia, SE Serbia

Prome *see* Pyay

Promyshlennyy *88 E3* Respublika Komi, NW Russia

Prościejów *see* Prostějov

Proskurov *see* Khmelnytskyi

Prossnitz *see* Prostějov

Prostějov *77 C5* *Ger.* Prossnitz, *Pol.* Prościejów. Olomoucký Kraj, E Czechia (Czech Republic)

Provence *69 D6* *cultural region* SE France

Providence *19 G3* *state capital* Rhode Island, NE USA

Providence *see* Fort Providence

Providencia, Isla de *31 F3* *island* NW Colombia, Caribbean Sea

Provideniya *133 B1* Chukotskiy Avtonomnyy Okrug, NE Russia

Provo *22 B4* Utah, W USA

Prudhoe Bay *14 D2* Alaska, USA

Prusa *see* Bursa

Pruszków *76 D3* *Ger.* Kaltdorf. Mazowieckie, C Poland

Prut *86 D4* *Ger.* Pruth. *river* E Europe

Pruth *see* Prut

Pružana *see* Pruzhany

Pruzhany *85 B6* *Pol.* Pružana. Brestskaya Voblasts', SW Belarus

Prychornomor'ska Nyzovyna *see* Black Sea Lowland

Prydniprovska Nyzovyna/Prydnyaprowskaya Nizina *see* Dnieper Lowland

Prydz Bay *132 D3* *bay* Antarctica

Pryluky *87 E2* *Rus.* Priluki. Chernihivs'ka Oblast', NE Ukraine

Prymorsk *87 G4* *prev.* Primorskoye. Zaporiz'ka Oblast', SE Ukraine

Prypiatski bolota *see* Pripyat Marshes

Pryp"yat'/Prypyats' *see* Pripet

Prypyatskiya baloty *see* Pripyat Marshes

Przemyśl *77 E5* *Rus.* Peremyshl. Podkarpackie, C Poland

Przheval'sk *see* Karakol

Psará *83 D5* *island* E Greece

Psel *87 F2* *Rus.* Psël. *river* Russia/Ukraine

Psël *see* Psel

Pskov *92 B2* *Ger.* Pleskau, *Latv.* Pleskava. Pskovskaya Oblast', W Russia

Pskov, Lake *84 E3* *Est.* Pihkva Järv, *Ger.* Pleskauer See, *Rus.* Pskovskoye Ozero. *lake* Estonia/Russia

Pskovskoye Ozero *see* Pskov, Lake

Ptich' *see* Ptsich

Ptsich *85 C7* *Rus.* Ptich'. Homyel'skaya Voblasts', SE Belarus

Ptsich *85 C7* *Rus.* Ptich'. *river* SE Belarus

Ptuj *73 E7* *Ger.* Pettau; *anc.* Poetovio. NE Slovenia

Pucallpa *38 C3* Ucayali, C Peru

Puck *76 C2* Pomorskie, N Poland

Pudasjärvi *62 D4* Pohjois-Pohjanmaa, C Finland

Puduchcheri *see* Puducherry

Puducherry *110 C2* *prev.* Pondicherry; *var.* Puduchcheri, *Fr.* Pondichéry. Pondicherry, SE India

Puebla *29 F4* *var.* Puebla de Zaragoza. Puebla, S Mexico

Puebla de Zaragoza *see* Puebla

Pueblo *22 D5* Colorado, C USA

Puerto Acosta *39 E4* La Paz, W Bolivia

Puerto Aisén *43 B6* Aisén, S Chile

Puerto Ángel *29 F5* Oaxaca, SE Mexico

Puerto Argentino *see* Stanley

Puerto Ayacucho *36 D3* Amazonas, SW Venezuela

Puerto Baquerizo Moreno *38 B5* *var.* Baquerizo Moreno. Galápagos Islands, Ecuador, E Pacific Ocean

Puerto Barrios *30 C2* Izabal, E Guatemala

Puerto Bello *see* Portobelo

Puerto Berrío *36 B2* Antioquia, C Colombia

Puerto Cabello *36 D1* Carabobo, N Venezuela

Puerto Cabezas *31 E2* *var.* Bilwi. Región Autónoma Atlántico Norte, NE Nicaragua

Puerto Carreño *36 D3* Vichada, E Colombia

Puerto Cortés *30 C2* Cortés, NW Honduras

Puerto Cumarebo *36 C1* Falcón, N Venezuela

Puerto Deseado *43 C7* Santa Cruz, SE Argentina

Puerto Escondido *29 F5* Oaxaca, SE Mexico

Puerto Francisco de Orellana *38 B1* *var.* Coca. NE Ecuador

Puerto Gallegos *see* Río Gallegos

Puerto Inírida *36 D3* *var.* Obando. Guainía, E Colombia

Puerto La Cruz *37 E1* Anzoátegui, NE Venezuela

Puerto Lempira *31 E2* Gracias a Dios, E Honduras

Puerto Limón *see* Limón

Puertollano *70 D4* Castilla-La Mancha, C Spain

Puerto López *36 C1* La Guajira, N Colombia

Puerto Maldonado *39 E3* Madre de Dios, E Peru

Puerto México *see* Coatzacoalcos

Puerto Montt *43 B5* Los Lagos, C Chile

Puerto Natales *43 B7* Magallanes, S Chile

Puerto Obaldía *31 H5* Kuna Yala, NE Panama

Puerto Plata *33 E3* *var.* San Felipe de Puerto Plata. N Dominican Republic

Puerto Presidente Stroessner *see* Ciudad del Este

Puerto Princesa *117 E2* *off.* Puerto Princesa City. Palawan, W Philippines

Puerto Princesa City *see* Puerto Princesa

Puerto Príncipe *see* Camagüey

Puerto Rico *33 F3* *off.* Commonwealth of Puerto Rico; *prev.* Porto Rico. *US commonwealth territory* C West Indies

Puerto Rico *34 B1* *island* C West Indies

Puerto Rico, Commonwealth of *see* Puerto Rico

Puerto Rico Trench *34 B1* *trench* NE Caribbean Sea

Puerto San José *see* San José

Puerto San Julián *43 B7* *var.* San Julián. Santa Cruz, SE Argentina

Puerto Suárez *39 H4* Santa Cruz, E Bolivia

Puerto Vallarta *28 D4* Jalisco, SW Mexico

Puerto Varas *43 B5* Los Lagos, C Chile

Puerto Viejo *31 E4* Heredia, NE Costa Rica

Puertoviejo *see* Portoviejo

Puget Sound *24 B1* *sound* Washington, NW USA

Puglia *75 E5* *var.* Le Puglie, *Eng.* Apulia. *region* SE Italy

Puhiwaero *see* South West Cape

Pukaki, Lake *129 B6* *lake* South Island, New Zealand

Pukekohe *128 D3* Auckland, North Island, New Zealand

Puket *see* Phuket

Pukhavichy *85 C6* *Rus.* Pukhovichi. Minskaya Voblasts', C Belarus

Pukhovichi *see* Pukhavichy

Pula *78 A3* *It.* Pola; *prev.* Pulj. Istra, NW Croatia

Pulaski *18 D5* Virginia, NE USA

Puławy *76 D4* *Ger.* Neu Amerika. Lubelskie, E Poland

Pul-e Khumrī *101 E4* *prev.* Pol-e Khomrī, *var.* Pul-i-Khumri. Baghlān, NE Afghanistan

Pul-i-Khumri *see* Pul-e Khumrī

Pulj *see* Pula

Pullman *24 C2* Washington, NW USA

Pułtusk *76 D3* Mazowieckie, C Poland

Puná, Isla *38 A2* *island* SW Ecuador

Pune *112 C5* *prev.* Poona. Mahārāshtra, W India

Punjab *112 C2* *prev.* West Punjab, Western Punjab. *province* E Pakistan

Puno *39 E4* Puno, SE Peru

Punta Alta *43 C5* Buenos Aires, E Argentina

Punta Arenas *43 B8* *prev.* Magallanes. Magallanes, S Chile

Punta Gorda *30 C2* Toledo, SE Belize

Punta Gorda *31 E4* Región Autónoma Atlántico Sur, SE Nicaragua

Puntarenas *30 D4* Puntarenas, W Costa Rica

Punto Fijo *36 C1* Falcón, N Venezuela

Pupuya, Nevado *39 E4* *mountain* W Bolivia

Puri *113 F5* *var.* Jagannath. Odisha, E India

Puriramya *see* Buriram

Purmerend *64 C3* Noord-Holland, C Netherlands

Pursat *115 D6* *Khmer.* Poŭthĭsăt. Pursat, W Cambodia

Purus, Rio *40 C2* *var.* Río Purús. *river* Brazil/Peru

Pusan *see* Busan

Pushkino *see* Biläsuvar

Püspökladány *77 D6* Hajdú-Bihar, E Hungary

Putorana, Gory/Putorana Mountains *see* Putorana, Plato

Putorana Mountains *93 E3* *var.* Gory Putorana, *Eng.* Putorana Mountains. *mountain range* N Russia

Putrajaya *116 B3* *administrative capital* (Malaysia) Kuala Lumpur, Peninsular Malaysia

Puttalam *110 C3* North Western Province, W Sri Lanka

Puttgarden *72 C2* Schleswig-Holstein, N Germany

Putumayo, Río *36 B5* *var.* Içá, Rio. *river* NW South America

Puurmani *84 D2* *Ger.* Talkhof. Jõgevamaa, E Estonia

Pyatigorsk *89 B7* Stavropol'skiy Kray, SW Russia

Pyatikhatki *see* Piatykhatky

P"yatykhatky *see* Piatykhatky

Pyay *114 B4* *var.* Prome, Pye. Bago, C Myanmar (Burma)

Pye *see* Pyay

Pyetrykaw *85 C7* *Rus.* Petrikov. Homyel'skaya Voblasts', SE Belarus

Pyin-Oo-Lwin *114 B3* *var.* Maymyo. Mandalay, C Myanmar (Burma)

Pýlos *83 B6* *var.* Pilos. Pelopónnisos, S Greece

P'yŏngyang *107 E3* *var.* P'yŏngyang-jikhalsi, *Eng.* Pyongyang. *country capital* (North Korea) SW North Korea

P'yŏngyang-jikhalsi *see* P'yŏngyang

Pyramid Lake *25 C5* *lake* Nevada, W USA

Pyrenaei Montes *see* Pyrenees

Pyrenees *80 B2* *Fr.* Pyrénées, *Sp.* Pirineos; *anc.* Pyrenaei Montes. *mountain range* SW Europe

Pýrgos *83 B6* *var.* Pírgos. Dytikí Ellás, S Greece

Pyriatyn *87 E2* *prev.* Pyryatyn, *Rus.* Piryatin. Poltavs'ka Oblast', NE Ukraine

Pyritz *see* Pyrzyce

Pyryatyn *see* Pyriatyn

Pyrzyce *76 B3* *Ger.* Pyritz. Zachodnio-pomorskie, NW Poland

Pyu *see* Phyu

Pyuntaza *114 B4* Bago, SW Myanmar (Burma)

Q

Qā' al Jafr *97 C7* *lake* S Jordan

Qaanaaq *60 D1* *var.* Qânâq, *Dan.* Thule. Avannaata, N Greenland

Qabāṭīyah *97 E6* N West Bank, Middle East

Qābis *see* Gabès

Qābis, Khalīj *see* Gabès, Golfe de

Qacentina *see* Constantine

Qafṣah *see* Gafsa

Qagan Us *see* Dulan

Qahremānshahr *see* Kermānshāh

Qaidam Pendi *104 C4* *basin* C China

Qal'aikhum *see* Qalaikhumb

Qalaikhumb *101 F3* *prev.* Qal'aikhum, *Rus.* Kalaikhum. S Tajikistan

Qalāt *101 E5 Per.* Kalāt. Zābol, S Afghanistan
Qal'at Bīshah *99 B5* 'Asīr, SW Saudi Arabia
Qalqiliya *see* Qalqīlyah
Qalqīlyah *97 D6 var.* Qalqiliya. Central, W West Bank, Middle East
Qamdo *104 D5* Xizang Zizhiqu, W China
Qamishly *see* Al Qāmishlī
Qânâq *see* Qaanaaq
Qaqortoq *60 C4 Dan.* Julianehåb. Kujalleq, S Greenland
Qaraghandy *92 C4 var.* Karagandy; *prev.* Karaganda. Karagandy, C Kazakhstan
Qara Qum *see* Garagum
Qarataū *see* Karatau, Zhambyl, Kazakhstan
Qarkilik *see* Ruoqiang
Qarokŭl *101 F3 Rus.* Karakul'. E Tajikistan
Qarqannah, Juzur *see* Kerkenah, Îles de
Qars *see* Kars
Qarshi *101 E3 Rus.* Karshi; *prev.* Bek-Budi. Qashqadaryo Viloyati, S Uzbekistan
Qasigianguit *see* Qasigiannguit
Qasigiannguit *60 C3 var.* Qasigianguit, *Dan.* Christianshåb. Qeqertalika, C Greenland
Qaşr al Farāfirah *50 B2 var.* Qasr Farâfra. W Egypt
Qasr Farâfra *see* Qaşr al Farāfirah
Qaţanā *97 B5 var.* Katana. Dimashq, S Syria
Qatar *98 C4 off.* State of Qatar, *Ar.* Dawlat Qaţar. *country* SW Asia
Qatar, State of *see* Qatar
Qattara Depression *see* Qaţţārah, Munkhafaḑ al
Qaţţâra, Monkhafad el *see* Qaţţārah, Munkhafaḑ al
Qaţţārah, Munkhafaḑ al *50 A1 var.* Monkhafad el Qaţţâra, *Eng.* Qattara Depression. *desert* NW Egypt
Qausuittuq *see* Resolute
Qazaqstan/Qazaqstan Respūblīkasy *see* Kazakhstan
Qazimämmäd *see* Hacıqabul
Qazris *see* Cáceres
Qazvīn *98 C2 var.* Kazvin. Qazvīn, N Iran
Qena *see* Qinā
Qeqertarsuaq *see* Qeqertarsuaq
Qeqertarsuaq *60 C3 var.* Qeqertarssuaq, *Dan.* Godhavn. Qeqertalik, S Greenland
Qeqertarsuaq *60 C3 island* W Greenland
Qeqertarsuup Tunua *60 C3 Dan.* Disko Bugt. *inlet* W Greenland
Qerveh *see* Qorveh
Qeshm *98 D4 var.* Jazīreh-ye Qeshm, Qeshm Island. *island* S Iran
Qeshm Island/Qeshm, Jazīreh-ye *see* Qeshm
Qilian Shan *104 D3 var.* Kilien Mountains. *mountain range* N China
Qimusseriarsuaq *60 C2 Dan.* Melville Bugt, *Eng.* Melville Bay. *bay* NW Greenland
Qinā *50 B2 var.* Qena; *anc.* Caene, Caenepolis. E Egypt
Qing *see* Qinghai
Qingdao *106 D4 var.* Ching-Tao, Ch'ing-tao, Tsingtao, Tsintao, *Ger.* Tsingtau. Shandong, E China
Qinghai *104 C4 var.* Chinghai, Koko Nor, Qing, Qinghai Sheng, Tsinghai. *province* C China
Qinghai Hu *104 D4 var.* Ch'ing Hai, Tsing Hai, *Mong.* Koko Nor. *lake* C China
Qinghai Sheng *see* Qinghai
Qingzang Gaoyuan *104 B4 var.* Xizang Gaoyuan, *Eng.* Plateau of Tibet. *plateau* W China
Qinhuangdao *106 D3* Hebei, E China
Qinzhou *106 B6* Guangxi Zhuangzu Zizhiqu, S China
Qiong *see* Hainan
Qiqihar *106 D2 var.* Ch'i-ch'i-ha-erh, Tsitsihar; *prev.* Lungkiang. Heilongjiang, NE China
Qira *104 B4* Xinjiang Uygur Zizhiqu, NW China
Qita Ghazzah *see* Gaza Strip
Qitai *104 C3* Xinjiang Uygur Zizhiqu, NW China
Qīzān *see* Jīzān
Qizil Orda *see* Qyzylorda
Qizil Qum/Qizilqum *see* Kyzylkum Desert
Qizilrabot *101 G3 Rus.* Kyzylrabot. SE Tajikistan
Qogir Feng *see* K2
Qom *98 C3 var.* Kum, Qum. Qom, N Iran
Qomolangma Feng *see* Everest, Mount
Qomul *see* Hami
Qo'qon *101 F2 var.* Khokand, *Rus.* Kokand. Farg'ona Viloyati, E Uzbekistan
Qorveh *98 C3 var.* Qerveh, Qurveh. Kordestān, W Iran
Qostanay *92 C4 var.* Kostanay, Kustanay. Kostanay, N Kazakhstan
Qoubaïyât *96 B4 var.* Al Qubayyāt. N Lebanon
Qoussantîna *see* Constantine
Quang Ngai *115 E5 var.* Quangngai, Quang Nghia. Quang Ngai, C Vietnam
Quangngai *see* Quang Ngai
Quang Nghia *see* Quang Ngai
Quan Long *see* Ca Mau
Quanzhou *106 D6 var.* Ch'uan-chou, Tsinkiang; *prev.* Chin-chiang. Fujian, SE China
Quanzhou *106 C6* Guangxi Zhuangzu Zizhiqu, S China
Qu'Appelle *15 F5 river* Saskatchewan, S Canada
Quarles, Pegunungan *117 E4 mountain range* Sulawesi, C Indonesia
Quarnero *see* Kvarner
Quartu Sant' Elena *75 A6* Sardegna, Italy, C Mediterranean Sea
Quba *95 H2 Rus.* Kuba. N Azerbaijan
Qubba *see* Ba'qūbah
Québec *17 E4 var.* Quebec. *province capital* Québec, SE Canada
Québec *16 D3 var.* Quebec. *province* SE Canada
Queen Charlotte Islands *see* Haida Gwaii
Queen Charlotte Sound *14 C5 sea area* British Columbia, W Canada
Queen Elizabeth Islands *15 E1 Fr.* Îles de la Reine-Élisabeth. *island group* Nunavut, N Canada
Queensland *126 B4 state* N Australia
Queenstown *129 B7* Otago, South Island, New Zealand
Queenstown *56 D5* Eastern Cape, S South Africa
Quelimane *57 E3 var.* Kilimane, Kilmain, Quilimane. Zambézia, NE Mozambique
Quelpart *see* Jeju-do
Quepos *31 E4* Puntarenas, S Costa Rica
Que Que *see* Kwekwe
Quera *see* Chur
Querétaro *29 E4* Querétaro de Arteaga, C Mexico
Quesada *31 E4 var.* Ciudad Quesada, San Carlos. Alajuela, N Costa Rica
Quetta *112 B2* Baluchisan, SW Pakistan
Quetzalcoalco *see* Coatzacoalcos
Quezaltenango *30 A2 var.* Quetzaltenango. Quezaltenango, W Guatemala
Quibdó *36 A3* Chocó, W Colombia
Quilimane *see* Quelimane
Quillabamba *38 D3* Cusco, C Peru
Quilon *see* Kollam
Quimper *68 A3 anc.* Quimper Corentin. Finistère, NW France
Quimper Corentin *see* Quimper
Quimperlé *68 A3* Finistère, NW France
Quincy *18 A4* Illinois, N USA
Qui Nhon/Quinhon *see* Quy Nhơn
Quissico *57 E4* Inhambane, S Mozambique
Quito *38 B1 country capital* (Ecuador) Pichincha, N Ecuador
Qulyndy Zhazyghy *see* Kulunda Steppe
Qum *see* Qom
Qurein *see* Al Kuwayt
Qŭrghonteppa *see* Bokhtar
Qurlurtuuq *see* Kugluktuk
Qurveh *see* Qorveh
Quşayr *see* Al Quşayr
Quxar *see* Lhazê
Quy Nhơn *115 E5 var.* Quinhon, Qui Nhon. Binh Đinh, C Vietnam
Qyteti Stalin *see* Kuçovë
Qyzylorda *92 B5 var.* Kzylorda, Kzyl-Orda, Qizil Orda; *prev.* Perovsk. Kyzylorda, S Kazakhstan
Qyzylqum *see* Kyzylkum Desert

R

Raab *78 B1 Hung.* Rába. *river* Austria/Hungary
Raab *see* Rába
Raab *see* Győr
Raahe *62 D4 Swe.* Brahestad. Pohjois-Pohjanmaa, W Finland
Raalte *64 D3* Overijssel, E Netherlands
Raamsdonksveer *64 C4* Noord-Brabant, S Netherlands
Raasiku *84 D2 Ger.* Rasik. Harjumaa, NW Estonia
Rába *77 B7 Ger.* Raab. *river* Austria/Hungary
Rába *see* Raab
Rabat *48 C2 var.* al Dar al Baida. *country capital* (Morocco) NW Morocco
Rabat *80 B5* W Malta
Rabat *see* Victoria
Rabbah Ammon/Rabbath Ammon *see* 'Ammān
Rabinal *30 B2* Baja Verapaz, C Guatemala
Rabka *77 D5* Małopolskie, S Poland
Râbniţa *see* Rîbniţa
Rabyānah, Ramlat *49 G4 var.* Rebiana Sand Sea, Şaḩrā' Rabyānah. *desert* SE Libya
Rabyānah, Şaḩrā' *see* Rabyānah, Ramlat
Răcari *see* Durankulak
Race, Cape *17 H3 headland* Newfoundland, Newfoundland and Labrador, E Canada
Rach Gia *115 D6* Kiên Giang, S Vietnam
Rach Gia, Vinh *115 D6 bay* S Vietnam
Racine *18 B3* Wisconsin, N USA
Rácz-Becse *see* Bečej
Rădăuţi *86 C3 Ger.* Radautz, *Hung.* Rádóc. Suceava, N Romania
Radautz *see* Rădăuţi
Rádeyilikóé *see* Fort Good Hope
Rádóc *see* Rădăuţi
Radom *76 D4* Mazowieckie, C Poland
Radomsko *76 D4 Rus.* Novoradomsk. Łódzkie, C Poland
Radomyshl *86 D2* Zhytomyrs'ka Oblast', N Ukraine
Radoviš *79 E6 prev.* Radovište. E North Macedonia
Radovište *see* Radoviš
Radviliškis *84 B4* Šiaulai, N Lithuania
Radzyń Podlaski *76 E4* Lubelskie, E Poland
Rae-Edzo *see* Edzo
Raetihi *128 D4* Manawatu-Wanganui, North Island, New Zealand
Rafa *see* Rafah
Rafaela *42 C3* Santa Fe, E Argentina
Rafah *97 A7 var.* Rafa, Rafaḩ, *Heb.* Rafiaḩ, Raphiah. SW Gaza Strip
Rafḩah *98 B4* Al Ḩudūd ash Shamālīyah, N Saudi Arabia
Rafiaḩ *see* Rafah
Raga *51 A5* W Bahr el Ghazal, W South Sudan
Ragged Island Range *32 C2 island group* S The Bahamas
Ragnit *see* Neman
Ragusa *75 C7* Sicilia, Italy, C Mediterranean Sea
Ragusa *see* Dubrovnik
Rahachow *85 D7 Rus.* Rogachëv. Homyel'skaya Voblasts', SE Belarus
Rahaeng *see* Tak
Rahaţ, Ḩarrat *99 B5 lava flow* W Saudi Arabia
Rahimyar Khan *112 C3* Punjab, SE Pakistan
Rahovec *79 D5 Serb.* Orahovac. W Kosovo
Raiatea *123 G4 island* Îles Sous le Vent, W French Polynesia
Rāichūr *110 C1* Karnātaka, C India
Raidestos *see* Tekirdağ
Rainier, Mount *12 A4 volcano* Washington, NW USA
Rainy Lake *16 A4 lake* Canada/USA
Raipur *113 E4* Chhattīsgarh, C India
Rājahmundry *113 E5* Andhra Pradesh, E India
Rajang *see* Rajang, Batang
Rajang, Batang *116 D3 var.* Rajang. *river* East Malaysia
Rājapālaiyam *110 C3* Tamil Nādu, SE India
Rājasthān *112 C3 cultural region* NW India
Rajin *107 E3 prev.* Najin. NE North Korea
Rājkot *112 C4* Gujarāt, W India
Rāj Nāndgaon *113 E4* Chhattīsgarh, C India
Rajshahi *113 G3 prev.* Rampur Boalia. Rajshahi, W Bangladesh
Rakahanga *123 F3 atoll* N Cook Islands
Rakaia *129 B6 river* South Island, New Zealand
Rakiura *see* Stewart Island
Rakka *see* Ar Raqqah
Rakke *84 E2* Lääne-Virumaa, NE Estonia
Rakvere *84 E2 Ger.* Wesenberg. Lääne-Virumaa, N Estonia
Raleigh *21 F1 state capital* North Carolina, SE USA
Ralik Chain *122 D1 island group* Ralik Chain, W Marshall Islands
Ramadi *see* Ar Ramādī
Ramallah *97 E7* C West Bank, Middle East
Râmnicul-Sărat *see* Râmnicu Sărat
Râmnicu Sărat *86 C4 prev.* Râmnicul-Sărat, Rimnicu-Sărat. Buzău, E Romania
Râmnicu Vâlcea *86 B4 prev.* Rimnicu Vîlcea. Vâlcea, C Romania
Rampur Boalia *see* Rajshahi
Ramree Island *114 A4 island* W Myanmar (Burma)
Ramtha *see* Ar Ramthā
Rancagua *42 B4* Libertador, C Chile
Rānchi *113 F4* Jhārkhand, N India
Randers *63 B7* Århus, C Denmark
Råneš *see* Ringvassøya
Rangiora *129 C6* Canterbury, South Island, New Zealand
Rangitikei *128 D4 river* North Island, New Zealand
Rangitoto ki te Tonga *128 C4 var.* D'Urville Island. *island* C New Zealand
Rangoon *see* Yangon
Rangpur *113 G3* Rajshahi, N Bangladesh
Rankin Inlet *15 G3* Nunavut, C Canada
Rankovićevo *see* Kraljevo
Ranong *115 B6* Ranong, SW Thailand
Rapa Nui *see* Pascua, Isla de
Raphiah *see* Rafah
Rapid City *22 D3* South Dakota, N USA
Rāpina *84 E3 Ger.* Rappin. Põlvamaa, SE Estonia
Rapla *84 D2 Ger.* Rappel. Raplamaa, NW Estonia
Rappel *see* Rapla
Rappin *see* Rāpina
Rarotonga *123 G5 island* S Cook Islands, C Pacific Ocean
Ras al 'Ain *see* Ra's al 'Ayn
Ra's al 'Ayn *96 D1 var.* Ras al'Ain. Al Ḩasakah, N Syria
Ra's an Naqb *97 B7* Ma'ān, S Jordan
Raseiniai *84 B4* Kaunas, C Lithuania
Rasht *98 C2 var.* Resht. Gīlān, NW Iran
Rasik *see* Raasiku
Râşnov *86 C4 prev.* Rîşno, Rozsnyó, *Hung.* Barcarozsnyó. Braşov, C Romania
Rastenburg *see* Kętrzyn
Ratak Chain *122 D1 island group* Ratak Chain, E Marshall Islands
Ratän *63 C5* Jämtland, C Sweden
Rat Buri *see* Ratchaburi
Ratchaburi *115 C5 var.* Rat Buri. Ratchaburi, W Thailand
Ratisbon/Ratisbona/Ratisbonne *see* Regensburg
Rat Islands *14 A2 island group* Aleutian Islands, Alaska, USA
Ratlām *112 D4 prev.* Rutlam. Madhya Pradesh, C India
Ratnapura *110 D4* Sabaragamuwa Province, S Sri Lanka
Raton *26 D1* New Mexico, SW USA
Rättvik *63 C5* Dalarna, C Sweden
Raudhatain *see* Ar Rawḑatayn
Raufarhöfn *61 E4* Nordhurland Eystra, NE Iceland
Raukawa *see* Cook Strait
Raukumara Range *128 E3 mountain range* North Island, New Zealand
Rāulakela *see* Rāurkela
Rauma *63 D5 Swe.* Raumo. Satakunta, SW Finland
Raumo *see* Rauma
Rāurkela *113 F4 var.* Rāulakela, Rourkela. Odisha, E India
Ravenna *74 C3* Emilia-Romagna, N Italy
Ravi *112 C2 river* India/Pakistan
Rawalpindi *112 C1* Punjab, NE Pakistan
Rawa Mazowiecka *76 D4* Łódzkie, C Poland
Rawicz *76 C4 Ger.* Rawitsch. Wielkopolskie, C Poland
Rawitsch *see* Rawicz
Rawlins *22 C3* Wyoming, C USA
Rawson *43 C6* Chubut, SE Argentina
Rayak *96 B4 var.* Rayaq, Riyāq. E Lebanon
Rayaq *see* Rayak
Rayong *115 C5* Rayong, S Thailand
Razazah, Buhayrat ar *98 B3 var.* Baḩr al Milḩ. *lake* C Iraq
Razdolnoye *see* Rozdolne
Razelm, Lacul *see* Razim, Lacul
Razgrad *82 D2* Razgrad, N Bulgaria
Razim, Lacul *86 D5 prev.* Lacul Razelm. *lagoon* NW Black Sea
Reading *67 D7* S England, United Kingdom
Reading *19 F4* Pennsylvania, NE USA
Realicó *42 C4* La Pampa, C Argentina
Reăng Kesei *115 D5* Battambang, W Cambodia
Greater Antarctica *see* East Antarctica
Rebecca, Lake *125 C6 lake* Western Australia
Rebiana Sand Sea *see* Rabyānah, Ramlat
Rebun-to *108 C2 island* NE Japan
Rechitsa *see* Rechytsa
Rechytsa *85 D7 Rus.* Rechitsa. Brestskaya Voblasts', SW Belarus
Recife *41 G2 prev.* Pernambuco. *state capital* Pernambuco, E Brazil
Recklinghausen *72 A4* Nordrhein-Westfalen, W Germany
Recogne *65 C7* Luxembourg, SE Belgium
Reconquista *42 D3* Santa Fe, C Argentina
Red Deer *15 E5* Alberta, SW Canada
Redding *25 B5* California, W USA
Redon *68 B4* Ille-et-Vilaine, NW France
Red River *23 E1 river* Canada/USA
Red River *114 C2 var.* Yuan, *Chin.* Yuan Jiang, *Vtn.* Sông Hông Hà. *river* China/Vietnam
Red River *13 C6 river* S USA
Red River *20 B3 river* Louisiana, S USA
Red Sea *50 C3 var.* Sinus Arabicus. *sea* Africa/Asia
Red Wing *23 G2* Minnesota, N USA
Reefton *129 C5* West Coast, South Island, New Zealand
Reese River *25 C5 river* Nevada, W USA
Refahiye *95 E3* Erzincan, C Turkey (Türkiye)
Regensburg *73 C6 Eng.* Ratisbon, *Fr.* Ratisbonne, *hist.* Ratisbona; *anc.* Castra Regina, Reginum. Bayern, SE Germany
Regenstauf *73 C6* Bayern, SE Germany
Rēgestān *see* Rēgistān
Reggane *48 D3* C Algeria
Reggio *see* Reggio nell'Emilia
Reggio Calabria *see* Reggio di Calabria
Reggio di Calabria *75 D7 var.* Reggio Calabria, *Gk.* Rhegion; *anc.* Regium, Rhegium. Calabria, SW Italy
Reggio Emilia *see* Reggio nell'Emilia
Reggio nell'Emilia *74 B2 var.* Reggio Emilia, *abbrev.* Reggio; *anc.* Regium Lepidum. Emilia-Romagna, N Italy
Reghin *86 C4 Ger.* Sächsisch-Reen, *Hung.* Szászrégen; *prev.* Reghinul Săsesc, *Ger.* Sächsisch-Regen. Mureş, C Romania
Reghinul Săsesc *see* Reghin
Regina *15 F5 province capital* Saskatchewan, S Canada
Reginum *see* Regensburg
Rēgistān *100 D5 var.* Rigestān, Rēgestān. *desert region* S Afghanistan
Regium *see* Reggio di Calabria
Regium Lepidum *see* Reggio nell'Emilia
Rehoboth *56 B3* Hardap, C Namibia
Rehovot *97 A6*; *prev.* Reḩovot. Central, C Israel
Reḩovot *see* Rehovot
Reichenau *see* Bogatynia, Poland
Reichenberg *see* Liberec
Reid *125 D6* Western Australia
Reikjavik *see* Reykjavík
Ré, Île de *68 A4 island* W France
Reims *68 D3 Eng.* Rheims; *anc.* Durocortorum, Remi. Marne, N France
Reindeer Lake *15 F4 lake* Manitoba/Saskatchewan, C Canada
Reine-Charlotte, Îles de la *see* Haida Gwaii
Reine-Élisabeth, Îles de la *see* Queen Elizabeth Islands
Reinga, Cape *128 C1 var.* Te Rerenga Wairua. *headland* North Island, New Zealand
Reinosa *70 D1* Cantabria, N Spain
Reka *see* Rijeka
Rekhovot *see* Rehovot
Reliance *15 F4* Northwest Territories, C Canada
Remi *see* Reims
Rendina *see* Rentína
Rendsburg *72 B2* Schleswig-Holstein, N Germany
Rengat *116 B4* Sumatera, W Indonesia
Reni *86 D4* Odes'ka Oblast', SW Ukraine
Rennell *122 C4 var.* Mu Nggava. *island* S Solomon Islands
Rennes *68 B3 Bret.* Roazon; *anc.* Condate. Ille-et-Vilaine, NW France
Reno *25 C5* Nevada, W USA
Renqiu *106 C4* Hebei, E China
Rentína *83 B5 var.* Rendina. Thessalía, C Greece
Reps *see* Rupea
Repulse Bay *see* Naujaat
Reschitza *see* Reşiţa
Resht *see* Rasht
Resicabánya *see* Reşiţa
Resistencia *42 D3* Chaco, NE Argentina
Reşiţa *86 A4 Ger.* Reschitza, *Hung.* Resicabánya. Caraş-Severin, W Romania
Resolute *15 F2 Inuit* Qausuittuq. Cornwallis Island, Nunavut, N Canada
Resolution Island *17 E1 island* Nunavut, NE Canada
Resolution Island *129 A7 island* SW New Zealand
Réunion *57 H4 off.* La Réunion. *French overseas department* W Indian Ocean
Réunion *119 B5 island* W Indian Ocean
Reus *71 F2* Cataluña, E Spain
Reutlingen *73 B6* Baden-Württemberg, S Germany
Reuver *65 D5* Limburg, SE Netherlands
Reval/Revel *see* Tallinn
Revillagigedo Island *28 B5 island* Alexander Archipelago, Alaska, USA
Rexburg *24 E3* Idaho, NW USA
Reyes *39 F3* Beni, NW Bolivia
Rey, Isla del *31 G5 island* Archipiélago de las Perlas, SE Panama
Reykjanes Basin *60 C5 var.* Irminger Basin. *undersea basin* N Atlantic Ocean
Reykjanes Ridge *58 A1 undersea ridge* N Atlantic Ocean
Reykjavík *61 E5 var.* Reikjavik. *country capital* (Iceland) Höfudhborgarsvaedhi, W Iceland
Reynosa *29 E2* Tamaulipas, C Mexico
Reẕā'īyeh, Daryācheh-ye *see* Orūmīyeh, Daryācheh-ye
Rezé *68 A4* Loire-Atlantique, NW France
Rēzekne *84 D4 Ger.* Rositten; *prev. Rus.* Rezhitsa. Rēzekne, SE Latvia
Rezhitsa *see* Rēzekne
Rezovo *82 E3 Turk.* Rezve. Burgas, E Bulgaria
Rezve *see* Rezovo
Rhaedestus *see* Tekirdağ
Rhegion/Rhegium *see* Reggio di Calabria
Rheims *see* Reims
Rhein *see* Rhine
Rheine *72 A3 var.* Rheine in Westfalen. Nordrhein-Westfalen, NW Germany
Rheine in Westfalen *see* Rheine
Rheinisches Schiefergebirge *73 A5 var.* Rhine State Uplands, *Eng.* Rhenish Slate Mountains. *mountain range* W Germany
Rhenish Slate Mountains *see* Rheinisches Schiefergebirge
Rhin *see* Rhine
Rhine *58 D4 Dut.* Rijn, *Fr.* Rhin, *Ger.* Rhein. *river* W Europe
Rhinelander *18 B2* Wisconsin, N USA
Rhine State Uplands *see* Rheinisches Schiefergebirge
Rho *74 B2* Lombardia, N Italy
Rhode Island *19 G3 off.* State of Rhode Island and Providence Plantations, *also known as* Little Rhody, Ocean State. *state* NE USA
Rhodes *83 E7 var.* Ródhos, *Eng.* Rhodes, *It.* Rodi; *anc.* Rhodos. *island* Dodekánisa, Greece, Aegean Sea
Rhodes *see* Ródos
Rhodesia *see* Zimbabwe
Rhodope Mountains *82 C3 var.* Rodópi Óri, *Bul.* Rodopi Planina, Rodopi, *Gk.* Oroseirá Rodópis, *Turk.* Dospad Dagh. *mountain range* Bulgaria/Greece
Rhône *58 C4 river* France/Switzerland
Rhum *66 B3 var.* Rum. *island* W Scotland, United Kingdom
Ribble *67 D5 river* NW England, United Kingdom
Ribeira *see* Santa Uxía de Ribeira
Ribeirão Preto *41 F4* São Paulo, S Brazil
Riberalta *39 F2* Beni, N Bolivia
Ribniţa *86 D3 var.* Râbniţa, *Rus.* Rybnitsa. NE Moldova
Rice Lake *18 A2* Wisconsin, N USA
Richard Toll *52 B3* N Senegal
Richfield *22 B4* Utah, W USA
Richland *24 C2* Washington, NW USA
Richmond *129 C5* Tasman, South Island, New Zealand
Richmond *18 C5* Kentucky, S USA
Richmond *19 E5 state capital* Virginia, NE USA
Richmond Range *129 C5 mountain range* South Island, New Zealand
Ricobayo, Embalse de *70 C2 reservoir* NW Spain
Ricomagus *see* Riom
Ridder/Ridder *92 D4 prev.* Leninogor, Leninogorsk. Vostochnyy Kazakhstan, E Kazakhstan
Ridgecrest *25 C7* California, W USA
Ried *see* Ried im Innkreis
Ried im Innkreis *73 D6 var.* Ried. Oberösterreich, NW Austria
Riemst *65 D6* Limburg, NE Belgium
Riesa *72 D4* Sachsen, E Germany
Rift Valley *see* Great Rift Valley
Rīga *84 C3 Eng.* Riga. *country capital* (Latvia) Rīga, C Latvia
Rigaer Bucht *see* Riga, Gulf of
Riga, Gulf of *84 C3 Est.* Liivi Laht, *Ger.* Rigaer Bucht, *Latv.* Rīgas Jūras Līcis, *Rus.* Rizhskiy Zaliv; *prev. Est.* Riia Laht. *gulf* Estonia/Latvia
Rīgas Jūras Līcis *see* Riga, Gulf of
Rīgestān *see* Rēgistān
Riia Laht *see* Riga, Gulf of
Riihimäki *63 D5* Kanta-Häme, S Finland
Rijeka *78 A2 Ger.* Sankt Veit am Flaum, *It.* Fiume, *Slvn.* Reka; *anc.* Tarsatica. Primorje-Gorski Kotar, NW Croatia
Rijn *see* Rhine
Rijssel *see* Lille
Rijssen *64 E3* Overijssel, E Netherlands
Rimah, Wadi ar *98 B4 var.* Wādī ar Rummah. *dry watercourse* C Saudi Arabia
Rimini *74 C3 anc.* Ariminum. Emilia-Romagna, N Italy
Rîmnicu-Sărat *see* Râmnicu Sărat
Rîmnicu Vîlcea *see* Râmnicu Vâlcea
Rimouski *17 E4* Québec, SE Canada
Ringebu *63 B5* Oppland, S Norway
Ringen *see* Rõngu
Ringkøbing Fjord *63 A7 fjord* W Denmark
Ringvassøya *62 C2 Lapp.* Ráneš. *island* N Norway
Rio *see* Rio de Janeiro
Riobamba *38 B1* Chimborazo, C Ecuador
Rio Branco *34 B3 state capital* Acre, W Brazil
Rio Branco, Território de *see* Roraima
Río Bravo *29 E2* Tamaulipas, C Mexico
Río Cuarto *42 C4* Córdoba, C Argentina
Rio de Janeiro *41 F4 var.* Rio. *state capital* Rio de Janeiro, SE Brazil
Río Gallegos *43 B7 var.* Gallegos, Puerto Gallegos. Santa Cruz, S Argentina
Rio Grande *41 E5 var.* São Pedro do Rio Grande do Sul. Rio Grande do Sul, S Brazil
Río Grande *28 D3* Zacatecas, C Mexico
Rio Grande do Norte *41 G2 off.* Estado do Rio Grande do Norte. *state/region* E Brazil
Rio Grande do Norte, Estado do *see* Rio Grande do Norte
Rio Grande do Sul *41 E5 off.* Estado do Rio Grande do Sul. *state/region* S Brazil
Rio Grande do Sul, Estado do *see* Rio Grande do Sul
Rio Grande Plateau *see* Rio Grande Rise
Rio Grande Rise *35 E6 var.* Rio Grande Plateau. *undersea plateau* SW Atlantic Ocean
Ríohacha *36 B1* La Guajira, N Colombia
Río Lagartos *29 H3* Yucatán, SE Mexico
Riom *69 C5 anc.* Ricomagus. Puy-de-Dôme, C France
Río Verde *29 E4 var.* Rioverde. San Luis Potosí, C Mexico
Rioverde *see* Río Verde
Ripoll *71 G2* Cataluña, NE Spain
Rishiri-to *108 C2 var.* Risiri Tô. *island* NE Japan
Risiri Tô *see* Rishiri-tō
Rîşno *see* Râşnov
Risti *84 D2 Ger.* Kreuz. Läänemaa, W Estonia
Rivas *30 D4* Rivas, SW Nicaragua
Rivera *42 D3* Rivera, NE Uruguay
River Falls *18 A2* Wisconsin, N USA
Riverside *25 C7* California, W USA
Riverton *129 A7 var.* Aparima. Southland, South Island, New Zealand
Riverton *22 C3* Wyoming, C USA
Rivière-du-Loup *17 E4* Québec, SE Canada
Rivne *86 C2 Pol.* Równe, *Rus.* Rovno. Rivnens'ka Oblast', NW Ukraine
Rivoli *74 A2* Piemonte, NW Italy
Riyadh/Riyāḑ, Minţaqat ar *see* Ar Riyāḑ
Riyāq *see* Rayak
Rize *95 E2* Rize, NE Turkey (Türkiye)
Rizhao *106 D4* Shandong, E China
Rizhskiy Zaliv *see* Riga, Gulf of
Rkîz *52 C3* Trarza, W Mauritania
Road Town *33 F3 dependent territory capital* (British Virgin Islands) Tortola, C British Virgin Islands
Roanne *69 C5 anc.* Rodunma. Loire, E France
Roanoke *19 E5* Virginia, NE USA
Roanoke River *21 F1 river* North Carolina/Virginia, SE USA
Roatán *30 C2 var.* Coxen Hole, Coxin Hole. Islas de la Bahía, N Honduras
Roat Kampuchea *see* Cambodia
Roazon *see* Rennes
Robbie Ridge *121 E3 undersea ridge* W Pacific Ocean
Robert Williams *see* Caála
Robinson Range *125 B5 mountain range* Western Australia
Robson, Mount *15 E5 mountain* British Columbia, SW Canada
Robstown *27 G4* Texas, SW USA
Roca Partida, Isla *28 B5 island* W Mexico
Rocas, Atol das *41 G2 island* E Brazil
Rochefort *65 C7* Namur, SE Belgium
Rochefort *68 B4 var.* Rochefort sur Mer. Charente-Maritime, W France
Rochefort sur Mer *see* Rochefort
Rochester *23 G3* Minnesota, N USA
Rochester *19 G2* New Hampshire, NE USA
Rocheuses, Montagnes/Rockies *see* Rocky Mountains
Rockall Bank *58 B2 undersea bank* N Atlantic Ocean
Rockall Trough *58 B2 trough* N Atlantic Ocean
Rockdale *126 E2* Texas, SW USA
Rockford *18 B3* Illinois, N USA
Rockhampton *126 D4* Queensland, E Australia
Rock Hill *21 E1* South Carolina, SE USA
Rockingham *125 A6* Western Australia
Rock Island *18 B3* Illinois, N USA

Rock Sound *32 C1* Eleuthera Island, C The Bahamas
Rock Springs *22 C3* Wyoming, C USA
Rockstone *37 F3* C Guyana
Rocky Mount *21 F1* North Carolina, SE USA
Rocky Mountains *12 B4 var.* Rockies, *Fr.* Montagnes Rocheuses. *mountain range* Canada/USA
Roden *64 E2* Drenthe, NE Netherlands
Rodez *69 C5 anc.* Segodunum. Aveyron, S France
Ródhos/Rodi *see* Ródos
Rodopi/ Rodópi Óri *see* Rhodope Mountains
Rodopi Planina *see* Rhodope Mountains
Rodosto *see* Tekirdağ
Rodunma *see* Roanne
Roermond *65 D5* Limburg, SE Netherlands
Roeselare *65 A6 Fr.* Roulers; *prev.* Rousselaere. West-Vlaanderen, W Belgium
Rogachëv *see* Rahachow
Rogatica *78 C4* Republika Srpska, SE Bosnia and Herzegovina
Rogers *20 A1* Arkansas, C USA
Roger Simpson Island *see* Abemama
Roi Ed *see* Roi Et
Roi Et *115 D5 var.* Muang Roi Et, Roi Ed. Roi Et, E Thailand
Roja *84 C2* Talsi, NW Latvia
Rokiškis *84 C4* Panevėžys, NE Lithuania
Rokycany *77 A5 Ger.* Rokytzan. Plzeňský Kraj, W Czechia (Czech Republic)
Rokytzan *see* Rokycany
Rôlas, Ilha das *54 E2 island* S Sao Tome and Principe, Africa, E Atlantic Ocean
Rolla *23 G5* Missouri, C USA
Röm *see* Rømø
Roma *74 C4 Eng.* Rome. *country capital* (Italy) Lazio, C Italy
Roma *127 D5* Queensland, E Australia
Roman *82 C2* Vratsa, NW Bulgaria
Roman *86 C4 Hung.* Románvásár. Neamţ, NE Romania
Romania *86 B4 Bul.* Rumŭniya, *Ger.* Rumänien, *Hung.* Románia, *Rom.* România, *Croatian* Rumunjska, *Ukr.* Rumuniya, *prev.* Republica Socialistă România, Roumania, Rumania, Socialist Republic of Romania, *prev.Rom.* Romînia. *country* SE Europe
România, Republica Socialistă *see* Romania
Romania, Socialist Republic of *see* Romania
Románvásár *see* Roman
Rome *20 D2* Georgia, SE USA
Rome *see* Roma
Rominia *see* Romania
Romny *87 F2* Sums'ka Oblast', NE Ukraine
Rømø *63 A7 Ger.* Röm. *island* SW Denmark
Roncador, Serra do *34 D4 mountain range* C Brazil
Ronda *70 D5* Andalucía, S Spain
Rondônia *40 D3 off.* Estado de Rondônia; *prev.* Território de Rondônia. *state/region* W Brazil
Rondônia, Estado de *see* Rondônia
Rondônia, Território de *see* Rondônia
Rondonópolis *41 E3* Mato Grosso, W Brazil
Rongelap Atoll *122 D1 var.* Rönlap. *atoll* Ralik Chain, NW Marshall Islands
Rõngu *84 D3 Ger.* Ringen. Tartumaa, SE Estonia
Rönlap *see* Rongelap Atoll
Rønne *63 B8* Bornholm, E Denmark
Ronne Ice Shelf *132 A3 ice shelf* Antarctica
Roosendaal *65 C5* Noord-Brabant, S Netherlands
Roosevelt Island *132 B4 island* Antarctica
Roraima *40 D1 off.* Estado de Roraima; *prev.* Território de Rio Branco, Território de Roraima. *state/region* N Brazil
Roraima, Estado de *see* Roraima
Roraima, Mount *37 E3 mountain* N South America
Roraima, Território de *see* Roraima
Røros *63 B5* Sør-Trøndelag, S Norway
Ross *129 B6* West Coast, South Island, New Zealand
Rosa, Lake *32 D2 lake* Great Inagua, S The Bahamas
Rosario *42 D4* Santa Fe, C Argentina
Rosario *42 D2* San Pedro, C Paraguay
Rosario *see* Rosarito
Rosarito *28 A1 var.* Rosario. Baja California Norte, NW Mexico
Roscianum *see* Rossano
Roscommon *18 C2* Michigan, N USA
Roseau *33 G4 prev.* Charlotte Town. *country capital* (Dominica) SW Dominica
Roseburg *24 B4* Oregon, NW USA
Rosenau *see* Rožňava
Rosenberg *27 G4* Texas, SW USA
Rosenberg *see* Ružomberok, Slovakia
Rosengarten *72 B3* Niedersachsen, N Germany
Rosenheim *73 C6* Bayern, S Germany
Rosia *71 H5* W Gibraltar Europe
Rosia Bay *71 H5 bay* SW Gibraltar Europe W Mediterranean Sea Atlantic Ocean
Roşiori de Vede *86 B5* Teleorman, S Romania
Rositten *see* Rēzekne
Roslavl' *89 A5* Smolenskaya Oblast', W Russia
Rosmalen *64 C4* Noord-Brabant, S Netherlands
Rossano *75 E6 anc.* Roscianum. Calabria, SW Italy
Ross Ice Shelf *132 B4 ice shelf* Antarctica
Rossiyskaya Federatsiya *see* Russia
Rosso *52 B3* Trarza, SW Mauritania
Rossosh' *89 B6* Voronezhskaya Oblast', W Russia
Ross Sea *132 B4 sea* Antarctica
Rostak *see* Ar Rustāq
Rostock *72 C2* Mecklenburg-Vorpommern, NE Germany
Rostov *see* Rostov-na-Donu
Rostov-na-Donu *89 B7 var.* Rostov, *Eng.* Rostov-on-Don. Rostovskaya Oblast', SW Russia
Rostov-on-Don *see* Rostov-na-Donu
Roswell *26 D2* New Mexico, SW USA
Rota *122 B1 island* S Northern Mariana Islands
Rotcher Island *see* Tamana
Rothera *132 A2 UK research station* Antarctica
Rotomagus *see* Rouen
Rotorua *128 D3* Bay of Plenty, North Island, New Zealand
Rotorua, Lake *128 D3 lake* North Island, New Zealand
Rotterdam *64 C4* Zuid-Holland, SW Netherlands
Rottweil *73 B6* Baden-Württemberg, S Germany
Rotuma *123 E4 island* NW Fiji Oceania, S Pacific Ocean
Roubaix *68 C2* Nord, N France
Rouen *68 C3 anc.* Rotomagus. Seine-Maritime, N France
Roulers *see* Roeselare
Roumania *see* Romania
Round Rock *27 G3* Texas, SW USA
Rourkela *see* Rāurkela
Rousselaere *see* Roeselare
Roussillon *69 C6 cultural region* S France
Rouyn-Noranda *16 D4* Québec, SE Canada
Rovaniemi *62 D3* Lappi, N Finland
Rovigno *see* Rovinj
Rovigo *74 C2* Veneto, NE Italy
Rovinj *78 A3 It.* Rovigno. Istra, NW Croatia
Rovno *see* Rivne
Rovuma, Rio *57 F2 var.* Ruvuma. *river* Mozambique/Tanzania
Rovuma, Rio *see* Ruvuma
Rôwne *see* Rivne
Roxas City *117 E2* Panay Island, C Philippines
Royale, Isle *18 B1 island* Michigan, N USA
Royan *69 B5* Charente-Maritime, W France
Rozdolne *87 F4 Rus.* Razdolnoye. Respublika Krym, S Ukraine
Rožňava *77 D6 Ger.* Rosenau, *Hung.* Rozsnyó. Košický Kraj, E Slovakia
Rózsahegy *see* Ružomberok
Rozsnyó *see* Râşnov, Romania
Rozsnyó *see* Rožňava, Slovakia
Ruanda *see* Rwanda
Ruapehu, Mount *128 D4 volcano* North Island, New Zealand
Ruapuke Island *129 B8 island* SW New Zealand
Ruatoria *128 E3* Gisborne, North Island, New Zealand
Ruawai *128 D2* Northland, North Island, New Zealand
Rubezhnoye *see* Rubizhne
Rubizhne *87 H3 Rus.* Rubezhnoye. Luhans'ka Oblast', E Ukraine
Ruby Mountains *25 D5 mountain range* Nevada, W USA
Rucava *84 B3* Liepāja, SW Latvia
Rudensk *see* Rudzyensk
Rūdiškės *85 B5* Vilnius, S Lithuania
Rudnik *see* Dolni Chiflik
Rudny *see* Rudnyy
Rudnyy *92 C4 var.* Rudny. Kostanay, N Kazakhstan
Rudolf, Lake *see* Turkana, Lake
Rudolfswert *see* Novo mesto
Rudzyensk *85 C6 Rus.* Rudensk. Minskaya Voblasts', C Belarus
Rufiji *51 C7 river* E Tanzania
Rufino *42 C4* Santa Fe, C Argentina
Rugāji *84 D4* Balvi, E Latvia
Rügen *72 D2 headland* NE Germany
Ruggell *72 E1* N Liechtenstein Europe
Ruhja *see* Rūjiena
Ruhnu *84 C2 var.* Ruhnu Saar, *Swe.* Runö. *island* SW Estonia
Ruhnu Saar *see* Ruhnu
Rujen *see* Rūjiena
Rūjiena *84 D3 Est.* Ruhja, *Ger.* Rujen. Valmiera, N Latvia
Rukwa, Lake *51 B7 lake* SE Tanzania
Rum *see* Rhum
Ruma *78 D3* Vojvodina, N Serbia
Rumadiya *see* Ar Ramādī
Rumania/Rumänien *see* Romania
Rumbek *51 B5* El Buhayrat, C South Sudan
Rum Cay *32 D2 island* C The Bahamas
Rumia *76 C2* Pomorskie, N Poland
Rummah, Wādī ar *see* Rimah, Wādī ar
Rummelsburg in Pommern *see* Miastko
Rumuniya/Rumŭniya/Rumunjska *see* Romania
Runanga *129 B5* West Coast, South Island, New Zealand
Rundu *56 C3 var.* Runtu. Okavango, NE Namibia
Runö *see* Ruhnu
Runtu *see* Rundu
Ruoqiang *104 C3 var.* Jo-ch'iang, *Uigh.* Charkhlik, Charkhliq, Qarkilik. Xinjiang Uygur Zizhiqu, NW China
Rupea *86 C4 Ger.* Reps, *Hung.* Kőhalom; *prev.* Cohalm. Braşov, C Romania
Rupel *65 B5 river* N Belgium
Rupella *see* la Rochelle
Rupert, Rivière de *16 D3 river* Québec, C Canada
Rusaddir *see* Melilla
Ruschuk/Rusçuk *see* Ruse
Ruse *82 D1 var.* Ruschuk, Rustchuk, *Turk.* Rusçuk. Ruse, N Bulgaria
Rusaddir *see* Melilla
Russellville *20 A1* Arkansas, C USA
Russia *90 D2 off.* Russian Federation, *Latv.* Krievija, *Rus.* Rossiyskaya Federatsiya. *country* Asia/Europe
Russian America *see* Alaska
Russian Federation *see* Russia
Rustaq *see* Ar Rustāq
Rustavi *95 G2 prev.* Rust'avi. SE Georgia
Rust'avi *see* Rustavi
Rustchuk *see* Ruse
Ruston *20 B2* Louisiana, S USA
Rutanzige, Lake *see* Edward, Lake
Rutba *see* Ar Ruţbah
Rutlam *see* Ratlām
Rutland *19 F2* Vermont, NE USA
Rutog *104 A4 var.* Rutög, Rutok. Xizang Zizhiqu, W China
Rutok *see* Rutog
Ruvuma *see* Rovuma, Rio
Ruwenzori *55 E5 mountain range* Dem. Rep. Congo/Uganda
Ruzhany *85 B6* Brestskaya Voblasts', SW Belarus
Ružomberok *77 C5 Ger.* Rosenberg, *Hung.* Rózsahegy. Žilinský Kraj, N Slovakia
Rwanda *51 B6 off.* Republic of Rwanda; *prev.* Ruanda. *country* C Africa
Rwanda, Republic of *see* Rwanda
Ryazan' *89 B5* Ryazanskaya Oblast', W Russia
Rybach'ye *see* Balykchy
Rybinsk *88 B4 prev.* Andropov. Yaroslavskaya Oblast', W Russia
Rybnik *77 C5* Śląskie, S Poland
Rybnitsa *see* Rîbniţa
Ryde *126 E1* United Kingdom
Ryki *76 D4* Lubelskie, E Poland
Rykovo *see* Yenakiieve
Rypin *76 C3* Kujawsko-pomorskie, C Poland
Ryssel *see* Lille
Rysy *77 C5 mountain* S Poland
Ryukyu Islands *see* Nansei-shotō
Ryukyu Trench *103 F3 var.* Nansei Syotō Trench. *trench* S East China Sea
Rzeszów *77 E5* Podkarpackie, SE Poland
Rzhev *88 B4* Tverskaya Oblast', W Russia

S

Saale *72 C4 river* C Germany
Saalfeld *73 C5 var.* Saalfeld an der Saale. Thüringen, C Germany
Saalfeld an der Saale *see* Saalfeld
Saarbrücken *73 A6 Fr.* Sarrebruck. Saarland, SW Germany
Sääre *84 C2 var.* Sjar. Saaremaa, W Estonia
Saare *see* Saaremaa
Saaremaa *84 C2 Ger.* Oesel, Ösel; *prev.* Saare. *island* W Estonia
Saariselkä *62 D2 Lapp.* Suoločielgi. Lappi, N Finland
Sab' Ābār *96 C4 var.* Sab'a Biyar, Sa'b Bi'ār. Ḩimş, C Syria
Sab'a Biyar *see* Sab' Ābār
Šabac *78 D3* Serbia, W Serbia
Sabadell *71 G2* Cataluña, E Spain
Sabah *116 D3 prev.* British North Borneo, North Borneo. *state* East Malaysia
Sabanalarga *36 B1* Atlántico, N Colombia
Sabaneta *36 C1* Falcón, N Venezuela
Sabaria *see* Szombathely
Sab'atayn, Ramlat as *99 C6 desert* C Yemen
Sabaya *39 F4* Oruro, S Bolivia
Sa'b Bi'ār *see* Sab' Ābār
Saberi, Hamun-e *100 C5 var.* Daryācheh-ye Hāmun, Daryācheh-ye Sīstān. *lake* Afghanistan/Iran
Sabhā *49 F3* C Libya
Sabi *see* Save
Sabinas *29 E2* Coahuila, NE Mexico
Sabinas Hidalgo *29 E2* Nuevo León, NE Mexico
Sabine River *27 H3 river* Louisiana/Texas, SW USA
Sabkha *see* As Sabkhah
Sable, Cape *21 E5 headland* Florida, SE USA
Sable Island *17 G4 island* Nova Scotia, SE Canada
Şabyā *99 B6* Jīzān, SW Saudi Arabia
Sabzawar *see* Sabzevār
Sabzevār *98 D2 var.* Sabzawar. Khorāsān-Razavī, NE Iran
Sachsen *72 D4 Eng.* Saxony, *Fr.* Saxe. *state* E Germany
Sachs Harbour *15 E2 var.* Ikaahuk. Banks Island, Northwest Territories, N Canada
Sächsisch-Reen/Sächsisch-Regen *see* Reghin
Sacramento *25 B5 state capital* California, W USA
Sacramento Mountains *26 D2 mountain range* New Mexico, SW USA
Sacramento River *25 B5 river* California, W USA
Sacramento Valley *25 B5 valley* California, W USA
Sá da Bandeira *see* Lubango
Şa'dah *99 B6* NW Yemen
Sado *109 C5 var.* Sadoga-shima. *island* C Japan
Sadoga-shima *see* Sado
Saena Julia *see* Siena
Safad *see* Tsefat
Şafāqis *see* Sfax
Şafāshahr *98 D3 var.* Deh Bīd. Fārs, C Iran
Safed *see* Tsefat
Safēd Kōh, Silsilah-ye *100 D4 prev.* Selseleh-ye Safīd Kūh, *Eng.* Paropamisus Range. *mountain range* W Afghanistan
Säffle *63 B6* Värmland, C Sweden
Safford *26 C3* Arizona, SW USA
Safi *48 B2* W Morocco
Safīd Kuh, Selseleh-ye *see* Safēd Kōh, Silsilah-ye
Sagaing *114 B3* Sagaing, C Myanmar (Burma)
Sagami-nada *109 D6 inlet* SW Japan
Sagan *see* Żagań
Sāgar *112 D4 prev.* Saugor. Madhya Pradesh, C India
Sagarmāthā *see* Everest, Mount
Sagebrush State *see* Nevada
Saghez *see* Saqqez
Saginaw *18 C3* Michigan, N USA
Saginaw Bay *18 D2 lake bay* Michigan, N USA
Sagua la Grande *32 B2* Villa Clara, C Cuba
Sagunto/Saguntum *see* Sagunt
Sagunt *71 F3 var.* Sagunto, *Ar.* Murviedro; *anc.* Saguntum. Comunitat Valenciana, E Spain
Sahara *46 B3 desert* Libya/Algeria
Sahara el Gharbîya *see* Şaḩrā' al Gharbīyah
Saharan Atlas *see* Atlas Saharien
Sahel *52 D3 physical region* C Africa
Sāḩilīyah, Jibāl as *96 B3 mountain range* NW Syria
Sahiwal *112 C2 prev.* Montgomery. Punjab, E Pakistan
Şaḩrā' al Gharbīyah *50 B2 var.* Sahara el Gharbîya, *Eng.* Western Desert. *desert* C Egypt
Şaḩrā' ash Sharqīyah *81 H5 Eng.* Arabian Desert, Eastern Desert. *desert* E Egypt
Saïda *97 A5 var.* Şaydā, Sayida; *anc.* Sidon. W Lebanon
Sa'īdābād *see* Sīrjān
Saidpur *113 G3 var.* Syedpur. Rajshahi, NW Bangladesh
Saidu Sharif *112 C1 var.* Mingora, Mongora. North-West Frontier Province, N Pakistan
Saigon *see* Hô Chi Minh
Saimaa *63 E5 lake* SE Finland
St Albans *67 E6 anc.* Verulamium. E England, United Kingdom
Saint Albans *18 D5* West Virginia, NE USA
St Andrews *66 C4* E Scotland, United Kingdom
Saint Anna Trough *see* Svyataya Anna Trough
St. Ann's Bay *32 B4* C Jamaica
St. Anthony *17 G3* Newfoundland and Labrador, SE Canada
Saint Augustine *21 E3* Florida, SE USA
St Austell *67 C7* SW England, United Kingdom
St Barthélemy *33 G3 French overseas collectivity,* E West Indies
St. Botolph's Town *see* Boston
St-Brieuc *68 A3* Côtes d'Armor, NW France
St. Catharines *16 D5* Ontario, S Canada
St-Chamond *69 D5* Loire, E France
Saint Christopher and Nevis, Federation of *see* Saint Kitts and Nevis
Saint Christopher-Nevis *see* Saint Kitts and Nevis
Saint Clair, Lake *18 D3 var.* Lac à L'Eau Claire. *lake* Canada/USA
St-Claude *69 D5 anc.* Condate. Jura, E France
Saint Cloud *23 F2* Minnesota, N USA
Saint Croix *33 F3 island* S Virgin Islands (US)
Saint Croix River *18 A2 river* Minnesota/ Wisconsin, N USA
St David's Island *20 B5 island* E Bermuda
St-Denis *57 G4 dependent territory capital* (Réunion) NW Réunion
St-Dié *68 E4* Vosges, NE France
St-Egrève *69 D5* Isère, E France
Sainte Marie, Cap *see* Vohimena, Tanjona
Saintes *69 B5 anc.* Mediolanum. Charente-Maritime, W France
St-Étienne *69 D5* Loire, E France
St-Flour *69 C5* Cantal, C France
St-Gall/Saint Gall/St. Gallen *see* Sankt Gallen
St-Gaudens *69 B6* Haute-Garonne, S France
Saint George *127 D5* Queensland, E Australia
St George *20 B4* N Bermuda
Saint George *22 A5* Utah, W USA
St. George's *33 G5 country capital* (Grenada) SW Grenada
St-Georges *17 E4* Québec, SE Canada
St-Georges *37 H3* E French Guiana
Saint George's Channel *67 B6 channel* Ireland/ Wales, United Kingdom
St George's Island *20 B4 island* E Bermuda
St Helena *see* St Helena, Ascension and Tristan da Cunha
St Helena, Ascension and Tristan da Cunha *47 A6 UK Overseas territory* C Atlantic Ocean
St Helier *67 D8 dependent territory capital* (Jersey) S Jersey, Channel Islands
St.Iago de la Vega *see* Spanish Town
Saint Ignace *18 C2* Michigan, N USA
St-Jean, Lac *17 E4 lake* Québec, SE Canada
Saint Joe River *24 D2 river* Idaho, NW USA North America
St. John *17 F4* New Brunswick, SE Canada
Saint-John *see* Saint John
Saint John *19 H1 Fr.* Saint-John. *river* Canada/USA
St John's *33 G3 country capital* (Antigua and Barbuda) Antigua, Antigua and Barbuda
St. John's *17 H3 province capital* Newfoundland and Labrador, E Canada
Saint Joseph *23 F4* Missouri, C USA
St Julian's *see* San Giljan
St Kilda *66 A3 island* NW Scotland, United Kingdom
Saint Kitts and Nevis *33 F3 off.* Federation of Saint Christopher and Nevis, *var.* Saint Christopher-Nevis. *country* E West Indies
St-Laurent *see* St-Laurent-du-Maroni
St-Laurent-du-Maroni *37 H3 var.* St-Laurent. NW French Guiana
St-Laurent, Fleuve *see* St. Lawrence
St. Lawrence *17 E4 Fr.* Fleuve St-Laurent. *river* Canada/USA
St. Lawrence, Gulf of *17 F3 gulf* NW Atlantic Ocean
Saint Lawrence Island *14 B2 island* Alaska, USA
St-Lô *68 B3 anc.* Briovera, Laudus. Manche, N France
St-Louis *68 E4* Haut-Rhin, NE France
Saint Louis *52 B3* NW Senegal
Saint Louis *23 G4* Missouri, C USA
Saint Lucia *33 E1 country* SE West Indies
Saint Lucia Channel *33 H4 channel* Martinique/ Saint Lucia
St-Malo *68 B3* Ille-et-Vilaine, NW France
St-Malo, Golfe de *68 A3 gulf* NW France
Saint Martin *see* Sint Maarten
St Martin *33 G3 French overseas collectivity.* E West Indies
St.Matthew's Island *see* Zadetkyi Kyun
St.Matthias Group *122 B3 island group* NE Papua New Guinea
St. Moritz *73 B7 Ger.* Sankt Moritz, *Rmsch.* San Murezzan. Graubünden, SE Switzerland
St-Nazaire *68 A4* Loire-Atlantique, NW France
Saint Nicholas *see* São Nicolau
Saint-Nicolas *see* Sint-Niklaas
St-Omer *68 C2* Pas-de-Calais, N France
Saint Paul *23 F2 state capital* Minnesota, N USA
St-Paul, Île *119 C6 var.* St.Paul Island. *island* Île St-Paul, NE French Southern and Antarctic Lands Antarctica Indian Ocea
St.Paul Island *see* St-Paul, Île
St Peter Port *67 D8 dependent territory capital* (Guernsey) C Guernsey, Channel Islands
Saint Petersburg *21 E4* Florida, SE USA
Saint Petersburg *see* Sankt-Peterburg
St-Pierre and Miquelon *17 G4 Fr.* Îles St-Pierre et Miquelon. *French overseas collectivity* NE North America
St-Quentin *68 C3* Aisne, N France
Saint Thomas *see* São Tomé, Sao Tome and Principe
Saint Thomas *see* Charlotte Amalie, Virgin Islands (US)
Saint Ubes *see* Setúbal
Saint Vincent *33 G4 island* N Saint Vincent and the Grenadines
Saint Vincent *see* São Vicente
Saint Vincent and the Grenadines *33 H4 country* SE West Indies
Saint Vincent, Cape *see* São Vicente, Cabo de
Saint Vincent Passage *33 H4 passage* Saint Lucia/ Saint Vincent and the Grenadines
Saint Yves *see* Setúbal
Saipan *120 B1 island/country capital* (Northern Mariana Islands) S Northern Mariana Islands
Saishū *see* Jeju-do
Sajama, Nevado *39 F4 mountain* W Bolivia
Sajószentpéter *77 D6* Borsod-Abaúj-Zemplén, NE Hungary
Sakākah *98 B4* Al Jawf, NW Saudi Arabia
Sakakawea, Lake *22 D1 reservoir* North Dakota, N USA
Sakartvelo *see* Georgia
Sakata *108 D4* Yamagata, Honshū, C Japan
Sakhalin *93 G4 var.* Sakhalin. *island* SE Russia
Sakhalin *see* Sakhalin, Ostrov
Sakhon Nakhon *see* Sakon Nakhon
Şäki *95 G2 Rus.* Sheki; *prev.* Nukha. NW Azerbaijan
Saki *see* Saky
Sakishima-shoto *108 A3 var.* Sakisima Syotô. *island group* SW Japan
Sakisima Syotô *see* Sakishima-shotō
Sakiz *see* Saqqez
Sakiz-Adasi *see* Chíos
Sakon Nakhon *114 D4 var.* Muang Sakon Nakhon, Sakhon Nakhon. Sakon Nakhon, E Thailand
Saky *87 F5 Rus.* Saki. Respublika Krym, S Ukraine
Sal *52 A3 island* Ilhas de Barlavento, NE Cape Verde (Cabo Verde)
Sala *63 C6* Västmanland, C Sweden
Salacgrīva *84 C3 Est.* Salatsi. Limbaži, N Latvia
Sala Consilina *75 D5* Campania, S Italy
Salado, Río *40 D5 river* E Argentina
Salado, Río *42 C3 river* C Argentina
Şalālah *99 D6* SW Oman
Salamá *30 B2* Baja Verapaz, C Guatemala
Salamanca *42 B4* Coquimbo, C Chile
Salamanca *70 D2 anc.* Helmantica, Salmantica. Castilla y León, NW Spain
Salamīyah *96 B3 var.* As Salamīyah. Ḩamāh, W Syria
Salang *see* Phuket
Salantai *84 B3* Klaipėda, NW Lithuania
Salatsi *see* Salacgrīva
Salavan *115 D5 var.* Saravan, Saravane. Salavan, S Laos
Salavat *89 D6* Respublika Bashkortostan, W Russia
Sala y Gomez *131 F4 island* Chile, E Pacific Ocean
Sala y Gomez Fracture Zone *see* Sala y Gomez Ridge
Sala y Gomez Ridge *131 G4 var.* Sala y Gomez Fracture Zone. *fracture zone* SE Pacific Ocean
Salazar *see* N'Dalatando
Šalčininkai *85 C5* Vilnius, SE Lithuania
Salduba *see* Zaragoza
Saldus *84 B3 Ger.* Frauenburg. Saldus, W Latvia
Sale *127 C7* Victoria, SE Australia
Salé *48 C2* NW Morocco
Salekhard *92 D3 prev.* Obdorsk. Yamalo-Nenetskiy Avtonomnyy Okrug, N Russia
Salem *110 C2* Tamil Nādu, SE India
Salem *24 B3 state capital* Oregon, NW USA
Salerno *75 D5 anc.* Salernum. Campania, S Italy
Salerno, Gulf of *75 C5 Eng.* Gulf of Salerno. *gulf* S Italy
Salerno, Gulf of *see* Salerno, Golfo di
Salernum *see* Salerno
Salfit *97 E6* C West Bank, Middle East
Salihorsk *85 C7 Rus.* Soligorsk. Minskaya Voblasts', S Belarus
Salima *57 E2* Central, C Malawi
Salina *23 E5* Kansas, C USA
Salina Cruz *29 F5* Oaxaca, SE Mexico
Salinas *38 A2* Guayas, W Ecuador
Salinas *25 B6* California, W USA
Salisbury *67 D7 var.* New Sarum. S England, United Kingdom
Salisbury *see* Harare
Sállan *see* Sørøya
Salliq *see* Coral Harbour
Sallyana *see* Şalyān
Salmantica *see* Salamanca
Salmon River *24 D3 river* Idaho, NW USA
Salmon River Mountains *24 D3 mountain range* Idaho, NW USA
Salo *63 D6* Länsi-Suomi, SW Finland
Salon-de-Provence *69 D6* Bouches-du-Rhône, SE France
Salonica/Salonika *see* Thessaloníki
Salonta *86 A3 Hung.* Nagyszalonta. Bihor, W Romania
Sal'sk *89 B7* Rostovskaya Oblast', SW Russia
Salt *see* As Salţ
Salta *42 C2* Salta, NW Argentina
Saltash *67 C7* SW England, United Kingdom
Saltillo *29 E3* Coahuila, NE Mexico
Salt Lake City *22 B4 state capital* Utah, W USA
Salto *42 D4* Salto, N Uruguay
Salton Sea *25 D8 lake* California, W USA
Salvador *41 G3 prev.* São Salvador. *state capital* Bahia, E Brazil
Salween *102 C2 Bur.* Thanlwin, *Chin.* Nu Chiang, Nu Jiang. *river* SE Asia
Şalyān *113 E3 var.* Sallyana. Mid Western, W Nepal
Salzburg *73 D6 anc.* Juvavum. Salzburg, N Austria
Salzgitter *72 C4 prev.* Watenstedt-Salzgitter. Niedersachsen, C Germany
Salzwedel *72 C3* Sachsen-Anhalt, N Germany
Šamac *see* Bosanski Šamac
Samakhixai *see* Attapu
Samalayuca *28 C1* Chihuahua, N Mexico
Samar *117 F2 island* C Philippines
Samara *92 B3 prev.* Kuybyshev. Samarskaya Oblast', W Russia
Samarang *see* Semarang
Samarinda *116 D4* Borneo, C Indonesia
Samarkand *see* Samarqand
Samarkandski/Samarkandskoye *see* Temirtau
Samarobriva *see* Amiens
Samarqand *101 E2 Rus.* Samarkand. Samarqand Viloyati, C Uzbekistan
Samawa *see* As Samāwah
Şamaxı *95 H2* E Azerbaijan
Sambalpur *113 F4* Odisha, E India
Sambava *57 G2* Antsiranana, NE Madagascar
Sambir *86 B2 Rus.* Sambor. L'vivs'ka Oblast', NW Ukraine
Sambor *see* Sambir
Sambre *68 D2 river* Belgium/France
Samfya *56 D2* Luapula, N Zambia
Saminatal *72 E2 valley* Austria/Liechtenstein, Europe
Samnān *see* Semnān
Sam Neua *see* Xam Nua
Samoa *123 E4 off.* Independent State of Western Samoa, *var.* Sāmoa; *prev.* Western Samoa. *country* W Polynesia
Sāmoa *see* Samoa
Samoa Basin *121 E3 undersea basin* W Pacific Ocean
Samobor *78 A2* Zagreb, N Croatia
Sámos *83 E6 prev.* Limín Vathéos. Sámos, Dodekánisa, Greece, Aegean Sea
Sámos *83 D6 island* Dodekánisa, Greece, Aegean Sea
Samothrace *see* Samothráki
Samothráki *82 D4* Samothráki, NE Greece
Samothraki *82 C4 anc.* Samothrace. *island* NE Greece
Sampit *116 C4* Borneo, C Indonesia
Samraong *115 D5 prev.* Phumĭ Sâmraông, Phum Samrong. Oddar Meanchey, NW Cambodia
Samsun *94 D2 anc.* Amisus. Samsun, N Turkey (Türkiye)
Samt'redia *95 F2* W Georgia
Samui, Ko *115 C6 island* SW Thailand
Samut Prakan *115 C5 var.* Muang Samut Prakan, Paknam. Samut Prakan, C Thailand

San *52 D3* Ségou, C Mali
San *77 E5 river* SE Poland
Şan'ā' *99 B6 Eng.* Sanaa. *country capital* (Yemen) W Yemen
Sana *78 B3 river* NW Bosnia and Herzegovina
Sanaa *see* Şan'ā'
Sanae *132 B2 South African research station* Antarctica
Sanaga *55 B5 river* C Cameroon
San Ambrosio, Isla *35 A5 Eng.* San Ambrosio Island. *island* W Chile
San Ambrosio Island *see* San Ambrosio, Isla
Sanandaj *98 C3 prev.* Sinneh. Kordestān, W Iran
San Andrés, Isla de *31 F3 island* NW Colombia, Caribbean Sea
San Andrés Tuxtla *29 F4 var.* Tuxtla. Veracruz-Llave, E Mexico
San Angelo *27 F3* Texas, SW USA
San Antonio *30 B2* Toledo, S Belize
San Antonio *42 B4* Valparaíso, C Chile
San Antonio *27 F4* Texas, SW USA
San Antonio Oeste *43 C5* Río Negro, E Argentina
San Antonio River *27 G4 river* Texas, SW USA
Sanāw *99 C6 var.* Sanaw. NE Yemen
San Benedicto, Isla *28 B4 island* W Mexico
San Benito *30 B1* Petén, N Guatemala
San Benito *27 G5* Texas, SW USA
San Bernardino *25 C7* California, W USA
San Blas *28 C3* Sinaloa, C Mexico
San Blas, Cape *20 D3 headland* Florida, SE USA
San Blas, Cordillera de *31 G4 mountain range* NE Panama
San Carlos *30 D4* Río San Juan, S Nicaragua
San Carlos *26 B2* Arizona, SW USA
San Carlos *see* Quesada, Costa Rica
San Carlos de Ancud *see* Ancud
San Carlos de Bariloche *43 B5* Río Negro, SW Argentina
San Carlos del Zulia *36 C2* Zulia, W Venezuela
San Clemente Island *25 B8 island* Channel Islands, California, W USA
San Cristóbal *36 C2* Táchira, W Venezuela
San Cristobal *122 C4 var.* Makira. *island* SE Solomon Islands
San Cristóbal *see* San Cristóbal de Las Casas
San Cristóbal de Las Casas *29 G5 var.* San Cristóbal. Chiapas, SE Mexico
San Cristóbal, Isla *38 B5 var.* Chatham Island. *island* Galápagos Islands, Ecuador, E Pacific Ocean
Sancti Spíritus *32 B2* Sancti Spíritus, C Cuba
Sandakan *116 D3* Sabah, East Malaysia
Sandalwood Island *see* Sumba, Pulau
Sandanski *82 C3 prev.* Sveti Vrach. Blagoevgrad, SW Bulgaria
Sanday *66 D2 island* NE Scotland, United Kingdom
Sanders *26 C2* Arizona, SW USA
Sand Hills *22 D3 mountain range* Nebraska, C USA
San Diego *25 C8* California, W USA
Sandnes *63 A6* Rogaland, S Norway
Sandomierz *76 D4 Rus.* Sandomir. Świętokrzyskie, C Poland
Sandomir *see* Sandomierz
Sandoway *see* Thandwe
Sandpoint *24 C1* Idaho, NW USA
Sand Springs *27 G1* Oklahoma, C USA
Sandusky *18 D3* Ohio, N USA
Sandvika *63 A6* Akershus, S Norway
Sandviken *63 C6* Gävleborg, C Sweden
Sandwich Island *see* Efate
Sandwich Islands *see* Hawaiian Islands
Sandy Bay *71 H5* Saskatchewan, C Canada
Sandy City *22 B4* Utah, W USA
Sandy Lake *16 B3 lake* Ontario, C Canada
San Esteban *30 D2* Olancho, C Honduras
San Eugenio/San Eugenio del Cuareim *see* Artigas
San Felipe *36 D1* Yaracuy, NW Venezuela
San Felipe de Puerto Plata *see* Puerto Plata
San Félix, Isla *35 A5 Eng.* San Felix Island. *island* W Chile
San Felix Island *see* San Félix, Isla
San Fernando *70 C5 prev.* Isla de León. Andalucía, S Spain
San Fernando *33 H5* Trinidad, Trinidad and Tobago
San Fernando *24 D1* California, W USA
San Fernando *36 D2 var.* San Fernando de Apure. Apure, C Venezuela
San Fernando de Apure *see* San Fernando
San Fernando del Valle de Catamarca *42 C3 var.* Catamarca. Catamarca, NW Argentina
San Fernando de Monte Cristi *see* Monte Cristi
San Francisco *25 B6* California, W USA
San Francisco del Oro *28 C2* Chihuahua, N Mexico
San Francisco de Macorís *33 E3* C Dominican Republic
San Fructuoso *see* Tacuarembó
San Gabriel *38 B1* Carchi, N Ecuador
San Gabriel Mountains *24 E1 mountain range* California, USA
Sangihe, Kepulauan *see* Sangir, Kepulauan
San Giljan *80 B5 var.* St Julian's. N Malta
Sangir, Kepulauan *117 F3 var.* Kepulauan Sangihe. *island group* N Indonesia
Sāngli *110 B1* Mahārāshtra, W India
Sangmélima *55 B5* Sud, S Cameroon
Sangre de Cristo Mountains *26 D1 mountain range* Colorado/New Mexico, C USA
San Ignacio *30 B1 prev.* Cayo, El Cayo. Cayo, W Belize
San Ignacio *39 F3* Beni, N Bolivia
San Ignacio *28 B2* Baja California Sur, NW Mexico
San Joaquin Valley *25 B7 valley* California, W USA
San Jorge, Golfo *43 C6 var.* Gulf of San Jorge. *gulf* S Argentina
San Jorge, Gulf of *see* San Jorge, Golfo
San José *31 E4 country capital* (Costa Rica) San José, C Costa Rica
San José *39 G3 var.* San José de Chiquitos. Santa Cruz, E Bolivia
San José *30 B3 var.* Puerto San José. Escuintla, S Guatemala
San Jose *25 B6* California, W USA
San José *see* San José del Guaviare, Colombia
San José de Chiquitos *see* San José
San José de Cúcuta *see* Cúcuta
San José del Guaviare *36 C4 var.* San José. Guaviare, S Colombia
San Juan *42 B4* San Juan, W Argentina
San Juan *33 F3 dependent territory capital* (Puerto Rico) NE Puerto Rico
San Juan *see* San Juan de los Morros
San Juan Bautista *42 D3* Misiones, S Paraguay
San Juan Bautista *see* Villahermosa
San Juan Bautista Tuxtepec *see* Tuxtepec
San Juan de Alicante *see* Sant Joan d'Alacant
San Juan del Norte *31 E4 var.* Greytown. Río San Juan, SE Nicaragua
San Juan de los Morros *36 D2 var.* San Juan. Guárico, N Venezuela
San Juanito, Isla *28 C4 island* C Mexico
San Juan Mountains *26 D1 mountain range* Colorado, C USA
San Juan, Río *31 E4 river* Costa Rica/Nicaragua
San Juan River *26 C1 river* Colorado/Utah, W USA
San Julián *see* Puerto San Julián
Sankt-Bartholomäi *see* Palamuse
Sankt Gallen *73 B7 var.* St. Gallen, *Eng.* Saint Gall, *Fr.* St-Gall. Sankt Gallen, NE Switzerland
Sankt-Georgen *see* Sfântu Gheorghe
Sankt-Jakobi *see* Pärnu-Jaagupi, Pärnumaa, Estonia
Sankt Martin *see* Martin
Sankt Moritz *see* St. Moritz
Sankt-Peterburg *88 B4 prev.* Leningrad, Petrograd, *Eng.* Saint Petersburg, *Fin.* Pietari. Leningradskaya Oblast', NW Russia
Sankt Pölten *73 E6* Niederösterreich, N Austria
Sankt Veit am Flaum *see* Rijeka
Sankuru *55 D6 river* C Dem. Rep. Congo
Şanlıurfa *95 E4 prev.* Sanli Urfa, Urfa; *anc.* Edessa. Şanlıurfa, S Turkey (Türkiye)
Sanli Urfa *see* Şanlıurfa
San Lorenzo *39 G5* Tarija, S Bolivia
San Lorenzo *38 A1* Esmeraldas, N Ecuador
San Lorenzo, Isla *38 C4 island* W Peru
Sanlúcar de Barrameda *70 C5* Andalucía, S Spain
San Luis *42 C4* San Luis, C Argentina
San Luis *30 B2* Petén, NE Guatemala
San Luis *see* San Luis Río Colorado
San Luis Obispo *25 B7* California, W USA
San Luis Potosí *29 E3* San Luis Potosí, C Mexico
San Luis Río Colorado *28 A1 var.* San Luis Río Colorado. Sonora, NW Mexico
San Marcos *30 A2* San Marcos, W Guatemala
San Marcos *27 G4* Texas, SW USA
San Marcos de Arica *see* Arica
San Marino *74 E1 country capital* (San Marino) C San Marino
San Marino *71 D1 off.* Republic of San Marino. *country* S Europe
San Marino, Republic of *see* San Marino
San Martín *132 A2 Argentinian research station* Antarctica
San Mateo *37 E2* Anzoátegui, NE Venezuela
San Matías *39 H3* Santa Cruz, E Bolivia
San Matías, Gulf of *43 C5 var.* Gulf of San Matías. *gulf* E Argentina
San Matías, Gulf of *see* San Matías, Golfo
Sanmenxia *106 C4 var.* Shan Xian. Henan, C China
Sânmiclăuş Mare *see* Sânnicolau Mare
San Miguel *30 C3* San Miguel, SE El Salvador
San Miguel *28 D2* Coahuila, N Mexico
San Miguel de Ibarra *see* Ibarra
San Miguel de Tucumán *42 C3 var.* Tucumán. Tucumán, N Argentina
San Miguelito *31 G4* Panamá, C Panama
San Miguel, Río *39 G3 river* E Bolivia
San Murezzan *see* St. Moritz
Sannār *see* Sennar
Sânnicolaul-Mare *see* Sânnicolau Mare
Sânnicolau Mare *86 A4 var.* Sânnicolaul-Mare, *Hung.* Nagyszentmiklós; *prev.* Sânmiclăuş Mare, Sînnicolau Mare. Timiş, W Romania
Sanok *77 E5* Podkarpackie, SE Poland
San Pablo *39 F5* Potosí, S Bolivia
San Pedro *30 C1* Corozal, NE Belize
San-Pédro *52 D5* S Ivory Coast
San Pedro *28 D3 var.* San Pedro de las Colonias. Coahuila, NE Mexico
San Pedro de la Cueva *28 C2* Sonora, NW Mexico
San Pedro de las Colonias *see* San Pedro
San Pedro de Lloc *38 B3* La Libertad, NW Peru
San Pedro Mártir, Sierra *28 A1 mountain range* NW Mexico
San Pedro Sula *30 C2* Cortés, NW Honduras
San Rafael *42 B4* Mendoza, W Argentina
San Rafael Mountains *25 C7 mountain range* California, W USA
San Ramón de la Nueva Orán *42 C2* Salta, N Argentina
San Remo *74 A3* Liguria, NW Italy
San Salvador *30 B3 country capital* (El Salvador) San Salvador, SW El Salvador
San Salvador *32 D2 prev.* Watlings Island. *island* E The Bahamas
San Salvador de Jujuy *42 C2 var.* Jujuy. Jujuy, N Argentina
San Salvador, Isla *38 A4 island* Ecuador
Sansanné-Mango *see* Mango
San Sebastián *71 E1* País Vasco, N Spain *see also* Donostia
Sansepolcro *74 C3* Toscana, C Italy
San Severo *75 D5* Puglia, SE Italy
Santa Ana *39 F3* Beni, N Bolivia
Santa Ana *30 B3* Santa Ana, NW El Salvador
Santa Ana *24 D2* California, W USA
Santa Ana de Coro *see* Coro
Santa Ana Mountains *24 E2 mountain range* California, W USA
Santa Barbara *28 C2* Chihuahua, N Mexico
Santa Barbara *25 C7* California, W USA
Santa Cataliña de Armada *70 B1 var.* Santa Comba. Galicia, NW Spain
Santa Catalina Island *25 B8 island* Channel Islands, California, W USA
Santa Catarina *41 E5 off.* Estado de Santa Catarina. *state/region* S Brazil
Santa Catarina, Estado de *see* Santa Catarina
Santa Clara *32 B2* Villa Clara, C Cuba
Santa Clarita *24 D1* California, USA
Santa Comba *see* Santa Cataliña de Armada
Santa Cruz *54 E2* São Tomé, S Sao Tome and Principe, Africa
Santa Cruz *25 B6* California, W USA
Santa Cruz *39 G4 department* E Bolivia
Santa Cruz Barillas *see* Barillas
Santa Cruz del Quiché *30 B2* Quiché, W Guatemala
Santa Cruz de Tenerife *48 A3* Tenerife, Islas Canarias, Spain, NE Atlantic Ocean
Santa Cruz, Isla *38 B5 var.* Indefatigable Island, Isla Chávez. *island* Galápagos Islands, Ecuador, E Pacific Ocean
Santa Cruz Islands *122 D3 island group* E Solomon Islands
Santa Cruz, Río *43 B7 river* S Argentina
Santa Elena *30 B1* Cayo, W Belize
Santa Fe *42 C4* Santa Fe, C Argentina
Santa Fe *26 D1 state capital* New Mexico, SW USA
Santa Fe *see* Bogotá
Santa Fe de Bogotá *see* Bogotá
Santa Genoveva *28 B3 mountain* NW Mexico
Santa Isabel *122 C3 var.* Bughotu. *island* N Solomon Islands
Santa Isabel *see* Malabo
Santa Lucia Range *25 B7 mountain range* California, W USA
Santa Margarita, Isla *28 B3 island* NW Mexico
Santa Maria *41 E5* Rio Grande do Sul, S Brazil
Santa Maria *25 B7* California, USA
Santa Maria *70 A5 island* Azores, Portugal, NE Atlantic Ocean
Santa Maria del Buen Aire *see* Buenos Aires
Santa María, Isla *38 A5 var.* Isla Floreana, Charles Island. *island* Galápagos Islands, Ecuador, E Pacific Ocean
Santa Marta *36 B1* Magdalena, N Colombia
Santa Maura *see* Lefkáda
Santa Monica *24 D1* California, W USA
Santana *54 E2* São Tomé, C Sao Tome and Principe, Africa
Santander *70 D1* Cantabria, N Spain
Santarém *41 E2* Pará, N Brazil
Santarém *70 B3 anc.* Scalabis. Santarém, W Portugal
Santa Rosa *42 C4* La Pampa, C Argentina
Santa Rosa *see* Santa Rosa de Copán
Santa Rosa de Copán *30 C2 var.* Santa Rosa. Copán, W Honduras
Santa Rosa Island *25 B8 island* California, W USA
Santa Uxía de Ribeira *70 B1 var.* Ribeira NW Spain
Sant Carles de la Rápida *see* Sant Carles de la Ràpita
Sant Carles de la Ràpita *71 F3 var.* Sant Carles de la Rápida. Cataluña, NE Spain
Santiago *42 B4 var.* Gran Santiago. *country capital* (Chile) Santiago, C Chile
Santiago *33 E3 var.* Santiago de los Caballeros. N Dominican Republic
Santiago *31 F5* Veraguas, S Panama
Santiago *see* Santiago de Compostela
Santiago *52 A3 var.* São Tiago. *island* Ilhas de Sotavento, S Cape Verde (Cabo Verde)
Santiago *see* Santiago de Cuba, Cuba
Santiago de Compostela *70 B1 var.* Santiago, *Eng.* Compostella; *anc.* Campus Stellae. Galicia, NW Spain
Santiago de Cuba *32 C3 var.* Santiago. Santiago de Cuba, E Cuba
Santiago de Guayaquil *see* Guayaquil
Santiago del Estero *42 C3* Santiago del Estero, C Argentina
Santiago de los Caballeros *see* Santiago, Dominican Republic
Santiago de los Caballeros *see* Ciudad de Guatemala, Guatemala
Santiago Pinotepa Nacional *see* Pinotepa Nacional
Santiago, Río *38 B2 river* N Peru
Santi Quaranta *see* Sarandë
Santissima Trinidad *see* Keelung
San Joan d'Alacant *71 F4 Cast.* San Juan de Alicante. Comunitat Valenciana, E Spain
Sant Julià de Lòria *69 A8* Sant Julià de Lòria, SW Andorra Europe
Santo *see* Espiritu Santo
Santo Antão *52 A2 island* Ilhas de Barlavento, N Cape Verde (Cabo Verde)
Santo António *54 E1* Príncipe, N Sao Tome and Principe, Africa
Santo Domingo *33 D3 prev.* Ciudad Trujillo. *country capital* (Dominican Republic) SE Dominican Republic
Santo Domingo de los Colorados *38 B1* Pichincha, NW Ecuador
Santo Domingo Tehuantepec *see* Tehuantepec
Santorini *see* Thíra
Santorini *83 D7 island* Kykládes, Greece, Aegean Sea
San Tomé de Guayana *see* Ciudad Guayana
Santos *41 F4* São Paulo, S Brazil
Santos Plateau *35 D5 undersea plateau* SW Atlantic Ocean
Santo Tomé *42 D3* Corrientes, NE Argentina
Santo Tomé de Guayana *see* Ciudad Guayana
San Valentín, Cerro *43 A6 mountain* S Chile
San Vicente *30 C3* San Vicente, C El Salvador
São Francisco, Rio *41 F3 river* E Brazil
Sao Hill *51 C7* Iringa, S Tanzania
São João da Madeira *70 B2* Aveiro, N Portugal
São Jorge *70 A5 island* Azores, Portugal, NE Atlantic Ocean
São Luís *41 F2 state capital* Maranhão, NE Brazil
São Mandol *see* São Manuel, Rio
São Manuel, Rio *41 E3 var.* São Mandol, Teles Pirés. *river* C Brazil
São Marcos, Baía de *41 F1 bay* N Brazil
São Miguel *70 A5 island* Azores, Portugal, NE Atlantic Ocean
Saona, Isla *33 E3 island* SE Dominican Republic
Saône *69 D5 river* E France
São Nicolau *52 A3 Eng.* Saint Nicholas. *island* Ilhas de Barlavento, N Cape Verde (Cabo Verde)
São Paulo *41 E4 state capital* São Paulo, S Brazil
São Paulo *41 E4 off.* Estado de São Paulo. *state/region* S Brazil
São Paulo de Loanda *see* Luanda
São Paulo, Estado de *see* São Paulo
São Pedro do Rio Grande do Sul *see* Rio Grande
São Roque, Cabo de *41 G2 headland* E Brazil
São Salvador *see* Salvador, Brazil
São Salvador/São Salvador do Congo *see* M'Banza Congo, Angola
São Tiago *see* Santiago
São Tomé *55 A5 country capital* (Sao Tome and Principe) São Tomé, S Sao Tome and Principe
São Tomé *54 E2 Eng.* Saint Thomas. *island* S Sao Tome and Principe
Sao Tome and Principe *54 D1 off.* Democratic Republic of Sao Tome and Principe. *country* E Atlantic Ocean
Sao Tome and Principe, Democratic Republic of *see* Sao Tome and Principe
São Tomé, Pico de *54 D2 mountain* São Tomé, C Sao Tome and Principe, Africa
São Vicente *52 A3 Eng.* Saint Vincent. *island* Ilhas de Barlavento, N Cape Verde (Cabo Verde)
São Vicente, Cabo de *70 B5 Eng.* Cape Saint Vincent, *Port.* Cabode São Vicente. *cape* S Portugal
São Vicente, Cabo de *see* São Vicente, Cabo de
Sápai *see* Sápes
Sapele *53 F5* Delta, S Nigeria
Sápes *82 D3 var.* Sápai. Anatolikí Makedonía kai Thráki, NE Greece
Sapir *97 B7 prev.* Sappir. Southern, S Israel
Sa Pobla *71 G3* Mallorca, Spain, W Mediterranean Sea
Sappir *see* Sapir
Sapporo *108 D2* Hokkaidō, NE Japan
Sapri *75 D6* Campania, S Italy
Sapulpa *27 G1* Oklahoma, C USA
Saqqez *98 C2 var.* Saghez, Sakiz, Saqqiz. Kordestān, NW Iran
Saqqiz *see* Saqqez
Sara Buri *115 C5 var.* Saraburi. Saraburi, C Thailand
Saraburi *see* Sara Buri
Saragossa *see* Zaragoza
Saragt *see* Sarahs
Saraguro *38 B2* Loja, S Ecuador
Sarahs *100 D3 var.* Saragt, *Rus.* Serakhs. Ahal Welaýaty, S Turkmenistan
Sarajevo *78 C4 country capital* (Bosnia and Herzegovina) Federacija Bosna I Hercegovina, SE Bosnia and Herzegovina
Sarakhs *98 E2* Khorāsān-Razavī, NE Iran
Saraktash *89 D6* Orenburgskaya Oblast', W Russia
Saran' *92 C4 Kaz.* Saran. Karagandy, C Kazakhstan
Saranda *see* Sarandë
Sarandë *79 C7 var.* Saranda, *It.* Porto Edda; *prev.* Santi Quaranta. Vlorë, S Albania
Saransk *89 C5* Respublika Mordoviya, W Russia
Sarasota *21 E4* Florida, SE USA
Saratov *92 B3* Saratovskaya Oblast', W Russia
Saravan/Saravane *see* Salavan
Sarawak *116 D3 state* East Malaysia
Sarawak *see* Kuching
Sarcelles *68 D1* Val-d'Oise, Île-de-France, N France Europe
Sardegna *75 A5 Eng.* Sardinia. *island* Italy, C Mediterranean Sea
Sardinia *see* Sardegna
Sarera, Teluk *see* Cenderawasih, Teluk
Sargasso Sea *44 B4 sea* W Atlantic Ocean
Sargodha *112 C2* Punjab, NE Pakistan
Sarh *54 C4 prev.* Fort-Archambault. Moyen-Chari, S Chad
Sārī *98 D2 var.* Sari, Sāri. Māzandarān, N Iran
Saría *83 E7 island* SE Greece
Sarıkamış *95 F3* Kars, NE Turkey (Türkiye)
Sarikol Range *101 G3 Rus.* Sarykol'skiy Khrebet. *mountain range* China/Tajikistan
Sark *67 D8 Fr.* Sercq. *island* Channel Islands
Şarkışla *94 D3* Sivas, C Turkey (Türkiye)
Sarmiento *43 B6* Chubut, S Argentina
Sarnia *16 C5* Ontario, S Canada
Sarny *86 C1* Rivnens'ka Oblast', NW Ukraine
Sarochyna *85 D5 Rus.* Sorochino. Vitsyebskaya Voblasts', N Belarus
Sarov *89 C5 prev.* Sarova. Respublika Mordoviya, SW Russia
Sarova *see* Sarov
Sarpsborg *63 B6* Østfold, S Norway
Sarrebruck *see* Saarbrücken
Sartène *69 E7* Corse, France, C Mediterranean Sea
Sarthe *68 B4 river* N France
Sárti *82 C4* Kentrikí Makedonía, N Greece
Saruhan *see* Manisa
Saryarqa *92 C4 var.* Kazakhskiy Melkosopochnik. *uplands* C Kazakhstan
Sarykol'skiy Khrebet *see* Sarikol Range
Sary-Tash *101 F2* Oshskaya Oblast', SW Kyrgyzstan
Saryyesik-Atyrau, Peski *101 G1 desert* E Kazakhstan
Sasebo *109 A7* Nagasaki, Kyūshū, SW Japan
Saskatchewan *15 F5 province* SW Canada
Saskatchewan *15 F5 river* Manitoba/ Saskatchewan, C Canada
Saskatoon *15 F5* Saskatchewan, S Canada
Sasovo *89 B5* Ryazanskaya Oblast', W Russia
Sassandra *52 D5* S Ivory Coast
Sassandra *52 D5 var.* Ibo, Sassandra Fleuve. *river* S Ivory Coast
Sassandra Fleuve *see* Sassandra
Sassari *75 A5* Sardegna, Italy, C Mediterranean Sea
Sassenheim *64 C3* Zuid-Holland, W Netherlands
Sassnitz *72 D2* Mecklenburg-Vorpommern, NE Germany
Sathmar *see* Satu Mare
Sátoraljaújhely *77 D6* Borsod-Abaúj-Zemplén, NE Hungary
Satpura Range *112 D4 mountain range* C India
Satsuma-Sendai *109 A8* Kagoshima, Kyūshū, SW Japan
Satsunan-shoto *108 A3 island group* Nansei-shotō, SW Japan Asia
Sattanen *62 D3* Lappi, NE Finland
Satu Mare *86 B3 Ger.* Sathmar, *Hung.* Szatmárnémeti. Satu Mare, NW Romania
Sau *see* Sava
Saudi Arabia *99 B5 off.* Kingdom of Saudi Arabia, Al 'Arabīyah as Su'ūdīyah, *Ar.* Al Mamlakah al 'Arabīyah as Su'ūdīyah. *country* SW Asia
Saudi Arabia, Kingdom of *see* Saudi Arabia
Sauer *see* Sûre
Saugor *see* Sāgar
Saulkrasti *84 C3* Rīga, C Latvia
Sault Sainte Marie *16 C4* Michigan, N USA
Sault Sainte Marie *18 C1* Michigan, N USA
Sault Ste. Marie *16 C4* Ontario, S Canada
Saumur *68 B4* Maine-et-Loire, NW France
Saurimo *56 C1 Port.* Henrique de Carvalho, Vila Henrique de Carvalho. Lunda Sul, NE Angola
Sava *85 E6* Mahilyowskaya Voblasts', E Belarus
Sava *78 B3 Eng.* Save, *Ger.* Sau, *Hung.* Száva. *river* SE Europe
Savá *30 D2* Colón, N Honduras
Savai'i *123 E4 island* NW Samoa
Savannah *21 E2* Georgia, SE USA
Savannah River *21 E2 river* Georgia/South Carolina, SE USA
Savannakhét *see* Khanthabouli
Savanna-La-Mar *32 A5* W Jamaica
Savaria *see* SzombathelySave *see* Sava
Save, Rio *57 E3 var.* Sabi. *river* Mozambique/ Zimbabwe
Saverne *68 E3 var.* Zabern; *anc.* Tres Tabernae. Bas-Rhin, NE France
Savigliano *74 A2* Piemonte, NW Italy
Savigsivik *see* Savissivik
Savinski *see* Savinskiy
Savinskiy *88 C3 var.* Savinski. Arkhangel'skaya Oblast', NW Russia
Savissivik *60 D1 var.* Savigsivik. Avannaata, N Greenland
Savoie *69 D5 cultural region* E France
Savona *74 A2* Liguria, NW Italy
Savu Sea *117 E5 Ind.* Laut Sawu. *sea* S Indonesia
Sawakin *see* Suakin
Sawdirī *see* Sodiri
Sawhāj *see* Sūhāj
Şawqirah *99 D6 var.* Suqrah. S Oman
Sawu, Laut *see* Savu Sea
Saxe *see* Sachsen
Saxony *see* Sachsen
Sayaboury *see* Xaignabouli
Sayanskiy Khrebet *90 D3 mountain range* S Russia
Saýat *100 D3 Rus.* Sayat. Lebap Welaýaty, E Turkmenistan
Sayaxché *30 B2* Petén, N Guatemala
Şaydā/Sayida *see* Saïda
Sayḥūt *99 D6* E Yemen
Saynshand *105 E2* Dornogovĭ, SE Mongolia
Sayre *19 E3* Pennsylvania, NE USA
Say'ūn *99 C6 var.* Saywūn. C Yemen
Saywūn *see* Say'ūn
Scalabis *see* Santarém
Scandinavia *44 D2 geophysical region* NW Europe
Scarborough *67 D5* N England, United Kingdom
Scarpanto *see* Kárpathos
Scebeli *see* Shebeli
Schaan *72 E1* W Liechtenstein Europe
Schaerbeek *65 C6* Brussels, C Belgium
Schaffhausen *73 B7 Fr.* Schaffhouse. Schaffhausen, N Switzerland
Schaffhouse *see* Schaffhausen
Schagen *64 C2* Noord-Holland, NW Netherlands
Schaulen *see* Šiauliai
Schebschi Mountains *see* Shebshi Mountains
Scheessel *72 B3* Niedersachsen, NW Germany
Schefferville *17 E2* Québec, E Canada
Schelde *see* Scheldt
Scheldt *65 B5 Dut.* Schelde, *Fr.* Escaut. *river* W Europe
Schell Creek Range *25 D5 mountain range* Nevada, W USA
Schenectady *19 F3* New York, NE USA
Schertz *27 G4* Texas, SW USA
Schiermonnikoog *64 D1 Fris.* Skiermûntseach. *island* Waddeneilanden, N Netherlands
Schijndel *64 D4* Noord-Brabant, S Netherlands
Schil *see* Jiu
Schiltigheim *68 E3* Bas-Rhin, NE France
Schivelbein *see* Świdwin
Schleswig *72 B2* Schleswig-Holstein, N Germany
Schleswig-Holstein *72 B2 state* N Germany
Schlettstadt *see* Sélestat
Schlochau *see* Człuchów
Schneekoppe *see* Sněžka
Schneidemühl *see* Piła
Schoden *see* Skuodas
Schönebeck *72 C4* Sachsen-Anhalt, C Germany
Schönlanke *see* Trzcianka
Schooten *see* Schoten
Schoten *65 C5 var.* Schooten. Antwerpen, N Belgium
Schouwen *64 B4 island* SW Netherlands
Schwabenalb *see* Schwäbische Alb
Schwäbische Alb *73 B6 var.* Schwabenalb, *Eng.* Swabian Jura. *mountain range* S Germany
Schwandorf *73 C5* Bayern, SE Germany
Schwaz *73 C7* Tirol, W Austria
Schweidnitz *see* Świdnica
Schweinfurt *73 B5* Bayern, SE Germany
Schweiz *see* Switzerland
Schwerin *72 C3* Mecklenburg-Vorpommern, N Germany
Schwertberg *see* Świecie
Schwiebus *see* Świebodzin
Schwyz *73 B7 var.* Schwiz. Schwyz, C Switzerland
Schyl *see* Jiu
Scio *see* Chíos
Scoresby Sound/Scoresbysund *see* Ittoqqortoormiit
Scoresby Sund *see* Kangertittivaq
Scotia Sea *35 C8 sea* SW Atlantic Ocean
Scotland *66 C3 cultural region* Scotland, United Kingdom
Scott Base *132 B4 NZ research station* Antarctica
Scott Island *132 B5 island* Antarctica
Scottsbluff *22 D3* Nebraska, C USA
Scottsboro *20 D1* Alabama, S USA
Scottsdale *26 B2* Arizona, SW USA
Scranton *19 F3* Pennsylvania, NE USA
Scrobesbyrig' *see* Shrewsbury
Scupi *see* Skopje
Scutari *see* Shkodër
Scutari, Lake *79 C5 Alb.* Liqeni i Shkodrës, *Croatian* Skadarsko Jezero. *lake* Albania/ Montenegro
Scyros *see* Skýros
Searcy *20 B1* Arkansas, C USA
Seattle *24 B2* Washington, NW USA
Sébaco *30 D3* Matagalpa, W Nicaragua
Sebaste/Sebastia *see* Sivas
Sebastián Vizcaíno, Bahía *28 A2 bay* NW Mexico
Sebastopol *see* Sevastopol
Sebenico *see* Šibenik
Sechura, Bahía de *38 A3 bay* NW Peru
Secunderābād *112 D5 var.* Sikandarabad. Telangana, C India
Sedan *68 D3* Ardennes, N France
Seddon *129 D5* Marlborough, South Island, New Zealand
Seddonville *129 C5* West Coast, South Island, New Zealand
Sédhiou *52 B3* SW Senegal
Sedlez *see* Siedlce
Sedona *26 B2* Arizona, SW USA
Sedunum *see* Sion

Seeland see Sjælland
Seenu Atoll see Addu Atoll
Seesen 72 B4 Niedersachsen, C Germany
Segestica see Sisak
Segezha 88 B3 Respublika Kareliya, NW Russia
Seghedin see Szeged
Segna see Senj
Segodunum see Rodez
Ségou 52 D3 var. Segu. Ségou, C Mali
Segovia 70 D2 Castilla y León, C Spain
Segoviao Wangkí see Coco, Río
Segu see Ségou
Séguédine 53 H2 Agadez, NE Niger
Seguin 27 G4 Texas, SW USA
Segura 71 E4 river S Spain
Seinäjoki 63 D5 Swe. Östermyra. Etelä-Pohjanmaa, W Finland
Seine 68 D1 river N France
Seine, Baie de la 68 B3 bay N France
Sejong 106 E4 var. Sejong City. administrative capital (South Korea) C South Korea
Sejong City see Sejong
Sekondi see Sekondi-Takoradi
Sekondi-Takoradi 53 E5 var. Sekondi. S Ghana
Selânik see Thessaloníki
Selenga 105 E1 Mong. Selenge Mörön. river Mongolia/Russia
Selenge Mörön see Selenga
Sélestat 68 E4 Ger. Schlettstadt. Bas-Rhin, NE France
Seleucia see Silifke
Selfoss 61 E5 Sudhurland, SW Iceland
Sélibabi 52 C3 var. Sélibaby. Guidimaka, S Mauritania
Sélibaby see Sélibabi
Selma 25 C6 California, W USA
Selway River 24 D2 river Idaho, NW USA
Selwyn Range 126 B3 mountain range Queensland, C Australia
Selzaete see Zelzate
Semarang 116 C5 var. Samarang. Jawa, C Indonesia
Sembé 55 B5 Sangha, NW Congo
Semendria see Smederevo
Semey 92 D4 prev. Semipalatinsk. Vostochnyy Kazakhstan, E Kazakhstan
Semechevo see Syemyezhava
Seminole 27 E3 Texas, SW USA
Seminole, Lake 20 D3 reservoir Florida/Georgia, SE USA
Semipalatinsk see Semey
Semnān 98 D3 var. Samnān. Semnān, N Iran
Semois 65 C8 river SE Belgium
Sendai 108 D4 Miyagi, Honshū, C Japan
Sendai-wan 108 D4 bay E Japan
Senec 77 C6 Ger. Wartberg, Hung. Szenc; prev. Szempcz. Bratislavský Kraj, W Slovakia
Senegal 52 B3 off. Republic of Senegal, Fr. Sénégal. country W Africa
Senegal 52 C3 Fr. Sénégal. river W Africa
Senegal, Republic of see Senegal
Senftenberg 72 D4 Brandenburg, E Germany
Senia see Senj
Senica 77 C6 Ger. Senitz, Hung. Szenice. Trnavský Kraj, W Slovakia
Seniça see Sjenica
Senitz see Senica
Senj 78 A3 Ger. Zengg, It. Segna; anc. Senia. Lika-Senj, NW Croatia
Senja 62 C2 prev. Senjen. island N Norway
Senjen see Senja
Senkaku Islands see Senkaku-shoto
Senkaku-shoto 108 A3 var. Senkaku Islands, Chin. Diaoyutai Lieyu, Diaoyutai Qundao. disputed island group SW Japan
Senlis 68 C3 Oise, N France
Sennar 50 C4 var. Sannār. Sinnar, C Sudan
Senones see Sens
Sens 68 C3 anc. Agendicum, Senones. Yonne, C France
Sensburg see Mrągowo
Sên, Stœng 115 D5 river C Cambodia
Senta 78 D3 Hung. Zenta. Vojvodina, N Serbia
Seo de Urgel see La See d'Urgel
Seoul 107 E4 off. Seoul Teukbyeolsi, prev. Sŏul, Jap. Keijō; prev. Kyŏngsŏng. country capital (South Korea) NW South Korea
Seoul Teukbyeolsi see Seoul
Şepşi-Sângeorz/Sepsiszentgyőrgy see Sfântu Gheorghe
Sept-Îles 17 E3 Québec, SE Canada
Seraing 65 D6 Liège, E Belgium
Serakhs see Sarahs
Seram, Laut 117 F4 Eng. Ceram Sea. sea E Indonesia
Pulau Seram 117 F4 var. Serang, Eng. Ceram. island Maluku, E Indonesia
Serang 116 C5 Jawa, C Indonesia
Serang see Seram, Pulau
Serasan, Selat 116 C3 strait Indonesia/Malaysia
Serbia 78 D4 off. Republic of Serbia; prev. Federal Republic of Serbia, Yugoslavia, Serb. Srbija, Republika Srbija. country SE Europe
Serbia, Federal Republic of see Serbia
Serbia, Republic of see Serbia
Sercq see Sark
Serdar 100 C2 prev. Rus. Gyzyrlabat, Kizyl-Arvat. Balkan Welaýaty, W Turkmenistan
Serdica see Sofia
Serdobol' see Sortavala
Serenje 56 D2 Central, E Zambia
Seres see Sérres
Seret/Sereth see Siret
Serhetabat 100 D4 prev. Rus. Gushgy, Kushka. Mary Welaýaty, S Turkmenistan
Sérifos 83 C6 anc. Seriphos. island Kykládes, Greece, Aegean Sea
Seriphos see Sérifos
Serov 92 C3 Sverdlovskaya Oblast', C Russia
Serowe 56 D3 Central, SE Botswana
Serpa Pinto see Menongue
Serpent's Mouth, The 37 F2 Sp. Boca de la Serpiente. strait Trinidad and Tobago/Venezuela
Serpiente, Boca de la see Serpent's Mouth, The
Serpukhov 89 B5 Moskovskaya Oblast', W Russia
Sérrai see Sérres
Serrana, Cayo de 31 F2 island group NW Colombia South America
Serranilla, Cayo de 31 F2 island group NW Colombia South America Caribbean Sea
Serravalle 74 E1 N San Marino
Sérres 82 C3 var. Seres; prev. Sérrai. Kentrikí Makedonía, NE Greece
Sesdlets see Siedlce
Sesto San Giovanni 74 B2 Lombardia, N Italy
Sesvete 78 B2 Zagreb, N Croatia
Setabis see Xàtiva
Sète 69 C6 prev. Cette. Hérault, S France
Setesdal 63 A6 valley S Norway
Sétif 49 E2 var. Stif. N Algeria
Setté Cama 55 A6 Ogooué-Maritime, SW Gabon
Setúbal 70 B4 Eng. Saint Ubes, Saint Yves. Setúbal, W Portugal
Setúbal, Baía de 70 B4 bay W Portugal
Seul, Lac 16 B3 lake Ontario, S Canada
Sevan 95 G2 C Armenia
Sevana Lich 95 G3 Eng. Lake Sevan, Rus. Ozero Sevan. lake E Armenia
Sevan, Lake/Sevan, Ozero see Sevana Lich
Sevastopol 87 F5 Eng. Sebastopol. Misto Sevastopol, S Ukraine
Severn 16 B2 river Ontario, S Canada
Severn 67 D6 Wel. Hafren. river England/Wales, United Kingdom
Severna Makedonija see North Macedonia
Severnaya Dvina 88 C4 var. Northern Dvina. river NW Russia
Severnaya Zemlya 93 E2 var. Nicholas II Land. island group N Russia
Severnyy 88 E3 Respublika Komi, NW Russia
Severodonetsk see Sievierodonetsk
Severodvinsk 88 C3 prev. Molotov, Sudostroy. Arkhangel'skaya Oblast', NW Russia
Severomorsk 88 C2 Murmanskaya Oblast', NW Russia
Seversk 92 D4 Tomskaya Oblast', C Russia
Sevier Lake 22 A4 lake Utah, W USA
Sevilla 70 C4 Eng. Seville; anc. Hispalis. Andalucía, SW Spain
Seville see Sevilla
Sevlievo 82 D2 Gabrovo, N Bulgaria
Sevluš/Sevlyush see Vynohradiv
Seward's Folly see Alaska
Seychelles 57 G1 off. Republic of Seychelles. country W Indian Ocean
Seychelles, Republic of see Seychelles
Seyðisfjörður 61 E5 Austurland, E Iceland
Seydi 100 D2 Rus. Seydi; prev. Neftezavodsk. Lebap Welaýaty, E Turkmenistan
Seyhan see Adana
Sfákia see Chóra Sfakíon
Sfântu Gheorghe 86 C4 Ger. Sankt-Georgen, Hung. Sepsiszentgyőrgy; prev. Şepşi-Sângeorz, Sfintu Gheorghe. Covasna, C Romania
Sfax 49 F2 Ar. Şafāqis. E Tunisia
Sfintu Gheorghe see Sfântu Gheorghe
's-Gravenhage 64 B4 var. Den Haag, Eng. The Hague, Fr. La Haye. country capital (Netherlands-seat of government) Zuid-Holland, W Netherlands
's-Gravenzande 64 B4 Zuid-Holland, W Netherlands
Shaan/Shaanxi Sheng see Shaanxi
Shaanxi 106 B5 var. Shaan, Shaanxi Sheng, Shan-hsi, Shenshi, Shensi. province C China
Shabani see Zvishavane
Shabeelle, Webi see Shebeli
Shache 104 A3 var. Yarkant. Xinjiang Uygur Zizhiqu, NW China
Shacheng see Huailai
Shackleton Ice Shelf 132 D3 ice shelf Antarctica
Shaddādī see Ash Shadādah
Shāhābād see Eslāmābād
Sha Hi see Orūmīyeh, Daryācheh-ye
Shahjahanabad see Delhi
Shahr-e Kord 98 C3 var. Shahr Kord. Chahār Maḩall va Bakhtiārī, C Iran
Shahr Kord see Shahr-e Kord
Shāhrūd 98 D2 prev. Emāmrūd, Emāmshahr. Semnān, N Iran
Shalkar see Shalqar
Shalqar 92 B4 var. Shalkar, Chelkar. Aktyubinsk, W Kazakhstan
Shām, Bādiyat ash see Syrian Desert
Shana see Kuril'sk
Shandī see Shendi
Shandong 106 D4 var. Lu, Shandong Sheng, Shantung. province E China
Shandong Sheng see Shandong
Shanghai 106 D5 var. Shang-hai. Shanghai Shi, E China
Shangrao 106 D5 Jiangxi, S China
Shan-hsi see Shaanxi, China
Shan-hsi see Shanxi, China
Shannon 67 A6 Ir. An tSionainn. river W Ireland
Shan Plateau 114 B3 plateau E Myanmar (Burma)
Shansi see Shanxi
Shantar Islands see Shantarskiye Ostrova
Shantarskiye Ostrova 93 G3 Eng. Shantar Islands. island group E Russia
Shantou 106 D6 var. Shan-t'ou, Swatow. Guangdong, S China
Shan-t'ou see Shantou
Shantung see Shandong
Shanxi 106 C4 var. Jin, Shan-hsi, Shansi, Shanxi Sheng. province C China
Shan Xian see Sanmenxia
Shanxi Sheng see Shanxi
Shaoguan 106 C6 var. Shao-kuan, Cant. Kukong; prev. Ch'u-chiang. Guangdong, S China
Shao-kuan see Shaoguan
Shaqrā' 98 B4 Ar Riyāḑ, C Saudi Arabia
Shaqrā see Shuqrah
Shar 92 D5 var. Charsk. Vostochnyy Kazakhstan, E Kazakhstan
Shari 108 D2 Hokkaidō, NE Japan
Shari see Chari
Sharjah see Ash Shāriqah
Shark Bay 125 A5 bay Western Australia
Sharqī, Al Jabal ash/Sharqi, Jebel esh see Anti-Lebanon
Shashe 56 D3 var. Shashi. river Botswana/Zimbabwe
Shashi see Shashe
Shatskiy Rise 103 G1 undersea rise N Pacific Ocean
Shawnee 27 G1 Oklahoma, C USA
Shaykh, Jabal ash see Hermon, Mount
Shchadryn 85 D7 Rus. Shchedrin. Homyel'skaya Voblasts', SE Belarus
Shchedrin see Shchadryn
Shcheglovsk see Kemerovo
Shchëkino 89 B5 Tul'skaya Oblast', W Russia
Shchors see Snovsk
Shchuchin see Shchuchyn
Shchuchinsk 92 C4 prev. Shchuchye. Akmola, N Kazakhstan
Shchuchye see Shchuchinsk
Shchuchyn 85 B5 Pol. Szczuczyn Nowogródzki, Rus. Shchuchin. Hrodzyenskaya Voblasts', W Belarus
Shebekino 89 A6 Belgorodskaya Oblast', W Russia
Shebelē Wenz, Wabē see Shebeli
Shebeli 51 D5 Amh. Wabē Shebelē Wenz, It. Scebeli, Som. Webi Shabeelle. river Ethiopia/Somalia
Sheberghān see Shibirghān
Sheboygan 18 B2 Wisconsin, N USA
Shebshi Mountains 54 A4 var. Schebschi Mountains. mountain range E Nigeria
Shechem see Nablus
Shedadi see Ash Shadādah
Sheffield 67 D5 N England, United Kingdom
Shekhem see Nablus
Sheki see Şäki
Shelby 22 B1 Montana, NW USA
Sheldon 23 F3 Iowa, C USA
Shelekhov Gulf see Shelikhova, Zaliv
Shelikhova, Zaliv 93 G2 Eng. Shelekhov Gulf. gulf E Russia
Shendi 50 C4 var. Shandī. River Nile, NE Sudan
Shengking see Liaoning
Shenking see Liaoning
Shenshi/Shensi see Shaanxi
Shenyang 106 D3 Chin. Shen-yang, Eng. Moukden, Mukden; prev. Fengtien. province capital Liaoning, NE China
Shen-yang see Shenyang
Shepetivka 86 D2 Rus. Shepetovka. Khmel'nyts'ka Oblast', NW Ukraine
Shepetovka see Shepetivka
Shepparton 127 C7 Victoria, SE Australia
Sherbrooke 17 E4 Québec, SE Canada
Shereik 50 C3 River Nile, N Sudan
Sheridan 22 C2 Wyoming, C USA
Sherman 27 G2 Texas, SW USA
's-Hertogenbosch 64 C4 Fr. Bois-le-Duc, Ger. Herzogenbusch. Noord-Brabant, S Netherlands
Shetland Islands 66 D1 island group NE Scotland, United Kingdom
Shevchenko see Aqtaū
Shiberghān/Shiberghan see Shibirghān
Shibirghān 101 E3 var. Sheberghān, Shiberghan, Shiberghān. Jowzjān, N Afghanistan
Shibetsu 108 D2 var. Sibetu. Hokkaidō, NE Japan
Shibh Jazīrat Sīnā' 50 C2 var. Sinai Peninsula, Ar. Shibh Jazirat Sīnā', Sīnā'. physical region NE Egypt
Shibushi-wan 109 B8 bay SW Japan
Shigatse see Xigazê
Shih-chia-chuang/Shihmen see Shijiazhuang
Shihezi 104 C2 Xinjiang Uygur Zizhiqu, NW China
Shiichi see Shyichy
Shijiazhuang 106 C4 var. Shih-chia-chuang; prev. Shihmen. province capital Hebei, E China
Shikarpur 112 B3 Sindh, S Pakistan
Shikoku 109 C7 var. Sikoku. island SW Japan
Shikoku Basin 103 F2 var. Sikoku Basin. undersea basin N Philippine Sea
Shikotan, Ostrov 108 E2 Jap. Shikotan-tō. island NE Russia
Shikotan-tō see Shikotan, Ostrov
Shilabo 51 D5 Sumalē, E Ethiopia
Shiliguri 113 F3 prev. Siliguri. West Bengal, NE India
Shilka 93 F4 river S Russia
Shillong 113 G3 state capital Meghālaya, NE India
Shimanto see Nakamura
Shimbir Berris see Shimbiris
Shimbiris 50 E4 var. Shimbir Berris. mountain N Somalia
Shimoga see Shivamogga
Shimonoseki 109 A7 var. Simonoseki, hist. Akamagaseki, Bakan. Yamaguchi, Honshū, SW Japan
Shinano-gawa 109 C5 var. Sinano Gawa. river Honshū, C Japan
Shīndand 100 D4 prev. Shīndand. Herāt, W Afghanistan
Shindand see Shīndand
Shingū 109 C6 var. Singû. Wakayama, Honshū, SW Japan
Shinjō 108 D4 var. Sinzyô. Yamagata, Honshū, C Japan
Shinyanga 51 C7 Shinyanga, NW Tanzania
Shiprock 26 C1 New Mexico, SW USA
Shīrāz 98 D4 var. Shirāz. Fārs, S Iran
Shishchitsy see Shyshchytsy
Shivamogga 110 C2 prev. Shimoga. Karnātaka, W India
Shivpuri 112 D3 Madhya Pradesh, C India
Shizugawa 108 D4 Miyagi, Honshū, NE Japan
Shizuoka 109 D6 var. Sizuoka. Shizuoka, Honshū, S Japan
Shklov see Shklow
Shklow 85 D6 Rus. Shklov. Mahilyowskaya Voblasts', E Belarus
Shkodër 79 C5 var. Shkodra, It. Scutari, Croatian Skadar. Shkodër, NW Albania
Shkodra see Shkodër
Shkodrës, Liqeni i see Scutari, Lake
Shkumbinit, Lumi i 79 C6 var. Shkumbî, Shkumbin. river C Albania
Shkumbî/Shkumbin see Shkumbinit, Lumi i
Sholāpur see Solāpur
Shostka 87 F1 Sums'ka Oblast', NE Ukraine
Show Low 26 B2 Arizona, SW USA
Show Me State see Missouri
Shpola 87 E3 Cherkas'ka Oblast', N Ukraine
Shqipëria/Shqipërisë, Republika e see Albania
Shreveport 20 A2 Louisiana, S USA
Shrewsbury 67 D6 hist. Scrobesbyrig'. W England, United Kingdom
Shu 92 C5 Kaz. Shū. Zhambyl, SE Kazakhstan
Shuang-liao see Liaoyuan
Shū, Kazakhstan see Shu
Shumagin Islands 14 B3 island group Alaska, USA
Shumen 82 D2 Shumen, NE Bulgaria
Shumilina 85 E5 Rus. Shumilino. Vitsyebskaya Voblasts', NE Belarus
Shumilino see Shumilina
Shunsen see Chuncheon
Shuqrah 99 B7 var. Shaqrā. SW Yemen
Shwebo 114 B3 Sagaing, C Myanmar (Burma)
Shyichy 85 C7 Rus. Shiichi. Homyel'skaya Voblasts', SE Belarus
Shymkent 92 B5 prev. Chimkent. Türkistan/Turkestan, S Kazakhstan
Shyshchytsy 85 C6 Rus. Shishchitsy. Minskaya Voblasts', C Belarus
Siam see Thailand
Siam, Gulf of see Thailand, Gulf of
Sian see Xi'an
Siang see Brahmaputra
Siangtan see Xiangtan
Šiauliai 84 B4 Ger. Schaulen. Šiauliai, N Lithuania
Siazan' see Siyäzän
Sibay 89 D6 Respublika Bashkortostan, W Russia
Šibenik 78 B4 It. Sebenico. Šibenik-Knin, S Croatia
Siberia see Sibir'
Siberoet see Siberut, Pulau
Siberut, Pulau 116 A4 prev. Siberoet. island Kepulauan Mentawai, W Indonesia
Sibi 112 B2 Baluchistan, SW Pakistan
Sibir' 93 E3 var. Siberia. physical region NE Russia
Sibiti 55 B6 Lékoumou, S Congo
Sibiu 86 B4 Ger. Hermannstadt, Hung. Nagyszeben. Sibiu, C Romania
Sibolga 116 B3 Sumatera, W Indonesia
Sibu 116 D3 Sarawak, East Malaysia
Sibut 54 C4 prev. Fort-Sibut. Kémo, S Central African Republic
Sibuyan Sea 117 E2 sea W Pacific Ocean
Sichon 115 C6 var. Ban Sichon, Si Chon. Nakhon Si Thammarat, SW Thailand
Si Chon see Sichon
Sichuan 106 B5 var. Chuan, Sichuan Sheng, Ssu-ch'uan, Szechuan, Szechwan. province C China
Sichuan Pendi 106 B5 basin C China
Sichuan Sheng see Sichuan
Sicilian Channel see Sicily, Strait of
Sicily 75 C7 Eng. Sicily; anc. Trinacria. island Italy, C Mediterranean Sea
Sicily, Strait of 75 B7 var. Sicilian Channel. strait C Mediterranean Sea
Sicuani 39 E4 Cusco, S Peru
Sidári 82 A4 Kérkyra, Iónia Nisiá, Greece, C Mediterranean Sea
Sidas 116 C4 Borneo, C Indonesia
Siderno 75 D7 Calabria, SW Italy
Sidhirókastron see Sidirókastro
Sidi Barrâni 50 A1 NW Egypt
Sidi Bel Abbès 48 D2 var. Sidi bel Abbès, Sidi-Bel-Abbès. NW Algeria
Sidirókastro 82 C3 prev. Sidhirókastron. Kentrikí Makedonía, NE Greece
Sidley, Mount 132 B4 mountain Antarctica
Sidney 22 D1 Montana, NW USA
Sidney 22 D4 Nebraska, C USA
Sidney 18 C4 Ohio, N USA
Sidon see Saïda
Sidra see Surt
Sidra/Sidra, Gulf of see Surt, Khalīj, N Libya
Siebenbürgen see Transylvania
Siedlce 76 E3 Ger. Sedlez, Rus. Sesdlets. Mazowieckie, C Poland
Siegen 72 B4 Nordrhein-Westfalen, W Germany
Siemiatycze 76 E3 Podlaskie, NE Poland
Siena 74 B3 Fr. Sienne; anc. Saena Julia. Toscana, C Italy
Sienne see Siena
Sieradz 76 C4 Sieradz, C Poland
Sierpc 76 D3 Mazowieckie, C Poland
Sierra Leone 52 C4 off. Republic of Sierra Leone. country W Africa
Sierra Leone Basin 44 C4 undersea basin E Atlantic Ocean
Sierra Leone, Republic of see Sierra Leone
Sierra Leone Ridge see Sierra Leone Rise
Sierra Leone Rise 44 C4 var. Sierra Leone Ridge, Sierra Leone Schwelle. undersea rise E Atlantic Ocean
Sierra Leone Schwelle see Sierra Leone Rise
Sierra Vista 26 B3 Arizona, SW USA
Sievierodonetsk 87 H3 prev. Syeverodonets'k, Rus. Severodonetsk. Luhans'ka Oblast', E Ukraine
Sífnos 83 C6 anc. Siphnos. island Kykládes, Greece, Aegean Sea
Sigli 116 A3 Sumatera, W Indonesia
Siglufjörður 61 E4 Nordhurland Vestra, N Iceland
Signal Peak 26 A2 mountain Arizona, SW USA
Signan see Xi'an
Siguatepeque 30 C2 Comayagua, W Honduras
Siguiri 52 D4 NE Guinea
Sihanoukville 115 D6 Khmer. Preăh Seihânŭ; prev. Kompong Som. Sihanoukville, SW Cambodia
Siilinjärvi 62 E4 Pohjois-Savo, C Finland
Siirt 95 F4 var. Sert; anc. Tigranocerta. Siirt, SE Turkey (Türkiye)
Sikandarabad see Secunderābād
Sikasso 52 D4 Sikasso, S Mali
Sikeston 23 H5 Missouri, C USA
Sikhote-Alin', Khrebet 93 G4 mountain range SE Russia
Siking see Xi'an
Siklós 77 C7 Baranya, SW Hungary
Sikoku see Shikoku
Sikoku Basin see Shikoku Basin
Šilalė 84 B4 Tauragė, W Lithuania
Silchar 113 G3 Assam, NE India
Silesia 76 B4 physical region SW Poland
Silifke 94 C4 anc. Seleucia. İçel, S Turkey (Türkiye)
Siliguri see Shiliguri
Siling Co 104 C5 lake W China
Silinhot see Xilinhot
Silistra 82 E1 var. Silistria; anc. Durostorum. Silistra, NE Bulgaria
Silistria see Silistra
Sillamäe 84 E2 Ger. Sillamäggi. Ida-Virumaa, NE Estonia
Sillamäggi see Sillamäe
Sillein see Žilina
Šilutė 84 B4 Ger. Heydekrug. Klaipėda, W Lithuania
Silvan 95 E4 Dıyarbakır, SE Turkey (Türkiye)
Silva Porto see Kuito
Silver State see Colorado
Silver State see Nevada
Simanichy 85 C7 Rus. Simonichi. Homyel'skaya Voblasts', SE Belarus
Simav 94 B3 Kütahya, W Turkey (Türkiye)
Simav Çayı 94 A3 river NW Turkey (Türkiye)
Simbirsk see Ul'yanovsk
Simeto 75 C7 river Sicilia, Italy, C Mediterranean Sea
Simeulue, Pulau 116 A3 island NW Indonesia
Simferopol 87 F5 Respublika Krym, S Ukraine
Simitla 82 C3 Blagoevgrad, SW Bulgaria
Şimlăul Silvaniei/Şimleul Silvaniei see Şimleu Silvaniei
Şimleu Silvaniei 86 B3 Hung. Szilágysomlyó; prev. Şimlăul Silvaniei, Şimleul Silvaniei. Sălaj, NW Romania
Simonichi see Simanichy
Simonoseki see Shimonoseki
Simpelveld 65 D6 Limburg, SE Netherlands
Simplon Pass 73 B8 pass S Switzerland
Simpson see Fort Simpson
Simpson Desert 126 B4 desert Northern Territory/South Australia
Sīnā' see Sīnā', Shibh Jazirat
Sīnā', Shibh Jazirat 50 C2 var. Sinai Peninsula, Sinai; Ar. Sīnā'. physical region NE Egypt
Sinai/Sinai Peninsula see Sīnā', Shibh Jazirat
Sinaia 86 C4 Prahova, SE Romania
Sinano Gawa see Shinano-gawa
Sincelejo 36 B2 Sucre, NW Colombia
Sind see Sindh
Sindelfingen 73 B6 Baden-Württemberg, SW Germany
Sindh 112 B3 var. Sind. province SE Pakistan
Sindi 84 D2 Ger. Zintenhof. Pärnumaa, SW Estonia
Sines 70 B4 Setúbal, S Portugal
Singan see Xi'an
Singapore 116 B3 country capital (Singapore) S Singapore
Singapore 116 A1 off. Republic of Singapore. country SE Asia
Singapore, Republic of see Singapore
Singen 73 B6 Baden-Württemberg, S Germany
Singida 51 C7 Singida, C Tanzania
Singkang 117 E4 Sulawesi, C Indonesia
Singkawang 116 C3 Borneo, C Indonesia
Singora see Songkhla
Singû see Shingū
Sining see Xining
Siniscola 75 A5 Sardegna, Italy, C Mediterranean Sea
Sinj 78 B4 Split-Dalmacija, SE Croatia
Sinkiang/Sinkiang Uighur Autonomous Region see Xinjiang Uygur Zizhiqu
Sinnamarie see Sinnamary
Sinnamary 37 H3 var. Sinnamarie. N French Guiana
Sinneh see Sanandaj
Sînnicolau Mare see Sânnicolau Mare
Sinoe, Lacul see Sinoie, Lacul
Sinoie, Lacul 86 D5 prev. Lacul Sinoe. lagoon SE Romania
Sinop 94 D2 anc. Sinope. Sinop, N Turkey (Türkiye)
Sinope see Sinop
Sinsheim 73 B6 Baden-Württemberg, SW Germany
Sint Maarten 33 G3 Eng. Saint Martin. Self-governing country of the Netherlands. E West Indies
Sint-Michielsgestel 64 C4 Noord-Brabant, S Netherlands
Sîn-Miclăuş see Gheorgheni
Sint-Niklaas 65 B5 Fr. Saint-Nicolas. Oost-Vlaanderen, N Belgium
Sint-Pieters-Leeuw 65 B6 Vlaams Brabant, C Belgium
Sintra 70 B3 prev. Cintra. Lisboa, W Portugal
Sinujiif 51 E5 Nugaal, NE Somalia
Sinus Aelaniticus see Aqaba, Gulf of
Sinus Gallicus see Lion, Golfe du
Sinyang see Xinyang
Sinzyô see Shinjō
Sion 73 A7 Ger. Sitten; anc. Sedunum. Valais, SW Switzerland
Sioux City 23 F3 Iowa, C USA
Sioux Falls 23 F3 South Dakota, N USA
Sioux State see North Dakota
Siphnos see Sífnos
Siping 106 D3 var. Ssu-p'ing, Szeping; prev. Ssu-p'ing-chieh. Jilin, NE China
Siple, Mount 132 A4 mountain Siple Island, Antarctica
Siquirres 31 E4 Limón, E Costa Rica
Siracusa 75 D7 Eng. Syracuse. Sicilia, Italy, C Mediterranean Sea
Sir Edward Pellew Group 126 B2 island group Northern Territory, NE Australia
Siret 86 C3 var. Siretul, Ger. Sereth, Rus. Seret. river Romania/Ukraine
Siretul see Siret
Siria see Syria
Sirikit Reservoir 114 C4 lake N Thailand
Sīrjān 98 D4 prev. Sa'īdābād. Kermān, S Iran
Sirna see Sýrna
Şırnak 95 F4 Şırnak, SE Turkey (Türkiye)
Síros see Sýros
Sirte see Surt
Sirte, Gulf of see Surt, Khalīj
Sirti, Gulf of see Surt, Khalīj
Şirvan 95 H3 prev. Äli-Bayramı. SE Azerbaijan
Sisak 78 B3 var. Siscia, Ger. Sissek, Hung. Sziszek; anc. Segestica. Sisak-Moslavina, C Croatia
Siscia see Sisak
Sisimiut 60 C3 var. Holsteinborg, Holsteinsborg, Holstenborg, Holstensborg. Qeqqata, S Greenland
Sissek see Sisak
Sīstān, Daryācheh-ye see Şāberī, Hāmūn-e
Sitaş Cristuru see Cristuru Secuiesc
Siteía 83 D8 var. Sitía. Kriti, Greece, E Mediterranean Sea
Sitges 71 G2 Cataluña, NE Spain
Sitia see Siteía
Sittang see Sittaung
Sittard 65 D5 Limburg, SE Netherlands
Sittaung 114 B4 var. Sittoung, Sittang. river S Myanmar (Burma)
Sitten see Sion
Sittoung see Sittaung
Sittwe 114 A3 var. Akyab. Rakhine State, W Myanmar (Burma)
Siuna 30 D3 Región Autónoma Atlántico Norte, NE Nicaragua
Siut see Asyūţ

Sivas *94 D3 anc.* Sebastia, Sebaste. Sivas, C Turkey (Türkiye)
Siverek *95 E4* Şanlıurfa, S Turkey (Türkiye)
Severskiy Donets *see* Siverskyi Donets
Siverskyi Donets *87 G2 var.* Donets, *Rus.* Severskiy Donets. *river* E Ukraine
Siwa *see* Sīwah
Sīwah *50 A2 var.* Siwa. NW Egypt
Six Counties, The *see* Northern Ireland
Six-Fours-les-Plages *69 D6* Var, SE France
Siyäzän *95 H2 Rus.* Siazan'. NE Azerbaijan
Sjar *see* Sääre
Sjenica *79 D5 Turk.* Seniça. Serbia, SW Serbia
Skadar *see* Shkodër
Skadarsko Jezero *see* Scutari, Lake
Skagerak *see* Skagerrak
Skagerrak *63 A6 var.* Skagerak. *channel* N Europe
Skagit River *24 B1 river* Washington, NW USA
Skalka *62 C3 lake* N Sweden
Skarżysko-Kamienna *76 D4* Świętokrzyskie, C Poland
Skaudvilė *84 B4* Tauragė, SW Lithuania
Skegness *67 E6* E England, United Kingdom
Skellefteå *62 D4* Västerbotten, N Sweden
Skellefteälven *62 C4 river* N Sweden
Ski *63 B6* Akershus, S Norway
Skiáthos *83 C5* Skiáthos, Vóreies Sporádes, Greece, Aegean Sea
Skidal' *85 B5 Rus.* Skidel'. Hrodzyenskaya Voblasts', W Belarus
Skidel' *see* Skidal'
Skiermûntseach *see* Schiermonnikoog
Skierniewice *76 D3* Łódzkie, C Poland
Skiftet *84 C1 strait* Finland Atlantic Ocean Baltic Sea Gulf of Bothnia/Gulf of Finland
Skíros *see* Skýros
Skópelos *83 C5* Skópelos, Vóreies Sporádes, Greece, Aegean Sea
Skopje *79 D6 var.* Üsküb, *Turk.* Üsküp, *prev.* Skoplje; *anc.* Scupi. *country capital* (North Macedonia) N North Macedonia
Skoplje *see* Skopje
Skovorodino *93 F4* Amurskaya Oblast', SE Russia
Skudnesfjorden *63 A6 fjord* S Norway
Skuodas *84 B3 Ger.* Schoden, *Pol.* Szkudy. Klaipėda, NW Lithuania
Skye, Isle of *66 B3 island* NW Scotland, United Kingdom
Skylge *see* Terschelling
Skýros *83 C5 var.* Skíros. Skńyros, Vóreies Sporádes, Greece, Aegean Sea
Skýros *83 C5 var.* Skíros; *anc.* Scyros. *island* Vóreies Sporádes, Greece, Aegean Sea
Slagelse *63 B7* Vestsjælland, E Denmark
Slatina *78 C3 Hung.* Szlatina; *prev.* Podravska Slatina. Virovitica-Podravina, NE Croatia
Slatina *86 B5* Olt, S Romania
Slavgorod *see* Slawharad
Slavonski Brod *78 C3 Ger.* Brod, *Hung.* Bród; *prev.* Brod, Brod na Savi. Brod-Posavina, NE Croatia
Slavuta *86 C2* Khmel'nyts'ka Oblast', NW Ukraine
Slavyansk *see* Sloviansk
Slawharad *85 E7 Rus.* Slavgorod. Mahilyowskaya Voblasts', E Belarus
Sławno *76 C2* Zachodnio-pomorskie, NW Poland
Slêmanî *see* As Sulaymānīyah
Sliema *80 B5* N Malta
Sligo *67 A5 Ir.* Sligeach. Sligo, NW Ireland
Sliven *82 D2 var.* Slivno. Sliven, C Bulgaria
Slivnitsa *82 B2* Sofiya, W Bulgaria
Slivno *see* Sliven
Slobozia *86 C5* Ialomiţa, SE Romania
Slonim *85 B6 Pol.* Słonim. Hrodzyenskaya Voblasts', W Belarus
Słonim *see* Slonim
Slovakia *77 C6 off.* Slovak Republic, *Ger.* Slowakei, *Hung.* Szlovákia, *Slvk.* Slovensko, Slovenská Republika. *country* C Europe
Slovak Ore Mountains *see* Slovenské rudohorie
Slovak Republic *see* Slovakia
Slovenia *73 D8 off.* Republic of Slovenia, *Ger.* Slowenien, *Slvn.* Slovenija. *country* SE Europe
Slovenia, Republic of *see* Slovenia
Slovenija *see* Slovenia
Slovenská Republika *see* Slovakia
Slovenské rudohorie *77 D6 Eng.* Slovak Ore Mountains, *Ger.* Slowakisches Erzgebirge, Ungarisches Erzgebirge. *mountain range* C Slovakia
Slovensko *see* Slovakia
Sloviansk *87 G3 prev.* Slov''yans'k, *Rus.* Slavyansk. Donets'ka Oblast', E Ukraine
Slov''yans'k *see* Sloviansk
Slowakei *see* Slovakia
Slowakisches Erzgebirge *see* Slovenské rudohorie
Slowenien *see* Slovenia
Słubice *76 B3 Ger.* Frankfurt. Lubuskie, W Poland
Sluch *86 D1 river* NW Ukraine
Słupsk *76 C2 Ger.* Stolp. Pomorskie, N Poland
Slutsk *85 C6* Minskaya Voblasts', S Belarus
Smallwood Reservoir *17 F2 lake* Newfoundland and Labrador, S Canada
Smara *48 B3 var.* Es Semara. N Western Sahara
Smarhon' *85 C5 Pol.* Smorgonie, *Rus.* Smorgon'. Hrodzyenskaya Voblasts', W Belarus
Smederevo *78 D4 Ger.* Semendria. Serbia, N Serbia
Smederevska Palanka *78 D4* Serbia, C Serbia
Smela *see* Smila
Smila *87 E2 Rus.* Smela. Cherkas'ka Oblast', C Ukraine
Smilten *see* Smiltene
Smiltene *84 D3 Ger.* Smilten. Valka, N Latvia
Smøla *62 A4 island* W Norway
Smolensk *89 A5* Smolenskaya Oblast', W Russia
Smorgon'/Smorgonie *see* Smarhon'
Smyrna *see* İzmir
Snake *12 B4 river* Yukon, NW Canada
Snake River *24 C3 river* NW USA
Snake River Plain *24 D4 plain* Idaho, NW USA
Sneek *64 D2 var.* Snits. Fryslân, N Netherlands
Sneeuw-gebergte *see* Maoke, Pegunungan
Sněžka *76 B4 Ger.* Schneekoppe, *Pol.* Śnieżka. *mountain* N Czechia (Czech Republic) /Poland
Śniardwy, Jezioro *76 D2 Ger.* Spirdingsee. *lake* NE Poland
Sniečkus *see* Visaginas
Śnieżka *see* Sněžka
Snina *77 E5 Hung.* Szinna. Prešovský Kraj, E Slovakia
Snits *see* Sneek
Snovsk *87 E1 Rus.* Shchors. Chernihivs'ka Oblast', N Ukraine
Snowdonia *67 C6 mountain range* NW Wales, United Kingdom
Snowdrift *see* Łutselk'e
Snow Mountains *see* Maoke, Pegunungan
Snyder *27 F3* Texas, SW USA
Sobradinho, Barragem de *see* Sobradinho, Represa de
Sobradinho, Represa de *41 F2 var.* Barragem de Sobradinho. *reservoir* E Brazil
Sochi *89 A7* Krasnodarskiy Kray, SW Russia
Société, Îles de la/Society Islands *see* Société, Archipel de la
Society Islands *123 G4 var.* Archipel de Tahiti, Îles de la Société, *Eng.* Society Islands. *island group* W French Polynesia
Soconusco, Sierra de *see* Madre, Sierra
Socorro *26 D2* New Mexico, SW USA
Socorro, Isla *28 B5 island* W Mexico
Socotra *see* Suquṭrá
Soc Trang *115 D6 var.* Khanh Hung. Soc Trăng, S Vietnam
Socuéllamos *71 E3* Castilla-La Mancha, C Spain
Sodankylä *62 D3* Lappi, N Finland
Sodari *see* Sodiri
Söderhamn *63 C5* Gävleborg, C Sweden
Södertälje *63 C6* Stockholm, C Sweden
Sodiri *50 B4 var.* Sawdirī, Sodari. Northern Kordofan, C Sudan
Soekaboemi *see* Sukabumi
Soemba *see* Sumba, Pulau
Soengaipenoeh *see* Sungaipenuh
Soerabaja *see* Surabaya
Soerakarta *see* Surakarta
Sofia *82 C2 var.* Sophia, Sofiya, *Lat.* Serdica. *country capital* (Bulgaria) Sofia-Grad, W Bulgaria
Sofiya *see* Sofia
Sogamoso *36 B3* Boyacá, C Colombia
Sognefjorden *63 A5 fjord* NE North Sea
Sohag *see* Sūhāj
Sohar *see* Ṣuḥār
Sohm Plain *44 B3 abyssal plain* NW Atlantic Ocean
Sohrau *see* Żory
Sokal *86 C2* L'vivs'ka Oblast', NW Ukraine
Söke *94 A4* Aydın, SW Turkey (Türkiye)
Sokhumi *95 E1 Rus.* Sukhumi. NW Georgia
Sokodé *53 F4* C Togo
Sokol *88 C4* Vologodskaya Oblast', NW Russia
Sokółka *76 E3* Podlaskie, NE Poland
Sokolov *77 A5 Ger.* Falkenau an der Eger; *prev.* Falknov nad Ohří. Karlovarský Kraj, W Czechia (Czech Republic)
Sokone *52 B3* W Senegal
Sokoto *53 F3* Sokoto, NW Nigeria
Sokoto *53 F4 river* NW Nigeria
Sokotra *see* Suquṭrá
Solāpur *102 B3 var.* Sholāpur. Mahārāshtra, W India
Solca *86 C3 Ger.* Solka. Suceava, N Romania
Sol, Costa del *70 D5 coastal region* S Spain
Soldeu *69 B7* NE Andorra Europe
Solec Kujawski *76 C3* Kujawsko-pomorskie, C Poland
Soledad *36 B1* Atlántico, N Colombia
Isla Soledad *see* East Falkland
Soligorsk *see* Salihorsk
Solikamsk *92 C3* Permskaya Oblast', NW Russia
Sol'-Iletsk *89 D6* Orenburgskaya Oblast', W Russia
Solingen *72 A4* Nordrhein-Westfalen, W Germany
Solka *see* Solca
Sollentuna *63 C6* Stockholm, C Sweden
Solo *see* Surakarta
Solok *116 B4* Sumatera, W Indonesia
Solomon Islands *122 C3 prev.* British Solomon Islands Protectorate. *country* W Solomon Islands N Melanesia W Pacific Ocean
Solomon Islands *122 C3 island group* Papua New Guinea/Solomon Islands
Solomon Sea *122 B3 sea* W Pacific Ocean
Soltau *72 B3* Niedersachsen, NW Germany
Sol'tsy *88 A4* Novgorodskaya Oblast', W Russia
Solun *see* Thessaloníki
Solwezi *56 D2* North Western, NW Zambia
Sōma *108 D4* Fukushima, Honshū, C Japan
Somalia *51 D5 off.* Somali Democratic Republic, *Som.* Jamhuuriyadda Federaalka Soomaaliya, Soomaaliya; *prev.* Italian Somaliland, Somaliland Protectorate. *country* E Africa
Somali Basin *47 E5 undersea basin* W Indian Ocean
Somali Democratic Republic *see* Somalia
Somaliland *51 D5 disputed territory* N Somalia
Somaliland Protectorate *see* Somalia
Sombor *78 C3 Hung.* Zombor. Vojvodina, NW Serbia
Someren *65 D5* Noord-Brabant, SE Netherlands
Somerset *20 A5 var.* Somerset Village. W Bermuda
Somerset *18 C5* Kentucky, S USA
Somerset Island *20 A5 island* W Bermuda
Somerset Island *15 F2 island* Queen Elizabeth Islands, Nunavut, NW Canada
Somerset Village *see* Somerset
Somers Islands *see* Bermuda
Somerton *26 A2* Arizona, SW USA
Someş *86 B3 river* Hungary/Romania Europe
Somme *68 C2 river* N France
Sommerfeld *see* Lubsko
Somotillo *30 C3* Chinandega, NW Nicaragua
Somoto *30 D3* Madriz, NW Nicaragua
Songea *51 C8* Ruvuma, S Tanzania
Songjin *see* Kimch'aek
Songkhla *115 C7 var.* Songkla, *Mal.* Singora. Songkhla, SW Thailand
Songkla *see* Songkhla
Sonoran Desert *26 A3 var.* Desierto de Altar. *desert* Mexico/USA
Sonsonate *30 B3* Sonsonate, W El Salvador
Soochow *see* Suzhou
Soomaaliya/Soomaaliya, Jamhuuriyadda Federaalka *see* Somalia
Soome Laht *see* Finland, Gulf of
Sop Hao *114 D3* Houaphan, N Laos
Sophia *see* Sofia
Sopianae *see* Pécs
Sopot *76 C2 Ger.* Zoppot. Pomorskie, N Poland
Sopron *77 B6 Ger.* Ödenburg. Győr-Moson-Sopron, NW Hungary
Sorau/Sorau in der Niederlausitz *see* Żary
Sorgues *69 D6* Vaucluse, SE France
Sorgun *94 D3* Yozgat, C Turkey (Türkiye)
Soria *71 E2* Castilla y León, N Spain
Soroca *86 D3 Rus.* Soroki. N Moldova
Sorochino *see* Sarochyna
Soroki *see* Soroca
Sorokyne *87 H3 Rus.* Krasnodon. Luhans'ka Oblast', E Ukraine
Sorong *117 F4* Papua, E Indonesia
Sørøy *see* Sørøya
Sørøya *62 C2 var.* Sørøy, *Lapp.* Sállan. *island* N Norway
Sortavala *88 B3 prev.* Serdobol'. Respublika Kareliya, NW Russia
Sotavento, Ilhas de *52 A3 var.* Leeward Islands. *island group* S Cape Verde (Cabo Verde)
Sotkamo *62 E4* Kainuu, C Finland
Souanké *55 B5* Sangha, NW Congo
Soueida *see* As Suwaydā'
Souflí *82 D3 prev.* Souflíon. Anatolikí Makedonía kai Thráki, NE Greece
Souflíon *see* Souflí
Soufrière *33 F2* W Saint Lucia
Soukhné *see* As Sukhnah
Sŏul *see* Seoul
Soûr *97 A5 var.* Ṣūr; *anc.* Tyre. SW Lebanon
Souris River *23 E1 var.* Mouse River. *river* Canada/USA
Soúrpi *83 B5* Thessalía, C Greece
Sousse *49 F2 var.* Sūsah. NE Tunisia
South Africa *56 C4 off.* Republic of South Africa, *Afr.* Suid-Afrika. *country* S Africa
South Africa, Republic of *see* South Africa
South America *34 continent*
Southampton *67 D7 hist.* Hamwih, *Lat.* Clausentum. S England, United Kingdom
Southampton Island *15 G3 island* Nunavut, NE Canada
South Andaman *111 F2 island* Andaman Islands, India, NE Indian Ocean
South Australia *127 A5 state* S Australia
South Australian Basin *120 B5 undersea basin* SW Indian Ocean
South Bend *18 C3* Indiana, N USA
South Beveland *see* Zuid-Beveland
South Bruny Island *127 C8 island* Tasmania, SE Australia
South Carolina *21 E2 off.* State of South Carolina, *also known as* The Palmetto State. *state* SE USA
South Carpathians *see* Carpaţii Meridionali
South China Basin *103 E4 undersea basin* SE South China Sea
South China Sea *103 E4 sea* SE Asia
South Dakota *22 D2 off.* State of South Dakota, *also known as* The Coyote State, Sunshine State. *state* N USA
Southeast Indian Ridge *119 D7 undersea ridge* Indian Ocean/Pacific Ocean
Southeast Pacific Basin *131 E5 var.* Belling Hausen Mulde. *undersea basin* SE Pacific Ocean
South East Point *127 C7 headland* Victoria, S Australia
Southend-on-Sea *67 E6* E England, United Kingdom
Southern Alps *129 B6 var.* Kā Tiritiri o Te Moana. *mountain range* South Island, New Zealand
Southern Cook Islands *123 F4 island group* S Cook Islands
Southern Cross *125 B6* Western Australia
Southern Indian Lake *15 F4 lake* Manitoba, C Canada
Southern Ocean *45 B7 ocean* Atlantic Ocean/ Indian Ocean/Pacific Ocean
Southern Uplands *66 C4 mountain range* S Scotland, United Kingdom
South Fiji Basin *120 D4 undersea basin* S Pacific Ocean
South Geomagnetic Pole *132 B3 pole* Antarctica
South Georgia *35 D8 island* South Georgia and the South Sandwich Islands, SW Atlantic Ocean
South Georgia and the South Sandwich Islands *35 D8 UK Overseas Territory* SW Atlantic Ocean
South Goulburn Island *124 E2 island* Northern Territory, N Australia
South Huvadhu Atoll *110 A5 atoll* S Maldives
South Indian Basin *119 D7 undersea basin* Indian Ocean/Pacific Ocean
South Island *129 C6 var.* Te Waipounamu. *island* S New Zealand
South Korea *107 E4 off.* Republic of Korea, *Kor.* Taehan Min'guk. *country* E Asia
South Lake Tahoe *25 C5* California, W USA
South Orkney Islands *132 A2 island group* Antarctica
South Ossetia *95 F2 former autonomous region* SW Georgia
South Pacific Basin *see* Southwest Pacific Basin
South Platte River *22 D4 river* Colorado/ Nebraska, C USA
South Pole *132 B3 pole* Antarctica
South Sandwich Islands *35 D8 island group* SW Atlantic Ocean
South Sandwich Trench *35 E8 trench* SW Atlantic Ocean
South Shetland Islands *132 A2 island group* Antarctica
South Shields *66 D4* NE England, United Kingdom
South Sioux City *23 F3* Nebraska, C USA
South Sudan *50 B5 off.* Republic of South Sudan, *country* N Africa
South Taranaki Bight *128 C4 bight* SE Tasman Sea
South Tasmania Plateau *see* Tasman Plateau
South Uist *66 B3 island* NW Scotland, United Kingdom
South-West Africa/South West Africa *see* Namibia
South West Cape *129 A8 var.* Puhiwaero. *headland* Stewart Island, New Zealand
Southwest Indian Ocean Ridge *see* Southwest Indian Ridge
Southwest Indian Ridge *119 B6 var.* Southwest Indian Ocean Ridge. *undersea ridge* SW Indian Ocean
Southwest Pacific Basin *121 E4 var.* South Pacific Basin. *undersea basin* SE Pacific Ocean
Sovereign Base Area *80 C5 uk military installation* S Cyprus
Soweto *56 D4* Gauteng, NE South Africa
Sōya-kaikyō *see* La Pérouse Strait
Spain *70 D3 off.* Kingdom of Spain, *Sp.* España; *anc.* Hispania, Iberia, *Lat.* Hispana. *country* SW Europe
Spain, Kingdom of *see* Spain
Spalato *see* Split
Spanish Town *32 B5 hist.* St.Iago de la Vega. C Jamaica
Sparks *25 C5* Nevada, W USA
Sparta *see* Spárti
Spartanburg *21 E1* South Carolina, SE USA
Spárti *83 B6 Eng.* Sparta. Pelopónnisos, S Greece
Spearfish *22 D2* South Dakota, N USA
Speightstown *33 G1* NW Barbados
Spencer *23 F3* Iowa, C USA
Spencer Gulf *127 B6 gulf* South Australia
Spey *66 C3 river* NE Scotland, United Kingdom
Spice Islands *see* Maluku
Spiess Seamount *45 C7 seamount* S Atlantic Ocean
Spijkenisse *64 B4* Zuid-Holland, SW Netherlands
Spíli *83 C8* Kríti, Greece, E Mediterranean Sea
Spīn Bōldak *101 E5* prev. Spīn Būldak. Kandahār, S Afghanistan
Spīn Būldak *see* Spīn Bōldak
Spirdingsee *see* Śniardwy, Jezioro
Spitsbergen *61 F2 island* NW Svalbard
Split *78 B4 It.* Spalato. Split-Dalmacija, S Croatia
Špoģi *84 D4* Daugvapils, SE Latvia
Spokane *24 C2* Washington, NW USA
Spratly Islands *116 B2 disputed territory* SE Asia
Spree *72 D4 river* E Germany
Springbok *56 B5* NE South Africa
Springfield *18 B4 state capital* Illinois, N USA
Springfield *19 G3* Massachusetts, NE USA
Springfield *23 G5* Missouri, C USA
Springfield *18 C4* Ohio, N USA
Springfield *24 B3* Oregon, NW USA
Spring Garden *37 F2* NE Guyana
Spring Hill *21 E4* Florida, SE USA
Springs Junction *129 C5* West Coast, South Island, New Zealand
Springsure *126 D4* Queensland, E Australia
Sprottau *see* Szprotawa
Spruce Knob *19 E4 mountain* West Virginia, NE USA
Srbija/Republika Srbija *see* Serbia
Srbinje *see* Foča
Srbobran *78 D3 var.* Bácsszenttamás, *Hung.* Szenttamás. Vojvodina, N Serbia
Srebrenica *78 C4* Republika Srpska, E Bosnia and Herzegovina
Sredets *82 D2 prev.* Syulemeshlii. Stara Zagora, C Bulgaria
Sredets *82 E2 prev.* Grudovo. Burgas, E Bulgaria
Srednerusskaya Vozvyshennost' *87 G1 Eng.* Central Russian Upland. *mountain range* W Russia
Sremska Mitrovica *78 C3 prev.* Mitrovica, *Ger.* Mitrowitz. Vojvodina, NW Serbia
Srepok, Sông *see* Srêpôk, Tônle
Srêpôk, Tônle *115 E5 var.* Sông Srepok. *river* Cambodia/Vietnam
Sri Aman *116 C3* Sarawak, East Malaysia
Sri Jayawardenapura Kotte *110 D3 administrative capital* (Sri Lanka) Western Province, W Sri Lanka
Srīkākulam *113 F5* Andhra Pradesh, E India
Sri Lanka *110 D3 off.* Democratic Socialist Republic of Sri Lanka; *prev.* Ceylon. *country* S Asia
Sri Lanka, Democratic Socialist Republic of *see* Sri Lanka
Srinagarind Reservoir *115 C5 lake* W Thailand
Srpska, Republika *78 B3 republic* Bosnia and Herzegovina
Ssu-ch'uan *see* Sichuan
Ssu-p'ing/Ssu-p'ing-chieh *see* Siping
Stabroek *65 B5* Antwerpen, N Belgium
Stade *72 B3* Niedersachsen, NW Germany
Stadskanaal *64 E2* Groningen, NE Netherlands
Stafford *67 D6* C England, United Kingdom
Staicele *84 D3* Limbaži, N Latvia
Ştaierdorf-Anina *see* Anina
Stájerlakanina *see* Anina
Stakhanov *see* Kadiivka
Stalin *see* Varna
Stalinabad *see* Dushanbe
Stalingrad *see* Volgograd
Stalino *see* Donets'k
Stalinobod *see* Dushanbe
Stalinsk *see* Novokuznetsk
Stalinski Zaliv *see* Varnenski Zaliv
Stalin, Yazovir *see* Iskar, Yazovir
Stalowa Wola *76 E4* Podkarpackie, SE Poland
Stamford *19 F3* Connecticut, NE USA
Stampalia *see* Astypálaia
Stanislau *see* Ivano-Frankivsk
Stanislav *see* Ivano-Frankivsk
Stanisławów *see* Ivano-Frankivsk
Stanke Dimitrov *see* Dupnitsa
Stanley *43 D7 var.* Port Stanley, Puerto Argentino. *dependent territory capital* (Falkland Islands) East Falkland, Falkland Islands
Stanleyville *see* Kisangani
Stann Creek *see* Dangriga
Stanovoy Khrebet *91 E3 mountain range* SE Russia
Stanthorpe *127 D5* Queensland, E Australia
Staphorst *64 D2* Overijssel, E Netherlands
Starachowice *76 D4* Świętokrzyskie, C Poland
Stara Kanjiža *see* Kanjiža
Stara Pazova *78 D3 Ger.* Altpasua, *Hung.* Ópazova. Vojvodina, N Serbia
Stara Planina *see* Balkan Mountains
Stara Zagora *82 D2 Lat.* Augusta Trajana. Stara Zagora, C Bulgaria
Starbuck Island *123 G3 prev.* Volunteer Island. *island* E Kiribati
Stargard in Pommern *see* Stargard Szczeciński
Stargard Szczeciński *76 B3 Ger.* Stargard in Pommern. Zachodnio-pomorskie, NW Poland
Stari Bečej *see* Bečej
Starobel'sk *see* Starobilsk
Starobilsk *87 H2 Rus.* Starobel'sk. Luhans'ka Oblast', E Ukraine
Starobin *85 C7 var.* Starobyn. Minskaya Voblasts', S Belarus
Starobyn *see* Starobin
Starogard Gdański *76 C2 Ger.* Preussisch-Stargard. Pomorskie, N Poland
Starokonstantinov *see* Starokostiantyniv
Starokostiantyniv *86 D2 prev.* Starokostyantyniv, *Rus.* Starokonstantinov. Khmel'nyts'ka Oblast', NW Ukraine
Starokostyantyniv *see* Starokostiantyniv
Starominskaya *89 A7* Krasnodarskiy Kray, SW Russia
Staryya Darohi *85 C6 Rus.* Staryye Dorogi. Minskaya Voblasts', S Belarus
Staryye Dorogi *see* Staryya Darohi
Staryy Oskol *89 B6* Belgorodskaya Oblast', W Russia
State College *19 E4* Pennsylvania, NE USA
Staten Island *see* Estados, Isla de los
Statesboro *21 E2* Georgia, SE USA
States, The *see* United States of America
Station Nord *61 F1* N Greenland
Staunton *19 E5* Virginia, NE USA
Stavanger *63 A6* Rogaland, S Norway
Stavers Island *see* Vostok Island
Stavropol' *89 B7 prev.* Voroshilovsk. Stavropol'skiy Kray, SW Russia
Stavropol' *see* Tol'yatti
Steamboat Springs *22 C4* Colorado, C USA
Steenwijk *64 D2* Overijssel, N Netherlands
Steier *see* Steyr
Steierdorf/Steierdorf-Anina *see* Anina
Steinamanger *see* Szombathely
Steinkjer *62 B4* Nord-Trøndelag, C Norway
Stejarul *see* Karapelit
Stendal *72 C3* Sachsen-Anhalt, C Germany
Stepanakert *see* Xankändi
Stephenville *27 F3* Texas, SW USA
Sterling *22 D4* Colorado, C USA
Sterling *18 B3* Illinois, N USA
Sterlitamak *92 B3* Respublika Bashkortostan, W Russia
Stettin *see* Szczecin
Stettiner Haff *see* Szczeciński, Zalew
Stevenage *67 E6* E England, United Kingdom
Stevens Point *18 B2* Wisconsin, N USA
Stewart Island *129 A8 var.* Rakiura. *island* S New Zealand
Steyerlak-Anina *see* Anina
Steyr *73 D6 var.* Steier. Oberösterreich, N Austria
St. Helena Bay *56 B5 bay* SW South Africa
Stif *see* Sétif
Stillwater *27 G1* Oklahoma, C USA
Štip *79 E6* E North Macedonia
Stirling *66 C4* C Scotland, United Kingdom
Stjørdalshalsen *62 B4* Nord-Trøndelag, C Norway
St-Maur-des-Fossés *68 E2* Val-de-Marne, Île-de-France, N France Europe
Stockach *73 B6* Baden-Württemberg, S Germany
Stockholm *63 C6 country capital* (Sweden) Stockholm, C Sweden
Stockmannshof *see* Pļaviņas
Stockton *25 B6* California, W USA
Stockton Plateau *27 E4 plain* Texas, SW USA
Stœng Trĕng *see* Stung Treng
Stoke *see* Stoke-on-Trent
Stoke-on-Trent *67 D6 var.* Stoke. C England, United Kingdom
Stolbce *see* Stowbtsy
Stolbtsy *see* Stowbtsy
Stolp *see* Słupsk
Stolpmünde *see* Ustka
Stómio *82 B4* Thessalía, C Greece
Store Bælt *see* Storebælt
Storebelt *see* Storebælt
Støren *63 B5* Sør-Trøndelag, S Norway
Storfjorden *61 G2 fjord* S Norway
Storhammer *see* Hamar
Stornoway *66 B2* NW Scotland, United Kingdom
Storsjön *63 B5 lake* C Sweden
Storuman *62 C4* Västerbotten, N Sweden
Storuman *62 C4 lake* N Sweden
Stowbtsy *85 C6 Pol.* Stolbce, *Rus.* Stolbtsy. Minskaya Voblasts', C Belarus
Strabane *67 B5 Ir.* An Srath Bán. W Northern Ireland, United Kingdom
Strakonice *77 A5 Ger.* Strakonitz. Jihočeský Kraj, S Czechia (Czech Republic)
Strakonitz *see* Strakonice
Stralsund *72 D2* Mecklenburg-Vorpommern, NE Germany
Stranraer *67 C5* S Scotland, United Kingdom
Strasbourg *68 E3 Ger.* Strassburg; *anc.* Argentoratum. Bas-Rhin, NE France
Străşeni *86 D3 var.* Strasheny. C Moldova
Strasheny *see* Străşeni
Strassburg *see* Strasbourg, France
Strassburg *see* Aiud, Romania
Stratford *128 D4* Taranaki, North Island, New Zealand
Strathfield *126 E2* New South Wales, E Australia
Straubing *73 C6* Bayern, SE Germany
Strehaia *86 B5* Mehedinţi, SW Romania
Strelka *92 D4* Krasnoyarskiy Kray, C Russia
Strigonium *see* Esztergom
Strofilia *see* Strofyliá
Strofyliá *83 C5 var.* Strofilia. Évvoia, C Greece
Stromboli *75 D6 island* Isole Eolie, S Italy
Stromeferry *66 C3* N Scotland, United Kingdom
Strömstad *63 B6* Västra Götaland, S Sweden
Strömsund *62 C4* Jämtland, C Sweden
Struga *79 D6* SW North Macedonia
Struma *see* Strymónas
Strumica *79 E6* E North Macedonia
Strumyani *82 C3* Blagoevgrad, SW Bulgaria
Strymónas *82 C3 Bul.* Struma. *river* Bulgaria/ Greece
Stryi *86 B2 prev.* Stryy. L'vivs'ka Oblast', NW Ukraine
Stryy *see* Stryi
Studholme *129 B6* Canterbury, South Island, New Zealand
Stuhlweissenberg *see* Székesfehérvár
Stung Treng *115 D5 Khmer.* Stœng Trĕng. Stung Treng, NE Cambodia
Sturgis *22 D3* South Dakota, N USA
Stuttgart *73 B6* Baden-Württemberg, SW Germany
Stykkishólmur *61 E4* Vesturland, W Iceland
Styr *86 C1 Rus.* Styr'. *river* Belarus/Ukraine
Su *see* Jiangsu
Suakin *50 C3 var.* Sawakin. Red Sea, NE Sudan
Subačius *84 C4* Panevėžys, NE Lithuania
Subaykhān *96 E3* Dayr az Zawr, E Syria
Subotica *78 D2 Ger.* Maria-Theresiopel, *Hung.* Szabadka. Vojvodina, N Serbia
Suceava *86 C3 Ger.* Suczawa, *Hung.* Szucsava. Suceava, NE Romania
Su-chou *see* Suzhou
Suchow *see* Suzhou, Jiangsu, China
Suchow *see* Xuzhou, Jiangsu, China
Sucker State *see* Illinois

Sucre 39 F4 *hist.* Chuquisaca, La Plata. *country capital* (Bolivia-legal capital) Chuquisaca, S Bolivia
Suczawa *see* Suceava
Sudak 87 F5 S Ukraine
Sudan 50 A4 *off.* Republic of Sudan, *Ar.* Jumhuriyat as-Sudan; *prev.* Anglo-Egyptian Sudan. *country* N Africa
Sudanese Republic *see* Mali
Sudan, Jumhuriyat as- *see* Sudan
Sudan, Republic of *see* Sudan
Sudbury 16 C4 Ontario, S Canada
Sudd 51 B5 *swamp region* N South Sudan
Sudeten 76 B4 *var.* Sudetes, Sudetic Mountains, *Cz./Pol.* Sudety. *mountain range* Czechia (Czech Republic) /Poland
Sudetes/Sudetic Mountains/Sudety *see* Sudeten
Südkarpaten *see* Carpaţii Meridionali
Südliche Morava *see* Južna Morava
Sudong, Pulau 116 A2 *island* SW Singapore Asia
Sudostroy *see* Severodvinsk
Sue 51 B5 *river* S South Sudan
Sueca 71 F3 Comunitat Valenciana, E Spain
Sue Wood Bay 20 B5 *bay* W Bermuda North America W Atlantic Ocean
Suez *see* As Suways
Suez Canal *see* Suways, Qanāt as
Suez, Gulf of *see* Khalīj as Suways
Suğla Gölü 94 C4 *lake* SW Turkey (Türkiye)
Sūhāj 50 B2 *var.* Sawhāj, Suliag; *Eng.* Sohag. C Egypt
Şuḩār 99 D5 *var.* Sohar. N Oman
Sühbaatar 105 E1 Selenge, N Mongolia
Suhl 73 C5 Thüringen, C Germany
Suicheng *see* Suixi
Suid-Afrika *see* South Africa
Suidwes-Afrika *see* Namibia
Suixi 106 C6 *var.* Suicheng. Guangdong, S China
Sujawal 112 B3 Sindh, SE Pakistan
Sukabumi 116 C5 *prev.* Soekaboemi. Jawa, C Indonesia
Sukagawa 109 D5 Fukushima, Honshū, C Japan
Sukarnapura *see* Jayapura
Sukarno, Puntjak *see* Jaya, Puncak
Sukhne *see* As Sukhnah
Sukhona 88 C4 *var.* Tot'ma. *river* NW Russia
Sukhumi *see* Sokhumi
Sukkertoppen *see* Maniitsoq
Sukkur 112 B3 Sindh, SE Pakistan
Sukumo 109 B7 Kōchi, Shikoku, SW Japan
Sulaimaniya *see* As Sulaymānīyah
Sulaiman Range 112 C2 *mountain range* C Pakistan
Sula, Kepulauan 117 E4 *island group* C Indonesia
Sulawesi 117 E4 *Eng.* Celebes. *island* C Indonesia
Sulawesi, Laut *see* Celebes Sea
Sulechów 76 B3 *Ger.* Züllichau. Lubuskie, W Poland
Suliag *see* Sūhāj
Sullana 38 B2 Piura, NW Peru
Sullivan Island *see* Lanbi Kyun
Sulphur Springs 27 G2 Texas, SW USA
Sultānābād *see* Arāk
Sulu Archipelago 117 E3 *island group* SW Philippines
Sülüktü *see* Sulyukta
Sulu, Laut *see* Sulu Sea
Sulu Sea 117 E2 *var.* Laut Sulu. *sea* SW Philippines
Sulyukta 101 E2 *Kir.* Sülüktü. Batkenskaya Oblast', SW Kyrgyzstan
Sumatera 115 B8 *Eng.* Sumatra. *island* W Indonesia
Sumatra *see* Sumatera
Šumava *see* Bohemian Forest
Sumba, Pulau 117 E5 *Eng.* Sandalwood Island; *prev.* Soemba. *island* Nusa Tenggara, C Indonesia
Sumba, Selat 117 E5 *strait* Nusa Tenggara, S Indonesia
Sumbawanga 51 B7 Rukwa, W Tanzania
Sumbe 56 B2 *var.* N'Gunza, *Port.* Novo Redondo. Cuanza Sul, W Angola
Sumeih 51 B5 Southern Darfur, S Sudan
Sumgait *see* Sumqayıt, Azerbaijan
Summer Lake 24 B4 *lake* Oregon, NW USA
Summit 71 H5 Alaska, USA
Sumqayıt 95 H2 *Rus.* Sumgait. E Azerbaijan
Sumy 87 F2 Sums'ka Oblast', NE Ukraine
Sunbury 127 C7 Victoria, SE Australia
Sunda Islands *see* Greater Sunda Islands
Sunda, Selat 116 B5 *strait* Jawa/Sumatera, SW Indonesia
Sunda Trench *see* Java Trench
Sunderland 66 D4 *var.* Wearmouth. NE England, United Kingdom
Sundsvall 63 C5 Västernorrland, C Sweden
Sunflower State *see* Kansas
Sungaipenuh 116 B4 *prev.* Soengaipenoeh. Sumatera, W Indonesia
Sunnyvale 25 A6 California, W USA
Sunset State *see* Oregon
Sunshine State *see* Florida
Sunshine State *see* New Mexico
Sunshine State *see* South Dakota
Suntar 93 F3 Respublika Sakha (Yakutiya), NE Russia
Sunyani 53 E5 W Ghana
Suoločielgi *see* Saariselkä
Suomenlahti *see* Finland, Gulf of
Suomen Tasavalta/Suomi *see* Finland
Suomussalmi 62 E4 Kainuu, E Finland
Suong 115 D6 Tbong Khmum, C Cambodia
Suoyarvi 88 B3 Respublika Kareliya, NW Russia
Supe 38 C3 Lima, W Peru
Supérieur, Lac *see* Superior, Lake
Superior 18 A1 Wisconsin, N USA
Superior, Lake 18 B1 *Fr.* Lac Supérieur. *lake* Canada/USA
Suqrah *see* Şawqirah
Suquṭrá 99 C7 *var.* Sokotra, *Eng.* Socotra. *island* SE Yemen
Şūr 99 E5 NE Oman
Şūr *see* Soûr
Surabaja *see* Surabaya
Surabaya 116 D5 *prev.* Surabaja, Soerabaja. Jawa, C Indonesia
Surakarta 116 C5 *Eng.* Solo; *prev.* Soerakarta. Jawa, S Indonesia
Šurany 77 C6 *Hung.* Nagysurány. Nitriansky Kraj, SW Slovakia
Sūrat 112 C4 Gujarāt, W India
Suratdhani *see* Surat Thani
Surat Thani 115 C6 *var.* Suratdhani. Surat Thani, SW Thailand
Surazh 85 E5 Vitsyebskaya Voblasts', NE Belarus
Surdulica 79 E5 Serbia, SE Serbia
Sûre 65 D7 *var.* Sauer. *river* W Europe
Surendranagar 112 C4 Gujarāt, W India
Surfers Paradise 127 E5 Queensland, E Australia
Surgut 92 D3 Khanty-Mansiyskiy Avtonomnyy Okrug-Yugra, C Russia
Surin 115 D5 Surin, E Thailand
Surinam *see* Suriname
Suriname 37 G3 *off.* Republic of Suriname, *var.* Surinam; *prev.* Dutch Guiana, Netherlands Guiana. *country* N South America
Suriname, Republic of *see* Suriname
Sūrīyah/Sūrīyah, Al-Jumhūrīyah al-'Arabīyah as- *see* Syria
Surkhab, Darya-i- *see* Kahmard, Daryā-ye
Surkhob 101 F3 *river* C Tajikistan
Surt 49 G2 *var.* Sidra, Sirte. N Libya
Surt, Khalīj 49 F2 *var.* Gulf of Sirte, Gulf of Sidra, Gulf of Sirti, Sidra. *gulf* N Libya
Surtsey 61 E5 *island* S Iceland
Suruga-wan 109 D6 *bay* SE Japan
Susa 74 A2 Piemonte, NE Italy
Sūsah *see* Sousse
Susanville 25 B5 California, W USA
Susitna 14 C3 Alaska, USA
Susteren 65 D5 Limburg, SE Netherlands
Susuman 93 G3 Magadanskaya Oblast', E Russia
Sutlej 112 C2 *river* India/Pakistan
Suur Munamägi 84 D3 *var.* Munamägi, *Ger.* Eier-Berg. *mountain* SE Estonia
Suur Väin 84 C2 *Ger.* Grosser Sund. *strait* W Estonia
Suva 123 E4 *country capital* (Fiji) Viti Levu, W Fiji
Suvalkai/Suvalki *see* Suwałki
Suvorovo 82 E2 *prev.* Vetrino. Varna, E Bulgaria
Suwałki 76 E2 *Lith.* Suvalkai, *Rus.* Suvalki. Podlaskie, NE Poland
Şuwār *see* Aş Şuwār
Suways, Qanāt as 50 B1 *Eng.* Suez Canal. *canal* NE Egypt
Suweida *see* As Suwaydā'
Suzhou 106 D5 *var.* Soochow, Su-chou, Suchow; *prev.* Wuhsien. Jiangsu, E China
Svalbard 61 E1 *constituent part of Norway. island group* Arctic Ocean
Svartisen 62 C3 *glacier* C Norway
Svay Rieng 115 D6 *Khmer.* Svay Riĕng. Svay Rieng, S Cambodia
Svay Riĕng *see* Svay Rieng
Sveg 63 B5 Jämtland, C Sweden
Svenstavik 63 C5 Jämtland, C Sweden
Sverdlovsk *see* Yekaterinburg
Sverige *see* Sweden
Sveti Vrach *see* Sandanski
Svetlogorsk *see* Svietlahorsk
Svetlograd 89 B7 Stavropol'skiy Kray, SW Russia
Svetlovodsk *see* Svitlovodsk
Svetozarevo *see* Jagodina
Svilengrad 82 D3 *prev.* Mustafa-Pasha. Haskovo, S Bulgaria
Svitlovodsk 87 F3 *Rus.* Svetlovodsk. Kirovohrads'ka Oblast', C Ukraine
Svizzera *see* Switzerland
Svobodnyy 93 G4 Amurskaya Oblast', SE Russia
Svyataya Anna Trough 133 C4 *var.* Saint Anna Trough. *trough* N Kara Sea
Svyetlahorsk 85 D7 *Rus.* Svetlogorsk. Homyel'skaya Voblasts', SE Belarus
Swabian Jura *see* Schwäbische Alb
Swakopmund 56 B3 Erongo, W Namibia
Swan Islands 31 E1 *island group* NE Honduras North America
Swansea 67 C7 *Wel.* Abertawe. S Wales, United Kingdom
Swarzędz 76 C3 Poznań, W Poland
Swatow *see* Shantou
Swaziland *see* Eswatini
Sweden 62 B4 *off.* Kingdom of Sweden, *Swe.* Sverige. *country* N Europe
Sweden, Kingdom of *see* Sweden
Sweetwater 27 F3 Texas, SW USA
Świdnica 76 B4 *Ger.* Schweidnitz. Wałbrzych, SW Poland
Świdwin 76 B2 *Ger.* Schivelbein. Zachodnio-pomorskie, NW Poland
Świebodzice 76 B4 *Ger.* Freiburg in Schlesien, Swiebodzice. Walbrzych, SW Poland
Świebodzin 76 B3 *Ger.* Schwiebus. Lubuskie, W Poland
Świecie 76 C3 *Ger.* Schwertberg. Kujawsko-pomorskie, C Poland
Swindon 67 D7 S England, United Kingdom
Swinemünde *see* Świnoujście
Świnoujście 76 B2 *Ger.* Swinemünde. Zachodnio-pomorskie, NW Poland
Swiss Confederation *see* Switzerland
Switzerland 73 A7 *off.* Swiss Confederation, *Fr.* La Suisse, *Ger.* Schweiz, *It.* Svizzera; *anc.* Helvetia. *country* C Europe
Sycaminum *see* Hefa
Sydenham Island *see* Nonouti
Sydney 126 D1 *state capital* New South Wales, SE Australia
Sydney 17 G4 Cape Breton Island, Nova Scotia, SE Canada
Sydney Island *see* Manra
Syedpur *see* Saidpur
Syemyezhava 85 C6 *Rus.* Semechevo. Minskaya Voblasts', C Belarus
Syene *see* Aswān
Syeverodonets'k *see* Sievierodonetsk
Syktyvkar 88 D4 *prev.* Ust'-Sysol'sk. Respublika Komi, NW Russia
Sylhet 113 G3 Sylhet, NE Bangladesh
Synelnykove 87 G3 Dnipropetrovska Oblast, E Ukraine
Syowa 132 C2 *Japanese research station* Antarctica
Syracuse 19 E3 New York, NE USA
Syracuse *see* Siracusa
Syrdar'ya 92 B4 Sirdaryo Viloyati, E Uzbekistan
Syria 96 B3 *off.* Syrian Arab Republic, *var.* Siria, Syrie, *Ar.* Al-Jumhūrīyah al-'Arabīyah as-Sūrīyah, Sūrīyah. *country* SW Asia
Syrian Arab Republic *see* Syria
Syrian Desert 97 D5 *Ar.* Al Hamad, Bādiyat ash Shām. *desert* SW Asia
Syrie *see* Syria
Sýrna 83 E7 *var.* Sirna. *island* Kykládes, Greece, Aegean Sea
Sýros 83 C6 *var.* Síros. *island* Kykládes, Greece, Aegean Sea
Syulemeshlii *see* Sredets
Syvash, Zaliv *see* Syvash, Zatoka
Syvash, Zatoka 87 F4 *Rus.* Zaliv Syvash. *inlet* S Ukraine
Syzran' 89 C6 Samarskaya Oblast', W Russia
Szabadka *see* Subotica
Szamotuły 76 B3 Poznań, W Poland
Szászrégen *see* Reghin
Szatmárrnémeti *see* Satu Mare
Száva *see* Sava
Szczecin 76 B3 *Eng./Ger.* Stettin. Zachodnio-pomorskie, NW Poland
Szczecinek 76 B2 *Ger.* Neustettin. Zachodnio-pomorskie, NW Poland
Szczeciński, Zalew 76 A2 *var.* Stettiner Haff, *Ger.* Oderhaff. *bay* Germany/Poland
Szczuczyn Nowogródzki *see* Shchuchyn
Szczytno 76 D3 *Ger.* Ortelsburg. Warmińsko-Mazurskie, NE Poland
Szechuan/Szechwan *see* Sichuan
Szeged 77 D7 *Ger.* Szegedin, *Rom.* Seghedin. Csongrád, SE Hungary
Szegedin *see* Szeged
Székelykeresztúr *see* Cristuru Secuiesc
Székesfehérvár 77 C6 *Ger.* Stuhlweissenberg; *anc.* Alba Regia. Fejér, W Hungary
Szeklerburg *see* Miercurea-Ciuc
Szekler Neumarkt *see* Târgu Secuiesc
Szekszárd 77 C7 Tolna, S Hungary
Szempcz/Szenc *see* Senec
Szenice *see* Senica
Szenttamás *see* Srbobran
Szeping *see* Siping
Szilágysomlyó *see* Şimleu Silvaniei
Szinna *see* Snina
Sziszek *see* Sisak
Szitás-Keresztúr *see* Cristuru Secuiesc
Szkudy *see* Skuodas
Szlatina *see* Slatina
Szlovákia *see* Slovakia
Szolnok 77 D6 Jász-Nagykun-Szolnok, C Hungary
Szombathely 77 B6 *Ger.* Steinamanger; *anc.* Sabaria, Savaria. Vas, W Hungary
Szprotawa 76 B4 *Ger.* Sprottau. Lubuskie, W Poland
Sztálinváros *see* Dunaújváros
Szucsava *see* Suceava

T

Tabariya, Bahrat *see* Kinneret, Yam
Table Rock Lake 27 G1 *reservoir* Arkansas/ Missouri, C USA
Tábor 77 B5 Jihočeský Kraj, S Czechia (Czech Republic)
Tabora 51 B7 Tabora, W Tanzania
Tabrīz 98 C2 *var.* Tebriz; *anc.* Tauris. Āzarbāyjān-e Sharqī, NW Iran
Tabuaeran 123 G2 *prev.* Fanning Island. *atoll* Line Islands, E Kiribati
Tabūk 98 A4 Tabūk, NW Saudi Arabia
Täby 63 C6 Stockholm, C Sweden
Tachau *see* Tachov
Tachov 77 A5 *Ger.* Tachau. Plveňský Kraj, W Czechia (Czech Republic)
Tacloban 117 F2 *off.* Tacloban City. Leyte, C Philippines
Tacloban City *see* Tacloban
Tacna 39 E4 Tacna, SE Peru
Tacoma 24 B2 Washington, NW USA
Tacuarembó 42 D4 *prev.* San Fructuoso. Tacuarembó, C Uruguay
Tademaït, Plateau du 48 D3 *plateau* C Algeria
Tadmor *see* Tadmur
Tadmur 96 C3 *var.* Tamar, *Gk.* Palmyra, *Bibl.* Tadmor. Ḩimş, C Syria
Tādpatri 110 C2 Andhra Pradesh, E India
Tadzhikistan *see* Tajikistan
Taegu *see* Daegu
Taehan-haehyŏp *see* Korea Strait
Taehan Min'guk *see* South Korea
Taejŏn *see* Daejeon
Tafassâsset, Ténéré du 53 G2 *desert* N Niger
Tafila/Ţafilah, Muḩāfaẓat aţ *see* Aţ Ţafilah
Taganrog 89 A7 Rostovskaya Oblast', SW Russia
Taganrog, Gulf of 87 G4 *Rus.* Taganrogskiy Zaliv, *Ukr.* Tahanroz'ka Zatoka. *gulf* Russia/Ukraine
Taganrogskiy Zaliv *see* Taganrog, Gulf of
Taguatinga 41 F3 Tocantins, C Brazil
Tagus 70 C3 *Port.* Rio Tejo, *Sp.* Río Tajo. *river* Portugal/Spain
Tagus Plain 58 A4 *abyssal plain* E Atlantic Ocean
Tahanroz'ka Zatoka *see* Taganrog, Gulf of
Tahat 49 E4 *mountain* SE Algeria
Tahiti 123 H4 *island* Îles du Vent, W French Polynesia
Tahiti, Archipel de *see* Société, Archipel de la
Tahlequah 27 G1 Oklahoma, C USA
Tahoe, Lake 25 B5 *lake* California/Nevada, W USA
Tahoua 53 F3 Tahoua, W Niger
Taibei *see* Taipei
Taichū *see* Taichung
Taichung 106 D6 *Jap.* Taichū; *var.* Taizhong, Taiwan. C Taiwan
Taiden *see* Daejeon
Taieri 129 B7 *river* South Island, New Zealand
Taihape 128 D4 Manawatu-Wanganui, North Island, New Zealand
Taihoku *see* Taibei
Taikyū *see* Daegu
Tailem Bend 127 B7 South Australia
T'ainan *see* Tainan
Tainan 106 D6 *prev.* T'ainan, Dainan. S Taiwan
Taipei 106 D6 *var.* Taibei, T'aipei; *Jap.* Taihoku; *prev.* Daihoku. *capital* (Taiwan) N Taiwan
Taiping 116 B3 Perak, Peninsular Malaysia
Taitetimu 129 A7 *var.* Caswell Sound. *sound* South Island, New Zealand
Taiwan 106 D6 *off.* Republic of China, *var.* Formosa, Formo'sa. *country* E Asia
Taiwan *see* Taichung
T'aiwan Haihsia/Taiwan Haixia *see* Taiwan Strait
Taiwan Strait 106 D6 *var.* Formosa Strait, *Chin.* T'aiwan Haihsia, Taiwan Haixia. *strait* China/ Taiwan
Taiyuan 106 C4 *var.* T'ai-yuan, T'ai-yüan; *prev.* Yangku. *province capital* Shanxi, C China
T'ai-yuan/T'ai-yüan *see* Taiyuan
Taizhong *see* Tiachung
Ta'izz 99 B7 SW Yemen
Tajikistan 101 E3 *off.* Republic of Tajikistan, *Rus.* Tadzhikistan, *Taj.* Jumhurii Tojikiston; *prev.* Tajik S.S.R. *country* C Asia
Tajikistan, Republic of *see* Tajikistan
Tajik S.S.R *see* Tajikistan
Tajo, Río *see* Tagus
Tak 114 C4 *var.* Rahaeng. Tak, W Thailand
Takao *see* Kaohsiung
Takaoka 109 C5 Toyama, Honshū, SW Japan
Takapuna 128 D2 Auckland, North Island, New Zealand
Takeshima *see* Liancourt Rocks
Takhiatash *see* Taxiatosh
Takhtakupyr *see* Taxtako'pir
Takikawa 108 D2 Hokkaidō, NE Japan
Takla Makan Desert *see* Taklimakan Shamo
Taklimakan Shamo 104 B3 *Eng.* Takla Makan Desert. *desert* NW China
Takow *see* Kaohsiung
Takutea 123 G4 *island* S Cook Islands
Talabriga *see* Aveiro, Portugal
Talabriga *see* Talavera de la Reina, Spain
Talachyn 85 D6 *Rus.* Tolochin. Vitsyebskaya Voblasts', NE Belarus
Talamanca, Cordillera de 31 E5 *mountain range* S Costa Rica
Talara 38 B2 Piura, NW Peru
Talas 101 F2 Talasskaya Oblast', NW Kyrgyzstan
Talaud, Kepulauan 117 F3 *island group* E Indonesia
Talavera de la Reina 70 D3 *anc.* Caesarobriga, Talabriga. Castilla-La Mancha, C Spain
Talca 42 B4 Maule, C Chile
Talcahuano 43 B5 Bío Bío, C Chile
Taldykorgan *see* Taldyqorghan
Taldy-Kurgan *see* Taldyqorghan
Taldyqorghan 92 C5 *var.* Taldykorgan; *prev.* Taldy-Kurgan. Taldykorgan, SE Kazakhstan
Ta-lien *see* Dalian
Taliq-an *see* Tāluqān
Tal'ka 85 C6 Minskaya Voblasts', C Belarus
Talkhof *see* Puurmani
Tall Abyaḑ 96 C2 *var.* At Tall al Abyaḑ, Tell Abyad, *Fr.* Tell Abiad. Ar Raqqah, N Syria
Tallahassee 20 D3 *prev.* Muskogean. *state capital* Florida, SE USA
Tallin *see* Tallinn
Tallinn 84 D2 *Ger.* Reval, *Rus.* Tallin; *prev.* Revel. *country capital* (Estonia) Harjumaa, NW Estonia
Tall Kalakh 96 B4 *var.* Tell Kalakh. Ḩimş, C Syria
Tallulah 20 B2 Louisiana, S USA
Talnakh 92 D3 Taymyrskiy (Dolgano-Nenetskiy) Avtonomnyy Okrug, N Russia
Tal'ne 87 E3 *Rus.* Tal'noye. Cherkas'ka Oblast', C Ukraine
Tal'noye *see* Talne
Taloga 27 F1 Oklahoma, C USA
Tāloqān *see* Tāluqān
Tāluqān 101 E3 *var.* Tāloqān, Taliq-an. Takhār, NE Afghanistan
Talsen *see* Talsi
Talsi 84 C3 *Ger.* Talsen. Talsi, NW Latvia
Taltal 42 B2 Antofagasta, N Chile
Talvik 62 D2 Finnmark, N Norway
Tamabo, Banjaran 116 D3 *mountain range* East Malaysia
Tamale 53 E4 C Ghana
Tamana 123 E3 *prev.* Rotcher Island. *atoll* Tungaru, W Kiribati
Tamanrasset 49 E4 *var.* Tamenghest. S Algeria
Tamar 67 C7 *river* SW England, United Kingdom
Tamar *see* Tadmur
Tamatave *see* Toamasina
Tamazunchale 29 E4 San Luis Potosí, C Mexico
Tambacounda 52 C3 SE Senegal
Tambov 89 B6 Tambovskaya Oblast', W Russia
Tambura 51 B5 W Equatoria, SW South Sudan
Tâmchaket *see* Tâmchekkeţ
Tâmchekkeţ 52 C3 *var.* Tamchaket. Hodh el Gharbi, S Mauritania
Tamenghest *see* Tamanrasset
Tamil Nādu 110 C3 *prev.* Madras. *cultural region* SE India
Tam Ky 115 E5 Quang Nam-Ɗa Nang, C Vietnam
Tammerfors *see* Tampere
Tampa 21 E4 Florida, SE USA
Tampa Bay 21 E4 *bay* Florida, SE USA
Tampere 63 D5 *Swe.* Tammerfors. Pirkanmaa, W Finland
Tampico 29 E3 Tamaulipas, C Mexico
Tamworth 127 D6 New South Wales, SE Australia
Tanabe 109 C7 Wakayama, Honshū, SW Japan
Tana Bru 62 D2 Finnmark, N Norway
T'ana Hāyk' 50 C4 *var.* Lake Tana. *lake* NW Ethiopia
Tanais *see* Don
Tana, Lake *see* T'ana Hāyk'
Tanami Desert 124 D3 *desert* Northern Territory, N Australia
Tananarive *see* Antananarivo
Țăndărei 86 D5 Ialomița, SE Romania
Tandil 43 D5 Buenos Aires, E Argentina
Tandjoengkarang *see* Bandar Lampung
Tanega-shima 109 B8 *island* Nansei-shotō, SW Japan
Tanen Taunggyi *see* Tane Range
Tane Range 114 B4 *Bur.* Tanen Taunggyi. *mountain range* W Thailand
Tanezrouft 48 D4 *desert* Algeria/Mali
Ţanf, Jabal aţ 96 D4 *mountain* SE Syria
Tanga 51 C7 Tanga, E Tanzania
Tanganyika and Zanzibar *see* Tanzania
Tanganyika, Lake 51 B7 *lake* E Africa
Tanger 48 C2 *var.* Tangiers, Tangier, *Fr./Ger.* Tangerk, *Sp.* Tánger; *anc.* Tingis. NW Morocco
Tangerk *see* Tanger
Tanggula Shan 104 C4 *mountain* W China
Tangier *see* Tanger
Tangiers *see* Tanger
Tangra Yumco 104 B5 *var.* Tangro Tso. *lake* W China
Tangro Tso *see* Tangra Yumco
Tangshan 106 D3 *var.* T'ang-shan. Hebei, E China
T'ang-shan *see* Tangshan
Tanimbar, Kepulauan 117 F5 *island group* Maluku, E Indonesia
Tanintharyi 115 B6 *prev.* Tenasserim. S Myanmar (Burma)
Tanjungkarang/Tanjungkarang-Telukbetung *see* Bandar Lampung
Tanna 122 D4 *island* S Vanuatu
Tannenhof *see* Krynica
Tan-Tan 48 B3 SW Morocco
Tan-tung *see* Dandong
Tanzania 51 C7 *off.* United Republic of Tanzania, *Swa.* Jamhuri ya Muungano wa Tanzania; *prev.* German East Africa, Tanganyika and Zanzibar. *country* E Africa
Tanzania, Jamhuri ya Muungano wa *see* Tanzania
Tanzania, United Republic of *see* Tanzania
Taoudenit *see* Taoudenni
Taoudenni *see* Tombouctou
Tapa 84 E2 *Ger.* Taps. Lääne-Virumaa, NE Estonia
Tapachula 29 G5 Chiapas, SE Mexico
Tapaiu *see* Gvardeysk
Tapajós, Rio 41 E2 *var.* Tapajóz. *river* NW Brazil
Tapajóz *see* Tapajós, Rio
Taps *see* Tapa
Ţarābulus 49 F2 *var.* Ţarābulus al Gharb, *Eng.* Tripoli. *country capital* (Libya) NW Libya
Ţarābulus al Gharb *see* Ţarābulus
Tarābulus/Ţarābulus ash Shām *see* Tripoli
Taraclia 86 D4 *Rus.* Tarakilya. S Moldova
Tarakilya *see* Taraclia
Taranaki, Mount 128 C4 *var.* Egmont. *volcano* North Island, New Zealand
Tarancón 71 E3 Castilla-La Mancha, C Spain
Taranto 75 E5 *var.* Tarentum. Puglia, SE Italy
Taranto, Gulf of 75 E6 *Eng.* Gulf of Taranto. *gulf* S Italy
Taranto, Gulf of *see* Taranto, Golfo di
Tarapoto 38 C2 San Martín, N Peru
Tarare 69 D5 Rhône, E France
Tarascon 69 D6 Bouches-du-Rhône, SE France
Tarawa 122 D2 *atoll and capital* (Kiribati) Tungaru, W Kiribati
Taraz 92 C5 *prev.* Aulie Ata, Auliye-Ata, Dzhambul, Zhambyl. Zhambyl, S Kazakhstan
Tarazona 71 E2 Aragón, NE Spain
Tarbes 69 B6 *anc.* Bigorra. Hautes-Pyrénées, S France
Tarcoola 127 A6 South Australia
Taree 127 D6 New South Wales, SE Australia
Tarentum *see* Taranto
Târgovişte 86 C5 *prev.* Tîrgovişte. Dâmboviţa, S Romania
Targu Jiu 86 B4 *prev.* Tîrgu Jiu. Gorj, W Romania
Târgul-Neamţ *see* Târgu-Neamţ
Târgul-Săcuiesc *see* Târgu Secuiesc
Târgu Mureş 86 B4 *prev.* Oşorhei, Tîrgu Mures, *Ger.* Neumarkt, *Hung.* Marosvásárhely. Mureş, C Romania
Târgu-Neamţ 86 C3 *var.* Târgul-Neamţ; *prev.* Tîrgu-Neamţ. Neamţ, NE Romania
Târgu Ocna 86 C4 *Hung.* Aknavásár; *prev.* Tîrgu Ocna. Bacău, E Romania
Târgu Secuiesc 86 C4 *Ger.* Neumarkt, Szekler Neumarkt, *Hung.* Kezdivásárhely; *prev.* Chezdi-Oşorheiu, Târgul-Săcuiesc, Tîrgu Secuiesc. Covasna, E Romania
Tar Heel State *see* North Carolina
Tarija 39 G5 Tarija, S Bolivia
Tarīm 99 C6 C Yemen
Tarim Basin *see* Tarim Pendi
Tarim Pendi 102 C2 *Eng.* Tarim Basin. *basin* NW China
Tarim He 104 B3 *river* NW China
Tarma 38 C3 Junín, C Peru
Tarn 69 C6 *cultural region* S France
Tarn 69 C6 *river* S France
Tarnobrzeg 76 D4 Podkarpackie, SE Poland
Tarnopol *see* Ternopil
Tarnów 77 D5 Małopolskie, S Poland
Tarraco *see* Tarragona
Tarragona 71 G2 *anc.* Tarraco. Cataluña, E Spain
Tarrasa *see* Terrassa
Tàrrega 71 F2 *var.* Tarrega. Cataluña, NE Spain
Tarsatica *see* Rijeka
Tarsus 94 C4 İçel, S Turkey (Türkiye)
Tartous/Tartouss *see* Ţarţūs
Tartu 84 D3 *Ger.* Dorpat; *prev. Rus.* Yurev, Yury'ev. Tartumaa, SE Estonia
Ţarţūs 96 A3 *off.* Muḩāfaẓat Ţarţūs, *var.* Tartous, Tartus. *governorate* W Syria
Ţarţūs, Muḩāfaẓat *see* Ţarţūs
Ta Ru Tao, Ko 115 B7 *island* S Thailand Asia
Tarvisio 74 D2 Friuli-Venezia Giulia, NE Italy
Tarvisium *see* Treviso
Tashauz *see* Daşoguz
Tashi Chho Dzong *see* Thimphu
Tashkent *see* Toshkent
Tash-Kömür *see* Tash-Kumyr
Tash-Kumyr 101 F2 *Kir.* Tash-Kömür. Dzhalal-Abadskaya Oblast', W Kyrgyzstan
Tashqurghan *see* Khulm
Tasiilaq 60 D4 *var.* Angmagssalik. Semersooq, S Greenland
Tasikmalaja *see* Tasikmalaya
Tasikmalaya 116 C5 *prev.* Tasikmalaja. Jawa, C Indonesia
Tasman Basin 120 C5 *var.* East Australian Basin. *undersea basin* S Tasman Sea
Tasman Bay 129 C5 *var.* Te Tai-o-Aorere. *inlet* South Island, New Zealand
Tasmania 127 B8 *prev.* Van Diemen's Land. *state* SE Australia
Tasmania 130 B4 *island* SE Australia
Tasman Plateau 120 C5 *var.* South Tasmania Plateau. *undersea plateau* SW Tasman Sea
Tasman Sea 120 C5 *sea* SW Pacific Ocean
Tassili-n-Ajjer 49 E4 *plateau* E Algeria
Tatabánya 77 C6 Komárom-Esztergom, NW Hungary
Tatar Pazardzhik *see* Pazardzhik
Tathlīth 99 B5 'Asīr, S Saudi Arabia
Tatra Mountains 77 D5 *Ger.* Tatra, *Hung.* Tátra, *Pol./Slvk.* Tatry. *mountain range* Poland/Slovakia
Tatra/Tátra *see* Tatra Mountains
Tatry *see* Tatra Mountains
Ta-t'ung/Tatung *see* Datong
Tatvan 95 F3 Bitlis, SE Turkey (Türkiye)
Ta'ū 123 F4 *var.* Tau. *island* Manua Islands, E American Samoa
Taukum, Peski 101 G1 *desert* SE Kazakhstan
Taumarunui 128 D4 Manawatu-Wanganui, North Island, New Zealand
Taungdwingyi 114 B3 Magway, C Myanmar (Burma)
Taunggyi 114 B3 Shan State, C Myanmar (Burma)
Taungoo 114 B4 Bago, C Myanmar (Burma)
Taunton 67 C7 SW England, United Kingdom

Taupo *128 D3* Waikato, North Island, New Zealand
Taupo, Lake *128 D3 lake* North Island, New Zealand
Tauragė *84 B4 Ger.* Tauroggen. Tauragė, SW Lithuania
Tauranga *128 D3* Bay of Plenty, North Island, New Zealand
Tauris *see* Tabrīz
Tauroggen *see* Tauragė
Taurus Mountains *see* Toros Dağları
Tavas *94 B4* Denizli, SW Turkey (Türkiye)
Tavastehus *see* Hämeenlinna
Tavira *70 C5* Faro, S Portugal
Tavoy *see* Dawei
Tavoy Island *see* Mali Kyun
Ta Waewae Bay *129 A7 bay* South Island, New Zealand
Tawakoni, Lake *27 G2 reservoir* Texas, SW USA
Tawau *116 D3* Sabah, East Malaysia
Ṭawkar *see* Tokar
Tawzar *see* Tozeur
Taxco *29 E4 var.* Taxco de Alarcón. Guerrero, S Mexico
Taxco de Alarcón *see* Taxco
Taxiatosh *100 C2 Rus.* Takhiatash. Qoraqalpog'iston Respublikasi, W Uzbekistan
Taxtako'pir *100 D1 Rus.* Takhtakupyr. Qoraqalpog'iston Respublikasi, NW Uzbekistan
Tay *66 C3 river* C Scotland, United Kingdom
Taylor *27 G3* Texas, SW USA
Taymā' *98 A4* Tabūk, NW Saudi Arabia
Taymyr, Ozero *93 E2 lake* N Russia
Taymyr, Poluostrov *93 E2 peninsula* N Russia
Taz *92 D3 river* N Russia
Tbilisi *95 G2 var.* T'bilisi, *Eng.* Tiflis. *country capital* (Georgia) SE Georgia
T'bilisi *see* **Tbilisi**
Tchad *see* Chad
Tchad, Lac *see* Chad, Lake
Tchien *see* Zwedru
Tchongking *see* Chongqing
Tczew *76 C2 Ger.* Dirschau. Pomorskie, N Poland
Te Anau *129 A7* Southland, South Island, New Zealand
Te Anau, Lake *129 A7 lake* South Island, New Zealand
Teapa *29 G4* Tabasco, SE Mexico
Teate *see* Chieti
Tebingtinggi *116 B3* Sumatera, N Indonesia
Tebriz *see* Tabrīz
Techirghiol *86 D5* Constanţa, SE Romania
Tecomán *28 D4* Colima, SW Mexico
Tecpan *29 E5 var.* Tecpan de Galeana. Guerrero, S Mexico
Tecpan de Galeana *see* Tecpan
Tecuci *86 C4* Galaţi, E Romania
Tedzhen *see* Harī Rōd
Tees *67 D5 river* N England, United Kingdom
Tefé *40 D2* Amazonas, N Brazil
Tegal *116 C4* Jawa, C Indonesia
Tegelen *65 D5* Limburg, SE Netherlands
Tegucigalpa *30 C3 country capital* (Honduras) Francisco Morazán, SW Honduras
Te Hauturu-o-Toi *128 D2 var.* Little Barrier Island. *island* N New Zealand
Teheran *see* Tehrān
Te Houhou *129 A7 var.* Gerorge Sound. *sound* South Island, New Zealand
Tehrān *98 C3 var.* Teheran. *country capital* (Iran) Tehrān, N Iran
Tehuacán *29 F4* Puebla, S Mexico
Tehuantepec *29 F5 var.* Santo Domingo Tehuantepec. Oaxaca, SE Mexico
Tehuantepec, Golfo de *29 F5 var.* Gulf of Tehuantepec. *gulf* S Mexico
Tehuantepec, Gulf of *see* Tehuantepec, Golfo de
Tehuantepec, Isthmus of *see* Tehuantepec, Istmo de
Tehuantepec, Istmo de *29 F5 var.* Isthmus of Tehuantepec. *isthmus* SE Mexico
Te Ika-a-Māui *see* North Island
Tejen *100 C3 Rus.* Tedzhen. Ahal Welaýaty, S Turkmenistan
Tejen *see* Harī Rōd
Tejo, Rio *see* Tagus
Te Kao *128 C1* Northland, North Island, New Zealand
Tekax *29 H4 var.* Tekax de Álvaro Obregón. Yucatán, SE Mexico
Tekax de Álvaro Obregón *see* Tekax
Tekeli *92 C5* Almaty, SE Kazakhstan
Tekirdağ *94 A2 It.* Rodosto; *anc.* Bisanthe, Raidestos, Rhaedestus. Tekirdağ, NW Turkey (Türkiye)
Te Kuiti *128 D3* Waikato, North Island, New Zealand
Tela *30 C2* Atlántida, NW Honduras
Telanaipura *see* Jambi
Telangana *112 D5 cultural region* SE India
Tel Aviv-Jaffa *see* Tel Aviv-Yafo
Tel Aviv-Yafo *97 A6 var.* Tel Aviv-Jaffa. Tel Aviv, C Israel
Teles Pirés *see* São Manuel, Rio
Telish *82 C2 prev.* Azizie. Pleven, N Bulgaria
Tell Abiad/Tell Abyad *see* Tall Abyaḍ
Tell Kalakh *see* Tall Kalakh
Tell Shedadi *see* Ash Shadādah
Tel'man/Tel'mansk *see* Gubadag
Teloekbetoeng *see* Bandar Lampung
Telo Martius *see* Toulon
Telschen *see* Telšiai
Telšiai *84 B3 Ger.* Telschen. Telšiai, NW Lithuania
Telukbetung *see* Bandar Lampung
Temerin *78 D3* Vojvodina, N Serbia
Temeschburg/Temeschwar *see* Timişoara
Temesvár/Temeswar *see* Timişoara
Temirtau *92 C4 prev.* Samarkandski, Samarkandskoye. Karagandy, C Kazakhstan
Tempio Pausania *75 A5* Sardegna, Italy, C Mediterranean Sea
Temple *27 G3* Texas, SW USA
Temuco *43 B5* Araucanía, C Chile
Temuka *129 B6* Canterbury, South Island, New Zealand
Tenasserim *see* Tanintharyi
Ténenkou *52 D3* Mopti, C Mali
Ténéré *53 G3 physical region* C Niger
Tenerife *48 A3 island* Islas Canarias, Spain, NE Atlantic Ocean
Tengger Shamo *105 E3 desert* N China
Tengréla *52 D4 var.* Tingréla. N Ivory Coast
Tenkodogo *53 E4* S Burkina
Tennant Creek *126 A3* Northern Territory, C Australia
Tennessee *20 C1 off.* State of Tennessee, *also known as* The Volunteer State. *state* SE USA
Tennessee River *20 C1 river* S USA
Tenos *see* Tínos
Te-Oneroa-a-Tōhē *128 C1 var.* Ninety Mile Beach. *beach* North Island, New Zealand
Tepelena *see* Tepelenë
Tepelenë *79 C7 var.* Tepelena, *It.* Tepeleni. Gjirokastër, S Albania
Tepeleni *see* Tepelenë
Tepic *28 D4* Nayarit, C Mexico
Teplice *76 A4 Ger.* Teplitz; *prev.* Teplice-Šanov, Teplitz-Schönau. Ústecký Kraj, NW Czechia (Czech Republic)
Teplice-Šanov/Teplitz/Teplitz-Schönau *see* Teplice
Tequila *28 D4* Jalisco, SW Mexico
Teraina *123 G2 prev.* Washington Island. *atoll* Line Islands, E Kiribati
Teramo *74 C4 anc.* Interamna. Abruzzi, C Italy
Tercan *95 E3* Erzincan, NE Turkey (Türkiye)
Terceira *70 A5 var.* Ilha Terceira. *island* Azores, Portugal, NE Atlantic Ocean
Terceira, Ilha *see* Terceira
Terekhovka *see* Tsyerakhowka
Te Rerenga Wairua *see* Reinga, Cape
Teresina *41 F2 var.* Therezina. *state capital* Piauí, NE Brazil
Termez *see* Termiz
Termia *see* Kýthnos
Términos, Laguna de *29 G4 lagoon* SE Mexico
Termiz *101 E3 Rus.* Termez. Surkhondaryo Viloyati, S Uzbekistan
Termoli *74 D4* Molise, C Italy
Terneuzen *65 B5 var.* Neuzen. Zeeland, SW Netherlands
Terni *74 C4 anc.* Interamna Nahars. Umbria, C Italy
Ternopil *86 C2 Pol.* Tarnopol, *Rus.* Ternopol'. Ternopil's'ka Oblast', W Ukraine
Ternopol' *see* Ternopil
Terracina *75 C5* Lazio, C Italy
Terranova di Sicilia *see* Gela
Terranova Pausania *see* Olbia
Terrassa *71 G2 Cast.* Tarrasa. Cataluña, E Spain
Terre Adélie *132 C4 physical region* Antarctica
Terre Haute *18 B4* Indiana, N USA
Terre Neuve *see* Newfoundland and Labrador
Terschelling *64 C1 Fris.* Skylge. *island* Waddeneilanden, N Netherlands
Teruel *71 F3 anc.* Turba. Aragón, E Spain
Tervel *82 E1 prev.* Kurtbunar, *Rom.* Curtbunar. Dobrich, NE Bulgaria
Tervueren *see* Tervuren
Tervuren *65 C6 var.* Tervueren. Vlaams Brabant, C Belgium
Teseney *50 C4 var.* Tessenei. W Eritrea
Tessalit *53 E2* Kidal, NE Mali
Tessaoua *53 G3* Maradi, S Niger
Tessenderlo *65 C5* Limburg, NE Belgium
Tessenei *see* Teseney
Testigos, Islas los *37 E1 island group* N Venezuela
Te Tai-o-Aorere *see* Tasman Bay
Tete *57 E2* Tete, NW Mozambique
Teterow *72 C3* Mecklenburg-Vorpommern, NE Germany
Tétouan *48 C2 var.* Tetouan, Tetuán. N Morocco
Tetovo *79 D5* Razgrad, N Bulgaria
Tetschen *see* Děčín
Tetuán *see* Tétouan
Teverya *see* Tverya
Te Waewae Bay *129 A7 bay* South Island, New Zealand
Te Waipounamu *see* South Island
Texarkana *20 A2* Arkansas, C USA
Texarkana *27 H2* Texas, SW USA
Texas *27 F3 off.* State of Texas, *also known as* Lone Star State. *state* S USA
Texas City *27 H4* Texas, SW USA
Texel *64 C2 island* Waddeneilanden, NW Netherlands
Texoma, Lake *27 G2 reservoir* Oklahoma/ Texas, C USA
Teziutlán *29 F4* Puebla, S Mexico
Thaa Atoll *see* Kolhumadulu
Thai, Ao *see* Thailand, Gulf of
Thai Binh *114 D3* Thai Binh, N Vietnam
Thailand *115 C5 off.* Kingdom of Thailand, *Th.* Prathet Thai; *prev.* Siam. *country* SE Asia
Thailand, Gulf of *115 C6 var.* Gulf of Siam, *Th.* Ao Thai, *Vtn.* Vinh Thai Lan. *gulf* SE Asia
Thailand, Kingdom of *see* Thailand
Thai Lan, Vinh *see* Thailand, Gulf of
Thai Nguyên *114 D3* Băc Thai, N Vietnam
Thakhèk *114 D4 var.* Muang Khammouan. Khammouan, C Laos
Thamarīd *see* Thamarīt
Thamarīt *99 D6 var.* Thamarīd, Thumrayt. SW Oman
Thames *128 D3* Waikato, North Island, New Zealand
Thames *67 B8 river* S England, United Kingdom
Thandwe *114 A4 var.* Sandoway. Rakhine State, W Myanmar (Burma)
Thanh Hoa *114 D3* Thanh Hoa, N Vietnam
Thanintari Taungdan *see* Bilauktaung Range
Thanlwin *see* Salween
Thar Desert *112 C3 var.* Great Indian Desert, Indian Desert. *desert* India/Pakistan
Tharthar, Buhayrat ath *98 B3 lake* C Iraq
Thásos *82 C4* Thásos, E Greece
Thásos *82 C4 island* E Greece
Thaton *114 B4* Mon State, S Myanmar (Burma)
Thayet *114 A4 var.* Thayetmyo. Magway, C Myanmar (Burma)
Thayetmyo *see* Thayet
The Crane *33 H2 var.* Crane. S Barbados
The Dalles *24 B3* Oregon, NW USA
The Flatts Village *see* Flatts Village
The Hague *see* 's-Gravenhage
Theodosia *see* Feodosiia
The Pas *15 F5* Manitoba, C Canada
Therezina *see* Teresina
Thérma *83 D6* Ikaría, Dodekánisa, Greece, Aegean Sea
Thermaic Gulf/Thermaicus Sinus *see* Thermaïkós Kólpos
Thermaïkós Kólpos *82 B4 Eng.* Thermaic Gulf; *anc.* Thermaicus Sinus. *gulf* N Greece
Thermiá *see* Kýthnos
Thérmo *83 B5* Dytikí Ellás, C Greece
The Rock *71 H4* New South Wales, SE Australia
The Sooner State *see* Oklahoma
Thessaloníki *82 C3 Eng.* Salonica, Salonika, *Croatian* Solun, *Turk.* Selânik. Kentrikí Makedonía, N Greece
The Valley *33 G3 dependent territory capital* (Anguilla) E Anguilla
The Village *27 G1* Oklahoma, C USA
The Volunteer State *see* Tennessee
Thiamis *see* Thýamis
Thian Shan *see* Tien Shan
Thibet *see* Xizang Zizhiqu
Thief River Falls *23 F1* Minnesota, N USA
Thienen *see* Tienen
Thiers *69 C5* Puy-de-Dôme, C France
Thiès *52 B3* W Senegal
Thikombia *see* Cikobia
Thimbu *see* Thimphu
Thimphu *113 G3 var.* Thimbu; *prev.* Tashi Chho Dzong. *country capital* (Bhutan) W Bhutan
Thionville *68 D3 Ger.* Diedenhofen. Moselle, NE France
Thíra *83 D7 var.* Santorini. Kykládes, Greece, Aegean Sea
Thiruvananthapuram *110 C3 var.* Trivandrum, Tiruvantapuram. *state capital* Kerala, SW India
Thitu Island *106 C8 island* NW Spratly Islands
Tholen *64 B4 island* SW Netherlands
Thomasville *20 D3* Georgia, SE USA
Thompson *15 F4* Manitoba, C Canada
Thonon-les-Bains *69 D5* Haute-Savoie, E France
Thoothukudi *see* Tuticorin
Thorenburg *see* Turda
Thorlákshöfn *61 E5* Sudhurland, SW Iceland
Thorn *see* Toruń
Thornton Island *see* Millennium Island
Thorshavn *see* Tórshavn
Thospitis *see* Van Gölü
Thouars *68 B4* Deux-Sèvres, W France
Thoune *see* Thun
Thracian Sea *82 D4 Gk.* Thrakikó Pélagos; *anc.* Thracium Mare. *sea* Greece/Turkey (Türkiye)
Thracium Mare/Thrakikó Pélagos *see* Thracian Sea
Three Gorges Reservoir *107 C5 reservoir* C China
Three Kings Islands *see* Manawatāwhi
Thrissur *110 C3 var.* Trichūr. Kerala, SW India
Thuin *65 B7* Hainaut, S Belgium
Thule *see* Qaanaaq
Thumrayt *see* Thamarīt
Thun *73 A7 Fr.* Thoune. Bern, W Switzerland
Thunder Bay *16 B4* Ontario, S Canada
Thuner See *73 A7 lake* C Switzerland
Thung Song *115 C7 var.* Cha Mai. Nakhon Si Thammarat, SW Thailand
Thurso *66 C2* N Scotland, United Kingdom
Thýamis *82 A4 var.* Kalamás; *prev.* Thiamis. *river* W Greece
Tianjin *106 D4 var.* Tientsin. Tianjin Shi, E China
Tianjin *see* Tianjin Shi
Tianjin Shi *106 D4 var.* Jin, Tianjin, T'ien-ching, Tientsin. *municipality* E China
Tian Shan *see* Tien Shan
Tianshui *106 B4* Gansu, C China
Tiba *see* Chiba
Tiber *74 C4 Eng.* Tiber. *river* C Italy
Tiber *see* Tevere, Italy
Tiber *see* Tivoli, Italy
Tiberias *see* Tverya
Tiberias, Lake *see* Yam Kinneret
Tibesti *54 C2 var.* Tibesti Massif, *Ar.* Tibistī. *mountain range* N Africa
Tibesti Massif *see* Tibesti
Tibet *see* Xizang Zizhiqu
Tibetan Autonomous Region *see* Xizang Zizhiqu
Tibet, Plateau of *see* Qingzang Gaoyuan
Tibistī *see* Tibesti
Tibnī *see* At Tibnī
Tiburón, Isla *28 B2 var.* Isla del Tiburón. *island* NW Mexico
Tiburón, Isla del *see* Tiburón, Isla
Tichau *see* Tychy
Tichit *52 D2 var.* Tichitt. Tagant, C Mauritania
Tichitt *see* Tîchît
Ticinum *see* Pavia
Ticul *29 H3* Yucatán, SE Mexico
Tidjikdja *see* Tidjikja
Tidjikja *52 C2 var.* Tidjikdja; *prev.* Fort-Cappolani. Tagant, C Mauritania
T'ien-ching *see* Tianjin Shi
Tienen *65 C6 var.* Thienen, *Fr.* Tirlemont. Vlaams Brabant, C Belgium
Tiên Giang, Sông *see* Mekong
Tien Shan *104 B3 Chin.* Thian Shan, Tian Shan, T'ien Shan, *Rus.* Tyan'-Shan'. *mountain range* C Asia
Tientsin *see* Tianjin
Tierp *63 C6* Uppsala, C Sweden
Tierra del Fuego *43 B8 island* Argentina/Chile
Tiflis *see* T'bilisi
Tifton *20 D3* Georgia, SE USA
Tifu *117 F4* Pulau Buru, E Indonesia
Tighina *see* Bender
Tigranocerta *see* Siirt
Tigris *98 B2 Ar.* Dijlah, *Turk.* Dicle. *river* Iraq/Syria/Turkey (Türkiye)
Tiguentourine *49 E3* E Algeria
Ti-hua/Tihwa *see* Ürümqi
Tijuana *28 A1* Baja California Norte, NW Mexico
Tikapa Moana *see* Hauraki Gulf
Tikhoretsk *89 A7* Krasnodarskiy Kray, SW Russia
Tikhvin *88 B4* Leningradskaya Oblast', NW Russia
Tikiarjuaq *see* Whale Cove
Tiki Basin *121 G3 undersea basin* S Pacific Ocean
Tikinsso *52 C4 river* C Guinea
Tiksi *93 F2* Respublika Sakha (Yakutiya), NE Russia
Tilburg *64 C4* Noord-Brabant, S Netherlands
Tilimsen *see* Tlemcen
Tilio Martius *see* Toulon
Tillabéri *53 F3 var.* Tillabéry. Tillabéri, W Niger
Tillabéry *see* Tillabéri
Tílos *83 E7 island* Dodekánisa, Greece, Aegean Sea
Timan Ridge *see* Timanskiy Kryazh
Timanskiy Kryazh *88 D3 Eng.* Timan Ridge. *ridge* NW Russia
Timaru *129 B6* Canterbury, South Island, New Zealand
Timbaki/Timbákion *see* Tympáki
Timbedgha *52 D3 var.* Timbédra. Hodh ech Chargui, SE Mauritania
Timbédra *see* Timbedgha
Timbuktu *see* Tombouctou
Timiş *86 A4 county* SW Romania
Timişoara *86 A4 Ger.* Temeschwar, Temeswar, *Hung.* Temesvár; *prev.* Temeschburg. Timiş, W Romania
Timmins *16 C4* Ontario, S Canada
Timor *103 F5 island* Nusa Tenggara, C Indonesia
Timor-Leste *see* East Timor
Timor Lorosa'e *see* East Timor
Timor Sea *103 F5 sea* E Indian Ocean
Timor Timur *see* East Timor
Timor Trench *see* Timor Trough
Timor Trough *103 F5 var.* Timor Trench. *trough* NE Timor Sea
Timrå *63 C5* Västernorrland, C Sweden
Tindouf *48 C3* W Algeria
Tineo *70 C1* Asturias, N Spain
Tingis *see* Tanger
Tingo María *38 C3* Huánuco, C Peru
Tingréla *see* Tengréla
Tinhosa Grande *54 E2 island* N Sao Tome and Principe, Africa, E Atlantic Ocean
Tinhosa Pequena *54 E1 island* N Sao Tome and Principe, Africa, E Atlantic Ocean
Tinian *122 B1 island* S Northern Mariana Islands
Tínos *83 D6* Tínos, Kykládes, Greece, Aegean Sea
Tínos *83 D6 anc.* Tenos. *island* Kykládes, Greece, Aegean Sea
Tip *79 E6* Papua, E Indonesia
Tipitapa *30 D3* Managua, W Nicaragua
Tip Top Mountain *16 C4 mountain* Ontario, S Canada
Tirana *see* Tiranë
Tiranë *79 C6 var.* Tirana. *country capital* (Albania) Tiranë, C Albania
Tiraspol *86 D4 Rus.* Tiraspol'. E Moldova
Tiraspol' *see* Tiraspol
Tiree *66 B3 island* W Scotland, United Kingdom
Tîrgovişte *see* Târgovişte
Tîrgu Jiu *see* Targu Jiu
Tîrgu Mures *see* Târgu Mureş
Tîrgu-Neamţ *see* Târgu-Neamţ
Tîrgu Ocna *see* Târgu Ocna
Tîrgu Secuiesc *see* Târgu Secuiesc
Tirlemont *see* Tienen
Tírnavos *see* Týrnavos
Tirnovo *see* Veliko Tarnovo
Tirol *73 C7 off.* Land Tirol, *var.* Tyrol, *It.* Tirolo. *state* W Austria
Tirol, Land *see* Tirol
Tirolo *see* Tirol
Tirreno, Mare *see* Tyrrhenian Sea
Tiruchchirāppalli *110 C3 prev.* Trichinopoly. Tamil Nādu, SE India
Tiruppattūr *110 C2* Tamil Nādu, SE India
Tiruvantapuram *see* Thiruvanathapuram
Tisa *see* Tisza
Tisza *81 F1 Ger.* Theiss, *Rom./Slvn./Croatian* Tisa, *Rus.* Tissa, *Ukr.* Tysa. *river* SE Europe
Tiszakécske *77 D7* Bács-Kiskun, C Hungary
Titano, Monte *74 E1 mountain* C San Marino
Tītī *129 A8 var.* Muttonbird Islands. *island group* SW New Zealand
Titicaca, Lake *39 E4 lake* Bolivia/Peru
Titograd *see* Podgorica
Titose *see* Chitose
Titova Mitrovica *see* Mitrovicë
Titovo Užice *see* Užice
Titu *86 C5* Dâmboviţa, S Romania
Titule *55 D5* Orientale, N Dem. Rep. Congo
Tiverton *67 C7* SW England, United Kingdom
Tivoli *74 C4 anc.* Tiber. Lazio, C Italy
Tizimín *29 H3* Yucatán, SE Mexico
Tizi Ouzou *49 E1 var.* Tizi-Ouzou. N Algeria
Tizi-Ouzou *see* Tizi Ouzou
Tiznit *48 B3* SW Morocco
Tjilatjap *see* Cilacap
Tjirebon *see* Cirebon
Tlaquepaque *28 D4* Jalisco, C Mexico
Tlascala *see* Tlaxcala
Tlaxcala *29 F4 var.* Tlascala, Tlaxcala de Xicohténcatl. Tlaxcala, C Mexico
Tlaxcala de Xicohténcatl *see* Tlaxcala
Tlemcen *48 D2 var.* Tilimsen, Tlemsen. NW Algeria
Tlemsen *see* Tlemcen
Toamasina *57 G3 var.* Tamatave. Toamasina, E Madagascar
Toba, Danau *116 B3 lake* Sumatera, W Indonesia
Tobago *33 H5 island* NE Trinidad and Tobago
Toba Kakar Range *112 B2 mountain range* NW Pakistan
Tobol *92 C4 Kaz.* Tobyl. *river* Kazakhstan/Russia
Tobol'sk *92 C3* Tyumenskaya Oblast', C Russia
Tobruch/Tobruk *see* Ṭubruq
Tobyl *see* Tobol
Tocantins *41 E3 off.* Estado do Tocantins. *state/ region* C Brazil
Tocantins, Estado do *see* Tocantins
Tocantins, Rio *41 F2 river* N Brazil
Tocoa *30 D2* Colón, N Honduras
Tocopilla *42 B2* Antofagasta, N Chile
Todi *74 C4* Umbria, C Italy
Todos os Santos, Baía de *41 G3 bay* E Brazil
Toetoes Bay *129 B8 bay* South Island, New Zealand
Tofua *123 E4 island* Ha'apai Group, C Tonga
Togo *53 E4 off.* Togolese Republic; *prev.* French Togoland. *country* W Africa
Togolese Republic *see* Togo
Tojikiston, Jumhurii *see* Tajikistan
Tokanui *129 B7* Southland, South Island, New Zealand
Tokar *50 C3 var.* Ṭawkar. Red Sea, NE Sudan
Tokat *94 D3* Tokat, N Turkey (Türkiye)
Tokelau *123 E3 NZ overseas territory* W Polynesia
Tőketerebes *see* Trebišov
Tokio *see* Tōkyō
Tokmak *101 G2 Kir.* Tokmok. Chuyskaya Oblast', N Kyrgyzstan
Tokmak *87 G4 var.* Velykyy Tokmak. Zaporiz'ka Oblast', SE Ukraine
Tokmok *see* Tokmak
Tokoroa *128 D3* Waikato, North Island, New Zealand
Tokounou *52 C4* C Guinea
Tokushima *109 C6 var.* Tokusima. Tokushima, Shikoku, SW Japan
Tōkyō *108 A1 var.* Tokio. *country capital* (Japan) Tōkyō, Honshū, S Japan
Tōkyō-wan *108 A2 bay* S Japan
Tolbukhin *see* Dobrich
Toledo *70 D3 anc.* Toletum. Castilla-La Mancha, C Spain
Toledo *18 D3* Ohio, N USA
Toledo Bend Reservoir *27 G3 reservoir* Louisiana/ Texas, SW USA
Toletum *see* Toledo
Toliara *57 F4 var.* Toliary; *prev.* Tuléar. Toliara, SW Madagascar
Toliary *see* Toliara
Tolmein *see* Tolmin
Tolmin *73 D7 Ger.* Tolmein, *It.* Tolmino. W Slovenia
Tolmino *see* Tolmin
Tolna *77 C7 Ger.* Tolnau. Tolna, S Hungary
Tolnau *see* Tolna
Tolochin *see* Talachyn
Tolosa *71 E1* País Vasco, N Spain
Tolosa *see* Toulouse
Toluca *29 E4 var.* Toluca de Lerdo. México, S Mexico
Toluca de Lerdo *see* Toluca
Tol'yatti *89 C6 prev.* Stavropol'. Samarskaya Oblast', W Russia
Tomah *18 B2* Wisconsin, N USA
Tomakomai *108 D2* Hokkaidō, NE Japan
Tomar *70 B3* Santarém, W Portugal
Tomaschow *see* Tomaszów Mazowiecki
Tomaschow *see* Tomaszów Lubelski
Tomaszów *see* Tomaszów Mazowiecki
Tomaszów Lubelski *76 E4 Ger.* Tomaschow. Lubelskie, E Poland
Tomaszów Mazowiecka *see* Tomaszów Mazowiecki
Tomaszów Mazowiecki *76 D4 var.* Tomaszów Mazowiecka; *prev.* Tomaszów, *Ger.* Tomaschow. Łódzkie, C Poland
Tombigbee River *20 C3 river* Alabama/ Mississippi, S USA
Tombouctou *53 E3 Eng.* Timbuktu. *var.* Taoudenni, N Mali
Tombua *56 A2 Port.* Porto Alexandre. Namibe, SW Angola
Tomelloso *71 E3* Castilla-La Mancha, C Spain
Tomini, Gulf of *see* Teluk Tomini
Tomini, Teluk *117 E4 Eng.* Gulf of Tomini; *prev.* Teluk Gorontalo. *bay* Sulawesi, C Indonesia
Tomsk *92 D4* Tomskaya Oblast', C Russia
Tömür Feng *104 B3 pre. Pik Pobedy; Kyrg.* Jengish Chokusu. *mountain* China/Kyrgyzstan
Tonezh *see* Tonyezh
Tonga *123 E4 off.* Kingdom of Tonga, *var.* Friendly Islands. *country* SW Pacific Ocean
Tonga, Kingdom of *see* Tonga
Tongatapu *123 E5 island* Tongatapu Group, S Tonga
Tongatapu Group *123 E5 island group* S Tonga
Tonga Trench *121 E3 trench* S Pacific Ocean
Tongchuan *106 C4* Shaanxi, C China
Tongeren *65 D6 Fr.* Tongres. Limburg, NE Belgium
Tongking, Gulf of *see* Tonkin, Gulf of
Tongliao *105 G2* Nei Mongol Zizhiqu, N China
Tongres *see* Tongeren
Tongshan *see* Xuzhou, Jiangsu, China
Tongtian He *104 C4 river* C China
Tonj *51 B5* Warab, C South Sudan
Tonkin, Gulf of *106 B7 var.* Tongking, *Gulf of, Chin.* Beibu Wan, *Vtn.* Vinh Băc Bô. *gulf* China/Vietnam
Tônlé Sap *115 D5 Eng.* Great Lake. *lake* W Cambodia
Tonopah *25 C6* Nevada, W USA
Tonyezh *85 C7 Rus.* Tonezh. Homyel'skaya Voblasts', SE Belarus
Tooele *22 B4* Utah, W USA
Toowoomba *127 E5* Queensland, E Australia
Topeka *23 F4 state capital* Kansas, C USA
Toplicza *see* Topliţa
Topliţa *86 C3 Ger.* Töplitz, *Hung.* Marosheviz; *prev.* Topliţa Română, *Hung.* Oláh-Toplicza, Toplicza. Harghita, C Romania
Topliţa Română/Töplitz *see* Topliţa
Topoľčany *77 C6 Hung.* Nagytapolcsány. Nitriansky Kraj, W Slovakia
Topolovgrad *82 D3 prev.* Kavakli. Haskovo, S Bulgaria
Topolya *see* Bačka Topola
Top Springs Roadhouse *124 E3* Northern Territory, N Australia
Tor *132 C2 Norwegian research station* Antarctica
Torda *see* Turda
Torez *see* Chystiakove
Torgau *72 D4* Sachsen, E Germany
Torhout *65 A5* West-Vlaanderen, W Belgium
Torino *74 A2 Eng.* Turin. Piemonte, NW Italy
Tornacum *see* Tournai
Torneå *see* Tornio
Torneträsk *62 C3 lake* N Sweden
Tornio *62 D4 Swe.* Torneå. Lappi, NW Finland
Tornionjoki *62 D3 river* Finland/Sweden
Toro *70 D2* Castilla y León, N Spain
Toronto *16 D5 province capital* Ontario, S Canada
Toros Dağları *94 C4 Eng.* Taurus Mountains. *mountain range* S Turkey (Türkiye)
Torquay *67 C7* SW England, United Kingdom
Torrance *24 D2* California, W USA
Torre, Alto da *70 B3 mountain* C Portugal
Torre del Greco *75 D5* Campania, S Italy
Torrejón de Ardoz *71 E3* Madrid, C Spain
Torrelavega *70 D1* Cantabria, N Spain
Torrens, Lake *127 A6 salt lake* South Australia
Torrent *71 F3 Cas.* Torrente, *var.* Torrent de l'Horta. Comunitat Valenciana, E Spain
Torrent de l'Horta/Torrente *see* Torrent
Torreón *28 D3* Coahuila, NE Mexico
Torres Strait *126 C1 strait* Australia/Papua New Guinea
Torres Vedras *70 B3* Lisboa, C Portugal
Torrington *22 D3* Wyoming, C USA
Tórshavn *61 F5 Dan.* Thorshavn. *Dependent territory capital* Faroe Islands
To'rtko'l *100 D2 var.* Türtkül, *Rus.* Turtkul'; *prev.* Petroaleksandrovsk. Qoraqalpog'iston Respublikasi, W Uzbekistan
Tortoise Islands *see* Galápagos Islands
Tortosa *71 F2 anc.* Dertosa. Cataluña, E Spain
Tortue, Montagne *37 H3 mountain range* C French Guiana
Tortuga, Isla *see* La Tortuga, Isla

Toruń 76 C3 Ger. Thorn. Toruń, Kujawsko-pomorskie, C Poland
Törva 84 D3 Ger. Törwa. Valgamaa, S Estonia
Törwa see Törva
Torzhok 88 B4 Tverskaya Oblast', W Russia
Tosa-wan 109 B7 bay SW Japan
Toscana 74 B3 Eng. Tuscany. region C Italy
Toscano, Archipelago 74 B4 Eng. Tuscan Archipelago. island group C Italy
Toshkent 101 E2 Eng./Rus. Tashkent. country capital (Uzbekistan) Toshkent Viloyati, E Uzbekistan
Totana 71 E4 Murcia, SE Spain
Tot'ma see Sukhona
Totness 37 G3 Coronie, N Suriname
Tottori 109 B6 Tottori, Honshū, SW Japan
Touâjîl 52 C2 Tiris Zemmour, N Mauritania
Touggourt 49 E2 NE Algeria
Toukoto 52 C3 Kayes, W Mali
Toul 68 D3 Meurthe-et-Moselle, NE France
Toulon 69 D6 anc. Telo Martius, Tilio Martius. Var, SE France
Toulouse 69 B6 anc. Tolosa. Haute-Garonne, S France
Toungoo see Taungoo
Touraine 68 B4 cultural region C France
Tourane see Đà Nẵng
Tourcoing 68 C2 Nord, N France
Tournai 65 A6 var. Tournay, Dut. Doornik; anc. Tornacum. Hainaut, SW Belgium
Tournay see Tournai
Tours 68 B4 anc. Caesarodunum, Turoni. Indre-et-Loire, C France
Tovarkovskiy 89 B5 Tul'skaya Oblast', W Russia
Tower Island see Genovesa, Isla
Townsville 126 D3 Queensland, NE Australia
Towoeti Meer see Towuti, Danau
Towraghoudi 100 D4 Herāt, NW Afghanistan
Towson 19 F4 Maryland, NE USA
Towuti, Danau 117 E4 Dut. Towoeti Meer. lake Sulawesi, C Indonesia
Toyama 109 C5 Toyama, Honshū, SW Japan
Toyama-wan 109 B5 bay W Japan
Toyohara see Yuzhno-Sakhalinsk
Toyota 109 C6 Aichi, Honshū, SW Japan
Tozeur 49 E2 var. Tawzar. W Tunisia
Trâblous see Tripoli
Trabzon 95 E2 Eng. Trebizond; anc. Trapezus. Trabzon, NE Turkey (Türkiye)
Traiectum ad Mosam/Traiectum Tungorum see Maastricht
Traiskirchen 73 E6 Niederösterreich, NE Austria
Trajani Portus see Civitavecchia
Trajectum ad Rhenum see Utrecht
Trakai 85 C5 Ger. Traken, Pol. Troki. Vilnius, SE Lithuania
Traken see Trakai
Tralee 67 A6 Ir. Trá Lí. SW Ireland
Trá Lí see Tralee
Tralles Aydin see Aydın
Tran 82 B2 var. Trŭn. Pernik, W Bulgaria
Trang 115 C7 Trang, S Thailand
Transantarctic Mountains 132 B3 mountain range Antarctica
Transilvania see Transylvania
Transilvaniei, Alpi see Carpaţii Meridionali
Transjordan see Jordan
Transnistria 86 D3 disputed territory NE Moldova
Transsylvanische Alpen/Transylvanian Alps see Carpaţii Meridionali
Transylvania 86 B4 Eng. Ardeal, Transilvania, Ger. Siebenbürgen, Hung. Erdély. cultural region NW Romania
Trapani 75 B7 anc. Drepanum. Sicilia, Italy, C Mediterranean Sea
Trâpeăng Vêng see Kampong Thom
Trapezus see Trabzon
Traralgon 127 C7 Victoria, SE Australia
Trasimenischersee see Trasimeno, Lago
Trasimeno, Lago 74 C4 Eng. Lake of Perugia, Ger. Trasimenischersee. lake C Italy
Traù see Trogir
Traverse City 18 C2 Michigan, N USA
Tra Vinh 115 D6 var. Phu Vinh. Tra Vinh, S Vietnam
Travis, Lake 27 F3 reservoir Texas, SW USA
Travnik 78 C4 Federacija Bosna I Hercegovina, C Bosnia and Herzegovina
Trbovlje 73 E7 Ger. Trifail. C Slovenia
Treasure State see Montana
Třebíč 77 B5 Ger. Trebitsch. Vysočina, C Czechia (Czech Republic)
Trebinje 79 C5 Republika Srpska, S Bosnia and Herzegovina
Trebišov 77 D6 Hung. Tőketerebes. Košický Kraj, E Slovakia
Trebitsch see Třebíč
Trebnitz see Trzebnica
Tree Planters State see Nebraska
Trélazé 68 B4 Maine-et-Loire, NW France
Trelew 43 C6 Chubut, SE Argentina
Tremelo 65 C5 Vlaams Brabant, C Belgium
Trenčín 77 C5 Ger. Trentschin, Hung. Trencsén. Trenčiansky Kraj, W Slovakia
Trencsén see Trenčín
Trengganu, Kuala see Kuala Terengganu
Trenque Lauquen 42 C4 Buenos Aires, E Argentina
Trent see Trento
Trento 74 C2 Eng. Trent, Ger. Trient; anc. Tridentum. Trentino-Alto Adige, N Italy
Trenton 19 F4 state capital New Jersey, NE USA
Trentschin see Trenčín
Tres Arroyos 43 D5 Buenos Aires, E Argentina
Treskavica 78 C4 mountain range SE Bosnia and Herzegovina
Tres Tabernae see Saverne
Treves/Trèves see Trier
Treviso 74 C2 anc. Tarvisium. Veneto, NE Italy
Trichinopoly see Tiruchchirāppalli
Trichūr see Thrissur
Tridentum/Trient see Trento
Trier 73 A5 Eng. Treves, Fr. Trèves; anc. Augusta Treverorum. Rheinland-Pfalz, SW Germany
Triesen 72 E2 SW Liechtenstein Europe
Triesenberg 72 E2 SW Liechtenstein
Trieste 74 D2 Slvn. Trst. Friuli-Venezia Giulia, NE Italy
Trifail see Trbovlje
Tríkala 82 B4 prev. Trikkala. Thessalía, C Greece
Trikkala see Tríkala
Trimontium see Plovdiv
Trinacria see Sicilia
Trincomalee 110 D3 var. Trinkomali. Eastern Province, NE Sri Lanka
Trindade, Ilha da 45 C5 island Brazil, W Atlantic Ocean
Trinidad 39 F3 Beni, N Bolivia
Trinidad 42 D4 Flores, S Uruguay
Trinidad 22 D5 Colorado, C USA
Trinidad 33 H5 island C Trinidad and Tobago
Trinidad and Tobago 33 H5 off. Republic of Trinidad and Tobago. country SE West Indies
Trinidad and Tobago, Republic of see Trinidad and Tobago
Trinité, Montagnes de la 37 H3 mountain range C French Guiana
Trinity River 27 G3 river Texas, SW USA
Trinkomali see Trincomalee
Trípoli 83 B6 prev. Trípolis. Pelopónnisos, S Greece
Tripoli 96 B4 var. Tarābulus, Ţarābulus ash Shām, Trâblous; anc. Tripolis. N Lebanon
Tripoli see Ţarābulus
Trípolis see Trípoli, Greece
Tripolis see Tripoli, Lebanon
Tripolitania 49 F3 region NW Libya
Tristan da Cunha see St Helena, Ascension and Tristan da Cunha
Triton Island 106 B7 island S Paracel Islands
Trivandrum see Thiruvananthapuram
Trnava 77 C6 Ger. Tyrnau, Hung. Nagyszombat. Trnavský Kraj, W Slovakia
Trnovo see Veliko Tarnovo
Trogir 78 B4 It. Traù. Split-Dalmacija, S Croatia
Troglav 78 B4 mountain Bosnia and Herzegovina/Croatia
Trois-Rivières 17 E4 Québec, SE Canada
Troki see Trakai
Troll 132 C2 Norwegian research station Antarctica
Trollhättan 63 B6 Västra Götaland, S Sweden
Tromsø 62 C2 Fin. Tromssa. Troms, N Norway
Tromssa see Tromsø
Trondheim 62 B4 Ger. Drontheim; prev. Nidaros, Trondhjem. Sør-Trøndelag, S Norway
Trondheimsfjorden 62 B4 fjord S Norway
Trondhjem see Trondheim
Troódos 80 C5 var. Troodos Mountains. mountain range C Cyprus
Troodos Mountains see Troódos
Troppau see Opava
Troy 20 D3 Alabama, S USA
Troy 19 F3 New York, NE USA
Troyan 82 C2 Lovech, N Bulgaria
Troyes 68 D3 anc. Augustobona Tricassium. Aube, N France
Trst see Trieste
Trstenik 78 E4 Serbia, C Serbia
Trucial States see United Arab Emirates
Trujillo 30 D2 Colón, NE Honduras
Trujillo 38 B3 La Libertad, NW Peru
Trujillo 70 C3 Extremadura, W Spain
Truk Islands see Chuuk Islands
Trŭn see Tran
Truro 17 F4 Nova Scotia, SE Canada
Truro 67 C7 SW England, United Kingdom
Trzcianka 76 B3 Ger. Schönlanke. Pila, Wielkopolskie, C Poland
Trzebnica 76 C4 Ger. Trebnitz. Dolnośląskie, SW Poland
Tsalka 95 F2 S Georgia Asia
Tsamkong see Zhanjiang
Tsangpo see Brahmaputra
Tsarevo 82 E2 prev. Michurin. Burgas, E Bulgaria
Tsarigrad see İstanbul
Tsaritsyn see Volgograd
Tschakathurn see Čakovec
Tschaslau see Čáslav
Tschenstochau see Częstochowa
Tsefat 97 B5 var. Safed, Ar. Safad; prev. Zefat. Northern, N Israel
Tselinograd see Nur-Sultan
Tsetsen Khan see Öndörhaan
Tsetserleg 104 D2 Arhangay, C Mongolia
Tshela 55 B6 Bas-Congo, W Dem. Rep. Congo
Tshikapa 55 C7 Kasai-Occidental, SW Dem. Rep. Congo
Tshuapa 55 D6 river C Dem. Rep. Congo
Tsinan see Jinan
Tsing Hai see Qinghai Hu, China
Tsinghai see Qinghai, China
Tsingtao/Tsingtau see Qingdao
Tsinkiang see Quanzhou
Tsintao see Qingdao
Tsitsihar see Qiqihar
Tsu 109 C6 var. Tu. Mie, Honshū, SW Japan
Tsugaru-kaikyo 108 C3 strait N Japan
Tsumeb 56 B3 Otjikoto, N Namibia
Tsuruga 109 C6 var. Turuga. Fukui, Honshū, SW Japan
Tsiurupynsk see Oleshky
Tsuruoka 108 D4 var. Turuoka. Yamagata, Honshū, C Japan
Tsushima 109 A7 var. Tsushima-tō, Tusima. island group SW Japan
Tsushima-tō see Tsushima
Tsyerakhowka 85 D8 Rus. Terekhovka. Homyel'skaya Voblasts', SE Belarus
Tu see Tsu
Tuamotu, Archipel des see Tuamotu, Îles
Tuamotu Fracture Zone 121 H3 fracture zone E Pacific Ocean
Tuamotu, Îles 123 H4 var. Archipel des Tuamotu, Dangerous Archipelago, Tuamotu Islands. island group N French Polynesia
Tuamotu Islands see Tuamotu, Îles
Tuapi 31 E2 Región Autónoma Atlántico Norte, NE Nicaragua
Tuapse 89 A7 Krasnodarskiy Kray, SW Russia
Tuba City 26 B1 Arizona, SW USA
Ţūbās 97 E6 N West Bank, Middle East
Tubbergen 64 E3 Overijssel, E Netherlands
Tubeke see Tubize
Tubize 65 B6 Dut. Tubeke. Walloon Brabant, C Belgium
Tubmanburg 52 C5 NW Liberia
Ţubruq 49 H2 Eng. Tobruk, It. Tobruch. NE Libya
Tubuai, Îles/Tubuai Islands see Australes, Îles
Tucker's Town 20 B5 E Bermuda
Tuckum see Tukums
Tucson 26 B3 Arizona, SW USA
Tucumán see San Miguel de Tucumán
Tucumcari 27 E2 New Mexico, SW USA
Tucupita 37 E2 Delta Amacuro, NE Venezuela
Tucuruí, Represa de 41 F2 reservoir NE Brazil
Tudela 71 E2 Basq. Tutera; anc. Tutela. Navarra, N Spain
Tuguegarao 117 E1 Luzon, N Philippines
Tuktoyaktuk 15 E3 Northwest Territories, NW Canada
Tukums 84 C3 Ger. Tuckum. Tukums, W Latvia
Tula 89 B5 Tul'skaya Oblast', W Russia
Tulancingo 29 E4 Hidalgo, C Mexico
Tulare Lake Bed 25 C7 salt flat California, W USA
Tulcán 38 B1 Carchi, N Ecuador
Tulcea 86 D5 Tulcea, E Romania
Tul'chin see Tulchyn
Tulchyn 86 D3 Rus. Tul'chin. Vinnyts'ka Oblast', C Ukraine
Tuléar see Toliara
Tulia 27 E2 Texas, SW USA
Ţūlkarm 97 D6 West Bank, Middle East
Tulle 69 C5 anc. Tutela. Corrèze, C France
Tulln 73 E6 var. Oberhollabrunn. Niederösterreich, NE Austria
Tully 126 D3 Queensland, NE Australia
Tulsa 27 G1 Oklahoma, C USA
Tuluá 36 B3 Valle del Cauca, W Colombia
Tulun 93 E4 Irkutskaya Oblast', S Russia
Tumaco 36 A4 Nariño, SW Colombia
Tumakūru 110 C2 prev. Tumkūr. Karnātaka, W India
Tumba, Lac see Ntomba, Lac
Tumbes 38 A2 Tumbes, NW Peru
Tumkūr see Tumakūru
Tumuc-Humac Mountains 41 E1 var. Serra Tumucumaque. mountain range N South America
Tumucumaque, Serra see Tumuc-Humac Mountains
Tunca Nehri see Tundzha
Tunduru 51 C8 Ruvuma, S Tanzania
Tundzha 82 D3 Turk. Tunca Nehri. river Bulgaria/Turkey (Türkiye)
Tungabhadra Reservoir 110 C2 lake S India
Tungaru 123 E2 prev. Gilbert Islands. island group W Kiribati
T'ung-shan see Xuzhou
Tungsten 14 D4 Northwest Territories, W Canada
Tung-t'ing Hu see Dongting Hu
Tunis 49 E1 var. Tūnis. country capital (Tunisia) NE Tunisia
Tunis, Golfe de 80 D3 Ar. Khalīj Tūnis. gulf NE Tunisia
Tunisia 49 F2 off. Republic of Tunisia, Ar. Al Jumhūrīyah at Tūnisīyah, Fr. République Tunisienne. country N Africa
Tunisia, Republic of see Tunisia
Tunisienne, République see Tunisia
Tūnisīyah, Al Jumhūrīyah at see Tunisia
Tūnis, Khalīj see Tunis, Golfe de
Tunja 36 B3 Boyacá, C Colombia
Tuong Buong see Tương Đương
Tương Đương 114 D4 var. Tuong Buong. Nghê An, N Vietnam
Tüp see Tyup
Tupelo 20 C2 Mississippi, S USA
Tupiza 39 G5 Potosí, S Bolivia
Turabah 99 B5 Makkah, W Saudi Arabia
Tūranganui-a-Kiwa 128 E4 var. Poverty bay. inlet North Island, New Zealand
Turangi 128 D4 Waikato, North Island, New Zealand
Turan Lowland 100 C2 var. Turan Plain, Kaz. Turan Oypaty, Rus. Turanskaya Nizmennost', Turk. Turan Pesligi, Uzb. Turan Pasttekisligi. plain C Asia
Turan Oypaty/Turan Pesligi/Turan Plain/Turanskaya Nizmennost' see Turan Lowland
Turan Pasttekisligi see Turan Lowland
Ţurayf 98 A3 Al Ḩudūd ash Shamālīyah, NW Saudi Arabia
Turba see Teruel
Turbat 112 A3 Baluchistan, SW Pakistan
Turčianský Svätý Martin see Martin
Turda 86 B4 Ger. Thorenburg, Hung. Torda. Cluj, NW Romania
Turek 76 C3 Wielkopolskie, C Poland
Turfan see Turpan
Turin see Torino
Turkana, Lake 51 C6 var. Lake Rudolf. lake N Kenya
Turkestan see Türkistan/Turkistan
Turkey 94 B3 off. Republic of Türkiye, var. Türkiye, Turk. Türkiye Cumhuriyeti. country SW Asia
Turkish Republic of Northern Cyprus 80 D5 disputed territory administered by Turkey Cyprus
Türkistan/Turkistan 92 B5 prev. Turkestan. Türkistan/Turkestan, S Kazakhstan
Türkiye see Turkey
Türkiye, Republic of see Turkey
Türkiye Cumhuriyeti see Turkey
Türkmenabat 100 D3 prev. Rus. Chardzhev, Chardzhou, Chardzhui, Lenin-Turkmenski, Turkm. Chärjew. Lebap Welaýaty, E Turkmenistan
Türkmen Aylagy 100 B2 Rus. Turkmenskiy Zaliv. lake gulf W Turkmenistan
Turkmenbashi see Türkmenbaşy
Türkmenbaşy 100 B2 Rus. Turkmenbashi; prev. Krasnovodsk. Balkan Welaýaty, W Turkmenistan
Türkmenbasy Aylagy 100 A2 prev. Rus. Krasnovodskiy Zaliv, Turkm. Krasnowodsk Aylagy. lake Gulf W Turkmenistan
Turkmenistan 100 B2; prev. Turkmenskaya Soviet Socialist Republic. country C Asia
Turkmenskaya Soviet Socialist Republic see Turkmenistan
Turkmenskiy Zaliv see Türkmen Aylagy
Turks and Caicos Islands 33 E2 UK Overseas Territory N West Indies
Turku 63 D6 Swe. Åbo. Varsinais-Suomi, SW Finland
Turlock 25 B6 California, W USA
Turnagain, Cape 128 D4 headland North Island, New Zealand
Turnau see Turnov
Turnhout 65 C5 Antwerpen, N Belgium
Turnov 76 B4 Ger. Turnau. Liberecký Kraj, N Czechia (Czech Republic)
Tŭrnovo see Veliko Tarnovo
Turnu Măgurele 86 B5 var. Turnu-Măgurele. Teleorman, S Romania
Turnu Severin see Drobeta-Turnu Severin
Turócszentmárton see Martin
Turoni see Tours
Turpan 104 C3 var. Turfan. Xinjiang Uygur Zizhiqu, NW China
Turpan Depression see Turpan Pendi
Turpan Pendi 104 C3 Eng. Turpan Depression. depression NW China
Turpentine State see North Carolina
Türtkŭl/Turtkul' see To'rtkok'l
Turuga see Tsuruga
Turuoka see Tsuruoka
Tuscaloosa 20 C2 Alabama, S USA
Tuscan Archipelago see Toscano, Archipelago
Tuscany see Toscana
Tusima see Tsushima
Tutela see Tulle, France
Tutela see Tudela, Spain
Tutera see Tudela
Tuticorin 110 C3 var. Thoothukudi. Tamil Nādu, SE India
Tutrakan 82 D1 Silistra, NE Bulgaria
Tutuila 123 F4 island W American Samoa
Tuvalu 123 E3 prev. Ellice Islands. country SW Pacific Ocean
Tuwayq, Jabal 99 C5 mountain range C Saudi Arabia
Tuxpan 28 D4 Jalisco, C Mexico
Tuxpán 29 F4 var. Tuxpán de Rodríguez Cano. Veracruz-Llave, E Mexico
Tuxpán de Rodríguez Cano see Tuxpán
Tuxtepec 29 F4 var. San Juan Bautista Tuxtepec. Oaxaca, S Mexico
Tuxtla 29 G5 var. Tuxtla Gutiérrez. Chiapas, SE Mexico
Tuxtla see San Andrés Tuxtla
Tuxtla Gutiérrez see Tuxtla
Tuy Hoa 115 E5 Phu Yên, S Vietnam
Tuz, Lake 94 C3 lake C Turkey (Türkiye)
Tver' 88 B4 prev. Kalinin. Tverskaya Oblast', W Russia
Tverya 97 B5 var. Tiberias; prev. Teverya. Northern, N Israel
Twin Falls 24 D4 Idaho, NW USA
Tyan'-Shan' see Tien Shan
Tychy 77 D5 Ger. Tichau. Śląskie, S Poland
Tyler 27 G3 Texas, SW USA
Tylos see Bahrain
Tympáki 83 C8 var. Timbaki; prev. Timbákion. Kríti, Greece, E Mediterranean Sea
Tynda 93 F4 Amurskaya Oblast', SE Russia
Tyne 66 D4 river N England, United Kingdom
Tyôsi see Chōshi
Tyras see Bilhorod-Dnistrovskyi
Tyras see Dniester
Tyre see Soûr
Tyrnau see Trnava
Týrnavos 82 B4 var. Tírnavos. Thessalía, C Greece
Tyrol see Tirol
Tyros see Bahrain
Tyrrhenian Sea 75 B6 It. Mare Tirreno. sea N Mediterranean Sea
Tyumen' 92 C3 Tyumenskaya Oblast', C Russia
Tyup 101 G2 Kir. Tüp. Issyk-Kul'skaya Oblast', NE Kyrgyzstan
Tywyn 67 C6 W Wales, United Kingdom
Tzekung see Zigong
Tziá see Kéa

U

Uaco Cungo 56 B1 C Angola
UAE see United Arab Emirates
Uanle Uen see Wanlaweyn
Uaupés, Rio see Vaupés, Río
Ubangi-Shari see Central African Republic
Ube 109 B7 Yamaguchi, Honshū, SW Japan
Úbeda 71 E4 Andalucía, S Spain
Uberaba 41 F4 Minas Gerais, SE Brazil
Uberlândia 41 F4 Minas Gerais, SE Brazil
Ubol Rajadhani/Ubol Ratchathani see Ubon Ratchathani
Ubon Ratchathani 115 D5 var. Muang Ubon, Ubol Rajadhani, Ubol Ratchathani, Udon Ratchathani. Ubon Ratchathani, E Thailand
Ubrique 70 D5 Andalucía, S Spain
Ubsu-Nur, Ozero see Uvs Nuur
Ucayali, Río 38 D3 river C Peru
Uchiura-wan 108 D3 bay NW Pacific Ocean
Uchkuduk see Uchquduq
Uchquduq 100 D2 Rus. Uchkuduk. Navoiy Viloyati, N Uzbekistan
Uchtagan Gumy/Uchtagan, Peski see Uçtagan Gumy
Uçtagan Gumy 100 C2 var. Uchtagan Gumy, Rus. Peski Uchtagan. desert NW Turkmenistan
Udaipur 112 C3 prev. Oodeypore. Rājasthān, N India
Uddevalla 63 B6 Västra Götaland, S Sweden
Udine 74 D2 anc. Utina. Friuli-Venezia Giulia, NE Italy
Udintsev Fracture Zone 132 A5 tectonic feature S Pacific Ocean
Udipi see Udupi
Udon Ratchathani see Ubon Ratchathani
Udon Thani 114 C4 var. Ban Mak Khaeng, Udorndhani. Udon Thani, N Thailand
Udorndhani see Udon Thani
Udupi 110 B2 var. Udipi. Karnātaka, SW India
Uele 55 D5 var. Welle. river NE Dem. Rep. Congo
Uelzen 72 C3 Niedersachsen, N Germany
Ufa 89 D6 Respublika Bashkortostan, W Russia
Ugāle 84 C2 Ventspils, NW Latvia
Uganda 51 B6 off. Republic of Uganda. country E Africa
Uganda, Republic of see Uganda
Uhorshchyna see Hungary
Uhuru Peak see Kilimanjaro
Uíge 56 B1 Port. Carmona, Vila Marechal Carmona. Uíge, NW Angola
Uinta Mountains 22 B4 mountain range Utah, W USA
Uitenhage see Kariega
Uithoorn 64 C3 Noord-Holland, C Netherlands
Ujda see Oujda
Ujelang Atoll 122 C1 var. Wujlān. atoll Ralik Chain, W Marshall Islands
Újgradiska see Nova Gradiška
Újmoldova see Moldova Nouă
Ujungpandang see Makassar
Ujung Salang see Phuket
Újvidék see Novi Sad
UK see United Kingdom
Ukhta 92 C3 Respublika Komi, NW Russia
Ukiah 25 B5 California, W USA
Ukmergė 84 C4 Pol. Wiłkomierz. Vilnius, C Lithuania
Ukraine 86 C2 off. Ukraine, Rus. Ukraina, Ukr. Ukrayina; prev. Ukrainian Soviet Socialist Republic, Ukrainskay S.S.R. country SE Europe
Ukraine see Ukraine
Ukrainian Soviet Socialist Republic see Ukraine
Ukrainskay S.S.R/Ukrayina see Ukraine
Ulaanbaatar 105 E2 Eng. Ulan Bator; prev. Urga. country capital (Mongolia) Töv, C Mongolia
Ulaangom 104 C2 Uvs, NW Mongolia
Ulan Bator see Ulaanbaatar
Ulanhad see Chifeng
Ulan-Ude 93 E4 prev. Verkhneudinsk. Respublika Buryatiya, S Russia
Uleälv see Oulujoki
Uleträsk see Oulujärvi
Ulft 64 E4 Gelderland, E Netherlands
Ulianovka see Blahovishchenske
Ullapool 66 C3 N Scotland, United Kingdom
Ulm 73 B6 Baden-Württemberg, S Germany
Ulsan 107 E4 Jap. Urusan. SE South Korea
Ulster 67 B5 province Northern Ireland, United Kingdom/Ireland
Ulungur Hu 104 B2 lake NW China
Uluṟu 125 D5 var. Ayers Rock. monolith Northern Territory, C Australia
Ulyanivka see Blahovishchenske
Ul'yanovsk 89 C5 prev. Simbirsk. Ul'yanovskaya Oblast', W Russia
Umán 29 H3 Yucatán, SE Mexico
Uman 87 E3 Cherkas'ka Oblast', C Ukraine
Umanak/Umanaq see Uummannaq
'Umān, Khalīj see Oman, Gulf of
'Umān, Salṭanat see Oman
Umbrian-Machigian Mountains see Umbro-Marchigiano, Appennino
Umbro-Marchigiano, Appennino 74 C3 Eng. Umbrian-Machigian Mountains. mountain range C Italy
Umeå 62 C4 Västerbotten, N Sweden
Umeälven 62 C4 river N Sweden
Umiat 14 D2 Alaska, USA
Umm Buru 50 A4 Western Darfur, W Sudan
Umm Durmān see Omdurman
Umm Ruwaba 50 C4 var. Umm Ruwābah, Um Ruwāba. Northern Kordofan, C Sudan
Umm Ruwābah see Umm Ruwaba
Umnak Island 14 A3 island Aleutian Islands, Alaska, USA
Um Ruwāba see Umm Ruwaba
Umtali see Mutare
Umtata see Mthatha
Una 78 B3 river Bosnia and Herzegovina/Croatia
Unac 78 B3 river W Bosnia and Herzegovina
Unalaska Island 14 A3 island Aleutian Islands, Alaska, USA
'Unayzah 98 B4 var. Anaiza. Al Qaşīm, C Saudi Arabia
Unci see Almería
Uncía 39 F4 Potosí, C Bolivia
Uncompahgre Peak 22 B5 mountain Colorado, C USA
Undur Khan see Öndörhaan
Ungaria see Hungary
Ungarisches Erzgebirge see Slovenské rudohorie
Ungarn see Hungary
Ungava Bay 17 E1 bay Québec, E Canada
Ungava Peninsula see Ungava, Péninsule d'
Ungava, Péninsule d' 16 D1 Eng. Ungava Peninsula. peninsula Québec, SE Canada
Ungeny see Ungheni
Ungheni 86 D3 Rus. Ungeny. W Moldova
Unguja see Zanzibar
Üngüz Angyrsyndaky Garagum 100 C2 Rus. Zaunguzskiye Garagumy. desert N Turkmenistan
Ungvár see Uzhhorod
Unimak Island 14 B3 island Aleutian Islands, Alaska, USA
Union 21 E1 South Carolina, SE USA
Union City 20 C1 Tennessee, S USA
Union of Myanmar see Myanmar
United Arab Emirates 99 C5 Ar. Al Imārāt al 'Arabīyah al Muttaḩidah, abbrev. UAE; prev. Trucial States. country SW Asia
United Arab Republic see Egypt
United Kingdom 67 B5 off. United Kingdom of Great Britain and Northern Ireland, abbrev. UK. country NW Europe
United Kingdom of Great Britain and Northern Ireland see United Kingdom
United Mexican States see Mexico
United Provinces see Uttar Pradesh
United States of America 13 B5 off. United States of America, var. America, The States, abbrev. U.S., USA. country North America
Unst 66 D1 island NE Scotland, United Kingdom
Ünye 94 D2 Ordu, W Turkey (Türkiye)
Upala 30 D4 Alajuela, NW Costa Rica
Upata 37 E2 Bolívar, E Venezuela
Upemba, Lac 55 D7 lake SE Dem. Rep. Congo
Upernavik 60 C2 var. Upernivik. Avannaata, C Greenland
Upernivik see Upernavik
Upington 56 C4 Northern Cape, W South Africa
'Upolu 123 F4 island SE Samoa
Upper Klamath Lake 24 A4 lake Oregon, NW USA
Upper Lough Erne 67 A5 lake SW Northern Ireland, United Kingdom
Upper Red Lake 23 F1 lake Minnesota, N USA
Upper Volta see Burkina
Uppsala 63 C6 Uppsala, C Sweden
Uqsuqtuuq see Gjoa Haven
Ural 90 B3 Kaz. Zhayyk. river Kazakhstan/Russia
Ural Mountains see Ural'skiye Gory
Ural'sk see Oral
Ural'skiye Gory 92 C3 var. Ural'skiy Khrebet, Eng. Ural Mountains. mountain range Kazakhstan/Russia
Ural'skiy Khrebet see Ural'skiye Gory
Uraricoera 40 D1 Roraima, N Brazil
Ura-Tyube see Istaravshan
Urbandale 23 F3 Iowa, C USA
Urdun see Jordan
Uren' 89 C5 Nizhegorodskaya Oblast', W Russia
Urga see Ulaanbaatar
Urganch 100 D2 Rus. Urgench; prev. Novo-Urgench. Xorazm Viloyati, W Uzbekistan
Urgench see Urganch

Urgut 101 E3 Samarqand Viloyati, C Uzbekistan
Urmia, Lake see Orūmīyeh, Daryācheh-ye
Uroševac see Ferizaj
Ŭroteppa see Istaravshan
Uruapan 29 E4 var. Uruapan del Progreso. Michoacán, SW Mexico
Uruapan del Progreso see Uruapan
Uruguai, Rio see Uruguay
Uruguay 42 D4 off. Oriental Republic of Uruguay; prev. La Banda Oriental. country E South America
Uruguay 42 D3 var. Rio Uruguai, Río Uruguay. river E South America
Uruguay, Oriental Republic of see Uruguay
Uruguay, Río see Uruguay
Urumchi see Ürümqi
Urumi Yeh see Orūmīyeh, Daryācheh-ye
Ürümqi 104 C3 var. Tihwa, Urumchi, Urumqi, Urumtsi, Wu-lu-k'o-mu-shi, Wu-lu-mu-ch'i; prev. Ti-hua. Xinjiang Uygur Zizhiqu, NW China
Urumtsi see Ürümqi
Urundi see Burundi
Urup, Ostrov 93 H4 island Kuril'skiye Ostrova, SE Russia
Urusan see Ulsan
Urziceni 86 C5 Ialomiţa, SE Romania
Usa 88 E3 river NW Russia
Uşak 94 B3 prev. Ushak. Uşak, W Turkey (Türkiye)
Ushak see Uşak
Ushant see Ouessant, Île d'
Ushuaia 43 B8 Tierra del Fuego, S Argentina
Usinsk 88 E3 Respublika Komi, NW Russia
Üsküb/Üsküp see Skopje
Usmas Ezers 84 B3 lake NW Latvia
Usol'ye-Sibirskoye 93 E4 Irkutskaya Oblast', C Russia
Ussel 69 C5 Corrèze, C France
Ussuriysk 93 G5 prev. Nikol'sk, Nikol'sk-Ussuriyskiy, Voroshilov. Primorskiy Kray, SE Russia
Ustica 75 B6 island S Italy
Ust'-Ilimsk 93 E4 Irkutskaya Oblast', C Russia
Ústí nad Labem 76 A4 Ger. Aussig. Ústecký Kraj, NW Czechia (Czech Republic)
Ustinov see Izhevsk
Ustka 76 C2 Ger. Stolpmünde. Pomorskie, N Poland
Ust'-Kamchatsk 93 H2 Kamchatskaya Oblast', E Russia
Ust'-Kamenogorsk see Öskemen
Ust'-Kut 93 E4 Irkutskaya Oblast', C Russia
Ust'-Olenëk 93 E3 Respublika Sakha (Yakutiya), NE Russia
Ustrzyki Dolne 77 E5 Podkarpackie, SE Poland
Ust'-Sysol'sk see Syktyvkar
Ust Urt see Ustyurt Plateau
Ustyurt Plateau 100 B1 var. Ust Urt, Uzb. Ustyurt Platosi. plateau Kazakhstan/Uzbekistan
Ustyurt Platosi see Ustyurt Plateau
Usulután 30 C3 Usulután, SE El Salvador
Usumacinta, Río 30 B1 river Guatemala/Mexico
Usumbura see Bujumbura
U.S./USA see United States of America
Utah 22 B4 off. State of Utah, also known as Beehive State, Mormon State. state W USA
Utah Lake 22 B4 lake Utah, W USA
Utena 84 C4 Utena, E Lithuania
Utica 19 F3 New York, NE USA
Utina see Udine
Utrecht 64 C4 Lat. Trajectum ad Rhenum. Utrecht, C Netherlands
Utsunomiya 109 D5 var. Utunomiya. Tochigi, Honshū, S Japan
Uttarakhand 113 E2 cultural region N India
Uttar Pradesh 113 E3 prev. United Provinces, United Provinces of Agra and Oudh. cultural region N India
Utunomiya see Utsunomiya
Uulu 84 D2 Pärnumaa, SW Estonia
Uummannaq 60 C3 var. Umanak, Umanaq. Avannaata, C Greenland
Uummannarsuaq see Nunap Isua
Uvalde 27 F4 Texas, SW USA
Uvaravichy 85 D7 Rus. Uvarovichi. Homyel'skaya Voblasts', SE Belarus
Uvarovichi see Uvaravichy
Uvea, Île 123 E4 island N Wallis and Futuna
Uviéu see Oviedo
Uvs Nuur 104 C1 var. Ozero Ubsu-Nur. lake Mongolia/Russia
'Uwaynāt, Jabal al 66 A3 var. Jebel Uweinat. mountain Libya/Sudan
Uweinat, Jebel see 'Uwaynāt, Jabal al
Uyo 53 G5 Akwa Ibom, S Nigeria
Uyuni 39 F5 Potosí, W Bolivia
Uzbekistan 100 D2 off. Republic of Uzbekistan. country C Asia
Uzbekistan, Republic of see Uzbekistan
Uzhgorod see Uzhhorod
Uzhhorod 86 B2 Rus. Uzhgorod; prev. Ungvár. Zakarpats'ka Oblast', W Ukraine
Užice 78 D4 prev. Titovo Užice. Serbia, W Serbia

V

Vaal 56 D4 river C South Africa
Vaals 65 D6 Limburg, SE Netherlands
Vaasa 63 D5 Swe. Vasa; prev. Nikolainkaupunki. Österbotten, W Finland
Vaassen 64 D3 Gelderland, E Netherlands
Vác 77 C6 Ger. Waitzen. Pest, N Hungary
Vadodara 112 C4 prev. Baroda. Gujarāt, W India
Vaduz 72 E2 country capital (Liechtenstein) W Liechtenstein
Vág see Váh
Vágbeszterce see Považská Bystrica
Váh 77 C5 Ger. Waag, Hung. Vág. river W Slovakia
Váhtjer see Gällivare
Väinameri 84 C2 prev. Muhu Väin, Ger. Moon-Sund. sea E Baltic Sea
Vajdahunyad see Hunedoara
Valachia see Wallachia
Valday 88 B4 Novgorodskaya Oblast', W Russia
Valdecañas, Embalse de 70 D3 reservoir W Spain
Valdepeñas 71 E4 Castilla-La Mancha, C Spain
Valdez 14 C3 Alaska, USA
Valdia see Weldiya
Valdivia 43 B5 Los Lagos, C Chile
Val-d'Or 16 D4 Québec, SE Canada
Valdosta 21 E3 Georgia, SE USA
Valence 69 D5 anc. Valentia, Valentia Julia, Ventia. Drôme, E France
València 71 F3 var. Valencia. Comunitat Valenciana, E Spain
Valencia see València
Valencia 24 D1 California, USA
Valencia 36 D1 Carabobo, N Venezuela
Valencia, Gulf of 71 F3 var. Gulf of Valencia. gulf E Spain
Valencia, Gulf of see Valencia, Golfo de
Valencia/València see Valenciana, Comunitat
Valenciana, Comunitat 71 F3 var. Valencia, Cat. València; anc. Valentia. autonomous community NE Spain
Valenciennes 68 D2 Nord, N France
Valentia see Valence, France
Valentia see Valenciana, Comunitat
Valentia Julia see Valence
Valentine State see Oregon
Valera 36 C2 Trujillo, NW Venezuela
Valetta see Valletta
Valga 84 D3 Ger. Walk, Latv. Valka. Valgamaa, S Estonia
Valira 69 A8 river Andorra/Spain Europe
Valjevo 78 C4 Serbia, W Serbia
Valjok see Válljohka
Valka 84 D3 Ger. Walk. Valka, N Latvia
Valka see Valga
Valkenswaard 65 D5 Noord-Brabant, S Netherlands
Valladolid 29 H3 Yucatán, SE Mexico
Valladolid 70 D2 Castilla y León, NW Spain
Vall D'Uxó see La Vall d'Uixó
Valle de La Pascua 36 D2 Guárico, N Venezuela
Valledupar 36 B1 Cesar, N Colombia
Vallejo 25 B6 California, W USA
Vallenar 42 B3 Atacama, N Chile
Valletta 75 C8 prev. Valetta. country capital (Malta) E Malta
Valley City 23 E2 North Dakota, N USA
Válljohka 62 D2 var. Valjok. Finnmark, N Norway
Valls 71 G2 Cataluña, NE Spain
Valmiera 84 D3 Est. Volmari, Ger. Wolmar. Valmiera, N Latvia
Valona see Vlorë
Valozhyn 85 C5 Pol. Wołożyn, Rus. Volozhin. Minskaya Voblasts', C Belarus
Valparaíso 42 B4 Valparaíso, C Chile
Valparaiso 18 C3 Indiana, N USA
Valverde del Camino 70 C1 Andalucía, S Spain
Van 95 F3 Van, E Turkey (Türkiye)
Vanadzor 95 F2 prev. Kirovakan. N Armenia
Vancouver 14 D5 British Columbia, SW Canada
Vancouver 24 B3 Washington, NW USA
Vancouver Island 14 D5 island British Columbia, SW Canada
Vanda see Vantaa
Van Diemen Gulf 124 D2 gulf Northern Territory, N Australia
Van Diemen's Land see Tasmania
Vaner, Lake see Vänern
Vänern 63 B6 Eng. Lake Vaner; prev. Lake Vener. lake S Sweden
Vangaindrano 57 G4 Fianarantsoa, SE Madagascar
Van Gölü 95 F3 Eng. Lake Van; anc. Thospitis. salt lake E Turkey (Türkiye)
Van Horn 26 D3 Texas, SW USA
Van, Lake see Van Gölü
Vannes 68 A3 anc. Dariorigum. Morbihan, NW France
Vantaa 63 D6 Swe. Vanda. Uusimaa, S Finland
Vanua Levu 123 E4 island N Fiji
Vanuatu 122 C4 off. Republic of Vanuatu; prev. New Hebrides. country SW Pacific Ocean
Vanuatu, Republic of see Vanuatu
Van Wert 18 C4 Ohio, N USA
Vapincum see Gap
Varakļāni 84 D4 Madona, C Latvia
Vārānasi 113 E3 prev. Banaras, Benares, hist. Kasi. Uttar Pradesh, N India
Varangerfjorden 62 E2 Lapp. Várjjatvuotna. fjord N Norway
Varangerhalvøya 62 D2 Lapp. Várnjárga. peninsula N Norway
Varannó see Vranov nad Topl'ou
Varasd see Varaždin
Varaždin 78 B2 Ger. Warasdin, Hung. Varasd. Varaždin, N Croatia
Varberg 63 B7 Halland, S Sweden
Vardar 79 E6 Gk. Áxios. river North Macedonia/Greece
Varde 63 A7 Ribe, W Denmark
Vareia see Logroño
Varėna 85 B5 Pol. Orany. Alytus, S Lithuania
Varese 74 B2 Lombardia, N Italy
Vârful Moldoveanu 86 B4 var. Moldoveanul; prev. Virful Moldoveanu. mountain C Romania
Várjjatvuotna see Varangerfjorden
Varkaus 63 E5 Pohjois-Savo, C Finland
Varna 82 E2 prev. Stalin; anc. Odessus. Varna, E Bulgaria
Varnenski Zaliv 82 E2 prev. Stalinski Zaliv. bay E Bulgaria
Várnjárga see Varangerhalvøya
Varshava see Warszawa
Vasa see Vaasa
Vasilikí 83 A5 Lefkáda, Iónia Nisiá, Greece, C Mediterranean Sea
Vasilishki 85 B5 Pol. Wasiliszki. Hrodzyenskaya Voblasts', W Belarus
Vasil'kov see Vasylkiv
Vaslui 86 D4 Vaslui, C Romania
Västerås 63 C6 Västmanland, C Sweden
Vasylkiv 87 E2 var. Vasil'kov. Kyivska Oblast, N Ukraine
Vatican City 75 A7 off. Vatican City State. country S Europe
Vatican City State see Vatican City
Vatnajökull 61 E5 glacier SE Iceland
Vatter, Lake see Vättern
Vättern 63 B6 Eng. Lake Vatter; prev. Lake Vetter. lake S Sweden
Vaughn 26 D2 New Mexico, SW USA
Vaupés, Río 36 C4 var. Rio Uaupés. river Brazil/Colombia
Vava'u Group 123 E4 island group N Tonga
Vavuniya 110 D3 Northern Province, N Sri Lanka
Vawkavysk 85 B6 Pol. Wołkowysk, Rus. Volkovysk. Hrodzyenskaya Voblasts', W Belarus
Växjö 63 C7 var. Vexiö. Kronoberg, S Sweden
Vaygach, Ostrov 88 E2 island NW Russia
Veendam 64 E2 Groningen, NE Netherlands
Veenendaal 64 D4 Utrecht, C Netherlands
Vega 62 B4 island C Norway
Veglia see Krk
Veisiejai 85 B5 Alytus, S Lithuania
Vejer de la Frontera 70 C5 Andalucía, S Spain
Veldhoven 65 D5 Noord-Brabant, S Netherlands
Velebit 78 A3 mountain range C Croatia
Velenje 73 E7 Ger. Wöllan. N Slovenia
Veles 79 E6 Turk. Köprülü. C North Macedonia
Velho see Porto Velho
Velika Kikinda see Kikinda
Velika Morava 78 D4 var. Glavn'a Morava, Morava, Ger. Grosse Morava. river C Serbia
Velikaya 91 G2 river NE Russia
Veliki Bečkerek see Zrenjanin
Velikiye Luki 88 A4 Pskovskaya Oblast', W Russia
Velikiy Novgorod 88 B4 prev. Novgorod. Novgorodskaya Oblast', W Russian Federation
Veliko Tarnovo 82 D2 prev. Tirnovo, Trnovo, Tŭrnovo. Veliko Tarnovo, N Bulgaria
Velingrad 82 C3 Pazardzhik, C Bulgaria
Vel'ký Krtíš 77 D6 Banskobystrický Kraj, C Slovakia
Vellore 110 C2 Tamil Nādu, SE India
Velobriga see Viana do Castelo
Velsen see Velsen-Noord
Velsen-Noord 64 C3 var. Velsen. Noord-Holland, W Netherlands
Vel'sk 88 C4 var. Velsk. Arkhangel'skaya Oblast', NW Russia
Velvendós see Velvéntos
Velvéntos 82 B4 var. Velvendós. C Greece
Velykyy Tokmak see Tokmak
Vendôme 68 C4 Loir-et-Cher, C France
Venedig see Venezia
Vener, Lake see Vänern
Venetia see Venezia
Venezia 74 C2 Eng. Venice, Fr. Venise, Ger. Venedig; anc. Venetia. Veneto, NE Italy
Venezia, Golfo di see Venice, Gulf of
Venezuela 36 D2 off. Bolivarian Republic of Venezuela; prev. Republic of Venezuela, Estados Unidos de Venezuela, United States of Venezuela. country N South America
Venezuela, Estados Unidos de see Venezuela
Venezuela, Gulf of 36 C1 Eng. Gulf of Maracaibo, Gulf of Venezuela. gulf NW Venezuela
Venezuela, Gulf of see Venezuela, Golfo de
Venezuelan Basin 34 B1 undersea basin E Caribbean Sea
Venezuela, Bolivarian Republic of see Venezuela
Venezuela, Republic of see Venezuela
Venezuela, United States of see Venezuela
Venice 20 C4 Louisiana, S USA
Venice see Venezia
Venice, Gulf of 74 C2 It. Golfo di Venezia, Slvn. Beneški Zaliv. gulf N Adriatic Sea
Venise see Venezia
Venlo 65 D5 prev. Venloo. Limburg, SE Netherlands
Venloo see Venlo
Venta 84 B3 Ger. Windau. river Latvia/Lithuania
Venta Belgarum see Winchester
Ventia see Valence
Ventimiglia 74 A3 Liguria, NW Italy
Ventspils 84 B2 Ger. Windau. Ventspils, NW Latvia
Vera 42 D3 Santa Fe, C Argentina
Veracruz 29 F4 var. Veracruz Llave. Veracruz-Llave, E Mexico
Veracruz Llave see Veracruz
Vercellae see Vercelli
Vercelli 74 A2 anc. Vercellae. Piemonte, NW Italy
Verdal see Verdalsøra
Verdalsøra 62 B4 var. Verdal. Nord-Trøndelag, C Norway
Verde, Cabo see Cape Verde
Verde, Costa 70 D1 coastal region N Spain
Verden 72 B3 Niedersachsen, NW Germany
Veria see Véroia
Verkhnedvinsk see Vyerkhnyadzvinsk
Verkhneudinsk see Ulan-Ude
Verkhoyanskiy Khrebet 93 F3 mountain range NE Russia
Vermillion 23 F3 South Dakota, N USA
Vermont 19 F2 off. State of Vermont, also known as Green Mountain State. state NE USA
Vernadsky 132 A2 Ukrainian research station Antarctica
Vernal 22 B4 Utah, W USA
Vernon 27 F2 Texas, SW USA
Verőcze see Virovitica
Véroia 82 B4 var. Veria, Vérroia, Turk. Karaferiye. Kentrikí Makedonía, N Greece
Verona 74 C2 Veneto, NE Italy
Vérroia see Véroia
Versailles 68 D1 Yvelines, N France
Versecz see Vršac
Verulamium see St Albans
Verviers 65 D6 Liège, E Belgium
Vesdre 65 D6 river E Belgium
Veselinovo 82 D2 Shumen, NE Bulgaria
Vesontio see Besançon
Vesoul 68 D4 anc. Vesulium, Vesulum. Haute-Saône, E France
Vesterålen 62 B2 island group N Norway
Vestfjorden 62 C3 fjord C Norway
Vestmannaeyjar 61 E5 Sudhurland, S Iceland
Vesulium/Vesulum see Vesoul
Vesuna see Périgueux
Vesuvio 75 D5 Eng. Vesuvius. volcano S Italy
Vesuvius see Vesuvio
Veszprém 77 C7 Ger. Veszprim. Veszprém, W Hungary
Veszprim see Veszprém
Vetrino see Suvorovo
Vetrino see Vyetryna
Vetter, Lake see Vättern
Veurne 65 A5 var. furnes. West-Vlaanderen, W Belgium
Vexiö see Växjö
Viacha 39 F4 La Paz, W Bolivia
Viana de Castelo see Viana do Castelo
Viana do Castelo 70 B2 var. Viana de Castelo; anc. Velobriga. Viana do Castelo, NW Portugal
Vianen 64 C4 Utrecht, C Netherlands
Viangchan 114 C4 Eng./Fr. Vientiane. country capital (Laos) C Laos
Viangphoukha 114 C3 var. Vieng Pou Kha. Louang Namtha, N Laos
Viareggio 74 B3 Toscana, C Italy
Viborg 63 A7 Viborg, NW Denmark
Vic 71 G2 var. Vich; anc. Ausa, Vicus Ausonensis. Cataluña, NE Spain
Vicentia see Vicenza
Vicenza 74 C2 anc. Vicentia. Veneto, NE Italy
Vich see Vic
Vichy 69 C5 Allier, C France
Vicksburg 20 B2 Mississippi, S USA
Victoria 57 H1 country capital (Seychelles) Mahé, SW Seychelles
Victoria 14 D5 province capital Vancouver Island, British Columbia, SW Canada
Victoria 80 A5 var. Rabat. Gozo, NW Malta
Victoria 27 G4 Texas, SW USA
Victoria 127 C7 state SE Australia
Victoria see Masvingo, Zimbabwe
Victoria Bank see Vitória Seamount
Victoria de Durango see Durango
Victoria de las Tunas see Las Tunas
Victoria Falls 56 C3 Matabeleland North, W Zimbabwe
Victoria Falls 56 C2 waterfall Zambia/Zimbabwe
Victoria Falls see Iguaçu, Saltos do
Victoria Island 15 F3 island Northwest Territories/Nunavut, NW Canada
Victoria, Lake 51 B6 var. Victoria Nyanza. lake E Africa
Victoria Land 132 C4 physical region Antarctica
Victoria Nyanza see Victoria, Lake
Victoria River 124 D3 river Northern Territory, N Australia
Victorville 25 C7 California, W USA
Vicus Ausonensis see Vic
Vicus Elbii see Viterbo
Vidalia 21 E2 Georgia, SE USA
Videm-Krško see Krško
Vídeň see Wien
Vidin 82 B1 anc. Bononia. Vidin, NW Bulgaria
Vidzy 85 C5 Vitsyebskaya Voblasts', NW Belarus
Viedma 43 C5 Río Negro, E Argentina
Vieja, Sierra 26 D3 mountain range Texas, SW USA
Vieng Pou Kha see Viangphoukha
Vienna see Wien, Austria
Vienna see Vienne, France
Vienne 69 D5 anc. Vienna. Isère, E France
Vienne 68 B4 river W France
Vientiane see Viangchan
Vientos, Paso de los see Windward Passage
Vierzon 68 C4 Cher, C France
Viesīte 84 C4 Ger. Eckengraf. Jēkabpils, S Latvia
Vietnam 114 D4 off. Socialist Republic of Vietnam, Vtn. Công Hoa Xa Hôi Chu Nghia Việt Nam. country SE Asia
Vietnam, Socialist Republic of see Vietnam
Vietri see Viêt Tri
Viêt Tri 114 D3 var. Vietri. Vinh Phu, N Vietnam
Vieux Fort 33 F2 S Saint Lucia
Vigo 70 B2 Galicia, NW Spain
Viipuri see Vyborg
Vijayawāda 110 D1 prev. Bezwada. Andhra Pradesh, SE India
Vila see Port-Vila
Vila Artur de Paiva see Cubango
Vila da Ponte see Cubango
Vila de João Belo see Xai-Xai
Vila de Mocímboa da Praia see Mocímboa da Praia
Vila do Conde 70 B2 Porto, NW Portugal
Vila do Zumbo 56 D2 prev. Vila do Zumbu, Zumbo. Tete, NW Mozambique
Vila do Zumbu see Vila do Zumbo
Vilafranca del Penedès 71 G2 var. Villafranca del Panadés. Cataluña, NE Spain
Vila General Machado see Camacupa
Vila Henrique de Carvalho see Saurimo
Viļaka 84 D4 Ger. Marienhausen. Balvi, NE Latvia
Vilalba 70 C1 Galicia, NW Spain
Vila Marechal Carmona see Uíge
Vila Nova de Gaia 70 B2 Porto, NW Portugal
Vila Nova de Portimão see Portimão
Vila Pereira de Eça see N'Giva
Vila Real 70 C2 var. Vila Rial. Vila Real, N Portugal
Vila Rial see Vila Real
Vila Robert Williams see Caála
Vila Salazar see N'Dalatando
Vila Serpa Pinto see Menongue
Vileyka see Vilyeyka
Vilhelmina 62 C4 Västerbotten, N Sweden
Vilhena 40 D3 Rondônia, W Brazil
Vília 83 C5 Attikí, C Greece
Viliya 85 C5 Lith. Neris. river W Belarus
Viliya see Neris
Viljandi 84 D2 Ger. Fellin. Viljandimaa, S Estonia
Vilkaviškis 84 B4 Pol. Wyłkowyszki. Marijampolė, SW Lithuania
Villa Acuña 28 D2 var. Ciudad Acuña. Coahuila, NE Mexico
Villa Bella 39 F2 Beni, N Bolivia
Villacarrillo 71 E4 Andalucía, S Spain
Villa Cecilia see Ciudad Madero
Villach 73 D7 Slvn. Beljak. Kärnten, S Austria
Villacidro 75 A5 Sardegna, Italy, C Mediterranean Sea
Villa Concepción see Concepción
Villa del Pilar see Pilar
Villafranca de los Barros 70 C4 Extremadura, W Spain
Villafranca del Panadés see Vilafranca del Penedès
Villahermosa 29 G4 prev. San Juan Bautista. Tabasco, SE Mexico
Villajoyosa see La Vila Joiosa
Villa María 42 C4 Córdoba, C Argentina
Villa Martín 39 F5 Potosí, SW Bolivia
Villa Mercedes 42 C4 San Juan, Argentina
Villanueva 28 D3 Zacatecas, C Mexico
Villanueva de la Serena 70 C3 Extremadura, W Spain
Villanueva de los Infantes 71 E4 Castilla-La Mancha, C Spain
Villarrica 42 D2 Guairá, SE Paraguay
Villavicencio 36 B3 Meta, C Colombia
Villaviciosa 70 D1 Asturias, N Spain
Villazón 39 G5 Potosí, S Bolivia
Villena 71 F4 Comunitat Valenciana, E Spain
Villeurbanne 69 D5 Rhône, E France
Villingen-Schwenningen 73 B6 Baden-Württemberg, S Germany
Villmanstrand see Lappeenranta
Vilna see Vilnius
Vilnius 85 C5 Pol. Wilno, Ger. Wilna; prev. Rus. Vilna. country capital (Lithuania) Vilnius, SE Lithuania
Vilvoorde 65 C6 Fr. Vilvorde. Vlaams Brabant, C Belgium
Vilvorde see Vilvoorde
Vilyeyka 85 C5 Pol. Wilejka, Rus. Vileyka. Minskaya Voblasts', NW Belarus
Vilyuy 93 F3 river NE Russia
Viña del Mar 42 B4 Valparaíso, C Chile
Vinaròs 71 F3 Comunitat Valenciana, E Spain
Vincennes 18 B4 Indiana, N USA
Vindhya Mountains see Vindhya Range
Vindhya Range 112 D4 var. Vindhya Mountains. mountain range N India
Vindobona see Wien
Vineland 19 F4 New Jersey, NE USA
Vinh 114 D4 Nghê An, N Vietnam
Vinh Loi see Bac Liêu
Vinishte 82 C2 Montana, NW Bulgaria
Vinita 27 G1 Oklahoma, C USA
Vinkovci 78 C3 Ger. Winkowitz, Hung. Vinkovcze. Vukovar-Srijem, E Croatia
Vinkovcze see Vinkovci
Vinnitsa see Vinnytsia
Vinnytsia 86 D2 prev. Vinnytsya, Rus. Vinnitsa. Vinnyts'ka Oblast', C Ukraine
Vinnytsya see Vinnytsia
Vinogradov see Vynohradiv
Vinson Massif 132 A3 mountain Antarctica
Viranşehir 95 E4 Şanlıurfa, SE Turkey (Türkiye)
Virful Moldoveanu see Vârful Moldoveanu
Virginia 23 G1 Minnesota, N USA
Virginia 19 E5 off. Commonwealth of Virginia, also known as Mother of Presidents, Mother of States, Old Dominion. state NE USA
Virginia Beach 19 F5 Virginia, NE USA
Virgin Islands see British Virgin Islands
Virgin Islands (US) 33 F3 var. Virgin Islands of the United States; prev. Danish West Indies. US unincorporated territory E West Indies
Virgin Islands of the United States see Virgin Islands (US)
Virôchey 115 E5 Ratanakiri, NE Cambodia
Virovitica 78 C2 Ger. Virovititz, Hung. Verőcze; prev. Ger. Werowitz. Virovitica-Podravina, NE Croatia
Virovititz see Virovitica
Virton 65 D8 Luxembourg, SE Belgium
Virtsu 84 D2 Ger. Werder. Läänemaa, W Estonia
Vis 78 B4 It. Lissa; anc. Issa. island S Croatia
Vis see Fish
Visaginas 84 C4 prev. Sniečkus. Utena, E Lithuania
Visākhapatnam 113 E5 var. Vishakhapatnam. Andhra Pradesh, SE India
Visalia 25 C6 California, W USA
Visby 63 C7 Ger. Wisby. Gotland, SE Sweden
Viscount Melville Sound 15 F2 prev. Melville Sound. sound Northwest Territories, N Canada
Visé 65 D6 Liège, E Belgium
Viseu 70 C2 prev. Vizeu. Viseu, N Portugal
Vishakhapatnam see Visākhapatnam
Vislinskiy Zaliv see Vistula Lagoon
Visoko 78 C4 Federacija Bosna I Hercegovina, C Bosnia and Herzegovina
Visttasjohka 62 D3 river N Sweden
Vistula 76 C2 Eng. Vistula, Ger. Weichsel. river C Poland
Vistula see Wisła
Vistula Lagoon 76 C2 Ger. Frisches Haff, Pol. Zalew Wiślany, Rus. Vislinskiy Zaliv. lagoon Poland/Russia
Vitebsk see Vitsyebsk
Viterbo 74 C4 anc. Vicus Elbii. Lazio, C Italy
Viti see Fiji
Viti Levu 123 E4 island W Fiji
Vitim 93 F4 river C Russia
Vitória 41 F4 state capital Espírito Santo, SE Brazil
Vitoria see Vitoria-Gasteiz
Vitoria Bank see Vitória Seamount
Vitória da Conquista 41 F3 Bahia, E Brazil
Vitoria-Gasteiz 71 E1 var. Vitoria, Eng. Vittoria. País Vasco, N Spain
Vitória Seamount 45 B5 var. Victoria Bank, Vitoria Bank. seamount C Atlantic Ocean
Vitré 68 B3 Ille-et-Vilaine, NW France
Vitsyebsk 85 E5 Rus. Vitebsk. Vitsyebskaya Voblasts', NE Belarus
Vittoria 75 C7 Sicilia, Italy, C Mediterranean Sea
Vittoria see Vitoria-Gasteiz
Vizcaya, Golfo de see Biscay, Bay of
Vizianagaram 113 E5 var. Vizianagram. Andhra Pradesh, E India
Vizianagram see Vizianagaram
Vjosës, Lumi i 79 C7 var. Vijosa, Vijosë, Gk. Aóos. river Albania/Greece
Vlaanderen see Flanders
Vlaardingen 64 B4 Zuid-Holland, SW Netherlands
Vladikavkaz 89 B8 prev. Dzaudzhikau, Ordzhonikidze. Respublika Severnaya Osetiya, SW Russia
Vladimir 89 B5 Vladimirskaya Oblast', W Russia
Vladimirovka see Yuzhno-Sakhalinsk
Vladimir-Volynskiy see Volodymyr-Volynskyi
Vladivostok 93 G5 Primorskiy Kray, SE Russia
Vlagtwedde 64 E2 Groningen, NE Netherlands
Vlasotince 79 E5 Serbia, SE Serbia
Vlieland 64 C1 Fris. Flylân. island Waddeneilanden, N Netherlands
Vlijmen 64 C4 Noord-Brabant, S Netherlands
Vlissingen 65 B5 Eng. Flushing, Fr. Flessingue. Zeeland, SW Netherlands
Vlodava see Włodawa
Vlonë/Vlora see Vlorë
Vlorë 79 C7 prev. Vlonë, It. Valona, Vlora. Vlorë, SW Albania
Vlotslavsk see Włocławek
Vöcklabruck 73 D6 Oberösterreich, NW Austria
Vogelkop see Doberai, Jazirah
Vohimena, Tanjona 57 F4 Fr. Cap Sainte Marie. headland S Madagascar
Voiron 69 D5 Isère, E France
Vojvodina 78 D3 Ger. Wojwodina. Vojvodina, N Serbia
Volga 89 B7 river NW Russia
Volga Uplands see Privolzhskaya Vozvyshennost'
Volgodonsk 89 B7 Rostovskaya Oblast', SW Russia
Volgograd 89 B7 prev. Stalingrad, Tsaritsyn. Volgogradskaya Oblast', SW Russia
Volkhov 88 B4 Leningradskaya Oblast', NW Russia
Volkoysk see Vawkavysk

Volmari *see* Valmiera
Volnovakha *87 G3* Donets'ka Oblast', SE Ukraine
Volodymyr-Volynskyi *86 C1 prev.* Volodymyr-Volyns'kyy, *Pol.* Włodzimierz, *Rus.* Vladimir-Volynskiy. Volyns'ka Oblast', NW Ukraine
Volodymyr-Volyns'kyy *see* Volodymyr-Volynskyi
Vologda *88 B4* Vologodskaya Oblast', W Russia
Vólos *83 B5* Thessalía, C Greece
Volozhin *see* Valozhyn
Vol'sk *89 C6* Saratovskaya Oblast', W Russia
Volta *53 E5 river* SE Ghana
Volta Blanche *see* White Volta
Volta, Lake *53 E5 reservoir* SE Ghana
Volta Noire *see* Black Volta
Volturno *75 D5 river* S Italy
Volunteer Island *see* Starbuck Island
Volzhskiy *89 B6* Volgogradskaya Oblast', SW Russia
Võnnu *84 E3 Ger.* Wendau. Tartumaa, SE Estonia
Voorst *64 D3* Gelderland, E Netherlands
Voranava *85 C5 Pol.* Werenów, *Rus.* Voronovo. Hrodzyenskaya Voblasts', W Belarus
Vorderrhein *73 B7 river* SE Switzerland
Vóreies Sporádes *83 C5 var.* Vóreioi Sporádes, Vórioi Sporádhes, *Eng.* Northern Sporades. *island group* E Greece
Vóreioi Sporádes *see* Vóreies Sporádes
Vórioi Sporádhes *see* Vóreies Sporádes
Vorkuta *92 C2* Respublika Komi, NW Russia
Vormsi *84 C2 var.* Vormsi Saar, *Ger.* Worms, *Swed.* Ormsö. *island* W Estonia
Vormsi Saar *see* Vormsi
Voronezh *89 B6* Voronezhskaya Oblast', W Russia
Voronovo *see* Voranava
Voroshilov *see* Ussuriysk
Voroshilovgrad *see* Luhansk
Voroshilovsk *see* Stavropol', Russia
Võru *84 D3 Ger.* Werro. Võrumaa, SE Estonia
Vosges *68 E4 mountain range* NE France
Vostochno-Sibirskoye More *93 F1 Eng.* East Siberian Sea. *sea* Arctic Ocean
Vostochnyy Sayan *93 E4 Mong.* Dzüün Soyonï Nuruu, *Eng.* Eastern Sayans. *mountain range* Mongolia/Russia
Vostock Island *see* Vostok Island
Vostok *132 C3 Russian research station* Antarctica
Vostok Island *123 G3 var.* Vostock Island; *prev.* Stavers Island. *island* Line Islands, SE Kiribati
Voznesensk *87 E3* Mykolayivs'ka Oblast', S Ukraine
Vranje *79 E5* Serbia, SE Serbia
Vranov *see* Vranov nad Topl'ou
Vranov nad Topl'ou *77 D5 var.* Vranov, *Hung.* Varannó. Prešovský Kraj, E Slovakia
Vratsa *82 C2* Vratsa, NW Bulgaria
Vrbas *78 C3* Vojvodina, NW Serbia
Vrbas *78 C3 river* N Bosnia and Herzegovina
Vršac *78 E3 Ger.* Werschetz, *Hung.* Versecz. Vojvodina, NE Serbia
Vsetín *77 C5 Ger.* Wsetin. Zlínský Kraj, E Czechia (Czech Republic)
Vučitrn *see* Vushtrri
Vukovar *78 C3 Hung.* Vukovár. Vukovar-Srijem, E Croatia
Vulcano, Isola *75 C7 island* Isole Eolie, S Italy
Vung Tau *115 E6 prev. Fr.* Cape Saint Jacques, Cap Saint-Jacques. Ba Ria-Vung Tau, S Vietnam
Vushtrri *79 D5 Serb.* Vučitrn. N Kosovo
Vyatka *89 C5 river* NW Russia
Vyatka *see* Kirov
Vyborg *88 B3 Fin.* Viipuri. Leningradskaya Oblast', NW Russia
Vyerkhnyadzvinsk *85 D5 Rus.* Verkhnedvinsk. Vitsyebskaya Voblasts', N Belarus
Vyetryna *85 D5 Rus.* Vetrino. Vitsyebskaya Voblasts', N Belarus
Vynohradiv *86 B3 Cz.* Sevluš, *Hung.* Nagyszöllös, *Rus.* Vinogradov; *prev.* Sevlyush. Zakarpats'ka Oblast', W Ukraine

W

Wa *53 E4* NW Ghana
Waag *see* Váh
Waagbistritz *see* Považská Bystrica
Waal *64 C4 river* S Netherlands
Wabash *18 C4* Indiana, N USA
Wabash River *18 B5 river* N USA
Waco *27 G3* Texas, SW USA
Wad Al-Hajarah *see* Guadalajara
Waddān *49 F3* NW Libya
Waddeneilanden *64 C1 Eng.* West Frisian Islands. *island group* N Netherlands
Waddenzee *64 C1 var.* Wadden Zee. *sea* SE North Sea
Wadden Zee *see* Waddenzee
Waddington, Mount *14 D5 mountain* British Columbia, SW Canada
Wādī as Sīr *97 B6 var.* Wadi es Sir. 'Ammān, NW Jordan
Wadi es Sir *see* Wādī as Sīr
Wadi Halfa *50 B3 var.* Wādī Ḥalfā'. Northern, N Sudan
Wādī Mūsā *97 B7 var.* Petra. Ma'ān, S Jordan
Wad Madanī *see* Wad Medani
Wad Medani *50 C4 var.* Wad Madanī. Gezira, C Sudan
Waflia *117 F4* Pulau Buru, E Indonesia
Wagadugu *see* Ouagadougou
Wagga Wagga *127 C7* New South Wales, SE Australia
Wagin *125 B7* Western Australia
Wah *112 C1* Punjab, NE Pakistan
Wahai *117 F4* Pulau Seram, E Indonesia
Wahaybah, Ramlat Al *see* Wahībah, Ramlat Āl
Wahiawā *25 A8 var.* Wahiawa. O'ahu, Hawaii, USA, C Pacific Ocean
Wahībah, Ramlat Ahl *see* Wahībah, Ramlat Āl
Wahibah Sands *99 E5 var.* Ramlat Ahl Wahībah, Ramlat Al Wahaybah, *Eng.* Wahībah Sands. *desert* N Oman
Wahībah Sands *see* Wahībah, Ramlat Āl
Wahpeton *23 F2* North Dakota, N USA
Wahran *see* Oran
Waiau *129 A7 river* South Island, New Zealand
Waigeo, Pulau *117 G4 island* Maluku, E Indonesia
Waikaremoana, Lake *128 E4 lake* North Island, New Zealand
Wailuku *25 B8* Maui, Hawaii, USA, C Pacific Ocean
Waimate *129 B6* Canterbury, South Island, New Zealand
Waiouru *128 D4* Manawatu-Wanganui, North Island, New Zealand
Waipara *129 C6* Canterbury, South Island, New Zealand
Waipawa *128 E4* Hawke's Bay, North Island, New Zealand
Waipukurau *128 D4* Hawke's Bay, North Island, New Zealand
Wairau *129 C5 river* South Island, New Zealand
Wairoa *128 E4* Hawke's Bay, North Island, New Zealand
Wairoa *128 D2 river* North Island, New Zealand
Waitaki *129 B6 river* South Island, New Zealand
Waitara *128 D4* Taranaki, North Island, New Zealand
Waitzen *see* Vác
Waiuku *128 D3* Auckland, North Island, New Zealand
Wakasa-wan *109 C6 bay* C Japan
Wakatipu, Lake *129 A7 lake* South Island, New Zealand
Wakayama *109 C6* Wakayama, Honshū, SW Japan
Wake Island *130 C2 US unincorporated territory* NW Pacific Ocean
Wake Island *120 D1 atoll* NW Pacific Ocean
Wakkanai *108 C1* Hokkaidō, NE Japan
Walachei/Walachia *see* Wallachia
Wałbrzych *76 B4 Ger.* Waldenburg, Waldenburg in Schlesien. Dolnośląskie, SW Poland
Walcourt *65 C7* Namur, S Belgium
Wałcz *76 B3 Ger.* Deutsch Krone. Zachodnio-pomorskie, NW Poland
Waldenburg/Waldenburg in Schlesien *see* Wałbrzych
Waldia *see* Weldiya
Wales *14 C2* Alaska, USA
Wales *67 C6 Wel.* Cymru. *cultural region* Wales, United Kingdom
Walgett *127 D5* New South Wales, SE Australia
Walk *see* Valga, Estonia
Walk *see* Valka, Latvia
Walker Lake *25 C5 lake* Nevada, W USA
Wallachia *86 B5 var.* Walachia, *Ger.* Walachei, *Rom.* Valachia. *cultural region* S Romania
Walla Walla *24 C2* Washington, NW USA
Wallenthal *see* Haţeg
Wallis and Futuna *123 E4 Fr.* Territoire de Wallis et Futuna. *French overseas collectivity* C Pacific Ocean
Wallis et Futuna, Territoire de *see* Wallis and Futuna
Walnut Ridge *20 B1* Arkansas, C USA
Waltenberg *see* Zalău
Walthamstow *67 B7* Waltham Forest, SE England, United Kingdom
Walvisbaai *see* Walvis Bay
Walvis Bay *56 A4 Afr.* Walvisbaai. Erongo, NW Namibia
Walvish Ridge *see* Walvis Ridge
Walvis Ridge *47 B7 var.* Walvish Ridge. *undersea ridge* E Atlantic Ocean
Wan *see* Anhui
Wanaka *129 B6* Otago, South Island, New Zealand
Wanaka, Lake *129 A6 lake* South Island, New Zealand
Wanchuan *see* Zhangjiakou
Wandel Sea *61 E1 sea* Arctic Ocean
Wandsworth *67 A8* Wandsworth, SE England, United Kingdom
Wanganui *128 D4* Manawatu-Wanganui, North Island, New Zealand
Wangaratta *127 C7* Victoria, SE Australia
Wankie *see* Hwange
Wanki, Río *see* Coco, Río
Wanlaweyn *51 D6 var.* Wanle Weyn, *It.* Uanle Uen. Shabeellaha Hoose, SW Somalia
Wanle Weyn *see* Wanlaweyn
Wanxian *see* Wanzhou
Wanzhou *106 B5 var.* Wanxian. Chongqing, C China
Warangal *113 E5* Telangana, C India
Warasdin *see* Varaždin
Warburg *72 B4* Nordrhein-Westfalen, W Germany
Ware *15 E4* British Columbia, W Canada
Waremme *65 C6* Liège, E Belgium
Waren *72 C3* Mecklenburg-Vorpommern, NE Germany
Wargla *see* Ouargla
Warkworth *128 D2* Auckland, North Island, New Zealand
Warnemünde *72 C2* Mecklenburg-Vorpommern, NE Germany
Warner *27 G1* Oklahoma, C USA
Warnes *39 G4* Santa Cruz, C Bolivia
Warrego River *127 C5 seasonal river* New South Wales/Queensland, E Australia
Warren *18 D3* Michigan, N USA
Warren *18 D3* Ohio, N USA
Warren *19 E3* Pennsylvania, NE USA
Warri *53 F5* Delta, S Nigeria
Warrnambool *127 B7* Victoria, SE Australia
Warsaw/Warschau *see* Warszawa
Warszawa *76 D3 Eng.* Warsaw, *Ger.* Warschau, *Rus.* Varshava. *country capital* (Poland) Mazowieckie, C Poland
Warta *76 B3 Ger.* Warthe. *river* W Poland
Wartberg *see* Senec
Warthe *see* Warta
Warwick *127 E5* Queensland, E Australia
Washington *22 A2* NE England, United Kingdom
Washington D.C. *19 E4 country capital* (USA) District of Columbia, NE USA
Washington Island *see* Teraina
Washington, Mount *19 G2 mountain* New Hampshire, NE USA
Wash, The *67 E6 inlet* E England, United Kingdom
Wasiliszki *see* Vasilishki
Waspam *31 E2 var.* Waspán. Región Autónoma Atlántico Norte, NE Nicaragua
Waspán *see* Waspam
Watampone *117 E4 var.* Bone. Sulawesi, C Indonesia
Watenstedt-Salzgitter *see* Salzgitter
Waterbury *19 F3* Connecticut, NE USA
Waterford *67 B6 Ir.* Port Láirge. Waterford, S Ireland
Waterloo *23 G3* Iowa, C USA
Watertown *19 F2* New York, NE USA
Watertown *23 F2* South Dakota, N USA
Waterville *19 G2* Maine, NE USA
Watford *67 A7* E England, United Kingdom
Watlings Island *see* San Salvador
Watsa *55 E5* Orientale, NE Dem. Rep. Congo
Watts Bar Lake *20 D1 reservoir* Tennessee, S USA
Wau *51 B5 var.* Wāw. Western Bahr el Ghazal, C South Sudan
Waukegan *18 B3* Illinois, N USA
Waukesha *18 B3* Wisconsin, N USA
Wausau *18 B2* Wisconsin, N USA
Waverly *23 G3* Iowa, C USA
Wavre *65 C6* Walloon Brabant, C Belgium
Wāw *see* Wau
Wawa *16 C4* Ontario, S Canada
Waycross *21 E3* Georgia, SE USA
Wearmouth *see* Sunderland
Webfoot State *see* Oregon
Webster City *23 F3* Iowa, C USA
Weddell Plain *132 A2 abyssal plain* SW Atlantic Ocean
Weddell Sea *132 A2 sea* SW Atlantic Ocean
Weener *72 A3* Niedersachsen, NW Germany
Weert *65 D5* Limburg, SE Netherlands
Weesp *64 C3* Noord-Holland, C Netherlands
Węgorzewo *76 D2 Ger.* Angerburg. Warmińsko-Mazurskie, NE Poland
Weimar *72 C4* Thüringen, C Germany
Weissenburg *see* Alba Iulia, Romania
Weissenburg in Bayern *73 C6* Bayern, SE Germany
Weissenstein *see* Paide
Weisskirchen *see* Bela Crkva
Weiswampach *65 D7* Diekirch, N Luxembourg
Wejherowo *76 C2* Pomorskie, NW Poland
Welchman Hall *33 G1* C Barbados
Weldiya *50 C4 var.* Waldia, *It.* Valdia. Āmara, N Ethiopia
Welkom *56 D4* Free State, C South Africa
Welle *see* Uele
Wellesley Islands *126 B2 island group* Queensland, N Australia
Wellington *129 D5 country capital* (New Zealand) Wellington, North Island, New Zealand
Wellington *23 F5* Kansas, C USA
Wellington *see* Wellington, Isla
Wellington, Isla *43 A7 var.* Wellington. *island* S Chile
Wells *24 D4* Nevada, W USA
Wellsford *128 D2* Auckland, North Island, New Zealand
Wells, Lake *125 C5 lake* Western Australia
Wels *73 D6 anc.* Ovilava. Oberösterreich, N Austria
Wembley *67 A8* Alberta, W Canada
Wemmel *65 B6* Vlaams Brabant, C Belgium
Wenatchee *24 B2* Washington, NW USA
Wenchi *53 E4* W Ghana
Wen-chou/Wenchow *see* Wenzhou
Wendau *see* Võnnu
Wenden *see* Cēsis
Wenzhou *106 D5 var.* Wen-chou, Wenchow. Zhejiang, SE China
Werda *56 C4* Kgalagadi, S Botswana
Werder *see* Virtsu
Werenów *see* Voranava
Werkendam *64 C4* Noord-Brabant, S Netherlands
Werowitz *see* Virovitica
Werro *see* Võru
Werschetz *see* Vršac
Wesenberg *see* Rakvere
Weser *72 B3 river* NW Germany
Wessel Islands *126 B1 island group* Northern Territory, N Australia
West Antarctica *132 A3 var.* Lesser Antarctica. *physical region* Antarctica
West Australian Basin *see* Wharton Basin
West Bank *97 A6 disputed region* SW Asia
West Bend *18 B3* Wisconsin, N USA
West Bengal *113 F4 cultural region* NE India
West Cape *129 A7 headland* South Island, New Zealand
West Des Moines *23 F3* Iowa, C USA
Westerland *72 B2* Schleswig-Holstein, N Germany
Western Australia *124 B4 state* W Australia
Western Bug *see* Bug
Western Carpathians *77 E7 mountain range* W Romania Europe
Western Desert *see* Şaḩrā' al Gharbīyah
Western Dvina *63 E7 Bel.* Dzvina, *Ger.* Düna, *Latv.* Daugava, *Rus.* Zapadnaya Dvina. *river* W Europe
Western Ghats *112 C5 mountain range* SW India
Western Isles *see* Outer Hebrides
Western Punjab *see* Punjab
Western Sahara *48 B3 disputed territory administered by Morocco* N Africa
Western Samoa *see* Samoa
Western Samoa, Independent State of *see* Samoa
Western Sayans *see* Zapadnyy Sayan
Western Scheldt *see* Westerschelde
Western Sierra Madre *see* Madre Occidental, Sierra
Westerschelde *65 B5 Eng.* Western Scheldt; *prev.* Honte. *inlet* S North Sea
West Falkland *43 C7 var.* Gran Malvina, Isla Gran Malvina. *island* W Falkland Islands
West Fargo *23 F2* North Dakota, N USA
West Frisian Islands *see* Waddeneilanden
West Irian *see* Papua
Westliche Morava *see* Zapadna Morava
West Mariana Basin *120 B1 var.* Perece Vela Basin. *undersea feature* W Pacific Ocean
West Memphis *20 B1* Arkansas, C USA
West New Guinea *see* Papua
Weston-super-Mare *67 D7* SW England, United Kingdom
West Palm Beach *21 F4* Florida, SE USA
West Papua *see* Papua
Westport *129 C5* West Coast, South Island, New Zealand
West Punjab *see* Punjab
West River *see* Xi Jiang
West Siberian Plain *see* Zapadno-Sibirskaya Ravnina
West Virginia *18 D4 off.* State of West Virginia, *also known as* Mountain State. *state* NE USA
Wetar, Pulau *117 F5 island* Kepulauan Damar, E Indonesia
Wetzlar *73 B5* Hessen, W Germany
Wevok *14 C2 var.* Wewuk. Alaska, USA
Wewuk *see* Wevok
Wexford *67 B6 Ir.* Loch Garman. SE Ireland
Weyburn *15 F5* Saskatchewan, S Canada
Weymouth *67 D7* S England, United Kingdom
Wezep *64 D3* Gelderland, E Netherlands
Whakatane *128 E3* Bay of Plenty, North Island, New Zealand
Whale Cove *15 G3 var.* Tikiarjuaq. Nunavut, C Canada
Whangarei *128 D2* Northland, North Island, New Zealand
Wharton Basin *119 D5 var.* West Australian Basin. *undersea feature* E Indian Ocean
Whataroa *129 B6* West Coast, South Island, New Zealand
Wheatland *22 D3* Wyoming, C USA
Wheeler Peak *26 D1 mountain* New Mexico, SW USA
Wheeling *18 D4* West Virginia, NE USA
Whenua Hou *see* Codfish Island
Whitby *67 D5* N England, United Kingdom
Whitefish *22 B1* Montana, NW USA
Whitehaven *67 C5* NW England, United Kingdom
Whitehorse *14 D4 territory capital* Yukon, W Canada
White Nile *50 B4 Ar.* Al Baḩr al Abyaḑ, An Nīl al Abyaḑ, Bahr el Jebel. *river* C South Sudan
White River *22 D3 river* South Dakota, N USA
White Sea *see* Beloye More
White Volta *53 E4 var.* Nakambé, *Fr.* Volta Blanche. *river* Burkina/Ghana
Whitianga *128 D2* Waikato, North Island, New Zealand
Whitney, Mount *25 C6 mountain* California, W USA
Whitsunday Group *126 D3 island group* Queensland, E Australia
Whyalla *127 B6* South Australia
Wichita *23 F5* Kansas, C USA
Wichita Falls *27 F2* Texas, SW USA
Wichita River *27 F2 river* Texas, SW USA
Wickenburg *26 B2* Arizona, SW USA
Wicklow *67 B6 Ir.* Cill Mhantáin. *county* E Ireland
Wicklow Mountains *67 B6 Ir.* Sléibhte Chill Mhantáin. *mountain range* E Ireland
Wieliczka *77 D5* Małopolskie, S Poland
Wieluń *76 C4* Sieradz, C Poland
Wien *73 E6 Eng.* Vienna, *Hung.* Bécs, *Slvk.* Vídeň, *Slvn.* Dunaj; *anc.* Vindobona. *country capital* (Austria) Wien, NE Austria
Wiener Neustadt *73 E6* Niederösterreich, E Austria
Wierden *64 E3* Overijssel, E Netherlands
Wiesbaden *73 B5* Hessen, W Germany
Wieselburg and Ungarisch-Altenburg/Wieselburg-Ungarisch-Altenburg *see* Mosonmagyaróvár
Wiesenhof *see* Ostrołęka
Wight, Isle of *67 D7 island* United Kingdom
Wigorna Ceaster *see* Worcester
Wijchen *64 D4* Gelderland, SE Netherlands
Wijk bij Duurstede *64 D4* Utrecht, C Netherlands
Wilcannia *127 C6* New South Wales, SE Australia
Wilejka *see* Vilyeyka
Wilhelm, Mount *122 B3 mountain* C Papua New Guinea
Wilhelm-Pieck-Stadt *see* Guben
Wilhelmshaven *72 B3* Niedersachsen, NW Germany
Wilia/Wilja *see* Neris
Wilkes Barre *19 F3* Pennsylvania, NE USA
Wilkes Land *132 C4 physical region* Antarctica
Wiłkomierz *see* Ukmergė
Willard *26 D2* New Mexico, SW USA
Willcox *26 C3* Arizona, SW USA
Willebroek *65 B5* Antwerpen, C Belgium
Willemstad *33 E5 dependent territory capital* (Curaçao) Lesser Antilles, S Caribbean Sea
Williston *22 D1* North Dakota, N USA
Wilmington *19 F4* Delaware, NE USA
Wilmington *21 F2* North Carolina, SE USA
Wilmington *18 C4* Ohio, N USA
Wilna/Wilno *see* Vilnius
Wilrijk *65 C5* Antwerpen, N Belgium
Winchester *67 D7 hist.* Wintanceaster, *Lat.* Venta Belgarum. S England, United Kingdom
Winchester *19 E4* Virginia, NE USA
Windau *see* Ventspils, Latvia
Windau *see* Venta, Latvia/Lithuania
Windhoek *56 B3 Ger.* Windhuk. *country capital* (Namibia) Khomas, C Namibia
Windhuk *see* Windhoek
Windorah *126 C4* Queensland, C Australia
Windsor *16 C5* Ontario, S Canada
Windsor *67 D7* S England, United Kingdom
Windsor *19 G3* Connecticut, NE USA
Windward Islands *33 H4 island group* E West Indies
Windward Islands *see* Barlavento, Ilhas de, Cape Verde (Cabo Verde)
Windward Passage *32 D3 Sp.* Paso de los Vientos. *channel* Cuba/Haiti
Winisk *16 C2 river* Ontario, C Canada
Winkowitz *see* Vinkovci
Winnebago, Lake *18 B2 lake* Wisconsin, N USA
Winnemucca *25 C5* Nevada, W USA
Winnipeg *15 G5 province capital* Manitoba, S Canada
Winnipeg, Lake *15 G5 lake* Manitoba, C Canada
Winnipegosis, Lake *16 A3 lake* Manitoba, C Canada
Winona *23 G3* Minnesota, N USA
Winschoten *64 E2* Groningen, NE Netherlands
Winsen *72 B3* Niedersachsen, N Germany
Winston Salem *21 E1* North Carolina, SE USA
Winsum *64 D1* Groningen, NE Netherlands
Wintanceaster *see* Winchester
Winterswijk *64 E4* Gelderland, E Netherlands
Winterthur *73 B7* Zürich, NE Switzerland
Winton *126 C4* Queensland, E Australia
Winton *129 A7* Southland, South Island, New Zealand
Wisby *see* Visby
Wisconsin *18 A2 off.* State of Wisconsin, *also known as* Badger State. *state* N USA
Wisconsin Rapids *18 B2* Wisconsin, N USA
Wisconsin River *18 B3 river* Wisconsin, N USA
Wisła *76 C2 var.* Vistula. *river* N Poland
Wiślany, Zalew *see* Vistula Lagoon
Wismar *72 C2* Mecklenburg-Vorpommern, N Germany
Wittenberge *72 C3* Brandenburg, N Germany
Wittlich *73 A5* Rheinland-Pfalz, SW Germany
Wittstock *72 C3* Brandenburg, NE Germany
W. J. van Blommesteinmeer *37 G3 reservoir* E Suriname
Władysławowo *76 C2* Pomorskie, N Poland
Włocławek *76 C3 Ger./Rus.* Vlotslavsk. Kujawsko-pomorskie, C Poland
Włodawa *76 E4 Rus.* Vlodava. Lubelskie, SE Poland
Włodzimierz *see* Volodymyr-Volynskyi
Wlotzkasbaken *56 B3* Erongo, W Namibia
Wodonga *127 C7* Victoria, SE Australia
Wodzisław Śląski *77 C5 Ger.* Loslau. Śląskie, S Poland
Wojerecy *see* Hoyerswerda
Wōjjā *see* Wotje Atoll
Wojwodina *see* Vojvodina
Woking *67 D7* SE England, United Kingdom
Wolf, Isla *38 A4 island* Galápagos Islands, W Ecuador South America
Wolfsberg *73 D7* Kärnten, SE Austria
Wolfsburg *72 C3* Niedersachsen, N Germany
Wolgast *72 D2* Mecklenburg-Vorpommern, NE Germany
Wołkowysk *see* Vawkavysk
Wöllan *see* Velenje
Wollaston Lake *15 F4* Saskatchewan, C Canada
Wollongong *127 D6* New South Wales, SE Australia
Wolmar *see* Valmiera
Wołożyn *see* Valozhyn
Wolvega *64 D2 Fris.* Wolvegea. Fryslân, N Netherlands
Wolvegea *see* Wolvega
Wolverhampton *67 D6* C England, United Kingdom
Wolverine State *see* Michigan
Wŏnsan *107 E3* SE North Korea
Woodburn *24 B3* Oregon, NW USA
Woodland *25 B5* California, W USA
Woodruff *18 B2* Wisconsin, N USA
Woods, Lake of the *16 A3 Fr.* Lac des Bois. *lake* Canada/USA
Woodville *128 D4* Manawatu-Wanganui, North Island, New Zealand
Woodward *27 F1* Oklahoma, C USA
Worcester *56 C5* Western Cape, SW South Africa
Worcester *67 D6 hist.* Wigorna Ceaster. W England, United Kingdom
Worcester *19 G3* Massachusetts, NE USA
Workington *67 C5* NW England, United Kingdom
Worland *22 C3* Wyoming, C USA
Wormatia *see* Worms
Worms *73 B5 anc.* Augusta Vangionum, Borbetomagus, Wormatia. Rheinland-Pfalz, SW Germany
Worms *see* Vormsi
Worthington *23 F3* Minnesota, N USA
Wotje Atoll *122 D1 var.* Wōjjā. *atoll* Ratak Chain, E Marshall Islands
Woudrichem *64 C4* Noord-Brabant, S Netherlands
Wrangel Island *93 F1 Eng.* Wrangel Island. *island* NE Russia
Wrangel Island *see* Vrangelya, Ostrov
Wrangel Plain *133 B2 undersea feature* Arctic Ocean
Wrocław *76 C4 Eng./Ger.* Breslau. Dolnośląskie, SW Poland
Września *76 C3* Wielkopolskie, C Poland
Wsetin *see* Vsetín
Wuchang *see* Wuhan
Wuday'ah *99 C6 spring/well* S Saudi Arabia
Wuhai *105 E3 var.* Haibowan. Nei Mongol Zizhiqu, N China
Wuhan *106 C5 var.* Han-kou, Han-k'ou, Hanyang, Wuchang, Wu-han; *prev.* Hankow. *province capital* Hubei, C China
Wu-han *see* Wuhan
Wuhsien *see* Suzhou
Wuhsi/Wu-his *see* Wuxi
Wuhu *106 D5 var.* Wu-na-mu. Anhui, E China
Wujlān *see* Ujelang Atoll
Wukari *53 G4* Taraba, E Nigeria
Wuliang Shan *106 A6 mountain range* SW China
Wu-lu-k'o-mu-shi/Wu-lu-mu-ch'i *see* Ürümqi
Wu-na-mu *see* Wuhu
Wuppertal *72 A4 prev.* Barmen-Elberfeld. Nordrhein-Westfalen, W Germany
Würzburg *73 B5* Bayern, SW Germany
Wusih *see* Wuxi
Wuxi *106 D5 var.* Wuhsi, Wu-hsi, Wusih. Jiangsu, E China
Wuyi Shan *103 E3 mountain range* SE China
Wye *67 C6 Wel.* Gwy. *river* England/Wales, United Kingdom
Wyłkowyszki *see* Vilkaviškis
Wyndham *124 D3* Western Australia
Wyoming *18 C3* Michigan, N USA
Wyoming *22 B3 off.* State of Wyoming, *also known as* Equality State. *state* C USA
Wyszków *76 D3 Ger.* Probstberg. Mazowieckie, NE Poland

X

Xaafuun, Raas *50 E4 var.* Ras Hafun. *cape* NE Somalia
Xaçmaz *95 H2 Rus.* Khachmas. N Azerbaijan
Xaignabouli *114 C4 prev.* Muang Xaignabouri, *Fr.* Sayaboury. Xaignabouli, N Laos
Xai-Xai *57 E4 prev.* João Belo, Vila de João Belo. Gaza, S Mozambique
Xalapa *29 F4* Veracruz-Llave, Mexico
Xam Nua *114 D3 var.* Sam Neua. Houaphan, N Laos
Xankändi *95 G3 Rus.* Khankendi; *prev.* Stepanakert. SW Azerbaijan
Xánthi *82 C3* Anatolikí Makedonía kai Thráki, NE Greece
Xàtiva *71 F3 Cas.* Xátiva; *anc.* Setabis, *var.* Jativa. Comunitat Valenciana, E Spain
Xauen *see* Chefchaouen
Xäzär Dänizi *see* Caspian Sea
Xeres *see* Jeréz de la Frontera
Xiaguan *see* Dali
Xiamen *106 D6 var.* Hsia-men; *prev.* Amoy. Fujian, SE China
Xi'an *106 C4 var.* Changan, Sian, Signan, Siking, Singan, Xian. *province capital* Shaanxi, C China
Xiang *see* Hunan
Xiangkhoang *see* Phônsaven
Xiangtan *106 C5 var.* Hsiang-t'an, Siangtan. Hunan, S China
Xiao Hinggan Ling *106 D2 Eng.* Lesser Khingan Range. *mountain range* NE China

Xichang 106 B5 Sichuan, C China
Xieng Khouang see Phônsaven
Xieng Ngeun see Muong Xiang Ngeun
Xigazê 104 C5 var. Jih-k'a-tse, Shigatse, Xigaze. Xizang Zizhiqu, W China
Xi Jiang 102 D3 var. Hsi Chiang, Eng. West River. river S China
Xilinhot 105 F2 var. Silinhot. Nei Mongol Zizhiqu, N China
Xilokastro see Xylókastro
Xin see Xinjiang Uygur Zizhiqu
Xingkai Hu see Khanka, Lake
Xingu, Rio 41 E2 river C Brazil
Xingxingxia 104 D3 Xinjiang Uygur Zizhiqu, NW China
Xining 105 E4 var. Hsining, Hsi-ning, Sining. province capital Qinghai, C China
Xinjiang see Xinjiang Uygur Zizhiqu
Xinjiang Uygur Zizhiqu 104 B3 var. Sinkiang, Sinkiang Uighur Autonomous Region, Xin, Xinjiang. autonomous region NW China
Xinpu see Lianyungang
Xinxiang 106 C4 Henan, C China
Xinyang 106 C4 var. Hsin-yang, Sinyang. Henan, C China
Xinzo de Limia 70 C2 Galicia, NW Spain
Xiqing Shan 102 D2 mountain range C China
Xiva 100 D2 Rus. Khiva, Khiwa. Xorazm Viloyati, W Uzbekistan
Xixón see Gijón
Xizang see Xizang Zizhiqu
Xizang Gaoyuan see Qingzang Gaoyuan
Xizang Zizhiqu 104 B4 var. Thibet, Tibetan Autonomous Region, Xizang, Eng. Tibet. autonomous region W China
Xolotlán see Managua, Lago de
Xucheng see Xuwen
Xuddur 51 D5 var. Hudur, It. Oddur. Bakool, SW Somalia
Xuwen 106 C7 var. Xucheng. Guangdong, S China
Xuzhou 106 D4 var. Hsu-chou, Suchow, Tongshan; prev. T'ung-shan. Jiangsu, E China
Xylókastro 83 B5 var. Xilokastro. Pelopónnisos, S Greece

Y

Ya'an 106 B5 var. Yaan. Sichuan, C China
Yabēlo 51 C5 Oromīya, C Ethiopia
Yablis 31 E2 Región Autónoma Atlántico Norte, NE Nicaragua
Yablonovyy Khrebet 93 F4 mountain range S Russia
Yabrai Shan 105 E3 mountain range NE China
Yafran 49 F2 NW Libya
Yaghan Basin 45 B7 undersea feature SE Pacific Ocean
Yagotin see Yahotyn
Yahotyn 87 E2 Rus. Yagotin. Kyivska Oblast, N Ukraine
Yahualica 28 D4 Jalisco, SW Mexico
Yakima 24 B2 Washington, NW USA
Yakima River 24 B2 river Washington, NW USA
Yakoruda 82 C3 Blagoevgrad, SW Bulgaria
Yaku-shima 109 B8 island Nansei-shotō, SW Japan
Yakutat 14 D4 Alaska, USA
Yakutsk 93 F3 Respublika Sakha (Yakutiya), NE Russia
Yakymivka 87 F4 Zaporizka Oblast, S Ukraine
Yala 115 C7 Yala, SW Thailand
Yalizava 85 D6 Rus. Yelizovo. Mahilyowskaya Voblasts', E Belarus
Yalong Jiang 106 A5 river C China
Yalova 94 B3 Yalova, NW Turkey (Türkiye)
Yalpug, Ozero see Yalpuh, Ozero
Yalpuh, Ozero 86 D4 Rus. Ozero Yalpug. lake SW Ukraine
Yalta 87 F5 Respublika Krym, S Ukraine
Yalu 110 E2 Chin. Yalu Jiang, Jap. Oryokko, Kor. Amnok-kang. river China/North Korea
Yalu Jiang see Yalu
Yamaguchi 109 B7 var. Yamaguti. Yamaguchi, Honshū, SW Japan
Yamal, Poluostrov 92 D2 peninsula N Russia
Yamaniyah, Al Jumhūrīyah al see Yemen
Yambio 51 B5 var. Yambiyo. Western Equatoria, S South Sudan
Yambiyo see Yambio
Yambol 82 D2 Turk. Yanboli. Yambol, E Bulgaria
Yamdena, Pulau 117 G5 prev. Jamdena. island Kepulauan Tanimbar, E Indonesia
Yamoussoukro 52 D5 country capital (Ivory Coast) C Ivory Coast
Yamuna 112 D3 prev. Jumna. river N India
Yana 93 F2 river NE Russia
Yanboli see Yambol
Yanbu 'al Bahr 99 A5 Al Madīnah, W Saudi Arabia
Yangambi 55 D5 Orientale, N Dem. Rep. Congo
Yangchow see Yangzhou
Yangi'yo'l 101 E2 Rus. Yangiyul'. Toshkent Viloyati, E Uzbekistan
Yangiyul' see Yangi'yo'l
Yangku see Taiyuan
Yangon 114 B4 Eng. Rangoon. Yangon, S Myanmar (Burma)
Yangtze 106 B5 var. Yangtze Kiang, Eng. Yangtze. river C China
Yangtze see Chang Jiang
Yangtze Kiang see Chang Jiang
Yangzhou 106 D5 var. Yangchow. Jiangsu, E China
Yankton 23 E3 South Dakota, N USA
Yany Kapu 87 F4 Rus. Krasnoperekopsk. Respublika Krym, S Ukraine
Yannina see Ioánnina
Yanskiy Zaliv 91 F2 bay N Russia
Yantai 106 D4 var. Yan-t'ai; prev. Chefoo, Chih-fu. Shandong, E China
Yaoundé 55 B5 var. Yaunde. country capital (Cameroon) Centre, S Cameroon
Yap 120 A1 island Caroline Islands, W Micronesia
Yapanskoye More see East Sea/Japan, Sea of
Yapen, Pulau 117 G4 prev. Japen. island E Indonesia
Yap Trench 120 B2 var. Yap Trough. undersea feature SE Philippine Sea
Yap Trough see Yap Trench
Yapurá, Río see Caquetá, Río, Brazil/Colombia
Yapurá see Japurá, Rio, Brazil/Colombia

Yaqui, Río 28 C2 river NW Mexico
Yaransk 89 C5 Kirovskaya Oblast', NW Russia
Yarega 88 D4 Respublika Komi, NW Russia
Yaren 122 D2 de facto country capital (Nauru) Nauru, SW Pacific
Yarkant see Shache
Yarlung Zangbo Jiang see Brahmaputra
Yarmouth 17 F5 Nova Scotia, SE Canada
Yarmouth see Great Yarmouth
Yaroslav see Jarosław
Yaroslavl' 88 B4 Yaroslavskaya Oblast', W Russia
Yarumal 36 B2 Antioquia, NW Colombia
Yasel'da 85 B7 river Brestskaya Voblasts', SW Belarus Europe
Yatsushiro 109 A7 var. Yatusiro. Kumamoto, Kyūshū, SW Japan
Yatusiro see Yatsushiro
Yaunde see Yaoundé
Yavarí, Rio see Javari, Rio
Yavari, Río 40 C2 var. Yavarí. river Brazil/Peru
Yaviza 31 H5 Darién, SE Panama
Yavoriv 86 B2 Pol. Jaworów, Rus. Yavorov. L'vivs'ka Oblast', W Ukraine
Yavorov see Yavoriv
Yazd 97 D3 var. Yezd. Yazd, C Iran
Yazoo City 20 B2 Mississippi, S USA
Yding Skovhøj 63 A7 hill C Denmark
Ye 115 B5 Mon State, S Myanmar (Burma)
Yecheng 104 A3 var. Kargilik. Xinjiang Uygur Zizhiqu, NW China
Yedy Kuiu 87 G5 prev. Lenine, Rus. Lenino. Respublika Krym, S Ukraine
Yefremov 89 B5 Tul'skaya Oblast', W Russia
Yekaterinburg 92 C3 prev. Sverdlovsk. Sverdlovskaya Oblast', C Russia
Yekaterinodar see Krasnodar
Yekaterinoslav see Dnipro
Yelets 89 B5 Lipetskaya Oblast', W Russia
Yelisavetpol see Gäncä
Yelizavetgrad see Kropyvnytskyi
Yelizovo see Yalizava
Yell 66 D1 island NE Scotland, United Kingdom
Yellowhammer State see Alabama
Yellowknife 15 E4 territory capital Northwest Territories, W Canada
Yellow River see Huang He
Yellow Sea 106 D4 Chin. Huang Hai, Kor. Hwang-Hae. sea E Asia
Yellowstone River 22 C2 river Montana/Wyoming, NW USA
Yel'sk 85 C7 Homyel'skaya Voblasts', SE Belarus
Yelwa 53 F4 Kebbi, W Nigeria
Yemen 99 C7 off. Republic of Yemen, Ar. Al Jumhūrīyah al Yamanīyah, Al Yaman. country SW Asia
Yemen, Republic of see Yemen
Yemva 88 D4 prev. Zheleznodorozhnyy. Respublika Komi, NW Russia
Yenakiieve 87 G3 prev. Yenakiyeve, Ordzhonikidze, Rykovo; Rus. Yenakiyevo. Donets'ka Oblast', E Ukraine
Yenakiyeve see Yenakiieve
Yenakiyevo see Yenakiieve
Yenangyaung 114 A3 Magway, W Myanmar (Burma)
Yendi 53 E4 NE Ghana
Yengisar 104 A3 Xinjiang Uygur Zizhiqu, NW China
Yenierenköy 80 D4 var. Yialousa, Gk. Agialoúsa. NE Cyprus
Yenipazar see Novi Pazar
Yenisey 92 D3 river Mongolia/Russia
Yenping see Nanping
Yeovil 67 D7 SW England, United Kingdom
Yeppoon 126 D4 Queensland, E Australia
Yerevan 95 F3 Eng. Erivan. country capital (Armenia) C Armenia
Yeriho see Jericho
Yerushalayim see Jerusalem
Yeso see Hokkaidō
Yeu, Île d' 68 A4 island NW France
Yevlakh see Yevlax
Yevlax 95 G2 Rus. Yevlakh. C Azerbaijan
Yevpatoriia 87 F5 prev. Yevpatoriya. Respublika Krym, S Ukraine
Yevpatoriya see Yevpatoriia
Yeya 87 H4 river S Russia
Yezerishche see Yezyaryshcha
Yezo see Hokkaidō
Yezyaryshcha 85 E5 Rus. Yezerishche. Vitsyebskaya Voblasts', NE Belarus
Yialousa see Yenierenköy
Yiannitsá see Giannitsá
Yichang 106 C5 Hubei, C China
Yıldızeli 94 D3 Sivas, N Turkey (Türkiye)
Yinchuan 106 B4 var. Yinch'uan, Yin-ch'uan, Yinchwan. province capital Ningxia, N China
Yinchwan see Yinchuan
Yindu Ni see Indus
Yin-hsien see Ningbo
Yining 104 B2 var. I-ning, Uigh. Gulja, Kuldja. Xinjiang Uygur Zizhiqu, NW China
Yin-tu Ho see Indus
Yisrael/Yisra'el see Israel
Yíthion see Gýtheio
Yogyakarta 116 C5 prev. Djokjakarta, Jogjakarta, Jokyakarta. Jawa, C Indonesia
Yokohama 109 D5 Aomori, Honshū, C Japan
Yokohama 108 A2 Kanagawa, Honshū, S Japan
Yokote 108 D4 Akita, Honshū, C Japan
Yola 53 H4 Adamawa, E Nigeria
Yonago 109 B6 Tottori, Honshū, SW Japan
Yong'an 106 D6 var. Yong'an. Fujian, SE China
Yongzhou 107 C6 var. Lengshuitan. Hunan, S China
Yonkers 19 F3 New York, NE USA
Yonne 68 C4 river C France
Yopal 36 C3 var. El Yopal. Casanare, C Colombia
York 67 D5 anc. Eboracum, Eburacum. N England, United Kingdom
York 23 E4 Nebraska, C USA
York, Cape 126 C1 headland Queensland, NE Australia
York, Kap see Innaanganeq
Yorkton 15 F5 Saskatchewan, S Canada
Yoro 42 C2 Yoro, C Honduras
Yoshkar-Ola 89 C5 Respublika Mariy El, W Russia
Yōsōnbulag see Altay
Youngstown 18 D4 Ohio, N USA

Youth, Isle of see Juventud, Isla de la
Ypres see Ieper
Yreka 24 B4 California, W USA
Yrendagüé 42 D2 de facto country capital (Nauru) Nauru, SW Pacific
Yssel see IJssel
Ysyk-Köl see Issyk-Kul', Ozero
Ysyk-Köl see Balykchy
Yu see Henan
Yuan see Red River
Yuan Jiang see Red River
Yuba City 25 B5 California, W USA
Yucatán, Canal de see Yucatan Channel
Yucatan Channel 29 H3 Sp. Canal de Yucatán. channel Cuba/Mexico
Yucatán Peninsula see Yucatán, Península de
Yucatán, Península de 13 C7 Eng. Yucatan Peninsula. peninsula Guatemala/Mexico
Yuci see Jinzhong
Yue see Guangdong
Yueyang 106 C5 Hunan, S China
Yugoslavia see Serbia
Yukhavichy 85 D5 Rus. Yukhovichi. Vitsyebskaya Voblasts', N Belarus
Yukhovichi see Yukhavichy
Yukon 14 D3 prev. Yukon Territory, Fr. Territoire du Yukon. territory NW Canada
Yukon River 14 C2 river Canada/USA
Yukon, Territoire du see Yukon
Yukon Territory see Yukon
Yulin 106 C6 Guangxi Zhuangzu Zizhiqu, S China
Yuma 26 A2 Arizona, SW USA
Yun see Yunnan
Yungki see Jilin
Yung-ning see Nanning
Yunjinghong see Jinghong
Yunki see Jilin
Yunnan 106 A6 var. Yun, Yunnan Sheng, Yünnan, Yun-nan. province SW China
Yunnan see Kunming
Yunnan Sheng see Yunnan
Yünnan/Yun-nan see Yunnan
Yurev see Tartu
Yurihonjō see Honjō
Yuruá, Río see Juruá, Rio
Yury'ev see Tartu
Yushu 104 D4 var. Gyêgu. Qinghai, C China
Yuty 42 D3 Caazapá, S Paraguay
Yuzhno-Sakhalinsk 93 H4 Jap. Toyohara; prev. Vladimirovka. Ostrov Sakhalin, Sakhalinskaya Oblast', SE Russia
Yuzhnyy Bug see Pivdennyi Buh
Yuzhou see Chongqing
Ýylanly see Gurbansoltan Eje

Z

Zaandam see Zaanstad
Zaanstad 64 C3 prev. Zaandam. Noord-Holland, C Netherlands
Zabaykal'sk 93 F5 Chitinskaya Oblast', S Russia
Zabern see Saverne
Zabid 99 B7 W Yemen
Ząbkowice see Ząbkowice Śląskie
Ząbkowice Śląskie 76 B4 var. Ząbkowice, Ger. Frankenstein, Frankenstein in Schlesien. Dolnośląskie, SW Poland
Zábřeh 77 C5 Ger. Hohenstadt. Olomoucký Kraj, E Czechia (Czech Republic)
Zacapa 30 B2 Zacapa, E Guatemala
Zacatecas 28 D3 Zacatecas, C Mexico
Zacatepec 29 E4 Morelos, S Mexico
Zacháro 83 B6 var. Zaharo, Zakháro. Dytikí Ellás, S Greece
Zadar 78 A3 It. Zara; anc. Iader. Zadar, SW Croatia
Zadetkyi Kyun 115 B6 var. St.Matthew's Island. island Myeik Archipelago, S Myanmar (Burma)
Zafra 70 C4 Extremadura, W Spain
Żagań 76 B4 var. Zagań, Żegań, Ger. Sagan. Lubuskie, W Poland
Zagazig see Az Zaqāzīq
Zágráb see Zagreb
Zagreb 78 B2 Ger. Agram, Hung. Zágráb. country capital (Croatia) Zagreb, N Croatia
Zagros Mountains 98 C3 Eng. Zagros Mountains. mountain range W Iran
Zagros Mountains see Zāgros, Kūhhā-ye
Zaharo see Zacháro
Zāhedān 98 E4 var. Zahidan; prev. Duzdab. Sīstān va Balūchestān, SE Iran
Zahidan see Zāhedān
Zaḥlah see Zahlé
Zahlé 96 B4 var. Zaḥlah. C Lebanon
Záhony 77 E6 Szabolcs-Szatmár-Bereg, NE Hungary
Zaire see Congo (river)
Zaire see Congo (Democratic Republic of)
Zaječar 78 E4 Serbia, E Serbia
Zakataly see Zaqatala
Zakháro see Zacháro
Zakhidnyi Buh/Zakhodni Buh see Bug
Zākhō 98 B2 var. Zākhū, Zaxo. Dahūk/Dihok, N Iraq
Zākhū see Zākhō
Zakopane 77 D5 Małopolskie, S Poland
Zákynthos 83 A6 var. Zákinthos, It. Zante. island Iónia Nísoi, Greece, C Mediterranean Sea
Zalaegerszeg 77 B7 Zala, W Hungary
Zalău 86 B3 Ger. Waltenberg, Hung. Zilah; prev. Ger. Zillenmarkt. Sălaj, NW Romania
Zalim 99 B5 Makkah, W Saudi Arabia
Zambesi/Zambeze see Zambezi
Zambezi 56 C2 North Western, W Zambia
Zambezi 56 D2 var. Zambesi, Port. Zambeze. river S Africa
Zambia 56 C2 off. Republic of Zambia; prev. Northern Rhodesia. country S Africa
Zambia, Republic of see Zambia
Zamboanga 117 E3 off. Zamboanga City. Mindanao, S Philippines
Zamboanga City see Zamboanga
Zambrów 76 E3 Łomża, E Poland
Zamora de Hidalgo 28 D4 Michoacán, SW Mexico
Zamość 76 E4 Rus. Zamoste. Lubelskie, E Poland
Zamoste see Zamość
Zancle see Messina
Zanda 104 A4 Xizang Zizhiqu, W China

Zanesville 18 D4 Ohio, N USA
Zanjān 98 C2 var. Zenjan, Zinjan. Zanjān, NW Iran
Zante see Zákynthos
Zanthus 125 C6 Western Australia, S Australia Oceania
Zanzibar 51 D7 Zanzibar, E Tanzania
Zanzibar 51 D7 Swa. Unguja. island E Tanzania
Zaozhuang 106 D4 Shandong, E China
Zapadna Morava 78 D4 Ger. Westliche Morava. river C Serbia
Zapadnaya Dvina 88 A4 Tverskaya Oblast', W Russia
Zapadnaya Dvina see Western Dvina
Zapadno-Sibirskaya Ravnina 92 C3 Eng. West Siberian Plain. plain C Russia
Zapadnyy Bug see Bug
Zapadnyy Sayan 93 D4 Eng. Western Sayans. mountain range S Russia
Zapala 43 B5 Neuquén, W Argentina
Zapiola Ridge 45 B6 undersea feature SW Atlantic Ocean
Zapolyarnyy 88 C2 Murmanskaya Oblast', NW Russia
Zaporizhia 87 F3 prev. Aleksandrovsk, Zaporizhzhya; Rus. Zaporozh'ye. Zaporiz'ka Oblast', SE Ukraine
Zaporizhzhya see Zaporizhia
Zaporozh'ye see Zaporizhia
Zapotiltic 28 D4 Jalisco, SW Mexico
Zaqatala 95 G2 Rus. Zakataly. NW Azerbaijan
Zara 94 D3 Sivas, C Turkey (Türkiye)
Zara see Zadar
Zarafshan see Zarafshon
Zarafshon 100 D2 Rus. Zarafshan. Navoiy Viloyati, N Uzbekistan
Zarafshon see Zeravshan
Zaragoza 71 F2 Eng. Saragossa; anc. Caesaraugusta, Salduba. Aragón, NE Spain
Zarand 98 D3 Kermān, C Iran
Zaranj 100 D5 Nīmrūz, SW Afghanistan
Zarasai 84 C4 Utena, E Lithuania
Zárate 42 D4 prev. General José F.Uriburu. Buenos Aires, E Argentina
Zarautz 71 E1 var. Zara
Zaxo see Zākhō
Zelenogradsk 84 A4 Ger. Cranz, Kranz. Kaliningradskaya Oblast', W Russia
Zelle see Celle
Zelzate 65 C5 var. Selzaete. Oost-Vlaanderen, NW Belgium
Zemaiciu Aukštumas 84 B4 physical region W Lithuania
Zemst 65 C5 Vlaams Brabant, C Belgium
Zemun 78 D3 Serbia, N Serbia
Zengg see Senj
Zenica 78 C4 Federacija Bosna I Hercegovina, C Bosnia and Herzegovina
Zenta see Senta
Zeravshan 101 E3 Taj./Uzb. Zarafshon. river Tajikistan/Uzbekistan
Zevenaar 64 D4 Gelderland, SE Netherlands
Zevenbergen 64 C4 Noord-Brabant, S Netherlands
Zeya 91 E3 river SE Russia
Zgerzh see Zgierz
Zgierz 76 B4 Ger. Neuhof, Rus. Zgerzh. Łódź, C Poland
Zgorzelec 76 B4 Ger. Görlitz. Dolnośląskie, SW Poland
Zhabinka 85 A6 Pol. Żabinka. Brestskaya Voblasts', SW Belarus
Zhambyl see Taraz
Zhanaozen 92 A4 var. Zhanaozen; prev. Novyy Uzen'. Mangistau, W Kazakhstan
Zhangaqazaly see Ayteke Bi
Zhang-chia-k'ou see Zhangjiakou
Zhangdian see Zibo
Zhangjiakou 106 C3 var. Changkiakow, Zhang-chia-k'ou, Eng. Kalgan; prev. Wanchuan. Hebei, E China
Zhangzhou 106 D6 Fujian, SE China
Zhanjiang 106 C7 var. Chanchiang, Chan-chiang, Cant. Tsamkong, Fr. Fort-Bayard. Guangdong, S China
Zhaoqing 106 C6 Guangdong, S China
Zhayyk see Ural
Zhdanov see Mariupol
Zhe see Zhejiang
Zhejiang 106 D5 var. Che-chiang, Chekiang, Zhe, Zhejiang Sheng. province SE China
Zhejiang Sheng see Zhejiang
Zheleznodorozhny 84 A4 Kaliningradskaya Oblast', W Russia
Zheleznodorozhnyy see Yemva
Zheleznogorsk 89 A5 Kurskaya Oblast', W Russia
Zheltyye Vody see Zhovti Vody
Zhengzhou 106 C4 var. Ch'eng-chou, Chengchow; prev. Chenghsien. province capital Henan, C China
Zhezkazgan see Zhezqazghan
Zhezqazghan 92 C4 var. Zhezkazgan; prev. Dzhezkazgan. Karagandy, C Kazakhstan
Zhidachov see Zhydachiv
Zhitkovichi see Zhytkavichy
Zhitomir see Zhytomyr
Zhlobin 85 D7 Homyel'skaya Voblasts', SE Belarus
Zhmerinka see Zhmerynka
Zhmerynka 86 D2 Rus. Zhmerinka. Vinnyts'ka Oblast', C Ukraine
Zhodino see Zhodzina
Zhodzina 85 D6 Rus. Zhodino. Minskaya Voblasts', C Belarus
Zholkev/Zholkva see Zhovkva
Zhongba see Jiangyou
Zhonghua Renmin Gongheguo see China
Zhongshan 132 D3 Chinese research station Antarctica
Zhosaly 92 B4 prev. Dzhusaly. Kzylorda, SW Kazakhstan
Zhovkva 86 B2 Pol. Żółkiew, Rus. Zholkev, Zholkva; prev. Nesterov. L'vivs'ka Oblast', NW Ukraine
Zhovti Vody 87 F3 Rus. Zheltyye Vody. Dnipropetrovsk Oblast', E Ukraine
Zhydachiv 86 B2 Pol. Żydaczów, Rus. Zhidachov. L'vivs'ka Oblast', NW Ukraine
Zhytkavichy 85 C7 Rus. Zhitkovichi. Homyel'skaya Voblasts', SE Belarus

Zhytomyr 86 D2 Rus. Zhitomir. Zhytomyrs'ka Oblast', NW Ukraine
Zibo 106 D4 var. Zhangdian. Shandong, E China
Zichenau see Ciechanów
Zielona Góra 76 B4 Ger. Grünberg, Grünberg in Schlesien, Grüneberg. Lubuskie, W Poland
Zierikzee 64 B4 Zeeland, SW Netherlands
Zigong 106 B5 var. Tzekung. Sichuan, C China
Ziguinchor 52 B3 SW Senegal
Zilah see Zalău
Žilina 77 C5 Ger. Sillein, Hung. Zsolna. Zlínský Kraj, N Slovakia
Zillenmarkt see Zalău
Zimbabwe 56 D3 off. Republic of Zimbabwe; prev. Rhodesia. country S Africa
Zimbabwe, Republic of see Zimbabwe
Zimnicea 86 C5 Teleorman, S Romania
Zimovniki 89 B7 Rostovskaya Oblast', SW Russia
Zinder 53 G3 Zinder, S Niger
Zinov'yevsk see Kropyvnytskyi
Zintenhof see Sindi
Zipaquirá 36 B3 Cundinamarca, C Colombia
Zittau 72 D4 Sachsen, E Germany
Zlatni Pyasatsi 82 E2 var. Zlatni Pyasŭtsi. Dobrich, NE Bulgaria
Zlatni Pyasŭtsi see Zlatni Pyasatsi
Zlín 77 C5 prev. Gottwaldov. Zlínský Kraj, E Czechia (Czech Republic)
Złoczów see Zolochiv
Złotów 76 C3 Wielkopolskie, C Poland
Znamenka see Znamianka
Znamianka 87 F3 prev. Znam"yanka, Rus. Znamenka. Kirovohrads'ka Oblast', C Ukraine
Znam"yanka see Znamianka
Żnin 76 C3 Kujawsko-pomorskie, C Poland
Zoetermeer 64 C4 Zuid-Holland, W Netherlands
Żółkiew see Zhovkva
Zolochev 87 G2 Rus. Zolochev. Kharkiv's'ka Oblast', E Ukraine
Zolochiv see Zolochev
Zolote 87 H3 Rus. Zolotoye. Luhans'ka Oblast', E Ukraine
Zolotonosha 87 E2 Cherkas'ka Oblast', C Ukraine
Zolotoye see Zolote
Zólyom see Zvolen
Zomba 57 E2 Southern, S Malawi
Zombor see Sombor
Zongo 55 C5 Equateur, N Dem. Rep. Congo
Zonguldak 94 C2 Zonguldak, NW Turkey (Türkiye)
Zonhoven 65 D5 Limburg, NE Belgium
Zoppot see Sopot
Żory 77 C5 var. Zory, Ger. Sohrau. Śląskie, S Poland
Zouar 52 C2 Borkou-Ennedi-Tibesti, N Chad
Zouérat 52 C2 var. Zouérate, Zouïrât. Tiris Zemmour, N Mauritania
Zouérate see Zouérat
Zouïrât see Zouérat
Zrenjanin 78 D3 prev. Petrovgrad, Veliki Bečkerek, Ger. Grossbetschkerek, Hung. Nagybecskerek. Vojvodina, N Serbia
Zsil/Zsily see Jiu
Zsolna see Žilina
Zsombolya see Jimbolia
Zsupanya see Županja
Zubov Seamount 45 D5 undersea feature E Atlantic Ocean
Zueila see Zawīlah
Zug 73 B7 Fr. Zoug. Zug, C Switzerland
Zugspitze 73 C7 mountain S Germany
Zuid-Beveland 65 B5 var. South Beveland. island SW Netherlands
Zuider Zee see IJsselmeer
Zuidhorn 64 E1 Groningen, NE Netherlands
Zuidlaren 64 E2 Drenthe, NE Netherlands
Zula 50 C4 E Eritrea
Züllichau see Sulechów
Zumbo see Vila do Zumbo
Zundert 65 C5 Noord-Brabant, S Netherlands
Zunyi 106 B5 Guizhou, S China
Županja 78 C3 Hung. Zsupanya. Vukovar-Srijem, E Croatia
Zürich 73 B7 Eng./Fr. Zurich, It. Zurigo. Zürich, N Switzerland
Zurich see Zürich
Zurich, Lake see Zürichsee
Zürichsee 73 B7 Eng. Lake Zurich. lake NE Switzerland
Zurigo see Zürich
Zutphen 64 D3 Gelderland, E Netherlands
Zuwärah 49 F2 NW Libya
Zuwaylah see Zawīlah
Zuyevka 89 D5 Kirovskaya Oblast', NW Russia
Zvenigorodka see Zvenyhorodka
Zvenyhorodka 87 E2 Rus. Zvenigorodka. Cherkas'ka Oblast', C Ukraine
Zvishavane 56 D3 prev. Shabani. Matabeleland South, S Zimbabwe
Zvolen 77 C6 Ger. Altsohl, Hung. Zólyom. Banskobystrický Kraj, C Slovakia
Zvornik 78 C4 E Bosnia and Herzegovina
Zwedru 52 D5 var. Tchien. E Liberia
Zwettl 73 E6 Wien, NE Austria
Zwevegem 65 A6 West-Vlaanderen, W Belgium
Zwickau 72 C5 Sachsen, E Germany
Zwolle 64 D3 Overijssel, E Netherlands
Żydaczów see Zhydachiv
Zyóetu see Jōetsu
Żyrardów 76 D3 Mazowieckie, C Poland
Zyryanovsk 92 D5 Vostochnyy Kazakhstan, E Kazakhstan